Psychology

EIGHTH EDITION IN MODULES

Custom Edition for
Solano Community College

Psychology

EIGHTH EDITION IN MODULES

David G. Myers

Hope College
Holland, Michigan

—WORTH—
Custom Publishing

ISBN-13: 978-1-4292-1229-8
ISBN-10: 1-4292-1229-2

Printed in the United States of America

Custom Publishing Division
Worth Publishers
41 Madison Avenue
New York, NY 10010

www.worthpublishers.com/custompub

Solano Community College

Psychology 1
Introduction to Psychology: Personal and Social Behavior

Instructor: Robert DaPrato, M.A.
Office location: Room 747 Humanities Bldg.
Office hours: MWF _____
      T TH _____

Contact Data:	**Phone**	864-7000 X 469	(24/7 messages!)
	E-mail:	robert.daprato@solano.edu	

Course Description: A **survey** of the field of Psychology, including an overview of the history and methods in human behavior. This is an **ACADEMIC class** which is comparable to most 4 year Colleges and Universities. Areas of emphasis will include: Research methods, history of psychology, sensation and perception, learning, memory, cognition and language, intelligence, life span development, motivation and emotions, sexuality & gender, personality theory and assessment, health & stress, psychological disorders, psychotherapy and social psychology.

Class Objectives:
(These are what I expect you as the student to accomplish after this semester)

(1) to gain a general understanding of human behavior as seen from the psychological perspective;
(2) to become more "fully functioning persons" by developing or sharpening skills that aid in human awareness;
(3) to appreciate the importance of psychology as a contribution to your everyday lives!

Methods of study: This course is a **traditional college level introductory** class that will take an objective approach to the study of human and animal behavior. We will study a variety of data based on theory, experiments, observations, case histories and other scientific research methods. Your textbook is a good example of the professionalism found in the field of the Behavioral Sciences, and the author is an authority in many current fields of research.

Read the preface of the text & see companion web site at www.worthpublishers.com/myers.

In order to understand these methods and the data from the text and class, various techniques of learning will be used, such as: lectures, discussion groups, multi-media presentations, random assignments as needed and independent research. **Success in this class depends on your prior reading and comprehension of assignments throughout the semester.**

Success Guidelines: Qualification for English 1 and / or English 62 is <u>a basic requirement</u>. There will be extensive reading (40 pages per week) and writing in order to complete the course with a passing grade. I am serious about this as those who have not achieved this level of reading and comprehension have had a high failure rate in the past. You will be given an informal psychology assessment test to pretest your abilities.
"There is no substitute for individual student efforts!" ....my quote and experience!

Class requirements: There will be **4 exams worth 140 points each**. Each exam will be based on data covered primarily in the classroom presentations and text, lectures or other assignments. Each exam will be a combination of 60 multiple choice questions and six essay questions. The essays will be given out to you in advance and two will be <u>chosen at random by me</u> during the exam. You are advised to prepare answers to ALL of the questions as they serve as study aides for the whole test as well as a "guaranteed" 20 points on the test!!
NO NOTES OF ANY KIND ARE TO BE USED DURING THE EXAM.

Grades: Your academic performance will be based on a contract system of evaluation, which is based on the following requirements: **(based on maximum possible 560 points!)**

- A =   4 exams @ 85%   (476+ pt), minimal absences* & term project required.
- B =   4 exams @ 75%   (420+ pts), average absences**, project optional
- C =   4 exams @ 65 %   (364+ pts), reasonable attendance*** / participation.
- D =   4 exams @ 55%   (308+ pts), reasonable attendance / participation.
- F =   less than what is noted above <u>and they will be given if you qualify</u>!

Note: * minimal = no more than 3 absences for a 3 unit course
          ** average = 4 -6 absences throughout the semester
          ***reasonable= more than the above with special circumstances (see Catalogue)

Text:

Psychology in Modules (8th Edition) David G. Myers, Worth Publishers 2007
*Optional – Study Guide to Accompany Text (Insurance for a good grade!)

Added needs: **(1) Notebook for lectures/ assignments – bring daily!**
          (4) <u>Scantron test forms #886E</u>

Term Project: This is an opportunity for you to show your special skills at a designated topic of current concern to the discipline. I have chosen the topic of **"Aging Issues"** and you will be required to prepare a detailed outline within 4 weeks with **your specific focus**. Your project may be a traditional research paper, an experiment, or survey research. **You must choose** the topic's focus and method to be used and this <u>must be submitted for approval to the instructor.</u> This one page outline / proposal will include the topic, hypothesis, points of emphasis, and any references you will have obtained from your search.

<u>Start with the American Psychological Association website @ http:www.apa.org.</u>

You must also <u>attend a Library Research Class (1 hour) or show proof of similar skills</u> must be presented to the instructor. **Once the proposal is approved**, you will have until 15th week of the semester to complete the project. All traditional papers will be typed and MUST follow either APA or MLA formats. (see APA.ORG for this style manual)

NOTE: THIS PROJECT WILL BE GRADED ON A CREDIT / NO-CREDIT BASIS AND CAN <u>ONLY RAISE</u> YOUR FINAL GRADE BY ONE WHOLE LETTER.
Also: This is the only extra credit possible in this course

Administrative items:
  - Roll sheets and Attendance & Participation Policy
  - Academic Regulations (see College Catalog pg 31-36)
  - Classroom behavior, Cell phones, pagers and MP3's OFF or your out!
  - Class hours and advancement in the course is measured by attendance and performance.
  - Contract grade form & data sheet for student file. (Separate form on day 2)
  - Term Project topic description & Sample Assignment-Assessment (day 2)

Any Questions? Ask now !

Psychology

Fine & Applied Arts/Behavioral Sciences Division

Program Description

The psychology program provides academic instruction in basic psychological concepts, theories, terminology, and research methods, and promotes students' life skills, personal growth, and interpersonal effectiveness.

Associate in Arts Degree

The Associate in Arts Degree can be obtained by completing a total of 60 units, including the 18-unit major, general education requirements and electives.

Required Courses

	Units
PSYCH 1 & 2—Intro. to Psych (3 & 3 units)	6
PSYCH 4—Research Methods in Behavl Science OR	
PSYCH 30—Intro to Social Psych.	3
PSYCH 20—Personal & Social Behavior OR	
PSYCH 5—Abnormal Psychology OR	
PSYCH 34—Human Sexual Behavior	3
PSYCH 10—Psych of Women OR	
PSYCH 24—Psych of African-Amer. OR	

	Units
PSYCH 65—Intro. to Psych of Aging OR	
SOCSC 22-Ethnic, Racial, and Minority Group Relations in Harmony and Conflict	3
One other course from the above list	3
	18

Recommended Electives:
ANTH 2
BIOSC 5, 6, 10
MATH 11
PSYCH 40, 49
SOCIO 1
SOCSC 23

PSYCH 1 3 Units

Introduction to Psychology: Individual & Social Processes

Course Advisories: SCC minimum English and math standards. Introduction to psychology as the scientific study of human behavior. Major topics include history of field, scientific method, sensation and perception, development, learning, cognitive skills, motivation, emotion, personality, tests and measurements, behavior disorders and treatment, and social psychology. *Three hours lecture.*

PSYCH 1H 3 Units

Honors Introduction to Psychology -Individual and Social Processes

Prerequisites: Eligibility for Honors Program. Completion of English 1 with a grade of "B" or higher. An honors course in the introduction to psychology as the scientific study of human behavior. Major topics include history of field, scientific method, sensation, and perception, development, learning, cognitive skills, motivation, emotion, personality, tests and measurements, behavior disorders and treatment, and social psychology. *Three hours lecture.*

PSYCH 2 3 Units

Introduction to Psychology: Biological Bases of Behavior

Course Advisories: SCC minimum English and math standards. Presents the relationship of genetic and physiological factors to behavior. Topics include neural mechanisms underlying sensory and perceptual processes, emotions, motivation, mental disorders, states of consciousness, learning and memory. (CAN PSY 2). *Three hours lecture.*

PSYCH 4 3 Units

Research Methods in Behavioral Science

Prerequisites: PSYCH 1 or PSYCH 2 or SOCIO 1. Course Advisories: Eligibility for ENGL 1; MATH 11. Introduction to basic methods in the behavioral sciences. Assumptions and goals of science are considered as well as several specific research techniques or designs. The ethics of research with human and animal subjects will be covered. *Three hours lecture.*

PSYCH 5 3 Units

Abnormal Psychology

Prerequisite: PSYCH 1. Course Advisories: ENGL 62, eligibility for ENGL 1, and SCC minimum math standard. Theoretical approaches to the explanation of psychological disorders. Survey of selected disorders in DSM IV, including psychoses, anxiety disorders, and depression. Survey of major therapeutic methods. *Three hours lecture.*

PSYCH 10 3 Units

Psychology of Women

Course Advisory: PSYCH 1. Study of contemporary women from a biological, psychological and sociological perspective. Theory and research pertaining to female development will be presented and critically examined. Open to all students. *Three hours lecture.*

PSYCH 20 3 Units

Personal and Social Behavior

Course Advisories: SCC minimum English and math standards. Study of human behavior in the process of adjusting to life's changes. The emphasis is on normal and abnormal adaptations to the various challenges which life presents. Issues related to the major schools of thought and their views towards a healthy personality effective and ineffective behavior, behavioral disorders, psychotherapy, relationship, careers and personal growth. *Three hours lecture.*

PSYCH 24 3 Units

Psychology of African Americans

Course Advisory: SCC minimum English standard. Examination of the principles and findings of psychology as they relate to the behavior and experience of African Americans. Emphasis upon theories and dimensions of personality, self-concept, normality, and the psychological effects of racism. *Three hours lecture.*

PSYCH 30 3 Units

Introduction to Social Psychology

Course Advisories: PSYCH 1; eligibility for ENGL 1; SCC minimum math standard. An attempt to understand and explain how the thoughts, feelings, and behavior of individuals are influenced by the actual, imagined, or implied presence of others. Focus will be on the social factors that influence human behavior; other people, institutions, situations and social and physical structures people have created. A review of the various perspectives unique to social psychologists and a variety of classical research studies will also be studied. *Three hours lecture.*

PSYCH 34 3 Units

Human Sexual Behavior

Course Advisory: SCC minimum English standard. Objective exploration of the various issues pertaining to human sexual behavior from the perspective of the behavioral and social sciences. Some of the major topics to be discussed include history of sexuality, attitudes, behaviors, life styles, psychosexual development, role and identity, sexual dysfunctions, therapy and treatment. *Three hours lecture.*

PSYCH 40 3 Units

Drugs, Society and Behavior

Course Advisories: Eligibility for ENGL 1 and SCC minimum math standard. The course will cover the historical, sociological, psychological, physiological, pharmacological and legal aspects of drugs. Emphasis will be placed on the effects of stimulants, sedative-hypnotics, narcotics, hallucinogens, alcohol, marijuana and inhalants. Various education, prevention and treatment approaches will be discussed. *Three hours lecture.*

PSYCH 49 1-3 Units

Psychology Honors

Prerequisites: Completion of 24 units of college credit with a minimum GPA of 3.3; a minimum of 5 units in the discipline with a grade of "B" or better; an ability to work independently; permission of the division Dean based on instructor availability. Independent study designed for honor students who intend to major in psychology. May be repeated to a maximum of 6 units, including initial enrollment. *Three to nine hours weekly by arrangement.*

PSYCH 65 3 Units

Introduction to the Psychology of Aging

Course Advisories: SCC minimum English and math standards. Introductory course on the psychological aspects of aging covering the physical, emotional, sexual and intellectual processes that occur as an individual matures. The course is designed for those people who work with older adults, for aging individuals or those who must relate to aging adults and/or parents. *Three hours lecture.*

Special Topics

These courses, number 48 or 98 depending upon their transferability, are courses of contemporary interest centered on changing knowledge and important issues in the field. Announcements of Special Topics courses appear in the Schedule of Classes.

HOW TO WRITE A PSYCHOLOGY RESEARCH PAPER

I. GETTING STARTED
- a. Focusing on Your Objective (quid est?)
- b. Scheduling Time (Try index of topics in text)
- c. Choosing a Topic (see instructor's handout)

II. FINDING AND USING REFERENCE MATERIAL
- a. Using the College Library & reference librarians!
- b. Using Reference Resources (see handouts from SCC)
- c. PsycINFO, PsycLIT, and ProQuest!

III. DRAFTING THE PROPOSAL
- a. Tempus Fugit* (time flies)
- b. Template for Writing and Note Taking

IV. PLANNING THE RESEARCH PAPER
- a. The Basic Structure
- b. Abstract
- c. Introduction
- d. Method
- e. Discussion
- f. References
- g. End Material
- h. Organizing Your Thoughts

V. WRITING AND REVISING
- a. Ethics of Writing and Reporting
- b. Avoiding Plagiarism
- c. Tone
- d. Nonsexist Language
- e. Voice
- f. Punctuation
- g. Quotations
- h. Revising

VI. PRODUCING THE FINAL DRAFT
- a. Title Page Format
- b. Headings
- c. Citations in Text
- d. Proofing and Correcting!

VII. APA or MLA Style Manuals
- a. APA Style Manual (see http://apastyle.apa.org/)

Adapted from: Writing Papers in Psychology, Ralph L Rosnow and Mimi Rosnow, 5th ed., 2001

Psychology Club & Psi Beta

Solano Community College

<u>Mission Statement</u>: "To encourage professional development of psychology students through the promotion and recognition of excellence in scholarship, leadership, research and community service."

Open to all majors

Activities Proposed:
- a. Careers in Psychology
- b. Napa State Hospital tour
- c. Movies & Socials
- d. Guest Speakers
- e. Scholarship Opportunities!
- f. Networking to other Colleges.

Next meeting date:

Look in the ASSC Newsletter or ask your teacher!

If any suggestions, feel free to email Robert DaPrato at
robertdaprato@solano.edu

ROBERT M. DA PRATO

EDUCATION

B.A. Degree, San Francisco State University, January 1970
        Majors (dual): Sociology and Psychology
M.A. Degree, San Francisco State University, June 1971
        Major: Psychology
Post Graduate Education:
        Advanced Group Processes, University of California, Santa Clara, 1972
        Basic Pharmacology, University of California, Davis, 1973
        Autogenic Biofeedback Training, University of California, Berkeley, 1975
        Human Sexuality, N.S.F., Stanford University, 1976
        Principles of Sex Counseling, University of California, San Francisco, 1978
        Holistic Health, N.S.F., Stanford University, 1979
        Abnormal Behavior; Research Methods; Environmental Studies; U.C. Davis 1989
        Business Law, Solano Community College 1991
        Issues in Aging, Chapman University, 2007

FOR MELINDA

About the Author

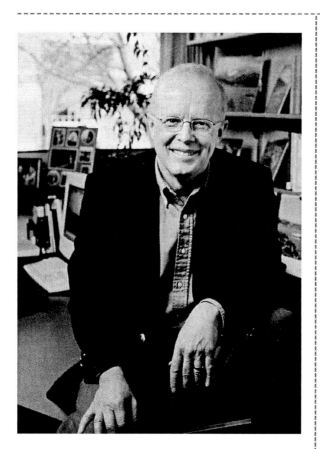

David Myers received his psychology Ph.D. from the University of Iowa. He has spent his career at Hope College, Michigan, where he is the John Dirk Werkman Professor of Psychology and has taught dozens of introductory psychology sections. Hope College students have invited him to be their commencement speaker and voted him "outstanding professor."

Myers' scientific articles have, with support from National Science Foundation grants, appeared in more than two dozen scientific periodicals, including *Science, American Scientist, Psychological Science,* and the *American Psychologist.* In addition to his scholarly writing and his textbooks for introductory and social psychology, he also digests psychological science for the general public. His writings have appeared in three dozen magazines, from *Today's Education* to *Scientific American.* He also has authored five general audience books, including *The Pursuit of Happiness* and *Intuition: Its Powers and Perils.*

David Myers has chaired his city's Human Relations Commission, helped found a thriving assistance center for families in poverty, and spoken to hundreds of college and community groups. He bikes to work year-round and plays daily pick-up basketball. David and Carol Myers have raised two sons and a daughter.

Contents

Preface

Two decades of time's ever rolling stream have flowed swiftly by since publication of the first edition of *Psychology*. And what an amazing two decades it has been. Hardly a day goes by without my feeling gratitude for the privilege of assisting with the teaching of psychology to so many students, in so many countries, through so many different languages. To be entrusted with discerning and communicating the wisdom of this humanly significant discipline is both an exciting honor and a great responsibility.

What sustains my motivation is, first, my continuing appreciation for psychological science and its ever-expanding understandings, and, second, my commitment to the students and teaching colleagues with whom this book enables me to have conversation. I love the mind-expanding learning that comes from my day-to-day reading of psychological science, and I love connecting with so many people (many hundreds of whom have written to share their experiences and gentle words of advice).

It is a rare day in between editions when I do not harvest new information about the field I love and its application to everyday life. Week by week, new information surprises us with discoveries about, for example, the neuroscience of our moods and memories, the reach of our adaptive unconscious, and the shaping power of our social and cultural context. No wonder this book has changed dramatically since I set to work on the first edition 23 years ago. Today's psychological science is more attuned to the relative effects of nature and nurture, to gender and cultural diversity, to our conscious and unconscious information processing, and to the biology that underlies our behavior (see **TABLES 1** and **2,** page xviii). We today can also harness new ways to present information, both in books and via electronic media. These changes are exhilarating! Keeping up with new discoveries fills each day and connects me with many colleagues and friends.

The thousands of instructors and millions of students across the globe who have studied this book have contributed immensely to its development. Much of this has occurred spontaneously, through correspondence and conversations. For *Psychology,* Eighth Edition, we also formally involved over 800 researchers and teaching psychologists, along with many students, in our efforts to gather accurate and up-to-date information about the field of psychology and the content, pedagogy, and supplements needs of instructors and students in the introductory course. Moreover, we look forward to continuing feedback as we strive, over future editions, to create an ever better book.

Why a Modular Book?

This 58-module text has been a longtime wish come true for me. It breaks out of the box by restructuring the material into a buffet of (a) short, digestible chapters (called modules) that (b) can be selected and assigned in any order.

Have we not all heard the familiar student complaint: "The chapters are too long!" A text's typical 30- to 50-page chapters cannot be read in a single sitting before the eyes grow weary and the mind wanders. So why not parse the material into readable units? Ask your students whether they would prefer a 700-page book to be organized as fourteen 50-page chapters or as fifty 14-page chapters. You may be surprised at their overwhelming support for shorter chapters. Indeed, students digest material better when they process it in smaller chunks—as "spaced" rather than massed practice.

TABLE 1 **Evolutionary Psychology and Behavior Genetics**

*In addition to the coverage found in Modules 6 and 7, the **evolutionary perspective** is covered on the following pages:*

*In addition to the coverage found in Modules 6 and 7, **behavior genetics** is covered on the following pages:*

TABLE 2 **Neuroscience**

*In addition to coverage found in Modules 4 and 5, **neuroscience** can be found on the following pages:*

I have equally often heard from instructors bemoaning the fact that they "just can't get to everything" in the book. Sometimes instructors want to cover certain sections in a traditional, long chapter but not others. For example, in the typical States of Consciousness chapter, someone may want to cover Sleep and Hypnosis but not Drugs. In *Psychology Eighth Edition in Modules,* instructors could easily choose to cover Module 18, Waking and Sleeping Rhythms, and Module 19, Hypnosis, but not Module 20, Drugs and Consciousness.

How Is This Different From *Psychology, Eighth Edition?*

The primary differences between this book and my *Psychology,* Eighth Edition, text are organization and module independence.

Organization

This book really IS *Psychology,* Eighth Edition—just in a different format. So, this modular version contains all the updated research and innovative new coverage from *Psychology,* Eighth Edition. A very few sections have moved around to accommodate the modular structure. For example, "Rates of Psychological Disorders" is a separate section at the end of the Psychological Disorders chapter in *Psychology,* Eighth Edition, but it is covered in the first of the Psychological Disorders modules in this modular version. And "Selective Attention" is covered at the beginning of the Perception chapter in *Psychology,* Eighth Edition, but it is covered at the beginning of the Sensation/Perception group of modules in this modular version (in Module 12, Introduction to Sensation and Perception).

The Modules Are Independent

Each module in this book is self-standing rather than dependent upon the others for understanding. Cross references to other parts of the book have been replaced with brief explanations. In some cases, illustrations or key terms are repeated to avoid possible confusion. No assumptions are made about what students have read prior to each module. This independence gives instructors ultimate flexibility in deciding which modules to use, and in what order. Connections among psychology's subfields and findings are still made—they are just made in a way that does not assume knowledge of other parts of the book.

What's New Since *Psychology Seventh Edition in Modules?*

In addition to updates everywhere and 900 new references—comprising 24 percent of the bibliography—I have introduced the following major changes to *Psychology Eighth Edition in Modules:*

Increased Coverage of Cultural and Gender Diversity

This edition presents an even more thoroughly cross-cultural perspective on psychology (see **TABLE 3**, page xx)—reflected in research findings and text and photo examples. Coverage of the psychology of women and men is thoroughly integrated (see **TABLE 4**, page xxi). In addition, I am working to offer a world-based psychology for our worldwide student readership. Thus, I continually search the world for research findings and text and photo examples, conscious that readers may be in Melbourne, Sheffield, Vancouver, or Nairobi. North American and European examples come easily, given that I re-

Table 3 Cultural and Multicultural Experience

*Coverage of **culture and multiculture experience** can be found on the following pages:*

Aging population, pp. 173–174

Aggression, pp. 753, 756, 757–758

AIDS, pp. 186, 407, 559

Alcoholism, pp. 294–296

Anger, pp. 536–538

Animal research ethics, p. 25

Attractiveness, pp. 104–106, 765–769

Behavioral effects of culture, pp. 23–24, 99

Categorization, p. 397

Conformity, pp. 734, 736, 737

Corporal punishment practices, pp. 329–330

Cultural norms, pp. 115–116, 125–126

Culture and the self, pp. 117–119

Culture context effects, p. 255

Culture shock, pp. 115–116, 554

Deaf culture, pp. 79–80, 83, 220–222, 413, 414, 415, 419, 421

Depression, pp. 669–670

Development:

  adolescence, p. 160

  attachment, pp. 152–155

  child-rearing, pp. 119–120

  cognitive development, p. 149

  developmental similarities, p. 120

  moral development, p. 164

motor development, p. 136

social development, p. 152

Dieting, p. 584

Drugs, psychological effects of, p. 296

Emotion:

  emotion-detecting ability, pp. 524–525

  expressing, pp. 526, 528–531, 537, 538

  experiencing, pp. 535–536, 538, 541–543

Enemy perceptions, p. 762

Flynn effect, p. 447

Gender:

  roles, pp. 125–126

  social connectedness, p. 166

Grief, expressing, pp. 186–187

Happiness, pp. 540–543, 544–545

Hindsight bias, p. 17

History of psychology, pp. 3–7

Homosexuality, views on, p. 31

Human diversity/kinship, pp. 23–24, 114–120

Hunger, pp. 477–478

Individualism/collectivism, pp. 117–120

Intelligence, pp. 446–447, 458–461

  bias, pp. 464–466

Language, pp. 114–115, 413, 416–417, 419–421

Leaving the nest, p. 169

Life-expectancy, pp. 172–174

Life satisfaction, pp. 539–543

Management styles, p. 510

Marijuana use, p. 305

Marriage, pp. 182–183

Medical risk, p. 460

Meditation, pp. 571–573

Memory, encoding, p. 357

Mental illness rate, pp. 650–651

Need to belong, pp. 495–497

Obesity, pp. 588–590

Observational learning:

  television viewing, p. 154

  television and aggression, pp. 341–343

Pace of life, pp. 33, 116

Parapsychology, pp. 258, 262

Participative management, p. 510

People with disabilities, p. 540

Perception, pp. 191, 246

Personal space, p. 116

Poverty and inequality, p. 34

Prejudice, pp. 747–753

Prejudice prototypes, p. 397

Psychological disorders:

  antisocial personality disorder, pp. 665–666

  dissociative personality disorder, p. 663

  eating disorders, pp. 479–480, 645

rates of, pp. 650–651

  schizophrenia, p. 645

  susto, p. 645

  taijin-kyofusho, p. 645

Psychotherapy:

  EMDR training, pp. 708–709

  Psychoanalysis, p. 688

Psychotherapists and values, pp. 711–713

Puberty and adult independence, p. 169

Self-esteem, pp. 544–545, 635

Self-serving bias, p. 636

Sexual attraction, pp. 105–106

Sexual orientation, pp. 488–489

Size-distance relationship, pp. 245–246

Smoking, pp. 578–584

Social-cultural perspective, pp. 8–11

Social clock, pp. 181–182

Stress:

  adjusting to a new culture, p. 554

  poverty and inequality/ life-expectancy, pp. 564, 565, 566

Suicide, p. 672

Teen sexuality, pp. 486–487

Testing bias, pp. 464–466

See also Modules 54–58, pp. 725–728

---

side in the United States, maintain contact with friends and colleagues in Canada, subscribe to several European periodicals, and live periodically in the U.K. This edition, for example, offers 82 explicit Canadian and 142 British examples, and 82 mentions of Australia and New Zealand. We are all citizens of a shrinking world, thanks to increased migration and the growing global economy. Thus, American students, too, benefit from information and examples that internationalize their world-consciousness. And if psychology seeks to explain *human* behavior (not just American or Canadian or Australian behavior), the broader the scope of studies presented, the more accurate is our picture of this world's people. My aim is to expose all students to the world beyond their own culture. Thus, I continue to welcome input and suggestions from all readers. Thoroughly revised Module 6 (Behavior Genetics and Evolutionary Psychology) and Module 7 (Environmental Influences on Behavior) encourage students to appreciate cultural and gender differences and commonalities, and to consider the interplay of nature and nurture.

Each part-opening art page now includes a **brief literary excerpt from varied cultural perspectives.** These excerpts, from Maya Angelou, Judith Ortiz Cofer, Jhumpa Lahiri, Faiz Ahmed Faiz, Gwendolyn Brooks, and others offer "Another Voice" on the modules' topics. In addition, **many new photos** showcase the diversity of cultures

TABLE 4 The Psychology of Men and Women

*Coverage of the **psychology of men and women** can be found in the following pages:*

ADHD, p. 643
Aggression, pp. 753–754
Alcohol use, pp. 294–295
Autism, p. 147
Behavioral effects of gender, p. 24
Biological sex/gender, pp. 123–125
Body image, pp. 479–480
Changes in physical development, pp. 172–173
Depression, pp. 669, 676
Dieting, pp. 584–585, 590–591
Dream content, pp. 280–283
Drugs and addiction, pp. 294–295, 296
Eating disorders, pp. 478–480
Emotion-detecting ability, pp. 463–464, 527–528
Emotional expression, pp. 185, 524–527
Empty nest, p. 183
Father care, pp. 152, 488

Fear, p. 534
Freud's views, pp. 598–599, 604
Gender and child-rearing, pp. 126–127, 479
Gender roles, pp. 125–126
Gender prejudice, pp. 748–749
Gendered brain, pp. 125, 479, 483, 486, 493
Generic pronoun "he," pp. 420–421
Happiness, p. 545
Heart disease, pp. 555–557
Help-receiving, p. 773
Hormones and:
  aggression, pp. 754–755
  sexual behavior, pp. 483–484
  sexual development, pp. 124–125, 161–162
Immune system, p. 558
Intelligence, pp. 461–464
  bias, p. 465

Life expectancy, p. 174
Marriage, p. 567
Maturation, pp. 161–162
Menarche, p. 161
Menopause, pp. 172–173
Midlife crisis, p. 181
Obesity, pp. 584–585
Pornography, pp. 485, 757–758
Prejudice, pp. 397, 750–751
Psychological disorders, rates of, pp. 650–651
Rape, pp. 321, 757–759
REM sleep, arousal in, p. 272
Risk taking, p. 106
Savant syndrome, pp. 432–433
Schizophrenia, pp. 678, 680
Sense of smell, p. 232
Sexual abuse, pp. 105, 153, 295, 567
Sexual attraction, pp. 105–106

Sexual disorders, p. 483
Sexual fantasies, pp. 486, 487
Sexual orientation, pp. 488–494
Sexuality, pp. 104–106, 482–486
Sleep, pp. 274, 275–276
Smoking, pp. 106, 136, 582
Social connectedness, pp. 565–567
Stereotyping, p. 256
Stress, pp. 555–557
  response, p. 553
  in marriage, p. 567
  sexual abuse, p. 567
Suicide, pp. 672–673
Weight discrimination, p. 586
Women and work, p. 184
Women in psychology, p. 5
See also Modules 54–58, pp. 725–777

within North America, as well as across the globe. In addition to significant cross-cultural examples and research presented within the narrative, these new photos with informative captions freshen each module and broaden students' perspectives in applying psychological science to their own world and to the worlds across the globe.

A Revised and Thoroughly Considered Pedagogical Program

In addition to the new part-opening literary excerpts, this edition includes the following new study aids.

- *New numbered Learning Objectives* (2 to 17 per module) introduce significant sections of text and direct student reading. These Learning Objectives also organize the Study Guide and the Test Banks and are included in the Instructor's Resources.
- *New Learning Outcomes,* found at the end of each module, repeat the Learning Objectives and address them with a narrative summary.
- The Learning Outcomes sections also include at least one *Ask Yourself* question (which encourages students to apply new concepts to their own experiences), one or more *Test Yourself* questions (with answers in an appendix) that assess student mastery and encourage big-picture thinking, and page-referenced *Terms and Concepts to Remember.*

Greater Emphasis on the Biological-Psychological-Social/Cultural Levels of Analysis Approach in Psychology

This edition now systematically includes coverage of the biological, psychological, and social-cultural influences on our behavior. A significant new section in Module 1 introduces the levels-of-analysis approach, and new levels-of-analysis figures in many modules help students understand concepts in the biopsychosocial context. Richard Straub's new, accompanying interactive Visual Concept Review booklet also includes charts that provide levels-of-analysis reviews.

Greater Sensitivity to the Clinical Perspective

With helpful guidance from clinical psychologist colleagues, I have been more mindful in this edition of the clinical angle on various concepts within psychology, which has sensitized and improved the Personality, Psychological Disorders, and Therapy discussions, among others. For example, I now cover problem-focused and emotion-focused coping strategies in Module 42, and Modules 32–33 include several mentions of how intelligence tests are used in clinical settings.

New Teaching and Learning Resources

Our supplements and media have been celebrated for their quality, abundance, and accuracy. The package available for *Psychology Eighth Edition in Modules* raises the bar even higher. New media items include the *ActivePsych* classroom activity CD-ROMs, the new Online Study Center 2.0 for students, and enhanced course management solutions. New print supplements include Martin Bolt's Instructor's Media Guide, Richard Straub's Visual Concept Reviews, and a thoroughly revised Test Bank. See pages xxiv–xxxi for details.

New Careers in Psychology Appendix, by Dr. Jennifer Lento, University of San Diego

This appendix provides guidance to students considering a psychology major and/or career. Topics include the benefits of studying psychology and obtaining a psychology degree, psychology careers available and the job market landscape for students at all levels (bachelors, masters, doctorate), career options within the subfields in psychology (such as clinical, counseling, community, school, forensic, and sports psychology), and early preparation tips for those considering graduate school.

Enhanced Critical Thinking Coverage

I aim to introduce students to critical thinking in a very natural way throughout the book, with even more in the narrative that encourages active learning of psychology's key concepts. In addition to the new Learning Objectives and Learning Outcomes, which encourage critical reading to glean an understanding of important concepts, this edition includes the following opportunities for students to learn or practice their critical thinking skills.

- *Modules 2 and 3 take a unique, critical thinking approach to introducing students to psychology's research methods,* emphasizing the fallacies of our everyday intuition and common sense and, thus, the need for psychological science. Critical thinking is introduced as a key term in Module 2 (page 16). The discussions of Statistical Reasoning encourage students to "focus on thinking smarter by applying simple statistical principles to everyday reasoning" (pp. 41–42).
- *"Thinking Critically About . . ." boxes* are found throughout the book, modeling for students a critical approach to some key issues in psychology. For example, see the new box "Thinking Critically About: ADHD—Pathologizing Rambunctiousness or Genuine Disorder?" on page 643.
- *Detective-style stories* throughout the narrative get students thinking critically about psychology's key research questions.
- *"Apply this"* and *"Think about it"*-style discussions keep students active in their study of each module.
- *Critical examinations of pop psychology* spark interest and provide important lessons in thinking critically about everyday topics.

See **TABLE 5** for a complete list of this text's coverage of critical thinking topics and Thinking Critically About boxes.

Table 5 Critical Thinking and Research Emphasis

Critical thinking coverage, and in-depth stories of psychology's **scientific research** process, can be found on the following pages:

Thinking Critically About . . . boxes:

Desegregation and the Death Penalty—When Beliefs Collide With Psychological Science, p. 28

Left Brain/Right Brain, p. 84

The Fear Factor—Do We Fear the Right Things?, pp. 404–405

Lie Detection, pp. 517–518

Alternative Medicine: New Ways to Health or Old Snake Oil?, pp. 570–571

How to Be a "Successful" Astrologer or Palm Reader, pp. 620–621

ADHD—Pathologizing Rambunctiousness or Genuine Disorder?, p. 693

Insanity and Responsibility, p. 650

Dissociation and Multiple Personalities, pp. 662–663

"Regressing" from Unusual to Usual, p. 704

Critical Examinations of Pop Psychology:

Do Video Games Teach or Release Violence?, pp. 759–760

Perceiving order in random events, pp. 37–38

Do we use only 10 percent of our brains?, p. 76

Critiquing the evolutionary perspective, pp. 106–107

How great is the power of parenting?, pp. 112–113

Sensory restriction, pp. 250–251

Is there extrasensory perception?, pp. 258–262

Can hypnosis enhance recall? Coerce action? Be therapeutic? Alleviate pain?, pp. 287–289

Has the concept of "addiction" been stretched too far?, p. 293

Near-death experiences, pp. 300–301

Do animals exhibit language?, pp. 425–428

Is aerobic exercise therapeutic?, pp. 569–570

Spirituality and faith communities, pp. 573–576

How valid is the Rorschach test?, p. 603

Is repression a myth?, pp. 606–607

Is Freud credible?, pp. 606–609

Post-traumatic stress disorder, pp. 657–658

Is psychotherapy effective?, pp. 702–707

Evaluating alternative therapies, pp. 707–709

Thinking Critically with Psychological Science:

The limits of intuition and common sense, pp. 16–19

"Critical thinking" introduced as a key term, p. 20

The scientific attitude, pp. 19–21

The scientific method, pp. 21–22

Correlation and causation, pp. 35–36

Illusory correlation, pp. 36–37

Exploring cause and effect, pp. 38–39

Evaluating therapies, pp. 39–40

Statistical reasoning, pp. 41–42

Making inferences, pp. 44–45

Scientific Detective Stories:

Is breast milk better than formula?, pp. 38–39

Language in the brain, pp. 77–79

Our divided brains, pp. 80–84

The twin and adoption studies, pp. 93–97

How a child's mind develops, pp. 141–149

Aging and intelligence, pp. 178–181

Parallel processing, pp. 208–210

How do we see in color?, pp. 210–212

Why do we sleep?, pp. 273–277

Why do we dream?, pp. 281–283

Is hypnosis an altered state of consciousness?, pp. 289–291

How do we store memories in our brains?, pp. 363–368

Memory construction, pp. 382–390

Do animals exhibit language?, pp. 425–428

Why do we feel hunger?, pp. 474–477

What determines sexual orientation?, pp. 489–495

The pursuit of happiness: Who is happy, and why?, pp. 538–546

Why—and in whom—does stress contribute to heart disease?, pp. 555–557

How and why is social support linked with health?, pp. 565–568

Self-esteem versus self-serving bias, pp. 633–636

What causes mood disorders?, pp. 667–676

Do prenatal viral infections increase risk of schizophrenia?, pp. 682–683

Is psychotherapy effective?, pp. 702–707

Why do people fail to help in emergencies?, pp. 772–774

What Continues?

Throughout its eight editions, my vision for *Psychology* has not wavered: *to merge rigorous science with a broad human perspective in a book that engages both mind and heart.* My aim has been to create a state-of-the-art introduction to psychology, written with sensitivity to students' needs and interests. I aspire to help students understand and appreciate the wonder of important phenomena of their lives. I also want to convey the inquisitive spirit in which psychologists *do* psychology. The study of psychology, I believe, enhances our abilities to restrain intuition with critical thinking, judgmentalism with compassion, and illusion with understanding.

Believing with Thoreau that "Anything living is easily and naturally expressed in popular language," I seek to communicate psychology's scholarship with crisp narrative and vivid storytelling. Writing as a solo author, I hope to tell psychology's story in a way that is warmly personal as well as rigorously scientific. I love to reflect on connections between psychology and other realms, such as literature, philosophy, history, sports, religion, politics, and popular culture. And I love to provoke thought, to play with words, and to laugh.

Although supplemented by added story telling, this new edition retains its predecessors' voice and much of their content and organization. It also retains the goals—the guiding principles—that have animated the previous seven editions:

1. *To exemplify the process of inquiry* I strive to show students not just the outcome of research, but how the research process works. Throughout, the book tries to excite the reader's curiosity. It invites readers to imagine themselves as participants in classic experiments. Several modules introduce research stories as mysteries that progressively unravel as one clue after another falls into place. (See, for example, the historical story of research on the brain's processing of language on pages 415–419.)

2. *To teach critical thinking* By presenting research as intellectual detective work, I exemplify an inquiring, analytical mind-set. Whether students are studying development, cognition, or statistics, they will become involved in, and see the rewards of, critical reasoning. Moreover, they will discover how an empirical approach can help them evaluate competing ideas and claims for highly publicized phenomena—ranging from subliminal persuasion, ESP, and alternative therapies to astrology, hypnotic regression, and repressed and recovered memories.

3. *To put facts in the service of concepts* My intention is not to fill students' intellectual file drawers with facts, but to reveal psychology's major concepts—to teach students how to think, and to offer psychological ideas worth thinking about. In each module, I place emphasis on those concepts I hope students will carry with them long after they have completed the course. Always, I try to follow Albert Einstein's dictum that "Everything should be made as simple as possible, but not simpler."

4. *To be as up-to-date as possible* Few things dampen students' interest as quickly as the sense that they are reading stale news. While retaining psychology's classic studies and concepts, I also present the discipline's most important recent developments. Nearly 500 references in this edition are dated 2004 or 2005.

5. *To integrate principles and applications* Throughout—by means of anecdotes, case histories, and the posing of hypothetical situations—I relate the findings of basic research to their applications and implications. Where psychology can illuminate pressing human issues—be they racism and sexism, health and happiness, or violence and war—I have not hesitated to shine its light.

6. *To enhance comprehension by providing continuity* Because the book has a single author, many significant issues—such as behavior genetics, cultural diversity, the bold thinking of intellectual pioneers, human rationality and irrationality, empathy for and understanding of troubled lives—weave throughout many modules, and students hear a consistent voice. "The uniformity of a work," observed Edward Gibbon, "denotes the hand of a single artist."

7. *To reinforce learning at every step* Everyday examples and rhetorical questions encourage students to process the material actively. Concepts are presented and then frequently applied to reinforce learning. Learning Objectives, Learning Outcomes, self-tests, a marginal glossary, and end-of-module key terms lists help students master important concepts and terminology.

8. *To convey respect for human unity and diversity* Throughout the book, readers will see evidence of our human kinship—our shared biological heritage, our common mechanisms of seeing and learning, hungering and feeling, loving and hating. They will also better understand the dimensions of our diversity—our *individual* diversity in development and aptitudes, temperament and personality, and disorder and health; and our *cultural* diversity in attitudes and expressive styles, childrearing and care for the elderly, and life priorities.

Innovative Multimedia Supplements Package

Psychology Eighth Edition in Modules boasts a host of new electronic and print supplements titles.

Media Supplements

New! ActivePsych Instructor's Classroom Exercise CD-ROMs include interactive activities designed for in-class presentation and group participation, as well as a robust library of new clips and animations. These activities require very little instructor preparation (just load the CD and launch the activity) and are designed to foster class discussion and critical thinking. The ActivePsych suite of instructor presentation CD-ROMs includes the following:

* *More than 30 interactive activities,* including animations, video clips, illustrations, photographs, and critical thinking questions. A number of activities have been adapted from Martin Bolt's Instructor's Resources and Thomas Ludwig's Psych-Sim 5.0 (and are now classroom presentation-friendly). ActivePsych also includes a significant number of completely original, creative activities, all authored (and class-tested) by veteran introductory psychology teachers.
* *Approximately 30 completely new short video clips,* drawn from a variety of sources, and numerous new animations.
* *New! Scientific American Frontiers Teaching Modules, Third Edition,* which have been housed in ActivePsych and edited by Martin Bolt. The Third Edition offers you 15 edited clips from Scientific American Frontiers segments produced between 2003 and 2005.

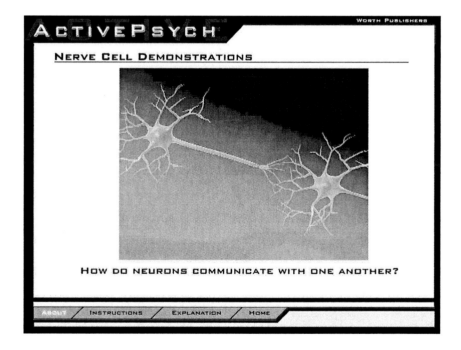

New! Instructor's Media Guide (based on the work of trusted *Instructor's Resources* author Martin Bolt) expands the Lecture Guides and offers instructors a simple way to incorporate instructor media, presentation, and video resources into their course.

New! Online Study Center 2.0 for *Psychology Eighth Edition in Modules* The customized Online Study Center (OSC) offers students a variety of tools to help them master the course:

* *A Module-by-Module Self-Guided Study Plan with Diagnostic Tests.* Students may take a 20–25 question Self-Test to assess their current knowledge of a particular module, then view a Study Plan that identifies areas of weakness and offers a variety of resources for learning those concepts.

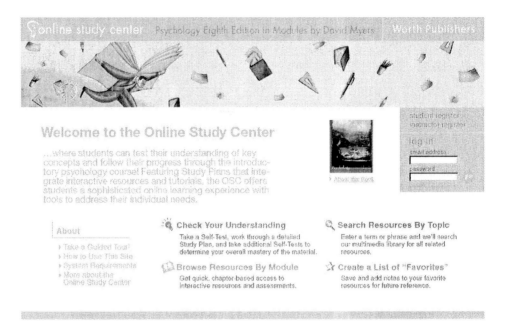

- *Self-Paced Tutorials* that allow students to revisit and master course concepts on their own.
- *Multiple Assessment and Review Tools,* organized by module. In addition to the Study Plan, students can "Search by Topic" or "Browse by Module" to access interactive demonstrations and review materials.
- *Dozens of Hands-On Activities.* Your students will be able to tackle classic experiments (condition a rat, probe the hypothalamus electronically), encounter perceptual illusions, test their memory, interpret facial expressions, and more.
- *Digitized Video Demonstrations* (for example, the effects of teratogens on development) *and Animations* (such as neural communication) bring text concepts to life.
- *A Sophisticated Search Engine* (similar to Google®) that allows students to search quickly by topic (not just by module).
- *Interactive Study Tools.* Students are able to add resources to their Favorites and even add Notes to specific resources.

New! Enhanced Course Management Solutions (WebCT, Blackboard, Desire2Learn, Angel) allow adopters to access all of this edition's teaching and learning resources in one, central location (through their course management system) through one, seamless, guided experience.

New! eLibrary for Psychology *Eighth Edition in Modules* brings together the supplementary resources, such as the *Instructor's Resources, PsychSim 5.0,* and *PsychOnline,* in a single, easy-to-use Web site. Through sophisticated and seamless search and browse functions, the eLibrary allows instructors to quickly build free, premium student Web pages, construct lectures, and organize resources.

New! Expanded and Improved Book Companion Site The *Psychology Eighth Edition in Modules* Book Companion Site offers students a virtual study guide, twenty-four hours a day, seven days a week. Best of all, these resources are free and do not require any special access codes or passwords. In addition to self-tests, review materials, annotated Web links, simulations, and demonstrations, the site now includes an interactive, historical timeline, a new Spanish-English glossary, and Spanish-English flashcards. The ***password-protected Instructor Site*** offers a full array of teaching resources, including a new suite of PowerPoint slides, electronic Lecture Guides, an online quiz grade book, and links to additional tools.

New! iclicker Radio Frequency Classroom Response System Offered by Worth Publishers, in partnership with iClicker and available for fall 2006 classes, iClicker is Worth's new polling system, created by educators for educators. This radio frequency system is the hassle-free way to make your class time more interactive. The system allows you to pause to ask questions and instantly record responses, as well as take attendance, direct students through lectures, gauge your students' understanding of the material, and much more.

Revised! Instructor's Resource CD-ROM Customized for *Psychology Eighth Edition in Modules,* this CD-ROM contains pre-built PowerPoint presentation slide sets for each chapter, a digital photograph library, an electronic version of Martin Bolt's *Instructor's Resources and Lecture Guides,* and a complete illustration and photo library.

* *Chapter Art PowerPoint® Slides* feature all of the text art and illustrations (including tables, charts, and graphs) within the PowerPoint format.
* *Revised! Lecture PowerPoint® Presentation Slides* Developed by a longtime adopter of *Psychology* and informed by 20 reviewers, these slides focus on key concepts and themes from the text. The slides feature tables, graphs and figures from the text and from outside sources. Also included are PDF handouts of the slides, which include spaces for note-taking.
* *New! Step Up to Psychology: A PowerPoint Review Game by John Schulte, University of North Carolina—Wilmington and Cape Fear Community College.* This PowerPoint-based review adopts a game-show approach where students divide into teams to compete for points by answering questions related to text material. The questions are ranked for difficulty (four levels), and include both factual/definitional and conceptual/application questions.
* *New! Digital Photo Library* gives you access to all of the photographs from the eighth edition, organized by module.

PsychSim 5.0, Thomas Ludwig, Hope College, CD-ROM and Booklet These 42 interactive simulations involve students in the practice of psychological research by having them play the role of experimenter (conditioning a rat, probing the hypothalamus electrically, working in a sleep lab) or participant (responding to tests of memory or visual illusions, interpreting facial expressions). Other simulations provide dynamic tutorials or demonstrations. In addition, five-question multiple choice quizzes are available for each activity on the Book Companion Site.

PsychInquiry for *Psychology Eighth Edition in Modules:* Student Activities in Research and Critical Thinking CD-ROM, Thomas Ludwig, Hope College Customized to work specifically with this new edition, this CD-ROM contains dozens of interactive activities designed to help students learn about psychological research and to improve their critical thinking skills.

PsychOnline (Course Management Version), Thomas Ludwig, Hope College Housed in both WebCT and Blackboard, *PsychOnline* is a comprehensive instructor and student online solution for introductory psychology. Designed for use as a supplement for either Web-enhanced lecture courses or complete online courses, *PsychOnline* offers a rich, Web-based collection of interactive tutorials and activities for introductory psychology.

PsychOnline 2.0 (Web-Based Version), Thomas Ludwig, Hope College *PsychOnline 2.0* is a comprehensive online resource for introductory psychology. *PsychOnline 2.0* looks like a Worth Web site, includes more than 100 interactive tutorials and over 250 activities, and also contains the following new features:

* A Web-based interface that is easy to use and incorporate within your course.
* A self-guided study plan that includes a multiple-choice Diagnostic Test for each topic. After the student completes the Diagnostic Test, the student is given a

Diagnostic Test Report that offers test results and suggestions for re-examining and studying material.

- 20 modules from Thomas Ludwig's *PsychSim* 5.0.

Diploma Computerized Test Bank (Available in Windows and Macintosh on One CD-ROM) The CD-ROM allows you to add an unlimited number of questions, edit questions, format a test, scramble questions, and include pictures, equations, or multimedia links. With the accompanying grade book, you can record students' grades throughout a course, sort student records and view detailed analyses of test items, curve tests, generate reports, add weights to grades, and more. This CD-ROM is the access point for Diploma Online Testing. Blackboard and WebCT formatted versions of the Test Bank are also available within the Course Cartridge and ePack.

Diploma Online Testing at www.brownstone.net With Diploma, you can easily create and administer exams over the Internet, with questions that incorporate multimedia and interactivity. Students receive instant feedback and can take the quizzes multiple times. Instructors can sort and view results, take advantage of various grade book and result-analysis features, and restrict tests to specific computers or time blocks.

Online Quizzing at www.worthpublishers.com/myers Now you can easily and securely quiz students online using prewritten multiple-choice questions for each module. Students receive instant feedback and can take the quizzes multiple times. As the instructor, you can view results by quiz, student, or question, or you can get weekly results via e-mail.

Worth Image and Lecture Gallery at www.worthpublishers.com/ilg Using the *Image and Lecture Gallery,* you can browse or search and download text art, illustrations, outlines, and pre-built PowerPoint slides for ALL Worth titles. Users can also create personal folders for easy organization of the materials.

Video/DVD Resources

New! Moving Images: Exploring Psychology Through Film Available in VHS and DVD and edited by Martin Bolt (Calvin College), this completely new series (drawn from the Films for the Humanities and Sciences) contains 25 one-to-eight minute clips of real people, real experiments, and real patients. The series combines historical footage with cutting-edge research and news programming. Highlights include: "Brain and Behavior: A Contemporary Phineas Gage," "Firewalking: Mind Over Matter," and "Social Rejection: The Need to Belong."

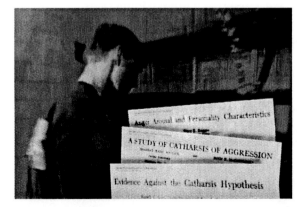

**Moving Images:
Exploring Psychology Through Film
(edited by Martin Bolt)**

New! Scientific American Frontiers Teaching Modules, Third Edition Housed on ActivePsych Instructor's Classroom Exercise CD-ROMs and also available separatttely on CD-ROM, DVD, and VHS, this series was edited by Martin Bolt (Calvin College). The Third Edition of this acclaimed series offers you 15 new clips from contemporary segments produced between 2003 and 2005. Featuring Alan Alda, the series presents both current research and real-world applications, and offers yet another terrific way to encourage discussion and debate in your introductory psychology course.

Worth Digital Media Archive (available in dual platform CD-ROMs, VHS, and DVD) This rich presentation tool contains 42 digitized video clips of classic experiments and research. Footage includes Bandura's Bobo doll experiment, Takooshian's bystander studies, Piaget's conservation experiment, Harlow's monkey experiments, and Milgram's obedience studies. The Digital Media Archive CD-ROM clips are available in MPEG for optimal visual presentation, and are compatible with PowerPoint.

Psychology: The Human Experience Teaching Modules This series includes more than 3 hours of footage from the Introductory Psychology telecourse, *Psychology: The Human Experience*, produced by Coast Learning Systems in collaboration with Worth Publishers. Footage contains noted scholars, the latest research, and striking animations.

The Many Faces of Psychology Video (available in VHS and DVD) Created and written by Frank J. Vattano, Colorado State University, and Martin Bolt, Calvin College (produced by the Office of Instructional Services, Colorado State University), this video is a terrific way to begin your psychology course. *The Many Faces of Psychology* introduces psychology as a science and a profession, illustrating basic and applied methods. The 22-minute video presents some of the major areas in which psychologists work and teach.

Scientific American Frontiers Video Collection, Second Edition (available in VHS and DVD) Hosted by Alan Alda, these 8- to 12-minute teaching modules from the highly praised Scientific American series feature the work of such notable researchers as Steven Suomi, Renée Baillargeon, Carl Rosengren, Laura Pettito, Steven Pinker, Barbara Rothbaum, Bob Stickgold, Irene Pepperberg, Marc Hauser, Linda Bartoshuk, and Michael Gazzaniga.

The Mind Video Teaching Modules, Second Edition (available in VHS and DVD) Edited by Frank J. Vattano, Colorado State University, with the consultation of

Charles Brewer, Furman University, and myself in association with WNET, these 35 brief, engaging video clips dramatically enhance and illustrate your lectures. Examples include segments on language processing, infant cognitive development, genetic factors in alcoholism, and living without memory (featuring a dramatic interview with Clive Wearing).

The Brain Video Teaching Modules, Second Edition (available in VHS and DVD) Edited by Frank J. Vattano and Thomas L. Bennet from Colorado State University, and Michelle Butler, from the United States Air Force Academy, this collection of 32 short clips provides vivid examples for myriad topics in introductory psychology.

Print Supplements for Instructors

New! Significantly Revised and Enhanced Printed Test Bank, Volumes 1 and 2, John Brink, Calvin College Broken down into two volumes of tests, the Test Bank provides approximately 6000 multiple-choice factual/definitional, conceptual/application, and conceptual questions, plus essay questions. In response to review input from over a dozen reviewers, Brink has changed the number of distracters from 5 to 4 to avoid confusion, and he has carefully edited each question for effectiveness and comprehension. As a result, this eighth edition set includes over 20 percent new and significantly revised questions. Each question is keyed to a learning objective from the text and rated for level of difficulty. Also included are copies of the Student Book Companion site quizzes. The first Test Bank includes optional questions from the Study Guide (for instructors who incorporate or require the Study Guide in their courses). The second Test Bank includes optional questions on key Worth media tools, such as *PsychSim 5.0, The Brain* and *The Mind* video series, and *Moving Images: Exploring Psychology Through Film.*

New! Instructor's Media Guide This handy guide quickly and visually organizes the extensive instructor and student media resources available for *Psychology Eighth Edition in Modules,* including every video, animation, student Web activity (including PsychSim), PowerPoint® presentation, and more—all organized by module.

Instructor's Resources, Martin Bolt, Calvin College (also available electronically within the eLibrary) Well-known in the psychology community for its comprehensiveness and innovative teaching ideas, Martin Bolt's revised Instructor's Resources feature more than 30 percent new, revised, and updated material and include the following:

* Outline of Resources, organized by text topic, includes the relevant Instructor Resource items by type (classroom exercise, lecture/discussion topic, etc.) with appropriate Instructor Resource page number.
* Learning Objectives from the text highlight main concepts and terms and detail the key points of each text module. They can be used as essay questions in classroom examinations. The test objectives also organize the Test Bank and Study Guide.
* Module Outlines follow the major text section headings (with page references), providing relevant instructional materials for each topic—including dozens of ready-to-use detailed lecture/discussion ideas, student projects, classroom exercises (many with ready-to-use handouts for in- or out-of-class use), and suggestions about how to use the videos provided by Worth Publishers (see above), PsychSim modules, and feature films (as they apply to psychological concepts discussed in the text). Note that the films and videos from other sources are outlined in the Book Companion Site. Other Web sites are also listed and described here and the feature film descriptions are repeated on the Book Companion Site.

Martin Bolt's Lecture Guides, available in both print and easily modifiable Microsoft Word formats (as well as at the end of the Instructor's Resources), offer you a terrific integrating resource for lecture preparation. For each text module, the Lecture Guides summarize the main ideas by major section and by Learning Objective. The Lecture Guides also list the lecture/discussion topics, exercises, projects, feature films, transparencies, PsychSim modules, and video segments (from the Worth library) that complement the topics within each major section.

Overhead Transparencies Our transparency set includes over 150 text images, charts, and tables from *Psychology,* Eighth Edition, and other sources.

Print Supplements for Students

New! Visual Concept Reviews, Richard Straub, University of Michigan-Dearborn This full-color booklet—available for free when shrink-wrapped with the book or Study Guide—offers fill-in-the-blank style concept charts that allow students to apply their understanding of the concepts to real-life situations (with answers in an appendix). Some of the Concept Reviews focus on the biopsychosocial approach, thus extending the levels of analysis theme that I have further applied in the text for this edition.

Study Guide, Richard Straub, University of Michigan-Dearborn Following the text's content, Richard Straub offers a Module Overview and Module Review, divided by major section. (Each group of fill-in-the-blank and short-essay questions is preceded by the relevant Learning Objective from the text.) The Study Guide also includes three self-tests (one of which encourages students to think critically about the chapter's concepts), answers (with page references for the self-tests and explanations of why a choice is correct or incorrect), and a Focus on Language and Vocabulary section, which explains idioms and other phrases from the text that may not be clear to some readers.

***Pursuing Human Strengths: A Positive Psychology Guide,* Martin Bolt, Calvin College** By using the scientific method in its efforts to assess, understand, and then build human strengths, positive psychology balances the investigation of weakness and damage with a study of strength and virtue. This brief *Positive Psychology Guide* gives instructors and students alike the means to learn more about this relevant approach to psychology.

***Critical Thinking Companion,* Second Edition, Jane Halonen, University of West Florida, and Cynthia Gray, Alverno College** Tied to the main topics in *Psychology Eighth Edition in Modules,* this engaging handbook includes six categories of critical thinking exercises: pattern recognition, practical problem solving, creative problem solving, scientific critical thinking, psychological reasoning, and perspective taking, which connect to the six categories used in the Critical Thinking Exercises available in the Student Study Guide.

Scientific American Reader I hand picked these 14 classic and current articles to provide another tool for enhancing lectures, encouraging discussions, and emphasizing the relevance of psychology to everyday life.

Scientific American Mind This special issue explores riveting breakthroughs in neuroscience and related fields, and investigates, analyzes, and reveals new thinking on: Dreaming and Consciousness, Intelligence and Cognition, Imagination and Emotions, Depression and Mental Illness, and Perception and Understanding.

***Improving the Mind and Brain:* A Scientific American Special Issue** This single-topic issue from Scientific American magazine features findings from the most distinguished researchers in the field.

***Scientific American Explores The Hidden Mind:* A Collector's Edition** This collector's edition includes feature articles that explore and reveal the mysterious inner workings of our minds and brains.

In Appreciation

If it is true that "whoever walks with the wise becomes wise" then I am wiser for all the wisdom and advice received from expert colleagues. Aided by nearly a thousand consultants and reviewers over the last two decades, this has become a better, more accurate book than one author alone (this author, at least) could write. As my editors and I keep reminding ourselves, all of us together are smarter than any one of us.

My indebtedness continues to each of the teacher-scholars whose influence I acknowledged in the seven previous editions, and also to the innumerable researchers who have been so willing to share their time and talent to help me accurately report their research. This new edition also benefited from the creative input and assistance of Jennifer Peluso, Florida Atlantic University, in revising Modules 24 through 30, which examine memory, thinking, and language.

My gratitude extends to the colleagues who contributed criticism, corrections, and creative ideas related to the content, pedagogy, and format of *Psychology*, Eighth Edition, and its supplements package. For their expertise and encouragement, and the gifts of their time to the teaching of psychology, I thank the *Psychology*, Eighth Edition reviewers, consultants, and focus group participants listed below. For this modular edition, I am also grateful to Richard Jackson Harris (Kansas State University) for his contributions in formulating the table of contents.

Julie Allison,
Pittsburg State University

Aneeq Ahmad,
Henderson State University

Emir Andrews,
Memorial University

Willow Aureala,
University of Hawaii Center, West Hawaii

Debra K. Bagley,
Mount Aloysius College

David Barkmeier,
Northeastern University

Marcelle Bartolo-Abela,
Holyoke Community College

Scott Bates,
Utah State University

Rochelle Battersby,
Sanford H. Calhoun High School

Susan Becker,
Mesa State University

Stefanie Bell,
Pikes Peak Community College

Suzanne T. Bell,
DePaul University

Sheryl Bereziuk,
Grande Prairie Regional College

Denise Berg,
Santa Monica College

Kathleen Bey,
Palm Beach Community College

Patricia Bishop,
Cleveland State Community College

Marilyn Blumenthal
Farmingdale State University

Linda Bradford,
Community College of Aurora

Suzanne Brayer,
North Canyon High School

June Breninger,
Cascade College

Gayle Brosnan-Watters,
Slippery Rock University

Jay Brown,
Southwest Missouri State University

Michelle A. Butler,
United States Air Force Academy

Hazel Caldwell,
Central Georgia Technical College

Cari Cannon,
Santiago Canyon College

William Canu,
University of Missouri-Rolla

Maureen Carrigan,
University of South Carolina Aiken

Pamela Carroll,
Three Rivers Community College

Richard G. Cavasina,
California University of Pennsylvania

Gabriela Chavira and her graduate student teachers,
California State University-Northridge

Dorothy Chin,
Santa Monica College

Stephen M. Colarelli,
Central Michigan University

Kaye Cook,
Gordon College

Mary Coplen,
Hutchinson Community College

Pamela Costa,
Tacoma Community College

Kathleen Cramm,
Community College of Aurora

Katherine Demtrakis,
Albuquerque Technical Vocational Institute

Vicki DiLillo,
Ohio Wesleyan University

Ellie Ezatti,
Santa Monica College

Gaithri Fernando,
California State University, Los Angeles

Gloria Fisher,
Mississippi College

Jim Frailing,
Neenah High School

Sue Frantz,
Highline Community College

Rick Froman,
John Brown University

Gary Gargano,
Merced College

Carol B. George,
St. Johns School

Andrew R. Getzfeld,
New Jersey City University

Kristy Gould,
Luther College

David Gramling,
Austin Preparatory School

Nicholas Greco,
College of Lake County

Toby Green,
Santa Monica College

Laura Gruntmeir,
Redlands Community College

Mary Hannah,
University of Detroit Mercy

Peg Hanson,
College of Lake County

Chris Heavey,
University of Nevada-Las Vegas

Paul Hillock,
Algonquin College

Len Hudzinski,
Lake Tahoe Community College

Steven Isonio,
Golden West College

Charles Ivey,
Winter Park High School

Maria Janicki,
Douglas College

Robert Jensen,
California State University-Sacramento

Andrew T. Johnson
Park University

Suzanne R. Jones,
Webster University

Oscar Joseph Harm,
University of South Carolina Aiken

Misty Hull,
Pikes Peak Community College

Wendy Kallina,
Macon State College

Cindy Kamilar,
Pikes Peak Community College

Jeffry Kellogg,
Marian College

Arthur D. Kemp,
Central Missouri State University

Raymond Kilduff,
Community College of Rhode Island

Rosalyn King,
Northern Virginia Community College-Loudon

Kristina T. Klassen,
North Idaho College

Gary Klatsky,
SUNY Oswego

Timothy Klitz,
Washington and Jefferson College

Jean E. Kubeck,
Adams State College

Samuel H. Lamb III,
Tidewater Community College

Claudia Lampman,
University of Alaska

Jackie Lanum,
Santa Monica College

Elizabeth Levin,
Laurentian University

Deborah Licht,
Pikes Peak Community College

Rachelle Lipschultz,
Anne Arundel Community College

Nancey Lobb,
Alvin Community College

Jann Longman,
Liberty High School

Wade C. Lueck,
College of Eastern Utah

Angie Mackewn,
University of Tennessee at Martin

Laura Madson,
New Mexico State University

Brian Malley,
University of Michigan

Nancy B. Mann,
Southern Wesleyan University

Cindy Marriot,
Schoolcraft College

Jerry Marshall,
Green River Community College

Diane Martichuski,
University of Colorado Boulder

Cathy Matresse,
North Idaho College and Bay Mills Community College

Donna Wood McCarty,
Clayton State University

David McCone,
United States Air Force Academy

Lisa McCone,
Pine Creek High School

Donna McEwen,
Friends University

Lesley McIntyre,
SUNY Cobleskill

Polly McMahon,
Spokane Falls Community College

Jennifer Meehan Brennom,
Kirkwood Community College

Joni Mihura,
University of Toledo

Antoinette Miller,
Clayton College and State University

Jeannie Mitchell,
Rend Lake College

Mark Mitchell,
Clarion University of Pennsylvania

Marta Mohr,
Kilian Community College

Joann Morgan,
Albuquerque Technical Vocational Institute

Karlyn Musante,
Santa Monica College

Barbara Nash,
Bentley College

Nathaniel Naughton,
Arlington Catholic High School

Michael Nelson,
University of Missouri-Rolla

Benjamin Newberry,
Kent State University

Cynthia O'Dell,
Indiana University Northwest

Peggy O'Neil-Chromey,
Northfield Mount Hermon School

William H. Overman,
University of North Carolina, Wilmington

Dan Patanella,
John Jay College of Criminal Justice

Marcus D. Patterson,
University of Massachusetts-Boston

Marilyn Patterson,
Lindenwood University

Andrew Peck,
Pennsylvania State University

Jennifer Peluso,
Florida Atlantic University

Pete Petersen,
Johnson County Community College

John Petraitis,
University of Alaska

Stephen Phillips,
Broward Community College

Michelle Pilati,
Rio Hondo College

Colleen Pilgrim,
Schoolcraft College

Debbie Podwika,
Kankakee Community College

Scott Plous,
Wesleyan University

Kathryn Potoczak,
Saint Lawrence University

Michael Poulin,
University of California-Irvine

Psi Chi Honors Society and other students,
Montana State University

Jennifer Puente,
William Rainey Harper College

Diane Quartarolo,
Union Institute and University

Christopher Randall,
Troy University, Montgomery Campus

Louise Rasmussen,
Wright State University

Judith S. Rauenzahn,
Kutztown University

Celia Reaves,
Monroe Community College

Brad Redburn,
Johnson County Community College

Darrel Regier,
American Psychiatric Association

Leonard Riley,
Pikes Peak Community College

Alan Roberts,
Indiana University

June Rosenberg,
Lyndon State College

Steve Rouse,
Pepperdine University

Lisa Routh,
Pikes Peak Community College

Patricia Sampson,
University of Maryland Eastern Shore

Don Saucier,
Kansas State University

Sherry Schnake,
Saint Mary of the Woods College

John Schwoebel,
Cazenovia College

Eric Seelau,
Indiana University of Pennsylvania

Jane Sheldon,
University of Michigan–Dearborn

Mark Sibicky,
Marietta College

Cynthia Silovich,
Fargo South High School

David Simpson,
Valparaiso University

Stephanie Smith,
Indiana University Northwest

Ross B. Steinman,
Rowan University

Betsy Stern,
Milwaukee Area Technical College

Robby Stewart,
Oakland University

Christine Sutow,
Rio Hondo College

Amy Sweetman,
Los Angeles City College

Patricia Toney,
Sandhills Community College

Meral Topcu-LeCroix,
Ferris State University

Michael Trumbull,
Pikes Peak Community College

Gopakumar Venugopalan,
University of Alaska

Jeanne M. Viviani,
LaGuardia Community College

Steven L. Voss,
Moberly Area Community College

Dennis Wanamaker,
Bellevue Community College

Kathryn M. Wescott,
Juniata College

Fred Whitford,
Montana State University

Gordon Whitman,
Tidewater Community College

Eric Wiertelak,
Macalester College

Jacquie Witsberger,
Wheeling Jesuit University

Leland Woodson,
Kwantlen University College

At Worth Publishers a host of people played key roles in creating this eighth edition.

Although the information gathering is never ending, the formal planning began as the author-publisher team gathered for a two-day retreat in October 2004. This happy and creative gathering included John Brink, Martin Bolt, Thomas Ludwig, Richard Straub, and me from the author team, along with my assistant Kathryn Brownson and manuscript developer Phyllis Vandervelde. We were joined by Worth Publishers' publisher Catherine Woods; editors Christine Brune, Renee Altier, Nancy Fleming, Tracey Kuehn, and Betty Probert; and sales and marketing executives Kate Nurre, Tom Kling, Guy Geraghty, Greg David, and Chuck Linsmeier. The input and brainstorming during this meeting of minds gave birth, among other things, to the new pedagogy in this edition, and to the thoroughly revised Modules 6 and 7 on behavior genetics, evolutionary psychology, culture, and gender.

Christine Brune, chief editor for the last six editions, is a wonder worker. She offers just the right mix of encouragement, gentle admonition, attention to detail, and passion for excellence. An author could not ask for more.

Renee Altier, who is now the Director of Product and New Business Development for Bedford, Freeman, and Worth Publishers, helped connect me with many colleagues throughout the revision process, and she spearheaded a creative new photo program. Renee also played an essential role in expanding and improving the impressive multimedia supplements that accompany this edition. As Renee's supportive role shifted, she passed the baton for editorial management of our teaching package to acquisitions editor Kevin Feyen, with whom we are pleased to now be working.

Development editor Nancy Fleming is one of those rare editors who is gifted both at "thinking big" about a chapter—and with a kindred spirit to my own—while also applying her sensitive, graceful, line-by-line touches. Nancy also displayed her gifts in leading the creation of the new Learning Objectives and Learning Outcomes.

Publisher Catherine Woods helped construct and execute the plan for this new edition and its supplements. Catherine was also a trusted sounding board as we faced the myriad discrete decisions along the way. Media Editor Andrea Musick coordinated production of the huge supplements package for this edition. Betty Probert efficiently edited and produced the print supplements, and, in the process, also helped fine-tune the whole book. Editorial Assistants Sarah Berger and Matthew Driskill provided invaluable support in commissioning and organizing the multitude of reviews, mailing information to professors, and numerous other daily tasks related to the book's development and production. Lee Mahler did a splendid job of laying out each page. Patricia Marx, Bianca Moscatelli, Christina Micek, and Julie Tesser worked together to locate the myriad new photographic illustrations.

Associate Managing Editor Tracey Kuehn displayed tireless tenacity, commitment, and impressive organization in leading Worth's gifted artistic production team and coordinating editorial input throughout the production process. Production Manager Sarah Segal masterfully kept the book to its tight schedule, and Babs Reingold skillfully directed creation of the distinctive design and art program. Production Manager Stacey Alexander, along with Supplements Production Editor Eve Conte, did their usual excellent work of producing the many supplements.

To achieve our goal of supporting the teaching of psychology, this teaching package not only must be authored, reviewed, edited, and produced, but also made available to teachers of psychology. For their exceptional success in doing that, our author team is grateful to Worth Publishers' professional sales and marketing team. We are especially grateful to Associate Marketing Director Carlise Stembridge and Senior Marketing Manager Kate Nurre both for their tireless efforts to inform our teaching colleagues of our efforts to assist their teaching, and for the joy of working with them.

At Hope College, the supporting team members for this edition included Kathryn Brownson, who researched countless bits of information, proofed hundreds of pages, and, with the assistance of Sara Neevel and Megan Rapelje, prepared the bibliography and name index. Kathryn has become a knowledgeable and sensitive adviser on many matters. With diligence and delight, Travis Goldwire and Erin Darlington supported all of Kathryn's efforts by sleuthing information, photocopying, and proofreading. Laura Luchies helped compile the cross-reference table on new coverage of gender in this edition, and Laura Myers updated, with page citations, all the cross-reference tables.

Manuscript developers Phyllis and Richard Vandervelde worked faithfully to enter or revise every one of the more than 400,000 words. Over more than two decades they have processed some 10 million words of my two dozen text editions and trade books with timely diligence, a passion for excellence, a guiding voice, and an infectious joy. Amid the pleasures of creating this new edition was the enormous sadness, after four decades of close family and professional friendship, of losing Phyllis to cancer. Even its associated pain could not, however, deter her from sending me her last work package less than two weeks before her death.

Because of this unexpected loss, we are especially grateful to Marilyn Essink and Sara Neevel for so ably stepping in to meticulously complete this text project.

Again, I gratefully acknowledge the influence and editing assistance of my writing coach, poet Jack Ridl, whose influence resides in the voice you will be hearing in the pages that follow. He, more than anyone, cultivated my delight in dancing with the language, and taught me to approach writing as a craft that shades into art.

After hearing countless dozens of people say that this book's supplements have taken their teaching to a new level, I reflect on how fortunate I am to be a part of a team on which everyone has produced on-time work marked by the highest professional standards. For their remarkable talents, their long-term dedication, and their friendship, I thank Martin Bolt, John Brink, Thomas Ludwig, and Richard Straub.

Finally, my gratitude extends to the many students and instructors who have written to offer suggestions, or just an encouraging word. It is for them, and those about to begin their study of psychology, that I have done my best to introduce the field I love.

The day this book went to press was the day I started gathering information and ideas for the ninth edition. Your input will again influence how this book continues to evolve. So, please, do share your thoughts.

David Myers

Hope College
Holland, Michigan 49422-9000 USA
davidmyers.org

Timeline

The Story of Psychology: A Timeline

by Charles L. Brewer, Furman University

B.C.

387 — Plato, who believed in innate ideas, suggests that the brain is the seat of mental processes.

335 — Aristotle, who denied the existence of innate ideas, suggests that the heart is the seat of mental processes.

A.D.

1604 — Johannes Kepler describes inverted image on the retina.

1605 — Francis Bacon publishes *The Proficiency and Advancement of Learning.*

1636 — Harvard College is founded.

1637 — René Descartes, the French philosopher and mathematician who proposed mind-body interaction and the doctrine of innate ideas, publishes *A Discourse on Method.*

1690 — John Locke, the British philosopher who rejected Descartes' notion of innate ideas and insisted that the mind at birth is a "blank slate" (*tabula rasa*), publishes *An Essay Concerning Human Understanding,* which stresses empiricism over speculation.

1774 — Franz Mesmer, an Austrian physician, performs his first supposed cure using "animal magnetism" (later called Mesmerism and hypnosis). In **1777** he was expelled from the practice of medicine in Vienna.

1793 — Philippe Pinel releases the first mental patients from their chains at the Bicêtre asylum in France and advocates more humane treatment of mental patients.

1802 — Thomas Young publishes *A Theory of Color Vision* in England (his theory was later called the trichromatic theory).

1808 — Franz Joseph Gall, a German physician, describes phrenology, the belief that the shape of a person's skull reveals mental faculties and character traits.

1834 — Ernst Heinrich Weber publishes *The Sense of Touch,* in which he discusses the just noticeable difference (*jnd*) and what we now call Weber's Law.

1848 — Phineas Gage suffers massive brain damage when a large iron rod accidentally pierces his brain, leaving his intellect and memory intact but altering his personality.

1859 — Charles Darwin publishes *On the Origin of Species by Means of Natural Selection,* synthesizing much previous work on the theory of evolution, including that of Herbert Spencer, who coined the phrase "survival of the fittest."

1861 — Paul Broca, a French physician, discovers an area in the left frontal lobe of the brain (now called Broca's area) that is criti-

1905 — Ivan Petrovich Pavlov begins publishing studies of conditioning in animals.

1913 — Alfred Binet and Théodore Simon produce the first intelligence test for assessing the abilities and academic progress of Parisian schoolchildren.

1914 — John B. Watson outlines the tenets of behaviorism in a *Psychological Review* article, "Psychology as the Behaviorist Views It."

During World War I, Robert Yerkes and his staff develop a group intelligence test for evaluating U.S. military personnel, which increases the U.S. public's acceptance of psychological testing.

1920 — Leta Stetter Hollingworth publishes *The Psychology of Subnormal Children,* an early classic. In **1921** she was cited in *American Men of Science* for her research on the psychology of women.

Francis Cecil Sumner receives a Ph.D. degree in psychology from Clark University, becoming the first African-American to earn a psychology doctorate.

John B. Watson and Rosalie Rayner report conditioning a fear reaction in a child called "Little Albert."

1921 — Hermann Rorschach, a Swiss psychiatrist, introduces the Rorschach inkblot test.

1923 — Developmental psychologist Jean Piaget publishes *The Language and Thought of the Child.*

1924 — Mary Cover Jones reports reconditioning a fear reaction in a child (Peter), a forerunner of systematic desensitization developed by Joseph Wolpe.

1927 — In *Introduction to the Technique of Child Analysis,* Anna Freud discusses psychoanalysis in the treatment of children.

1929 — Wolfgang Köhler publishes *Gestalt Psychology,* which criticizes behaviorism and outlines essential elements of the Gestalt position and approach.

1931 — Margaret Floy Washburn becomes the first female psychologist (and the second female scientist in any discipline) elected to the U.S. National Academy of Sciences.

1932 — In *The Wisdom of the Body,* Walter B. Cannon coins the term *homeostasis,* discusses the fight-or-flight response, and identifies hormonal changes associated with stress.

1933 — Inez Beverly Prosser becomes the first African-American woman to receive a doctoral degree in psychology from a U.S. institution (Ed.D., University of Cincinnati).

Genius, in which he claims that intelligence is inherited. In **1876** he coined the expression "nature and nurture" to correspond with "heredity and environment."

1874 — Carl Wernicke, a German neurologist and psychiatrist, shows that damage to a specific area in the left temporal lobe (now called Wernicke's area) disrupts ability to comprehend or produce spoken or written language.

1878 — G. Stanley Hall receives from Harvard University the first Ph.D. degree in psychology awarded in the United States.

1879 — Wilhelm Wundt establishes at the University of Leipzig, Germany, the first psychology laboratory, which becomes a Mecca for psychology students from all over the world.

1883 — G. Stanley Hall, student of Wilhelm Wundt, establishes the first formal U.S. psychology laboratory at Johns Hopkins University.

1885 — Hermann Ebbinghaus publishes On Memory, summarizing his extensive research on learning and memory, including the "forgetting curve."

1889 — Alfred Binet and Henri Beaunis establish the first psychology laboratory in France at the Sorbonne, and the first International Congress of Psychology meets in Paris.

1890 — William James, Harvard University philosopher and psychologist, publishes The Principles of Psychology, describing psychology as "the science of mental life."

1891 — James Mark Baldwin establishes the first psychology laboratory in the British Commonwealth at the University of Toronto.

1892 — G. Stanley Hall spearheads the founding of the American Psychological Association (APA) and becomes its first president.

1893 — Mary Whiton Calkins (pictured) and Christine Ladd-Franklin are the first women elected to membership in the APA.

1894 — Margaret Floy Washburn is the first woman to receive a Ph.D. degree in psychology (Cornell University).

Harvard University denies Mary Whiton Calkins admission to doctoral candidacy because of her gender, despite Hugo Münsterberg's claim that she was the best student he had ever had there.

1896 — John Dewey publishes "The Reflex Arc Concept in Psychology," helping to formalize the school of psychology called functionalism.

1898 — In "Animal Intelligence," Edward L. Thorndike, Columbia University, describes his learning experiments with cats in "puzzle boxes." In **1905**, he proposed the "law of effect."

1900 — Sigmund Freud publishes The Interpretation of Dreams, his major theoretical work on psychoanalysis.

1901 — Ten founders establish the British Psychological Society.

1905 — Mary Whiton Calkins becomes the first woman president of the APA.

Christiana Morgan and Henry Murray introduce the Thematic Apperception Test to elicit fantasies from people undergoing psychoanalysis.

1936 — Egas Moniz, Portuguese physician, publishes work on the first frontal lobotomies performed on humans.

1938 — B. F. Skinner publishes The Behavior of Organisms, which describes operant conditioning of animals.

In Primary Mental Abilities, Louis L. Thurstone proposes seven such abilities.

Ugo Cerletti and Lucino Bini use electroshock treatment with a human patient.

1939 — David Wechsler publishes the Wechsler-Bellevue intelligence test, forerunner of the Wechsler Intelligence Scale for Children (WISC) and the Wechsler Adult Intelligence Scale (WAIS).

Mamie Phipps Clark receives a master's degree from Howard University. In collaboration with Kenneth B. Clark, she later extended her thesis, "The Development of Consciousness of Self in Negro Preschool Children," providing joint research cited in the U.S. Supreme Court's **1954** decision to end racial segregation in public schools.

Edward Alexander Bott helps found the Canadian Psychological Association. He becomes its first president in **1940.**

World War II provides many opportunities for psychologists to enhance the popularity and influence of psychology, especially in applied areas.

1943 — Psychologist Starke Hathaway and physician J. Charnley McKinley publish the Minnesota Multiphasic Personality Inventory (MMPI).

1945 — Karen Horney, who criticized Freud's theory of female sexual development, publishes Our Inner Conflicts.

1946 — Benjamin Spock's first edition of The Commonsense Book of Baby and Child Care appears; the book will influence child rearing in North America for several decades.

1948 — Alfred Kinsey and his colleagues publish Sexual Behavior in the Human Male.

B. F. Skinner's novel, Walden Two, describes a Utopian community based on positive reinforcement, which becomes a clarion call for applying psychological principles in everyday living, especially communal living.

Ernest R. Hilgard publishes Theories of Learning, which was required reading for several generations of psychology students in North America.

1949 — Raymond B. Cattell publishes the Sixteen Personality Factor Questionnaire (16PF).

Continued

1949 In *The Organization of Behavior: A Neuropsychological Theory*, Canadian psychologist Donald O. Hebb outlines a new and influential conceptualization of how the nervous system functions.

1950 Solomon Asch publishes studies of effects of conformity on judgments of line length.

In *Childhood and Society*, Erik Erikson outlines his stages of psychosocial development.

1951 Carl Rogers publishes *Client-Centered Therapy*.

1952 The American Psychiatric Association publishes *Diagnostic and Statistical Manual of Mental Disorders*, an influential book that will be updated periodically.

1953 Eugene Aserinski and Nathaniel Kleitman describe rapid eye movements (REM) that occur during sleep.

Janet Taylor's Manifest Anxiety Scale appears in the *Journal of Abnormal Psychology*.

1954 In *Motivation and Personality*, Abraham Maslow proposes a hierarchy of motives ranging from physiological needs to self-actualization.

James Olds and Peter Milner, McGill University neuropsychologists, describe rewarding effects of electrical stimulation of the hypothalamus in rats.

Gordon Allport publishes *The Nature of Prejudice*.

1956 In his *Psychological Review* article titled "The Magical Number Seven, Plus or Minus Two: Some Limits on Our Capacity for Processing Information," George Miller coins the term *chunk* for memory researchers.

1957 Robert Sears, Eleanor Maccoby, and Harry Levin publish *Patterns of Child Rearing*.

Charles Ferster and B. F. Skinner publish *Schedules of Reinforcement*.

1959 Noam Chomsky's critical review of B. F. Skinner's *Verbal Behavior* appears in the journal *Language*.

Eleanor Gibson and Richard Walk report their research on infants' depth perception in "The Visual Cliff."

Harry Harlow outlines "The Nature of Love," his work on attachment in monkeys.

Lloyd Peterson and Margaret Peterson in the *Journal of Experimental Psychology* article, "Short-Term Retention of Individual Verbal Items," highlight the importance of rehearsal in memory.

John Thibaut and Harold Kelley publish *The Social Psychology of Groups*.

1969 In his APA presidential address, "Psychology as a Means of Promoting Human Welfare," George Miller emphasizes the importance of "giving psychology away."

1971 Kenneth B. Clark becomes the first African-American president of the American Psychological Association.

Albert Bandura publishes *Social Learning Theory*.

Allan Paivio publishes *Imagery and Verbal Processes*.

B. F. Skinner publishes *Beyond Freedom and Dignity*.

1972 Elliot Aronson publishes *The Social Animal*.

Fergus Craik and Robert Lockhart's "Levels of Processing: A Framework for Memory Research" appears in the *Journal of Verbal Learning and Verbal Behavior*.

Robert Rescorla and Allan Wagner publish their associative model of Pavlovian conditioning.

Under the leadership of Derald Sue and Stanley Sue, the Asian-American Psychological Association is founded.

1973 Ethologists Karl von Frisch, Konrad Lorenz, and Nikolaas Tinbergen receive the Nobel Prize for their research on animal behavior.

1974 APA's Division 2 first publishes its journal, *Teaching of Psychology*, with Robert S. Daniel as editor.

Eleanor Maccoby (pictured) and Carol Jacklin publish *The Psychology of Sex Differences*.

1975 Biologist Edward O. Wilson's *Sociobiology* appears; it will be a controversial precursor to evolutionary psychology.

1976 Sandra Wood Scarr and Richard A. Weinberg publish "IQ Test Performance of Black Children Adopted by White Families" in *American Psychologist*.

1978 Psychologist Herbert A. Simon, Carnegie-Mellon University, wins a Nobel Prize for pioneering research on computer simulations of human thinking and problem solving.

1979 James J. Gibson publishes *The Ecological Approach to Visual Perception*.

Elizabeth Loftus publishes *Eyewitness Testimony*.

1981 Ellen Langer is the first woman to be granted tenure in Harvard University's Department of Psychology.

David Hubel and Torsten Wiesel receive a Nobel Prize for research on single-cell recordings that identified feature detector cells in the visual cortex.

Roger Sperry receives a Nobel Prize for research on split-brain patients.

...Paleontologist Stephen Jay Gould publishes *The Mismeasure of Man*, highlighting the debate concerning biological determination of intelligence.

1984 — The American Psychological Association creates Division 44 (Society for the Psychological Study of Lesbian and Gay Issues).

1986 — In *Intelligence Applied*, Robert Sternberg proposes the triarchic theory of intelligence.

1987 — Elizabeth Scarborough and Laurel Furumoto (pictured) publish *Untold Lives: The First Generation of American Women Psychologists*.

— Fluoxetine (Prozac) is introduced as a treatment for depression.

— Wilbert J. McKeachie, University of Michigan, receives the first APA Award for Distinguished Career Contributions to Education and Training in Psychology.

1988 — The American Psychological Society is founded. It changes its name to Association of Psychological Science in 2006.

1990 — Psychiatrist Aaron Beck receives the Distinguished Scientific Award for the Applications of Psychology for advancing understanding and treatment of psychopathology, including pivotal contributions to the development of cognitive therapy.

1990 — B. F. Skinner receives APA's first Citation for Outstanding Lifetime Contributions to Psychology and presents his last public address, "Can Psychology Be a Science of Mind?" (He died a few days later at age 86.)

1991 — The U.S. National Conference on Enhancing the Quality of Undergraduate Education in Psychology is held at St. Mary's College of Maryland, and suggestions from participants produce many salutary changes in numerous psychology programs.

— Martin Seligman publishes *Learned Optimism*, which foreshadows the "positive psychology" movement.

1992 — Teachers of Psychology in Secondary Schools (TOPSS) is established as part of the APA.

— About 3,000 U.S. secondary school students take the first Advanced Placement Examination in Psychology, hoping to earn exemption from an introductory psychology course at the post-secondary level.

1993 — Psychologist Judith Rodin is elected president of the University of Pennsylvania, becoming the first female president of an Ivy League school.

— In his *Frames of Mind*, Howard Gardner outlines his theory of multiple intelligences.

2002 — New Mexico becomes the first U.S. state to allow qualified clinical psychologists to prescribe certain drugs.

— The first International Conference on Education in Psychology is held in St. Petersburg, Russia, with Wilbert J. McKeachie and Charles L. Brewer as keynote speakers.

— Psychologist Daniel Kahneman, Princeton University, receives a Nobel Prize for research on decision making.

... Visual Presentations."

1961 — Georg von Békésy receives a Nobel Prize for research on the physiology of hearing.

— David McClelland publishes *The Achieving Society*.

1962 — Jerome Kagan and Howard Moss publish *Birth to Maturity*.

— Stanley Schachter and Jerome Singer publish findings that support the two-factor theory of emotion.

— Albert Ellis' *Reason and Emotion in Psychotherapy* appears; it is a milestone in the development of rational-emotive therapy (RET).

1963 — Raymond B. Cattell distinguishes between *fluid* and *crystallized* intelligence.

— Stanley Milgram's "Behavioral Study of Obedience" appears in the *Journal of Abnormal and Social Psychology*.

1965 — Canadian researcher Ronald Melzack and British researcher Patrick Wall propose the gate control theory of pain.

— Robert Zajonc's "Social Facilitation" is published in *Science*.

1966 — Nancy Bayley becomes the first woman to receive the APA's Distinguished Scientific Contribution Award.

— Jerome Bruner and colleagues at Harvard University's Center for Cognitive Studies publish *Studies in Cognitive Growth*.

— William Masters and Virginia Johnson publish results of their research in *Human Sexual Responses*.

— Allen Gardner and Beatrix Gardner begin training a chimpanzee (Washoe) in American Sign Language at the University of Nevada, Reno.

— John Garcia (pictured) and Robert Koelling publish a study on taste aversion in rats.

— David M. Green and John A. Swets publish *Signal Detection Theory and Psychophysics*.

— Julian Rotter publishes research on locus of control.

1967 — Ulric Neisser's *Cognitive Psychology*, helps to steer psychology away from behaviorism and toward cognitive processes.

— Martin Seligman and Steven Maier publish the results of their research with "learned helplessness" in dogs.

1968 — Richard Atkinson and Richard Shiffrin's influential three-stage memory model appears in *The Psychology of Learning and Motivation*.

— Neal E. Miller's article in *Science*, describing instrumental conditioning of autonomic responses, stimulates research on biofeedback.

1969 — Albert Bandura publishes *Principles of Behavior Modification*.

ANOTHER VOICE ON: THE HISTORY AND SCIENCE OF PSYCHOLOGY

MAYA ANGELOU (b. 1928), FROM "HUMAN FAMILY," 1994, *THE COMPLETE COLLECTED POEMS OF MAYA ANGELOU*

I note the obvious differences
in the human family.
Some of us are serious,
some thrive on comedy.

Some declare their lives are lived
as true profundity,
and others claim they really live
the real reality.

The variety of our skin tones
can confuse, bemuse, delight,
brown and pink and beige and purple,
tan and blue and white.

I've sailed upon the seven seas
and stopped in every land,

I've seen the wonders of the world,
not yet one common man.

I know ten thousand women
called Jane and Mary Jane,
but I've not seen any two
who really were the same.

Mirror twins are different
although their features jibe,
and lovers think quite different thoughts
while lying side by side.

We love and lose in China,
we weep on England's moors,
and laugh and moan in Guinea,
and thrive on Spanish shores.

We seek success in Finland,
are born and die in Maine,
In minor ways we differ,
in major we're the same.

I note the obvious differences
between each sort and type,
but we are more alike, my friends,
than we are unalike.

We are more alike, my friends,
than we are unalike.

We are more alike, my friends,
than we are unalike.

Introduction to the History and Science of Psychology

"What's it like being married to a psychologist?" people occasionally ask my wife. "Does he use his psychology on you?"

"So, does your Dad, like, analyze you?" my children have been asked many times.

"What do you think of me?" asked one barber, hoping for a personality analysis after learning that I am a psychologist.

For most people whose exposure to psychology comes from popular books, magazines, and TV, psychologists analyze personality, offer counseling, and dispense childrearing advice.

Do they? Yes, and much more. Consider some of psychology's questions that from time to time you may wonder about:

Have you ever found yourself reacting to something just as one of your biological parents would—perhaps in a way you vowed you never would—and then wondered how much of your personality you inherited? *To what extent is personality predisposed by one's genes? To what extent by one's environments?*

Have you ever wondered why a baby finds a game of peekaboo so delightful? The infant reacts as if, when you move behind a door, you disappear—only to reappear later out of thin air. *What do babies actually perceive and think?*

Have you ever awakened from a nightmare and, with great relief, wondered why you had such a crazy dream? *How often, and why, do we dream?*

Have you ever wondered what leads to success? Are some people just born smarter? *Does sheer intelligence explain why some people get richer, think more creatively, or relate more sensitively?*

Have you ever become depressed or anxious and wondered whether you'll ever feel "normal"? *What triggers our bad moods—and our good ones?*

Have you ever worried about how to act among people of a different culture, race, or gender? *In what ways are we alike as members of the human family? How do we differ?*

Such questions provide grist for psychology's mill because psychology is a science that seeks to answer all sorts of questions about us all: how we think, feel, and act. In Module 1, we trace psychology's roots and survey its scope. In Module 2, we consider how psychological science can help you to think critically in everyday life and to understand some dangers in relying too heavily on intuition and common sense. In Module 3, we survey psychology's methods—how psychologists ask and answer questions.

A smile is a smile the world around
Throughout this book, you will see examples not only of our cultural and gender diversity but also of the similarities that define our shared human nature. People in different cultures vary in when and how often they smile, but a smile *means* the same thing anywhere in the world.

© Stock Image/Alamy

Sally Cassidy/The Picture Cube/Index Stock Imagery

Robert Caputo/Stock, Boston

1-1

MODULE

1

The History and Scope of Psychology

Psychology's Roots

OBJECTIVE **1-1** | Define *psychology*.

Once upon a time, on a planet in your neighborhood of the universe, there came to be people. Soon thereafter, these creatures became intensely interested in themselves and in one another. They wondered, *"Who are we? From where come our thoughts? Our feelings? Our actions? And how are we to understand—and to master or manage—those around us?"* Psychology's answers to these wonderings have developed from international roots in philosophy and biology into a science that aims to describe and explain how we think, feel, and act. Today we define **psychology** as *the scientific study of behavior and mental processes.* Let's unpack this definition. *Behavior* is anything an organism *does*—any action we can observe and record. Yelling, smiling, blinking, sweating, talking, and questionnaire marking are all observable behaviors. *Mental processes* are the internal, subjective experiences we infer from behavior—sensations, perceptions, dreams, thoughts, beliefs, and feelings.

The key word in psychology's definition is *science. Psychology is less a set of findings than a way of asking and answering questions.* As science, psychology evaluates competing ideas with careful observation and rigorous analysis. In its attempt to describe and explain human nature, psychological science welcomes hunches and plausible-sounding theories. And it puts them to the test. If a theory works—if the data support its predictions—so much the better for that theory. If the predictions fail, the theory will be revised or rejected.

My aim in this text, then, is not merely to report results but also to show you how psychologists play their game. You will see how researchers evaluate conflicting opinions and ideas. And you will learn how all of us, whether scientists or simply curious people, can think smarter when describing and explaining the events of our lives.

But first, let's consider the roots of today's psychology to help us appreciate psychologists' varied perspectives.

Prescientific Psychology

OBJECTIVE **1-2** | Trace psychology's prescientific roots, from early understandings of mind and body to the beginnings of modern science.

We can trace many of psychology's current questions back through human history. These early thinkers wondered: How do our minds work? How do our bodies relate to our minds? How much of what we know comes built in? How much is acquired through experience? In India, for example, Buddha pondered how sensations and perceptions combine to form ideas. In China, Confucius stressed the power of ideas and of an educated mind. In ancient Israel, Hebrew scholars anticipated today's psychology by linking mind and emotion to the body; people were said to think with their hearts and feel with their bowels.

In ancient Greece, the philosopher-teacher Socrates (469–399 B.C.) and his student Plato (428–348 B.C.) concluded that mind is separable from body and continues after the body dies, and that knowledge is innate—born within us. As Socrates lay dying, Plato's future student, a teenager named Aristotle (384–322 B.C.), was developing a sharp mind in another part of Greece. Aristotle's love of data distinguished him from Socrates and Plato, who derived principles by logic. An intellectual ancestor of today's scientists, Aristotle derived principles from careful observations. His observations told him that "the soul is not separable from the body, and the same holds good of particular parts of the soul" (*De Anima*). Moreover, he said knowledge is *not* preexisting (sorry, Socrates and Plato); instead, it grows from the experiences stored in our memories.

The next 2000 years brought few enduring new insights into human nature, but that changed in the 1600s, when modern science began to flourish. With it came new theories of human behavior, and new versions of the ancient debates. A frail but brilliant Frenchman named René Descartes (1595–1650) agreed with Socrates and Plato about the existence of innate ideas and the mind's being "entirely distinct from the body" and able to survive its death. Descartes' concept of mind forced him to conjecture, as people have ever since, how the immaterial mind and physical body communicate. A scientist as well as a philosopher, Descartes dissected animals and concluded that the fluid in the brain's cavities contained "animal spirits." These spirits, he surmised, flowed from the brain through what we call the nerves (which he thought were hollow) to the muscles, provoking movement. Memories formed as experiences opened pores in the brain, into which the animal spirits also flowed.

A seventeenth-century view of nerves In his *Treatise of Man*, Descartes proposed the hydraulics of a simple reflex.

Descartes was right that nerve paths are important and that they enable reflexes. Yet, genius though he was, and standing upon the knowledge accumulated from 99+ percent of our human history, he hardly had a clue of what today's average 12-year-old knows. Indeed, most of the scientific story of our self-exploration—the story told in this book's modules—has been written in but the last historical eyeblink of human time.

Meanwhile, across the English channel in Britain, science was taking a more down-to-earth form, centered on experiment, experience, and common-sense judgment. Francis Bacon (1561–1626) became one of the founders of modern science, and his influence lingers in the experiments of today's psychological science. Bacon also was fascinated by the human mind and its failings. Anticipating what we have come to appreciate about our mind's hunger to perceive patterns even in random events, he wrote that "the human understanding, from its peculiar nature, easily supposes a greater degree of order and equality in things than it really finds" (*Novum Organuum*). He also foresaw research findings on our noticing and remembering events that confirm our beliefs: "All superstition is much the same whether it be that of astrology, dreams, omens . . . in all of which the deluded believers observe events which are fulfilled, but neglect and pass over their failure, though it be much more common."

Some 50 years after Bacon's death, John Locke (1632–1704), a British political philosopher, sat down to write a one-page essay on "our own abilities" for an upcoming discussion with friends. After 20 years and hundreds of pages, Locke had completed one of history's latest and greatest late papers (*An Essay Concerning Human Understanding*), in which he famously argued that the mind at birth is a blank slate—a "white paper"—on which experience writes. This idea, adding to Bacon's ideas, helped form modern **empiricism,** the view that knowledge originates in experience and that science should, therefore, rely on observation and experimentation.

Psychological Science Is Born

OBJECTIVE 1-3 | Explain how the early psychologists sought to understand the mind's structure and functions, and identify some leading psychologists who worked in these areas.

Philosophers' thinking about thinking continued until the birth of psychology as we know it, on a December day in 1879, in a small room on the third floor of a shabby building at Germany's University of Leipzig. There, two young men were helping an

■ **psychology** the scientific study of behavior and mental processes.

■ **empiricism** the view that (a) knowledge comes from experience via the senses, and (b) science flourishes through observation and experiment.

Wilhelm Wundt
Wundt (far left) established the first psychology laboratory at the University of Leipzig, Germany.

Information sources are cited in parentheses, with name and date, then provided fully in the References section at the book's end.

austere, middle-aged professor, Wilhelm Wundt, create an experimental apparatus. Their machine measured the time lag between people's hearing a ball hit a platform and their pressing a telegraph key. Later, the researchers compared this lag with the time required for slightly more complex tasks. Curiously, people responded in about one-tenth of a second when asked to press the key as soon as the sound occurred—and in about two-tenths of a second when asked to press the key as soon as they were consciously aware of perceiving the sound. (To be aware of one's awareness takes a little longer.) Wundt was seeking to measure "atoms of the mind"—the fastest and simplest mental processes (Hunt, 1993). Thus began what many consider psychology's first experiment, launching the first psychological laboratory, staffed by Wundt and psychology's first graduate students.

Before long this new science of psychology became organized into different branches, or schools of thought, each promoted by pioneering thinkers. These early schools included *structuralism* and *functionalism,* described here, and Gestalt psychology, behaviorism, and psychoanalysis, described in other modules.

Thinking About the Mind's Structure

Soon after receiving his Ph.D. in 1892, Wundt's student Edward Bradford Titchener joined the Cornell University faculty and introduced **structuralism.** As physicists and chemists discerned the structure of matter, so Titchener aimed to discover the elements of mind. His method was to engage people in self-reflective *introspection* (looking inward), training them to report elements of their experience as they looked at a rose, listened to a metronome, smelled a scent, or tasted a substance. What were their immediate sensations, their images, their feelings? And how did these relate to one another? Titchener shared with the English essayist C. S. Lewis (1960, pp. 18–19) the view that "there is one thing, and only one in the whole universe which we know more

Edward Bradford Titchener
Used introspection to search for the mind's structural elements.

The rose is smooth-petaled, sweetly aromatic,...

about than we could learn from external observation." That one thing, Lewis said, is ourselves. "We have, so to speak, inside information."

Alas, structuralism waned as introspection waned. Introspection required smart, verbal people. It also proved somewhat unreliable, its results varying from person to person and experience to experience. Moreover, recent studies indicate that people's recollections frequently err. So do their self-reports about what, for example, has caused them to help or hurt another (Myers, 2002). Often we just don't know why we feel what we feel and do what we do.

"You don't know your own mind."
Jonathan Swift, *Polite Conversation*, 1738

Thinking About the Mind's Functions

Unlike those hoping to assemble the structure of mind from simple elements—which was rather like trying to understand a car by examining its disconnected parts—philosopher-psychologist William James thought it more fruitful to consider the evolved *functions* of our thoughts and feelings. Smelling is what the nose does; thinking is what the brain does. But why do the nose and brain do these things? Under the influence of evolutionary theorist Charles Darwin, James assumed that thinking, like smelling, developed because it was adaptive—it contributed to our ancestors' survival. Consciousness serves a function. It enables us to consider our past, adjust to our present circumstances, and plan our future. As a **functionalist,** James encouraged explorations of down-to-earth emotions, memories, will power, habits, and moment-to-moment streams of consciousness.

James' greatest legacy, however, came less from his laboratory than from his Harvard teaching and his writing. When not plagued by ill health and depression, James was an impish, outgoing, and joyous man, who once recalled that "the first lecture on psychology I ever heard was the first I ever gave." During one of his wise-cracking lectures, a student interrupted and asked him to get serious (Hunt, 1993). He was reportedly one of the first American professors to solicit end-of-course student evaluations of his teaching. He loved his students, his family, and the world of ideas, but tired of painstaking chores such as proofreading. "Send me no proofs!" he once told an editor. "I will return them unopened and never speak to you again" (Hunt, 1993, p. 145).

James displayed the same spunk in 1890, when—over the objections of Harvard's president—he admitted Mary Calkins into his graduate seminar (Scarborough & Furumoto, 1987). When Calkins joined, all the other students dropped. (In those years women lacked even the right to vote.) So James tutored her alone. Later she finished all the requirements for a Harvard Ph.D., outscoring all the male students on the qualifying exams. Alas, Harvard denied her the degree she had earned, offering her instead a degree from Radcliffe College, its undergraduate sister school for women. Calkins resisted the unequal treatment and refused the degree. More than a century later, psychologists and psychology students were lobbying Harvard to posthumously award the Ph.D. she earned (*Feminist Psychologist,* 2002).

Calkins nevertheless became a distinguished memory researcher and the American Psychological Association's (APA's) first female president in 1905. What a different world from the recent past—1996 to 2005—when women claimed two-thirds or more of new psychology Ph.D.s and were 5 of the 10 elected presidents of the science-oriented American Psychological Society. In Canada and Europe, too, most recent psychology doctorates have been earned by women.

When Harvard denied Calkins the claim to being psychology's first female psychology Ph.D., that honor fell to Margaret Floy Washburn, who later wrote an influential book, *The Animal Mind,* and became the second female APA president in 1921. Although Washburn's thesis was the first foreign study Wundt published in his journal, her gender meant she was barred from joining the organization of experimental psychologists founded by Titchener, her own graduate adviser (Johnson, 1997).

James' influence reached even further through his dozens of well-received articles, which moved the publisher Henry Holt to offer a contract for a textbook of the new science of psychology. James agreed and began work in 1878, with an apology for requesting two years to finish his writing. The work proved an unexpected chore and actually took him 12 years. (Why am I not surprised?) More than a century later, people still read the resulting *Principles of Psychology* and marvel at the brilliance and elegance with which James introduced psychology to the educated public.

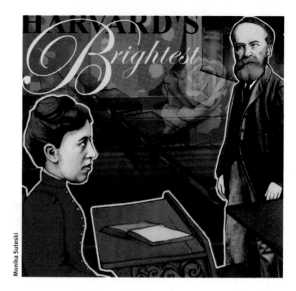

Monika Suteski

**William James and
Mary Whiton Calkins**
James, legendary teacher-writer, mentored Calkins, who became a pioneering memory researcher and American Psychological Association president.

■ **structuralism** an early school of psychology that used introspection to explore the elemental structure of the human mind.

■ **functionalism** a school of psychology that focused on how mental and behavioral processes function—how they enable the organism to adapt, survive, and flourish.

Margaret Floy Washburn
The first woman to receive a psychology Ph.D.; synthesized animal behavior research in *The Animal Mind.*

Monika Suteski

Sigmund Freud
Famed personality theorist and therapist, whose controversial ideas influenced humanity's self-understanding.

Psychological Science Develops

OBJECTIVE 1-4 | Describe the evolution of psychology as defined from the 1920s through today.

This young science of psychology developed from the more established fields of philosophy and biology. Wundt was both a philosopher and a physiologist. James was an American philosopher. Ivan Pavlov, who pioneered the study of learning, was a Russian physiologist. Sigmund Freud, who developed an influential theory of personality, was an Austrian physician. Jean Piaget, the last century's most influential observer of children, was a Swiss biologist. This list of pioneering psychologists—"Magellans of the mind," as Morton Hunt (1993) has called them—illustrates psychology's origins in many disciplines and countries.

The rest of the story of psychology—the subject of this book—develops at many levels. With activities ranging from psychotherapy to the study of nerve cell activity, *psychology* is not easily defined. Wundt and Titchener focused on *inner* sensations, images, and feelings. James, too, engaged in introspective examination of the stream of consciousness and of emotion. Freud emphasized the ways emotional responses to childhood experiences and our unconscious thought processes affect our behavior. Thus, until the 1920s, *psychology* was defined as "the science of mental life."

From the 1920s into the 1960s, American psychologists, initially led by flamboyant and provocative John B. Watson and later by the equally provocative B. F. Skinner, dismissed introspection and redefined *psychology* as "the scientific study of observable behavior." After all, said these *behaviorists,* science is rooted in observation. You cannot observe a sensation, a feeling, or a thought, but you *can* observe and record people's *behavior* as they respond to different situations.

Humanistic psychology was a softer, 1960s response to Freudian psychology and to behaviorism, which pioneers Carl Rogers and Abraham Maslow found too mechanistic. Rather than calling up childhood memories or focusing on learned behaviors, Rogers and Maslow both emphasized the importance of current environmental influences on our growth potential, and the importance of meeting our needs for love and acceptance.

In the 1960s, psychology began to recapture its initial interest in mental processes through studies of how our mind processes and retains information. This *cognitive*

■ **humanistic psychology** historically significant perspective that emphasized the growth potential of healthy people; used personalized methods to study personality in hopes of fostering personal growth.

John B. Watson and Rosalie Rayner
Working with Rayner, Watson championed psychology as the science of behavior and demonstrated conditioned responses on a baby who became famous as "Little Albert."

B. F. Skinner
A leading behaviorist, who rejected introspection and studied how consequences shape behavior.

revolution supported ideas developed by earlier psychologists, such as the importance of considering internal thought processes, but it expanded upon those ideas to explore scientifically the ways we perceive, process, and remember information. Cognitive psychology and more recently *cognitive neuroscience* (the study of the interaction of thought processes and brain function) have been especially beneficial in expanding the understanding and treatment of disorders such as depression.

To encompass psychology's concern with observable behavior *and* with inner thoughts and feelings, we define *psychology* today as the scientific study of behavior *and* mental processes.

Courtesy Nancy S. Breland

Psychology's scope and history
In her quilt, "Crazy About Psychology," Nancy S. Breland, a psychology professor at the College of New Jersey, captures images and people from psychology's first century.

Contemporary Psychology

Like its pioneers, today's psychologists are citizens of many lands. The International Union of Psychological Science has 69 member nations, from Albania to Zimbabwe. Nearly everywhere, membership in psychological societies is mushrooming—from 4183 American Psychological Association members and affiliates in 1945 to more than 160,000 today, with similarly rapid growth in Britain (from 1100 to 34,000). In China, five universities had psychology departments in 1985; by the century's end, there were 50 (Jing, 1999). Worldwide, some 500,000 people have been trained as psychologists, and 130,000 of them belong to European psychological organizations (Tikkanen, 2001). Moreover, thanks to international publications, joint meetings, and the Internet, collaboration and communication cross borders more now than ever: "We are moving rapidly towards a single world of psychological science," reports Robert Bjork (2000). Psychology is *growing* and it is *globalizing*.

Today's psychologists debate some enduring issues and view behavior from differing perspectives. They also teach, work, and do research in many different subfields.

Psychology's Big Debate

OBJECTIVE 1-5 | Summarize the nature-nurture debate in psychology, and describe the principle of natural selection.

During its short history, psychology has wrestled with some issues that will reappear throughout this book. The biggest and most persistent issue concerns *the relative contributions of biology and experience.* As we have seen, the origins of this **nature-nurture** debate are ancient. Do our human traits develop through experience, or do we come equipped with them? The ancient Greeks debated this, with Plato assuming that character and intelligence are largely inherited and that certain ideas are also inborn, and Aristotle countering that there is nothing in the mind that does not first come in from the external world through the senses. In the 1600s, philosophers rekindled the debate. Locke rejected the notion of inborn ideas, offering his notion that the mind is a blank sheet on which experience writes. Descartes disagreed, believing that some ideas are innate.

Two centuries later, Descartes' views gained support from a curious naturalist. In 1831, an indifferent student but ardent collector of beetles, mollusks, and shells set sail on what was to prove a historic round-the-world journey. The 22-year-old voyager was Charles Darwin, and for some time afterward, he pondered the incredible species variation he had encountered, including tortoises on one island that differed from those on other islands of the region. Darwin's 1859 *Origin of Species* explained this diversity of life by proposing an evolutionary process. From among chance variations in organisms, he believed, nature selects those that best enable an organism to survive and reproduce in a particular environment. Darwin's principle of **natural selection**—"the single best idea anyone has ever had," says philosopher Daniel Dennett (1996)—is still with us nearly 150 years later as an organizing principle of biology. Evolution also has become an important principle for twenty-first century psychology. This would surely have pleased Darwin, for he believed his theory

■ **nature-nurture issue** the longstanding controversy over the relative contributions that genes and experience make to the development of psychological traits and behaviors.

■ **natural selection** the principle that, among the range of inherited trait variations, those contributing to reproduction and survival will most likely be passed on to succeeding generations.

Charles Darwin
Argued that natural selection shapes behaviors as well as bodies.

Monika Suteski

A nature-made nature-nurture experiment
Because identical twins have the same genes, they are ideal participants in studies designed to shed light on hereditary and environmental influences on temperament, intelligence, and other traits. Studies of identical and fraternal twins provide a rich array of findings that underscore the importance of both nature and nurture.

explained not only animal structures (such as why polar bear coats are white) but also animal behaviors (such as the emotional expressions associated with lust and rage).

The nature-nurture debate weaves a thread from the distant past to our time. Today's psychologists have continued the debate by asking:

- How are differences in intelligence, personality, and psychological disorders influenced by heredity and by environment?
- Is children's grammar mostly innate or formed by experience?
- Are sexual behaviors more "pushed" by inner biology or "pulled" by external incentives?
- Should we treat depression as a disorder of the brain or a disorder of thought—or both?
- How are we humans alike (because of our common biology and evolutionary history) and different (because of our differing environments)?
- Are gender differences biologically predisposed or socially constructed?

The debate continues. Yet over and over again we will see that in contemporary science the nature-nurture tension dissolves: *Nurture works on what nature endows.* Our species is biologically endowed with an enormous capacity to learn and adapt. Moreover, every psychological event (every thought, every emotion) is simultaneously a biological event. Thus depression can be *both* a thought disorder and a brain disorder.

Psychology's Three Main Levels of Analysis

OBJECTIVE 1-6 | Identify the three main levels of analysis in the biopsychosocial approach, and explain why psychology's varied perspectives are complementary.

Each of us is a complex system that is part of a larger social system, but each of us is also composed of smaller systems, such as our nervous system and body organs, which are composed of still smaller systems—cells, molecules, and atoms.

These different systems suggest different **levels of analysis,** which offer complementary outlooks. It's like explaining why grizzly bears hibernate. Is it because hibernation enhanced their ancestors' survival and reproduction? Because their inner physiology drives them to do so? Because cold environments hinder food gathering during winter? Such perspectives are complementary, because "everything is related to everything else" (Brewer, 1996). Together, different levels of analysis form an integrated **biopsychosocial approach,** which considers the influences of biological, psychological, and social-cultural factors (**FIGURE 1.1**). Each level provides a valuable vantage point for looking at behavior, yet each by itself is incomplete.

FIGURE 1.1
Biopsychosocial approach
This integrated viewpoint incorporates various levels of analysis and offers a more complete picture of any given behavior or mental process.

Biological influences:
- genetic predispositions
- genetic mutations
- natural selection of adaptive physiology and behaviors
- genes responding to the environment

Psychological influences:
- learned fears and other learned expectations
- emotional responses
- cognitive processing and perceptual interpretations

Behavior or mental process

Social-cultural influences:
- presence of others
- cultural, societal, and family expectations
- peer and other group influences
- compelling models (such as the media)

TABLE **1.1**

PSYCHOLOGY'S CURRENT PERSPECTIVES

Perspective	Focus	Sample Questions
Neuroscience	How the body and brain enable emotions, memories, and sensory experiences	How are messages transmitted within the body? How is blood chemistry linked with moods and motives?
Evolutionary	How the natural selection of traits promotes the perpetuation of one's genes	How does evolution influence behavior tendencies?
Behavior genetics	How much our genes and our environment influence our individual differences	To what extent are psychological traits such as intelligence, personality, sexual orientation, and vulnerability to depression attributable to our genes? To our environment?
Psychodynamic	How behavior springs from unconscious drives and conflicts	How can someone's personality traits and disorders be explained in terms of sexual and aggressive drives or as the disguised effects of unfulfilled wishes and childhood traumas?
Behavioral	How we learn observable responses	How do we learn to fear particular objects or situations? What is the most effective way to alter our behavior, say, to lose weight or stop smoking?
Cognitive	How we encode, process, store, and retrieve information	How do we use information in remembering? Reasoning? Solving problems?
Social-cultural	How behavior and thinking vary across situations and cultures	How are we—as Africans, Asians, Australians, or North Americans—alike as members of one human family? As products of different environmental contexts, how do we differ?

Consider, for example, how psychology's varied perspectives described in **TABLE 1.1** can supplement one another and shed light on anger.

- Someone working from a *neuroscience perspective* might study brain circuits that produce the physical state of being "red in the face" and "hot under the collar."
- Someone working from the *evolutionary perspective* might analyze how anger facilitated the survival of our ancestors' genes.
- Someone working from the *behavior genetics perspective* might study how heredity and experience influence our individual differences in temperament.
- Someone working from the *psychodynamic perspective* might view an outburst as an outlet for unconscious hostility.
- Someone working from the *behavioral perspective* might study the facial expressions and body gestures that accompany anger, or might attempt to determine which external stimuli result in angry responses or aggressive acts.
- Someone working from the *cognitive perspective* might study how our interpretation of a situation affects our anger and how our anger affects our thinking.
- Someone working from the *social-cultural perspective* might explore which situations produce the most anger, and how expressions of anger vary across cultural contexts.

This important point—that different perspectives can complement one another—is also true of the different academic disciplines. Each academic perspective has its questions and its limits. A perfume manufacturer needs chemistry to create its products, psychology to know what will sell, and marketing and business to turn a profit. Differing academic perspectives are like different two-dimensional views of a three-dimensional object. Each two-dimensional perspective is helpful, but by itself fails to reveal the whole picture.

So bear in mind psychology's limits. Don't expect it to answer the ultimate questions, such as those posed by Russian novelist Leo Tolstoy (1904): "Why should I live? Why should I do anything? Is there in life any purpose which the inevitable death that awaits me does not undo and destroy?" Instead, expect that psychology will help you understand why people think, feel, and act as they do. Then you should find the study of psychology fascinating and useful.

Gabe Palmer/Corbis

Views of anger
How would each of psychology's levels of analysis (see Figure 1.1) explain what's going on here?

Want to learn more? See Appendix A, Careers in Psychology, at the end of this book for more information about psychology's subfields and to learn about the many interesting options available to those with bachelor's, master's, and doctoral degrees in psychology.

■ **levels of analysis** the differing complementary views, from biological to psychological to social-cultural, for analyzing any given phenomenon.

■ **biopsychosocial approach** an integrated perspective that incorporates biological, psychological, and social-cultural levels of analysis.

■ **basic research** pure science that aims to increase the scientific knowledge base.

■ **applied research** scientific study that aims to solve practical problems.

■ **counseling psychology** a branch of psychology that assists people with problems in living (often related to school, work, or marriage) and in achieving greater well-being.

■ **clinical psychology** a branch of psychology that studies, assesses, and treats people with psychological disorders.

■ **psychiatry** a branch of medicine dealing with psychological disorders; practiced by physicians who sometimes provide medical (for example, drug) treatments as well as psychological therapy.

Psychology's Subfields

OBJECTIVE 1-7 | Identify some of psychology's subfields, and explain the difference between clinical psychology and psychiatry.

Psychology is a collection of diverse subfields. Some psychologists do basic research, some do applied research, and some provide professional services. Picturing a chemist at work, you probably envision a white-coated scientist surrounded by glassware and high-tech equipment. Picture a psychologist at work and you would be right to envision

- a white-coated scientist probing a rat's brain.
- an intelligence researcher measuring how quickly an infant becomes bored with (looks away from) a familiar picture.
- an executive evaluating a new "healthy life-styles" training program for employees.
- someone at a computer keyboard analyzing data on whether adopted teens' temperaments more closely resemble those of their adoptive parents or those of their biological parents.
- a therapist listening carefully to a client's depressed thoughts.
- a traveler en route to another culture to collect data on variations in human values and behaviors.
- a teacher or writer sharing the joy of psychology with others.

The cluster of subfields we call psychology has less unity than most other sciences. But there is a payoff: Psychology is a meeting ground for different disciplines and is thus a perfect home for those with wide-ranging interests. In their diverse activities, from biological experimentation to cultural comparisons, a common quest unites the tribe of psychology: to describe and explain behavior and the mind underlying it.

Some psychologists conduct **basic research** that builds psychology's knowledge base. In the pages that follow we will meet a wide variety of such researchers:

- *Biological psychologists* exploring the links between brain and mind
- *Developmental psychologists* studying our changing abilities from womb to tomb
- *Cognitive psychologists* experimenting with how we perceive, think, and solve problems
- *Personality psychologists* investigating our persistent traits
- *Social psychologists* exploring how we view and affect one another

These psychologists also may conduct **applied research** that tackles practical problems. So do other psychologists, such as *industrial/organizational psychologists* as they study and advise on behavior in the workplace. They use psychology's concepts and methods to help organizations and companies select and train employees more effectively, to boost morale and productivity, to design products, and to implement systems.

Although most psychology textbooks focus on psychological science, psychology is also a helping profession devoted to such practical issues as how to have a happy marriage, how to overcome anxiety or depression, and how to raise thriving children. **Counseling psychologists** help people cope with challenges (including academic, vocational, and marital issues) by recognizing their strengths and resources. **Clinical psychologists** assess and treat mental, emotional, and behavior disorders (APA, 2003). Both counseling and clinical psychologists administer and interpret tests, provide counseling and therapy, and sometimes conduct basic and applied research. By contrast, **psychiatrists,** who also often provide psychotherapy, are medical doctors licensed to prescribe drugs and otherwise treat physical causes of psychological disorders. (Some clinical psychologists are lobbying for a similar right to prescribe mental health–related drugs, and in 2002 New Mexico was the first state to grant that right to specially trained and licensed psychologists.)

With perspectives ranging from the biological to the social, and with settings from the laboratory to the clinic, psychology relates to many disciplines. More and more, psychology connects with fields ranging from mathematics to biology to sociology to philosophy. And more and more, psychology's methods and findings aid other disciplines.

"I'm a social scientist, Michael. That means I can't explain electricity or anything like that, but if you ever want to know about people I'm your man."

Michael Newman/Photo Edit

Jeff Greenberg/PhotoEdit

Psychologists teach in medical schools, law schools, and theological seminaries, and they work in hospitals, factories, and corporate offices. They engage in interdisciplinary studies, such as psychohistory (the psychological analysis of historical characters), psycholinguistics (the study of language and thinking), and psychoceramics (the study of crackpots).[1]

Psychology also influences modern culture. Knowledge transforms us. Learning about the solar system and the germ theory of disease alters the way people think and act. Learning psychology's findings also changes people: They less often judge psychological disorders as a moral failing, treatable by punishment and ostracism. They less often regard and treat women as men's mental inferiors. They less often view and rear children as ignorant, willful beasts in need of taming. "In each case," notes Morton Hunt (1990, p. 206), "knowledge has modified attitudes, and, through them, behavior." Once aware of psychology's well-researched ideas— about how body and mind connect, how a child's mind grows, how we construct our perceptions, how we remember (and misremember) our experiences, how people across the world differ (and are alike)—your mind may never again be quite the same.

Michael Newman/Photo Edit

Psychology:
A science and a profession
Psychologists experiment with, observe, test, and treat behavior. Here we see psychologists testing a child, recording children's behavior through a two-way mirror, and doing face-to-face therapy.

"Once expanded to the dimensions of a larger idea, [the mind] never returns to its original size."

Oliver Wendell Holmes, 1809–1894

[1]Confession time: I wrote the last part of this sentence on April Fools' Day.

Laura Dwight

I see you!
A biological psychologist might view this child's delighted response as evidence of brain maturation. A cognitive psychologist might see it as a demonstration of the baby's growing knowledge of his surroundings. For a cross-cultural psychologist, the role of grandparents in different societies might be the issue of interest. As you will see throughout this book, these and other perspectives offer complementary views of behavior.

CLOSE-UP:

YOUR STUDY OF PSYCHOLOGY

OBJECTIVE 1-8 | Describe some effective study techniques.

The investment you are making in studying psychology should enrich your life and enlarge your vision. Although many of life's significant questions are beyond psychology, some very important ones are illuminated by even a first psychology course. Through painstaking research, psychologists have gained insights into brain and mind, depression and joy, dreams and memories. Even the unanswered questions can enrich us, by renewing our sense of mystery about "things too wonderful" for us yet to understand. What is more, your study of psychology can help teach you *how to ask and answer important questions*—how to think critically as you evaluate competing ideas and claims.

Having your life enriched and your vision enlarged (and getting a decent grade) requires effective study. To master information you must *actively process* it. Your mind is not like your stomach, something to be filled passively; it is more like a muscle that grows stronger with exercise. Countless experiments reveal that people learn and remember material best when they put it in their own words, rehearse it, and then review and rehearse it again.

A simple study method incorporates these principles. You can remember it as SQ3R: *Survey, Question, Read, Review,* and *Reflect.*

First, *survey* what you're about to read, including module outlines and section heads. Note a section's main topic, as indicated by the learning objective at the beginning. This will focus your reading and study.

Keep the learning objective in mind as a *question* you will attempt to answer as you *read* the section. Usually a single module—sometimes just a main section within a module—will be as much as you can absorb without tiring. Read actively and critically. Ask questions. Make notes. Consider implications: How does what you've read support or challenge your assumptions? How convincing is the evidence? How does it relate to your own life?

Finally, *review* and *reflect*. To root a module's organization more deeply in your memory, rescan the module

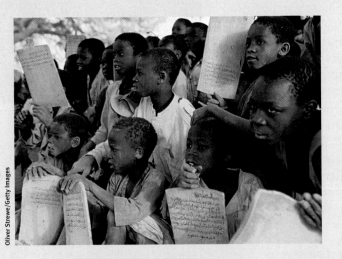

Learning how to ask and answer important questions
The basic study tips in this box are beneficial to students at all levels and in all places, including these children at a village school in Niger.

and the marginal definitions of key terms. Study the Learning Outcomes at the end of each module. Quiz yourself with the end-of-module Test Yourself questions and, perhaps, by taking quizzes in the book's accompanying study guide and on-line learning resources (at www.worth publishers.com/myers). Glance over your notes or highlighting. Then stop and let it all sink in. Better yet, summarize the material for a friend or lecture about it to an imaginary audience.

Survey, question, read, review, reflect. I have organized the modules to facilitate your using the SQ3R study method. Each module begins with an outline that helps you survey what is upcoming, and each main section begins with a learning objective. I have divided modules into shorter sections of readable length. To assist your reviewing, each module ends with a Learning Outcomes narrative summary, followed by an organized reminder of key terms and a big-picture Test Yourself question. Finally, an Ask Yourself question is designed to help you reflect—applying what you've learned to your own life to make the material more meaningful and memorable. Survey, question, read, review, reflect.

Five additional study hints may further boost your learning:

Distribute your study time: One of psychology's oldest findings is that spaced practice promotes better retention than massed practice. You'll remember material better if you space your time over several study periods—perhaps one hour a day, six days a week—rather than cram it into one long study blitz. Spacing your study sessions requires a disciplined approach to managing your time. (Richard O. Straub explains time management in the helpful *Study Guide* that accompanies this text.)

In class, listen actively: As psychologist William James urged some 100 years ago, *"No reception without reaction, no impression without . . . expression."* Listen for the main idea and sub-ideas in lectures. *Write them down.* Ask questions during and after class. In class, as in your private study, process the information actively and you will understand and retain it better.

Overlearn. Psychology tells us that "overlearning improves retention." The more often students read assigned material and the fewer classes they miss, the better their exam scores are (Woehr & Cavell, 1993). Students frequently stop short of overlearning and overestimate how much they know. Really *learning* something requires more than momentarily understanding it. You may understand a module as you read it, but if you devote extra study time to rereading, to testing yourself, and to reviewing what you think you know, you will actually *learn* the material and retain your new knowledge longer.

Focus on the big ideas. It helps to step back periodically and see the big picture so that you know how all the facts and research fit together. To understand and appreciate psychology's lessons, for example, it's important to read about the research that informs them, but it is also important to watch for the bigger concepts and themes that psychologists construct from these smaller findings. Among this book's big ideas are these:

- Critical thinking and scientific scrutiny help us think smarter about many things.

- We gain understanding by viewing a phenomenon from the biological, psychological, and social-cultural levels. Everything psychological is simultaneously biological. Yet our behavior is often influenced by our environment and our culture.

- Nature (our genes and our biological makeup) and nurture (our environment, our culture, and the world around us) work together in forming our traits and behaviors.

- We are creatures of our culture and gender, yet we are far more alike than different.

- Much of our human information processing is unconscious, below the radar screen of our awareness.

Be a smart test-taker. If a test contains both multiple-choice questions and an essay question, turn first to the essay. Read the question carefully, noting exactly what the instructor is asking. On the back of a page, pencil in a list of points you'd like to make, and then organize them. Before writing, put the essay aside and work through the multiple-choice questions. (As you do so, you may continue to mull over the essay question. Sometimes the objective questions will bring pertinent thoughts to mind.) Then reread the essay question, rethink your answer, and start writing. When you finish, proofread your work to eliminate spelling and grammatical errors that make you look less competent than you are.

When reading multiple-choice questions, don't confuse yourself by trying to imagine how each choice might be the right one. Try instead to answer the question as if it were a fill-in-the-blank. First, cover the answers, recall what you know, and complete the sentence in your mind. Then read the answers on the test and find the alternative that best matches your own answer.

As you read psychology, you will learn much more than effective study techniques. Psychology teaches us how to ask important questions—how to think critically as we evaluate competing ideas and popular claims. It deepens our appreciation for how we humans perceive, think, feel, and act. By so doing, it informs our living and enlarges our compassion. Through this book I hope to help guide you toward that end. As educator Charles Eliot said a century ago, "Books are the quietest and most constant of friends, and the most patient of teachers."

>> LEARNING OUTCOMES

The History and Scope of Psychology

OBJECTIVE 1-1 | Define *psychology.*

Psychology is the scientific study of behavior (anything an organism does) and mental processes (subjective experiences inferred from behavior). The key word in this definition is *science.*

OBJECTIVE 1-2 | **Trace psychology's prescientific roots, from early understandings of mind and body to the beginnings of modern science.**

Psychology traces its roots back through recorded history to India, China, the Middle East, and Europe, where scholars tried to understand how our minds work and how our bodies relate to our minds. More than 2000 years ago, Buddha and Confucius focused on the powers and origin of ideas. The ancient Hebrews, Socrates, his student Plato, and Plato's student Aristotle pondered whether mind and body are connected or distinct, and whether human ideas are innate or result from experience. In the 1600s, René Descartes and John Locke reengaged aspects of those ancient debates, and Locke coined his famous description of the mind as a "white paper." The ideas of Francis Bacon and John Locke were important ingredients in the development of modern *empiricism,* the view that knowledge comes from experience through the senses and that science should rely on observation and experimentation.

OBJECTIVE 1-3 | **Explain how the early psychologists sought to understand the mind's structure and functions, and identify some leading psychologists who worked in these areas.**

In Germany in the late 1800s, Wilhelm Wundt ran the first true experiments in psychology's first lab. Soon, the new discipline formed branches. Edward Bradford Titchener and other *structuralists* searched for the basic elements of the mind by training people to look inward and describe the smallest units of their experiences. Focusing on how mental and behavioral processes help us to adapt, survive, and flourish, William James and other functionalists tried to explain why we do what we do. James also wrote a popular text for the new discipline.

OBJECTIVE 1-4 | **Describe the evolution of psychology as defined from the 1920s through today.**

Until the 1920s, psychology was a "science of mental life" studied through introspection. Then American behaviorists, led by John B. Watson and later by B. F. Skinner, changed psychology's focus to the study of observable behavior. In the 1960s, humanistic psychologists drew attention to the importance of environmental influences, personal growth, and the needs for love and acceptance. Also in the 1960s, the cognitive revolution began to refocus psychology's interest in mental processes, with special attention to perception, information processing, and memory. Cognitive neuroscientists are broadening our understanding of these and other processes in today's psychology, which views itself as a "science of behavior and mental processes."

OBJECTIVE 1-5 | **Summarize the nature-nurture debate in psychology, and describe the principle of natural selection.**

Psychology's biggest and most enduring issue concerns the balance between the influences of nature (genes) and nurture (all other influences, from conception to death). A great deal of research, including studies of identical and fraternal twins, sheds light on the relative importance of these two sets of influences on such traits as personality and intelligence. Psychologists now believe that in most cases, every psychological event is simultaneously a biological event. Charles Darwin proposed a mechanism—the principle of natural selection—by which nature selects chance variations that enable organisms to survive and reproduce in particular environments.

OBJECTIVE 1-6 | **Identify the three main levels of analysis in the biopsychosocial approach, and explain why psychology's varied perspectives are complementary.**

The biopsychosocial approach integrates information from the biological, psychological, and social-cultural levels of analysis. Psychologists study human behaviors and mental processes from many different perspectives (including the neuroscientific, evolutionary, behavior genetics, psychodynamic, behavioral, cognitive, and social-cultural perspectives). Melding the information gathered from these many lines of research creates a more complete understanding of behaviors and mental processes than would be available from any one viewpoint alone.

OBJECTIVE 1-7 | **Identify some of psychology's subfields, and explain the difference between clinical psychology and psychiatry.**

Psychology's subfields encompass basic research (often done by biological, developmental, cognitive, personality, and social psychologists), applied research (sometimes conducted by industrial/organizational psychologists), and clinical applications (the work of counseling and clinical psychologists). Clinical psychologists study, assess, and treat (with psychotherapy) people with psychological disorders; psychiatrists also study, assess, and treat people with disorders, but they are medical doctors who can prescribe medication as well as offer psychotherapy.

OBJECTIVE 1-8 | **Describe some effective study techniques.**

SQ3R is an effective study method in which you *survey* material before reading it, keep in mind a *question* you will try to answer as you *read,* and then *review* the material you have read, and *reflect* on it to make it meaningful and memorable. Five additional tips are to distribute study time, listen actively in class, overlearn, focus on big ideas, and be a smart test-taker.

TERMS AND CONCEPTS TO REMEMBER

psychology, p. 1-0	levels of analysis, p. 1-6
empiricism, p. 1-1	biopsychosocial approach, p. 1-7
structuralism, p. 1-2	basic research, p. 1-8
functionalism, p. 1-3	applied research, p. 1-8
humanistic psychology, p. 1-4	counseling psychology, p. 1-8
nature-nurture issue, p. 1-5	clinical psychology, p. 1-8
natural selection, p. 1-5	psychiatry, p. 1-8

TEST YOURSELF*

1. What events defined the founding of scientific psychology?

2. What are psychology's major levels of analysis?

ASK YOURSELF**

1. How do you think psychology might change as more people from non-Western countries contribute their ideas to the field?

2. When you signed up for this course, what did you think psychology would be all about?

>WEB

Multiple-choice *self-tests* and more may be found at www.worthpublishers.com/myers.

*The Test Yourself questions offer you a handy self-test on the material you have just read. Answers to these questions can be found in Appendix B at the back of the book.

**The Ask Yourself questions will help you reflect on key issues and connect them to your own life. Making these issues personally meaningful will make them memorable.

2

Thinking Critically With Psychological Science

What good fortune for those in power that people do not think.

Adolf Hitler, 1889-1945

Hoping to satisfy their curiosity about people and to remedy their own woes, millions turn to "psychology." They listen to talk-radio counseling, read articles on psychic powers, attend stop-smoking hypnosis seminars, and absorb self-help books on the meaning of dreams, the path to ecstatic love, and the roots of personal happiness.

Others, intrigued by claims of psychological truth, wonder: Do mothers and infants bond in the first hours after birth? Should we trust childhood sexual abuse memories that get "recovered" in adulthood—and prosecute the alleged predators? Are first-born children more driven to achieve? Does handwriting offer clues to personality? Does psychotherapy heal?

In working with such questions, how can we separate uninformed opinions from examined conclusions? *How can we best use psychology to understand why people think, feel, and act as they do?*

The Need for Psychological Science

As we familiarize ourselves with psychological science's strategies and incorporate its underlying principles into our daily thinking, our thinking becomes smarter. Two phenomena—hindsight bias and judgmental overconfidence—illustrate why we cannot rely solely on intuition and common sense. The critical inquiry that flows from a scientific approach—undergirded by curiosity, skepticism, and humility—helps winnow sense from nonsense.

The Limits of Intuition and Common Sense

Some people think psychology merely documents what people already know and dresses it in jargon: "So what else is new—you get paid for using fancy methods to prove what my grandmother knew?" Others scorn a scientific approach because of their faith in human intuition. Advocates of "intuitive management" urge us to distrust statistical predictors and tune into our hunches when hiring, firing, and investing. Like *Star Wars'* Luke Skywalker, should we trust the force within?

Actually, notes writer Madeleine L'Engle, "The naked intellect is an extraordinarily inaccurate instrument" (1972). Our intuition can lead us astray.

- Imagine (or ask someone to imagine) folding a sheet of paper on itself 100 times. Roughly how thick would it then be?
- A rope is placed around the Earth at the equator. How much more rope would have to be added for the rope to be 1 foot above the Earth all the way around? (See this module's final page for the answers.)

Our notions of common sense similarly err. We're all wise after the fact, presuming that we could have foreseen what happened.

The limits of intuition
Personnel interviewers tend to be overconfident of their gut feelings about job applicants. Their confidence stems partly from their recalling cases where their favorable impression proved right, and partly from their ignorance about rejected applicants who succeeded elsewhere.

Taxi/Getty Images

Did We Know It All Along? Hindsight Bias

OBJECTIVE 2-1 | Describe *hindsight bias,* and explain how it can make research findings seem like mere common sense.

How easy it is to seem astute when drawing the bull's eye after the arrow has struck. *After* each stock market downswing—after the bursting of the dot-com bubble, for example—investment gurus say "the market was obviously overdue for a correction." After the first World Trade Center tower in New York was hit on September 11, 2001 (9/11), commentators said people in the second tower *should* have immediately evacuated (it became obvious only later that it was not an accident). And after physicians receive case information *plus* an autopsy report, they find the cause of death to be self-evident—something they presume they easily could have foreseen, knowing the symptoms. But *before* the arrow strikes, the stock market drops, the terrorists attack, and death occurs, these results are anything but obvious. Causes of death, for example, are not so clear to doctors told the same symptoms without the autopsy report (Dawson & others, 1988). Finding that something has happened makes it seem inevitable. Psychologists Paul Slovic and Baruch Fischhoff (1977) have called this 20/20 hindsight vision **hindsight bias,** also known as the *I-knew-it-all-along phenomenon.*

This phenomenon is easy to demonstrate: Give half the members of a group some purported psychological finding, and the other half an opposite result. Tell the first group, "Psychologists have found that separation weakens romantic attraction. As the saying goes, 'Out of sight, out of mind.'" Ask them to imagine why this might be true. Most people can, and nearly all will then regard this true finding as unsurprising.

Tell the second group just the opposite—that "psychologists have found that separation strengthens romantic attraction. As the saying goes, 'Absence makes the heart grow fonder.'" People given this untrue result can also easily explain it, and they overwhelmingly see it as unsurprising common sense. Obviously, when both a supposed finding and its opposite seem like common sense, there is a problem.

Such errors in our recollections and explanations show why we need psychological research. Just asking people how and why they felt or acted as they did can sometimes be misleading—*not* because common sense is usually wrong, but because it is after the fact. Common sense describes what has happened more easily than it predicts what will happen. As physicist Neils Bohr reportedly said, "Prediction is very difficult, especially about the future."

The phenomenon is widespread. Some 100 studies have observed hindsight bias in various countries and among both children and adults (Bernstein & others, 2004; Guilbault & others, 2004). Nevertheless, Grandmother is often right. As Yogi Berra once said, "You can observe a lot by watching." (We have Berra to thank for other gems, such as "Nobody ever comes here—it's too crowded," and "If the people don't want to come out to the ballpark, nobody's gonna stop 'em.") Because we're all

> "Life is lived forwards, but understood backwards."
> Philosopher Søren Kierkegaard, 1813–1855

> "History is written through a rearview mirror, but it unfolds through a foggy windshield."
> Samuel Berger, President Clinton's national security adviser, in testimony before the 9/11 Commission, 2004

> "Anything seems commonplace, once explained."
> Dr. Watson to Sherlock Holmes

Non Sequitur

Reprinted by permission of Universal Press Syndicate. © 1997 Wiley.

■ **hindsight bias** the tendency to believe, after learning an outcome, that one would have foreseen it. (Also known as the *I-knew-it-all-along phenomenon.*)

TABLE 2.1

TRUE OR FALSE?

Psychological research has either confirmed or refuted each of these statements (adapted, in part, from Furnham & others, 2003).

1. If you want to teach a habit that persists, reward the desired behavior every time, not just intermittently.

2. Patients whose brains are surgically split down the middle survive and function much as they did before the surgery.

3. Traumatic experiences, such as sexual abuse or surviving the Holocaust, are typically "repressed" from memory.

4. Most abused children do *not* become abusive adults.

5. Most infants recognize their own reflection in a mirror by the end of their first year.

6. Adopted siblings tend not to develop similar personalities, even though reared by the same parents.

7. Fears of harmless objects, such as flowers, are just as easy to acquire as fears of potentially dangerous objects, such as snakes.

8. Lie detection tests often lie.

(For answers, see this module's final page.)

Hindsight bias *After* the horror of 9/11, it seemed obvious that the U.S. intelligence analysts should have taken advance warnings more seriously, that airport security should have anticipated box-cutter–wielding terrorists, that occupants of the second World Trade Center tower should have known to play it safe and leave. With 20/20 hindsight, everything seems obvious. Thus we now spend billions to protect ourselves against what the terrorists did last time.

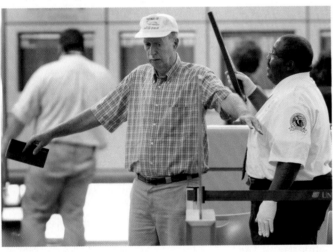

Tim Boyle/Getty Images

behavior watchers, it would be surprising if many of psychology's findings had *not* been foreseen. Many people believe that love breeds happiness, and they are right, according to researchers who have found we have a deep "need to belong" to others. Indeed, note Daniel Gilbert, Brett Pelham, and Douglas Krull (2003), "Good ideas in psychology usually have an oddly familiar quality, and the moment we encounter them we feel certain that we once came close to thinking the same thing ourselves and simply failed to write it down."

But sometimes Grandmother's intuition has it wrong. Informed by countless casual observations, our intuition may tell us that familiarity breeds contempt, that dreams predict the future, and that emotional reactions coincide with menstrual phase. The available evidence suggests that these common-sense ideas are wrong, wrong, and wrong. Do you know which of the popular ideas in **TABLE 2.1** have been confirmed by psychology's research, and which have been refuted? Throughout this book we will see how research has both inspired and overturned popular ideas—about aging, about sleep and dreams, about personality. And we will also see how it has surprised us with discoveries about how the brain's chemical messengers control our moods and memories, about animal abilities, and about the effects of stress on our capacity to fight disease.

Overconfidence

OBJECTIVE 2-2 | Describe how overconfidence contaminates our everyday judgments.

Our everyday thinking is limited not only by our after-the-fact common sense but also by our human tendency toward overconfidence—we tend to think we know more than we do. Asked how sure we are of our answers to factual questions (Is Boston north or south of Paris?), we tend to be more confident than correct.[1]

[1]Boston is south of Paris.

Or consider these three anagrams, which Richard Goranson (1978) asked people to unscramble:

WREAT → WATER
ETRYN → ENTRY
GRABE → BARGE

Reflect for a moment: About how many seconds do you think it would have taken you to unscramble each of these?

Once people know the target word, hindsight makes it seem obvious—so much so that they become overconfident. They think they would have seen the solution in only 10 seconds or so, when in reality the average problem solver spends 3 minutes, as you also might, given a similar anagram without the solution: OCHSA (see this module's final page to check your answer).

Are we any better at predicting our social behavior? To find out, Robert Vallone and his associates (1990) had students predict at the beginning of the school year whether they would drop a course, vote in an upcoming election, call their parents more than twice a month, and so forth. On average, the students felt 84 percent confident in making these self-predictions. Later quizzes about their actual behavior showed their predictions were correct only 71 percent of the time. Even when they were 100 percent sure of themselves, their self-predictions erred 15 percent of the time.

It's not just collegians. For a dozen years, Ohio State University psychologist Philip Tetlock (1998) collected experts' predictions of political, economic, and military situations. In the late 1980s, for example, he invited expert professors, think-tank analysts, government experts, and journalists to project the governance of the Soviet Union or of South Africa five years later, and to rate how confident they felt. Others did the same for the future of Canada in 1992. After the five years had elapsed (and Communism had collapsed in the Soviet Union, South Africa had become a multiracial democracy, and the Canadian constitution continued), Tetlock invited the experts to recall and reflect on their predictions—which, as in laboratory studies, were far more confident than correct. Experts who had felt more than 80 percent confident were right less than 40 percent of the time.

Despite their lackluster predictions, those who erred were nearly as likely as those who got it right to convince themselves that their initial analysis was *still basically right*. I was "almost right," many of them felt. "The hardliners almost succeeded in their coup attempt against Gorbachev." "The Quebecois separatists almost won the secessionist referendum." "But for the coincidence of de Klerk and Mandela, the transition to black majority rule in South Africa would have been a lot bloodier." The overconfidence of political experts (and stock market forecasters and sports prognosticators) is therefore hard to dislodge, no matter what the outcome.

The point to remember: Hindsight bias and overconfidence often lead us to overestimate our intuition. But scientific inquiry, fed by curious skepticism and by humility, can help us sift reality from illusions.

The Scientific Attitude

OBJECTIVE 2-3 | Explain how the scientific attitude encourages critical thinking.

Underlying all science is, first, a hard-headed *curiosity,* a passion to explore and understand without misleading or being misled. Some questions (Is there life after death?) are beyond science. To answer them in any way requires a leap of faith. With many other ideas (Can some people demonstrate ESP?), the proof is in the pudding. No matter how sensible or crazy-sounding an idea, the hard-headed question is, Does it work? When put to the test, can its predictions be confirmed?

Fun anagram solutions from Wordsmith.org:
Elvis = lives
Dormitory = dirty room
Slot machines = cash lost in 'em

"We don't like their sound. Groups of guitars are on their way out."
Decca Records, in turning down a recording contract with the Beatles in 1962

"Computers in the future may weigh no more than 1.5 tons."
Popular Mechanics, 1949

"The telephone may be appropriate for our American cousins, but not here, because we have an adequate supply of messenger boys."
British expert group evaluating the invention of the telephone

"They couldn't hit an elephant at this dist—."
General John Sedgwick's last words, uttered during a U.S. Civil War battle, 1864

Courtesy of the James Randi Education Foundation

The amazing Randi The magician James Randi exemplifies skepticism. He has tested and debunked a variety of psychic phenomena.

This scientific approach has a long history. As ancient a figure as Moses used such an approach. How do you evaluate a self-proclaimed prophet? His answer: Put the prophet to the test. If the predicted event "does not take place or prove true," then so much the worse for the prophet (*Deuteronomy* 18:22). Magician James Randi uses Moses' approach when testing those claiming to see auras around people's bodies:

Randi: Do you see an aura around my head?
Aura-seer: Yes, indeed.
Randi: Can you still see the aura if I put this magazine in front of my face?
Aura-seer: Of course.
Randi: Then if I were to step behind a wall barely taller than I am, you could determine my location from the aura visible above my head, right?

Randi has told me that no aura-seer has agreed to take this simple test.

When subjected to such scrutiny, crazy-sounding ideas sometimes find support. During the 1700s, scientists scoffed at the notion that meteorites had extraterrestrial origins. When two Yale scientists dared to deviate from the conventional opinion, Thomas Jefferson jeered, "Gentlemen, I would rather believe that those two Yankee Professors would lie than to believe that stones fell from heaven." Sometimes scientific inquiry refutes skeptics.

More often, science relegates crazy-sounding ideas to the mountain of forgotten claims of perpetual motion machines, miracle cancer cures, and out-of-body travels into centuries past. To sift reality from fantasy, sense from nonsense, therefore requires a scientific attitude: being skeptical but not cynical, open but not gullible.

As scientists, psychologists approach the world of behavior with a *curious skepticism*. They persistently ask two questions: What do you mean? How do you know? In business, the motto is "Show me the money." In science, it is "Show me the evidence."

Do parental behaviors determine their children's sexual orientation? Can astrologers analyze your character and predict your future based on the position of the planets at your birth? As you will see in the pages that follow, putting such claims to the test has led most psychologists to doubt them. In the arena of competing ideas, skeptical testing can reveal which ones best match the facts. "To believe with certainty," says a Polish proverb, "we must begin by doubting."

Putting a scientific attitude into practice requires not only skepticism but also *humility*, because we may have to reject our own ideas. In the last analysis, what matters is not my opinion or yours, but the truths nature reveals in response to our questioning. If people don't behave as our ideas predict, then so much the worse for our ideas. This is the humble attitude expressed in one of psychology's early mottos: "The rat is always right."

Historians of science tell us that these attitudes of curiosity, skepticism, and humility helped make modern science possible. Many of its founders, including Copernicus and Newton, were people whose religious convictions made them humble before nature and skeptical of mere human authority (Hooykaas, 1972; Merton, 1938). Today's deeply religious people sometimes view science, especially psychological science, as a threat. Yet, notes sociologist Rodney Stark (2003a,b), the scientific revolution was led mostly by deeply religious people acting on the religious idea that "in order to love and honor God, it is necessary to fully appreciate the wonders of his handiwork."

Of course, scientists, like anyone else, can have big egos and may cling to their preconceptions. We all view nature through the spectacles of our preconceived ideas. Nevertheless, the ideal that unifies psychologists with all scientists is the curious, skeptical, humble scrutiny of competing ideas. As a community, scientists check and recheck one another's findings and conclusions.

This scientific attitude prepares us to think smarter. Smart thinking, called **critical thinking,** examines assumptions, discerns hidden values, evaluates evidence, and assesses conclusions. Whether reading a news report or listening to a conversation, critical thinkers ask questions. Like scientists, they wonder, How do they know that?

What is this person's agenda? Is the conclusion based on anecdote and gut feelings, or on evidence? Does the evidence justify a cause-effect conclusion? What alternative explanations are possible? Carried to an extreme, healthy skepticism can degenerate into a negative cynicism that scorns any unproven idea. Better to have a critical attitude that produces humility—an awareness of our own vulnerability to error and an openness to surprises and new perspectives.

Has psychology's critical inquiry been open to surprising findings? The answer is plainly yes. Believe it or not . . .

- massive losses of brain tissue early in life may have minimal long-term effects.
- within days, newborns can recognize their mother's odor and voice.
- brain damage can leave a person able to learn new skills, yet be unaware of such learning.
- diverse groups—men and women, old and young, rich and working class, those with disabilities and without—report roughly comparable levels of personal happiness.
- electroconvulsive therapy (delivering an electric shock to the brain) is often a very effective treatment for severe depression.

And has critical inquiry convincingly debunked popular presumptions? The answer is again yes. The evidence indicates that . . .

- sleepwalkers are *not* acting out their dreams and sleeptalkers are *not* verbalizing their dreams.
- our past experiences are *not* all recorded verbatim in our brains; with brain stimulation or hypnosis, one *cannot* simply "play the tape" and relive long-buried or repressed memories.
- most people do *not* suffer from unrealistically low self-esteem, and high self-esteem is not all good.
- opposites do *not* generally attract.

In each of these instances and more, what has been learned is not yet what is widely believed.

The Scientific Method

OBJECTIVE 2-4 | Describe how psychological theories guide scientific research.

Psychologists arm their scientific attitude with the *scientific method:* They make observations, form theories, and then refine their theories in the light of new observations. In everyday conversation, we tend to use *theory* to mean "mere hunch." In science, however, *theory* is linked with observation. A scientific **theory** *explains* through an integrated set of principles that *organizes* and *predicts* behaviors or events. By organizing isolated facts, a theory simplifies things. There are too many facts about behavior to remember them all. By linking facts and bridging them to deeper principles, a theory offers a useful summary. When we connect the observed dots, we may discover a coherent picture.

A good theory of depression, for example, helps us organize countless observations concerning depression into a short list of principles. Imagine we observe over and over that people with depression describe their past, present, and future in gloomy terms. We might therefore theorize that low self-esteem contributes to depression. So far so good: Our self-esteem principle neatly summarizes a long list of facts about people with depression.

Yet no matter how reasonable a theory may sound—and low self-esteem seems a reasonable explanation of depression—we must put it to the test. A good theory doesn't just sound appealing. It must produce testable predictions, called **hypotheses.** By enabling us to test and reject or revise the theory, such predictions give direction to research. They specify what results would support the theory and what results would disconfirm it. To test our self-esteem theory of depression, we might assess people's self-esteem by having them indicate their agreement to statements such as "I

"The real purpose of the scientific method is to make sure Nature hasn't misled you into thinking you know something you don't actually know."
Robert M. Pirsig, *Zen and the Art of Motorcycle Maintenance*, 1974

■ **critical thinking** thinking that does not blindly accept arguments and conclusions. Rather, it examines assumptions, discerns hidden values, evaluates evidence, and assesses conclusions.

■ **theory** an explanation using an integrated set of principles that organizes and predicts observations.

■ **hypothesis** a testable prediction, often implied by a theory.

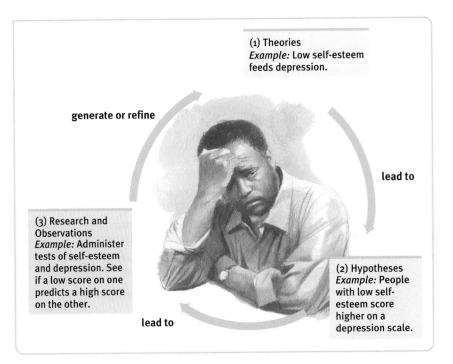

(1) Theories
Example: Low self-esteem feeds depression.

generate or refine

lead to

(3) Research and Observations
Example: Administer tests of self-esteem and depression. See if a low score on one predicts a high score on the other.

lead to

(2) Hypotheses
Example: People with low self-esteem score higher on a depression scale.

FIGURE 2.1

The scientific method A self-correcting process for asking questions and observing nature's answer.

have good ideas" and "I am fun to be with." Then we could see whether, as we hypothesized, people who report poorer self-images also score higher on a depression scale (**FIGURE 2.1**).

In testing our theory, we should be aware that it can bias subjective observations. Having theorized that depression springs from low self-esteem, we may see what we expect. We may perceive depressed people's neutral comments as self-disparaging. The urge to see what we expect is an ever-present temptation for all of us. For example, according to the bipartisan U.S. Senate Select Committee on Intelligence (2004), preconceived expectations that Iraq had weapons of mass destruction led intelligence analysts to wrongly interpret ambiguous observations as confirming that theory, and this theory-driven conclusion then led to the preemptive U.S. invasion of Iraq.

As a check on their biases, psychologists report their research—with precise **operational definitions** of concepts that allow anyone to **replicate** (repeat) their observations. If other researchers re-create a study with different participants and materials and get similar results, then our confidence in the finding's reliability grows. The first study of hindsight bias aroused psychologists' curiosity. Now, after many successful replications with differing people and questions, we feel sure of the phenomenon's power.

In the end, our theory will be useful if it (1) effectively *organizes* a range of self-reports and observations and (2) implies clear *predictions* that anyone can use to check the theory or to derive practical applications. (If we boost people's self-esteem, will their depression lift?) Eventually, our research will probably lead to a revised theory that better organizes and predicts what we know about depression.

Good theories explain by
1. organizing and linking observed facts.
2. implying hypotheses that offer testable predictions and, sometimes, practical applications.

Frequently Asked Questions About Psychology

You are now prepared to think critically about psychological matters. Yet, even knowing this much, you may still be approaching psychology with a mixture of curiosity and apprehension. So before we move ahead, let's address some frequently asked questions.

Can Laboratory Experiments Illuminate Everyday Life?

OBJECTIVE 2-5 | Explain the value of simplified laboratory conditions in discovering general principles of behavior.

When you see or hear about psychological research, do you ever wonder whether people's behavior in the lab will predict their behavior in real life? For example, does detecting the blink of a faint red light in a dark room have anything useful to say about flying a plane at night? Does our tendency to remember best the first and last items in a list of unrelated words tell us anything about why we remember the names of certain people we meet at a party? After viewing a violent, sexually explicit film, does an aroused man's increased willingness to push buttons that he thinks will electrically shock a woman really say anything about whether violent pornography makes a man more likely to abuse a woman?

Before you answer, consider: The experimenter *intends* the laboratory environment to be a simplified reality—one that simulates and controls important features of everyday life to allow focused study of one or two specific behaviors. Laboratory experiments have the advantage of allowing researchers to rule out effects from other factors. Just as an aeronautical wind tunnel enables an engineer to re-create atmospheric forces under controlled conditions, a laboratory experiment enables a psychologist to re-create psychological forces under controlled conditions.

People in the lab are not different creatures from their out-of-lab selves. For example, Cecilia Cheng (2001) observed that Hong Kong adults who coped flexibly with laboratory stresses also coped flexibly with stress in their marriages. In aggression studies, deciding whether to push a button that delivers a shock may not be the same as slapping someone in the face, but the *principle* is the same. And the experiment's purpose, notes Douglas Mook (1983), is not to re-create the exact behaviors of everyday life but to test theoretical principles. *It is the resulting principles—not the specific findings—that help explain everyday behaviors.*

When psychologists apply laboratory research on aggression to actual violence, they are applying theoretical *principles* of aggressive behavior, principles they have refined through many experiments. Similarly, it is the principles of the visual system, developed from experiments in artificial settings (such as looking at red lights in the dark), that we apply to more complex behaviors such as night flying. And many investigations show that principles derived in the laboratory *do* typically generalize to the everyday world (Anderson & others, 1999).

The point to remember: As psychologists, our concerns lie less with particular behaviors than with the general principles that help explain many behaviors.

Does Behavior Depend on One's Culture?

OBJECTIVE 2-6 | Discuss whether psychological research can be generalized across cultures and genders.

If culture shapes behavior, what can psychological studies done in one culture, often with white Europeans or North Americans, really tell us about people in general? As we will see time and again, **culture**—shared ideas and behaviors that one generation passes on to the next—matters. Our culture influences our standards of promptness and frankness, our attitudes toward premarital sex and varying body shapes, our tendency to be casual or formal, our eye contact, our conversational distance, and much, much more. Being aware of such differences, we can restrain our assumptions that others will think and act as we do. Given the growing mixing and clashing of cultures, our need for such awareness is urgent.

■ **operational definition** a statement of the procedures (operations) used to define research variables. For example, *human intelligence* may be operationally defined as what an intelligence test measures.

■ **replication** repeating the essence of a research study, usually with different participants in different situations, to see whether the basic finding extends to other participants and circumstances.

■ **culture** the enduring behaviors, ideas, attitudes, and traditions shared by a large group of people and transmitted from one generation to the next.

A cultured greeting Because culture shapes people's understanding of social behavior, actions that seem ordinary to us may seem quite odd to visitors from far away. Yet underlying these differences are powerful similarities. Supporters of newly elected leaders everywhere typically greet them with pleased deference, though not necessarily with bows and folded hands, as in India. Here influential and popular politician Sonia Gandhi greets some of her constituents shortly after her election.

Ami Vitale/Getty Images

Our shared biological heritage does, however, unite us as a universal human family. The same underlying processes guide people everywhere:

- People diagnosed with dyslexia, a reading disorder, exhibit the same brain malfunction whether they are Italian, French, or British (Paulesu & others, 2001).
- Variation in languages—spoken and gestured—may impede communication across cultures. Yet all languages share deep principles of grammar, and people from opposite hemispheres can communicate with a smile or a frown.
- People in different cultures do vary in feelings of loneliness. But across cultures, loneliness is magnified by shyness, low self-esteem, and being unmarried (Jones & others, 1985; Rokach & others, 2002).
- Most Japanese prefer their fish raw and most North Americans prefer theirs cooked. But the same principles of hunger and taste influence all of us when we sit down to a meal. We are each in certain respects like all others, like some others, and like no other. Studying people of all races and cultures helps us discern our similarities and our differences, our human kinship and our diversity.

The point to remember: Even when specific attitudes and behaviors vary across cultures, as they often do, the underlying processes are much the same.

Does Behavior Vary With Gender?

At your birth, friends and family immediately wondered which of the two human types you were: male or female. Given how important gender is to our identity and to others' perceptions of us, do we need a different psychology for women and for men?

You will see throughout this book that gender issues permeate psychology. Researchers report gender differences in what we dream, in how we express and detect emotions, and in our risk for alcoholism, depression, and eating disorders. Not only is studying such differences interesting, it also is potentially beneficial. For example, many researchers believe that women carry on conversations more readily to build relationships, while men talk more to give information and advice (Tannen, 1990). Knowing this difference can help us prevent conflicts and misunderstandings in everyday relationships.

Nevertheless, it's important to remember that psychologically as well as biologically, women and men are overwhelmingly similar. Whether female or male, we learn to walk at about the same age. We experience the same sensations of light and sound. We feel the same pangs of hunger, desire, and fear. We exhibit similar overall intelligence and well-being. We also tend to exhibit and perceive the very behaviors our culture expects of males and females.

So, gender matters. Biology determines our sex, and then culture further bends the genders. Yet in many ways female and male are similarly human.

Why Do Psychologists Study Animals?

OBJECTIVE 2-7 | Explain why psychologists study animals, and discuss the ethics of experimentation with both animals and humans.

Many psychologists study animals because they find them fascinating. They want to understand how different species learn, think, and behave. Psychologists also study animals to learn about people, by doing experiments that are permissible only with animals. Human physiology resembles that of many other animals. We humans are not *like* animals; we *are* animals. Animal experiments have therefore led to treatments for human diseases—insulin for diabetes, vaccines to prevent polio and rabies, transplants to replace defective organs.

Likewise, the same processes by which humans see, exhibit emotion, and become obese are present in rats and monkeys. To discover more about the basics of human learning, researchers even study sea slugs. To understand how a combustion engine

"All people are the same; only their habits differ."

Confucius, 551–479 B.C.

"Rats are very similar to humans except that they are not stupid enough to purchase lottery tickets."

Dave Barry, July 2, 2002

Animal research benefiting animals
Thanks partly to research on the benefits of novelty, control, and stimulation, these Bronx Zoo gorillas are enjoying improved quality of life.

works, you would do better to study a lawn mower's engine than a Mercedes'. Like Mercedes engines, humans are complex. But the simplicity of the sea slug's nervous system is precisely what makes it so revealing of the neural mechanisms of learning.

Is It Ethical to Experiment on Animals?

If we share important similarities with other animals, then should we not respect them? "We cannot defend our scientific work with animals on the basis of the similarities between them and ourselves and then defend it morally on the basis of differences," noted Roger Ulrich (1991). The animal protection movement protests the use of animals in psychological, biological, and medical research. Researchers remind us that the world's 30 million mammals used each year in research are but a fraction of 1 percent of the billions of animals killed annually for food (which means the average person eats 20 animals a year). While researchers each year conduct experiments on some 200,000 dogs and cats cared for under humane regulations, humane animal shelters are forced to kill 50 times that many (Goodwin & Morrison, 1999).

Animal protection organizations, such as Psychologists for the Ethical Treatment of Animals, advocate naturalistic observation of animals rather than laboratory manipulation. Animal researchers have responded that the issue is not the morality of good versus evil but of compassion for animals versus compassion for people. How many of us would have attacked Pasteur's experiments with rabies, which caused some dogs to suffer but led to a vaccine that spared millions of people (and dogs) from agonizing death? And would we really wish to have deprived ourselves of the animal research that led to effective methods of training children with mental disorders; of understanding aging; of relieving fears and depression; and of controlling obesity, alcoholism, and stress-related pain and disease? The answers to such questions vary by culture. In Gallup surveys in Canada and the United States, about 6 in 10 adults deem medical testing on animals "morally acceptable." In Britain, only 37 percent do (Mason, 2003).

Out of this heated debate, two issues emerge. The basic one is whether it is right to place the well-being of humans above that of animals. In experiments on stress and cancer, is it right that mice get tumors in hopes that people might not? Should some monkeys be exposed to an HIV-like virus in the search for an AIDS vaccine? Is our use of other animals as natural as the behavior of carnivorous hawks, cats, and whales? Defenders of research on animals argue that anyone who has eaten a hamburger, worn leather shoes, tolerated hunting and fishing, or supported the extermination of crop-destroying or plague-carrying pests has already agreed that, yes, it is sometimes permissible to sacrifice animals for the sake of human well-being.

Scott Plous (1993) notes, however, that our compassion for animals varies, as does our compassion for people—based on their perceived similarity to us. We feel more attraction, give more help, and act less aggressively toward similar others. Likewise,

> I believe that to prevent, cripple, or needlessly complicate the research that can relieve animal and human suffering is profoundly inhuman, cruel, and immoral."
>
> Psychologist Neal Miller, 1983

> Please do not forget those of us who suffer from incurable diseases or disabilities who hope for a cure through research that requires the use of animals."
>
> Psychologist Dennis Feeney (1987)

we value animals according to their perceived kinship with us. Thus, primates and companion pets get top priority. (Western people raise or trap mink and foxes for their fur, but not dogs or cats.) Other mammals occupy the second rung on the privilege ladder, followed by birds, fish, and reptiles on the third rung, with insects at the bottom. In deciding which animals have rights, we each draw our own cut-off line somewhere across the animal kingdom.

If we give human life first priority, the second issue is the priority we give to the well-being of animals in research. What safeguards should protect them? Most researchers today feel ethically obligated to enhance the well-being of captive animals and protect them from needless suffering. In one survey of animal researchers, 98 percent or more supported government regulations protecting primates, dogs, and cats, and 74 percent supported regulations providing for the humane care of rats and mice (Plous & Herzog, 2000). Many professional associations and funding agencies now have guidelines for the humane use of animals. For example, British Psychological Society guidelines call for housing animals under reasonably natural living conditions, with companions for social animals (Lea, 2000). American Psychological Association (2002) guidelines mandate ensuring the "comfort, health, and humane treatment" of animals, and of minimizing "infection, illness, and pain of animal subjects." Humane care also leads to more effective science, because pain and stress would distort the animals' behavior during experiments.

Animals have themselves benefited from animal research. One Ohio team of research psychologists measured stress hormone levels in samples of millions of dogs brought each year to animal shelters, and they devised methods of handling and stroking them that reduced stress and eased their transition to adoptive homes (Tuber & others, 1999). Thanks to animal behavior studies, formerly idle Bronx Zoo animals are now staving off listless boredom by working for their supper, as would their counterparts in the wild (Stewart, 2002). Other studies have helped improve care and management in animals' natural habitats. By revealing our behavioral kinship with animals and the remarkable intelligence of chimpanzees, gorillas, and other animals, experiments have also led to increased empathy and protection for them. At its best, a psychology concerned for humans and sensitive to animals serves the welfare of both.

Is It Ethical to Experiment on People?

If the image of animals or people receiving supposed electric shocks troubles you, you may be relieved to know that most psychological research involves no such stress. With people, blinking lights, flashing words, and pleasant social interactions are more common.

Occasionally, though, researchers do temporarily stress or deceive people, but only when they believe it is essential to a justifiable end, such as understanding and controlling violent behavior or studying mood swings. Such experiments wouldn't work if the participants knew all there was to know about the experiment beforehand. Either the procedures would be ineffective or the participants, wanting to be helpful, might try to confirm the researchers' predictions.

Ethical principles developed by the American Psychological Association (1992) and the British Psychological Society (1993) urge investigators to (1) obtain the informed consent of potential participants, (2) protect them from harm and discomfort, (3) treat information about individual participants confidentially, and (4) fully explain the research afterward. Moreover, most universities today screen research proposals through an ethics committee that safeguards the well-being of every participant.

Much research, however, occurs outside of university laboratories, in places where there may be no ethics committees. For example, retail stores routinely survey people, photograph their purchasing behavior, track their buying patterns, and test the effectiveness of advertising. Curiously, such research attracts less attention than the scientific research done to advance human understanding.

"The righteous know the needs of their animals."
Proverbs 12:10

"The greatness of a nation can be judged by the way its animals are treated."
Mahatma Gandhi, 1869–1948

Is Psychology Free of Value Judgments?

OBJECTIVE 2-8 | Describe how personal values can influence psychologists' research and its application, and discuss psychology's potential to manipulate people.

Psychology is definitely not value-free. Values affect what we study, how we study it, and how we interpret results. Consider: Researchers' values influence their choice of research topics—whether to study worker productivity or worker morale, sex discrimination or gender differences, conformity or independence. Values can also color "the facts." As we noted earlier, our preconceptions can bias our observations and interpretations; sometimes we see what we want or expect to see (FIGURE 2.2).

FIGURE **2.2**
What do you see? People interpret ambiguous information to fit their preconceptions. Did you see a duck or a rabbit? Before showing some friends this image, ask them if they can see the duck lying on its back (or the bunny in the grass). (From Shepard, 1990.)

Even the words we use to describe a phenomenon can reflect our values. Labeling the sex acts we do not practice as "perversions" or as "sexual variations" conveys a value judgment. The same holds true in everyday speech, when one person's "rigidity" is another's "consistency," or one person's "faith" is another's "fanaticism." Our labeling someone as "firm" or "stubborn," "careful" or "picky," "discreet" or "secretive" reveals our feelings. Both in and out of psychology, labels describe and labels evaluate.

Popular applications of psychology also contain hidden values. If you defer to "professional" guidance about how to live—how to raise children, how to achieve self-fulfillment, what to do with sexual feelings, how to get ahead at work—you are accepting value-laden advice. A science of behavior and mental processes can certainly help us reach our goals, but it cannot decide what those goals should be. (See Thinking Critically About Desegregation and the Death Penalty, on the next page.)

" It is doubtless impossible to approach any human problem with a mind free from bias."

Simone de Beauvoir, *The Second Sex*, 1953

Is Psychology Potentially Dangerous?

If some people see psychology as merely common sense, others have a different concern—that it is becoming dangerously powerful. Is it an accident that astronomy is the oldest science and psychology the youngest? Exploring the external universe is one thing, but exploring our own inner universe seems more dangerous and threatening. Might psychology be used to manipulate people?

Knowledge, like all power, can be used for good or evil. Nuclear power has been used to light up cities—and to demolish them. Persuasive power has been used to educate people—and to deceive them. The power of mind-altering drugs has been used to restore sanity—and to destroy it.

Although psychology does indeed have the power to deceive, its purpose is to enlighten. Every day, psychologists are exploring ways to enhance learning, creativity, and compassion. Psychology also speaks to many of our world's great problems—war, overpopulation, prejudice, family dysfunction, crime—all of which involve attitudes and behaviors. And psychology speaks to our deepest longings—for nourishment, for love, for happiness. True, psychology cannot address all of life's great questions, but it speaks to some mighty important ones.

DESEGREGATION AND THE DEATH PENALTY— WHEN BELIEFS COLLIDE WITH PSYCHOLOGICAL SCIENCE

An influential modern viewpoint, ironically called *postmodernism*, questions scientific objectivity. Rather than mirroring the real world, say postmodernists, scientific concepts are socially constructed fictions. Like all knowledge, they reflect the culture that formed them. "Intelligence," for instance, is a concept psychologists created and defined. Because personal values guide theory and research, "truth" is said to be personal and subjective. (What behaviors shall we call "intelligent"?) In our quest for truth, we cannot help following our hunches, our biases, our cultural bent.

Psychological scientists agree that many important questions lie beyond the reach of science. And they agree that personal beliefs often shape perceptions. But they also believe that there is a real world out there, and that we advance truth by checking our hunches against it. Marie Curie did not just construct the concept of radium, she *discovered* radium. It really exists. In the behavioral sciences, pure objectivity, like pure love, may be unattainable. Yet most would argue that it is better to humble ourselves before reliable evidence than to cling to untested presumptions.

Humbling itself before the evidence is what the U.S. Supreme Court did in making its historic 1954 decision declaring segregated schools unconstitutional. This was the Court's first case in which social psychologists participated actively. They did so as expert witnesses and as authors, led by Kenneth Clark (1952), of an influential social science brief that formed part of the case presented. The Court found it noteworthy that when Kenneth Clark and Mamie Phipps Clark

Psychologists Mamie Phipps Clark and Kenneth B. Clark
Their work was cited in the historic U.S. Supreme Court school desegregation decision in 1954.

Office of Public Affairs at Columbia University

(1947) gave African-American children a choice between Black dolls and White dolls, most chose the White, which suggested that under segregation Black children were internalizing anti-Black prejudice.

This social science success inspired hundreds more studies that researchers hoped would inform future judicial decisions. More recently, however, the Court has joined postmodernists in discounting behavioral science research. In deciding whether the death penalty falls under the Constitution's ban on "cruel and unusual punishment," the Court wrestled with whether society defines execution as cruel and unusual, whether courts inflict the penalty arbitrarily, whether they apply it with racial bias, and whether execution deters crime more than all other available punishments. The behavioral science answers to each of these questions, note psychologists Mark Costanzo (1997) and Craig Haney and Deana

Logan (1994), could hardly be clearer. And yet, on two of these issues—the fairness of the death penalty and its effectiveness—the Court has disregarded social science research.

Is the death penalty applied fairly? Studies show that those eligible to serve as jurors in capital punishment cases— namely, those who accept the death penalty—do not represent the greater population. Compared with people excluded by virtue of their qualms about capital punishment, those chosen as jurors are less likely to be minorities and women. They are also more likely to believe the prosecution's arguments, and they are more conviction-prone.

Does the death penalty work—does it deter crime? The evidence is consistent: States with a death penalty do not have lower homicide rates. After instituting the death penalty, these states did not see their rates drop. And homicide has not risen in states that have abandoned the death penalty. A person committing a crime of passion doesn't pause to calculate the consequences (and, if she or he did, would likely consider life in a prison cell an ample deterrent). Yet the Court persists in its belief that "the death penalty undoubtedly is a significant deterrent."

Beliefs guide perceptions. And that, say psychological scientists responding to postmodernists, is why we *need* to think smarter—to restrain our hunches, our biases, and our cultural leanings by checking them against available evidence. Why not put our testable beliefs to the test? If they find support, so much the better for them. If they collide against a wall of observation, so much the worse for them. These ideals of skeptical scrutiny and humility fuel all scientific endeavor.

Thinking Critically With Psychological Science

OBJECTIVE 2-1 | **Describe *hindsight bias,* and explain how it can make research findings seem like mere common sense.**

Hindsight bias (also called the *I-knew-it-all-along phenomenon*) is the tendency to believe, after learning an outcome, that we would have foreseen it. Thus, learning the outcome of a study can make it seem like obvious common sense. Scientific inquiry and critical thinking can help us overcome this tendency to overestimate our unaided intuition.

OBJECTIVE 2-2 | **Describe how overconfidence contaminates our everyday judgments.**

We are routinely *overconfident* of our judgments, thanks partly to our bias to seek information that confirms them. Science, with its procedures for gathering and sifting evidence, restrains error by taking us beyond the limits of our intuition and common sense.

OBJECTIVE 2-3 | **Explain how the scientific attitude encourages critical thinking.**

Although limited by the testable questions it can address, a scientific approach helps us sift reality from illusion. Scientific inquiry begins with an attitude—a curious eagerness to *skeptically* scrutinize competing ideas and an open-minded *humility* before nature. This attitude carries into everyday life as *critical thinking,* which examines assumptions, discerns hidden values, evaluates evidence, and assesses outcomes. Putting ideas, even crazy-sounding ideas, to the test helps us winnow sense from nonsense.

OBJECTIVE 2-4 | **Describe how psychological theories guide scientific research.**

Psychological *theories* organize *observations* and imply predictive *hypotheses.* After constructing precise operational definitions of their procedures, researchers test their hypotheses (predictions), validate and refine the theory, and, sometimes, suggest practical applications. If other researchers can replicate the study with similar results, we can then place greater confidence in the conclusion.

OBJECTIVE 2-5 | **Explain the value of simplified laboratory conditions in discovering general principles of behavior.**

Researchers test theoretical principles by creating a controlled, simplified environment in the lab. Their concern is not the particular behavior being studied, but rather the underlying principles that help explain many behaviors.

OBJECTIVE 2-6 | **Discuss whether psychological research can be generalized across cultures and genders.**

Behaviors, ideas, attitudes, and traditions vary across cultures, but the principles that underlie them are shared, in part because of our common biological heritage. Biology also determines our sex, but our culture sets up expectations about what it means to be male or female. Males and females do differ in some ways, but they are biologically and psychologically much more alike than different.

OBJECTIVE 2-7 | **Explain why psychologists study animals, and discuss the ethics of experimentation with both animals and humans.**

Some psychologists study animals out of an interest in animal behavior. Others do so because knowledge of other animals' physiological and psychological processes helps them understand similar human processes.

Under ethical and legal guidelines, animals used in psychological experiments rarely experience pain. Nevertheless, animal rights groups raise an important issue: Even if it leads to the relief of human suffering, is an animal's temporary suffering justified?

Occasionally researchers temporarily stress or deceive people to learn something important. Professional ethical standards, enforced by university ethics committees, safeguard research participants' well-being.

OBJECTIVE 2-8 | **Describe how personal values can influence psychologists' research and its application, and discuss psychology's potential to manipulate people.**

Psychologists' own values influence their choice of research topics, their theories and observations, their labels for behavior, and their professional advice. Psychology has the power to deceive, but so far, applications of psychology's principles have been overwhelmingly for the good. Psychology can help us reach our goals, but it cannot decide what those goals should be.

TERMS AND CONCEPTS TO REMEMBER

hindsight bias, p. 2-1
critical thinking, p. 2-4
theory, p. 2-5
hypothesis, p.2-5

operational definition, p. 2-6
replication, p. 2-6
culture, p. 2-7

TEST YOURSELF

1. What is the scientific attitude, and why is it important for critical thinking?

2. How are human and animal research subjects protected?

(Answers in Appendix B.)

ASK YOURSELF

1. How might the scientific method help us understand the roots of terrorism?

2. Were any of the Frequently Asked Questions your questions? Do you have other questions or concerns about psychology?

ANSWERS TO QUESTIONS WITHIN THE MODULE

Q. Which of the popular ideas in Table 2.1 have been confirmed or refuted by psychological research?

A. The odd-numbered statements have been refuted. The even-numbered statements have been confirmed.

Q. Roughly how thick would a sheet of paper be if you folded it on itself 100 times?

A. Given a 0.1-millimeter-thick sheet, the thickness after 100 folds would be 800 trillion times the distance between the Earth and the Sun (Gilovich, 1991).

Q. If a rope were placed around the Earth at the equator, how much additional rope would be needed for the rope to be 1 foot above the Earth all the way around?

A. About 6 more feet of rope. The circumference of a circle, or of the Earth, is $2\pi r$. The circumference of a rope elevated one foot is $2\pi(r + 1)$. Thus the added length is $2\pi(r + 1) - 2\pi r = 2\pi$, or about 6 feet.

Q. Can you unscramble this anagram? OCHSA.

A. Did you figure it out? The answer is CHAOS.

>WEB

Multiple-choice **self-tests** and more may be found at www.worthpublishers.com/myers.

3

Research Strategies: How Psychologists Ask and Answer Questions

Description

The starting point of any science is description. In everyday life, all of us observe and describe people, often drawing conclusions about why they behave as they do. Professional psychologists do much the same, though more objectively and systematically.

The Case Study

OBJECTIVE 3-1 | Identify an advantage and a disadvantage of using case studies to study behavior.

Among the oldest research methods is the **case study,** in which psychologists study one individual in great depth in the hope of revealing things true of us all. Some examples: Much of our early knowledge about the brain came from case studies of individuals who suffered a particular impairment after damage to a certain brain region. Jean Piaget taught us about children's thinking after carefully observing and questioning but a few children. Studies of only a few chimpanzees have revealed their capacity for understanding and language. Intensive case studies are sometimes very revealing.

Case studies can suggest hypotheses for further study. They also show us what *can* happen. In everyday life, however, individual cases sometimes mislead us: An individual may be atypical. Unrepresentative information can lead to mistaken judgments and false conclusions. Indeed, anytime a researcher mentions a finding ("Smokers die younger: 95 percent of men over 85 are nonsmokers") someone is sure to offer a contradictory case ("Well, I have an uncle who smoked two packs a day and lived to be 89"). Anecdotal cases—dramatic stories, personal experiences, even psychological case examples—have a way of overwhelming general truths. Highly publicized school shootings can raise alarm about school violence even while school violence rates are subsiding. Numbers can be numbing (in one study [Murray & Wheeler, 1937] of 1300 dream reports concerning a kidnapped child, only 5 percent correctly envisioned the child as dead). Anecdotes are often more startling. ("But I know a man who dreamed his sister was in a car accident, and two days later she was.") As psychologist Gordon Allport (1954, p. 9) said, "Given a thimbleful of [dramatic] facts we rush to make generalizations as large as a tub."

The point to remember: Individual cases can suggest fruitful ideas. What's true of all of us can be glimpsed in any one of us. But to discern the general truths that cover individual cases, we must answer questions with other methods.

"'Well my dear,' said Miss Marple, 'human nature is very much the same everywhere, and of course, one has opportunities of observing it at closer quarters in a village.'"

Agatha Christie, *The Tuesday Club Murders,* 1933

The case of the conversational chimpanzee In intensive case studies of chimpanzees, psychologists have explored the intriguing question of whether language is uniquely human. Here Nim Chimpsky signs *hug* as his trainer, psychologist Herbert Terrace, shows him the puppet Ernie. But is Nim really capable of using language? Cognitive theorists continue to debate that issue.

Susan Kuklin/Photo Researchers

The Survey

OBJECTIVE 3-2 | Identify the advantages and disadvantages of using surveys to study behavior and mental processes, and explain the importance of wording effects and random sampling.

The **survey** method looks at many cases in less depth. A survey asks people to report their behavior or opinions. Questions about everything from sexual practices to political opinions get put to the public. It's hard to think of a significant question that survey researchers have not asked. For example, Harris and Gallup polls have revealed that 72 percent of Americans think there is too much TV violence, 84 percent favor equal job opportunities for homosexual people, 89 percent say they face high stress, 95 percent believe in God, and 96 percent would like to change something about their appearance. In Britain, seven in ten 18- to 29-year-olds support gay marriage; among those over 50, about the same percentage oppose it (a generation gap found in many Western countries). But asking questions is tricky, and the answers may well depend on your wording and your choice of respondents.

Wording Effects

Even subtle changes in the order or wording of questions can have major effects. Should cigarette ads or pornography be allowed on television? People are much more likely to approve "not allowing" such things than "forbidding" or "censoring" them. In one national survey, only 27 percent of Americans approved of "government censorship" of media sex and violence, though 66 percent approved of "more restrictions on what is shown on television" (Lacayo, 1995). People are similarly much more approving of "aid to the needy" than of "welfare," of "affirmative action" than of "preferential treatment," and of "revenue enhancers" than of "taxes." Because wording is such a delicate matter, critical thinkers will reflect on how the phrasing of a question might have affected the opinions respondents expressed.

Random Sampling

In our everyday experience we spend most of our time with a biased sample of people—mostly those who share our attitudes and habits. Thus, when we wonder how many people hold a particular belief, those who think as we do come to mind most readily. This tendency to overestimate others' agreement with us is the **false consensus effect** (Ross & others, 1977). Vegetarians will think more people are vegetarians than will meat-eaters, and conservatives will perceive more support for conservative views than will liberals.

You can describe human experience using your estimates of others, perhaps supplemented by dramatic anecdotes and personal experience. But for an accurate picture of the experiences and attitudes of a whole population, there's only one game in town—the representative sample.

We can extend this point to everyday thinking, as we generalize from samples we observe, especially vivid cases. Given (a) a statistical summary of a professor's student evaluations and (b) the vivid comments of two irate students, an administrator's impression of the professor may be influenced as much by the two unhappy students as by the many favorable evaluations in the statistical summary. Standing in the checkout line at the supermarket, George sees the woman in front of him pay with government-provided food stamps and then watches with dismay as she drives away in a fancy car. In both situations, the temptation to generalize from a few vivid but unrepresentative cases is nearly irresistible.

The point to remember: The best basis for generalizing is from a representative sample of cases.

If you wish to survey the students at your college or university, how could you survey a representative sample of the total student **population**—the whole group you want to study and describe? Typically, you would choose a **random sample,** one in which every person in the entire group has an equal chance of participating.

This Modern World by Tom Tomorrow © 1991.

To sample the students randomly, you would *not* send each of them a questionnaire. (The conscientious people who return it would not be a random sample.) Rather, you would aim for a representative sample by, say, using a table of random numbers to pick participants from a student listing and then making sure you involve as many as possible. Large representative samples are better than small ones, but a small representative sample of 100 is better than an unrepresentative sample of 500.

The point to remember: Before believing survey findings, think critically: Consider the sample. You cannot compensate for an unrepresentative sample by simply adding more people.

The random-sampling principle also works in national surveys. Imagine that you had a giant barrel containing 60 million white beans mixed with 40 million red beans. A scoop that randomly sampled 1500 of them would contain about 60 percent white and 40 percent red beans, give or take 2 or 3 percent. Sampling voters in a national election survey is like sampling the beans; 1500 randomly sampled people, drawn from all areas of a country, provide a remarkably accurate snapshot of the opinions of a nation. Without random sampling, large samples—including call-in phone samples and TV Web site polls—often merely give misleading results.

With very large samples, estimates become quite reliable. *E* is estimated to represent 12.7 percent of the letters in written English. *E*, in fact, is 12.3 percent of the 925,141 letters in Melville's *Moby Dick*, 12.4 percent of the 586,747 letters in Dickens' *A Tale of Two Cities*, and 12.1 percent of the 3,901,021 letters in 12 of Mark Twain's works (*Chance News*, 1997).

Naturalistic Observation

OBJECTIVE 3-3 | Identify an advantage and a disadvantage of using naturalistic observation to study behavior.

A third descriptive research method involves watching and recording the behavior of organisms in their natural environment. These **naturalistic observations** range from watching chimpanzee societies in the jungle, to unobtrusively videotaping (and later systematically analyzing) parent-child interactions in different cultures, to recording students' self-seating patterns in the lunchrooms of multiracial schools.

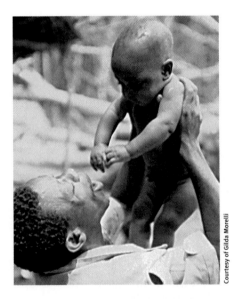

Naturalistic observation
For more than 20 years, psychologist Gilda Morelli has lived among and observed the Efe people of Central Africa, including the man and baby shown here, studying paternal and maternal care and observing children's development.

Courtesy of Gilda Morelli

Like the case study and survey methods, naturalistic observation does not *explain* behavior. It *describes* it. Nevertheless, descriptions can be revealing. We once thought, for example, that only humans use tools. Then naturalistic observation revealed that chimpanzees sometimes insert a stick in a termite mound and withdraw it, eating the stick's load of termites. Such unobtrusive naturalistic observations, recalls chimpanzee observer Jane Goodall (1998), paved the way for later studies of animal thinking, language, and emotion: "Observations, made in the natural habitat, helped to show that the societies and behavior of animals are far more complex than previously supposed," thus expanding our understanding of our fellow animals. We later learned that chimps and baboons also use deception to achieve their aims. Psychologists Andrew Whiten and Richard Byrne (1988) repeatedly saw one young baboon pretending to have been attacked by another as a tactic to get its mother to drive the other baboon away from its food.

Naturalistic observations are also done with humans. Here are three examples I think you will enjoy.

- *A funny finding.* We humans laugh 30 times more often in social situations than in solitary situations. (Have you noticed how seldom you laugh when alone?) When we do laugh, 17 muscles contort our mouth and squeeze our eyes, and we emit a series of 75-millisecond vowel-like sounds that are spaced about one-fifth of a second apart (Provine, 2001).

- *Sounding out students.* What, really, are introductory psychology students saying and doing during their everyday lives? To find out, Matthias Mehl and James Pennebaker (2003) equipped 52 such University of Texas students with a belt-worn tape recorder that, for up to four days, captured 30 seconds of their waking hours every 12.5 minutes—thus enabling the researchers to eavesdrop on more than 10,000 half-minute life slices. On what percentage of the slices do you suppose they found the students talking with someone? What percentage captured the students at a computer keyboard? The answers: 28 and 9 percent, respectively. (What percentage of *your* waking hours are spent in these activities?)

"How would you like me to answer that question? As a member of my ethnic group, educational class, income group, or religious category?"

■ **naturalistic observation** observing and recording behavior in naturally occurring situations without trying to manipulate and control the situation.

■ **correlation** a measure of the extent to which two factors vary together, and thus of how well either factor predicts the other. The *correlation coefficient* is the mathematical expression of the relationship, ranging from –1 to +1.

■ **scatterplot** a graphed cluster of dots, each of which represents the values of two variables. The slope of the points suggests the direction of the relationship between the two variables. The amount of scatter suggests the strength of the correlation (little scatter indicates high correlation). (Also called a *scattergram* or *scatter diagram*.)

- *Culture, climate, and the pace of life.* Naturalistic observation also enabled Robert Levine and Ara Norenzayan (1999) to compare the pace of life in 31 countries. By operationally defining *pace of life* as walking speed, the speed with which postal clerks completed a simple request, and the accuracy of public clocks, they concluded that life is fastest paced in Japan and Western Europe, and slower paced in economically less-developed countries. People in colder climates also tend to live at a faster pace (and are more prone to die from heart disease). Naturalistic observation describes behavior more than it explains it. But this study illustrates how naturalistic observation can also be used with correlational research, our next topic.

Correlation

OBJECTIVE 3-4 | Describe positive and negative correlations, and explain how correlational measures can aid the process of prediction.

Describing behavior is a first step toward predicting it. When surveys and naturalistic observations reveal that one trait or behavior accompanies another, we say the two **correlate.** The *correlation coefficient* is a statistical measure of a relationship (**FIGURE 3.1**): It reveals how closely two things vary together and thus how well either one *predicts* the other. Knowing how much aptitude test scores *correlate* with school success tells us how well the scores *predict* school success.

Throughout this book we will often ask how strongly two things are related: For example, how closely related are the personality scores of identical twins? How well do intelligence test scores predict achievement? How closely is stress related to disease?

FIGURE 3.2 on the next page illustrates perfect positive and negative correlations, which rarely occur in the "real world." These graphs are called **scatterplots,** because each point *plots* the value of two variables. A positive correlation means that two sets of scores, such as height and weight, tend to rise or fall together. A correlation's being negative has nothing to do with its strength or weakness; a negative correlation means two things relate inversely (one set of scores goes up as the other goes down). As toothbrushing goes up from zero, tooth decay goes down; brushing and decay correlate (negatively). A weak correlation, indicating little or no relationship, has a coefficient near zero.

FIGURE 3.1
How to read a correlation coefficient

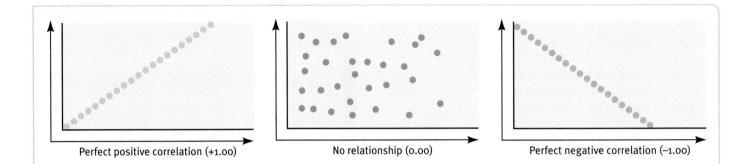

Perfect positive correlation (+1.00)   No relationship (0.00)   Perfect negative correlation (−1.00)

FIGURE 3.2

Scatterplots, showing patterns of correlation Correlations can range from +1.00 (scores on one measure increase in direct proportion to scores on another) to −1.00 (scores on one measure decrease precisely as scores rise on the other).

Here are some recent news reports of correlational research. Can you spot which are reporting positive correlations, which negative?

- The more TV is on in the homes of young children, the less time they spend reading (Kaiser, 2003).
- The more sexual content teens see on TV, the more likely they are to have sex (Collins & others, 2004).
- The longer children are breast-fed, the greater their later academic achievement (Horwood & Fergusson, 1998).
- The more income rose among a sample of poor families, the fewer psychiatric symptoms their children experienced (Costello & others, 2003).

(These are negative, positive, positive, and negative correlations, respectively.)

Statistics can help us see what the naked eye sometimes misses. To demonstrate this for yourself, try an imaginary project. Wondering if tall men are more or less easygoing, you collect two sets of scores: men's heights and men's temperaments. You measure the heights of 20 men, and have someone else independently assess their temperaments (from zero for extremely calm to 100 for highly reactive).

With all the relevant data (**TABLE 3.1**) right in front of you, can you tell whether there is (1) a positive correlation between height and reactive temperament, (2) very little or no correlation, or (3) a negative correlation?

Comparing the columns in Table 3.1, most people detect very little relationship between height and temperament. In fact, the correlation in this imaginary example is moderately positive, +0.63, as we can see if we display the data as a scatterplot. In **FIGURE 3.3**, moving from left to right, the upward, oval-shaped slope of the cluster of points shows that our two imaginary sets of scores (height and reactivity) tend to rise together.

If we fail to see a relationship when data are presented as systematically as in Table 3.1, how much less likely are we to notice them in everyday life? To see what is right in front of us, we sometimes need statistical illumination. We can easily see evidence of gender discrimination when given statistically summarized information about job level, seniority, performance, gender, and salary. But we often see no discrimination when the same information dribbles in, case by case (Twiss & others, 1989).

Though informative, psychology's correlations usually leave most of the variation among individuals unpredicted. For example, research shows there is a correlation between parents' abusiveness and their children's later abusiveness when they become parents. But this does not mean that most abused children become abusive. The correlation simply indicates a statistical relationship: Although most abused children do not grow into abusers, nonabused children are even less likely to become abusive.

The point to remember: A correlation coefficient helps us see the world more clearly by revealing the extent to which two things relate.

TABLE 3.1

HEIGHT AND TEMPERAMENT OF 20 MEN

Height	Height in Inches	Temperament
1	80	75
2	63	66
3	61	60
4	79	90
5	74	60
6	69	42
7	62	42
8	75	60
9	77	81
10	60	39
11	64	48
12	76	69
13	71	72
14	66	57
15	73	63
16	70	75
17	63	30
18	71	57
19	68	84
20	70	39

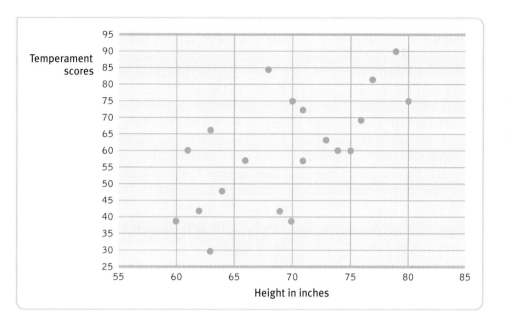

FIGURE 3.3
Scatterplot for height and temperament This display of data from 20 imagined people (each represented by a data point) reveals an upward slope, indicating a positive correlation. The considerable scatter of the data indicates the correlation is much lower than +1.0.

Correlation and Causation

OBJECTIVE 3-5 | Explain why correlational research fails to provide evidence of cause-effect relationships.

Correlations help us predict, and they restrain the illusions of our flawed intuition. Watching violence correlates with (and therefore predicts) aggression. But does that mean it *causes* aggression? Does low self-esteem *cause* depression? If, based on the correlational evidence, you assume that they do, you have much company. A nearly irresistible thinking error is assuming that correlation proves causation. But no matter how strong the relationship, it does not!

For example, what about the negative correlation between self-esteem and depression? Perhaps low self-esteem does cause depression. But as **FIGURE 3.4** suggests, we'd get the same correlation between low self-esteem and depression if depression caused people to be down on themselves, or if something else—a third factor such as heredity or brain chemistry—caused both low self-esteem and depression. Among men, length of marriage correlates positively with hair loss—because both are associated with a third factor, age. And people who wear hats are *more* likely to suffer skin cancer—because both are associated with fair-skinned people (who are vulnerable to skin cancer and more likely to wear protective hats).

Correlation need not mean causation Length of marriage correlates with hair loss in men. Does this mean that marriage causes men to lose their hair (or that balding men make better husbands)? In this case, as in many others, a third factor obviously explains the correlation: Golden anniversaries and baldness both accompany aging.

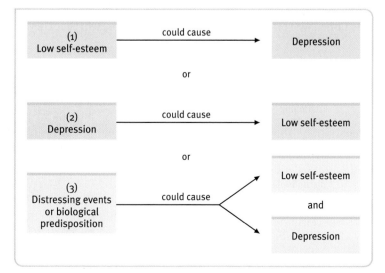

FIGURE 3.4
Three possible cause-effect relationships People low in self-esteem are more likely to report depression than are those high in self-esteem. One possible explanation of this negative correlation is that a bad self-image causes depressed feelings. But, as the diagram indicates, other cause-effect relationships are possible.

This point is so important—so basic to thinking smarter with psychology—that it merits one more example, from a survey of over 12,000 adolescents: The more teens feel loved by their parents, the less likely they are to behave in unhealthy ways—having early sex, smoking, abusing alcohol and drugs, exhibiting violence (Resnick & others, 1997). "Adults have a powerful effect on their children's behavior right through the high school years," gushed an Associated Press (AP) story on the study. But the correlation comes with no built-in cause-effect arrow. Said differently (turn the volume up here), *correlation does not prove causation*. Thus, the AP could as well have said, "Well-behaved teens feel their parents' love and approval; out-of-bounds teens more often think their parents are disapproving jerks."

The point to remember: Correlation indicates the *possibility* of a cause-effect relationship, *but it does not prove causation*. Knowing that two events are correlated need not tell us anything about causation. Remember this principle and you will be wiser as you read and hear news of scientific studies.

Illusory Correlations

OBJECTIVE 3-6 | Describe how people form illusory correlations.

Correlations make visible the relationships we might otherwise miss. They also restrain our "seeing" relationships that actually do not exist. A perceived nonexistent correlation is an **illusory correlation.** When we *believe* there is a relationship between two things, we are likely to *notice* and *recall* instances that confirm our belief (Trolier & Hamilton, 1986).

Illusory correlations help explain many a superstitious belief, such as the presumption that more babies are born when the moon is full or that infertile couples who adopt become more likely to conceive (Gilovich, 1991). Those who conceive after adopting capture our attention. We're less likely to notice those who adopt and never conceive, or those who conceive without adopting. In other words, illusory correlations occur when we over-rely on the top left cell of **FIGURE 3.5**, ignoring equally essential information in the other cells.

Such illusory thinking helps explain why for so many years people believed (and many still do) that sugar made children hyperactive, that getting cold and wet caused one to catch a cold, and that weather changes trigger arthritis pain. Physician Donald Redelmeier, working with psychologist Amos Tversky (1996), followed 18 arthritis patients for 15 months. The researchers recorded both the patients' pain reports and the daily weather—temperature, humidity, and barometric pressure. Despite patients' beliefs, the weather was uncorrelated with their discomfort, either on the same day or up to two days earlier or later. Shown columns of random numbers labeled "arthritis pain" and "barometric pressure," even college students saw a correlation where there was none. We seem prone to perceiving patterns, whether they're there or not.

A *New York Times* writer reported a massive survey showing that "adolescents whose parents smoked were 50 percent more likely than children of nonsmokers to report having had sex." He concluded (would you agree?) that the survey indicated a causal effect—that "to reduce the chances that their children will become sexually active at an early age" parents might "quit smoking" (O'Neil, 2002).

FIGURE 3.5
Illusory correlation in everyday life
Many people believe infertile couples become more likely to conceive a child after adopting a baby. This belief arises from their attention being drawn to such cases. The many couples who adopt without conceiving or conceive without adopting grab less attention. To determine whether there actually is a correlation between adoption and conception, we need data from all four cells in this figure. (From Gilovich, 1991)

	Conceive	Do not conceive
Adopt	confirming evidence	disconfirming evidence
Do not adopt	disconfirming evidence	confirming evidence

Michael Newman Jr./PhotoEdit

Because we are sensitive to dramatic or unusual events, we are especially likely to notice and remember the occurrence of two such events in sequence—say, a premonition of an unlikely phone call followed by the call. When the call does not follow the premonition, we are less likely to note and remember the nonevent.

Likewise, instances of positive-thinking people being cured of cancer impress those who believe that positive attitudes counter disease. But to assess whether positive thinking actually affects cancer, we need three more types of information. We need an estimate of how many positive thinkers were *not* cured. Then we need to know how many cancer patients were and were not cured among those not using positive thinking. Without these comparison figures, the positive examples of a few tell us nothing about the actual correlation between attitudes and disease.

The point to remember: When we notice random coincidences, we may forget that they are random and instead see them as correlated. Thus, we can easily deceive ourselves by seeing what is not there.

Perceiving Order in Random Events

OBJECTIVE 3-7 | Explain the human tendency to perceive order in random sequences.

Illusory correlations arise from our natural eagerness to make sense of our world—what poet Wallace Stevens called our "rage for order." Given even random data, we look for order, for meaningful patterns. And we usually find such, because *random sequences often don't look random.* Consider a random coin flip: If someone flipped a coin six times, which of the following sequences of heads (H) and tails (T) would be most likely: HHHTTT or HTTHTH or HHHHHH?

Daniel Kahneman and Amos Tversky (1972) found that most people believe HTTHTH would be the most likely random sequence. Actually, all three are equally likely (or, you might say, equally unlikely) to occur. A bridge or poker hand of 10 through Ace, all of hearts, would seem extraordinary; actually, it would be no more or less likely than any other specific hand of cards (**FIGURE 3.6**).

In actual random sequences, patterns and streaks (such as repeating digits) occur more often than people expect. To demonstrate this phenomenon for myself (as you can do), I flipped a coin 51 times, with these results:

1. H	11. T	21. T	31. T	41. H	51. T
2. T	12. H	22. T	32. T	42. H	
3. T	13. H	23. H	33. T	43. H	
4. T	14. T	24. T	34. T	44. H	
5. H	15. T	25. T	35. T	45. T	
6. H	16. H	26. T	36. H	46. H	
7. H	17. T	27. H	37. T	47. H	
8. T	18. T	28. T	38. T	48. T	
9. T	19. H	29. H	39. H	49. T	
10. T	20. H	30. T	40. T	50. T	

Looking over the sequence, patterns jump out: Tosses 10 to 22 provided an almost perfect pattern of pairs of tails followed by pairs of heads. On tosses 30 to 38 I had a "cold hand," with only one head in eight tosses. But my fortunes immediately reversed with a "hot hand"—seven heads out of the next nine tosses. Similar streaks happen, about as often as one would expect in random sequences, in basketball shooting, baseball hitting, and mutual fund stock pickers' selections (Gilovich & others, 1985; Malkiel, 1989, 1995; Myers, 2002). Whether flipping coins, watching basketball, or monitoring investment adviser performance, random sequences often don't look random, and so get overinterpreted ("When you're hot, you're hot—give her the ball!").

■ **illusory correlation** the perception of a relationship where none exists.

FIGURE 3.6
Two random sequences Your chances of being dealt either of these hands are precisely the same: 1 in 2,598,960.

Bizarre-looking, perhaps. But actually no more unlikely than any other number sequence.

Given enough random events, something weird will happen Angelo and Maria Gallina were the beneficiaries of one of those extraordinary chance events when they won two California lottery games on the same day.

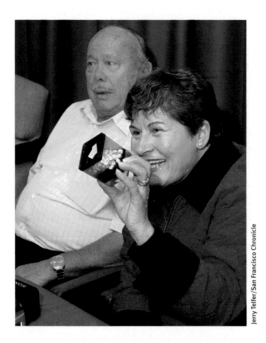

Jerry Telfer/San Francisco Chronicle

On March 11, 1998, Utah's Ernie and Lynn Carey gained three new grandchildren when three of their daughters gave birth—on the same day (*Los Angeles Times*, 1998).

What explains these streaky patterns? Was I exercising some sort of paranormal control over my coin? Did I snap out of my tails funk and get in a heads groove? No such explanations are needed, for these are the sorts of streaks found in any random data. Comparing each toss to the next, 24 of the 50 comparisons yielded a changed result—just the sort of near 50-50 result we expect from coin tossing. Despite the seeming patterns in these data, the outcome of one toss gives no clue to the outcome of the next toss.

However, some happenings seem so extraordinary that we struggle to conceive an ordinary, chance-related explanation (as applies to our coin-tosses). In such cases, statisticians often are less mystified. When Evelyn Marie Adams won the New Jersey lottery *twice*, newspapers reported the odds of her feat as 1 in 17 trillion. Bizarre? Actually, 1 in 17 trillion are the odds that a given person who buys a single ticket for two New Jersey lotteries will win both times. But statisticians Stephen Samuels and George McCabe (1989) report that, given the millions of people who buy U.S. state lottery tickets, it was "practically a sure thing" that someday, somewhere, someone would hit a state jackpot twice. Indeed, say fellow statisticians Persi Diaconis and Frederick Mosteller (1989), "with a large enough sample, any outrageous thing is likely to happen." "The really unusual day would be one where nothing unusual happens," adds Diaconis (2002). An event that happens to but one in 1 billion people every day occurs about six times a day, 2000 times a year.

Experimentation

Happy are they, remarked the Roman poet Virgil, "who have been able to perceive the causes of things." We endlessly wonder and debate *why* we act as we do. Why do people smoke? Have babies while they are still children? Do stupid things when drunk? Become troubled teens and open fire on their classmates? Though psychology cannot answer these questions directly, it has helped us to understand what influences drug use, sexual behaviors, thinking when drinking, and aggression.

Exploring Cause and Effect

OBJECTIVE 3-8 | Explain how experiments help researchers isolate cause and effect.

Many factors influence our everyday behavior. To isolate cause and effect—say, in looking for causes of depression—psychologists statistically control for other factors. For example, many studies have found that breast-fed infants grow up with somewhat higher intelligence scores than those of infants bottle-fed with cow's milk (Angelsen & others, 2001; Mortensen & others, 2002; Quinn & others, 2001). Mother's milk correlates modestly but positively with later intelligence. But does this mean that smarter mothers (who more often breast-feed) have smarter children? Or, as some researchers believe, do the nutrients of mother's milk contribute to brain development? To help answer this question, researchers have "controlled for" (statistically removed differences in) maternal age, education, and intelligence. Still, breast-fed infants exhibit slightly higher intelligence as young children.

The clearest and cleanest way to isolate cause and effect is, however, to **experiment.** Experiments enable a researcher to focus on the possible effects of one or more factors by (1) *manipulating the factors of interest* and (2) *holding constant ("controlling") other factors.* Knowing that correlations of infant nutrition and later intelligence can't possibly control for all other possible factors, a British research team led by Alan Lucas (1998) decided to experiment, using 424 hospital preterm infants. With parental permission, the researchers randomly assigned some infants to the usual infant formula feedings and others to donated breast milk feedings. When given intelligence tests at age 8, the children nourished with breast milk had significantly higher intelligence scores than their formula-fed counterparts. No single experiment is conclusive, of course, but by randomly assigning infants to a feeding condition, these researchers were able to hold constant all factors except nutrition. This eliminated alternative explanations and supported the conclusion that, so far as the developing intelligence of preterm infants is concerned, breast is best. (*Note:* The other infants were not harmed by the experiment, because they received the standard feeding.)

If a behavior (such as test performance) changes when we vary an experimental factor (such as infant nutrition), then we know the factor is having an effect. *The point to remember:* Unlike correlational studies, which uncover naturally occurring relationships, an experiment manipulates a factor to determine its effect.

Understanding experimentation is central to thinking critically with psychological science. So, let's consider further how we experiment.

Evaluating Therapies

OBJECTIVE **3-9** | Explain why the double-blind procedure and random assignment build confidence in research findings.

Our tendency to seek new remedies when we are ill or emotionally down can produce misleading testimonies. If three days into a cold we start taking vitamin C tablets and find our cold symptoms lessening, we may credit the pills rather than the cold naturally subsiding. If, after nearly failing the first exam, we listen to a "peak learning" subliminal tape and then improve on the next exam, we may credit the tape rather than conclude that our performance has returned to our average. In the 1700s, blood-letting *seemed* effective. Sometimes people improved after the treatment; when they didn't, the practitioner inferred the disease was just too advanced to be reversed. (We, of course, now know that blood-letting is a *bad* treatment.) So, whether or not a remedy is truly effective, enthusiastic users will probably endorse it. To find out whether it actually is effective, we must experiment.

And that is precisely how new drug treatments and new methods of psychological therapy are evaluated. In many of these studies, the participants are *blind* (uninformed) about what treatment, if any, they are receiving. One group receives the treatment. Others receive a pseudotreatment—an inert *placebo* (perhaps a pill with no drug in it). Often, neither the participant nor the research assistant collecting the data knows whether the participant's group is receiving the treatment. This **double-blind procedure** enables researchers to check a treatment's actual effects apart from the research participants' (and their own) enthusiasm for it and from the healing power of belief. The **placebo effect** is well documented in reducing pain, depression, and anxiety (Kirsch & Sapirstein, 1998). Just *believing* you are getting a treatment can boost your spirits, relax your body, and relieve your symptoms.

The double-blind procedure is one way to create an **experimental condition** in which people receive the treatment and a contrasting **control condition** without the treatment. By **randomly assigning** people to these conditions, researchers can be

■ **experiment** a research method in which an investigator manipulates one or more factors (independent variables) to observe the effect on some behavior or mental process (the dependent variable). By random assignment of participants, the experimenter aims to control other relevant factors.

■ **double-blind procedure** an experimental procedure in which both the research participants and the research staff are ignorant (blind) about whether the research participants have received the treatment or a placebo. Commonly used in drug-evaluation studies.

■ **placebo** [pluh-SEE-bo; Latin for "I shall please"] **effect** experimental results caused by expectations alone; any effect on behavior caused by the administration of an inert substance or condition, which is assumed to be an active agent.

■ **experimental condition** the condition of an experiment that exposes participants to the treatment, that is, to one version of the independent variable.

■ **control condition** the condition of an experiment that contrasts with the experimental condition and serves as a comparison for evaluating the effect of the treatment.

■ **random assignment** assigning participants to experimental and control conditions by chance, thus minimizing preexisting differences between those assigned to the different groups.

■ **independent variable** the experimental factor that is manipulated; the variable whose effect is being studied.

■ **dependent variable** the outcome factor; the variable that may change in response to manipulations of the independent variable.

fairly certain the two groups are otherwise identical. Random assignment roughly equalizes the two groups in age, attitudes, and every other characteristic. With random assignment, as occurred with the infants in the breast milk experiment, we also can know that any later differences between people in the experimental and control conditions will usually be the result of the treatment.

Another example: On the advice of their physicians, millions of postmenopausal women turned to hormone replacement therapy after correlational studies found that women on replacement hormones had lower rates of heart disease, stroke, and colon cancer. But these women may also have been more likely to receive medical care, to exercise, and to eat well. So, did the hormones make women healthy or did healthy women take the hormones? In 2002, the National Institutes of Health announced the surprising results of a massive experiment that randomly assigned 16,608 healthy women to either replacement hormones or a placebo. The shocking result: Compared with women in the control condition, women receiving the hormones had *more* health problems (Love, 2002).

Independent and Dependent Variables

OBJECTIVE 3-10 | Explain the difference between an independent and a dependent variable.

Here is an even more potent example: The drug Viagra was approved for use after 21 clinical trials, including an experiment in which researchers randomly assigned 329 men with impotence to either an experimental condition (Viagra) or a control condition (a placebo). It was a double-blind procedure—neither the men nor the person who gave them the pills knew which drug they were receiving. The result: At peak doses, 69 percent of Viagra-assisted attempts at intercourse were successful, compared with 22 percent for men receiving the placebo (Goldstein & others, 1998). Viagra had an effect.

This simple experiment manipulated just one drug factor. We call this experimental factor the **independent variable** because we can vary it independently of other factors, such as the men's age, weight, and personality (which random assignment should control). Experiments examine the effect of one or more independent variables on some measurable behavior, called the **dependent variable** because it can vary *depending* on what takes place during the experiment. Both variables are given precise operational definitions, which specify the procedures that manipulate the independent variable (the precise drug dosage and timing in this study) or measure the dependent variable (the questions that assessed the men's responses). These definitions answer the "What do you mean?" question with a level of precision that enables others to repeat the study. (See **FIGURE 3.7** for another experiment's design.)

FIGURE 3.7
Experimentation To discern causation, psychologists may randomly assign some participants to an experimental treatment, others to a control condition. Measuring the dependent variable (child's intelligence score) will determine the effect of the independent variable (type of milk received in first 12 months).

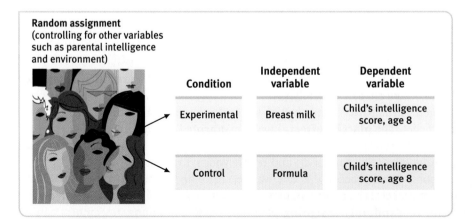

TABLE **3.2**

COMPARING RESEARCH METHODS

Research Method	Basic Purpose	How Conducted	What Is Manipulated	Weaknesses
Descriptive	To observe and record behavior	Do case studies, surveys, or naturalistic observations	Nothing	No control of variables; single cases may be misleading
Correlational	To detect naturally occurring relationships; to assess how well one variable predicts another	Compute statistical association, sometimes among survey responses	Nothing	Does not specify cause and effect
Experimental	To explore cause and effect	Manipulate one or more factors; use random assignment	The independent variable(s)	Sometimes not feasible; results may not generalize to other contexts; not ethical to manipulate certain variables

Experiments can also help us evaluate social programs. Do early childhood education programs boost impoverished children's chances for success? What are the effects of different anti-smoking campaigns? Do school sex-education programs reduce teen pregnancies? To answer these questions, we can experiment: If an intervention is welcomed but resources are scarce, we could use a lottery to randomly assign some people (or regions) to experience the new program and others to a control condition. If later the two groups differ, the intervention's effect will be confirmed (Passell, 1993).

Let's recap. A variable is anything that can vary (infant nutrition, intelligence, TV exposure—anything within the bounds of what is feasible and ethical). Experiments aim to *manipulate* an *independent* variable, *measure* the *dependent* variable, and *control* all other variables. An experiment has at least two different conditions: an experimental condition and a comparison or control condition. Random assignment works to equate the conditions before any treatment effects. In this way, an experiment tests the effect of at least one independent variable (what we manipulate) on at least one dependent variable (the outcome we measure). **TABLE 3.2** compares the features of psychology's research methods.

Note the distinction between random sampling *(typically associated with surveys) and random* assignment *in experiments. Random sampling helps us generalize to a larger population. Random assignment controls extraneous influences, which helps us infer cause and effect.*

Statistical Reasoning

OBJECTIVE 3-11 | Explain the importance of statistical principles, and give an example of their use in everyday life.

Having gathered data, we must next organize, summarize, and make inferences from it, using statistics. Today's statistics are tools that help us see and interpret what the unaided eye might miss.

Off-the-top-of-the-head estimates often misread reality and then mislead the public. Someone throws out a big round number. Others echo it and before long the big round number becomes public misinformation. A few examples:

- *One percent of Americans (2.7 million) are homeless.* Or is it 300,000, an earlier estimate by the federal government? Or 600,000, an estimate by the Urban Institute (Crossen, 1994)?
- *Ten percent of people are lesbians or gay men.* Or is it 2 to 3 percent, as suggested by various national surveys?
- *We ordinarily use but 10 percent of our brain.* Or is it closer to 100 percent? (Which 90 percent, or even 10 percent, would you be willing to sacrifice?)

"Figures can be misleading—so I've written a song which I think expresses the real story of the firm's performance this quarter."

© Patrick Hardincord

■ **mode** the most frequently occurring score(s) in a distribution.

■ **mean** the arithmetic average of a distribution, obtained by adding the scores and then dividing by the number of scores.

■ **median** the middle score in a distribution; half the scores are above it and half are below it.

■ **range** the difference between the highest and lowest scores in a distribution.

■ **standard deviation** a computed measure of how much scores vary around the mean score.

• *We remember 10 percent of what we read, 20 percent of what we hear, 30 percent of what we see, and 80 percent of what we say.* So reported the British Audio Visual Society (Genovese, 2004). Or is it, as a book on accelerated learning declares, 20 percent of what we read, 30 percent of what we hear, 40 percent of what we see, and 50 percent of what we say?

The point to remember: Doubt big, round, undocumented numbers. Rather than swallow top-of-the-head estimates, focus on thinking smarter by applying simple statistical principles to everyday reasoning.

Describing Data

OBJECTIVE 3-12 | Explain how bar graphs can misrepresent data.

Once researchers have gathered their data, their first task is to *organize* them. One way is to use a simple *bar graph,* as in **FIGURE 3.8**, which displays a distribution of trucks of different brands still on the road after a decade. When reading statistical graphs such as this, take care. As you can see, people can design a graph to make a difference look small or big, depending on what they want to emphasize.

The point to remember: Think smart. When viewing figures in magazines and on television, read the scale labels and note their range.

Measures of Central Tendency

OBJECTIVE 3-13 | Describe the three measures of central tendency, and tell which is most affected by extreme scores.

The next step is to summarize the data using some *measure of central tendency,* a single score that represents a whole set of scores. The simplest measure is the **mode,** the most frequently occurring score or scores. The most commonly reported is the **mean,** or arithmetic average—the total sum of all the scores divided by the number of scores. On a divided highway, the median is the middle. So, too, with data: The **median** is the midpoint—the 50th percentile. If you arrange all the scores in order from the highest to the lowest, half will be above the median and half will be below it.

FIGURE 3.8
Read the scale labels An American truck manufacturer offered a graph (a)—with actual brand names included—to suggest the much greater durability of its trucks. Note, however, how the apparent difference shrinks as the vertical scale changes (graph b).

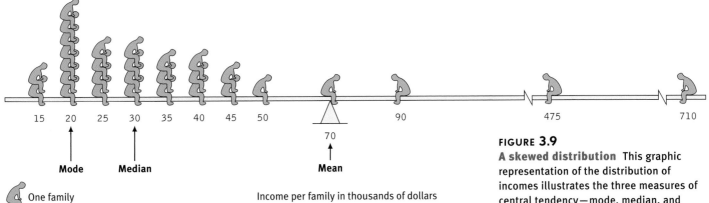

15   20   25   30   35   40   45   50   70   90   475   710

↑ Mode   ↑ Median   ↑ Mean

One family   Income per family in thousands of dollars

FIGURE 3.9
A skewed distribution This graphic representation of the distribution of incomes illustrates the three measures of central tendency—mode, median, and mean. Note how just a few high incomes make the mean—the fulcrum point that balances the incomes above and below—deceptively high.

Measures of central tendency neatly summarize data. But consider what happens to the mean when a distribution is lopsided or *skewed*. With income data, for example, the mode, median, and mean often tell very different stories (**FIGURE 3.9**). This happens because the mean is biased by a few extreme scores. When Microsoft founder Bill Gates sits down in an intimate cafe, its average (mean) patron instantly becomes a billionaire. Understanding this, you can see how a British newspaper could accurately run the headline "Income for 62% Is Below Average" (Waterhouse, 1993). Because the bottom *half* of British income earners receive only a *quarter* of the national income cake, most British people, like most people everywhere, make less than the mean.

In the United States, advocates and critics described the 2003 tax cut with different statistics, both true. The White House explained that "92 million Americans will receive an average tax cut of $1083." Critics agreed, but also noted that 50 million taxpayers got no cut, and half of the 92 million who did benefit received less than $100 (Krugman, 2003). Mean and median tell different true stories.

The point to remember: Always note which measure of central tendency is reported. Then, if it is a mean, consider whether a few atypical scores could be distorting it.

The average person has one ovary and one testicle.

Measures of Variation

OBJECTIVE 3-14 | Describe two measures of variation.

Knowing the value of an appropriate measure of central tendency can tell us a great deal. But it also helps to know something about the amount of *variation* in the data—how similar or diverse the scores are. Averages derived from scores with low variability are more reliable than averages based on scores with high variability. Consider a basketball player who scored between 13 and 17 points in each of her first 10 games in a season. Knowing this, we would be more confident that she would score near 15 points in her next game than if her scores had varied from 5 to 25 points.

The **range** of scores—the gap between the lowest and highest scores—provides only a crude estimate of variation because a couple of extreme scores in an otherwise uniform group, such as the $475,000 and $710,000 incomes in Figure 3.9, will create a deceptively large range.

The more useful standard for measuring how much scores deviate from one another is the **standard deviation.** It better gauges whether scores are packed together or dispersed, because it uses information from each score (**TABLE 3.3** on the next page). (The computation assembles information about how much individual scores differ from the mean.) If your college or university attracts students of a certain ability level, their intelligence scores will have a smaller standard deviation than the one found in the more diverse community population outside your school.

"The poor are getting poorer, but with the rich getting richer it all averages out in the long run."

TABLE **3.3**

STANDARD DEVIATION IS MUCH MORE INFORMATIVE THAN MEAN ALONE

Note that the test scores in Class A and Class B have the same mean (80), but very different standard deviations, which tell us more about how the students in each class are really faring.

Test Scores in Class A			Test Scores in Class B		
Score	Deviation From the Mean	Squared Deviation	Score	Deviation From the Mean	Squared Deviation
72	−8	64	60	−20	400
74	−6	36	60	−20	400
77	−3	9	70	−10	100
79	−1	1	70	−10	100
82	+2	4	90	+10	100
84	+4	16	90	+10	100
85	+5	25	100	+20	400
87	+7	49	100	+20	400
Total = 640	Sum of (deviations)² =	204	Total = 640	Sum of (deviations)² =	2000
Mean = 640 ÷ 8 = 80			Mean = 640 ÷ 8 = 80		

Standard deviation =

$$\sqrt{\frac{Sum\ of\ (deviations)^2}{Number\ of\ scores}} = \sqrt{\frac{204}{8}} = 5.0$$

Standard deviation =

$$\sqrt{\frac{Sum\ of\ (deviations)^2}{Number\ of\ scores}} = \sqrt{\frac{2000}{8}} = 15.8$$

Making Inferences

Data are "noisy." One group's average score (breast-fed babies' intelligence scores) could conceivably differ from another's (the formula-fed babies) not because of any real difference but merely because of chance fluctuations in the people sampled. How confidently, then, can we infer that an observed difference accurately estimates the true difference?

When Is an Observed Difference Reliable?

OBJECTIVE 3-15 | Identify three principles for making generalizations from samples.

In deciding when it is safe to generalize from a sample, we should keep three principles in mind. Let's look at each in turn.

1. *Representative samples are better than biased samples.* The best basis for generalizing is not from the exceptional and memorable cases one finds at the extremes (remember Bill Gates' income?) but from a representative sample of cases. No research involves a representative sample of the whole human population. Thus, it pays to keep in mind what population a study has sampled.

2. *Less-variable observations are more reliable than those that are more variable.* As we noted in the example of the basketball player whose points scored were consistent, an average is more reliable when it comes from scores with low variability.

3. *More cases are better than fewer.* An eager prospective university student visits two college campuses, each for a day. At the first, the student randomly attends two classes and discovers both instructors to be witty and engaging. At the next campus, the two sampled instructors seem dull and uninspiring. Returning home, the student (discounting the small sample size of only two teachers at each institution) tells friends about the "great teachers" at the first school, and the "bores" at the second. Again, we know it but we ignore it: *Averages based on many cases are more reliable* (less variable) than averages based on only a few cases.

The point to remember: Don't be overly impressed by a few anecdotes. Generalizations based on a few unrepresentative cases are unreliable.

When Is a Difference Significant?

OBJECTIVE 3-16 | Explain how psychologists decide whether differences are meaningful.

■ statistical significance a statistical statement of how likely it is that an obtained result occurred by chance.

Statistical tests also help us determine whether differences are meaningful. Here is the underlying logic: When *averages* from two samples are each *reliable* measures of their respective populations (as when each is based on many observations that have small variability), then their difference (sometimes even a very small difference) is likely to be reliable as well. (The less the variability in women's and in men's aggression scores, the more confidence we would have that any observed gender difference is reliable.) But when the *difference* between the sample averages is *large,* we have even more confidence that the difference between them reflects a real difference in their populations.

In short, *when the sample averages are reliable and the difference between them is relatively large*, we say the difference has **statistical significance.** This simply means that the difference we observed is probably not due to chance variation between the samples.

In judging statistical significance, psychologists are conservative. They are like juries who must presume innocence until guilt is proven. For most psychologists, proof beyond a reasonable doubt means not making much of a finding unless the odds of its occurring by chance are less than 5 percent (an arbitrary criterion).

Given large enough or homogeneous enough samples, a difference between them may be "statistically significant" yet have little practical significance. For example, comparisons of intelligence test scores among hundreds of thousands of first-born and later-born individuals indicate a highly significant tendency for first-born individuals to have higher average scores than their later-born siblings (Zajonc & Markus, 1975). But because the scores differ by only one or two points, the difference has little practical importance. Such findings have caused some psychologists to advocate alternatives to significance testing (Hunter, 1997). Better, they say, to use other ways to express a finding's "effect size"—its magnitude and reliability.

The point to remember: Statistical significance indicates the *likelihood* that a result will happen by chance. It does not indicate the *importance* of the result.

Using the principles we have discussed here will help us to think critically—to see more clearly what we might otherwise miss or misinterpret, and to generalize more accurately from our observations. We do think smarter when we understand and use the principles of research methods and statistics (Fong & others, 1986; Lehman & others, 1988; VanderStoep & Shaughnessy, 1997). It requires training and practice, but developing clear and critical thinking abilities is part of becoming an educated person. The report of the Project on Redefining the Meaning and Purpose of Baccalaureate Degrees (1985) eloquently asserts why there are few higher priorities in a college education:

> If anything is paid attention to in our colleges and universities, thinking must be it. Unfortunately, thinking can be lazy. It can be sloppy. . . . It can be fooled, misled, bullied. . . . Students possess great untrained and untapped capacities for logical thinking, critical analysis, and inquiry, but these are capacities that are not spontaneous: They grow out of wide instruction, experience, encouragement, correction, and constant use.

PEANUTS

>> LEARNING OUTCOMES

Research Strategies: How Psychologists Ask and Answer Questions

OBJECTIVE 3-1 | **Identify an advantage and a disadvantage of using case studies to study behavior.**

Researchers using case studies focus in depth on one individual, in the hope of revealing universal principles. Case studies describe behavior. They can suggest hypotheses, but studying an unrepresentative individual may lead to false conclusions.

OBJECTIVE 3-2 | **Identify the advantages and disadvantages of using surveys to study behavior and mental processes, and explain the importance of wording effects and random sampling.**

Surveys describe behavior by gathering information from a large number of people. This technique relies on people giving accurate self-reports of their attitudes or behaviors. Wording effects—subtle influences in the sequence or phrasing of questions—can affect responses. Random sampling helps researchers achieve a sample that fairly represents the population under study. Because random sampling chooses people by chance, each person in the entire group has an equal chance of participating.

OBJECTIVE 3-3 | **Identify an advantage and a disadvantage of using naturalistic observation to study behavior.**

Naturalistic observation gives researchers an opportunity to watch and record behavior in naturally occurring situations. Like other forms of description, naturalistic observation cannot explain behaviors, but it can expand our understanding and lead to hypotheses that can be studied by other methods.

OBJECTIVE 3-4 | **Describe positive and negative correlations, and explain how correlational measures can aid the process of prediction.**

A *correlation coefficient* is a statistical measure of the strength and duration of the relationship between two factors. In a *positive correlation* (ranging from 0 to +1.00), the two factors rise or fall together. In a *negative correlation* (ranging from 0 to −1.00), one item rises as the other falls. Scatterplots and the correlations they reveal help us to see relationships that the naked eye might miss.

OBJECTIVE 3-5 | **Explain why correlational research fails to provide evidence of cause-effect relationships.**

A correlation indicates the *possibility* of a cause-effect relationship, but it does not prove causation or, if causation exists, the direction of the influence. A third factor may be the cause of the correlation.

OBJECTIVE 3-6 | **Describe how people form illusory correlations.**

Illusory correlations are random (often dramatic or unusual) events that we notice and falsely assume are related. Once we believe two things are related, we tend to notice and recall instances that confirm this belief.

OBJECTIVE 3-7 | **Explain the human tendency to perceive order in random sequences.**

We search for patterns in an attempt to make sense of the world around us. Patterns or sequences occur naturally in sets of random data, but we tend to interpret these patterns as meaningful connections.

OBJECTIVE 3-8 | **Explain how experiments help researchers isolate cause and effect.**

To discover cause-effect relationships, psychologists conduct *experiments*. By manipulating one or more factors of interest, and controlling other factors, experimenters can determine the effect on some behavior or mental process.

OBJECTIVE 3-9 | **Explain why the double-blind procedure and random assignment build confidence in research findings.**

In a *double-blind procedure*, neither the researchers nor the participants know whether participants are receiving the treatment or a placebo. This counteracts the possibility that a placebo effect or researchers' expectations will unintentionally influence the study's results. *Random assignment* minimizes preexisting differences between the groups by selecting people by chance for the *experimental condition* (the group exposed to the treatment) or the *control condition* (a group that experiences no treatment or a different version of the treatment).

OBJECTIVE 3-10 | **Explain the difference between an independent and a dependent variable.**

The *independent variable* is the factor you manipulate to study its effect. The *dependent variable* is the factor you measure to discover any changes that occur in response to these manipulations.

OBJECTIVE 3-11 | **Explain the importance of statistical principles, and give an example of their use in everyday life.**

Statistics help us to organize, summarize, and make inferences from data. We need not remember complicated formulas to think more clearly and critically about the data we encounter in everyday life. For example, understanding statistical concepts teaches us the importance of doubting big, round, undocumented numbers.

OBJECTIVE 3-12 | **Explain how bar graphs can misrepresent data.**

Scale labels and ranges used in bar graphs can be designed to minimize or maximize differences. When looking at statistical graphs in books and magazines and on TV and the Internet, think critically.

OBJECTIVE 3-13 | **Describe the three measures of central tendency, and tell which is most affected by extreme scores.**

The *median* is the middle score in a group of data. The *mode* is the most frequently occurring score. The *mean*, the arithmetic average, is most easily distorted by a few very high or very low scores.

OBJECTIVE 3-14 | **Describe two measures of variation.**

Measures of variation tell us how similar or diverse data are. A *range* describes the gap between the highest and lowest scores. The more useful measure, the *standard deviation,* states how much scores vary around the mean, or average, score.

OBJECTIVE 3-15 | **Identify three principles for making generalizations from samples.**

1. Representative samples are better than biased samples.
2. Less-variable observations are more reliable than those that are more variable.
3. More cases are better than fewer.

OBJECTIVE 3-16 | Explain how psychologists decide whether differences are meaningful.

When averages from two samples are each reliable measures of their own populations, and the difference between them is relatively large, we can assume the difference is *significant*—that the result did not occur by chance alone. Statistical significance indicates the likelihood of a result's occurring, not the importance of the result.

TERMS AND CONCEPTS TO REMEMBER

case study, p. 3-0	experimental condition, p. 3-9
survey, p. 3-1	control condition, p. 3-9
false consensus effect, p. 3-1	random assignment, p. 3-9
population, p. 3-1	independent variable, p. 3-10
random sample, p. 3-1	dependent variable, p. 3-10
naturalistic observation, p. 3-2	mode, p. 3-12
correlation, p. 3-3	mean, p. 3-12
scatterplot, p. 3-3	median, p. 3-12
illusory correlation, p. 3-6	range, p. 3-13
experiment, p. 3-9	standard deviation, p. 3-13
double-blind procedure, p. 3-9	statistical significance, p. 3-15
placebo effect, p. 3-9	

TEST YOURSELF

1. What are the strengths and weaknesses of the three different methods psychologists use to describe behavior—case studies, surveys, and naturalistic observation?

2. Here are some recently reported correlations, with interpretations drawn by journalists. Further research, often including experiments, has clarified cause and effect in each case. Knowing just these correlations, can you come up with other possible explanations for each of these?

   a. Alcohol use is associated with violence. (One interpretation: Drinking triggers or unleashes aggressive behavior.)

   b. Educated people live longer, on average, than less-educated people. (One interpretation: Education lengthens life and enhances health.)

   c. Teens engaged in team sports are less likely to use drugs, smoke, have sex, carry weapons, and eat junk food than are teens who do not engage in team sports. (One interpretation: Team sports encourage healthy living.)

   d. Adolescents who frequently see smoking in movies are more likely to smoke. (One interpretation: Movie stars' behavior influences impressionable teens.)

3. Why, when testing a new drug for blood pressure, would we learn more about its effectiveness from giving it to half of the participants in a group of 1000 than to all 1000 participants?

4. Consider a question posed by Christopher Jepson, David Krantz, and Richard Nisbett (1983) to University of Michigan introductory psychology students:

   > The registrar's office at the University of Michigan has found that usually about 100 students in Arts and Sciences have perfect marks at the end of their first term at the University. However, only about 10 to 15 students graduate with perfect marks. What do you think is the most likely explanation for the fact that there are more perfect marks after one term than at graduation?

(Answers in Appendix B.)

ASK YOURSELF

1. Can you recall examples of misleading surveys you have experienced or read about? What principles for a good survey did they violate?

2. Can you think of an example of correlational research that you recently heard about from a friend or on the news? Was an unwarranted conclusion drawn?

3. If you were to become a research psychologist, what questions would you like to explore with experiments?

4. Find a graph in a popular magazine ad. How does the advertiser use (or abuse) statistics to make a point?

>WEB

Multiple-choice *self-tests* and more may be found at www.worthpublishers.com/myers.

ANOTHER VOICE ON: NEUROSCIENCE AND BEHAVIOR

FROM "THE BRAIN IS WIDER THAN THE SKY," *THE COMPLETE POEMS OF EMILY DICKINSON*. BOSTON: LITTLE, BROWN, 1924.

The brain is wider than the sky,
For, put them side by side,
The one the other will include
With ease, and you beside.

The brain is deeper than the sea,
For, hold them, blue to blue,
The one the other will absorb,
As sponges, buckets do.

Nature, Nurture, and Human Diversity

OBJECTIVE 6-1 | Give examples of differences and similarities within the human family.

What makes you you? In important ways, we are each unique. We look different. We sound different. We have varying personalities, interests, and cultural and family backgrounds. But how different are we really?

We are also the leaves of one tree. Our human family shares not only a common biological heritage—cut us and we bleed—but also common behavioral tendencies. Our shared brain architecture predisposes us to sense the world, develop language, and feel hunger through identical mechanisms. Whether we live in the Arctic or the tropics, we prefer sweet tastes to sour. We divide the color spectrum into similar colors. And we feel drawn to behaviors that produce and protect offspring.

Our kinship appears in our social behaviors as well. Whether our last name is Wong, Nkomo, Smith, or Gonzales, at about eight months we start fearing strangers, and as adults we prefer the company of those whose attitudes and attributes are similar to our own. Coming from different parts of the globe, we know how to read one another's smiles and frowns. As members of one species, we affiliate, conform, reciprocate favors, punish offenses, organize hierarchies of status, and grieve a child's death. A visitor from outer space could drop in anywhere and find humans dancing and feasting, singing and worshiping, playing sports and games, laughing and crying, living in families, and forming groups. Taken together, such universal behaviors reveal our human nature.

What causes our striking diversity and our shared human nature? Modules 6 and 7 begin to tell this complex story. In Module 6, we start with *behavior genetics,* which studies the relative effects of our genes *(nature)* and our environments *(nurture)* on our individual differences in behavior and mental processes. Together, our genes and environments design our unique body-mind system and define the things that make us different. Genes matter. But in Module 7, we'll see that culture, and everything we experience from womb to tomb, matter, too. We will also consider how nature and nurture together shape us.

In Module 6, we'll focus on *evolutionary psychology,* which studies behaviors, emotions, and thinking capacities that seemingly allowed our distant ancestors to survive, reproduce, and send their genes into the future. We humans tend to fear snakes and spiders, and to avoid heights and bitter-tasting foods, because such fears and behaviors helped our ancestors to survive.

Then in Module 7, we'll take a close look at some ways *parents, peers, and culture* influence our beliefs and values, our interests and food tastes, and our language and appearance. (Even before hearing their accent, my Scottish friends can spot American tourists by the way they look and walk.) And we'll also consider the influences of *gender* and all its associated expectations, which affect how others perceive us and how we think about ourselves. Yet for all their publicized differences, women and men are, as we will see, more alike than different.

Jeffrey W. Myers/Stock, Boston

The nurture of nature

Parents everywhere wonder: Will my baby grow up to be peaceful or aggressive? Homely or attractive? Successful or struggling at every step? What comes built in, and what is nurtured—and how? Research reveals that nature and nurture together shape our development—every step of the way.

Behavior Genetics: Predicting Individual Differences

Evolutionary Psychology: Understanding Human Nature

"Thanks for almost everything, Dad."

■ **environment** every nongenetic influence, from prenatal nutrition to the people and things around us.

■ **behavior genetics** the study of the relative power and limits of genetic and environmental influences on behavior.

■ **chromosomes** threadlike structures made of DNA molecules that contain the genes.

■ **DNA (deoxyribonucleic acid)** a complex molecule containing the genetic information that makes up the chromosomes.

■ **genes** the biochemical units of heredity that make up the chromosomes; a segment of DNA capable of synthesizing a protein.

■ **genome** the complete instructions for making an organism, consisting of all the genetic material in that organism's chromosomes.

■ **identical twins** twins who develop from a single fertilized egg that splits in two, creating two genetically identical organisms.

■ **fraternal twins** twins who develop from separate fertilized eggs. They are genetically no closer than brothers and sisters, but they share a fetal environment.

6

Behavior Genetics and Evolutionary Psychology

Behavior Genetics: Predicting Individual Differences

OBJECTIVE **6-2** | Describe the types of questions that interest behavior geneticists.

How much are our behavior differences shaped by our genetic differences? And how much by our **environment**—every external influence, from maternal nutrition while in the womb to social support while nearing the tomb—reacting to our genetic traits? More specifically, to what extent are we formed by our upbringing? By our culture? By our current circumstances? If Jaden Agassi, son of tennis stars Andre Agassi and Stephanie Graf, grows up to be a tennis star, should we attribute his talent to his Grand Slam genes? To his growing up in a tennis-rich environment? To high expectations? Equally to all three? **Behavior geneticists** study our differences and weigh the relative effects of heredity and environment.

Genes: Our Codes for Life

OBJECTIVE **6-3** | Define *chromosome, DNA, gene,* and *genome,* and describe their relationships.

Behind the story of our body and of our brain—surely the most awesome thing on our little planet—is the heredity that interacts with our experience to create both our universal human nature and our individual and social diversity. Barely more than a century ago, few would have guessed that every cell nucleus in your body contains the genetic master code for your entire body. It's as if every room in the Empire State Building had a book containing the architect's plans for the entire structure. The plans for your own book of life run to 46 chapters—23 donated by your mother (from her egg) and 23 by your father (from his sperm). These chapters, called **chromosomes,** are each composed of a coiled chain of the molecule **DNA** (*deoxyribonucleic acid*). **Genes,** small segments of the giant DNA molecules, form the words of these chromosome books (**FIGURE 6.1**). All told, each of us has 30,000 or so of these gene words, each a self-replicating unit capable of synthesizing proteins. Genes do not directly guide our behavior. They simply, when "turned on," provide the code for creating protein molecules, the building blocks of our physical development.

Genetically speaking, every other human is close to being your identical twin. Even the person you like least is your near-clone, sharing about 99.9 percent of your DNA (Plomin & Crabbe, 2000). But that 0.1 percent difference, in interaction with differing environments, can give us a Nelson Mandela or an Adolf Hitler.

Human **genome** researchers have discovered the common sequence within human DNA. It is this shared genetic profile that makes us humans, rather than chimpanzees or tulips. Actually, we aren't all that different from our chimpanzee cousins; with them we share, depending on how the count is done, 96 percent of our DNA sequence (Mikkelsen & others, 2005). At "functionally important" DNA sites, reports one molecular genetics team, the human–chimpanzee DNA similarity is 99.4

Nucleus
(the inner area of a cell that houses chromosomes and genes)

Chromosome
(threadlike structure made largely of DNA molecules)

Gene
(segment of DNA containing the code for a particular protein; determines our individual biological development)

Cell
(the basic structural unit of a living thing)

DNA
(a spiraling, complex molecule containing genes)

FIGURE 6.1
The genes: Their location and composition
Contained in the nucleus of each of the trillions of cells in your body are chromosomes. Each chromosome contains a coiled chain of the molecule DNA. Genes are DNA segments that, when expressed (turned on), form templates for the production of proteins. By directing the manufacture of proteins, the genes determine our individual biological development.

percent (Wildman & others, 2003). Yet that wee difference matters. Despite some remarkable abilities, chimpanzees grunt. Shakespeare intricately wove some 24,000 words to form his literary masterpieces. And small differences matter among chimpanzees, too. Two species that differ by much less than 1 percent of their genomes also display obvious behavior differences. Common chimpanzees are aggressive and male-dominated. Bonobos are peaceable and female led.

Geneticists and psychologists are interested in the occasional variations found at particular gene sites in the DNA—variations that in their many combinations define each person's uniqueness. Slight person-to-person variations from the common pattern give clues to why one person has a disease that another does not, why one person is short and another tall, why one is happy and another depressed.

Human traits are influenced by *gene complexes*—many genes acting in concert. How tall you are, for example, reflects the height of your face, the size of your vertebrae, the length of your leg bones, and so forth—each of which may be influenced by different genes interacting with your environment. Complex human traits such as intelligence, happiness, and aggressiveness are similarly influenced by groups of genes. Thus our genetic predispositions help explain both our shared human nature and our human diversity.

Twin Studies

OBJECTIVE 6-4 | Explain how identical and fraternal twins differ, and cite ways that behavior geneticists use twin studies to understand the effects of environment and heredity.

To disentangle the threads of heredity and environment, behavior geneticists often use two sets of tweezers: twin studies and adoption studies.

Identical Versus Fraternal Twins

To scientifically tease apart the influences of environment and heredity, we would need to control the home environment while varying heredity. Happily for our purposes, nature has given us ready-made subjects for this experiment: identical versus fraternal twins. **Identical twins,** who develop from a single fertilized egg that splits in two, are *genetically* identical (**FIGURE 6.2** on the next page). They are nature's own human clones—indeed, clones who share not only the same genes but the same conception, uterus, birth date, and usually the same cultural history.

Fraternal twins, who develop from separate fertilized eggs, are genetically no more similar than ordinary brothers and sisters. A person whose identical twin has Alzheimer's disease has a 60 percent risk of

We share half our genes with the banana."

Evolutionary biologist Robert May, president of Britain's Royal Society, 2001

Identical?
Twins Morgan Hamm (left) and Paul Hamm (right), world-class gymnasts, are identical, yet their achievements are not. In the 2004 Olympics, Paul won more medals than the brother with whom he grew up. This small difference suggests the influence of slightly different environments (perhaps even prenatal environments) as well as the influence of their individual interactions with their environments after birth.

Adrian Dennis/AFP/Getty Images

FIGURE 6.2
Same fertilized egg, same genes; different eggs, different genes
Identical twins develop from a single fertilized egg, fraternal twins from two.

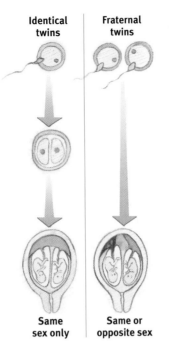

Identical twins

Fraternal twins

Same sex only

Same or opposite sex

Curiously, twinning rates vary by race. The rate among Caucasians is roughly twice that of Asians and half that of Africans. In Africa and Asia, most twins are identical. In Western countries, most twins are fraternal, and fraternal twins are increasing with the use of fertility drugs (Hall, 2003; Steinhauer, 1999).

sharing the disease; if the affected twin is fraternal, the risk is only 30 percent (Plomin & others, 1997a). Such a difference suggests a genetic influence. But behavior geneticists also work to tease out the influences of siblings' unique experiences and shared environments (such as being in the same family, neighborhood, and schools); see **FIGURE 6.3**.

Are identical twins, being genetic clones of one another, behaviorally more similar than fraternal twins (Bouchard, 2004)? Studies of nearly 13,000 pairs of Swedish twins, of 7000 Finnish twin pairs, and of 3810 Australian twin pairs provide a consistent answer: On both extraversion (outgoingness) and neuroticism (emotional instability), identical twins are much more similar than fraternal twins. In explaining individual differences, genes matter.

If genes influence traits such as emotional instability, might they also influence the social effects of such traits? To find out, Matt McGue and David Lykken (1992) studied divorce rates among 1500 same-sex, middle-age twin pairs. Their result: If you have a fraternal twin who has divorced, the odds of your divorcing go up 1.6 times (compared with having a not-divorced twin). If you have an identical twin who has divorced, the odds of your divorcing go up 5.5 times. From such data, McGue and Lykken estimate that people's differing divorce risks are about 50 percent attributable to genetic factors.

Other dimensions also reflect genetic influences. When John Loehlin and Robert Nichols (1976) gave a battery of questionnaires to 850 U.S. twin pairs, identical twins were much more similar than fraternals in many ways—in abilities, personal traits, and interests. However, the identical twins, more than fraternal twins, also reported being treated alike. So, did their experience rather than their genes account for their similarity? No, said Loehlin and Nichols; identical twins whose parents treated them alike were *not* psychologically more alike than identical twins who were treated less similarly.

FIGURE 6.3
Twin studies
Behavior geneticists have used twin studies to disentangle the influence of *genes*, the *shared environment*, and the unique or *nonshared environment*. (Adapted from Lisa Legrand, William Iacono, and Matt McGue, 2005.)

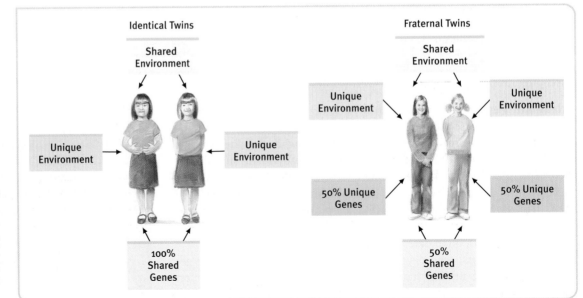

Identical Twins

Shared Environment

Unique Environment

Unique Environment

100% Shared Genes

Fraternal Twins

Shared Environment

Unique Environment

Unique Environment

50% Unique Genes

50% Unique Genes

50% Shared Genes

Separated Twins

Imagine the following science fiction experiment: A mad scientist decides to separate identical twins at birth, then rear them in differing environments. Better yet, consider a true story:

On a chilly Ohio Saturday morning in February 1979, some time after divorcing his first wife, Linda, Jim Lewis awoke in his modest, middle-class home next to his second wife, Betty. Jim—a romantic, affectionate type—was determined that this marriage would work and made a habit of leaving love notes to Betty around the house. As Jim lay in bed he thought about others he had loved, including his son, James Alan, and his faithful dog, Toy.

Having outfitted a workshop in a corner of his basement, Jim looked forward to spending some of the day's free time on his woodworking hobby. He had derived many hours of satisfaction from building furniture, picture frames, and an assortment of other items, including a circular white bench around a tree in his front yard. Jim also liked to spend free time driving his Chevy, watching stock-car racing, and drinking Miller Lite beer.

Jim was basically healthy. Having undergone a vasectomy, he was done having children. His blood pressure was a little high, perhaps related to his chain-smoking habit. He chewed his fingernails to the nub. And he suffered occasional half-day migraine headaches—"like somebody's hitting you with a two-by-four in the back of the neck." He had become overweight a while back but had shed some of the pounds.

What was extraordinary about Jim Lewis, however, was that at that same moment (I am not making this up) there existed another man—also named Jim—for whom all these things (right down to the dog's name) were also true.[1] This other Jim—Jim Springer—just happened, 38 years earlier, to have been his womb-mate. Thirty-seven days after their birth, these two genetically identical twins were separated, adopted by blue-collar families, and reared with no contact or knowledge of each other's whereabouts until one February day when Jim Lewis' phone rang. The caller was his genetic clone (who, having been told he had a twin, set out to find him).

One month after that fateful encounter, the brothers became the first twin pair tested by University of Minnesota psychologist Thomas Bouchard and his colleagues, thus beginning a study of separated twins that extends to the present (Holden, 1980a,b; Wright, 1998). When given tests measuring their personality, intelligence, heart rate, and brain waves, the Jim twins—despite 38 years of separation—were virtually as alike as the same person tested twice. Their voice intonations and inflections were so similar that, hearing a playback of an earlier interview, Jim Springer guessed "That's me." Wrong—it was his brother.

Identical twins Oskar Stohr and Jack Yufe presented equally striking similarities. One was raised by his grandmother in Germany as a Catholic and a Nazi, while the other was raised by his father in the Caribbean as a Jew. Nevertheless, they share traits and habits galore. They like spicy foods and sweet liqueurs, have a habit of falling asleep in front of the television, flush the toilet before using it, store rubber bands on their wrists, and dip buttered toast in their coffee. Stohr is domineering toward women and yells at his wife, as did Yufe before he and his wife separated. Both married women named Dorothy Jane Scheckelburger. Okay, the last item is a joke. But as Judith Rich Harris (2006) notes, it is hardly weirder than some other reported coincidences.

Aided by publicity in magazine and newspaper stories, Bouchard and his colleagues (1990; DiLalla & others, 1996; Segal, 1999) have located and studied 80 pairs of identical twins reared apart. They continue to find similarities not only of tastes and physical attributes but also of personality, abilities, attitudes, interests, and even fears.

Sweden has the world's largest national twin registry—140,000 living and dead twin pairs—which form part of a massive European registry of 600,000 twins currently being sampled in the world's largest twin study (Wheelwright, 2004). www.genomeutwin.org

Twins Lorraine and Levinia Christmas, driving to deliver Christmas presents to each other near Flitcham, England, collided (Shepherd, 1997).

"In some domains it looks as though our identical twins reared apart are . . . just as similar as identical twins reared together. Now that's an amazing finding and I can assure you none of us would have expected that degree of similarity."

Thomas Bouchard (1981)

[1] Actually, this description of the two Jims errs in one respect: Jim Lewis named his son James Alan. Jim Springer named his James Allan.

Identical twins are people two
Identical twins Gerald Levey and Mark Newman were separated at birth and raised in different homes. When reunited at age 31, they discovered that they both volunteered as firefighters. Research has shown remarkable similarities in the life choices of separated identical twins, lending support to the idea that genes influence personality.

Bob Sacha

Coincidences are not unique to twins. Patricia Kern of Colorado was born March 13, 1941, and named Patricia Ann Campbell. Patricia DiBiasi of Oregon also was born March 13, 1941, and named Patricia Ann Campbell. Both had fathers named Robert, worked as bookkeepers, and at the time of this comparison had children ages 21 and 19. Both studied cosmetology, enjoyed oil painting as a hobby, and married military men, within 11 days of each other. They are not genetically related (from an AP report, May 2, 1983).

In Sweden, Nancy Pedersen and her co-workers (1988) identified 99 separated identical twin pairs and more than 200 separated fraternal twin pairs. Compared with equivalent samples of identical twins reared together, the separated identical twins had more dissimilar *personalities*—characteristic patterns of thinking, feeling, and acting. Still, separated twins were more alike if genetically identical than if fraternal. Separation shortly after birth (rather than, say, at age 8) didn't amplify their personality differences.

The stories of startling twin similarity do not impress Bouchard's critics, who remind us that "the plural of anecdote is not data." They contend that if any two strangers were to spend hours comparing their behaviors and life histories, they would probably discover many coincidental similarities. If researchers created a control group of biologically unrelated pairs of the same age, sex, and ethnicity, who had not grown up together but who were as similar to one another in economic and cultural background as are many of the separated twin pairs, wouldn't these pairs also exhibit striking similarities (Joseph, 2001)? (Bouchard replies that separated fraternal twins do not exhibit similarities comparable to those of separated identical twins, and twin researcher Nancy Segal [2000] notes that "virtual twins"—same-age, biologically unrelated siblings—are also much more dissimilar.)

Even the more impressive data from the personality assessments are clouded by the reunion of many of the separated twins some years before they were tested. Moreover, separated twins share an appearance, and the responses it evokes. And adoption agencies tend to place separated twins in similar homes. Despite these criticisms, the striking twin study results have helped shift scientific thinking toward a greater appreciation of genetic influences.

Adoption Studies

OBJECTIVE 6-5 | Cite ways that behavior geneticists use adoption studies to understand the effects of environment and heredity.

Family ties
Studies of adoptive families have provided clues to hereditary and environmental influences. Adopted children share many values and attitudes with their adoptive parents, but adopted children's *personalities* tend to display the genetic legacy of their biological parents.

David Young-Wolff/PhotoEdit, Inc.

For behavior geneticists, another handy real-life experiment—adoption—creates two groups of relatives: the adoptees' genetic relatives (biological parents and siblings) and their environmental relatives (adoptive parents and siblings). For any given trait we can therefore ask whether adopted children are more like their adoptive parents, who contribute a home environment, or their biological parents, who contributed their genes. While sharing the same home environment, do adopted siblings come to share traits?

The stunning finding from studies of hundreds of adoptive families is that people who grow up together, whether biologically related or not, do not much resemble one another in personality (McGue & Bouchard, 1998; Plomin & others, 1998; Rowe, 1990). Adoptees' traits (their outgoingness, agreeableness, and so forth) bear more similarities to their biological parents than to their caregiving adoptive parents.

The finding is important enough to bear repeating: Environmental factors shared by a family's children have virtually no impact on their personalities. Two adopted children reared in the same home are no more likely to share personality traits with each other than with the child down the block. Heredity shapes other primates' personalities, too. For chimpanzees, being raised in the same zoo hardly matters (Weiss & others, 2000). Similarly, macaque monkeys raised by foster mothers exhibit social behaviors that resemble their biological, rather than foster, mothers (Maestripieri, 2003). Add all this to the finding that identical twins are about as similar as we would expect from their shared genes, whether they grow up together or apart, and the effect of a shared rearing environment seems shockingly modest.

What we have here is perhaps "the most important puzzle in the history of psychology," contends Steven Pinker (2002): Why are children in the same family so different? (Even biological siblings tend to be strikingly different.) Why do the shared genes and the shared family environment (the family's social class, the parents' personalities and marital status, day care versus home care, the neighborhood) have so little discernible effect on children's personalities? Is it because each sibling nevertheless has differing experiences—differing peer influences and life events? Is it because sibling relationships ricochet off each other, amplifying their differences? Is it because siblings—despite sharing half their genes—have very different combinations of genes? Does parental influence therefore affect an easygoing child one way, an emotionally reactive child another? "Child-rearing is not something a parent does to a child," notes Judith Rich Harris (1998). "It is something the parent and the child do together. . . . I would have been pegged as a permissive parent with my first child, a bossy one with my second."

So is adoptive parenting a fruitless venture? No. The genetic leash may limit the family environment's influence on personality, but parents do influence their children's attitudes, values, manners, faith, and politics (Brodzinsky & Schechter, 1990). A pair of adopted children or identical twins *will* have more similar religious beliefs, especially while still at home during adolescence, if reared together (Kelley & De Graaf, 1997; Koenig & others, 2005; Rohan & Zanna, 1996). Parenting matters!

Moreover, in adoptive homes, child neglect and abuse and even parental divorce are rare. (Adoptive parents are carefully screened; natural parents are not.) So it is not surprising that, despite a somewhat greater risk of psychological disorder, most adopted children thrive, especially when adopted as infants (Benson & others, 1994; Wierzbicki, 1993). They score higher than their biological parents on intelligence tests. Seven in eight report feeling strongly attached to one or both adoptive parents. As children of self-giving parents, they grow up to be more self-giving and altruistic than average (Sharma & others, 1998). And they generally become happier and more stable people than they would have been in a stressed or neglectful environment. In one Swedish study, infant adoptees grew up with fewer problems than were experienced by children whose biological mothers had initially registered them for adoption but then decided to raise the children themselves (Bohman & Sigvardsson, 1990). Regardless of personality differences between parents and their adoptees, children benefit from adoption.

Temperament Studies

OBJECTIVE **6-6** | Discuss how the relative stability of our temperament illustrates the influence of heredity on development.

As most parents will tell you after having their second child, babies differ even before gulping their first breath. Consider one quickly apparent aspect of personality. An infant's **temperament** is its emotional excitability—whether reactive, intense, and fidgety, or easygoing, quiet, and placid. From the first weeks of life, *difficult* babies are more irritable, intense, and unpredictable. *Easy* babies are cheerful, relaxed, and predictable in feeding and sleeping (Chess & Thomas, 1987).

■ **temperament** a person's characteristic emotional reactivity and intensity.

❝ Mom may be holding a full house while Dad has a straight flush, yet when Junior gets a random half of each of their cards his poker hand may be a loser."
David Lykken (2001)

The greater uniformity of adoptive homes—mostly healthy, nurturing homes—helps explain the lack of striking differences when comparing child outcomes of different adoptive homes (Stoolmiller, 1999).

"Oh, he's cute, all right, but he's got the temperament of a car alarm."

■ **heritability** the proportion of variation among individuals that we can attribute to genes. The heritability of a trait may vary, depending on the range of populations and environments studied.

Parents, being keenly sensitive to their children's differences, perceive their temperaments as even more different than they are (Saudino & others, 2004). Yet actual temperament differences do exist and do persist. Consider these findings:

- The most emotionally reactive newborns tend also to be the most reactive 9-month-olds (Wilson & Matheny, 1986; Worobey & Blajda, 1989).
- Four-month-olds who react to changing scenes with arched back, pumping legs, and crying are usually fearful and inhibited in their second year. Those who react with relaxed smiles are usually fearless and sociable in their second year (Kagan, 1990).
- Exceptionally inhibited and fearful 2-year-olds often are still relatively shy as 8-year-olds; about half will become introverted adolescents (Kagan & others, 1992, 1994).
- The most emotionally intense preschoolers tend to be relatively intense as young adults (Larsen & Diener, 1987). In one ongoing study of more than 900 New Zealanders, emotionally reactive and impulsive 3-year-olds have developed into somewhat more impulsive, aggressive, and conflict-prone 21-year-olds (Caspi, 2000).

Compared with fraternal twins, identical twins have more similar temperaments, indicating that heredity may predispose temperament differences (Emde & others, 1992; Gabbay, 1992; Robinson & others, 1992). Another line of evidence comes from physiological tests which reveal that anxious, inhibited infants have high and variable heart rates and a reactive nervous system, and that they become more physiologically aroused when facing new or strange situations (Kagan & Snidman, 2004). Such evidence adds to the emerging conclusion that our biologically rooted temperament helps form our enduring personality (McCrae & others, 2000; Rothbart & others, 2000).

Heritability

OBJECTIVE 6-7 | Discuss heritability's application to individuals and groups, and explain what we mean when we say genes are *self-regulating*.

Using the twin and adoption methods, behavior geneticists can mathematically estimate the **heritability** of a trait—the extent to which variation among individuals can be attributed to their differing genes. If the heritability of intelligence is, say, 50 percent, this does *not* mean that your intelligence is 50 percent genetic. (If the heritability of height is 90 percent, this does not mean that a 60-inch-tall woman can credit her genes for 54 inches and her environment for the other 6 inches.) Rather, it means that we can attribute to genetic influence 50 percent of the observed variation among people. This point is so often misunderstood that I repeat: We can never say what percentage of an *individual's* personality or intelligence is inherited. It makes no sense to say that your personality is due *x* percent to your heredity and *y* percent to your environment. Heritability refers instead to the extent to which *differences among people* are attributable to genes.

Even this conclusion must be qualified, because heritability can vary from study to study. If we were to follow humorist Mark Twain's (1835–1910) proposal to raise boys in barrels to age 12, feeding them through a hole, they would emerge with lower-than-normal intelligence scores. Yet, given their equal environments, their individual IQ score differences at age 12 could be explained only by their heredity. In other words, heritability for their differences would be near 100 percent. *As environments become more similar, heredity as a source of differences necessarily becomes more important.* If all schools were of uniform quality, all families equally loving, and all neighborhoods equally

"The title of my science project is 'My Little Brother: Nature or Nurture.'"

healthy, heritability—differences due to genes—would *increase* (because differences due to environment would decrease). At the other extreme, if all people had similar heredities but were raised in drastically different environments (some in barrels, some in luxury homes), heritability would be much lower.

Group Differences

If genetic influences help explain individual diversity in traits such as aggressiveness, can the same be said of group differences between men and women, or between people of different races? Not necessarily. Individual differences in height and weight, for example, are highly heritable; yet nutritional rather than genetic influences explain why, as a group, today's adults are taller and heavier than those of a century ago. The two groups differ, but not because human genes have changed in a mere century's eyeblink of time.

As with height and weight, so with personality and intelligence scores: Heritable individual differences need not imply heritable group differences. If some *individuals* are genetically disposed to be more aggressive than others, that doesn't explain why some *groups* are more aggressive than others. Putting people in a new social context can change their aggressiveness. Today's peaceful Scandinavians carry many genes inherited from their Viking ancestors.

Nature *and* Nurture

Among our similarities, the most important—the behavioral hallmark of our species—is an enormous adaptive capacity. Some human traits, such as having two eyes, develop the same in virtually every environment. But most psychologically interesting traits are expressed in particular environments. We all are driven to eat, but depending on our culturally learned tastes, we may have a yen for fish eyes, black bean salad, or chicken legs. Go barefoot for a summer and you will develop toughened, callused feet—a biological adaptation to friction. Meanwhile, your shod neighbor will remain a tenderfoot. The difference between the two of you is, of course, an effect of environment. But it is also the product of a biological mechanism. Our shared biology enables our developed diversity (Buss, 1991).

An analogy may help: Genes and environment—nature and nurture—work together like two hands clapping. Genes not only code for particular proteins, they also respond to environments. An African butterfly that is green in summer turns brown in fall, thanks to a temperature-controlled genetic switch. "The genome is giving the butterfly two different choices, two different opportunities. It's not dictating, 'You must take this form,'" Gary Marcus (2004) explains. "It's saying, 'If you're in this situation you can take this form, if you're in this other situation you can take this other form.'" Thus, genes are *self-regulating*. Rather than acting as blueprints that lead to the same result no matter the context, genes react. People with identical genes but differing experiences therefore have similar though not identical minds. One twin may fall in love with someone quite different from the co-twin's love. And at least one known gene will, in response to major life stresses, code for a protein that controls neurotransmitter functions underlying depression. By itself, the gene doesn't cause depression, but it is part of the recipe.

Thus, asking whether your personality is more a product of your genes or your environment is like asking whether water's wetness is due more to its hydrogen or its oxygen, or whether the area of a field is more the result of its length or its width. We could, however, ask whether the *differing* areas of various fields are more the result of differences in their length or width and whether person-to-person personality *differences* are influenced more by nature or nurture. For psychological phenomena, human differences are nearly always the result of both genetic and environmental influences. Eating disorders, for example, are genetically influenced: Some individuals are more at risk than others. But culture also bends the twig, for eating disorders are primarily a contemporary Western cultural phenomenon.

Men's natures are alike; it is their habits that carry them far apart."
Confucius, *Analects*, 500 B.C.

Genes are as important to the brain as sparking plugs are to car engines, but there is a big difference between something being necessary and sufficient. The potential of a sparking plug is only realized when it is placed in an engine, the engine is in a car, and the car has a driver."
Neuroscientist Susan Greenfield, "Alcohol on the Brain," 2002

Gene-environment interaction
People respond differently to a Rowan Atkinson (left, playing Mr. Bean) than to fellow actor Orlando Bloom.

Gene-Environment Interaction

OBJECTIVE 6-8 | Give an example of a genetically influenced trait that can evoke responses in others, and give another example of an environment that can trigger gene activity.

To say that genes and experience are *both* important is true. But more precisely, they interact. Imagine two babies, one genetically predisposed to be attractive, sociable, and easygoing, the other less so. Assume further that the first baby attracts more affectionate and stimulating care than the second and so develops into a warmer and more outgoing person. As the two children grow older, the more naturally outgoing child more often seeks activities and friends that encourage further social confidence.

What has caused their resulting personality differences? Neither heredity nor experience dances alone. Environments trigger gene activity. And our genetically influenced traits *evoke* significant responses in others. Thus, a child's impulsivity and aggression may evoke an angry response from a teacher who reacts warmly to the child's model classmates. Parents, too, may treat their children differently; one child elicits punishment, another does not. In such cases, the child's nature and the parents' nurture interact. Neither operates apart from the other. Gene and scene dance together.

Evocative interactions may help explain why identical twins reared in different families recall their parents' warmth as remarkably similar—almost as similar as if they had had the same parents (Plomin & others, 1988, 1991, 1994). Fraternal twins recall greater variations in their early family life—even if reared in the same family! "Children experience us as different parents, depending on their own qualities," notes Sandra Scarr (1990). Moreover, as we grow older we also *select* environments well suited to our natures.

So, from conception onward, we are the product of a cascade of **interactions** between our genetic predispositions and our surrounding environments. Our genes affect how people react to and influence us. Biological appearances have social consequences. Asking whether genes or experiences are more important is therefore like asking whether an engine or a steering wheel is more important for driving a car. So, forget nature *versus* nurture; think nurture *via* nature.

The New Frontier: Molecular Genetics

OBJECTIVE 6-9 | Identify the potential promise and perils of molecular genetics research.

Behavior geneticists have progressed beyond asking, "Do genes influence behavior?" The new frontier of behavior-genetics research is the "bottom-up" **molecular genetics** quest to identify *specific genes* influencing behavior. As psychologist Robert Plomin (1997) observes, "The DNA train [is] pulling out of the station," and psychologists are climbing aboard.

"Heredity deals the cards; environment plays the hand."
Psychologist Charles L. Brewer (1990)

"We predict that DNA will revolutionize psychological research and treatment early in the twenty-first century."
Robert Plomin and John Crabbe (2000)

We now know that most human traits are influenced by teams of genes. For example, twin and adoption studies tell us that heredity influences body weight, but there is no single "obesity gene." More likely, some genes influence how quickly the stomach tells the brain, "I'm full." Others might dictate how much fuel the muscles need, how many calories are burned off by fidgeting, and how efficiently the body converts the extra calories into fat (Vogel, 1999). The goal of molecular behavior genetics is to find some of the many genes that influence normal human traits, such as body weight, sexual orientation, and extraversion.

"I thought that sperm-bank donors remained anonymous."

Genetic tests can now reveal at-risk populations for at least a dozen diseases. The search continues in labs worldwide, where molecular geneticists are teaming with psychologists to pinpoint genes that put people at risk for such genetically influenced disorders as learning disabilities, depression, schizophrenia, aggressiveness, and alcoholism. In one notable example, a worldwide research effort is under way to sleuth the genes that make some people vulnerable to the emotional swings of bipolar disorder (formerly known as manic-depressive disorder). To tease out the implicated genes, molecular geneticists seek links between certain genes or chromosome segments and specific disorders. First, they find families that have had the disorder across several generations. Then they draw blood or take cheek swabs from both affected and unaffected family members and examine their DNA, looking for differences. "The most powerful potential for DNA," note Robert Plomin and John Crabbe (2000), "is to predict risk so that steps can be taken to prevent problems before they happen."

Aided by inexpensive DNA-scanning techniques, medical personnel may soon be able to give would-be parents a read out on how their fetus' genes differ from the normal pattern and what this might mean. With this benefit come risks. Might labeling a fetus, for example, "at risk for a learning disorder" lead to discrimination? Prenatal screening poses ethical dilemmas. In China and India, where boys are highly valued, testing for an offspring's sex has enabled selective abortions resulting in millions—yes, millions—of "missing women." A new technique for sorting sperm carrying male or female chromosomes can provide expectant parents a reasonable chance of success at choosing a child's sex before conception.

Blueprints for "designer babies" are, of course, constrained by the reality that it takes many genes to influence behavior in combination with complex environments. But assuming it were possible, should prospective parents take their eggs and sperm to a genetics lab for screening before combining them to produce an embryo? Before scoffing at this possibility, recall that a quarter century ago people were horrified at the prospect of in vitro fertilization ("test-tube" conception). Today, infertile couples demand it. A half-century ago, people worried about the kind of control that novelist Aldous Huxley imagined in his *Brave New World,* in which government social engineers bred hothouse babies genetically assigned to roles, such as clever "Alphas" and dim-witted "Epsilons." In today's more plausible new world, notes Robert Wright (1999), millions of parents will freely select for health, and perhaps for brains, beauty, and athleticism. But as always, progress is a two-edged sword, raising both hopeful possibilities and difficult problems. By selecting out certain traits, we may deprive ourselves of future Handels and van Goghs, Churchills and Lincolns, Tolstoys and Dickinsons—troubled people all.

■ **interaction** in psychology, occurs when the effect of one factor (such as environment) depends on another factor (such as heredity).

■ **molecular genetics** the subfield of biology that studies the molecular structure and function of genes.

■ **evolutionary psychology** the study of the evolution of behavior and the mind, using principles of natural selection.

■ **natural selection** the principle that, among the range of inherited trait variations, those that lead to increased reproduction and survival will most likely be passed on to succeeding generations.

■ **mutation** a random error in gene replication that leads to a change.

Evolutionary Psychology: Understanding Human Nature

OBJECTIVE 6-10 | Describe the area of psychology that interests evolutionary psychologists.

Molecular genetics involves a here-and-now way to select for certain behaviors and traits that make individuals distinct. **Evolutionary psychologists** instead focus mostly on what makes us so much alike as humans. To understand how these principles work, let's first consider a straightforward example in foxes.

Natural Selection

OBJECTIVE 6-11 | State the principle of natural selection, and point out some possible effects of natural selection in the development of human characteristics.

A fox is a wild and wary animal. If you capture a fox and try to befriend it, be careful. Stick your hand in the cage and, if the timid fox cannot flee, it probably will make a snack of your fingers. Familiar with foxes, Dmitry Belyaev, of the Russian Academy of Science's Institute of Cytology and Genetics, wondered how our human ancestors had domesticated dogs from their equally wild wolf forebears. Might he, within a comparatively short stretch of time, accomplish a similar feat by transforming the fearful fox into a friendly fox?

To find out, Belyaev set to work with 30 male and 100 female foxes. From their offspring he selected and mated the tamest 5 percent of males and 20 percent of females. (He measured tameness by the foxes' responses to attempts to feed, handle, and stroke them.) Over more than 30 generations of foxes, Belyaev and his successor, Lyudmila Trut, repeated that simple procedure. Today, more than 40 years and 45,000 foxes later, they have a new breed of foxes that, in Trut's (1999) words, are "docile, eager to please, and unmistakably domesticated. . . . Before our eyes, 'the Beast' has turned into 'beauty,' as the aggressive behavior of our herd's wild [ancestors] entirely disappeared." So friendly and eager for human contact are they, so inclined to whimper to attract attention and to lick people like affectionate cats, that the cash-strapped institute seized on a way to raise funds—marketing its foxes to people as house pets.

As Belyaev and Trut demonstrated, when certain traits are *selected*—by conferring a reproductive advantage to an individual or a species—those traits, over time, will prevail. Over many generations, wild wolves can become tame dogs, and wary foxes can have cuddly descendants. Dog breeders, as Robert Plomin and his colleagues (1997b) remind us, have given us sheepdogs that herd, retrievers that retrieve, trackers that track, and pointers that point. Psychologists, too, have bred dogs, mice, and rats whose genes predispose them to be serene or reactive, quick learners or slow learners.

In life outside the laboratory, the same selection process confers an advantage on other organisms. Deep in the sea, many years ago, a mutant shark with keener-than-normal smell was able to find more prey, enabling it to live longer and leave more offspring. As nature continued over countless generations to give an edge to sharks best suited to their ecological niche, an exquisitely effective predator came into being. A much smaller predator has developed in your lifetime. Bacteria that resist a hospital's antibiotics will multiply rapidly, as less-resistant bacteria die off. Over time, the natural result has been many hospitals plagued by antibiotic-resistant bacteria.

Does **natural selection** also explain our human tendencies? Nature has indeed selected advantageous variations from among the **mutations** (random

From beast to beauty
More than 40 years into the fox-breeding experiment, most of the offspring are devoted, affectionate, and capable of forming strong bonds with people.

errors in gene replication) and the new gene combinations produced at each human conception. Do we, as suggested earlier, fear snakes and heights because our ancestors who feared them were more likely to survive and spread their genes?

Perhaps. But the tight genetic leash that predisposes a dog's retrieving, a cat's pouncing, or an ant's nest building is looser on humans. The genes selected during our ancestral history provide more than a long leash; they endow us with a great capacity to learn and therefore to adapt to life in varied environments, from the tundra to the jungle. Genes and experience together wire the brain. Our adaptive flexibility in responding to different environments contributes to our fitness—our ability to survive and reproduce.

Yet in the big picture, our lives are remarkably alike. Visit the international arrivals area at London's Heathrow Airport, a world hub where arriving passengers meet their excited loved ones. There you will see the same delighted joy in the faces of Jamaican grandmothers, Chinese children, and homecoming Britons. Although human differences grab our attention, our deep similarities also demand explanation. Evolutionary psychologist Steven Pinker (2002, p. 73) believes our shared human traits "were shaped by natural selection acting over the course of human evolution." No wonder, then, that our emotions, drives, and reasoning "have a common logic across cultures."

Our behavioral and biological similarities arise from our shared human genome. No more than 5 percent of the genetic differences among humans arise from population group differences. Some 95 percent of genetic variation exists within populations (Rosenberg & others, 2002). The typical genetic difference between two Icelandic villagers or between two Kenyans is much greater than the *average* difference between the two groups. Thus, noted geneticist Richard Lewontin (1982), if after a worldwide catastrophe only Icelanders or Kenyans survived, the human species would suffer only "a trivial reduction" in its genetic diversity.

Why are we all so much alike? At the dawn of human history, our ancestors faced certain questions: Who is my ally, who my foe? What food should I eat? With whom should I mate? Some individuals answered those questions more successfully than others. For example, some women's experience of nausea in the critical first three months of pregnancy predisposes their avoiding certain bitter, strongly flavored, and novel foods. Avoiding such foods has survival value, since they are the very foods most often toxic to embryonic development (Schmitt & Pilcher, 2004). Those disposed to eat nourishing rather than poisonous food survived to contribute their genes to later generations. Those who deemed leopards "nice to pet" often did not.

Similarly successful were those who mated with someone with whom they could produce and nurture offspring. Over generations, the genes of individuals not so disposed tended to be lost from the human gene pool. As further mutations occurred, genes providing an adaptive edge continued to be selected. The result, say evolutionary psychologists, is behavioral tendencies and thinking and learning capacities that prepared our Stone Age ancestors to survive, reproduce, and send their genes into the future. Nature selected the fittest adaptations, which also include the human diversity that allows Arctic and equatorial dwellers to thrive in their distinct environments.

As inheritors of this prehistoric genetic legacy, we are predisposed to behave in ways that promoted our ancestors' surviving and reproducing. We love the taste of sweets and fats, which once were hard to come by but which prepared our ancestors to survive famines. Ironically, with famine rare in Western cultures, and sweets and fats beckoning us from store shelves, fast-food outlets, and vending machines, obesity has become a growing problem. Our natural dispositions, rooted deep in history, are mismatched with today's junk-food environment (Colarelli & Dettman, 2003). We are, in some ways, biologically prepared for a world that no longer exists.

Evolution has been an organizing principle for biology for a long time. Jared Diamond (2001) notes that "virtually no contemporary scientists believe that Darwin was basically wrong." Darwin's theory lives on as an organizing principle for biology and, more recently, in "the second Darwinian revolution," in psychology. Charles Darwin (1859) anticipated this application of evolutionary principles to psychology. In concluding *On the Origin of Species,* he foresaw "open fields for far more important researches. Psychology will be based on a new foundation" (p. 346).

Evolutionary psychologists are now exploring such questions as these:

- Why do infants start to fear strangers about the time they become mobile?
- Why are biological fathers so much less likely than unrelated boyfriends to abuse and murder the children with whom they share a home?
- Why are most parents so passionately devoted to their children?
- Why do so many more people have phobias about spiders and snakes than about more dangerous threats, such as guns and electricity?
- How are men and women alike? How and why do men and women differ? For example, why are men quicker than women to perceive friendliness as sexual interest, to initiate sexual relations, and to feel jealous rage over a mate's having sex with someone else?

To see how evolutionary psychologists think and reason, let's pause to explore this last question: How—and why, according to evolutionary psychology—do women's and men's sexuality differ?

An Evolutionary Explanation of Human Sexuality

Gender Differences in Sexuality

OBJECTIVE 6-12 | Identify some gender differences in sexuality.

Having faced many similar challenges throughout history, men and women have adapted in similar ways. Whether male or female, we eat the same foods, fear the same heights, avoid the same predators, and perceive, learn, and remember similarly. It is only in those domains where we have faced differing adaptive challenges—most obviously in behaviors related to reproduction—that we differ, say evolutionary psychologists. And differ we do, report psychologists Roy Baumeister, Kathleen Catanese, and Kathleen Vohs (2001). They invite us to consider whether women or men have the stronger sex drive. Who desires more frequent sex, thinks more about sex, masturbates more often, initiates more sex, and makes more sacrifices to gain sex? The answers, they report, are men, men, men, men, and men. Indeed, "with few exceptions anywhere in the world," agree cross-cultural psychologist Marshall Segall and his colleagues (1990, p. 244), "males are more likely than females to initiate sexual activity." This difference is among the largest of **gender** differences in sexuality, but there are others:

- In a 2004 survey of 289,452 entering U.S. college students, 60 percent of men but only 35 percent of women agreed that "if two people really like each other, it's all right for them to have sex even if they've known each other for a very short time" (Sax & others, 2004). "I can imagine myself being comfortable and enjoying 'casual' sex with different partners," agreed 48 percent of men and 12 percent of women in another survey of 4901 Australians (Bailey & others, 2000).
- In one careful survey of 3432 U.S. 18- to 59-year-olds, 48 percent of the women but only 25 percent of the men cited affection as a reason for first intercourse. And how often do they think about sex? "Every day" or "several times a day," acknowledged 19 percent of the women and 54 percent of the men (Laumann & others, 1994).

Those who are troubled by an apparent conflict between scientific and religious accounts of human origins may find it helpful to recall that different perspectives of life can be complementary. For example, the scientific account attempts to tell us *when* and *how;* religious creation stories usually aim to tell about an ultimate *who* and *why.* As Galileo explained to the Grand Duchess Christina, "The Bible teaches how to go to heaven, not how the heavens go."

■ **gender** in psychology, the biologically and socially influenced characteristics by which people define *male* and *female.*

- Such gender differences characterize both heterosexual and homosexual people. Gay men report more interest in uncommitted sex, more responsiveness to visual sexual stimuli, and more concern with their partner's physical attractiveness than do lesbians (Bailey & others, 1994). Compared with their gay male counterparts, American lesbians are nearly twice as likely to have partners (24 percent versus 47 percent, respectively [Doyle, 2005]).

Gender differences in attitudes extend to differences in behavior. Casual, impulsive sex is most frequent among males with traditional masculine attitudes (Pleck & others, 1993). Russell Clark and Elaine Hatfield (1989) observed this striking gender difference in 1978 when they sent some average-looking student research assistants strolling across the Florida State University quadrangle. Spotting an attractive person of the other sex, a researcher would approach and say, "I have been noticing you around campus and I find you to be very attractive. Would you go to bed with me tonight?" The women all declined, some obviously irritated ("What's wrong with you, creep! Leave me alone"). But 75 percent of the men readily agreed, often replying with comments such as "Why do we have to wait until tonight?" Somewhat astonished by their result, Clark and Hatfield repeated their study in 1982 and twice more during the late-1980s U.S. AIDS era (Clark, 1990). Each time, virtually no women, but half or more of the men, agreed to go to bed with a stranger.

Men also have a lower threshold for perceiving warm responses as a sexual come-on. In study after study, men more often than women attribute a woman's friendliness to sexual interest (Abbey, 1987; Johnson & others, 1991). Misattributing women's cordiality as a come-on helps explain, but does not excuse, men's greater sexual assertiveness (Kenrick & Trost, 1987). The unfortunate results can range from sexual harassment to date rape.

Natural Selection and Mating Preferences

OBJECTIVE 6-13 | Describe evolutionary explanations for gender differences in sexuality.

As biologists use natural selection to explain the mating behaviors of many species, so evolutionary psychologists use natural selection to explain women's more relational and men's more recreational approaches to sex. Their explanation goes like this: While a woman normally incubates and nurses one infant, a male can spread his genes through other females. Our natural yearnings are our genes' way of reproducing themselves. In our ancestral history, women most often sent their genes into the future by pairing wisely, men by pairing widely. "Humans are living fossils—collections of mechanisms produced by prior selection pressures," says evolutionary psychologist David Buss (1995).

And what do heterosexual men and women find attractive in the other sex? Some aspects of attractiveness cross place and time. Men in 37 cultures, from Australia to Zambia, judge women as more attractive if they have a youthful appearance. Evolutionary psychologists say that men who were drawn to healthy, fertile-appearing women—women with smooth skin and a youthful shape suggesting many childbearing years to come—stood a better chance of sending their genes into the future. Regardless of cultural

"I had a nice time, Steve. Would you like to come in, settle down, and raise a family?"

> "It's not that gay men are oversexed; they are simply men whose male desires bounce off other male desires rather than off female desires."
>
> Steven Pinker, *How the Mind Works*, 1997

Canada's famed Starbuck Holstein bull sired more than 200,000 offspring.

FIGURE **6.4**
Worldwide mating preferences
If men more than women prefer attractive physical features suggesting youth and health—and reproductive potential—and if women more than men prefer mates with resources and social status, we can credit (or blame) natural selection. (The red dots indicate the 37 cultures studied [Buss, 1994].)

variations in ideal weight, men everywhere feel most attracted to women whose waists are roughly a third narrower than their hips—a sign of future fertility (Singh, 1993).

Women also feel attracted to healthy-looking men, but especially to those who seem mature, dominant, bold, and affluent (Singh, 1995). Such attributes, say the evolutionary psychologists, connote a capacity to support and protect (Buss, 1996, 2000; Geary, 1998). Some 150 studies of gender and risk taking reveal that in 14 of 16 realms (including intellectual risk taking, physical skills, smoking, and sex) men are the greater risk takers (Byrnes & others, 1999). They also tend to be more optimistic about the stock market and more aggressive in trading stocks (Jacobe, 2003; Myers, 2002). In explaining why 16- to 24-year-old men show more bravado—and are therefore nearly three times more likely than young women to die in auto crashes—Victor Nell (2002) speculates that "young men who do crazy things are saying in one voice with the peacock and the buck that prances when the lion approaches, 'Look at me! I have so much strength and skill that I am fearless, I will survive no matter how much I drink or how fast I drive.'"

Evolutionary psychologists note that women also prefer mates with the potential for long-term mating and investment in their joint offspring (Gangestad & Simpson, 2000). They prefer stick-around dads over likely cads. Long-term mates contribute protection and support, which give their offspring greater survival prospects. Thus, for men there are genetic tradeoffs between seeking to distribute one's genes widely and being willing to co-parent.

There is a principle at work here, say evolutionary psychologists: Nature selects behaviors that increase the likelihood of sending one's genes into the future (**FIGURE 6.4**). As mobile gene machines, we are designed to prefer whatever worked for our ancestors in their environments. They were predisposed to act in ways that would leave grandchildren—had they not been, we wouldn't be here. And as carriers of their genetic legacy, we are similarly predisposed.

Critiquing the Evolutionary Perspective

OBJECTIVE 6-14 | Summarize the criticisms of evolutionary explanations of human behaviors, and describe the evolutionary psychologists' responses to those criticisms.

Without disputing nature's selection of traits that enhance gene survival, critics see problems with evolutionary psychology. It often, they say, starts with an effect (such as the gender sexuality difference) and works backward to propose an explanation. So let's imagine a different observation and reason backward. If men were uniformly loyal to their mates, might we not reason that the children of committed, supportive fathers more often survived to perpetuate their genes? Might not men also be better off bonded to one woman—both to increase the otherwise slim odds of impregnation and to keep her from the advances of competing men? Might not a ritualized bond—a marriage—also spare women from chronic male harassment? Such suggestions are, in fact, evolutionary explanations for why humans tend to pair off monogamously.

Lynn Carol Miller and her colleagues (2002) note, for example, that more men than women desire multiple sexual partners, but the things men and women seek in a mate "are remarkably similar." And what about those species, such as common bonobo chimpanzees, in which ardent females mate with numerous males? Does this ensure that the males, not knowing the true paternity of a female's offspring, will join in tolerating or protecting them? One can hardly lose at hindsight explanation, which is, said paleontologist Stephen Jay Gould (1997), mere "speculation [and] guesswork in the cocktail party mode."

Some worry about the social consequences of evolutionary psychology. Does it suggest a genetic determinism that strikes at the heart of progressive efforts to re-make society (Rose, 1999)? Does it undercut ethical theory and moral responsibility? Could it be used to rationalize "high-status men marrying a series of young, fertile women" (Looy, 2001)? Much of who we are is *not* hard-wired (which evolutionary psychologists do not dispute). Cultural expectations bend the genders, and what's considered attractive does vary somewhat with time and place. The voluptuous Marilyn Monroe ideal of the 1950s has been replaced by the turn-of-the-century leaner, athletic female image. Moreover, if socialized to value lifelong commitment, men may sexually bond with one partner; if socialized to accept casual sex, women may willingly have sex with many partners.

To some extent, gender differences in mate preferences are universal across cultures. But gender differences do vary within a culture's social and family structures. Show Alice Eagly and Wendy Wood (1999; Wood & Eagly, 2002) a culture with gender inequality—where men are providers and women are homemakers—and they will show you a culture where men strongly desire youth and domestic skill in their potential mates, and where women seek status and earning potential in their mates. Show Eagly and Wood a culture with gender equality, and they will show you a culture with smaller gender differences in mate preferences. They draw their conclusions from an analysis of the same 37 cultures studied earlier by David Buss (1994).

Evolutionary psychologists reassure us that the sexes, having faced similar adaptive problems, are far more alike than different. They stress that humans have a great capacity for learning and social progress. (We come equipped to adapt and survive, whether living in igloos or tree houses.) They point to the coherence and explanatory power of evolutionary principles, especially those offering testable predictions (for example, that we will favor others to the extent they share our genes or can later reciprocate our favors). And they remind us that the study of how we came to be who we are need not dictate how we ought to act. Sometimes understanding our propensities helps us overcome them.

>> LEARNING OUTCOMES

Behavior Genetics and Evolutionary Psychology

OBJECTIVE 6-1 | **Give examples of differences and similarities within the human family.**
We humans differ in personality, interests, physical appearance, family background, culture, and native language. Our similarities include our biological heritage and needs, our shared brain architecture, our ability to use language, the senses with which we explore the world around us, and our social behaviors.

OBJECTIVE 6-2 | **Describe the types of questions that interest behavior geneticists.**
Behavior geneticists are especially interested in the extent to which genetics and environment influence our behavior, creating individual differences. In this context, *environment* means every external, nongenetic aspect of our lives, from prenatal nutrition to the people and things around us now.

OBJECTIVE 6-3 | **Define *chromosome, DNA, gene,* and *genome,* and describe their relationships.**
We have 46 chromosomes in each cell—23 from our mother and 23 from our father. *Chromosomes* are threadlike structures made of *DNA,* a spiraling complex molecule containing genes. Our approximately 30,000 *genes* are DNA segments that, when "turned on" (expressed) form templates for the creation of various protein molecules, the building blocks of our physical and behavioral development. A *genome* is an organism's genetic profile—the complete set of instructions for making that organism, consisting of all the genetic material in its chromosomes. Combinations of variations at particular gene sites help define our differences. Most human traits are influenced by many genes acting together, not by the influence of a single gene acting alone.

OBJECTIVE 6-4 | **Explain how identical and fraternal twins differ, and cite ways that behavior geneticists use twin studies to understand the effects of environment and heredity.**
Identical twins develop from one egg that splits after being fertilized. They share the same set of genes, a similar prenatal environment, and—usually—the same family and culture after birth. *Fraternal twins* develop from separate fertilized eggs so are genetically no more similar than any other two siblings. They do share a prenatal environment, family, and social-cultural environment after birth. When some trait (such as extraversion) is present in both members of identical twin pairs but in only one member of fraternal twin pairs, researchers have a clue that heredity may be important in the development of that trait. Such comparisons are especially rich sources of information when twins have been separated at (or shortly after) birth, letting researchers see more clearly the effects of heredity in different environments.

OBJECTIVE 6-5 | **Cite ways that behavior geneticists use adoption studies to understand the effects of environment and heredity.**
Adopted children carry the genetic inheritance from their biological parents into an environment created by their adoptive families. Similarities between the child and the biological relatives give clues to the influence of heredity. Similarities between the child and the adoptive relatives give clues to the influence of environment. Adopted children tend to resemble their biological parents in their personality (their characteristic pattern of thinking, feeling, and acting), and their adoptive parents in their values, attitudes, manners, faith, and politics.

OBJECTIVE 6-6 | **Discuss how the relative stability of our temperament illustrates the influence of heredity on development.**
Temperament, a person's characteristic level of emotional reactivity and intensity, is apparent soon after birth and tends to continue relatively unchanged into adulthood. This suggests that heredity plays a much larger role than environment in the development of temperament.

OBJECTIVE 6-7 | **Discuss heritability's application to individuals and groups, and explain what we mean when we say genes are *self-regulating.***
Heritability describes the extent to which variation among individuals can be attributed to genes. It applies only to differences *among individuals*—never to any one person's traits. Saying that genes are *self-regulating* means that genes are not blueprints; they can react differently in different environments.

OBJECTIVE 6-8 | **Give an example of a genetically influenced trait that can evoke responses in others, and give another example of an environment that can trigger gene activity.**
Many important psychological traits are a product of the interaction of our genetic predispositions and our surrounding environment. For example, a genetic predisposition that causes a child to be restless and hyperactive can evoke angry responses from parents or teachers. And a stressful environment can trigger genes that affect the production of neurotransmitters contributing to depression.

OBJECTIVE 6-9 | **Identify the potential promise and perils of molecular genetics research.**
Psychologists and molecular geneticists are cooperating in a search to identify specific genes—or more often, teams of genes—that put people at risk for disorders. Knowledge of such links will enable medical personnel to inform expectant parents of some situations in which a fetus deviates from normal patterns. The ethical implications of such choices will be debated if parents choose to abort children who do not conform to their image of an ideal child.

OBJECTIVE 6-10 | **Describe the area of psychology that interests evolutionary psychologists.**
Evolutionary psychologists attempt to understand how natural selection has shaped behaviors found throughout the human species.

OBJECTIVE 6-11 | **State the principle of natural selection, and point out some possible effects of natural selection in the development of human characteristics.**
The principle of natural selection states that, among the range of possible variations in an inherited trait, the variations most likely to be passed on to future generations are those that increase the odds of reproducing and surviving. Genes that enabled a capacity to learn and to adapt had survival value for our

ancestors, as did those that prepared people to survive in feast-or-famine conditions. We suffer the effects of famine less often, thanks to modern technology, but with a genetic legacy that causes us to store fat and with a decrease in rigorous exercise, we become obese. Charles Darwin, whose theory of evolution has for a long time been an organizing principle in biology, anticipated the contemporary application of evolutionary principles in psychology.

OBJECTIVE 6-12 | **Identify some gender differences in sexuality.**
Gender refers to the biologically and socially influenced characteristics by which we define *male* and *female*. Men and women differ in their attitudes toward sex: Men are more approving of casual sex, think about sex more often, and are more likely to misinterpret friendliness as sexual interest. Women are more likely to cite affection as a reason for first intercourse and to have a relational view of sexual activity. Similar differences appear in sexual behavior.

OBJECTIVE 6-13 | **Describe evolutionary explanations for gender differences in sexuality.**
Evolutionary psychologists interpret human sexual behavior in terms of its survival value. In this view, being attracted to multiple healthy, fertile-appearing partners increases men's chances of spreading their genes widely and reproducing. Because women incubate and nurse babies, they increase their own and their children's chances of survival by searching for mates with economic resources and social status, who have the potential for long-term mating and investment in their joint offspring.

OBJECTIVE 6-14 | **Summarize the criticisms of evolutionary explanations of human behaviors, and describe the evolutionary psychologists' responses to those criticisms.**
(1) Evolutionary psychologists start with an effect and work backward to an explanation. (2) The evolutionary perspective underestimates cultural expectations and socialization. (3) The evolutionary viewpoint absolves people from taking ethical and moral responsibility for their sexual behavior. Evolutionary psychologists respond that understanding our predispositions can help us overcome them. They also cite the value of testable predictions based on evolutionary principles, and the coherence and explanatory power of those principles

TERMS AND CONCEPTS TO REMEMBER

environment, p. 6-0	temperament, p. 6-5
behavior genetics, p. 6-0	heritability, p. 6-6
chromosomes, p. 6-0	interaction, p. 6-8
DNA p. 6-0	molecular genetics, p. 6-8
genes, p. 6-0	evolutionary psychology, p. 6-10
genome, p. 6-0	natural selection, p. 6-10
identical twins, p. 6-1	mutation, p. 6-10
fraternal twins, p. 6-1	gender, p. 6-12

TEST YOURSELF

1. What is *heritability*?

2. What are the three main criticisms of the evolutionary explanation of human sexuality?

(Answers in Appendix B.)

ASK YOURSELF

1. Would you want genetic tests on your unborn offspring, in the uterus? What would you do if you knew your child would be destined for hemophilia? A learning disability? Would society benefit or lose if such embryos were aborted?

2. Whose reasoning do you find most persuasive—that of evolutionary psychologists or their critics? Why?

>WEB

Multiple-choice *self-tests* and more may be found at www.worthpublishers.com/myers.

Environmental Influences on Behavior

Parents and Peers

Our genes, as expressed in specific environments, influence our developmental differences. But what about the part of us that is *not* hard wired? If we are formed by nature *via* nurture, what are the most influential components of our nurture? How do our prenatal environment, our early experiences, our family, our friends, and our culture guide our development and contribute to our diversity?

Parents and Early Experiences

The formative nurture that conspires with nature begins at conception, with the prenatal environment. After birth, it extends into our family and peer relationships, and to all our other experiences.

Prenatal Environment

OBJECTIVE 7-1 | Describe some of the conditions that can affect development before birth.

Nurture begins in the womb, as embryos receive differing nutrition and varying levels of exposure to toxic agents. Even identical twins may receive not-so-identical prenatal nurture. Two-thirds of identical twins share the same placenta, and thus a more similar prenatal environment (although one might get a richer blood supply and weigh more at birth). Other identical twins have separate placentas (**FIGURE 7.1**). In this arrangement, one placenta sometimes has a more advantageous placement that provides better nourishment and a better placental barrier against viruses. Early indications are that, compared with same-placenta identical twins, those who develop with separate placentas are somewhat less similar in their psychological traits, such as self-control and social competence (Phelps & others, 1997; Sokol & others, 1995).

(a)   (b)

FIGURE 7.1
Two placental arrangements in identical twins
Identical twins may (a) have separate placentas and blood sources, as do all fraternal twins. Or they may (b) share the same placental blood. Researchers are now studying how this variation predicts later differences between identical twins. (From Davis & others, 1995.)

Experience and Brain Development

OBJECTIVE 7-2 | Describe how experience can modify the brain.

Nurture continues outside the womb, where our early experiences foster brain development. Experience helps develop our brain's neural connections. This early learning prepares our brains for thought and language, and also for later experiences. But how do early experiences leave their "marks" in the brain? Mark Rosenzweig and David Krech reared some young rats in solitary confinement and others in a communal playground (**FIGURE 7.2**). When their brains were then analyzed, the rats who died with the most toys had won. Those living in the enriched environment, which simulated a natural environment, usually developed a heavier and thicker brain cortex.

Rosenzweig (1984; Renner & Rosenzweig, 1987) was so surprised by this discovery that he repeated the experiment several times before publishing his findings. The effects are great enough that, shown brief video clips of rats, you could tell from their

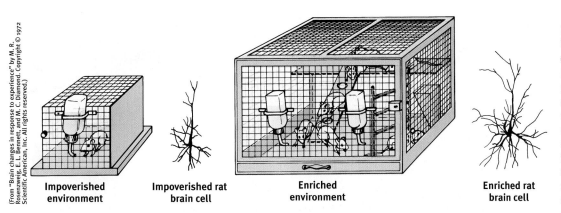

**Impoverished
environment**

**Impoverished rat
brain cell**

**Enriched
environment**

**Enriched rat
brain cell**

FIGURE 7.2
**Experience affects brain
development**
Mark Rosenzweig and David Krech
reared rats either alone in an
environment without playthings, or
with others in an environment
enriched with playthings that were
changed daily. In 14 of 16 repetitions of this basic experiment, the
rats placed in the enriched environment developed significantly more
cerebral cortex (relative to the rest
of the brain's tissue) than did those
in the impoverished environment.

activity and curiosity whether their rearing was impoverished or enriched (Renner & Renner, 1993). After rats have been housed for 60 days in enriched environments, re- port Bryan Kolb and Ian Whishaw (1998), the rats' brain weight increases 7 to 10 percent and the number of synapses mushrooms by about 20 percent—"an extraordi- nary change!" Such results have motivated improvements in the environments we provide for laboratory, farm, and zoo animals—and for children in institutions.

Several research teams have found that the stimulation of touch or massage bene- fits infant rats and premature babies (Field, 2001; Field & others, 2004). "Handled" infants of both species gain weight more rapidly and develop faster neurologically. Neonatal intensive care units now apply this finding by giving preemies massage therapy, enabling them to develop faster and go home sooner. William Greenough and his University of Illinois colleagues (1987) further discovered that repeated expe- riences modify a rat's neural tissue—at the very spot in the brain that processes the experience. After brain maturation provides us with an abundance of neural
connections, experience preserves our
activated connections while allowing
our unused connections to degenerate.
The result by puberty is a massive loss of
unemployed connections (a process
known as *pruning*).

Here, then, at the juncture of nurture
and nature, is where a child's enriched
environment activates and preserves
connections that, given impoverished
experiences, might have died off from
disuse. There is a biological reality to early childhood education. During early child- hood—while the excess connections are still on call—youngsters can most easily mas- ter the grammar and accent of another language. Lacking any exposure to written or signed language before adolescence, a person will never master any language.

Likewise, lacking visual experience during the early years, people whose vision is restored by cataract removal never achieve normal perceptions. The brain cells nor- mally assigned to vision have died or been diverted to other uses. For us to have opti- mum brain development, normal stimulation during the early years is critical. The maturing brain seems governed by a rule: Use it or lose it.

The brain's development does not, however, end with childhood. Throughout life our neural tissue is changing. Both nature and nurture sculpt our synapses. Sights and smells, touches and tugs activate and strengthen some neural pathways while others weaken from disuse. Similar to pathways through a forest, less-traveled paths gradually disappear and popular paths are broadened. Our genes dictate our overall

Courtesy of C. Brune

Stringing the circuits young
String musicians who started playing before age 12 have larger and more complex neural circuits controlling the note-making left-hand fingers than do string musicians whose training started later (Elbert & others, 1995).

"Genes and experiences are just two ways of doing the same thing—wiring synapses."
Joseph LeDoux, *The Synaptic Self*, 2002

FIGURE **7.3**
A trained brain
A well-learned finger-tapping task activates more motor cortex neurons (orange area, right) than were active in the same brain before training (left). (From Karni & others, 1998.)

brain architecture, but experience directs the details. If a monkey is trained to push a lever with a finger several thousand times a day, the brain tissue that controls the finger changes to reflect the experience. Human brains work similarly. Whether learning to keyboard or skateboard, we perform with increasing skill as our brain incorporates the learning (**FIGURE 7.3**).

How Much Credit (or Blame) Do Parents Deserve?

OBJECTIVE 7-3 | Explain why we should be careful about attributing children's successes and failures to their parents' influence.

It may be scary to realize how risky it is to have and raise children. In procreation, a woman and a man shuffle their gene decks and deal a life-forming hand to their child-to-be, who is then subjected to countless influences beyond their control. Parents, nonetheless, feel enormous satisfaction in their children's successes, and guilt or shame over their failures. They beam over the child who wins an award. They wonder where they went wrong with the child repeatedly called into the principal's office. Freudian psychiatry and psychology have been among the sources of such ideas, by blaming problems from asthma to schizophrenia on "bad mothering." And society reinforces such parent-blaming: Believing that parents shape their offspring as a potter molds clay, people readily praise parents for their children's virtues and blame them for their children's vices. Popular culture has endlessly proclaimed the psychological harm toxic parents inflict on their fragile children. "The major source of human misery" is the "neglected, wounded child" within each of us, claimed author-lecturer John Bradshaw (1990, p. 7).

But do parents really produce future adults with an inner wounded child by being (take your pick from the toxic-parent lists) overbearing—or uninvolved? Pushy—or ineffectual? Overprotective—or distant? Are children really so easily wounded? If so, should we then blame our parents for our failings, and ourselves for our children's failings? Should we pass city ordinances that punish parents for their children's misdeeds? Or does all the talk of wounding fragile children through normal parental mistakes trivialize the brutality of real abuse?

Peter Neubauer and Alexander Neubauer (1990, pp. 20-21) illustrate how, with hindsight, we may inappropriately credit or blame our parents:

> Identical twin men, now age 30, were separated at birth and raised in different countries by their respective adoptive parents. Both kept their lives neat—neat to the point of pathology. Their clothes were preened, appointments met precisely on time, hands scrubbed regularly to a raw, red color. When the first was asked why he felt the need to be so clean, his answer was plain.

Even among chimpanzees, when one infant is hurt by another, the victim's mother will often attack the offender's mother (Goodall, 1968).

"So I blame you for everything—whose fault is that?"

"My mother. When I was growing up she always kept the house perfectly ordered. She insisted on every little thing returned to its proper place, the clocks—we had dozens of clocks—each set to the same noonday chime. She insisted on this, you see. I learned from her. What else could I do?"

The man's identical twin, just as much a perfectionist with soap and water, explained his own behavior this way: "The reason is quite simple. I'm reacting to my mother, who was an absolute slob."

Parents do matter (Collins & others, 2000; Eisenberg & others, 1998a,b; Vandell, 2000). The power of parenting to shape our differences is clearest at the extremes—the abused who become abusive, the neglected who become neglectful, the loved but firmly handled children who become self-confident and socially competent. The power of the family environment also frequently shows up in children's political attitudes, religious beliefs, and personal manners. And it appears in the remarkable academic and vocational successes of children of the refugee "boat people" fleeing Vietnam and Cambodia—successes attributed to close-knit, supportive, even demanding families (Caplan & others, 1992).

Yet in personality measures, at least, shared environmental influences—including the home influences that siblings share—typically account for less than 10 percent of children's differences. In the words of behavior geneticists Robert Plomin and Denise Daniels (1987), "Two children in the same family [are on average] as different from one another as are pairs of children selected randomly from the population." To developmental psychologist Sandra Scarr (1993), this implies that "parents should be given less credit for kids who turn out great and blamed less for kids who don't." Although environments matter, "extreme environmentalism is cruel," contends Michael Gazzaniga (1992, p. 202). Why? "Because it suggests to the parents that their child has been warped by something they did."

Parental nurture is like nutrition. It may not matter much whether we get our protein from eating chicken or beans, but we must have food. Likewise, it may not matter whether we grew up with parents who toilet trained us early or late, but it sure helps to have someone we belong to, someone who cares about us.

Miquel L. Fairbanks

Who's to blame?
These teens risk all by riding atop high-speed trains. Why? The surprising differences among children raised in the same home reveal the limits of parental influence. Genetic predispositions and social influences also shape children's lives.

" If you want to blame your parents for your own adult problems, you are entitled to blame the genes they gave you, but you are not entitled—by any facts I know—to blame the way they treated you. . . . We are not prisoners of our past."
Martin Seligman, *What You Can Change and What You Can't*, 1994

Peer Influence

OBJECTIVE 7-4 | Evaluate the importance of peer influence on development.

As children mature, what other experiences do the work of nurturing? We are subject to group influences at all ages, as we seek to establish ourselves and to be accepted in various school and other groups. The conformity behavior of children seeking to fit in with various groups is a significant influence on day-to-day behaviors. For example:

- Preschoolers who disdain a certain food despite parents' urgings often will eat the food if put at a table with a group of children who like it.
- A child who hears English spoken with one accent at home and another in the neighborhood and at school will invariably adopt the accent of the peers, not the parents.
- Direct parental influences on smoking are less important than many people suppose. Rather, teens who start smoking typically have *friends* who model smoking, who suggest its pleasures, and who offer cigarettes (Rose & others, 1999, 2003). Part of the similarity to peers may result from a *selection effect,* as kids seek out peers with similar attitudes and interests. Those who smoke (or don't) may select as friends those who also smoke (or don't).

" Men resemble the times more than they resemble their fathers."
Ancient Arab proverb

Peer power
As we develop, we play, mate, and partner with peers. No wonder children and youths are so sensitive and responsive to peer influences.

" It takes a village to raise a child."

African proverb

Uniform requirements
People in individualist Western cultures sometimes see traditional Japanese culture as confining. But from the Japanese perspective the same tradition expresses a "serenity that comes to people who know exactly what to expect from each other" (Weisz & others, 1984).

Knowing that lives are formed by influences partly beyond parents' control suggests caution in crediting parents for their children's achievements and blaming them for their children's troubling traits. And if our children are not easily sculpted by parental nurture, then perhaps we parents can relax a bit more and love our children for who they are.

Powerful parental influence may, however, occur indirectly. A group of parents can influence the culture that shapes the peer group. Culture is transmitted across generations partly by what Judith Rich Harris (2000b) calls "parents'-group-to-children's-group effects." That being so, parental influence occurs when parents help select their children's neighborhood and peers. Neighborhood influences matter (Kalff & others, 2001; Leventhal & Brooks-Gunn, 2000). Intervention programs for youth had therefore best be aimed at a whole school or neighborhood and not just at isolated individuals. If the vapors of a toxic climate are seeping into a child's life, that climate—not just the child—needs reforming.

Howard Gardner (1998) concludes that parents and peers are complementary:

Parents are more important when it comes to education, discipline, responsibility, orderliness, charitableness, and ways of interacting with authority figures. Peers are more important for learning cooperation, for finding the road to popularity, for inventing styles of interaction among people of the same age. Youngsters may find their peers more interesting, but they will look to their parents when contemplating their own futures. Moreover, parents [often] choose the neighborhoods and schools that supply the peers.

Cultural Influences

OBJECTIVE 7-5 | Discuss the survival benefits of culture.

Compared with the narrow path taken by flies, fish, and foxes, nature has built for us a longer, wider road along which environment drives us. The mark of our species—nature's great gift to us—is our ability to learn and adapt. We come equipped with a huge cerebral hard drive ready to receive many gigabytes of cultural software.

Culture is the behaviors, ideas, attitudes, values, and traditions shared by a group of people and transmitted from one generation to the next (Brislin, 1988). Human nature, notes Roy Baumeister (2005), seems designed for culture. We are social animals, but more. Wolves are social animals; they live and hunt in packs. Ants are incessantly social, never alone. But "culture is a better way of being social," notes Baumeister. Culture supports survival and reproduction with social and economic systems that enable us to eat fruit in the winter, surf the Internet, and accumulate information. Wolves function pretty much as they did 10,000 years ago. You and I enjoy things unknown to most of our century-ago ancestors, including electricity, indoor plumbing, and antibiotics. Culture works.

Primates exhibit the rudiments of culture, with local customs of tool use, grooming, and courtship. Younger chimpanzees and macaque monkeys sometimes invent customs—potato washing, in one famous example—and pass them on to their peers and offspring. But human culture does more. Thanks to our mastery of *language,* we humans not only know how to clean our food, we also enjoy one of culture's hallmarks: the *preservation of innovation.* Within the span of this day, I have, thanks to my culture, made good use of Post-It notes, Google, and a single-shot skinny latté. We also have culture's accumulated knowledge to thank for the last century's extension of our life expectancy from 47 to 76 years. Moreover, culture enables an efficient *division of labor.* Although one lucky person gets his name on this book's cover, the product actually results from the coordination and commitment of a team of women and men, no one of whom is capable of producing it alone.

Across cultures, we differ in our language, our monetary system, our sports, which fork—if any—we eat with, even which side of the road we drive on. But beneath these differences is our great similarity—our capacity for culture, for the shared and transmitted customs and beliefs that enable us to communicate, to exchange money for things, to play, to eat, and to drive with agreed-upon rules and without crashing into one another. This shared capacity for culture enables our striking differences. Human nature manifests human diversity.

If we all lived in homogeneous ethnic groups in separate regions of the world, as some people still do, cultural diversity would be less relevant. In Japan, 99 percent of the country's 126 million people are of Japanese descent. Internal cultural differences are therefore minimal compared with those found in Los Angeles, where the public schools recently taught 82 different languages, or in Toronto or Vancouver, where minorities are one-third of the population and many are immigrants (as are 17 percent of all Canadians and 24 percent of Australians) (Iyer, 1993; Statistics Canada, 2002; Trewin, 2001). I am ever mindful that the readers of this book are culturally diverse. You and your ancestors reach from Australia to Africa and from Singapore to Sweden.

Variation Across Cultures

OBJECTIVE 7-6 | Describe some ways that cultures differ.

We see our adaptability in cultural variations among our beliefs and our values, in how we raise our children and bury our dead, and in what we wear (or whether we wear anything at all). Riding along with a unified culture is like biking with the wind: As it carries us along, we hardly notice it is there. When we try riding *against* the wind we feel its force. Face to face with a different culture, we become aware of the cultural winds. Visiting Europe, most North Americans notice the smaller cars, the left-handed use of the fork, the uninhibited attire on the beaches. Stationed in Iraq, Afghanistan, and Kuwait, European and American soldiers alike realized how liberal their home cultures were. A decade of working with refugee immigrants sensitized psychologist Mary Pipher (2002) to her own culture:

> Like most Americans I only speak English fluently. I value freedom and personal space. I am time-conscious. I am comfortable with only certain forms of touch. A certain amount of eye contact and distance between bodies seems right to me. Some things seem much more edible than others. Certain clothes—jeans and T-shirts—feel best to me. I do not cover my head when I go out and I wear shoes inside my house. I like to talk.

Arriving in North America, visitors from Japan and India struggle to understand why many people wear their dirty *street* shoes in the house, and others wonder why people find it fun to eat a picnic lunch out in the woods amid flies and ants.

Each cultural group evolves its own **norms**—the rules for accepted and expected behavior. Many South Asians, for example, use only the right hand's fingers for eating. The British have a norm for orderly waiting in line. Sometimes social expectations seem oppressive: "Why should it matter how I dress?" Yet, norms grease the social machinery. Prescribed, well-learned behaviors free us from self-preoccupation.

■ **culture** the enduring behaviors, ideas, attitudes, values, and traditions shared by a group of people and transmitted from one generation to the next.

■ **norm** an understood rule for accepted and expected behavior. Norms prescribe "proper" behavior.

Cultures differ

Behavior seen as appropriate in one culture may violate the norms of another group. In Arab societies, but not in Western cultures, men often greet one another with a kiss, or hold hands as a sign of friendship, as U.S. President George W. Bush did in 2005 while strolling with Saudi Crown Prince Abdullah.

Jason Reed/Reuters/Corbis

Knowing when to clap or bow, which fork to pick up first at a dinner party, and what sorts of gestures and compliments are appropriate, we can relax and enjoy one another without fear of embarrassment or insult. Likewise, having a well-understood norm for greeting people in one's culture—by shaking hands or kissing each cheek—precludes awkward moments of indecision about whether to lead with one's hand or cheek.

When cultures collide, their differing norms often befuddle. For example, if someone invades our **personal space**—the portable buffer zone we like to maintain around our bodies—we feel uncomfortable. Scandinavians, North Americans, and the British prefer more personal space than do Latin Americans, Arabs, and the French (Sommer, 1969). At a social gathering, a Mexican seeking a comfortable conversation distance may end up walking around a room with a backpedaling American. (You can experience this at a party by playing Space Invader as you talk with someone.) To the American, the Mexican may seem intrusive; to the Mexican, the American may seem standoffish.

Cultures also vary in their expressiveness. Those with roots in northern European culture often perceive people from Mediterranean cultures as warm and charming but inefficient. The Mediterraneans, in turn, see northern Europeans as efficient but cold and preoccupied with punctuality (Triandis, 1981).

Cultures vary in their pace of life, too. A British businessperson may feel frustrated by a Latin American client who arrives 30 minutes after the time set for lunch. People from time-conscious Japan—where bank clocks keep exact time, pedestrians walk briskly, and postal clerks fill requests speedily—may find themselves growing impatient when visiting Indonesia, where clocks keep less accurate time and the pace of life is more leisurely (Levine & Norenzayan, 1999). In adjusting to their host countries, the first wave of U.S. Peace Corps volunteers reported that two of their greatest culture shocks, after the language differences, were the differing pace of life and the people's differing sense of punctuality (Spradley & Phillips, 1972).

Variation Over Time

OBJECTIVE 7-7 | Explain why changes in the human gene pool cannot account for culture change over time.

Consider, too, how rapidly cultures may change over time. English poet Geoffrey Chaucer (1342–1400) is separated from a modern Briton by only 20 generations, but the two would converse with great difficulty. In the thinner slice of history since 1960, most Western cultures have changed with remarkable speed. Middle-class people fly to places they once only read about, e-mail those they once snail-mailed, and work in air-conditioned comfort where they once sweltered. They enjoy the convenience of on-line holiday shopping, cell-phone calling, and—enriched by doubled per-person real income—eating out more than twice as often as did their parents back in the culture of 1960. With greater economic independence, today's women are more likely to marry for love and less likely to endure abusive relationships out of economic need. Many minority groups enjoy expanded human rights.

But some changes seem not so wonderfully positive. Had you fallen asleep in the United States in 1960 and awakened a third of a century later, you would have opened your eyes to a culture with a doubled rate of divorce, a nearly tripled rate of teen suicide, a quadrupled rate of reported juvenile violent crime, a quintupled prison population, and an escalating incidence of depression (Myers, 2000). (Thankfully, the teen suicide and crime rates began subsiding after 1993.) You would also find Americans spending more hours at work, fewer hours sleeping, and fewer hours with friends and family (Frank, 1999; Putnam, 2000). Similar cultural transformations have occurred in Canada, Britain, Australia, and New Zealand.

■ **personal space** the buffer zone we like to maintain around our bodies.

■ **individualism** giving priority to one's own goals over group goals and defining one's identity in terms of personal attributes rather than group identifications.

■ **collectivism** giving priority to the goals of one's group (often one's extended family or work group) and defining one's identity accordingly.

Whether we love or loathe these changes, we cannot fail to be impressed by their breathtaking speed. And we cannot explain them by changes in the human gene pool, which evolves far too slowly to account for high-speed cultural transformations. Cultures vary. Cultures change. And cultures shape our lives.

Culture and the Self

OBJECTIVE 7-8 | Identify some ways a primarily individualist culture differs from a primarily collectivist culture, and compare their effects on personal identity.

Cultures vary in the event to which they give priority to the nurturing and expression of one's personal identity or of one's group identity. To grasp the difference, imagine that someone were to rip away your social connections, making you a solitary refugee in a foreign land. How much of your identity would remain intact? The answer would depend in large part on whether you give greater priority to the independent self that marks **individualism** or to the interdependent self that marks **collectivism.**

If as our solitary traveler you were an individualist, a great deal of your identity would remain intact—the very core of your being, the sense of "me," the awareness of your personal convictions and values. Individualists give relatively greater priority to personal goals and define their identity mostly in terms of personal attributes. They strive for personal control and individual achievement. In American culture, with its relatively big "I" and small "we," 85 percent of people say it is possible "to pretty much be who you want to be" (Sampson, 2000). Being more self-contained, individualists more easily move in and out of social groups. They feel relatively free to switch places of worship, leave one job for another, or even leave their extended families and migrate to a new place. Marriage is often for as long as they both shall love.

Individualism varies from person to person within any culture. In the movie *Antz*, Woody Allen gave voice to an individualist ant who resisted the extreme collectivism of his colony's culture: "It's this whole gung-ho, superorganism thing that—that, you know, I can't get. I try, but I don't get it. I mean, what is it? I'm supposed to do everything for the colony? And—and what about my needs? What about me?"

If set adrift in a foreign land as a collectivist, you might experience a much greater loss of identity than as an individualist. Cut off from family, groups, and loyal friends, you would lose the connections that have defined who you are. In a collectivist culture, group identifications provide a sense of belonging, a set of values, a network of caring individuals, an assurance of security. In return, collectivists give priority to the goals of their groups, often their family, clan, or company, and define their identity accordingly—not as "me" but as "we." In Korea, for example, people place less value on expressing a consistent, unique self-concept, and more on tradition and shared practices (Choi & Choi, 2002).

Collectivists may act shy in new groups and are more easily embarrassed than their individualist counterparts (Singelis & others, 1995, 1999). Compared with Westerners, people in Japanese and Chinese cultures, for example, exhibit greater shyness toward strangers and greater concern for social harmony and loyalty (Bond, 1988; Cheek & Melchior, 1990; Triandis, 1994). They have deeper, more stable attachments to their familiar groups and families. Duty to one's family may trump personal career preference. Compared with students in the United States, for example, students in Japan, China, and India are much less likely to complete the sentence "I am . . ." with personal traits ("I am sincere," "I am confident") and are more likely to declare their social identities ("I am a Keio University student," "I am the third son in my family") (Cousins, 1989; Dhawan & others, 1995; Triandis, 1989a,b).

Like athletes who take more pleasure in their team's victory than in their own performance, collectivists find satisfaction in advancing their groups' interests, even at the expense of personal needs.

Collectivism

By identifying with family and other groups, these women and children in Pakistan have gained a sense of "we," a set of values, a network of care. This collectivist support system may have helped these people struggle through the devastation of the October 2005 Kashmir earthquake, which leveled the house behind them.

Kyodo News

"One needs to cultivate the spirit of sacrificing the *little me* to achieve the benefits of the *big me*."

Chinese saying

Individualist proverb: "The squeaky wheel gets the grease."
Collectivist proverb: "The quacking duck gets shot."

"My parents will be disappointed in me" has been a concern expressed by 7 percent of American and Italian teenagers and 14 percent of Australian teens, but by nearly 25 percent of teens in Taiwan and Japan (Atkinson, 1988).

Relationships are long-term. Loyalties run strong between employer and employees. No wonder, says Harry Triandis (1989b), that modern world colonization was led not by Asians, who were reluctant to cut social and family ties, but by the more individualist Europeans. And no wonder that some countries colonized by Europeans willing to leave friends and family are today highly individualistic. People wanting to resettle in a new country express more concern for work and achievement, and less concern for relationships and family, than do those wanting to remain (Boneva & Frieze, 2001).

Individuals within a culture vary and cultures include varying subgroups (Oyserman & others, 2002a,b). Yet cross-cultural psychologists have discovered some variations across cultures, ranging from the individualism of the United States outside the Deep South to the collectivism of rural Asia (Hofstede, 1980; Triandis, 1994; Vandello & Cohen, 1999). Valuing communal solidarity, people in collectivist cultures place a premium on maintaining harmony and making sure others never lose face. What people say reflects both what they feel (their inner attitudes) and what they presume others feel (Kashima & others, 1992). Elders and superiors are given respect. To preserve group spirit, people avoid direct confrontation, blunt honesty, and uncomfortable topics; they defer to others' wishes and display a polite, self-effacing humility (Markus & Kitayama, 1991). Thus, that individualized latté—"decaf, single shot, skinny, extra hot"— that feels so good to a North American in an espresso shop might sound more like a selfish demand in Seoul, note Heejung Kim and Hazel Markus (1999). And Korean ads are also less likely to emphasize personal choice, freedom, and uniqueness, and they more often feature people together (Markus, 2001). In collectivist cultures, people remember those who have done them favors, and reciprocity becomes a social art. The collectivist self is not independent but *inter*dependent (**TABLE 7.1**). Among collectivists—especially those influenced by the Confucian idea of self as embedded in "a web of interrelatedness"—no one is an island (Kim & Lee, 1994). Happiness is being attuned to others (Kitayama & Markus, 2000).

TABLE 7.1

VALUE CONTRASTS BETWEEN INDIVIDUALISM AND COLLECTIVISM

Concept	Individualism	Collectivism
Self	Independent (identity from individual traits)	Interdependent (identity from belonging)
Life task	Discover and express one's uniqueness	Maintain connections, fit in, perform role
What matters	Me—personal achievement and fulfillment; rights and liberties; self-esteem	Us—group goals and solidarity; social responsibilities and relationships; family duty
Coping method	Change reality	Accommodate to reality
Morality	Defined by individuals (self-based)	Defined by social networks (duty-based)
Relationships	Many, often temporary or casual; confrontation acceptable	Few, close and enduring; harmony valued
Attributing behavior	Behavior reflects one's personality and attitudes	Behavior reflects social norms and roles

Sources: Adapted from Thomas Schoeneman (1994) and Harry Triandis (1994).

Both individualism and collectivism offer benefits and come at a cost. People in competitive, individualist cultures have more personal freedom, take more pride in personal achievements, are less geographically bound to their families, and enjoy more privacy. Their less-unified cultures offer a smorgasbord of life-styles and invite individuals to construct their own identities. These cultures also celebrate innovation and creativity, and they tend to respect individual human rights. Such may help explain Ed Diener, Marissa Diener, and Carol Diener's (1995) finding that people in individualist cultures report experiencing greater happiness than do those in collectivist cultures. When individualists pursue their own ends and all goes well, life can seem rewarding.

Curiously, though, within individualist cultures, people with the strongest social ties express greatest satisfaction with their lives (Bettencourt & Door, 1997). Moreover, the seeming benefits of individualism can come at the cost of more loneliness, more divorce, more homicide, and more stress-related disease (Popenoe, 1993; Triandis & others, 1988). People in individualist cultures express more self-focused "narcissism," by agreeing, for example, that "I find it easy to manipulate people" (Foster & others, 2003). Individualists also demand more romance and personal fulfillment in marriage, which subjects the marriage relationship to more pressure (Dion & Dion, 1993). In one survey, "keeping romance alive" was rated as important to a good marriage by 78 percent of U.S. women but only 29 percent of Japanese women (*American Enterprise,* 1992). In China, love songs often express enduring commitment and friendship (Rothbaum & Tsang, 1998). As one song put it, "We will be together from now on . . . I will never change from now to forever."

Culture and Child-Rearing

OBJECTIVE 7-9 | Describe some ways that child-rearing differs in individualist and collectivist cultures.

Child-rearing practices are not immune to the variations in cultural values from one time and place to another. Do you prefer children who are independent or children who comply with what others think?

If you live in a Westernized culture, the odds are you prefer the former. Most parents in Western societies want their children to think for themselves. "You are responsible for yourself," Western families and schools tell their children. "Follow your conscience. Be true to yourself. Discover your gifts. Think through your personal needs." But these cultural values represent change over time. A half-century ago, Western parents placed greater priority on obedience, respect, and sensitivity to others (Alwin, 1990; Remley, 1988). "Be true to your traditions," they taught their children. "Be loyal to your heritage and country. Show respect toward your parents and other superiors."

Unlike most Westerners, who now raise their children to be independent, many Asians and Africans live in cultures that focus on cultivating emotional closeness. Rather than being given their own bedrooms and entrusted to day care, infants and toddlers have typically slept with their mothers and spent their days close to a family member (Morelli & others, 1992; Whiting & Edwards, 1988). Children in these cultures grow up with a stronger sense of *family self*—a feeling that what shames the child shames the family, and what brings honor to the family brings honor to the self.

Cultures vary
In Scotland's Orkney Islands' town of Stromness, social trust has enabled parents to park their toddlers outside of shops.

Parental involvement promotes development
Parents in every culture facilitate their children's discovery of their world, but cultures differ in what they deem important. Asian cultures place more emphasis on school and hard work than does North American culture. This may help explain why Japanese and Taiwanese children get higher scores on mathematics achievement tests.

"We recognize that we are the products of many cultures, traditions, and memories; that mutual respect allows us to study and learn from other cultures; and that we gain strength by combining the foreign with the familiar."

U.N. Secretary-General Kofi Annan, Nobel Peace Prize lecture, 2001

Children across place and time have thrived under various child-rearing systems. Upper-class British parents traditionally handed off routine caregiving to nannies, then sent their children off to boarding school at about age 10. These children generally grew up to be pillars of British society, just like their parents and their boarding-school peers. In the African Gusii society, babies nurse freely but spend most of the day on their mother's back—with lots of body contact but little face-to-face and language interaction. When the mother becomes pregnant, the toddler is weaned and handed over to someone else, often an older sibling. Westerners may wonder about the negative effects of this lack of verbal interaction, but then the African Gusii would in turn wonder about Western mothers pushing their babies around in strollers and leaving them in playpens and car seats (Small, 1997). Such diversity in child-rearing cautions us against presuming that our culture's way is the only way to rear children successfully.

Developmental Similarities Across Groups

OBJECTIVE 7-10 | Describe some ways that humans are similar, despite their cultural differences.

Because we are so mindful of how others differ from us, we often fail to notice the similarities predisposed by our shared biology. Cross-cultural research can help us by leading us to appreciate both our cultural diversity *and* our human kinship. Compared with the person-to-person differences within groups, the differences between groups are small. Regardless of our culture—and culture is itself something that shapes and guides us all—we humans share the same life cycle. We all speak to our infants in similar ways and respond similarly to their coos and cries (Bornstein & others, 1992a,b). All over the world, the children of parents who are warm and supportive feel better about themselves and are less hostile than are the children of parents who are punitive and rejecting (Rohner, 1986; Scott & others, 1991).

Within a culture, ethnic subgroups may behave differently and yet be influenced similarly. Differences sometimes attributed to race may therefore actually result from other factors. David Rowe and his colleagues (1994, 1995) illustrate this with an analogy: Black men tend to have higher blood pressure than white men. Suppose that (1) in both groups salt consumption correlates with blood pressure, and (2) salt consumption is higher among black men than among white men. What then might we expect? A blood pressure "race difference" that may actually be, at least partly, a *diet* difference.

And that, say Rowe and his colleagues, parallels psychological findings: Behavior differences, like blood pressure differences, can result from differing inputs to the same process. Although American Hispanic, Asian, Black, and White ethnic groups differ in school achievement and delinquency, the differences are "no more than skin deep." To the extent that family structure, peer influences, and parental education predict behavior in one ethnic group, they do so for other groups as well.

So in surface ways we may differ, but as members of one species we seem subject to the same psychological forces. As members of different ethnic and cultural groups, our languages vary, yet they reflect universal principles of grammar. Our tastes vary, yet they reflect common principles of hunger. Our social behaviors vary, but they reflect pervasive principles of human influence.

"When someone has discovered why men in Bond Street wear black hats he will at the same moment have discovered why men in Timbuctoo wear red feathers."

G. K. Chesterton, *Heretics*, 1908

Gender Development

Cognitive psychologists have demonstrated that we humans have an irresistible urge to organize our worlds into simple categories. Among the ways we classify people (and ourselves)—as tall or short, slim or fat, smart or dull—two stand out: race and, especially, sex. At your birth, the one thing everyone wanted to know was, "Boy or girl?" Our biological sex then helps define our *gender,* our assumed characteristics as male or female. In considering how nature and nurture together create social diversity, gender is the prime case example. Let's recap one of psychology's main themes—that nature and nurture together create our differences and commonalities—by considering some gender variations.

Gender Similarities and Differences

OBJECTIVE 7-11 | Identify some biological and psychological differences between males and females.

In most ways, males and females, having faced similar adaptive challenges, are alike. Men and women are not from different planets—Mars and Venus—but from the same planet Earth. Tell me whether you are male or female and you give me virtually no clues to your vocabulary, your intelligence, your self-esteem, your happiness, or the mechanisms by which you see, hear, learn, and remember. Your "opposite" sex is, in reality, your very similar sex. And should we be surprised? Among your 46 chromosomes, 45 are unisex.

But there also are some differences, and differences we notice. Diversity commands attention. Ask people to describe themselves, and their unique features often come to mind. Redheads will mention their hair color. Tall people will mention their height. In situations where you are the only person of your race or gender, you will be mindful of those unique features (McGuire & others, 1978).

Some male-female differences are obvious. Compared with the average man, the average woman has 70 percent more fat, possesses 40 percent less muscle, and is 5 inches shorter. She also enters puberty two years sooner and will outlive her male counterparts by five years. However, it's worth noting that the women's world records in the 400-meter dash and the marathon are now within 10 percent of men's record times (Leonhardt, 2004). Throughout this book, we will also see some less obvious gender differences. Women are more likely to dream equally of men and women, to become sexually re-aroused immediately after orgasm, to smell faint odors, to express emotions freely, and in some situations to be offered help. They also are doubly vulnerable to depression and anxiety and are at 10 times greater risk for eating disorders. But then men are some four times more likely to commit suicide or suffer alcoholism, and are far more likely to be diagnosed with autism, color-blindness, hyperactivity (as children), and antisocial personality disorder (as adults). Choose your gender and pick your vulnerability.

Let's look more closely at gender and social behavior. Researchers have found differences in aggression, social power, and social connectedness. How much does biology bend the genders, and what portion of such differences are socially constructed—by the gender roles that culture assigns us, and by how we are socialized as children?

Gender and Aggression

OBJECTIVE 7-12 | Summarize the gender gap in aggression.

In surveys, men admit to more **aggression** than do women, and experiments confirm that men tend to behave more aggressively, such as by administering what they believe are more painful electric shocks (Bettencourt & Kernahan, 1997). The aggression gender gap, which pertains to *physical* rather than verbal aggression, also appears in everyday life in various cultures and at various ages (Archer, 2004). Violent crime rates illustrate the difference. The male-to-female arrest ratio for murder, for example, is 9 to 1 in the United States and 7 to 1 in Canada (FBI, 2004; Statistics Canada, 2003).

■ **aggression** physical or verbal behavior intended to hurt someone

Throughout the world, hunting, fighting, and warring are primarily men's activities (Wood & Eagly, 2002). Men also express more support for war. In one 2005 survey, 51 percent of American men but only 34 percent of American women expressed approval of George Bush's Iraq initiative (Gallup, 2005).

Gender and Social Power

OBJECTIVE 7-13 | Describe some gender differences in social power.

Around the world, from Nigeria to New Zealand, people perceive men as more dominant, forceful, and independent, women as more deferential, nurturant, and affiliative (Williams & Best, 1990). Indeed, in most societies men *are* socially dominant. When groups form, whether as juries or companies, leadership tends to go to males (Colarelli & others, 2005). As leaders, men tend to be more directive, even autocratic; women tend to be more democratic, more welcoming of subordinates' participation in decision making (Eagly & Johnson, 1990; van Engen & Willemsen, 2004). When people interact, men are more likely to utter opinions, women to express support (Aries, 1987; Wood, 1987). In everyday behavior, men are more likely to act as powerful people often do—to talk assertively, to interrupt, to initiate touching, to smile less, to stare (Hall, 1987; Major & others, 1990).

Such behaviors help sustain the inequities of social power. When political leaders are elected, they usually are men, who held 84 percent of the seats in the world's governing parliaments in 2005 (IPU, 2005). When salaries are paid, those in traditionally male occupations receive more. Gender differences in power do appear to lessen with maturity, however, as middle-aged women become more assertive and men more empathic (Maccoby, 1998).

Women's 2005 representations in national parliaments ranged from 7 percent in the Arab States to 40 percent in Scandinavia (IPU, 2005).

" In the long years liker must they grow;
The man be more of woman, she of man."
Alfred Lord Tennyson, *The Princess*, 1847

Gender and Social Connectedness

OBJECTIVE 7-14 | Discuss gender differences in connectedness, or the ability to "tend and befriend."

To Carol Gilligan and her colleagues (1982, 1990), the "normal" struggle to create one's separate identity describes individualist males more than relationship-oriented females. Gilligan believes females differ from males both in being less concerned with viewing themselves as separate individuals and in being more concerned with "making connections."

These gender differences surface early, in children's play. Boys typically play in large groups with an activity focus and little intimate discussion. Girls usually play in smaller groups, often with one friend. Their play is less competitive than boys' and more imitative of social relationships. Both in play and other settings, females are more open and responsive to feedback than are males (Maccoby, 1990; Roberts,

Every man for himself, or tend and befriend? Gender differences in the way we interact with others begin to appear at a very young age.

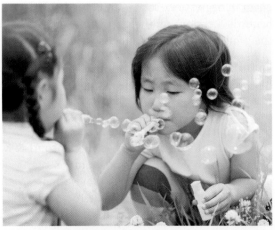

1991). Asked difficult questions—"Do you have any idea why the sky is blue?" "Do you have any idea why shorter people live longer?"—men are more likely than women to hazard answers rather than admit they don't know, a phenomenon Traci Giuliano and her colleagues (1998a,b) call the *male answer syndrome.*

As teens, girls spend more time with friends and less time alone (Wong & Csik-szentmihalyi, 1991). The gender difference in connectedness continues through adulthood. Women, being more *interdependent,* use conversation more to explore re-lationships; men use it to communicate solutions (Tannen, 1990). New studies from several countries confirm gender differences in communication:

- *New Zealand:* Given a sample of students' e-mail notes, people correctly guessed the writer's gender 66 percent of the time (Thomson & Murachver, 2001). (Males less often disclosed emotion and personal information, offered apologies, and used such hedges as "it was *sort of* interesting.")
- *United States:* When using computers, girls spend less time playing games and more time e-mailing friends (Crabtree, 2002).
- *France:* Women make 63 percent of telephone calls, and when talking to a woman stay connected longer (7.2 minutes) than men do when talking to other men (4.6 minutes) (Smoreda & Licoppe, 2000).

Women emphasize caring and provide most of the care to the very young and the very old. Women also purchase 85 percent of greeting cards (*Time,* 1997). Although 69 percent of people say they have a close relationship with their father, 90 percent feel close to their mother (Hugick, 1989).

Like empowered people generally, men emphasize freedom and self-reliance. That helps explain why at all ages men worldwide assign less importance to religion and pray less often than their female counterparts (Benson, 1992; Stark, 2002). In a 2003 U.S. Gallup Poll, 53 percent of men and 69 percent of women said religion was "very important" in their life (Saad, 2003). Men also dominate the ranks of profes-sional skeptics. Nearly 4 in 5 respondents to one Skeptics Society survey were men (Shermer, 1999). Likewise, the two dozen winners and runners-up on the *Skeptical Inquirer's* list of outstanding twentieth-century rationalist skeptics were all men. In the Science and the Paranormal section of the 2004–2005 catalog of Prometheus Books (the leading publisher of skepticism), I counted 104 male authors and only 4 female authors. Women, it appears, are more open to spirituality (and are far more likely to author books on spirituality than on skepticism).

Bonds and feelings of support are also stronger among women than among men (Rossi & Rossi, 1993). Women's ties—as mothers, daughters, sisters, aunts, and grandmothers—bind families together. As friends, women are more intimate than men; they talk more often and more openly (Berndt, 1992; Dindia & Allen, 1992). While men enjoy doing activities *side-by-side,* women take more pleasure in talking *face-to-face* (Wright, 1989). And when coping with stress, women more often turn to others for support—they *tend and befriend* (Tamres & others, 2002; Taylor, 2002).

Both men and women report their friendships with women to be more intimate, enjoyable, and nurturing (Rubin, 1985; Sapadin, 1988). When wanting understand-ing and someone with whom to share worries and hurts, both men and women usu-ally turn to women.

Question: Why does it take 200 million sperm to fertilize one egg?
Answer: Because they won't stop for directions.

Sex brought us together, but gender drove us apart.

The Nature of Gender

OBJECTIVE 7-15 | Explain how biological sex is determined, and describe the role of sex hormones in biological development and gender differences.

What explains our gender diversity? Is biology destiny? Are we shaped by our cul-tures? A biopsychosocial view suggests it is both, thanks to the interplay among what Wendy Wood and Alice Eagly (2002) call "the evolved character of the sexes," our de-velopmental experiences, and our current situations.

Courtesy of Nick Downes.

In domains where men and women have faced similar challenges—regulating heat with sweat, developing tastes that nourish, growing calluses where the skin meets friction—the sexes are similar. Even when describing the ideal mate, both men and women put traits such as "kind," "honest," and "intelligent" at the top of their lists. But in domains pertinent to mating, evolutionary psychologists contend, guys act like guys whether they are elephants or elephant seals, rural peasants or corporate presidents. Such gender differences may be influenced genetically, by our differing *sex chromosomes* and, physiologically, from our differing concentrations of *sex hormones*.

Males and females are variations on a single form. Seven weeks after conception, you were anatomically indistinguishable from someone of the other sex. Then your genes activated your biological sex. Your sex was determined by your twenty-third pair of chromosomes, the two sex chromosomes. From your mother you received an **X chromosome.** From your father, you received the one chromosome out of 46 that is not unisex. This was either an X chromosome, making you a girl, or a **Y chromosome,** making you a boy. The Y chromosome includes a single gene that throws a master switch triggering the testes to develop and produce the principal male hormone, **testosterone,** which about the seventh week starts the development of external male sex organs. Females also have testosterone, but less of it. Another key period for sexual differentiation falls during the fourth and fifth prenatal months, when different brain-wiring patterns for males and females develop under the influence of the male's greater testosterone and the female's ovarian hormones (Hines, 2004; Udry, 2000).

What do you suppose happens when glandular malfunction or hormone injections expose a female embryo to excess testosterone? These genetically female infants are born with masculine-appearing genitals, which can be corrected surgically. Until puberty, such females tend to act in more aggressive "tomboyish" ways than do most girls, and they dress and play in ways more typical of boys than of girls (Berenbaum & Hines, 1992; Ehrhardt, 1987). Given a choice of toys, they (like boys) are more likely to play with cars and guns than with dolls and crayons. Some develop into lesbians, but most—like nearly all girls with traditionally feminine interests—become heterosexual. Moreover, the hormones do not reverse their gender identity; they view themselves as girls, not boys (Berenbaum & Bailey, 2004).

Is the tomboyish behavior of these girls due to the prenatal hormones? If so, may we conclude that biological sex differences produce behavioral gender differences? Like humans, male vervet monkeys spend more time with "masculine" toys such as trucks, and females with "feminine" toys such as dolls (Hines, 2004). And experiments with many species, from rats to monkeys, confirm that female embryos given male hormones will later exhibit atypically masculine appearance and more aggressive behavior (Hines & Green, 1991). But among humans, such girls frequently *look* masculine and are known to be "different," so perhaps people also treat them more like boys. Early exposure to sex hormones thus affects us both directly, in our biological appearance, and indirectly, by influencing social experiences that shape us. Like a sculptor's two hands shaping a lump of clay, nature and nurture work together.

Further evidence that biology influences gender development comes from studies of genetic males who, despite normal male hormones and testes, are born without penises or with very small ones. In one study of 14 who underwent early sex-reassignment surgery and were raised as girls, six later declared themselves as male, five were living as female, and three had unclear sexual identity (Reiner & Gearhart, 2004). In one famous case, the parents of a Canadian boy who lost his penis to a botched circumcision followed advice to raise him as a girl rather than as a damaged boy. Alas, "Brenda" was not like other girls. "She" didn't like dolls. She tore her dresses with rough-and-tumble play. At puberty she wanted no part of kissing boys. Finally, Brenda's parents explained what had happened, whereupon Brenda immediately rejected her female identity, cut her hair, took a male name, and ended up marrying a woman, becoming a stepfather,

"Genes, by themselves, are like seeds dropped onto pavement: powerless to produce anything."
Primatologist Frans B. M. de Waal (1999)

and, sadly, later committing suicide (Colapinto, 2000). Although socially influenced, gender is not written on a biologically blank slate.

Sex chromosomes control sex hormones that bathe the fetal brain and influence its wiring. Recent research confirms male–female differences during development in brain areas with abundant sex hormone receptors (Cahill, 2005). In adulthood, part of the frontal lobes, an area involved in verbal fluency, is reportedly thicker in women. Part of the parietal cortex, a key area for space perception, is thicker in men. Other studies report gender differences in the hippocampus, the amygdala, and the volume of brain gray matter (the neural bodies) versus white matter (the axons and dendrites). Although further research is needed to confirm these findings and sort out their implications, this much seems clear, reports the National Academy of Sciences (2001): "Sex matters." In combination with the environment, sex-related genes and physiology "result in behavioral and cognitive differences between males and females."

The Nurture of Gender

OBJECTIVE 7-16 | Discuss the importance of environment in the development of gender roles, and describe two theories of gender-typing.

Although biologically influenced, gender is also socially constructed. What biology initiates, culture accentuates.

Gender Roles

Sex matters. But from a biopsychosocial perspective, culture and the immediate situation matter, too. Culture, as we noted earlier, is everything that is shared by a group and transmitted across generations. We can see culture's shaping power in the social expectations that guide men's and women's behavior. In psychology, as in the theater, a **role** refers to a cluster of prescribed actions—the behaviors we expect of those who occupy a particular social position. One set of norms defines our culture's **gender roles**—our expectations about the way men and women behave. Thirty years ago, it was standard for men to initiate dates, drive the car, and pick up the check, and for women to decorate the home, buy and care for the children's clothes, and select the wedding gifts. Gender roles exist outside the home, too. In the United States, employed men spend about an hour more per day working than do employed women, and about an hour a day less on household activities and in caregiving (Bureau of Labor Statistics, 2004). And, I do not have to tell you which parent, about 90 percent of the time in two-parent families, still stays home with a sick child, arranges for the baby-sitter, or calls the doctor (Maccoby, 1995). In Australia, women devote 54 percent more time to unpaid household work and 71 percent more time to child care than do men (Trewin, 2001).

Gender roles can smooth social relations, saving awkward decisions about who does the laundry this week and who mows the lawn. But they often do so at a cost: If we deviate from such conventions, we may feel anxious.

Do gender roles reflect what is biologically natural for men and women? Or do cultures construct them? The diversity of gender roles across cultures and over time indicates that culture has a big influence. Nomadic societies of food-gathering people have only a minimal division of labor by sex. Boys and girls receive much the same upbringing. However, in agricultural societies, women remain close to home, working in the fields and staying with the children; men often roam more freely, herding cattle or sheep. Such societies typically socialize their children into more distinct gender roles (Segall & others, 1990; Van Leeuwen, 1978).

Among the industrialized countries, gender roles and attitudes nevertheless vary widely. Would you say that life is more satisfying when both spouses work and share child care? A Pew Global Attitudes survey (2003)

▪ **X chromosome** the sex chromosome found in both men and women. Females have two X chromosomes; males have one. An X chromosome from each parent produces a female child.

▪ **Y chromosome** the sex chromosome found only in males. When paired with an X chromosome from the mother, it produces a male child.

▪ **testosterone** the most important of the male sex hormones. Both males and females have it, but the additional testosterone in males stimulates the growth of the male sex organs in the fetus and the development of the male sex characteristics during puberty.

▪ **role** a set of expectations (norms) about a social position, defining how those in the position ought to behave.

▪ **gender role** a set of expected behaviors for males and for females.

The gendered tsunami
In Sri Lanka, Indonesia, and India, the gendered division of labor helps explain the excess of female deaths from the 2004 tsunami. In some villages, 80 percent of those killed were women, who were mostly at home while the men were more likely to be out at sea fishing or doing out-of-the-home chores (Oxfam, 2005).

(c) DPA/The Image Works

FIGURE 7.4
Changing attitudes about gender roles
U.S. college students' endorsement of the traditional view of women's role has declined dramatically. Men's and women's attitudes have also converged. (From Dey & others, 1991; Sax & others, 2004.)

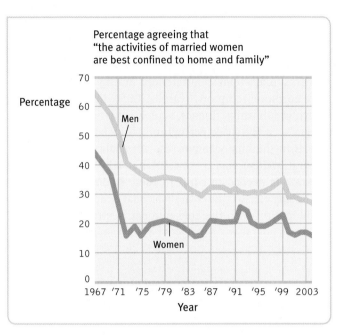

revealed that in 41 of 44 countries, most people agreed that shared work and child care is most satisfying (rather than women staying home while the husband provides). But the culture-to-culture differences were huge, ranging from Egypt, where people disagreed 2 to 1, to Vietnam, where people concurred by 11 to 1.

Gender roles also vary over time:

- As we began the last century, only one country—New Zealand—granted women the right to vote. As we ended it, only one democracy—Kuwait—did not (Briscoe, 1997).
- With the flick of an apron, the number of U.S. college women hoping to be full-time homemakers plunged during the late 1960s and early 1970s (**FIGURE 7.4**). In 1960, one in 30 entering U.S. law students were women; by the early twenty-first century, half were (Glater, 2001).
- Over the decades since 1930, women's assertiveness has increased and decreased with their social status—up until the end of World War II, then down until the mid-1960s, then up again (Twenge, 2001). It is "all right for a girl to telephone a boy to ask for a date," agreed 29 percent of Americans in a 1950 Gallup poll, and 70 percent a half-century later.

Gender ideas also vary across generations. When families emigrate from Asia to Canada and the United States, the immigrant children often grow up with peers who assume gender roles different from those of the immigrant parents. Daughters, especially, may feel torn between competing sets of norms (Dion & Dion, 2001).

Gender and Child-Rearing

Society assigns each of us to a gender, the social category of male or female. The inevitable result is our strong **gender identity,** our sense of being male or female. To varying extents, we also become **gender-typed.** That is, some boys more than others exhibit traditionally masculine traits and interests, and some girls more than others become distinctly feminine.

Social learning theory assumes that children learn gender-linked behaviors by observing and imitating and by being rewarded or punished. "Nicole, you're such a good mommy to your dolls"; "Big boys don't cry, Alex." But modeling and rewarding is not done by parents alone, because the differences in the way parents rear boys and girls aren't enough to explain gender-typing (Lytton & Romney, 1991). In fact, even when their families discourage traditional gender-typing, children organize themselves into "boy worlds" and "girl worlds," each guided by rules for what boys and girls do.

Gender roles have changed, but not every male has changed with them.

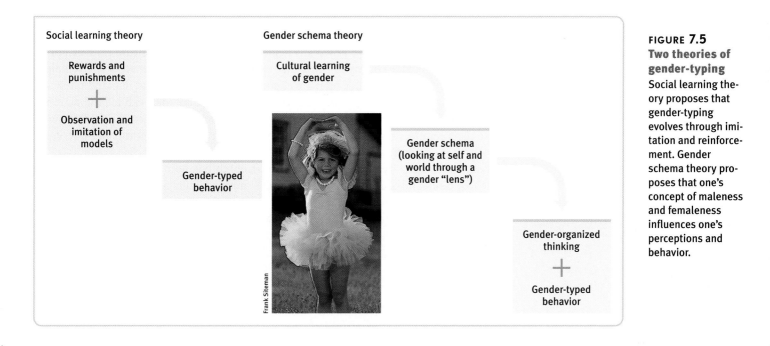

FIGURE **7.5**
Two theories of gender-typing Social learning theory proposes that gender-typing evolves through imitation and reinforcement. Gender schema theory proposes that one's concept of maleness and femaleness influences one's perceptions and behavior.

Gender schema theory combines social learning theory with cognition: In your own childhood, as you struggled to comprehend the world, you—like other children—formed concepts, or *schemas,* including a schema for your own gender (Bem, 1987, 1993). Gender then became a lens through which you viewed your experiences (**FIGURE 7.5**). Before age 1, children begin to discriminate male and female voices and faces (Martin & others, 2002). After age 2, language forces children to begin organizing their worlds on the basis of gender. English, for example, uses the pronouns *he* and *she;* other languages classify objects as masculine ("*le train*") or feminine ("*la table*"). Through language, dress, toys, and songs, social learning shapes gender schemas. Children then compare themselves with their concept of gender ("I am male—thus, masculine, strong, aggressive," or "I am female—therefore, feminine, sweet, and helpful") and adjust their behavior accordingly.

Young children are "gender detectives," explain Carol Lynn Martin and Diane Ruble (2004). Once they grasp that two sorts of people exist—and they are of one sort—they search for cues about gender. Girls, they may decide, are the ones with long hair. Having divided the human world in half, 3-year-olds will then like their own sex better and seek out their own kind for play. The rigidity of their stereotypes about boys and girls increases to a peak at about age 5 or 6. If the new neighbor is a boy, a 6-year-old girl may just assume that he cannot share her interests. For young children, gender schemas loom large.

"How is it gendered?"

Reflections on Nature and Nurture

OBJECTIVE **7-17** | Describe the biopsychosocial approach to development.

"There are trivial truths and great truths," reflected the physicist Niels Bohr on some of the paradoxes of modern science. "The opposite of a trivial truth is plainly false. The opposite of a great truth is also true." It appears true that our ancestral history helped form us as a species. Where there is variation, natural selection, and heredity, there will be, on some scale, evolution. The unique gene combination created when our mother's egg engulfed our father's sperm also helped form us, as individuals. Genes predispose both our shared humanity and our individual differences. This is a great truth about human nature. Genes form us.

But it also is true that our experiences form us. In the womb, in our families, and in our peer social relationships, we learn ways of thinking and acting. Even differences

■ **gender identity** one's sense of being male or female.

■ **gender-typing** the acquisition of a traditional masculine or feminine role.

■ **social learning theory** the theory that we learn social behavior by observing and imitating and by being rewarded or punished.

■ **gender schema theory** the theory that children learn from their cultures a concept of what it means to be male and female and that they adjust their behavior accordingly.

initiated by our nature may be amplified by our nurture. If their genes and hormones predispose males to be more physically aggressive than females, culture may magnify this gender difference through norms that encourage males to be macho and females to be the kinder, gentler sex. If men are encouraged toward roles that demand physical power, and women toward more nurturing roles, each may then exhibit the actions expected of those who fill such roles and find themselves shaped accordingly. Roles remake their players. Presidents in time become more presidential, servants more servile. Gender roles similarly shape us.

But gender roles are converging. As brute strength has become increasingly irrelevant to power and status (think Bill Gates), both women and men have become "fully capable of effectively carrying out organizational roles at all levels," note Wendy Wood and Alice Eagly (2002). And as women's employment in formerly male occupations has increased, gender differences in traditional masculinity/femininity and in what one seeks in a mate have diminished (Twenge, 1997). As the roles we play change over time, we change with them.

* * * * *

If nature and nurture jointly form us, are we "nothing but" the product of nature and nurture? Are we rigidly determined?

We *are* the product of nature and nurture (**FIGURE 7.6**), but we are also an open system. Genes are all-pervasive but not all-powerful. Sometimes people defy their genetic bent to reproduce, by electing celibacy. Culture, too, is all-pervasive but not all-powerful. Sometimes people defy peer pressures, by asserting their freedom and doing the opposite of the expected. When the crowd goes one way, they remember who they are and go another. To excuse our failings by blaming our nature and nurture is what philosopher-novelist Jean-Paul Sartre called "bad faith"—attributing responsibility for one's fate to bad genes or bad influences.

In reality, we are both the creatures and the creators of our worlds. We are—it is a great truth—the products of our genes and environments. Nevertheless—another great truth—the stream of causation that shapes the future runs through our present choices. Our decisions today design our environments tomorrow. Mind matters. The human environment is not like the weather—something that just happens. We are its architects. Our hopes, goals, and expectations influence our future. And that is what enables cultures to vary and to change so quickly.

* * * * *

I know from my mail and from public opinion surveys that some readers feel troubled by the naturalism and evolutionism of contemporary science. They worry that a science

FIGURE 7.6
The biopsychosocial approach to development

of behavior (and evolutionary science in particular) will destroy our sense of the beauty, mystery, and spiritual significance of the human creature. For those concerned, I offer some reassuring thoughts.

When Isaac Newton explained the rainbow in terms of light of differing wavelengths, the poet Keats feared that Newton had destroyed the rainbow's mysterious beauty. Yet, notes Richard Dawkins (1998) in *Unweaving the Rainbow,* Newton's analysis led to Maxwell's theory of electromagnetism and onward to an even deeper mystery—Einstein's theory of special relativity. Moreover, nothing about Newton's optics need diminish our appreciation for the dramatic elegance of a rainbow arching across a rain-darkened sky.

When Galileo assembled evidence that the Earth revolved around the Sun, not vice versa, he did not offer irrefutable proof for his theory. Rather he offered a coherent explanation for a variety of observations, such as the changing shadows cast by the Moon's mountains. His explanation eventually won the day because it described and explained things in a way that made sense, that hung together. Darwin's theory of evolution likewise is a coherent view of natural history. It offers an organizing principle that unifies various observations.

Although some people of faith may find the scientific idea of human origins troubling, many others find it congenial with their spirituality. In the fifth century, St. Augustine (quoted by Wilford, 1999) wrote, "The universe was brought into being in a less than fully formed state, but was gifted with the capacity to transform itself from unformed matter into a truly marvelous array of structures and life forms." Some 1600 years later, Pope John Paul II in 1996 welcomed a science-religion dialogue, finding it noteworthy that evolutionary theory "has been progressively accepted by researchers, following a series of discoveries in various fields of knowledge."

Meanwhile, many people of science are awestruck at the emerging understanding of the universe and the human creature. It boggles the mind—the entire universe popping out of a point some 14 billion years ago, and instantly inflating to cosmological size. Had the energy of this Big Bang been the tiniest bit less, the universe would have collapsed back on itself. Had it been the tiniest bit more, the result would have been a soup too thin to support life. Had gravity been a teeny bit stronger or weaker, or had the weight of a carbon proton been a wee bit different, our universe just wouldn't have worked.

What caused this almost-too-good-to-be-true, finely tuned universe? Why is there something rather than nothing? How did it come to be, in the words of Harvard-Smithsonian astrophysicist Owen Gingerich (1999), "so extraordinarily right, that it seemed the universe had been expressly designed to produce intelligent, sentient beings"? Is there a benevolent superintelligence behind it all? Have there instead been an infinite number of universes born and we just happen to be the lucky inhabitants of one that, by chance, was exquisitely fine-tuned to give birth to us? Or does that idea violate *Occam's razor,* the principle that we should prefer the simplest of competing explanations? On most of these matters, science is silent. Faced with such mind-boggling questions, a humble, awed, scientific silence is appropriate, suggested philosopher Ludwig Wittgenstein: "Whereof one cannot speak, thereof one must be silent."

Rather than fearing or restraining science, we can welcome its enlarging our understanding and awakening our sense of awe. In *The Fragile Species,* Lewis Thomas (1992) described his utter amazement that the Earth in time gave rise to bacteria and eventually to Bach's *Mass in B-Minor.* In a short 4 billion years, life on Earth has come from nothing to structures as complex as a 6-billion-unit strand of DNA and the incomprehensible intricacy of the human brain. Nature, says cosmologist Paul Davies (1992, 1999, 2004), seems cunningly and ingeniously devised to produce extraordinary, self-replicating, information-processing systems—us. Although we appear to have been created from dust, over eons of time, the end result is a priceless creature, one rich with potentials beyond our imagining.

"Let's hope that it's not true; but if it is true, let's hope that it doesn't become widely known."
Lady Ashley, commenting on Darwin's theory

"Is it not stirring to understand how the world actually works—that white light is made of colors, that color measures light waves, that transparent air reflects light . . . ? It does no harm to the romance of the sunset to know a little about it."
Carl Sagan, *Skies of Other Worlds,* 1988

"The causes of life's history [cannot] resolve the riddle of life's meaning."
Stephen Jay Gould, *Rocks of Ages: Science and Religion in the Fullness of Life,* 1999

>> LEARNING OUTCOMES

Environmental Influences on Behavior

OBJECTIVE 7-1 | **Describe some of the conditions that can affect development before birth.**

Prenatal environments differ in terms of nutrition and exposure to toxic agents. Even identical twins sharing a placenta can, because of their differing locations, have unequal access to nourishment and protection from viruses.

OBJECTIVE 7-2 | **Describe how experience can modify the brain.**

During maturation, a child's neural connections increase in areas associated with repetitive activities (vision, for example), and degenerate in unused areas. Though the process is most evident in the brains of young children, growth and pruning of synapses continue throughout life.

OBJECTIVE 7-3 | **Explain why we should be careful about attributing children's successes and failures to their parents' influence.**

Freudian psychiatry and extreme environmentalism in early psychology contributed to the idea that parents shape their children's futures. Parents do influence some areas of their children's lives, such as their manners and political and religious beliefs. But in other areas, such as personality, the home environment accounts for less than 10 percent of siblings' differences.

OBJECTIVE 7-4 | **Evaluate the importance of peer influence on development.**

Children, like adults, attempt to fit into groups by conforming. But children also select peers who share their attitudes and interests. Parents are important models for education, discipline, responsibility, orderliness, charitableness, and ways of interacting with authorities. Peers are influential in learning to cooperate with others, achieving popularity, and finding appropriate styles of interaction with people of a similar age. By choosing the neighborhoods in which their children live, parents can exert some influence over the peer group culture that helps shape children.

OBJECTIVE 7-5 | **Discuss the survival benefits of culture.**

Culture is a set of enduring behaviors, ideas, attitudes, values, and traditions shared by a group of people and transmitted from one generation to the next. Culture and our capacity for language let us preserve innovations and pass them on to the next generation, a process that encourages diversity between groups. Despite cultural differences, the human species shares a capacity for culture.

OBJECTIVE 7-6 | **Describe some ways that cultures differ.**

Cultures vary in their ideas, attitudes, values, and traditions. Those variations are embedded in each culture's *norms*, its rules for accepted and expected behavior. In a culture different from our own, we may experience *culture shock*—confusion or frustration about differing norms for observing personal space, expressing personal feelings, maintaining a certain pace of life, or educating and caring for children.

OBJECTIVE 7-7 | **Explain why changes in the human gene pool cannot account for culture change over time.**

Cultures change rapidly. Western cultures, for example, have changed as they have discovered and adapted to new forms of technology. Cultures also change in their values, attitudes, and behaviors. The speed at which such changes occur is much faster than the slow pace of evolutionary changes in the human gene pool.

OBJECTIVE 7-8 | **Identify some ways a primarily individualist culture differs from a primarily collectivist culture, and compare their effects on personal identity.**

Cultures based on *individualism,* like those of most of the United States, Canada, and Western Europe, value personal independence and individual achievement. Relationships tend to be more temporary and casual, confrontation is acceptable, and morality is self-defined. Individualist cultures tend to define identity in terms of self-esteem, personal goals and attributes, and personal rights and liberties. Cultures based on *collectivism,* like those of many parts of Asia and Africa, value interdependence, tradition, and harmony. Relationships tend to be few, close, and enduring, and morality is based on duty to one's social network. Collectivist cultures tend to define identity in terms of group goals and commitments and belonging to one's group.

OBJECTIVE 7-9 | **Describe some ways that child-rearing differs in individualist and collectivist cultures.**

Individualist cultures expect their members to be independent and to think for themselves, and child-rearing practices in those cultures reflect these values. Collectivist cultures, which emphasize a stonger sense of family self, tend to focus more on developing a sense of emotional closeness.

OBJECTIVE 7-10 | **Describe some ways that humans are similar, despite their cultural differences.**

Although we humans differ in our cultures, we share the same genetic profile, life cycle, capacity for language, biological needs, and need to belong. To the extent that biology and social forces predict behavior in individuals in one group, they often predict similar behaviors in those in other groups.

OBJECTIVE 7-11 | **Identify some biological and psychological differences between males and females.**

Although similar in their genetic makeup, males and females differ biologically in body fat, muscle, height, age of onset of puberty, and life expectancy. They also differ psychologically, for example, in their vulnerability to certain disorders: More women are diagnosed with depression, more men with antisocial personality disorder.

OBJECTIVE 7-12 | **Summarize the gender gap in aggression.**

Men more than women behave aggressively and describe themselves as aggressive. The aggression gender gap appears in many cultures and at various ages, especially for physical aggression.

OBJECTIVE 7-13 | **Describe some gender differences in social power.**

In most societies, men are socially dominant and are perceived as such. Men tend to occupy more leadership positions, and their leadership style is more directive than women's.

OBJECTIVE 7-14 | **Discuss gender differences in connectedness, or the ability to "tend and befriend."**

Women, more than men, are concerned with making connections with others. This difference is noticeable in young children's play, and it continues throughout the teen years and into adulthood. Women tend and befriend—they emphasize caring, often being responsible for the very young and very old. Bonds between women seem stronger and more supportive than those between men. Men tend to emphasize freedom and self-reliance.

OBJECTIVE 7-15 | **Explain how biological sex is determined, and describe the role of sex hormones in biological development and gender differences.**

Biological sex is determined by the twenty-third pair of chromosomes. In this pair, the mother's contribution is always an X chromosome. The father may contribute either an X or a Y. An XX combination produces a female; an XY combination produces a male. The Y chromosome contains a master switch for the production of the hormone testosterone, which triggers the growth of external male sex organs in the seventh week of prenatal development. (Females also produce testosterone, but less of it.) The fourth and fifth prenatal months are a second key period for sexual differentiation, influenced by a male fetus' greater testosterone or a female fetus' ovarian hormones. *Gender* is the set of biologically and socially influenced characteristics by which people define *male* and *female*. Sex-related genes and hormones do influence gender differences in behavior, possibly by influencing brain development, but many gender differences are learned.

OBJECTIVE 7-16 | **Discuss the importance of environment in the development of gender roles, and describe two theories of gender-typing.**

Cultures shape *gender roles*—expectations about how men and women should behave. Gender roles can vary from one place to another, and from one time to another within the same culture. A person's sense of being male or female is called *gender identity,* and some people more than others exhibit *gender-typed* (traditionally masculine or feminine) behavior. *Social learning theory* proposes that we learn gender behavior as we learn other things—through reinforcement, punishment, and observation. *Gender schema theory* proposes that we learn a cultural "recipe" of how to be male or female, which influences our behaviors and perceptions of what is appropriate for "people like us."

OBJECTIVE 7-17 | **Describe the biopsychosocial approach to development.**

Our biology—established through natural selection as members of the human species or through our unique genetic combination at the time of our conception—provides us with certain abilities and places limits on others. The people and customs in our social environment direct us toward specific roles and reward us for conforming (or punish us for not conforming) to cultural expectations. Our individual biological and psychological characteristics also evoke reactions from those around us, which then influence our behavior. But our choices matter, too. We can study development from any point on this biopsychosocial continuum. Rather than diminishing us, science can enlarge our understanding of ourselves and our appreciation of the world around us.

TERMS AND CONCEPTS TO REMEMBER

culture, p. 7-4	testosterone, p. 7-14
norm, p. 7-5	role, p. 7-15
personal space, p. 7-6	gender role, p. 7-15
individualism, p. 7-7	gender identity, p. 7-16
collectivism, p. 7-7	gender-typing, p. 7-16
aggression, p. 7-11	social learning theory, p. 7-16
X chromosome, p. 7-14	gender schema theory, p. 7-17
Y chromosome, p. 7-14	

TEST YOURSELF

1. To predict whether a teenager smokes, ask how many of the teen's friends smoke. One explanation for this correlation is peer influence. What's another?

2. How do individualist and collectivist cultures differ?

3. What are gender roles, and what do their variations tell us about our human capacity for learning and adaptation?

(Answers in Appendix B.)

ASK YOURSELF

1. To what extent, and in what ways, have your peers and your parents helped shape who you are?

2. Which concept best describes you—collectivist or individualist? Do you fit completely in either category, or are you sometimes a collectivist and sometimes an individualist?

3. Do you consider yourself strongly gender-typed or *not* strongly gender-typed? What factors do you think have contributed to your feelings of masculinity or femininity?

4. Do you believe your heredity and your environment *determined* who you are today or *influenced* who you are today? Can you recall an important time when you determined your own fate in a way that was at odds with your heredity and your environment?

❯WEB

Multiple-choice *self-tests* and more may be found at www.worthpublishers.com/myers.

JHUMPA LAHIRI (b. 1967), FROM *THE NAMESAKE*, 2003

Ashima Ganguli ... is in labor.... She is alone, cut off by curtains from the three other women in the room. ... It is the first time in her life she has slept alone, surrounded by strangers; all her life she has slept either in a room with her parents, or with Ashoke at her side. She wishes the curtains were open, so that she could talk to the American women. Perhaps one of them has given birth before, can tell her what to expect. But she has gathered that Americans, in spite of their public declarations of affections, in spite of their miniskirts and bikinis, in spite of their hand-holding on the street and lying on top of each other on the Cambridge Common, prefer their privacy. She spreads her fingers over the taut, enormous drum her middle has become, wondering where the baby's feet and hands are at this moment. The child is no longer restless; for the past few days, apart from the occasional flutter, she has not felt it punch or kick or press against her ribs. She wonders if she is the only Indian person in the hospital, but a gentle twitch from the baby reminds her that she is, technically speaking, not alone. Ashima thinks it is strange that her child will be born in a place most people enter to either suffer or to die .... In India, she thinks to herself, women go home to their parents to give birth, away from husbands and in-laws and household cares, retreating briefly to childhood when the baby arrives.

Developing Through the Life Span

OBJECTIVE 8-1 | State the three areas of change that developmental psychologists study, and identify the three major issues in developmental psychology.

As we journey through life—from womb to tomb—when, how, and why do we develop? We can't help but notice how people differ. However, to **developmental psychologists,** who study physical, cognitive, and social changes throughout the human life cycle, discerning our commonalities is just as important. Virtually all of us began walking around age 1 and talking by age 2. As children, we engaged in social play in preparation for life's work. As adults, we all smile and cry, love and loathe, and occasionally ponder the fact that someday we will die. Psychology's developmental perspective examines how people are continually developing, from infancy through old age. Much of its research centers on three major issues:

1. *Nature/nurture:* How do genetic inheritance (*our nature*) and experience (*the nurture we receive*) influence our development?

2. *Continuity/stages:* Is development a gradual, continuous process like riding an escalator, or does it proceed through a sequence of separate stages, like climbing rungs on a ladder?

3. *Stability/change:* Do our early personality traits persist through life, or do we become different persons as we age?

In other modules, we engaged the nature/nurture issue. In the modules in this part, we will reflect on the continuity and stability issues throughout the life span.

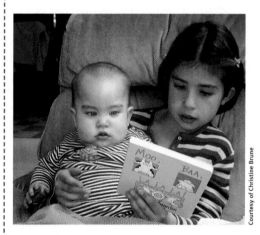

Courtesy of Christine Brune

"Nature is all that a man brings with him into the world; nurture is every influence that affects him after his birth."

Francis Galton, *English Men of Science,* 1874

■ **developmental psychology** a branch of psychology that studies physical, cognitive, and social change throughout the life span.

MODULE

8

Prenatal Development and the Newborn

How, over time, did we come to be who we are? From the union of sperm and egg to the birth of the newborn, development progresses in an orderly, though fragile, sequence. We begin with a look at what developmental biologists have learned about life before birth, and we then turn to some of the findings of *developmental psychology* about the newborn.

Conception

OBJECTIVE 8-2 | Describe the union of sperm and egg at conception.

Nothing is more natural than a species reproducing itself. Yet nothing is more wondrous. Consider human reproduction. The process starts when a woman's ovary releases a mature egg, a cell roughly the size of the period at the end of this sentence, and when the 200 million or more sperm deposited during intercourse begin their race upstream toward it. The woman was born with all the immature eggs she would ever have, although only 1 in 5000 will ever mature and be released. A man, in contrast, begins producing sperm cells at puberty. The manufacturing process continues 24 hours a day for the rest of his life, although the rate of production—in the beginning more than 1000 sperm during the second it takes to read this phrase—slows with age.

Like space voyagers approaching a huge planet, the sperm approach a cell 85,000 times their own size. The relatively few that make it to the egg release digestive enzymes that eat away the egg's protective coating, allowing a sperm to penetrate (**FIGURE 8.1**). But the egg is hardly passive. As soon as one sperm begins to penetrate, the egg's surface blocks out the others. Meanwhile, fingerlike projections sprout around the successful sperm and pull it in. Before half a day elapses, the egg nucleus and the sperm nucleus fuse. The two have become one. Consider it your most fortunate of moments. Among 200 million sperm, the one needed to make you, in combination with that one particular egg, won the race. Physician and author Lewis Thomas (1979) appreciated the wonder when the first "test tube baby" was born:

> In mid-1978, the newest astonishment in medicine . . . was the birth of an English baby nine months after conception in a dish. The older surprise, which should still be fazing us all, is that a solitary sperm and a single egg

FIGURE **8.1**
Life is sexually transmitted
(a) Sperm cells surround an ovum.
(b) As one sperm penetrates the egg's jellylike outer coating, a series of chemical events begins that will cause sperm and egg to fuse into a single cell. If all goes well, that cell will subdivide again and again to emerge 9 months later as a 100-trillion-cell human being.

(a)

(b)

can fuse and become a human being. . . . This has been going on under our eyes for so long a time that we've gotten used to it; hence the outcries of amazement at this really minor technical modification of the general procedure—nothing much, really, beyond relocating the beginning of the process from the fallopian tube to a plastic container.

Prenatal Development

OBJECTIVE 8-3 | Define *zygote, embryo,* and *fetus,* and explain how teratogens can affect development.

Fewer than half of all fertilized eggs, called **zygotes,** survive beyond the first 2 weeks (Grobstein, 1979; Hall, 2004). But for you and me, good fortune prevailed. Beginning as one cell, each of us became 2 cells, then 4—each cell just like the first. Then, within the first week, when this cell division had produced a zygote of some 100 cells, the cells began to *differentiate*—to specialize in structure and function. How identical cells do this—as if one decides "I'll become a brain, you become intestines!"—is a scientific puzzle that developmental biologists are just beginning to solve.

About 10 days after conception, the increasingly diverse cells attach to the mother's uterine wall, beginning approximately 37 weeks of the closest human relationship. The zygote's outer part attaches to the uterine wall, forming the placenta, through which nourishment passes. The inner cells become the **embryo** (FIGURE 8.2). Over the next 6 weeks, organs begin to form and function. The heart begins to beat.

■ **zygote** the fertilized egg; it enters a 2-week period of rapid cell division and develops into an embryo.

■ **embryo** the developing human organism from about 2 weeks after fertilization through the second month.

" From the very moment that the sperm hits the egg, a precarious trip on the thin edge of biological extinction has begun."
Ralph Blair, *Nevertheless Joy!* 1989

(a)   (b)

(c)   (d)

FIGURE 8.2
Prenatal development
(a) The embryo grows and develops rapidly. At 40 days, the spine is visible and the arms and legs are beginning to grow. (b) Five days later, the inch-long embryo's proportions have begun to change. The rest of the body is now bigger than the head, and the arms and legs have grown noticeably. (c) By the end of the second month, when the fetal period begins, facial features, hands, and feet have formed. (d) As the fetus enters the fourth month, its 3 ounces could fit in the palm of your hand.

Prenatal development

zygote: conception to 2 weeks

embryo: 2 weeks through 8 weeks

fetus: 9 weeks to birth.

By 9 weeks after conception, the embryo looks unmistakably human. It is now a **fetus** (Latin for "offspring" or "young one"). During the sixth month, organs such as the stomach are sufficiently formed and functional to allow a prematurely born fetus a chance of survival. At this point, the fetus is also responsive to sound. Microphone readings taken inside the uterus have revealed that the fetus is exposed to the sound of its mother's muffled voice (Ecklund-Flores, 1992). Immediately after birth, infants prefer this voice to another woman's voice or their father's (Busnel & others, 1992; DeCasper & others, 1984, 1986, 1994).

At each prenatal stage, genetic *and* environmental factors affect our development. The placenta transfers nutrients and oxygen from mother to fetus, while screening out many potentially harmful substances. But some substances slip by. The placental screen can admit **teratogens**—harmful agents such as certain viruses and drugs. If the mother is a heroin addict, her baby will be born a heroin addict. If she carries the AIDS virus, her baby may also. A pregnant woman never smokes alone; she and her fetus both experience reduced blood oxygen and a shot of nicotine. If she is a heavy smoker, her fetus may receive fewer nutrients and be born underweight and at risk for various problems (Pringle & others, 2005).

There is no known safe amount of alcohol for a pregnant woman. Even light drinking can affect the fetal brain, and even a single drinking binge can kill millions of fetal brain cells (Braun, 1996; Ikonomidou & others, 2000). Alcohol enters the woman's bloodstream—and her fetus'—and depresses activity in both their central nervous systems. If she drinks heavily, her baby will be at risk for birth defects and mental retardation. For 1 in 750 infants, the effects are visible as **fetal alcohol syndrome (FAS),** marked by a small, misproportioned head and lifelong brain abnormalities. FAS is now the leading cause of mental retardation (Niccols, 1994; Streissguth & others, 1991). More children suffer from it where maternal drinking has been commonplace (Dorozyaski, 1993; Dorris, 1989). Children of alcoholic mothers are especially at risk. About 4 in 10 alcoholic mothers who drink during pregnancy have babies with FAS.

"You shall conceive and bear a son. So then drink no wine or strong drink."

Judges 13:7

In many parts of the world, people believe that a woman's psychological state during pregnancy affects her fetus. Exploring this possibility in experiments that stressed pregnant rodents and nonhuman primates, researchers have found that stress does lead to offspring with delayed motor development, increased emotionality, learning deficits, and alterations in neurotransmitter systems associated with human psychological disorders, such as depression (DiPietro, 2004; Huizink & others, 2004). It remains for future studies to determine whether prenatal maternal stress similarly influences human development and, if so, at what level of stress.

The Competent Newborn

OBJECTIVE 8-4 | Describe some abilities of the newborn, and explain how researchers use habituation to assess infant sensory and cognitive abilities.

Having survived prenatal hazards, we as newborns came equipped with reflexes ideally suited for our survival. We withdrew our limbs to escape pain. If a cloth over our face interfered with our breathing, we turned our head from side to side and swiped at it.

New parents are often in awe of the coordinated sequence of reflexes by which their baby gets food. The **rooting reflex** illustrates this: When something touches their cheek, babies turn toward that touch, open their mouth, and vigorously "root" for a nipple. Finding one, they automatically close on it and begin sucking—which itself requires a coordinated sequence of tonguing, swallowing, and breathing. Failing to find satisfaction, the hungry baby may cry—a behavior parents are predisposed to find highly unpleasant and very rewarding to relieve.

■ **fetus** the developing human organism from 9 weeks after conception to birth.

■ **teratogens** agents, such as chemicals and viruses, that can reach the embryo or fetus during prenatal development and cause harm.

■ **fetal alcohol syndrome (FAS)** physical and cognitive abnormalities in children caused by a pregnant woman's heavy drinking. In severe cases, symptoms include noticeable facial misproportions.

■ **rooting reflex** a baby's tendency, when touched on the cheek, to turn toward the touch, open the mouth, and search for the nipple.

Prepared to feed and eat
Animals are predisposed to respond to their offsprings' cries for nourishment.

The pioneering American psychologist William James presumed that the newborn experiences a "blooming, buzzing confusion." Until the 1960s, few people disagreed. It was said that, apart from a blur of meaningless light and dark shades, newborns could not see. But these scientists themselves saw the light, thanks to new investigative techniques that enhance infant studies. They discovered that babies can tell you a lot—if you know how to ask. (See Close-Up: Research Strategies for Understanding Infants' Thinking on the next page.) To ask, you must capitalize on what the baby can do—gaze, suck, turn her head. So, equipped with eye-tracking machines and pacifiers wired to electronic gear, researchers set out to answer parents' age-old questions: What can my baby see, hear, smell, and think?

What they discovered was fascinating. We are born preferring sights and sounds that facilitate social responsiveness. As newborns, we turn our heads in the direction of human voices. We gaze longer at a drawing of a facelike image (**FIGURE 8.3**) than at a bull's-eye pattern; yet we gaze more at a bull's-eye pattern—which has contrasts much like those of the human eye—than at a solid disk (Fantz, 1961). We prefer to look at objects 8 to 12 inches away, which, wonder of wonders, just happens to be the approximate distance between a nursing infant's eyes and its mother's (Maurer & Maurer, 1988).

Our perceptual abilities develop continuously during the first months of life. Within days after birth, our brain's neural networks were stamped with the smell of our mother's body. Thus, a week-old nursing baby, placed between a gauze pad from its mother's bra and one from another nursing mother, will usually turn toward the smell of its own mother's pad (MacFarlane, 1978). At 3 weeks, if given a pacifier that sometimes turns on recordings of its mother's voice and sometimes that of a female stranger's, an infant will suck more vigorously when it hears its now-familiar mother's voice (Mills & Melhuish, 1974). So not only can we as young infants see what we need to see, and smell and hear well, but we are already using our sensory equipment to learn.

FIGURE 8.3
Newborns' preference for faces
When shown these two stimuli with the same elements, Italian newborns spent nearly twice as many seconds looking at the facelike image (Johnson & Morton, 1991). Canadian newborns—average age 53 minutes in one study—display the same apparently inborn preference to look toward faces (Mondloch & others, 1999).

CLOSE-UP:

RESEARCH STRATEGIES FOR UNDERSTANDING INFANTS' THINKING

Can a newborn see well enough to distinguish shapes? Can a 3-month-old recognize faces? Does a 5-month-old have a concept of number? If babies could talk, we would ask them. But they can't, so psychologists let behavior do the talking. Developmental researchers, for example, exploit a simple form of learning called **habituation**—a decrease in responding with repeated stimulation. A novel stimulus gets attention when first presented. But the more often the stimulus is presented, the weaker the response becomes. This seeming boredom with familiar stimuli gives us a way to ask infants what they see and remember.

Janine Spencer, Paul Quinn, and their colleagues (1997; Quinn, 2002) used a novelty preference procedure to ask 4-month-olds how they recognize cats and dogs. The researchers first showed the infants a series of images of

FIGURE 8.4
Quick—which is the cat?
Researchers used cat-dog hybrid images such as these to test how infants categorize animals.

Courtesy Paul Quinn, © John Wiley & Sons

cats or dogs. Which of the two animals in **FIGURE 8.4** do you think the infants would find more novel (measured in looking time) after seeing a series of cats? It was the hybrid animal with the dog's head (or with a cat's head, if they had previously viewed a series of dogs). This suggests that infants, like adults, focus first on the face, not the body.

Other researchers using the habituation phenomenon report that infants

can also discriminate colors, shapes, and sounds and can understand some basic concepts of numbers and physics (for example, that two solid objects cannot occupy the same space).

Why have such elegantly simple studies been done only recently? Researcher Alan Slater (1994) explains: To recognize a new stimulus as different, an infant must remember the initial stimulus. Until the early 1980s, researchers assumed a newborn's brain was too immature to enable such memory. Then, as their appreciation for a newborn's abilities grew, they devised new ways to test the scope of infant cognition.

■ **habituation** decreasing responsiveness with repeated stimulation. As infants gain familiarity with repeated exposure to a visual stimulus, their interest wanes and they look away sooner.

>> LEARNING OUTCOMES

Prenatal Development and the Newborn

OBJECTIVE 8-1 | State the three areas of change that developmental psychologists study, and identify the three major issues in developmental psychology.

Developmental psychologists study physical, mental, and social changes throughout the life span. The three major issues are the relative influence of nature (heredity) and nurture (experience); whether development is a continuous process or a series of discrete stages; and whether personality is stable or changes as we age.

OBJECTIVE 8-2 | Describe the union of sperm and egg at conception.

At conception, only one sperm can penetrate the egg's outer coating before all others are blocked out. Within about 12 hours, the nuclei of the sperm and egg fuse into a single cell.

OBJECTIVE 8-3 | Define *zygote, embryo,* and *fetus,* and explain how teratogens can affect development.

A *zygote* is a fertilized egg, which becomes increasingly diverse. After about 10 days, the outer part of the cell mass attaches to the mother's uterine wall and the inner cells soon become the *embryo,* beginning a stage of development when major organs form and begin to function. From 9 weeks after fertilization until birth, the organism, now known as a *fetus,* continues to develop and grow. *Teratogens* are potentially harmful agents that can pass through the placental screen and harm the developing embryo or fetus.

OBJECTIVE 8-4 | Describe some abilities of the newborn, and explain how researchers use habituation to assess infant sensory and cognitive abilities.

Infants are born with a number of automatic responses (*reflexes*) that aid survival, including the rooting reflex that helps them locate food. Newborns' rapidly developing senses of sight and hearing seem tuned to social events, such as a caretaker's face or voice. Researchers can discover some of what preverbal infants sense, think, and remember by observing how they react to novel stimuli (such as colors, shapes, and forms) and grow bored with (habituate to) familiar stimuli.

TERMS AND CONCEPTS TO REMEMBER

developmental psychology, p. P4-1

zygote, p. 8-1

embryo, p. 8-1

fetus, p. 8-2

teratogens, p. 8-2

fetal alcohol syndrome (FAS), p. 8-2

rooting reflex, p. 8-2

habituation, p. 8-4

TEST YOURSELF

1. Your friend—a heavy smoker—hopes to become pregnant soon and has stopped smoking. Why is this a good idea? What negative effect does smoking during pregnancy have on the fetus? (Answer in Appendix B.)

ASK YOURSELF

1. Are you surprised by the news of infants' competencies? Or did you "know it all along"?

MODULE

Infancy and Childhood

During infancy, a baby grows from newborn to toddler, and during childhood from toddler to teenager. We all traveled this path, developing physically, cognitively, and socially. From infancy on, brain and mind, neural hardware and cognitive software, develop together.

Physical Development

Infants' biological development underlies their psychological development. To understand the emergence of motor skills and memory, we must understand the developing brain.

Brain Development

OBJECTIVE 9-1 | Describe some developmental changes in a child's brain, and explain why maturation accounts for many of our similarities.

While you resided in your mother's womb, your body was forming nerve cells at the explosive rate of nearly one-quarter million per *minute*. The developing brain cortex actually overproduces neurons, with the number peaking at 28 weeks and then subsiding to a stable 23 billion or so at birth (Rabinowicz & others, 1996, 1999; de Courten-Myers, 2002). On the day you were born, you had most of the brain cells you would ever have. However, at birth your nervous system was immature: After birth, the neural networks that eventually enabled you to walk, talk, and remember had a wild growth spurt (**FIGURE 9.1**). From ages 3 to 6, the brain's neural network is sprouting most rapidly in the frontal lobes, which enable rational planning (and which continue developing into adolescence and beyond). The association areas of the cortex—those linked with thinking, memory, and language—are the last brain areas to develop. As they do, mental abilities surge ahead (Chugani & Phelps, 1986; Thatcher & others, 1987). Fiber pathways supporting language and agility proliferate into puberty, after which a pruning process shuts down excess connections, while strengthening others (Paus & others, 1999; Thompson & others, 2000).

A flower unfolds in accord with its genetic instructions. So do we, experiencing an orderly sequence of genetically designed biological growth processes called **maturation.** Maturation decrees many of our commonalities—from standing before walking, to using nouns before adjectives. Severe deprivation or abuse will retard development, and ample experiences with parents who talk and read to the child will help sculpt neural connections. Yet the genetic growth tendencies are inborn. Maturation sets the basic course of development; experience adjusts it.

Motor Development

OBJECTIVE 9-2 | Outline four events in the motor development sequence from birth to toddlerhood, and evaluate the effects of maturation and experience on that sequence.

The developing brain enables physical coordination. As an infant's muscles and nervous system mature, more complicated skills emerge. With minor exceptions, the sequence of physical (motor) development is universal. Babies roll over before they sit unsupported, and they usually creep on all fours

> " It is a rare privilege to watch the birth, growth, and first feeble struggles of a living human mind."
>
> Annie Sullivan, in Helen Keller's *The Story of My Life*, 1903

■ **maturation** biological growth processes that enable orderly changes in behavior, relatively uninfluenced by experience.

FIGURE 9.1
Drawings of human cerebral cortex sections
In humans, the brain is immature at birth. As the child matures, the neural networks grow increasingly more complex.

At birth   3 months   15 months

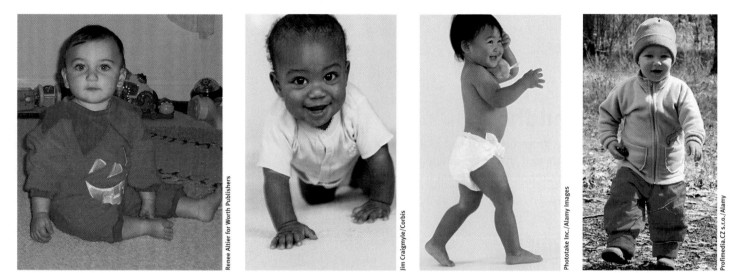

FIGURE 9.2
Triumphant toddlers
Sit, crawl, walk, run—the sequence of these motor development milestones is the same the world around, though babies reach them at varying ages.

"This is the path to adulthood. You're here."

Can you recall your first day of preschool (or your third birthday party)?

Still building a sense of self
What will Evan remember from his infant experience? Nothing *consciously*, but conscious memories are not everything. His neural networks are wildly expanding with the stimulating experiences his caregivers are providing, and he is busy learning all about his new world.

before they walk (**FIGURE 9.2**). These behaviors reflect not imitation but a maturing nervous system; blind children, too, crawl before they walk.

There are, however, individual differences in the timing of this sequence. In the United States, for example, 25 percent of all babies walk by age 11 months, 50 percent within a week after their first birthday, and 90 percent by age 15 months (Frankenburg & others, 1992). The recommended infant "back-to-sleep" position (putting babies to sleep on their backs to reduce the risk of a smothering crib death) has been associated with somewhat later crawling but not with later walking (Davis & others, 1998; Lipsitt, 2003).

Genes play a major role. Identical twins typically begin sitting up and walking on nearly the same day (Wilson, 1979). Biological maturation—including the rapid development of the cerebellum at the back of the brain—creates our readiness to learn walking at about age 1. Experience before that time has a limited effect. This is true for other physical skills, including bowel and bladder control. Before necessary muscular and neural maturation, no pleading, harassment, or punishment will produce successful toilet training.

Maturation and Infant Memory

OBJECTIVE 9-3 | Explain why we have few memories of experiences during our first three years of life.

Our earliest memories seldom predate our third birthdays. We see this "infantile amnesia" in the memories of some preschoolers who experienced an emergency fire evacuation caused by a burning popcorn maker. Seven years later they were able to recall the alarm and what caused it—*if* they were 4 to 5 years old at the time. Those who experienced the event as 3-year-olds could not remember the cause and usually misrecalled being already outside when the alarm sounded (Pillemer, 1995).

Other studies confirm that the average age of earliest conscious memory is 3.5 years (Bauer, 2002). By 4 to 5 years, childhood amnesia is giving way to remembered experiences (Bruce & others, 2000).

Memories of our preschool years are very few because we organize our memories differently after age 3 or 4. As the brain cortex matures, toddlers gain a sense of self and their long-term storage increases (Howe, 2003). Trying to access memories of those first 4 years is like trying to read a document formatted by an earlier version of a computer operating system (Hayne, 2004; Loftus & Kaufman, 1992). Infants' preverbal memories do not easily translate into their later language.

For parents, children's blank memory for infancy can be disconcerting. After all, we parents spend countless hours with our babies—frolicking on the rug, diapering, feeding, and rocking them to sleep. But what will they consciously remember of us if we die before they reach age 4? Virtually nothing!

Although we consciously recall little from before age 4, some memories exist during and beyond those early years. Given occasional reminders, 3-month-old infants who learn that moving their leg propels a mobile will remember the association for at least a month (**FIGURE 9.3**). Ten-year-olds shown photos of former classmates they had not seen since preschool recognize (amid other photos of preschoolers) only 1 in 5 of their onetime compatriots. Yet their physiological responses (measured as skin perspiration) are greater to their former classmates, whether or not they consciously recognize them (Newcombe & others, 2000). What the conscious mind does not know and cannot express in words, the nervous system somehow remembers.

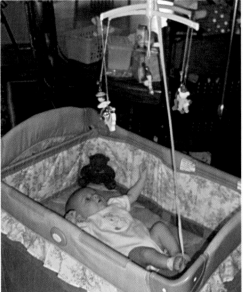

Courtesy of Carolyn Rovee-Collier

FIGURE 9.3
Infant at work
Babies only 3 months old can learn that kicking moves a mobile—and can retain that learning for a month. (From Rovee-Collier, 1989, 1997.)

Cognitive Development

OBJECTIVE 9-4 | State Piaget's understanding of how the mind develops, and discuss the importance of assimilation and accommodation in this process.

"Who knows the thoughts of a child?" wondered poet Nora Perry. As much as anyone of his generation, developmental psychologist Jean Piaget (pronounced Pee-ah-ZHAY) knew. His interest began in 1920, when he was working in Paris to develop questions for children's intelligence tests. While administering tests to find out at what age children could answer certain questions correctly, Piaget became intrigued by children's *wrong* answers. Where others saw childish mistakes, Piaget saw intelligence at work. The errors made by children of a given age, he noted, were often strikingly similar.

A half-century spent with children convinced Piaget that a child's mind is not a miniature model of an adult's. Piaget revolutionized our understanding of children's minds, much as Copernicus revolutionized our understanding of the solar system, suggests William Damon (1995). Until Piaget, most people—forgetting their own preschool days—assumed children "simply knew less, not *differently*, than adults" (p. 100). Thanks partly to his work, we now understand that "children reason in wildly illogical ways about problems whose solutions are self-evident to adults" (Brainerd, 1996).

Piaget further believed that a child's mind develops through a series of stages, in an upward march from the newborn's simple reflexes to the adult's abstract reasoning power. An 8-year-old child comprehends things a 3-year-old cannot. An 8-year-old might grasp the analogy "getting an idea is like having a light turn on in your head." Trying to teach the same analogy to a 3-year-old would be fruitless. An 8-year-old also understands what the 2-year-olds in **FIGURE 9.4** on the next page do not—that the miniature slide is too small for sliding, and the miniature car is much too small to get into. But our adult minds likewise engage in reasoning uncomprehended by 8-year-olds.

Piaget believed the driving force behind this intellectual progression is our unceasing struggle to make sense of our experiences. His core idea is that "children are active thinkers, constantly trying to construct more advanced understandings of the

"Childhood has its own way of seeing, thinking, and feeling, and there is nothing more foolish than the attempt to put ours in its place."

Philosopher Jean-Jacques Rousseau, 1798

FIGURE 9.4
Scale errors
Psychologists Judy DeLoache, David Uttal, and Karl Rosengren (2004) report that 18- to 30-month-old children may fail to take the size of an object into account when trying to perform impossible actions with it. At left, a 21-month-old attempts to slide down a miniature slide. At right, a 24-month-old opens the door to a miniature car and tries to step inside.

world" (Siegler & Ellis, 1996). To this end, the maturing brain builds concepts, which Piaget called **schemas.** Schemas (or schemes) are mental molds into which we pour our experiences. By adulthood we have built countless schemas, ranging from cats and dogs to our concept of love (**FIGURE 9.5**).

FIGURE 9.5
An impossible object
Look carefully at the "devil's tuning fork" at left. Now look away—no, better first study it some more—and then look away and draw it. . . . Not so easy, is it? Because this tuning fork is an impossible object, you have no schema for such an image.

To explain how we use and adjust our schemas, Piaget proposed two processes. First, we **assimilate** new experiences—we interpret them in terms of our current understandings (schemas). Having a simple schema for *dog*, for example, a toddler may call all four-legged animals *doggies*. But we also adjust, or **accommodate,** our schemas to fit the particulars of new experiences. The child soon learns that the original *doggie* schema is too broad and accommodates by refining the category (focusing especially on the head). As children interact with the world, they construct and modify their schemas (**FIGURE 9.6**).

Piaget's Theory and Current Thinking

OBJECTIVE 9-5 | Outline Piaget's four main stages of cognitive development, and comment on how children's thinking changes during these four stages.

Cognition refers to all the mental activities associated with thinking, knowing, remembering, and communicating. Piaget believed that children experience spurts of change followed by greater stability as they move from one cognitive developmental plateau to the next. These plateaus form four stages (**TABLE 9.1**), each with distinctive

FIGURE 9.6
Pouring experience into mental molds
We use our existing schemas to assimilate new experiences. But sometimes we need to accommodate (adjust) our schemas to include new experiences.

Two-year-old Gabriella has learned the schema for "cow" from her picture books.

Gabriella sees a moose and calls it a "cow." She is trying to assimilate this new animal into an existing schema. Her mother tells her, "No, it's a moose."

Gabriella accommodates her schema for large, shaggy animals and continues to modify that schema to include "mommy moose," "baby moose," and so forth.

TABLE **9.1**

PIAGET'S STAGES OF COGNITIVE DEVELOPMENT

Typical Age Range	Description of Stage	Developmental Phenomena
Birth to nearly 2 years	*Sensorimotor* Experiencing the world through senses and actions (looking, touching, mouthing, and grasping)	• Object permanence • Stranger anxiety
2 to about 6 or 7 years	*Preoperational* Representing things with words and images; use intuitive rather than logical reasoning	• Pretend play • Egocentrism • Language development
About 7 to 11 years	*Concrete operational* Thinking logically about concrete events; grasping concrete analogies and performing arithmetical operations	• Conservation • Mathematical transformations
About 12 through adulthood	*Formal operational* Abstract reasoning	• Abstract logic • Potential for mature moral reasoning

Milt and Patti Putnam/Corbis

characteristics that permit specific kinds of thinking. To appreciate how a child's mind grows, let's look at Piaget's stages in the light of our current thinking about cognitive development.

Sensorimotor Stage

During Piaget's **sensorimotor stage,** from birth to nearly age 2, babies take in the world through their sensory and motor interactions with objects—through looking, hearing, touching, mouthing, and grasping.

Very young babies seem to live in the present: What is out of sight is out of mind. In one of his tests, Piaget would show an infant an appealing toy and then flop his beret over it to see whether the infant searched for the toy. Before the age of 6 months, the infant did not. Young infants lack **object permanence**—the awareness that objects continue to exist when not perceived (**FIGURE 9.7** on the next page). By 8 months, infants begin exhibiting memory for things no longer seen. If you hide a toy, the infant will momentarily look for it. Within another month or two, the infant will look for it even after being restrained for several seconds.

But does object permanence in fact blossom at 8 months, much as tulips blossom in spring? Today's researchers see development as more continuous than Piaget did, and they now view object permanence as unfolding gradually. Even young infants will at least momentarily look for a toy where they saw it hidden a second before.

Researchers believe that Piaget and his followers underestimated young children's competence. Piaget assumed that before age 2, infants cannot think. They can recognize things, smile at them, crawl to them, manipulate them. But they have no abstract concepts or ideas. Theirs is a life lived, but not thought about.

Consider, however, some simple experiments that demonstrate baby logic:

• Like adults staring in disbelief at a magic trick (the "Whoa!" look), infants look longer at an unexpected scene of a car seeming to pass through a solid object, a ball stopping in midair, or an object violating object permanence by magically disappearing (Baillargeon, 1995, 1998, 2004; Wellman & Gelman, 1992). Babies seem to have a more intuitive grasp of simple laws of physics than Piaget realized.

Bill Anderson/Photo Researchers, Inc.

Jean Piaget
"If we examine the intellectual development of the individual or of the whole of humanity, we shall find that the human spirit goes through a certain number of stages, each different from the other" (1930).

■ **schema** a concept or framework that organizes and interprets information.

■ **assimilation** interpreting one's new experience in terms of one's existing schemas.

■ **accommodation** adapting one's current understandings (schemas) to incorporate new information.

■ **cognition** all the mental activities associated with thinking, knowing, remembering, and communicating.

■ **sensorimotor stage** in Piaget's theory, the stage (from birth to about 2 years of age) during which infants know the world mostly in terms of their sensory impressions and motor activities.

■ **object permanence** the awareness that things continue to exist even when not perceived.

Doug Goodman

FIGURE 9.7
Object permanence
Infants younger than 6 months seldom understand that things continue to exist when they are out of sight. But for this infant, out of sight is definitely not out of mind.

- Babies also have a head for numbers. Karen Wynn (1992, 2000) showed 5-month-olds one or two objects. Then she hid the objects behind a screen, and then visibly removed or added one (**FIGURE 9.8**). When she lifted the screen, the infants sometimes did a double take, staring longer when shown a wrong number of objects. But were they just responding to a greater or smaller mass of objects, rather than a change in number (Feigenson & others, 2002)? Later experiments showed that babies' number sense extends to larger numbers and such things as drumbeats and motions (Lipton & Spelke, 2003; McCrink & Wynn, 2004; Spelke, 2000; Wynn & others, 2002). If accustomed to a Daffy Duck puppet jumping three times on stage, they show surprise if it jumps only twice. Clearly, infants are smarter than Piaget appreciated. Even as babies, we had a lot on our minds.

FIGURE 9.8
Baby math
Shown a numerically impossible outcome, infants stare longer. (From Wynn, 1992.)

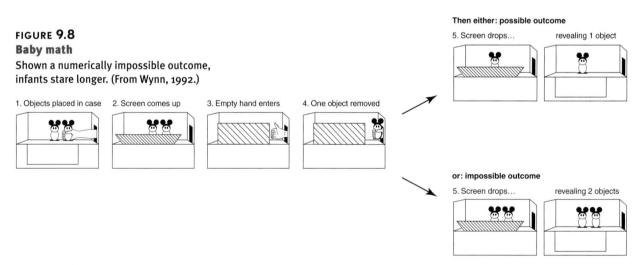

1. Objects placed in case   2. Screen comes up   3. Empty hand enters   4. One object removed

Then either: possible outcome
5. Screen drops…   revealing 1 object

or: impossible outcome
5. Screen drops…   revealing 2 objects

■ **preoperational stage** in Piaget's theory, the stage (from about 2 to 6 or 7 years of age) during which a child learns to use language but does not yet comprehend the mental operations of concrete logic.

■ **conservation** the principle (which Piaget believed to be a part of concrete operational reasoning) that properties such as mass, volume, and number remain the same despite changes in the forms of objects.

■ **egocentrism** in Piaget's theory, the preoperational child's difficulty taking another's point of view.

Preoperational Stage

Piaget believed that during the preschool period and up to about age 6 or 7, children are in a **preoperational stage**—too young to perform mental operations. For a 5-year-old, the milk that seems "too much" in a tall, narrow glass may become an acceptable amount if poured into a short, wide glass. Focusing only on the height dimension the child is incapable of performing the *operation* of mentally pouring the milk back. This preoperational child lacks the concept of **conservation**—the principle that quantity remains the same despite changes in shape (**FIGURE 9.9**). Closed beakers with identical volumes seem suddenly to hold different amounts after one is merely inverted.

FIGURE **9.9**
Piaget's test of conservation
This preoperational child does not yet understand the principle of conservation of substance. Closed beakers with identical volumes seem suddenly to hold different amounts after one is merely inverted.

Piaget did not view the stage transitions as abrupt. Even so, symbolic thinking appears at an earlier age than he supposed. Judy DeLoache (1987) discovered this when she showed children a model of a room and hid a model toy in it (a miniature stuffed dog behind a miniature couch). The 2½-year-olds easily remembered where to find the miniature toy, but they could not use the model to locate an actual stuffed dog behind a couch in a real room. Three-year-olds—only 6 months older—usually went right to the actual stuffed animal in the real room, showing that they *could* think of the model as a symbol for the room. Piaget probably would have been surprised.

Egocentrism Piaget contended that preschool children are **egocentric:** They have difficulty perceiving things from another's point of view. Asked to "show Mommy your picture," 2-year-old Gabriella holds the picture up facing her own eyes. Three-year-old Gray makes himself "invisible" by putting his hands over his eyes, assuming that if he can't see someone, they can't see him. Children's conversations also reveal their egocentrism, as one young boy demonstrated (Phillips, 1969, p. 61):

> *"Do you have a brother?"*
> *"Yes."*
> *"What's his name?"*
> *"Jim."*
> *"Does Jim have a brother?"*
> *"No."*

TV-watching preschoolers who block your view of the television assume that you see what they see. When relating to a young child, remember that such behaviors reflect a cognitive limitation: The egocentric preschoolers are not intentionally "selfish" or "inconsiderate." They simply have not developed the ability to take another's viewpoint. We never, however, fully outgrow our early childhood egocentrism. Even as adults, we often overestimate the extent to which others share our opinions and perspective, as when we assume that something will be clear to others if it is clear to us (Epley & others, 2004). Children, however, are even more susceptible to this "curse of knowledge" (Birch, 2005).

Parents who abuse their children generally have no understanding of children's greater egocentrism. They see their children as junior adults able to control their behavior (Larrance & Twentyman, 1983). Thus, they misperceive an egocentric child who stands in the way, spills food, disobeys negative instructions, or cries as willfully malicious.

Theory of Mind When Little Red Riding Hood realizes her "grandmother" is really a wolf, she swiftly revises her ideas about the creature's intentions and races away. Preschoolers, although still egocentric, develop this ability to infer others' mental

Question: If most 2½-year-olds do not understand how miniature dolls and toys can symbolize real objects, should anatomically correct dolls be used when questioning such children about alleged physical or sexual abuse? Judy DeLoache (1995) reports that "very young children do not find it natural or easy to use a doll as a representation of themselves."

FAMILY CIRCUS ® BIL KEANE

"Don't you remember, Grandma? You were in it with me."

■ **theory of mind** people's ideas about their own and others' mental states—about their feelings, perceptions, and thoughts and the behavior these might predict.

states when they begin forming a **theory of mind** (a term coined by psychologists David Premack and Guy Woodruff to describe chimpanzees' seeming ability to read intentions).

As their ability to infer others' mental states develops, children will seek to understand what made a playmate angry, when a sibling will share, and what might make a parent buy a toy. The preschooler's growing ability to tease, empathize, and persuade stems from this growing ability to take another's perspective. Between about 3½ and 4½, for example, children worldwide come to realize that others may hold false beliefs (Callaghan & others, 2005; Wellman & others, 2001; Zimmer, 2003). Jennifer Jenkins and Janet Astington (1996) showed Toronto children a Band Aids box and asked them what was inside. Expecting Band Aids, the children were surprised to discover that the box actually contained pencils. Asked what a child who had never seen the box would think was inside, 3-year-olds typically answered "pencils." By age 4 to 5, the children's "theory of mind" had leapt forward, and they delighted in anticipating their friends' false belief that the box would hold Band Aids.

Our theory of mind also enables us to infer others' feelings. Even young preschoolers understand that sad events cause sad feelings, report John Flavell and his Stanford colleagues (2001). Next, children come to understand that thoughts can cause feelings—for example, that reminders of an earlier sad event can trigger a sad feeling. Finally, between ages 5 and 8, children learn that spontaneous self-produced thoughts can also create feelings. If someone's mood suddenly changes for no apparent reason, an 8-year-old will assume the occurrence of a thought.

This is Sally.   This is Anne.

Sally puts her ball in the red cupboard.

Sally goes away.

Anne moves the ball to the blue cupboard.

Where will Sally look for her ball?

FIGURE 9.10
Testing children's theory of mind
This simple problem illustrates how researchers explore children's presumptions about others' mental states. (Inspired by Baron-Cohen & others, 1985.)

Researchers explore children's ability to take another person's perspective with seemingly simple experiments. In one experiment (**FIGURE 9.10**), children see a doll named Sally leaving her ball in a red cupboard. Another doll, Anne, then moves the ball to a blue cupboard. Researchers then pose a question: When Sally returns, where will she look for the ball? Children with *autism* (see Close-Up: Autism) have difficulty understanding that Sally's state of mind differs from their own—that Sally, not knowing the ball has been moved, will return to the red cupboard. They also have difficulty reflecting on their own mental states. They are, for example, less likely to use the personal pronouns *I* and *me*. Deaf children who have hearing parents and minimal opportunities for communication have similar difficulty inferring others' states of mind (Peterson & Siegal, 1999).

Our abilities to perform mental operations, to think symbolically, and to take another's perspective are not absent in the

CLOSE-UP

AUTISM

Autism, a disorder characterized by deficient communication and social interaction, is marked by an impaired theory of mind (Klein & Kihlstrom, 1998; Yirmiya & others, 1998). People with autism are said to be "mind blind." They have difficulty inferring others' thoughts and feelings. They do not appreciate that playmates and parents might view things differently. Mindreading that you do intuitively—is that face conveying a happy smile, a self-satisfied smirk, or a contemptuous sneer?—is difficult for those with autism. Most children learn that another child's pouting mouth signals sadness, and that twinkling eyes mean happiness or mischief. A child with autism (which is related to malfunctions of brain areas that enable attending to others) fails to understand these signals (Frith & Frith, 2001). *Asperger syndrome,* which is sometimes classified as a "high functioning" form of autism, is marked by normal intelligence, often accompanied by exceptional skill or talent in a specific area, but deficient social and communication skills (and thus an inability to form normal peer relationships).

Autism

Both of Bobbie Gallagher's children were diagnosed with autism, which is marked by deficient social communication and difficulty in grasping others' states of mind.

Symptoms of autism, which can also include speech difficulty and clumsiness, range from mild to severe, and for reasons still debated, diagnoses of autism have increased in recent years. The underlying cause—altered brain circuitry involving the fibers that connect distant neurons and enable communication among brain regions—appears to result from an unknown number of genes interacting with the environment (Blakeslee, 2005; Wickelgren, 2005).

In a provocative new theory, psychologist Simon Baron-Cohen (2004, 2005) proposes that autism represents an "extreme male brain." Girls are naturally predisposed to be "empathizers," he contends. They are better at reading facial expressions and gestures—a task that challenges those with autism. Although the sexes overlap, boys, he believes, tend to be "systemizers"—of understanding things according to rules or laws, as in mathematical and mechanical systems. "If two 'systemizers' have a child, this will increase the risk of the child having autism," he theorizes. And because of "assortative mating"—people's tendency to seek spouses who share their interests—two systemizers will indeed often mate, he notes. "I do not discount environmental factors; I'm just saying, don't forget about biology." Elizabeth Spelke (2005), however, is skeptical of the supposed inborn, male-systemizing tendency. From other research, she sees "no male advantage for perceiving objects or learning about mechanical systems. In most studies, male and female infants are found to discover the same things at the same times." So, is there any merit to the idea that children with autism (most of whom are male) have extreme male brains? Stay tuned for more research to come.

preoperational stage, and then miraculously present later. Rather, these abilities begin early and develop gradually (Wellman & others, 2001) (**FIGURE 9.11** on the next page).

By age 7, children become increasingly capable of thinking in words and of using words to work out solutions to problems. They do this, noted the Russian psychologist Lev Vygotsky (1896–1934), by no longer thinking aloud. Instead they internalize their culture's language and rely on inner speech. Parents who say "No" when pulling a child's hand away from a cake are giving the child a self-control tool. When later needing to resist temptation the child may likewise say "No." Second-graders who mutter to themselves while doing math problems grasp third-grade math better the following year (Berk, 1994). Whether out loud or inaudible, talking to themselves helps children control their behavior and emotions and master new skills. And when parents give children words, they provide, in Vygotsky's words, a *scaffold* upon which children can step to higher levels of thinking.

■ **autism** a disorder that appears in childhood and is marked by deficient communication, social interaction, and understanding of others' states of mind.

(a)

(b)

(c)

FIGURE **9.11**
Piaget's stages
(a) Sensorimotor stage
Infants try to get to know their dog by tasting and touching it.
(b) Preoperational stage
Preschoolers see the family pet as yet another playmate, existing purely for them to play with.
(c) Concrete and formal operational stages
Older children begin to understand the level of responsibility and work that is associated with keeping a pet.

Concrete Operational Stage

By the time children are about 6 or 7 years of age, said Piaget, they enter the **concrete operational stage.** Given concrete materials, they begin to grasp conservation—that change in shape does not mean change in quantity. They can mentally pour milk back and forth between glasses of different shapes. They also enjoy jokes that allow them to use their new understanding of conservation:

> Mr. Jones went into a restaurant and ordered a whole pizza for his dinner. When the waiter asked if he wanted it cut into 6 or 8 pieces, Mr. Jones said, "Oh, you'd better make it 6, I could never eat 8 pieces!" (McGhee, 1976)

During the concrete operational stage, said Piaget, children fully gain the mental ability to comprehend mathematical transformations and conservation. When my daughter Laura was 6, I was astonished at her inability to reverse arithmetic operations. Asked, "What is 8 plus 4?" she required 5 seconds to compute "12," and another 5 seconds to then compute 12 minus 4. By age 8, she could answer the second question instantly.

Formal Operational Stage

By age 12, our reasoning expands from the purely concrete (involving actual experience) to encompass abstract thinking (involving imagined realities and symbols). As children approach adolescence, said Piaget, many become capable of solving hypothetical propositions and deducing consequences: *If* this, *then* that. Systematic reasoning, what Piaget called **formal operational** thinking, is now within their grasp.

Although full-blown logic and reasoning await adolescence, the rudiments of formal operational thinking begin earlier than Piaget realized. Consider this simple problem:

> If John is in school, then Mary is in school. John is in school. What can you say about Mary?

Formal operational thinkers have no trouble answering correctly. But neither do most 7-year-olds (Suppes, 1982).

■ **concrete operational stage** in Piaget's theory, the stage of cognitive development (from about 6 or 7 to 11 years of age) during which children gain the mental operations that enable them to think logically about concrete events.

■ **formal operational stage** in Piaget's theory, the stage of cognitive development (normally beginning about age 12) during which people begin to think logically about abstract concepts.

■ **stranger anxiety** the fear of strangers that infants commonly display, beginning by about 8 months of age.

Reflecting on Piaget's Theory

OBJECTIVE 9-6 | Discuss psychologists' current views on Piaget's theory of cognitive development.

Piaget's stage theory has been influential. In some respects, it gets high marks. Studies around the globe, from aboriginal Australia to Algeria to North America, have supported his idea that human cognition unfolds basically in the sequence Piaget proposed (Segall & others, 1990). However, today's researchers see development as more continuous than did Piaget. By detecting the beginnings of each type of thinking at earlier ages, they have revealed conceptual abilities Piaget missed. Moreover, they see formal logic as a smaller part of cognition than he did.

What remains of Piaget's ideas about the child's mind? Plenty—enough to merit his being singled out in 1999 by *Time* magazine as one of the century's 20 most influential scientists and thinkers and rated in a survey of British psychologists as the greatest twentieth-century psychologist (*Psychologist*, 2003). Piaget identified significant cognitive milestones and stimulated worldwide interest in how the mind develops. His emphasis was less on the ages at which children typically reach specific milestones than on their sequence—a sequence that later research has shown is pretty much as he described (Lourenco & Machado, 1996). Piaget would not be surprised that today, as part of our own cognitive development, we are adapting his ideas to accommodate new findings.

What are the implications of all this for parents and teachers? Piaget contended that children construct their understandings from their *interactions* with the world. This implies that children are not passive receptacles waiting to be filled with a teacher's knowledge. Teachers would do better to build on what children already know, engaging them in concrete demonstrations and stimulating them to think for themselves. Future parents and teachers, remember: Young children are incapable of adult logic. Realize that what is simple and obvious to you—that getting off a teeter-totter will cause a friend on the other end to crash—may be incomprehensible to a 3-year-old. And accept children's cognitive immaturity as adaptive. It is nature's strategy for keeping children close to protective adults and providing time for learning and socialization (Bjorklund & Green, 1992).

> "Assessing the impact of Piaget on developmental psychology is like assessing the impact of Shakespeare in English literature."
>
> Developmental psychologist Harry Beilin (1992)

Social Development

OBJECTIVE 9-7 | Define *stranger anxiety.*

A human is, as Aristotle said, "a social animal," destined to live in close relationship with important others. How then do the bonds of attachment form? What happens when they form securely, or when they are missing or broken?

From birth, babies are social creatures. In all cultures, infants develop an intense bond with their caregivers. Beginning with a newborn's attraction to humans in general, infants soon come to prefer familiar faces and voices, then to coo and gurgle when given their mother's or father's attention. Soon after object permanence emerges and children become mobile, a curious thing happens: In most cultures, they develop a fear of strangers, called **stranger anxiety.** Beginning at about 8 months, they may greet strangers by crying and reaching for their familiar caregivers. "No! Don't leave me!" their distress seems to say. At about this age, children have schemas for familiar faces; when they cannot assimilate the new face into these remembered schemas, they become distressed (Kagan, 1984). This illustrates an important principle: The brain, mind, and social-emotional behavior develop together.

Stranger anxiety
A newly emerging ability to evaluate people as unfamiliar and possibly threatening helps protect babies 8 months and older.

© Christina Kennedy/PhotoEdit

FIGURE 9.12
The Harlows' mothers
Psychologists Harry Harlow and Margaret Harlow reared monkeys with two artificial mothers—one a bare wire cylinder with a wooden head and an attached feeding bottle, the other a cylinder with no bottle but covered with foam rubber and wrapped with terry cloth. The Harlows' discovery surprised many psychologists: The monkeys much preferred contact with the comfortable cloth mother, even while feeding from the nourishing mother.

Lee Kirkpatrick (1999) reports that for some people a perceived relationship with God functions as do other attachments—by providing a secure base for exploration and a safe haven when threatened.

At 12 months, many infants cling tightly to a parent when they are frightened or expect separation. Reunited after being separated, they shower the parent with smiles and hugs. No social behavior is more striking than this intense and mutual infant-parent bond.

Origins of Attachment

OBJECTIVE 9-8 | Discuss the effects of nourishment, body contact, and familiarity on infant social attachment.

The **attachment** bond is a powerful survival impulse that keeps infants close to their caregivers. Infants become attached to those—typically their parents—who are comfortable and familiar. For many years, developmental psychologists had reasoned that infants became attached to those who satisfied their need for nourishment. It made sense. But an accidental finding overturned this explanation.

Body Contact

During the 1950s, University of Wisconsin psychologists Harry Harlow and Margaret Harlow bred monkeys for their learning studies. To equalize the infant monkeys' experiences and to isolate any disease, they separated them from their mothers shortly after birth and raised them in sanitary individual cages, which included a cheesecloth baby blanket (Harlow & others, 1971). Surprisingly, the infants became intensely attached to their blankets: When the blankets were taken to be laundered, the monkeys became distressed.

The Harlows recognized that this attachment to the blanket contradicted the idea that attachment derives from an association with nourishment. But how could they show this more convincingly? To pit the drawing power of a food source against the contact comfort of the blanket, they created two artificial mothers. One was a bare wire cylinder with a wooden head, the other a cylinder wrapped with terry cloth. By attaching a bottle they could associate either with nourishment.

When reared with both a nourishing wire mother and a non-nourishing cloth mother, the monkeys overwhelmingly preferred the comfy cloth mother (**FIGURE 9.12**). Like human infants clinging to their mothers, the monkeys would cling to their cloth mothers when anxious. They also used her as a secure base from which to venture into the environment, as if attached to the mother by an invisible elastic band that stretched so far and then pulled the infant back. Further studies revealed other qualities—rocking, warmth, and feeding—that made the cloth mother even more appealing.

Human infants, too, become attached to parents who are soft and warm and who rock, feed, and pat. Much of the parent-infant emotional communication occurs via touch (Hertenstein, 2002), which can be either soothing (snuggles) or arousing (tickles). Human attachment also consists of one person providing another with a *safe haven* when distressed and a *secure base* from which to explore. As we mature, our secure base and safe haven shift—from parents to peers and partners (Cassidy & Shaver, 1999). But at all ages we are social creatures. We gain strength when someone offers, by words and actions, a safe haven: "I will be here. I am interested in you. Come what may, I will actively support you" (Crowell & Waters, 1994).

Familiarity

Contact is one key to attachment. Another is familiarity. In many animals, attachments based on familiarity likewise form during a **critical period**—an optimal period shortly after birth when certain events must take place to facilitate proper development (Bornstein, 1989). The first moving object a gosling, duckling, or chick sees during the hours shortly after hatching is normally its mother. From then on, the young fowl follows her, and her alone.

This rigid attachment process, called **imprinting,** was explored by Konrad Lorenz (1937). He wondered: What would ducklings do if *he* was the first moving creature they observed? What they did was follow him around: Everywhere that Konrad went, the ducks were sure to go. Further tests revealed that although baby birds imprint best to their own species, they also will imprint to a variety of moving objects—an animal of another species, a box on wheels, a bouncing ball (Colombo, 1982; Johnson, 1992). And, once formed, this attachment is difficult to reverse.

Children—unlike ducklings—do not imprint. However, they do become attached to what they've known. "Mere exposure" to people and things fosters fondness—children like to reread the same books, rewatch the same movies, reenact family traditions. They prefer to eat familiar foods, live in the same familiar neighborhood, attend school with the same old friends. Familiarity is a safety signal. Familiarity breeds content.

Attachment
When French pilot Christian Moullec takes off in his microlight plane, his imprinted geese, which he reared since their hatching, follow closely.

Attachment Differences

OBJECTIVE 9-9 | Contrast secure and insecure attachment, and discuss the roles of parents and infants in the development of attachment and an infant's feelings of basic trust.

What accounts for attachment differences? Placed in a *strange situation* (usually a laboratory playroom), about 60 percent of infants display *secure attachment*. In their mother's presence they play comfortably, happily exploring their new environment. When she leaves, they are distressed; when she returns, they seek contact with her. Other infants show *insecure attachment*. They are less likely to explore their surroundings; they may even cling to their mother. When she leaves, they either cry loudly and remain upset or seem indifferent to their mother's going and returning (Ainsworth, 1973, 1989; Kagan, 1995; van IJzendoorn & Kroonenberg, 1988).

One possible source of these differences is the mother's behavior. Female rats reared by relaxed, attentive adoptive mothers become more relaxed and attentive to their offspring than do those reared by stress-prone, inattentive adoptive mothers (Francis & others, 1999). Do human infants likewise pick up their mothers' tendencies?

Mary Ainsworth (1979) studied attachment differences by observing mother-infant pairs at home during their first six months. Later she observed the 1-year-old infants in a strange situation without their mothers. Sensitive, responsive mothers—those who noticed what their babies were doing and responded appropriately—had infants who exhibited secure attachment. Insensitive, unresponsive mothers—mothers who attended to their babies when they felt like doing so but ignored them at other times—had infants who often became insecurely attached. The Harlows' monkey studies, in which the artificial structures were certainly the ultimate unresponsive mothers, produced even more striking effects. When put in strange situations without their artificial mothers, the deprived infants were terrified (**FIGURE 9.13**).

Follow-up studies have confirmed that sensitive mothers—and fathers—tend to have securely attached infants (De Wolff & van IJzendoorn, 1997; van IJzendoorn, 1997). But is attachment style the result of parenting, as children's early experiences form their thinking about relationships? Or is attachment style the result of genetically influenced *temperament*—one's characteristic emotional reactivity and intensity? Shortly after birth, some babies are noticeably "difficult"—irritable, intense, and unpredictable. Others are "easy"—cheerful, relaxed, and feeding and sleeping on predictable schedules (Chess & Thomas, 1987). By neglecting such inborn differences, chides Judith Harris (1998), the parenting studies are like "comparing foxhounds reared in kennels with poodles reared in apartments." So, to separate nature and nurture, Dutch researcher Dymphna van den Boom (1990) varied parenting while controlling temperament. (Pause and think: If you were the researcher, how might you have done this?)

■ **attachment** an emotional tie with another person; shown in young children by their seeking closeness to the caregiver and showing distress on separation.

■ **critical period** an optimal period shortly after birth when an organism's exposure to certain stimuli or experiences produces proper development.

■ **imprinting** the process by which certain animals form attachments during a critical period very early in life.

FIGURE 9.13
Social deprivation and fear
Monkeys raised by artificial mothers were terror-stricken when placed in strange situations without their surrogate mothers. (Today's climate of greater respect for animal welfare prevents such primate studies.)

■ **basic trust** according to Erik Erikson, a sense that the world is predictable and trustworthy; said to be formed during infancy by appropriate experiences with responsive caregivers.

Further discussions of Father Care and Children and Divorce can be found at the Web site accompanying this text (www.worthpublishers.com/myers).

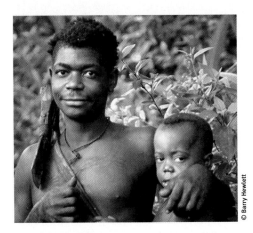

Fantastic father
Among the Aka people of Central Africa, fathers form an especially close bond with their infants, even suckling the babies with their own nipples when hunger makes the child impatient for Mother's return. According to anthropologist Barry Hewlett (1991), fathers in this culture are holding or within reach of their babies 47 percent of the time.

"Out of the conflict between trust and mistrust, the infant develops hope, which is the earliest form of what gradually becomes faith in adults."

Erik Erikson, 1983

Van den Boom's solution was to randomly assign one hundred 6- to 9-month-old temperamentally difficult infants to either an experimental condition, in which mothers received personal training in sensitive responding, or to an untreated control condition in which they did not. At 12 months of age, 68 percent of the experimental-condition infants were rated securely attached; only 28 percent of the control-condition infants received this rating. Other studies have also found that intervention programs can increase parental sensitivity and, to a lesser extent, infant attachment security (Bakermans-Kranenburg & others, 2003).

As these examples indicate, researchers have more often studied mother care than father care. Infants who lack a caring mother are said to suffer "maternal deprivation"; those lacking the care of a father are said merely to experience "father absence."

"Fathering a child" has meant impregnating; "mothering" has meant nurturing. But evidence increasingly indicates that fathers are more than just mobile sperm banks. Across nearly 100 studies worldwide, a father's love and acceptance have been comparable to a mother's love in predicting offsprings' health and well-being (Rohner & Veneziano, 2001). In one mammoth British study following 7259 children from birth to adulthood, those whose fathers were most involved in parenting (including outings, reading to them, and taking an interest in their education) tended to achieve more in school, even after controlling for many other factors such as parental education and family wealth (Flouri & Buchanan, 2004).

Whether children stay home or attend a day-care center, whether they live in North America, Guatemala, or the Kalahari Desert, anxiety over separation from parents peaks at around 13 months, then gradually declines (FIGURE 9.14). Does this mean our need for and love of others also fades away? Hardly. Our capacity for love grows, and our pleasure in touching and holding those we love never ceases. The power of early attachment does nonetheless gradually relax, allowing us to move out into a wider range of situations, communicate with strangers more freely, and stay attached emotionally to loved ones despite distance.

Developmental theorist Erik Erikson (1902–1994) would not have been surprised. Erikson, in collaboration with his wife, Joan Erikson, said that securely attached children approach life with a sense of **basic trust**—a sense that the world is predictable and reliable. He attributed basic trust not to one's continuing positive environment or inborn temperament, but to early parenting. He theorized that infants blessed with sensitive, loving caregivers form a lifelong attitude of trust rather than fear. Nor would Erikson have been surprised that our adult styles of romantic love exhibit either secure, trusting attachment; insecure, anxious attachment; or the avoidance of attachment (Feeney & Noller, 1990; Mikulincer & Shaver, 2005; Rholes & Simpson, 2004). Although debate continues, many researchers now believe that our early attachments form the foundation for our adult relationships (Fraley, 2002).

FIGURE 9.14
Infants' distress over separation from parents
In an experiment, groups of infants were left by their mothers in an unfamiliar room. In both groups, the percentage who cried when the mother left peaked at about 13 months. (From Kagan, 1976.) Whether the infant had experienced day care made little difference.

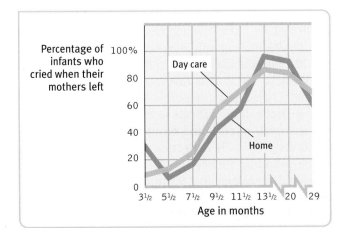

Deprivation of Attachment

OBJECTIVE 9-10 | Assess the impact of parental neglect, family disruption, and day care on attachment patterns and development.

If secure attachment nurtures social competence, what happens when circumstances prevent a child from forming attachments? In all of psychology, there is no sadder research literature. Babies reared in institutions without the stimulation and attention of a regular caregiver, or locked away at home under conditions of abuse or extreme neglect, are often withdrawn, frightened, even speechless. Those abandoned in Romanian orphanages during the 1980s looked "frighteningly like Harlow's monkeys" (Carlson, 1995). If institutionalized more than 8 months, they often bore lasting emotional scars (Chisholm, 1998; Malinosky-Rummell & Hansen, 1993; Rutter & others, 1998).

Harlow's monkeys similarly bore scars if reared in total isolation, without even an artificial mother. As adults, when placed with other monkeys their age, they either cowered in fright or lashed out in aggression. When they reached sexual maturity, most were incapable of mating. If artificially impregnated, females often were neglectful, abusive, even murderous toward their first-born.

In humans, too, the unloved sometimes become the unloving. Most abusive parents report having been neglected or battered as children (Kempe & Kempe, 1978). Many condemned murderers report the same. One study of 14 young men awaiting execution for juvenile crimes found that all but two had histories of brutal physical abuse (Lewis & others, 1988).

But does this mean that today's victim is predictably tomorrow's victimizer? The answer is no. Though most abusers were indeed abused, most abused children do *not* later become violent criminals or abusive parents. Most children growing up under adversity, as did the surviving children of the Holocaust, are resilient; they become normal adults (Helmreich, 1992; Masten, 2001). One study followed 1000 youths who had been maltreated. If the abuse had been restricted to early childhood, its manifestation as delinquency waned by late adolescence (Ireland & others, 2002).

But other children, especially those who experience no sharp break from their abusive past, are not so dramatically resilient. Some 30 percent of those abused do abuse their children—a rate four times higher than the national rate of child abuse (Kaufman & Zigler, 1987; Widom, 1989a, b). Moreover, young children terrorized through physical abuse or wartime atrocities (being beaten, witnessing torture, and living in constant fear) may suffer other lasting wounds—often nightmares, depression, and an adolescence troubled by substance abuse, binge eating, or aggression (Kendall-Tackett & others, 1993; Polusny & Follette, 1995; Trickett & McBride-Chang, 1995). Child sexual abuse, especially if severe and prolonged, places children at increased risk for health problems, psychological disorders, substance abuse, and criminality (Freyd & others, 2005; Tyler, 2002).

Although children are resilient, extreme childhood trauma can leave footprints on the brain. Baby rats deprived of their care-giving adult for several hours a day form fewer new brain neurons later in life (Mirescu & others, 2004). Normally placid golden hamsters that are repeatedly threatened and attacked while young grow up to be cowards when caged with same-sized hamsters, or bullies when caged with weaker ones (Ferris, 1996). Such animals show changes in the brain chemical serotonin, which calms aggressive impulses. A similarly sluggish serotonin response has been found in abused children who become aggressive teens and adults. "Stress can set off a ripple of hormonal changes that permanently wire a child's brain to cope with a malevolent world," concludes abuse researcher Martin Teicher (2002).

Might abuse victims' problems result from something else—perhaps other family troubles, a dysfunctional neighborhood, or a vulnerable temperament? Studies of

"What is learned in the cradle, lasts to the grave."

French proverb

American and Australian twins reveal that women who suffered child sexual abuse that included intercourse have greater risk of depression, anxiety, and alcohol abuse than do their nonabused identical twins (Kendler & others, 2000; Nelson & others, 2002). Given the same genes, same parents, and same neighborhood, the badly abused twin lives with the aftereffects. Nevertheless, researchers caution against inferring past sexual abuse from current symptoms (Sbraga & O'Donohue, 2003). Although child sex abuse increases the risk of depression, for example, many abused people do not suffer depression and most depressed people have not been sexually abused.

Disruption of Attachment

What happens to an infant when attachment is disrupted? Separated from their families, both monkey and human infants become upset and, before long, withdrawn and even despairing (Bowlby, 1973; Mineka & Suomi, 1978). Fearing that the stress of separation might cause lasting damage (and when in doubt, acting to protect parents' rights), courts are usually reluctant to remove children from their homes.

If placed in a more positive and stable environment, most infants recover from the separation distress. In studies of adopted children, Leon Yarrow and his co-workers (1973) found that when children between 6 and 16 months of age were removed from their foster mothers, they initially had difficulties eating, sleeping, and relating to their new mothers. But when these children were studied at age 10, little visible effect remained. Thus, they fared no worse than children placed before the age of 6 months (with little accompanying distress). Likewise, socially deprived but adequately nourished Romanian orphans who were adopted into a loving home during infancy or early childhood usually progressed rapidly, especially in their cognitive development. If removed and adopted after age 2, however, they were at risk for attachment problems. Foster care that prevents attachment by moving a child through a series of foster families can be very disruptive. So can repeated and prolonged removals from a mother.

Adults also suffer when attachment bonds are severed. Whether it occurs through death or separation, the break produces a predictable sequence of agitated preoccupation with the lost partner, followed by deep sadness and, eventually, the beginnings of emotional detachment and a return to normal living (Hazan & Shaver, 1994). Newly separated couples who have long ago ceased feeling affection are sometimes surprised at their desire to be near the former partner. Deep and longstanding attachments seldom break quickly. Detaching is a process, not an event.

Does Day Care Affect Attachment?

In the mid-twentieth century, when Mom-at-home was the social norm, researchers asked, "Is day-care bad for children? Does it disrupt children's attachments to their parents?" For the high-quality day-care programs usually studied, the answer was no (Belsky, 1990). In *Mother Care/Other Care,* developmental psychologist Sandra Scarr (1986) explained that children are "biologically sturdy individuals . . . who can thrive in a wide variety of life situations." Scarr spoke for many developmental psychologists, whose research has uncovered no major impact of maternal employment on children's development (Erel & others, 2000).

Research then shifted to the effects of differing quality of day care on different types and ages of children. Scarr (1997) explained: Around the world, "high-quality child care consists of warm, supportive interactions with adults in a safe, healthy, and stimulating environment. . . . Poor care is boring and unresponsive to children's needs." Newer research not only confirms that day-care quality matters, but also finds that family poverty often consigns children to lower-quality day care, as well as more family instability and turmoil, more authoritarian parenting, more time in front of the television, and less access to books (Love & others, 2003; Evans, 2004).

One ongoing study in 10 American cities has followed 1100 children since the age of 1 month. The researchers found that at ages 4½ to 6, those children who had spent the most time in day care had slightly advanced thinking and language skills. They also had an increased rate of aggressiveness and defiance (NICHHD, 2002; NICHHD, 2003). To developmental psychologist Eleanor Maccoby (2003), the positive correlation between increased rate of problem behaviors and time spent in child care suggests "some risk for some children spending extended time in some day-care settings as they're now organized." But the child's temperament, the mother's sensitivity, and the family's economic and educational level mattered more than time spent in day care. Other recent research offers a mixed bag of findings:

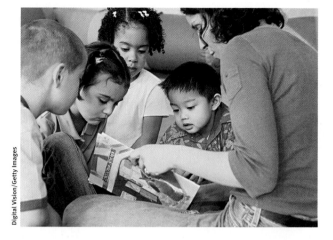

An example of high-quality day care
Research has shown that young children thrive socially and intellectually in safe, stimulating environments with a ratio of one caregiver for every three or four children.

- Toddler's stress hormone levels tend to rise during days spent in day care and to diminish during days spent at home (Watamura & others, 2003).
- When mothers transition from welfare to work, their preschool children do not suffer negative outcomes (Chase-Lansdale & others, 2003).
- Although working mothers spend less total time with their infants, they tend to partially compensate by sacrificing other activities (such as socializing) during their off hours, including weekends. As a result, they spend more time during those hours playing with, talking to, and holding their infants than do their nonworking counterparts (Huston & Aronson, 2005).

To be a day-care researcher and "to follow the data" can be controversial, notes researcher Jay Belsky (2003). Both opponents and advocates of day care have strong feelings. "As a result," says Belsky, "the scientist who is willing to report unpopular results is all too frequently blamed for generating them." Just as weather forecasters can report rain but love sunshine, so scientists aim to reveal and report the way things are, even when they wish it were otherwise.

Children's ability to thrive under varied types of responsive caregiving should not surprise us, given cultural variations in attachment patterns. Westernized attachment features one or two caregivers and their offspring. In other cultures, such as the Efe of Zaire, multiple caregivers are the norm (Field, 1996; Whaley & others, 2002). Even before the mother holds her newborn, the baby is passed among several women. In the weeks to come, the infant will be constantly held (and fed), by other women. The result is strong multiple attachments. As the now-famous African proverb says, "It takes a village to raise a child."

There is little disagreement that the many preschool children left *alone* for part of their parents' working hours deserve better. So do the children who merely exist for 9 hours a day in minimally equipped, understaffed centers. What all children need is a consistent, warm relationship with people whom they can learn to trust.

Self-Concept

OBJECTIVE **9-11** | Trace the onset and development of children's self-concept.

Infancy's major social achievement is attachment. *Childhood's* major social achievement is a positive sense of self. By the end of childhood, at about age 12, most children have developed a **self-concept**—a sense of their own identity and personal worth. Parents often wonder when and how this sense of self develops. "Is my baby girl aware of herself—does she know she is a person distinct from everyone else?"

Of course we cannot ask the baby directly, but we can again capitalize on what she can do—letting her *behavior* provide clues to the beginnings of her self-awareness. In 1877, biologist Charles Darwin offered one idea: Self-awareness begins when we recognize ourselves in a mirror. By this indicator, self-recognition emerges gradually over

■ **self-concept** a sense of one's identity and personal worth.

Self-awareness
Mirror images fascinate infants from the age of about 6 months. Only at about 18 months, however, does the child recognize that the image in the mirror is "me."

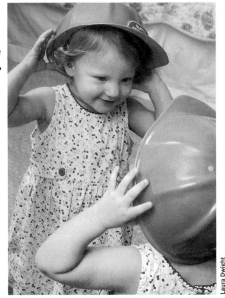

Laura Dwight

After prolonged exposure to mirrors, four other species—chimpanzees, orangutans, gorillas, and dolphins—have similarly demonstrated self-recognition of their mirror image (Marino & others, 1994; Wright, 1996). Capuchin monkeys display partial self-recognition (de Waal & others, 2005).

about a year, starting in roughly the sixth month as the child reaches toward the mirror to touch her image as if it were another child (Courage & Howe, 2002; Damon & Hart, 1982, 1988).

But how can we know when the child recognizes that the girl in the mirror is indeed herself, not just an agreeable playmate? In a simple variation of the mirror procedure, researchers sneakily dabbed rouge on children's noses before placing them in front of the mirror. At about 15 to 18 months, children will begin to touch their own noses when they see the red spot in the mirror (Butterworth, 1992; Gallup & Suarez, 1986). Apparently, 18-month-olds have a schema of how their faces should look, and they wonder, "What is that spot doing on *my* face?"

Beginning with this simple self-recognition, the child's self-concept gradually strengthens. By school age, children start to describe themselves in terms of their gender, group memberships, and psychological traits, and they compare themselves with other children (Newman & Ruble, 1988; Stipek, 1992). They come to see themselves as good and skillful in some ways but not others. They form a concept of which traits, ideally, they would like to have. By age 8 or 10, their self-images are quite stable.

Children's views of themselves affect their actions. Children who form a positive self-concept are more confident, independent, optimistic, assertive, and sociable (Maccoby, 1980). This then raises important questions: Can parents encourage a positive yet realistic self-concept? Does parenting style affect children?

Child-Rearing Practices

OBJECTIVE 9-12 | Describe three parenting styles, and offer three potential explanations for the link beween authoritative parenting and social competence.

Parenting styles vary. Some parents spank, some reason. Some are strict, some are lax. Some show little affection, some liberally hug and kiss. Do such differences affect children?

The most heavily researched aspect of parenting has been how, and to what extent, parents seek to control their children. Investigators have identified three parenting styles:

1. *Authoritarian* parents impose rules and expect obedience: "Don't interrupt." "Do keep your room clean." "Don't stay out late or you'll be grounded." "Why? Because I said so."

2. *Permissive* parents submit to their children's desires, make few demands, and use little punishment.

3. *Authoritative* parents are both demanding and responsive. They exert control not only by setting rules and enforcing them but also by explaining the reasons and, especially with older children, encouraging open discussion and allowing exceptions when making the rules.

Too hard, too soft, and just right, these styles have been called. Studies by Stanley Coopersmith (1967), Diana Baumrind (1996), and John Buri and others (1988) reveal that children with the highest self-esteem, self-reliance, and social competence usually have warm, concerned, *authoritative* parents. (Those with authoritarian parents tend to have less social skill and self-esteem, and those with permissive parents tend to be more aggressive and immature.) Although the participants in most studies have been middle-class white families, studies with families of other races and in more than 200 cultures worldwide confirm the social and academic correlates of loving and authoritative parenting (Rohner & Veneziano, 2001; Steinberg & Morris, 2001).

But wait. Before jumping to conclusions about the results of different parenting styles, heed this caution: *Correlation is not causation.* The association between certain parenting styles (being firm but open) and certain childhood outcomes (social competence) is correlational. There are other possible explanations for this parenting-competence link (**FIGURE 9.15**).

- Perhaps children's traits influence parenting more than vice versa. Parental warmth and control vary somewhat from child to child even in the same family (Holden & Miller, 1999). So perhaps socially mature, agreeable, easygoing children *evoke* greater trust and warmth from their parents, and less competent and less cooperative children elicit less. Twin studies support this possibility (Kendler, 1996).

- Perhaps there may be some underlying third factor. Maybe, for example, competent parents and their competent children share genes that predispose social competence.

Parents struggling with conflicting advice and with the stresses of child-rearing should remember that *all advice reflects the advice-giver's values.* For those who prize unquestioning obedience from a child, an authoritarian style may have the desired effect. For those who value children's sociability and self-reliance, authoritative firm-but-open parenting is advisable.

The investment in raising a child buys many years not only of joy and love but of worry and irritation. Yet for most parents, a child is one's biological and social legacy—one's personal investment in the human future. Remind young adults of their mortality and they will express increased desire for children (Wisman & Goldenberg, 2005). To paraphrase psychiatrist Carl Jung, we reach backward into our parents and forward into our children, and through their children into a future we will never see, but about which we must therefore care.

"You are the bows from which your children as living arrows are sent forth."

Kahlil Gibran, *The Prophet*, 1923

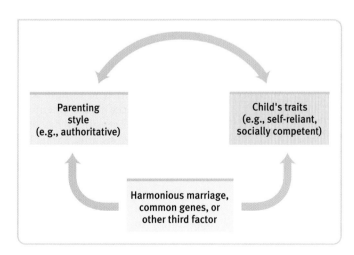

FIGURE 9.15

The correlation between authoritative parenting and social competence in children

Three possible explanations are: (1) parenting may influence children's competence; (2) children's social competence may influence parenting; or (3) both may be influenced by an underlying third factor.

>> Learning Outcomes

Infancy and Childhood

OBJECTIVE 9-1 | **Describe some developmental changes in a child's brain, and explain why maturation accounts for many of our similarities.**

In a rapid growth spurt, neural networks proliferate in the newborn's brain. Between ages 3 and 6, growth is most pronounced in the frontal lobes. Development in the association areas of the cortex enables thinking, memory, and language. Brain pathways develop and strengthen with use until puberty, when pruning eliminates excess connections. In the absence of severe abuse or neglect, *maturation*—the orderly sequence of genetically determined biological processes—guides all infants along the same general course of development.

OBJECTIVE 9-2 | **Outline four events in the motor development sequence from birth to toddlerhood, and evaluate the effects of maturation and experience on that sequence.**

The timing may vary, but most babies follow the same sequence: rolling over, sitting unsupported, crawling, and then walking. Experience has little influence; maturation, including that of the cerebellum, enables these events.

OBJECTIVE 9-3 | **Explain why we have few memories of experiences during our first three years of life.**

"Infantile amnesia"—an inability to consciously recall events that happened before age 3—results from a change in the way the brain organizes memories at about that age. As the cortex matures, long-term storage increases; also, children's preverbal memories are not easily transformed into language.

OBJECTIVE 9-4 | **State Piaget's understanding of how the mind develops, and discuss the importance of assimilation and accommodation in this process.**

Piaget proposed that children's reasoning develops in stages, and that children actively construct and modify their understanding of the world as they interact with it. They form *schemas* (concepts or frameworks for organizing experience), which they use to *assimilate* (interpret) information. If new information does not conform to the schema, they *accommodate* (adjust) the schema.

OBJECTIVE 9-5 | **Outline Piaget's four main stages of cognitive development, and comment on how children's thinking changes during these four stages.**

In the *sensorimotor stage* (birth to age 2), children experience the world through their senses and actions. In the first six months, infants lack *object permanence*, or the awareness that things exist when out of sight. In the *preoperational stage* (age 2 to about 6 or 7), children learn to use language and can represent things with words and images, but they are unable to reason logically. They lack a *theory of mind*, are *egocentric*, and have no concept of *conservation* (the understanding that things can change form but retain their mass, volume, or number). In the *concrete operational stage* (about age 7 to 11), children can think logically about concrete events, grasp analogies, and perform arithmetical operations. In the *formal operational stage* (12 through adulthood), they gain the ability to reason abstractly. Piaget viewed the ages connected with these stages as approximate, but the sequence as universal.

OBJECTIVE 9-6 | **Discuss psychologists' current views on Piaget's theory of cognitive development.**

Formal logic plays a smaller part in cognitive development than Piaget believed, and the development of cognitive abilities is more continuous, with stages starting earlier. Nevertheless, Piaget's views about the *sequence* of development of children's cognitive abilities have been supported repeatedly.

OBJECTIVE 9-7 | **Define *stranger anxiety.***

Stranger anxiety is the fear of strangers that infants begin to display at about 8 months of age. Children of this age have formed schemas for familiar faces, and they become distressed when faces do not match their schemas.

OBJECTIVE 9-8 | **Discuss the effects of nourishment, body ontact, and familiarity on infant social attachment.**

Until the Harlows' research in the mid-1950s, many psychologists believed that, through a conditioning process, children become attached (form an emotional tie) to those who provide nourishment. The Harlows' experiments showed that infant monkeys would search out a non-nourishing "mother" that provided comfort in preference to one that provided nourishment without comfort. Ducks and other animals imprint, forming an attachment to a significant organism or object during a *critical period* (a time shortly after birth when proper development depends on exposure to certain stimuli or experiences). Humans do not imprint, but they do become attached to familiar people and things, which provide feelings of safety.

OBJECTIVE 9-9 | **Contrast secure and insecure attachment, and discuss the roles of parents and infants in the development of attachment and an infant's feelings of basic trust.**

Strange situation experiments monitor children's reactions as their mother leaves and returns. *Securely attached* children play and explore comfortably in the mother's presence, are distressed when she leaves, and seek contact when she returns. *Insecurely attached* children explore less in the mother's presence and may cling to her, cry loudly when she leaves, and remain upset or act indifferent when she returns. Other studies show that sensitive responsive parents tend to have securely attached children. Genetically influenced temperament may evoke responsive parenting, but parental sensitivity has been taught and does increase infant attachment security. Father love as well as mother love is a predictor of children's health and well-being.

OBJECTIVE 9-10 | **Assess the impact of parental neglect, family disruption, and day care on attachment patterns and development.**

When parental neglect or other trauma deprives children of the opportunity to form attachments, children become withdrawn and frightened and may not develop speech. Prolonged childhood abuse places children at risk for a variety of physical, psychological, and social problems and may alter the brain's production of serotonin. Disruption of attachment bonds, as happens when children are placed in foster care, appears to inflict minimal damage before 16 months of age, but children who do not form attachments by age 2 may be at risk for attachment problems. Quality day care, with responsive adults interacting with children in a safe and stimulating environment, does not appear to harm children's thinking and language skills, but extensive time in day care may increase aggressiveness and defiance.

OBJECTIVE 9-11 | Trace the onset and development of children's self-concept.

Self-concept, a sense of one's identity and personal worth, emerges gradually, beginning at about 6 months. At 15 to 18 months, children recognize themselves in a mirror. By school age, they can describe many of their own traits, and by age 8 to 10, their self-image is stable.

OBJECTIVE 9-12 | Describe three parenting styles, and offer three potential explanations for the link between authoritative parenting and social competence.

Authoritarian parents impose rules and expect obedience. *Permissive* parents submit to children's demands, ask little, and punish rarely. *Authoritative* parents are demanding but responsive to their children. Authoritative parenting correlates with social competence, but the cause-effect relationship is not clear. This style of parenting may produce socially competent children, or agreeable easygoing children may evoke authoritative parenting. Or a third factor, such as shared genes, may lead to a temperament that is comfortable with an authoritative parenting style and that manifests itself in agreeable easygoing social interactions.

TERMS AND CONCEPTS TO REMEMBER

maturation, p. 9-1
schema, p. 9-4
assimilation, p. 9-4
accommodation, p. 9-4
cognition, p. 9-4
sensorimotor stage, p. 9-5
object permanence, p. 9-5
preoperational stage, p. 9-6
conservation, p. 9-6
egocentrism, p. 9-7
theory of mind, p. 9-8
autism, p. 9-9
concrete operational stage, p. 9-10
formal operational stage, p. 9-10
stranger anxiety, p. 9-11
attachment, p. 9-12
critical period, p. 9-12
imprinting, p. 9-12
basic trust, p. 9-14
self-concept, p. 9-17

TEST YOURSELF

1. Use Piaget's first three stages of cognitive development to explain why young children are *not* just miniature adults in the way they think.

(Answer in Appendix B.)

ASK YOURSELF

1. Can you recall a time when you have misheard some song lyrics, by *assimilating* them into your own *schema?* (For hundreds of examples of such, visit www.kissthisguy.com.)

>WEB

Multiple-choice *self-tests* and more may be found at www.worthpublishers.com/myers.

10

Adolescence

OBJECTIVE 10-1 | Define *adolescence*.

Many psychologists once believed that childhood sets our traits. Today's developmental psychologists see development as lifelong. At a five-year high school reunion, former soul mates may be surprised at their divergence; a decade later, they may have trouble sustaining a conversation.

As this life-span perspective emerged, psychologists began to look at how maturation and experience shape us not only in infancy and childhood, but also in adolescence and beyond. **Adolescence** is life between childhood and adulthood. It starts with the physical beginnings of sexual maturity and ends with the social achievement of independent adult status.

What are the teen years like? In Leo Tolstoy's *Anna Karenina,* the teen years were "that blissful time when childhood is just coming to an end, and out of that vast circle, happy and gay, a path takes shape." But in her diary, written while hiding from the Nazis, teenager Anne Frank described tumultuous teen emotions:

> My treatment varies so much. One day Anne is so sensible and is allowed to know everything; and the next day I hear that Anne is just a silly little goat who doesn't know anything at all and imagines that she's learned a wonderful lot from books. . . . Oh, so many things bubble up inside me as I lie in bed, having to put up with people I'm fed up with, who always misinterpret my intentions.

To G. Stanley Hall (1904), one of the first psychologists to describe adolescence, the tension between biological maturity and social dependence created a period of "storm and stress." Indeed, after age 30, many who grow up in independence-fostering Western cultures look back on their teenage years as a time they would not want to relive, a time when their peers' social approval was imperative, their sense of direction in life was in flux, and their feeling of alienation from their parents was deepest (Arnett, 1999; Macfarlane, 1964). Humorist Dave Barry (1996) is one such person:

> When my dad pulled up, wearing his poodle hat and driving his Nash Metropolitan—a comically tiny vehicle resembling those cars outside supermarkets that go up and down when you put in a quarter, except the Metropolitan looked sillier and had a smaller motor—I was mortified. I might as well have been getting picked up by a flying saucer piloted by some bizarre multi-tentacled stalk-eyed slobber-mouthed alien being that had somehow got hold of a Russian hat. I was horrified at what my peers might think of my dad; it never occurred to me that my peers didn't even notice my dad, because they were too busy being mortified by THEIR parents.
>
> Of course eventually my father stopped being a hideous embarrassment to me, and I, grasping the Torch of Dorkhood, became a hideous embarrassment to my son.

Embarrassment is just one of the many adolescent moods. Despite the mood swings, adolescence can also be a time of vitality without the cares of adulthood, a time of rewarding friendships, of heightened idealism and a growing sense of life's exciting possibilities (Coleman, 1980).

How will you look back on your life 10 years from now? Are you making choices that someday you will recollect with satisfaction?

■ **adolescence** the transition period from childhood to adulthood, extending from puberty to independence.

■ **puberty** the period of sexual maturation, during which a person becomes capable of reproducing.

■ **primary sex characteristics** the body structures (ovaries, testes, and external genitalia) that make sexual reproduction possible.

■ **secondary sex characteristics** nonreproductive sexual characteristics, such as female breasts and hips, male voice quality, and body hair.

■ **menarche** [meh-NAR-key] the first menstrual period.

Physical Development

OBJECTIVE 10-2 | Identify the major physical changes during adolescence.

Adolescence begins with **puberty,** the time when one is maturing sexually. Puberty follows a surge of hormones, which may intensify moods and which trigger a two-year period of rapid physical development, usually beginning at about age 11 in girls and at about age 13 in boys. About the time of puberty, boys' growth propels them to greater height than their female counterparts (**FIGURE 10.1**). During this growth spurt, the **primary sex characteristics**—the reproductive organs and external genitalia—develop dramatically. So do **secondary sex characteristics,** the nonreproductive traits such as breasts and hips in girls, facial hair and deepened voice in boys, pubic and underarm hair in both sexes (**FIGURE 10.2**). A year or two before puberty, however, boys and girls often feel the first stirrings of attraction toward those of the other (or their own) sex (McClintock & Herdt, 1996).

In girls, puberty starts with breast development, which now often begins by age 10 (Brody, 1999). But puberty's landmarks are the first ejaculation in boys, usually by about age 14, and the first menstrual period in girls, usually within a year of age 12. The first menstrual period, called **menarche** (meh-NAR-key), is a memorable event. Nearly all adult women recall it and remember experiencing a mixture of feelings—pride, excitement, embarrassment, and apprehension (Greif & Ulman, 1982; Woods & others, 1983). Girls who have been prepared for menarche usually experience it as a positive life transition. Most men similarly recall their first ejaculation (*spermarche*), which usually occurs as a nocturnal emission (Fuller & Downs, 1990).

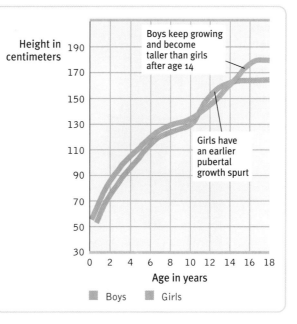

Height in centimeters

Boys keep growing and become taller than girls after age 14

Girls have an earlier pubertal growth spurt

Age in years

☐ Boys   ☐ Girls

FIGURE 10.1
Height differences
Throughout childhood, boys and girls are similar in height. At puberty, girls surge ahead briefly, but then boys overtake them at about age 14. (Data from Tanner, 1978.) Recent studies suggest that sexual development and growth spurts are beginning somewhat earlier than was the case a half-century ago (Herman-Giddens & others, 2001).

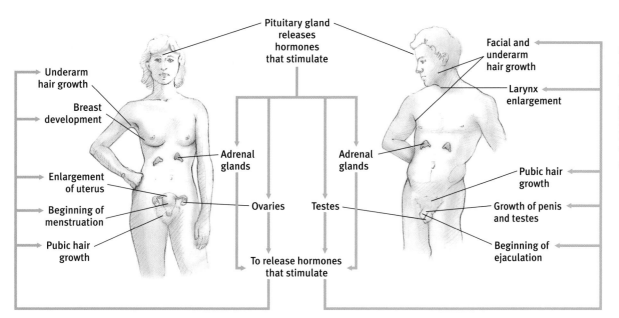

Pituitary gland releases hormones that stimulate

Underarm hair growth

Breast development

Adrenal glands

Enlargement of uterus

Ovaries

Beginning of menstruation

Pubic hair growth

To release hormones that stimulate

Facial and underarm hair growth

Larynx enlargement

Adrenal glands

Testes

Pubic hair growth

Growth of penis and testes

Beginning of ejaculation

FIGURE 10.2
Body changes at puberty
At about age 11 in girls and age 13 in boys, a surge of hormones triggers a variety of physical changes.

Young rockers
Children are now doing things that have in the past been reserved for their older peers. Chloe, age 11 (left), and her sister Asya, age 13, are the nationally known indie rock duo Smoosh, joining dozens of other similarly young but famous musicians who have hit the rock scene in recent years.

AP Photo/Jeff Chiu

"If a gun is put in the control of the prefrontal cortex of a hurt and vengeful 15-year-old, and it is pointed at a human target, it will very likely go off."
National Institutes of Health brain scientist Daniel R. Weinberger, "A Brain Too Young for Good Judgment," 2001

Just as in the earlier life stages, the *sequence* of physical changes in puberty (for example, breast buds and visible pubic hair before menarche) is far more predictable than their *timing*. Some girls start their growth spurt at 9, some boys as late as age 16. Though such variations have little effect on height at maturity, they may have psychological consequences. Early maturation pays dividends for boys. Early developing boys, being stronger and more athletic during their early teen years, tend to be more popular, self-assured, and independent, though also more at risk for alcohol use and premature sexual activity (Steinberg & Morris, 2001). But for girls, early maturation can be stressful. If a young girl's body is out of sync with her own emotional maturity and her friends' physical development and experiences, she may begin associating with older adolescents or may suffer teasing or sexual harassment. It is not only when we mature that counts, but how people react to our genetically influenced physical development. Remember: *Heredity and environment interact.*

Adolescents' brains are also a work in progress. Until puberty, brain cells increase their connections, like trees growing more roots and branches. Then, during adolescence, comes a selective pruning of unused neurons and connections (Durston & others, 2001). What we don't use, we lose. It's rather like traffic engineers reducing congestion by eliminating certain streets and constructing new beltways that move traffic more efficiently.

Frontal lobe development during adolescence also includes the continuing growth of *myelin,* the fatty tissue around axons that speeds neurotransmission. This frontal lobe maturation lags the emotional limbic system. The pubertal hormonal surge and limbic system development helps explain teens' occasional impulsiveness, risky behaviors, emotional storms—slamming doors and turning up the music. With frontal lobe maturation during the teens and early twenties comes improved judgment, impulse control, and the ability to plan for the long term. When university students choose immediate rewards, fMRI scans show their limbic reward system activating; when electing a bigger delayed reward, a part of their calculating frontal lobe area more strongly activates (McClure & others, 2004). No wonder younger teens (whose unfinished frontal lobes aren't yet fully equipped for making long-term plans and curbing impulses) so often succumb to the lure of smoking, which most adult smokers could tell them they will later regret.

So, when Junior drives recklessly and academically self-destructs, should his parents reassure themselves that "he can't help it; his frontal cortex isn't yet fully grown"? They can at least take hope: The brain with which Junior begins his teens differs from the brain with which he will end his teens, and which will continue maturing until about age 25 (Beckman, 2004). In 2004, the American Psychological Association joined seven other medical and mental health associations in filing U.S. Supreme Court briefs, arguing against the death penalty for 16- and 17-years olds. The briefs documented the teen brain's immaturity "in areas that bear upon adolescent decision-making." Teens are "less guilty by reason of adolescence," suggested psychologist Laurence Steinberg and law professor Elizabeth Scott (2003). In 2005, by a 5-to-4 margin, the Court concurred, declaring juvenile death penalties unconstitutional.

Cognitive Development

Adolescents' developing ability to reason gives them a new level of social awareness and moral judgment. As young teenagers become capable of thinking about their thinking, and of thinking about other people's thinking, they begin imagining what other people are thinking about *them*. (Adolescents might worry less about what others think of them if they knew how similarly self-preoccupied their peers are.) As their cognitive abilities mature, many adolescents think about what is ideally possible and criticize their society, their parents, and even their own shortcomings.

> "When the pilot told us to brace and grab our ankles, the first thing that went through my mind was that we must all look pretty stupid."
> Jeremiah Rawlings, age 12, after a 1989 DC-10 crash in Sioux City, Iowa

Developing Reasoning Power

OBJECTIVE 10-3 | Describe the changes in reasoning abilities that Piaget called formal operations.

During the early teen years, reasoning is often self-focused. Adolescents may think their private experiences are unique. They may assume their parents just can't understand what it feels like to be dating or to hate school: "But, Mom, *you* don't really know how it feels to be in love" (Elkind, 1978).

Gradually, though, most achieve the intellectual summit that Piaget called *formal operations*. Preadolescents reason concretely, but adolescents become more capable of abstract logic: *If* this, *then* that. We can see this new abstract reasoning power as adolescents ponder and debate human nature, good and evil, truth and justice. Having perhaps envisioned God as an old man in the clouds when they were first capable of symbolic thinking in early childhood, they may now seek a deeper conception of God and existence (Elkind, 1970; Worthington, 1989). Adolescents' ability to reason hypothetically and deduce consequences also enables them to detect inconsistencies in others' reasoning and to spot hypocrisy. This can lead to heated debates with parents and silent vows never to lose sight of their own ideals (Peterson & others, 1986).

"Ben is in his first year of high school, and he's questioning all the right things."

Demonstrating their reasoning ability Although on opposite sides of the Iraq War debate, these teens demonstrate their newfound ability to think logically about abstract topics. According to Piaget, they are in the final cognitive stage, formal operations.

Developing Morality

OBJECTIVE 10-4 | Discuss moral development from the perspectives of moral thinking, moral feeling, and moral action.

A crucial task of childhood and adolescence is discerning right from wrong and developing character—the psychological muscles for controlling impulses. To be a moral person is to *think* morally and *act* accordingly.

Moral Thinking

Piaget (1932) believed that children's moral judgments build on their cognitive development. Agreeing with Piaget, Lawrence Kohlberg (1981, 1984) sought to describe the development of *moral reasoning,* the thinking that occurs as we consider right and wrong.

> "It is a delightful harmony when doing and saying go together."
> Michel Eyquem de Montaigne (1533–1592)

Moral reasoning
New Orleans hurricane and flood victims were faced with a moral dilemma: Should they steal household necessities? Their reasoning likely reflected different levels of moral thinking, even if they behaved similarly.

AP Photo/Dave Martin

Kohlberg posed moral dilemmas (for example, whether a person should steal medicine to save a loved one's life), and asked children, adolescents, and adults if the action was right or wrong. He then analyzed their answers for evidence of stages of moral thinking.

His findings led him to believe that as we develop intellectually, we pass through three basic levels of moral thinking:

- **Preconventional morality** Before age 9, most children have a preconventional morality of self-interest: They obey either to avoid punishment or to gain concrete rewards.

- **Conventional morality** By early adolescence, morality usually evolves to a more conventional level that cares for others and upholds laws and social rules simply because they are the laws and rules.

- **Postconventional morality** Some of those who develop the abstract reasoning of formal operational thought may come to a third level. Postconventional morality affirms people's agreed-upon rights or follows what one personally perceives as basic ethical principles.

Kohlberg's claim was that these levels form a moral ladder (**FIGURE 10.3**), from the bottom rung of a young child's immature, preconventional morality, to the top rung of an adult's self-defined ethical principles, which only some attain. As with all stage theories, the sequence is unvarying. We begin on the bottom rung and ascend to varying heights.

Research confirms that children in various cultures progress from the level Kohlberg called preconventional, then into his conventional level (Edwards, 1981, 1982; Snarey, 1985, 1987). And as our *thinking* matures, our *behavior* also becomes less selfish and more caring (Krebs & Van Hesteren, 1994; Miller & others, 1996). However, the postconventional level is more controversial. It appears mostly in the European and North American educated middle class, which prizes individualism—giving priority to one's own goals rather than to group goals (Eckensberger, 1994; Miller & Bersoff, 1995). Critics therefore contend that the theory is biased against the moral reasoning of those in communal societies such as China and India—and also against Western women, whose morality may be based slightly less on abstract, impersonal principles and more on caring relationships.

"I am a bit suspicious of any theory that says that the highest moral stage is one in which people talk like college professors."
James Q. Wilson, *The Moral Sense*, 1993

Moral Feeling

The mind makes moral judgments as it makes aesthetic judgments—quickly and automatically. We feel disgust when seeing people engaged in degrading or subhuman acts, and we feel *elevation*—a tingly, warm, glowing feeling in the chest—when seeing people display exceptional generosity, compassion, or courage.

One woman recalled driving through her snowy neighborhood with three young men as they passed "an elderly woman with a shovel in her driveway. I did not think much of it, when one of the guys in the back asked the driver to let him off there. . . .

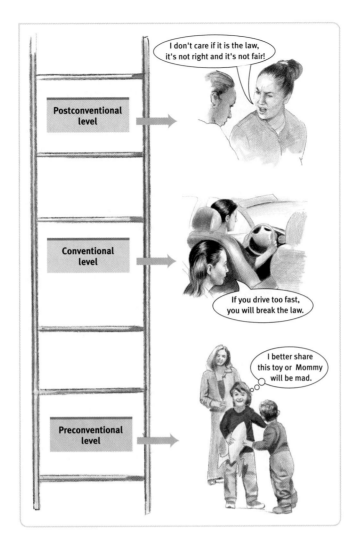

FIGURE 10.3
Kohlberg's moral ladder
As moral development progresses, the focus of concern moves from the self to the wider social world. Kohlberg contended that postconventional moral thinking, embodied by Martin Luther King, Jr., may be rejected by those who do not comprehend it.

When I saw him jump out of the back seat and approach the lady, my mouth dropped in shock as I realized that he was offering to shovel her walk for her." Witnessing this unexpected goodness triggered elevation: "I felt like jumping out of the car and hugging this guy. I felt like singing and running, or skipping and laughing. I felt like saying nice things about people" (Haidt, 2000).

In Jonathan Haidt's (2001, 2002) *social intuitionist* account of morality, moral feelings precede moral reasoning. "Could human morality really be run by the moral emotions," he wonders, "while moral reasoning struts about pretending to be in control?" Indeed, he surmises, "moral judgment involves quick gut feelings, or affectively laden intuitions, which then trigger moral reasoning." Moral reasoning—our mind's press secretary—aims to convince others of what we intuitively feel.

The social intuitionist explanation of morality finds support from a study of moral paradoxes. Imagine a runaway trolley headed for five people. All will certainly be killed unless you throw a switch that diverts the trolley onto another track, where it will kill one person. Should you throw the switch?

Most say yes. Kill one, save five. Now imagine the same dilemma, except that your opportunity to save the five requires you to push a large stranger onto the tracks, where he will die as his body stops the trolley. Kill one, save five?

The logic is the same, but most say no. Seeking to understand why, a Princeton research team led by Joshua Greene (2001) used brain imaging to spy on people's neural responses as they contemplated such dilemmas. Only when given the body-pushing type of moral dilemma did their brain's emotion areas light up. Despite the identical logic, the personal dilemma engaged emotions that altered moral judgment. Moral judgment is more than thinking; it is also gut-level feeling.

"This might not be ethical. Is that a problem for anybody?"

Moral Action

Our moral thinking and feeling surely affect our moral talk. But sometimes talk is cheap and emotions are fleeting. Morality involves *doing* the right thing, and what we do also depends on social influences. As political theorist Hannah Arendt (1963) observed, many Nazi concentration camp guards during World War II were ordinary "moral" people who were corrupted by a powerfully evil situation.

Today's character education programs tend to focus both on discussions of moral issues and their implications and on *doing* the right thing. Thus, they teach children *empathy* for others' feelings, and also the self-discipline needed to restrain one's own impulses—to delay small gratifications now to enable bigger rewards later. Those who do learn to *delay gratification* become more socially responsible, academically successful, and productive (Funder & Block, 1989; Mischel & others, 1988, 1989). They often engage students in responsible action through *service learning*. When teens tutor, clean up their neighborhoods, and assist the elderly, their sense of competence and desire to serve increases and their school absenteeism and drop-out rates diminish (Andersen, 1998; Piliavin, 2003). Moral action feeds moral attitudes.

Social Development

OBJECTIVE 10-5 | Identify Erikson's eight stages of psychosocial development and their accompanying issues.

Theorist Erik Erikson (1963) contended that each stage of life has its own *psychosocial task,* a crisis that needs resolution. Young children wrestle with issues of *trust,* then *autonomy* (independence), then *initiative* (TABLE 10.1). School-age children strive for *competence,* feeling able and productive. The adolescent's task, said Erikson, is to synthesize past, present, and future possibilities into a clearer sense of self. Adolescents wonder "Who am I as an individual? What do I want to do with my life? What values should I live by? What do I believe in?" Erikson called this quest the adolescent's *search for identity.*

TABLE 10.1

ERIKSON'S STAGES OF PSYCHOSOCIAL DEVELOPMENT

Stage (approximate age)	Issues	Description of Task
Infancy (to 1 year)	*Trust vs. mistrust*	If needs are dependably met, infants develop a sense of basic trust.
Toddlerhood (1 to 2 years)	*Autonomy vs. shame and doubt*	Toddlers learn to exercise will and do things for themselves, or they doubt their abilities.
Preschooler (3 to 5 years)	*Initiative vs. guilt*	Preschoolers learn to initiate tasks and carry out plans, or they feel guilty about efforts to be independent.
Elementary school (6 years to puberty)	*Competence vs. inferiority*	Children learn the pleasure of applying themselves to tasks, or they feel inferior.
Adolescence (teen years into 20s)	*Identity vs. role confusion*	Teenagers work at refining a sense of self by testing roles and then integrating them to form a single identity, or they become confused about who they are.
Young adulthood (20s to early 40s)	*Intimacy vs. isolation*	Young adults struggle to form close relationships and to gain the capacity for intimate love, or they feel socially isolated.
Middle adulthood (40s to 60s)	*Generativity vs. stagnation*	In middle age, people discover a sense of contributing to the world, usually through family and work, or they may feel a lack of purpose.
Late adulthood (late 60s and up)	*Integrity vs. despair*	When reflecting on his or her life, the older adult may feel a sense of satisfaction or failure.

As sometimes happens in psychology, Erikson's interests were bred by his own life experience. As the son of a Jewish mother and a Danish father, Erikson was "doubly an outsider," reports Morton Hunt (1993, p. 391). He was "scorned as a Jew in school but mocked as a Gentile in the synagogue because of his blond hair and blue eyes." Such episodes fueled his interest in the adolescent struggle for identity.

Forming an Identity

OBJECTIVE **10-6** | Explain how the search for identity affects us during adolescence, and discuss how forming an identity prepares us for intimacy.

To refine their sense of identity, adolescents in Western cultures usually try out different "selves" in different situations—perhaps acting out one self at home, another with friends, and still another at school and work. If two of these situations overlap—as when a teenager brings home friends—the discomfort can be considerable. The teen asks, "Which self should I be? Which is the real me?" This role confusion usually gets resolved by forming a self-definition that unifies the various selves into a consistent and comfortable sense of who one is—an **identity.**

But not always. Erikson noticed that some adolescents forge their identity early, simply by taking on their parents' values and expectations. (Traditional, less individualistic cultures inform adolescents about who they are, rather than letting them decide on their own.) Other adolescents may adopt a negative identity defined in opposition to parents and society but in conformity with a particular peer group—the jocks, the preppies, the geeks, the goths.

Most young people do develop a sense of contentment with their lives. When American teens were asked whether a series of statements described them, 80 percent said yes to "I would choose my life the way it is right now." But others never quite seem to find themselves: About 20 percent agreed with "I wish I were somebody else," and 28 percent with "I often wonder why I exist" (Lyons, 2004). Reflecting on their existence, 75 percent of American collegians say they "discuss religion/spirituality" with friends, "pray," and agree that "we are all spiritual beings" and "search for meaning/purpose in life" (HERI, 2005). This would not surprise Stanford psychologist William Damon and his colleagues (2003), who contend that a key task of adolescent development is to achieve a purpose—a desire to accomplish something personally meaningful that makes a difference to the world beyond oneself.

The late teen years, when many people begin attending college or working full time, provide new opportunities for trying out possible roles. As seniors, many college students have achieved a clearer identity than they had as first-year students (Waterman, 1988). Their identity typically incorporates an increasingly positive self-concept. In several nationwide studies, researchers have given young Americans tests of self-esteem. (Sample item: "I am able to do things as well as most other people.") During the early to mid-teen years, self-esteem falls and for girls, depression scores often increase, but then self-image rebounds during the late teens and twenties (Robins & others, 2002; Twenge & Campbell, 2001; Twenge & Nolen-Hoeksema, 2002).

Identity also becomes more personalized. Daniel Hart (1988) asked youths of various ages to imagine a machine that would clone (*a*) what you think and feel, (*b*) your appearance, or (*c*) your relationships with friends and family. When he then asked which clone would be "closest to being you?" three-fourths of the seventh-graders chose (*c*), the clone with the same social network. In contrast, three-fourths of the ninth-graders chose (*a*), the one with their individual thoughts and feelings.

Erikson contended that the adolescent identity stage is followed in young adulthood by a developing capacity for **intimacy,** the ability to form emotionally close

■ **identity** one's sense of self; according to Erikson, the adolescent's task is to solidify a sense of self by testing and integrating various roles.

■ **intimacy** in Erikson's theory, the ability to form close, loving relationships; a primary developmental task in late adolescence and early adulthood.

Who shall I be today?
By varying the way they look, adolescents try out different "selves." Although we eventually form a consistent and stable sense of identity, the self we present may change with the situation.

" I am becoming still more independent of my parents; young as I am, I face life with more courage than Mummy; my feeling for justice is immovable, and truer than hers. I know what I want, I have a goal, an opinion, I have a religion, and love. Let me be myself and then I am satisfied. I know that I'm a woman, a woman with inward strength and plenty of courage."
Anne Frank, *Diary of a Young Girl,* 1947

"How was my day? How was my day? Must you micromanage my life?"

Compared with teens in other Western nations, teens in the United States spend more time watching TV and hanging out with friends (both predictors of negative outcomes) and less time on schoolwork (Larson, 2001).

FIGURE 10.4
The changing parent-child relationship
Interviews from a large, national study of Canadian families reveal that the typically close, warm relationships between parents and preschoolers loosen among children of older ages. (Data from Statistics Canada, 1999.)

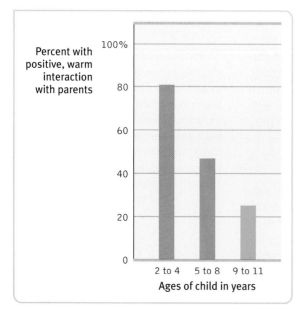

relationships. Once you have a clear and comfortable sense of who you are, said Erikson, you are ready for close relationships. Such relationships are, for most of us, a source of great pleasure. When Mihaly Csikszentmihalyi (pronounced chick-SENT-me-hi) and Jeremy Hunter (2003) used a beeper to sample the daily experiences of American teens, they found them unhappiest when alone and happiest when with friends. As Aristotle long ago recognized, we humans are "the social animal."

Parent and Peer Influence

OBJECTIVE **10-7** | Contrast parental and peer influences during adolescence.

As adolescents in Western cultures seek to form their own identities, they begin to separate themselves from their parents (Paikoff & Brooks-Gunn, 1991). The preschooler who can't be close enough to her mother, who loves to touch and cling to her, becomes the 14-year-old who wouldn't be caught dead holding hands with Mom. The transition occurs gradually (**FIGURE 10.4**). By adolescence, arguments occur more often, usually over mundane things—household chores, bedtime, homework (Tesser & others, 1989). From early to late adolescence, parent-adolescent conflicts become temporarily (during early adolescence) more intense but progressively less frequent.

For a minority of parents and their adolescents, differences lead to estrangement and to great stress (Steinberg & Morris, 2001). But for most, disagreement at the level of bickering is not destructive. One study of 6000 adolescents in 10 countries, from Australia to Bangladesh to Turkey, found that most liked their parents (Offer & others, 1988). "We usually get along but . . . ," adolescents often report (Galambos, 1992; Steinberg, 1987). Positive relations with parents support positive peer relations. High school girls who have the most affectionate relationships with their mothers tend also to enjoy the most intimate friendships with girlfriends (Gold & Yanof, 1985). And teens who feel close to their parents tend to be healthy and happy and to do well in school (Resnick & others, 1997). Of course, we can state this correlation the other way: Misbehaving teens are more likely to have tense parental relationships.

Adolescence is typically a time of diminishing parental influence and growing peer influence. Asked in a survey if they had "ever had a serious talk" with their child about illegal drugs, 85 percent of American *parents* answered yes. But the teens sometimes tuned out this earnest advice, for only 45 percent could recall such a serious talk (Morin & Brossard, 1997). Instead, what their friends are—what "everybody's doing"—they often become.

Heredity does much of the heavy lifting in forming individual differences in character and personality, and parent and peer influences do much of the rest. Teens are herd animals. They talk, dress, and act more like their peers than their parents. In teen calls to hotline counseling services, peer relationships are the most discussed topic (Boehm & others, 1999). For those who feel excluded, the pain is acute. "The social atmosphere in most high schools is poisonously clique-driven and exclusionary," observes social psychologist Elliot Aronson (2001). Most excluded "students suffer in silence. . . . A small number act out in violent ways against their classmates." When rejected adolescents withdraw, they are vulnerable to loneliness, low self-esteem, and depression (Steinberg & Morris, 2001). Peer approval matters.

Teens see their parents as having more influence in other areas—for example, in shaping their religious faith and practices and in thinking about college and career choices (*Emerging Trends*, 1997). A Gallup Youth Survey reveals that most share their parent's political views, too (Lyons, 2005).

Emerging Adulthood

OBJECTIVE 10-8 | Discuss the characteristics of emerging adulthood.

As people mature in young adulthood, their emotional ties with parents loosen. During their early twenties, many still lean heavily on their parents. By their late twenties, most feel more comfortably independent of their parents and better able to empathize with them as fellow adults (Frank, 1988; White, 1983). This graduation from adolescence to adulthood is now taking longer.

In the Western world, adolescence now roughly corresponds to the teen years, but at earlier times—and in some developing countries today—adolescence was a brief interlude between the dependence of childhood and the responsibilities of adulthood (Baumeister & Tice, 1986). Shortly after sexual maturity, society bestowed adult responsibilities and status on the young person, often marking the event with an elaborate initiation. The new adult then worked, married, and had children. With compulsory schooling, adult independence began occurring later. In industrialized cultures from Europe to Australia, adolescents are taking more time to finish college, to leave the nest, and to establish careers. In the United States, for example, the average age at first marriage has increased more than 4 years since 1960 (to 27 for men, 25 for women). Today's earlier sexual maturity is related both to increased body fat (which can support pregnancy and nursing) and to weakened parent-child bonds, including absent fathers (Ellis, 2004). Together, later independence and earlier sexual maturity have widened the once-brief interlude between biological maturity and social independence (**FIGURE 10.5**). That gap—the years spent morphing from child to adult—is adolescence.

The time from 18 to the mid-twenties is an increasingly not-yet-settled phase of life, which some now call *emerging adulthood* (Arnett, 2000). These emerging adults are no longer adolescents, but they have not yet taken on adult-level responsibilities and independence, either. Unlike some non-Western cultures that have public rites of passage marking an abrupt transition to adulthood, Westerners typically have a more gradual transition. Those who leave home for college, for example, are separated from parents and, more than ever before, managing their time and priorities. Yet they may remain dependent on their parents' financial and emotional support and may return home for holidays. For many others out of school, their parents' home may be the only affordable place to live. Adulthood emerges, gradually.

FIGURE 10.5
Adolescence is being stretched from both ends
In the 1890s the average interval between a woman's first menstrual period and marriage, which typically marked a transition to adulthood, was about 7 years; today in industrialized countries it is about 12 years (Guttmacher, 1994, 2000). Although many adults are unmarried, later marriage combines with prolonged education and earlier menarche to help stretch out adolescence.

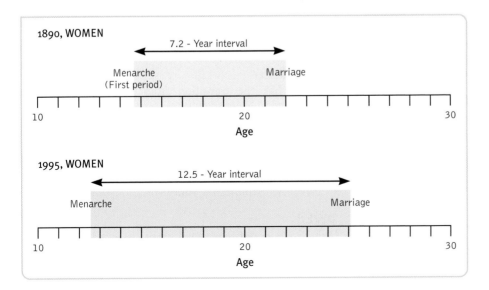

1890, WOMEN
7.2 - Year interval
Menarche (First period)   Marriage
10   20   30
Age

1995, WOMEN
12.5 - Year interval
Menarche   Marriage
10   20   30
Age

Ariel Skelley/Corbis

>> Learning Outcomes

Adolescence

Objective 10-1 | Define *adolescence*.

Adolescence is the transition period from childhood to adulthood, extending from puberty to independence.

Objective 10-2 | Identify the major physical changes during adolescence.

Just before *puberty*, a surge of hormones triggers a two-year growth spurt, beginning at about age 11 in girls and age 13 in boys. During puberty, *primary sex characteristics* (the reproductive organs and external genitalia) and *secondary sex characteristics* (nonreproductive sexual characteristics such as a girl's breasts and a boy's deepened voice) develop. For most girls, *menarche* happens within a year of age 12. For most boys, *spermarche* occurs by about age 14. Individual onset of puberty varies, depending on heredity and environment, and other people's reactions to early or late maturation can influence adolescents' adjustment. During adolescence, frontal lobes mature and unused neurons and their connections are pruned.

Objective 10-3 | Describe the changes in reasoning abilities that Piaget called formal operations.

With the development of formal operations, adolescents gain the ability to reason abstractly. This ability lets them form hypotheses and deduce consequences.

Objective 10-4 | Discuss moral development from the perspectives of moral thinking, moral feeling, and moral action.

Building on Piaget's idea that moral judgments reflect the developing child's reasoning powers, Lawrence Kohlberg proposed three levels of *moral thinking: preconventional morality* (self-interested, based on reasoning that attempts to avoid punishment or gain concrete rewards); *conventional morality* (law-abiding, based on reasoning that existing laws must be upheld), and *postconventional morality* (self-defined, based on abstract reasoning about what is ethical, right, and fair). The *social intuitionist* view of morality proposes that *moral feelings* precede moral thinking and judgments. The *moral action* perspective focuses on social influences on decisions to do the right thing; this is the basis of some programs for teaching children to empathize with others and to delay gratification.

Objective 10-5 | Identify Erikson's eight stages of psychosocial development and their accompanying issues.

Erik Erikson proposed that we pass through eight stages in life (loosely associated with age), each with its own psychosocial task. In infancy (to 1 year), the issue is trust versus mistrust; in toddlerhood (1 to 2 years), the issue is autonomy versus shame and doubt. Preschoolers (3 to 5) learn initiative or guilt, and elementary school children (6 to puberty), competence or inferiority. A chief task of adolescence (teens to twenties) is solidifying one's sense of self—one's identity. For young adults (twenties to early forties), the issue is intimacy versus isolation, and for middle adulthood (forties to sixties), generativity versus stagnation. Late adulthood's (late sixties and up) task is integrity versus despair.

Objective 10-6 | Explain how the search for identity affects us during adolescence, and discuss how forming an identity prepares us for intimacy.

Most Western adolescents try out different selves before settling into a consistent identity. A smaller number unthinkingly adopt their parents' identity or, rejecting parental and social values, take on the identity of peers. Erikson believed that having a clear and comfortable identity is a precondition for forming close relationships.

Objective 10-7 | Contrast parental and peer influences during adolescence.

Adolescents in Western cultures do tend to become increasingly independent of their parents, but most teenagers relate to their parents reasonably well. Teens talk, dress, and act like their peers and value peer approval and relationships. Parents continue to influence teens in such areas as religiosity and college and career choices.

Objective 10-8 | Discuss the characteristics of emerging adulthood.

Emerging adulthood refers to the period from about age 18 to the mid-twenties, when many young people in Western cultures are no longer adolescents but have not yet achieved full independence as adults. During this time, many young people attend college or work but continue to live in their parents' home. In the United States, the age of first marriage now extends into the mid-twenties for men and women.

TERMS AND CONCEPTS TO REMEMBER

adolescence, p. 10-0

puberty, p. 10-1

primary sex characteristics, p. 10-1

secondary sex characteristic p. 10-1

menarche [meh-NAR-key], p. 10-1

identity, p. 10-7

intimacy, p. 10-7

TEST YOURSELF

1. How has the transition from childhood to adulthood changed in Western cultures in the last 100 years?

(Answer in Appendix B.)

ASK YOURSELF

1. What are the most positive and most negative things you remember about your own adolescence? And who do you credit or blame more—your parents or your peers?

>WEB

Multiple-choice *self-tests* and more may be found at www.worthpublishers.com/myers.

MODULE

Adulthood, and Reflections on Developmental Issues

At one time, psychologists viewed the center-of-life years between adolescence and old age as one long plateau. No longer. Those who follow the unfolding of people's adult lives now believe our development continues.

It is more difficult to generalize about adulthood stages than about life's early years. If you know that James is a 1-year-old and Jamal is a 10-year-old, you could say a great deal about each child. Not so with adults who differ by a similar number of years. The boss may be 30 or 60; the marathon runner may be 20 or 50; a 19-year-old can be a parent who supports a child or a child who gets an allowance. Yet our life courses are in some ways similar. Physically, cognitively, and especially socially, we are at age 50 different from our 25-year-old selves. Although our bodies, minds, and relationships undergo some changes in common with those of our childhood friends, in other ways, we may now seem very different.

Rick Doyle / Corbis

"
I am still learning."

Michelangelo, 1560, at age 85

Adult abilities vary widely
Eighty-seven-year-olds: Don't try this. In 2002, George Blair became the world's oldest barefoot water skier, 18 days after his eighty-seventh birthday.

Physical Development

Our physical abilities—muscular strength, reaction time, sensory keenness, and cardiac output—all crest by the mid-twenties. Like the declining daylight after the summer solstice, the decline of physical prowess begins imperceptibly. Athletes are often the first to notice. World-class sprinters and swimmers peak by their early twenties. Women, because they mature earlier than men, also peak earlier. But most of us—especially those of us whose daily lives do not require top physical performance—hardly perceive the early signs of decline.

Physical Changes in Middle Adulthood

OBJECTIVE 11-1 | Identify the major physical changes that occur in middle adulthood.

Middle-age (post-40) athletes know all too well that physical decline gradually accelerates (**FIGURE 11.1** on the next page). As a 63-year-old who regularly plays basketball, I now find myself occasionally wondering whether my team really needs me down court. But even diminished vigor is sufficient for normal activities. Moreover, during early and middle adulthood, physical vigor has less to do with age than with a person's health and exercise habits. Many of today's physically fit 50-year-olds run 4 miles with ease, while sedentary 25-year-olds find themselves huffing and puffing up two flights of stairs.

How old does a person have to be before you think of him or her as old? The average 18- to 29-year-old says 67. The average person 60 and over says 76 (Yankelovich Partners, 1995).

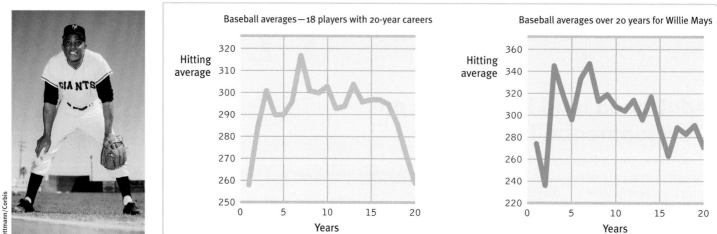

Baseball averages—18 players with 20-year careers

Baseball averages over 20 years for Willie Mays

FIGURE 11.1
Gradually accelerating decline
An analysis of aging and batting averages of all twentieth-century major league baseball players revealed a gradual but accelerating decline in players' later years (Schall & Smith, 2000). The career performance record of the great Willie Mays is illustrative.

"There are no life-style changes, surgical procedures, vitamins, antioxidants, hormones or techniques of genetic engineering available today that have been demonstrated to influence the processes of aging."
Position Statement on Human Aging signed by 51 scientists who study aging, 2002

"If the truth were known, we'd have to diagnose [older women] as having P.M.F.— Post-Menstrual Freedom."
Social psychologist Jacqueline Goodchilds (1987)

"Happy fortieth. I'll take the muscle tone in your upper arms, the girlish timbre of your voice, your amazing tolerance for caffeine, and your ability to digest french fries. The rest of you can stay."

The physical changes of adult life may trigger psychological responses, which vary depending on how one views growing older. In some Eastern cultures, where respect and power come with age, outward signs of advancing years are accepted and even welcomed. In Western cultures, where the perceived ideal is smooth skin and a slim torso, middle-age wrinkles and bulges can threaten self-esteem. Millions therefore spend billions in hopes of slowing or reversing the process. But nature will not be denied; inevitably the lines appear (or reappear) and the youthful form changes shape.

For women, aging means a gradual decline in fertility. Among women 35 to 39, a single act of intercourse is half as likely to produce a pregnancy as it would be for a woman 19 to 26 (Dunson & others, 2002). But women's foremost biological sign of aging is **menopause,** the ending of the menstrual cycle, usually beginning within a few years of age 50. Menopause and its physical symptoms accompany a reduction in the hormone estrogen. For 4 or 5 in 10 Canadian and U.S. women, but only 1 in 7 Japanese women, these symptoms include occasional hot flashes (Goode, 1999; Lock, 1998). But the stereotype of menopausal emotionality and depression clashes with reality: Menopause usually does *not* create psychological problems for women. Studies following thousands of American and Australian middle-aged women for up to 10 years have all found them no more or less depressed if experiencing menopause (Avis, 2003; Dennerstein & others, 2000).

A woman's expectations and attitudes influence the emotional impact of menopause. Does she see it as a sign that she is losing her femininity and sexual attractiveness and growing old? Or does she view it as liberation from menstrual periods, fears of pregnancy, and children's demands? To learn women's attitudes toward menopause, Bernice Neugarten and her colleagues (1963) did what, a half-century before, no one had ever done: They questioned women whose experience of menopause had *not* led them to seek treatment. When asked whether it is true that after menopause "women generally feel better than they have for years," only one-fourth of the premenopausal women under age 45 guessed yes. Of the older women who had experienced menopause, two-thirds said yes. As one woman said, "I can remember my mother saying that after her menopause she really got her vigor, and I can say the same thing myself." In one MacArthur Foundation study of 3000 midlife adults, most postmenopausal women recalled "only relief" when their periods stopped; just 2 percent felt "only regret" (Goode, 1999).

Men experience no equivalent to menopause—no cessation of fertility, no sharp drop in sex hormones. They do experience a more gradual decline in sperm count, testosterone level, and speed of erection and ejaculation. If testosterone levels plummet too fast and far, the result may be depression, irritability, insomnia, impotence, or weakness, which can be treated by testosterone replacement therapy (Sternbach,

Perception Laboratory, University of St. Andrews

The aging face
Psychologists Michael Burt and David Perrett (1995) created computer composite images averaged from 20- to 24-year-old and 50- to 54-year-old Caucasian males. Then they applied the age changes to other faces, projecting, for example, what an older Marilyn Monroe would have looked like.

1998). Some may also experience psychological distress related to their perception of decreased virility and declining physical capacities. But most men age without such problems. After middle age, most men and women remain capable of satisfying sexual activity. When people over 60 were surveyed by the National Council on Aging, 39 percent expressed satisfaction with the amount of sex they were having and 39 percent said they wished for sex more frequently (Leary, 1998).

> "The things that stop you having sex with age are exactly the same as those that stop you riding a bicycle (bad health, thinking it looks silly, no bicycle)."
> Alex Comfort, *The Joy of Sex,* 2002

Physical Changes in Later Life

OBJECTIVE 11-2 | Compare life expectancy in the mid-twentieth and early twenty-first centuries, and discuss changes in sensory abilities and health (including frequency of dementia) in older adults.

Is old age "more to be feared than death" (Juvenal, *Satires*)? Or is life "most delightful when it is on the downward slope" (Seneca, *Epistulae ad Lucilium*)? What is it like to grow old? To gauge your own understanding, take the following true/false quiz:

■ **menopause** the time of natural cessation of menstruation; also refers to the biological changes a woman experiences as her ability to reproduce declines.

1. Older people become more susceptible to short-term illnesses.
2. During old age many of the brain's neurons die.
3. If they live to be 90 or older, most elderly people eventually become senile.
4. Recognition memory—the ability to identify things previously experienced— declines with age.
5. Life satisfaction peaks in the fifties and then gradually declines after age 65.

The above statements—all false—are among the misconceptions about aging exploded by recent research on the world's most rapidly growing population group.

Life Expectancy

Worldwide, life expectancy at birth increased from 49 years in 1950 to 67 in 2004—and to 80 and beyond in some developed countries (PRB, 2004; Sivard, 1996). This increasing life expectancy (humanity's greatest achievement, say some) combines with decreasing birthrates to make the elderly a bigger and bigger population segment. By 2050, about 35 percent of Europe's population likely will be over age 60 (Fernández-Ballesteros, 2003). Clearly, countries that have depended on children to care for the aged are destined for major social changes. Russia and Western Europe are also headed for depopulation—146 million to 104 million people in Russia by 2050, projects the

Swaziland has the world's shortest life expectancy (33 years). Andorrans enjoy the longest expectation of life—almost 84 years (CIA Factbook, 2005).

World record for longevity?
French woman Jeanne Calment, the oldest human in history with authenticated age, died in 1998 at age 122. At age 100, she was still riding a bike. At age 114, she became the oldest film actor ever, by portraying herself in *Vincent and Me*.

After age 30, the risk of death doubles every 8 years. A 48-year-old's risk of dying is twice that of a 40-year-old's (National Center for Health Statistics, 1992; Olshansky & others, 1993).

Most stairway falls taken by older people occur on the top step, precisely where the person typically descends from a window-lit hallway into the darker stairwell (Fozard & Popkin, 1978). Our knowledge of aging could be used to design environments that would reduce such accidents (National Research Council, 1990).

United Nations (Brooks, 2005). "When an entire continent, healthier, wealthier, and more secure than ever before, fails to create the human future in the most elemental sense—by creating the next generation—something very serious is afoot," surmises George Weigel (2005).

Life expectancy differs for males and females; males are more prone to dying. Although 126 male embryos begin life for every 100 females who do so, the sex ratio is down to 105 males for every 100 females at birth (Strickland, 1992). During the first year, male infants' death rates exceed females' by one-fourth. Women outlive men by 4 years worldwide and by 5 to 6 years in Canada, the United States, and Australia. (Rather than marrying a man older than themselves, 20-year-old women who want a husband who shares their life expectancy should wait for the 15-year-old boys to mature.) By age 100, females outnumber males 5 to 1.

But few of us live to 100. Even if no one died before age 50, and cancer, heart disease, and infectious illness were eliminated, average life expectancy would still increase only to about 85 or a few years beyond (Barinaga, 1991). The body ages. Its cells stop reproducing. It becomes frail. It becomes vulnerable to tiny insults—hot weather, a fall, a mild flu bug—that at age 20 would have been trivial.

Why do we eventually wear out? Why don't we, like the bristlecone pine trees, rockfish, and some social insect queens, grow older without withering? One theory, proposed by evolutionary biologists, speculates that the answer relates to our survival as a species: We pass on our genes most successfully when we raise our young and then stop consuming resources. Once we've fulfilled our gene-reproducing task, there are no natural selection pressures against genes that cause degeneration in later life (Olshansky & others, 1993; Sapolsky & Finch, 1991).

Sensory Abilities

As we have seen, physical decline begins in early adulthood, but we are not usually acutely aware of it until later life. Visual sharpness diminishes, and adaptation to changes in light level slows. Muscle strength, reaction time, and stamina also diminish noticeably, as do hearing, distance perception, and the sense of smell (**FIGURE 11.2**). In later life, the stairs get steeper, the print gets smaller, and people seem to mumble more.

FIGURE 11.2
The aging senses
Sight, smell, and hearing all are less acute among those over age 70. (From Doty & others, 1984.)

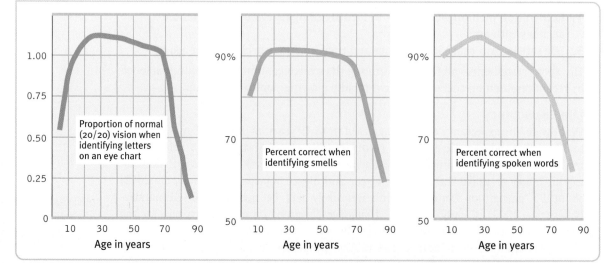

With age, the eye's pupil shrinks and its lens becomes less transparent, reducing the amount of light reaching the retina. In fact, a 65-year-old retina receives only about one-third as much light as its 20-year-old counterpart (Kline & Schieber, 1985). Thus, to see as well as a 20-year-old when reading or driving, a 65-year-old needs three times as much light—a reason for buying cars with untinted windshields. This also explains why older people sometimes ask younger people, "Don't you need better light for reading?"

Health

For those growing older, there is both bad and good news about health. The bad news: The body's disease-fighting immune system weakens, making the elderly more susceptible to life-threatening ailments such as cancer and pneumonia. The good news: Thanks partly to a lifetime's accumulation of antibodies, older people *less* often suffer short-term ailments, such as common flu and cold viruses. For example, those over 65 are half as likely as 20-year-olds and one-fifth as likely as preschoolers to suffer upper respiratory flu each year (National Center for Health Statistics, 1990). This helps explain why older workers have lower absenteeism rates (Rhodes, 1983).

Aging levies a tax on the brain by slowing our neural processing. Up to the teen years, we process information with greater and greater speed (Fry & Hale, 1996; Kail, 1991). But compared with teens and young adults, older people take a bit more time to react, to solve perceptual puzzles, even to remember names (Bashore & others, 1997; Verhaeghen & Salthouse, 1997). The lag is greatest when tasks become complex (Cerella, 1985; Poon, 1987). At video games, most 70-year-olds are no match for a 20-year-old. And, as **FIGURE 11.3** indicates, fatal accident rates per mile driven increase sharply after age 75. By age 85, they exceed the 16-year-old level. Nevertheless, because older people drive less, they account for less than 10 percent of crashes (Coughlin & others, 2004).

Brain regions important to memory begin to atrophy during aging (Schacter, 1996). In young adulthood, a small, gradual net loss of brain cells begins, contributing by age 80 to a brain-weight reduction of 5 percent or so. Aging may proceed more slowly in women. Not only do women worldwide live four years longer than men, their brains shrink more slowly than men's (Coffey & others, 1998).

Exercising the body feeds the brain. The birth of new cells and the proliferation of neural connections, especially in those who remain active, helps compensate for the cell loss (Coleman & Flood, 1986). Physical exercise enhances muscles, bones, and energy and helps prevent obesity and heart disease. It also stimulates brain cell development and connections, thanks perhaps to increased oxygen and nutrient flow

> "For some reason, possibly to save ink, the restaurants had started printing their menus in letters the height of bacteria."
>
> Dave Barry, *Dave Barry Turns Fifty*, 1998

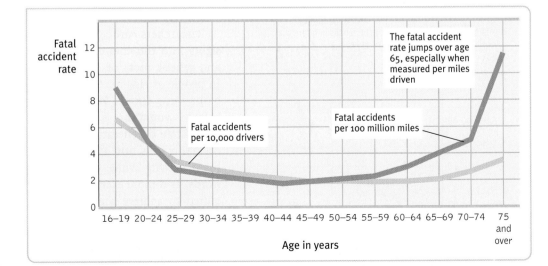

FIGURE 11.3
Age and driver fatalities
Slowing reactions contribute to increased accident risks among those 75 and older, and their greater fragility increases their risk of death when accidents happen (NHTSA, 2000). Would you favor driver exams based on performance, not age, to screen out those whose slow reactions or sensory impairments indicate accident risk?

Keeping the biological clock running smoothly How quickly people age depends in part on their health habits. As these members of the Young@Heart Chorus make clear, the more active people remain, the more vigor they retain. Here Jeanne Hatch sings solo as the chorus dances and provides backup vocals.

© Asia Kepka

■ **Alzheimer's disease** a progressive and irreversible brain disorder characterized by gradual deterioration of memory, reasoning, language, and, finally, physical functioning.

(Kempermann & others, 1998). And that may explain why active older adults tend to be mentally quick older adults, and why, across 20 studies, sedentary older adults randomly assigned to aerobic exercise programs have exhibited enhanced memory and sharpened judgment (Colcombe & Kramer, 2003; Colcombe & others, 2004; Weuve & others, 2004). We are more likely to rust from disuse than to wear out from overuse. "Use it or lose it" is sound advice.

Dementia and Alzheimer's Disease

Some adults do, unfortunately, suffer a substantial loss of brain cells. Up to age 95, the incidence of mental disintegration doubles roughly every 5 years (**FIGURE 11.4**). A series of small strokes, a brain tumor, or alcoholism can progressively damage the brain, causing that mental erosion we call *dementia*. So, too, can the most feared of all brain ailments, **Alzheimer's disease,** which strikes 3 percent of the world's population by age 75. Alzheimer's symptoms are *not* the same as normal aging. (Occasionally forgetting where you laid the car keys is no cause for alarm; forgetting how to get home does suggest Alzheimer's.)

Alzheimer's destroys even the brightest of minds. First memory, then reasoning, deteriorates. Robert Sayre (1979) recalls his father shouting at his afflicted mother to "think harder," while his mother, confused, embarrassed, on the verge of tears, randomly searched the house for lost objects. As Alzheimer's runs its course, after 5 to 20 years, the person becomes emotionally flat, then disoriented and disinhibited, then incontinent, and finally mentally vacant—a sort of living death, a mere body stripped of its humanity.

Underlying the symptoms of Alzheimer's is a loss of brain cells and deterioration of neurons that produce the neurotransmitter acetylcholine. Deprived of this vital chemical messenger, memory and thinking suffer. An autopsy reveals two telltale abnormalities in these acetylcholine-producing neurons: shriveled protein filaments in the cell body and plaques (globs of degenerating tissue) at the tips of neuron branches. In one line of research, scientists are working to develop drugs that will block proteins from aggregating into plaques (Ingram, 2003).

Researchers are gaining insights into the chemical, neural, and genetic roots of Alzheimer's. In people at risk for this disease, brain scans (**FIGURE 11.5**) reveal—before symptoms appear—both the telltale degeneration of critical brain cells and more diffuse brain activity while memorizing words, as if more exertion was required to achieve the same performance (Bookheimer & others, 2000; Fox & others, 2001). Physically active, nonobese people are

FIGURE 11.4
Incidence of dementia (mental disintegration) by age
Risk of dementia due to Alzheimer's disease or a series of strokes doubles about every 5 years in later life. (From Jorm & others, 1987, based on 22 studies in industrial nations.)

Alan Oddie/PhotoEdit

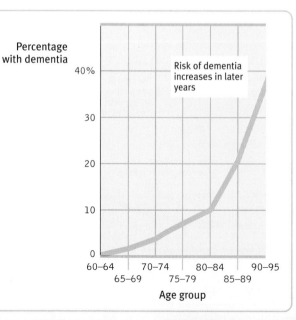

Percentage with dementia

Risk of dementia increases in later years

40%

30

20

10

0

60–64 | 70–74 | 80–84 | 90–95
65–69 | 75–79 | 85–89

Age group

Susan Bookheimer

FIGURE 11.5
Predicting Alzheimer's disease
During a memory test, MRI scans of the brains of people at risk for Alzheimer's (left) revealed more intense activity (yellow, followed by orange and red) when compared with normal brains (right). As brain scans and genetic tests make it possible to identify those likely to suffer Alzheimer's, would you want to be tested? At what age?

less at risk for Alzheimer's (Abbott & others, 2004; Gustafson & others, 2003; Marx, 2005). So, too, are those with an active, challenged mind—often the mind of an educated, active reader (Wilson & Bennett, 2003). As with muscles, so with the brain: Those who use it, less often lose it.

Cognitive Development

Among the most controversial questions in the study of the human life span is whether adult cognitive abilities, such as memory, creativity, and intelligence, parallel the gradually accelerating decline of physical abilities.

Aging and Memory

OBJECTIVE 11-3 | Assess the impact of aging on recall and recognition in adulthood.

As we age, we remember some things well. Looking back in later life, people most vividly recall not only recent happenings but also their experiences in life's second two decades (Conway & others, 2005; Rubin & others, 1998). Asked to recall the one or two most important events over the last half-century, they tend to name events from their teens or twenties. Whatever one experienced around this stage of life—World War II, the civil rights movement, the Vietnam war, or the events of 9/11—becomes pivotal (Pillemer, 1998; Schuman & Scott, 1989). Our teens and twenties are also the time when we experience so many of life's memorable "firsts"—first date, first job, first going to college, first meeting your parents-in-law.

For some types of learning and remembering, early adulthood is indeed a peak time. In one experiment, Thomas Crook and Robin West (1990) invited 1205 people to learn some names. Fourteen videotaped people said their names, using a common format: "Hi, I'm Larry." Then the same individuals reappeared and said, for example, "I'm from Philadelphia"—thus providing a visual and voice cue for remembering the person's name. As **FIGURE 11.6** shows, everyone remembered more names after a second and third replay of the introductions, but younger adults consistently surpassed older adults in their name recall. Similar results appear in other studies. Within hours after Prime Minister Margaret Thatcher announced her resignation, young and old British people recalled how they heard the news. When asked again 11 months later, 90 percent of the younger group, but only 42 percent of the older group, told the same story (Cohen & others, 1994). Perhaps it is not surprising, then, that nearly two-thirds of people over age 40 say their memory is worse than it was 10 years ago (KRC, 2001).

But consider another experiment. David Schonfield and Betty-Anne Robertson (1966) asked adults of various ages to learn a list of 24 words. Without giving any clues, the researchers asked some to *recall* as many words as they could from the list, and others simply to *recognize* words, using multiple-choice questions. Again, younger

If you are within five years of 20, what experiences from your last year will you likely never forget? (This is the time of your life you may best remember when you are 50.)

FIGURE 11.6
Tests of recall
Recalling new names introduced once, twice, or three times is easier for younger adults than for older ones. (Data from Crook & West, 1990.)

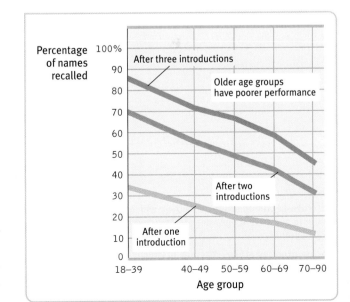

Percentage of names recalled

After three introductions

Older age groups have poorer performance

After two introductions

After one introduction

Age group

18–39   40–49   50–59   60–69   70–90

FIGURE 11.7
Recall and recognition in adulthood

In this experiment, the ability to *recall* new information declined during early and middle adulthood, but the ability to *recognize* new information did not. (From Schonfield & Robertson, 1966.)

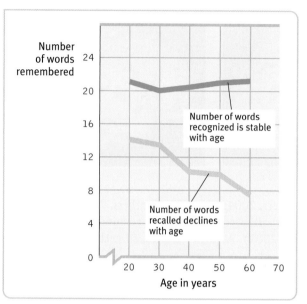

Number of words recognized is stable with age

Number of words recalled declines with age

Taking several pills several times each day can be a challenge for an older adult's declining prospective memory. The simple solution is an external aid: Putting each week's pills into a box that has slots for all the days and times removes confusion about whether one has taken the pills or only thought about doing so. (Pharmacies offer these.)

■ **cross-sectional study** a study in which people of different ages are compared with one another.

■ **longitudinal study** research in which the same people are restudied and retested over a long period.

adults had better recall (**FIGURE 11.7**). But the researchers found no similar memory decline with age on the recognition tests. Tests also reveal that, unless given a jolt of caffeine, recognition memory is better for older adults early in the day rather than late (May & others, 1993; Ryan & others, 2002). So, how well older people remember depends: Are they being asked simply to *recognize* what they have tried to memorize (minimal decline) or to *recall* it without clues (greater decline)?

Forgetting seems also to depend on the type of information you are trying to remember. If asked to recall meaningless information—nonsense syllables or unimportant events—then the older you are, the more errors you are likely to make. If the information is meaningful, older people's rich web of existing knowledge will help them to catch it, though they may take longer than younger adults to *produce* the words and things they know (Burke & Shafto, 2004). (Quick-thinking game show winners are usually younger to middle-age adults.) Older people's capacity to learn and remember skills also decline less than their verbal recall (Graf, 1990; Labouvie-Vief & Schell, 1982; Perlmutter, 1983).

Prospective memory ("Remember to. . .") remains strong when events help trigger memories, as when walking by a convenience store triggers a ". . . pick up milk" memory. Time-based tasks ("Remember the 3 P.M. meeting") prove somewhat more challenging for older people. Habitual tasks, such as remembering to take medications three times daily, can be especially challenging, report Gilles Einstein, Mark McDaniel, and their colleagues (1990, 1995, 1998). To minimize problems associated with declining prospective memory, older adults rely more on time management and on using reminder cues, such as notes to themselves (Henry & others, 2004).

Those who study our capacity to learn and remember are aware of one other important complication: Right through our later years, we continue to diverge. Twenty-year-olds differ widely in their abilities to learn and remember, but 70-year-olds differ much more. Some 70-year-olds perform below nearly all 20-year-olds; other 70-year-olds match or outdo the average 20-year-old.

Aging and Intelligence

OBJECTIVE **11-4** | Summarize the contributions of cross-sectional and longitudinal studies to our understanding of the normal effects of aging on adult intelligence.

What happens to our broader intellectual powers as we age? Do they gradually decline, as does our ability to recall new material? Or do they remain constant, as does our ability to recognize meaningful material? The evolving answer to this question makes an interesting research story, one that illustrates psychology's self-correcting process (Woodruff-Pak, 1989).

Phase I: Cross-Sectional Evidence for Intellectual Decline

In **cross-sectional studies,** researchers test and compare people of various ages. When giving intelligence tests to representative samples of people, researchers consistently find that older adults give fewer correct answers than do younger adults. David Wechsler (1972), creator of the most widely used adult intelligence test, therefore concluded that "the decline of mental ability with age is part of the general [aging] process of the organism as a whole."

For a long time, this rather dismal view of mental decline went unchallenged. Many corporations established mandatory retirement policies, assuming the companies would benefit by replacing aging workers with younger, presumably more capable, employees. As everyone "knew," you couldn't teach an old dog new tricks.

Phase II: Longitudinal Evidence for Intellectual Stability

After colleges began giving intelligence tests to entering students about 1920, several psychologists saw their chance to study intelligence **longitudinally**—retesting the same people over a period of years. What they expected to find was a decrease in intelligence after about age 30 (Schaie & Geiwitz, 1982). What they actually found was a surprise: Until late in life, intelligence remained stable (**FIGURE 11.8**). On some tests, it even increased.

How then are we to account for the findings from the cross-sectional studies? In retrospect, researchers saw the problem. When cross-sectional studies compared 70-year-olds and 30-year-olds, it compared people not only of two different ages but of two different eras. It compared generally less-educated people (born, say, in the early 1900s) with better-educated people (born after 1950), people raised in large families with people raised in smaller families, people growing up in less affluent families with people raised in more affluent families.

According to this more optimistic view, the myth that intelligence sharply declines with age is laid to rest. As everyone "knows," given good health you're never too old to learn. At age 70, John Rock developed the birth control pill. At age 78, Grandma Moses took up painting, and she was still painting after age 100. At age 81—and 17 years from the end of his college football coaching career—Amos Alonzo Stagg was named coach of the year. At age 89, architect Frank Lloyd Wright designed New York City's Guggenheim Museum.

Phase III: It All Depends

But the controversy continues. For one thing, longitudinal studies have their own pitfalls. Those who survive to the end of longitudinal studies may be bright, healthy people whose intelligence is least likely to decline. (Perhaps people who died younger and were removed from the study had declining intelligence.) Adjusting for the loss of subjects, as did a study following more than 2000 people over 75 in Cambridge, England, reveals a steeper intelligence decline. This is especially so as people age after 85 (Brayne & others, 1999).

Research is further complicated by the finding that intelligence is not a single trait, but rather a number of distinct skills and abilities. Intelligence tests that assess speed of thinking may place older adults at a disadvantage because of their slower neural mechanisms for processing information. Meeting old friends on the street, names rise to the mind's surface more slowly—"like air bubbles in molasses," says David Lykken (1999). But slower need not mean less intelligent. When given tests that assess general vocabulary, knowledge, and ability to integrate information, older adults generally fare well (Craik, 1986). Older Canadians surpass younger Canadians at answering questions such as, "Which province was once called New Caledonia?" In four studies, the highest average performance on *New York Times* crossword puzzles (given 15 minutes to fill in words) was achieved by adults in their fifties, sixties, and seventies (**FIGURE 11.9** on the next page).

German researcher Paul Baltes and his colleagues (1993, 1994, 1999) have developed "wisdom" tests that assess "expert knowledge about life in general and good judgment and advice about how to conduct oneself in the face of complex, uncertain circumstances." Their results suggest that older adults more than hold their own on such tests. Thus, despite 30-year-olds' quick-thinking smarts, we usually select older

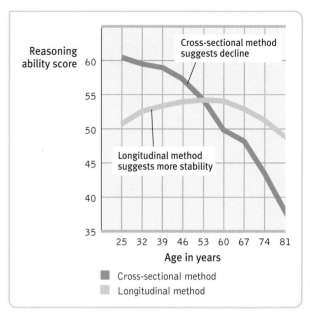

FIGURE 11.8
Cross-sectional versus longitudinal testing of intelligence at various ages
In this test of one type of verbal intelligence (inductive reasoning), the cross-sectional method produced declining scores with age. The longitudinal method (in which the same people were retested over a period of years) produced a slight *rise* in scores well into adulthood. (Adapted from Schaie, 1994.)

"In youth we learn, in age we understand."
Marie Von Ebner-Eschenbach, *Aphorisms*, 1883

FIGURE 11.9
Word power grows with age
In four studies summarized by Timothy Salthouse (2004), older crossword puzzle players excelled when given 15 minutes with a *New York Times* puzzle.

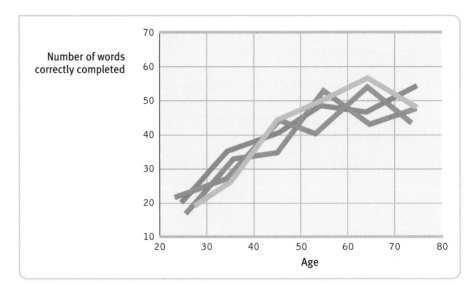

people to be president of the company, the college, or the country. Age is sage. To paraphrase one 60-year-old, "Forty years ago I had a great memory, but I was a fool."

So, whether intelligence increases or decreases with age depends on the type of intellectual performance we measure. **Crystallized intelligence**—one's accumulated knowledge as reflected in vocabulary and analogies tests—*increases* up to old age. **Fluid intelligence**—one's ability to reason speedily and abstractly, as when solving novel logic problems—*decreases* slowly up to age 75 or so, then more rapidly, especially after age 85 (Cattell, 1963; Horn, 1982). We can see this pattern in the intelligence scores of a national sample of adults. After adjustments for education, verbal scores (reflecting crystallized intelligence) held relatively steady from ages 20 to 74. Nonverbal, puzzle-solving intelligence declined. Thus, Denise Park and her colleagues (2002) confirm, with age we lose and we win (**FIGURE 11.10**). We lose recall memory and processing speed, but we gain vocabulary and knowledge.

FIGURE 11.10
The downs and ups of aging
Using a variety of reliable measures of processing capacity (such as speed of processing, working memory, and long-term memory) and world knowledge (such as vocabulary), Denise Park and her colleagues (2002) consistently illustrated that with age, our processing capacity declines but our vocabulary and general knowledge increase.

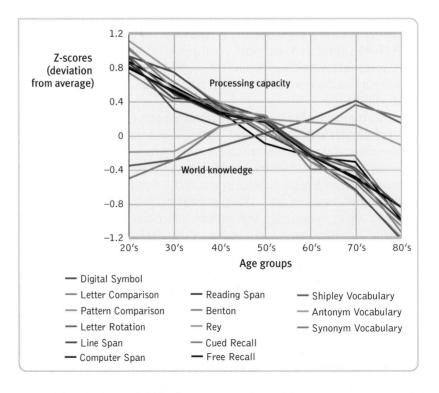

These cognitive differences help explain why mathematicians and scientists produce much of their most creative work during their late twenties or early thirties, whereas those in literature, history, and philosophy tend to produce their best work in their forties, fifties, and beyond, after accumulating more knowledge (Simonton, 1988, 1990). For example, poets (who depend on fluid intelligence) reach their peak output earlier than prose authors (who need a deeper knowledge reservoir), a finding observed in every major literary tradition, for both living and dead languages. So, intellectual performance can either increase or decrease with age, depending on what we assess and how we assess it.

Social Development

Many differences between younger and older adults are created not by the physical and cognitive changes that accompany aging but by life events associated with family relationships and work. A new job means new relationships, new expectations, and new demands. Marriage brings the joy of intimacy and the stress of merging your life with another's. The birth of a child introduces responsibilities and significantly alters your life focus. The death of a loved one creates an irreplaceable loss and a need to reaffirm your own life. Do these normal events of adult life shape a predictable sequence of life changes?

Adulthood's Ages and Stages

OBJECTIVE 11-5 | Explain why the path of adult development need not be tightly linked to one's chronological age.

As people enter their forties, they undergo a transition to middle adulthood, a time when they realize that life will soon be mostly behind them instead of ahead of them. Some psychologists have argued that for many the *midlife transition* is a crisis, a time of great struggle, of regret, or even of feeling struck down by life. The popular image of the midlife crisis is an early-forties man who forsakes his family for a younger girlfriend and a hot sports car. But the fact—reported by large samples of people—is that unhappiness, job dissatisfaction, marital dissatisfaction, divorce, anxiety, and suicide do *not* surge during the early forties (Hunter & Sundel, 1989; Mroczek & Kolarz, 1998). Divorce, for example, is most common among those in their twenties, suicide among those in their seventies and eighties. One study of emotional instability in nearly 10,000 men and women found "not the slightest evidence" that distress peaks anywhere in the midlife age range (**FIGURE 11.11**). For the 1 in 4 adults who does report experiencing a life crisis, the trigger is not age, but a major event such as illness, divorce, or job loss (Lachman, 2004).

There is another reason skeptics question age-linked stages such as the "midlife crisis." The **social clock**—the cultural prescription of "the right time" to leave home, get a job, marry, have children, and retire—varies from culture to culture and era to era. In Jordan, 40 percent of brides are in their teens; in Hong Kong, only 3 percent are (United Nations,

crystallized intelligence one's accumulated knowledge and verbal skills; tends to increase with age.

fluid intelligence one's ability to reason speedily and abstractly; tends to decrease during late adulthood.

social clock the culturally preferred timing of social events such as marriage, parenthood, and retirement.

"Midway in the journey of our life I found myself in a dark wood, for the straight way was lost."

Dante, *The Divine Comedy,* 1314

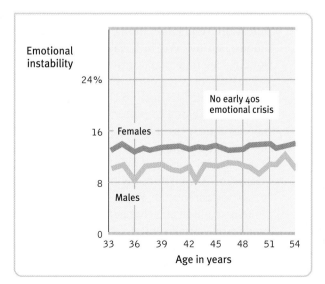

FIGURE **11.11**
Early forties midlife crises?
Among 10,000 people responding to a national health survey, there was no early forties increase in emotional instability ("neuroticism") scores. (From McCrae & Costa, 1990.)

Resetting the social clock
The social clock once prescribed that university graduation should occur around age 22. Today, more students are earning degrees at other ages.

"The important events of a person's life are the products of chains of highly improbable occurrences."

Joseph Traub, "Traub's Law," 2003

"One can live magnificently in this world if one knows how to work and how to love."

Leo Tolstoy, 1856

Love
Intimacy, attachment, commitment—love by whatever name—is central to healthy and happy adulthood.

1992). In Western Europe, fewer than 10 percent of men over 65 remain in the work force, as do 16 percent in the United States, 36 percent in Japan, and 69 percent in Mexico (Davies & others, 1991). And the once rigid sequence for Western women—of student to worker to wife to at-home mom to worker again—has loosened. Contemporary women occupy these roles in any order or all at once.

Life Events and Chance Encounters

For women and men, life events—marriage, parenthood, vocational changes, divorce, nest emptying, relocation, and retirement—mark transitions to new life stages whenever they occur, and they are occurring at increasingly unpredictable ages. The social clock still ticks, but people feel freer about being out of sync with it.

Even chance events can have lasting significance because they often deflect us down one road rather than another (Bandura, 1982). Romantic attraction, for example, is often influenced by chance encounters. Albert Bandura (2004) recalls the ironic true story of a book editor who came to one of his lectures on the "Psychology of Chance Encounters and Life Paths"—and ended up marrying the woman who happened to sit next to him.

Consider one study of identical twins and their spouses. Twins, especially identical twins, make similar choices of friends, clothes, vacations, jobs, and so on. So, if your identical twin became engaged to someone, wouldn't you (being in so many ways the same as your twin) expect to also feel attracted to this person? Surprisingly, only half the identical twins recalled really liking their co-twin's selection, and only 5 percent said, "I could have fallen for my twin's partner." Researchers David Lykken and Auke Tellegen (1993) surmise that romantic love is rather like ducklings' imprinting: Given repeated exposure to someone after childhood, you may form a bond (infatuation) with almost any available person who has a roughly similar background and level of attractiveness and who reciprocates your affections.

Adulthood's Commitments

OBJECTIVE 11-6 | Discuss the importance of love, marriage, and children in adulthood, and comment on the contribution of one's work to feelings of self-satisfaction.

Two basic aspects of our lives do, however, dominate adulthood. Erik Erikson called them *intimacy* (forming close relationships) and *generativity* (being productive and supporting future generations). Researchers have chosen various terms—*affiliation* and *achievement*, *attachment* and *productivity*, *commitment* and *competence*. Sigmund Freud (1935) put it most simply: The healthy adult, he said, is one who can *love* and *work*.

Love

Across time and place, human societies have nearly always included relatively monogamous pairing. We flirt, fall in love, and commit—one person at a time. "Pair-bonding is a trademark of the human animal," observed anthropologist Helen Fisher (1993). From an evolutionary perspective, the arrangement makes sense: Parents who cooperated to nurture their children to maturity were more likely to have their genes passed along to posterity than parents who didn't. Rivaling or exceeding adult pair-bonding is the love of parent for child. "I feel an overwhelming love for my children unlike anything I feel for anyone else," agreed 93 percent of American mothers in a national survey (Erickson & Aird, 2005). Many fathers feel the same. A few weeks after the birth of my first child I was suddenly struck by a realization: "So *this* is how my parents felt about me!"

Research indicates that adult bonds of love are most satisfying and enduring when marked by a similarity of interests and values, a sharing of emotional and material support, and intimate self-disclosure. Marriage bonds are also likely to last when couples marry after age 20 and are well educated. Compared with their counterparts of 40 years ago, people in Western countries *are* better educated and marrying later. Yet, ironically, they are twice as likely to divorce. This partly reflects women's lessened economic dependence and men and women's rising expectations. We now hope not only for an enduring bond, but also for a mate who is a wage earner, caregiver, intimate friend, and warm and responsive lover. To judge from the divorce rate—both Canada and the United States now have about one divorce for every two marriages—marriage has become a union that often defies management (Bureau of the Census, 2004). In Europe, divorce is only slightly less common.

Might test-driving life together in a "trial marriage" minimize divorce risk? In a 2001 Gallup survey of American twenty-somethings, 62 percent thought it would (Whitehead & Popenoe, 2001). In reality, studies in Europe, Canada, and the United States have repeatedly found that those who cohabited before marriage actually had *higher* rates of divorce and marital dysfunction than those who did not (Dush & others, 2003; Popenoe & Whitehead, 2002). The risk of poor marital outcomes appears greatest for those who cohabit prior to engagement (Kline & others, 2004). Cohabiters tend to be initially less committed to the ideal of enduring marriage, and they become even less marriage-supporting while cohabiting.

Nonetheless, the institution of marriage endures. Worldwide, reports the United Nations, 9 in 10 heterosexual adults marry (Lowy, 2000). In Western countries, 3 in 4 who divorce will remarry—and their second marriages will be virtually as happy as the average first marriage (Vemer & others, 1989). They are not alone. Surveys of more than 40,000 Americans since 1972 reveal that 40 percent of married adults, though only 23 percent of unmarried adults, report being "very happy." Lesbian couples, too, report greater well-being than those who are alone (Wayment & Peplau, 1995). Marriage is a predictor not only of happiness but also of health, sexual satisfaction, and income. Moreover, neighborhoods with high marriage rates typically have low rates of social pathologies such as crime, delinquency, and emotional disorders among children (Myers & Scanzoni, 2005).

Marriages that last are not always devoid of conflict. Some couples fight but also shower one another with affection. Other couples never raise their voices yet also seldom praise one another or nuzzle. Both styles can last. After observing the interactions of 2000 couples, John Gottman (1994) reported one indicator of marital success: at least a five-to-one ratio of positive to negative interactions. Stable marriages provide five times more instances of smiling, touching, complimenting, and laughing than of sarcasm, criticism, and insults. So, if you want to predict which newlyweds will stay together, do not pay attention to how passionately they are in love. The couples who make it are more often those who restrain putting down their partners. To prevent a cancerous negativity, successful couples learn to fight fair (to state feelings without insulting) and to steer conflict away from chaos with comments like "I know it's not your fault" or "I'll just be quiet for a moment and listen."

Often, love bears children. For most people, the most enduring of life changes, having a child, is a happy event. However, when children begin to absorb time, money, and emotional energy, satisfaction with the marriage itself may decline. This is especially likely among employed women who, more than they expected, carry the traditional burden of doing the chores at home. Putting effort into creating an equitable relationship can thus pay double dividends: a more satisfying marriage, which breeds better parent-child relations (Erel & Burman, 1995).

Although love bears children, children eventually leave home. This departure is a significant event, and a sometimes difficult separation. But national surveys reveal that the empty nest is for most people a happy place (Adelmann & others, 1989; Glenn, 1975). Compared with middle-aged women with children at home, those living in an empty nest report greater happiness and greater enjoyment of their marriage. Many parents experience what sociologists Lynn White and John Edwards (1990) call a "postlaunch honeymoon," especially if they maintain close relationships with their children.

What do you think? Does marriage correlate with happiness because marital support and intimacy breed happiness, because happy people more often marry and stay married, or both?

If you have left home, did your parents suffer the "empty nest syndrome"—a feeling of distress focusing on a loss of purpose and relationship? Did they mourn the lost joy of listening for you in the wee hours of Saturday morning? Or did they seem to discover a new freedom, relaxation, and (if still married) renewed satisfaction with their own relationship?

Job satisfaction and life satisfaction
Work can provide us with a sense of identity and competence and opportunities for accomplishment. Perhaps this is why challenging and interesting occupations enhance people's happiness.

Work

For many adults, the answer to "Who are you?" depends a great deal on the answer to "What do you do?" Was Freud right that work, including a career, contributes to self-fulfillment and life satisfaction? It does for those who enter the working world with a positive disposition that helps engender success which, over time, reinforces a positive approach to life. "Alienated and hostile adolescents," on the other hand, tend to have less satisfying work experiences that undermine their achieving a positive transition into the working world (Roberts & others, 2003).

Researchers have also studied the work–satisfaction relationship by comparing the roughly equal numbers of North American women who are or are not employed. From their studies at the Wellesley College Center for Research on Women, Grace Baruch and Rosaline Barnett (1986) concluded that what matters is not which roles a woman occupies—paid worker, wife, and/or mother—but the quality of her experience in those roles.

For women and men, choosing a career path is difficult, especially in today's changing work environment. During the first two years of college or university, few students can predict their later careers. Most shift from their initially intended majors, many find their postcollege employment in fields not directly related to their majors, and most will change careers (Rothstein, 1980). In the end, happiness is about having work that fits your interests and provides you with a sense of competence and accomplishment. And for those who choose to marry, it is having a partner who is a close, supportive companion and who sees you as special, and—for some—it includes having loving children whom you like and feel proud of.

Well-Being Across the Life Span

OBJECTIVE 11-7 | Describe trends in people's life satisfaction across the life span.

We're all aging. This moment marks the oldest you have ever been and the youngest you will henceforth be. To live is to grow older. That means we all can look back with satisfaction or regret, and forward with hope or dread. When people are asked what they would have done differently if they could relive their lives, their most common answer is "taken my education more seriously and worked harder at it" (Kinnier & Metha, 1989). How will you look back on your life 10 years from now? Are you making choices that someday you will recollect with satisfaction? Other regrets—"I should have told my father I loved him," "I regret that I never went to Europe"—also focus less on mistakes made than on the things one *failed* to do (Gilovich & Medvec, 1995).

From early adulthood to midlife, people typically experience a strengthening sense of identity, confidence, and self-esteem (Miner-Rubino & others, 2004; Robins & Trzesniewski, 2005). In later life, challenges arise: Income shrinks, work is often taken away, the body deteriorates, recall fades, energy wanes, family members and friends die or move away, and the great enemy, death, looms ever closer. Small wonder that many presume the over-65 years to be the worst of times (Freedman, 1978). But they are not, as Ronald Inglehart (1990) discovered when he amassed interviews conducted during the 1980s with representative samples of nearly 170,000 people in 16 nations. Older people report as much happiness and satisfaction with life as younger people do (**FIGURE 11.12**).

If anything, positive feelings grow after midlife and negative feelings subside (Charles & others, 2001; Mroczek, 2001). Older adults increasingly use words that convey positive emotions (Pennebaker & Stone, 2003). They attend less and less to negative information. For example, they are slower than younger adults to perceive negative faces (Mather & Carstensen, 2003). Their amygdala, a neural processing center for emotions, shows diminishing activity in response to negative events while maintaining its responsiveness to positive events (Mather & others, 2004). Moreover, the bad feelings we associate with negative events fade faster than do the good feelings we associate with positive events (Walker & others, 2003). This contributes to most older people's sense that life, on balance, has been mostly good. Given that growing older is an outcome of living (an outcome nearly all of us prefer to early dying), the positivity of later life is comforting (**FIGURE 11.13**).

The astonishing stability of well-being across the life span obscures some interesting age-related emotional differences. As the years go by, feelings mellow (Costa & others, 1987; Diener & others, 1986). Highs become less high, lows less low. Thus, although the *average* feeling level may remain stable, with age we find ourselves less often feeling excited, intensely proud, and on top of the world, but also less often depressed. Compliments provoke less elation and criticisms less despair, as both become merely additional feedback atop a mountain of accumulated praise and blame. Psychologists Mihaly Csikszentmihalyi and Reed Larson (1984) mapped people's emotional terrain by periodically signaling them with electronic beepers to report their current activities and feelings. They found that teenagers typically come down from elation or up from gloom in less than an hour. Adult moods are less extreme but more enduring. For most people, old age offers less intense joy but greater contentment and increased spirituality, especially for those who remain socially engaged (Harlow & Cantor, 1996; Wink & Dillon, 2002). As we age, life becomes less an emotional roller coaster, more like paddling a canoe.

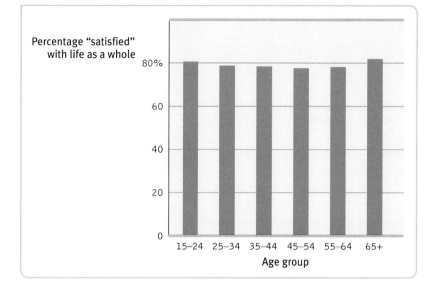

FIGURE 11.12
Age and life satisfaction
With the tasks of early adulthood behind them, many older adults have more time to pursue personal interests. No wonder their satisfaction with life remains high, and may even rise if they are healthy and active. As this graph based on multinational surveys shows, age differences in life satisfaction are trivial. (Data from Inglehart, 1990.)

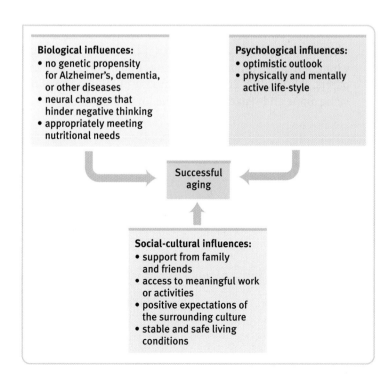

FIGURE 11.13
Biopsychosocial influences on successful aging
Numerous biological, psychological, and social-cultural factors affect the way we age. With the right genes, we have a good chance of aging successfully if we maintain a positive outlook and stay mentally and physically active as well as connected to family and friends in the community.

Death and Dying

OBJECTIVE 11-8 | Describe the range of reactions to the death of a loved one.

Most of us will suffer and cope with the deaths of relatives and friends. Usually, the most difficult separation is from one's spouse—a loss suffered by five times more women than men. When, as usually happens, death comes at an expected late-life time, the grieving may be relatively short-lived. (**FIGURE 11.14** shows the typical emotions before and after a spouse's death.) Grief is especially severe when the death of a loved one comes suddenly and before its expected time on the social clock. The accidental death of a child or the sudden illness that claims a 45-year-old life partner may trigger a year or more of mourning flooded with memories, eventually subsiding to a mild depression that sometimes continues for several years (Lehman & others, 1987). For some, the loss is unbearable. One study, following more than 1 million Danes over the last half of the twentieth century, found that more than 17,000 people had suffered the death of a child under 18. In the five years following that death, their 3 percent rate of first psychiatric hospitalization was 67 percent higher than the rate recorded for parents who had not lost a child (Li & others, 2005).

AIDS, which so often strikes down people in midlife and younger, has left countless grief-stricken partners experiencing bereavement, as well as millions of orphaned children. In 2004, the disease killed more than 3 million people worldwide (UNAIDS, 2005). In sub-Saharan Africa, which is home to 1 in 10 of the world's people and 6 in 10 of those carrying the HIV virus, the resulting death and treatment needs are sapping social resources. In nine African countries, life expectancy at birth has dropped below 40 years (UNAIDS, 2004).

The normal range of reactions to a loved one's death is wider than most suppose. Some cultures encourage public weeping and wailing; others hide grief. Within any culture, some individuals grieve more intensely and openly. Contrary to popular misconceptions, however,

- those who express the strongest grief immediately do not purge their grief more quickly (Bonanno & Kaltman, 1999; Wortman & Silver, 1989).
- for most people, bereavement therapy and self-help groups do little to enhance the healing power of time and supportive friends. Grieving spouses who talk often with others or who receive grief counseling adjust no better than those who grieve more privately (Bonanno, 2001, 2004; Genevro, 2003; Stroebe & others, 2001, 2002, 2005). No amount of talking can eliminate the feeling of being alone and separated from the loved one.

"The best thing about being 100 is *no peer pressure*."

Lewis W. Kuester, 2005, on turning 100

Death comes too young for too many in AIDS-ravaged Africa

"Do not go gentle into that good night,
Old age should burn and rave at close of day;
Rage, rage against the dying of the light."

Dylan Thomas, "Do not go gentle into that good night," 1952, poem written to his father, who lay dying peacefully

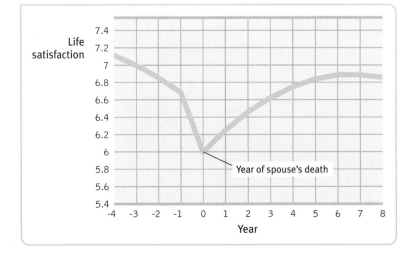

FIGURE **11.14**
Life satisfaction before, during the year of, and after a spouse's death Richard Lucas and his collaborators (2003) examined longitudinal annual surveys of more than 30,000 Germans. The researchers identified 513 married people who experienced the death of a spouse and did not remarry. They found that life satisfaction began to dip during the prewidowhood year, dropped significantly during the year of the spouse's death, and then eventually rebounded to nearly the earlier level. (*Source:* Richard Lucas.)

- terminally ill and bereaved people do not go through predictable stages, such as denial, anger, and so forth (Nolen-Hoeksema & Larson, 1999). Given similar losses, some people grieve hard and long, others more lightly and briefly.

We can be grateful for the waning of death-denying attitudes. Facing death with dignity and openness helps people complete the life cycle with a sense of life's meaningfulness and unity—the sense that their existence has been good and that life and death are parts of an ongoing cycle. Although death may be unwelcome, life itself can be affirmed even at death. This is especially so for people who review their lives not with despair but with what Erik Erikson called a sense of *integrity*—a feeling that one's life has been meaningful and worthwhile.

> "Consider, friend, as you pass by, as you are now, so once was I. As I am now, you too shall be. Prepare, therefore, to follow me."
>
> Scottish tombstone epitaph

Reflections on Two Major Developmental Issues

OBJECTIVE 11-9 | Summarize current views on continuity versus stages and stability versus change in lifelong development.

Any survey of developmental psychology must consider three pervasive issues. The first—how development is steered by the interaction of genes and experience—recurs throughout this text. But let's stop now and consider the second issue, whether development is a gradual, continuous process or a series of discrete stages, and the third, whether development is characterized more by stability over time or by change.

Continuity and Stages

Adults are vastly different from infants. But do they differ as a giant redwood differs from its seedling—a difference created by gradual, cumulative growth? Or do they differ as a butterfly differs from a caterpillar—a difference of distinct stages?

Generally speaking, researchers who emphasize experience and learning see development as a slow, continuous shaping process. Those who emphasize biological maturation tend to see development as a sequence of genetically predisposed stages or steps: Although progress through the various stages may be quick or slow, everyone passes through the stages in the same order.

Are there clear-cut stages of psychological development, as there are physical stages such as walking before running? The stage theories of Jean Piaget on cognitive development, Lawrence Kohlberg on moral development, and Erik Erikson on psychosocial development propose that such stages do exist. But some research casts doubt on the idea that life proceeds through neatly defined, age-linked stages. Young children have some abilities Piaget attributed to later stages. Kohlberg's work reflected a worldview characteristic of educated males in individualistic cultures and emphasized thinking over acting. Adult life does not progress through the fixed, predictable series of steps Erikson envisioned.

Nevertheless, the concept of stage remains useful. The human brain does experience growth spurts during childhood and puberty that correspond roughly to Piaget's stages (Thatcher & others, 1987). And stage theories contribute a developmental perspective on the whole life span, by suggesting how people of one age think and act differently when they arrive at a later age.

Stability and Change

This leads us to the second question: Over time, are people's personalities consistent, or do they change? If reunited with a long-lost grade school friend, would you instantly recognize that "it's the same old Andy"? Or does a person during one period of life seem like a different person at a later period?

TOO MUCH COFFEE MAN BY SHANNON WHEELER

LIFE:

PLAY, SCHOOL, PLAY, SCHOOL, PLAY, SCHOOL, PLAY, SCHOOL, FIRST LOVE, BRIEF HAPPINESS, BREAK UP, REGRET, SCHOOL, SCHOOL, SCHOOL, SCHOOL, SCHOOL, SCHOOL, SCHOOL, SCHOOL, SCHOOL, SCHOOL, SCHOOL, SCHOOL, SCHOOL, SCHOOL, PLAY, WORK, PLAY, WORK, PLAY, WORK, PLAY, WORK, IDEALISM, EFFORT, REJECTION, FAILURE, WORK, EFFORT, FAILURE, COMPROMISE, WORK, WORK, WORK, WORK, WORK, WORK, PLAY, COMMITMENT, WORK, WORK, WORK, WORK, WORK, WORK, PLAY, WORK, WORK, WORK, WORK, WORK, WORK, WORK, WORK, PLAY, WORK, WORK, WORK, WORK, WORK, WORK, WORK, WORK, PLAY, WORK, WORK, WORK, WORK, WORK, WORK, WORK, WORK, PLAY, WORK, WORK, WORK, WORK, WORK, WORK, WORK, WORK, PLAY, WORK, WORK, WORK, WORK, WORK, WORK, WORK, WORK, PLAY, WORK, WORK, WORK, WORK, WORK, WORK, WORK, WORK, PLAY, WORK, WORK, WORK, WORK, WORK, WORK, WORK, WORK, PLAY, WORK, WORK, WORK, WORK, WORK, WORK, WORK, WORK, PLAY, WORK, WORK, WORK, WORK, WORK, WORK, WORK, WORK, PLAY, WORK, WORK, WORK, WORK, WORK, WORK, WORK, WORK, PLAY, WORK, WORK, WORK, WORK, WORK, WORK, WORK, WORK, PLAY, WORK, WORK, WORK, WORK, WORK, WORK, WORK, WORK, PLAY, RETIRE, PLAY, DIE.

©Shannon Wheeler

Stages of the life cycle

As adults grow older, there is continuity of self.

" At 70, I would say the advantage is that you take life more calmly. You know that 'this, too, shall pass'!"

Eleanor Roosevelt, 1954

Researchers who have followed lives through time have found evidence for both stability and change. There is continuity to personality and yet, happily for troubled children and adolescents, life is a process of becoming: The struggles of the present may be laying a foundation for a happier tomorrow. More specifically, researchers generally agree on the following points:

1. The first two years of life provide a poor basis for predicting a person's eventual traits (Kagan & others, 1978, 1998). Older children and adolescents also change. Although delinquent children have elevated rates of work problems, substance abuse, and crime, many confused and troubled children have blossomed into mature, successful adults (Moffitt & others, 2002; Roberts & others, 2001; Thomas & Chess, 1986). As people grow older, however, personality does gradually stabilize (Johnson & others, 2005; Vaidya & others, 2002).

2. Some characteristics, such as temperament, are more stable than others, such as social attitudes (Moss & Susman, 1980). When a research team led by Avshalom Caspi (2003) studied 1000 New Zealanders from age 3 to 26, they were struck by the consistency of temperament and emotionality across time. But attitudes, too, become more stable with age (Krosnick & Alwin, 1989). For most people, life goals, such as whether one seeks status, pleasure, or close relationships, also are quite stable (Roberts & others, 2004).

3. In some ways, we all change with age. Most shy, fearful toddlers begin opening up by age 4, and most people become calmer and more self-disciplined, agreeable, and self-confident in the years after adolescence (McCrae & Costa, 1994; Roberts & others, 2003). Conscientiousness increases especially during the twenties, and agreeableness during the thirties (Srivastava & others, 2003). Many a 20-year-old goof-off has matured into a 40-year-old business or cultural leader. Such changes can occur without changing a person's position *relative* to others of the same age. The hard-driving young adult may mellow by later life yet still be a relatively hard-driving senior citizen.

Finally, we should remember that life requires *both* stability and change. Stability enables us to depend on others, provides our identity, and motivates our concern for the healthy development of children. Change motivates our concerns about present influences, sustains our hope for a brighter future, and lets us adapt and grow with experience.

>> LEARNING OUTCOMES

Adulthood, and Reflections on Developmental Issues

OBJECTIVE 11-1 | Identify the major physical changes that occur in middle adulthood.

Muscular strength, reaction time, sensory abilities, and cardiac output begin to decline in the late twenties. Around age 50, menopause ends women's period of fertility, but they may continue to enjoy a satisfying sex life. Most women do not experience depression or other psychological problems with menopause. Men do not undergo a similar sharp drop in hormone levels or fertility.

OBJECTIVE 11-2 | Compare life expectancy in the mid-twentieth and early twenty-first centuries, and discuss changes in sensory abilities and health (including frequency of dementia) in older adults.

Worldwide, life expectancy has increased from 49 years in the mid-twentieth century to 67 in the early twenty-first century, and it exceeds 80 in some developed countries. Women outlive

men and outnumber men at most ages past early infancy. In late adulthood, especially after age 70, hearing, distance perception, and the sense of smell diminish, as do muscle strength, reaction time, and stamina. Life-threatening diseases such as cancer and pneumonia increase, but short-term ailments decrease. Neural processes slow, but physical exercise can stimulate the development of some new brain cells and connections. With age, the incidence of dementia increases, but dementia is not a normal part of the aging process.

OBJECTIVE 11-3 | Assess the impact of aging on recall and recognition in adulthood.

The ability to recall new information declines during early and middle adulthood, but the ability to recognize such information does not. Older adults recall meaningful information more easily than meaningless information. Prospective memory ("remember to . . .") remains strong when cues are available.

OBJECTIVE **11-4** | **Summarize the contributions of cross-sectional and longitudinal studies to our understanding of the normal effects of aging on adult intelligence.**

Cross-sectional studies (comparing people of different ages with one another) suggested that intelligence declines steadily after early adulthood, but this research failed to consider generational differences in education and other life experiences. *Longitudinal studies* (retesting the same people over a long period of time) suggested intelligence was stable until very late in life, but that research failed to account for the characteristics of those who dropped out of the studies. Today's view is that *fluid intelligence* (the ability to reason speedily and abstractly) declines in later life, but *crystallized intelligence* (accumulated knowledge and skills) does not.

OBJECTIVE **11-5** | **Explain why the path of adult development need not be tightly linked to one's chronological age.**

Adults do not pass through an orderly sequence of age-bound stages. Major events (such as divorce) or chance occurrences (such as meeting a future partner) tend to trigger life crises. The *social clock* (the cultural prescription of the "right time" for social events) varies from place to place and from time to time.

OBJECTIVE **11-6** | **Discuss the importance of love, marriage, and children in adulthood, and comment on the contribution of one's work to feelings of self-satisfaction.**

Commitment had survival value for our ancestors; parents who stayed together and raised children to a child-bearing age had a better chance of passing along their genes to posterity. Women's increased economic independence, and men's and women's increased expectations of acceptable qualities in a life partner, have contributed to rising divorce rates. Most people still expect to marry, and those who do tend to be happier than their single counterparts. The birth of a child is usually a welcome event but may strain a couple's financial and emotional resources. Settling into a career path is difficult and time-consuming, but work that gives a sense of competence and accomplishment also correlates with life satisfaction.

OBJECTIVE **11-7** | **Describe trends in people's life satisfaction across the life span.**

Well-being and people's feelings of satisfaction are stable across the life span. As we age, highs may be less high and lows less low, but the average level of satisfaction remains stable.

OBJECTIVE **11-8** | **Describe the range of reactions to the death of a loved one.**

There is no "normal" reaction or series of grief stages after the death of a loved one. Grief is most severe when the death is sudden or before its expected time, as in the death of a child. People who in old age achieve a sense of integrity, in Erikson's terms, may meet death by affirming that their own life was meaningful and worthwhile.

OBJECTIVE **11-9** | **Summarize current views on continuity versus stages and stability versus change in lifelong development.**

Researchers viewing development as a slow continuous process are generally those who emphasize experience and learning. Researchers who emphasize biological maturation see development as a series of genetically predisposed steps. Later studies have modified the stage theories of Piaget (cognitive development), Kohlberg (moral development), and Erikson (psychosocial development), but these theorists have enriched psychology by alerting us to ways people differ at various points in the life span. Lifelong development features both stability and change.

TERMS AND CONCEPTS TO REMEMBER

menopause, p. 11-2	crystallized intelligence, p. 11-10
Alzheimer's disease, p. 11-6	fluid intelligence, p. 11-10
cross-sectional study, p. 11-8	social clock, p. 11-11
longitudinal study, p. 11-9	

TEST YOURSELF

1. Research has shown that living together before marriage predicts an increased likelihood of future divorce. Can you imagine two possible explanations for this correlation?

2. What findings in psychology support the stage theory of development and the idea of stability in personality across the life span? What findings challenge these ideas?

(Answers in Appendix B.)

ASK YOURSELF

1. As you reflect on your last four years—four formative years if you are a young adult—what do you most regret? What do you feel best about?

2. Are you the same person you were as a preschooler? A 10-year-old? A mid-teen? How are you different? How are you the same?

>WEB

Multiple-choice *self-tests* and more may be found at www.worthpublishers.com/myers.

ANOTHER VOICE ON: SENSATION

HELEN KELLER (1880–1968), FROM "BEFORE THE SOUL DAWN"

Perhaps my sun shines not as yours. The colors that glorify my world, the blue of the sky, the green of the fields, may not correspond exactly with those you delight in; but they are none the less color to me. The sun does not shine for my physical eyes, nor does the lightning flash, nor do the trees turn green in the spring; but they have not therefore ceased to exist; any more than the landscape is annihilated when you turn your back on it.

I understand how scarlet can differ from crimson because I know the smell of an orange is not the smell of a grapefruit. I can also conceive that colors have shades, and guess what shades are. . . . Odors in certain grasses fade as real to my sense as certain colors do to yours in the sun. I make use of analogies like these to enlarge my conceptions of colors. Some analogies which I draw between qualities in surface and vibration, taste and smell, are drawn by others between sight, hearing, and touch. This fact encourages me to persevere, to try to bridge the gap between the eye and the hand.

Sensation and Perception

Meriwether Lewis, leader of the nineteenth-century Lewis and Clark expedition, was exploring ahead of his group. Startled by an aggressive grizzly bear charging out of the bush, Lewis jumped into a river to escape, and the bear withdrew. While traveling the 12 miles back to his group, the shaken Lewis found himself perceiving other animals as threatening, and he preemptively shot several. "It now seemed to me that all the beasts of the neighborhood had made a league to destroy me" (Larsen, 2004). Primed by his frightening encounter, Lewis was perceiving the world differently.

Two centuries later, Amadou Diallo, an unarmed West African immigrant, was approached by four New York City police officers on the stoop of his Bronx apartment complex. As he pulled his wallet and identification out of his pocket, the officers—apparently feeling threatened by their own previous encounters—mistook his wallet for a gun. Diallo, a street vendor, died in a hail of 41 bullets.

Some 2400 years ago, Plato rightly discerned the principle that these cases illustrate—that we perceive objects through our senses, with our mind.

Twenty-four hours a day, stimuli from the outside world bombard your body. Meanwhile, in a silent, cushioned, inner world, your brain floats in utter darkness. By itself, it sees nothing. It hears nothing. It feels nothing. This raises a question that predates psychology by thousands of years and helped inspire its beginnings more than a century ago: *How does the world out there get in?*

To modernize the question: How do we construct our representations of the external world? How do a campfire's flicker, crackle, and smoky scent activate neural connections? And how, from this living neurochemistry, do we create our conscious experience of the fire's motion and temperature, its aroma and beauty?

To represent the world in our head, we must transform physical energy from our environment into neural signals, a process traditionally called *sensation*. And we must interpret sensory information, a process traditionally called *perception*. In our everyday experiences, sensation and perception blend into one continuous process. In Modules 12 through 17, we slow down that process to study its parts.

In Modules 12 through 15, we start with the sensory receptors and work up to higher levels of processing. Psychologists refer to sensory analysis that starts at the entry level as *bottom-up processing*. Modules 16 and 17 focus on how our mind interprets what our senses detect. We construct perceptions drawing both on sensations coming bottom-up to the brain and on our experience and expectations, which psychologists call *top-down processing*.

Failures of perception may occur anywhere between sensory detection and perceptual interpretation. After losing a temporal lobe area essential to recognizing faces, patient "E.H." suffers from a condition called *prosopagnosia*. She has complete sensation but incomplete perception. She can sense visual information—indeed may accurately report the features of a face—yet she is unable to recognize it. Shown an unfamiliar face, she does not react. Shown a familiar face, her autonomic nervous system responds with measurable perspiration. Still, she hasn't a clue who the person is. Shown her own face in a mirror, she is again stumped. Because of her brain damage, she cannot process top-down—she cannot relate her stored knowledge to the sensory input.

M O D U L E

12

Introduction to Sensation and Perception

OBJECTIVE 12-1 | Contrast sensation and perception, and explain the difference between bottom-up and top-down processing.

To construct the outside world inside our heads we must detect physical energy from the environment and then encode it as neural signals (a process traditionally called **sensation**). We must also select, organize, and interpret our sensations (a process traditionally called **perception**). We not only sense raw sights and sounds, tastes and smells, we *perceive*. We hear not just a mix of pitches and rhythms but a child's cry, the traffic's hum, a symphony's crescendo. Our perceptions are affected by the biology of our sensory systems, but also by our previous experiences and cultural expectations. In transforming sensations into perceptions, *we* create the meaning (FIGURE **12.1**).

Our sensory and perceptual processes work together to help us sort out the complex images in the FIGURE **12.2** painting. Through **bottom-up processing**, which begins with our sense receptors, we detect the lines, angles, and colors that form the horse, rider, and surroundings. But we also apply **top-down processing**, drawing on our experience and expectations, when we consider the painting's title, notice the apprehensive expressions, and then direct our attention to aspects of the painting that will give those observations meaning.

We begin our introduction to sensation and perception with a look at some basic principles by which we experience the world.

FIGURE **12.1**
**Sensation and perception:
One continuous process**

FIGURE 12.2
Top-down and bottom-up processing: The Forest Has Eyes
(Detail, "The Forest Has Eyes" by Bev Doolittle © The Greenwich Workshop, Inc., Trumbull, CT.)

Thresholds

OBJECTIVE 12-2 | Distinguish between absolute and difference thresholds, and discuss whether we can sense stimuli below our absolute thresholds and be influenced by them.

We exist in a sea of energy. At this moment, you and I are being struck by x-rays and radio waves, ultraviolet and infrared light, and sound waves of very high and very low frequencies. To all of these we are blind and deaf. Other animals detect the world that lies beyond human experience (Hughes, 1999). Birds use their magnetic compass. Bats and dolphins locate prey with sonar (bouncing echoing sound off objects). On a cloudy day, bees navigate by detecting polarized light from an invisible (to us) sun.

The shades on our own senses are open just a crack, allowing us only a restricted awareness of this vast sea of energy. **Psychophysics** is the study of how this physical energy relates to our psychological experience. What stimuli can we detect? At what intensity? How sensitive are we to changing stimulation?

Absolute Thresholds

To some kinds of stimuli we are exquisitely sensitive. Standing atop a mountain on an utterly dark, clear night, most of us could see a candle flame atop another mountain 30 miles away. We could feel the wing of a bee falling on our cheek. We could even smell a single drop of perfume in a three-room apartment (Galanter, 1962).

Our awareness of these faint stimuli illustrates our **absolute thresholds**—the minimum stimulation necessary to detect a particular light, sound, pressure, taste, or odor 50 percent of the time. To test your absolute threshold for sounds, a hearing specialist would expose each of your ears to varying sound levels. For each tone, the test would define where half the time you correctly detect the sound and half the time you do not. For each of your senses, that 50-50 recognition point defines your absolute threshold.

■ **sensation** the process by which our sensory receptors and nervous system receive and represent stimulus energies from our environment.

■ **perception** the process of organizing and interpreting sensory information, enabling us to recognize meaningful objects and events.

■ **bottom-up processing** analysis that begins with the sensory receptors and works up to the brain's integration of sensory information.

■ **top-down processing** information processing guided by higher-level mental processes, as when we construct perceptions drawing on our experience and expectations.

■ **psychophysics** the study of relationships between the physical characteristics of stimuli, such as their intensity, and our psychological experience of them.

■ **absolute threshold** the minimum stimulation needed to detect a particular stimulus 50 percent of the time.

■ **signal detection theory** a theory predicting how and when we detect the presence of a faint stimulus ("signal") amid background stimulation ("noise"). Assumes there is no single absolute threshold and that detection depends partly on a person's experience, expectations, motivation, and level of fatigue.

■ **subliminal** below one's absolute threshold for conscious awareness.

■ **priming** the activation, often unconsciously, of certain associations, thus predisposing one's perception, memory, or response.

Signal Detection

Nature's sensory gifts suit each recipient's needs. They enable each organism to obtain the information it needs. Consider:

- A frog, which feeds on flying insects, has eyes with receptor cells that fire only in response to small, dark, moving objects. A frog could starve to death knee-deep in motionless flies. But let one zoom by and the frog's "bug detector" cells snap awake.
- A male silkworm moth has receptors so sensitive to the female sex-attractant odor that a single female need release only a billionth of an ounce per second to attract every male silkworm moth within a mile. That is why there continue to be silkworms.
- We are similarly designed to detect what are, for us, the important features of our environment. Our ears are most sensitive to sound frequencies that include human voice consonants and a baby's cry.

For people, detecting a weak stimulus, or signal, depends not only on the signal's strength (such as the hearing-test tone), but also on our psychological state—our experience, expectations, motivation, and alertness. **Signal detection theory** predicts when we will detect weak signals, measured as our ratio of "hits" to "false alarms." Signal detection theorists seek to understand why people respond differently to the same stimuli, and why the same person's reactions vary as circumstances change. Exhausted parents of a newborn will notice the faintest whimper from the cradle while failing to notice louder, unimportant sounds. Responsiveness also increases in a horror-filled wartime situation, where failure to detect an intruder may mean death. Mindful of many comrades' deaths, soldiers and police in Iraq probably became more likely to notice—and fire at—an almost imperceptible noise. With such heightened responsiveness come more false alarms, as when the American military fired on an approaching car that was rushing an Italian journalist to freedom, killing the Italian intelligence officer who had rescued her. In peacetime, when survival is not threatened, the same soldiers require a stronger signal before sensing danger.

Signal detection can also have life-or-death consequences when people are responsible for watching an airport scanner for weapons, monitoring patients from an intensive-care nursing station, or detecting radar blips. Studies have shown, for example, that people's ability to catch a faint signal diminishes after about 30 minutes. But this diminishing response depends on the task, on the time of day, and even on whether the participants periodically exercise (Warm & Dember, 1986). Experience matters, too. In one experiment, 10 hours of action video game playing—scanning for and instantly responding to any intrusion—increased novice players' signal detection skills (Green & Bavelier, 2003).

Try out this old riddle on a couple of friends. "You're driving a bus with 12 passengers. At your first stop, 6 passengers get off. At the second stop, 3 get off. At the third stop, 2 more get off but 3 new people get on. What color are the bus driver's eyes?" Do your friends detect the signal—who is the bus driver?—amid the accompanying noise?

Signal detection
How soon would you notice the radar blips of an approaching object? Fairly quickly if (1) you *expect* an attack, (2) it is *important* that you detect it, and (3) you are *alert*.

Carol Lee / Tony Stone Images

Subliminal Stimulation

In 1956, a national controversy erupted over a report (later shown to be false) that New Jersey movie audiences were unwittingly being influenced by imperceptible flashed messages to DRINK COCA-COLA and EAT POPCORN (Pratkanis, 1992).

Many years later, the controversy erupted anew. Rock recordings were said to contain "satanic messages" that could be heard if the recordings were played backward and that, even when played forward, could unconsciously persuade the unwitting listener (Vokey, 2002). Hoping to penetrate our unconscious, entrepreneurs offer audiotapes to help us lose weight, stop smoking, or improve our memories. These tapes contain soothing ocean sounds that mask unheard messages such as, "I am thin," "Smoke tastes bad," or "I do well on tests. I have total recall of information." Such claims make two assumptions: We can unconsciously sense **subliminal** (literally, "below threshold") stimuli, and without our awareness, these stimuli have extraordinary suggestive powers. Can we? Do they?

Can we sense stimuli below our absolute thresholds? In one sense, the answer is clearly yes. Remember that the "absolute" threshold is merely the point at which we detect a stimulus half the time (**FIGURE 12.3**). At or slightly below this threshold we will still detect the stimulus some of the time. The answer is yes in another sense, too. People who plead total ignorance when asked to make some perceptual judgment—for example, when deciding which of two very similar weights is heavier—usually beat chance. Sometimes we know more than we think we do.

Can we be affected by stimuli so weak as to be unnoticed? Under certain conditions, the answer is again yes. An invisible image or word can briefly **prime** your response to a later question. In a typical experiment, the image or word is quickly flashed, then replaced by a "masking" stimulus that interrupts the brain's processing before conscious perception. For example, one experiment subliminally flashed either emotionally positive scenes (kittens, a romantic couple) or negative scenes (a werewolf, a dead body) an instant before participants viewed slides of people (Krosnick & others, 1992). Although the participants consciously perceived only a flash of light, they gave more positive ratings to people whose photos had been associated with positive scenes. People somehow looked nicer if their photo immediately followed unperceived kittens rather than an unperceived werewolf.

This experiment illustrates an intriguing aspect of the priming effect: Sometimes we *feel* what we do not know and cannot describe. An imperceptibly brief stimulus

How to think uncritically without psychology: James Vicary, an unemployed marketing researcher, masterminded the EAT POPCORN subliminal advertising hoax with the help of uncritical reporters and broadcasters. Vicary reportedly collected big fees from advertising firms for his promised services—and then disappeared (Rogers, 1993, 1994).

FIGURE 12.3
Absolute threshold
Do I taste it or not? When stimuli are detectable less than 50 percent of the time, they are "subliminal." Absolute threshold is the intensity at which we can detect a stimulus half the time.

Kurt Scholz/Superstock

"The heart has its reasons which reason does not know."

Pascal, *Pensées*, 1670

Subliminal persuasion?
Although subliminally presented stimuli *can* subtly influence people, experiments discount attempts at subliminal advertising and self-improvement. (The playful message here is not actually subliminal—because you can easily perceive it.)

The difference threshold
In this computer-generated copy of the Twenty-third Psalm, each line of the typeface changes imperceptibly. How many lines are required for you to experience a just noticeable difference?

The LORD is my shepherd;
        I shall not want.
He maketh me to lie down
            in green pastures:
        he leadeth me
            beside the still waters.
He restoreth my soul:
        he leadeth me
            in the paths of righteousness
            for his name's sake.
Yea, though I walk through the valley
            of the shadow of death,
        I will fear no evil:
for thou art with me;
        thy rod and thy staff
        they comfort me.
Thou preparest a table before me
            in the presence of mine enemies:
    thou anointest my head with oil,
        my cup runneth over.
Surely goodness and mercy
            shall follow me
        all the days of my life:
    and I will dwell
        in the house of the LORD
            for ever.

evidently triggers a weak response that *can* be detected by brain scanning (Blankenburg & others, 2003). That small brain response may evoke a feeling, though not a conscious awareness of the stimulus. This subliminal priming phenomenon joins much other evidence in pointing to the powers of intuition (Myers, 2002). The conclusion (turn up the volume here): *Much of our information processing occurs automatically, out of sight, off the radar screen of our conscious mind.*

But does the fact of subliminal *sensation* verify entrepreneurial claims of subliminal *persuasion*? Can advertisers really manipulate us with "hidden persuasion"? The near-consensus among research psychologists is no. Their verdict is similar to that of astronomers who say of astrologers, yes, they are right that stars and planets are out there, but no, the celestial bodies don't directly affect us. The laboratory research reveals a *subtle, fleeting* effect. Priming thirsty people with the subliminal word *thirst* might therefore, for a brief interval, make a thirst-quenching beverage ad more persuasive (Strahan & others, 2002). But the subliminal tape hucksters claim something different: a *powerful, enduring* effect on *behavior*.

To test whether commercial subliminal tapes have an effect beyond that of a placebo—the effect of one's belief in them—Anthony Greenwald and his colleagues (1991) randomly assigned university students to listen daily for five weeks to commercial subliminal tapes claiming to improve either self-esteem or memory. On half the tapes they played a very practical joke and switched the labels. Some students *thought* they were receiving affirmations of self-esteem when they actually were hearing the memory enhancement tape. Others got the self-esteem tape but *thought* their memory was being recharged.

Were the tapes effective? Students' scores on tests for both self-esteem and memory, taken before and after the five weeks, revealed no effects. And yet, those who *thought* they had heard a memory tape *believed* their memories had improved. A similar result occurred for those who thought they had heard a self-esteem tape. The tapes had no effects, yet the students *perceived* themselves receiving the benefits they *expected*. When reading this research, one hears echoes of the testimonies that ooze from the mail-order tape catalogs. Some customers, having bought what is not supposed to be heard (and having indeed not heard it!) offer testimonials like, "I really know that your tapes were invaluable in reprogramming my mind." Over a decade, Greenwald conducted 16 double-blind experiments evaluating subliminal self-help tapes. His results were uniform: Not one had any therapeutic effect (Greenwald, 1992). His conclusion: "Subliminal procedures offer little or nothing of value to the marketing practitioner" (Pratkanis & Greenwald, 1988).

Difference Thresholds

To function effectively, we need absolute thresholds low enough to allow us to detect important sights, sounds, textures, tastes, and smells. We also need to detect small differences among stimuli. A musician must detect minute discrepancies in an instrument's tuning. A wine taster must detect the slight flavor difference between two vintage wines. Parents must detect the sound of their own child's voice amid other children's voices.

The **difference threshold** (also called the *just noticeable difference*, or *jnd*) is the minimum difference a person can detect between any two stimuli half the time. The difference threshold increases with the magnitude of the stimulus. Thus, if you add 10 grams to a 100-gram weight, you will detect the difference; add 10 grams to a 1-*kilogram* weight and you will not, because the difference threshold has increased. More than a century ago, Ernst Weber noted that regardless of their magnitude, two stimuli must differ by a constant proportion for their difference to be perceptible. This principle—that the difference threshold is not a constant amount but some constant *proportion* of the stimulus—is so simple and so widely applicable that we still refer to it as **Weber's law**. The exact proportion varies, depending on the stimulus. For the average person to perceive their differences, two lights must differ in intensity by 8 percent. Two objects must differ in weight by 2 percent. And two tones must differ in frequency by only 0.3 percent (Teghtsoonian, 1971).

Weber's law is a rough approximation. It works well for nonextreme sensory stimuli, and it parallels some of our life experiences. If the price of a $1 chocolate bar goes up by 10 cents, shoppers might notice the change; similarly, it might take a £4000 price hike in a £40,000 Mercedes to raise the eyebrows of its potential buyers. In both cases, the price went up by 10 percent. Weber's principle: Our thresholds for detecting differences are a roughly constant proportion of the size of the original stimulus.

Sensory Adaptation

OBJECTIVE 12-3 | Describe sensory adaptation, and explain how we benefit from being unaware of unchanging stimuli.

Entering your neighbors' living room, you smell a musty odor. You wonder how they can stand it, but within minutes you no longer notice it. Jumping into a swimming pool, you shiver and complain about how cold it is. A short while later a friend arrives and you exclaim, "C'mon in. Water's fine!" These examples illustrate **sensory adaptation**—our diminishing sensitivity to an unchanging stimulus. (To experience this phenomenon, move your watch up your wrist an inch: You will feel it—but only for a few moments.) After constant exposure to a stimulus, our nerve cells fire less frequently.

Why, then, if we stare at an object without flinching, does it not vanish from sight? Because, unnoticed by us, our eyes are always moving, quivering just enough to guarantee that stimulation on the eyes' receptors continually changes.

But what if we actually could stop our eyes from moving? Would sights seem to vanish, as odors do? To find out, psychologists have devised ingenious instruments for maintaining a constant image on the eye's inner surface. Imagine that we have fitted a volunteer, Mary, with one of these instruments—a miniature projector mounted on a contact lens (**FIGURE 12.4a**). When Mary's eye moves, the image from the projector moves as well. So everywhere that Mary looks, the scene is sure to go.

If we project the profile of a face through such an instrument, what will Mary see? At first, she will see the complete profile. But within a few seconds, as her sensory receptors begin to fatigue, things get weird. Bit by bit, the image vanishes, only later to reappear and then disappear—in recognizable fragments or as a whole (**FIGURE 12.4b**). Interestingly, the disappearance and reappearance of an image occurs in meaningful units. If a person is shown a word, it will disappear, and new words made up of parts of that word will appear and then vanish. This phenomenon illustrates one of psychology's major conclusions: Our perceptions are organized by the meanings that our minds impose.

■ **difference threshold** the minimum difference between two stimuli required for detection 50 percent of the time. We experience the difference threshold as a just noticeable difference. (Also called *just noticeable difference* or *jnd*.)

■ **Weber's law** the principle that, to be perceived as different, two stimuli must differ by a constant minimum percentage (rather than a constant amount).

■ **sensory adaptation** diminished sensitivity as a consequence of constant stimulation.

"We need above all to know about changes; no one wants or needs to be reminded 16 hours a day that his shoes are on."

Neuroscientist David Hubel (1979)

For 9 in 10 people—but, curiously, for only 1 in 3 of those with schizophrenia—this eye flutter turns off when the eye is following a moving target (Holzman & Matthyss, 1990).

"My suspicion is that the universe is not only queerer than we suppose, but queerer than we can suppose."

J. B. S. Haldane, *Possible Worlds*, 1927

(a)

(b)

FIGURE 12.4
Sensory adaptation: Now you see it, now you don't!
(a) A projector mounted on a contact lens makes the projected image move with the eye. (b) Initially the person sees the stabilized image, but soon she sees fragments fading and reappearing. (From "Stabilized images on the retina" by R. M. Pritchard. Copyright © 1961 Scientific American, Inc. All Rights Reserved.)

■ **selective attention** the focusing of conscious awareness on a particular stimulus, as in the cocktail party effect.

■ **inattentional blindness** failing to see visible objects when our attention is directed elsewhere.

Although sensory adaptation reduces our sensitivity, it offers an important benefit: It enables us to focus on *informative* changes in our environment without being distracted by the uninformative constant stimulation of garments, odors, and street noise. Our sensory receptors are alert to novelty; bore them with repetition and they free our attention for more important things. This reinforces a fundamental lesson: We perceive the world not exactly as it is, but as it is useful for us to perceive it.

Our sensitivity to changing stimulation helps explain television's attention-getting power. Cuts, edits, zooms, pans, and sudden noises demand attention. Even television researchers marvel at the attention-grabbing power of TV. During interesting conversations, notes media researcher Percy Tannenbaum (2002), "I cannot for the life of me stop from periodically glancing over to the screen."

Sensory thresholds and adaptation are not the only phenomena that influence what we sense and perceive. Another is our capacity to attend to stimuli.

Selective Attention

OBJECTIVE 12-4 | Describe the interplay between attention and perception.

Perceptions come to us moment by moment, one perception vanishing as the next appears. Note how the Necker cube in **FIGURE 12.5** evokes more than one perception. The circles can be organized into several coherent images, each equally plausible, and your mind switches back and forth from one to the next. You *know* that alternative interpretations of this figure are possible, but you can consciously experience only one at any moment. This illustrates an important principle: Our conscious attention is *selective*.

Selective attention means that at any moment our awareness focuses, like a flashlight beam, on only a limited aspect of all that we experience. Indeed, a *very* limited aspect: By one estimate, our five senses take in 11,000,000 bits of information per second, of which we consciously process about 40 (Wilson, 2002). Yet we intuitively make great use of the other 10,999,960 bits. Until reading this sentence, you have been unaware that your shoes are pressing against your feet or that your nose is in your line of vision. Now, suddenly, your attentional spotlight shifts. Your feet feel encased, your nose stubbornly intrudes on the page before you. While attending to these words, you've also been blocking from awareness information coming from your peripheral vision. But you can change that. While staring at the X below, notice what surrounds the book (the edges of the page, your desktop, and so forth).

X

Another example of selective attention, the *cocktail party effect*, is your ability to attend to only one voice among many (though let another voice speak your name and your cognitive radar will instantly bring that voice into consciousness). This focused listening comes at a cost. Imagine hearing two conversations over a headset, one in each ear, and being asked to repeat the message in your left ear while it is spoken. When paying attention to what is being said in your left ear, you won't perceive what is said in your right. Asked later what language your right ear heard, you may draw a blank (though you could report the speaker's gender and loudness).

At the level of conscious awareness, our attention is divided. Talk while driving and your attention will shift back and forth from the road to the phone. That explains why drivers typically stop talking when demanding situations require their full attention. The process of switching attentional gears also costs a bit of time, especially when shifting to complex tasks (Rubenstein & others, 2001). But even shifting from cell-phone talking to a driving crisis can entail a slight delay in coping. In University of Utah driving-simulation experiments, students conversing on cell phones were slower to detect and respond to traffic signals, billboards, and other cars (Strayer &

FIGURE 12.5
Selective attention
What do you see: circles with white lines, or a cube? If you stare at the cube, you may notice that it reverses location, moving the tiny X in the center from the front edge to the back. At times the cube may seem to float in front of the page, with circles behind it; other times the circles may become holes in the page through which the cube appears, as though it were floating behind the page. Because attention is selective, you see only one interpretation at a time. (From Bradley & others, 1976.)

Sally Forth

Driven to distraction

In one driving-simulation experiment, students whose attention was diverted by cell-phone conversation (rather than merely listening to a radio) missed twice as many traffic signals as did those not talking on the phone.

Johnston, 2001; Strayer & others, 2003). Some experienced airline pilots, while attending to data displayed on a flight simulator's console and windshield, have similarly failed to notice visible airplanes blocking their landing path (Haines, 1991).

From the immense array of visual stimuli constantly before us, we select just a few to process. Ulric Neisser (1979) and Robert Becklen and Daniel Cervone (1983) demonstrated this dramatically. They showed people a one-minute videotape in which the images of three men in black shirts tossing a basketball were superimposed over the images of three men in white shirts doing the same thing. They asked the viewers to press a key every time the black-shirted players passed the ball. Midway through the tape, a young woman carrying an umbrella sauntered across the screen. Most had focused their attention so completely on the black-shirted players that they failed to notice the woman. When the researchers replayed the tape for them, they were astonished to see her. In a recent repeat of the experiment, smart-aleck researchers Daniel Simons and Christopher Chabris (1999) sent a gorilla-suited assistant through the swirl of players (**FIGURE 12.6**). During its 5- to 9-second cameo appearance, the gorilla paused to thump its chest. Still, half the conscientious pass-counting participants exhibited **inattentional blindness**. They failed to see it.

In other experiments, people also exhibit a remarkable lack of awareness of happenings in their visual environment. After a brief visual interruption, a big Coke bottle may disappear from the scene, a railing may rise, clothing color may change, and, more often than not, viewers don't notice (Resnick & others, 1997; Simons, 1996; Simons & Ambinder, 2005). This form of inattentional blindness, also called *change blindness*, has occurred among people giving directions to a construction worker who, unnoticed by two-thirds of them, is replaced by another construction worker (**FIGURE 12.7**). Out of sight, out of mind. *Change deafness* can also occur. In one experiment, 40 percent of people focused on repeating a list of sometimes challenging words failed to notice a change in the person speaking (Vitevitch, 2003).

FIGURE 12.6
Gorillas in our midst
When attending to one task (counting basketball passes by one of the three-person teams) about half the viewers display inattentional blindness by failing to notice a clearly visible gorilla passing through.

FIGURE 12.7
Change blindness
While a man (wearing glasses) provides directions to a construction worker, two experimenters rudely pass between them carrying a door. During this interruption, the original construction worker switches places with a different person wearing different colored clothing. Most people, focused on their direction giving, do not notice the switch. (From Daniel Simons.)

FIGURE 12.8
The pop-out phenomenon

An equally astonishing form of inattentional blindness is the phenomenon of *choice blindness* discovered by a Swedish research team. Petter Johansson and his colleagues (2005) showed 120 volunteers two female faces for 2 to 5 or more seconds and asked them which they thought was more attractive. They then put the photos face down and handed them the one they had chosen, inviting them to explain their choice. On 3 of 15 occasions, the tricky researchers used sleight-of-hand to switch the photos—showing them the face they had *not* chosen. Not only did the people seldom notice the deception (on only 13 percent of the switches), they readily explained why they preferred the face they had actually rejected. "I chose her because she smiled," said one person (after having picked the solemn-faced one). When asked after the experiment whether, in a "hypothetical experiment," they would notice such a switch, 84 percent insisted they would. They exhibit a blindness to the phenomenon that the researchers call (can you see the twinkle in their eyes?) *choice-blindness blindness*.

Yet some stimuli are so powerful that we experience *pop-out,* when a strikingly distinct stimulus, such as the only smiling face in **FIGURE 12.8** draws our eye. We don't choose to attend to these stimuli; they demand our attention. Meriwether Lewis couldn't have missed the attacking bear.

>> LEARNING OUTCOMES

Introduction to Sensation and Perception

OBJECTIVE 12-1 | Contrast sensation and perception, and explain the difference between bottom-up and top-down processing.
Sensation is the process by which our sensory receptors and nervous system receive and represent stimulus energies from our environment. *Perception* is the process by which we organize and interpret this information. Although we view sensation and perception separately to analyze and discuss them, they are actually parts of one continuous process. *Bottom-up processing* is sensory analysis that begins at the entry level, with information flowing from the sensory receptors to the brain. *Top-down processing* is analysis that begins with the brain and flows down, filtering information through our experience and expectations to produce perceptions.

OBJECTIVE 12-2 | Distinguish between absolute and difference thresholds, and discuss whether we can sense stimuli below our absolute thresholds and be influenced by them.
The *absolute threshold* for any stimulus is the minimum stimulation necessary to be consciously aware of it 50 percent of the time. Signal detection theory demonstrates that individual absolute thresholds vary, depending on the strength of the signal and also on experience, expectations, motivation, and alertness. The *difference threshold* (also called *just noticeable difference,* or *jnd*) is the barely noticeable difference we discern between two stimuli 50 percent of the time. Weber's law states that, to be perceptibly different, two stimuli must differ by a constant proportion (such as a 2 percent difference in weight), not a constant amount, of the original stimulus. Although we *can* process some information from stimuli below our absolute threshold for conscious awareness, the effect is too restricted to enable unscrupulous opportunists to exploit us with subliminal messages.

OBJECTIVE 12-3 | Describe sensory adaptation, and explain how we benefit from being unaware of unchanging stimuli.
Sensory adaptation is our diminished sensitivity to constant or routine odors, sounds, and touches. We benefit from this phenomenon because it focuses our attention on informative changes in stimulation, rather than on unchanging elements in our environment.

OBJECTIVE 12-4 | Describe the interplay between attention and perception.
Our senses of vision, hearing, taste, smell, and touch detect physical energy from the environment and encode it as neural signals. Aided by knowledge and expectations, our brain perceives meaning in these signals. We selectively attend to, and process, a limited number of the stimuli bombarding our senses and block out the others.

TERMS AND CONCEPTS TO REMEMBER

sensation, p. 12-0	subliminal, p. 12-3
perception, p. 12-0	priming, p. 12-3
bottom-up processing, p. 12-0	difference threshold, p. 12-4
top-down processing, p. 12-0	Weber's law, p. 12-5
psychophysics, p. 12-1	sensory adaptation, p. 12-5
absolute threshold, p. 12-1	selective attention, p. 12-6
signal detection theory, p. 12-2	inattentional blindness, p. 12-7

TEST YOURSELF

1. What is the rough distinction between sensation and perception?

2. Your friend insists that he *did* call you to dinner as you intently watched TV. What principle explains your not perceiving him?

(Answers in Appendix B.)

ASK YOURSELF

1. What types of sensory adaptation have you experienced in the last 24 hours?

>WEB

Multiple-choice *self-tests* and more may be found at www.worthpublishers.com/myers.

16

Perceptual Organization

Our yen for assembling visual features into complete forms involves bottom-up processing, starting with entry-level sensory analysis, as well as top-down processing that uses our experiences and expectations to interpret those sensations. But the more we learn about this information-processing system, the fuzzier the distinction grows between *sensation* and *perception*. Sensation is not just bottom-up processing, and perception is not just top-down processing. Sensation and perception blend into one continuous process, progressing upward from specialized detector cells and downward from our assumptions. This module considers some top-down principles of how we organize our perceptions, which appear in some striking perceptual illusions.

Perceptual Illusions

OBJECTIVE 16-1 | Explain how illusions help us to understand some of the ways we organize stimuli into meaningful perceptions.

Perceptual illusions have long fascinated scientists: Why, even when we know better, do we see illusions? Illusions reveal the ways we normally organize and interpret our sensations. Illusions illuminate. Consider six such perceptual illusions, which we will refer to in later discussions in this module:

Illusion 1 To the right is an adaptation of a classic illusion created in 1889 by Franz Müller-Lyer. Does either line segment—AB or BC—appear longer? To most

people the two segments appear to be the same length. Surprise! They are not. As your ruler can verify, line AB is more than one-fourth longer than line BC. Why did your eyes deceive you? (Later in this module, you will discover one explanation.)

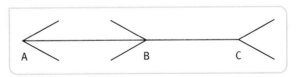

Illusion 2 Below we have two unretouched photos of the same two girls, in the same room. The camera shows you these scenes much as you would see them if you were viewing the room through a peephole. Why do the girls seem to change size when they switch places? (Hint: The answer lies in our assumptions, as you will see later.)

Both photos: S. Schwartzenberg/The Exploratorium

Illusion 3 Is the St. Louis Gateway Arch—the world's largest human-made illusion—taller than it is wide? Or wider than it is tall? To most it appears taller. In truth, its height and width are equal. Once again, seeing is deceiving. Why? (Keep this in mind: Everything is relative.)

Illusion 4 Here is another brain construction of virtual reality, described in 1935 by Hans Wallach. Do you see, below, a glowing blue worm curving through the black lines? The illusory worm is merely the short blue lines of the left figure with black lines added. Anything else you perceive is a product of your "creative genius" (Hoffman, 1998). (You will hear more about this in the discussion of grouping principles.)

> "Has your visual system gone off the deep end? It constructs from whole cloth a ripple in space and then proceeds to embellish it with mutable parts. Shall we henceforth distrust the witness of vision, knowing now its penchant to perjure?"
>
> Donald Hoffman,
> *Visual Intelligence*, 1998

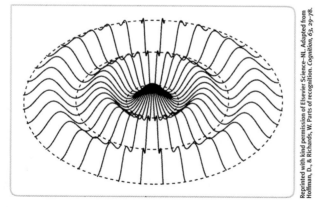

Illusion 5 The real creators of virtual reality are not software developers, but the brains that developers trick into constructing virtual realities. Donald Hoffman's (1998) ripple is a flat, two-dimensional drawing. But can you perceive it as flat? Not easily. Your brain will persist in creating a ripple that is not there. And it will construe it quite differently if you turn the book upside down. The ripple illusion is in part an assumption about light sources.

Illusion 6 Illusions occur with the other senses, too, as the German psychologist Wilhelm Wundt pointed out more than a century ago. Wundt was puzzled by people's hearing the steady beat of a metronome or clock as if it were a repeating rhythm of two, three, or four beats. Rather than hearing an unaccented click-click-click-click, one might, for example, hear CLICK-click CLICK-click.

Although a steady beat strikes the ear, each listener unconsciously shapes an auditory pattern. What perceptual principle is at work here? (By the end of this module, you'll know the answer to that question.)

Psychology's emphasis on *visual* illusions reflects vision's preeminence among our senses. When vision competes with other senses, vision usually wins—a phenomenon called **visual capture.** If the sound of a movie comes from a projector behind us, we nevertheless perceive it as coming from the screen, where we *see* the actors talking (much as we perceive a voice from a ventriloquist's dummy). While watching a roller coaster ride on a wraparound movie screen, we may brace ourselves, though our other senses tell us we're not moving. In each case, vision *captures* the other senses.

Hearing can also capture another sense. Kirsten Hötting and Brigitte Röder (2004) invited volunteers to count mechanical touches of their fingers while also hearing multiple tones. When one touch was accompanied by more than one tone, people often reported perceiving more than a single touch. There is more to touch than meets the skin.

Organizational Principles

OBJECTIVE **16-2** | Describe Gestalt psychology's contribution to our understanding of perception.

To transform sensory information into meaningful perceptions, we must organize it: We must perceive objects as distinct from their surroundings, see them as having a meaningful and constant form, and discern their distance and motion. The brain's rules for constructing perceptions explain some of the puzzling illusions we've considered.

Early in the twentieth century, a group of German psychologists became intrigued with how the mind organizes sensations into perceptions. They noticed that when given a cluster of sensations, we tend to organize them into a **gestalt,** a German word meaning a "form" or a "whole." The Gestalt psychologists provided compelling demonstrations of gestalt perception and described principles by which we organize our sensations into perceptions. For example, look at **FIGURE 16.1**. Note that the individual elements of the figure are really nothing but eight blue circles, each containing three converging white lines. When we view them all together, however, we see a *whole*, a form, a Necker cube.

The Gestalt psychologists were fond of saying that in perception the whole may exceed the sum of its parts. Combine sodium, a corrosive metal, with chlorine, a poisonous gas, and something very different emerges—table salt. Likewise, a unique perceived form emerges from a stimulus' components (Rock & Palmer, 1990).

As you read further about the Gestalt psychologists' organizational principles, keep in mind the fundamental truth they illustrate: Our brains do more than merely register information about the world. Perception is not just opening a shutter and letting a picture print itself on the brain. We constantly filter sensory information and infer perceptions in ways that make sense to us. Mind matters.

> **visual capture** the tendency for vision to dominate the other senses.
>
> **gestalt** an organized whole. Gestalt psychologists emphasized our tendency to integrate pieces of information into meaningful wholes.

FIGURE 16.1
Necker cube
What do you see: circles with white lines, or a cube? If you stare at the cube, you may notice that it reverses location, moving the tiny X in the center from the front edge to the back. At times the cube may seem to float in front of the page, with circles behind it; other times the circles may become holes in the page through which the cube appears, as though it were floating behind the page. But note how our perceptual system always interprets this collection of lines and shading as a *gestalt* or whole form of some sort. (From Bradley & others, 1976.)

Form Perception

OBJECTIVE 16-3 | Explain the figure-ground relationship, and identify principles of perceptual grouping in form perception.

Imagine designing a video/computer system that, like your eye/brain system, could recognize faces at a glance. What abilities will it need?

Figure and Ground

To start with, the system needs to recognize the faces as distinct from their backgrounds. Likewise, our first perceptual task is to perceive any object, called the figure, as distinct from its surroundings, called the ground. Among the voices you hear at a party, the one you attend to becomes the figure; all others, part of the ground. As you read, the words are the figure; the white paper, the ground. In **FIGURE 16.2**, the **figure-ground** relationship continually reverses—but always we organize the stimulus into a figure seen against a ground. Such reversible figure-and-ground illustrations demonstrate again that the same stimulus can trigger more than one perception.

FIGURE 16.2
Reversible figure and ground

Time Saving Suggestion, © 2003 Roger Shepherd.

Grouping

Having discriminated figure from ground, we (and our video/computer system) now have to organize the figure into a meaningful form. Some basic features of a scene—such as color, movement, and light/dark contrast—we process instantly and automatically (Treisman, 1987). To bring order and form to these basic sensations, our minds follow certain rules for **grouping** stimuli together (**FIGURE 16.3**). These rules, identified by the Gestalt psychologists and applied even by infants, illustrate the idea that the perceived whole differs from the sum of its parts (Quinn & others, 2002; Rock & Palmer, 1990):

Proximity We group nearby figures together. We see not six separate lines, but three sets of two lines.

Similarity We group together figures that are similar to each other. We see the triangles and circles as vertical columns of similar shapes, not as horizontal rows of dissimilar shapes.

Continuity We perceive smooth, continuous patterns rather than discontinuous ones. The pattern at lower left could be a series of alternating semicircles, but we perceive it as two continuous lines—one wavy, one straight.

Connectedness Because they are uniform and linked, we perceive the two dots and the line between them as a single unit.

Closure We fill in gaps to create a complete, whole object.

FIGURE 16.3
Organizing stimuli into groups
We could perceive the stimuli shown here in many ways, yet people everywhere see them similarly. The Gestalt psychologists believed this shows that the brain follows rules to order sensory information into wholes.

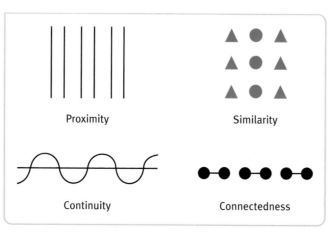

Proximity

Similarity

Continuity

Connectedness

Thus we assume that the circles (right) are complete but partially blocked by the (illusory) triangle. Add nothing more than little line segments that close off the circles and now your brain stops constructing a triangle.

Usually, these grouping principles help us construct reality. Sometimes, however, they lead us astray, as with our perception of the neon worm we saw earlier in Illusion 4, or of the doghouse in **FIGURE 16.4.**

FIGURE 16.4
What's the secret to this impossible doghouse?
You probably perceive this doghouse as a gestalt—a whole (though impossible) structure. Actually, your brain imposes this sense of wholeness on the picture. As the photo on this module's final page shows, Gestalt grouping principles are at work here.

Depth Perception

OBJECTIVE 16-4 | Explain the importance of depth perception, and discuss the contribution of visual cliff research to our understanding of this ability.

Two-dimensional images fall on our retinas, yet we somehow organize three-dimensional perceptions. Seeing objects in three dimensions, called **depth perception,** enables us to estimate their distance from us. At a glance, we estimate the distance of an oncoming car or the height of a house. This ability is partly innate. Eleanor Gibson and Richard Walk (1960) discovered this using a miniature cliff with a drop-off covered by sturdy glass. Gibson's inspiration for these experiments occurred while she was picnicking on the rim of the Grand Canyon. She wondered: Would a toddler peering over the rim perceive the dangerous drop-off and draw back?

Back in their Cornell University laboratory, Gibson and Walk placed 6- to 14-month-old infants on the edge of a safe canyon—a **visual cliff** (**FIGURE 16.5** on the next page). Their mothers then coaxed them to crawl out onto the glass. Most refused to do so, indicating that they could perceive depth. Perhaps by crawling age the infants had *learned* to perceive depth. Yet newborn animals with virtually no visual experience—including young kittens, a day-old goat, and newly hatched chicks—respond similarly.

■ **figure-ground** the organization of the visual field into objects (the *figures*) that stand out from their surroundings (the *ground*).

■ **grouping** the perceptual tendency to organize stimuli into coherent groups.

■ **depth perception** the ability to see objects in three dimensions although the images that strike the retina are two-dimensional; allows us to judge distance.

■ **visual cliff** a laboratory device for testing depth perception in infants and young animals.

FIGURE **16.5**
Visual cliff
Eleanor Gibson and Richard Walk devised this miniature cliff with a glass-covered drop-off to determine whether crawling infants and newborn animals can perceive depth. Even when coaxed, infants are reluctant to venture onto the glass over the cliff.

Each species, by the time it is mobile, has the perceptual abilities it needs. What is more, by 3 months of age, infants are using Gestalt perception principles, by looking more at novel groupings of objects (Quinn & others, 2002). But if biological maturation predisposes our wariness of heights, experience amplifies it. Infants' wariness increases with their experiences of crawling, no matter when they begin to crawl.

How do we do it? How do we transform two differing two-dimensional retinal images into a single three-dimensional perception? The process begins with depth cues, some that depend on the use of two eyes, and others that are available to each eye separately.

Binocular Cues

OBJECTIVE **16-5** | Describe two binocular cues for perceiving depth, and explain how they help the brain to compute distance.

Try this: With both eyes open, hold two pens or pencils in front of you and touch their tips together. Now do so with one eye closed. With one eye the task becomes noticeably more difficult, demonstrating the importance of **binocular cues** in judging the distance of nearby objects. Two eyes are better than one.

Because our eyes are about 2½ inches apart, our retinas receive slightly different images of the world. When the brain compares these two images, the difference between them—their **retinal disparity**—provides an important cue to the relative distance of different objects. When you hold your finger directly in front of your nose, your retinas receive quite different views. (You can see this if you close one eye and then the other, or create a finger sausage as in **FIGURE 16.6**.) At a greater distance—say, when you hold your finger at arm's length—the disparity is smaller.

The creators of three-dimensional (3-D) movies simulate or exaggerate retinal disparity by photographing a scene with two cameras placed a few inches apart (a feature we might want to build into our seeing computer). When we view the movie through spectacles that allow the left eye to see only the image from the left camera and the right eye only the image from the right camera, the 3-D effect mimics normal retinal disparity. Similarly, twin cameras in airplanes can take photos of terrain for integration into 3-D maps.

FIGURE **16.6**
The floating finger sausage
Hold your two index fingers about 5 inches in front of your eyes, with their tips half an inch apart. Now look beyond them and note the weird result. Move your fingers out farther and the retinal disparity—and the finger sausage—will shrink.

Another binocular cue to distance is **convergence,** a neuromuscular cue caused by the eyes' greater inward turn when they view a near object. The brain notes the angle of convergence, then computes whether you are focusing on this printed page or on something else across the room. The greater the inward strain, the closer the object.

Monocular Cues

OBJECTIVE **16-6** | Explain how monocular cues differ from binocular cues, and describe several monocular cues for perceiving depth.

How do we judge whether a person is 10 or 100 meters away? In both cases, the retinal disparity and convergence while looking straight ahead are slight. At such distances we depend on **monocular cues** (available to each eye separately), such as the following:

Relative size If we assume that two objects are similar in size, we perceive the one that casts the smaller retinal image as farther away. To a driver, distant pedestrians appear smaller, which also means that small-looking pedestrians (children) may sometimes be misperceived as more distant than they are (Stewart, 2000).

Relative size
(providing *most* people a cue to distance)

Interposition If one object partially blocks our view of another, we perceive it as closer. Rene Magritte's painting of a woman on horseback purposely confuses figure and ground by interposition.

Relative clarity Because light from distant objects passes through more atmosphere, we perceive hazy objects as farther away than sharp, clear objects. In fog or snow, the car in front of you may therefore seem farther away than it is.

Rene Magritte, *The Blank Signature*, oil on canvas, National Gallery of Art, Washington. Collection of Mr. and Mrs. Paul Mellon. Photo by Richard Carafelli.

Interposition

■ **binocular cues** depth cues, such as retinal disparity and convergence, that depend on the use of two eyes.

■ **retinal disparity** a binocular cue for perceiving depth: By comparing images from the two eyeballs, the brain computes distance—the greater the disparity (difference) between the two images, the closer the object.

■ **convergence** a binocular cue for perceiving depth; the extent to which the eyes converge inward when looking at an object. The greater the inward strain, the closer the object.

■ **monocular cues** depth cues, such as interposition and linear perspective, available to either eye alone.

Texture gradient
Here, artist Victor Vaserly used texture gradient to depict depth.

© Erich Lessing/Art Resource, NY

Texture gradient A gradual change from a coarse, distinct texture to a fine, indistinct texture signals increasing distance. Objects far away appear smaller and more densely packed.

Relative height We perceive objects higher in our field of vision as farther away. Because we perceive the lower part of a figure-ground illustration as closer, we perceive it as figure (Vecera & others, 2002). Invert the illustration below (right) and the black becomes ground, like a night sky.

Relative height may contribute to the illusion that vertical dimensions are longer than identical horizontal dimensions (as we saw in Illusion 3, the St. Louis Gateway Arch). No wonder people pour less juice when given a tall, thin glass rather than a short, wide glass (Wansink & van Ittersum, 2003). A tall glass looks as though it has more liquid than it actually does. Is the vertical line in the diagram below (left) longer, shorter, or equal in length to the horizontal line? Measure and see.

Figure this
Thanks to relative height, lower objects seem closer—and thus are usually perceived as figure.

Relative height

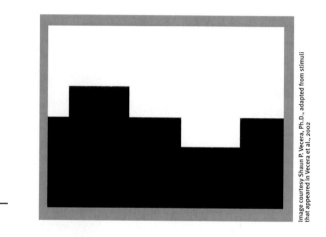

Image courtesy Shaun P. Vecera, Ph.D., adapted from stimuli that appeared in Vecera et al., 2002

Relative motion   ⟶ Direction of passenger's motion

Relative motion (motion parallax) As we move, objects that are actually stable may appear to move. If while riding on a bus you fix your gaze on some object—say, a house—the objects closer than the house (the fixation point) appear to move backward. The nearer the object is to you, the faster it seems to move.

Objects beyond the fixation point appear to move with you, and the farther away those objects are, the faster they will move. Your brain uses these speed and direction clues to compute the objects' relative distances.

THE FREIGHT ELEVATOR FOR THE MAN WHO HAS EVERYTHING

Linear perspective

Light and shadow

Linear perspective Parallel lines, such as railroad tracks, appear to converge with distance. The more the lines converge, the greater their perceived distance. Linear perspective can contribute to rail-crossing accidents by leading people to overestimate a train's distance (Leibowitz, 1985).

Light and shadow Nearby objects reflect more light to our eyes. Given two identical objects, the dimmer one seems farther away. This illusion can also contribute to accidents, as when a fog-shrouded vehicle, or one with only its parking lights on, seems farther away than it is. Shading, too, produces a sense of depth consistent with the assumed light source. (Recall the ripples of Illusion 5.) Invert the the Light and Shadow illustration (above right) and the hollow becomes a hill, because our brain follows a simple rule that works well on Planet Earth: *Assume that light comes from above.*

Artists use monocular cues to convey depth on a flat canvas (**FIGURE 16.7**). To you and me, the drawing in **FIGURE 16.8** clearly indicates that the elephant is far away, rather than about to be speared—which is how it was perceived a half-century ago by many South African Bantus who had minimal experience with photos and drawings (Deregowski, 1972; Hudson, 1960).

FIGURE 16.7
Perspective techniques

By the time that "Bristol, Broad Quay" was painted (c. 1730, Anonymous), techniques for depicting three dimensions on a flat surface were well established. Note the effective use of distance cues such as texture gradient, interposition, linear perspective, and relative size and height.

FIGURE 16.8
What's for dinner?

Monocular depth cues such as relative size and distance indicate to people familiar with artistic and photographic use of such cues that it's *not* the elephant. (From Deregowski, 1972.)

Motion Perception

OBJECTIVE **16-7** | State the basic assumption we make in our perceptions of motion, and explain how these perceptions can be deceiving.

Imagine that you could perceive the world as having color, form, and depth but that you could not see motion. Not only would you be unable to bike or drive, you might even have trouble writing, eating, and walking.

Computing motion
Venus Williams' brain automatically uses available cues to compute motion.

Fortunately, you can perceive motion. Normally your brain computes motion based partly on its assumption that shrinking objects are retreating (not getting smaller) and enlarging objects are approaching. But you are imperfect at motion perception. Large objects, such as trains, appear to move more slowly than smaller objects, such as cars moving at the same speed. (Perhaps at an airport you've noticed that jumbo jets seem to land more slowly than little jets going the same speed or slower.)

To catch a fly ball, softball or cricket players (unlike drivers) *want* to achieve a collision—with the ball that's flying their way. To accomplish that, they follow a simple rule: By keeping the ball at a constant angle of gaze, a fielder will run through the point of its return as it arrives (McBeath & others, 1995). A dog catching a Frisbee does the same (Shaffer & others, 2004).

As film animation artists know well, the brain will also perceive continuous movement in a rapid series of slightly varying images (a phenomenon called *stroboscopic movement*). A motion picture creates this illusion by flashing 24 still pictures each second. The motion we see is not in the film, which merely presents a superfast slide show. The motion is constructed in our heads.

Marquees and holiday lights create another illusion of movement using the **phi phenomenon.** When two adjacent stationary lights blink on and off in quick succession, we perceive a single light moving back and forth between them. Lighted signs exploit the phi phenomenon with a succession of lights that creates the impression of, say, a moving arrow. This reinforces a fundamental lesson: Perception is not merely projecting the world onto our brain. Rather, sensations are disassembled into information bits that the brain then reassembles into its own functional model of the external world. *Our brain constructs our perceptions.*

Perceptual Constancy

OBJECTIVE **16-8** | Explain the importance of perceptual constancy.

So far, we have noted that our video/computer system must first perceive objects as we do—as having a distinct form, location, and perhaps motion. Its next task is even more challenging: to recognize the object without being deceived by changes in its shape, size, brightness, or color. **Perceptual constancy** enables us to perceive an object as unchanging despite a changing stimulus. Thanks to this top-down process, we can identify things regardless of the angle, distance, and illumination by which we view them. You glance at someone ahead of you on the sidewalk and instantly recognize a classmate. In less time than it takes to draw a breath, information reaching your eyes has been sent to your brain, where work teams comprising millions of neurons have extracted the essential features, compared them with stored images, and identified the person. Replicating this human perceptual feat, which has intrigued perception researchers for decades, provides a monumental challenge for our perceiving computer.

■ **phi phenomenon** an illusion of movement created when two or more adjacent lights blink on and off in quick succession.

■ **perceptual constancy** perceiving objects as unchanging (having consistent lightness, color, shape, and size) even as illumination and retinal images change.

Shape and Size Constancies

OBJECTIVE 16-9 | Describe the shape and size constancies, and explain how our expectations about perceived size and distance contribute to some visual illusions.

Sometimes an object whose actual shape cannot change *seems* to change shape with the angle of our view (**FIGURE 16.9**). More often, thanks to *shape constancy,* we perceive the form of familiar objects as constant even while our retinal images of them change. When a door opens, it casts a changing shape on our retinas, yet we still manage to perceive the door as having a constant doorlike shape (**FIGURE 16.10**).

Thanks to *size constancy* we perceive objects as having a constant size, even while our distance from them varies. Size constancy leads us to perceive a car as large enough to carry people, even when we see its tiny image from two blocks away. This illustrates the close connection between an object's perceived *distance* and perceived *size.* Perceiving an object's distance gives us cues to its size. Likewise, knowing its general size—that the object is, say, a car—provides us with cues to its distance.

FIGURE 16.9
Perceiving shape
Do the tops of these tables have different dimensions? They appear to. But—believe it or not—they are identical. (Measure and see.) With both tables we adjust our perceptions relative to our viewing angle.

Shepard's tables, © 2003 Roger Shepard.

FIGURE 16.10
Shape constancy
A door casts an increasingly trapezoidal image on our retinas as it opens, yet we still perceive it as rectangular.

Size-Distance Relationship It is a marvel how effortlessly size perception occurs. Given an object's perceived distance and the size of its image on our retinas, we instantly and unconsciously infer the object's size. Although the monsters in **FIGURE 16.11a** cast the same retinal images, the linear perspective tells our brain that the monster in pursuit is farther away. We therefore perceive it as larger.

This interplay between perceived size and perceived distance helps explain several well-known illusions. For example, can you imagine why the Moon looks up to 50 percent larger near the horizon than when high in the sky? For at least 22 centuries, scholars have wondered and have argued about reasons for the *Moon illusion* (Hershenson, 1989). One reason is that cues to objects' distances at the horizon make the Moon behind them seem farther away than the Moon high in the night sky (Kaufman & Kaufman, 2000). Thus, the horizon Moon—like the distant monster in Figure 16.11a and the distant bar in the *Ponzo illusion* in **FIGURE 16.11b**—seems larger. Take away these distance cues—by looking at the horizon Moon (or each monster or each bar) through a paper tube—and the object immediately shrinks.

From Shepard, (1990)

(a)

Alan Choisnet/The Image Bank

(b)

FIGURE 16.11
The interplay between perceived size and distance
(a) The monocular cues for distance (such as linear perspective and relative height) make the pursuing monster look larger than the pursued. It isn't.
(b) This visual trick, called the Ponzo illusion, is based on the same principle as the fleeing monsters. The two red bars cast identical-sized images on our retinas. But experience tells us that a more distant object can create the same-sized image as a nearer one only if it is actually larger. As a result, we perceive the bar that seems farther away as larger.

FIGURE **16.12**
The Müller-Lyer illusion
Richard L. Gregory (1968) suggested that the corners in our rectangularly carpentered world teach us to interpret "outward" or "inward" pointing arrowheads at the ends of a line as a cue to the line's distance from us and so to its length. The red line defined by the corner at the ticket booth looks shorter than the red line defined by the room corner. But if you measure them, you will see that both are the same length.

The size-distance relationship helps us understand two illusions demonstrated earlier. Illusion 1, the Müller-Lyer illusion concerning the lengths of straight lines between arrow tips, has been the subject of more than 1250 scientific publications, yet psychologists still debate its explanation. One is that our experience with the corners of rooms or buildings prompts us to interpret the vertical line on the ticket booth in **FIGURE 16.12** as closer to us and therefore shorter, and the same-length vertical line by the door as farther away and therefore longer. Thus, what appears as an illusion when isolated in a line drawing actually enables correct depth perception in our three-dimensional world.

Experience supports this theory. People have been more susceptible to the Müller-Lyer illusion if, unlike some mid–twentieth-century rural Africans, they have lived in a carpentered world of rectangular shapes (Segall & others, 1990). The phenomenon reflects cultural experience, not race. Africans who live in cities are more vulnerable to the illusion than are their rural counterparts in uncarpentered environments. Our experience in rectangular contexts helps us construct our perceptions, top-down.

Culture and perception
Rural Africans who did not live in an environment of constructed rectangular buildings—such as people in South African Zulu round houses shown here—were less vulnerable to the Müller-Lyer illusion.

Ed Kashi / Corbis

FIGURE 16.13
The illusion of the shrinking and growing girls
This distorted room, designed by Adelbert Ames, appears to have a normal rectangular shape when viewed through a peephole with one eye. The girl in the near corner appears disproportionately large because we judge her size based on the false assumption that she is the same distance away as the girl in the far corner.

Size-distance relationships also explain Illusion 2, the shrinking and growing girls you saw at the beginning of this module. As **FIGURE 16.13** reveals, the room is distorted. Viewed with one eye through a peephole, its trapezoidal walls produce the same images as those of a normal rectangular room viewed with both eyes. Presented with the camera's one-eyed view, the brain makes the reasonable assumption that the room *is* normal and that each of the girls is therefore the same distance from us. And given the different sizes of the images on the retina, our brain ends up calculating that the girls are very different in size.

Our occasional misperceptions reveal the workings of our normally effective perceptual processes. The perceived relationship between distance and size is generally valid, but under special circumstances it can lead us astray—as when helping to create the Moon illusion, the Müller-Lyer illusion, and the distorted-room illusion.

Lightness Constancy

OBJECTIVE 16-10 | Discuss lightness constancy and its similarity to color constancy.

White paper reflects 90 percent of the light falling on it; black paper, only 10 percent. In sunlight a black paper may reflect 100 times more light than does a white paper viewed indoors, but it still looks black (McBurney & Collings, 1984). This illustrates *lightness constancy* (also called *brightness constancy*); we perceive an object as having a constant lightness even while its illumination varies. Perceived lightness depends on *relative luminance*—the amount of light an object reflects relative to its surroundings. If you view sunlit black paper through a narrow tube so nothing else is visible, it may look gray, because in bright sunshine it reflects a fair amount of light. View it without the tube and it is again black, because it reflects much less light than the objects around it. The phenomenon is similar to that of *color constancy:* As light changes, a red apple in a fruit bowl retains its redness, because our brain computes the light reflected by any object relative to its surrounding objects.

Perceived lightness stays roughly constant, given an unchanging context. But what happens when the surrounding context changes? As **FIGURE 16.14** shows, the visual system computes brightness and color relative to surrounding objects. Thus, perceived lightness changes with context.

FIGURE 16.14
Brightness contrast
Squares A and B are identical in color, believe it or not. (If you don't believe me, photocopy the illustration, cut out the squares, and compare.) But we perceive B as lighter.

Form perception, depth perception, motion perception, and perceptual constancy illuminate how we organize our visual experiences. Perceptual organization applies to other senses, too. It explains why we group a clock's steady clicking into patterns (Illusion 6). Listening to an unfamiliar language, we have trouble hearing where one word stops and the next one begins. Listening to our own language, we automatically hear distinct words. This, too, is a form of perceptual organization. But it is more, for we even organize a string of letters—THEDOGATEMEAT—into words that make an intelligible phrase, more likely "The dog ate meat" than "The do gate me at" (McBurney & Collings, 1984). This process involves not only organization but interpretation—discerning meaning in what we perceive.

>> Learning Outcomes

Perceptual Organization

OBJECTIVE 16-1 | Explain how illusions help us to understand some of the ways we organize stimuli into meaningful perceptions.
Perceptual illusions fascinate psychologists because they reveal how we normally organize and interpret sensations. When visual and other sensory information conflict, our brain usually resolves the disagreement by accepting the visual data, a tendency known as *visual capture*. In contests between hearing and touch, hearing may dominate.

OBJECTIVE 16-2 | Describe Gestalt psychology's contribution to our understanding of perception.
Gestalt psychologists searched for rules by which the brain organizes fragments of sensory data into *gestalts* (from the German word for "whole"), or meaningful forms. In pointing out that the whole is more than the sum of its parts, these researchers showed that we constantly filter sensory information and infer perceptions in ways that make sense to us. This truth remains valid, even though contemporary research demonstrates that sensation and perception are parts of a continuous information processing system, involving both bottom-up and top-down processing.

OBJECTIVE 16-3 | Explain the figure-ground relationship, and identify principles of perceptual grouping in form perception.
To recognize an object, we must first perceive it (see it as a *figure*) as distinct from its surroundings (the *ground*). We bring order and form to stimuli by organizing them into meaningful groups, following the rules of *proximity, similarity, continuity, connectedness,* and *closure.*

OBJECTIVE 16-4 | Explain the importance of depth perception, and discuss the contribution of visual cliff research to our understanding of this ability.
Depth perception is our ability to see objects in three dimensions, even though our retinas receive two-dimensional images. Without depth perception, we would be unable to judge distance, height, or depth. The *visual cliff research* with 6- to 14-month-olds demonstrated that depth perception is in part innate. Many species perceive the world in three dimensions at, or very soon after, birth.

OBJECTIVE 16-5 | Describe two binocular cues for perceiving depth, and explain how they help the brain to compute distance.
Binocular cues are depth cues that rely on information from both eyes. In the *retinal disparity cue,* the brain computes the relative distance of an object by comparing the slightly different images the object casts on our two retinas. The greater the difference, the closer the object must be. In the *convergence cue,* the brain calculates the degree of neuromuscular strain when our two eyes turn inward to look at a nearby object. The greater the strain (or the angle of convergence), the closer the object.

OBJECTIVE 16-6 | Explain how monocular cues differ from binocular cues, and describe several monocular cues for perceiving depth.
Monocular cues let us judge depth using information transmitted by only one eye; *binocular cues* require information from both eyes. Monocular cues include

- *relative size* (smaller is more distant).
- *interposition* (an object that blocks another is closer than the blocked object).
- *relative clarity* (a hazy object is farther away than an object seen clearly).
- *texture gradient* (when texture changes, coarse distinct objects are close and fine indistinct objects are distant).
- *relative height* (objects higher in our field of vision are farther away).
- *relative motion* or *motion parallax* (when you are moving, objects closer than a fixation point appear to move backward—the nearer the object, the faster it moves; objects beyond the fixation point appear to move with you).
- *linear perspective* (the more two parallel lines converge, the farther away they are).
- *light and shadow* (nearby objects reflect more light than faraway objects).

OBJECTIVE **16-7** | **State the basic assumption we make in our perceptions of motion, and explain how these perceptions can be deceiving.**

As objects move across or toward our retinas, our basic assumption is that shrinking objects are retreating, and enlarging objects are approaching. But sometimes we misperceive. We may miscalculate the speed of movement of large objects or objects picked up by our peripheral vision. A quick succession of images on the retina can create an illusion of movement, as in *stroboscopic movement* (triggered by a rapid series of slightly varying images) or the *phi phenomenon* (triggered by the rapid on-off blinking of two adjacent stationary lights).

OBJECTIVE **16-8** | **Explain the importance of perceptual constancy.**

Perceptual constancy, the ability to recognize an object regardless of its changing angle, distance, or illumination, lets us perceive objects as having unchanging characteristics despite the changing images they cast on our retinas.

OBJECTIVE **16-9** | **Describe the shape and size constancies, and explain how our expectations about perceived size and distance contribute to some visual illusions.**

Shape constancy is our ability to perceive familiar objects (such as an opening door) as unchanging in shape, and *size constancy* is perceiving objects as unchanging in size, despite the changing images they cast on our retinas. There is a close relationship between perceived size and perceived distance. Knowing an object's size gives us clues to its distance; knowing its distance gives clues about its size. This interplay sometimes misleads us, as when we misread monocular distance cues and reach the wrong conclusions, as in the Moon, Ponzo, and Müller-Lyer illusions.

OBJECTIVE **16-10** | **Discuss lightness constancy and its similarity to color constancy.**

Lightness (or *brightness*) *constancy* is our ability to perceive an object as having a constant lightness even when its illumination—the light cast upon it—changes. *Color constancy* enables us to perceive the color of an object as unchanging even when its illumination changes. In both cases, the brain perceives the quality (lightness or color) relative to surrounding objects.

TERMS AND CONCEPTS TO REMEMBER

visual capture, p. 16-3	binocular cues, p. 16-6
gestalt, p. 16-3	retinal disparity, p. 16-6
figure-ground, p. 16-4	convergence, p. 16-7
grouping, p. 16-4	monocular cues, p. 16-7
depth perception, p. 16-5	phi phenomenon, p. 16-10
visual cliff, p. 16-5	perceptual constancy, p. 16-10

TEST YOURSELF

1. How does the study of illusions inform our understanding of normal perceptions?

2. What do we mean when we say that, in perception, the whole is greater than the sum of its parts?

(Answers in Appendix B.)

ASK YOURSELF

1. Have you ever watched a movie where spoken words and people's facial expressions were out of sync? Which did you think needed to be adjusted—the visual image you were seeing, or the sounds you were hearing?

2. Try drawing a realistic depiction of the scene from your window. How many monocular cues will you use in your drawing?

ANSWERS TO QUESTIONS WITHIN THE MODULE

Q. What's the secret of this impossible doghouse?

A. Another view of the impossible doghouse in Figure 16.4 reveals the secrets of this illusion. From the photo angle in Figure 16.4, the grouping principle of closure leads us to perceive the boards as continuous.

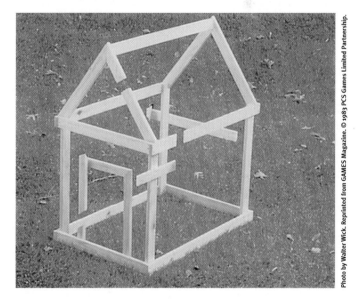

Photo by Walter Wick. Reprinted from GAMES Magazine. © 1983 PCS Games Limited Partnership.

>WEB

Multiple-choice *self-tests* and more may be found at www.worthpublishers.com/myers.

17

Perceptual Interpretation

Philosophers have debated whether our perceptual ability should be credited to our nature or our nurture. To what extent do we *learn* to perceive? German philosopher Immanuel Kant (1724–1804) maintained that knowledge comes from our *inborn* ways of organizing sensory experiences. Indeed, we come equipped to process sensory information. But British philosopher John Locke (1632–1704) argued that through our experiences we also *learn* to perceive the world. Indeed, we learn to link an object's distance with its size. So, just how important is experience? How radically does it shape our perceptual interpretations?

Sensory Deprivation and Restored Vision

OBJECTIVE 17-1 | Describe the contribution of restored-vision and sensory deprivation research in our understanding of the nature-nurture interplay in our perceptions.

Writing to John Locke, William Molyneux wondered whether "a man *born* blind, and now adult, taught by his *touch* to distinguish between a cube and a sphere" could, if made to see, visually distinguish the two. Locke's answer was no, because the man would never have *learned* to see the difference.

Molyneux' hypothetical case has since been put to the test with a few dozen adults who, though blind from birth, have gained sight (Gregory, 1978; von Senden, 1932). Most had been born with cataracts—clouded lenses that allowed them to see only diffused light, rather as you or I might see a diffuse fog through a Ping-Pong ball sliced in half. When their cataracts were surgically removed, the patients could distinguish figure from ground and could sense colors—suggesting that these aspects of perception are innate. But much as Locke supposed, the formerly blind patients often could not recognize by sight objects that were familiar by touch.

You and I perceive and recognize individual faces as a whole. Show us the same top half of a face paired with two different bottom halves (as in **FIGURE 17.1**), and the

"Let us then suppose the mind to be, as we say, white paper void of all characters, without any ideas: How comes it to be furnished? . . . To this I answer, in one word, from EXPERIENCE."

John Locke, *An Essay Concerning Human Understanding*, 1690

FIGURE 17.1
Perceiving composite faces
To most people, the top halves of these two faces, created by Richard Le Grand and his colleagues (2004), look different. Actually, they are the same, though paired with two different lower face halves. People deprived of visual experience early in life have more difficulty perceiving whole faces, which ironically enables their superiority at recognizing that the top halves of these faces are identical.

Courtesy of Richard LeGrand

identical top halves will seem different. People deprived of visual experience during infancy surpass the rest of us at recognizing that the top halves are the same, because they didn't learn to process faces as a whole (Le Grand & others, 2004). For example, one 43-year-old man, whose sight was recently restored after 40 years of blindness, could associate people with distinct features ("Mary's the one with red hair") but could not instantly recognize a face. He also lacked perceptual constancy: As people walk away from him they seem to be shrinking in size (Bower, 2003). Vision, such cases make clear, is partly an acquired sense.

Seeking to gain more control than is provided by clinical cases, researchers have conducted Molyneux' imaginary experiment with infant kittens and monkeys. In one experiment, they outfitted them with goggles through which the animals could see only diffuse, unpatterned light (Wiesel, 1982). After infancy, when their goggles were removed, these animals exhibited perceptual limitations much like those of humans born with cataracts. They could distinguish color and brightness, but not the form of a circle from that of a square. Their eyes had not degenerated; their retinas still relayed signals to their visual cortex. But lacking stimulation, the cortical cells had not developed normal connections. Thus, the animals remained functionally blind to shape.

In both humans and animals, a similar period of sensory restriction does no permanent harm if it occurs later in life. Cover the eye of an animal for several months during adulthood, and its vision will be unaffected after the eye patch is removed. Remove cataracts that develop after early childhood, and a human, too, will enjoy normal vision. The effects of visual experiences during infancy in cats, monkeys, and humans suggest there is a *critical period* shortly after birth—an optimal time when certain events must take place—for normal sensory and perceptual development. Experience guides, sustains, and maintains the brain's neural organization.

Human infants born today with an opaque lens (cataract) will typically have corrective surgery within a few months. The brain network responsible for the corrected eye then rapidly develops, enabling improved visual acuity with as little as one hour's visual experience (Maurer & others, 1999). Congenitally deaf kittens and infants given cochlear implants exhibit a similar "awakening" of the pertinent brain area (Klinke & others, 1999; Sirenteanu, 1999). Nurture sculpts what nature has endowed.

Experiments on perceptual limitations and advantages produced by early sensory deprivation provide a partial answer to an important question: Does the effect of early experience last a lifetime? For some aspects of visual perception, the answer is clearly yes: "Use it *soon* or lose it." We retain the imprint of early visual experiences far into the future.

Learning to see
At age 3, Mike May lost his vision in an explosion. On March 7, 2000, after a new cornea restored vision to his right eye, he got his first look at his wife and children. Alas, although signals were reaching his long dormant visual cortex, it lacked the experience to interpret them. Faces, apart from features such as hair, were not recognizable. Expressions eluded him. Yet he can see an object in motion and is gradually learning to navigate his world and to marvel at such things as dust floating in sunlight (Abrams, 2002).

Perceptual Adaptation

OBJECTIVE 17-2 | Explain how the research on distorting goggles increases our understanding of the adaptability of perception.

Given a new pair of glasses, we may feel slightly disoriented, even dizzy. Within a day or two, we adjust. Our **perceptual adaptation** to changed visual input makes the world seem normal again. But imagine a far more dramatic new pair of glasses—one that shifts the apparent location of objects 40 degrees to the left. When you first put them on and toss a ball to a friend, it sails off to the left. Walking forward to shake hands with the person, you veer to the left.

Could you adapt to this distorted world? Chicks cannot. When fitted with such lenses, they continue to peck where food grains *seem* to be (Hess, 1956; Rossi, 1968).

■ **perceptual adaptation** in vision, the ability to adjust to an artificially displaced or even inverted visual field.

Perceptual adaptation
"Oops, missed," thinks researcher Hubert Dolezal as he views the world through inverting goggles. Yet, believe it or not, kittens, monkeys, and humans can adapt to an inverted world.

But we humans adapt to distorting lenses quickly. Within a few minutes your throws would again be accurate, your stride on target. Remove the lenses and you would experience an aftereffect: At first your throws would err in the *opposite* direction, sailing off to the right; but again, within minutes you would readapt.

Indeed, given an even more radical pair of glasses—one that literally turns the world upside down—you could still adapt. Psychologist George Stratton (1896) experienced this when he invented, and for eight days wore, optical headgear that flipped left to right *and* up to down, making him the first person to experience a right-side-up retinal image while standing upright. The ground was up, the sky was down.

At first, Stratton felt disoriented. When he wanted to walk, he found himself searching for his feet, which were now "up." Eating was nearly impossible. He became nauseated and depressed. But Stratton persisted, and by the eighth day he could comfortably reach for something in the right direction and walk without bumping into things. When Stratton finally removed the headgear, he readapted quickly.

Later experiments replicated Stratton's experience (Dolezal, 1982; Kohler, 1962). After a period of adjustment, people wearing the optical gear have even been able to ride a motorcycle, ski the Alps, and fly an airplane. Did all these people adjust by perceptually converting their strange worlds to "normal" views? No. Actually, the world around them still seemed above their heads or on the wrong side of them. But by actively moving about in these topsy-turvy worlds, they adapted to the context and learned to coordinate their movements.

Perceptual Set

OBJECTIVE 17-3 | Define *perceptual set,* and explain how it influences what we do or do not perceive.

As everyone knows, to see is to believe. As we also know, but less fully appreciate, to believe is to see. Our experiences, assumptions, and expectations may give us a **perceptual set,** or mental predisposition, that greatly influences what we perceive (top-down). People perceive an adult-child pair as looking more alike when told they are parent and child (Bressan & Dal Martello, 2002). And consider: Is the image in the center picture of **FIGURE 17.2** a man playing a saxophone or a woman's face? What we see in such a drawing can be influenced by first looking at either of the two unambiguous versions (Boring, 1930).

Once we have formed a wrong idea about reality, we have more difficulty seeing the truth. Even scientists, striving for objectivity, perceive reality through the lenses of their theories. When first viewing the "canals" on Mars through telescopes, some people perceived them as the product of intelligent life. They were—but the intelligence was on the viewing end of the telescope.

Everyday examples of perceptual set abound. In 1972, a British newspaper published genuine, unretouched photographs of a "monster" in Scotland's Loch Ness—

IT'S AMAZING HOW PEOPLE SLOW DOWN WHEN YOU POINT A HAIR DRYER AT THEM.

"The temptation to form premature theories upon insufficient data is the bane of our profession."

Sherlock Holmes, in Arthur Conan Doyle's *The Valley of Fear,* 1914

FIGURE 17.2
Perceptual set
What do you see in the center picture: a male saxophonist or a woman's face? Glancing first at one of the two unambiguous versions of the picture is likely to influence your interpretation.

Frank Searle, photo Adams/Corbis-Sygma

Dick Ruhl

(a)   (b)

FIGURE 17.3
Believing is seeing
What do you perceive in these photos? (a) Is this Nessie, the Loch Ness monster, or a log? (b) Are these flying saucers or clouds? We often perceive what we expect to see.

"the most amazing pictures ever taken," stated the paper. If this information creates in you the same perceptual set it did in most of the paper's readers, you, too, will see the monster in the photo reproduced in **FIGURE 17.3a**. But when Steuart Campbell (1986) approached the photos with a different perceptual set, he saw a curved tree trunk—very likely the same tree trunk others had seen in the water the day the photo was shot. Moreover, with this different perceptual set, you may now notice that the object is floating motionless, without any rippling water or wake around it—hardly what we would expect of a lively monster. Apparently aided by perceptual set, thousands of others have marveled at a face on the Moon, Mother Teresa on a cinnamon bun, and Jesus on a pancake.

Perceptual set can also influence what we hear. Consider the kindly airline pilot who, on a takeoff run, looked over at his depressed co-pilot and said, "Cheer up." The co-pilot heard the usual "Gear up" and promptly raised the wheels—before they left the ground (Reason & Mycielska, 1982). Clearly, much of what we perceive comes not just from the world "out there" but also from what's behind our eyes and between our ears.

What determines our perceptual set? Through experience we form concepts, or *schemas*, that organize and interpret unfamiliar information. Our preexisting schemas for male saxophonists and women's faces, for monsters and tree trunks, for airplane lights and UFOs all influence how we interpret ambiguous sensations with top-down processing. Confronted with an ambiguous moving object in the sky, different people may therefore apply different schemas: "It's a bird." "It's a plane." "It's Superman!"

Children's drawings give us a way to glimpse their developing perceptual schemas. A preschooler can draw circles and angled lines but cannot combine them to create an elaborate human figure. The child's difficulty is not clumsiness. A right-handed adult asked to draw with the left hand will create an awkward drawing, but it will be unlike the child's drawing in **FIGURE 17.4**. Part of the difference lies in the challenge

■ **perceptual set** a mental predisposition to perceive one thing and not another.

When shown the phrase:
  Mary had a
  a little lamb
many people perceive what they expect, and miss the repeated word. Did you?

Courtesy of Anna Elizabeth Voskuil

FIGURE 17.4
Schemas
Children's drawings reflect their schemas of reality, as well as their abilities to represent what they see. This drawing by 4-year-old Anna illustrates that the face has far greater importance than the body in young children's schemas of essential human characteristics.

Anticaricature   Actual   Caricature

FIGURE 17.5
Recognizing faces
When briefly flashed, a caricature of Arnold Schwarzenegger was more accurately recognized than Schwarzenegger himself. Ditto for other familiar male faces.

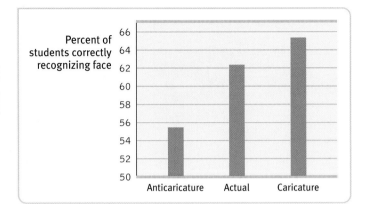

for children to represent visually what they see. The main difference, however, lies in the child's simplified schema for essential human characteristics. To 3- and 4-year-olds, a face is a more important human feature than a body. From ages 3 to 8, children's schemas for bodies become more elaborate, and so do their drawings.

Our schemas for faces prime us to see facial patterns even in random configurations, such as the lunar landscape. Kieran Lee, Graham Byatt, and Gillian Rhodes (2000) demonstrated how we recognize people by facial features that cartoonists can caricature. For but a fraction of a second they showed University of Western Australia students three versions of familiar faces—the actual face, a computer-created caricature that accentuated the differences between this face and the average face, and an "anticaricature" that muted the distinctive features. As **FIGURE 17.5** shows, the students more accurately recognized the caricatured faces than the actual ones. A caricatured Arnold Schwarzenegger is more recognizably Schwarzenegger than Schwarzenegger himself!

FIGURE 17.6
Aye for an eye
Christopher Tyler (1998) discovered that artists, when trying to capture a sense of the person, consciously or unconsciously place one eye on the painting's centerline.

FIGURE 17.7
Face schemas
Which of these is the real Madonna? Slowly rotate the page to find out. As you do so, you will reach a point where you suddenly cannot assimilate her mouth and eyes into your schema for faces.

Peter Thompson (1980) at the University of York discovered that our face recognition is especially attuned to the expressive eyes and mouth. Portrait artists seem to understand this. Two-thirds of portraits sampled from the last five centuries have an eye at or within 5 percent of the painting's exact centerline (**FIGURE 17.6**). We are so attuned to eyes that we have trouble imagining what Madonna's inverted eyes and mouth will look like when we turn her face upright (**FIGURE 17.7**).

Context Effects

OBJECTIVE 17-4 | Explain why the same stimulus can evoke different perceptions in different contexts.

A given stimulus may trigger radically different perceptions, partly because of our differing schemas, but also because of the immediate context. Two examples:

● Imagine hearing a noise interrupted by the words "eel is on the wagon." Likely, you would actually perceive the first word as *wheel*. Given "eel is on the orange," you would hear *peel*. This curious phenomenon, discovered by Richard Warren, suggests that the brain can work backward in time to allow a later stimulus to determine how we perceive an earlier one. The context creates an expectation that, top-down, influences our perception as we match our bottom-up signal against it (Grossberg, 1995).

● Is the "magician's cabinet" in **FIGURE 17.8** sitting on the floor or hanging from the ceiling? How we perceive it depends on the context defined by the rabbits.

FIGURE 17.8
Context effects: The magician's cabinet
Is the box in the far left frame lying on the floor or hanging from the ceiling? What about the one on the far right? In each case, the context defined by the inquisitive rabbits guides our perceptions. From Shepard, 1990.

Soviet film director Lew Kulechov believed that skilled directors evoke emotion in an audience by defining a context in which viewers interpret an actor's expressions. He once produced three short films, each depicting one of three contexts, followed by identical clips of an actor with a neutral expression (Wallbott, 1988). Shown a film of a dead woman, viewers of the clip were struck by the actor's sadness. Shown a dish of soup, viewers judged the actor thoughtful. Shown a playing child, viewers said the actor appeared happy. Even hearing sad rather than happy music can predispose people to perceive a sad meaning in spoken homophonic words—*mourning* rather than *morning*, *die* rather than *dye*, *pain* rather than *pane* (Halberstadt & others, 1995).

Culture and context effects
What is above the woman's head? In one study, nearly all the East Africans who were questioned said the woman was balancing a metal box or can on her head and that the family was sitting under a tree. Westerners, for whom corners and boxlike architecture are more common, were more likely to perceive the family as being indoors, with the woman sitting under a window. (Adapted from Gregory & Gombrich, 1973.)

Given a perceptual set — "this is a girl" — people see a more feminine baby.

"Have you ever noticed that anyone driving slower than you is an idiot, and anyone going faster is a maniac?"

George Carlin, *George Carlin on Campus*, 1984

Biological influences:
• entry-level sensory analysis
• unlearned visual phenomena
• critical period for sensory development

Psychological influences:
• selective attention
• learned schemas
• Gestalt principles
• emotional context effects
• perceptual set

Perception: Our version of reality

Social-cultural influences:
• cultural assumptions and expectations
• physical context effects

FIGURE 17.9
Perception is a biopsychosocial phenomenon
Psychologists study how we perceive with different levels of analysis, from the biological to the social-cultural.

■ **human factors psychology** a branch of psychology that explores how people and machines interact and how machines and physical environments can be made safe and easy to use.

Emotional contexts also color our social perceptions. Spouses who feel loved and appreciated perceive less threat in stressful marital events—"He's just having a bad day" (Murray & others, 2003). If told a soccer team has a history of aggressive behavior, professional referees will assign more penalty cards after watching videotaped fouls (Jones & others, 2002). Lee Ross invites us to recall our own perceptions in different contexts: "Ever notice that when you're driving you hate pedestrians, the way they saunter through the crosswalk, almost daring you to hit them, but when you're walking you hate drivers?" (Jaffe, 2004).

The effects of perceptual set and context show how experience helps us construct perception. "We hear and apprehend only what we already half know," said Thoreau. In everyday life, for example, stereotypes about gender (another instance of perceptual set) can color the context. Without the obvious cues of pink or blue, people will struggle over whether to call the new baby "he" or "she." But told an infant is "David," people (especially children) may perceive "him" as bigger and stronger than if the same infant is called "Diana" (Stern & Karraker, 1989). Some differences, it seems, exist merely in the eyes of their beholders.

To return to the question "Is perception innate or learned?" we can answer: It's both. The river of perception is fed by two streams: sensation and cognition. And that is why we need multiple levels of analysis (**FIGURE 17.9**). "Simple" perceptions are the brain's creative products.

Perception and the Human Factor

OBJECTIVE **17-5** | Describe the role human factors psychologists play in creating user-friendly machines and work settings.

I love my new bedside clock-radio, though I struggle to remember which buttons are Snooze, Alarm Off, and Radio On. Our stove is also wonderful, except for the moments I spend puzzling over which control works which burner. The push-bar doors on our campus buildings are sturdy, though occasionally frustrating when I push the wrong end. The extra buttons on my phone are handy, though when transferring a call I still must look up which buttons to press.

Human factors psychologists help to design appliances, machines, and work settings that fit our natural perceptions. Psychologist Donald Norman (1988) suggests how simple design changes could reduce some of our frustrations. For example, by exploiting *natural mapping*, we could design stove controls that require no labels (**FIGURE 17.10**). ATM machines are internally more complex than VCRs ever were, yet, thanks to human factors psychologists working with engineers, ATMs are easier to operate. TiVo has solved the TV recording problem with a simple point-and-click menu system ("record that one").

(a)   (b)

FIGURE 17.10
Natural mapping
(a) With traditionally positioned stove controls, a person must read the labels to figure out which knob works which burner. (b) By positioning the controls in a natural map, which the brain understands at a glance, we can eliminate the need to ponder written instructions just to boil water.

Norman (2001), who hosts a Web site (jnd.org) on designing equipment to fit people, bemoaned the complexity of assembling his new high-definition TV, receiver, speakers, digital recorder, DVD player, VCR, and seven remotes into a usable home theater system. "I was VP of Advanced Technology at Apple," says Norman, an MIT alumnus with a Ph.D. "I can program dozens of computers in dozens of languages. I understand television, really, I do. . . . It doesn't matter: I am overwhelmed." If only the makers of home entertainment equipment would minimize cords and cables by bundling audio, visual, control, and power lines into a single cable. If only a single control could operate a point-and-click menu. If only engineers would routinely work with human factors psychologists to test their designs and instructions on real people.

Technology developers often suffer the "curse of knowledge," which leads them to mistakenly assume that others share their expertise—that what's clear to them will similarly be clear to others (Camerer & others, 1989; Nickerson, 1999). When you know a thing, it's hard to mentally simulate what it's like not to know.

Understanding human factors can do more than enable us to design for reduced frustration; it can help avoid disaster. Two-thirds of commercial air accidents, for example, have been caused by human error (Nickerson, 1998). After beginning commercial flights in the late 1960s, the Boeing 727 was involved in several landing accidents caused by pilot error. Psychologist Conrad Kraft (1978) noted a common setting for these accidents: All took place at night, and all involved landing short of the runway after crossing a dark stretch of water or unilluminated ground. Kraft reasoned that, beyond the runway, city lights would project a larger retinal image if on a rising terrain. This would make the ground seem farther away than it was. By recreating these conditions in flight simulations, Kraft discovered that pilots were deceived into thinking they were flying higher than their actual altitudes (**FIGURE 17.11**). Aided by Kraft's finding, the airlines began requiring the co-pilot to monitor the altimeter—calling out altitudes during the descent—and the accidents diminished.

FIGURE 17.11
The human factor in misperception
Lacking distance cues when approaching a runway from over a dark surface, pilots simulating a night landing tended to fly too low. (From Kraft, 1978.)

FIGURE 17.12
How not to go mad while going to Mars
Future astronauts headed to Mars will be confined in conditions of monotony, stress, and weightlessness for months on end. To help design and evaluate a workable human environment, such as for this Transit Habitation (Transhab) Module, NASA engages human factors psychologists (Weed, 2001; Wichman, 1992).

Courtesy of NASA

Later Boeing psychologists worked on other human factors problems (Murray, 1998): How should airlines best train and manage mechanics to reduce the maintenance errors that underlie about 50 percent of flight delays and 15 percent of accidents? What illumination and typeface would make on-screen flight data easiest to read? How would warning messages be most effectively worded—as an action statement ("Pull Up") rather than a problem statement ("Ground Proximity")?

In studying human factors issues, psychologists' most powerful tool is research. If an organization wonders what sort of Web design (emphasizing content? speed? graphics?) would most effectively draw in visitors and entice them to return, the psychologist will want to test responses to several alternatives. If NASA (National Aeronautics and Space Administration) wonders what sort of spacecraft design would best facilitate sleeping, work, and morale, their human factors psychologists will want to test the alternatives (**FIGURE 17.12**).

Consider, finally, the available "assistive listening" technologies in various auditoriums, places of worship, and theaters. One technology, commonly available in the United States, requires people with hearing loss to use a headset attached to a pocket-sized receiver that detects infrared or FM signals from the room's sound system. The well-meaning people who design, purchase, and install these systems correctly understand that the technology puts sound directly into the user's ears. Alas, few people with hearing loss undergo the hassle and embarrassment of locating, requesting, wearing, and returning a conspicuous headset. Most such units therefore sit in closets. Britain, the Scandinavian countries, and Australia have instead installed "loop systems" that broadcast customized sound directly through a person's own hearing aid. When suitably equipped, a discrete touch of a switch can transform hearing aids into in-the-ear loudspeakers. A loop system (a special amplifier attached to a wire encircling an audience) can also work in homes, enabling TV sound or phone conversation to broadcast directly through hearing aids (see www.hearingloop.org). When offered convenient, inconspicuous, personalized sound, many more people elect to use assistive listening.

The point to remember: Designers and engineers should consider the human factor, by designing things to fit people, being mindful of the curse of knowledge, and user-testing their inventions before production and distribution.

Is There Extrasensory Perception?

OBJECTIVE 17-6 | Identify the three most testable forms of ESP, and explain why most research psychologists remain skeptical of ESP claims.

Can we perceive only what we sense? Or, without sensory input, are we capable of **extrasensory perception (ESP)?** Are there indeed people—any people—who can read minds, see through walls, or foretell the future? Five British universities have **parapsychology** units staffed by Ph.D. graduates of Edinburgh University's parapsychology program (Turpin, 2005). Sweden's Lund University, the Netherlands' Utrecht University, and Australia's University of Adelaide also have added faculty chairs or research units for parapsychology. But other research psychologists and scientists—including 96 percent of the scientists in the U.S. National Academy of Sciences—are skeptical (McConnell, 1991). If ESP is real, we would need to overturn the scientific

SNAPSHOTS

understanding that we are creatures whose minds are tied to our physical brains and whose perceptual experiences of the world are built of sensations. Sometimes new evidence does overturn our scientific preconceptions. Science, as we will see throughout this book, offers us various surprises—about the extent of the unconscious mind, about the effects of emotion on health, about what heals and what doesn't, and much more. Before we evaluate claims of ESP, let's review them.

Claims of ESP

Claims of paranormal phenomena include astrological predictions, psychic healing, communication with the dead, and out-of-body experiences. But the most testable and (in the study of perception) most relevant claims are for three varieties of ESP:

Telepathy, or mind-to-mind communication—one person sending thoughts to another or perceiving another's thoughts.

Clairvoyance, or perceiving remote events, such as sensing that a friend's house is on fire.

Precognition, or perceiving future events, such as a political leader's death or a sporting event's outcome.

Closely linked with these are claims of *psychokinesis*, or "mind over matter," such as levitating a table or influencing the roll of a die (**FIGURE 17.13**). (The claim is illustrated by the wry request, "Will all those who believe in psychokinesis please raise my hand?")

FIGURE 17.13
Parapsychological concepts

Premonitions or Pretensions?

Can psychics see into the future? Although one might wish for a psychic stock forecaster, the tallied forecasts of "leading psychics" reveal meager accuracy. No greedy—or charitable—psychic has been able to predict the outcome of a lottery jackpot, or to make billions on the stock market. During the 1990s, tabloid psychics were all wrong in predicting surprising events. (Madonna did not become a gospel singer, the Statue of Liberty did not lose both its arms in a terrorist blast, Queen Elizabeth did not abdicate her throne to enter a convent.) And the new-century psychics missed the big-news events such as the Florida presidential ballot controversy, the whereabouts and capture of Saddam Hussein, and the horror of 9/11. (Where were the precogs on 9/10 when we needed them?) Gene Emery (2004), who has tracked annual psychic forecasts for 26 years, reports that almost never have unusual predictions come true and virtually never have psychics anticipated any of the year's headline events.

Analyses of psychic visions offered to police departments reveal that these, too, are no more accurate than guesses made by others (Reiser, 1982). Psychics working with the police do, however, generate hundreds of predictions. This increases the odds of an occasional correct guess, which psychics can then report to the media. Moreover, vague predictions can later be interpreted ("retrofitted") to match events that provide a perceptual set for interpreting them. Nostradamus, a sixteenth-century French psychic, explained in an unguarded moment that his ambiguous prophecies "could not possibly be understood till they were interpreted after the event and by it."

Police departments are wise to all this. When Jane Ayers Sweat and Mark Durm (1993) asked the police departments of America's 50 largest cities whether they ever used psychics, 65 percent said they never had. Of those that had, not one had found it helpful. Thousands of psychics reportedly overwhelmed police with mispredictions

"A person who talks a lot is sometimes right."

Spanish proverb

BIZARRO   By DAN PIRARO

Which supposed psychic ability does Psychic Pizza claim? (See this module's final page for the answer.)

of the whereabouts of Washington, D.C., intern Chandra Levy, whose body was discovered by a jogger on a wooded hill a year after her disappearance (Radford, 2002).

Are the spontaneous "visions" of everyday people any more accurate? Consider our dreams. Do they foretell the future, as about half of university students have believed (Messer & Griggs, 1989)? Or do they only seem to do so because we are more likely to recall or reconstruct dreams that seem to have come true? Two Harvard psychologists (Murray & Wheeler, 1937) tested the prophetic power of dreams after aviator Charles Lindbergh's baby son was kidnapped and murdered in 1932, but before the body was discovered. When the researchers invited the public to report their dreams about the child, 1300 visionaries submitted dream reports. How many accurately envisioned the child dead? Five percent. And how many also correctly anticipated the body's location—buried among trees? Only 4 of the 1300. Although this number was surely no better than chance, to those 4 dreamers the accuracy of their *apparent* precognitions must have seemed uncanny.

Throughout the day, each of us imagines many events. Given the billions of events in the world each day, and given enough days, some stunning coincidences are sure to occur. By one careful estimate, chance alone would predict that more than a thousand times a day someone on Earth will think of someone and then within the ensuing five minutes will learn of the person's death (Charpak & Broch, 2004). With enough time or people, the improbable becomes inevitable.

That has been the experience of comics writer John Byrne (2003). Six months after his Spider-Man story about a New York blackout appeared, New York suffered its massive blackout. A subsequent Spider-Man storyline involved a major earthquake in Japan "and again," he recalls, "the real thing happened in the month the issue hit the stands." Later, when working on a Superman comic book, he "had the Man of Steel fly to the rescue when disaster beset the NASA space shuttle. The *Challenger* tragedy happened almost immediately thereafter" (with time for the issue to be redrawn). "Most recently, and chilling, came when I was writing and drawing Wonder Woman and did a story in which the title character was killed as a prelude to her becoming a goddess." The issue cover "was done as a newspaper front page, with the headline 'Princess Diana Dies.' (Diana is Wonder Woman's real name.) That issue went on sale on a Thursday. The following Saturday . . . I don't have to tell you, do I?"

> "Things that happen by chance are events in search of causes."
>
> K. C. Cole, *The Universe and the Teacup*, 1998

Putting ESP to Experimental Test

In the past, there have been all kinds of strange ideas—that bumps on the head reveal character traits, that bloodletting is a cure-all, that each sperm cell contains a miniature person. When faced with such claims—or with claims of mind reading or out-of-body travel or communication with the dead—how can we separate bizarre ideas from those that sound bizarre but are true? At the heart of science is a simple answer: *Test them to see if they work.* If they do, so much the better for the ideas. If they don't, so much the better for our skepticism.

> "At the heart of science is an essential tension between two seemingly contradictory attitudes—an openness to new ideas, no matter how bizarre or counterintuitive they may be, and the most ruthless skeptical scrutiny of all ideas, old and new."
>
> Carl Sagan (1987)

Courtesy of Claire Cole

Testing psychic powers in the British population
Hertfordshire University psychologist Richard Wiseman created a "mind machine" to see if people can influence or predict a coin toss. Using a touch-sensitive screen, visitors to festivals around the country were given four attempts to call heads or tails. Using a random-number generator, a computer then decided the outcome. When the experiment concluded in January 2000, nearly 28,000 people had predicted 110,972 tosses—with 49.8 percent correct.

This scientific attitude has led both believers and skeptics to agree that what parapsychology needs to give it credibility is a reproducible phenomenon and a theory to explain it. Parapsychologist Rhea White (1998) acknowledges that "the image of parapsychology that comes to my mind, based on nearly 44 years in the field, is that of a small airplane [that] has been perpetually taxiing down the runway of the Empirical Science Airport since 1882 . . . its movement punctuated occasionally by lifting a few feet off the ground only to bump back down on the tarmac once again. It has never taken off for any sustained flight."

Seeking a reproducible phenomenon, how might we test ESP claims in a controlled experiment? An experiment differs from a staged demonstration. In the laboratory, the experimenter controls what the "psychic" sees and hears. On stage, the psychic controls what the audience sees and hears. Time and again, skeptics note, so-called psychics have exploited unquestioning audiences with mind-blowing performances in which they *appeared* to communicate with the spirits of the dead, read minds, or levitate objects—only to have it revealed that their acts were nothing more than the illusions of stage magicians.

The search for a valid and reliable test of ESP has resulted in thousands of experiments. One controlled procedure has invited "senders" to telepathically transmit one of four visual images to "receivers" deprived of sensation in a nearby chamber (Bem & Honorton, 1994). The result? A reported 32 percent accurate response rate, surpassing the chance rate of 25 percent. But follow-up studies have (depending on who was summarizing the results) failed to replicate the phenomenon or produced mixed results (Bem & others, 2001; Milton & Wiseman, 2002; Storm, 2000, 2003).

One skeptic, magician James Randi, has a longstanding offer—now U.S. $1 million—"to anyone who proves a genuine psychic power under proper observing conditions" (Randi, 1999). French, Australian, and Indian groups have parallel offers of up to 200,000 euros to anyone with demonstrable paranormal abilities (CFI, 2003). And $50 million was available for information leading to Osama bin Laden's capture. Large as these sums are, the scientific seal of approval would be worth far more to anyone whose claims could be authenticated. To refute those who say there is no ESP, one need only produce a single person who can demonstrate a single, reproducible ESP phenomenon. (To refute those who say pigs can't talk would take but one talking

"A psychic is an actor playing the role of a psychic."

Psychologist-magician Daryl Bem (1984)

"People's desire to believe in the paranormal is stronger than all the evidence that it does not exist."

Susan Blackmore, "Blackmore's first law," 2004

"So, how *does* the mind work? I don't know. You don't know. Pinker doesn't know. And, I rather suspect, such is the current state of the art, that if God were to tell us, we wouldn't understand."

Jerry Fodor, "Reply to Steven Pinker," 2005

pig.) So far, no such person has emerged. Randi's offer has been publicized for three decades and dozens of people have been tested, sometimes under the scrutiny of an independent panel of judges. Still, nothing.

Why, then, are so many people predisposed to believe that ESP exists? In part, such beliefs may stem from understandable misperceptions, misinterpretations, and selective recall. But some people also have an unsatisfied hunger for wonderment, an itch to experience the magical. In Britain and the United States, the founders of parapsychology were mostly people who, having lost their religious faith, began searching for a scientific basis for believing in the meaning of life and in life after death (Alcock, 1985; Beloff, 1985). In the upheaval after the collapse of autocratic rule in Russia, there came an "avalanche of the mystical, occult, and pseudoscientific" (Kapitza, 1991). In Russia as elsewhere, "extrasensorial" healers and seers have fascinated the awestruck public. "Many people," declared a statement by 32 leading Russian scientists in 1999, "believe in clairvoyance, astrology, and other superstitions to compensate for the psychological discomforts of our time."

To feel awe and to gain a deep reverence for life, we need look no further than our own perceptual system and its capacity for organizing formless nerve impulses into colorful sights, vivid sounds, and evocative smells. As Shakespeare's Hamlet recognized, "There are more things in Heaven and Earth, Horatio, than are dreamt of in your philosophy." Within our ordinary perceptual experiences lies much that is truly extraordinary—surely much more than has so far been dreamt of in our psychology. A century of research has revealed many of the secrets of sensation and perception, yet for future generations of researchers there remain profound and genuine mysteries to solve. Between our sensing and acting lies an unimaginably complex information system that, more than ever, beckons explorers of our mind's inner space.

>> LEARNING OUTCOMES

Perceptual Interpretation

OBJECTIVE 17-1 | **Describe the contribution of restored-vision and sensory deprivation research in our understanding of the nature-nurture interplay in our perceptions.**

If all aspects of visual perception were entirely inborn, people who were born blind but regained sight after surgery should have normal visual perception. They do not. After cataract surgery, for example, adults who had been blind from birth are able to distinguish figure from ground and to perceive colors, but they lack the experience to recognize shapes, forms, and complete faces. Animals reared with severely restricted visual input suffered enduring visual handicaps when returned to a normal visual environment. A critical period exists for some aspects of sensory and perceptual development. Without the stimulation provided by early visual experiences, the brain's neural organization does not develop normally.

OBJECTIVE 17-2 | **Explain how the research on distorting goggles increases our understanding of the adaptability of perception.**

The experiences of people who have worn distorting goggles demonstrates our ability to adjust to an artificially altered visual field and coordinate our movements in response to that new world.

OBJECTIVE 17-3 | **Define *perceptual set*, and explain how it influences what we do or do not perceive.**

Perceptual set is a mental predisposition that functions as a lens through which we perceive the world. Because our learned concepts (schemas) prime us to organize and interpret sensory input, especially ambiguous stimuli, in certain ways, our perceptions reflect our version of reality. Thus, some of us "see" monsters, faces, and UFOs or "hear" messages that others do not.

OBJECTIVE 17-4 | **Explain why the same stimulus can evoke different perceptions in different contexts.**

Context creates expectations that guide our perceptions of a given stimulus. Emotional context can color our interpretation of other people's behaviors—and our own. Perceptual set and context effects interact to help us construct our perceptions.

OBJECTIVE 17-5 | **Describe the role human factors psychologists play in creating user-friendly machines and work settings.**

Human factors psychologists encourage developers and designers to consider human perceptual abilities, to avoid the *curse of knowledge* (the mistaken assumption that others share our expertise and will behave as we would), and to schedule user-testing to reveal perception-based problems before production and distribution. Human factors psychologists have contributed to improved safety in air and space travel; better-designed appliances, equipment, and workplaces; and easier-to-use assistive listening.

OBJECTIVE 17-6 | **Identify the three most testable forms of ESP, and explain why most research psychologists remain skeptical of ESP claims.**

ESP (extrasensory perception) is one form of purported paranormal phenomena. (Another form is psychokinesis [PK].) The three most testable forms of ESP are *telepathy* (mind-to-mind communication), *clairvoyance* (perceiving remote events), and *precognition* (perceiving future events). Most research psychologists are skeptical of ESP claims because (1) they do not believe the brain is capable of perceiving without sensory input, and (2) parapsychologists have been unable to replicate (reproduce) ESP phenomena under controlled conditions.

TERMS AND CONCEPTS TO REMEMBER

perceptual adaptation, p. 17-1
perceptual set, p. 17-2
human factors psychology, p. 17-6

extrasensory perception (ESP), p. 17-8
parapsychology, p. 17-8

TEST YOURSELF

1. What type of evidence shows that, indeed, "there is more to perception than meets the senses"?

(Answer in Appendix B.)

ASK YOURSELF

1. Can you recall a time when your expectations have predisposed how you perceived a person (or group of people)?

2. Have you ever had an ESP experience? Can you think of an explanation other than ESP for that experience?

ANSWER TO QUESTION WITHIN THE MODULE

Q. Which supposed psychic ability does Psychic Pizza claim?

A. Psychic Pizza claims to fill customer orders by telepathy—mind-to-mind communication.

>WEB

Multiple-choice *self-tests* and more may be found at www.worthpublishers.com/myers.

Faiz Ahmed Faiz (Pakistan) (1911–1984), From "A Prison Daybreak," *Rebel's Silhouette*

Night wasn't over when the moon stood beside my bed
and said, "You've drunk your sleep to the dregs,
your share of that wine is finished for this night."

My eyes tore themselves from a dream of passion–
they said farewell to my lover's image, still
lingering in the night's stagnant waters
that were spread, like a sheet, over the earth.

Silver whirlpools began their dervish dance
as lotuses of stars fell from the moon's hands.
Some sank. Some rose to the surface, floated, and opened their petals.
Night and daybreak had fallen desperately
into each other's arms.

States of Consciousness

Now playing at an inner theater near you: the premiere showing of a sleeping person's vivid dream. This never-before-seen mental movie features captivating characters wrapped in a plot so original and unlikely, yet so intricate and so seemingly real, that the viewer later marvels at its creation.

Waking from a troubling dream, wrenched by its emotions, who among us has not wondered about this weird state of consciousness? How does our brain so creatively, colorfully, and completely construct this alternative, conscious world? In the shadowland between our dreaming and waking consciousness, we may even wonder for a moment which is real. And what shall we make of other altered states of consciousness, such as hypnosis, drug-altered hallucinations, and near-death visions?

Module 18 presents a historical view of consciousness, a discussion of conscious and unconscious information processing, and an in-depth look at sleep and dreams.

Module 19 discusses various beliefs about hypnosis, including research support for some of the claims related to hypnosis.

Module 20 details dependence, addiction, and the three main categories of psychoactive drugs.

States of consciousness
In addition to normal, waking awareness, consciousness comes to us in altered states, note Dieter Vaitl and colleagues (2005), including daydreaming, sleeping, meditating, and drug-induced hallucinating.

MODULE

Consciousness and
Information Processing

Sleep and Dreams

18

Waking and Sleeping Rhythms

Consciousness and Information Processing

OBJECTIVE 18-1 | Discuss the history of psychology's study of consciousness, and contrast conscious and unconscious information processing.

> "Neither [psychologist] Steve Pinker nor I can explain human subjective consciousness. . . . We don't understand it."
> Evolutionary biologist Richard Dawkins (1999)

> "Psychology must discard all reference to consciousness."
> Behaviorist John B. Watson (1913)

What is consciousness? In every science there are concepts so fundamental they are nearly impossible to define. Biologists agree on what is alive but not on precisely what life is. In physics, matter and energy elude simple definition. In psychology, consciousness is similarly a fundamental yet slippery concept.

Psychologists have long explored consciousness, at first eagerly, then warily, and now with renewed vigor. At its beginning, *psychology* was "the description and explanation of states of consciousness" (Ladd, 1887). But the difficulty of scientifically studying consciousness led many psychologists during the first half of the last century to turn to direct observations of behavior—an approach favored by an emerging school of psychology called *behaviorism*. By the 1960s, psychology no longer defined itself as the study of consciousness or "mental life" but rather as the science of behavior. Psychology had nearly lost consciousness. Consciousness was viewed as resembling a car's speedometer: "It doesn't make the car go, it just reflects what's happening" (Seligman, 1991, p. 24).

After 1960, mental concepts began to reenter psychology. Advances in neuroscience made it possible to relate brain activity to various mental states—waking, sleeping, dreaming. Researchers began studying consciousness altered by hypnosis and drugs. Psychologists of all persuasions were affirming the importance of mental processes (cognition). Psychology was regaining consciousness.

For most psychologists today, **consciousness** is our awareness of ourselves and our environment. Consciousness brings varied information to the surface, enabling us to reflect and plan. When we learn a complex concept or behavior—say, driving a car—consciousness focuses our concentration on the car and the traffic. This awareness varies with our attentional spotlight. With practice, driving becomes automatic and no longer requires our undivided attention—freeing our consciousness to focus on other things. If I ask you to pay attention to the weight of your body pressing on your buttocks as you sit reading, you will momentarily stop reading.

Conscious awareness enables us to exert voluntary control and to communicate our mental states to others, yet consciousness is but the tip of the information-processing iceberg. Research reported throughout this book reveals that we process a great deal of information outside our awareness. We register and react to stimuli we do not consciously perceive. We perform well-learned tasks automatically, as when keyboarding without attending to where the letters are. We change our attitudes and reconstruct our memories with no awareness of doing so. When we meet people, we instantly and unconsciously react to their gender, age, and appearance, and *then* become aware of our response.

Beneath the surface, unconscious information processing occurs simultaneously on many parallel tracks. When we look at a bird flying, we are consciously aware of the result of our cognitive processing ("It's a hummingbird!") but not of our subprocessing of the bird's color, form, movement, distance, and identity.

■ **consciousness** our awareness of ourselves and our environment.

TABLE 18.1

STATES OF CONSCIOUSNESS

Some Occur Spontaneously	Some Are Physiologically Induced	Some Are Pyschologically Induced
Daydreaming	Hallucinations	Sensory Deprivation
Drowsiness	Orgasm	Hypnosis
Dreaming	Food or Oxygen Starvation	Meditation

According to one theory, when reverberating brain activity among interconnected brain areas crosses a threshold of intensity, it triggers consciousness (Sergent & Dehaene, 2004). Stephen Kosslyn and Olivier Koenig (1992) suggest that brain events are to consciousness what a guitar's individual notes are to a chord. As a chord emerges from the interaction of different notes, so consciousness emerges from the interaction of individual brain events.

Today's neuroscientists are identifying neurological activity linked with consciousness. In some provocative experiments, Benjamin Libet (1985, 2004) observed that we experience the chord an instant *after* all the notes are present, so consciousness is known to lag behind the brain events that evoke it. For example, when you move a wrist at will, you consciously experience the decision to move about 0.2 seconds before the actual movement. No surprise there. But your brain waves jump about 0.35 seconds ahead of your conscious perception of the decision (**FIGURE 18.1**)! Thus, before you become aware of it, your brain seems headed toward your decision to move your wrist. Likewise, if asked to press a button when you feel a tap, you can respond in 1/10th of a second—less time than it takes to become conscious that you have responded (Wegner, 2002). The startling conclusion from these experiments is that consciousness sometimes arrives late to the decision-making party.

Unlike the processing of unconscious information, which occurs simultaneously on multiple parallel tracks, conscious processing takes place in sequence (serially). Consciousness is relatively slow and has limited capacity but is skilled at solving novel problems. It is like a chief executive, whose many assistants automatically take care of routine business. Traveling a familiar route, your hands and feet do the driving while your mind is elsewhere. Running on automatic pilot allows consciousness—the mind's CEO—to monitor the whole system and deal with new challenges.

Novel tasks require our conscious attention. Try this: If you are right-handed, you can move your right foot in a smooth counterclockwise circle, and you can write the number 3 repeatedly with your right hand—but probably not at the same time. (If you are musically inclined, try something equally difficult: Tap a steady three times with your left hand while tapping four times with your right hand.) Both tasks require conscious attention, which can be in only one place at a time. If time is nature's way of keeping everything from happening at once, then consciousness is nature's way of keeping us from thinking and doing everything at once.

FIGURE 18.1

Is the brain ahead of the mind?

In research by Benjamin Libet, unconscious brain activity precedes conscious awareness of a simple decision preceding an action. A person watches a computer clock that sweeps a revolution every 2.56 seconds, and notes the time at which she decides to move her wrist. About one-third of a second before the person decides to move, brain wave activity jumps, indicating a "readiness potential" to move. Thus, watching a slow motion replay, the researchers can predict when the person is about to decide to move (following which the wrist does move).

Sleep and Dreams

Sleep—the irresistible tempter to whom we inevitably succumb. Sleep—the equalizer of presidents and peasants. Sleep—sweet, renewing, mysterious sleep. Sleep's age-old mysteries have intrigued scientists for centuries.

Now, some of these mysteries are being solved. In laboratories throughout the world, thousands have slept attached to recording devices while others observe. By recording sleepers' brain waves and muscle movements, and by observing and waking them from time to time, the sleep watchers glimpse things that a thousand years of common sense never told us. Perhaps you can anticipate some of their discoveries. Are the following statements true or false?

1. When people dream of performing some activity, their limbs often move in concert with the dream.
2. Older adults sleep more than young adults.
3. Sleepwalkers are acting out their dreams.
4. Sleep experts recommend treating insomnia with an occasional sleeping pill.
5. Some people dream every night; others seldom dream.

All these statements (adapted from Palladino & Carducci, 1983) are false. To see why, read on.

Biological Rhythms

OBJECTIVE 18-2 | Distinguish four types of biological rhythms, and give an example of each.

Like the ocean, life has its rhythmic tides. Over varying time periods our bodies fluctuate, and with them our minds. These **biological rhythms,** controlled by internal "biological clocks," include

- *Annual cycles* On an annual cycle, geese migrate, grizzly bears hibernate, and humans may experience seasonal variations in appetite, sleep length, and moods. For some people, especially in far northern regions, a depressed mood during winter's dark months may define a *seasonal affective disorder.*
- *Twenty-eight–day cycles* The female menstrual cycle averages 28 days. Does that cycle cause fluctuating moods? Many believe it indeed does, but some research psychologists are skeptical (**FIGURE 18.2**).

"I love to sleep. Do you? Isn't it great? It really is the best of both worlds. You get to be alive and unconscious."
Comedian Rita Rudner, 1993

"When a man can't explain a woman's actions, the first thing he thinks about is the condition of her uterus."
Clare Boothe Luce, *Slam the Door Softly,* 1970

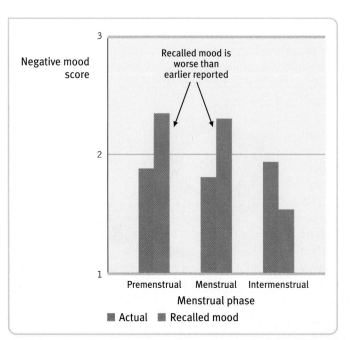

FIGURE 18.2
Menstruation, actual mood, and perceived mood
Cathy McFarland and her colleagues (1989) found that Ontario women's daily mood reports did not vary across their menstrual cycle. Yet they *perceived* that their moods were generally worse just before and after menstruation and better at others times of the cycle.

- *Twenty-four–hour cycles* Humans experience 24-hour cycles of varying alertness, body temperature, and growth hormone secretion. And not just humans. All mammals and birds sleep (Siegel, 2002).
- *Ninety-minute cycles* This chapter explores how we move through various stages of sleep in 90-minute cycles. Curiously, small animals have shorter sleep cycles (rats, 9 minutes; cats and dogs, 25 minutes) than big animals (elephants, 100+ minutes) (Hobson, 1989; Morrison, 2003).

The Rhythm of Sleep

Let's look more closely at two of those biological rhythms—our 24-hour biological clock and our 90-minute sleep cycle.

Circadian Rhythm

OBJECTIVE **18-3** | Describe the cycle of our circadian rhythm, and identify some events that can disrupt this biological clock.

The rhythm of the day parallels the rhythm of life—from our waking to a new day's birth to our nightly return to what Shakespeare called "death's counterfeit." Our bodies roughly synchronize with the 24-hour cycle of day and night through a biological clock called the **circadian rhythm** (from the Latin *circa,* "about," and *diem,* "day"). Our body temperature rises as morning approaches, peaks during the day, dips for a time in early afternoon (when many people take siestas), and then begins to drop again before we go to sleep. Awake at 4:00 A.M., body depressed, we may fret over concerns: Does a lovers' spat signal a split? Does a child's moodiness mean more trouble ahead? By mid-day, our body energized, we fret less. Pulling an all-nighter, we feel groggiest about 4:00 A.M., and then we get a second wind after our normal wake-up time arrives.

Recent evidence suggests that thinking is sharpest and memory most accurate when people are at their daily peak in circadian arousal. With age, we tend to shift from being evening-energized "owls" to being morning-loving "larks." Most university students are owls (May & Hasher, 1998); their performance typically improves across the day. Most older adults are larks, with their performance declining as the day wears on. In retirement homes, all is quiet by mid-evening; in university dorms, the day is far from over. The transition from sleeping later to sleeping earlier begins about age 20—though slightly earlier for women, who also enter puberty earlier and stop growing earlier than men (Roenneberg & others, 2004).

A transcontinental flight disrupts our circadian rhythm and we experience jet lag, mainly because we are awake when our circadian rhythm cries "Sleep!" Studies in the laboratory and with shift workers reveal that bright light helps reset our biological clocks (Czeisler & others, 1986, 1989; Eastman & others, 1995). Thus, to speed the resetting of your biological clock after a long flight, spend the first day outdoors. Bright light in the morning facilitates awakening (and protects against depression). Bright light at night helps delay sleep (Oren & Terman, 1998).

Light tweaks the circadian clock by activating light-sensitive retinal proteins. These proteins trigger signals to the brain's *suprachiasmatic nucleus*—a pair of pinhead-sized clusters of 20,000 cells that control the circadian clock (Foster, 2004). It does so partly by causing the brain's pineal gland to decrease (in the morning) or increase (in the evening) its production of the sleep-inducing hormone *melatonin* (**FIGURE 18.3**). The longer we are awake, the more our active brain produces

■ **biological rhythms** periodic physiological fluctuations.

■ **circadian** [ser-KAY-dee-an] **rhythm** the biological clock; regular bodily rhythms (for example, of temperature and wakefulness) that occur on a 24-hour cycle.

Dolphins can sleep while moving.

FIGURE 18.3
The biological clock
Light striking the retina causes the suprachiasmatic nucleus (a tiny neural center in the hypothalamus) to alter the production of biologically active substances, such as melatonin production by the pineal gland.

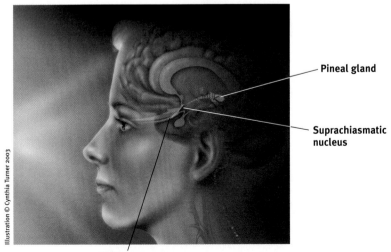

Illustration © Cynthia Turner 2003

Pineal gland

Suprachiasmatic nucleus

Optic nerve

and accumulates the chemical *adenosine,* which inhibits certain neurons, making us sleepy. (Caffeine blocks adenosine's activity.) During sleep, adenosine concentration declines (Porkka-Heiskanen & others, 1997).

We can unwittingly reset our biological clocks by adjusting our sleep schedules. If we stay up late and sleep in on weekends, we may end up with "Sunday night insomnia" and "Monday morning blues." Those who sleep till noon on Sunday and then go to bed just 11 hours later in preparation for the new workweek often find sleep elusive. They are like New Yorkers whose biology is on California time, or like someone who has just flown east from Perth to Sydney.

Curiously—given that our ancestors' body clocks were attuned to the rising and setting sun of the 24-hour day—many of today's young adults adopt something closer to a 25-hour day, by staying up too late to get 8 hours of sleep. For this, we can thank (or blame) Thomas Edison, inventor of the light bulb. Being bathed in light, even in a cave, is like traveling one time zone west—it nudges our 24-hour biological clock back (Czeisler & others, 1999; Dement, 1999). This helps explain why rotating shift workers and store clerks servicing a 24/7 culture adapt better to progressively later shifts than to earlier ones, and why until our later years we must discipline ourselves to go to bed on time and force ourselves to get up. Most animals, too, when placed under unnatural constant illumination will exceed a 24-hour day. Artificial light delays sleep.

If our natural circadian rhythm were attuned to a 23-hour cycle, would we instead need to discipline ourselves to stay up later at night and sleep in longer in the morning? Do older adults, who typically prefer earlier waking and bedtime than university students, have a shorter circadian rhythm?

Sleep Stages

OBJECTIVE 18-4 | List the stages of the sleep cycle, and explain how they differ.

As sleep overtakes us and different parts of the cortex stop communicating, consciousness fades (Massimini & others, 2005). But the still-active sleeping brain does not emit a constant dial tone, for there is also a biological rhythm during sleep. About every 90 minutes we pass through a cycle of five distinct sleep stages. This elementary fact apparently was unknown until 8-year-old Armond Aserinsky went to bed one night in 1952. His father, Eugene, a University of Chicago graduate student, needed to test an electroencephalograph he had been repairing during the day (Aserinsky, 1988; Seligman & Yellen, 1987). He placed electrodes near Armond's eyes to record the rolling eye movements believed to occur during sleep. Before long, the machine went wild, tracing deep zigzags on the graph paper. Aserinsky thought the machine was still broken. But as the night proceeded, the activity periodically recurred. This indicated, Aserinsky finally realized, fast, jerky eye movements accompanied by energetic brain activity. When he awakened Armond during one such episode, the boy reported he was having a dream. Aserinsky had discovered what we now know as **REM sleep** (rapid *eye* movement sleep).

To find out if similar cycles occur during adult sleep, Nathaniel Kleitman (1960) and Aserinsky pioneered procedures that have now been used with thousands of volunteers. To appreciate both their methods and findings, imagine yourself as a participant. As the hour grows late, you begin to fight sleepiness and yawn in response to reduced brain metabolism. Yawning stretches your neck muscles and increases your heart rate, which increases your alertness (Moorcroft, 2003). When you are ready for bed, the researcher glues electrodes to your scalp (to detect your brain waves), just outside the corners of your eyes (to detect eye movements), and on your chin (to detect muscle tension) (**FIGURE 18.4**). Other devices allow the researcher to record your heart rate, your respiration rate, and the degree of your genital arousal.

Left eye movements

Right eye movements

EMG (muscle tension)

EEG (brain waves)

FIGURE 18.4
Measuring sleep activity
Sleep researchers measure brain-wave activity, eye movements, and muscle tension by electrodes that pick up weak electrical signals from the brain, eye, and facial muscles. (From Dement, 1978.)

Hank Morgan/Rainbow

When you are in bed with your eyes closed, the researcher in the next room sees on the EEG the relatively slow **alpha waves** of your awake but relaxed state (**FIGURE 18.5**). As you adapt to all this equipment and grow tired, you slip into **sleep**. Sleep is a state we do not know we are in until we leave it. Our dive into sleep—marked by the slowed breathing and the irregular brain waves of Stage 1—happens in an unremembered moment (**FIGURE 18.6**).

In one of his 15,000 sleep research participants, William Dement (1999) observed the moment the perceptual door between the brain and outside world slammed shut. Dement asked this sleep-deprived young man, lying on his back with eyelids taped open, to press a button every time a strobe light flashed in his eyes (averaging about every 6 seconds). After a few minutes the subject missed one. Asked why, he said, "Because there was no flash." But there was a flash—which he missed because (as his brain activity revealed) he had fallen asleep for 2 seconds. Unaware that he had done so, he had missed not only the flash 6 inches from his nose but also the abrupt moment of his entry into sleep.

During this brief Stage 1 sleep you may experience fantastic images, resembling **hallucinations**—sensory experiences that occur without a sensory stimulus. You may have a sensation of falling (at which moment your body may suddenly jerk) or of floating weightlessly. Such *hypnagogic* sensations may later be incorporated into memories. People who claim to have been abducted by aliens—often shortly after getting into bed—commonly recall being floated off their beds.

Soon, you relax more deeply and begin about 20 minutes of Stage 2 sleep, characterized by the periodic appearance of *sleep spindles*—bursts of rapid, rhythmic brain-wave activity. Although you can still be awakened without too much difficulty during this phase, you are now clearly asleep. Sleeptalking—usually garbled or nonsensical—can occur during this or any other sleep stage (Mahowald & Ettinger, 1990).

Then for the next few minutes you go through the transitional Stage 3 to the deep sleep of Stage 4. First in Stage 3, and increasingly in Stage 4, your brain emits large, slow **delta waves.** These two *slow-wave sleep* stages last for about 30 minutes, during which you are hard to awaken. Curiously, it is at the end of the deep sleep of Stage 4 that children may wet the bed or begin walking in their sleep. About 20 percent of 3- to 12-year-olds have at least one episode of sleepwalking, usually lasting 2 to 10 minutes; some 5 percent have repeated episodes (Giles & others, 1994).

Even when you are deeply asleep, your brain somehow processes certain stimuli. You move around on your bed, but you manage not to fall out of it. If you sleep with your babies, you will not roll over and suffocate them (assuming you are not intoxicated). The occasional roar of passing vehicles may leave deep sleep undisturbed, but the cry from a baby's nursery quickly interrupts it. So does the sound of your name—a stimulus our selective attention is ever alert for. EEG recordings confirm that the brain's auditory cortex responds to sound stimuli even during sleep (Kutas, 1990).

FIGURE 18.5
Brain waves and sleep stages
The regular alpha waves of an awake, relaxed state are quite different from the slower, larger delta waves of deep Stage 4 sleep. Although the rapid REM sleep waves resemble the near-waking Stage 1 sleep waves, the body is more aroused during REM sleep than during Stage 1 sleep. (From Dement, 1978.)

■ **REM sleep** rapid eye movement sleep, a recurring sleep stage during which vivid dreams commonly occur. Also known as *paradoxical sleep*, because the muscles are relaxed (except for minor twitches) but other body systems are active.

■ **alpha waves** the relatively slow brain waves of a relaxed, awake state.

■ **sleep** periodic, natural, reversible loss of consciousness—as distinct from unconsciousness resulting from a coma, general anesthesia, or hibernation. (Adapted from Dement, 1999.)

■ **hallucinations** false sensory experiences, such as seeing something in the absence of an external visual stimulus.

■ **delta waves** the large, slow brain waves associated with deep sleep.

FIGURE 18.6
The moment of sleep
We seem unaware of the moment we fall into sleep, but someone eavesdropping on our brain waves could tell. (From Dement, 1999.)

"Boy are my eyes tired! I had REM sleep all night long."

Question: Does eating spicy foods cause one to dream more?
Answer: Any food that causes you to awaken more increases your chance of *recalling* a dream (Moorcroft, 2003).

All this reminds us of one of this book's basic lessons: *We process most information outside our conscious awareness.*

About an hour after you first fall asleep, a strange thing happens. Rather than continuing in deep slumber, you ascend from your initial sleep dive. Returning through Stage 3 and Stage 2 (where you spend about half your night), you enter the most intriguing sleep phase of all—REM sleep (**FIGURE 18.7**). For about 10 minutes, your brain waves become rapid and saw-toothed, more like those of the nearly awake Stage 1 sleep. But unlike Stage 1 sleep, during REM sleep your heart rate rises, your breathing becomes rapid and irregular, and every half-minute or so your eyes dart around in a momentary burst of activity behind closed lids. Because anyone watching a sleeper's eyes can notice these REM bursts, it is amazing that science was ignorant of REM sleep until 1952.

Except during very scary dreams, your genitals become aroused during REM sleep, and you have an erection or increased vaginal lubrication and clitoral engorgement, regardless of whether the dream's content is sexual (Karacan & others, 1966). The phenomenon has been studied mostly in men, from whom measurements are more easily recorded and for whom the common "morning erection" stems from the night's last REM period, often just before waking. In young men, sleep-related erections outlast REM periods, lasting 30 to 45 minutes on average (Karacan & others, 1983; Schiavi & Schreiner-Engel, 1988). A typical 25-year-old man therefore has an erection during nearly half his night's sleep, a 65-year-old man for one-quarter. Many men troubled by *erectile dysfunction* (impotence) have morning erections, suggesting that the problem is not between their legs.

Although your brain's motor cortex is active during REM sleep, your brainstem blocks its messages, leaving your muscles relaxed—so relaxed that, except for an occasional finger, toe, or facial twitch, you are essentially paralyzed. (That explains why horses, which spend 92 percent of each day standing and can sleep standing, must lie down for REM sleep [Morrison, 2003].) Moreover, you cannot easily be awakened. Thus, REM sleep is sometimes called *paradoxical* sleep; the body is internally aroused and externally calm.

More intriguing than the paradoxical nature of REM sleep is what the rapid eye movements announce: the beginning of a dream. Even those who claim they never dream will, more than 80 percent of the time, recall a dream after being awakened during REM sleep. Unlike the fleeting images of Stage 1 sleep ("I was thinking about

FIGURE 18.7
The stages in a typical night's sleep
Most people pass through the five-stage sleep cycle (graph a) several times, with the periods of Stage 4 sleep and then Stage 3 sleep diminishing and REM sleep periods increasing in duration. Graph b plots this increasing REM sleep and decreasing deep sleep based on data from 30 young adults. (From Cartwright, 1978; Webb, 1992.)

Luc Delahaye/Magnum Photos

Some sleep deeply, some not
The fluctuating sleep cycle enables safe sleep for these soldiers on the battlefield. One benefit of communal sleeping is that someone will probably be awake or easily roused in the event of a threat during the night.

my exam today," or "I was trying to borrow something from someone"), REM sleep dreams are often emotional, usually storylike, and more richly hallucinatory:

> My husband and I were at some friends' house, but our friends weren't there. Their TV had been left on, but otherwise it was very quiet. After we wandered around for a while, their dogs finally noticed us and barked and growled loudly, with bared teeth.

PET scans of sleeping people's brains (if sleepy enough, you, too, could sleep while lying in a brain-scanning machine) show that visual and auditory brain areas are relatively active during REM sleep and inactive during other sleep stages (Fosse & others, 2001).

Are the eye movements linked to a dream's visual aspects? Is the dreamer "watching" the dream as if it were a private movie projected in the mind's inner theater? Most researchers believe that is not the case: Darting eyes, like the occasional twitching of muscles, seem merely to reflect the overflow of the dreamer's active nervous system (Chase & Morales, 1983).

Fantasy-prone people are especially likely to recall dreams from the previous night (Watson, 2003)

The sleep cycle repeats itself about every 90 minutes. As the night wears on, deep Stage 4 sleep gets progressively briefer and then disappears. The REM sleep period gets longer (see Figure 18.7b). By morning, 20 to 25 percent of our average night's sleep—some 100 minutes—has been REM sleep. Thirty-seven percent of people report rarely or never having dreams "that you can remember the next morning" (Moore, 2004). Unknown to those people, they spend about 600 hours a year experiencing some 1500 dreams, or more than 100,000 dreams over a typical lifetime—dreams swallowed by the night but never acted out, thanks to REM's protective paralysis.

People rarely snore during dreams. When REM starts, snoring stops.

Why Do We Sleep?

OBJECTIVE 18-5 | Explain why sleep patterns and duration vary from person to person.

The idea that "everyone needs 8 hours of sleep" is untrue. Newborns spend nearly two-thirds of their day asleep, most adults no more than one-third. Age-related differences in average time spent sleeping are rivaled by differences in the normal amount of sleep among individuals at any age. Some people thrive with fewer than 6 hours of sleep per night; others regularly sleep 9 hours or more. Such sleep patterns may be genetically influenced. When Wilse Webb and Scott Campbell (1983) checked the pattern and duration of sleep among fraternal and identical twins, only the identical twins were strikingly similar.

Gallup poll:
"Usually, how many hours sleep do you get at night?"

5 or less	16%
6	27
7	28
8	28

2001 average = 6.7 hours
1942 average = 7.6 hours

Sleep patterns are also culturally influenced. Because of modern light bulbs, shift work, and social diversions, people in industrialized nations sleep less than they did a century ago. People who would have gone to bed at 9:00 P.M. are now up until 11:00 P.M. Thomas Edison (1948, pp. 52, 178) was pleased to accept credit for this. For him, less sleep meant more productive time and greater opportunities:

> When I went through Switzerland in a motor-car, so that I could visit little towns and villages, I noted the effect of artificial light on the inhabitants. Where water power and electric light had been developed, everyone seemed normally intelligent. When these appliances did not exist, and the natives went to bed with the chickens, staying there till daylight, they were far less intelligent.

Allowed to sleep unhindered, most humans will sleep at least 9 hours a night, reports Stanley Coren (1996). With that much sleep, we do not become groggy. We awake refreshed, sustain better moods, and perform more efficient and accurate work than do those who get less sleep. With a succession of 5-hour nights, however, we accumulate a sleep debt that is not paid off by one 10-hour sleep—which explains why we can feel sleepy even after a long sleep. "The brain keeps an accurate count of sleep debt for at least two weeks," says William Dement (1999, p. 64). Deprived of sleep, we also begin to feel terrible, as our bodies yearn for sleep. Try to stay awake and eventually we will lose. In the tiredness battle, sleep always wins.

Obviously, then, we need sleep. Sleep commands roughly one-third of our lives—some 25 years, on average. But why? It seems an easy question to answer: Just keep people awake for several days and note how they deteriorate. If you were a volunteer in such an experiment, how do you think it would affect your body and mind?

Of course, you would become terribly drowsy at times—especially during the hours when your biological clock programs you to sleep. But could a lack of sleep physically damage you? Would it noticeably alter your biochemistry or body organs? Would you become emotionally disturbed? Mentally disoriented?

The Effects of Sleep Deprivation

OBJECTIVE **18-6** | Discuss several risks associated with sleep deprivation.

Good news! Psychologists have discovered a treatment that strengthens memory, increases concentration, boosts mood, moderates hunger and obesity, fortifies the disease-fighting immune system, and lessens the risk of fatal accidents. Moreover, while supplies last, it's available free!

Even better news: The treatment feels good, it can be self-administered, and the supplies are limitless. If you are a typical university-age student, often going to bed near 2:00 A.M. and dragged out of bed six hours later by the dreaded alarm, the treatment is simple: Each night just add an hour to your sleep.

A major effect of lessened sleep is not only sleepiness but a general malaise (Mikulincer & others, 1989). People today more than ever suffer from sleep patterns that thwart their having an energized feeling of well-being. Teenagers typically need 8 or 9 hours of sleep, but they now average less than 7 hours, which is nearly 2 hours less sleep a night than their counterparts of 80 years ago (Holden, 1993; Maas, 1999). Many fill this need by using their first class for an early siesta and after-lunch study hall for a slumber party. When the going gets boring, the students start snoring. Even when awake, students often function below their peak. And they know it: Four in five American teens and three in five 18- to 29-year-olds wish they could get more sleep on weekdays (Mason, 2003, 2005).

At Stanford University, William Dement (1997) reports, 80 percent of students are "dangerously sleep deprived." Such individuals "are at high risk for some sort of accident. . . . Sleep deprivation [entails] difficulty studying, diminished productivity,

In 1989, Michael Doucette was named America's Safest Driving Teen. In 1990, while driving home from college, he fell asleep at the wheel and collided with an oncoming car, killing both himself and the other driver. Michael's driving instructor later acknowledged never having mentioned sleep deprivation and drowsy driving (Dement, 1999).

Jose Luis Pelaez, Inc./Corbis

Sleepless and suffering
This fatigued, sleep-deprived person may also experience a depressed immune system, impaired concentration, and greater vulnerability to accidents.

"Tiger Woods said that one of the best things about his choice to leave Stanford for the professional golf circuit was that he could now get enough sleep."
Stanford sleep researcher William Dement, 1997

tendency to make mistakes, irritability, fatigue." A large sleep debt "makes you stupid," says Dement (1999, p. 231). But let's put this positively: To manage your life with enough sleep to awaken naturally and well rested is to be more alert, productive, healthy, and happy. For teens, that's easier said than done. The one who staggers glumly out of bed in response to an unwelcome alarm, yawns through morning classes, and feels half-depressed much of the day may be energized at 11 P.M. and mindless of the next day's looming sleepiness (Carskadon, 2002). Are *you* a sleep-deprived student? Find out by taking the test in **TABLE 18.2**.

In experiments, the U.S. Navy and the National Institutes of Health have paid volunteers to spend 14 hours daily in bed for at least a week. For the first few days, the volunteers in both experiments averaged 12 hours sleep a day or more, apparently paying off a sleep debt that averaged 25 to 30 hours. That accomplished, they then settled back to 7.5 to 9 hours of sleep a night and, with no sleep debt, felt energized and happier. "What this means to me," reflected Dement (1999, p. 72) "is that millions of us are living a less than optimal life and performing at a less than optimal level, impaired by an amount of sleep debt that we're not even aware we carry." When Daniel Kahneman and his colleagues (2004) invited 909 working women to report on their daily moods, they were struck by what mattered little, such as money (so long as they were not battling poverty) and job security, and what mattered a lot—less time pressure at work and a good night's sleep. In a Gallup survey (Mason, 2005), 63 percent of adults who report getting the sleep they need also report being "very satisfied" with their personal life (as do only 36 percent of those needing more sleep).

In a 2001 Gallup poll, 61 percent of men, but only 47 percent of women, said they got enough sleep.

TABLE 18.2

ARE YOU SLEEP DEPRIVED?

Cornell University psychologist James Maas reports that most college students suffer the consequences of sleeping less than they should. To see if you are in that group, answer the following true-false questions:

True	False	
☐	☐	1. I need an alarm clock in order to wake up at the appropriate time.
☐	☐	2. It's a struggle for me to get out of bed in the morning.
☐	☐	3. Weekday mornings I hit the snooze bar several times to get more sleep.
☐	☐	4. I feel tired, irritable, and stressed out during the week.
☐	☐	5. I have trouble concentrating and remembering.
☐	☐	6. I feel slow with critical thinking, problem solving, and being creative.
☐	☐	7. I often fall asleep watching TV.
☐	☐	8. I often fall asleep in boring meetings or lectures or in warm rooms.
☐	☐	9. I often fall asleep after heavy meals or after a low dose of alcohol.
☐	☐	10. I often fall asleep while relaxing after dinner.
☐	☐	11. I often fall asleep within five minutes of getting into bed.
☐	☐	12. I often feel drowsy while driving.
☐	☐	13. I often sleep extra hours on weekend mornings.
☐	☐	14. I often need a nap to get through the day.
☐	☐	15. I have dark circles around my eyes.

If you answered "true" to three or more items, you probably are not getting enough sleep. To determine your sleep needs, Maas recommends that you "go to bed 15 minutes earlier than usual every night for the next week—and continue this practice by adding 15 more minutes each week—until you wake without an alarm clock and feel alert all day." (Quiz reprinted with permission from James B. Maas, *Power sleep: The revolutionary program that prepares your mind and body for peak performance* [New York: HarperCollins, 1999].)

As a demonstration of the costs of sleep deprivation, Stanley Coren capitalized on what is, for many North Americans, a semi-annual sleep-manipulation experiment—the "spring forward" to "daylight savings" time and "fall backward" to "standard" time. Searching millions of records, he found that in both Canada and the United States, accidents increase immediately after the shortened sleep associated with the spring time change. In Canada, for example, traffic accidents during 1991 and 1992 were 7 percent higher on the Monday after the spring time change than on the Monday before, and they were 7 percent *lower* on the Monday following the extra sleep bestowed by the fall time change (**FIGURE 18.8**).

> "Drowsiness is red alert!"
> William Dement, *The Promise of Sleep*, 1999

Similar effects were seen in accident patterns in the United States, though with more effect in the spring than fall. Coren (1996) speculates that we lose more sleep at the spring shift than we gain in the fall.

Sleep deprivation experiments reveal slowed reaction times and increased errors on visual tasks similar to those involved in airport baggage screening, performing surgery, and reading X-rays (Horowitz & others, 2003). And sleep deprivation can be devastating for driving and piloting. Some 30 percent of Australian highway deaths occur when drivers fall asleep on long, monotonous roads (Maas, 1999). Driver fatigue similarly contributes to an estimated 20 percent of American traffic accidents (Brody, 2002). "Rest. That's what I need is rest," said Eastern Airlines Captain James Reeves to the control tower on a September 1974 morning—30 minutes before crashing his airliner at low altitude, killing the crew and all 68 passengers (Moorcroft, 1993). Consider also the 1989 *Exxon Valdez* oil spill; Union Carbide's 1984 Bhopal, India, disaster; and the 1979 Three Mile Island and 1986 Chernobyl nuclear accidents—they all occurred after midnight, when operators in charge were likely to be drowsiest. Severely sleep-deprived, the *Exxon Valdez* mate at the helm was unresponsive to clear signals to turn his vessel back into the shipping lanes.

Sleep loss also affects us in more subtle ways, including suppression of the disease-fighting immune system (Beardsley, 1996; Irwin & others, 1994). Sleep deprivation suppresses immune cells that fight off viral infections and cancer, which helps explain why people who sleep 7 to 8 hours a night tend to outlive those who are chronically sleep deprived, and why older adults who have no difficulty falling or staying asleep tend to live longer (Dement, 1999; Dew & others, 2003). When infections do set in, we typically sleep more, boosting our immune cells. Chronic sleep debt also alters metabolic and hormonal functioning in ways that mimic aging and are conducive to obesity, hypertension, and memory impairment (Spiegel & others, 1999;

FIGURE 18.8
Canadian traffic accidents, 1991 and 1992
On the Monday after the spring time change, when people lose one hour of sleep, accidents increased as compared with the Monday before. In the fall, traffic accidents normally increase because of greater snow, ice, and darkness, but they diminish after the time change. (Adapted from Coren, 1996.)

Taheri, 2004). Other effects include irritability, slowed performance, and impaired creativity, concentration, and communication (Harrison & Horne, 2000). When sleepy frontal lobes confront an unexpected situation, misfortune often results.

Sleep Theories

OBJECTIVE **18-7** | Identify four theories of why we sleep.

So, nature charges us for our sleep debt. But why do we have this need for sleep?

We have very few answers, but sleep may have evolved for four reasons: First, sleep *protects*. When darkness precluded our ancestors' hunting and food gathering and made travel treacherous, they were better off asleep in a cave, out of harm's way. Our distant ancestors who didn't try to navigate around rocks and cliffs at night were more likely to leave descendants. Our sleep suits our ecological niche. Animals with the most need to graze and the least ability to hide tend to sleep less. Elephants and horses sleep 3 to 4 hours a day, gorillas 12 hours, and cats 14 hours. For bats and eastern chipmunks, both of which sleep 20 hours, to live is hardly more than to eat and to sleep (Moorcroft, 2003).

Second, sleep helps us recuperate. It helps *restore and repair* brain tissue. Bats and other animals with high waking metabolism burn a lot of calories, producing a lot of molecules, called free radicals, that are toxic to neurons. Sleeping a lot gives resting neurons time to repair themselves, while allowing unused connections to weaken (Siegel, 2003). Think of it this way: When consciousness leaves your house, brain construction workers come in for a makeover.

But sleep is not just for keeping us safe and for repairing our brain. Sleep is also for *remembering*. New research reveals that sleep restores and rebuilds our fading memories of the day's experiences. People trained to perform tasks recall them better after a night's sleep than after several hours awake (Fenn & others, 2003). And in both humans and rats, neural activity during slow-wave sleep reenacts and promotes recall of prior novel experiences (Peigneux & others, 2004; Ribeiro & others, 2004). Sleep also feeds creative thinking. After working on a task, then sleeping on it, people solve problems more insightfully than do those who stay awake (Wagner & others, 2004).

Finally, sleep may play a role in the *growth* process. During deep sleep, the pituitary gland releases a growth hormone. As adults grow older, they release less of this hormone, and they spend less time in deep sleep (Pekkanen, 1982). These discoveries are beginning to solve the ongoing riddle of sleep.

Sleep Disorders

OBJECTIVE **18-8** | Identify the major sleep disorders.

No matter what their normal need for sleep, some 10 to 15 percent of adults complain of **insomnia**—persistent problems in falling or staying asleep. True insomnia is not the occasional inability to sleep that we experience when anxious or excited. For any stressed organism, being vigilant is natural and adaptive. A personal conflict during the day often means a fitful sleep that night (Brisette & Cohen, 2002). Moreover, from middle age on, sleep is seldom uninterrupted. Being occasionally awakened becomes the norm, not something to fret over or treat with medication.

Some people fret unnecessarily about their sleep (Coren, 1996). In laboratory studies, insomnia complainers do get less sleep than others, but they typically overestimate—by about double—how long it took them to fall asleep. They also underestimate by nearly half how long they actually slept. Even if we have been awake only an hour or two, we may *think* we have had very little sleep, because it's the waking part we remember. When researchers awaken people repeatedly during the night, some, after quickly falling back to sleep, recall having slept soundly.

■ **insomnia** recurring problems in falling or staying asleep.

"Sleep faster, we need the pillows."
Yiddish proverb

"Corduroy pillows make headlines."
Anonymous

"The lion and the lamb shall lie down together, but the lamb will not be very sleepy."
Woody Allen, in the movie *Love and Death*, 1975

"In 1757 Benjamin Franklin gave us the axiom, 'Early to bed, early to rise, makes a man healthy, wealthy, and wise.' It would be more accurate to say 'consistently to bed and consistently to rise . . .'"
James B. Maas, *Power Sleep*, 1999

Stress robs sleep
Urban police officers, especially those under stress, report poorer sleep quality and less sleep than average (Neylan & others, 2002).

Dwayne Newton/PhotoEdit

The most common quick fixes for true insomnia—sleeping pills and alcohol—can aggravate the problem. Alcohol and some sleep medications reduce REM sleep and can leave a person with next-day blahs. Relying on such, a person may need increasing doses to get an effect. Then, when the drug is discontinued, the insomnia can worsen.

Scientists are searching for natural chemicals that are abundant during sleep, hoping they might be synthesized as a sleep aid without side effects. In the meantime, sleep experts offer other natural alternatives:

- Relax before bedtime, using dimmer light.
- Avoid caffeine (this includes chocolate) after late afternoon, and avoid rich foods before bedtime. A glass of milk may help. (Milk provides raw materials for the manufacture of serotonin, a neurotransmitter that facilitates sleep.)
- Sleep on a regular schedule (rise at the same time even after a restless night) and avoid naps. A regular sleep schedule boosts daytime alertness, too, as shown in an experiment in which University of Arizona students averaged 7.5 hours of sleep a night on either a varying or consistent schedule (Manber & others, 1996).
- Exercise regularly but not in the late evening (late afternoon is best).
- Reassure yourself that a temporary loss of sleep causes no great harm, certainly nothing worth losing sleep over. "Sleep is like love or happiness," notes Wilse Webb (1992, p. 170). "If you pursue it too ardently it will elude you."
- Hide the clock face so you aren't tempted to check it repeatedly.
- If nothing else works, aim for less sleep; go to bed later or get up earlier.

■ **narcolepsy** a sleep disorder characterized by uncontrollable sleep attacks. The sufferer may lapse directly into REM sleep, often at inopportune times.

■ **sleep apnea** a sleep disorder characterized by temporary cessations of breathing during sleep and repeated momentary awakenings.

■ **night terrors** a sleep disorder characterized by high arousal and an appearance of being terrified; unlike nightmares, night terrors occur during Stage 4 sleep, within two or three hours of falling asleep, and are seldom remembered.

Rarer but also more troublesome than insomnia are the sleep disorders narcolepsy and sleep apnea. People who suffer **narcolepsy** (from *narco,* "numbness," and *lepsy,* "seizure") experience periodic, overwhelming sleepiness. This usually lasts less than 5 minutes, but sometimes occurs at the most inopportune times, perhaps just after taking a terrific swing at a softball or when laughing loudly, shouting angrily, or having sex (Dement, 1978, 1999). In severe cases, the person may collapse directly into a brief period of REM sleep, with its accompanying loss of muscular tension.

Those who suffer from narcolepsy—1 in 2000 people, estimates the Stanford University Center for Narcolepsy (2002)—must live with extra caution. As a traffic menace, "snoozing is second only to boozing," says the American Sleep Disorders Association, and those with narcolepsy are especially at risk (Aldrich, 1989). Curiously, studies in Canada, France, and the United States have found that September babies are at 37 percent less than average risk for narcolepsy, and March babies 45 percent more so (Dauvilliers & others, 2003; Picchioni & others, 2004). Perhaps, researchers speculate, the March risk relates to the fall cold and flu season, which occurs during the critical second trimester of fetal development.

Imagine observing a person with narcolepsy in medieval times. Might such symptoms and their associated hallucinations have seemed like demon possession?

At the century's end, researchers discovered a gene causing narcolepsy in dogs (Lin & others, 1999; Taheri, 2004). Genes help sculpt the brain, and neuroscientists are searching the brain for abnormalities linked with narcolepsy. One team of researchers discovered a relative absence of a hypothalamic neural center that produces *hypocretin,* an alerting neurotransmitter (Taheri & others, 2002; Thannickal & others, 2000). Narcolepsy, it is now clear, is a brain disease; it is not just "in your mind." And this gives hope that narcolepsy might be effectively relieved by a drug that mimics the missing hypocretin and can sneak through the blood-brain barrier (Fujiki & others, 2003; Siegel, 2000). In the meantime, physicians are prescribing other drugs to relieve narcolepsy's sleepiness in humans.

Another sleep disorder—**sleep apnea**—leaves millions of people (mostly overweight men) tired and sometimes irritable during the day and therefore, like those who suffer narcolepsy, at increased risk of traffic accidents (Teran-Santos & others, 1999). The National Institutes of Health reports that 1 person in 20 suffers from this condition, which was unknown before modern sleep research. They intermittently stop breathing during sleep. (*Apnea* means "with no breath.") After an airless minute or so, decreased blood oxygen arouses the sleeper to awaken and snort in air for a few seconds. The process can repeat more than 400 times a night, depriving the person of slow-wave sleep. Apart from complaints of sleepiness and irritability during the day—and their mates' complaints about their loud "snoring"—apnea sufferers are often unaware of their disorder. (The next morning they have no recall of these episodes.)

As the number of obese people in the United States has increased, so has sleep apnea. Anyone who snores at night, who feels tired during the day, and who possibly has high blood pressure as well (putting them at risk for a stroke or heart attack), should be checked for apnea (Dement, 1999). For serious cases, physicians often give the sleeper a masklike device with an air pump that keeps the airway open and breathing regular. If one doesn't mind looking a little goofy in the dark (imagine a snorkeler at a slumber party), the treatment is often effective.

Unlike sleep apnea, **night terrors** target mostly children, who may sit up or walk around, talk incoherently, experience a doubling of heart and breathing rates, and appear terrified (Hartmann, 1981). They seldom wake up fully during an episode and recall little or nothing the next morning—at most, a fleeting, frightening image. Night terrors are not nightmares (which, like other dreams, typically occur during early morning REM sleep); night terrors usually occur during the first few hours of Stage 4 (**FIGURE 18.9**).

Children also are most prone to sleepwalking—another Stage 4 sleep disorder—and to sleeptalking, conditions that run in families. Finnish twin studies reveal that occasional childhood sleepwalking occurs for about one-third of those with a sleepwalking fraternal twin and half of those with a sleepwalking identical twin. The same is true for sleeptalking (Hublin & others, 1997, 1998). Sleepwalking is usually harmless and unrecalled the next morning. Sleepwalkers typically return to bed on their own or are guided there by a family member. Young children, who have the deepest and lengthiest Stage 4 sleep, are the most likely to experience both night terrors and sleepwalking. As we grow older and deep Stage 4 sleep diminishes, so do night terrors and sleepwalking. After age 40, sleepwalking is rare.

Did Brahms need his own lullabies? Cranky, overweight, and nap-prone, Johannes Brahms exhibited common symptoms of sleep apnea (Margolis, 2000).

FIGURE 18.9
Night terrors and nightmares
Night terrors occur within two or three hours of falling asleep, during Stage 4 sleep. Nightmares occur toward morning, during REM sleep. (From Hartmann, 1984.)

Dreams

Discovering the link between REM sleep and dreaming opened a new era in dream research. Instead of relying on someone's hazy recall hours or days after having a dream, researchers could catch dreams as they happened. They could awaken people during or within 3 minutes after a REM sleep period and hear a vivid account.

What Do We Dream?

OBJECTIVE 18-9 | Describe the most common content of dreams.

REM **dreams**—"hallucinations of the sleeping mind"—are vivid, emotional, and bizarre. They are unlike daydreams, which tend to involve the familiar details of our lives—perhaps imagining an alternative approach to something we have to do, or picturing ourselves explaining to an instructor why a paper will be late, or replaying in our minds personal encounters that we relish or regret. The dreams of REM sleep are so vivid we may confuse them with reality. Awakening from a nightmare, a 4-year-old may complain of a bear in the house.

Occasionally, we may be sufficiently aware during a dream to wonder whether we are, in fact, dreaming. When experiencing such *lucid dreams*, some people are able to test their state of consciousness. If they can perform some absurd act, such as floating in the air, then they know they are dreaming.

Would you suppose that people dream if blind from birth? Studies of blind people in France, Hungary, Egypt, and the United States all found them dreaming of using their nonvisual senses—hearing, touching, smelling, tasting (Buquet, 1988; Taha, 1972; Vekassy, 1977). Yet even congenitally blind people can experience visual images in dreams (Bértolo & others, 2003).

We spend six years of our life in dreams, many of which are anything but sweet. For both women and men, 8 in 10 dreams are marked by negative emotions (Domhoff, 1999). People commonly dream of repeatedly failing in an attempt to do something; of being attacked, pursued, or rejected; or of experiencing misfortune (Hall & others, 1982). When awakened during REM sleep, people report dreams with sexual imagery less often than you might think. In one study, only 1 in 10 dreams among young men and 1 in 30 among young women had sexual overtones (Domhoff, 1996). More commonly, we dream of events in our daily lives, a meeting at work, taking an exam, or relating to a family member or friend. Across the world, people of all ages show an unexplainable gender difference in dream content. Women dream of males and females equally often, whereas 65 percent of the characters in men's dreams are males. No one is sure why (Hall, 1984).

"I do not believe that I am now dreaming, but I cannot prove that I am not."

Philosopher Bertrand Russell (1872–1970)

A popular sleep myth: If you dream you are falling and hit the ground (or if you dream of dying), you die. (Unfortunately, those who could confirm these ideas are not around to do so. Some people, however, have had such dreams and are alive to report them.)

MAXINE

© 2001 Mariam Henley

www.maxine.net — © 2001 Mariam Henley — mkhenley@prodigy.net

The story line of our dreams—what Sigmund Freud called their **manifest content**—sometimes incorporates traces of previous days' experiences and preoccupations (De Koninck, 2000):

- After suffering a trauma, people commonly report nightmares.
- Robert Stickgold and his colleagues (2000) had people play the computer game "Tetris" for seven hours and then repeatedly awakened them during their first hour of sleep; three-fourths reported experiencing images of the game's falling blocks.
- People in hunter-gatherer societies often dream of animals; urban Japanese rarely do (Mestel, 1997).

The sensory stimuli of our sleeping environment may also intrude. A particular odor or the telephone's ringing may be instantly and ingeniously woven into the dream story. In a classic experiment, William Dement and Edward Wolpert (1958) lightly sprayed cold water on dreamers' faces. Compared with sleepers who did not get the cold-water treatment, these people were more likely to dream about water—about a waterfall, a leaky roof, or even about being sprayed by someone. Even while in REM sleep, focused on internal stimuli, we maintain some awareness of changes in our external environment.

So, could we learn a foreign language by listening to tapes while we sleep? If only it were so easy. While sleeping we can learn to associate a sound with a mild electric shock (and to react to the sound accordingly). But we do not remember taped information played while we are soundly asleep (Eich, 1990; Wyatt & Bootzin, 1994). In fact, anything that happens during the 5 minutes just before we fall asleep is typically lost from memory (Roth & others, 1988). This explains why sleep apnea patients, who repeatedly awaken with a gasp and then immediately fall back to sleep, do not recall the episodes. It also explains why dreams that momentarily awaken us are mostly forgotten by morning. To remember a dream, get up and stay awake for a few minutes.

Why Do We Dream?

OBJECTIVE **18-10** | Compare the major perspectives on why we dream.

Dream theorists have proposed several possible explanations of why we dream, including these:

To satisfy our own wishes. In his landmark book *The Interpretation of Dreams,* published in 1900, Freud offered what he thought was "the most valuable of all the discoveries it has been my good fortune to make." He argued that by fulfilling wishes, a dream provides a psychic safety valve that discharges otherwise unacceptable feelings. According to Freud, a dream's manifest, or apparent, content is a censored, symbolic version of its **latent content,** which consists of unconscious drives and wishes that would be threatening if expressed directly. Although most dreams have no overt sexual imagery, Freud nevertheless believed that most adult dreams can be "traced back by analysis to *erotic wishes*." Thus, a gun might be a disguised representation of a penis.

Freud considered dreams the key to understanding our inner conflicts. However, his critics say it is time to wake up from Freud's dream theory, which is a scientific nightmare. Based on the accumulated science, "there is no reason to believe any of Freud's specific claims about dreams and their purposes," notes dream researcher William Domhoff (2000). Some contend that even if dreams are symbolic, they could be interpreted any way one wished. Others maintain that dreams hide nothing. A dream about a gun is a dream about a gun. Legend has it that even Freud, who loved to smoke cigars, remarked that "sometimes, a cigar is just a cigar."

To file away memories. Freud's wish-fulfillment theory of dreams has in large part given way to other theories. Researchers who see dreams as *information processing* believe that dreams may help sift, sort, and fix the day's experiences in our memory.

> "For what one has dwelt on by day, these things are seen in visions of the night."
> Menander of Athens (342–292 B.C.), *Fragments*

dream a sequence of images, emotions, and thoughts passing through a sleeping person's mind. Dreams are notable for their hallucinatory imagery, discontinuities, and incongruities, and for the dreamer's delusional acceptance of the content and later difficulties remembering it.

manifest content according to Freud, the remembered story line of a dream (as distinct from its latent, or hidden, content).

latent content according to Freud, the underlying meaning of a dream (as distinct from its manifest content). Freud believed that a dream's latent content functions as a safety valve.

> "When people interpret [a dream] as if it were meaningful and then sell those interpretations, it's quackery."
> Sleep researcher J. Allan Hobson (1995)

We have known for some time that REM sleep facilitates memory (McGrath & Cohen, 1978). In experiments, people have heard unusual phrases or learned to find hidden visual images before bedtime. If awakened every time they began REM sleep, they remembered less the next morning than if awakened during other sleep stages (Empson & Clarke, 1970; Karni & Sagi, 1994).

Moreover, it's true that people tested the next day generally improved on a learned task after a night of memory consolidation. But even after two nights of recovery sleep, those deprived of both slow-wave and REM sleep didn't do as well as those who slept undisturbed on their new learning (Stickgold & others, 2000, 2001).

Other studies confirm that we experience REM sleep, in part, to remember. The brain regions that buzz as rats learn to navigate a maze, or as people learn to perform a visual-discrimination task, buzz again later during REM sleep (Louie & Wilson, 2001; Maquet, 2001). So precise were the activity patterns that the scientists could tell where in the maze the rat would be if awake. Deep, slow-wave sleep, it seems, helps stabilize our memories of experiences. And REM sleep helps convert memories into long-term learning.

So, a night of solid sleep (and dreaming) has an important place in our lives: To sleep, perchance to remember. This is important news for teens and college students, researcher Robert Stickgold (2000) believes. Many students suffer from a kind of sleep bulimia, binge-sleeping on the weekend. "But if you don't get good sleep and enough sleep after you learn new stuff, you won't integrate it effectively into your memories," Stickgold notes. That may help explain why high-achieving secondary students with high grades average 25 minutes more sleep a night and go to bed 40 minutes earlier than their lower-achieving classmates (Wolfson & Carskadon, 1998).

To develop and preserve neural pathways. Dreams may also serve a *physiological function.* Perhaps dreams—or the associated brain activity of REM sleep—provide the sleeping brain with periodic stimulation. We know that stimulating experiences develop and preserve the brain's neural pathways. This brain-stimulation theory of dreaming makes sense from a developmental point of view. Infants, whose neural networks are fast developing, spend a great deal of time in REM sleep (**FIGURE 18.10**).

To make sense of neural static. Other physiological theories propose that dreams erupt from neural activity that spreads upward from the brainstem (Antrobus, 1991; Hobson, 2003, 2004). According to one version—the *activation-synthesis* theory—this neural activity is random, and dreams are the brain's attempt to make sense of it. Much as a neurosurgeon can produce hallucinations by stimulating different parts of

Rapid eye movements also stir the liquid behind the cornea; this delivers fresh oxygen to corneal cells, preventing their suffocation.

FIGURE 18.10
Sleep across the life span
As we age, our sleep patterns change. During our first few months, we spend progressively less time in REM sleep. During our first 20 years, we spend progressively less time asleep. (Adapted from Snyder & Scott, 1972.)

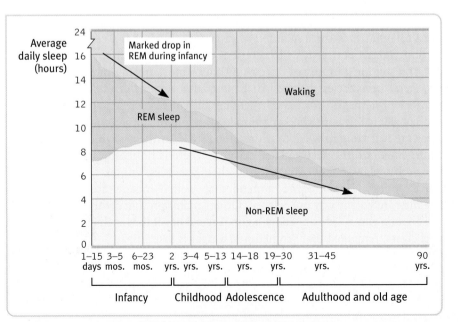

TABLE **18.3**

DREAM THEORIES

Theory	Explanation	Critical Considerations
Freud's wish-fulfillment	Dreams provide a "psychic safety valve"—expressing otherwise unacceptable feelings; contain manifest (remembered) content and a deeper layer of latent content—a hidden meaning.	Lacks any scientific support; dreams may be interpreted in many different ways.
Information-processing	Dreams help us sort out the day's events and consolidate our memories.	But why do we sometimes dream about things we have not experienced?
Physiological function	Regular brain stimulation from REM sleep may help develop and preserve neural pathways.	This may be true, but it does not explain why we experience *meaningful* dreams.
Activation-synthesis	REM sleep triggers neural activity that evokes random visual memories, which our sleeping brain weaves into stories.	The individual's brain is weaving the stories, which still tells us something about the dreamer.
Cognitive theory	Dream content reflects dreamers' cognitive development—their knowledge and understanding.	Does not address the neuroscience of dreams.

a patient's cortex, so can stimulation originating within the brain. These internal stimuli activate brain areas that process visual images, but not the visual cortex area, which receives raw input from the eyes. As Freud might have expected, PET scans of sleeping people also reveal increased activity in the emotion-related limbic system (in the amygdala) during REM sleep. In contrast, frontal lobe regions responsible for inhibition and logical thinking seem to idle, which may explain why our dreams are less inhibited than we are (Maquet & others, 1996). Add the limbic system's emotional tone to the brain's visual bursts and—voilà!—we dream. Damage either the limbic system or the visual centers active during dreaming, and dreaming itself may be impaired (Domhoff, 2003).

To reflect cognitive development. Some dream researchers dispute both the Freudian and activation-synthesis theories, preferring instead to see dreams as part of brain maturation and cognitive development. For example, prior to age 9, children's dreams seem more like a slide show and less like an active story in which the dreamer is an actor (Domhoff, 2003; Foulkes, 1999). Dreams also overlap with waking cognition, note those who favor a cognitive theory of dreams. Dreams feature coherent speech. They draw on our concepts and knowledge. And they share some commonalities with the mind's occasional flights during waking reverie. Moreover, some dream images appear outside REM sleep, when brainstem activation is minimal. **TABLE 18.3** compares major dream theories.

There is one thing dream theorists agree on: We *need* REM sleep. Deprived of it by repeatedly being awakened, people return more and more quickly to the REM stage after falling back to sleep. When finally allowed to sleep undisturbed, they literally sleep like babies—with increased REM sleep, a phenomenon called **REM rebound.** Withdrawing REM-suppressing sleeping medications also increases REM sleep, but with accompanying nightmares.

Most other mammals also experience REM sleep and REM rebound. Animals' need for REM sleep suggests that its causes and functions are deeply biological. That REM sleep occurs in mammals—and not in animals such as fish, whose behavior is less influenced by learning—also fits the information-processing theory of dreams. All of this reminds us once again of a basic lesson: *Biological and psychological explanations of behavior are partners, not competitors.*

But if dreams lack the disguised meanings that Freud supposed and instead serve physiological functions and extend normal cognition, are they therefore psychologically meaningless? Not necessarily. Every psychologically meaningful experience involves an active brain. Moreover, say advocates of dream reflection, dreams may be akin to abstract art—amenable to more than one meaningful interpretation, and illuminating to ponder.

■ **REM rebound** the tendency for REM sleep to increase following REM sleep deprivation (created by repeated awakenings during REM sleep).

"Those dreams that on the silent night intrude, and with false flitting shapes our minds delude . . . are mere productions of the brain. And fools consult interpreters in vain."

Jonathan Swift, "On Dreams," 1727

>> LEARNING OUTCOMES

Waking and Sleeping Rhythms

OBJECTIVE 18-1 | Discuss the history of psychology's study of consciousness, and contrast conscious and unconscious information processing.

Consciousness, currently defined as our awareness of ourselves and our environment, occurs in the normal states of seeing and hearing, reasoning and remembering, but also in the altered consciousness of sleep, hypnotic states, and chemically induced hallucinations. Psychology began as the study of consciousness, then, under the behaviorists, turned to the study of observable behavior. Neuroscience and cognitive psychology have refocused psychologists' interest in the scientific investigation of states of mind. Our conscious processing is serial and relatively slow, but this focused state of awareness enables us to perform voluntary acts, solve novel problems, and communicate with others. In unconscious processing, we perform familiar tasks automatically, and our sensory systems and neural pathways register stimuli rapidly and simultaneously on multiple tracks (parallel processing).

OBJECTIVE 18-2 | Distinguish four types of biological rhythms, and give an example of each.

Our internal "biological clocks" create periodic physiological fluctuations. These cycles occur annually (as in seasonal variations in appetite and mood), every 28 days (as in women's menstrual periods), every 24 hours (as in daily cycles of alertness), and every 90 minutes (as in human sleep stages).

OBJECTIVE 18-3 | Describe the cycle of our circadian rhythm, and identify some events that can disrupt this biological clock.

The circadian rhythm's 24-hour cycle regulates our daily schedule of sleeping and waking. This cycle is in part a response to light striking the retina, signaling the suprachiasmatic nucleus to trigger alterations in the level of biochemical substances, including sleep-inducing melatonin. Time changes, long flights, shifts in sleep schedules, and exposure to bright light can reset this biological clock.

OBJECTIVE 18-4 | List the stages of the sleep cycle, and explain how they differ.

Leaving the alpha waves of the awake, relaxed stage, we descend into transitional *Stage 1 sleep,* often with the sensation of falling or floating. *Stage 2 sleep* (in which we spend the most time) follows about 20 minutes later, with its characteristic sleep spindles. Then follow *Stages 3 and 4,* together lasting about 30 minutes with large, slow delta waves. Reversing course, we retrace our path through these stages—with one difference: About an hour after falling asleep, we begin approximately 10 minutes of *REM (rapid eye movement) sleep,* in which most dreaming occurs. In this fifth stage (also known as *paradoxical sleep*), we are internally aroused but outwardly paralyzed. As this 90-minute cycle repeats during a normal night's sleep, periods of Stage 4 and then Stage 3 sleep progressively shorten and dreaming REM sleep lengthens.

OBJECTIVE 18-5 | Explain why sleep patterns and duration vary from person to person.

Most people, if allowed to sleep as long as they want, will average about 9 hours. But sleep is affected by age (newborns, for example, sleep twice as much as adults), by individual sleep requirements (which may be partly genetic), and by cultural expectations about "the perfect sleep."

OBJECTIVE 18-6 | Discuss several risks associated with sleep deprivation.

Sleep deprivation puts people at risk not only for fatigue, but also for a depressed immune system; impaired concentration, creativity, and communication; irritability; and slowed performance (with greater vulnerability to accidents). Chronic sleep deprivation can alter metabolic and hormonal functioning, creating conditions that may contribute to obesity, hypertension, and memory impairment.

OBJECTIVE 18-7 | Identify four theories of why we sleep.

Sleep may have played a protective role in human evolution by keeping people safe during potentially dangerous periods. Sleep gives the brain time to heal, as it restores and repairs damaged neurons. During sleep, we restore and rebuild memories of the day's experiences, and a good night's sleep promotes insightful problem-solving the next day. Sleep also encourages growth; the pituitary gland secretes a growth hormone in Stage 4 sleep.

OBJECTIVE 18-8 | Identify the major sleep disorders.

The disorders of sleep include *insomnia* (recurring wakefulness), *narcolepsy* (sudden uncontrollable sleepiness or lapsing into REM sleep), *sleep apnea* (the stopping of breathing while asleep), *night terrors* (high arousal and the appearance of being terrified), *sleepwalking,* and *sleeptalking.* Sleep apnea mainly targets overweight men. Children are most prone to night terrors, sleepwalking, and sleeptalking.

OBJECTIVE 18-9 | Describe the most common content of dreams.

We usually dream of ordinary events and everyday experiences, 80 percent of them involving some anxiety or misfortune. Fewer than 10 percent of dreams (and less among women) have any sexual content. Most dreams occur during REM sleep; those that happen during non-REM sleep tend to be vague fleeting images.

OBJECTIVE 18-10 | Compare the major perspectives on why we dream.

(1) Freud believed that dreams provide a safety valve, because their manifest content (or story line) is a censored version of latent content (some underlying meaning that gratifies our unconscious wishes). (2) The information-processing perspective proposes that dreams help us sort out the day's experiences and fix them in memory. (3) Other physiological theories propose that REM-induced regular brain stimulation helps develop and preserve neural pathways in the brain. (4) The activation-synthesis explanation is that REM sleep triggers impulses in the

visual cortex, evoking random visual images that our brain tries to weave into a story line. (5) The brain-maturation/cognitive-development perspective believes dreams represent the dreamer's level of development, knowledge, and understanding. Most sleep theorists agree that REM sleep serves an important function, as shown by REM rebound following REM deprivation.

TERMS AND CONCEPTS TO REMEMBER

consciousness, p. 18-0
biological rhythms, p. 18-2
circadian [ser-KAY-dee-an]
  rhythm, p. 18-3
REM sleep, p. 18-4
alpha waves, p. 18-5
sleep, p. 18-5
hallucinations, p. 18-5
delta waves, p. 18-5

insomnia, p. 18-11
narcolepsy, p. 18-12
sleep apnea, p. 18-13
night terrors, p. 18-13
dream, p. 18-14
manifest content, p. 18-15
latent content, p. 18-15
REM rebound, p. 18-17

TEST YOURSELF

1. During psychology's history, what were the ups and downs of "consciousness"?

2. Are you getting enough sleep? What might you ask yourself to answer this question?

(Answers in Appendix B.)

ASK YOURSELF

1. Have you ever wondered how horses, dogs, and cats experience the world? Do you think they are consciously aware? If yes, are they also aware of being aware of the world?

2. In some countries, such as Britain, the school day for teenagers runs from about 9:00 A.M. to 4:00 P.M. In other countries, such as the United States, the teen school day often runs from 8:00 A.M. to 3:00 P.M., or even 7:30 A.M. to 2:30 P.M. Early to rise isn't making kids wise, say critics—it's making them sleepy. For optimal alertness and well-being, teens need 8 to 9 hours of sleep a night. So, should early-start schools move to a later start time, even if it requires buying more buses or switching start times with elementary schools? Or is this impractical, and would it do little to remedy the tired-teen problem?

⟩WEB

Multiple-choice *self-tests* and more may be found at www.worthpublishers.com/myers.

Learning

OBJECTIVE **21-1** | Define *learning*, and identify two forms of learning.

> "Learning is the eye of the mind."
> Thomas Drake, *Bibliotheca Scholastica Instructissima*, 1633

When a chinook salmon first emerges from its egg in a stream's gravel bed, its genes provide most of the behavioral instructions it needs for life. It knows instinctively how and where to swim, what to eat, and how to protect itself from predators. Following a built-in plan, the young salmon soon begins its trek to the sea. After some four years in the ocean, the mature salmon returns to its birthplace. It navigates hundreds of miles to the mouth of its home river and then, guided by the scent of its home stream, begins an upstream odyssey to its ancestral spawning ground. Once there, the salmon seeks out the exact conditions of temperature, gravel, and water flow that will facilitate its breeding. It then mates and, its life mission accomplished, dies.

"Actually, sex just isn't that important to me."

Unlike the salmon, we are not born with a genetic blueprint for life. Much of what we do we learn from experience. Although we struggle to find the life direction a salmon is born with, our learning gives us more flexibility. We can learn how to build grass huts or snow shelters, submarines or space stations, and thereby adapt to almost any environment. Indeed, nature's most important gift to us may be our *adaptability*—our capacity to learn new behaviors that enable us to cope with changing circumstances.

Learning breeds hope. What is learnable we can potentially teach—a fact that encourages parents, educators, coaches, and animal trainers. What has been learned we can potentially change by new learning—an assumption that underlies counseling, psychotherapy, and rehabilitation programs. No matter how unhappy, unsuccessful, or unloving we are, that need not be the end of our story.

No topic is closer to the heart of psychology than **learning,** *a relatively permanent change in an organism's behavior due to experience.* Psychologists study the learning of visual perceptions, of moral ideas, of a drug's expected effect. They also consider how learning shapes our thought and language, our motivations and emotions, our personalities and attitudes. Modules 21 through 23 examine some of the processes of learning.

How Do We Learn?

More than 200 years ago, philosophers such as John Locke and David Hume echoed Aristotle's conclusion from 2000 years earlier: We learn by association. Our minds naturally connect events that occur in sequence. If, after seeing and smelling freshly baked bread, you eat some and find it satisfying, then the next time you see and smell fresh bread, your experience will lead you to expect that eating it will be satisfying again. And if you associate a sound with a frightening consequence, then your fear may be aroused by the sound itself. As one 4-year-old exclaimed after watching a TV character get mugged, "If I had heard

■ **learning** a relatively permanent change in an organism's behavior due to experience.

Most of us would be unable to name the order of the songs on our favorite CD. Yet hearing the end of one piece cues (by association) an anticipation of the next. Likewise, when singing your national anthem, you associate the end of each line with the beginning of the next. (Pick a line out of the middle and notice how much harder it is to recall the *previous* line.)

that music, I wouldn't have gone around the corner!" (Wells, 1981).

Simpler animals can learn simple associations. When disturbed by a squirt of water, the sea snail *Aplysia* will protectively withdraw its gill. If the squirts continue, as happens naturally in choppy water, the withdrawal response diminishes. (The snail's response *habituates*.) But if the sea snail repeatedly receives an electric shock just after being squirted, its withdrawal response to the squirt instead becomes stronger. The animal relates the squirt to the impending shock. Complex animals can learn more response-outcome associations. Seals in an aquarium will repeat behaviors, such as slapping and barking, that prompt people to toss them a herring.

By linking two events that occur close together, both the sea snail and the seals exhibit *associative learning*. The sea snail associates the squirt with impending shock; the seals associate slapping and barking with receiving a herring. In both cases, the animals learned something important to their survival: to predict the immediate future.

The significance of an animal's learning is illustrated by the challenges captive-bred animals face when introduced to the wild. After being bred and raised in captivity, 11 Mexican gray wolves—extinct in the United States since 1977—were released in Arizona's Apache National Forest in 1998. Eight months later, the lone survivor of this initial effort was recaptured. The pen-reared wolves had learned how to hunt—and to move 100 feet away from people—but had not learned to run from a human with a gun. The gray wolves' experience is not unusual. Of 145 documented reintroductions of 115 species in the twentieth century, only 11 percent produced self-sustaining populations in the wild. Successful adaptation requires both nature (the needed genetic predispositions) and nurture (a history of appropriate learning).

Conditioning is the process of learning associations. In *classical conditioning*, the topic of Module 21, we learn to associate two stimuli and thus to anticipate events.

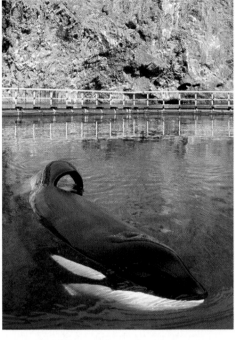

Nature without appropriate nurture
Keiko—the killer whale of *Free Willy* fame—had all the right genes for being dropped right back into his Icelandic home waters. But lacking life experience, he required caregivers to his life's end in a Norwegian fjord.

We learn that a flash of lightning signals an impending crack of thunder, and so we start to brace ourselves when lightning flashes nearby (**FIGURE 1**).

In *operant conditioning*, Module 22's focus, we learn to associate a response (our behavior) and its consequence and thus to repeat acts followed by good results (**FIGURE 2**) and avoid acts followed by bad results.

To simplify, we will consider these two types of associative learning separately in Modules 21 and 22, but you should be aware that they often occur together in the same situation. A clever Japanese rancher reportedly herds cattle by outfitting them with electronic pagers, which he calls from his cell phone. After a week of training, the animals learn to associate two stimuli—the beep on their pager and the arrival of food (classical conditioning). But they also learn to associate their hustling to the food trough with the pleasure of eating (operant conditioning).

FIGURE 1
Classical conditioning

Two related events:

Stimulus 1:
Lightning

+

Stimulus 2:
Thunder

Result after repetition:

Stimulus:
We see
lightning

Response:
We wince,
anticipating
thunder

The concept of association by conditioning, however, provokes questions: What principles influence the learning and the loss of associations? How can these principles be applied? And what really are the associations: Does the beep on a steer's pager evoke a mental representation of food, to which the steer responds by coming to the trough? Or does it make little sense to explain conditioned associations in terms of cognitive processes? (These questions are among the many being studied by researchers exploring how the brain stores and retrieves learning.)

Conditioning is not the only form of learning. As Module 23 explains, we also learn from others' experiences and examples, through *observational learning.* Complex animals, such as chimpanzees, sometimes learn behaviors merely by observing others perform them. If one animal watches another learn to solve a puzzle that gains a food reward, the observing animal may perform the trick more quickly.

By conditioning and by observation we humans learn and adapt to our environments. We learn to expect and prepare for significant events such as food or pain (classical conditioning). We also learn to repeat acts that bring good results and to avoid acts that bring bad results (operant conditioning). By watching others we learn new behaviors (observational learning). And through language we also learn things we have neither experienced nor observed.

FIGURE 2
Operant conditioning

(a) Response: balancing a ball

(b) Consequence: receiving food

(c) Behavior strengthened

MODULE

21

Classical Conditioning

OBJECTIVE **21-2** | Define *classical conditioning* and *behaviorism,* and describe the basic components of classical conditioning.

Although **associative learning** had long generated philosophical discussion, only in the early twentieth century did psychology's most famous research verify it. For many people, the name Ivan Pavlov (1849–1936) rings a bell. His experiments are classics, and the phenomenon he explored we justly call **classical conditioning.**

Pavlov's work also laid the foundation for many of psychologist John B. Watson's ideas. In searching for laws underlying **learning,** Watson (1913) urged his colleagues to discard reference to inner thoughts, feelings, and motives. The science of psychology should instead study how organisms respond to stimuli in their environments, said Watson. "Its theoretical goal is the prediction and control of behavior. Introspection forms no essential part of its methods." Simply said, psychology should be an objective science based on *observable behavior.* This view, which influenced North American psychology during the first half of the twentieth century, Watson called **behaviorism.** Watson and Pavlov shared both a disdain for "mentalistic" concepts such as consciousness and a belief that the basic laws of learning were the same for all animals—whether dogs or humans. Although today's researchers generally agree that psychology should study mental processes, they would also agree that classical conditioning is a basic form of learning by which all organisms adapt to their environment.

Pavlov's Experiments

Pavlov was driven by a lifelong passion for research. After setting aside his initial plan to follow his father into the Russian Orthodox priesthood, Pavlov received a medical degree at age 33 and spent the next two decades studying the digestive system. This work earned him Russia's first Nobel prize in 1904. But it was his novel experiments on learning, to which he devoted the last three decades of his life, that earned this feisty scientist his place in history.

Pavlov's new direction came when his creative mind seized on an incidental finding. After studying salivary secretion in dogs, he knew that when he put food in a dog's mouth the animal would invariably salivate. He also noticed that when he worked with the same dog repeatedly, the dog began salivating to stimuli associated with food—the mere sight of the food, the food dish, the presence of the person who regularly brought the food, or even the sound of that person's approaching footsteps. Because these "psychic secretions" interfered with his experiments on digestion, Pavlov considered them an annoyance—until he realized they pointed to a simple but important form of learning. From that time on, Pavlov studied learning, which he hoped might enable him to better understand the brain's workings.

At first, Pavlov and his assistants tried to imagine what the dog was thinking and feeling as it drooled in anticipation of the food. This only led them into fruitless debates. So to explore the phenomenon more objectively, they experimented. To eliminate the possible influence of extraneous stimuli, they isolated the dog in a small room, secured it in a harness, and attached a device that diverted its saliva to a measuring instrument. From an adjacent room they could present food—at first by sliding in a food bowl, later by blowing meat powder into the dog's mouth at a precise moment. They then paired various neutral stimuli—something the dog could see or

■ **associative learning** learning that certain events (two stimuli, in classical conditioning) occur together.

■ **classical conditioning** a type of learning in which an organism comes to associate stimuli. A neutral stimulus that signals an unconditioned stimulus (US) begins to produce a response that anticipates and prepares for the unconditioned stimulus. Also called *Pavlovian* or *respondent conditioning.*

■ **learning** a relatively permanent change in an organism's behavior due to experience.

■ **behaviorism** the view that psychology (1) should be an objective science that (2) studies behavior without reference to mental processes. Most research psychologists today agree with (1) but not with (2).

Ivan Pavlov
"Experimental investigation . . . should lay a solid foundation for a future true science of psychology" (1927).

Sovfoto

BEFORE CONDITIONING

US (food in mouth) → UR (salivation)

An unconditioned stimulus (US) produces an unconditioned response (UR).

Neutral stimulus (tone) → No salivation

A neutral stimulus produces no salivation response.

DURING CONDITIONING

Neutral stimulus (tone) + US (food in mouth) → UR (salivation)

The unconditioned stimulus is repeatedly presented just after the neutral stimulus. The unconditioned stimulus continues to produce an unconditioned response.

AFTER CONDITIONING

CS (tone) → CR (salivation)

The neutral stimulus alone now produces a conditioned response (CR), thereby becoming a conditioned stimulus (CS).

FIGURE 21.1
Pavlov's classic experiment
Pavlov presented a neutral stimulus (a tone) just before an unconditioned stimulus (food in mouth). The neutral stimulus then became a conditioned stimulus, producing a conditioned response.

hear—with food in the dog's mouth. If the neutral stimulus regularly signaled the arrival of food, would the dog associate the two stimuli? If so, would it begin salivating to the neutral stimulus in anticipation of the food?

The answers proved to be yes and yes. Just before placing food in the dog's mouth to produce salivation, Pavlov sounded a tone. After several pairings of tone and food, the dog began salivating to the tone alone, in anticipation of the meat powder. Using this procedure, Pavlov conditioned dogs to salivate to other stimuli—a buzzer, a light, a touch on the leg, even the sight of a circle. It works with people, too. When Jay Gottfried and his colleagues (2003) showed some hungry young Londoners abstract figures before exposing them to the aroma of peanut butter or vanilla, their brains soon were responding in anticipation to the abstract images alone.

Because salivation in response to food in the mouth was unlearned, Pavlov called it an **unconditioned response (UR).** Food in the mouth automatically, *unconditionally,* triggers a dog's salivary reflex (**FIGURE 21.1**). Thus, Pavlov called the food stimulus an **unconditioned stimulus (US).**

Salivation in response to the tone was *conditional* upon the dog's learning the association between the tone and the food. One translation of Pavlov therefore calls the salivation the *conditional reflex* (Todes, 1997). Today we call this learned response the **conditioned response (CR).** The previously irrelevant tone stimulus that now triggered the conditional salivation we call the **conditioned stimulus (CS).** It's easy to distinguish these two kinds of stimuli and responses. Just remember: conditioned = learned; *unconditioned = unlearned.*

PEANUTS

PEANUTS reprinted by permission of United Feature Syndicate, Inc.

© 1989 United Feature Syndicate, Inc.

THE EARS HEAR THE CAN OPENER..

RIGHT AWAY THE STOMACH KNOWS THAT SUPPER IS COMING..

HOW DO THE EARS TELL THE STOMACH?

I'VE NEVER BEEN ABLE TO FIGURE THAT OUT..

■ **unconditioned response (UR)** in classical conditioning, the unlearned, naturally occurring response to the unconditioned stimulus (US), such as salivation when food is in the mouth.

■ **unconditioned stimulus (US)** in classical conditioning, a stimulus that unconditionally—naturally and automatically—triggers a response.

■ **conditioned response (CR)** in classical conditioning, the learned response to a previously neutral (but now conditioned) stimulus (CS).

■ **conditioned stimulus (CS)** in classical conditioning, an originally irrelevant stimulus that, after association with an unconditioned stimulus (US), comes to trigger a conditioned response.

Question: If the aroma of cake baking sets your mouth to watering, what is the US? The CS? The CR? (See this module's final page.)

Remember:
US = Unconditioned Stimulus
UR = Unconditioned Response
CS = Conditioned Stimulus
CR = Conditioned Response

A second example, drawn from more recent experiments, may help. An experimenter sounds a tone just before delivering an air puff to your eye. After several repetitions, you blink to the tone alone. What is the US? The UR? The CS? The CR?[1]

If Pavlov's demonstration of associative learning was so simple, what did he do for the next three decades? What discoveries did his research factory publish in his 532 papers on salivary conditioning (Windholz, 1997)? He and his associates explored the causes and effects of classical conditioning. Their experiments identified five major conditioning processes: *acquisition, extinction, spontaneous recovery, generalization,* and *discrimination.*

Acquisition

OBJECTIVE **21-3** | Describe the timing requirements for the initial learning of a stimulus-response relationship.

To understand the **acquisition,** or initial learning, of the stimulus-response relationship, Pavlov and his associates first had to confront the question of timing: How much time should elapse between presenting the neutral stimulus (the tone, the light, the touch) and the unconditioned stimulus? They found that, in most cases, the answer was not much. With many species and procedures, half a second works well. What do you suppose would happen if the food (US) appeared *before* the tone (CS) rather than after? Would conditioning occur?

Not likely. Although there are exceptions, conditioning seldom occurs when the CS follows the US. This finding fits the presumption that classical conditioning is biologically adaptive. It helps organisms *prepare* for good or bad events. Pavlov's tone (CS) signals an important biological event—the arrival of food (US). To a deer in the forest, the sound of a snapping twig (CS) may come to signal a predator (US). If the good or bad event had already occurred, the CS would not likely signal anything significant.

Michael Domjan (1992, 1994, 2005) showed how the CS signals an important biological event by conditioning the sexual arousal of male Japanese quail. Just before presenting an approachable female, the researchers turned on a red light. Over time, with the red light continuing to herald a female's impending arrival, it caused the male quail to become excited (and to copulate with her more quickly when she arrived). Moreover, the male quail developed a preference for their cage's red-light district. Exposure to sexually conditioned stimuli also caused them to release more semen and sperm (Domjan & others, 1998). All in all, the quail's capacity for classical conditioning gives it a reproductive edge. This illustrates the larger lesson that conditioning serves a function: It helps an animal survive and reproduce—by responding to cues that help it gain food, avoid dangers, defeat rivals, locate mates, and produce offspring (Hollis, 1997).

In humans, too, objects, smells, and sights associated with sexual pleasure—even a geometric figure in one experiment—can become conditioned stimuli for sexual arousal (Byrne, 1982). Psychologist Michael Tirrell (1990) recalls: "My first girlfriend loved onions, so I came to associate onion breath with kissing. Before long, onion breath sent tingles up and down my spine. Oh what a feeling!" (*Questions:* What is the unconditioned stimulus here? What is the conditioned response? See **FIGURE 21.2**.)

Associations, even associations not consciously noticed, can also give rise to attitudes (De Houwer & others, 2001). Michael Olson and Russell Fazio (2001) discovered this when they classically conditioned people's attitudes toward little-known Pokemon characters. The participants, playing the role of a security guard monitoring a video screen, were shown a stream of words, images, and Pokemon characters; they were told to respond to one target Pokemon character by pressing a button.

■ **acquisition** the initial stage in classical conditioning; the phase associating a neutral stimulus with an unconditioned stimulus so that the neutral stimulus comes to elicit a conditioned response.

■ **extinction** the diminishing of a conditioned response; occurs in classical conditioning when an unconditioned stimulus (US) does not follow a conditioned stimulus (CS).

■ **spontaneous recovery** the reappearance, after a pause, of an extinguished conditioned response.

[1]US = air puff; UR = blink to air puff; CS = tone; CR = blink to tone.

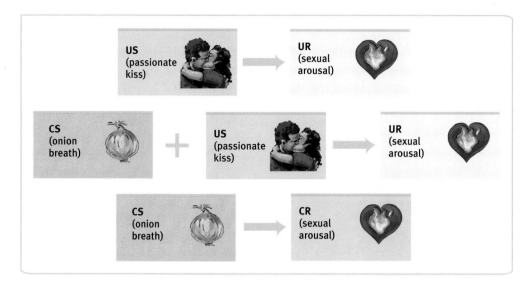

FIGURE 21.2
An unexpected CS
Onion breath does not usually produce sexual arousal. But when repeatedly paired with a passionate kiss, it can become a CS and do just that.

Unnoticed by the participants, when two other Pokemon characters appeared on the screen one was consistently associated with various positive words and images (such as *awesome* or a hot fudge sundae) and the other with negative words and images (such as *awful* or a cockroach). Afterward, asked to evaluate all Pokemon characters, people preferred those associated with the positive stimuli. Without any conscious memory for the pairings, the participants had formed gut-level positive or negative attitudes.

Extinction and Spontaneous Recovery

OBJECTIVE 21-4 | Summarize the processes of extinction, spontaneous recovery, generalization, and discrimination.

After conditioning, what happens if the CS occurs repeatedly without the US? Will the CS continue to elicit the CR? Pavlov found that when he sounded the tone again and again without presenting food, the dogs salivated less and less. Their declining salivation illustrates **extinction,** the diminished responding that occurs when the CS (tone) no longer signals an impending US (food).

Pavlov found, however, that if he allowed several hours to elapse before sounding the tone again, the salivation to the tone would reappear spontaneously (**FIGURE 21.3**). This **spontaneous recovery**—the reappearance of a (weakened) CR after a pause—suggested to Pavlov that extinction was suppressing the CR rather than eliminating it.

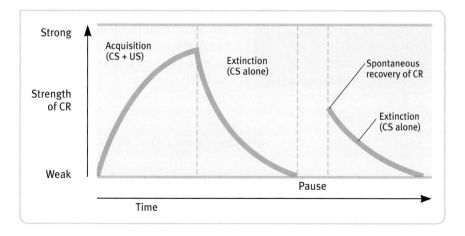

FIGURE 21.3
Idealized curve of acquisition, extinction, and spontaneous recovery
The rising curve shows that the CR rapidly grows stronger as the CS and US are repeatedly paired (acquisition), then weakens as the CS is presented alone (extinction). After a pause, the CR reappears (spontaneous recovery).

After breaking up with his fire-breathing heartthrob, Tirrell also experienced extinction and spontaneous recovery. He recalls that "the smell of onion breath (CS), no longer paired with the kissing (US), lost its ability to shiver my timbers. Occasionally, though, after not sensing the aroma for a long while, smelling onion breath awakens a small version of the emotional response I once felt."

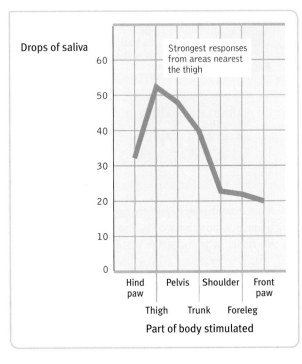

FIGURE 21.4
Generalization
Pavlov demonstrated generalization by attaching miniature vibrators to various parts of a dog's body. After conditioning salivation to stimulation of the thigh, he stimulated other areas. The closer a stimulated spot was to the thigh, the stronger the conditioned response. (From Pavlov, 1927.)

Generalization

Pavlov and his students noticed that a dog conditioned to the sound of one tone also responded somewhat to the sound of a different tone never paired with food. Likewise, a dog conditioned to salivate when rubbed would also salivate somewhat when scratched (Windholz, 1989) or when stimulated on a different body part (**FIGURE 21.4**). This tendency to respond to stimuli similar to the CS is called **generalization.**

Generalization can be adaptive, as when toddlers taught to fear moving cars in the street respond similarly to trucks and motorcycles. So automatic is generalization that one Argentine writer who underwent torture still recoils with fear when he sees black shoes—his first glimpse of his torturers when they approached his cell. Generalization has been brought to the laboratory in studies comparing abused with nonabused children. Shown an angry face on a computer screen, abused children's brain-wave responses are dramatically stronger and longer lasting (Pollak & others, 1998).

Why child abuse puts children at risk
Seth Pollak (University of Wisconsin-Madison) reports that abused children's sensitized brains react more strongly to angry faces. This generalized anxiety response may help explain their greater risk of psychological disorder.

Because of generalization, stimuli that are similar to naturally disgusting or appealing objects will, by association, evoke some disgust or liking. Normally desirable foods, such as fudge, are unappealing when presented in a disgusting form, as when shaped to resemble dog feces (Rozin & others, 1986). We perceive adults with childlike facial features (round face, large forehead, small chin, large eyes) as having childlike warmth, submissiveness, and naiveté (Berry & McArthur, 1986). In both cases, people's emotional reactions to one stimulus generalize to similar stimuli.

Discrimination

OBJECTIVE 21-5 | Discuss the survival value of generalization and discrimination.

Pavlov's dogs also learned to respond to the sound of a particular tone and *not* to other tones. **Discrimination** is the learned ability to *distinguish* between a conditioned stimulus (which predicts the US) and other irrelevant stimuli. Like generalization, discrimination has survival value. Slightly different stimuli are at times followed by vastly different consequences. Being able to recognize these differences is adaptive. Confronted by a pit bull, your heart may race; confronted by a golden retriever, it probably will not.

Extending Pavlov's Understanding

Pavlov's and Watson's disdain for "mentalistic" concepts such as consciousness has given way to a growing realization that they underestimated the importance of *cognitive processes* (thoughts, perceptions, expectations) and *biological constraints* on an organism's learning capacity.

Cognitive Processes

OBJECTIVE 21-6 | Discuss the importance of cognitive processes in classical conditioning.

The early behaviorists believed that the learned behaviors of various organisms could be reduced to mindless mechanisms. Any presumption of cognition in rats and dogs therefore struck many psychologists as unnecessary. No longer. Robert Rescorla and Allan Wagner (1972) argued that when two significant events occur close together in time, an animal learns the *predictability* of the second event. If a shock always is preceded by a tone, and then sometimes also by a light that accompanies the tone, a rat will react with fear to the tone but not to the light. Although the light is always followed by the shock, it adds no new information; the tone better predicts impending shock. The more predictable the association, the stronger the conditioned response. It's as if the animal learns an *expectancy,* an awareness of how likely it is that the US will occur. Classical conditioning "is not a stupid process by which the organism willy-nilly forms associations between any two stimuli that happen to occur," added Rescorla (1988).

This principle helps explain why classical conditioning treatments that ignore cognition often have limited success. For example, people receiving therapy for alcoholism sometimes are given alcohol spiked with a nauseating drug. Will they then associate alcohol with sickness? If classical conditioning were merely a matter of "stamping in" stimulus associations, we might hope so, and to some extent this does occur. However, those receiving the drink are aware that they can blame their nausea on the drug, not on the alcohol. This cognition often weakens the association between alcohol and feeling sick. So, even in classical conditioning, it is, especially with humans, not only the simple CS–US association but also the thought that counts.

Biological Predispositions

OBJECTIVE 21-7 | Describe some of the ways that biological predispositions can affect learning by classical conditioning.

Ever since Charles Darwin, scientists have assumed that all animals share a common evolutionary history and resulting commonalities in their makeup and functioning. Pavlov and Watson, for example, believed the basic laws of learning were essentially similar in all animals. So it should make little difference whether one studied pigeons or people. Moreover, it seemed that any natural response could be conditioned to any neutral stimulus. As learning researcher Gregory Kimble proclaimed in 1956, "Just about any activity of which the organism is capable can be conditioned and . . . these responses can be conditioned to any stimulus that the organism can perceive" (p. 195).

Discrimination failure

"I don't care if she's a tape dispenser. I love her."

"All brains are, in essence, anticipation machines."
Daniel C. Dennett, *Consciousness Explained,* 1991

■ **generalization** the tendency, once a response has been conditioned, for stimuli similar to the conditioned stimulus to elicit similar responses.

■ **discrimination** in classical conditioning, the learned ability to distinguish between a conditioned stimulus and stimuli that do not signal an unconditioned stimulus.

John Garcia
As the laboring son of California farmworkers, Garcia attended school only in the off-season during his early childhood years. After entering junior college in his late twenties, and earning his Ph.D. in his late forties, he received the American Psychological Association's Distinguished Scientific Contribution Award "for his highly original, pioneering research in conditioning and learning." He was also elected to the National Academy of Sciences.

Taste aversion
If you became violently ill after eating mussels, you probably would have a hard time eating them again. Their smell and taste would have become a CS for nausea. This learning occurs readily because our biology prepares us to learn taste aversions to toxic foods.

Twenty-five years later, Kimble (1981) humbly acknowledged that "half a thousand" scientific reports had proven him wrong. More than the early behaviorists realized, an animal's capacity for conditioning is constrained by its biology. Each species' predispositions prepare it to learn the associations that enhance its survival. Environments are not the whole story.

John Garcia was among those who challenged the prevailing idea that any associations can be learned equally well. While researching the effects of radiation on laboratory animals, Garcia and Robert Koelling (1966) noticed that rats began to avoid drinking water from the plastic bottles in radiation chambers. They wondered whether classical conditioning might be the culprit. Might the rats have linked the plastic-tasting water (a CS) to the sickness (UR) triggered by the radiation (US)?

To test their hunch, Garcia and Koelling gave the rats a particular taste, sight, or sound (CS) and later also gave them radiation or drugs (US) that led to nausea and vomiting (UR). Two startling findings emerged: First, even if sickened as late as several hours after tasting a particular novel flavor, the rats thereafter avoided that flavor. This appeared to violate the notion that for conditioning to occur, the US must immediately follow the CS.

Second, the sickened rats developed aversions to tastes but not to sights or sounds. This contradicted the behaviorists' idea that any perceivable stimulus could serve as a CS. But it made adaptive sense, because for rats the easiest way to identify tainted food is to taste it. (If sickened after sampling a new food, they thereafter avoid the food—which makes it difficult to eradicate a population of "bait-shy" rats by poisoning.) Birds, which hunt by sight, appear biologically primed to develop aversions to the *sight* of tainted food (Nicolaus & others, 1983). And remember those Japanese quail that were conditioned to get excited by a red light that signaled a receptive female's arrival? Michael Domjan and his colleagues (2004) report that such conditioning is even speedier, stronger, and more durable when the CS is "ecologically relevant"—something similar to stimuli associated with sexual activity in the natural environment, such as the stuffed head of a female quail. In the real world, observes Domjan (2005), conditioned stimuli have a natural association with the unconditioned stimuli they predict. No wonder organisms are predisposed to learn those associations.

Humans, too, seem biologically prepared to learn some things rather than others. If you become violently ill four hours after eating contaminated mussels, you will probably develop an aversion to the taste of mussels but not to the sight of the associated restaurant, its plates, the people you were with, or the music you heard there. Similarly, we more easily learn to fear snakes and spiders than to fear flowers (Cook & others, 1986). Again, it makes sense: Such animals harm us more frequently than do flowers.

All these cases support Darwin's principle that natural selection favors traits that aid survival. Nature prepares the members of each species to learn those things crucial to their survival. Someone who readily learns a taste aversion is unlikely to eat the same toxic food again and is more likely to survive and leave descendants. Indeed, all sorts of bad feelings, from nausea to anxiety to pain, serve good purposes. Like the low-oil light on a car dashboard, each alerts the body to a threat (Neese, 1991).

The German philosopher Arthur Schopenhauer (1788–1860) once said that important ideas are first ridiculed, then attacked, and finally taken for granted. So it was with Garcia's findings on taste aversion. At first, the leading journals refused to publish his work. The findings were impossible, said some critics. But as often happens in science, Garcia and Koelling's provocative research stimulated new experiments, which confirmed the surprising findings and extended them to other species. In one well-known study, coyotes and wolves that were tempted into eating sheep carcasses laced with a sickening poison developed an aversion to sheep meat (Gustavson & others, 1974, 1976). Two wolves later penned with a live sheep seemed actually to fear it.

Such research suggests possible humane ways for controlling predators and agricultural pests. This is but one instance in which psychological research that began with the discomfort of some laboratory animals enhanced the welfare of many more animals. In this case, the research saved the sheep from the coyotes. The coyotes in turn were saved from angry ranchers and farmers who, with their livestock no longer endangered, were less adamant about destroying the coyotes. Later experiments revealed that conditioned taste aversion could successfully prevent baboons from raiding African gardens, raccoons from attacking chickens, and ravens and crows from feeding on crane eggs—all while preserving predators who occupy an important ecological niche (Garcia & Gustavson, 1997).

The discovery of biological constraints affirms the value of different levels of analysis (including the biological and cognitive) when seeking to understand phenomena such as learning. It also affirms a deep principle: *Learning enables animals to adapt to their environments.* Adaptation shows us why animals would be responsive to stimuli that announce significant events, such as food or pain. And it helps us understand why animals are generally predisposed to associate a CS with a US that follows predictably and immediately: Causes often immediately precede effects.

Adaptation also sheds light on exceptions, such as the taste-aversion finding. In this case, effect need not follow cause immediately—poisoned food usually causes sickness quite a while after the food has been eaten. Similarly, when chemotherapy triggers nausea and vomiting more than an hour following treatment, cancer patients often develop classically conditioned nausea to stimuli associated with taking the drug (**FIGURE 21.5**). After four or five treatments, the patients may react with anxiety and anticipatory nausea to the sights, sounds, and smells associated with the clinic (Hall, 1997). Merely returning to the clinic's waiting room or seeing the nurses can provoke these feelings (Burish & Carey, 1986; Davey, 1992). (Under normal circumstances, such revulsion to sickening stimuli is adaptive.) The conditioned stimuli elicit the associated nausea.

> "Once bitten, twice shy."
>
> G. F. Northall, *Folk-Phrases*, 1894

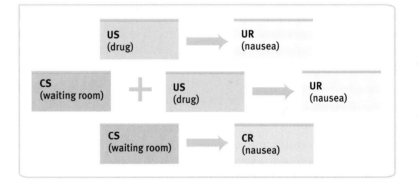

FIGURE 21.5
Nausea conditioning in cancer patients

Pavlov's Legacy

OBJECTIVE 21-8 | Summarize Pavlov's contribution to our understanding of learning.

What, then, remains of Pavlov's ideas about conditioning? A great deal. All the researchers we have met so far agree that classical conditioning is a basic form of learning. Judged by today's knowledge of cognitive processes and biological predispositions, Pavlov's ideas were incomplete. But if we see further than Pavlov did, it is because we stand on his shoulders.

Why does Pavlov's work remain so important? If he had taught us only that old dogs can learn new tricks, his experiments would long ago have been forgotten. Why should anyone care that a dog can be conditioned to salivate at the sound of a tone? The importance lies first in this finding: Many other responses to many other stimuli can be classically conditioned in many other organisms—in fact, in every species tested, from earthworms to fish to dogs to monkeys to people (Schwartz, 1984). Thus, classical conditioning is one way that virtually all organisms learn to adapt to their environment.

"[Psychology's] factual and theoretical developments in this century—which have changed the study of mind and behavior as radically as genetics changed the study of heredity—have all been the product of objective analysis—that is to say, behavioristic analysis."

Psychologist Donald Hebb (1980)

Question: In Watson and Rayner's experiment, what was the US? The UR? The CS? The CR? (See this module's final page.)

John B. Watson
Watson (1924) admitted to "going beyond my facts" when offering his famous boast: "Give me a dozen healthy infants, well-formed, and my own specified world to bring them up in and I'll guarantee to take any one at random and train him to become any type of specialist I might select—doctor, lawyer, artist, merchant-chief, and, yes, even beggar-man and thief, regardless of his talents, penchants, tendencies, abilities, vocations, and race of his ancestors."

Brown Brothers

Second, Pavlov showed us how a process such as learning can be studied objectively. Pavlov was proud that his methods involved virtually no subjective judgments or guesses about what went on in the dogs' minds. The salivary response is an overt behavior measurable in cubic centimeters of saliva. Pavlov's success therefore suggested a scientific model for how the young discipline of psychology might proceed—by isolating the elementary building blocks of complex behaviors and studying them with objective laboratory procedures.

Applications of Classical Conditioning

OBJECTIVE 21-9 | Describe some uses of classical conditioning to improve human health and well-being.

In countless areas of psychology, including consciousness, motivation, emotion, health, psychological disorders, and therapy, Pavlov's principles of classical conditioning are now used to improve human health and well-being. Some examples:

• Former crack cocaine users often feel a craving when they again encounter cues (people, places) associated with previous highs. Thus, drug counselors advise addicts to steer clear of settings and paraphernalia associated with the euphoria of previous drug use.

• Counselors sometimes provide people who abuse alcohol with aversive experiences that may partly reverse their positive associations with alcohol.

• Classical conditioning even works on the body's disease-fighting immune system. When a particular taste accompanies a drug that influences immune responses, the taste by itself may come to produce an immune response.

Pavlov's work also provided a basis for John Watson's (1913) idea that human emotions and behavior, though biologically influenced, are mainly a bundle of conditioned responses. In one famous study, Watson and Rosalie Rayner (1920; Harris, 1979) showed how specific fears might be conditioned. Their subject was an 11-month-old infant named Albert. Like most infants, "Little Albert" feared loud noises but not white rats. Watson and Rayner presented him with a white rat and, as he reached to touch it, struck a hammer against a steel bar just behind his head. After seven repetitions of seeing the rat and then hearing the frightening noise, Albert burst into tears at the mere sight of the rat (an ethically troublesome study by today's standards). What is more, five days later Albert showed generalization of his conditioned response by reacting with fear to a rabbit, a dog, and a sealskin coat, but not to dissimilar objects such as toys.

Although Little Albert's fate is unknown, Watson's is not. After losing his professorship at Johns Hopkins University over an affair with Rayner (whom he later married), he became the J. Walter Thompson advertising agency's resident psychologist. There he used his knowledge of associative learning to conceive many successful campaigns, including one for Maxwell House that helped make the "coffee break" an American custom (Hunt, 1993).

Some psychologists, noting that Albert's fear wasn't learned quickly, had difficulty repeating Watson and Rayner's findings with other children. Nevertheless, Little Albert's case has had legendary significance for many psychologists. Some have wondered if each of us might not be a walking repository of conditioned emotions (see Close-Up on the aftermath of trauma). Might our worst emotions be controlled by the application of extinction procedures or by conditioning new responses to emotion-arousing stimuli? One therapist told a patient, who for 30 years had feared going into an elevator alone, to force himself to enter 20 elevators a day. Within 10 days, his fear nearly vanished (Ellis & Becker, 1982). This dramatic turnaround is but one example of how psychologists use behavioral techniques to treat emotional disorders.

CLOSE-UP:

TRAUMA AS CLASSICAL CONDITIONING

"A burnt child dreads the fire," says a medieval proverb. Experiments with dogs reveal that, indeed, if a painful stimulus is sufficiently powerful, a single event is sometimes enough to traumatize the animal when it again faces the situation. The human counterparts to these experiments can be tragic, as illustrated by one woman's experience of being attacked and raped, and conditioned to a period of fear. Her fear (CR) was most powerfully associated with particular locations and people (CS), but it generalized to other places and people. Note, too, how her traumatic experience robbed her of the normally relaxing associations with such stimuli as home and bed.

Four months ago I was raped. In the middle of the night I awoke to the sound of someone outside my bedroom. Thinking my housemate was coming home, I called out her name. Someone began walking slowly toward me, and then I realized. I screamed and fought, but there

were two of them. One held my legs, while the other put a hand over my mouth and a knife to my throat and said, "Shut up, bitch, or we'll kill you." Never have I been so terrified and helpless. They both raped me, one brutally. As they then searched my room for money and valuables, my housemate came home. They brought her into my room, raped her, and left us both tied up on my bed.

We never slept another night in that apartment. We were too terrified. Still, when I go to bed at night—always with the bedroom light left on—the memory of them entering my room repeats itself endlessly. I was an independent person who had lived alone or with other women for four years; now I can't even think about spending a night alone. When I drive by our old apartment, or when I have to go into an empty house, my heart pounds

and I sweat. I am afraid of strangers, especially men, and the more they resemble my attackers the more I fear them. My housemate shares many of my fears and is frightened when entering our new apartment. I'm afraid to stay in the same town, I'm afraid it will happen again, I'm afraid to go to bed. I dread falling asleep.

Eleven years later this woman could report—as do many trauma victims (Gluhoski & Wortman, 1996)—that her conditioned fears had mostly extinguished:

The frequency and intensity of my fears have subsided. Still, I remain cautious about personal safety and occasionally have nightmares about my experience. But more important is my renewed ability to laugh, love, and trust—both old friends and new. Life is once again joyful. I have survived.

(From personal correspondence, with permission.)

>> LEARNING OUTCOMES

Classical Conditioning

OBJECTIVE 21-1 | Define *learning*, and identify two forms of learning.

Learning is a relatively permanent change in an organism's behavior due to experience. In *associative learning,* we learn to associate two stimuli (as in classical conditioning) or a response and its consequences (as in operant conditioning). In *observational learning,* we learn by watching others' experiences and examples.

OBJECTIVE 21-2 | Define *classical conditioning* and *behaviorism*, and describe the basic components of classical conditioning.

Classical conditioning is a type of learning in which an organism comes to associate stimuli. Pavlov's work on classical conditioning laid the foundation for *behaviorism,* the view that psychology should be an objective science that studies behavior without reference to mental processes. In classical conditioning, a *UR* is an event that occurs naturally (such as salivation), in response to some stimulus. A *US* is something that naturally and automatically

(without learning) triggers the unlearned response (as food in the mouth triggers salivation). A *CS* in classical conditioning is an originally neutral stimulus (such as a bell) that, through learning, comes to be associated with some unlearned response (salivating). A *CR* is the learned response (salivating) to the originally neutral but now conditioned stimulus.

OBJECTIVE 21-3 | Describe the timing requirements for the initial learning of a stimulus-response relationship.

Classical conditioning occurs most readily when a CS is presented just before (ideally, about a half-second before) a US, preparing the organism for the upcoming event. This finding supports the view that classical conditioning is biologically adaptive.

OBJECTIVE 21-4 | Summarize the processes of extinction, spontaneous recovery, generalization, and discrimination.

In classical conditioning, *extinction* is diminished responding when the CS no longer signals an impending US. *Spontaneous recovery* is the appearance of a formerly extinguished response, following a rest period. *Generalization* is the tendency to respond to stimuli that are similar to a CS. *Discrimination* is the learned ability to distinguish between a CS and other irrelevant stimuli.

OBJECTIVE 21-5 | **Discuss the survival value of generalization and discrimination.**

Generalization (our tendency to respond to stimuli similar to a CS) has survival value because it lets us extend a learned response to other stimuli in a given category—as in fleeing from all dangerous animals. *Discrimination* (our learned ability to distinguish between a CS and other irrelevant stimuli) also has survival value because it lets us limit our learned responses to appropriate stimuli—as in fleeing from a rampaging lion but not from a playful kitten.

OBJECTIVE 21-6 | **Discuss the importance of cognitive processes in classical conditioning.**

Conditioning principles are influenced by our thoughts, perceptions, and expectations. In classical conditioning, humans and other animals learn when to "expect" a US, and their awareness of the link between stimuli and responses can weaken associations.

OBJECTIVE 21-7 | **Describe some of the ways that biological predispositions can affect learning by classical conditioning.**

Early behaviorists believed that any natural response could be conditioned to any neutral stimulus in any living organism. We now know that each species is biologically prepared to learn associations—such as humans' fear of spiders and snakes, or rats' aversion to tastes associated with nausea—that enhance its survival. Outside the laboratory, a CS tends to have a natural association with the US it predicts.

OBJECTIVE 21-8 | **Summarize Pavlov's contribution to our understanding of learning.**

Pavlov taught us that significant psychological phenomena can be studied objectively, and that conditioning principles have important applications, as in treating phobias. He also demonstrated that principles of learning apply across species, although later research modified this finding somewhat to reflect the influence of cognition and biological predispositions.

OBJECTIVE 21-9 | **Describe some uses of classical conditioning to improve human health and well-being.**

Classical conditioning is used to treat people recovering from alcohol and other drug abuse and to condition more appropriate responses in therapy for emotional disorders. The immune system may also respond to classical conditioning.

TERMS AND CONCEPTS TO REMEMBER

associative learning, p. 21-0
classical conditioning, p. 21-0
learning, p. 21-0
behaviorism, p. 21-0
unconditioned response (UR), p. 21-1
unconditioned stimulus (US), p. 21-1
conditioned response (CR), p. 21-1

conditioned stimulus (CS), p. 21-1
acquisition, p. 21-2
extinction, p. 21-3
spontaneous recovery, p. 21-3
generalization, p. 21-4
discrimination, p. 21-4

TEST YOURSELF

1. As we develop, we learn cues that lead us to expect and prepare for good and bad events. We learn to repeat behaviors that bring rewards. And we watch others and learn. What do psychologists call these three types of learning?

2. In slasher movies, sexually arousing images of women are sometimes paired with violence against women. Based on classical conditioning principles, what might be an effect of this pairing?

(Answers in Appendix B.)

ASK YOURSELF

1. How have your emotions or behaviors been classically conditioned?

ANSWERS TO QUESTIONS WITHIN THE MODULE

Q. If the aroma of cake baking sets your mouth to watering, what is the US? The CS? The CR?

A. The cake (and its taste) is the US. The associated aroma is the CS. Salivation to the aroma is the CR.

Q. In Watson and Rayner's experiment, what was the US? The UR? The CS? The CR?

A. The US was the loud noise. The UR was the startled fear response. The CS was the rat. The CR was fear.

>WEB

Multiple-choice *self-tests* and more may be found at www.worthpublishers.com/myers.

MODULE

Operant Conditioning

OBJECTIVE 22-1 | Identify the two major characteristics that distinguish classical conditioning from operant conditioning.

It's one thing to classically condition an animal to salivate at the sound of a tone, or a child to fear cars in the street. In each case, the organism associates stimuli it does not control. It's something else to teach an elephant to walk on its hind legs or a child to say *please.* Another type of **associative learning** explains and trains such behaviors. Through **operant conditioning** organisms associate their own actions with consequences: Behaviors followed by reinforcers increase; those followed by punishers decrease.

Both classical and operant conditioning involve acquisition, extinction, spontaneous recovery, generalization, and discrimination (**TABLE 22.1**). Yet their difference is straightforward: Classical conditioning forms associations between stimuli (a CS and the US it signals). It also involves **respondent behavior**—behavior that occurs as an *automatic* response to some stimulus (such as salivating in response to meat powder and later in response to a tone). Operant conditioning involves **operant behavior,** so-called because the behavior *operates* on the environment to *produce* rewarding or punishing stimuli. We can therefore distinguish classical from operant conditioning by asking: *Is the organism learning associations between events that it doesn't control* (classical conditioning)? *Or is it learning associations between its behavior and resulting events* (operant conditioning)?

■ **associative learning** learning that certain events (a response and its consequences in operant conditioning) occur together.

■ **operant conditioning** a type of learning in which behavior is strengthened if followed by a reinforcer or diminished if followed by a punisher.

■ **respondent behavior** behavior that occurs as an automatic response to some stimulus; Skinner's term for behavior learned through classical conditioning.

■ **operant behavior** behavior that operates on the environment, producing consequences.

TABLE 22.1

SOME DIFFERENCES BETWEEN CLASSICAL AND OPERANT CONDITIONING

	Classical Conditioning	Operant Conditioning
Basic idea	Organism learns associations between events it doesn't control.	Organism learns associations between its behavior and resulting events.
Acquisition	Initial stage in which a neutral stimulus is associated with an unconditioned stimulus (US) and comes to elicit a conditioned response (CR).	The strengthening of a reinforced response.
Extinction	The diminishing of a conditioned response; occurs when a US does not follow a conditioned stimulus (CS).	The elimination of a response that is no longer reinforced.
Spontaneous recovery	The reappearance, after a rest period, of an extinguished CR.	The reappearance, after a rest period, of an extinguished response.
Generalization	The tendency, once a response has been conditioned, for stimuli similar to the CS to elicit similar responses.	Organism's response to stimuli that signal that a behavior will be reinforced.
Discrimination	The learned ability to distinguish between a CS and other stimuli that do not signal a US.	Organism's response to stimuli that do not signal that a behavior will be reinforced.

Skinner's Experiments

OBJECTIVE 22-2 | State Thorndike's law of effect, and explain its connection to Skinner's research on operant conditioning.

B. F. Skinner (1904–1990) was a college English major and an aspiring writer who, seeking a new direction, entered graduate school in psychology. He went on to become modern behaviorism's most influential and controversial figure. Skinner's

FIGURE 22.1
Cat in a puzzle box
Thorndike (1898) used a fish reward to entice cats to find their way out of a puzzle box (above left) through a series of maneuvers. The cats' performance tended to improve with successive trials (above right), illustrating Thorndike's *law of effect*. (Adapted from Thorndike, 1898.)

work elaborated a simple fact of life that psychologist Edward L. Thorndike (1874–1949) called the **law of effect:** *Rewarded behavior is likely to recur* (**FIGURE 22.1**). Using Thorndike's law of effect as a starting point, Skinner developed a "behavioral technology" that revealed principles of behavior control. These principles also enabled him to teach pigeons such unpigeonlike behaviors as walking in a figure 8, playing Ping-Pong, and keeping a missile on course by pecking at a target on a screen.

The law of effect at Stingray City
For 35 years, Cayman Islands fishing crews have gathered conch and cleaned them over this barrier reef. Stingrays gradually became accustomed to these yummy treats. Noticing the rays congregating, scuba divers then began feeding the increasingly friendly rays by hand. Today, tourists can do the same and can even pet the rays as they graze past them.

For his pioneering studies with rats (and later with pigeons), Skinner designed an **operant chamber,** popularly known as a *Skinner box* (**FIGURE 22.2**). The box has a bar or key that an animal presses or pecks to release a reward of food or water, and a device that records these responses. Operant conditioning experiments have done far more than teach us how to pull habits out of a rat. They have explored the precise conditions that foster efficient and enduring **learning.**

FIGURE 22.2
A Skinner box
Inside the box, the rat presses a bar for a food reward. Outside the box (not shown here), a measuring device records the animal's accumulated responses.

Shaping Behavior

OBJECTIVE 22-3 | Describe the shaping procedure, and explain how it can increase our understanding of what animals and babies can discriminate.

In his experiments, Skinner used **shaping,** a procedure in which *reinforcers,* such as food, gradually guide an animal's ations toward a desired behavior. Imagine that you wanted to condition a hungry rat to press a bar. After observing how the animal naturally behaves before training, you would build on its existing behaviors. You might give the rat a food reward each time it approaches the bar. Once the rat is approaching regularly, you would require it to move closer before rewarding it, then closer still. Finally, you would require it to touch the bar before you gave it the food. With this method of *successive approximations,* you reward responses that are ever-closer to the final desired behavior, and you ignore all other responses. By making rewards contingent on desired behaviors, researchers and animal trainers gradually shape complex behaviors.

By shaping nonverbal organisms to discriminate between stimuli, a psychologist can also determine what they perceive. Can a dog distinguish colors? Can a baby discriminate sounds? If we can shape them to respond to one stimulus and not to another, then obviously they can perceive the difference. Experiments show that some animals are remarkably capable of forming concepts; they demonstrate this by discriminating between classes of events or objects. If an experimenter reinforces a pigeon for pecking after seeing a human face, but not after seeing other images, the pigeon will learn to recognize human faces (Herrnstein & Loveland, 1964). In this experiment, a face is a *discriminative stimulus;* like a green traffic light, it signals that a response will be reinforced. After being trained to discriminate among flowers, people, cars, and chairs, pigeons can usually identify in which of these categories a new pictured object belongs (Bhatt & others, 1988; Wasserman, 1993). With training, pigeons have even been taught to discriminate between Bach's music and Stravinsky's (Porter & Neuringer, 1984).

In everyday life, too, we continually reward and shape the behavior of others, said Skinner, but we often do so unintentionally. Sometimes we unthinkingly reward behaviors we find annoying. Billy's whining, for example, annoys his mystified parents, but look how they typically deal with Billy:

> **Billy:** *Could you tie my shoes?*
> **Father:** *(Continues reading paper.)*
> **Billy:** *Dad, I need my shoes tied.*
> **Father:** *Uh, yeah, just a minute.*
> **Billy:** *DAAAAD! TIE MY SHOES!*
> **Father:** *How many times have I told you not to whine? Now, which shoe do we do first?*

Shaping rats to save lives
A Gambian giant pouched rat, having been shaped to sniff out land mines, receives a banana after successfully locating a mine during training in Mozambique.

■ **law of effect** Thorndike's principle that behaviors followed by favorable consequences become more likely, and that behaviors followed by unfavorable consequences become less likely.

■ **operant chamber** a chamber also known as a *Skinner box,* containing a bar or key that an animal can manipulate to obtain a food or water reinforcer, with attached devices to record the animal's rate of bar pressing or key pecking. Used in operant conditioning research.

■ **learning** a relatively permanent change in an organism's behavior due to experience.

■ **shaping** an operant conditioning procedure in which reinforcers guide behavior toward closer and closer approximations of the desired behavior.

A discriminating creature
University of Windsor psychologist Dale Woodyard uses a food reward to train this manatee to discriminate between objects of different shapes, colors, and sizes. A manatee can remember such responses for a year or more.

HI AND LOIS

Billy's whining is reinforced, because he gets something desirable—his dad's attention. Dad's response is reinforced because it gets rid of something aversive—Billy's whining.

Or consider a teacher who pastes gold stars on a wall chart after the names of children scoring 100 percent on spelling tests. All children take the same tests. As everyone can then see, some children, the academic all-stars, easily get 100 percent. The others get no stars. The teacher would be better advised to apply the principles of operant conditioning—to reinforce all spellers for gradual improvements (successive approximations toward perfect spelling of words they find challenging).

Types of Reinforcers

OBJECTIVE 22-4 | Compare positive and negative reinforcement, and give one example each of a primary reinforcer, a conditioned reinforcer, an immediate reinforcer, and a delayed reinforcer.

People often refer rather loosely to the power of "rewards." This idea gains a more precise meaning in Skinner's concept of **reinforcement:** any event that strengthens, or increases the frequency of, a preceding response. A *positive* reinforcer may be a tangible reward. It may be praise or attention. Or it may be an activity—being able to borrow the car when the dishes are done, or to have a break after an hour of study.

Positive reinforcement
A heat lamp positively reinforces this Taronga Zoo meerkat's behavior during a cold snap in Sydney, Australia.

Most people think of reinforcers as rewards. Actually, anything that serves to increase behavior is a reinforcer—even being yelled at, if yelling *increases* a child's offending behavior. Reinforcers vary with circumstances. What's reinforcing to one person (rock concert tickets) may not be to another. What's reinforcing in one situation (food when hungry) may not be in another.

There are two basic kinds of reinforcement (**TABLE 22.2**). One type (**positive reinforcement**) strengthens a response by *presenting* a typically pleasurable stimulus after a response. Food is a positive reinforcer for hungry animals; attention, approval, and money are positive reinforcers for most people. The other type (**negative reinforcement**) strengthens a response by reducing or *removing* an aversive (undesirable) stimulus. Taking aspirin may relieve a headache. Pushing the snooze button silences an annoying alarm. Dragging on a cigarette will reduce a nicotine addict's pangs. All these consequences provide negative reinforcement and increase the likelihood that the behavior will be repeated. For drug addicts, the negative reinforcement of escaping withdrawal pangs becomes compelling (Baker & others, 2004). When someone stops nagging or whining, that, too, is a negative reinforcer. (Note that contrary to popular usage, negative reinforcement is *not* punishment; rather, it *removes* a punishing aversive event.)

TABLE 22.2

WAYS TO INCREASE BEHAVIOR

Operant Conditioning Term	Description	Possible Examples
Positive reinforcement	*Add* a desirable stimulus	Getting a hug; receiving a paycheck
Negative reinforcement	*Remove* an aversive stimulus	Fastening seatbelt to turn off beeping

So imagine a worried student who, after goofing off and getting a bad exam grade, studies harder for the next exam. The student's studying may be reinforced by reduced anxiety (negative reinforcement) and by a better grade (positive reinforcement). Whether it works by giving something desirable or by reducing something aversive, *reinforcement is any consequence that strengthens behavior.*

Primary and Conditioned Reinforcers

Primary reinforcers—getting food when hungry or being relieved of electric shock—are innately satisfying. **Conditioned reinforcers,** also called *secondary reinforcers,* are learned. They get their power through their association with primary reinforcers. If a rat in a Skinner box learns that a light reliably signals that food is coming, the rat will work to turn on the light. The light has become a secondary reinforcer associated with food. Our lives are filled with secondary reinforcers—money, good grades, a pleasant tone of voice, a word of praise—each of which has been linked with more basic rewards. Secondary reinforcers greatly enhance our ability to influence one another.

"Oh, not bad. The light comes on, I press the bar, they write me a check. How about you?"

Immediate and Delayed Reinforcers

Let's return to the imaginary shaping experiment in which you were conditioning a rat to press a bar. Before performing this "wanted" behavior, the hungry rat will engage in a sequence of "unwanted" behaviors—scratching, sniffing, and moving around. When the food reinforcer immediately follows one of these behaviors, that response becomes more likely to recur. If the rat presses the bar, but you are distracted and delay the reinforcer for longer than 30 seconds, the rat will not learn to press the bar. Other incidental behaviors will intervene and be reinforced.

Unlike rats, humans do respond to reinforcers that are greatly delayed: the paycheck at the end of the week, the good grade at the end of the semester, the trophy at the end of the season. Indeed, to function effectively we must learn to postpone immediate rewards for greater long-term rewards. In laboratory testing, some 4-year-olds show an ability to delay gratification; in choosing a candy, they would rather have a big reward tomorrow than a small one right now. As they mature, these children tend to become socially competent and high achieving (Mischel & others, 1989). A big step toward maturity—and toward gaining the most satisfying life—is learning to delay gratification, to control one's impulses in order to achieve more valued rewards (Logue, 1998a,b).

But to our detriment, small but immediate consequences (the enjoyment of watching late-night TV, for example) are sometimes more alluring than big but delayed consequences (tomorrow's sluggishness). Smokers, alcoholics, and other drug users may know that their immediate pleasure—the kick that often comes within seconds—is more than offset by future ill effects, such as cancer in 30 years or a hangover in the morning. Still, immediate reinforcement prevails, and drugs such as nicotine and cocaine that provide the biggest kick are the most strongly addictive (Marlatt, 1991). And for many teens, the immediate gratification of risky, unprotected sex in passionate moments prevails over the delayed gratifications of safe sex or saved sex (Loewenstein & Furstenberg, 1991). Likewise, the immediate rewards of today's gas-guzzling vehicles prevail over the bigger consequences of tomorrow's global warming, rising seas, and extreme weather.

Reinforcement Schedules

OBJECTIVE 22-5 | Discuss the strengths and weaknesses of continuous and partial (intermittent) reinforcement schedules, and identify four schedules of partial reinforcement.

So far, most of our examples assume **continuous reinforcement:** The desired response is reinforced every time it occurs. Under such conditions, learning occurs rapidly. But extinction also occurs rapidly. When the reinforcement stops—when we disconnect the food delivery chute—the rat soon stops pressing the bar. If a normally dependable candy

■ **reinforcer** in operant conditioning, any event that *strengthens* the behavior it follows.

■ **positive reinforcement** increasing behaviors by presenting positive stimuli, such as food. A positive reinforcer is any stimulus that, when *presented* after a response, strengthens the response.

■ **negative reinforcement** increasing behaviors by stopping or reducing negative stimuli, such as shock. A negative reinforcer is any stimulus that, when *removed* after a response, strengthens the response. (Note: negative reinforcement is *not* punishment.)

■ **primary reinforcer** an innately reinforcing stimulus, such as one that satisfies a biological need.

■ **conditioned reinforcer** a stimulus that gains its reinforcing power through its association with a primary reinforcer; also known as *secondary reinforcer.*

■ **continuous reinforcement** reinforcing the desired response every time it occurs.

"The charm of fishing is that it is the pursuit of what is elusive but attainable, a perpetual series of occasions for hope."

Scottish author John Buchan (1875–1940)

machine fails to deliver a chocolate bar twice in a row, we stop putting money into it (although a week later we may exhibit spontaneous recovery by trying again).

Real life often does not provide continuous reinforcement. A salesperson does not make a sale with every pitch, nor does an angler get a bite with every cast. But they persist because their efforts have occasionally been rewarded. Researchers have explored several **partial (intermittent) reinforcement** schedules, in which responses are sometimes reinforced, sometimes not (Nevin, 1988). Initial learning is typically slower with intermittent reinforcement, which makes continuous reinforcement preferable until a behavior is mastered. But intermittent reinforcement produces greater persistence—greater *resistance to extinction*—than is found with continuous reinforcement. Imagine a pigeon that has learned to peck a key to obtain food. When the experimenter gradually phases out the delivery of food until it occurs only rarely and unpredictably, pigeons may peck 150,000 times without a reward (Skinner, 1953). With intermittent reinforcement, hope springs eternal.

Corresponding human examples come readily to mind:

- New York City's computer-controlled traffic lights made most of the city's 3250 pedestrian traffic-signal buttons at intersections obsolete. Yet occasionally, usually coincidentally, pedestrians are reinforced with a "Walk" light soon after pressing the button. So the mostly futile button pressing continues.
- Slot machines reward gamblers occasionally and unpredictably. This intermittent reinforcement affects them much as it affects pigeons: They keep trying, sometimes interminably.
- There is also a valuable lesson here for parents. *Occasionally* giving in to children's demanding tantrums for the sake of peace and quiet intermittently reinforces the tantrums. That is the very best procedure for making a behavior persist.

Skinner (1961) and his collaborators compared four schedules of partial reinforcement. Some are rigidly fixed, some unpredictably variable.

Fixed-ratio schedules reinforce behavior after a set number of responses. Like people paid on a piecework basis—say, for every 30 pieces—laboratory animals may be reinforced on a fixed ratio of, say, one reinforcer for every 30 responses. Once conditioned, the animal will pause only briefly after a reinforcer and will then return to a high rate of responding (**FIGURE 22.3**).

Question: Remember whining Billy? In that example, which behavior was positively reinforced and which was negatively reinforced? (See this module's final page.)

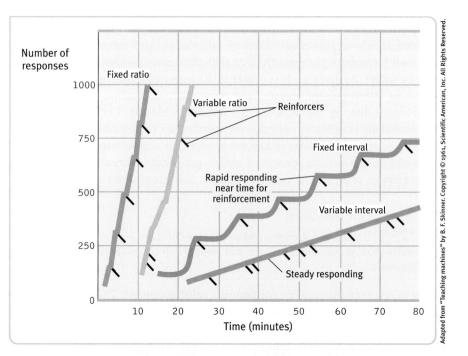

FIGURE 22.3
Intermittent reinforcement schedules Skinner's laboratory pigeons produced these response patterns to each of four reinforcement schedules. (Reinforcers are indicated by diagonal marks.) For people, as for pigeons, reinforcement linked to number of responses (a ratio schedule) produces a higher response rate than reinforcement linked to amount of time elapsed (an interval schedule). But the predictability of the reward also matters. An unpredictable (variable) schedule produces more consistent responding than does a predictable (fixed) schedule.

Variable-ratio schedules provide reinforcers after an unpredictable number of responses. This is what slot-machine players and fly-casting anglers experience—unpredictable reinforcement—and what makes gambling and fly fishing so hard to extinguish. Like the fixed-ratio schedule, the variable-ratio schedule produces high rates of responding, because reinforcers increase as the number of responses increases.

Fixed-interval schedules reinforce the first response after a fixed time period. Like people checking more frequently for the mail as the delivery time approaches, or checking to see if the Jell-O is set, pigeons on a fixed-interval schedule peck a key more frequently as the anticipated time for reward draws near, producing a choppy stop-start pattern (see Figure 22.3) rather than a steady rate of response.

Variable-interval schedules reinforce the first response after *varying* time intervals. Like the "You've got mail" that finally rewards persistence in rechecking for e-mail, variable-interval schedules tend to produce slow, steady responding. This makes sense, because there is no knowing when the waiting will be over.

Animal behaviors differ, yet Skinner (1956) contended that these reinforcement principles of operant conditioning are universal. It matters little, he said, what response, what reinforcer, or what species you use. The effect of a given reinforcement schedule is pretty much the same: "Pigeon, rat, monkey, which is which? It doesn't matter. . . . Behavior shows astonishingly similar properties."

Punishment

OBJECTIVE 22-6 | Discuss the ways negative punishment, positive punishment, and negative reinforcement differ, and list some drawbacks of punishment as a behavior-control technique.

The effect of **punishment** is opposite to that of reinforcement. Reinforcement increases a behavior; punishment decreases it. Thus, a punisher is any consequence that *decreases* the frequency of a preceding behavior, usually by administering an undesirable consequence or withdrawing a desirable one (see TABLE **22.3**). Swift and sure punishers can powerfully restrain unwanted behavior. The rat that is shocked after touching a forbidden object and the child who loses a treat after running into the street will learn not to repeat the behavior. Some punishments, though unintentional, are nevertheless quite effective: A dog that has learned to come running at the sound of the electric can opener will stop coming if its master starts running the machine to attract the dog and banish it to the basement.

Robert Larzelere (1996, 2000, 2004) notes a problem with human punishment studies, which often find that spanked children are at increased risk for aggression, depression, and low self-esteem. Well, yes, says Larzelere, just as people who have received radiation treatments are more likely to die of cancer, and people who have undergone psychotherapy are more likely to suffer depression—because they had preexisting problems that triggered the treatments. Physical punishment is followed by bad behavior. And bad behavior is followed by physical punishment. So which is the chicken and which is the egg? The correlation doesn't hand us an answer.

TABLE **22.3**

WAYS TO DECREASE BEHAVIOR

Type of Punisher	Description	Possible Examples
Positive punishment	Administer an aversive stimulus	Spanking; a parking ticket
Negative punishment	Withdraw a desirable stimulus	Time-out from privileges (such as time with friends); revoked driver's license

Question: Door-to-door salespeople are reinforced by which schedule? People checking the oven to see if the cookies are done are on which schedule? Airline frequent-flyer programs that offer a free flight after every 25,000 miles of travel use which reinforcement schedule? (See this module's final page.)

■ **partial (intermittent) reinforcement** reinforcing a response only part of the time; results in slower acquisition of a response but much greater resistance to extinction than does continuous reinforcement.

■ **fixed-ratio schedule** in operant conditioning, a reinforcement schedule that reinforces a response only after a specified number of responses.

■ **variable-ratio schedule** in operant conditioning, a reinforcement schedule that reinforces a response after an unpredictable number of responses.

■ **fixed-interval schedule** in operant conditioning, a reinforcement schedule that reinforces a response only after a specified time has elapsed.

■ **variable-interval schedule** in operant conditioning, a reinforcement schedule that reinforces a response at unpredictable time intervals.

■ **punishment** an event that *decreases* the behavior that it follows.

Children see, children do?
Children who often experience physical punishment tend to display more aggression.

If one adjusts for the preexisting conditions—cancer or depression or antisocial behavior—then the treatment (radiation, psychotherapy, or an occasional single swat or two to misbehaving 2- to 6-year-olds) looks more effective, note Larzelere and Diana Baumrind and her co-authors (2002). That is especially so if the swat is combined with a generous dose of reasoning and reinforcing parenting, and if it is used only as a backup to enhance the effectiveness of milder disciplinary tactics such as reasoning and time-out.

Nevertheless, say advocates of nonviolent parenting, physical punishment has drawbacks (Gershoff, 2002; Marshall, 2002). Punished behavior is not forgotten; it is suppressed. This temporary suppression may (negatively) reinforce the parents' punishing behavior. The child swears, the parent swats, the parent hears no more swearing from the child, and the parent feels the punishment was successful in stopping the behavior. No wonder spanking is a hit with so many U.S. parents of 3- and 4-year-olds—more than 9 in 10 of whom acknowledge spanking their children (Kazdin & Benjet, 2003).

But was the punishment effective? If the punishment is avoidable, the punished behavior may reappear in safe settings. The child may simply learn discrimination: It's not okay to swear around the house, but it is okay to swear elsewhere. The driver who gets a speeding ticket may buy a radar detector and speed freely when no radar patrol is around.

Physical punishment may increase aggressiveness by demonstrating that aggression is a way to cope with problems. This helps explain why so many aggressive delinquents and abusive parents come from abusive families (Straus & Gelles, 1980; Straus & others, 1997). Moreover, punishment can create fear; the person receiving the punishment may associate the fear not only with the undesirable behavior but also with the person who administers it or with the situation in which it occurs. Thus, a child may come to fear the punitive teacher and want to avoid school. Worse, when punishments are unpredictable and inescapable, both animals and people may develop the sense that events are beyond their control. As a result, they may come to feel helpless and depressed. For these reasons, most European countries have banned hitting children in schools and child-care institutions (Leach, 1993, 1994). Eleven countries, including those in Scandinavia, have further outlawed hitting by parents, thereby extending to children the same legal protection given to spouses (EPOCH, 2000).

Even though punishment suppresses unwanted behavior, it often does not guide one toward more desirable behavior. Punishment tells you what *not* to do; reinforcement tells you what *to* do. Thus, punishment combined with reinforcement is usually more effective than punishment alone. This approach has been used to change self-destructive behaviors by children who bite themselves or bang their heads. They may be mildly punished (say, with a squirt of water in the face) whenever they bite themselves, but also rewarded with positive attention and food when they behave well. The approach also works in the classroom. The teacher whose feedback on a paper says "No, but try this . . ." and "Yes, that's it!" reduces unwanted behavior by reinforcing alternative behaviors.

Parents of delinquent youth often lack this awareness of how to reinforce desirable behavior without screaming or hitting (Patterson & others, 1982). Training programs for such parents help them reframe contingencies from dire threats to positive incentives—from "You clean up your room this minute or no dinner!" to "You're welcome at the dinner table after you get your room cleaned up." When you stop to think about it, many threats of punishment are just as forceful, and perhaps more effective, if rephrased positively. Thus, "If you don't get your homework done, there'll be no car" would better be phrased as . . .

What punishment often teaches, said Skinner, is how to avoid it. Most psychologists now favor an emphasis on reinforcement: Notice people doing something right and affirm them for it.

Extending Skinner's Understanding

Skinner granted the existence of private thought processes and the biological underpinnings of behavior. Nevertheless, many psychologists criticized him for discounting the importance of these processes and predispositions.

Cognition and Operant Conditioning

OBJECTIVE **22-7** | Explain how latent learning and the effect of external rewards demonstrate that cognitive processing is an important part of learning.

A mere eight days before dying of leukemia, Skinner (1990) stood before the American Psychological Association convention for one final critique of "cognitive science," which he viewed as a throwback to early twentieth-century introspectionism. Skinner died resisting the growing belief that cognitive processes—thoughts, perceptions, expectations—have a necessary place in the science of psychology and even in our understanding of conditioning. (He regarded thoughts and emotions as behaviors that follow the same laws as other behaviors.) Yet we have seen several hints that cognitive processes might be at work in operant learning. For example, animals on a fixed-interval reinforcement schedule respond more and more frequently as the time approaches when a response will produce a reinforcer. The animals behave as if they expected that repeating the response would soon produce the reward. (To a strict behaviorist, however, talk of "expectations" is unnecessary; it is enough to say that when responses are reinforced under certain conditions they recur when those conditions recur.)

Latent Learning

Evidence of cognitive processes has also come from studying rats in mazes. Rats exploring a maze, with no obvious reward, are like people sightseeing in a new town. The rats seem to develop a **cognitive map,** a mental representation of the maze. When an experimenter then places a reward in the maze's goal box, the rats very quickly perform as well as rats that have been reinforced with food for running the maze (**FIGURE 22.4**).

During their explorations, the rats seemingly experience **latent learning**—learning that becomes apparent only when there is some incentive to demonstrate it.

■ **cognitive map** a mental representation of the layout of one's environment. For example, after exploring a maze, rats act as if they have learned a cognitive map of it.

■ **latent learning** learning that occurs but is not apparent until there is an incentive to demonstrate it.

For more information on animal behavior, see books by (I am not making this up) Robin Fox and Lionel Tiger.

"Bathroom? Sure, it's just down the hall to the left, jog right, left, another left, straight past two more lefts, then right, and it's at the end of the third corridor on your right."

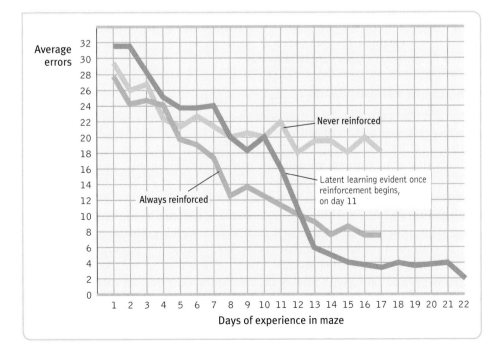

Average errors / Days of experience in maze

Never reinforced

Always reinforced

Latent learning evident once reinforcement begins, on day 11

FIGURE 22.4
Latent learning
Animals, like people, can learn from experience, with or without reinforcement. After exploring a maze for 10 days, rats received a food reward at the end of the maze. They quickly demonstrated their prior learning of the maze—by immediately doing as well as (and even better than) rats that had been reinforced for running the maze. (From Tolman & Honzik, 1930.)

■ **intrinsic motivation** a desire to perform a behavior for its own sake.

■ **extrinsic motivation** a desire to perform a behavior due to promised rewards or threats of punishment.

Children, too, may learn from watching a parent, but demonstrate the learning much later when needed. The conclusion: There is more to learning than associating a response with a consequence. There is also cognition, and psychologists have presented some striking evidence of animals' cognitive abilities in solving problems and in using aspects of language.

Intrinsic Motivation

The cognitive perspective has also led to an important qualification concerning the power of rewards: Unnecessary rewards sometimes carry hidden costs. Most people think that offering tangible rewards will boost anyone's interest in an activity (Boggiano & others, 1987). Actually, promising children a reward for a task they already enjoy can backfire. In experiments, children promised a payoff for playing with an interesting puzzle or toy later play with the toy less than do their unpaid counterparts (Deci & others, 1999; Tang & Hall, 1995). It is as if the children think, "If I have to be bribed into doing this, then it must not be worth doing for its own sake."

Excessive rewards can undermine **intrinsic motivation**—the desire to perform a behavior effectively and for its own sake. Intrinsically motivated people work and play in search of enjoyment, interest, self-expression, or challenge. **Extrinsic motivation** is the desire to behave in certain ways to receive external rewards or avoid threatened punishment. If youth sports coaches aim to promote enduring interest in an activity, and not just to pressure players into winning, they should focus on the intrinsic joy of play and reaching one's potential, note motivation researchers Edward Deci and Richard Ryan (1985, 1992, 2000).

To sense the difference between extrinsic and intrinsic motivation, you might reflect on your own current experience. Are you feeling pressured to get this reading finished before a deadline? Worried about your course grade? Eager for rewards that depend on your doing well? If yes, then you are extrinsically motivated (as, to some extent, almost all students must be). Are you also finding the course material interesting? Does learning it make you feel more competent? If there were no grade at stake, might you be curious enough to want to learn the material for its own sake? If yes, intrinsic motivation also fuels your efforts.

A person's interest often survives when a reward is used neither to bribe nor to control but to signal a job well done, as in a "most improved player" award (Boggiano & others, 1985). If a reward boosts your feeling of competence after doing good work, your enjoyment of the task may increase. Rewards, rightly administered, can motivate high performance and creativity (Eisenberger & Rhoades, 2001; Henderlong & Lepper, 2002). And extrinsic rewards (such as good scholarships, admissions, and jobs that often follow good grades) are here to stay.

Tiger Woods' intrinsic motivation
"I remember a daily ritual that we had: I would call Pop at work to ask if I could practice with him. He would always pause a second or two, keeping me in suspense, but he'd always say yes. . . . In his own way, he was teaching me initiative. You see, he never pushed me to play" (quoted in *USA Weekend*, 1997).

Biological Predispositions

OBJECTIVE 22-8 | Explain how biological predispositions place limits on what can be achieved through operant conditioning.

" Never try to teach a pig to sing. It wastes your time and annoys the pig."
Mark Twain (1835–1910)

As with classical conditioning, an animal's natural predispositions constrain its capacity for operant conditioning. When you reinforce a hamster's behavior with food, you can easily condition it to dig or to rear up, because these are among the animal's natural behaviors when searching for food. But it is difficult to use food as a reinforcer to shape other hamster behaviors, such as face washing, that aren't normally associated with food or hunger (Shettleworth, 1973). Similarly, pigeons easily learn to flap their wings to avoid being shocked, and to peck to obtain food, because fleeing with their wings and eating with their beaks are natural behaviors for them. However, pigeons have a hard time learning to peck to avoid a shock, or to flap their wings to obtain food (Foree & LoLordo, 1973). The principle: Biological constraints predispose organisms to learn associations that are naturally adaptive.

Skinner's former associates Keller Breland and Marian Breland (1961) observed biological predispositions while using operant procedures to train animals for circuses, TV shows, and movies. The Brelands had originally assumed that operant principles would work on almost any response that any animal could make. But after training 6000 animals of 38 different species, from chickens to whales, they concluded that biological predispositions were more important than they had supposed. In one act, they trained pigs to pick up large wooden "dollars" and deposit them in a piggy bank. After learning this behavior, however, the animals began to drift back to their natural ways. They would drop the coin, push it with their snouts as pigs are prone to do, pick it up again, and then repeat the sequence—delaying their food reinforcer. As this *instinctive drift* illustrates, "misbehaviors" occurred as the animals reverted to their biologically predisposed patterns.

Natural athletes
Animals can most easily learn and retain behaviors that draw on their biological predispositions, such as cats' inborn tendency to leap high and land on their feet.

Skinner's Legacy

OBJECTIVE 22-9 | Describe the controversy over Skinner's views of human behavior.

B. F. Skinner was one of the most controversial intellectual figures of the late twentieth century. He stirred a hornet's nest by repeatedly insisting that external influences (not internal thoughts and feelings) shape behavior and by urging the use of operant principles to influence people's behavior at school, work, and home. To help or manage people effectively, Skinner said, we should worry less about their illusions of freedom and dignity. Recognizing that behavior is shaped by its consequences, we should, he argued, administer rewards in ways that promote more desirable behavior.

Skinner's critics objected, saying that he dehumanized people by neglecting their personal freedom and by seeking to control their actions. Skinner's reply: People's behavior is already haphazardly controlled by external consequences, so why not administer those consequences for human betterment? In place of the punishments used in homes, schools, and prisons, would not reinforcers be more humanitarian? And if it is humbling to think that we are shaped by our histories, this very idea also gives us hope that we can shape our future.

B. F. Skinner
"I am sometimes asked, 'Do you think of yourself as you think of the organisms you study?' The answer is yes. So far as I know, my behavior at any given moment has been nothing more than the product of my genetic endowment, my personal history, and the current setting" (1983).

Applications of Operant Conditioning

OBJECTIVE 22-10 | Describe some ways to apply operant conditioning principles at school, in sports, at work, and at home.

Psychologists are applying operant conditioning principles to help people moderate high blood pressure or gain social skills. Reinforcement technologies are also at work in schools, sports, workplaces, and homes (Flora, 2004).

At School

A generation ago, Skinner and others advocated the use of teaching machines and textbooks that would shape learning in small steps and provide immediate reinforcement for correct responses. Such machines and texts, they said, would revolutionize education and free teachers to concentrate on their students' special needs.

To envision Skinner's idea, imagine two math teachers, each with a class of academically diverse students. Teacher A gives the whole class the same math lesson, knowing that some students will readily understand the concepts and that others will be frustrated. With so many different children, how can one teacher guide them individually? The whiz kids breeze through unchallenged; the slower learners experience failure. Faced

Computer-assisted learning
Computers have helped realize Skinner's goal of individually paced instruction with immediate feedback.

with a similar class, Teacher B paces the material according to each student's rate of learning and provides prompt feedback with positive reinforcement to both slow and fast learners. Does the individualized instruction of Teacher B seem unrealistic?

Although the predicted education revolution has not occurred, to the end of his life Skinner (1986, 1988, 1989) believed the ideal was achievable. "Good instruction demands two things," he said. "Students must be told immediately whether what they do is right or wrong and, when right, they must be directed to the step to be taken next." Computers were his final hope. For reading and math drills, the computer could be Teacher B—pacing material according to the student's rate of learning, quizzing the student to find gaps in understanding, providing immediate feedback, and keeping flawless records for the supervising teacher. Today's interactive student software, Web-based learning, and on-line testing bring us closer than ever before to achieving Skinner's ideal.

In Sports

Reinforcement principles can enhance athletic performance as well. Again, the key is to shape behavior, by first reinforcing small successes and then gradually increasing the challenge. Thomas Simek and Richard O'Brien (1981, 1988) applied these principles to teaching golf and baseball by starting with easily reinforced responses. Golf students learn putting by starting with very short putts. As they build mastery, they eventually step back farther and farther. Likewise, novice batters begin with half swings at an oversized ball pitched from 10 feet away, giving them the immediate pleasure of smacking the ball. As the hitters' confidence builds with their success and they achieve mastery at each level, the pitcher gradually moves back—to 15, then 22, 30, and 40.5 feet—and eventually introduces a standard baseball. Compared with children taught by conventional methods, those trained by this behavioral method show, in both testing and game situations, faster improvement in their skill.

At Work

Believing reinforcers influence productivity, business managers have capitalized on psychological research. Many companies now enable their employees to share profits and to participate in company ownership. When workers' productivity boosts rewards for everyone, their motivation, morale, and cooperative spirit often increase (Deutsch, 1991). Reinforcement for a job well done is especially effective in boosting productivity when the desired performance is *well-defined and achievable*. The message for managers? Reward specific behaviors, not vaguely defined merit. Even criticism triggers the least resentment and the greatest performance boost when specific and considerate (Baron, 1988).

It is also wise to make the reinforcement *immediate*. When IBM legend Thomas Watson observed an achievement, he would write the employee a check on the spot (Peters & Waterman, 1982). But rewards need not be material, nor should they be so substantial that they become political and a source of discouragement to those who don't receive them. An effective manager may simply walk the floor and sincerely affirm people for good work, or write notes of appreciation for a completed project. As Skinner said, "How much richer would the whole world be if the reinforcers in daily life were more effectively contingent on productive work?"

At Home

Many economists and psychologists believe people's spending behavior is controlled by its consequences (its costs and benefits). Compared with people who rent apartments in buildings where energy costs are paid by the landlord, those who live in comparable buildings but pay their own utility bills (therefore reaping the rewards of their own savings) use about 20 percent less energy. Similarly, those on an "energy diet" for their home electricity are helped by receiving frequent feedback showing current usage compared with past consumption (Darley & others, 1979). In homes, as elsewhere, immediate consequences most effectively influence behavior. Al Gore (1992, p. 348) suggested how U.S. tax policies might harness the power of consequences:

> There is an economic rule of thumb: Whatever we tax, we tend to get less of; whatever we subsidize, we tend to get more of. Currently, we tax work and we subsidize the depletion of natural resources—and both policies have contributed to high unemployment and the waste of natural resources. What if we lowered the tax on work and simultaneously raised it on the burning of fossil fuels?

"I wrote another five hundred words. Can I have another cookie?"

Parents can also take helpful advantage of operant conditioning. Parent-training researchers Michelle Wierson and Rex Forehand (1994) remind us that when parents say "get ready for bed" and then cave in to protests or defiance, they reinforce such behaviors. Eventually, exasperated, they may yell at their child or gesture menacingly, at which point the child's fearful compliance in turn reinforces the parents' angry behavior. Over time, a destructive parent-child relationship develops. To disrupt this cycle, Wierson and Forehand offer these tips:

- Give children attention and other reinforcers when they are behaving well. Target a specific behavior, reward it, and watch it increase.
- Ignore whining. If whining has triggered attention in the past, it may temporarily increase when ignored. Over time, if not reinforced, it will diminish.
- When children misbehave or are defiant, do not yell at or hit them. Simply explain the misbehavior and give them a *time-out*—for a specific time remove them from any reinforcing surroundings.

Finally, we can use operant conditioning on ourselves, by reinforcing our most desired behaviors and extinguishing those undesired. To take charge of your own behavior, psychologists suggest taking these steps:

1. *State your goal*—to stop smoking, eat less, or study or exercise more—in measurable terms, and make your intention public. You might, for example, aim to boost your study time by an hour a day and announce that goal to some supportive friends.
2. *Monitor* how often you engage in the behavior you wish to promote. You might log your current study time, noting under what conditions you do and don't study. (When I began writing textbooks, I logged how I spent my time throughout each day and was astonished to discover how much time I was wasting.)
3. *Reinforce* the desired behavior. To increase your study time, allow yourself a snack (or some other reinforcing activity) only after specified periods of study. Agree with your friends that you will join them for weekend activities only if you have met your realistic weekly studying goal.
4. *Reduce the incentives* gradually, as your new behaviors become more habitual, while giving yourself a mental pat on the back.

Contrasting Classical and Operant Conditioning

OBJECTIVE 22-11 | Identify the major similarities and differences between classical and operant conditioning.

Both classical and operant conditioning are forms of associative learning, and both involve acquisition, extinction, spontaneous recovery, generalization, and discrimination. The similarities are sufficient to make some researchers wonder if a single stimulus-response learning process might explain them both (Donahoe & Vegas, 2004). Their procedural difference is this: Through classical (Pavlovian) conditioning,

> "O! This learning, what a thing it is."
> William Shakespeare, *The Taming of the Shrew*, 1597

an organism associates different stimuli that it does not control and responds automatically (respondent behaviors). Through operant conditioning, an organism associates its operant behaviors—those that act on its environment to produce rewarding or punishing stimuli—with their consequences. Cognitive processes and biological predispositions influence both classical and operant conditioning (TABLE 22.4).

TABLE **22.4**

COMPARISON OF CLASSICAL AND OPERANT CONDITIONING

	Classical Conditioning	Operant Conditioning
Response	Involuntary, automatic.	Voluntary, operates on environment.
Acquisition	Associating events; CS announces US.	Associating response with a consequence (reinforcer or punisher).
Extinction	CR decreases when CS is repeatedly presented alone.	Responding decreases when reinforcement stops.
Cognitive processes	Organisms develop expectation that CS signals the arrival of US.	Organisms develop expectation that a response will be reinforced or punished; they also exhibit latent learning, without reinforcement.
Biological predispositions	Natural predispositions constrain what stimuli and responses can easily be associated.	Organisms best learn behaviors similar to their natural behaviors; unnatural behaviors instinctively drift back toward natural ones.

>> LEARNING OUTCOMES

Operant Conditioning

OBJECTIVE 22-1 | **Identify the two major characteristics that distinguish classical conditioning from operant conditioning.**
In *classical conditioning,* the organism forms associations between behaviors it does not control; this form of conditioning involves *respondent behavior* (automatic responses to some stimulus). In *operant conditioning,* the organism learns associations between its own behavior and resulting events; this form of conditioning involves *operant behavior* (behavior that operates on the environment, producing consequences).

OBJECTIVE 22-2 | **State Thorndike's law of effect, and explain its connection to Skinner's research on operant conditioning.**
Thorndike's law of effect asserts that rewarded behavior is likely to recur. Using this as his starting point, Skinner devoted his life to exploring the principles and conditions of learning through operant conditioning.

OBJECTIVE 22-3 | **Describe the shaping procedure, and explain how it can increase our understanding of what animals and babies can discriminate.**
In shaping, we use reinforcers to guide a person's or an animal's behavior toward a desired goal. Building on existing behaviors, we reward successive approximations to some desired behavior. Because nonverbal animals and babies can respond only to what they perceive, their reactions demonstrate which events they can discriminate.

OBJECTIVE 22-4 | **Compare positive and negative reinforcement, and give one example each of a primary reinforcer, a conditioned reinforcer, an immediate reinforcer, and a delayed reinforcer.**
Positive reinforcement *adds* something *desirable* to increase the frequency of a behavior. Negative reinforcement *removes* something *undesirable* to increase the frequency of a behavior. *Primary reinforcers* (such as receiving food when hungry or having nausea end during an illness) are innately satisfying—no learning is required. *Conditioned* (or secondary) *reinforcers* (such as cash) are satisfying because we have learned to associate them with more basic rewards (such as the food or medicine we buy with them). *Immediate reinforcers* (such as the nicotine addict's cigarette) offer immediate payback; *delayed reinforcers* (such as a weekly paycheck) require the ability to delay gratification.

OBJECTIVE 22-5 | **Discuss the strengths and weaknesses of continuous and partial (intermittent) reinforcement schedules, and identify four schedules of partial reinforcement.**
In *continuous reinforcement* (reinforcing desired responses every time they occur), learning is rapid, but so is extinction if rewards cease. Continuous reinforcement is preferable until a behavior is learned. In *partial reinforcement* (reinforcing responses only part of the time), initial learning is slower, but the behavior is much more resistant to extinction. Reinforcement schedules may vary according to the number of responses rewarded or the time gap between

responses. *Fixed-ratio schedules* offer rewards after a set number of responses; *variable-ratio schedules,* after an unpredictable number. *Fixed-interval schedules* offer rewards after set time periods; *variable-interval schedules,* after unpredictable time periods.

OBJECTIVE 22-6 | **Discuss the ways negative punishment, positive punishment, and negative reinforcement differ, and list some drawbacks of punishment as a behavior-control technique.**

Both positive punishment (*administering* an undesirable consequence, such as spanking) and negative punishment (*withdrawing* something desirable, such as taking away a favorite toy) attempt to *decrease* the frequency of a behavior (a child's disobedience). Negative reinforcement (such as taking aspirin) removes something undesirable (such as a headache) to *increase* the frequency of a behavior. Punishment's undesirable side effects may include suppressing rather than changing unwanted behaviors, teaching aggression, creating fear, encouraging discrimination (so that the undesirable behavior appears when the punisher is not present), and fostering depression and feelings of helplessness.

OBJECTIVE 22-7 | **Explain how latent learning and the effect of external rewards demonstrate that cognitive processing is an important part of learning.**

Latent learning, as shown in rats' learning of cognitive maps or children's delayed imitation of others' behavior, indicates that we can learn from experience, without apparent reinforcement. An external reward's ability to undermine our interest and pleasure in an activity weakens the idea that behaviors that are rewarded will increase in frequency.

OBJECTIVE 22-8 | **Explain how biological predispositions place limits on what can be achieved through operant conditioning.**

Biological constraints predispose organisms to learn associations that are naturally adaptive. Training that attempts to override these tendencies will probably not endure because the animals will revert to their biologically predisposed patterns.

OBJECTIVE 22-9 | **Describe the controversy over Skinner's views of human behavior.**

Many psychologists criticized Skinner for underestimating the importance of cognition and biological constraints on learning. They also engaged in a vigorous intellectual debate with him over the nature of human freedom and the strategies and ethics of managing people.

OBJECTIVE 22-10 | **Describe some ways to apply operant conditioning principles at school, in sports, at work, and at home.**

In school, teachers can use shaping techniques to guide students' behaviors, and interactive software and Web sites to provide immediate feedback to students. *In sports,* coaches can build players' skills and self-confidence by rewarding small improvements. *At work,* managers can boost productivity and morale by rewarding well-defined and achievable behaviors. *At home,* we can control our energy usage by comparing recent consumption with past consumption. Parents can reward behaviors they consider desirable, but not those that are undesirable. Individually, we can use these principles to reinforce our own desired behaviors and extinguish undesirable ones.

OBJECTIVE 22-11 | **Identify the major similarities and differences between classical and operant conditioning.**

Both classical and operant conditioning are forms of associative learning. Both involve acquisition, extinction, spontaneous recovery, generalization, and discrimination. And both are influenced—and sometimes constrained—by cognitive processes and biological predispositions. These forms of learning differ in an important way. In classical conditioning, an organism associates different stimuli that it does not control and responds automatically (respondent behaviors). In operant conditioning, an organism associates its own behaviors with their effects on the environment (operant behavior).

TERMS AND CONCEPTS TO REMEMBER

associative learning, p. 22-1
operant conditioning, p. 22-1
respondent behavior, p. 22-1
operant behavior, p. 22-1
law of effect, p. 22-2
operant chamber, p. 22-2
learning, p. 22-2
shaping, p. 22-3
reinforcer, p. 22-4
positive reinforcement, p. 22-4
negative reinforcement, p. 22-4
primary reinforcer, p. 22-5
conditioned reinforcer
 (*secondary reinforcer*), p. 22-5

continuous reinforcement,
 p. 22-5
partial (intermittent) reinforcement, p. 22-6
fixed-ratio schedule, p. 22-6
variable-ratio schedule, p. 22-7
fixed-interval schedule, p. 22-7
variable-interval schedule, p. 22-7
punishment, p. 22-7
cognitive map, p. 22-9
latent learning, p. 22-9
intrinsic motivation, p. 22-10
extrinsic motivation, p. 22-10

TEST YOURSELF

1. *Positive reinforcement, negative reinforcement,* and *punishment* are tricky concepts for many students. Can you fit the right term in the four boxes in this table? I'll do the first one (positive reinforcement) for you.

Type of Stimulus	Give It	Take It Away
Desired (for example, a compliment):	Positive reinforcement	
Undesired/aversive (for example, an insult):		

(Answer in Appendix B.)

ASK YOURSELF

1. Can you recall a time when a teacher, coach, family member, or employer helped you learn something by shaping your behavior in little steps until you achieved your goal?

>WEB

Multiple-choice *self-tests* and more may be found at www.worthpublishers.com/myers.

MODULE

23

Learning by Observation

OBJECTIVE **23-1** | Describe the process of observational learning, and explain the importance of the discovery of mirror neurons.

From drooling dogs, running rats, and pecking pigeons we have learned much about the basic processes of **learning.** But conditioning principles alone do not tell us the whole story. Among higher animals, especially humans, learning need not occur through direct experience. **Observational learning,** in which we observe and imitate others, also plays a big part. A child who sees his big sister burn her fingers on the stove has thereby learned not to touch it.

The process of observing and imitating a specific behavior is often called **modeling.** We learn all kinds of social behaviors by observing and imitating models. Lord Chesterfield (1694–1773) had the idea: "We are, in truth, more than half what we are by imitation."

We can glimpse the roots of observational learning in other species. Rats, pigeons, crows, and gorillas all observe others and learn (Byrne & Russon, 1998; Dugatkin, 2002). So do monkeys. Shortly after a fight, stumptail macaque monkeys often reconcile with one another by approaching their opponent and making friendly contact. Rhesus macaque monkeys rarely make up quickly—unless they grow up with forgiving older stumptails. Then, more often than not, their fights, too, are quickly followed by reconciliation (de Waal & Johanowicz, 1993). Monkey see, monkey do (**FIGURE 23.1**).

Imitation is all the more striking in humans. So many of our ideas, fashions, and habits travel by imitation that these transmitted cultural elements now have a name: *memes*. We humans are the supreme meme machines, notes Susan Blackmore (1999, 2000). Our catch-phrases, hem lengths, ceremonies, foods, traditions, vices, and fads (think Harry Potter) all spread by one person copying another.

Neuroscientists have discovered **mirror neurons** (in a frontal-lobe area adjacent to the brain's motor cortex) that provide a neural basis for observational learning. When a monkey performs a task such as grasping, holding, or tearing, these neurons fire (Rizzolatti & others, 2002). But they also fire when the monkey observes another monkey performing the same task. When one monkey sees, these neurons will mirror what another monkey does.

> "Children need models more than they need critics."
>
> Joseph Joubert, *Pensées,* 1842

■ **learning** a relatively permanent change in an organism's behavior due to experience.

■ **observational learning** learning by observing others.

■ **modeling** the process of observing and imitating a specific behavior.

■ **mirror neurons** frontal lobe neurons that fire when performing certain actions or when observing another doing so. The brain's mirroring of another's action may enable imitation, language learning, and empathy.

FIGURE 23.1
Cognitive imitation
When Monkey A, on the left, sees Monkey B touch four pictures on a display screen in a certain order to gain a banana, Monkey A learns to imitate that order, even when shown a different configuration (Subiaul & others, 2004).

Monkey A's screen   Monkey B's screen

Pain   Empathy

Reprinted with permission from The American Association for the Advancement of Science, Subiaul et al., Science 305:407-410 (2004) ©2004 AAAS.

FIGURE 23.2
Experienced and imagined pain in the brain
Brain activity related to actual pain (left) is mirrored in the brain of an observing loved one. Empathy in the brain involves emotional brain areas, but not the somatosensory cortex, which receives the physical pain input.

It's not just monkey business. PET scans reveal that humans, too, have mirror neurons in this brain area, which also serves language. Human mirror neurons help children learn by observation how to mime lip and tongue movements when forming new words. Mirror neurons also help give rise to children's empathy and to their ability to infer another's mental state (an ability known as *theory of mind*). As adults, we often feel what another feels, and we find it harder to frown when viewing a smile than when viewing a frown (Dimberg & others, 2000, 2002). Seeing a loved one's pain, it's not just our faces that mirror their emotion, but also our brains. As **FIGURE 23.2** shows, the pain imagined by an empathic romantic partner triggers some of the same brain activity experienced by the one actually having the pain (Singer & others, 2004).

The imitation of models shapes even very young children's behavior. Shortly after birth, an infant may imitate an adult who sticks out his tongue. By 9 months, infants will imitate novel play behaviors. And by age 14 months (**FIGURE 23.3**), children will imitate acts modeled on television (Meltzoff, 1988; Meltzoff & Moore, 1989, 1997). To persuade children to smoke, simply expose them to parents, older youth, and attractive media models who smoke. To encourage children to read, read to them and surround them with books and people who read. To increase the odds of your children practicing your religion, worship and attend other religious activities with them. Children see, children do.

Meltzoff, A. N. (1988). Imitation of televised models by infants. Child Development, 59, 1221-1229. Photos courtesy of A. N. Meltzoff and M. Hanuk.

FIGURE 23.3
Learning from observation
This 14-month-old boy in Andrew Meltzoff's laboratory is imitating behavior he has seen on TV. In the top photo the infant leans forward and carefully watches the adult pull apart a toy. In the middle photo he has been given the toy. In the bottom photo he pulls the toy apart, imitating what he has seen the adult do.

Bandura's Experiments

OBJECTIVE 23-2 | Describe Bandura's findings on what determines whether we will imitate a model.

Picture this scene from a famous experiment devised by Albert Bandura, the pioneering researcher of observational learning (Bandura & others, 1961). A preschool child is at work on a drawing. An adult in another part of the room is working with some Tinkertoys. The adult then gets up and for nearly 10 minutes pounds, kicks, and throws a large inflated Bobo doll around the room, while yelling such remarks as, "Sock him in the nose. . . . Hit him down. . . . Kick him."

After observing this outburst, the child is taken to another room where there are many appealing toys. Soon the experimenter interrupts the child's play and explains that she has decided to save these good toys "for the other children." She now takes

Albert Bandura

"The Bobo doll follows me wherever I go. The photographs are published in every introductory psychology text and virtually every undergraduate takes introductory psychology. I recently checked into a Washington hotel. The clerk at the desk asked, 'Aren't you the psychologist who did the Bobo doll experiment?' I answered, 'I am afraid that will be my legacy.' He replied, 'That deserves an upgrade. I will put you in a suite in the quiet part of the hotel'" (2005).

the frustrated child to an adjacent room containing a few toys, including a Bobo doll. Left alone, what does the child do?

Compared with children not exposed to the adult model, those who observed the model's aggressive outburst were much more likely to lash out at the doll. Apparently, observing the adult model beating up the doll lowered their inhibitions. But something more than lowered inhibitions was at work, for the children also imitated the very acts they had observed and used the very words they had heard.

What determines whether we will imitate a model? Bandura believes part of the answer is reinforcements and punishments—those received by the model as well as by the imitator. We look and we learn. By looking, we learn to anticipate a behavior's consequences in situations like those we are observing. We are especially likely to imitate people we perceive as similar to ourselves, as successful, or as admirable.

Applications of Observational Learning

The bad news from Bandura's studies is that antisocial models—in one's family or neighborhood, or on TV—may have antisocial effects. In the first eight days after the 1999 Columbine High School massacre, every U.S. state except Vermont had to deal with copycat threats or incidents. Pennsylvania alone had 60 threats of school violence (Cooper, 1999). By watching TV programs, children may "learn" that physical intimidation is an effective way to control others, that free and easy sex brings pleasure without later misery or disease, or that men are supposed to be tough and women gentle.

Observational learning also helps us understand how abusive parents might have aggressive children, and why many men who beat their wives had wife-battering fathers (Stith & others, 2000). The lessons we learn as children are not easily unlearned as adults, and they are sometimes visited on future generations. Critics note that the intergenerational transmission of abuse could be genetic. But with monkeys we know it can be environmental. In study after study, young monkeys that received high levels of aggression when reared apart from their mothers grew up to be perpetrators of aggression (Chamove, 1980).

Positive Observational Learning

OBJECTIVE 23-3 | Discuss the impact of prosocial modeling.

A model grandma
This boy is learning to cook by observing his grandmother. As the sixteenth-century proverb states, "Example is better than precept."

The good news is that **prosocial** (positive, helpful) models can have prosocial effects. People who exemplify nonviolent, helpful behavior can prompt similar behavior in others. India's Mahatma Gandhi and America's Martin Luther King, Jr., both drew on the power of modeling, making nonviolent action a powerful force for social change in both countries. Parents are also powerful models. European Christians who risked their lives to rescue Jews from the Nazis usually had a close relationship with at least one parent who modeled a strong moral or humanitarian concern; this was also true for U.S. civil rights activists in the 1960s (London, 1970; Oliner & Oliner, 1988). The observational learning of morality begins early. Socially responsive toddlers who readily imitate their parents tend to become preschoolers with a strong internalized conscience (Fordman & others, 2004).

Models are most effective when their actions and words are consistent. Sometimes, however, models say one thing and do another. Many parents seem to operate according to the principle "Do as I *say*, not as I do." Experiments suggest that children learn to do both (Rice & Grusec, 1975; Rushton, 1975). Exposed to a hypocrite, they tend to imitate the hypocrisy by doing what the model did and saying what the model said.

Television and Observational Learning

OBJECTIVE 23-4 | Explain why correlations cannot prove that watching violent TV causes violent behavior, and cite some experimental evidence that helps demonstrate a cause-effect link.

Wherever television exists, it becomes the source of much observational learning. During their first 18 years, most children in developed countries spend more time watching TV than they spend in school. In Australia, 99.2 percent of households have television and 56 percent have multiple sets (Trewin, 2001). In the United States, where 9 in 10 teens watch TV daily, someone who lives to 75 will have spent 9 years staring at the tube (Gallup, 2002; Kubey & Csikszentmihalyi, 2002). Two-thirds of U.S. homes have three or more sets, which helps explain why parents' reports of what their children watch hardly correlate with children's reports of what they watch (Donnerstein, 1998).

In urban homes across the world, including those of South America and Asia, television is now commonplace. With more than a billion TV sets now in homes worldwide, CNN reaching 150 countries, and MTV broadcasting in 17 languages, television has created a global pop culture (Gunderson, 2001; Lippman, 1992). One can watch American programs in Perth or Prague and catch the latest rock videos from Newfoundland to the tiny Himalayan kingdom of Bhutan, where television was introduced in 1999 and soon began influencing speech and children's behavior (Keys, 2001).

Does the reel world reflect the real world? Our data are limited because funding for ongoing media monitoring by social scientists waned after the early 1990s. But on evening dramas broadcast in the United States during the 1980s and early 1990s and often exported to the rest of the world, only one-third of the characters were women. Fewer than 3 percent were visibly old. One percent were Hispanic. Only 1 in 10 was married (Gerbner, 1993). U.S. network programs have offered about 3 violent acts per hour during prime time, and 18 per hour during children's Saturday morning programs (Gerbner & others, 1994). Unlike the real world, where 87 percent of crimes are nonviolent, in TV's world of "reality-based" police shows, 13 percent of crimes are nonviolent (Oliver, 1994).

Television viewers are learning about life from a rather peculiar storyteller, one who reflects the culture's mythology but not its reality. During the late twentieth century, the average child viewed some 8000 TV murders and 100,000 other acts of violence before finishing elementary school (Huston & others, 1992). If one includes cable programming and video rentals, the violence numbers escalate. (Popular rental films like *Die Hard 1,* with its 264 deaths, are much more violent than major network programs.) An analysis of more than 3000 network and cable programs aired during 1996/1997 revealed that nearly 6 in 10 featured violence, that 74 percent of the violence went unpunished, that 58 percent did not show the victims' pain, and that nearly half the incidents involved "justified" violence and nearly half involved an attractive perpetrator. These conditions define the recipe for the violence-viewing effect described below (Donnerstein, 1998).

Do you think viewing televised aggression influences some people to commit aggression? Was the judge who in 1993 tried two British 10-year-olds for their murder of a 2-year-old right to suspect that one possible influence was the aggressors' exposure to "violent video films"? Were the American media right to think that the teen assassins who killed 13 of their Columbine High School classmates had been influenced by repeated viewings of *Natural Born Killers* and by frequently playing splatter games such as *Doom?* To answer similar questions, researchers have conducted both correlational and experimental studies (Anderson & others, 2003).

■ **prosocial behavior** positive, constructive, helpful behavior. The opposite of antisocial behavior.

"The problem with television is that the people must sit and keep their eyes glued to a screen: The average American family hasn't time for it. Therefore the showmen are convinced that . . . television will never be a serious competitor of [radio] broadcasting."

New York Times, 1939

TV's greatest effect may stem from what it displaces. Children and adults who spend four hours a day watching TV spend four fewer hours in active pursuits—talking, studying, playing, reading, or socializing with friends. What would you have done with your extra time if you had never watched TV, and how might you therefore be different?

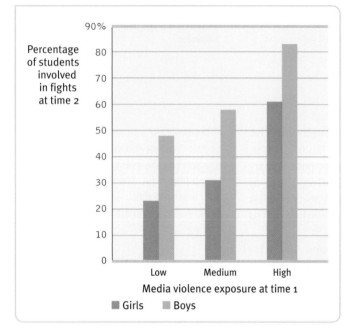

FIGURE 23.4
**Media violence viewing
predicts future aggressive behavior**
In a study of more than 400 third to fifth
graders, Douglas Gentile and his colleagues
(2004) reported increased aggression in
those heavily exposed to violent television, videos, and video games. The data
shown here were adjusted for the children's preexisting differences in hostility
and aggression.

"Thirty seconds worth of glorification of a
soap bar sells soap. Twenty-five minutes
worth of glorification of violence sells
violence."

U.S. Senator Paul Simon, Remarks to the
Communitarian Network, 1993

**Violence
viewing leads to
violent play**
Research has
shown that viewing
media violence
does lead to
increased expres-
sion of aggression
in the viewers, as
with these boys
imitating pro
wrestlers.

Correlational studies do link violence viewing with violent
behavior.

- The more hours elementary school children spend engaged
  with media violence (via television, videos, and video
  games), the more often they get in fights when restudied
  two to six months later (**FIGURE 23.4**).
- The more hours children spend watching violent programs,
  the more at risk they also are for aggression and crime as
  teens and adults (Eron, 1987; Turner & others, 1986). One
  study compared 16- and 22-year-olds who had watched less
  than an hour of TV daily at age 14 with those who had
  watched more than three hours. The heavy viewer group
  committed five times as many aggressive acts.
- In the United States and Canada, homicide rates doubled
  between 1957 and 1974, coinciding with the introduction
  and spread of TV. Moreover, census regions that were late in
  acquiring TV service had their homicide rate jump corre-
  spondingly later.
- White South Africans were first introduced to TV in 1975. A
  similar near-doubling of the homicide rate began after 1975
  (Centerwall, 1989).

"There is absolutely no doubt," concluded the 1993 American Psychological Association Commission on Violence and Youth, "that higher levels of viewing violence on
television are correlated with increased acceptance of aggressive attitudes and increased aggressive behavior."

But remember: *Correlation does not imply causation.* So these correlational studies do not prove that viewing violence *causes* aggression (Freedman, 1988;
McGuire, 1986). Maybe aggressive children prefer violent programs. Maybe children of neglectful or abusive parents are both more aggressive and more often left
in front of the TV. Maybe violent programs simply reflect, rather than affect, violent trends.

To pin down causation, experimenters have randomly assigned some viewers
to view violence and others to view entertaining nonviolence. Does viewing
cruelty prepare people, when irritated, to react more cruelly? To some extent,
it does. "The consensus among most of the research community," reported the
National Institute of Mental Health (1982), "is that violence on television does
lead to aggressive behavior by children and teenagers who watch the programs."
This is especially so when an attractive person commits seemingly justified, realistic violence that goes unpunished and causes no visible pain or harm (Donnerstein, 1998).

The violence effect seems to stem from a
combination of factors including *imitation*
(Geen & Thomas, 1986). As we noted earlier, children as young as 14 months will
imitate acts they observe on TV. One research team observed a sevenfold increase
in violent play immediately after children
viewed the "Power Rangers" (Boyatzis &
others, 1995). Boys often precisely imitated the characters' flying karate kicks
and other violent acts.

Prolonged exposure to violence also *de-
sensitizes* viewers; they become more indif-

ferent to it when later viewing a brawl, whether on TV or in real life (Rule & Ferguson, 1986). While spending three evenings watching sexually violent movies, male viewers in one experiment became progressively less bothered by the rapes and slashings. Compared with research participants who did not watch these films, they later expressed less sympathy for domestic violence victims, and they rated the victims' injuries as less severe (Mullin & Linz, 1995).

Indeed, suggested Edward Donnerstein and his co-researchers (1987), an evil psychologist could hardly imagine a better way to make people indifferent to brutality than to expose them to a graded series of scenes, from fights to killings to the mutilations in slasher movies. Watching cruelty fosters indifference.

Bandura's work—like that of Ivan Pavlov, John B. Watson, B. F. Skinner, and thousands of others who advanced our knowledge of learning principles—illustrates the impact that can result from single-minded devotion to a few well-defined problems and ideas. All of these researchers defined the issues and impressed on us the importance of learning. As their legacy demonstrates, intellectual history is often made by people who risk going to extremes in pushing ideas to their limits (Simonton, 2000).

Gallup surveys asked American teens (Mazzuca, 2002): "Do you feel there is too much violence in the movies, or not?"
1977:   42 percent said yes.
1999:   23 percent said yes.

"Don't you understand? This is life, this is what is happening. We can't switch to another channel."

>> LEARNING OUTCOMES

Learning by Observation

OBJECTIVE 23-1 | Describe the process of observational learning, and explain the importance of the discovery of mirror neurons.
In *observational learning,* we observe and imitate others. *Mirror neurons,* located in the brain's frontal lobes, demonstrate a neural basis for observational learning. They fire when we perform certain actions (such as responding to pain or moving our mouth to form words), or when we observe someone else performing those actions.

OBJECTIVE 23-2 | Describe Bandura's findings on what determines whether we will imitate a model.
Bandura and others demonstrated that we are likely to imitate actions that go unpunished. And we tend to imitate models we perceive as similar to us, successful, or admirable.

OBJECTIVE 23-3 | Discuss the impact of prosocial modeling.
Children tend to imitate what a model does and says, whether the behavior is *prosocial* (positive, constructive, and helpful) or *antisocial.* If a model's actions and words are inconsistent, children may imitate the hypocrisy they observe.

OBJECTIVE 23-4 | Explain why correlations cannot prove that watching violent TV causes violent behavior, and cite some experimental evidence that helps demonstrate a cause-effect link.
Correlations show relationships, but not the direction of influence. Correlational studies show that violence viewing and violent behavior are linked, but they do not prove that watching violent TV causes children to become violent. Children who behave violently may enjoy watching violence on TV, or some third factor may cause children both to behave violently and to prefer watching violent programs. Experiments designed to prove cause and effect show that people who have viewed violence tend later to be more aggressive and less sympathetic. Two factors—imitation and desensitization—seem to contribute to the violence effect.

TERMS AND CONCEPTS TO REMEMBER

learning, p. 23-0	mirror neurons, p. 23-0
observational learning, p. 23-0	prosocial behavior, p. 23-2
modeling, p. 23-0	

TEST YOURSELF

1. Jason's parents and older friends all smoke, but they advise him not to. Juan's parents and friends don't smoke, but they say nothing to deter him from doing so. Will Jason or Juan be more likely to start smoking?

(Answer in Appendix B.)

ASK YOURSELF

1. Who has been a significant role model for you? For whom are you a model?

>WEB

Multiple-choice *self-tests* and more may be found at www.worthpublishers.com/myers.

ANOTHER VOICE ON: MEMORY

GWENDOLYN BROOKS (1917–2000), FROM *THE BEAN EATERS*

They eat beans mostly, this old yellow
   pair.
Dinner is a casual affair.
Plain chipware on a plain and creaking
   wood,
Tin flatware.

Two who are Mostly Good.
Two who have lived their day,
But keep on putting on their clothes
And putting things away.

And remembering . . .

Remembering, with twinklings and
   twinges,
As they lean over the beans in their
   rented back room that is full of beads
   and receipts and dolls and cloths,
   tobacco crumbs, vases and fringes.

Memory

An event is such a little piece of time and space, leaving only a mindglow behind like the tail of a shooting star. For lack of a better word, we call that scintillation memory.

Diane Ackerman, *An Alchemy of Mind*, 2004

Be thankful for memory. We take it for granted, except when it malfunctions. But it is our memory, notes Rebecca Rupp (1998, p. xvii), that "allows us to recognize friends, neighbors, and acquaintances and call them by their names; to knit, type, drive, and play the piano; to speak English, Spanish, or Mandarin Chinese." It is our memory that accounts for time and defines our life. It is our memory that enables us to sing our national anthem, find our way home, and locate the food and water we need for survival. It is our shared memories that bind us together as Irish or Aussies, as Serbs or Albanians. And it is our memories that occasionally pit us against those whose offenses we cannot forget.

In large part, you are what you remember. Without memory, there would be no savoring joyful moments past, no guilt or anger over painful recollections. You would instead live in an enduring present. Each moment would be fresh. But each person would be a stranger, every language foreign, every task—dressing, cooking, biking—a novel challenge. You would even be a stranger to yourself, lacking that continuous sense of self that extends from your distant past to your momentary present. Memory researcher James McGaugh (2003) suggested, "If you lose the ability to recall your old memories then you have no life. You might as well be a rutabaga or a cabbage."

To think about memory, we first need a model of how it works. Module 24 introduces a modified version of Richard Atkinson and Richard Shiffrin's classic and influential three-stage model of memory. Modules 25 through 27 examine sensory memory, short-term/working memory, and long-term memory—thus reviewing how we move information into our memories, retain it, and later retrieve it. Module 28 looks at what happens when our memories fail us (as when we forget information, misremember it, or create false memories). That module concludes with some tips on how you can apply memory researchers' findings to your own education.

"Waiter, I'd like to order, unless I've eaten, in which case bring me the check."

Memory Loss and
Memory Feats

Information Processing

Introduction to Memory

OBJECTIVE 24-1 | Define *memory*, and explain how flashbulb memories differ from other memories.

Your memory is your mind's storehouse, the reservoir of your accumulated learning. To the Roman statesman Cicero, memory was "the treasury and guardian of all things." To a psychologist, **memory** is any indication that learning has persisted over time. It is our ability to store and retrieve information.

Memory Loss and Memory Feats

Studying memory's extremes has helped researchers understand how memory works. Some studies have explored the roots and fruits of memory loss. At age 92, my father suffered a small stroke that had but one peculiar effect. His genial personality was intact. He was as mobile as before. He knew us and while poring over family photo albums could reminisce in detail about his past. But he had lost most of his ability to lay down new memories of conversations and everyday episodes. He could not tell me what day of the week it was. Told repeatedly of his brother-in-law's death, he expressed surprise each time he heard the news.

MR. TOTAL RECALL

At the other extreme are some people who would be medal winners in a memory Olympics, such as Russian journalist Shereshevskii, or S, as psychologist Alexander Luria (1968) called him. S's memory not only allowed him merely to listen while other reporters were scribbling notes, it also earned him a place in virtually every modern book on memory. You and I can repeat back a string of about 7 digits—almost surely no more than 9. S could repeat up to 70 digits or words, provided they were read about 3 seconds apart in an otherwise silent room. Moreover, he could recall them backward as easily as forward. His accuracy was unerring, even when he was asked to recall a list as much as 15 years later, after having memorized hundreds of other lists. "Yes, yes," he might recall. "This was a series you gave me once when we were in your apartment. . . . You were sitting at the table and I in the rocking chair. . . . You were wearing a gray suit and you looked at me like this. . . ."

Do S's memory feats make your own memory seem feeble? If so, consider your own pretty staggering capacity for remembering countless voices, sounds, and songs; tastes, smells, and textures; faces, places, and happenings. Imagine viewing more than 2500 slides of faces and places, for only 10 seconds each. Later you see 280 of these slides one at a time, paired with a previously unseen slide. If you are like the participants in this experiment by Ralph Haber (1970), you would recognize 90 percent of those you saw before.

Your memory capacity is perhaps most apparent in your recall of unique and highly emotional moments in your past. One of my vivid memories is of my only hit in an entire season of Little League baseball. Perhaps yours is of a car accident, your first romantic kiss, your first day as an immigrant in a new country, or your surroundings when you heard some tragic news. Most Americans over 55 feel sure of exactly what they were doing when they heard the news of President Kennedy's

Which is more important—your experiences or your memories of them?

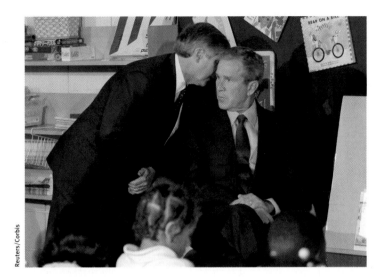

False flashbulb memory
After the second plane hit the World Trade Center on 9/11, U.S. President George W. Bush's then chief of staff, Andrew Card, whispered the news to him in a Florida classroom. But what about the first attack? Three months later, when asked how he had heard about the first attack, the president recalled "sitting outside the classroom waiting to go in, and I saw an airplane hit the tower—the TV was obviously on, and I used to fly myself, and I said, 'There's one terrible pilot.' And, I said, 'It must have been a horrible accident.'" But no one saw it on live TV, nor was there at that time any available footage of the first plane crashing (Paltrow, 2004). Hearing the story, some people perceived a blatant lie or even a conspiracy. But as psychologist Daniel Greenberg (2004) later noted, "we need only consider the frailty of human memory.... President Bush appears to be suffering from a near-textbook case of false recall."

assassination (Brown & Kulik, 1982). Seven months and even four years after Princess Diana's death, most British people could still recall their exact whereabouts on hearing that news (Kvavilashvili & others, 2003; Wynn & Gilhooly, 1999). Six decades after the Nazi invasion of Denmark, few younger Danish adults displayed any knowledge of the details of invasion day. But Danes over 72 years remembered. Seven in ten even recalled the day's weather (Berntsen & Thomsen, 2005). And you perhaps recall where you first heard the news on 9/11—that September day in 2001 that was, said the next morning's *New York Times,* "one of those moments in which history splits and we define the world as 'before and after.'" This perceived clarity for our memories of surprising, significant events leads some psychologists to call them **flashbulb memories.** It's as if the brain commands, "Capture this!" But like other memories, our flashbulb memories can err (Talarico & Rubin, 2003).

Why can even our flashbulb memories sometimes prove dead wrong? How do we accomplish other memory feats? How can we remember things we have not thought about for years, yet forget the name of someone we met a minute ago? How are memories stored in our brains? How can two people's memories of the same event be so different? How can we improve our memories? These will be among the questions we consider as we review more than a century of research on memory.

THE FAR SIDE® BY GARY LARSON

I was just getting ready to cross the interstate.

I was down by the edge of the lake at the time.

I was in the glen, just finishing a new burrow when I got the news.

I was looking for crawdads in my favorite creek.

I was under a rock, getting ready to shed.

More facts of nature: All forest animals, to this very day, remember exactly where they were and what they were doing when they heard that Bambi's mother had been shot.

Information Processing

OBJECTIVE 24-2 | Describe Atkinson-Shiffrin's classic three-stage processing model of memory, and explain how the contemporary model of working memory differs.

Building a memory is in some ways like my information processing in creating this book. For each edition, I first glimpse countless items of information, including some 100,000 journal article titles. Most of it I ignore, but some things merit temporary storage in my briefcase for more detailed processing later. Most of these items I eventually discard. The rest—typically about 3000 articles and news items—gets organized and filed for long-term storage. Later, I retrieve this information and draw from it as I spin the story of today's psychology. Very important current events jump into my long-term mental storage, from which I draw fresh examples of psychology in everyday life. In forming memories, you, too, must select, process, store, and retrieve information. You process information not only in the "cramming" you do to study in your courses, but also in the skills you learn and in your processing of countless daily events.

■ **memory** the persistence of learning over time through the storage and retrieval of information.

■ **flashbulb memory** a clear memory of an emotionally significant moment or event.

■ **encoding** the processing of information into the memory system—for example, by extracting meaning.

■ **storage** the retention of encoded information over time.

■ **retrieval** the process of getting information out of memory storage.

■ **sensory memory** the immediate, very brief recording of sensory information in the memory system.

■ **short-term memory** activated memory that holds a few items briefly, such as the seven digits of a phone number while dialing, before the information is stored or forgotten.

■ **long-term memory** the relatively permanent and limitless storehouse of the memory system. Includes knowledge, skills, and experiences.

■ **working memory** a newer understanding of short-term memory that involves conscious, active processing of incoming auditory and visual-spatial information, and of information retrieved from long-term memory.

FIGURE 24.1

A modified three-stage processing model of memory

Today's researchers recognize other ways long-term memories form. For example, as we will see, some information slips into long-term memory via a "back door," without our having consciously attended to it. And we have learned that short-term memory is more than passive rehearsal; it is better termed *working memory* to recognize the active processing that occurs there.

In some ways, our memory is like a computer's information-processing system. To remember any event, we must *get information into our brain* (**encoding**), *retain* that information (**storage**), and later *get it back out* (**retrieval**). Consider how a computer *encodes, stores,* and *retrieves* information. First, it translates input (keystrokes) into an electronic language, much as the brain encodes sensory information into a neural language. The computer permanently stores vast amounts of information on a disk, from which it can later be retrieved.

Like all analogies, the computer model has its limits. Our memories are less literal and more fragile than a computer's. Moreover, most computers process information speedily but sequentially, even while alternating between tasks. The brain is slower but does many things at once—in parallel.

Psychologists have proposed several information-processing models of memory. Richard Atkinson and Richard Shiffrin's classic *three-stage processing* model of memory (1968) suggests that we form memories through three stages. Atkinson and Shiffrin proposed that we first record to-be-remembered information as a fleeting **sensory memory,** from which it is processed into a **short-term memory** bin, where we encode it through rehearsal for **long-term memory** and later retrieval. This three-step process, though historically important and helpfully simple, is limited and fallible. Some information, as we will see, skips the first two stages and is processed into long-term memory automatically—without our conscious awareness. In addition, we now realize that because we are bombarded daily with sensory information, we cannot possibly focus on everything at once. Instead, we shine the flashlight beam of our attention on certain incoming stimuli—often novel or important stimuli. These incoming stimuli, along with information we retrieve from our long-term memory, become conscious short-term memories in a temporary construction zone. This zone is a work site where we rehearse and manipulate information (Engle, 2002). But unlike brick-and-mortar work sites, the content of **working memory** quickly fades unless we keep using or rehearsing it. It is here that we actively associate new and old information and solve problems. The modified version of the three-stage processing model of memory that we use in studying memory in this text incorporates this important working-memory concept (**FIGURE 24.1**).

Working memory includes both auditory and visual-spatial elements, coordinated by a *central executive* processor (**FIGURE 24.2**) (Baddeley, 1992, 2001, 2002). These separate mental subsystems allow us to process images and words simultaneously. This

Sensory memory registers incoming information, allowing your brain to capture for a fleeting moment a sea of faces.

We pay attention to and encode important or novel stimuli—in this case an angry face in the crowd.

If we stare at the face long enough (rehearsal), or if we're sufficiently disturbed by it (it's deemed "important"), we will encode it for long-term storage, and we may, an hour later, be able to call up an image of the face.

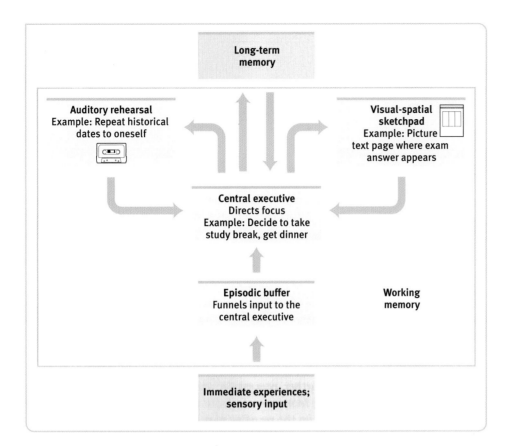

FIGURE 24.2
Working memory
Alan Baddeley's (1998, 2001, 2002) model of working memory, simplified here, contains auditory and visual-spatial processors, which are managed by a central executive. Information enters working memory from long-term storage or from immediate experience. The episodic buffer helps the central executive integrate input in a way we can comprehend.

explains why we can talk (verbal processing) while driving (visual-spatial processing). And working memory's limited capacity explains why it is so difficult to try to remember the melody for one song while we are listening to another. Brain activity underlies these working memory components (Jonides & others, 2005). Brain scans show that the frontal lobes are active when the central executive focuses on complex thinking, and that the parietal and temporal lobe areas that help us process auditory and visual information also are active when such information is in our working memory.

>> LEARNING OUTCOMES

Introduction to Memory

OBJECTIVE 24-1 | Define *memory,* and explain how flashbulb memories differ from other memories.

Memory is the persistence of learning over time, through the storage and retrieval of information. *Flashbulb memories,* which are attached to emotionally significant moments or events, differ from most other memories in their striking clarity.

OBJECTIVE 24-2 | Describe Atkinson-Shiffrin's classic three-stage processing model of memory, and explain how the contemporary model of working memory differs.

The Atkinson-Shiffrin classic three-stage model of memory suggests that we (1) register fleeting *sensory memories,* some of which are (2) processed into on-screen *short-term* memories, a tiny fraction of which are (3) encoded for *long-term memory* and, possibly, later retrieval. In pointing out the limits of this model, contemporary memory researchers note that we register some information automatically, bypassing the first two stages. And they prefer the term *working memory* (rather than *short-term memory*) because it emphasizes a more active role in this second processing stage, where we rehearse and manipulate information, associating new stimuli with our older stored memories. The working-memory model includes visual-spatial and auditory

subsystems, coordinated by a central executive processor that focuses attention where needed

TERMS AND CONCEPTS TO REMEMBER

memory, p. 24-0
flashbulb memory, p. 24-1
encoding, p. 24-1
storage, p. 24-2
retrieval, p. 24-2

sensory memory, p. 24-2
short-term memory, p. 24-2
long-term memory, p. 24-2
working memory, p. 24-2

TEST YOURSELF

1. Memory includes (in alphabetical order) long-term memory, sensory memory, and working/short-term memory. What's the correct order of these three memory stores?

(Answer in Appendix B.)

ASK YOURSELF

1. What flashbulb memory do you have for an emotion-laden experience in your past?

>WEB

Multiple-choice *self-tests* and more may be found at www.worthpublishers.com/myers.

25

Encoding: Getting Information In

How does sensory information, once registered, get encoded and transferred into the memory system? What types of information do we absorb unconsciously? What types require conscious processing?

How We Encode

We will use a modified version of Richard Atkinson and Richard Shiffrin's classic *three-stage processing model of memory* (1968) (**FIGURE 25.1**). We process some external stimuli consciously in our *sensory memory,* while other external events are processed beneath the radar of our conscious efforts. The events we notice and attend to are *encoded,* or processed in our *working memory* (which Atkinson and Shiffrin referred to as our *short-term memory*). Further processing and rehearsing encodes important parts of the event into our *long-term memory,* from which the information may later be retrieved. Here we will focus on the *encoding* part of that process. You encode some information, such as the route you walked to your last class, with great ease, freeing your memory system to focus on less familiar events. But to retain novel information, such as a friend's new cell-phone number, you need to pay attention and try hard.

FIGURE 25.1

A modified three-stage processing model of memory

Here we will focus on the "encoding" part of our memory processing.

Automatic Processing

OBJECTIVE 25-1 | Describe the types of information we encode automatically.

With little or no effort, you absorb an enormous amount of information. For example, without conscious effort you **automatically process** information about

- *space.* While reading your textbook, you often encode the place on a page where certain material appears; later, when struggling to recall the information, you may visualize its location.
- *time.* While going about your day, you unintentionally note the sequence of the day's events. Later, when you realize that you left your coat somewhere, you re-create the sequence of what you did that day and retrace your steps.
- *frequency.* You effortlessly keep track of how many times things happen, thus enabling you to realize "this is the third time I've run into her today."

Thanks to our brain's capacity for parallel processing, all of this processing and more goes on without our needing to pay attention to it. Automatic processing occurs so effortlessly that it is difficult to shut off. When you see words in your native language, such as on the side of a delivery truck, you cannot help but register their meanings.

Some forms of processing require attention and effort when we first perform them, but with experience and practice become automatic. When learning to read, you at first sounded out individual letters to figure out what words they made.

Later in this module, I'll ask you to recall this sentence: *"The angry rioter threw the rock at the window."*

With effort, you plodded slowly through a mere 20 to 50 words on a page. Now, however, after years of practice, you can read quickly and effortlessly. Imagine now learning to read reversed sentences like this:

.citamotua emoceb nac gnissecorp luftroffE

At first, this requires effort. But after enough practice, tasks like this can be performed much more automatically. We have developed many of our skills in this way: learning to drive, rollerblade, or find our way around town.

Effortful Processing

OBJECTIVE 25-2 | Contrast effortful processing with automatic processing, and discuss the next-in-line effect, the spacing effect, and the serial position effect.

We encode and retain vast amounts of information automatically, but we remember other types of information, such as this chapter's concepts, only with effort and attention (**FIGURE 25.2**). **Effortful processing** often produces durable and accessible memories.

When learning novel information such as names, we can boost our memory through **rehearsal,** or conscious repetition. This was shown long ago by the pioneering researcher of verbal memory, German philosopher Hermann Ebbinghaus (1850–1909). Ebbinghaus was to the study of memory what Ivan Pavlov was to the study of conditioning. Ebbinghaus became impatient with philosophical speculations about memory and decided to study it scientifically. To do so, he chose to study his own learning and forgetting of novel verbal materials.

Ebbinghaus needed to find verbal material that was not familiar. His solution was to form a list of all possible nonsense syllables created by sandwiching a vowel between two consonants. Then, for a particular experiment, he would randomly select a sample of the syllables. To get a feel for how Ebbinghaus tested himself, rapidly read aloud, eight times over, the following list (from Baddeley, 1982). Then try to recall the items:

JIH, BAZ, FUB, YOX, SUJ, XIR, DAX, LEQ, VUM, PID, KEL, WAV, TUV, ZOF, GEK, HIW.

■ **automatic processing** unconscious encoding of incidental information, such as space, time, and frequency, and of well-learned information, such as word meanings.

■ **effortful processing** encoding that requires attention and conscious effort.

■ **rehearsal** the conscious repetition of information, either to maintain it in consciousness or to encode it for storage.

FIGURE 25.2
Automatic versus effortful processing
Some information, such as where you ate dinner yesterday, you process automatically. Other information, such as this chapter's concepts, requires effort to encode and remember.

The day after learning such a list, Ebbinghaus could recall few of the syllables. But were they entirely forgotten? As **FIGURE 25.3** portrays, the more frequently he repeated the list aloud on day 1, the fewer repetitions he required to relearn the list on day 2. Here, then, was a simple beginning principle: *The amount remembered depends on the time spent learning.* Even after we learn material, additional rehearsal (*overlearning*) increases retention.

The point to remember is that for novel verbal information, practice—effortful processing—does indeed make perfect. And that helps us understand some other interesting phenomena:

- The *next-in-line effect*: When people go around a circle saying words or their names, and attempting to remember what was said by the others, their poorest memories are for what was said by the person just before them (Bond & others, 1991; Brenner, 1973). When we are next in line, we focus on our own performance and often fail to process the last person's words.
- Information presented in the seconds just before sleep is seldom remembered (Wyatt & Bootzin, 1994). When our consciousness fades before we've processed the information, all is lost. Information presented in the *hour* before sleep, however, is well remembered.
- Taped information played during sleep is registered by the ears but is not remembered (Wood & others, 1992). Without opportunity for rehearsal, "sleep learning" doesn't occur. We also retain information better when our rehearsal is distributed over time (as when learning classmates' names), a phenomenon called the **spacing effect** (Bjork, 1999; Dempster, 1988).

In a 9-year experiment, Harry Bahrick and three of his family members (1993) practiced foreign language word translations for a given number of times, at intervals ranging from 14 to 56 days. Their consistent finding: The longer the space between practice sessions, the better their retention up to 5 years later. Reflecting on the spacing effect, Bahrick saw a practical implication: Restudying material for comprehensive final exams, capstone review courses, and senior examinations will enhance lifelong retention. Spreading out learning—over a semester or a year, rather than over shorter terms—should also help. To paraphrase Ebbinghaus (1885), those who learn quickly also forget quickly. It is another point to remember: Spaced study beats cramming.

"He should test his memory by reciting the verses."
Abdur-Rahman Abdul Khaliq, "Memorizing the Quran"

"The mind is slow in unlearning what it has been long in learning."
Roman philosopher Seneca (4 B.C.–A.D. 65)

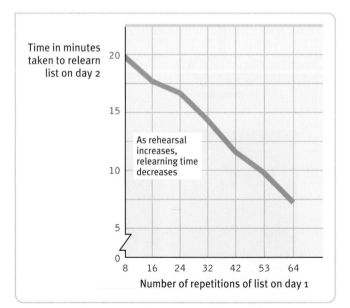

FIGURE 25.3
Ebbinghaus' retention curve
Ebbinghaus found that the more times he practiced a list of nonsense syllables on day 1, the fewer repetitions he required to relearn it on day 2. Said simply, the more time we spend learning novel information, the more we retain. (From Baddeley, 1982.)

To memorize such things as a phone number, "expanding" spaced rehearsal works well. Thomas Landauer (2001) explains: "Rehearse the name or number you are trying to memorize, wait a few seconds, rehearse again, wait a little longer, rehearse again, then wait longer still and rehearse yet again. The waits should be as long as possible without losing the information."

A phenomenon you have surely experienced further illustrates the benefits of rehearsal. Experimenters have shown people a list of items (words, names, dates, even odors) and then immediately asked them to recall the items in any order (Reed, 2000). As people struggle to recall the list, they often demonstrate the **serial position effect:** They remember the last and first items better than they do those in the middle (**FIGURE 25.4**). Perhaps because the last items are still in working memory, people briefly recall them especially quickly and well. But after a delay—after they shift their attention from the last items—their recall is best for the first items.

As an everyday parallel, imagine it's your first day in a new job, and your manager is introducing you to your co-workers. As you meet each one, you repeat (rehearse) all their names, starting from the beginning. By the time you meet the last person, you will have spent more time rehearsing the earlier names than the later ones; thus, the next day you will probably more easily recall the earlier names. Also, learning the first few names may interfere with your learning the later ones.

But sometimes merely repeating information, such as the new phone number we are about to dial, is not enough to store it for later recall (Craik & Watkins, 1973; Greene, 1987). How, then, do we encode information for processing into long-term memory? Processing our sensory input is like sorting through the day's mail. Some items we instantly discard. Others we process more thoughtfully: We open, read, and retain them. Our memory system processes information by encoding its significant features.

Percentage of words recalled

Immediate recall: last items best

Later recall: only first items recalled well

Position of word in list

Getty Images

FIGURE 25.4
The serial position effect
After being presented with a list of words or names, as Spain's King Juan Carlos I is in this greeting line, people immediately recall the last items well (perhaps because they are still "on-screen"), and quite often the first few items nearly as well. But later they recall the first items best. (From Craik & Watkins, 1973.)

What We Encode

We process information in three key ways—by encoding its meaning, by encoding its image, and by mentally organizing it. To some extent, we do these things automatically. But in each case, there are effortful strategies for enhancing memory.

Encoding Meaning

OBJECTIVE 25-3 | Compare the benefits of visual, acoustic, and semantic encoding in remembering verbal information, and describe a memory-enhancing strategy related to the self-reference effect.

When processing verbal information for storage, we usually encode its meaning, associating it with what we already know or imagine. Whether we hear "eye-screem" as "ice cream" or "I scream" depends on how the context and our experience guide us to interpret and encode the sounds. (Remember, our working memories interact with our long-term memories.)

■ **spacing effect** the tendency for distributed study or practice to yield better long-term retention than is achieved through massed study or practice.

■ **serial position effect** our tendency to recall best the last and first items in a list.

■ **visual encoding** the encoding of picture images.

■ **acoustic encoding** the encoding of sound, especially the sound of words.

■ **semantic encoding** the encoding of meaning, including the meaning of words.

■ **imagery** mental pictures; a powerful aid to effortful processing, especially when combined with semantic encoding.

Earlier in this module, I said I'd ask you to recall a sentence about a rioter. ("The angry rioter threw . . .") Perhaps, like the subjects in an experiment by William Brewer (1977), you recalled the rioter sentence by the meaning you encoded when you read it (for example, "The angry rioter threw the rock *through* the window") and not as it was written ("The angry rioter threw the rock *at* the window"). As such recall indicates, we tend not to remember things exactly as they were. Rather, *we remember what we encoded*. Studying for an exam, you may remember your lecture notes rather than the lecture itself. Gordon Bower and Daniel Morrow (1990) liken our minds to theater directors who, given a raw script, imagine a finished stage production. Asked later to recall what we heard or read, we recall not the literal text but the mental model we constructed from it.

What kind of encoding do you think yields the best memory of verbal information? **Visual encoding** of images? **Acoustic encoding** of sounds? **Semantic encoding** of meaning? Each has its own brain system (Poldrack & Wagner, 2004). And each can help. For example, acoustic encoding enhances the memorability and seeming truth of rhyming aphorisms. "What sobriety conceals, alcohol reveals" seems more accurate than "what sobriety conceals, alcohol unmasks" (McGlone & Tofighbakhsh, 2000). Attorney Johnnie Cochran's celebrated plea to O. J. Simpson's jury—"If the glove doesn't fit, you must acquit"—was also more easily remembered than had Cochran said, "If the glove doesn't fit, you must find him not guilty!"

To compare visual, acoustic, and semantic encoding, Fergus Craik and Endel Tulving (1975) flashed a word at people. Then they asked a question that required the people to process the words (1) visually (the appearance of the letters), (2) acoustically (the sound of the words), or (3) semantically (the meaning of the words). To experience the task yourself, rapidly answer the following questions:

Sample Questions to Elicit Processing	Word Flashed	Yes	No
1. Is the word in capital letters?	chair	___	___
2. Does the word rhyme with train?	BRAIN	___	___
3. Would the word fit in this sentence:			
The girl put the _____ on the table.	gun	___	___

Which type of processing would best prepare you to recognize the words at a later time? In Craik and Tulving's experiment, the deeper, semantic encoding—question 3—yielded much better memory than the "shallow processing" elicited by question 2 and especially by question 1 (**FIGURE 25.5**).

How many *F*s are in the following sentence?
FINISHED FILES ARE THE RESULTS OF YEARS OF SCIENTIFIC STUDY COMBINED WITH THE EXPERIENCE OF YEARS. (See this module's final page.)

FIGURE 25.5
Levels of processing
Processing a word deeply—by its meaning (semantic encoding)—produces better recognition of it at a later time than does shallow processing by attending to its appearance or sound. (From Craik & Tulving, 1975.)

But given too raw a script, we have trouble creating a mental model. Put yourself in the place of the students who John Bransford and Marcia Johnson (1972) asked to remember the following recorded passage:

> The procedure is actually quite simple. First you arrange things into different groups. Of course, one pile may be sufficient depending on how much there is to do. . . . After the procedure is completed one arranges the materials into different groups again. Then they can be put into their appropriate places. Eventually they will be used once more and the whole cycle will then have to be repeated. However, that is part of life.

When the students heard the paragraph you have just read, without a meaningful context, they remembered little of it. When told that the paragraph was about washing clothes (something meaningful to them), they remembered much more of it—as you probably could now after rereading it.

Such research suggests the benefits of rephrasing what we read and hear into meaningful terms. From his experiments on himself, Ebbinghaus estimated that, compared with learning nonsense material, learning meaningful material required one-tenth the effort. As memory researcher Wayne Wickelgren (1977, p. 346) noted, "The time you spend thinking about material you are reading and relating it to previously stored material is about the most useful thing you can do in learning any new subject matter." Thus, the amount remembered depends both on the time spent learning and on what we do while learning.

We have especially good recall for information we can relate to ourselves. Asked how well certain adjectives describe someone else, we often forget them; asked how well the adjectives describe ourselves, we remember the words well—a phenomenon called the *self-reference effect* (Symons & Johnson, 1997). So, you will profit from taking time to find personal meaning in what you are studying (for example, by taking the time to answer the Ask Yourself questions found at the end of each Learning Outcomes section in this book). Information deemed "relevant to me" is processed more deeply and remains more accessible.

> " Among the things which greatly aid the process of memorization is understanding the verses that one has memorized and knowing their relationship and link, one to another."
>
> Abdur-Rahman Abdul Khaliq, "Memorizing the Quran"

Visual Encoding

OBJECTIVE 25-4 | Explain how encoding imagery aids effortful processing, and describe some memory-enhancing strategies that use visual encoding.

> " A thing when heard, remember, strikes less keen on the spectator's mind than when 'tis seen."
>
> Horace, Ars *Poetica*, 8 B.C.

Why is it that we struggle to remember formulas, definitions, and dates, yet we can easily remember where we were yesterday, who was with us, where we sat, and what we wore? One difference relates to the greater ease of remembering mental pictures. Our earliest memories—probably of something that happened at age 3 or 4—involve visual **imagery.** Researchers have also documented that we remember concrete words that lend themselves to visual mental images better than we remember abstract, low-imagery words. (When I quiz you later, which three of these words—*typewriter, void, cigarette, inherent, fire, process*—will you most likely recall?) Similarly, you probably still recall the sentence about the rock-throwing rioter, not only because of the meaning you encoded, but also because the sentence lent itself to a visual image. Memory for

Both photos: Ho/AP Photo

The imagery principle
Plastic surgery researcher Darrick Antell observes that "you can talk until you're blue in the face about all the health hazards" of tanning and smoking. But show people photos of identical twins, only one of whom has aged under the influence of tanning and smoking, and they will learn and remember. Sixty-year-old Gay Black, left, was an avid tanner and onetime smoker, unlike her younger-looking identical twin, Gwen Sirota, right.

Rosy retrospection
A happy fact of life: For most people, the negative emotion recalled from bad events fades more rapidly than the positive emotion recalled from good events (Walker & others, 2003).

SALLY FORTH

concrete nouns is aided by encoding them *both* semantically and visually (Marschark & others, 1987; Paivio, 1986). Two codes are better than one.

Thanks to the durability of our most vivid images, we sometimes recall our experiences with mental snapshots of their best or worst moments. Thus, the best moment of a pleasure or joy, and the worst moment of a pain or frustration, often colors our memories (Fredrickson & Kahneman, 1993). Recalling the high points while forgetting the mundane moments may explain a phenomenon that Terrence Mitchell, Leigh Thompson, Erika Peterson, and Randy Cronk (1997) call *rosy retrospection*: People tend to recall events such as a camping holiday more positively than they evaluated them at the time. They remember their visit to Disney World less for the muggy heat and long lines than for the surroundings, food, and rides. And it is the experience we remember, not the experience we had, that predicts our future choices (Wirtz & others, 2003).

Imagery is at the heart of many memory aids. **Mnemonic** (nih-MON-ik) devices (so named after the Greek word for memory) were developed by ancient Greek scholars and orators as aids to remembering lengthy passages and speeches. Using the "method of loci," they imagined themselves moving through a familiar series of locations, associating each place with a visual representation of the to-be-remembered topic. Then, when speaking, the orator would mentally revisit each location and retrieve the associated image. A modern study of star performers in the World Memory Championships showed them not to have exceptional intelligence, but rather to be superior at using spatial mnemonic strategies (Maguire & others, 2003).

Other mnemonic devices involve both acoustic and visual codes. For example, the "peg-word" system requires that you first memorize a jingle: *"One is a bun; two is a shoe; three is a tree; four is a door; five is a hive; six is sticks; seven is heaven; eight is a gate; nine is swine; ten is a hen."* Without much effort, you will soon be able to count by peg-words instead of numbers: bun, shoe, tree ... and then to visually associate the peg-words with to-be-remembered items. Now you are ready to challenge anyone to give you a grocery list to remember. Carrots? Imagine them stuck into a bun. Milk? Fill the shoe with it. Paper towels? Drape them over the tree branch. Think "bun, shoe, tree" and you see their associated images: carrots, milk, paper towels. With few errors (Bugelski & others, 1968), you will be able to recall the items in any order and to name any given item. Such mnemonic systems are used by memory whizzes who repeat long lists of names and objects, and they can also help you.

Organizing Information for Encoding

OBJECTIVE 25-5 | Discuss the use of chunking and hierarchies in effortful processing.

"You simply associate each number with a word, such as 'table' and 3,476,029."

■ **mnemonics** [nih-MON-iks] memory aids, especially those techniques that use vivid imagery and organizational devices.

■ **chunking** organizing items into familiar, manageable units; often occurs automatically.

Meaning and imagery enhance our memory partly by helping us organize information. When Bransford and Johnson's laundry paragraph (described earlier in this module) became meaningful, we could mentally organize its sentences into a sequence. Mnemonic devices help organize material for our later retrieval.

Chunking

To experience the importance of organization, glance for a few seconds at row 1 of **FIGURE 25.6**, then look away and try to reproduce what you saw. Impossible, yes? But you can easily reproduce the second row, which is no less complex. Similarly, you will probably find row 4 much easier to remember than row 3, although both contain the same letters. And you could remember the sixth cluster more easily than the fifth, although both contain the same words.

1. ◁ ⊃ ⊃ ∿ ∠ ℵ ⊥
2. K L C I S N E

3. KLCISNE NVESE YNA NI CSTTIH TNDO
4. NICKELS SEVEN ANY IN STITCH DONT

5. NICKELS SEVEN ANY IN STITCH DONT SAVES AGO A SCORE TIME AND NINE WOODEN FOUR YEARS TAKE

6. DONT TAKE ANY WOODEN NICKELS FOUR SCORE AND SEVEN YEARS AGO A STITCH IN TIME SAVES NINE

FIGURE 25.6
Effects of chunking on memory
When we organize information into meaningful units, such as letters, words, and phrases, we recall it more easily. (From Hintzman, 1978.)

As this demonstrates, we more easily recall information when we can organize it into meaningful units, or chunks. **Chunking** occurs so naturally that we take it for granted. If you are a native English speaker, you can reproduce perfectly the 150 or so line segments that make up the words in the three phrases of item 6 in Figure 25.6. It would astonish someone unfamiliar with the language.

I am similarly awed at the ability of someone literate in Chinese to glance at **FIGURE 25.7** and then to reproduce all of the strokes; or of a chess master who, after a 5-second look at the board during a game, can recall the exact positions of most of the pieces (Chase & Simon, 1973); or of a varsity basketball player who, given a 4-second glance at a basketball play, can recall the positions of the players (Allard & Burnett, 1985). We all remember information best when we can organize it into personally meaningful arrangements.

Chunking also aids our recall of unfamiliar material. One mnemonic technique organizes it into a more familiar form by encoding the first letters of to-be-remembered words as sentences or as words (called *acronyms*). Want to remember the colors of the rainbow in order of wavelength? Think of the mnemonic ROY G. BIV (*red*, *orange*, *yellow*, *green*, *blue*, *indigo*, *violet*). Should you ever need to recall the names of North America's five Great Lakes, just remember HOMES (*Huron*, *Ontario*, *Michigan*, *Erie*, *Superior*).

With chunking, you can increase your recall of digits, too. An impossible string of 16 numbers—1-4-9-2-1-7-7-6-1-8-1-2-1-9-4-1—becomes easy for an American when chunked into 1492, 1776, 1812, 1941 (as would 1066, 1688, 1815, and 1914 for those familiar with British history). After more than 200 hours of practice in the laboratory of Anders Ericsson and William Chase (1982), two Carnegie-Mellon University students even managed to increase their memory span from the typical 7 digits to more than 80. In another testing session, student Dario Donatelli heard the researcher read one digit per second in a monotonous voice: "15185937655021578416658506120948856867727314181861054629748012949749965928." Motionless while learning the numbers, Donatelli then sprang alive. He whispered numbers, rubbed his chin, tapped his feet, counted on his fingers, and ran his hands through his hair. "Okay," he announced almost 2 minutes later. "The first set is 1518. Then 5937. . . ." He repeated all 73 digits, in groups of 3 and 4.

How did he do it? By increasing the capacity of his working memory? No. When asked to remember letters, Donatelli fell back to about a seven-item capacity. Rather, he had developed a sophisticated strategy for number chunking. "First set was a 3-mile time," reported Donatelli, an All-American cross-country runner. "Second set was a 10-mile time. Then a mile. Half-mile. Two-mile time. An age. . . . Two mile. Age. Age. Age. Two-mile. . . ." (Wells, 1983).

Memory researchers agree that Canada's postal codes, with alternating numbers and letters, are especially hard to memorize (Hebert, 2001). A1C 5S7 would be more easily remembered if chunked by letters and numbers, as ACS 157.

FIGURE 25.7
An example of chunking— for those who read Chinese
After looking at these characters, can you reproduce them exactly? If so, you are literate in Chinese.

Hierarchies

For Donatelli to reach his peak—106 digits—he retrieved the chunks of numbers by clustering them as a hierarchy (Waldrop, 1987). First came "three groups of four," he might think, and so forth. When people develop expertise in an area, they process information not only in chunks but also in hierarchies composed of a few broad concepts divided and subdivided into narrower concepts and facts. By organizing knowledge in hierarchies, we retrieve information efficiently. This module therefore aims not only to teach you the elementary facts of encoding but also to help you organize these facts around the broad principle of encoding; subprinciples, such as automatic and effortful processing; and still more specific concepts, such as meaning, imagery, and organization (**FIGURE 25.8**).

FIGURE 25.8

Organization benefits memory
When we organize words or concepts into hierarchical groups, as illustrated here with concepts in this module, we remember them better than when we see them presented randomly.

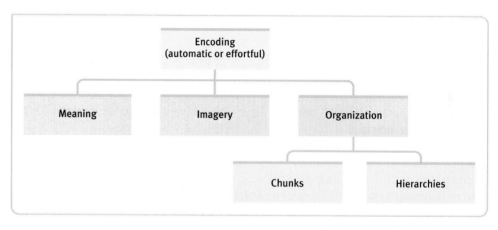

Gordon Bower and his colleagues (1969) demonstrated the benefits of hierarchical organization. They presented words either randomly or grouped into categories. When the words were organized into groups, recall was two to three times better. Such results show the benefits of organizing what you study—of giving special attention to module outlines, headings, Objectives, Learning Outcomes, and Test Questions. If you can master a module's concepts within their overall organization, your recall should be effective at test time. Taking lecture and text notes in outline format—a type of hierarchical organization—may also prove helpful.

In the discussion of encoding imagery, I gave you six words and told you I would quiz you about them later. How many of these words can you now recall? Of these, how many are high-imagery words? How many are low-imagery?

>> LEARNING OUTCOMES

Encoding: Getting Information In

OBJECTIVE 25-1 | Describe the types of information we encode automatically.

We unconsciously and automatically encode incidental information, such as space, time, and frequency. We also register well-learned information, such as words in our native language, by this form of processing.

OBJECTIVE 25-2 | Contrast effortful processing with automatic processing, and discuss the next-in-line effect, the spacing effect, and the serial position effect.

Automatic processing happens unconsciously, as we absorb information (space, time, frequency, well-learned material) in our environment. *Effortful processing* (of meaning, imagery, organization) requires conscious attention and deliberate effort (rehearsal). The *next-in-line effect* is our tendency to forget (through failure to encode) what the person ahead of us in line has said because we are focusing on what we will say in our upcoming turn. The *spacing effect* is our tendency to retain information more easily if we practice it repeatedly over time (spaced study) than if we practice it in one long session (cramming). The *serial position effect* is our tendency to recall the first and last items in a long list more easily than we recall the intervening items.

OBJECTIVE 25-3 | Compare the benefits of visual, acoustic, and semantic encoding in remembering verbal information, and describe a memory-enhancing strategy related to the self-reference effect.

Visual encoding (of picture images) and *acoustic encoding* (of sounds, especially of words) are shallower forms of processing than is *semantic encoding* (of meaning). We process verbal information best when we encode it semantically, especially if we apply the *self-reference effect,* making information "relevant to me."

OBJECTIVE 25-4 | Explain how encoding imagery aids effortful processing, and describe some memory-enhancing strategies that use visual encoding.

Encoding imagery aids effortful processing because vivid images are very memorable. We tend to remember concrete nouns better than abstract nouns because, for example, we can associate both an image and a meaning with *gorilla,* but only a meaning with *process.* Many *mnemonic devices* (memory strategies or aids) rely on imagery. Others trap items in memory by combining visual encoding (imagining a series of vivid images) and acoustic encoding (a memorable rhyme).

OBJECTIVE 25-5 | Discuss the use of chunking and hierarchies in effortful processing.

We remember organized information better than we do random data. In *chunking,* we organize information into familiar, manageable clusters, such as words into sentences. In *hierarchies,* we organize information by dividing it into logical levels, beginning with the most general and moving to the most specific.

TERMS AND CONCEPTS TO REMEMBER

automatic processing, p. 25-0

effortful processing, p. 25-1

rehearsal, p. 25-1

spacing effect, p. 25-2

serial position effect, p. 25-3

visual encoding, p. 25-4

acoustic encoding, p. 25-4

semantic encoding, p. 25-4

imagery, p. 25-5

mnemonics [nih-MON-iks], p. 25-6

chunking, p. 25-7

TEST YOURSELF

1. What would be the most effective strategy to learn and retain a list of names of key historical figures for a week? For a year?

(Answer in Appendix B.)

ASK YOURSELF

1. Can you think of three ways to employ the principles in this section to improve your own learning and retention of important things?

ANSWER TO QUESTION WITHIN THE MODULE

Q. How many Fs are in the following sentence?
FINISHED FILES ARE THE RESULTS OF YEARS OF SCIENTIFIC STUDY COMBINED WITH THE EXPERIENCE OF YEARS.

A. Partly because your initial processing of the letters was primarily acoustic rather than visual, you probably missed some of the six Fs, especially those that sound like a *V* rather than an *F.*

>WEB

Multiple-choice *self-tests* and more may be found at www.worthpublishers.com/myers.

26

Storage: Retaining Information

At the heart of memory is storage. If you later recall something you experienced, you must, somehow, have stored and retrieved it. Anything stored in long-term memory lies dormant, waiting to be reconstructed by a cue. What is our temporary and our long-term memory storage capacity? Let's start with the first memory store noted in the *modified three-stage processing model* outlined in **FIGURE 26.1** (Atkinson & Shiffrin, 1968)—our fleeting *sensory memory*.

FIGURE 26.1
A modified three-stage processing model of memory
Here we will focus on the storage aspects of our memory processing: sensory memory, working memory, and long-term memory.

Sensory Memory

OBJECTIVE 26-1 | Contrast two types of sensory memory.

Consider what one intriguing memory experiment revealed about our sensory memory—the initial recording of sensory information in the memory system. As part of his doctoral research, George Sperling (1960) showed people three rows of three letters each for only 1/20th of a second (**FIGURE 26.2**). It was harder than reading by lightning flashes. After the nine letters disappeared from the screen, people could recall only about half of them.

Was it because they had insufficient time to glimpse them? No, Sperling cleverly demonstrated that even at faster than lightning-flash speed, people actually *can* see and recall all the letters, but only momentarily. Rather than ask them to recall all nine letters at once, Sperling sounded a high, medium, or low tone immediately *after* flashing the nine letters. This cue directed participants to report only the letters of the top, middle, or bottom row, respectively. Now they rarely missed a letter, showing that all nine letters were momentarily available for recall.

Sperling's experiment revealed that we have a fleeting photographic memory called **iconic memory.** For an instant, our eyes register an exact representation of a scene and we can recall any part of it in amazing detail—but only for a few tenths of a second. If Sperling delayed the tone signal by more than half a second, the iconic memory was gone and participants once again recalled only about half the letters. Your visual screen clears quickly, as it must, so that new images can be superimposed over old ones.

We also have an impeccable, though fleeting, sensory memory for auditory stimuli, called **echoic memory** (Cowan, 1988; Lu & others, 1992). If partially interpreted, an auditory echo lingers for 3 or 4 seconds. Picture yourself in conversation, as your attention veers to the TV. If your mildly irked conversational partner tests your attention by asking, "What did I just say?" you can recover the last few words from your mind's echo chamber.

FIGURE 26.2
Momentary photographic memory
When George Sperling flashed a group of letters similar to this for 1/20th of a second, people could recall only about half of the letters. But when signaled to recall a particular row immediately after the letters had disappeared, they could do so with near-perfect accuracy.

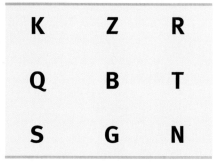

Working/Short-Term Memory

OBJECTIVE 26-2 | Describe the duration and working capacity of short-term memory.

Among the vast amounts of information registered by our sensory memory, we illuminate some with our attentional flashlight. We also retrieve information from long-term storage for "on-screen" display. But unless our working memory meaningfully encodes or rehearses that information, it quickly disappears from our short-term store. During your finger's trip from phone book to phone, your memory of a telephone number may evaporate.

To find out how quickly a short-term memory will disappear, Lloyd Peterson and Margaret Peterson (1959) asked people to remember three-consonant groups, such as *CHJ*. To prevent rehearsal of the letters, the researchers asked participants, for example, to start at 100 and count aloud backwards by threes. After 3 seconds, people recalled the letters only about half the time; after 12 seconds, they seldom recalled them at all (**FIGURE 26.3**). Without active processing, short-term memories have a limited life.

Short-term memory is limited not only in duration but also in capacity. Our short-term memory typically stores just seven or so bits of information (give or take two). George Miller (1956) enshrined this recall capacity as the *Magical Number Seven, plus or minus two*. Not surprisingly, when some phone companies began requiring all callers to dial a three-digit area code in addition to a seven-digit number, many people reported trouble retaining the just-looked-up number.

Our short-term recall is slightly better for random digits (as in a phone number) than for random letters, which sometimes have similar sounds. It is slightly better for what we hear than for what we see. Both children and adults have short-term recall for roughly as many words as they can speak in 2 seconds (Cowan, 1994; Hulme & Tordoff, 1989). With information chunks (for example, letters meaningfully grouped as ABC, BBC, FBI, KGB, CIA) and without rehearsal, the average person retains only about four chunks in short-term memory (Cowan, 2001). Suppressing rehearsal by saying "the the the" while hearing random digits also reduces memory to about four items. The basic principle: At any given moment, we can consciously process only a very limited amount of information.

■ **iconic memory** a momentary sensory memory of visual stimuli; a photographic or picture-image memory lasting no more than a few tenths of a second.

■ **echoic memory** a momentary sensory memory of auditory stimuli; if attention is elsewhere, sounds and words can still be recalled within 3 or 4 seconds.

The Magical Number Seven has become psychology's contribution to an intriguing list of magic sevens—the seven wonders of the world, the seven seas, the seven deadly sins, the seven primary colors, the seven musical scale notes, the seven days of the week—seven magical sevens.

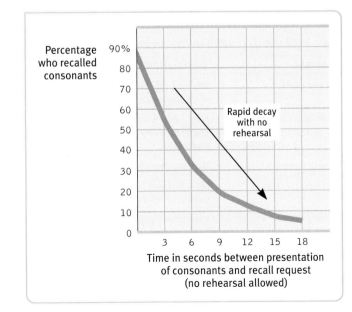

FIGURE 26.3
Short-term memory decay
Unless rehearsed, verbal information may be quickly forgotten. (From Peterson & Peterson, 1959.)

Clark's Nutcracker
Among animals, one contender for champion memorist would be a mere birdbrain—the Clark's Nutcracker—which during winter and early spring can locate up to 6000 caches of buried pine seeds (Shettleworth, 1993).

Pi in the sky: As this book went to press, the world record for memorizing pi was held by Japan's Akira Haraguchi, who in 2005 recited the first 83,431 digits correctly (BBC, 2005).

Long-Term Memory

OBJECTIVE 26-3 | Describe the capacity and duration of long-term memory.

In Arthur Conan Doyle's *A Study in Scarlet,* Sherlock Holmes offers a popular theory of memory capacity:

> I consider that a man's brain originally is like a little empty attic, and you have to stock it with such furniture as you choose. . . . It is a mistake to think that that little room has elastic walls and can distend to any extent. Depend upon it, there comes a time when for every addition of knowledge you forget something that you knew before.

Contrary to Holmes' belief, our capacity for storing long-term memories is essentially limitless. By one careful estimate, the average adult has about a billion bits of information in memory and a storage capacity that will accommodate probably a thousand to a million times that amount (Landauer, 1986). Given the number of brain synapses, one computer engineering group estimated that "the total memory capacity of computers all over the world is far less than that of a single brain" (Wang & others, 2003). Although even a single laptop beats our brain's capacity to remember literal text (What was that definition of negative reinforcement?), this much is sure: Our brains are *not* like attics, which once filled can store more items only if we discard old ones.

The point is vividly illustrated by those who have performed phenomenal memory feats (**TABLE 26.1**). Consider the 1990s tests of psychologist Rajan Mahadevan's memory. Give him a block of 10 digits from the first 30,000 or so digits of pi and, after a few moments of mental searching for the string, he would pick up the series from there, firing numbers like a machine gun (Delaney & others, 1999; Thompson & others, 1993). He could also repeat 50 random digits—backwards. It is not a genetic gift, he said; anyone could learn to do it. But given the genetic influence on so many human traits, and knowing that Rajan's father memorized Shakespeare's complete works, one wonders. So how does he do it? As with other psychological phenomena, researchers study memory using different levels of analysis, including the biological.

TABLE 26.1

WORLD MEMORY CHAMPIONSHIP RECORDS

From world memory competition, here are some current records, as of 2005:

Contest	Description	Record
Speed cards	Shortest time to memorize a shuffled pack of 52 playing cards	33 seconds
One-hour cards	Most cards memorized in one hour (52 points for every pack correct; 26 points if 1 mistake)	1170 cards
Speed numbers	Most random digits memorized in 5 minutes	324 digits
Names and faces	Most first and last names memorized in 15 minutes after being shown with faces	167.5 names
Binary digits	Most binary digits (101101, etc.) memorized in 30 minutes when presented in rows of 30 digits	3705

Sources: usamemoriad.com and worldmemorychampionship.com

Storing Memories in the Brain

I marveled at my aging mother-in-law, a retired pianist and organist. At age 88 her blind eyes could no longer read music. But let her sit at a keyboard and she would flawlessly play any of hundreds of hymns, including ones she had not thought of for 20 years. Where did her brain store those thousands of sequenced notes?

For a time, some memory researchers believed that brain stimulation during surgery provided evidence that our whole past, not just well-practiced music, is "in there," in complete detail, just waiting to be relived. To predict possible side effects of brain surgery, Wilder Penfield (1969) electrically stimulated different cortical regions of his patients' brains while they were wide awake. When his patients occasionally reported hearing things, such as a "mother calling her little boy," Penfield assumed he was activating long-lost experiences etched permanently on the brain. Analysis of these famous reports by Elizabeth Loftus and Geoffrey Loftus (1980) revealed that these reports were extremely rare, occurring in only a handful of Penfield's 1100 stimulated patients. Furthermore, the flashbacks appear to have been invented, not relived. (People would recall being in locations they had never visited.)

Psychologist Karl Lashley (1950) provided further evidence that memories do not reside in single, specific spots. He trained rats to solve a maze, then cut out pieces of their cortexes and retested their memory. Alas, no matter what small cortical section he removed, the rats retained at least a partial memory of how to solve the maze.

So, despite the brain's vast storage capacity, we do not seem to store most information with the exactness of a tape recorder. Rather, memory researchers argue, forgetting occurs as new experiences interfere with our retrieval and as the physical memory trace decays. But what is the *memory trace*?

Could the physical memory trace be rooted in the brain's ongoing electrical activity? If so, then temporarily shutting down that activity should eliminate them, much as a dead battery will eliminate the settings on a car radio. Testing that idea, Ralph Gerard (1953) first trained hamsters to turn right or left to get food, and then lowered their body temperature until the brains' electrical activity ceased. When the hamsters were revived and their brains were active again, would they remember which way to turn? Yes. Their long-term memories survived the electrical blackout. In commenting on the elusiveness of the memory trace, one memory researcher, with tongue only partly in cheek, said, "I must admit that memories are more of a spiritual than a physical reality. When you try to touch them, they turn to mist and disappear" (Loftus & Ketcham, 1994, p. 4). To know how our brain stores and effortlessly retrieves a flood of details "defies comprehension," said one awestruck neuroscientist (Doty, 1998).

Recently, the search for the physical basis of memory—for information incarnated in matter—has focused on the synapses.

Synaptic Changes

OBJECTIVE 26-4 | Discuss the synaptic changes that accompany memory formation and storage.

Neuroscientists are expanding the search for the location of memories by exploring changes within and between single neurons. Memories begin as impulses whizzing through brain circuits, somehow leaving permanent neural traces. Where does the neural change occur? The available clues point to the synapses—the sites where nerve cells communicate with one another through their neurotransmitter messengers. We know that experience modifies the brain's neural networks—given increased activity in a particular pathway, neural interconnections form or strengthen.

Eric Kandel and James Schwartz (1982) observed changes in the sending neurons of a simple animal, the California sea snail, *Aplysia*. Its mere 20,000 or so nerve cells

Aplysia
The much-studied California sea snail has increased our understanding of the neural basis of learning.

"Our memories are flexible and superimposable, a panoramic blackboard with an endless supply of chalk and erasers."
Elizabeth Loftus and Katherine Ketcham, *The Myth of Repressed Memory*, 1994

Both photos: From N. Toni et al., *Nature*, 402, Nov. 25, 1999. Courtesy of Dominique Muller

FIGURE 26.4
Doubled receptor sites
Electron microscope images show just one receptor site (gray) reaching toward a sending neuron before long-term potentiation (left) and two afterward (right). A doubling of the receptor sites means that the receiving neuron has increased sensitivity for detecting the presence of the neurotransmitter molecules that may be released by the sending neuron. (From Toni & others, 1999.)

> "The biology of the mind will be as scientifically important to this [new] century as the biology of the gene [was] to the twentieth century."
>
> Eric Kandel, acceptance remarks for the 2000 Nobel prize

Disrupted memory consolidation
After suffering a concussion in the accident that killed Princess Diana, her bodyguard, Trevor Rees-Jones (right), had no memory for the accident or the minutes before it (Riccio & others, 2003).

Orban/Segretain/Forestier/Corbis Sygma

are unusually large and accessible, enabling the researchers to observe synaptic changes during learning. The sea snail can be classically conditioned (with electric shock) to reflexively withdraw its gills when squirted with water, much as a shell-shocked soldier jumps at the sound of a snapping twig. By observing the snails' neural connections before and after conditioning, Kandel and Schwartz pinpointed changes. When learning occurs, the snail releases more of the neurotransmitter *serotonin* at certain synapses. These synapses then become more efficient at transmitting signals.

Increased synaptic efficiency makes for more efficient neural circuits. In experiments, rapidly stimulating certain memory-circuit connections has increased their sensitivity for hours or even weeks to come. The sending neuron now needs less prompting to release its neurotransmitter, and the receiving neuron's receptor sites may increase (**FIGURE 26.4**). This prolonged strengthening of potential neural firing, called **long-term potentiation (LTP),** a term coined by Gary Lynch (2002) and others, provides a neural basis for learning and remembering associations. We know now that drugs that block LTP interfere with learning (Lynch & Staubli, 1991). Mutant mice engineered to lack an enzyme needed for LTP can't learn their way out of a maze (Silva & others, 1992). And rats given a drug that enhances LTP will learn a maze with half the usual number of mistakes (Service, 1994).

Kandel, Lynch, and several other memory-biology explorers have each helped found pharmaceutical companies that are competing to develop and test memory-boosting drugs (*Economist,* 2004; Marshall, 2004). At least 40 "cognitive enhancers" are currently in some phase of development or clinical trial. Their target market includes millions of people with Alzheimer's disease, millions more with "mild cognitive impairment" that often becomes Alzheimer's, and countless millions who would love to turn back the clock on age-related memory decline. From shrinking memories perhaps will come bulging profits.

One approach is developing drugs that boost production of the protein CREB, which can switch genes off or on. Genes code the production of protein molecules. With repeated neural firing, a nerve cell's genes produce synapse-strengthening proteins, enabling long-term memories to form (Fields, 2005). Boosting CREB production might lead to increased production of proteins that help reshape synapses and consolidate a short-term memory into a long-term memory. Sea slugs, mice, and fruit flies with enhanced CREB production have displayed enhanced memories. Another approach is developing drugs that boost glutamate, a brain neurotransmitter that enhances synaptic communication (LTP). Whether such drugs can boost memory without nasty side effects and without cluttering our minds with trivia best forgotten remains to be seen. In the meantime, one effective, safe, and free memory enhancer is already available on college campuses: study followed by adequate sleep!

After long-term potentiation has occurred, passing an electric current through the brain won't disrupt old memories. But the current will wipe out very recent memories. Such is the experience both of laboratory animals and of depressed people given electroconvulsive therapy. A blow to the head can do the same. Like sleepers who can't remember what they heard just before losing consciousness, football players and boxers momentarily knocked unconscious typically have no memory of events just before the knock-out (Yarnell & Lynch, 1970). The information in short-term memory before the blow did not have time to consolidate into long-term memory.

Stress Hormones and Memory

OBJECTIVE 26-5 | Discuss some ways stress hormones can affect memory.

The stress hormones that humans and animals produce when excited or stressed make more glucose energy available to fuel brain activity, signaling the brain that something important has happened. Moreover, the *amygdala,* two emotion-processing clusters in the limbic system, boost activity in the brain's memory-forming areas (Dolcos & others, 2004; Hamann & others, 2002). The result? Arousal can sear certain events into the brain, while disrupting memory for neutral events around the same time (Birnbaum & others, 2004; Strange & Dolan, 2004).

The point to remember, according to James McGaugh (1994, 2003), is that "stronger emotional experiences make for stronger, more reliable memories." After traumatic experiences—a wartime ambush, a house fire, a rape—vivid recollections of the horrific event may intrude again and again. It is as if they were burned in.

Conversely, weaker emotion means weaker memories. People given a drug that blocks the effects of stress hormones will later have more trouble remembering the details of an upsetting story (Cahill & others, 1994). That connection is appreciated by those working to develop an optimum drug that, when taken after a traumatic experience, might blunt intrusive memories.

Emotion-triggered hormonal changes help explain why we long remember exciting or shocking events, such as our first kiss, an earthquake, or 9/11. People who experienced the 1989 San Francisco earthquake had perfect recall a year and a half later of where they were and what they were doing (as they had recorded within a day or two of the quake). Others' memories for the circumstances under which they merely *heard* about the quake were more prone to errors (Neisser & others, 1991; Palmer & others, 1991). (A second important reason for the durability of dramatic experiences is our reliving and rehearsing them—as did most people who experienced the earthquake and told their stories to countless others.)

There are, however, limits to stress-enhanced remembering. When stress is *prolonged*—as in sustained abuse or combat—it can act like acid, corroding neural connections and shrinking a brain area (the hippocampus) that is vital for laying down memories. Moreover, when sudden stress hormones are flowing, older memories may be blocked. It is true for rats trying to find their way to a hidden target (de Quervain & others, 1998). And it is true for those of us whose minds have gone blank while speaking in public.

Storing Implicit and Explicit Memories

OBJECTIVE 26-6 | Distinguish between implicit and explicit memory, and identify the main brain structure associated with each.

A memory-to-be enters the cortex through the senses, then wends its way into the brain's depths. Precisely where it goes depends on the type of information, as dramatically illustrated by those who suffer from a type of **amnesia** in which they are unable to form new memories.

Electroconvulsive therapy (ECT) for depression disrupts memory for recent experience but leaves most memory intact.

Scott Barbour/Getty Images

Severe stress sears in memories
Significantly stressful events, such as the tragic tsunami that struck Southeast Asia in late 2004, may be an indelible part of the memories of those who experience them.

■ **long-term potentiation (LTP)** an increase in a synapse's firing potential after brief, rapid stimulation. Believed to be a neural basis for learning and memory.

■ **amnesia** the loss of memory.

■ **implicit memory** retention independent of conscious recollection. (Also called *procedural memory*.)

■ **explicit memory** memory of facts and experiences that one can consciously know and "declare." (Also called *declarative memory*.)

■ **hippocampus** a neural center that is located in the limbic system and helps process explicit memories for storage.

Neurologist Oliver Sacks (1985, pp. 26–27) describes one such patient, Jimmie, who had brain damage. Jimmie had no memories—thus, no sense of elapsed time—beyond his injury in 1945. Asked in 1975 to name the U.S. President, he replied, "FDR's dead. Truman's at the helm."

When Jimmie gave his age as 19, Sacks set a mirror before him: "Look in the mirror and tell me what you see. Is that a 19-year-old looking out from the mirror?"

Jimmie turned ashen, gripped the chair, cursed, then became frantic: "What's going on? What's happened to me? Is this a nightmare? Am I crazy? Is this a joke?" When his attention was diverted to some children playing baseball, his panic ended, the dreadful mirror forgotten.

Sacks showed Jimmie a photo from *National Geographic*. "What is this?" he asked.

"It's the Moon," Jimmie replied.

"No, it's not," Sacks answered. "It's a picture of the Earth taken from the Moon."

"Doc, you're kidding? Someone would've had to get a camera up there!"

"Naturally."

"Hell! You're joking—how the hell would you do that?" Jimmie's wonder was that of a bright young man from 60 years ago reacting with amazement to his travel back to the future.

Careful testing of these unique people reveals something even stranger: Although incapable of recalling new facts or anything they have done recently, Jimmie and others with similar conditions can learn. Shown hard-to-find figures in pictures (in the *Where's Waldo?* series), they can quickly spot them again later. They can learn to read mirror-image writing or do a jigsaw puzzle, and they have even been taught complicated job skills (Schacter, 1992, 1996; Xu & Corkin, 2001). They can be classically conditioned. However, *they do all these things with no awareness of having learned them.*

These amnesia victims are in some ways like people with brain damage who cannot consciously recognize faces but whose physiological responses to familiar faces reveal an implicit (unconscious) recognition. Their behaviors challenge the idea that memory is a single, unified, conscious system. Instead, we seem to have two memory systems operating in tandem (**FIGURE 26.5**). Whatever has destroyed *conscious* recall in these individuals with amnesia has not destroyed their *unconscious* capacity for learning. They can learn *how* to do something—called **implicit memory** (*procedural memory*). But they may not know and declare *that* they know—called **explicit memory** (*declarative memory*).

Having read a story once, they will read it faster a second time, showing implicit memory. But there will be no explicit memory, for they cannot recall having seen the story before. If repeatedly shown the word *perfume*, they will not recall having seen it.

FIGURE 26.5
Memory subsystems We process and store our explicit and implicit memories separately. Thus, one may lose explicit memory (becoming amnesic), yet display implicit memory for material one cannot consciously recall.

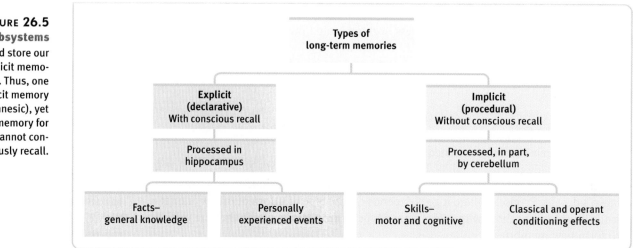

But if asked the first word that comes to mind in response to the letters *per,* they say *perfume,* readily displaying their learning. Performing such tasks, even Alzheimer's patients, whose explicit memories for people and events are lost, display an ability to form new implicit memories (Lustig & Buckner, 2004). They retain their new learning but do not explicitly recall it.

The Hippocampus

One way to discover how memory works is to study its malfunctions. For example, these remarkable stories provoke us to wonder: Do our explicit and implicit memory systems involve separate brain regions? Scans of the brain in action, and autopsies of people who had amnesia, reveal that new explicit memories of names, images, and events are laid down via the **hippocampus (FIGURE 26.6)**, a neural center in the limbic system. When brain scans capture the brain forming a memory, they reveal activity in the hippocampus as well as in certain areas of the frontal lobes (Wagner & others, 1998). The hippocampus again lights up on a PET scan when people recall words (using explicit memory) (Squire, 1992).

Damage to the hippocampus disrupts some types of memory. Chickadees and other birds can store food in hundreds of places and return to these unmarked caches months later, but not if their hippocampus has been removed (Sherry & Vaccarino, 1989). Like the cortex, the hippocampus is lateralized. (You've got two of them, one just above each ear and about an inch and a half straight in.) Damage to the left or right hippocampus seems to produce different results. Patients with left-hippocampus damage have trouble remembering verbal information, but they have no trouble recalling visual designs and locations. For those with right-hippocampus damage, the problem is reversed (Schacter, 1996).

New research also pinpoints the functions of different hippocampus subregions. One part is active as people learn to associate names with faces (Zeineh & others, 2003). Another part is active as memory whizzes engage in spatial mnemonics (Maguire & others, 2003b). The rear area, which processes spatial memory, also grows bigger the longer a London cabbie has been navigating the maze of city streets (Maguire & others, 2003a).

Monkeys and people who lose their hippocampus to surgery or disease also lose most of their recall for things learned during the preceding month, though their older memories remain intact (Bayley & others, 2005; McGaugh, 2000). The longer the hippocampus and its pathway to the cortex are left intact after training, the smaller the memory deficit (Remondes & Schuman, 2004). The hippocampus seems to act as a loading dock where the brain registers and temporarily stores the elements of a remembered episode—its smell, feel, sound, and location. But then, like older files shifted to a basement storeroom, memories migrate for storage elsewhere. The hippocampus is active during slow-wave sleep, as memories are processed and filed for later retrieval. The greater the hippocampus activity during sleep after a training experience, the better the next day's memory (Peigneux & others, 2004).

Our brain's librarian assigns different information to different regions. Brain scans reveal that, once stored, our mental encores of past experience activate various parts of the frontal and temporal lobes (Fink & others, 1996; Gabrieli & others, 1996; Markowitsch, 1995). Calling up a telephone number and holding it in working memory activates a region of the left frontal cortex; calling up a party scene would more likely activate a region of the right hemisphere.

The two-track memory system reinforces an important principle of the way the brain handles information via parallel processing: Mental feats such as vision, thinking, and memory may seem to be single abilities, but they are not. Rather, we split information into different components for separate and simultaneous processing.

[Brain-scanning] technologies are revolutionizing the study of the brain and mind in the same way that the telescope revolutionized the study of the heavens."

Endel Tulving (1996)

Weidenfield & Nicolson archives

FIGURE 26.6
The hippocampus
Explicit memories for facts and episodes are processed in the hippocampus and fed to other brain regions for storage.

There is no longer any doubt: Our memories are not in one place. Many brain regions are active as we encode, store, and retrieve different kinds of information. Savoring that memory of a successful performance requires a mental symphony conductor that retrieves snippets from various cortical storage sites and integrates them with the emotional associations provided by your amygdala. Amnesia patients may retain the distributed fragments of a memory—the sight, sound, smell, objects, people, actions, and emotions. But the connections that enable the patients to reassemble the fragments into an explicit memory of an event may be lost.

The Cerebellum

Although your hippocampus is a temporary processing site for your explicit memories, you could lose it and still lay down memories for skills and conditioned associations. Implicit memories require fewer connections among cortical storage areas, so people with hippocampal damage may retain those memories (Paller, 2004). Joseph LeDoux (1996) recounts the story of a brain-damaged patient whose amnesia left her unable to recognize her physician as, each day, he shook her hand and introduced himself. One day, after reaching for his hand, she yanked hers back, for the physician had pricked her with a tack in his palm. The next time he returned to introduce himself she refused to shake his hand but couldn't explain why. Having been classically conditioned, she just wouldn't do it.

The cerebellum, the brain region extending out from the rear of the brainstem, plays a key role in forming and storing the implicit memories created by classical conditioning. Humans with a damaged cerebellum are incapable of developing certain conditioned reflexes, such as associating a tone with an impending puff of air—and thus blinking in anticipation of the puff (Daum & Schugens, 1996; Green & Woodruff-Pak, 2000). By methodically disrupting the function of different pathways in the cortex and cerebellum of rabbits, Richard Thompson, David Krupa, and Judith Thompson showed that rabbits will also fail to learn a conditioned eyeblink response when the cerebellum is temporarily deactivated during training (Krupa & others, 1993; Steinmetz, 1999). Implicit memory formation needs the cerebellum.

Our dual explicit-implicit memory system helps explain infantile amnesia: The reactions and skills we learned during infancy reach far into our future, yet as adults we recall nothing (explicitly) of our first three years. Our conscious minds are blank, not only because we index so much of our explicit memory by words that nonspeaking children have not learned, but also because the hippocampus is one of the last brain structures to mature.

>> Learning Outcomes

Storage: Retaining Information

OBJECTIVE 26-1 | **Contrast two types of sensory memory.**

As information enters the memory system through our senses, we register and store visual images via *iconic memory,* in which picture images last no more than a few tenths of a second. We register and store sounds via *echoic memory,* where echoes of auditory stimuli may linger as long as 3 or 4 seconds.

OBJECTIVE 26-2 | **Describe the duration and working capacity of short-term memory.**

At any given time, we can focus on and process only about seven items of information (either new or retrieved from our memory store). Without rehearsal, information disappears within seconds from short-term memory and is forgotten.

OBJECTIVE 26-3 | **Describe the capacity and duration of long-term memory.**

Our capacity for storing information permanently in long-term memory is essentially unlimited.

OBJECTIVE 26-4 | **Discuss the synaptic changes that accompany memory formation and storage.**

Contemporary researchers are focusing on memory-related changes within and between single neurons. As experience strengthens the pathways between neurons, synapses transmit signals more efficiently. In a process known as *long-term potentiation (LTP),* sending neurons in these pathways release neurotransmitters more quickly, and receiving neurons may develop additional receptors, increasing their ability to detect the incoming neurotransmitters. LTP appears to be the neural basis for learning and memory.

OBJECTIVE 26-5 | **Discuss some ways stress hormones can affect memory.**

By enabling the production of extra glucose (which fuels brain activity), stress hormones alert the brain to important events. The amygdala, an emotion-processing structure in the brain's limbic system, arouses brain areas that process emotion. These emotion-triggered hormonal changes may produce indelible memories.

OBJECTIVE 26-6 | **Distinguish between implicit and explicit memory, and identify the main brain structure associated with each.**

We are often not aware of our *implicit (procedural) memories*—our memory of our own skills and operantly and classically conditioned responses. These memories are processed in part by the cerebellum, near the brainstem. We consciously recall our *explicit (declarative) memories*—our general knowledge, specific facts, and personally experienced events. Explicit memories are processed in various subregions of the hippocampus (a neural center in the limbic system) and sent for storage in other areas in the brain. The implicit and explicit memory systems are independent. Damage to the hippocampus may destroy the ability to consciously recall memories, without destroying skills or classically conditioned responses.

TERMS AND CONCEPTS TO REMEMBER

iconic memory, p. 26-0
echoic memory, p. 26-0
long-term potentiation (LTP), p. 26-4

amnesia, p. 26-5
implicit memory, p. 26-6
explicit memory, p. 26-6
hippocampus, p. 26-7

TEST YOURSELF

1. Your friend tells you that her father experienced brain damage in an accident. She wonders if psychology can explain why he can still play checkers very well but has a hard time holding a sensible conversation. What can you tell her?

(Answer in Appendix B.)

ASK YOURSELF

1. Can you name an instance where stress has helped you remember something, and another instance where stress has interfered with remembering something?

>WEB

Multiple-choice *self-tests* and more may be found at www.worthpublishers.com/myers.

MODULE

Recall, Recognition,
and Relearning

Retrieval Cues

27

Retrieval: Getting Information Out

OBJECTIVE 27-1 | Contrast the recall, recognition, and relearning measures of memory.

Recall, Recognition, and Relearning

To remember an event requires not only getting it in (encoding) and retaining it (storage), but also getting it out. To most people, memory is **recall**, the ability to retrieve information not in conscious awareness. To a psychologist, memory is any sign that something learned has been retained. So *recognizing* or more quickly *relearning* information also indicates memory (**FIGURE 27.1**).

Here is another sentence I will ask you about later: The fish attacked the swimmer.

Long after you cannot recall most of the people in your high school graduating class, you may still be able to **recognize** their yearbook pictures from a photographic lineup and pick their names from a list of names. Harry Bahrick and his colleagues (1975) reported that people who had graduated 25 years earlier could not *recall* many of their old classmates, but they could *recognize* 90 percent of their pictures and names. If you are like most students, you, too, could likely recognize more names of the Seven Dwarfs than you could recall (Miserandino, 1991).

Remembering things past
Even if Oprah Winfrey and Brad Pitt had not become famous, their high school classmates would most likely still recognize their yearbook photos.

Our speed at **relearning** can also reveal memory. If you once learned something and then forgot it, you probably will relearn it more quickly than you originally learned it. When you study for a final exam or resurrect a language used in early childhood, the relearning is easier. Tests of recognition and of time spent relearning reveal that we remember more than we can recall.

Our recognition memory is impressively quick and vast. "Is your friend wearing a new or old outfit?" "Old." "Is this five-second movie clip from a film you've ever seen?" "Yes." "Have you ever before seen this person—this minor variation on the same old human features (two eyes, one nose, and so on)?" "No." Before the mouth can form our answer to any of millions of such questions, the mind knows, and knows that it knows.

FIGURE 27.1
A modified three-stage processing model of memory
Here we will focus on the retrieval aspects of our memory processing.

CLOSE-UP:

RETRIEVING PASSWORDS

There's something that you need lots of, and that your grandparents at your age didn't: passwords. To log into your e-mail, retrieve your voice mail, draw cash from a machine, access your phone card, use the copy machine, or persuade the keypad to open the building door, you need to remember your password. A typical introductory psychology student faces eight demands for passwords, report Alan Brown and his colleagues (2004).

With so many passwords needed, what's a person to do? Memory researcher Henry Roediger takes a simple approach to storing all the important phone, PIN, and code numbers in his life: "I have a sheet in my shirt pocket with all the numbers I need," says Roediger (2001), adding that he can't mentally store them all, so why bother? Other strategies may help those who do not want to lose their PINS in the wash. First, duplicate. The average student uses four different passwords to meet those eight needs. Second, harness retrieval cues. Surveys in Britain and the United States reveal that about half of our passwords harness a familiar name or date. Others often involve familiar phone or identification numbers.

For on-line banking or other situations where security is essential, use a mix of letters and numbers, advise Brown and his colleagues. After composing such a password, rehearse it, then rehearse it a day later, and continue rehearsing at increasing intervals. In such ways, long-term memories will form and be retrievable at the cash and copy machines.

Retrieval Cues

OBJECTIVE 27-2 | Explain how retrieval cues help us access stored memories, and describe the process of priming.

Imagine a spider suspended in the middle of her web, held up by the many strands extending outward from her in all directions to different points (perhaps a window sill, a tree branch, a leaf on a shrub). If you were to trace a pathway to the spider, you would first need to create a path from one of these anchor points and then follow the strand attached to that point down into the web.

The process of retrieving a memory follows a similar principle, because memories are held in storage by a web of associations, each piece of information interconnected with others. When you encode into memory a target piece of information, such as the name of the person sitting next to you in class, you associate with it other bits of information about your surroundings, mood, seating position, and so on. These other bits of information are like tags, hints, or identifying marks on the target information. They act as *retrieval cues*, anchor points you can use to access the target information when you want to retrieve it later. The more retrieval cues you have, the better your chances of finding a route to the suspended memory (see Close-Up: Retrieving Passwords).

Questions:
Multiple-choice questions test our
a. recall.
b. recognition.
c. relearning.

Fill-in-the-blank questions test our
_____ . (See this module's final page for answers to these questions.)

"Memory is not like a container that gradually fills up; it is more like a tree growing hooks onto which memories are hung."
Peter Russell, *The Brain Book*, 1979

"Let me refresh your memory. It was the night before Christmas and all through the house not a creature was stirring until you landed a sled, drawn by reindeer, on the plaintiff's home, causing extensive damage to the roof and chimney."

■ **recall** a measure of memory in which the person must retrieve information learned earlier, as on a fill-in-the-blank test.

■ **recognition** a measure of memory in which the person need only identify items previously learned, as on a multiple-choice test.

■ **relearning** a memory measure that assesses the amount of time saved when learning material for a second time.

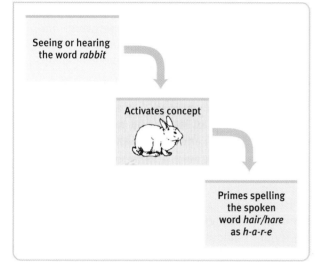

FIGURE 27.2
Priming—awakening associations
After seeing or hearing *rabbit,* we are later more likely to spell the spoken word as *h-a-r-e.* The spreading of associations unconsciously activates related associations. This phenomenon is called priming. (Adapted from Bower, 1986.)

Ask a friend two rapid-fire questions: (a) How do you pronounce the word spelled by the letters *s-h-o-p?* (b) What do you do when you come to a green light? If your friend answers "stop" to the second question, you have demonstrated priming.

■ **priming** the activation, often unconsciously, of particular associations in memory.

■ **déjà vu** that eerie sense that "I've experienced this before." Cues from the current situation may subconsciously trigger retrieval of an earlier experience.

Mnemonic devices (memory aids that use vivid images or organizational devices) provide us with handy retrieval cues. But the best retrieval cues come from the associations formed at the time we encode a memory, and those cues can be experiences as well as words. Tastes, smells, and sights often evoke our recall of associated episodes. To call up visual cues when trying to recall something, we may mentally place ourselves in the original context. For British theologian John Hull (1990, p. 174) this became difficult after losing his sight. On one occasion when his wife asked him what he had done that day he had difficulty recalling. "I knew I had been somewhere, and had done particular things with certain people, but where? I could not put the conversations I had had into a context. There was no background, no features against which to identify the place. Normally, the memories of people you have spoken to during the day are stored in frames which include the background."

To retrieve a specific memory from the web of associations, you first need to activate one of the strands that leads to it, a process called **priming.** Philosopher-psychologist William James referred to priming as the "wakening of associations." Often our associations are activated, or primed, without our awareness. As **FIGURE 27.2** indicates, seeing or hearing the word *rabbit* primes associations with *hare* even though we may not recall having seen or heard *rabbit.*

Priming is often "memoryless memory"—memory without explicit remembering, invisible memory. If, walking down a hallway, you see a poster of a missing child, you will then unconsciously be primed to interpret an ambiguous adult-child interaction as a possible kidnapping (James, 1986). Although you don't consciously remember the poster, it predisposes your interpretation. Even subliminal stimuli can briefly prime responses to later stimuli.

Context Effects

OBJECTIVE 27-3 | Cite some ways that context can affect retrieval.

Putting yourself back in the context where you experienced something can prime your memory retrieval. Duncan Godden and Alan Baddeley (1975) discovered this when they had scuba divers listen to a list of words in two different settings, either 10 feet underwater or sitting on the beach. As **FIGURE 27.3** illustrates, the divers recalled more words when they were retested in the same place.

Consider this scenario: While making notes in this book, you realize you need to sharpen your pencil. You get up and walk downstairs. When you get there, however, you cannot remember why you came. After trying to recall your purpose, you give up and return to your desk. As soon as you sit down to work again, it hits you: "I wanted to sharpen this pencil!" What happens to create this frustrating experience? In one context (desk, reading psychology), it occurs to you that you want the pencil sharpened. When you get up and go downstairs, you move into a different context where you have few cues to lead you to the thought that brought you there. When you give up and go back to your desk, you are back in the context in which you encoded the thought ("This pencil is dull").

You have probably experienced similar context effects. You return to where you once lived or to the school you once attended and are flooded with retrieval cues and memories. Even taking an exam in the same room where you are taught may help a little. In several experiments, Carolyn Rovee-Collier (1993) found that a familiar context activates memories even in 3-month-olds. After infants learned that kicking a crib mobile would make it move (via a connecting ribbon from the

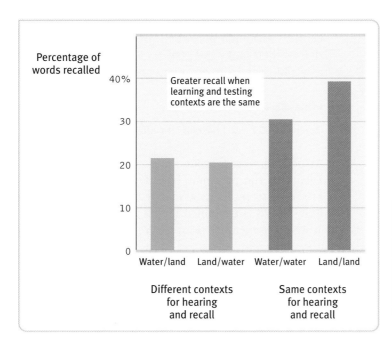

Percentage of words recalled

Greater recall when learning and testing contexts are the same

Water/land   Land/water   Water/water   Land/land

Different contexts for hearing and recall

Same contexts for hearing and recall

FIGURE 27.3
The effects of context on memory
Words heard underwater are best recalled underwater; words heard on land are best recalled on land. (Adapted from Godden & Baddeley, 1975.)

ankle), the infants kicked more when tested again in the same crib with the same bumper than when in a different context (**FIGURE 27.4**).

Sometimes, being in a context similar to one we've been in before may trigger the experience of **déjà vu** (French for "already seen")—that eerie sense that "I've been in this exact situation before." This fleeting experience happens most commonly to well-educated, imaginative young adults, especially when tired or stressed (Brown, 2003, 2004). The two-thirds of people who report having experienced déjà vu (McAneny, 1996) often wonder, "How could I recognize a situation I'm experiencing for the first time?" Those who suppose a paranormal explanation may think of rein-carnation ("I must have experienced this in a previous life") or precognition ("I viewed this scene in my mind before experiencing it").

Posing the question differently ("Why do I feel as if I recognize this situation?"), we can see how our memory system might produce déjà vu (Alcock, 1981). If we have previously been in a similar situation, the current situation may be loaded with cues that unconsciously retrieve the earlier ex-perience. (We take in and retain vast amounts of information while hardly noticing and often forgetting where it came from.) Thus, if in a similar context you see a stranger who looks and walks like one of your friends, the similarity may give rise to an eerie feeling of recognition. Having awakened a shadow of that earlier experience, you may think, "I've seen that person in this situation before."

Or perhaps, suggests James Lampinen (2002), a situation seems familiar when moderately similar to several events. Imagine you briefly encounter my dad, my brothers, my sister, my children, and a few weeks later meet me. Perhaps you might think, "I've been with this guy

"Do you ever get that strange feeling of vujà dé? Not déjà vu; vujà dé. It's the distinct sense that, somehow, something just happened that has never happened before. Nothing seems familiar. And then suddenly the feeling is gone. Vujà dé."

George Carlin, *Funny Times*, December 2001

FIGURE 27.4
Familiar context activates memory
After learning to move a mobile by kicking, infants had their learning reactivated most strongly when retested in the same rather than a different context. (From Butler & Rovee-Collier, 1989.)

before." Although no one in my family looks or acts just like me (lucky them), their looks and gestures are somewhat like mine and I might form a "global match" to what you had experienced.

Moods and Memories

OBJECTIVE 27-4 | Describe the effects of internal states on retrieval.

Associated words, events, and contexts are not the only retrieval cues. Events in the past may have aroused a specific *emotion* that later can prime us to recall its associated events. Cognitive psychologist Gordon Bower (1983) explained it this way: "An emotion is like a library room into which we place memory records. We best retrieve those records by returning to that emotional room." What we learn in one state—be it joyful or sad, drunk or sober—is sometimes more easily recalled when we are again in that state, a subtle phenomenon called *state-dependent memory.* What people learn when depressed or drunk they don't recall well in *any* state (depression disrupts encoding and alcohol disrupts storage). But they recall it slightly better when again depressed or drunk. Someone who hides money when drunk may forget the location until drunk again.

> "When a feeling was there, they felt as if it would never go; when it was gone, they felt as if it had never been; when it returned, they felt as if it had never gone."
>
> George MacDonald, *What's Mine's Mine,* 1886

Our moods similarly bias our memories. We seem to associate good or bad events with their accompanying emotions, which become retrieval cues (Fiedler & others, 2001). Thus, our memories are somewhat **mood-congruent.** Being depressed sours memories by priming negative associations, which we then use to explain our current mood. If put in a buoyant mood—whether under hypnosis or just by the day's events (a World Cup soccer victory for the German participants in one study)—people recall the world through rose-colored glasses (DeSteno & others, 2000; Forgas & others, 1984; Schwarz & others, 1987). They judge themselves competent and effective, other people benevolent, happy events more likely.

Knowing this connection, we should not be surprised that in some studies *currently* depressed people recall their parents as rejecting, punitive, and guilt-promoting, whereas *formerly* depressed people describe their parents much as do

CALLAHAN

"I wonder if you'd mind giving me directions. I've never been sober in this part of town before."

Mood and memory
Elated, we remember other happy times and expect more such times. Mood serves as a retrieval cue, activating other memories associated with the same emotion. These memories help sustain the current mood.

those who have never suffered depression (Lewinsohn & Rosenbaum, 1987; Lewis, 1992). No wonder Robert Bornstein and others (1991) report that adolescents' ratings of parental warmth give little clue to how the same adolescents will rate their parents six weeks later. When teenagers are down, their parents seem inhuman; as their mood brightens, their parents morph from devils into angels. You and I may nod our heads knowingly. Yet, in a good or bad mood, we persist in attributing to reality our own changing judgments and memories.

Moods also influence how we *interpret* other people's behavior. Being mindful of our feelings can help us correct for the mood bias (McFarland & others, 2003). Still, the phenomenon is hard to resist. In a bad mood we read someone's look as a glare; in a good mood we encode the same look as interest. How we perceive the world depends on our mood. Passions exaggerate.

Your mood's effect on retrieval helps explain why moods persist. When happy, you recall happy events and therefore see the world as a happy place, which helps prolong the good mood. When depressed, you recall sad events, which darkens your interpretations of current events. Unfortunately for those suffering from depression, this process can maintain depression's vicious cycle.

■ **mood-congruent memory** the tendency to recall experiences that are consistent with one's current good or bad mood.

Do you recall the gist of the sentence I asked you to remember at the beginning of this module? If not, does the word *shark* help? Experiments show that *shark* more readily cues the image you stored than does the sentence's actual word, *fish* (Anderson & others, 1976).

>> Learning Outcomes

Retrieval: Getting Information Out

OBJECTIVE 27-1 | Contrast the recall, recognition, and relearning measures of memory.

Recall is the ability to *retrieve* information not in conscious awareness; a fill-in-the-blank question tests recall. *Recognition* is the ability to *identify* items previously learned; a multiple-choice question tests recognition. *Relearning* is the ability to *master* previously stored information more quickly than you originally learned it.

OBJECTIVE 27-2 | Explain how retrieval cues help us access stored memories, and describe the process of priming.

Retrieval cues are bits of related information we encode while processing a target piece of information. These bits are linked in some way to the context of the target, and they become a part of a web of stored associations. When one of these associated bits catches our attention, it is as though we are pulling on a strand in the web of associations, retrieving the target information into our conscious awareness. This process of activating associations (often unconsciously) is *priming*.

OBJECTIVE 27-3 | Cite some ways that context can affect retrieval.

The context in which we originally experienced an event or encoded a thought can flood our memory with retrieval cues, leading us to the target memory. If we are in a different context very similar to the original one, we may experience *déjà vu*, as many of these cues return and trick us into unconsciously retrieving the target memory.

OBJECTIVE 27-4 | Describe the effects of internal states on retrieval.

Specific states or emotions can prime us to recall events associated with those states or emotions. While in a good mood, we

tend to retrieve memories consistent—or congruent—with that happy state. When depressed, we more easily recall negative memories. Moods also prime us to interpret others' behavior in ways consistent with our emotions.

TERMS AND CONCEPTS TO REMEMBER

recall, p. 27-0
recognition, p. 27-0
relearning, p. 27-0
priming, p. 27-2

déjà vu, p. 27-3
mood-congruent memory, p. 27-4

TEST YOURSELF

1. What is priming?

(Answer in Appendix B.)

ASK YOURSELF

1. What sort of mood have you been in lately? How has your mood colored your memories, perceptions, and expectations?

ANSWERS TO QUESTIONS WITHIN THE MODULE

Q. Multiple-choice questions test our
    a. recall.
    b. recognition.
    c. relearning.

    Fill-in-the-blank questions test our _____.

A. Multiple-choice questions test recognition. Fill-in-the-blank questions test recall.

>WEB

Multiple-choice **self-tests** and more may be found at www.worthpublishers.com/myers.

Forgetting

Memory Construction

Improving Memory

Forgetting, Memory Construction, and Memory Improvement

OBJECTIVE 28-1 | Explain why we should value our ability to forget, and distinguish three general ways our memory fails us.

Amid all the applause for memory—all the efforts to understand it, all the books on how to improve it—have any voices been heard in praise of forgetting? William James (1890, p. 680) was such a voice: "If we remembered everything, we should on most occasions be as ill off as if we remembered nothing." To discard the clutter of useless or out-of-date information—where we parked the car yesterday, a friend's old phone number, restaurant orders already cooked and served—is surely a blessing. Russian journalist and memory whiz Shereshevskii accumulated a junk heap of memories that haunted him. They dominated his consciousness. He had difficulty thinking abstractly—generalizing, organizing, evaluating. A good memory is helpful, but so is the ability to forget. If a memory-enhancing pill becomes available, it had better not be too effective.

More often, however, our memory dismays and frustrates us. Memories are quirky. My own memory can easily call up such episodes as that wonderful first kiss with the woman I love or trivial facts like the air mileage from London to Detroit. Then it abandons me when I'm trying to recall that new colleague's name or where I left my sunglasses, and discover that I have failed to encode, store, or retrieve the information. Memory researcher Daniel Schacter (1999) enumerates seven ways our memories fail us—the seven sins of memory, he calls them:

Three sins of forgetting:

- *Absent-mindedness*—inattention to details produces encoding failure (our mind is elsewhere as we lay down the car keys).
- *Transience*—storage decay over time (after we part ways with former classmates, unused information fades).
- *Blocking*—inaccessibility of stored information (seeing an old classmate, we may feel the name on the tip of our tongue, but we experience retrieval failure—we cannot get it out).

Three sins of distortion:

- *Misattribution*—confusing the source of information (putting words in someone else's mouth or remembering a movie scene as an actual happening).
- *Suggestibility*—the lingering effects of misinformation (a leading question—"Did Mr. Jones touch your private parts?"—later becomes a young child's false memory).
- *Bias*—belief-colored recollections (a friend's current feelings toward her fiancé may color her recalled initial feelings).

One sin of intrusion:

- *Persistence*—unwanted memories (being haunted by images of a sexual assault).

Let's first consider the sins of forgetting, then those of distortion and intrusion.

"Happiness is nothing more than health and a poor memory."
Physician Albert Schweitzer (1875–1965)

Cellist Yo-Yo Ma forgot his 266-year-old, $2.5 million cello in a New York taxi. (He later recovered it.)

"Amnesia seeps into the crevices of our brains, and amnesia heals."
Joyce Carol Oates, "Words Fail, Memory Blurs, Life Wins," 2001

Forgetting

Encoding Failure

OBJECTIVE 28-2 | Discuss the role of encoding failure in forgetting.

We cannot remember what we fail to encode, because the information never enters long-term memory (**FIGURE 28.1**). Age can affect encoding efficiency. The same brain areas that jump into action when young adults are encoding new information are less responsive among older adults. This slower encoding helps explain age-related memory decline (Grady & others, 1995). (Although older people tend to *recall* less than younger adults do, they usually remember as well as younger people when given reminders or a recognition test.)

But no matter how young we are, we selectively attend to few of the myriad sights and sounds continually bombarding us. Consider something you have looked at countless times: What letters accompany the number 5 on your telephone? For most of us, the question is surprisingly difficult.

> "Each of us finds that in [our] own life every moment of time is completely filled. [We are] bombarded every second by sensations, emotions, thoughts . . . nine-tenths of which [we] must simply ignore. The past [is] a roaring cataract of billions upon billions of such moments: Any one of them too complex to grasp in its entirety, and the aggregate beyond all imagination. . . . At every tick of the clock, in every inhabited part of the world, an unimaginable richness and variety of 'history' falls off the world into total oblivion."
>
> English novelist-critic C. S. Lewis (1967)

FIGURE 28.1
Forgetting as encoding failure
We cannot remember what we have not encoded.

Here's another example of encoding failure. If you live in North America, Britain, or Australia, you have looked at thousands of pennies in your lifetime. You can surely recall their color and size, but can you recall what the side with the head looks like? If not, let's make the memory test easier: If you are familiar with U.S. coins, can you recognize the real thing in **FIGURE 28.2**? Most people cannot (Nickerson & Adams, 1979). Of the eight critical features (Lincoln's head, date, "In God we trust," and so on), the average person spontaneously remembers only three. Likewise, few British people can draw from memory the one-pence coin (Richardson, 1993). The details of a penny are

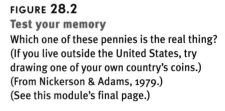

FIGURE 28.2
Test your memory
Which one of these pennies is the real thing? (If you live outside the United States, try drawing one of your own country's coins.) (From Nickerson & Adams, 1979.) (See this module's final page.)

not very meaningful—nor are they essential for distinguishing pennies from other coins—and few of us have made the effort to encode them. We encode some information (where we had dinner yesterday) automatically; other types of information (like the concepts in this module) require effort and attention. Without this effortful processing, many memories never form.

Storage Decay

OBJECTIVE 28-3 | Discuss the concept of storage decay, and describe Ebbinghaus' forgetting curve.

Even after encoding something well, we sometimes later forget it. To study the durability of our stored memories, Hermann Ebbinghaus (1885) learned lists of nonsense syllables and measured how much he retained when relearning each list, from 20 minutes to 30 days later. His famous *forgetting curve* (**FIGURE 28.3**) indicates that much of what we learn we may indeed quickly forget. Later experiments made the forgetting curve into one of psychology's laws: The course of forgetting is initially rapid, then levels off with time (Wixted & Ebbesen, 1991).

Harry Bahrick (1984) extended Ebbinghaus' finding. He examined the forgetting curve for Spanish vocabulary learned in school. Compared with those just completing a high school or college Spanish course, people who had been out of school for 3 years had forgotten much of what they had learned (**FIGURE 28.4**). However, after roughly 3 years, their forgetting leveled off; what people remembered then, they still remembered 25 and more years later, even if they had not used their Spanish at all.

FIGURE 28.3
Ebbinghaus' forgetting curve
After learning lists of nonsense syllables, Ebbinghaus studied how much he retained up to 30 days later. He found that memory for novel information fades quickly, then levels out. (Adapted from Ebbinghaus, 1885.)

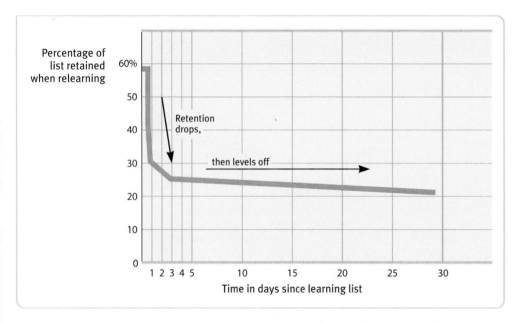

FIGURE 28.4
The forgetting curve for Spanish learned in school
Compared with people just completing a Spanish course, those 3 years out of the course remembered much less. Compared with the 3-year group, however, those who studied Spanish even longer ago did not forget much more. (Adapted from Bahrick, 1984.)

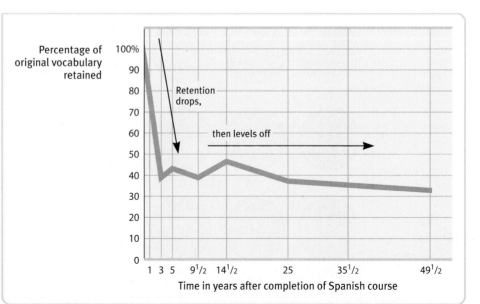

One explanation for these forgetting curves is a gradual fading of the physical memory trace. As we are learning more about the physical storage of memory, we are better understanding how memory storage can decay. But memories also fade because of the accumulation of other learning that disrupts our retrieval.

Retrieval Failure

We have seen that forgotten events are like books you can't find in your campus library—some because they were never acquired (not encoded), others because they were discarded (stored memories decay).

But there is a third possibility: Even if the book is stored and available, it may be inaccessible. Perhaps you lack the information needed to look it up and retrieve it. Information sometimes gets into our brain and, though we know it is there, we cannot get it out (**FIGURE 28.5**). A name may lie poised on the tip of the tongue, waiting to be retrieved. Given retrieval cues ("It begins with an *M*"), we may easily retrieve an elusive memory. Retrieval problems contribute to older adults' occasional memory failures. Forgetting is often not memories discarded but memories unretrieved.

Deaf persons fluent in sign language experience a parallel "tip of the fingers" phenomenon (Thompson & others, 2005).

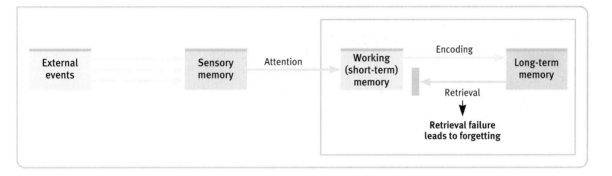

FIGURE 28.5
Retrieval failure
We store in long-term memory what's important to us or what we've rehearsed. But sometimes even stored information cannot be accessed, which leads to forgetting.

Interference

OBJECTIVE 28-4 | Contrast proactive and retroactive interference, and explain how they can cause retrieval failure.

Learning some items may interfere with retrieving others, especially when the items are similar. If someone gives you a phone number, you may be able to recall it later. But if two more people give you their numbers, each successive number will be more difficult to recall. Likewise, if you buy a new combination lock or get a new phone number, your memory of the old one may interfere. Such **proactive** (*forward-acting*) **interference** occurs when something you learned earlier disrupts your recall of something you experience later. As you collect more and more information, your mental attic never fills, but it certainly gets cluttered.

Benton Underwood (1957) found that those who learn different lists of words on successive days have more and more difficulty remembering each new list the next day. This proactive interference explains why Ebbinghaus, after memorizing countless lists of nonsense syllables during his career, could remember only about one-fourth of a new list of syllables on the day after he learned it—far fewer than you as a novice could remember after learning a single list.

Retroactive (*backward-acting*) **interference** occurs when new information makes it harder to recall something you learned earlier (**FIGURE 28.6** on the next page). For example, learning new students' names typically interferes with a teacher's recall of the names of previous students. It is rather like a second stone tossed in a pond, disrupting the waves rippling out from a first.

You can minimize retroactive interference by reducing the number of interfering events—say, by going for a walk or to sleep shortly after learning new information. Researchers John Jenkins and Karl Dallenbach (1924) discovered the sleep benefit in a

■ **proactive interference** the disruptive effect of prior learning on the recall of new information.

■ **retroactive interference** the disruptive effect of new learning on the recall of old information.

FIGURE 28.6 Proactive and retroactive interference

French, learned beforehand, interferes proactively

Study French — papier livre plume école

Study Spanish — papel libro pluma escuela

Spanish 101 Mid-term exam

proactive interference

Spanish, learned afterward, interferes retroactively

Study French — papier livre plume école

Study Spanish — papel libro pluma escuela

French 101 Mid-term exam

retroactive interference

now-classic experiment. Day after day, two people each learned some nonsense syllables, then tried to recall them after up to eight hours of being awake or asleep at night. As **FIGURE 28.7** shows, forgetting occurred more rapidly after being awake and involved with other activities. The investigators surmised that "forgetting is not so much a matter of the decay of old impressions and associations as it is a matter of interference, inhibition, or obliteration of the old by the new" (1924, p. 612). Later experiments have confirmed the benefits of sleep and found that the hour before a night's sleep (but not the minute before sleep) is a good time to commit information to memory (Benson & Feinberg, 1977; Fowler & others, 1973; Nesca & Koulack, 1994).

FIGURE 28.7 Retroactive interference
More forgetting occurred when a person stayed awake and experienced other new material. (From Jenkins & Dallenbach, 1924.)

Percentage of syllables recalled

Without interfering events, recall is better

After sleep

After remaining awake

Hours elapsed after learning syllables

Interference is an important cause of forgetting and may explain why ads viewed during violent or sexual TV programs are so forgettable (Bushman & Bonacci, 2002). But we should not overstate the point. Sometimes old information can facilitate our learning of new information. Knowing Latin may help us to learn French—a phenomenon called *positive transfer*. It is when old and new information compete with each other that interference occurs.

■ **repression** in psychoanalytic theory, the basic defense mechanism that banishes from consciousness anxiety-arousing thoughts, feelings, and memories.

Motivated Forgetting

OBJECTIVE **28-5** | Summarize Freud's concept of repression, and state whether this view is reflected in current memory research.

The huge cookie jar in our kitchen was jammed with freshly baked chocolate chip cookies. Still more were cooling across racks on the counter. Twenty-four hours later, not a crumb was left. Who had taken them? During that time, my wife, three children, and I were the only people in the house. So while memories were still fresh, I conducted a little memory test. Andy acknowledged wolfing down as many as 20. Peter admitted eating 15. Laura guessed she had stuffed her then-6-year-old body with 15 cookies. My wife, Carol, recalled eating 6, and I remembered consuming 15 and taking 18 more to the office. We sheepishly accepted responsibility for 89 cookies. Still, we had not come close; there had been 160.

In experiments that parallel the cookie-memory phenomenon, Michael Ross and his colleagues (1981) found that people unknowingly revise their own histories. After Ross persuaded a group of people that frequently brushing their teeth is desirable, they (more than other people) recalled having frequently brushed their teeth in the last two weeks. Having taken a highly touted study skills course, students later inflated their estimates of self-improvement. By *deflating* their evaluations of their previous study habits, they convinced themselves that they had really benefited (Conway & Ross, 1984). To remember our past is often to revise it.

Why do our memories fail us? Why did my family and I not encode, store, and retrieve the actual number of cookies each of us ate? As **FIGURE 28.8** reminds us, we automatically encode sensory information in amazing detail. So was it a storage problem? Might our memories of cookies, like Ebbinghaus' memory of nonsense syllables, have vanished almost as fast as the cookies themselves? Or might the information still be intact but irretrievable because it would be embarrassing to remember?[1]

With his concept of **repression**, Sigmund Freud proposed that our memory systems do indeed self-censor painful information. To protect our self-concept and to minimize anxiety, we supposedly repress painful memories. But the submerged memory lingers, said Freud, and with patience and effort may be retrieved by some later cue or during therapy. One reported case involved a woman with an intense, unexplained fear of running water. One day an aunt solved the mystery. She whispered, "I have never told."

"[It is] necessary to remember that events happened in the desired manner. And if it is necessary to rearrange one's memories . . . then it is necessary to forget that one has done so. The trick of doing this can be learned like any other mental technique. . . . It is called doublethink."

George Orwell, *Nineteen Eighty-Four,* 1948

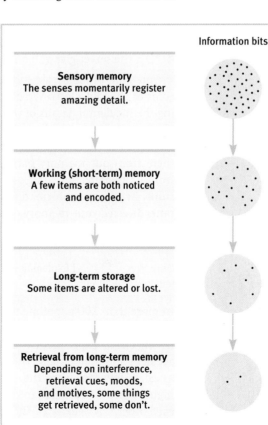

FIGURE 28.8
When do we forget?
Forgetting can occur at any memory stage. As we process information, we filter, alter, or lose much of it.

---

[1]One of my cookie-scarfing sons, on reading this in his father's textbook years later, confessed that he had fibbed "a little."

■ **misinformation effect** incorporating misleading information into one's memory of an event.

The words relit a blown-out candle in the mind; they cued the woman's memory of an incident when, as a disobedient young child, she wandered away from a family picnic and became trapped under a waterfall—until being rescued by her aunt, who promised not to tell her parents (Kihlstrom, 1990). Such stories have fed the now-common belief, shared by 9 in 10 university students, that "memories for painful experiences are sometimes pushed into unconsciousness" (Brown & others, 1996). Repression was central to Freud's psychology and became part of psychology's lore. Most everyone believes it. Therapists often assume it. Yet increasing numbers of memory researchers think repression rarely, if ever, occurs. Earlier we noted that emotions and associated stress hormones *strengthen* memories. But what about horrible happenings? Do people typically have trouble remembering traumatic experiences, or trouble forgetting them? Stay tuned.

Memory Construction

Picture yourself having this experience:

> You go to a fancy restaurant for dinner. You are seated at a table with a white tablecloth. You study the menu. You tell the server you want prime rib, medium rare, a baked potato with sour cream, and a salad with blue cheese dressing. You also order some red wine from the wine list. A few minutes later the server returns with your salad. Later the rest of the meal arrives. You enjoy it all, except the prime rib is a bit overdone.

Were I immediately to quiz you on this paragraph (adapted from Hyde, 1983), you could surely retrieve considerable detail. For example, without looking back, answer the following questions:

1. What kind of salad dressing did you order?
2. Was the tablecloth red checked?
3. What did you order to drink?
4. Did the server give you a menu?

You were probably able to recall exactly what you ordered, and maybe even the color of the tablecloth. We do have an enormous capacity for storing and reproducing the incidental details of our daily experience. But did the server give you a menu? Not in the paragraph given. Nevertheless, many answer yes. We often construct our memories as we encode them, and we may also alter our memories as we withdraw them from our memory bank. Like a scientist who infers a dinosaur's appearance from its remains, we infer our past from stored information plus what we now assume. By filtering information and filling in missing pieces, your schema for restaurants directed your memory construction.

Misinformation and Imagination Effects

OBJECTIVE 28-6 | Explain how misinformation and imagination can distort our memory of an event.

In more than 200 experiments, involving more than 20,000 people, Elizabeth Loftus has shown how eyewitnesses similarly reconstruct their memories when questioned. In one classic experiment with John Palmer, Loftus showed people a film of a traffic accident and then quizzed them about what they saw (Loftus & Palmer, 1974). Those asked, "How fast were the cars going when they *smashed* into each other?" gave higher speed estimates than those asked, "How fast were the cars going when they *hit* each other?" A week later, the researchers asked the viewers if they recalled seeing any broken glass. Compared with those asked the question with *hit,* those who had heard *smashed* were more than twice as likely to say they had seen broken glass (**FIGURE 28.9**). In fact, the film showed no broken glass.

Depiction of actual accident

Memory construction

Leading question:
"About how fast were the cars going when they *smashed* into each other?"

FIGURE **28.9**
Memory construction
When people who had seen the film of a car accident were later asked a leading question, they recalled a more serious accident than they had witnessed. (From Loftus, 1979.)

In many follow-up experiments around the world, people have witnessed an event, received or not received misleading information about it, and then taken a memory test. The repeated result is a **misinformation effect:** After exposure to subtle misinformation, many people misremember. They have misrecalled a yield (give way) sign as a stop sign, hammers as screwdrivers, Coke cans as peanut cans, *Vogue* magazine as *Mademoiselle,* "Dr. Henderson" as "Dr. Davidson," breakfast cereal as eggs, and a clean-shaven man as a man with a mustache (Loftus & others, 1992). As a memory fades with time following an event, the injection of misinformation becomes easier (Loftus, 1992).

So unwitting is the misinformation effect that people later find it nearly impossible to discriminate between their memories of real and suggested events (Schooler & others, 1986). As we recount an experience, we fill in memory gaps with plausible guesses and assumptions. After more retellings, we often recall the guessed details, which have now been absorbed into our memories, as if we had actually observed them (Roediger & others, 1993). Others' vivid retelling of an event may also implant false memories.

Even repeatedly *imagining* nonexistent actions and events can create false memories. In one laboratory experiment, students who repeatedly imagined simple acts such as breaking a toothpick or picking up a stapler later experienced "imagination inflation"; they were more likely to think they had actually done such things during the experiment's first phase (Goff & Roediger, 1998). Two other experiments invited

"Memory is insubstantial. Things keep replacing it. Your batch of snapshots will both fix and ruin your memory.... You can't remember anything from your trip except the wretched collection of snapshots."

Annie Dillard, "To Fashion a Text," 1988

DOONESBURY

■ **source amnesia** attributing to the wrong source an event we have experienced, heard about, read about, or imagined. (Also called *source misattribution*.) Source amnesia, along with the misinformation effect, is at the heart of many false memories.

American and British university students to imagine certain childhood events, such as breaking a window with their hand or having a nurse remove a skin sample from their little finger. In both, one-fourth came to recall that the imagined event really happened (Garry & others, 1996; Mazzoni & Memon, 2003). Imagination inflation occurs partly because visualizing something and actually perceiving it activate similar brain areas (Gonsalves & others, 2004).

Imagined events later seem more familiar, and familiar things seem more real. Thus the more vividly people can imagine things, the more likely they are to inflate their imaginations into memories (Loftus, 2001; Porter & others, 2000). People who believe they have been abducted by aliens for medical exams on spaceships tend to have powerful imaginations and, in memory tests, to be more susceptible to false memories (Clancy & others, 2002). Those who believe they have recovered memories of childhood sexual abuse likewise tend to have vivid imaginations and to score high on false memory tests (Clancy & others, 2000; McNally, 2003).

To see how far the mind's search for a fact will go in creating a fiction, Richard Wiseman and his University of Hertfordshire colleagues (1999) staged eight seances, each attended by 25 curious people. During the supposed seance, the medium—actually a professional actor and magician—asked everyone to concentrate on the moving table. Although it never moved, he suggested that it had: "That's good. Lift the table up. That's good. Keep concentrating. Keep the table in the air." When questioned two weeks later, 34 percent of the participants recalled having actually seen the table levitate.

We psychologists are not immune to memory construction. The psychologist Jean Piaget was startled as an adult to learn that his vivid, detailed memory of his nurse-maid's thwarting his kidnapping was utterly false. Piaget apparently constructed the memory from the many retellings of the story he had heard (which his nursemaid, after undergoing a religious conversion, later confessed to have been false).

"It isn't so astonishing, the number of things I can remember, as the number of things I can remember that aren't so."

Mark Twain (1835–1910)

Source Amnesia

OBJECTIVE 28-7 | Describe source amnesia's contribution to false memories.

Piaget remembered, but attributed his memory to the wrong sources (to his own experience rather than to his nursemaid's stories). When we encode memories, we distribute different aspects of them to different parts of the brain. Among the frailest parts of a memory is its source. Thus, we may recognize someone but have no idea where we have seen the person. Or we imagine or dream an event and later are unsure whether it really happened. Or we may hear something and later recall seeing it (Henkel & others, 2000). In all these cases, we retain the image, but not the context in which we acquired it.

Debra Poole and Stephen Lindsay (1995, 2001, 2002) replicated Piaget's **source amnesia** (also called *source misattribution*). They had preschoolers interact with "Mr. Science," who engaged them in demonstrations such as blowing up a balloon with baking soda and vinegar. Three months later, their parents on three successive days read them a story about themselves and Mr. Science. The stories described some things they had experienced and some they had not. When asked by a new interviewer what Mr. Science had done with them—"Did Mr. Science have a machine with ropes to pull?"—4 in 10 children spontaneously recalled Mr. Science doing things that were only in the story.

Authors and songwriters sometimes suffer source amnesia. They think an idea came from their own creative imagination, when in fact they are unintentionally plagiarizing something they earlier read or heard.

Discerning True and False Memories

OBJECTIVE 28-8 | List some differences and similarities between true and false memories.

Because memory is reconstruction as well as reproduction, we can't be sure whether a memory is real by how real it feels. Much as perceptual illusions may seem like real perceptions, unreal memories feel like real memories.

(a)   (b)

© Simon Niedenthal

FIGURE 28.10
Our assumptions alter our perceptual memories
Researchers Jamin Halberstadt and Paula Niedenthal showed people faces with computer-blended expressions, such as the angry/happy face in (a), then asked them to explain why the person was either angry or happy. Those asked to explain an "angry" expression later (when sliding a bar on a morphing movie to identify the earlier-seen face) remembered an angrier face, such as the one shown in (b).

Indeed, note today's researchers, memories are akin to perceptions—perceptions of the past (Koriat & others, 2000). And as Jamin Halberstadt and Paula Niedenthal (2001) show, people's initial interpretations influence their perceptual memories. They invited New Zealand university students to view morphed faces that expressed a mix of emotions, such as happiness and anger (**FIGURE 28.10a**), and to imagine and explain "why this person is feeling angry [or happy]." A half-hour later, the researchers asked the students to view a computer video showing a morphed transition from the angry to happy face, and to slide a bar to change the face's expression until it matched the expression they had seen earlier (**FIGURE 28.10b**). Students who had explained anger ("This woman is angry because her best friend has cheated on her with her boyfriend") recalled the face as angrier than did those who had explained happiness ("This woman is very happy that everyone remembered her birthday").

We also cannot judge a memory's reality by its persistence. Memory researchers Charles Brainerd and Valerie Reyna (Brainerd & others, 1995, 1998, 2002) note that memories we derive from experience have more detail than memories we derive from imagination. Memories of imagined experiences are more restricted to the *gist* of the supposed event—the meanings and feelings we associate with it. Because gist memories are durable, children's false memories sometimes outlast their true memories, especially as children mature and become better able to process the gist (Brainerd & Poole, 1997). And when therapists or investigators ask for the gist rather than the details, they run a greater risk of eliciting false memories.

False memories created by suggested misinformation and misattributed sources may *feel* as real as true memories and may be very persistent. Imagine that I were to read aloud a list of words such as *candy, sugar, honey,* and *taste.* Later, I ask you to recognize the presented words from a larger list. If you are at all like the people tested by Henry Roediger and Kathleen McDermott (1995), you would err three out of four times—by falsely remembering a nonpresented similar word such as *sweet.* We more easily remember the gist than the words themselves.

In experiments on eyewitness testimony, researchers have repeatedly found that the most confident and consistent eyewitnesses are the most persuasive; however, they often are not the most accurate. Eyewitnesses, whether right or wrong, express roughly similar self-assurance (Bothwell & others, 1987; Cutler & Penrod, 1989; Wells & Murray, 1984).

Memory construction helps explain why "hypnotically refreshed" memories of crimes so easily incorporate errors, some of which originate with the hypnotist's leading questions ("Did you hear loud noises?"). It explains why dating partners who fall in love *over*estimate their first impressions of one another ("It was love at first sight"), while those who break up *under*estimate their earlier liking ("We never really clicked") (McFarland & Ross, 1987). And it explains why people who are asked how they felt 10 years ago about marijuana or gender issues recall attitudes closer to their current views than to the views they actually reported a decade earlier (Markus, 1986).

Older adults' susceptibility to suggested false memories makes them vulnerable to scams, as when a repairperson overcharges by falsely claiming "I told you it would cost X and you agreed to pay" (Jacoby & others, 2005).

"Memory isn't like reading a book; it's more like writing a book from fragmentary notes."
Psychologist John F. Kihlstrom (1994)

Eyewitness recollections
Our memories of witnessed events are falli-ble, especially when prompted by misleading questions. Even our relatively good memories of faces are not photographic, as this police sketch and photo of convicted "Unabomber" killer Theodore Kaczynski show.

One research team interviewed 73 ninth-grade boys and then reinterviewed them 35 years later. When asked to recall how they had reported their attitudes, activities, and experiences, most men recalled statements that matched their actual prior responses at a rate no better than chance. One in three now remembered receiving physical punishment, though as ninth-graders 82 percent said they had (Offer & others, 2000). As George Vaillant (1977, p. 197) noted after following adult lives through time, "It is all too common for caterpillars to become but-terflies and then to maintain that in their youth they had been little butterflies. Maturation makes liars of us all."

Australian psychologist Donald Thompson found his own work on memory distor-tion ironically haunting him when authorities brought him in for questioning about a rape. Although he was a near-perfect match to the victim's memory of the rapist, he had an airtight alibi. Just before the rape occurred, Thompson was being interviewed on live television. He could not possibly have made it to the crime scene. Then it came to light that the victim had been watching the interview—ironically about face recognition—and had experienced source amnesia, confusing her memories of Thompson with those of the rapist (Schacter, 1996).

Recognizing that the misinformation effect can occur as police and attorneys ask questions framed by their own understandings of an event, Ronald Fisher, Edward Geiselman, and their colleagues (1987, 1992) train police interviewers to ask less suggestive, more effective questions. To activate retrieval cues, the detective first asks witnesses to visualize the scene—the weather, time of day, lighting, sounds, smells, positions of objects, and their mood. Then the witness tells in detail, and without in-terruption, every point recalled, no matter how trivial. Only then does the detective ask evocative follow-up questions: "Was there anything unusual about the person's appearance or clothing?" When this *cognitive interview technique* is used, Fisher and Geiselman report, accurate recall increases by some 50 percent.

Children's Eyewitness Recall

OBJECTIVE 28-9 | Give arguments supporting and rejecting the position that very young children's reports of abuse are reliable.

If memories can be sincere, yet sincerely wrong, might children's recollections of sex-ual abuse be prone to err? Who is most often victimized—abused children whose rec-ollections are disbelieved or falsely accused adults whose reputations are ruined?

At issue is the reliability of children's reports. As we have seen, interviewers who ask leading questions can plant false memories. We also know that although children are sometimes accurate eyewitnesses in criminal cases, they tend to be suggestible. Many young children have falsely reported that a nurse had licked their knee, a man had put "something yucky" in their mouth, their doctor had put a stick in their geni-tals, and someone had touched their private parts. When suggestive interview tech-niques are added, most preschoolers and many older children can be induced to report false events, such as seeing a thief steal food in their day-care center (Bruck & Ceci, 1999, 2004).

Nevertheless, if questioned about their experiences in neutral words they under-stand, children often accurately recall what happened and who did it (Goodman & others, 1990; Howe, 1997; Pipe, 1996). When the cognitive interview described ear-lier is used, even 4- to 5-year-old children produce more accurate recall (Holliday & Albon, 2004; Pipe & others, 2004). Children are especially accurate when involved adults have not talked with them prior to the interview and when their disclosure is made in a first interview with a neutral person who asks nonleading questions.

Studies of children's recollections of physical examinations illustrate both their reasonable accuracy and occasional lapses. Lynne Baker-Ward and her colleagues (1993) tested children's memories with general questions ("Tell me what the doctor did to check you") and specific questions ("Did the doctor shine a light in your eyes?"). Three to six weeks after the exam, 3-year-olds recalled about 60 percent and 7-year-olds about 90 percent of what the doctor did. Asked about things that didn't happen ("Did the doctor cut your hair?" "Did the nurse sit on top of you?"), 3-year-olds gave wrong answers nearly 30 percent of the time; 7-year-olds erred only about 15 percent of the time.

Stephen Ceci (1993) thinks "it would be truly awful to ever lose sight of the enormity of child abuse." Yet Ceci and Maggie Bruck's (1993, 1995) studies of children's memories have sensitized them to children's suggestibility. In one study, they asked 3-year-olds to show on anatomically correct dolls where a pediatrician had touched them. Fifty-five percent of the children who had not received genital examinations pointed to either genital or anal areas.

In another study, Ceci and Bruck had a child choose a card from a deck of possible happenings and an adult then read from the card. For example, "Think real hard, and tell me if this ever happened to you. Can you remember going to the hospital with a mousetrap on your finger?" After 10 weekly interviews, with the same adult repeatedly asking children to think about several real and fictitious events, a new adult asked the same question. The stunning result: 58 percent of preschoolers produced false (often vivid) stories regarding one or more events they had never experienced, as this little boy did (Ceci & others, 1994):

> My brother Colin was trying to get Blowtorch [an action figure] from me, and I wouldn't let him take it from me, so he pushed me into the wood pile where the mousetrap was. And then my finger got caught in it. And then we went to the hospital, and my mommy, daddy, and Colin drove me there, to the hospital in our van, because it was far away. And the doctor put a bandage on this finger.

Given such detailed stories, professional psychologists who specialize in interviewing children were often fooled. They could not reliably separate real memories from false ones. Nor could the children themselves. The above child, reminded that his parents had told him several times that the mousetrap incident never happened—that he had imagined it—protested, "But it really did happen. I remember it!"

Repressed or Constructed Memories of Abuse?

OBJECTIVE 28-10 | Discuss the controversy over reports of repressed and recovered memories of childhood sexual abuse.

During the 1990s, psychology's most intense controversy—the "memory wars"—concerned claims of repressed and recovered memories of childhood sexual abuse. During 2002, such claims surfaced again amid seemingly more credible accusations of sexual abuse by some priests. Are clinicians who have guided people in "recovering" memories of childhood abuse triggering false memories that damage innocent adults, or are they uncovering the truth?

Some therapists have reasoned with patients that "people who've been abused often have your symptoms, so you probably were abused. Let's see if, aided by hypnosis or drugs, or helped to dig back and visualize your trauma, you can recover it." In one American survey, the average therapist estimated that 11 percent of the population—some 34 million people—have repressed memories of childhood sexual abuse (Kamena, 1998). In another survey, of British and American doctoral-level therapists, 7 in 10 said they had used techniques such as hypnosis or drugs to help clients recover suspected repressed memories of childhood sexual abuse (Poole & others, 1995).

> "[The] research leads me to worry about the possibility of false allegations. It is not a tribute to one's scientific integrity to walk down the middle of the road if the data are more to one side."
>
> Stephen Ceci (1993)

As we might expect from the research on source amnesia and the misinformation effect, many patients exposed to such techniques do form an image of a threatening person. With further visualization, the image grows more vivid, leaving the patient stunned, angry, and ready to confront or sue the equally stunned and devastated parent, relative, or clergy member. As the therapist has predicted, the presumed abuser then vigorously denies the accusation. One woman in her thirty-second therapy session recalled that her father had abused her at age 15 months. After such aided recall, actress Roseanne Barr (1991) claimed to have recovered memories of sexual abuse beginning in infancy.

Without questioning the professionalism of most therapists, skeptics compare the uncorroborated accusations suggested by some therapists to a 1990s reenactment of the Salem witch trials. Clinicians who use "memory work" techniques such as "guided imagery," hypnosis, and dream analysis to recover memories "are nothing more than merchants of mental chaos, and, in fact, constitute a blight on the entire field of psychotherapy," charged some scientific critics (Loftus & others, 1995). Irate clinicians counter that those who dispute recovered memories of abuse add to abused people's trauma and play into the hands of child molesters.

In an effort to find a sensible common ground that might resolve this ideological battle, study panels have been convened and public statements made by the American Medical, American Psychological, and American Psychiatric Associations; the Australian Psychological Society; the British Psychological Society; and the Canadian Psychiatric Association. Those committed to protecting abused children and those committed to protecting wrongly accused adults agree on the following:

- *Injustice happens.* Some innocent people have been falsely convicted. Some guilty people have evaded responsibility by casting doubt on their truth-telling accusers.
- *Incest and other sexual abuse happen.* And it happens more often than we once supposed. There is no characteristic "survivor syndrome" (Kendall-Tackett & others, 1993). However, sexual abuse can leave its victims predisposed to problems ranging from sexual dysfunction to depression.
- *Forgetting happens.* Many of the abused were either very young when abused or may not have understood the meaning of their experience—circumstances under which forgetting is "utterly common." Forgetting isolated past events, both negative and positive, is an ordinary part of everyday life.
- *Recovered memories are commonplace.* Cued by a remark or an experience, we recover memories of long-forgotten events, both pleasant and unpleasant. What is debated is whether the unconscious mind sometimes forcibly represses painful experiences and, if so, whether these can be retrieved by certain therapist-aided techniques.
- *Memories "recovered" under hypnosis or the influence of drugs are especially unreliable.* "Age-regressed" hypnotized subjects incorporate suggestions into their memories, even memories of "past lives."
- *Memories of things happening before age 3 are also unreliable.* People do not reliably recall happenings of any sort from their first 3 years—a phenomenon called *infantile amnesia.* Most psychologists—including most clinical and counseling psychologists—therefore are skeptical of "recovered" memories of abuse during infancy (Gore-Felton & others, 2000; Knapp & VandeCreek, 2000). The older a child's age when suffering sexual abuse, and the more severe it was, the more likely it is to be remembered (Goodman & others, 2003).
- *Memories, whether real or false, can be emotionally upsetting.* If a false memory of abuse becomes a real part of one's history, both the accuser and the accused may suffer. What was born of mere suggestion can, like an actual trauma, become a stinging memory that may drive bodily stress (McNally, 2003). People

"When memories are 'recovered' after long periods of amnesia, particularly when extraordinary means were used to secure the recovery of memory, there is a high probability that the memories are false."
Royal College of Psychiatrists Working Group on Reported Recovered Memories of Child Sexual Abuse (Brandon & others, 1998)

TODAY'S SPECIAL GUEST

BRUNDAGE MORNALD, OF
BATTLE CREEK, MONTANA
UNDER HYPNOSIS, MR. MORNALD
RECOVERED LONG-BURIED
MEMORIES OF A PERFECTLY
NORMAL, HAPPY CHILDHOOD.

knocked unconscious by unremembered accidents sometimes later develop stress disorders when haunted by memories constructed from photos, news reports, and friends' accounts (Bryant, 2001).

To more closely approximate therapist-aided recall, Elizabeth Loftus and her colleagues (1996) have experimentally implanted false memories of childhood traumas. In one study, she had a trusted family member recall for a teenager three real childhood experiences and a false one—a vivid account of the child's being lost for an extended time in a shopping mall at age 5 until being rescued by an elderly person. Two days later, one participant, Chris, said, "That day I was so scared that I would never see my family again." Two days after that, he began to visualize the flannel shirt, bald head, and glasses of the old man who supposedly had found him. Told the story was made up, Chris was incredulous: "I thought I remembered being lost . . . and looking around for the guys. I do remember that, and then crying, and Mom coming up and saying, 'Where were you? Don't you . . . ever do that again.'" In other experiments, a third of participants have become wrongly convinced that they almost drowned as a child, and about half were led to falsely recall an awful experience, such as a vicious animal attack (Heaps & Nash, 2001; Porter & others, 1999).

Such is the memory construction process by which people can recall being abducted by UFOs, victimized by a satanic cult, molested in a crib, or living a past life. Thousands of reasonable, normally functioning human beings, notes Loftus, "speak in terror-stricken voices about their experience aboard flying saucers. They *remember*, clearly and vividly, being abducted by aliens" (Loftus & Ketcham, 1994, p. 66).

Loftus knows firsthand the phenomenon she studies. At a family reunion, an uncle told her that at age 14, she found her mother's drowned body. Shocked, she denied it. But the uncle was adamant, and over the next three days she began to wonder if *she* had a repressed memory. "Maybe that's why I'm so obsessed with this topic." As the now-upset Loftus pondered her uncle's suggestion, she "recovered" an image of her mother lying in the pool, face down, and of herself finding the body. "I started putting everything into place. Maybe that's why I'm such a workaholic. Maybe that's why I'm so emotional when I think about her even though she died in 1959."

Then her brother called and said there had been a mistake. Her uncle now remembered what other relatives also confirmed. Aunt Pearl, not Loftus, had found the body (Loftus & Ketcham, 1994; Monaghan, 1992).

But then again, Loftus also knows firsthand the reality of sexual abuse. A male baby-sitter molested her when she was 6 years old. She has not forgotten. And that makes her wary of those whom she sees as trivializing real abuse by suggesting and seeking out uncorroborated traumatic experiences, then accepting them uncritically as fact.

Although scorned by some trauma therapists, Loftus has been elected president of the science-oriented Association for Psychological Science, awarded psychology's biggest prize ($200,000), and elected to the U.S. National Academy of Sciences and the Royal Society of Edinburgh.

Elizabeth Loftus
"The research findings for which I am being honored now generated a level of hostility and opposition I could never have foreseen. People wrote threatening letters, warning me that my reputation and even my safety were in jeopardy if I continued along these lines. At some universities, armed guards were provided to accompany me during speeches." Elizabeth Loftus, on receiving the Association for Psychological Science's William James Fellow Award, 2001

The enemies of the truly victimized are not only those who prey and those who deny, she says, but those whose writings and allegations "are bound to lead to an increased likelihood that society in general will disbelieve the genuine cases of childhood sexual abuse that truly deserve our sustained attention" (Loftus, 1993).

So, does repression of threatening memories ever occur? Psychologists continue to have heated debates on this topic, which is the cornerstone of Freud's theory and a recurring theme in much popular psychology. But this much now appears certain: The most common response to a traumatic experience (witnessing a parent's murder, experiencing the horrors of a Nazi death camp, being terrorized by a hijacker or a rapist, escaping the collapsing World Trade Center towers, surviving the Asian tsunami) is not banishment of the experience into the unconscious. Rather, such experiences are typically etched on the mind as vivid, persistent, haunting memories. Playwright Eugene O'Neill understood. As one of the characters in his *Strange Interlude* (1928) exclaimed, "The devil! . . . what beastly incidents our memories insist on cherishing!"

Improving Memory

OBJECTIVE 28-11 | Explain how an understanding of memory can contribute to effective study techniques.

How might we apply memory principles in everyday situations—perhaps to better remember a person's name or even the material of this module?

Now and then we are dismayed at our forgetfulness—at our embarrassing inability to recall someone's name, at forgetting to bring up a point in conversation, at forgetting to bring along something important, at finding ourselves standing in a room unable to recall why we are there (Herrmann, 1982). Is there anything we can do to minimize such misdeeds of our memory system? Much as biology benefits medicine and botany benefits agriculture, so can the psychology of memory benefit education. Here for easy reference is a summary of concrete suggestions for improving memory. The SQ3R—*Survey, Question, Read, Rehearse, Review*—study technique used in this book incorporates several of these strategies.

Study repeatedly to boost long-term recall. Overlearn. To learn a name, say it to yourself after being introduced; wait a few seconds and say it again; wait longer and say it again. To learn a concept, provide yourself with many separate study sessions: Take advantage of life's little intervals—riding on the bus, walking across campus, waiting for class to start.

Spend more time rehearsing or actively thinking about the material. New memories are weak; exercise them and they will strengthen. Speed-reading (skimming) complex material—with minimal rehearsal—yields little retention. Rehearsal and critical reflection help more. It pays to study actively!

Make the material personally meaningful. To build a network of retrieval cues, take thorough text and class notes in your own words. Answer the Ask Yourself questions (at the end of each module) to apply the concepts to your own life. Mindlessly repeating someone else's words is relatively ineffective. It is better to form images, understand and organize information, relate the material to what you already know or have experienced, and put it in your own words. Without such cues, you may find yourself stuck when a question uses phrasing different from the rote forms you memorized. To increase retrieval cues, form as many associations as possible.

To remember a list of unfamiliar items, use mnemonic devices. Make up a story to associate items with memorable images or jingles. Vivid images or words

> "Horror sears memory, leaving . . . the consuming memories of atrocity."
>
> Robert Kraft, *Memory Perceived: Recalling the Holocaust*, 2002

> "I have discovered that it is of some use when you lie in bed at night and gaze into the darkness to repeat in your mind the things you have been studying. Not only does it help the understanding, but also the memory."
>
> Leonardo da Vinci (1452–1519)

> "Knit each new thing on to some acquisition already there."
>
> William James, *Principles of Psychology*, 1890

in familiar rhymes can act as pegs on which you can "hang" items. Chunk information into acronyms.

Refresh your memory by activating retrieval cues. Mentally re-create the situation and the mood in which the original learning occurred. Return to the same location. Jog your memory by allowing one thought to cue the next.

Recall events while they are fresh, before you encounter possible misinformation. If you are an eyewitness to an important event, record your memory before allowing others to suggest what may have occurred.

Minimize interference. Study before sleeping. Do not schedule back-to-back study times for topics that are likely to interfere with each other, such as Spanish and French.

Test your own knowledge, both to rehearse it and to help determine what you do not yet know. If you must recall information later, do not be lulled into overconfidence by your ability to recognize it. Test your recall using the learning objectives. Outline modules or shorter sections on a blank page. Define terms and concepts listed at each module's end before turning back to their definitions. Take practice tests (see the Test Yourself questions on the final page of each module). The printed study guide that accompanies this text and the companion Web site (www.worthpublishers.com/myers) are both good sources for such self-tests.

Thinking and memory
Most of what we know is not the result of efforts to memorize. We learn because we're curious and because we spend time thinking about our experiences. Actively thinking as we read, by rehearsing and relating ideas, yields the best retention.

Without self-testing, one can easily become overconfident, as John Shaughnessy and Eugene Zechmeister (1992) found in an experiment with two groups of students. A "reread group" repeatedly read dozens of factual statements, then judged the likelihood that they would remember each fact, and finally were tested on their recall. Students in this group felt fairly confident of their knowledge, even on the questions they later missed. Students in a "practice test group" also read the statements, but they then spent the rest of the time responding to tests that required them to retrieve the facts. Compared with the "reread" group, the practice-test group did just as well on the final recall test. What is more, they could better discriminate what they did and did not know. It is clear that self-testing enhances recall and can help you to know what you know—and thus enables you to focus your study time on what you do not yet know. As former British Prime Minister Benjamin Disraeli once said, "To be conscious that you are ignorant is a great step to knowledge."

>> LEARNING OUTCOMES

Forgetting, Memory Construction, and Memory Improvement

OBJECTIVE 28-1 | **Explain why we should value our ability to forget, and distinguish three general ways our memory fails us.**
Without an ability to forget, we would be overwhelmed by out-of-date and irrelevant information. Our memory can fail us through *forgetting* (absent-mindedness, transience, and blocking), *distortion* (misattribution, suggestibility, and bias), or *intrusion* (persistence of unwanted memories).

OBJECTIVE 28-2 | **Discuss the role of encoding failure in forgetting.**
What we encode (whether automatically or through effortful processing) is only a very limited portion of the sensory stimuli around us. And as we age, our encoding grows slower and less efficient. Without encoding, information does not enter our long-term memory store and cannot be retrieved.

OBJECTIVE 28-3 | **Discuss the concept of storage decay, and describe Ebbinghaus' forgetting curve.**
Encoded memories may fade after storage. Ebbinghaus' research on learning and retention showed that the course of forgetting is initially rapid, then levels off with time. This trend is known as the *forgetting curve.*

OBJECTIVE 28-4 | **Contrast proactive and retroactive interference, and explain how they can cause retrieval failure.**
Retrieval failure can happen when old and new information compete for retrieval. In *proactive interference,* something learned in the past (a friend's old phone number) interferes with our ability to recall something recently learned (the friend's new number). In *retroactive interference,* something recently learned (vocabulary in this semester's Spanish course) interferes with something learned in the past (vocabulary in last year's French course).

OBJECTIVE 28-5 | **Summarize Freud's concept of repression, and state whether this view is reflected in current memory research.**
Freud believed we banish from conscious thought anxiety-arousing thoughts, feelings, and memories. In his view, this motivated forgetting (*repression*) submerges memories but leaves them available for later retrieval under the right conditions. Memory researchers tend to believe repression rarely occurs.

OBJECTIVE 28-6 | **Explain how misinformation and imagination can distort our memory of an event.**
Memories are not stored or retrieved as exact copies of our experiences. Rather, we construct our memories, using both stored and new information. If children or adults are subtly exposed to misinformation after an event, or if they repeatedly imagine and rehearse an event that never occurred, they may incorporate the misleading details into their memory of what actually happened. Memory is thus best understood not only as a cognitive and a biological phenomenon, but also as a social-cultural phenomenon (see **FIGURE 28.11**)

FIGURE 28.11
Levels of analysis for the study of memory
As with other psychological phenomena, memory is fruitfully studied at biological, psychological, and social-cultural levels.

OBJECTIVE 28-7 | **Describe source amnesia's contribution to false memories.**
When we process memories, we encode and store various aspects of them in different locations in the brain. In reassembling a memory during retrieval, we may successfully retrieve something we have heard, read, or imagined, but attribute it to the wrong source. *Source amnesia* is one of two main components of false memories. (The other is the misinformation effect.)

OBJECTIVE 28-8 | **List some differences and similarities between true and false memories.**
False memories feel like true memories and are equally durable, so neither the sincerity nor the longevity of a memory signifies it is real. True memories contain more details than imagined ones, which tend to be the gist of an event—the meaning and feelings associated with it.

OBJECTIVE 28-9 | **Give arguments supporting and rejecting the position that very young children's reports of abuse are reliable.**
A supporting argument: Even very young children can accurately recall events (and the people involved) if a neutral person talks with them in words they can understand, asks nonleading questions, and uses the cognitive interview technique. *A rejecting*

argument: Preschoolers are more suggestible than older children or adults, and they can be induced, through suggestive questions, to report false events.

OBJECTIVE 28-10 | **Discuss the controversy over reports of repressed and recovered memories of childhood sexual abuse.**

Psychologists motivated to protect abused children and wrongly accused adults tend to agree on seven points: (1) Innocent people have been falsely convicted of abuse that never happened, and true abusers have used the controversy over recovered memories to avoid punishment. (2) Incest and abuse happen, and they can leave lasting scars. (3) Forgetting isolated past events, either good or bad, is an everyday occurrence for all of us. (4) Recovering good or bad memories, triggered by some memory cue, is commonplace, but memory researchers question whether we forcibly repress memories, in Freud's sense, to avoid anxiety or pain. (5) Memories obtained under the influence of hypnosis or drugs are unreliable. (6) Infantile amnesia—the inability to recall memories from the first three years of life—makes recovery of very early childhood memories unlikely. (7) Both real and false memories cause suffering and can lead to stress disorders.

OBJECTIVE 28-11 | **Explain how an understanding of memory can contribute to effective study techniques.**

The psychology of memory suggests concrete strategies for improving memory. These include scheduling spaced study times; actively rehearsing information to be learned; aiding encoding by making well-organized, vivid, and personally meaningful associations; using mnemonic techniques; returning to contexts and moods that are rich with associations; recording memories before misinformation can corrupt them; minimizing interference; and self-testing to rehearse information and find gaps in your memory.

TERMS AND CONCEPTS TO REMEMBER

proactive interference, p. 28-3   misinformation effect, p. 28-7
retroactive interference, p. 28-3   source amnesia, p. 28-8
repression, p. 28-5

TEST YOURSELF

1. Can you offer an example of proactive interference?
2. What—given the commonality of source amnesia—might life be like if we remembered all our waking experiences and all our dreams?
3. What are the recommended memory strategies you just read about? (One advised rehearsing to-be-remembered material. What were the others?)

(Answers in Appendix B.)

ASK YOURSELF

1. Most people, especially as they grow older, wish for a better memory. Is that true of you? Or do you more often wish you could discard old memories?
2. Could you be an impartial jury member in a trial of a parent accused of sexual abuse based on a recovered memory, or of a therapist being sued for creating a false memory of abuse?
3. Which of the study and memory strategies suggested in this section will work best for you?

ANSWER TO QUESTION WITHIN THE MODULE

Q. Which penny in Figure 28.2 is the real thing?
A. The first penny (a) is the real penny.

>WEB

Multiple-choice *self-tests* and more may be found at www.worthpublishers.com/myers.

ANOTHER VOICE ON: THINKING, LANGUAGE, AND INTELLIGENCE

ALLISON JOSEPH (B. 1967), FROM "ON BEING TOLD I DON'T SPEAK LIKE A BLACK PERSON," 1999

Now I realize there's nothing
more personal than speech,
that I don't have to defend
how I speak, how any person,
black, white, chooses to speak.
Let us speak. Let us talk
with the sounds of our mothers

and fathers still reverberating
in our minds, wherever our mothers
or fathers come from:
Arkansas, Belize, Alabama,
Brazil, Aruba, Arizona.
Let us simply speak
to one another,

listen and prize the inflections,
never assuming how any person will sound
until his mouth opens, until her
mouth opens, greetings welcome
in any language.

Thinking, Language, and Intelligence

Throughout history, we humans have both deplored our foolishness and celebrated our wisdom. The poet T. S. Eliot was struck by "the hollow men . . . Headpiece filled with straw." But Shakespeare's Hamlet extolled the human species as "noble in reason! . . . infinite in faculties! . . . in apprehension how like a god!" Throughout this text, we likewise marvel both at our capabilities and at our propensity to err.

We have studied the human brain—3 pounds of wet tissue the size of a small cabbage, yet containing circuitry more complex than the planet's telephone networks. We have appreciated the competence of newborn infants. We have relished the human sensory system, which disassembles visual stimuli into millions of nerve impulses, distributes them for parallel processing, and then reassembles them into clear and colorful perceived images. We have pondered our memory's seemingly limitless capacity and the ease with which we process information, consciously and unconsciously. Little wonder that our species has had the collective genius to invent the camera, the car, and the computer; to unlock the atom and crack the genetic code; to travel out to space and into the oceans' depths.

Yet we have also seen that our species is kin to the other animals, influenced by the same principles that produce learning in rats and pigeons. As one pundit said, echoing Pavlov, how like a dog! We have noted that we assimilate reality into our preconceptions and succumb to perceptual illusions. We have seen how easily we deceive ourselves about pseudopsychic claims, hypnotic feats, and false memories.

In Modules 29 and 30, we encounter further instances of these two images of the human condition—the rational and the irrational. We will see how we form concepts, solve problems, and make judgments. We will look at our flair for language and ask whether our species alone has this capability.

In Modules 31 through 33, we focus on an ongoing debate about *intelligence,* in which psychologists and others pick sides on two major questions: (1) Does each of us have an inborn general mental capacity (intelligence), and (2) can we quantify this capacity as a meaningful number?

Thinking

OBJECTIVE 29-1 | Define *cognition*.

Our brain receives, perceives, stores, and retrieves information. How then does our cognitive system use this information—logically and illogically—as we form concepts that organize our world, solve problems, and make efficient decisions and judgments? What strategies do we typically use? What biases put us at risk for error?

Thinking, or **cognition,** refers to all the mental activities associated with processing, understanding, remembering, and communicating. *Cognitive psychologists* study these mental activities. By thinking about thinking, and by alerting us to common errors in our thinking, cognitive psychologists help us think *smart.* Their research helps us appreciate both the powers and the limits of our intuition, and to reason more effectively when making practical decisions and everyday judgments.

We begin with the building blocks of thinking: concepts. As you read this discussion and others in this module, join me in reflecting on how deserving we are of our name, *Homo sapiens*—wise human.

Concepts

OBJECTIVE 29-2 | Describe the roles of categories, hierarchies, definitions, and prototypes in concept formation.

To think about the countless events, objects, and people in our world, we simplify things. We form **concepts**—mental groupings of similar objects, events, and people. The concept *chair* includes a variety of items—a baby's high chair, a reclining chair, the chairs around a dining room table, a dentist's chair—all of which are for sitting. Chairs vary, but it is their common features that define the concept of *chair.*

Imagine life without concepts. We would need a different name for every object and idea. We could not ask a child to "throw the ball" because there would be no concept of *ball* (or *throw*). Instead of saying, "They were angry," we would have to describe facial expressions, vocal intensities, gestures, and words. Such concepts as *ball* and *angry* provide us with much information without much cognitive effort.

To simplify things further, we organize concepts into category *hierarchies* (**FIGURE 29.1**). Cab drivers organize their cities into geographical sectors, which subdivide into neighborhoods and again into blocks. Once our categories exist, we use them efficiently. Shown a bird, car, or food, people need no more time to identify an item's category than to perceive that something is there. "As soon as you know it is there, you know what it is," report Kalanit Grill-Spector and Nancy Kanwisher (2005).

We form some concepts by *definition.* Told the rule that a triangle has three sides, we thereafter classify all three-sided geometric forms as triangles. More often, however, we form our concepts by developing **prototypes**—a mental image or best example that incorporates all the features we associate with a category (Rosch, 1978). The more closely something matches our prototype of a concept, the more readily we recognize it as an example of the concept. A robin and a goose both satisfy our definition of *bird:* a two-footed animal that has wings and feathers and hatches from an egg. Yet people

■ **cognition** the mental activities associated with thinking, knowing, remembering, and communicating.

■ **concept** a mental grouping of similar objects, events, ideas, or people.

■ **prototype** a mental image or best example of a category. Matching new items to the prototype provides a quick and easy method for including items in a category (as when comparing feathered creatures to a prototypical bird, such as a robin).

"Attention, everyone! I'd like to introduce the newest member of our family."

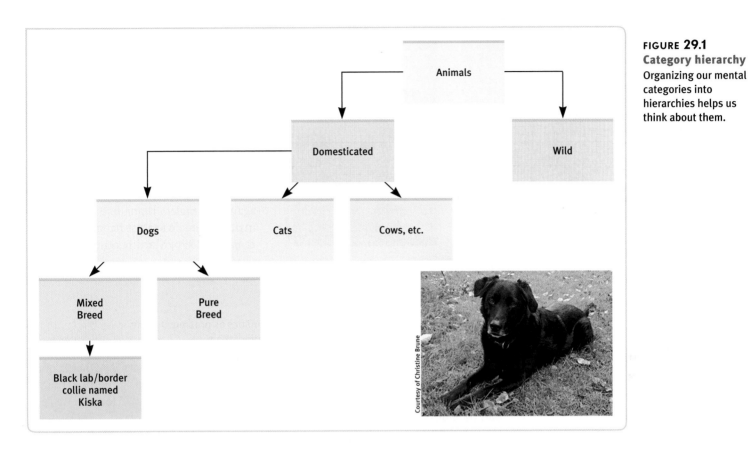

FIGURE **29.1**
Category hierarchy
Organizing our mental categories into hierarchies helps us think about them.

agree more quickly that "a robin is a bird" than that "a goose is a bird." For most of us, the robin, with its smaller beak and overall size, and its easier flight, is the birdier bird; it more closely resembles our bird prototype.

Once we place an item in a category, our memory for it later shifts toward the category prototype. Olivier Corneille and his colleagues (2004) found memory shifts after showing Belgian students ethnically mixed faces. For example, when shown a face that was a blend of 70 percent of the features of a Caucasian person and 30 percent of an Asian person, people categorized the face as Caucasian and later recalled having seen a more prototypically Caucasian person. (They were more likely to recall an 80 percent Caucasian face than the 70 percent Caucasian they actually saw.) If shown a 70 percent Asian face, they later recalled a more prototypically Asian face (**FIGURE 29.2**). A follow-up study found the phenomenon with gender as well. For example, those shown 70 percent male faces categorized them as male (no surprise there), and then later misrecalled them as even more prototypically male (Huart & others, 2005).

Move away from our prototypes, and categories may have fuzzy boundaries. Is a whale a mammal? Is a tomato a fruit? Is a 17-year-old female a girl or a woman? Are penguins and kiwis birds? Because these nonflying creatures fail to match our prototype, we are slower to recognize them as birds. Similarly, we are slow to perceive an illness when our symptoms don't fit one of our disease prototypes (Bishop, 1991).

FIGURE **29.2**
Face categorization influences our recollection
For example, shown a face that was 70 percent Caucasian, people tended to classify the person as Caucasian and to recollect the face as more Caucasian than it was. (From Corneille & others, 2004.)

90% CA   80% CA   70% CA   60% CA   50%/50%   60% AS   70% AS   80% AS   90% AS

People whose heart attack symptoms (shortness of breath, exhaustion, a dull weight in the chest) don't match their prototype of a heart attack (sharp chest pain) may not seek help. And when discrimination doesn't fit our prejudice prototypes—of White against Black, male against female, young against old—we often fail to notice it. People more easily detect male prejudice against females than female against males or female against females (Inman & Baron, 1996; Marti & others, 2000).

Solving Problems

OBJECTIVE 29-3 | Compare algorithms and heuristics as problem-solving strategies, and explain how insight differs from both of them.

One tribute to our rationality is our ability to form and use concepts. Another is our skill at solving problems as we cope with novel situations. What's the best route around this traffic jam? How shall we respond to a friend's criticism? How can we get into the house when we've lost our keys?

Some problems we solve through trial and error. Thomas Edison tried thousands of light bulb filaments before stumbling upon one that worked. For other problems, we may follow an **algorithm,** a step-by-step procedure that guarantees a solution. Told to find another word using all the letters in *SPLOYOCHYG,* we could try each letter in each position, but generating and examining the 907,200 resulting permutations would be exasperating. Because step-by-step algorithms can be laborious (well-suited to computers), we often solve problems with simple strategies called **heuristics.** Thus, in rearranging the letters of *SPLOYOCHYG,* we might exclude letter combinations such as two *Y*'s together. By using heuristics to reduce the number of options, and then applying trial and error, you may hit upon the answer (or see the final page of this module).

Heuristic searching
To search for guava juice you could search every supermarket aisle (an algorithm) or check the bottled beverage, natural foods, and produce sections (heuristics). The heuristic approach is often speedier, but an algorithmic search guarantees you will find it eventually.

Sometimes we are unaware of using any problem-solving strategy; the answer just comes to us. We can all recall occasions when we puzzled over a problem. Then, suddenly, the pieces fell together and we perceived the solution. Such sudden flashes of inspiration we call **insight.** Ten-year-old Johnny Appleton displayed insight in solving a problem that had stumped construction workers: how to rescue a young robin that had fallen into a narrow 30-inch-deep hole in a cement-block wall. Johnny's solution: to slowly pour in sand, giving the bird enough time to keep its feet on top of the constantly rising sand (Ruchlis, 1990).

A team of researchers, including psychologists Mark Jung-Beeman, John Kounios, and Edward Bowden (2004), have identified brain activity associated with sudden flashes of insight. They gave people sets of three words, such as *pine, crab, sauce,* and asked them to think of another word that could form a compound word or phrase with each. Participants pressed a button when they achieved the solution (in this case: *apple*). About half the solutions were by a sudden Aha! insight. The researchers mapped either the location of the brain's associated neural activity (using fMRI) or its electrical signature (using EEG). When the solutions occurred with sudden insight, both methods showed a burst of activity in the right temporal lobe, just above the ear (**FIGURE 29.3**). One type of brain activity, which seemingly corresponded to the unconscious processing popping into a conscious insight, preceded the button pressing by about 0.3 second.

FIGURE 29.3
The Aha! moment
A burst of right temporal lobe activity accompanies insight solutions to word problems.

Insight provides a sense of satisfaction. After solving a difficult problem or discovering how to resolve a conflict, we feel happy. The joy of a joke may similarly lie in our capacity for insight—our sudden comprehension of an unexpected ending or a double meaning, as illustrated in the two jokes rated funniest (among 2 million ratings of 40,000 submitted jokes) in an Internet humor study co-sponsored by Richard Wiseman (2002) and the British Association for the Advancement of Science. First, the runner-up:

> Sherlock Holmes and Dr. Watson are going camping. They pitch their tent under the stars and go to sleep. Sometime in the middle of the night Holmes wakes Watson up.
>
> **Holmes:** "Watson, look up at the stars, and tell me what you deduce."
> **Watson:** "I see millions of stars and even if a few of those have planets, it's quite likely there are some planets like Earth, and if there are a few planets like Earth out there, there might also be life. What does it tell you, Holmes?"
> **Holmes:** "Watson, you idiot, somebody has stolen our tent!"

And roll the drums for the winner:

> A couple of New Jersey hunters are out in the woods when one of them falls to the ground. He doesn't seem to be breathing, his eyes are rolled back in his head. The other guy whips out his cell phone and calls the emergency services. He gasps to the operator: "My friend is dead! What can I do?" The operator, in a calm, soothing voice says: "Just take it easy. I can help. First, let's make sure he's dead." There is a silence, then a shot is heard. The guy's voice comes back on the line: "OK, now what?"

Obstacles to Problem Solving

OBJECTIVE 29-4 | Contrast confirmation bias and fixation, and explain how they can interfere with effective problem solving.

Inventive as we can be in solving problems, the correct answer may elude us. Two cognitive tendencies—*confirmation bias* and *fixation*—often lead us astray.

Confirmation Bias

A major obstacle to problem solving is our eagerness to search for information that confirms our ideas, a phenomenon known as **confirmation bias.** Peter Wason (1960) demonstrated this tendency by giving British university students the three-number

■ **algorithm** a methodical, logical rule or procedure that guarantees solving a particular problem. Contrasts with the usually speedier—but also more error-prone—use of *heuristics*.

■ **heuristic** a simple thinking strategy that often allows us to make judgments and solve problems efficiently; usually speedier but also more error-prone than *algorithms*.

■ **insight** a sudden and often novel realization of the solution to a problem; it contrasts with strategy-based solutions.

■ **confirmation bias** a tendency to search for information that confirms one's preconceptions.

sequence 2-4-6 and asking them to guess the rule he had used to devise the series. (The rule was simple: any three ascending numbers.) Before submitting their answers, the students generated their own sets of three numbers, and each time Wason told them whether their sets conformed to his rule. Once they had done enough testing to feel *certain* they had the rule, they were to announce it. The result? Seldom right but never in doubt. Most of Wason's students convinced themselves of a wrong rule. Typically, they formed a wrong idea ("Maybe it's counting by twos") and then searched only for confirming evidence (by testing 6-8-10, 100-102-104, and so forth).

Such experiments reveal that we seek evidence verifying our ideas more eagerly than we seek evidence that might refute them (Klayman & Ha, 1987; Skov & Sherman, 1986). Business managers, for example, are more likely to follow the successful careers of those they once hired than to track the achievements of those they rejected, leading them to confirm their own perceived hiring ability. "Ordinary people," said Wason (1981), "evade facts, become inconsistent, or systematically defend themselves against the threat of new information relevant to the issue."

The results of doing so sometimes are momentous. The United States launched its war against Iraq on the assumption that Saddam Hussein possessed weapons of mass destruction (WMD) that posed an immediate threat. When that assumption turned out to be false, flaws in the judgment process identified by the bipartisan U.S. Senate Select Committee on Intelligence (2004) included confirmation bias. Administration analysts "had a tendency to accept information which supported [their presumptions] . . . more readily than information which contradicted" them. Sources denying such weapons were deemed "either lying or not knowledgeable about Iraq's problems, while those sources who reported ongoing WMD activities were seen as having provided valuable information."

Fixation

Try your hand at these two classic brainteasers:

* Arrange the six matches shown in **FIGURE 29.4** so they will form four equilateral triangles.
* How can you use the box of matches, thumbtacks, and candle shown in **FIGURE 29.5** to mount the candle on a bulletin board? (Read on after trying these problems.)

Fixation—the inability to see a problem from a fresh perspective—is a true impediment to problem solving. Once we incorrectly represent the problem, it's hard to restructure how we approach it. If your attempts to solve the matchstick problem were fixated on two-dimensional solutions, then the three-dimensional solution will have eluded you. (Turn the page and see **FIGURE 29.6**.)

> "The human understanding, when any proposition has been once laid down . . . forces everything else to add fresh support and confirmation."
>
> Francis Bacon, *Novum Organum*, 1620

■ **fixation** the inability to see a problem from a new perspective; an impediment to problem solving.

■ **mental set** a tendency to approach a problem in a particular way, often a way that has been successful in the past.

■ **functional fixedness** the tendency to think of things only in terms of their usual functions; an impediment to problem solving.

FIGURE 29.4
The matchstick problem
How would you arrange six matches to form four equilateral triangles?

FIGURE 29.5
The candle-mounting problem
Using these materials, how would you mount the candle on a bulletin board? (From Duncker, 1945.)

Two examples of fixation are *mental set* and *functional fixedness*. As a perceptual set predisposes what we perceive, a **mental set** predisposes how we think. Mental set refers to our tendency to approach a problem with the mindset of what has worked for us previously. Indeed, solutions that worked in the past often do work on new problems. Consider:

Given the sequence *O-T-T-F-?-?-?*, what are the final three letters? Most people have difficulty recognizing that the three final letters are *F*(ive), *S*(ix), and *S*(even). But solving this problem may make the next one easier:

Given the sequence *J-F-M-A-?-?-?*, what are the final three letters? (If you don't get this one, ask yourself what month it is.)

Sometimes, however, our mental set based on what worked in the past precludes our finding a new solution to a new problem. Our mental set from past experience with matchsticks predisposes our arranging them in two dimensions.

Another type of fixation—our tendency to think of only the familiar functions for objects, without imagining alternative uses—goes by the awkward but appropriate label **functional fixedness.** A person may ransack the house for a screwdriver when a dime would have turned the screw. Perhaps you experienced functional fixedness when you tried to solve the candle-mounting problem. If you thought of the matchbox as having only the function of holding matches, you may have overlooked its use shown in **FIGURE 29.7** (on next page). Perceiving and relating familiar things in new ways is part of creativity. Much as stereotypes constrain our perception of people (we may forget that firefighters are also first aid experts and may be good cooks), so fixation constrains our perceptions of objects. Both stereotypes and fixation limit our thinking.

Mental set
The mental set created by reading the first door may predispose how one reads the second door.

Making Decisions and Forming Judgments

When making each day's hundreds of judgments and decisions—Is it worth the bother to take an umbrella? Can I trust this person? Should I shoot the basketball or pass to the player who's hot?—we seldom take the time and effort to reason systematically. We just follow our intuition. After interviewing policymakers in government, business, and education, social psychologist Irving Janis (1986) concluded that they "often do not use a reflective problem-solving approach. How do they usually arrive at their decisions? If you ask, they are likely to tell you . . . they do it mostly by *the seat of their pants*."

Using and Misusing Heuristics

OBJECTIVE 29-5 | Contrast the representativeness and availability heuristics, and explain how they can cause us to underestimate or ignore important information.

Those mental shortcuts we call heuristics often do help us make reasonable seat-of-the-pants decisions. When quick action is needed, analysis can mean paralysis. Thanks to the mind's automatic information processing, intuitive judgments are

Amos Tversky, 1937–1996

Daniel Kahneman

"In creating these problems, we didn't set out to fool people. All our problems fooled us, too."

Amos Tversky (1985)

"Intuitive thinking [is] fine most of the time. . . . But sometimes that habit of mind gets us in trouble."

Nobel laureate Daniel Kahneman (2005)

■ **representativeness heuristic** judging the likelihood of things in terms of how well they seem to represent, or match, particular prototypes; may lead one to ignore other relevant information.

■ **availability heuristic** estimating the likelihood of events based on their availability in memory; if instances come readily to mind (perhaps because of their vividness), we presume such events are common.

■ **overconfidence** the tendency to be more confident than correct—to overestimate the accuracy of one's beliefs and judgments.

FIGURE 29.6
Solution to the matchstick problem
To solve this problem (see Figure 29.4), you must break the fixation of limiting your considerations to two-dimensional solutions.

FIGURE 29.7
Solution to the candle-mounting problem
Solving this problem (see Figure 29.5), requires recognizing that a box need not always serve as a container. (From Duncker, 1945.)

instantaneous. But the price we sometimes pay for this efficiency—quick but bad judgments—can be costly. To gain an idea of how heuristics determine our intuitive judgments—and how they occasionally lead even the smartest people into dumb decisions—consider two heuristics identified by cognitive psychologists Amos Tversky and Daniel Kahneman (1974): *representativeness* and *availability*.

The Representativeness Heuristic

To judge the likelihood of things in terms of how well they represent particular prototypes is to use the **representativeness heuristic.** To illustrate, consider:

> A stranger tells you about a person who is short, slim, and likes to read poetry, and then asks you to guess whether this person is more likely to be a professor of classics at an Ivy League university or a truck driver (adapted from Nisbett & Ross, 1980). Which would be the better guess?

If you are like most people, you answered "professor" because the description seems more *representative* of Ivy League scholars than of truck drivers. The representativeness heuristic enabled you to make a snap judgment. But it also led you to ignore other relevant information. When I help people think through this question, the conversation goes something like this:

"The information-processing shortcuts—called heuristics—which are normally both highly efficient and immensely time-saving in day-to-day situations, work systematically against us in the marketplace. . . . The tendency to underestimate or altogether ignore past probabilities in making a decision is undoubtedly the most significant problem of intuitive predictions."

David Dreman, *Contrarian Investment Strategy: The Psychology of Stock Market Success,* 1979

Question:	First, let's figure out how many professors fit the description. How many Ivy League universities do you suppose there are?
Answer:	Oh, about 10, I suppose.
Question:	How many classics professors would you guess there are at each?
Answer:	Maybe 4.
Question:	Okay, that's 40 Ivy League classics professors. What fraction of these are short and slim?
Answer:	Let's say half.
Question:	And, of these 20, how many like to read poetry?
Answer:	I'd say half—10 professors.
Question:	Okay, now let's figure how many truck drivers fit the description. How many truck drivers do you suppose there are?
Answer:	Maybe 400,000.
Question:	What fraction are short and slim?
Answer:	Not many—perhaps 1 in 8.
Question:	Of these 50,000, what percentage like to read poetry?
Answer:	Truck drivers who like poetry? Maybe 1 in 100—oh, oh, I can see where this is going—that leaves me with 500 short, slim, poetry-reading truck drivers.

Comment: Yup. So, although the person I've described may be much more representative of classics professors than of truck drivers, this person is still (even if we accept your stereotypes) 50 times more likely to be a truck driver than a classics professor.

The representativeness heuristic influences many of our daily decisions. To judge the likelihood of something, we intuitively compare it with our mental representation of that category—of, say, what truck drivers are like. If the two match, that fact usually overrides other considerations of statistics or logic.

The Availability Heuristic

The **availability heuristic** operates when we base our judgments on how mentally available information is. If instances of an event are easily available—if they come to mind quickly and with little effort—we presume such events are common. The faster people can remember an instance of some event ("a broken promise"), the more they expect it to recur (MacLeod & Campbell, 1992). Cognitively available events *are* more likely to recur—but not always. To see this, make a guess: Does the letter *k* appear more often as the first or third letter in English usage?

Because words beginning with *k* come to mind more easily than words having *k* as their third letter, most people guess that *k* occurs more frequently as the first letter. Actually, *k* is much more likely to appear as the third letter. So far in this module, words such as *know, kingdom,* and *kin* are outnumbered 46 to 13 by words such as *make, likely, asked,* and *acknowledged.*

Why does the availability heuristic lead us astray? Anything that increases the ease of our retrieving information can increase its perceived availability. Many factors enable information to "pop into mind." These include how recently you heard about it, its distinctiveness, and its concreteness. Thus, an event's availability to our memory need not indicate its likelihood in reality.

The judgmental errors influenced by the availability heuristic are not always harmless. A lot of important decisions involve judgments of risk (see Thinking Critically About: The Fear Factor on the next page). Whether we favor using nuclear power or burning coal to produce energy depends partly on our judgments of their risks to our health, our air, and our climate. Our efforts to prevent various deadly diseases depend on our judgments of the likelihood of their occurrence. Our choice to buy or not to buy a lottery ticket depends on our hunch of the odds of striking it rich. Casinos entice us to gamble by signaling even small wins with bells and lights—making them vividly memorable—while keeping big losses soundlessly invisible. In such ways, hucksters can manipulate the intuitive hopes and fears of anyone naive about statistics.

The availability heuristic also affects our social judgments, as Ruth Hamill and her co-workers demonstrated (1980). They presented people with a single, vivid case of welfare abuse, in which a long-term welfare recipient had several unruly children. Statistically, this case was exceptional: Most people who received welfare did so for four years or less (Duncan & others, 1988). Yet when the statistical reality was pitted against the single vivid case, the memorable case had greater influence on people's opinions about welfare recipients.

Overconfidence

OBJECTIVE 29-6 | Describe the drawbacks and advantages of overconfidence in decision making.

Our use of intuitive heuristics when forming judgments, our eagerness to confirm the beliefs we already hold, and our knack for explaining away failures combine to create **overconfidence,** a tendency to overestimate the accuracy of our knowledge and judgments. Across various tasks, people overestimate what their performance was, is, or will be (Metcalfe, 1998).

"The problem is I can't tell the difference between a deeply wise, intuitive nudge from the Universe and one of my own bone-headed ideas!"

Based on the roughly 10-million-to-1 odds against a bet's winning a state Lotto jackpot, one's chances are not much better than the odds of being struck by lightning. If you are an average British citizen and you place a bet in the National Lottery, the odds of your dying during the 20-minute National Lottery draw program on television are several times greater than the odds of your winning (*Chance News*, 1999).

"The human understanding is most excited by that which strikes and enters the mind at once and suddenly, and by which the imagination is immediately filled and inflated. It then begins almost imperceptibly to conceive and suppose that everything is similar to the few objects which have taken possession of the mind."

Francis Bacon, *Novum Organum*, 1620

THE FEAR FACTOR— DO WE FEAR THE RIGHT THINGS?

"Most people reason dramatically, not quantitatively," said Oliver Wendell Holmes. Especially since 9/11, many people fear flying more than driving. Yet National Safety Council (2005) data reveal that between 2000 and 2002, Americans were— mile for mile—39.5 times more likely to die in an automobile crash than on a commercial flight. In a late-2001 essay, I calculated that if—because of 9/11—we flew 20 percent less and instead drove half those unflown miles, about 800 more people would die in traffic accidents in the year after 9/11 (Myers, 2001). When German psychologist Gerd Gigerenzer (2004) later checked this estimate against accident data (why didn't I think of this?), he found that the last three months of 2001 indeed produced significantly more

U.S. traffic fatalities than the average for those months in the previous five years (**FIGURE 29.8**). Long after 9/11, the dead terrorists were still killing Americans. As air travel gradually recovered during 2002, 2003, and 2004, U.S. commercial flights carried nearly 2 billion passengers, with only 34 deaths—none on a major airline big jet (Miller, 2005). Meanwhile, 128,000 Americans died in traffic accidents.

Why do we fear the wrong things? Why do we fear terrorism more than accidents—which kill nearly as many per *week* in just the United States as did terrorism with its 2527 worldwide deaths in all of the 1990s (Johnson, 2001)? Even with the horror of 9/11, more Americans in 2001 died of food poisoning (which scares few) than of

terrorism (which scares many). And why do so many smokers (whose habit shortens their lives, on average, by about five years) fret before flying (which, averaged across people, shortens life by one day)?

Psychological science has identified four influences on our intuitions about risk. First, we fear *what our ancestral history has prepared us to fear*. Human emotions were road

FIGURE 29.8
Still killing Americans
Images of 9/11 etched a sharper image in our minds than did the millions of fatality-free flights on U.S. airlines during 2002 and after. Such dramatic events, being readily available to memory, shape our perceptions of risk. In the three months after 2001, those faulty perceptions led more people to travel, and some to die, by car. (Adapted from Gigerenzer, 2004.)

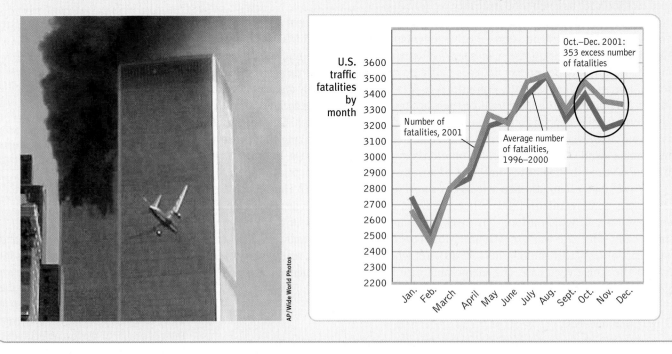

In a classic study of overconfidence, Kahneman and Tversky (1979) asked people to answer obscure factual questions with a wide enough range to surely include the actual answer. The questions had this format: "I feel 98 percent certain that the population of New Zealand is more than _____ but less than _____." Nearly one-third of the time, people's estimates, made with 98 percent confidence, failed to include tested in the Stone Age. Yesterday's risks prepare us to fear snakes, lizards, and spiders (although all three combined now kill virtually no one in developed countries). And they prepare us to fear confinement and heights, and therefore flying.

Second, we fear *what we cannot control*. Driving we control, flying we do not.

Third, we fear *what is immediate*. Threats related to flying are mostly telescoped into the moments of takeoff and landing, while the dangers of driving are diffused across many moments to come, each trivially dangerous. Teens are often indifferent to smoking's toxicity because they live more for the present than for the distant future.

Fourth, we fear *what is most readily available in memory*. Horrific images of United Flight 175 slicing into the World Trade Center form indelible memories. And powerful, available memories serve as our measuring rods as we intuitively judge risks. Thousands of safe car trips (for those who have survived to read this) have extinguished our anxieties about driving.

Vivid events also distort our comprehension of risks and probable outcomes. We comprehend Andrew "Jack" Whittaker's winning $315 million in a 2002 Powerball lottery. We do not comprehend each of the more than 560 million losing players who undramatically enabled his jackpot. We comprehend those 9/11 flights that ended in the deaths of 266 passengers and crew. We do not comprehend the vast numbers of

Dramatic deaths in bunches breed concern and fear
The memorable South Asian tsunami that killed some 300,000 people stirred an outpouring of concern and new tsunami-warning technology. Meanwhile, a "silent tsunami" of poverty-related malaria was killing about that many of the world's children every couple months, noted Jeffrey Sachs, the head of a United Nations project aiming to cut extreme poverty in half by 2015 (Dugger, 2005).

Ian Berry/Magnum Photos

accident-free flights—16 *million* consecutive fatality-free takeoffs and landings during one stretch of the 1990s (Tolchin, 1994). Dramatic outcomes capture our attention; probabilities we hardly grasp. The result: We overvalue lottery tickets, overestimate flight risk, and underestimate the dangers of driving.

We fear too much those things that have killed people dramatically, in bunches, and recently, and we fear too little those threats that will claim lives undramatically, one by one, and in the distant future. If a single 747 were taken down by a rocket-propelled grenade, the horror would be seared upon our minds. But as Bill Gates has noted, each year a half-million children worldwide—the equivalent of four 747s full of children every day—die quietly, one by one, from rotavirus, and we hear nothing of it (Glass, 2004).

We must "learn to protect ourselves and our families against future terrorist attacks," warns a U.S. Department of Homeland Security ad that has appeared periodically in my local newspapers. The ad advises us on the food supplies, duct tape, and battery-powered radios we'll need if "there's a terrorist attack on your city." With 4 in 10 Americans being at least somewhat worried "that you or someone in your family will become a victim of terrorism," the "Be afraid!" message—be afraid not just of a terrorist attack on somebody somewhere, but of one on you and your place—has been heard (Carroll, 2005).

The point to remember: It is perfectly normal to fear purposeful violence from those who hate us. When terrorists strike again, we will all recoil in horror. But smart thinkers will also want to check their fears against facts and to resist those who serve their own purposes by cultivating a culture of fear. By so doing, we can take away the terrorists' most omnipresent weapon: exaggerated fear.

the correct answer (4.1 million as of 2006, in this instance). Although very sure of themselves, they were often wrong. Warning people against overconfidence doesn't much reduce overconfidence.

People are also more confident than correct when answering such questions as, "Is absinthe a liqueur or a precious stone?" (It's a licorice-flavored liqueur.) On ques-

> "Don't believe everything you think."
> Bumper sticker

tions where only 60 percent of people answer correctly, respondents typically feel 75 percent confident. Even when people feel 100 percent certain of their answers to such questions, they err about 15 percent of the time (Fischhoff & others, 1977).

Overconfidence plagues decisions outside the laboratory, too. It was an overconfident Hitler who invaded Russia, an overconfident Lyndon Johnson who waged war with North Vietnam, an overconfident George W. Bush who marched into Iraq to eliminate supposed weapons of mass destruction. On a smaller scale, stockbrokers and investment managers market their services with confidence that they can outperform the market average in picking stocks, despite overwhelming evidence to the contrary (Malkiel, 2004). A purchase of stock X, recommended by a broker who judges this to be the time to buy, is usually balanced by a sale made by someone who judges this to be the time to sell. Despite their confidence, buyer and seller cannot both be right.

Students, too, are routinely overconfident about how quickly they can do assignments and write papers, report Roger Buehler and his colleagues (1994). They typically expect to finish projects ahead of schedule. But in fact, the projects generally get finished after about twice the number of days they predicted. Although we know we have often underestimated completion times, we remain overly confident of our next prediction. Moreover, presuming how much we're going to get done, we also overestimate our future free time (Zauberman & Lynch, 2005). We expect to be experiencing more free time a month from today than today. So we say yes to requests for our future time, only to discover it's just as busy.

Failing to appreciate one's potential for error when making military, economic, or political judgments can have devastating consequences, but so can a lack of self-confidence. Overconfidence does have adaptive value. People who err on the side of overconfidence live more happily, find it easier to make tough decisions, and seem more credible (Baumeister, 1989; Taylor, 1989). Moreover, if given prompt and clear feedback on the accuracy of their judgments—as weather forecasters are after each day's predictions—people soon learn to assess their accuracy more realistically (Fischhoff, 1982). The wisdom to know when we know a thing and when we do not is born of experience.

Framing Decisions

OBJECTIVE 29-7 | Describe how others can use framing to elicit from us the answers they want.

A further test of rationality is whether the same issue, presented in two different but logically equivalent ways, will elicit the same answer. For example, one surgeon tells

"When you know a thing, to hold that you know it; and when you do not know a thing, to allow that you do not know it; this is knowledge."

Confucius (551–479 B.C.), *Analects*

Predict your own behavior
When will you finish reading this module?

Worth Publishers photo by Nicole Villamora

someone that 10 percent of people die while undergoing a particular surgery. Another tells someone that 90 percent survive. The information is the same. The effect is not. To both patients and physicians, the risk seems greater to those who hear that 10 percent will die (Marteau, 1989; McNeil & others, 1988; Rothman & Salovey, 1997).

The way we present an issue is called **framing,** and its effects are sometimes striking. Consumers respond more positively to ground beef described as "75 percent lean" rather than "25 percent fat" (Levin & Gaeth, 1988; Sanford & others, 2002). Nine in 10 college students rate a condom as effective if it has a supposed "95 percent success rate" in stopping the AIDS virus; only 4 in 10 think it successful when given a "5 percent failure rate" (Linville & others, 1992). And people express more surprise when a "1 in 20" event happens than when an equivalent "10 in 200" event happens (Denes-Raj & others, 1995). To scare people, frame risks as numbers, not percentages. People told that a chemical exposure is projected to kill 10 of every 10 million people (imagine 10 dead people!) feel more frightened than if told the fatality risk is an infinitesimal .000001 (Kraus & others, 1992).

Consider how the framing effect influences economic and business decisions. Merchants mark up their "regular prices" to appear to offer huge savings on "sale prices." A $100 coat marked down from $150 by Store X can seem like a better deal than the same coat priced regularly at $100 by Store Y (Urbany & others, 1988). My dentist doesn't charge more if we pay later, though she does offer a 5 percent discount for immediate cash payment. She, like thousands of other service providers, knows to frame the price difference as a "cash discount" rather than a "credit-card surcharge."

That our judgments can flip-flop so dramatically is startling. It suggests that our judgments and decisions may not be well reasoned, and that those who understand the power of framing can use it to influence important decisions—for example, by framing survey questions to support or reject a particular viewpoint.

■ **framing** the way an issue is posed; how an issue is framed can significantly affect decisions and judgments.

"This CD player costs less than players selling for twice as much."

Belief Bias

OBJECTIVE 29-8 | Explain how our preexisting beliefs can distort our logic.

We have seen that part of psychology's thinking about thinking emphasizes that we are prone to bias as we seek confirmation of our hunches, rely on efficient but fallible heuristics, display overconfidence, and fall prey to the effects of framing. But would logic help us escape the bias inflicted by our beliefs?

Logic does help, but we still find it easier to accept conclusions that agree with our opinions. Consider this logical argument:

> *Premise 1:* Some communists are golfers.
> *Premise 2:* All golfers are Marxists.
> *Conclusion:* Some communists are Marxists.

In experiments, nearly everyone correctly recognized that the conclusion logically follows from the premises (Oakhill & others, 1989). But now consider this argument:

> *Premise 1:* Some communists are golfers.
> *Premise 2:* All golfers are capitalists.
> *Conclusion:* Some communists are capitalists.

Many people had a harder time seeing that, given the premises, this conclusion is equally valid. Judge this next conclusion for yourself (adapted from Hunt, 1982):

> *Premise 1:* Democrats support free speech.
> *Premise 2:* Dictators are not democrats.
> *Conclusion:* Dictators do not support free speech.

"God is love.
Love is blind.
Ray Charles is blind.
Ray Charles is God."
Anonymous graffiti

If that conclusion seems logical, you are experiencing **belief bias**—the tendency for our beliefs to distort our logic (Oakhill & others, 1990). (Premise 1 did not exclude the possibility that others, even dictators, can believe in free speech.) Consider another set of statements with *identical form and logic* and note how much easier it feels to refute the conclusion:

Premise 1: Robins have feathers.
Premise 2: Chickens are not robins.
Conclusion: Chickens do not have feathers.

Thus, belief bias: We more easily see the illogic of conclusions that run counter to our beliefs than of those that agree with our beliefs.

The Belief Perseverance Phenomenon

OBJECTIVE 29-9 | Describe the remedy for the belief perseverance phenomenon.

An additional source of irrationality is **belief perseverance,** our tendency to cling to our beliefs in the face of contrary evidence. Belief perseverance often fuels social conflict. Charles Lord and his colleagues (1979) revealed how this happens when they studied people with opposing views of capital punishment. Those on both sides studied two supposedly new research findings, one supporting and the other refuting the claim that the death penalty deters crime. Each side was more impressed by the study that supported its own beliefs, and each readily disputed the other study. Thus, showing the pro- and anti–capital-punishment groups the *same* mixed evidence actually *increased* their disagreement.

"Once you have a belief, it influences how you perceive all other relevant information. Once you see a country as hostile, you are likely to interpret ambiguous actions on their part as signifying their hostility."
Political scientist Robert Jervis (1985)

If you want to rein in the belief perseverance phenomenon, a simple remedy exists: *Consider the opposite.* When Lord and his colleagues (1984) repeated the capital-punishment study, they asked some of their participants to be "as *objective* and *unbiased* as possible." The plea did nothing to reduce the biased evaluation of evidence. They asked another group to consider "whether you would have made the same high or low evaluations had exactly the same study produced results on the *other* side of the issue." Having imagined and pondered *opposite* findings, these people became much less biased in their evaluations of the evidence.

"To begin with, it was only tentatively that I put forward the views I have developed . . . but in the course of time they have gained such a hold upon me that I can no longer think in any other way."
Sigmund Freud, *Civilization and Its Discontents*, 1930

The more we come to appreciate why our beliefs might be true, the more tightly we cling to them. Once people have explained to themselves why they believe a child is "gifted" or "learning disabled," or why candidate X or Y will be more likely to preserve peace, or why company Z is a stock worth owning, they tend to ignore the evidence that undermines that belief. Prejudice persists. Once beliefs form and get justified, it takes more compelling evidence to change them than it did to create them.

The Perils and Powers of Intuition

OBJECTIVE 29-10 | Describe the smart thinker's reaction to using intuition to solve problems.

We have seen how our irrational thinking can plague our efforts to solve problems, make wise decisions, form valid judgments, and reason logically. Moreover, these perils of intuition appear even when people are offered extra pay for thinking smart, even when they are asked to justify their answers, and even when they are expert physicians or clinicians (Shafir & LeBoeuf, 2002). All in all, these and many other findings (see **TABLE 29.1**) suggest "bleak implications for human rationality" (Nisbett & Borgida, 1975).

Truths often come in complementary pairs. It is true that unchecked intuition is perilous. But today's cognitive scientists also are revealing intuition's powers. Our

■ **belief bias** the tendency for one's preexisting beliefs to distort logical reasoning, sometimes by making invalid conclusions seem valid, or valid conclusions seem invalid.

■ **belief perseverance** clinging to one's initial conceptions after the basis on which they were formed has been discredited.

TABLE **29.1**

INTUITION'S PERILS AND POWERS

Intuition's Dozen Deadly Sins	Evidence of Intuition's Powers
• *Hindsight bias*—looking back on events, we falsely surmise that we knew it all along. • *Illusory correlation*—intuitively perceiving a relationship where none exists. • *Memory construction*—influenced by our present moods and by misinformation, we may form false memories. • *Representativeness and availability*—fast and frugal heuristics become quick and dirty when leading us into illogical and incorrect judgments. • *Overconfidence*—our intuitive assessments of our own knowledge are often more confident than correct. • *Belief perseverance and confirmation bias*—thanks partly to our preference for confirming information, beliefs are often resilient, even after their foundation is discredited. • *Framing*—judgments flip-flop, depending on how the same issue or information is posed. • *Interviewer illusion*—inflated confidence in one's discernment based on interview alone. • *Mispredicting our own feelings*—we often mispredict the intensity and duration of our emotions. • *Self-serving bias*—in various ways, we exhibit inflated self-assessments. • *Fundamental attribution error*—overly attributing others' behavior to their dispositions by discounting unnoticed situational forces. • *Mispredicting our own behavior*—our intuitive self-predictions often go astray.	• *Blindsight*—brain-damaged persons' "sight unseen" as their bodies react to things and faces not consciously recognized. • *Right-brain thinking*—split-brain persons displaying knowledge they cannot verbalize. • *Infants' intuitive learning*—of language and physics. • *Moral intuition*—quick gut feelings that precede moral reasoning. • *Divided attention and priming*—unattended information processed by the mind's downstairs radar watchers. • *Everyday perception*—the instant parallel processing and integration of complex information streams. • *Automatic processing*—the cognitive autopilot that guides us through most of life. • *Implicit memory*—learning *how* to do something without knowing *that* one knows. • *Heuristics*—those fast and frugal mental shortcuts that normally serve us well enough. • *Intuitive expertise*—phenomena of nonconscious learning, expert learning, and physical genius. • *Creativity*—the sometimes-spontaneous appearance of novel and valuable ideas. • *Social and emotional intelligence*—the intuitive know-how to comprehend and manage ourselves in social situations and to perceive and express emotions. • *The wisdom of the body*—when instant responses are needed, the brain's emotional pathways bypass the cortex; hunches sometimes precede rational understanding. • *Thin slices*—detecting traits from mere seconds of behavior. • *Dual attitude system*—as we have two ways of knowing (unconscious and conscious) and two ways of remembering (implicit and explicit), we also have gut-level and rational attitude responses.

cognition, for the most part, is wonderfully efficient and effective. Its instant, intuitive reactions enable us to react quickly and *usually* adaptively. Experienced nurses, firefighters, art critics, car mechanics, hockey players, and you, for anything in which you develop expertise, learn to size up many a situation in an eye blink.

In showing how everyday heuristics usually make us smart (and only sometimes make us dumb), Gerd Gigerenzer (2004) asked both American and German university students, "Which city has more inhabitants: San Diego or San Antonio?" Sixty-two percent of the Americans, after thinking a moment, guessed right: San Diego. In Germany, where many people have not heard of San Antonio (apologies to our Texas friends), students used a fast and frugal intuitive heuristic: Pick the one you recognize. With less knowledge but an adaptive heuristic, 100 percent of Gigerenzer's German respondents answered correctly.

Intuition is huge. More than we realize, thinking occurs off-screen, with the results occasionally displayed on-screen. Intuition is adaptive. It feeds our expertise, our creativity, our love, and our spirituality. And intuition, smart intuition, is born of experience. Chess masters can look at a board and intuitively know the right move. Playing "blitz chess," where every move is made after barely more than a glance, they display a hardly diminished skill (Burns, 2004). At every moment, skilled violin players know,

"I'm happy to say that my final judgment of a case is almost always consistent with my prejudgment of the case."

Chick sexing
When acquired expertise becomes an automatic habit, as it is for experienced chick sexers, it feels like intuition. At a glance, they just know.

Jean-Philippe Ksiazek/AFP

without thinking, just where to place the bow, at what angle, with what pressure. Experienced chicken sexers can tell you a chick's sex at a glance, yet cannot tell you how they do it. In each case, the immediate insight describes acquired, speedy expertise that feels like instant intuition. Intuition is recognition, observed Nobel laureate psychologist-economist Herbert Simon (2001). It is analysis "frozen into habit."

Mindful of intuition's perils and powers, smart thinkers will welcome their intuitions but also check them against available evidence. Our gut intuitions are terrific at some things, such as instantly reading emotions in others' faces, but not so good at others, such as assessing risks. Wisdom comes with knowing the difference.

In the discussion of decision making and overconfidence, I asked you to predict when you would finish this module. What time is it now? Did you underestimate or overestimate how quickly you would finish?

Let's pause to consider the question posed on the first page of this module—how deserving are we of our name *Homo sapiens*? If we were being graded on decision making and judgment, our error-prone species might rate a C+. On problem solving, where humans are inventive yet vulnerable to fixation, we would probably receive better marks, perhaps a B. On cognitive efficiency, our fallible but quick heuristics earn us an A.

>> LEARNING OUTCOMES

Thinking

OBJECTIVE 29-1 | Define *cognition*.
Cognition is a term covering all the mental activities associated with thinking, knowing, remembering, and communicating.

OBJECTIVE 29-2 | Describe the roles of categories, hierarchies, definitions, and prototypes in concept formation.
We use concepts to simplify and order the world around us. We divide clusters of objects, events, ideas, or people into *categories* based on their similarities. In creating *hierarchies,* we subdivide these categories into smaller and more detailed units. We form other concepts, such as triangles, by *definition* (three-sided objects). But we form most concepts around *prototypes*, or best examples of a category. Matching objects and ideas against prototypes is an efficient way of making snap judgments about what belongs in a specific category.

OBJECTIVE 29-3 | Compare algorithms and heuristics as problem-solving strategies, and explain how insight differs from both of them.
An *algorithm* is a time-consuming but thorough set of rules or procedures (such as a recipe for cookies, or a step-by-step description for evacuating a building during a fire) that guarantees a solution to a problem. A *heuristic* is a simpler thinking strategy (such as running for an exit if you smell heavy smoke) that may allow us to solve problems quickly, but sometimes leads us to incorrect solutions. *Insight* differs from both because it is not a strategy-based solution, but rather an Aha! reaction—a sudden flash of inspiration that solves a problem.

OBJECTIVE 29-4 | Contrast the confirmation bias and fixation, and explain how they can interfere with effective problem solving.
The *confirmation bias* predisposes us to verify rather than challenge our hypotheses. *Fixation,* such as mental set and functional fixedness, may leave us doggedly pursuing one line of reasoning and prevent us from taking the fresh perspective that would let us solve the problem.

OBJECTIVE 29-5 | Contrast the representativeness and availability heuristics, and explain how they can cause us to underestimate or ignore important information.
The *representativeness heuristic* leads us to judge the likelihood of things in terms of how they represent our prototype for a group of items. The *availability heuristic* leads us to judge the likelihood of things based on how vivid they are or how readily they come to mind. Either of these two thinking shortcuts can cause us to ignore important information or to underestimate the chances of something happening.

OBJECTIVE 29-6 | Describe the drawbacks and advantages of overconfidence in decision making.
The main drawback of overconfidence is that our tendencies to seek confirmation of our hypotheses and to use quick and easy heuristics can blind us to our vulnerability to error—a fault that can be tragic if we are in a position of responsibility. But on a personal level, overconfident people tend to live happier lives, make difficult decisions more easily, and seem more credible than their less confident counterparts.

OBJECTIVE 29-7 | **Describe how others can use framing to elicit from us the answers they want.**

An issue can be presented (or *framed*) in different but equally logical ways, but the subtle wording can nudge us in the direction the questioner wants us to take.

OBJECTIVE 29-8 | **Explain how our preexisting beliefs can distort our logic.**

We tend to judge conclusions that agree with our beliefs as more logical than those that do not match our beliefs. This *belief bias* can lead us to accept invalid conclusions and reject valid ones.

OBJECTIVE 29-9 | **Describe the remedy for the belief perseverance phenomenon.**

Belief perseverance is clinging to our ideas because the explanation we once accepted as valid lingers in our mind even after it has been discredited. The best remedy for this form of bias is considering evidence supporting the opposite position.

OBJECTIVE 29-10 | **Describe the smart thinker's reaction to using intuition to solve problems.**

Although it may lead us astray, human intuition can be efficient and adaptive, as when we gain expertise in a field and grow adept at making quick, shrewd judgments. Smart thinkers welcome their intuitions but check them against available evidence, hoping to avoid overconfidence and biased and illogical thinking.

TERMS AND CONCEPTS TO REMEMBER

cognition, p. 29-0	functional fixedness, p. 29-5
concept, p. 29-0	representativeness heuristic, p. 29-6
prototype, p. 29-0	
algorithm, p. 29-2	availability heuristic, p. 29-7
heuristic, p. 29-2	overconfidence, p. 29-7
insight, p. 29-2	framing, p. 29-11
confirmation bias, p. 29-3	belief bias, p. 29-12
fixation, p. 29-4	belief perseverance, p. 29-12
mental set, p. 29-5	

TEST YOURSELF

1. The availability heuristic is a quick-and-easy but sometimes misleading guide to judging reality. What is the availability heuristic?

(Answer in Appendix B.)

ASK YOURSELF

1. People's perceptions of risk, often biased by vivid images from movies or the news, are surprisingly unrelated to actual risks. (People may hide in the basement during thunderstorms but fail to buckle their seat belts in the car.) What are the things you fear? Are some of those fears out of proportion to statistical risk? Are you failing, in other areas of your life, to take reasonable precautions?

ANSWER TO QUESTION WITHIN THE MODULE

Q. Can you find another word using all the letters of *SPLOY-OCHYG?*

A. Psychology

>WEB

Multiple-choice *self-tests* and more may be found at www.worthpublishers.com/myers.

30

Language and Thought

The most tangible indication of our thinking power is **language**—our spoken, written, or signed words and the ways we combine them as we think and communicate. Humans have long and proudly proclaimed that language sets us above all other animals. "When we study human language," asserted linguist Noam Chomsky (1972), "we are approaching what some might call the 'human essence,' the qualities of mind that are, so far as we know, unique" to humans. To cognitive scientist Steven Pinker (1990), language is "the jewel in the crown of cognition."

Imagine an alien species that could pass thoughts from one head to another merely by pulsating air molecules in the space between them. Perhaps these weird creatures could inhabit a future Spielberg movie? Actually, we are those creatures! When we speak, our brain and voice box conjure up air pressure waves that we send banging against another's ear drum—enabling us to transfer thoughts from our brain into theirs. As Pinker (1998) notes, we sometimes sit for hours "listening to other people make noise as they exhale, because those hisses and squeaks contain *information*." And thanks to all those funny sounds created in our heads from the air pressure waves we send out, adds Bernard Guerin (2003), we get people's attention, we get them to do things, and we maintain relationships.

When the human vocal tract evolved the ability to utter vowels, our capacity for language exploded, catapulting our species forward (Diamond, 1989). Whether spoken, written, or signed, language enables us not only to communicate but to transmit civilization's accumulated knowledge across generations. Monkeys mostly know what they see. Thanks to language, we know much that we've never seen.

Language Structure

OBJECTIVE **30-1** | Describe the basic structural units of a language.

Consider how we might go about inventing a language. For a spoken language, we would need three building blocks. First, we would need a set of basic sounds, which linguists call **phonemes.** To say *bat* we utter the phoneme sounds *b, a,* and *t. Chat* also has three phonemes—*ch, a,* and *t.* Languages have varying numbers of phonemes. English has about 40; other languages have anywhere from half to more than twice that many. Linguists surveying nearly 500 languages have identified 869 different phonemes in human speech (Holt, 2002; Maddieson, 1984).

Changes in phonemes produce changes in meaning. In English, varying the vowel sound between *b* and *t* creates 12 different meanings: *bait, bat, beat/beet, bet, bit, bite, boat, boot, bought, bout,* and *but* (Fromkin & Rodman, 1983). Generally, though, consonant phonemes carry more information than do vowel phonemes. The treth ef thes stetement shed be evedent frem thes bref demenstretien.

People who grow up learning one set of phonemes usually have difficulty pronouncing those of another language. The native English speaker may smile at the native German speaker's difficulties with the *th* sound, which can make *this* sound like *dis.*

■ **language** our spoken, written, or signed words and the ways we combine them to communicate meaning.

■ **phoneme** in a language, the smallest distinctive sound unit.

■ **morpheme** in a language, the smallest unit that carries meaning; may be a word or a part of a word (such as a prefix).

■ **grammar** in a language, a system of rules that enables us to communicate with and understand others.

■ **semantics** the set of rules by which we derive meaning from morphemes, words, and sentences in a given language; also, the study of meaning.

■ **syntax** the rules for combining words into grammatically sensible sentences in a given language.

Language transmits culture
The actual words and grammar may differ from culture to culture, but every society has a history it transmits in story form to its children. Here, a group of Ivory Coast boys listens as an elder retells a tribal legend.

M. & E. Bernheim/Woodfin Camp & Associates

But the German speaker smiles back at the problems English speakers have rolling the German r or pronouncing the breathy *ch* in *Ich,* the German word for *I.*

Sign language also has phonemelike building blocks defined by hand shapes and movements. Like speakers, native signers of one of the 200+ sign languages may have difficulty with the phonemes of another. Chinese native signers who come to America and learn sign usually sign with an accent, notes researcher Ursula Bellugi (1994).

But sounds alone do not make a language. The second building block is the **morpheme,** the smallest unit of language that carries meaning. In English, a few morphemes are also phonemes—the personal pronoun *I* and the article *a,* for instance. But most morphemes are combinations of two or more phonemes. Some, like *bat,* are words, but others are only parts of words. Morphemes include prefixes and suffixes, such as the *pre -* in *preview* or the *-ed* that shows past tense. *Undesirables* has four morphemes—*un-desir-able-s*—each of which adds to the word's total meaning.

Finally, our new language must have a **grammar,** a system of rules (*semantics* and *syntax*) in a given language that enables us to communicate with and understand others. **Semantics** is the set of rules we use to derive meaning from morphemes, words, and even sentences. In English, for example, a semantic rule tells us that adding *-ed* to *laugh* means that it happened in the past. **Syntax** refers to the rules we use to order words into sentences. One rule of English syntax says that adjectives usually come before nouns, so we say *white house.* Spanish adjectives usually come after nouns, so a Spanish speaker says *casa blanca.* The English rules of syntax allow the sentence *They are hunting dogs.* Given the context, semantics will tell us whether it refers to dogs that seek animals or people who seek dogs.

In all 6000 human languages, the grammar is intricately complex. "There are 'stone age' societies," says Steven Pinker (1995), "but they do not have 'stone age' languages." Contrary to the illusion that less-educated people speak ungrammatically, they simply speak a different dialect. To a linguist, "ain't got none" is grammatically equal to "doesn't have any." (It has the same syntax.)

Note, however, that language becomes more complex as you move from phoneme to morpheme to word to sentence. In English, the relatively small number of 40 or so phonemes can be combined to form more than 100,000 morphemes, which alone or in combination produce the 616,500 word forms in the *Oxford English Dictionary* (including 290,500 main entries such as *meat* and 326,000 subentries such as *meat eater*). We can then use these words to create an infinite number of sentences, most of which (like this one) are original. Like life itself constructed from the genetic code's simple alphabet, language is complexity built of simplicity. I know that you can know why I worry that you think this sentence is starting to get too complex, but that complexity—and our capacity to communicate and comprehend it—is what distinguishes human language capacity (Hauser & others, 2002).

How many morphemes are in the word *cats*? How many phonemes? (See this module's final page.)

"Let me get this straight now. Is what you want to build a jean factory or a gene factory?"

A cultural universal: In every language, the commonest words are the shortest. As a word or phrase is used more and more, it often gets shortened. *Television* becomes *TV, compact disc* becomes *CD, electronic mail* becomes *e-mail* (Triandis, 1994).

Language Development

Make a quick guess: How many words did you learn in one average day during the years between your first birthday and your high school graduation?

The average secondary school graduate knows some 60,000 words (Bloom, 2000). That averages (after age 1) to nearly 3500 words learned each year, or 10 each day! How you did it—how the 3500 words a year you learned could so far outnumber the roughly 200 words a year that your schoolteachers consciously taught you—is one of the great human wonders.

Before children can add 2 + 2, they are creating their own original and grammatically appropriate sentences. Most parents would have trouble stating the rules of syntax. Yet their preschoolers comprehend and speak with a facility that puts to shame a college student struggling to learn a foreign language or a scientist struggling to

Although you probably know about 80,000 words, you use only 150 words for about half of what you say.

simulate natural language on a computer. But you, too, have an astonishing facility for language. With remarkable efficiency, you can selectively sample the tens of thousands of words in your memory, effortlessly combine them on the fly with near-perfect syntax, and spew them out three words a second (Vigliocco & Hartsuiker, 2002). It is amazing, given how many ways there are to mess up. You also adapt your language to your social context. You know your culture's rules for speaking and listening, such as how far apart to stand and how to take turns in conversation. Language is a social dance. So, how did your language ability unfold, and how can we explain it?

When Do We Learn Language?

OBJECTIVE 30-2 | Trace the course of language acquisition from the babbling stage through the two-word stage.

Children's language development mirrors language structure—it moves from simplicity to complexity. Infants start without language (*in fantis* means "not speaking"). Yet by 4 months of age, babies can read lips and discriminate speech sounds. They prefer to look at a face that matches a sound, so we know they can recognize that *ah* comes from wide open lips and *ee* from a mouth with corners pulled back (Kuhl & Meltzoff, 1982). This marks the beginning of the development of babies' *receptive language,* their ability to comprehend speech. Babies' receptive language abilities begin to mature before their *productive language,* their ability to produce words.

Around 4 months of age, babies enter a **babbling stage** in which they spontaneously utter a variety of sounds, such as *ah-goo.* Babbling is not an imitation of adult speech, for it includes sounds from various languages, even sounds that do not occur in the household's language. From this early babbling, a listener could not identify an infant as being, say, French, Korean, or Ethiopian. Deaf infants who observe their Deaf parents signing begin to babble more with their hands (Petitto & Marentette, 1991). It seems, then, that before nurture molds our speech, nature enables a wide range of possible phonemes. Many of these natural babbling sounds are consonant-vowel pairs formed by simply bunching the tongue in front of the mouth (*da-da, na-na, ta-ta*) or by opening and closing the lips (*ma-ma*), both of which babies do naturally for feeding (MacNeilage & Davis, 2000).

Eventually our babbling comes to resemble the characteristic sounds and intonations of our household language. By the time infants are about 10 months old, their babbling has changed so that a trained ear can identify the language of the household (de Boysson-Bardies & others, 1989). Phoneme sounds outside the infant's native tongue begin to disappear, as does the ability to discriminate those sounds.

Without exposure to other languages, we become functionally deaf to speech sounds outside our native languages (Pallier & others, 2001). Thus, by adulthood those who speak only English cannot discriminate certain Japanese phonemes within speech. Nor can Japanese adults with no training in English distinguish between the English *r* and *l*. Thus (believe it or not), *la-la-ra-ra* may sound like the same repeated syllable to a Japanese adult. This makes life challenging for the Japanese tourist who is told the train station is "just after the next light." The next what? After the street veering right, or farther down, after the traffic light?

■ **babbling stage** beginning at about 4 months, the stage of speech development in which the infant spontaneously utters various sounds at first unrelated to the household language.

■ **one-word stage** the stage in speech development, from about age 1 to 2, during which a child speaks mostly in single words.

■ **two-word stage** beginning about age 2, the stage in speech development during which a child speaks mostly two-word statements.

■ **telegraphic speech** early speech stage in which a child speaks like a telegram—"go car"—using mostly nouns and verbs and omitting auxiliary words.

Around the first birthday (the exact age varies from child to child), most children enter the **one-word stage.** They have already learned that sounds carry meanings, and if repeatedly trained to associate, say, *fish* with a picture of a fish, one-year-olds will look at a fish when a researcher says "Fish, fish! Look at the fish!" (Schafer, 2005). These one-year-olds also begin to use sounds to communicate meaning. Their first words usually contain only one syllable—*ma* or *da,* for instance—and may be barely recognizable. But family members quickly learn to understand the infant's language, and gradually it conforms more and more to the family's language. At this one-word stage, an inflected word may equal a sentence. "Doggy!" may mean "Look at the dog out there!"

Children typically use more and more single words during the second year. At about 18 months, their word learning expands from a word per week to a word per day. Before their second birthday, they usually enter the **two-word stage,** when they start uttering two-word sentences (**TABLE 30.1**). Language at this stage is characterized by **telegraphic speech:** Like telegrams (TERMS ACCEPTED. SEND MONEY), this early form of speech contains mostly nouns and verbs (*Want juice*). Also like telegrams, it follows rules of syntax; the words are in a sensible order. The English-speaking child typically says adjectives before nouns—*big doggy* rather than *doggy big.*

There seems to be no "three-word stage." Once children move out of the two-word stage, they quickly begin uttering longer phrases (Fromkin & Rodman, 1983). Although the sentences may still resemble a telegraphed message (*Mommy get ball*), they continue to follow the rules of syntax. By early elementary school, children understand complex sentences and begin to enjoy the humor conveyed by double meanings: "You never starve in the desert because of all the sand-which-is there."

"Got idea. Talk better. Combine words. Make sentences."

TABLE 30.1

SUMMARY OF LANGUAGE DEVELOPMENT

Month (approximate)	Stage
4	Babbles many speech sounds.
10	Babbling resembles household language.
12	One-word stage.
24	Two-word, telegraphic speech.
24+	Language develops rapidly into complete sentences.

Explaining Language Development

OBJECTIVE 30-3 | Discuss Skinner's and Chomsky's contributions to the nature-nurture debate over how children acquire language, and explain why statistical learning and critical periods are important concepts in children's language learning.

Those who study language acquisition inevitably wonder how we do it. Attempts to answer this question have sparked a spirited intellectual controversy. The controversy parallels the larger debate over the behaviorist view of the malleable organism versus the view that each organism comes biologically prepared to learn certain associations. The nature-nurture debate surfaces again and, here as elsewhere, appreciation for innate predisposition and the nature-nature interaction has grown.

Skinner: Operant Learning

Behaviorist B. F. Skinner (1957) believed that we can explain language development with familiar learning principles, such as association (of the sights of things with the sounds of words); imitation (of the words and syntax modeled by others); and reinforcement (with success, smiles, and hugs when the child says something right). Thus, Skinner (1985) argued, babies learn to talk in many of the same ways that animals learn to peck keys and press bars: "Verbal behavior evidently came into existence when, through a critical step in the evolution of the human species, the vocal musculature became susceptible to operant conditioning."

What happens when there is minimal reinforcement for speaking, as is often the case with hearing children of Deaf parents? Their exposure to spoken language, much of it via television, is more passive, and they learn spoken language more slowly. But they learn to sign on a normal time frame (Messer, 2000).

Chomsky: Inborn Universal Grammar

Linguist Noam Chomsky (1959, 1987) thinks Skinner's ideas were naive. Surely, Chomsky has said, a Martian scientist observing children in a single-language community would conclude that language is almost entirely inborn. But it isn't. Children do learn their environment's language. However, they acquire untaught words and grammar at a rate too extraordinary to be explained solely by learning principles. They generate all sorts of sentences they have never heard, sometimes with novel errors. (No parent teaches the sentence, "I hate you, Daddy.") Children begin using morphemes in a predictable order. English-speakers begin adding *-ing* to words. Then they start using the prepositions *in* and *on*. Then come *a* and *the*, followed by *is* (Brown, 1973). There are 3,628,800 ways to arrange this sentence's 10 words. Only a handful of them make any sense. Yet any 4-year-old could pick them out from among the 3,628,700+ nonsensical orderings.

Moreover, many of the errors young children make result from *overgeneralizing* logical grammatical rules, such as adding *-ed* to make the past tense (from de Cuevas, 1990):

Child: My teacher holded the baby rabbits and we petted them.
Mother: Did you say your teacher held the baby rabbits?
Child: Yes.
Mother: Did you say she held them tightly?
Child: No, she holded them loosely.

Chomsky (1987) likened the behaviorist view of how language develops to filling a bottle with water. The behaviorists, he believed, oversimplified. Developing language is not just being "filled up" with the right kinds of experiences. Chomsky instead has viewed language development much like "helping a flower to grow in its own way." Language will naturally occur, given adequate nurture; it just "happens to the child." He has contended that all human languages have the same grammatical building blocks, such as nouns and verbs, subjects and objects, negations and questions. Thus, there is a sort of *universal grammar* that underlies all human language. As Steven Pinker (2002) points out, there are no other conceivable ways to power a communication system.

Our 6000 human languages are, therefore, dialects of this universal grammar for which our brains are prewired (Baker, 2001). Thus, we learn readily the specific grammar of whatever language we experience, whether spoken or signed (Bavelier & others, 2003). And no matter what that language is, we start speaking mostly in nouns *(kitty, da-da)* rather than verbs and adjectives (Bornstein & others, 2004). It happens so naturally—as naturally as birds learning to fly—that training hardly helps.

Expose children to language and they will soak it up. Raise them in isolation, and they will develop without language. If not exposed to language, a *group* of children will, however, make up their own. Without exposure to language, deaf children, too, will over time create their own with gestures, complete with grammar (Sandler & others, 2005).

Chomsky maintains that our capacity for developing language is natural and quick because we come equipped with a sort of switch box—a *language acquisition device*—already in place. It is as if the switches need to be turned either "on" or "off" for us to understand and produce language. As we hear language, the switches get set for the language we are to learn.

Over time we grasp specific phonemes, morphemes, words, and sentences, and the rules by which we can combine them. These make up what Chomsky calls the *surface structure* of a language, which will vary from one human language to another. For instance, English-speaking children learn to put the object of a sentence last ("She ate an apple"). Japanese-speaking children learn to put the object before the verb ("She an apple ate"). While deciphering our

Slightly more than half the world's 6000 languages are spoken by fewer than 10,000 people. And slightly more than half the world's population speaks one of the top 20 languages (Gibbs, 2002).

Creating a language
Brought together as if on a desert island (actually a school), Nicaragua's young deaf children over time drew upon sign gestures from their own home to create their own Nicaraguan Sign Language, complete with words and intricate grammar. Our biological predisposition for language does not create language in a vacuum. But activated by a social context, nature and nurture work creatively together (Osborne, 1999; Senghas & Coppola, 2001).

Susan Meiselas/Magnum Photos

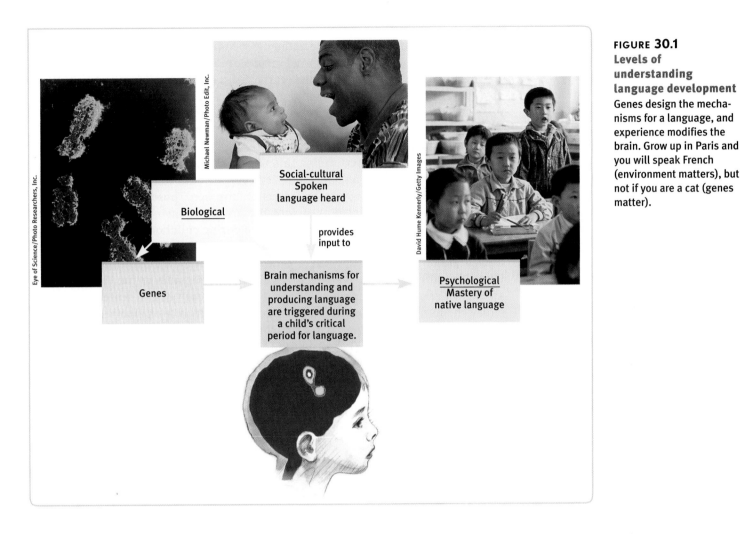

Biological

Social-cultural
Spoken
language heard

Genes

provides
input to

Brain mechanisms for
understanding and
producing language
are triggered during
a child's critical
period for language.

Psychological
Mastery of
native language

FIGURE 30.1
Levels of understanding language development
Genes design the mechanisms for a language, and experience modifies the brain. Grow up in Paris and you will speak French (environment matters), but not if you are a cat (genes matter).

language's surface structure we also learn to discern its meanings, which Chomsky calls its *deep structure*. In the English and Japanese examples above, the same deep structure is being conveyed through different surface structures. "Mario is easy to please" and "Mario is eager to please" have the same surface structure but different deep structures. (The first can be restructured to "It is easy to please Mario" but not the second.) According to Chomsky, then, it is as if we are born with the hardware and an operating system for language, and our linguistic experiences write the software (**FIGURE 30.1**).

Cognitive Scientists: Statistical Learning and Critical Periods

Human infants display a remarkable ability to learn statistical aspects of human speech. When you or I listen to an unfamiliar language, the syllables all run together. Someone unfamiliar with English might, for example, hear *United Nations* as "Uneye Tednay Shuns." Well before our first birthday, our brains were discerning word breaks by statistically analyzing which syllables, as in "hap-py-ba-by," most often go together. Jenny Saffran and her colleagues (1996) showed this by exposing 8-month-old infants to a computer voice speaking an unbroken, monotone string of nonsense syllables (*bidakupadotigolabubidaku . . .*). After just two minutes of exposure, the infants were able to recognize (as indicated by their attention) three-syllable sequences that appeared repeatedly. Others have found infants as young as 6 months able to similarly segment speech (Bortfield & others, 2005).

Little statistician
Human infants come with a remarkable capacity to statistically analyze language and discern words and grammatical rules. This is a tribute to both nature and nurture—to our biological machinery for learning language.

Brain scans reveal a difference in how the brain records a second language learned early versus a second language learned later in life. Adults who learned a second language early in life use the *same* patch of frontal lobe tissue when recounting an event in either the native or the second language. Those who learned their second tongue after childhood display activity in an *adjacent* brain area while using their second language (Kim & others, 1997).

Follow-up research offers further testimony to infants' surprising knack for soaking up language. For example, 7-month-old infants can learn simple sentence structures. After repeatedly hearing syllable sequences that follow one rule, such as *ga-ti-ga* and *li-na-li* (an ABA pattern), they listen longer to syllables in a different sequence, such as *wo-fe-fe* (an ABB pattern) rather than *wo-fe-wo*. Their detecting the difference between the two patterns suggests that babies come with a built-in readiness to learn grammatical rules (Marcus & others, 1999).

But are we capable of performing this same feat of statistical analysis throughout our life span? Many researchers believe not. Childhood seems to represent a *critical period* for mastering certain aspects of language. Those who learn a second language as adults usually speak it with the accent of their first language. (But people who often overhear a second language during childhood can later learn to speak it with a more nativelike accent [Au & others, 2002].) Do they master the foreign grammar better than the accent? To find out, Jacqueline Johnson and Elissa Newport (1991) gave Korean and Chinese immigrants to the United States an English grammar test, requiring them to identify each of 276 sentences ("Yesterday the hunter shoots a deer") as grammatically correct or incorrect. Some of the test-takers had immigrated in early childhood, others as adults. Regardless of their age at immigration, each had been in the United States for approximately 10 years. Nevertheless, as **FIGURE 30.2** reveals, those who learned their second language early learned it best. Chomsky would say that once the grammar switches are thrown during a child's developing years, mastering another grammar becomes more difficult. It is not impossible, but the older the age at which one emigrates to a new country, the harder it is to learn its language (Hakuta & others, 2003). During childhood and early adolescence, your language acquisition system pretty well mastered grammar and accent, and ever since it has been inclined to rest on its laurels.

"Childhood is the time for language, no doubt about it. Young children, the younger the better, are good at it; it is child's play. It is a onetime gift to the species."

Lewis Thomas, *The Fragile Species*, 1992

As a flower's growth will be stunted without nourishment, so, too, will children become linguistically stunted if isolated from language during the critical period for its acquisition. The window for learning language is wide open in our early years, then, after age 7, it gradually closes. The impact of early experience is evident in studies of deaf children receiving cochlear implants. Implants by age 2 lead to better oral speech than implants after age 4 (Greers, 2004).

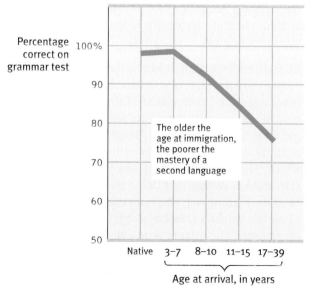

FIGURE 30.2
New language learning gets harder with age
Although there is no sharply defined critical period for second language learning, young children have a greater readiness to learn language than older children and adults. Ten years after coming to the United States, Asian immigrants took a grammar test. Those who arrived before age 8 understood American English grammar as well as native speakers did. Those who arrived later did not. (From Johnson & Newport, 1991.)

Percentage correct on grammar test

The older the age at immigration, the poorer the mastery of a second language

Native   3–7   8–10   11–15   17–39

Age at arrival, in years

Hearing children of hearing-speaking parents, and deaf children of Deaf-signing parents have much in common. As noted earlier, both groups babble as infants—hearing children by repeating sounds, deaf children by repeating elementary sign gestures. Both groups develop vocabularies at comparable rates (Bavelier & others, 2003). For both groups, later-than-usual exposure to language (at age 2 or 3) unleashes their brain's idle language capacity, producing a rush of language. But consider the 90+ percent of deaf children born to hearing-nonsigning parents. These children typically do not experience language during their early years. Compared with children exposed to sign language from birth, those who learn to sign as teens or adults are like immigrants who learn English after childhood. They can master the basic words and learn to order them, but they never become as fluent as native signers in producing and comprehending subtle grammatical differences (Newport, 1990). Moreover, the late-learners show less brain activity in right hemisphere regions that are active as native signers read sign language (Newman & others, 2002).

George Ancona

No means no—no matter how you say it!
Deaf children of Deaf-signing parents and hearing children of hearing parents have much in common. They develop language skills at about the same rate, and they are equally effective at opposing parental wishes and demanding their way.

Those not exposed to either a spoken or a signed language during their early years lose their ability to master *any* language. Natively deaf children who learn sign language after age 9 never learn it as well as those who become deaf at age 9 after learning English. They also never learn English as well as other natively deaf children who learned sign in infancy (Mayberry & others, 2002). The striking conclusion: When a young brain does not learn any language, its language-learning capacity never fully develops.

To summarize, children's genes design complex brain wiring that prepares them to learn language as they interact with their caregivers. Skinner's emphasis on learning helps explain how infants acquire their language as they interact with others. (So does infants' ability to learn statistical probabilities in speech.) Chomsky's emphasis on our built-in readiness to learn grammar rules helps explain why preschoolers acquire language so readily and use grammar so well. Once again, we see biology and experience working together.

Thinking and Language

Thinking and language intricately intertwine. Asking which comes first is one of psychology's chicken-and-egg questions. Do our ideas come first and we wait for words to name them? Or are our thoughts conceived in words and therefore unthinkable without them?

Language Influences Thinking

OBJECTIVE 30-4 | Summarize Whorf's linguistic determinism hypothesis, and comment on its standing in contemporary psychology.

Linguist Benjamin Lee Whorf contended that language determines the way we think. According to Whorf's (1956) **linguistic determinism** hypothesis, different languages impose different conceptions of reality: "Language itself shapes a man's basic ideas." The Hopi, Whorf noted, have no past tense for their verbs. Therefore, he contended, a Hopi could not so readily *think* about the past.

Whorf's hypothesis would probably not occur to people who speak only one language and view that language as simply a vehicle for thought. But to those who speak

■ **linguistic determinism** Whorf's hypothesis that language determines the way we think.

two dissimilar languages, such as English and Japanese, it seems obvious that a person thinks differently in different languages (Brown, 1986). Unlike English, which has a rich vocabulary for self-focused emotions such as anger, Japanese has more words for interpersonal emotions such as sympathy (Markus & Kitayama, 1991). Many bilinguals report that they have a different sense of self, depending on which language they are using (Matsumoto, 1994). After emigrating from Asia to North America, bilinguals may even reveal different personalities when taking the same personality test in their two languages (Dinges & Hull, 1992). Michael Ross, Elaine Xun, and Anne Wilson (2002) demonstrated this by inviting China-born, bilingual University of Waterloo students to describe themselves in English or Chinese. When describing themselves in English, their self-descriptions were typically Canadian: They expressed mostly positive self-statements and moods. When responding in Chinese, they were typically Chinese: They reported more agreement with Chinese values and roughly equal positive and negative self-statements and moods. Their language use seemed to shape how they thought of themselves.

Learn a language and you learn about a culture. When a language becomes extinct—the likely fate of most of the world's 6000 remaining languages—the world loses the culture and thinking that hang on that language. "To destroy a people, destroy their language," observed poet Joy Harjo.

To say that language *determines* the way we think is much too strong. A Papua New Guinean without our words for shapes and colors nevertheless perceives them much as we do (Rosch, 1974). Yet our words do *influence* what we think (Hardin & Banaji, 1993; Özgen, 2004). In Brazil, the isolated Piraha tribespeople have words for the numbers "1" and "2," but numbers above that are simply "many." Thus if shown seven nuts in a row, they find it very difficult to lay out the same number from their own pile (Gordon, 2004). Whether living in Britain, New Guinea, or Namibia, people also use their language when classifying and remembering colors (Davidoff, 2004; Roberson & others, 2004). If English is your native language, imagine that while viewing three colors you called two of them "yellow" and one of them "blue." Later you would likely see and recall the yellows as being more similar. People in Papua New Guinea's Berinmo tribe, which has words for two different shades of yellow, would better recall the distinctions between the two yellows. On the color spectrum, blue blends into green. But we find it relatively easy to distinguish two colors that are on either side of the dividing line between what we call "blue" and "green." Given the same degree of difference on the color spectrum (**FIGURE 30.3**), two different "blues" (or two different "greens") are, when given the same names, harder to distinguish (Özgen, 2004). The perceived difference grows when we assign different names to colors.

Given the subtle influence of words on thinking, we do well to choose our words carefully. Does referring to women as *girls*—as in "girls' night out"—assume women's lower status? What about the generic use of the pronoun *he*? Does it make any difference whether I write, "A child learns language as *he* interacts with *his* caregivers" or "Children learn language as *they* interact with *their* caregivers"? Some argue it makes no difference because every reader knows "the masculine gender shall be deemed and taken to include females" (as the British Parliament declared in 1850).

Before reading on, draw a picture of this idea "The girl pushes the boy," which I'll ask you about later.

"Language is not a straight jacket."
Psychologist Lila Gleitman, American Association for the Advancement of Science Convention, 2002

"All words are pegs to hang ideas on."
Henry Ward Beecher, *Proverbs from Plymouth Pulpit*, 1887

FIGURE 30.3
Language and perception
Emre Özgen (2004) reports that when shown equally different colors, those that carry different names seem more different. Thus the "green" and "blue" in contrast A may appear to differ more than the two similarly different blues in contrast B.

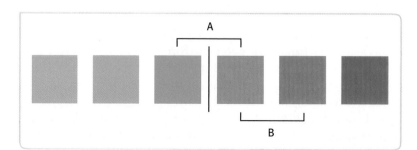

But many studies have found that when hearing the generic *he* (as in "the artist and his work") people are more likely to picture a male (Henley, 1989; Ng, 1990). Consider, too, that people use generic pronouns selectively, as in "the doctor . . . he" and "the secretary . . . she" (MacKay, 1983). If *he* and *his* were truly gender-free, we shouldn't skip a beat when hearing that "man, like other mammals, nurses his young."

To expand language is to expand the ability to think. In young children, thinking develops hand in hand with language (Gopnik & Meltzoff, 1986). Indeed, it is very difficult to think about or conceptualize certain abstract ideas (commitment, freedom, or rhyming) without language! And what is true for preschoolers is true for everyone: *It pays to increase your word power.* That's why most textbooks, including this one, introduce new words—to teach new ideas and new ways of thinking.

Increasing word power through sign language has had great benefits for deaf people, who for thousands of years were viewed by the hearing community as incompetent to inherit property, marry, be educated, or have challenging work (Sacks, 1990). Deaf people's competency is clear when they are exposed to signing as preschoolers and then schooled in their own language. Children of signing Deaf parents develop native sign fluency, and they outperform nonfluent deaf children on measures of intelligence and academic achievement (Isham & Kamin, 1993).

Increased word power helps explain what McGill University researcher Wallace Lambert (1992; Lambert & others, 1993) calls the *bilingual advantage*. Bilingual children, who learn to inhibit one language while using their other language, are also better able to inhibit their attention to irrelevant information. If asked to say whether a sentence is grammatically correct ("Why is the cat barking so loudly?") they can more efficiently focus on the grammar alone (Bialystok, 2001).

Lambert helped devise a Canadian program that immerses English-speaking children in French. (From 1981 to 1999, the number of non-Quebec Canadian children immersed in French rose from 65,000 to 280,000 [Commissioner, 1999].) For most of their first three years in school, the English-speaking children are taught entirely in French, and thereafter gradually shift by the end of their schooling to classes mostly in English. Not surprisingly, the children attain a natural French fluency unrivaled by other methods of language teaching. Moreover, compared with similarly capable children in control conditions, they do so without detriment to their English fluency, and with increased aptitude scores, math scores, and appreciation for French-Canadian culture (Genesee & Gándara, 1999).

So, for English-speaking Canadians, immersion followed by bilingual education pays dividends. Does bilingual education for children in a linguistic minority also pay dividends? Advocates of "English-only" education doubt it. They argue that bilingual programs are expensive, ineffective, and detrimental to non–English-speaking children's assimilation into their English-based cultures (Porter, 1998). But some researchers disagree (August & Hakuta, 1998; Padilla & Benavides, 1992; Thomas & Collier, 1998). Children in "two-way" schools where they, together with English-speaking children, experience half their classes in English and half in their native language, tend to develop higher self-esteem than do non–English-speaking children dropped into English-only schools. They drop out less frequently. And they eventually attain higher levels of academic achievement and English proficiency.

Stop now, and look at how you illustrated "the girl pushes the boy," which I asked you to do earlier in this module. Anne Maass and Aurore Russo (2003) report that people whose language reads from left to right mostly position the pushing girl on the left. Those who speak Arabic, a language that reads from right to left, mostly place her on the right. Whether we are deaf or hearing, language transforms experience. Language fuels our imagination. Language connects us to the past and the future. Language links us to one another.

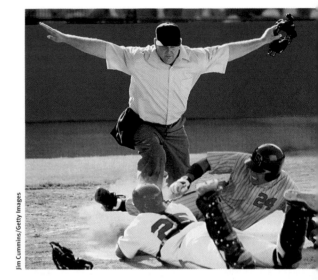

Jim Cummins/Getty Images

A safe sign
We have outfielder William Hoy to thank for baseball sign language. The first deaf player to join the major leagues (1892), he invented hand signals for "Strike!" "Safe!" (shown here) and "Yerr Out!" (Pollard, 1992). Such gestures worked so well that referees in all sports now use invented signs, and fans are fluent in sports sign language.

Many native English speakers, including most Americans, are monolingual. Most humans are bilingual or multilingual. Does monolingualism limit people's ability to comprehend the thinking of other cultures?

Thinking in Images

OBJECTIVE 30-5 | Discuss the value of thinking in images.

When you are alone, do you talk to yourself? Is "thinking" simply conversing with yourself? Without a doubt, words convey ideas. But aren't there times when ideas precede words? To turn on the cold water in your bathroom, in which direction do you turn the handle? To answer this question, you probably thought not in words but with procedural memory—a mental picture of how you do it. Indeed, we often think in images. Artists think in images. So do composers, poets, mathematicians, athletes, and scientists. Albert Einstein reported that he achieved some of his greatest insights through visual images and later put them into words.

Pianist Liu Chi Kung showed the value of thinking in images. One year after placing second in the 1958 Tchaikovsky piano competition, Liu was imprisoned during China's cultural revolution. Soon after his release, after seven years without touching a piano, he was back on tour, the critics judging his musicianship better than ever. How did he continue to develop without practice? "I did practice," said Liu, "every day. I rehearsed every piece I had ever played, note by note, in my mind" (Garfield, 1986). For someone who has learned a skill, such as ballet dancing, even just watching the activity will activate the brain's internal simulation of it, reports one British research team after collecting fMRI scans as people watched videos (Calvo-Merino & others, 2004).

For Olympic athletes, "mental practice has become a standard part of training," reports Richard Suinn (1997). In a laboratory test, Georgia Nigro (1984) demonstrated the wisdom of such practice. She had people actually throw darts 24 times at a target, then had half the people throw 24 darts mentally, and, finally, had everyone throw another 24 darts. Only those who had rehearsed the throws showed any improvement. Brain-imaging studies, such as the one shown in FIGURE 30.4, indicate that mentally simulating an action activates neural networks that are also active when performing the action (Grèzes & Decety, 2001).

Young figure skaters have exhibited similar improvement in their performance ratings for jumps and spins following mental practice while listening to their skating music (Garza & Feltz, 1998). One experiment on mental practice and basketball foul shooting tracked the University of Tennessee women's team over 35 games (Savoy & Beitel, 1996). During that time, the team's free-throw shooting increased from approximately 52 percent in games following standard physical practice to some 65 percent after mental practice. Players had repeatedly imagined making foul shots under various conditions, including being "trash-talked" by their opposition. In a dramatic conclusion, Tennessee won the national championship game in overtime, thanks in part to their foul shooting.

Mental rehearsal can also help you achieve an academic goal. In one study, Shelley Taylor and her UCLA colleagues (1998) engaged introductory psychology students who were a week away from facing a midterm exam. Some were told to visualize themselves scanning the posted grade list, seeing their A, beaming with joy, and feeling proud. Repeating this *outcome simulation* 5 minutes each day until the exam had little effect,

FIGURE 30.4
The power of imagination
Imagining a physical activity triggers action in the same brain areas that are triggered when actually performing that activity. These MRIs show a person imagining the experience of pain, which activates some of the same areas in the brain as the actual experience of pain.

© Jean Duffy Decety, September 2003

adding only 2 points to their exam scores, compared with scores of student counterparts not engaging in any mental simulation. But the researchers had another group visualize themselves effectively studying—reading the chapters, going over notes, eliminating distractions, declining an offer to go out. Repeating this *process simulation* for 5 minutes each day had a beneficial effect. Compared with the control students, this second group began studying sooner, spent more time at it, and beat the others' average by 8 points. From such experiments, the researchers conclude that it is better to spend your fantasy time planning how to get somewhere than to dwell on the imagined destination.

Courtesy Christine Brune

A thoughtful art
Playing the piano engages thinking without language. In the absence of a piano, mental practice can sustain one's skill.

More evidence of thinking without language comes from evidence of our information processing outside of consciousness. Inside the ever-active brain, many streams of activity flow in parallel, function automatically, are remembered implicitly, and only occasionally surface as conscious words. "Thinking lite," this unconscious processing has been called—"one-fourth the effort of regular thinking." So, yes, there is thinking, much thinking, without language.

What, then, should we say about the relationship between thinking and language? As we have seen, language does influence our thinking. But if thinking did not also affect language, there would never be any new words. And new words and new combinations of old words express new ideas. The basketball term *slam dunk* was coined after the act itself had become fairly common. So, let us say that *thinking affects our language, which then affects our thought* (**FIGURE 30.5**).

Psychological research on thinking and language demonstrates that the human mind is simultaneously capable of striking intellectual failures and of striking intellectual power. Misjudgments are common and can have disastrous consequences. So we do well to appreciate our capacity for error. Yet our efficient heuristics—our snap judgment strategies—often serve us well. Moreover, our ingenuity at problem solving and our extraordinary power of language mark humankind as almost "infinite in faculties."

Animal Thinking and Language

If in our use of language we humans are, as the psalmist long ago rhapsodized, "little lower than God," where do other animals fit in the scheme of things? Are they "little lower than human"? Do animals—in some sense we can identify with—think? Do they even exhibit language?

Do Animals Think?

OBJECTIVE 30-6 | List five cognitive skills shared by the great apes and humans.

Animals, especially the great apes, display remarkable capacities for thinking. They can, for example, form concepts. After monkeys learn to classify cats and dogs, certain frontal lobe neurons in their brains fire in response to new "catlike" images, others to new "doglike" images (Freedman & others, 2001). Pigeons—mere birdbrains—can sort objects according to their similarity. Shown pictures of cars, cats, chairs, and flowers, they readily learn to identify the categories. Shown a picture of a never-before-seen chair, the pigeon will reliably peck a key that represents "chairs" (Wasserman, 1995).

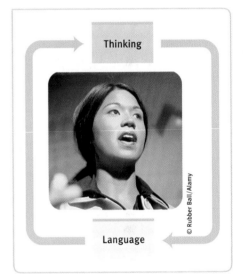

© Rubber Ball/Alamy

Thinking

Language

FIGURE 30.5
The interplay of thought and language
The traffic runs both ways between thinking and language. Thinking affects our language, which affects our thought.

Chimpanzee inventiveness

A wild chimpanzee shows ingenuity by using a stick to fish for ants living in the tree. Crows, too, have been observed to fashion a twig into a tool that can poke out insect larvae (Emery & Clayton, 2004).

Courtesy of Jennifer Byrne, c/o Richard Byrne, Department of Psychology, University of St. Andrews, Scotland

We also are not the only creatures to display insight. Psychologist Wolfgang Köhler (1925) observed apparent insight while studying chimpanzees placed on an island off the coast of Africa. In one experiment with a caged chimp named Sultan, Köhler placed a piece of fruit and a long stick well beyond reach, and a short stick inside the cage. Spying the short stick, Sultan grabbed it and tried to reach the fruit. But by design, the stick was too short. After several unsuccessful attempts, Sultan dropped the stick and paused to survey the situation. Then suddenly, as if thinking "Aha!" he jumped up, seized the short stick again, and used it to pull in the longer stick—which he then used to reach the fruit. Sultan's actions displayed animal cognition, claimed Köhler, and showed that there is more to learning than conditioning.

Thanks to problem solving shaped by reinforcement, forest-dwelling chimpanzees have become natural tool users (Boesch-Achermann & Boesch, 1993). They select appropriate branches or stones to use as hammers in cracking nuts. They also break off a reed or a stick, strip the twigs and leaves, carry it to a termite mound, fish for termites by twisting it just so, and then carefully remove it without scraping off many termites. They even select different tools for different purposes, including a heavy stick to puncture holes and a light, flexible stick for fishing (Sanz & others, 2004). One anthropologist, trying to mimic the chimpanzee's deft termite fishing, failed miserably.

Researchers have found at least 39 local customs related to chimp tool use, grooming, and courtship (Whiten & Boesch, 2001). One group may slurp ants directly from the stick, while another group plucks them off individually. One group may break nuts with a stone hammer, another with a wooden hammer. Such group differences, along with differing dialects and hunting styles, seem not to be genetic. Rather, they are the chimpanzee equivalent of cultural diversity. Like humans, chimpanzees—often younger ones—invent customs and pass them on to their peers and offspring. So do orangutans (van Schaik & others, 2003). And so do at least one group of Australian dolphins, which has learned to break off sponges and wear them on their snouts while probing the sea floor for fish (Krützen & others, 2005).

Chimpanzee culture

On the western bank of one Ivory Coast river, a mother uses a stone hammer to open a nut while a youngster watches. On the river's other side, a few miles away, chimps have not learned this trick.

Michael Nichols/National Geographic Image Collection

If primates can form concepts, exhibit insight, use tools, and transmit cultural innovations, do they have a "theory of mind"? Can they infer mental states in themselves and their peers? Chimps are not humans, Daniel Povinelli and Jesse Bering (2002) remind us. When choosing who should retrieve food for them, humans prefer someone who has witnessed it being hidden. Chimps do not. Chimps and orangutans have, however, been observed using mirrors to inspect themselves and

Cultural transmission in dolphins
This bottlenose dolphin in Shark Bay, Western Australia, is among a small group that has learned to use marine sponges as foraging tools.

touching a colored spot that a researcher has dabbed on their face (Gallup, 1998). Dolphins, too, pause by a mirror to examine ink marks placed on their bodies (Reiss & Marino, 2001).

Chimps and baboons have also been observed using deception, as when a young baboon feigns having been attacked as a seeming tactic for getting its mother to drive a competing baboon away from its food (Whiten & Byrne, 1988). Do such observations indicate that primates are capable of self-recognition and of comprehending others' perceptions? Many researchers think so. After reviewing great apes' capacity for reasoning, self-recognition, empathy, imitation, and understanding another's mind, Thomas Suddendorf and Andrew Whiten (2001) estimate their mental accomplishments as "very similar to that observed in 2-year-old humans."

Do Animals Exhibit Language?

OBJECTIVE 30-7 | Outline the arguments for and against the idea that animals and humans share the capacity for language.

Smart bird brain
Alex, an African gray parrot trained and tested by University of Arizona professor Irene Pepperberg (2002), displays numerical competence when shown novel assortments of objects. Asked, for example, "How many red blocks?" or "How many green balls?" Alex, with a brain the size of a walnut, answers correctly more than 80 percent of the time.

Without doubt, animals communicate. Vervet monkeys have different alarm cries for different predators: a barking call for a leopard, a cough for an eagle, and a chuttering for a snake. Hearing the leopard alarm, other vervets climb the nearest tree. Hearing the eagle alarm, they rush into the bushes. Hearing the snake chutter, they stand up and scan the ground (Byrne, 1991). Whales also communicate, with clicks and wails. Honeybees do a dance that informs other bees of the direction and distance of the food source.

And then there is Rico the border collie. He knows 200 items by name and can fetch any one of them (among a group of 10 items, and even when he can hear but cannot see his owner). Moreover, reports a team of psychologists at Leipzig's Max-Planck Institute, if asked to retrieve a novel toy with a name he has never heard, Rico will pick out the novel item from among a group of familiar items (Kaminski & others, 2004). And four weeks later, if this item is placed among other novel and familiar items, Rico, when hearing that novel word for the second time, will as often as not retrieve the object. Without question, such feats show animals' comprehension and communication. But is this language?

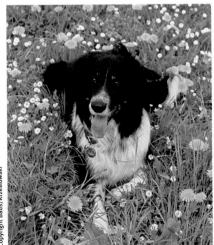

Comprehending canine
Rico, a border collie with a 200-word vocabulary, can infer that an unfamiliar sound refers to a novel object.

The Case of the Apes

The greatest challenge to humanity's claim to be the only language-using species has come from reports of apes that "talk" with people. Genetically speaking, our closest relatives are the chimpanzees, and the chimpanzees' closest relatives are not other apes, but us (Sagan & Druyan, 1992). Knowing that chimpanzees could not vocalize more than a few words, University of Nevada researchers Allen Gardner and Beatrix Gardner (1969) tried to teach sign language words to a chimpanzee named Washoe, as though she were a deaf human child. After four years, Washoe could use 132 signs. At age 32, Washoe had a vocabulary of 181 signs (Sanz & others, 1998). The Gardners' announcement of the success of their efforts aroused enormous scientific and public interest. One *New York Times* reporter, having learned sign language from his deaf parents, visited Washoe and exclaimed, "Suddenly I realized I was conversing with a member of another species in my native tongue."

Human language may have evolved from gestured communications (Corballis, 2002, 2003). If so, it is no wonder that our ape relatives have produced many gestured words but few spoken words. It is no wonder that gestures survive as part of people's speech (even when talking on the phone!). It is no wonder that signing so readily develops among Deaf people as an alternative to speech. It is no wonder that congenitally blind people produce gestures similar to those of sighted people, even if they believe the listener is also blind (Iverson & Goldin-Meadow, 1998). It is no wonder that prohibiting gestures disrupts speech that has spatial content (for example, describing an apartment layout). And it's therefore no wonder that gesturing lightens the cognitive load carried by speech. People told not to gesture put more effort into communicating with words alone, and are less able to remember recently learned information, such as lists of words or numbers (Goldin-Meadow & others, 2001). For both humans and apes, communication entails gestures.

Further evidence of gestured "ape language" surfaced during the 1970s. Usually apes sign just single words such as "that" or "gimme" (Bowman, 2003). But sometimes they have strung signs together to form intelligible sentences. Washoe signed, "You me go out, please." Apes even appeared to combine words creatively. Washoe designated a swan as a "water bird." Koko, a gorilla trained by Francine Patterson (1978), reportedly described a long-nosed Pinocchio doll as an "elephant baby." Lana, a "talking" chimpanzee that punches a crude computer keyboard which translates her entries into English, wanted her trainer's orange. She had no word for *orange,* but she did know her colors and the word for *apple,* so she improvised: "?Tim give apple which-is orange" (Rumbaugh, 1977).

As reports of ape language accumulated, it seemed that they might indeed be "little lower than human." Granted, their vocabularies and sentences are simple, rather like those of a 2-year-old child. Yet the apes do seem to share what we humans have considered our unique ability.

Seeing a doll floating in her water, Washoe signed, "Baby in my drink."

Gesture researcher Robert Krauss (1998) recalls his grandfather telling of two men walking on a bitter winter day. One chattered away while the second nodded, saying nothing. "Schmuel, why aren't you saying anything?" the first friend finally wondered. "Because," replied Schmuel, "I forgot my gloves."

Gestured communication
For hearing people, today's gestures may be less central to communication than for those who first used hand signals. Yet gestures remain naturally associated with spontaneous speech, especially speech that has spatial content.

But Can Apes Really Talk?

By the late 1970s, fascination with "talking apes" turned toward cynicism: Were the chimps language champs or were the researchers chumps? The ape language researchers were making monkeys of themselves, said the skeptics, who raised the following arguments:

- Apes gain their limited vocabularies only with great difficulty. They are hardly like speaking or signing children, who effortlessly soak up dozens of new words a week (Wynne, 2004). Saying that apes can learn language because they can sign words is like saying humans can fly because they can jump.
- Chimpanzees can make signs or push buttons in sequence to get a reward, just as Moscow circus bears can learn to ride unicycles. But pigeons, too, can peck a sequence of keys to get grain (Straub & others, 1979). No one says the pigeon is "talking."
- Apes can certainly use symbols meaningfully. But "Give orange me give eat orange me eat orange . . ." is a far cry from the exquisite syntax of a 3-year-old (Anderson, 2004; Pinker, 1995). To the child, "you tickle" and "tickle you" communicate different ideas. A chimpanzee, lacking human syntax, might sign the phrases interchangeably.
- After training a chimp he named Nim Chimsky, Herbert Terrace (1979) concluded that much of chimpanzees' signing is nothing more than apes aping their trainers' signs and learning that certain arm movements produce rewards.
- Presented with ambiguous information, people, thanks to their "perceptual set," tend to see what they want or expect to see. Interpreting chimpanzee signs as language may be little more than the trainers' wishful thinking, claimed Terrace. (When Washoe signed *water bird*, she perhaps was separately naming *water* and *bird*.)

"Chimps do not develop language," concludes Steven Pinker (1995). "But that is no shame on them; humans would surely do no better if trained to hoot and shriek like chimps, to perform the waggle-dance of the bee, or any of the other wonderful feats in nature's talent show."

In science as in politics, controversy can stimulate progress. The provocative claim that "apes share our capacity for language" and the skeptical rejoinder that "apes no use language" (as Washoe might have put it) have moved psychologists toward a greater appreciation of both apes' remarkable abilities and our own (Friend, 2004; Rumbaugh & Washburn, 2003). Everyone agrees: Humans alone possess language, if by the term we mean verbal or signed expression of complex grammar. If we mean, more simply, the ability to communicate through a meaningful sequence of symbols, then apes are indeed capable of language.

Although chimpanzees do not have our facility for language, their abilities to think and communicate continue to impress their trainers. After her second infant died, a depressed Washoe repeatedly asked, "Baby?" and became withdrawn when told, "Baby dead, baby gone, baby finished." Two weeks later, caretaker-researcher Roger Fouts (1992, 1997) had better news for Washoe: "I have baby for you." Washoe reacted to the signed news with instant excitement, her hair on end, swaggering and panting while signing over and again, "Baby, my baby." When Fouts then introduced the foster infant, Loulis, it took several hours for them to warm to each other, whereupon Washoe broke the ice by signing, "Come baby" and cuddling Loulis. In the months that followed, Loulis picked up 68 signs simply by observing Washoe and three other language-trained chimps.

Moreover, Washoe, Loulis, and the others now sign spontaneously. They ask one another to *chase, tickle, hug, come,* or *groom.* People who sign can actually eavesdrop on these chimp-to-chimp conversations with near-perfect agreement about what the chimps are saying, 90 percent of which pertains to social interaction, reassurance, or

"Although humans make sounds with their mouths and occasionally look at each other, there is no solid evidence that they actually communicate with each other."

"[Our] view that [we are] unique from all other forms of animal life is being jarred to the core."
Duane Rumbaugh and Sue Savage-Rumbaugh (1978)

Another "talking" chimpanzee
Sue Savage-Rumbaugh trains Kanzi, a very smart pygmy chimpanzee.

play (Fouts & Bodamer, 1987). The chimps are even modestly bilingual; they can translate spoken English words into signs (Shaw, 1989–1990).

More stunning is the claim by Sue Savage-Rumbaugh and her colleagues (1993) that pygmy chimpanzees can learn to comprehend the semantic nuances of spoken English. Kanzi, a pygmy chimpanzee with the seeming grammatical abilities of a human 2-year-old, happened onto language while observing his adoptive mother during language training. Kanzi has behaved intelligently whether asked, "Can you show me the light?" or "Can you bring me the [flash]light?" or "Can you turn the light on?" Kanzi also knows the spoken words *snake, bite,* and *dog.* Given stuffed animals and asked—for the first time—to "make the dog bite the snake," he put the snake to the dog's mouth. If Kanzi "had a vocal tract, he would be talking," exclaimed Duane Rumbaugh (1994). For chimps as for humans, early life is a critical time for learning language. If raised without early exposure to speech or word symbols, the chimps are unable as adults to gain language competence (Rumbaugh & Savage-Rumbaugh, 1994).

Believing that animals could not think, Descartes and other philosophers argued that they were living robots without any moral rights. Animals, it has been said at one time or another, cannot plan, conceptualize, count, use tools, show compassion, or use language (Thorpe, 1974). Today, we know better. Animal researchers have shown us that primates exhibit insight, show family loyalty, communicate with one another, display altruism, transmit cultural patterns across generations, and comprehend the syntax of human speech. Accepting and working out the moral implications of all this is an unfinished task for our own thinking species.

>> LEARNING OUTCOMES

Language and Thought

OBJECTIVE 30-1 | Describe the basic structural units of a language.

All languages have the same basic structural units. *Phonemes* are the basic units of sound in a language. *Morphemes* are the elementary units of meaning; some (such as *I*) are words, but most are elements such as prefixes (*anti-*) or suffixes (*-ing*). *Grammar* is the system of rules (mental rules, not those taught in English classes) that enable us to communicate and understand others. *Semantics,* which is part of grammar, is a set of rules for deriving meaning in a given language. *Syntax,* also a part of grammar, is a set of rules for ordering words into sentences.

OBJECTIVE 30-2 | Trace the course of language acquisition from the babbling stage through the two-word stage.

At about 4 months of age, infants babble, making a wide range of sounds found in languages all over the world. By about 10 months, their babbling contains only the sounds of their household language. By about 12 months, babies speak in single words, followed by two-word (telegraphic) utterances before their second birthday. Shortly after, children begin speaking in full sentences. The timing of these stages may vary, but all children follow this sequence.

OBJECTIVE 30-3 | Discuss Skinner's and Chomsky's contributions to the nature-nurture debate over how children acquire language, and explain why statistical learning and critical periods are important concepts in children's language learning.

Behaviorist B. F. Skinner (representing the nurture side of the language-development debate) proposed that we learn language by the familiar principles of association (of sights of things with sounds of words), imitation (of words and syntax modeled by others), and reinforcement (with smiles and hugs after saying something right). Challenging this claim, linguist Noam Chomsky (representing the nature position) argues that we are born with a language acquisition device that biologically prepares us to learn language. He cites as evidence the species-wide presence of language and its underlying universal grammar; children's amazing rate of acquiring vocabulary; and the uniform sequence of the stages of language development. *Statistical learning* is the ability to detect speech patterns (such as syllable breaks). Childhood is a *critical period* for learning spoken and signed language: Children who do not learn language during this early period lose their ability to fully master language.

OBJECTIVE 30-4 | Summarize Whorf's linguistic determinism hypothesis, and comment on its standing in contemporary psychology.

Whorf proposed that language *determines* thought. Contemporary psychologists believe it is more accurate to say that language *influences* thought. Research on bilingual people demonstrates that different languages embody different ways of thinking. Subtle prejudices can be conveyed by the words we choose to express our everyday thoughts.

OBJECTIVE 30-5 | Discuss the value of thinking in images.

We often think in images when we use procedural memory—our unconscious memory system for motor and cognitive skills and conditioned associations. Thinking in images is especially useful for mentally practicing upcoming events and can actually increase our skills.

OBJECTIVE 30-6 | List five cognitive skills shared by the great apes and humans.

Both humans and the great apes form concepts, display insight, use and create tools, transmit cultural innovations, and have a theory of mind (including the capacity for reasoning, self-recognition, empathy, imitation, and understanding another's mind).

OBJECTIVE 30-7 | Outline the arguments for and against the idea that animals and humans share the capacity for language.

Bees dance to communicate the direction and distance of food, parrots sort items by number, and dogs comprehend and respond to complicated human commands. Several species of apes have learned to communicate with humans by signing or by pushing buttons wired to a computer. These apes have developed vocabularies of hundreds of words, have communicated by stringing these words together, and have taught their skills to younger animals, who—like humans—tend to acquire the skills most easily and thoroughly if taught them at a very young age. Nevertheless, research reveals an important difference between apes' and humans' facilities with language: Only humans can master the verbal or signed expression of complex rules of syntax.

TERMS AND CONCEPTS TO REMEMBER

language, p. 30-0
phoneme, p. 30-0
morpheme, p. 30-1
grammar, p. 30-1
semantics, p. 30-1
syntax, p. 30-1

babbling stage, p. 30-2
one-word stage, p. 30-3
two-word stage, p. 30-3
telegraphic speech, p. 30-3
linguistic determinism, p. 30-7

TEST YOURSELF

1. If children are not yet speaking, is there any reason to think they would benefit from parents and other caregivers reading to them?

2. To say that "words are the mother of ideas" assumes the truth of what concept?

3. If your dog barks at a stranger at the front door, does this qualify as language? What if the dog yips in a telltale way to let you know she needs to go out?

(Answers in Appendix B.)

ASK YOURSELF

1. There has been controversy at some universities about allowing fluency in sign language to fulfill a second-language requirement for an undergraduate degree. What is your opinion?

2. Do you use certain words or gestures that only your family or closest circle of friends would understand? Can you envision using these words or gestures to construct a language, as the Nicaraguan children did in building their version of sign?

3. Can you think of a time when you felt an animal was communicating with you? How might you put such intuition to a test?

ANSWER TO QUESTION WITHIN THE MODULE

Q. How many morphemes are in the word *cats*?
A. Two—*cat* and *-s*

>WEB

Multiple-choice *self-tests* and more may be found at www.worthpublishers.com/myers.

New York Times *interviewer Deborah Solomon, 2004:*
"What is your IQ?"
Physicist Stephen Hawking:
"I have no idea. People who boast about their IQ are losers."

■ **intelligence** mental quality consisting of the ability to learn from experience, solve problems, and use knowledge to adapt to new situations.

Introduction to Intelligence

OBJECTIVE **31-1** | Discuss the difficulty of defining *intelligence,* and explain what it means to "reify intelligence."

School boards, courts, scientists, and clinicians debate the usefulness and fairness of tests that attempt to assess people's mental abilities, assign them a score, and compare them with the scores of others. Should we use such tests to rank people, to admit them to a particular college, to hire them for a particular job, to diagnose them with a particular psychological disorder? First, we'd better ask a more basic question: What *is* intelligence?

Psychologists debate: Should we consider intelligence as one aptitude or many? As linked to cognitive speed? As neurologically measurable? Yet, intelligence experts do agree on this: Intelligence is a concept and not a "thing." When we refer to someone's "IQ" (short for *intelligence quotient*) as if it were a fixed and objectively real trait like height, we commit a reasoning error called *reification*—viewing an abstract, immaterial concept as if it were a concrete thing. To reify is to invent a concept, give it a name, and then convince ourselves that such a thing objectively exists in the world. When someone says, "She has an IQ of 120," they are reifying IQ; they are imagining IQ to be a thing one *has,* rather than a score once obtained on a particular *intelligence test.* One should say, "Her score on the intelligence test was 120."

Intelligence is a socially constructed concept. Cultures deem "intelligent" whatever attributes enable success in those cultures (Sternberg & Kaufman, 1998). In the Amazon rain forest, intelligence may be a gift for discerning which native herbs effectively treat particular diseases. In Western countries, it may be superior performance on cognitive tasks. In each context, **intelligence** is the ability to learn from experience, solve problems, and use knowledge to adapt to new situations. In research studies, *intelligence* is whatever intelligence tests measure, which historically, as we will see, has tended to be school smarts.

Despite this general agreement, two controversies remain:

1. Is intelligence a single overall ability or several specific abilities?
2. With the tools neuroscience now offers, can we locate and measure intelligence within the brain?

Is Intelligence One General Ability or Several Specific Abilities?

You probably know some people with talents in science, others who excel at the humanities, and still others gifted in athletics, art, music, or dance. You may also know a talented artist who is dumbfounded by the simplest mathematical problems, or a brilliant math student with little aptitude for literary discussion. Perhaps you have wondered whether people's mental abilities are too diverse to justify labeling them with the single word *intelligence* or quantifying them with a number from some single scale. How might you test this idea?

General Intelligence

OBJECTIVE 31-2 | Present arguments for and against considering intelligence as one general mental ability.

To find out whether there might be a general ability factor that runs throughout our specific mental abilities, psychologists study how individual abilities relate to one another. The statistical procedure **factor analysis** enables researchers to identify clusters of test items that measure a common ability. For example, people who do well on vocabulary items often do well on paragraph comprehension, a cluster that helps define a verbal intelligence factor. Other clusters include a spatial ability factor and a reasoning ability factor.

Charles Spearman (1863–1945), who helped develop factor analysis, believed there is also a **general intelligence,** or **g,** factor that underlies the various clusters. Spearman granted that people often have special abilities that stand out. But he also noted that those who score high on one factor, such as verbal intelligence, typically score higher than average on other factors, such as spatial or reasoning ability. So there is at least a tendency for different abilities to come in the same package. Spearman believed that this commonality, the g factor, underlies all of our intelligent behavior, from navigating the sea to excelling in school.

This idea of a general mental capacity expressed by a single intelligence score was controversial in Spearman's day, and it remains so in our own. One of Spearman's early opponents was L. L. Thurstone (1887–1955). Thurstone gave 56 different tests to people and mathematically identified seven clusters of *primary mental abilities* (word fluency, verbal comprehension, spatial ability, perceptual speed, numerical ability, inductive reasoning, and memory). Thurstone did not rank his subjects on a single scale of general aptitude. But when other investigators studied the profiles of his subjects, they detected a small tendency for those who excelled in one of the seven clusters to score well on the others. So, they concluded, there was still some evidence of a g factor.

We might, then, liken mental abilities to physical abilities. Athleticism is not one thing but many. The ability to run fast is distinct from the strength needed for power lifting, which is distinct from the eye-hand coordination required to throw a ball on target. A champion weightlifter rarely has the potential to be a skilled ice skater. Yet there remains some tendency for good things to come packaged together—for running speed and throwing accuracy to correlate, thanks to general athletic ability. Similarly, intelligence involves several distinct abilities, which correlate enough to define a small general intelligence factor.

Satoshi Kanazawa (2004) argues that general intelligence evolved as a form of intelligence that helps people solve novel problems—how to stop a fire from spreading, how to find food during a drought, how to reunite with one's band on the other side of a flooded river. More common problems, such as how to mate or how to read strangers' faces or how to find one's way back to camp, require a different sort of intelligence. In fact, general intelligence scores *do* correlate with ability to solve various novel problems (like those found in academic and many vocational situations) but do *not* much correlate with individuals' skills in "evolutionarily familiar" situations—such as marrying and parenting, forming close friendships, displaying social competence, and navigating without maps.

■ **factor analysis** a statistical procedure that identifies clusters of related items (called *factors*) on a test; used to identify different dimensions of performance that underlie one's total score.

■ **general intelligence (g)** a general intelligence factor that according to Spearman and others underlies specific mental abilities and is therefore measured by every task on an intelligence test.

"g is one of the most reliable and valid measures in the behavioral domain . . . and it predicts important social outcomes such as educational and occupational levels far better than any other trait."
Behavior geneticist Robert Plomin (1999)

Athleticism, like intelligence, is many things
Some coaches have therefore encouraged players, such as this baseball player and golfer, to develop efficient movement as well as endurance, speed, and quickness by taking Pilates classes.

Stacey Valant/www.pilatescenterindy.net

■ **savant syndrome** a condition in which a person otherwise limited in mental ability has an exceptional specific skill, such as in computation or drawing.

Gardner (1998) also speculates about a ninth possible intelligence—*existential intelligence*—the ability "to ponder large questions about life, death, existence."

Contemporary Intelligence Theories

OBJECTIVE 31-3 | Compare Gardner's and Sternberg's theories of intelligence.

Since the mid-1980s some psychologists have sought to extend the definition of intelligence beyond Spearman's and Thurstone's academic smarts.

Multiple Intelligences

Howard Gardner (1983, 1999) supports Thurstone's idea that intelligence comes in different packages. He notes that brain damage may diminish one type of ability but not others. He observes that different abilities enabled our ancestors to cope with different environmental challenges (finding their way home, reading others' emotions, solving problems). And he studies people with exceptional abilities, including those who excel in only one. People with **savant syndrome,** for example, often score low on intelligence tests but have an island of brilliance—some incredible ability, as in computation, drawing, or musical memory (Treffert & Wallace, 2002). Some have virtually no language ability, yet are able to compute numbers as quickly and accurately as an electronic calculator, or identify almost instantly the day of the week that corresponds to any given date in history (Miller, 1999). About 4 in 5 people with this syndrome are males, and many also have autism, a developmental disorder afflicting more males than females. With or without savant syndrome, people with autism may excel in some areas, such as math, and fail at other tasks, such as reading facial expressions.

Using such evidence, Gardner argues that we do not have *an* intelligence, but instead have *multiple* intelligences, each relatively independent of the others. In addition to the verbal and mathematical aptitudes assessed by standard tests, he identifies distinct aptitudes for musical accomplishment, for spatially analyzing the visual world, for mastering movement skills (as in dance), and for insightfully understanding ourselves, others, and our natural environment (**TABLE 31.1**).

According to Gardner (1998), the computer programmer, the poet, the street-smart adolescent who becomes a crafty executive, and the point guard on the basketball team exhibit different kinds of intelligence. He notes,

> If a person is strong (or weak) in telling stories, solving mathematical proofs, navigating around unfamiliar terrain, learning an unfamiliar song, mastering a new game that entails dexterity, understanding others, or understanding himself, one simply does not know whether comparable strengths (or weaknesses) will be found in other areas.

TABLE 31.1

GARDNER'S EIGHT INTELLIGENCES

Aptitude	Exemplar
1. Linguistic	T. S. Eliot, poet
2. Logical-mathematical	Albert Einstein, scientist
3. Musical	Igor Stravinsky, composer
4. Spatial	Pablo Picasso, artist
5. Bodily-kinesthetic	Martha Graham, dancer
6. Intrapersonal (self)	Sigmund Freud, psychiatrist
7. Interpersonal (other people)	Mahatma Gandhi, leader
8. Naturalist	Charles Darwin, naturalist

Islands of genius: Savant syndrome Matt Savage, (left) a 13-year-old with autism, is also an award-winning jazz pianist. Matt has his own band—the Matt Savage Trio. Kim Peek (middle), the inspiration for the character Raymond Babbit in the movie *Rain Man*, depends on his father for many of his daily needs. Yet Peek knows more than 7600 books by heart, as well as all U.S. area codes, Zip codes, and TV stations. Alonzo Clemons (right), despite a developmental disability, can create perfect replicas of any animal he briefly sees. His bronze figures have earned him a national reputation.

Courtesy of Diane and Matt Savage

Ethan Hill

Ethan Hill

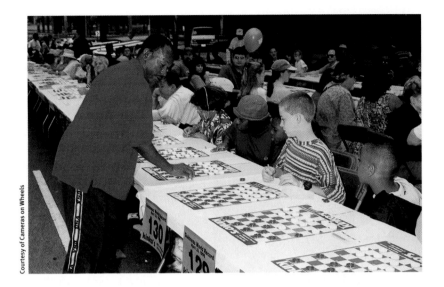

Spatial intelligence genius
In 1998, World Checkers Champion Ron "Suki" King of Barbados set a new record by simultaneously playing 385 players in 3 hours and 44 minutes. Thus, while his opponents often had hours to plot their game moves, King could only devote about 35 seconds to each game. Yet he still managed to win all 385 games!

A general intelligence score is therefore like the overall rating of a city—which doesn't give you much specific information about its schools, streets, or nightlife.

Wouldn't it be wonderful if the world were so just, responds intelligence researcher Sandra Scarr (1989), that being weak in any area would often be compensated by genius in some other area? Alas, the world is not just, for there remains some tendency for different skills to correlate. For example, people with mental disadvantages often have lesser physical abilities as well; Special Olympics gives them and others a chance to enjoy fair competition. Moreover, in one digest of 127 studies, an academic intelligence score that predicted graduate school success also predicted later job success (Kuncel & others, 2004). General intelligence scores likewise predict performance on various complex tasks and in various jobs; *g* matters (Gottfredson, 2002a,b, 2003a,b; Reeve & Hakel, 2002). It even matters for longevity. In studies controlling for income and education differences, the 11-year-old test-takers who scored low on an intelligence test in 1932 had in their adult years shorter average life spans and a higher likelihood of dying from lung cancer and cardiovascular diseases than did their higher-scoring counterparts (Hart & others, 2003; Whalley & Deary, 2001).

Gardner's critics have pointed out that, without tests for measuring all these intelligences, it is difficult to research his theory. Critics also question whether it really makes sense to lump all sorts of abilities under the concept of intelligence. Intelligence is *mental* ability, they say. The abilities we can manage without, as in music and athletics, are better considered *talents* than the more crucial verbal and reasoning skills. If people lack physical talent, do we consider them as lacking in *intelligence*? Gardner counters that all forms of intelligence have intrinsic value—it is one's culture and context that place greater value on some capacities than on others. Indeed, definitions of intelligence—whether the traditional predictor of school achievement or a broader definition—tend to express what people value in a human being.

Aspects of Successful Intelligence

Robert Sternberg (1985, 1999, 2003) agrees with Gardner's idea of multiple intelligences, but his *triarchic theory* (from *triarchy*—"a country under three rulers") distinguishes three, not eight, intelligences:

- *Analytical (academic problem-solving) intelligence*—assessed by intelligence tests, which present well-defined problems having a single right answer.
- *Creative intelligence*—demonstrated in reacting adaptively to novel situations and generating novel ideas.
- *Practical intelligence*—often required for everyday tasks, which are frequently ill-defined, with multiple solutions.

> You have to be careful, if you're good at something, to make sure you don't think you're good at other things that you aren't necessarily so good at. . . . Because I've been very successful at [software development] people come in and expect that I have wisdom about topics that I don't."
> Bill Gates (1998)

Street smarts
This child selling candy on the streets of Manaus, Brazil, is developing practical intelligence at a very young age.

Traditional intelligence tests assess academic intelligence. They predict school grades reasonably well but predict vocational success more modestly. People who demonstrate keen practical intelligence may or may not have distinguished themselves in school. Managerial success, for example, depends less on the academic abilities assessed by an intelligence test score (assuming the score is average or above) than on a shrewd ability to manage oneself, one's tasks, and other people.

Sternberg and Richard Wagner's (1993, 1995) test of practical managerial intelligence measures whether test-takers know how to write effective memos, how to motivate people, when to delegate tasks and responsibilities, how to read people, and how to promote their own careers. Business executives who score high on this test tend to earn higher salaries and receive better performance ratings than do those who score low. In a similar finding, Stephen Ceci and Jeffrey Liker (1986) reported that racetrack fans' expertise in handicapping horses—a practical but complex cognitive task—was unrelated to their intelligence test scores.

Although Sternberg (1998, 1999) and Gardner (1998) differ on specific points, they agree that multiple abilities can contribute to life success. (Neither candidate in the 2000 U.S. presidential election had scored exceptionally high on college entrance aptitude tests, notes Sternberg [2000], yet both, after college, have been successful.) They also agree that the differing varieties of giftedness add spice to life and challenges for education. Under Gardner's or Sternberg's influence, many teachers have been trained to appreciate the varieties of ability and to apply multiple intelligence theory in their classrooms.

Some critics contend that Sternberg's proposed three intelligences are not as independent of one another as he thinks, and actually share an underlying general intelligence (Brody, 2003). Much as the idea of practical intelligence appeals to the popular idea that "everyone can be smart in some way," argues Linda Gottfredson (2003a,b), "no one has yet demonstrated that practical intelligence . . . is even a useful concept." What predicts successful job performance is not so much practical intelligence, she contends, as general intelligence, personality, and motivation. Actually, replies Sternberg (2003), studies from Kenyan villages to rural Alaska show that *g* measures fail to tap important ability domains, and that the triarchic understanding of intelligence helps "pave the way for subsequent generations of better theories." (**TABLE 31.2** summarizes the four main theories discussed in this module.) As Sternberg understands, no one's ideas are the final word; today's best theories are often developed into or replaced by tomorrow's better ideas. So stay tuned.

Hands-on healing
Success for this folk healer in Peru may have less to do with general intelligence than with knowledge about his medicinal plants and an understanding of the people he is helping.

TABLE 31.2

COMPARING THEORIES OF INTELLIGENCE

Theory	Summary	Strengths	Other Considerations
Spearman's general intelligence (g)	A basic intelligence predicts our abilities in varied academic areas.	Different abilities, such as verbal and spatial, do have some tendency to correlate.	Human abilities are too diverse to be encapsulated by a single general intelligence factor.
Thurstone's primary mental abilities	Our intelligence may be broken down into seven factors: word fluency, verbal comprehension, spatial ability, perceptual speed, numerical ability, inductive reasoning, and memory.	A single g score is not as informative as scores for seven primary mental abilities.	Even Thurstone's seven mental abilities show a tendency to cluster, suggesting an underlying g factor.
Gardner's multiple intelligences	Our abilities are best classified into eight independent intelligences, which include a broad range of skills beyond traditional school smarts.	Intelligence is more than just verbal and mathematical skills. Other abilities are equally important to our human adaptability.	Should all of our abilities be considered *intelligences*? Shouldn't some of them be called less vital *talents* instead?
Sternberg's triarchic	Our intelligence is best classified into three areas that predict our real-world success: analytical, creative, and practical.	These three facets may be reliably measured.	1. These three facets may be less independent than Sternberg thought and may actually share an underlying g factor. 2. Additional testing is needed to determine whether these facets can reliably predict success.

Emotional Intelligence

OBJECTIVE 31-4 | Describe the four aspects of emotional intelligence, and discuss criticisms of this concept.

Also distinct from academic intelligence is what Nancy Cantor and John Kihlstrom (1987) first called *social intelligence*—the know-how involved in comprehending social situations and managing oneself successfully. Consistent with this distinction between academic and social intelligence is the repeated finding that college grades only modestly predict later work achievement (Bretz, 1989; Dye & Reck, 1989).

Seymour Epstein and Petra Meier (1989) have wondered why high-aptitude people are "not, by a wide margin, more effective . . . in achieving better marriages, in successfully raising their children, and in achieving better mental and physical well-being." The answer may lie in part in a critical part of social intelligence, which Peter Salovey and John Mayer (1990; Salovey & others, 2002) call **emotional intelligence**—the ability to perceive, understand, manage, and use emotions. One study, led by emotion researcher Carroll Izard (2001), assessed 5-year-olds' ability to recognize and label facial emotions. Even after controlling for verbal aptitude and temperament, researchers found that the 5-year-olds who had most accurately discerned emotions became 9-year-olds who easily made friends, cooperated with the teacher, and effectively managed their emotions.

Emotionally intelligent people are self-aware. Mayer, Salovey, and David Caruso (2002; Grewal & Salovey, 2005) have developed an emotional intelligence test to assess both overall emotional intelligence and its four components—the ability to *perceive* emotions (to recognize them in faces, music, and stories), to *understand* emotions (to predict them and how they change and blend), to *manage* emotions (to know how to express them in varied situations), and to *use* emotions to enable adaptive or creative thinking. In both the United States and Germany, those scoring high on managing emotions enjoy higher-quality interactions with friends of both sexes (Lopes & others, 2004). They avoid being hijacked by overwhelming depression, anxiety, or anger. Their empathy enables them to read others' emotions and to handle those emotions skillfully, knowing what to say to a grieving friend, how to encourage colleagues, and how to manage conflicts well. Across 69 studies in many countries,

"You're wise, but you lack tree smarts."

■ **emotional intelligence** the ability to perceive, understand, manage, and use emotions.

those scoring high in emotional intelligence also have exhibited modestly better job performance (Van Rooy & Viswesvaran, 2004). They can delay gratification in pursuit of long-range rewards, rather than being overtaken by immediate impulses. Simply said, they are emotionally smart, and thus they often succeed in career, marriage, and parenting situations where academically smarter (but emotionally less intelligent) people fail.

In extreme cases, brain damage may diminish emotional intelligence while leaving general intelligence intact. Antonio Damasio, a University of Iowa neuroscientist known for his registry of more than 2000 brain-damaged patients, tells of Elliot, a man with normal intelligence and memory. Since removal of a brain tumor, Elliot has lived without emotion. "I never saw a tinge of emotion in my many hours of conversation with him," Damasio (1994) reported, "no sadness, no impatience, no frustration." Shown disturbing pictures of injured people, destroyed communities, and natural disasters, Elliot shows—and realizes he feels—no emotion. Like Data, the human-appearing android of *Star Trek: The Next Generation,* he knows but he cannot feel. Unable to intuitively adjust his behavior in response to others' feelings, Elliot lost his job. He went bankrupt. His marriage collapsed. He remarried and divorced again. At last report, he was dependent on custodial care from a sibling and a disability check.

Some scholars, however—including even multiple-intelligence man Howard Gardner (1999)—are concerned that concepts such as "emotional intelligence" stretch *intelligence* too far. It is wise to stretch the concept to include our processing not only of words, numbers, and logic, but also of space, music, and information about ourselves and others, says Gardner. But let us also, he says, respect emotional sensitivity, creativity, and motivation as important but different. Stretch a word to include everything we prize and it will lose its meaning.

In defense of academic smarts—the *g* factor—researchers point to studies in which traditional intelligence scores *do* predict both occupational status and job performance (Brody, 1997; Schmidt & Hunter, 1998). For example, intelligence matters most in mentally demanding jobs. Meteorology more than meter reading requires intelligence to excel. However, once admitted to a vocation, those who become highly successful have other traits as well—they are conscientious, well-connected, and doggedly energetic. Thus, high intelligence does more to get you into a profession (via the schools and training programs that take you there) than it does to make you successful once there. The recipe for success combines talent with grit. Anders Ericsson (2002; Ericsson & Lehmann, 1996) reports a common ingredient of expert performance in chess, dancing, sports, computer programming, music, and medicine: "about 10 years of intense, daily practice."

So, the academic aptitude tapped by intelligence tests is indeed important. Yet our competence in everyday living requires much that traditional intelligence tests do not measure.

> " I worry about [intelligence] definitions that collapse assessments of our cognitive powers with statements about the kind of human beings we favor."
>
> Howard Gardner, "Rethinking the Concept of Intelligence," 2000

Emotional intelligence
Success in the real world is affected not just by book smarts, but also by our ability to perceive, understand, and express emotions. These prison inmates are trying to learn those traits by participating in a role-playing, parent-training program sponsored by Girl Scouts Beyond Bars.

Intelligence and Creativity

OBJECTIVE 31-5 | Identify the factors associated with creativity, and describe the relationship between creativity and intelligence.

> **creativity** the ability to produce novel and valuable ideas.

Pierre de Fermat, a seventeenth-century mischievous genius, challenged mathematicians of his day to match his solutions to various number theory problems. He offered his most famous challenge—his so-called last theorem, after mathematicians solved all his others. This problem baffled the greatest mathematical minds, even after a $2 million prize (in today's dollars) was offered in 1908 to whoever first created a proof.

Like countless others, Princeton mathematician Andrew Wiles had pondered the problem for more than 30 years and had come to the brink of a solution. Then, one morning, out of the blue, the "incredible revelation"—the fix to the one remaining difficulty—struck him. "It was so indescribably beautiful; it was so simple and so elegant. I couldn't understand how I'd missed it and I just stared at it in disbelief for 20 minutes. Then during the day I walked around the department, and I'd keep coming back to my desk looking to see if it was still there. It was still there. I couldn't contain myself, I was so excited. It was the most important moment of my working life" (Singh, 1997, p. 25).

Wiles' incredible moment illustrates **creativity**—the ability to produce ideas that are both novel and valuable. Studies of intelligence and creativity suggest that a certain level of aptitude is necessary but not sufficient for creativity. In general, people who do well on intelligence tests also do well on creativity tests ("How many uses can you think of for a brick?"). But beyond a certain level—a score of about 120—the correlation between intelligence scores and creativity shrivels. Exceptionally creative architects, mathematicians, scientists, and engineers usually score no higher on intelligence tests than do their less creative peers (MacKinnon & Hall, 1972; Simonton, 2000). So clearly there is more to creativity than what intelligence tests reveal. Indeed, the brain areas supporting the *convergent thinking* tested by intelligence tests (which demand a single correct answer) differ from those supporting the *divergent thinking* that imagines multiple possible answers to a problem (such as words beginning with the letter *s*). Injury to the left parietal lobe damages the convergent thinking required by intelligence test scores and for school success. Injury to certain areas of the frontal lobes can leave reading, writing, and arithmetic skills intact but destroy imagination (Kolb & Whishaw, 2006).

Studies of creative people suggest five components of creativity beyond a minimal level of aptitude (Sternberg, 1988; Sternberg & Lubart, 1991, 1992):

1. **Expertise** is a well-developed base of knowledge. "Chance favors only the prepared mind," observed Louis Pasteur. The more ideas, images, and phrases we have available through our accumulated learning, the more chances we have to combine these mental building blocks in novel ways. Wiles' well-developed base of knowledge put the needed theorems and methods at his disposal.

2. **Imaginative thinking skills** provide the ability to see things in novel ways, to recognize patterns, to make connections. Having mastered a problem's basic elements, we redefine or explore it in a new way. Copernicus first developed expertise regarding the solar system and its planets and then creatively defined the system as revolving around the Sun, not the Earth. Wiles' imaginative solution combined two important but incomplete solutions.

3. **A venturesome personality** tolerates ambiguity and risk, perseveres in overcoming obstacles, and seeks new experiences rather than following the pack. Inventors, for example, have a willingness to persist after failures. Thomas Edison tried countless substances for his light bulb filament. Wiles said he labored in isolation from the mathematics community partly to stay focused and avoid distraction.

After picking up a Nobel prize in Stockholm, physicist Richard Feynman stopped in Queens, New York, to look at his high school record. "My grades were not as good as I remembered," he reported, "and my IQ was [a good, though unexceptional] 124" (Faber, 1987).

" If you would allow me any talent, it's simply this: I can, for whatever reason, reach down into my own brain, feel around in all the mush, find and extract something from my persona, and then graft it onto an idea."

Cartoonist Gary Larson, *The Complete Far Side*, 2003

Imaginative thinking
Cartoonists often display creativity as they see things in new ways or make unusual connections.

FURIOUS GEORGE

Everyone held up their crackers as David threw the cheese log into the ceiling fan.

4. **Intrinsic motivation** is creativity's fourth component. As psychologist Teresa Amabile points out, "People will be most creative when they feel motivated primarily by the interest, enjoyment, satisfaction, and challenge of the work itself—rather than by external pressures" (Amabile & Hennessey, 1992). Creative people focus not so much on extrinsic motivators—meeting deadlines, impressing people, or making money—as on the intrinsic pleasure and challenge of their work. Asked how he solved such difficult scientific problems, Isaac Newton reportedly answered, "By thinking about them all the time." Wiles concurred: "I was so obsessed by this problem that for eight years I was thinking about it all the time—when I woke up in the morning to when I went to sleep at night" (Singh & Riber, 1997).

5. **A creative environment** sparks, supports, and refines creative ideas. After studying the careers of 2026 prominent scientists and inventors, Dean Keith Simonton (1992) noted that the most eminent among them were in fact not lone geniuses. Rather they were mentored, challenged, and supported by their relationships with colleagues. Such people often have the emotional intelligence needed to network effectively with peers. Even Wiles stood on the shoulders of others and wrestled his problem with the collaboration of a former student.

Amabile's (1983, 1987) experiments demonstrated that creative environments also free people from concern about social approval. In one experiment, she asked college students to make paper collages, telling half beforehand that experts would evaluate their work. Students, unaware that their work would be evaluated, produced collages that judges rated as more creative. Unworried about being evaluated, they felt freer to be creative.

Managers wanting to foster innovation at work should keep the intrinsic motivation principle in mind, observed Amabile (1988). They should set employees to work on what naturally interests them. And they can emulate managers who have successfully nurtured creativity—by providing their subordinates with time, freedom, and support to attain set goals. The 3M company, with an Eleventh Commandment of "Thou shalt not kill a new product idea," encouraged researchers to spend 15 percent of their time pursuing creative projects that have no immediate payoff. This creativity-nurturing environment produced such products as the now-commonplace Post-it notes (Kreitner, 1992).

Is Intelligence Neurologically Measurable?

OBJECTIVE 31-6 | Describe the relationship between intelligence and brain anatomy.

Using today's neuroscience tools, might we link differences in people's intelligence test performance to dissimilarities in the heart of smarts—the brain? Might we anticipate a future brain test of intelligence?

Brain Anatomy

After the brilliant English poet Lord Byron died in 1824, doctors discovered that his brain was a massive 5 pounds. Three years later, Beethoven died and his brain was found to have exceptionally numerous and deep convolutions. Such observations set brain scientists off studying the brains of other geniuses at their wits' end (Burrell, 2005). Do people with big brains have big smarts?

Alas, some geniuses had small brains, and some dim-witted criminals had brains like those of scientists. More recent studies that directly measure brain volume using MRI scans do reveal correlations of about +.40 between brain size (adjusted for body size) and intelligence score (Gignac & others, 2003; Rushton & Ankney, 1996). Moreover, as adults age, brain size and nonverbal intelligence test scores fall in concert (Bigler & others, 1995).

If intelligence does modestly correlate with brain size, the cause could be differing genes, nutrition, environmental stimulation, some combination of these, or perhaps something else. We now know that experience alters the brain. Rats raised in a stimulating rather than deprived environment develop thicker, heavier cortexes. And learning leaves detectable traces in the brain's neural connections. "Intelligence is due to the development of neural connections in response to the environment," notes University of Sydney psychologist Dennis Garlick (2003).

Postmortem brain analyses reveal that highly educated people die with more synapses—17 percent more in one study—than their less-educated counterparts (Orlovskaya & others, 1999). This does not tell us whether people grow synapses with education, or people with more synapses seek more education (or both). But other evidence suggests that highly intelligent people differ in their *neural plasticity*—their ability during childhood and adolescence to adapt and grow neural connections in response to their environment (Garlick, 2002, 2003).

Efforts to link brain structure with cognition continue. One research team, led by psychologist Richard Haier (2004), correlated intelligence scores from 47 adult volunteers with scans that measured their volume of gray matter (neural bodies) and white matter (axons and dendrites) in various brain regions. Higher intelligence scores were linked with more gray matter in some specific areas known to be involved in memory, attention, and language (**FIGURE 31.1**).

With the brains of 91 Canadians as a comparison base, Sandra Witelson and her colleagues (1999) seized an opportunity to study Einstein's brain. Although not notably heavier or larger in total size than the typical Canadian's brain, Einstein's brain was 15 percent larger in the parietal lobe's lower region—which just happens to be a center for processing mathematical and spatial information. Certain other areas were a tad smaller than average. With different mental functions competing for the brain's real estate, these observations may offer a clue to why Einstein, like some other great physicists such as Richard Feynman and Edward Teller, was slow in learning to talk (Pinker, 1999).

FIGURE 31.1
Gray matter matters
A frontal view of the brain shows some of the areas where gray matter is concentrated in people with high intelligence scores, and where *g* therefore may be concentrated. (From Haier & others, 2004.)

Brain Function

OBJECTIVE 31-7 | Discuss findings on the correlations between perceptual speed, neural processing speed, and intelligence.

Even if the modest correlations between brain anatomy and intelligence prove reliable, they only begin to explain intelligence differences. Searching for other explanations, neuroscientists are studying the brain's functioning.

A sperm whale's brain is about 6 times heavier than your brain.

Correlations do not indicate cause-effect, but they do tell us whether two things are associated in some way. A correlation of –1.0 represents perfect disagreement between two sets of scores—as one score goes up, the other goes down. A correlation of zero represents no association. A correlation of +1.0 represents perfect agreement—as the first score goes up, so does the second.

" I am, somehow, less interested in the weight and convolutions of Einstein's brain than in the near certainty that people of equal talent have lived and died in cotton fields and sweatshops."
Stephen Jay Gould, *The Panda's Thumb*, 1980

As people contemplate a variety of questions like those found on intelligence tests, a frontal lobe area just above the outer edge of the eyebrows becomes especially active—in the left brain for verbal questions, and on both sides for spatial questions (Duncan & others, 2000). Information from various brain areas seems to converge in this spot, suggesting to researcher John Duncan (2000) that it may be a "global workspace for organizing and coordinating information" and that some people may be "blessed with a workspace that functions very, very well."

Are more intelligent people literally more quick-witted, much as today's speedy computer chips enable more powerful computing than did their predecessors? On some tasks they seem to be. Earl Hunt (1983) found that verbal intelligence scores are predictable from the speed with which people retrieve information from memory. Those who recognize quickly that *sink* and *wink* are different words, or that *A* and *a* share the same name, tend to score high in verbal ability. Extremely precocious 12- to 14-year-old college students are especially quick in responding to such tasks (Jensen, 1989). To try to define "quick-wittedness," researchers are taking a close look at speed of perception and speed of neural processing of information.

Perceptual Speed Across many studies, the correlation between intelligence score and the speed of taking in perceptual information tends to be about +.4 to +.5 (Deary & Der, 2005; Grudnik & Kranzler, 2001). A typical experiment flashes an incomplete stimulus, as in **FIGURE 31.2**, then another image that overrides the lingering afterimage of the incomplete stimulus. The researcher then asks participants whether the long side appeared on the right or left. How much stimulus inspection time does one need to answer correctly 80 percent of the time? Perhaps .01 second? Or .02 second? Those who perceive quickly tend to score somewhat higher on intelligence tests, particularly on tests based on perceptual rather than verbal problem solving.

Neurological Speed Do the quicker processing and perceptions of highly intelligent people reflect greater neural processing speed? Repeated studies have found that their brain waves register a simple stimulus (such as a flash of light or a tone beep) more quickly and with greater complexity (Caryl, 1994; Deary & Caryl, 1993; Reed & Jensen, 1992). The evoked brain response also tends to be slightly faster when people with high rather than low intelligence scores perform a simple task, such as pushing a button when an *X* appears on a screen (McGarry-Roberts & others, 1992).

Neural processing speed on a simple task seems far removed from the untimed responses to complex intelligence test items, such as "In what way are *wool* and *cotton* alike?" As yet, notes intelligence expert Nathan Brody (1992, 2001), we have no firm understanding of *why* fast reactions on simple tasks should predict intelligence test performance, though he suspects they reflect one's "core information processing ability." Philip Vernon (1983) has speculated that "faster cognitive processing may allow more information to be acquired." Perhaps people who more quickly process information accumulate more information—about wool, cotton, and millions of other things.

The neurological approach to understanding intelligence (and so many other things in psychology) is currently in its heyday. Will this new research reduce what we now call the *g* factor to simple measures of underlying brain activity? Or are these efforts totally wrongheaded because what we call intelligence is not a single general trait but several culturally adaptive skills? The controversies surrounding the nature of intelligence are a long way from resolution.

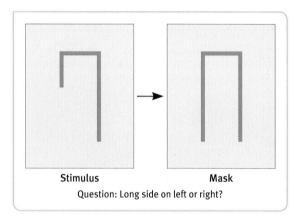

Stimulus   Mask
Question: Long side on left or right?

FIGURE 31.2
An inspection time task
A stimulus is flashed before being overridden by a masking image. How long would you need to glimpse the stimulus at the left to answer the question? People who can perceive the stimulus very quickly tend to score somewhat higher on intelligence tests. (Adapted from Deary & Stough, 1996.)

>> LEARNING OUTCOMES

Introduction to Intelligence

OBJECTIVE 31-1 | **Discuss the difficulty of defining** *intelligence,* **and explain what it means to "reify intelligence."**
Intelligence is a socially constructed concept that differs from culture to culture. The two big controversies in current research on intelligence are (1) whether it is one overall ability or many, and (2) whether neuroscientists can locate and measure intelligence within the brain. To *reify* intelligence is to treat it as though it were a real object, not an abstract concept. Most psychologists now define *intelligence* as the ability to learn from experience, solve problems, and adapt to new situations.

OBJECTIVE 31-2 | **Present arguments for and against considering intelligence as one general mental ability.**
Factor analysis, a statistical procedure, has been used to show that mental abilities tend to form clusters, and that people show about the same level of competence in all abilities in the cluster. In the mid-twentieth century, Charles Spearman (a developer of factor analysis) named this general mental ability the *g* factor. Some psychologists today agree with Spearman's idea that we have a common level of intelligence that can predict our abilities in all other academic areas, but others believe we have multiple intelligences.

OBJECTIVE 31-3 | **Compare Gardner's and Sternberg's theories of intelligence.**
Howard Gardner disputes the idea of one general intelligence. He proposes eight independent intelligences: *linguistic* (word smarts), *logical-mathematical* (number smarts), *musical* (music smarts), *spatial* (space smarts), *bodily-kinesthetic* (body smarts), *intrapersonal* (self smarts), *interpersonal* (people smarts), and *natural* (nature smarts). Robert Sternberg's triarchic theory proposes only three intelligences: *analytical* (academic problem solving), *creative,* and *practical* intelligences. (For more on the single-intelligence/multiple intelligences debate, see Table 31.2.)

OBJECTIVE 31-4 | **Describe the four aspects of emotional intelligence, and discuss criticisms of this concept.**
The four components of emotional intelligence are the ability to *perceive* emotions (to recognize them in faces, music, and stories), to *understand* emotions (to predict them and how they change and blend), to *manage* emotions (to know how to express them in varied situations), and to *use* emotions. Critics of the idea of emotional intelligence question whether we stretch the idea of intelligence too far when we apply it to emotions.

OBJECTIVE 31-5 | **Identify the factors associated with creativity, and describe the relationship between creativity and intelligence.**
Creativity is the ability to produce novel and valuable ideas. It correlates somewhat with intelligence test scores, but beyond a score of 120, that correlation dwindles. It also correlates with expertise, imaginative thinking skills, a venturesome personality, intrinsic motivation, and the support offered by a creative environment. Different brain areas are active when we engage in *convergent thinking* (the type required for intelligence test solutions) and *divergent thinking* (the type required for multiple imaginative solutions).

OBJECTIVE 31-6 | **Describe the relationship between intelligence and brain anatomy.**
There is some correlation between brain size (adjusted for body size) and intelligence score. But the direction of the relationship is not clear. Larger brain size may enable greater intelligence; greater intelligence may lead to experiences that exercise the brain and build more connections, thus increasing its size; or some third factor may be at work.

OBJECTIVE 31-7 | **Discuss findings on the correlations between perceptual speed, neural processing speed, and intelligence.**
People who score high on intelligence tests tend also to retrieve information from memory more quickly, and to perceive stimuli faster than others. These differences are reflected in neurological studies that show faster brain response times.

TERMS AND CONCEPTS TO REMEMBER

intelligence, p. 31-0	savant syndrome, p. 31-2
factor analysis, p. 31-1	emotional intelligence, p. 31-5
general intelligence (*g*), p. 31-1	creativity, p. 31-7

TEST YOURSELF

1. Joseph is a straight-A student at Harvard Law School, writes a small column for the *Harvard Law Review,* and will be working for a Supreme Court justice next year. Judith is very proud of her grandson and says he is way more intelligent than she ever was. But Joseph is also very proud of his grandmother, who had been imprisoned by the Nazis. When the war ended, she walked out of Germany, contacted a relief agency, traveled to the United States, and began a new life. According to the definition of intelligence in this module, is Joseph the only intelligent person in this story? Why or why not?

(Answer in Appendix B.)

ASK YOURSELF

1. The modern concept of multiple intelligences (as proposed by Gardner and Sternberg) assumes that the analytical word smarts and number smarts measured by traditional intelligence tests are important abilities but that other abilities are also important. Different people have different gifts. What are yours?

>WEB

Multiple-choice *self-tests* and more may be found at www.worthpublishers.com/myers.

Assessing Intelligence

OBJECTIVE 32-1 | Define *intelligence test,* and discuss the history of intelligence testing.

How do we assess intelligence? Movie hero Forrest Gump's answer, "Stupid is as stupid does," catches the spirit of psychology's simplest answer: Intelligent is as intelligent does on an IQ test. In other words, *intelligence* is whatever **intelligence tests** measure. So, what are these tests, and what makes a test credible? Answering those questions begins with a look at why psychologists created tests of mental abilities and how they have used those tests.

The Origins of Intelligence Testing

Some societies concern themselves with promoting the collective welfare of the family, community, and society. Other societies emphasize individual opportunity. Plato, a pioneer of the individualist tradition, wrote more than 2000 years ago in *The Republic* that "no two persons are born exactly alike; but each differs from the other in natural endowments, one being suited for one occupation and the other for another." As heirs to Plato's individualism, people in Western societies have pondered how and why individuals differ in mental ability.

Western attempts to assess such differences began in earnest about a century ago. The historical story of intelligence testing illustrates an important lesson: Although science itself strives for objectivity, individual scientists are affected by their own assumptions and attitudes.

Alfred Binet: Predicting School Achievement

The modern intelligence-testing movement began at the turn of the twentieth century when France passed a law requiring that all children attend school. Teachers soon faced an overwhelming range of individual differences. Some children, including many newcomers to Paris, seemed incapable of benefiting from the regular school curriculum and in need of special classes. But how could the schools objectively identify children with special needs?

The French government hesitated to trust teachers' subjective judgments of children's learning potential. Academic slowness might merely reflect inadequate prior education. Also, teachers might prejudge children on the basis of their social backgrounds. To minimize bias, France's minister of public education in 1904 commissioned Alfred Binet (1857–1911) and others to study the problem.

Binet and his collaborator, Théodore Simon, began by assuming that all children follow the same course of intellectual development but that some develop more rapidly. On tests, therefore, a "dull" child should perform as does a typical younger child, and a "bright" child as does a typical older child.

Binet and Simon set out to measure what came to be called a child's **mental age,** the chronological age typical of a given level of performance. The average 9-year-old has a mental age of 9. Children with below-average mental ages, such as 9-year-olds who perform at the level of a typical 7-year-old, would struggle with schoolwork considered normal for their age.

■ **intelligence test** a method for assessing an individual's mental aptitudes and comparing them with those of others, using numerical scores.

■ **mental age** a measure of intelligence test performance devised by Binet; the chronological age that most typically corresponds to a given level of performance. Thus, a child who does as well as the average 8-year-old is said to have a mental age of 8.

■ **Stanford-Binet** the widely used American revision (by Terman at Stanford University) of Binet's original intelligence test.

■ **intelligence quotient (IQ)** defined originally as the ratio of mental age (*ma*) to chronological age (*ca*) multiplied by 100 (thus, IQ = *ma/ca* x 100). On contemporary intelligence tests, the average performance for a given age is assigned a score of 100.

Alfred Binet

"The scale, properly speaking, does not permit the measure of intelligence, because intellectual qualities . . . cannot be measured as linear surfaces are measured" (Binet & Simon, 1905).

National Library of Medicine

To measure mental age, Binet and Simon theorized that mental aptitude, like athletic aptitude, is a general capacity that shows up in various ways. They then developed varied reasoning and problem-solving questions that might predict school achievement, and they tried many of them with Binet's two daughters. By then testing "bright" and "backward" Parisian schoolchildren on these questions, Binet and Simon succeeded: They found items that did predict how well the children would handle schoolwork.

Note that Binet and Simon made no assumptions concerning *why* a particular child was slow, average, or precocious. Binet personally leaned toward an environmental explanation. To raise the capacities of low-scoring children, he recommended "mental orthopedics" that would train them to develop their attention span and self-discipline. He refused to speculate about what the test was actually measuring, and insisted that it did not measure inborn intelligence as a meter stick measures height. Rather, the test had a single practical purpose: to identify French schoolchildren needing special attention. Binet hoped his test would be used to improve children's education, but he also feared it would be used to label children and limit their opportunities (Gould, 1981).

Lewis Terman: The Innate IQ

Binet might have been dismayed to discover that the test he designed as a practical guide for identifying slow learners in need of special help would soon be used as a numerical measure of inherited intelligence. After Binet's death in 1911, Stanford University professor Lewis Terman (1877–1956) attempted to use Binet's test but found that the Paris-developed age norms worked poorly with California schoolchildren. So Terman adapted some of Binet's original items, added others, established new age norms, and extended the upper end of the test's range from teenagers to "superior adults." Terman gave his revision the name it retains today—the **Stanford-Binet.**

From such tests, German psychologist William Stern derived the famous **intelligence quotient,** or **IQ.** The IQ was simply a person's mental age divided by chronological age and multiplied by 100 to get rid of the decimal point:

$$IQ = \frac{\text{mental age}}{\text{chronological age}} \times 100$$

Thus, an average child, whose mental and chronological ages are the same, has an IQ of 100. But an 8-year-old who answers questions as would a typical 10-year-old has an IQ of 125.

Most current intelligence tests, including the Stanford-Binet, no longer compute an IQ. The original IQ formula works fairly well for children but not for adults. (Should a 40-year-old who does as well on the test as an average 20-year-old be assigned an IQ of only 50?) Today's intelligence tests therefore produce a mental ability score based on the test-taker's performance *relative to the average performance of others the same age.* As on the original Stanford-Binet, current tests define this score so that 100 is average, with about two-thirds of all people scoring between 85 and 115. Although there is no longer any intelligence *quotient,* the term "IQ" still lingers in everyday vocabulary as a shorthand expression for "intelligence test score."

Terman promoted the widespread use of intelligence testing. His motive was to "take account of the inequalities of children in original endowment" by assessing their "vocational fitness." In sympathy with eugenics—a much-criticized nineteenth-century movement that proposed measuring human traits and using the results to encourage only smart and fit people to reproduce—Terman (1916, pp. 91–92) envisioned that the use of intelligence tests would "ultimately result in curtailing the reproduction of feeble-mindedness and in the elimination of an enormous amount of crime, pauperism, and industrial inefficiency" (p. 7).

> "The IQ test was invented to predict academic performance, nothing else. If we wanted something that would predict life success, we'd have to invent another test completely."
>
> Social psychologist Robert Zajonc (1984b)

Lewis Terman
"The children of successful and cultured parents test higher than children from wretched and ignorant homes for the simple reason that their heredity is better" (1916, p. 115).

THAT'S MY BOY, MARK... HE'S 39, BUT HE'S ALREADY READING AT A 42-YEAR OLD LEVEL...

Mrs. Randolph takes mother's pride too far.

> "Science must be understood as a social phenomenon, a gutsy, human enterprise, not the work of robots programmed to collect pure information."
>
> Stephen Jay Gould (1981)

With Terman's help, the U.S. government developed new tests to evaluate newly arriving immigrants and 1.7 million World War I army recruits—the world's first mass administration of an intelligence test. To some psychologists, the results indicated the inferiority of people not sharing their Anglo-Saxon heritage. Such findings were part of the cultural climate that led to a 1924 immigration law, which reduced immigration quotas for Southern and Eastern Europe to less than a fifth of those for Northern and Western Europe.

Binet probably would have been horrified that his test was adapted and used to draw such conclusions. Indeed, such sweeping judgments did become an embarrassment to most of those who championed testing. Even Terman, for instance, came to appreciate that test scores reflect not only people's innate mental abilities but also their education and their familiarity with the culture assumed by the test. Nevertheless, abuses of the early intelligence tests serve to remind us that science can be value-laden. Behind a screen of scientific objectivity, ideology sometimes lurks.

Modern Tests of Mental Abilities

OBJECTIVE 32-2 | Distinguish between aptitude and achievement tests, and describe modern tests of mental abilities, such as the WAIS.

By this point in your life, you've faced dozens of ability tests: school tests of basic reading and math skills, course examinations, intelligence tests, driver's license examinations, and college and university entrance examinations, to name just a few. Psychologists classify such tests as either **aptitude tests,** intended to *predict* your ability to learn a new skill, or **achievement tests,** intended to *reflect* what you have learned. Thus, a college entrance exam, which seeks to predict your ability to do college work, is an aptitude test—a "thinly disguised intelligence test," says Howard Gardner (1999). Indeed, report Meredith Frey and Douglas Detterman (2004), total scores on the U.S. SAT (Scholastic Assessment Test; formerly called the U.S. Scholastic Aptitude Test) correlated +.82 with general intelligence scores in a national sample of 14- to 21-year-olds (**FIGURE 32.1**). Exams covering what you have learned in this course are achievement tests.

Actually, the differences between aptitude tests and achievement tests are not so clear-cut. Your *achieved* vocabulary influences your score on most aptitude tests. Similarly, your *aptitudes* for learning and test-taking influence your grades on achievement

■ **aptitude test** a test designed to predict a person's future performance; *aptitude* is the capacity to learn.

■ **achievement test** a test designed to assess what a person has learned.

■ **Wechsler Adult Intelligence Scale (WAIS)** the WAIS is the most widely used intelligence test; contains verbal and performance (nonverbal) subtests.

FIGURE 32.1
Close cousins: Aptitude and intelligence scores
A scatterplot shows the close correlation between intelligence scores and verbal and quantitative SAT scores. (From Frey and Detterman, 2004.)

tests. Most tests, whether labeled aptitude or achievement, assess both ability and its development. Practically speaking, however, aptitude tests predict future performance and achievement tests assess current performance.

As a 6-year-old Romanian, David Wechsler arrived just ahead of other Eastern European immigrants who, during the early 1900s, took the Stanford-Binet test and were believed by some to be "feeble-minded." Many years later, Wechsler, then a psychologist, created what is now the most widely used intelligence test, the **Wechsler Adult Intelligence Scale (WAIS).** After creating the WAIS, Wechsler developed the *Wechsler Intelligence Scale for Children (WISC)* for school-age children, and still later a test for preschool children. As illustrated in **FIGURE 32.2,** the WAIS consists of 11 subtests. It yields not only an overall intelligence score, as does the Stanford-Binet, but also separate scores for verbal comprehension, perceptual organization, working memory, and processing speed. Striking differences among these scores alert the examiner to possible learning problems or brain disorders. For example, a verbal comprehension score much lower than the same person's other scores might indicate a reading or language disability. Comparing scores can also help a psychologist or psychiatrist to establish a rehabilitation plan for patients who have suffered a stroke or brain injury. In addition, the tests provide clues to cognitive strengths that a teacher, employer, or therapist might build upon.

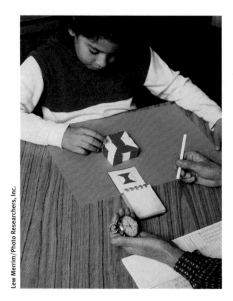

Matching patterns
Block design puzzles test the ability to analyze patterns. Wechsler's individually administered intelligence test comes in forms suited for adults (WAIS) and children (WISC).

FIGURE 32.2
Sample items from the Wechsler Adult Intelligence Scale (WAIS) subtests
(Adapted from Thorndike & Hagen, 1977.)

VERBAL

General Information
What day of the year is Independence Day?

Similarities
In what way are *wool* and *cotton* alike?

Arithmetic Reasoning
If eggs cost 60 cents a dozen, what does 1 egg cost?

Vocabulary
Tell me the meaning of corrupt.

Comprehension
Why do people buy fire insurance?

Digit Span
Listen carefully, and when I am through, say the numbers right after me.

7   3   4   1   8   6

Now I am going to say some more numbers, but I want you to say them backward.

3   8   4   1   6

PERFORMANCE

Picture Completion
I am going to show you a picture with an important part missing. Tell me what is missing.

Picture Arrangement
The pictures below tell a story. Put them in the right order to tell the story.

Block Design
Using the four blocks, make one just like this.

Object Assembly
If these pieces are put together correctly, they will make something. Go ahead and put them together as quickly as you can.

Digit-Symbol Substitution

■ **standardization** defining meaningful scores by comparison with the performance of a pretested standardization group.

■ **normal curve** the symmetrical bell-shaped curve that describes the distribution of many physical and psychological attributes. Most scores fall near the average, and fewer and fewer scores lie near the extremes.

Principles of Test Construction

To be widely accepted, psychological tests must meet three criteria: They must be *standardized, reliable,* and *valid.* The Stanford-Binet and Wechsler tests meet these requirements.

Standardization

OBJECTIVE 32-3 | Discuss the importance of standardizing psychological tests, and describe the distribution of scores in a normal curve.

The number of questions you answer correctly on an intelligence test would tell us almost nothing. To evaluate your performance, we need a basis for comparing it with others' performance. To enable meaningful comparisons, test-makers first give the test to a representative sample of people. When individuals later take the test following the same procedures, their scores can be compared with the standards defined by the sample. Recall that Lewis Terman and his colleagues recognized that items developed for Parisians did not provide a satisfactory standard for evaluating Americans. They revised the test and recalibrated the new version by testing 2300 native-born, white Americans of differing socioeconomic levels. Ironically, they then used this standard to evaluate nonwhite American and immigrant groups (Van Leeuwen, 1982). The process of defining meaningful scores relative to a pretested group is called **standardization.**

Standardized test results typically form a *normal distribution,* a bell-shaped pattern of scores that forms the **normal curve** (FIGURE **32.3**). No matter what we measure—people's heights, weights, or mental aptitudes—scores often form a roughly symmetrical, bell-shaped distribution clustered around the average. On an intelligence test, we call this average score 100. As we move out from the average (toward either extreme), we find fewer and fewer people. Within each age group, the Stanford-Binet and the Wechsler tests assign any person a score according to how much that person's performance deviates above or below the average. As Figure 32.3 shows, a performance higher than all but 2 percent of all scores earns an intelligence score of 130. A raw score that is comparably *below* 98 percent of all the scores earns an intelligence score of 70.

To keep the average score near 100, the Stanford-Binet and the Wechsler scales are periodically restandardized. If you took the WAIS Third Edition recently, your performance was compared with a standardization sample who took the test during 1996,

FIGURE 32.3
The normal curve
Scores on aptitude tests tend to form a normal, or bell-shaped, curve around an average score. For the Wechsler scale, for example, the average score is 100.

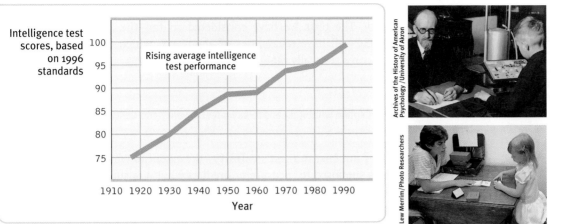

Intelligence test scores, based on 1996 standards

Rising average intelligence test performance

Year

FIGURE 32.4
Getting smarter?
In every country studied, intelligence test performance rose during the twentieth century, as shown here with American Wechsler and Stanford-Binet test performance between 1918 and 1989. In Britain, test scores have risen 27 points since 1942. (From Hogan, 1995.)

not to David Wechsler's initial 1930s sample. If you compared the performance of the most recent standardization sample with that of the 1930s sample, do you suppose you would find rising or declining test performance? Amazingly—given that college entrance aptitude scores were dropping during the 1960s and 1970s—intelligence test performance has been *improving*. This worldwide phenomenon is called the *Flynn effect* in honor of New Zealand researcher James Flynn (1987, 1999), who first calculated its magnitude. As **FIGURE 32.4** indicates, the average person's intelligence test score 80 years ago was—by today's standard—only a 76! Such rising performance has been observed in 20 countries, from Canada to rural Australia (Daley & others, 2003). Although the gains slowed during the 1990s and may now have ceased, the increase seems real and is now widely accepted as an important phenomenon (Sundet & others, 2004; Teasdale & Owen, 2000).

The Flynn effect's cause is a mystery (Neisser, 1997, 1998). Does it result from greater test sophistication? (But the gains began before testing was widespread.) Better nutrition? As the nutrition explanation would predict, people have gotten not only smarter but taller. Moreover, the increases have been greatest at the lowest economic levels, which have gained the most from improved nutrition (Colom & others, 2005). Or does the Flynn effect stem from more education? More stimulating environments? Less childhood disease? Smaller families and more parental investment?

Regardless of what combination of factors explains the rise in intelligence test scores, the phenomenon counters one concern of some hereditarians—that the higher twentieth-century birthrates among those with lower scores would shove human intelligence scores downward. Seeking to explain the rising scores and mindful of global mixing, one scholar has even speculated about the influence of a genetic phenomenon comparable to "hybrid vigor," which occurs in agriculture when cross-breeding produces corn or livestock superior to the parent plants or animals (Mingroni, 2004).

Reliability

OBJECTIVE 32-4 | Explain what it means to say a test is *reliable*.

Comparing your test scores to those of the standardizing group still won't tell us much about you unless the test has **reliability**. A good test must yield dependably consistent scores. To check a test's reliability, researchers retest people using either the same test or another form of it. If the two scores generally agree, or *correlate*, the test is reliable. As an alternative, the researcher may split a test in half and see whether scores derived from odd and even questions agree. Assuming that one's basic ability has not changed between two adjacent testings, any score difference reflects "error" variation related to such things as luck, fatigue, and anxiety.

■ **reliability** the extent to which a test yields consistent results, as assessed by the consistency of scores on two halves of the test, on alternate forms of the test, or on retesting.

■ **validity** the extent to which a test measures or predicts what it is supposed to. (See also *content validity* and *predictive validity*.)

■ **content validity** the extent to which a test samples the behavior that is of interest (such as a driving test that samples driving tasks).

■ **criterion** the behavior (such as future college grades) that a test (such as the SAT) is designed to predict; thus, the measure used in defining whether the test has predictive validity.

■ **predictive validity** the success with which a test predicts the behavior it is designed to predict; it is assessed by computing the correlation between test scores and the criterion behavior. (Also called *criterion-related validity*.)

The higher the correlation between the *test-retest* or the *split-half* scores, the higher the test's reliability. The tests we have considered so far—the Stanford-Binet, the WAIS, and the WISC—all have reliabilities of about +.9, which is very high. When retested, people's scores generally match their first score closely.

Validity

OBJECTIVE 32-5 | Explain what it means to say a test is *valid*, and describe two types of validity.

High reliability does not ensure a test's **validity**—the extent to which the test actually measures what it is supposed to measure or predicts what it is supposed to predict. If you use an inaccurate tape measure to measure people's heights, your height report would have high reliability (consistency) but low validity. It is enough for some tests that they have **content validity**, meaning the test taps the pertinent behavior. The road test for a driver's license has content validity because it samples the tasks a driver routinely faces. Course exams have content validity if they assess one's mastery of a representative sample of course material.

Other tests are evaluated in terms of how well they agree with some **criterion**, an independent measure of what the test aims to assess. For some tests, the criterion is future performance. For example, aptitude tests must have **predictive validity**, which means they predict future achievement.

Are general aptitude tests as predictive as they are reliable? As critics are fond of noting, the answer is plainly no. The predictive power of aptitude tests is fairly strong in the early school years, but later it weakens. Academic aptitude test scores are reasonably good predictors of achievement for children ages 6 to 12, where the correlation between intelligence score and school performance is about +.60 (Jensen, 1980). The SAT, used in the United States as a college entrance exam, is less successful in predicting first-year college performance; here, the correlation is less than +.50 (Willingham & others, 1990). By the time we get to the U.S. Graduate Record Examination (GRE; an aptitude test similar to the SAT but for those applying to graduate school), the correlation with graduate school performance is an even more modest +.30 (GRE, 1990).

Why does the predictive power of aptitude scores diminish as students move up the educational ladder? Consider a parallel situation: Among all American or Canadian football linemen, body weight correlates with success. A 300-pound player tends to overwhelm a 200-pound opponent. But within the narrow 260- to 300-pound range typically found at the professional level, the correlation between weight and success becomes negligible (**FIGURE 32.5**). The narrower the *range* of weights, the

FIGURE 32.5
Diminishing predictive power
Let's imagine a correlation between football linemen's body weight and their success on the field. Note how insignificant the relationship becomes when we narrow the range of weight to 260 to 300 pounds. As the range of data under consideration narrows, its predictive power diminishes.

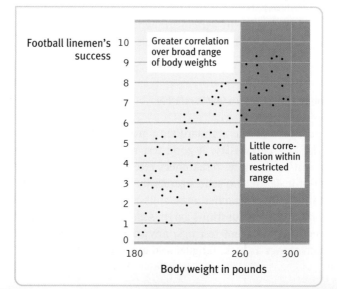

lower the predictive power of body weight becomes. If an elite university takes only those students who have very high aptitude scores, those scores cannot possibly predict much. This will be true even if the test has excellent predictive validity with a more diverse sample of students. So, when we validate a test using a wide range of people but then use it with a restricted range of people, it loses much of its predictive validity.

The Dynamics of Intelligence

We now can address some age-old questions about the dynamics of human intelligence—about its stability over the life span, and about the extremes of intelligence.

Stability or Change?

OBJECTIVE 32-6 | Describe the stability of intelligence scores over the life span.

If we retested people periodically throughout their lives, would their intelligence scores be stable? This question has led to a search for indicators of infants' later intelligence that has left few stones unturned. Unable to talk with infants, developmental researchers have assessed what they can observe—everything from birth weight, to whether the third toe was longer than the second, to age of sitting up alone. None of these measures provides any useful prediction of intelligence scores at much later ages (Bell & Waldrop, 1989; Broman, 1989). Perhaps, as developmental psychologist Nancy Bayley reflected in 1949, "we have not yet found the right tests." Someday, she speculated, we might find "infant behaviors which are characteristic of underlying intellectual functions" and which will predict later intelligence. Some studies have found that 2- to 7-month-old babies who quickly grow bored with a picture—who, given a choice, prefer to look at a new one—score higher on tests of brain speed and intelligence up to 11 years later, but the prediction is crude (Kavšek, 2004; Tasbihsazan & others, 2003).

So, new parents who are wondering about their baby's intelligence and anxiously comparing their baby to others can relax. Except for extremely impaired or very precocious children, casual observation and intelligence tests before age 3 predict children's future aptitudes only minimally (Humphreys & Davey, 1988). For example, children who are early talkers—speaking by age 20 months in sentences typical of 3-year-olds—are *not* especially likely to be reading by age 4½ (Crain-Thoreson & Dale, 1992). (A better predictor of early reading is having parents who have read lots of stories to their child.) Even Albert Einstein was slow in learning to talk (Quasha, 1980).

By age 4, however, children's performance on intelligence tests begins to predict their adolescent and adult scores. Moreover, high-scoring adolescents tend to have been early readers. One study surveyed the parents of 187 American seventh- and eighth-graders who had taken a college aptitude test as part of a seven-state talent search and had scored considerably higher than most high school seniors. If their parents' memories can be trusted, more than half of this precocious group of adolescents began reading by age 4 and more than 80 percent were reading by age 5 (Van Tassel-Baska, 1983). Not surprisingly, then, intelligence tests given 5-year-olds begin to predict school achievement (Tramontana & others, 1988).

After about age 7, intelligence test scores, though certainly not fixed, stabilize (Bloom, 1964). Thus, the consistency of scores over time increases with the age of the child. The remarkable stability of aptitude scores by late adolescence is seen in a U.S. Educational Testing Service study of 23,000 students who took the SAT and then later took the GRE (Angoff, 1988). On either test, verbal scores correlated only modestly with math scores—revealing that these two aptitudes are distinct. Yet scores on the SAT verbal test correlated +.86 with the scores on the GRE verbal tests taken four to five years later. An equally astonishing +.86 correlation occurred between the two math tests. Given the time lapse and differing educational experiences of these 23,000 students, the stability of their aptitude scores is remarkable.

> "My dear Adele, I am 4 years old and I can read any English book. I can say all the Latin Substantives and Adjectives and active verbs besides 52 lines of Latin poetry."
> Francis Galton, Letter to his sister, 1827

Ironically, SAT and GRE scores correlate better with each other than either does with its intended criterion, school achievement. Thus, their reliability far exceeds their predictive validity. If either test was much affected by coaching, luck, or how one feels on the test day (as so many people believe), such reliability would be impossible.

FIGURE 32.6
FIGURE 32.6
Intelligence endures
When Ian Deary and his colleagues (2004) gave 80-year-old Scots an intelligence test they had taken as 11-year-olds, their scores across seven decades correlated +.66.

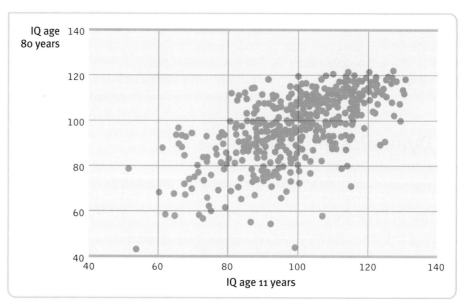

■ **mental retardation** a condition of limited mental ability, indicated by an intelligence score of 70 or below and difficulty in adapting to the demands of life; varies from mild to profound.

■ **Down syndrome** a condition of retardation and associated physical disorders caused by an extra chromosome in one's genetic makeup.

A young man with Down syndrome
In the past, people with this condition were often institutionalized. Today, with a supportive family environment and special education, many people with Down syndrome learn to care for themselves and hold a job.

Ian Deary and his colleagues (2004) recently set a record for long-term follow-up. When the intelligence test administered to 11-year-old Scots in 1932 was readministered to 542 survivors as turn-of-the-millennium 80-year-olds, the correlation between the two sets of scores—after some 70 years of varied life experiences—was striking (**FIGURE 32.6**). High-scoring 11-year-olds also were more likely to be living independently as 77-year-olds and less likely to have suffered late-onset Alzheimer's disease (Starr & others, 2000; Whalley & others, 2000). Another study that followed 93 nuns confirmed that those exhibiting less verbal ability in written essays when entering their convent in their teens were more at risk for Alzheimer's disease after age 75 (Snowdon & others, 1996).

Extremes of Intelligence

OBJECTIVE 32-7 | Discuss the two extremes of the normal distribution of intelligence.

One way to glimpse the validity and significance of any test is to compare people who score at the two extremes of the normal curve. The two groups should differ noticeably, and they do.

The Low Extreme

At one extreme of the normal curve are those whose intelligence test scores fall at 70 or below. To be labeled as having **mental retardation,** a child must have both a low test score and difficulty adapting to the normal demands of independent living. Only about 1 percent of the population meets both criteria, with males outnumbering females by 50 percent (American Psychiatric Association, 1994). As **TABLE 32.1** indicates, most individuals with mental retardation can, with support, live in mainstream society.

Mental retardation sometimes has a known physical cause. **Down syndrome,** for example, is a disorder of varying severity caused by an extra chromosome 21 in the person's genetic makeup.

During the last two centuries, the pendulum of opinion about how best to care for people with mental retardation has made a complete swing. Until the mid-nineteenth century, they were cared for at home. Many of those with the most severe disabilities died, but people with milder forms of retardation often found a place in a farm-based society. Then, residential schools for slow learners were established. By the twentieth century, many of these institutions had become warehouses, providing residents little attention, no privacy, and no hope. Parents often were told to separate themselves permanently from their impaired child before they became attached.

TABLE **32.1**

DEGREES OF MENTAL RETARDATION

Level	Approximate Intelligence Scores	Percentage of Persons with Retardation	Adaptation to Demands of Life
Mild	50–70	85%	May learn academic skills up to sixth-grade level. Adults may, with assistance, achieve self-supporting social and vocational skills.
Moderate	35–50	10%	May progress to second-grade level academically. Adults may contribute to their own support by laboring in sheltered workshops.
Severe	20–35	3–4%	May learn to talk and to perform simple work tasks under close supervision but are generally unable to profit from vocational training.
Profound	Below 20	1–2%	Require constant aid and supervision.

Source: Reprinted with permission from the *Diagnostic and Statistical Manual of Mental Disorders*, Fourth Edition, text revision. Copyright 2000 American Psychiatric Association.

In the last half of the twentieth century, the pendulum swung back to normalization—encouraging people to live in their own communities as normally as their functioning permits. Children with mild retardation are educated in less restrictive environments, and many are integrated, or *mainstreamed*, into regular classrooms. Most grow up with their own families, then move into a protected living arrangement, such as a group home. The hope, and often the reality, is a happier and more dignified life.

But think about another reason people diagnosed with mild retardation—those just below the 70 score used to define retardation with an intelligence test—might be better able to live independently today than many decades ago. Recall that, thanks to the Flynn effect, the tests have been periodically restandardized. When that has happened, individuals who scored near 70 suddenly lose about 6 IQ points, and the number of people diagnosed with retardation suddenly jumps (Kanaya & others, 2003). Two people with the same ability level could now be classified differently, depending on when they were tested. With the new norms, more people suddenly become eligible for special education, and for Social Security payments for those with a mental disability, and in the United States (one of only a few countries with the death penalty) fewer for execution. (The U.S. Supreme Court ruled in 2002 that the execution of people with mental retardation is "cruel and unusual punishment.") For people near that score of 70, intelligence testing can be high stakes.

The High Extreme

In one famous project begun in 1921, Lewis Terman studied more than 1500 California schoolchildren with IQ scores over 135. Contrary to the popular notion that intellectually gifted children are frequently maladjusted because they are "in a different world" from their nongifted peers, Terman's high-scoring children, like those in later studies, were healthy, well-adjusted, and unusually successful academically (Lubinski & Benbow, 2000; Stanley, 1997). When restudied over the next seven decades, most people in Terman's group had attained high levels of education (Austin & others, 2002; Holahan & Sears, 1995). They included many doctors, lawyers, professors, scientists, and writers, but no Nobel prize winners. (Terman did test one future Nobel laureate in physics but excluded him from the gifted sample because his measured IQ wasn't high enough [Cassandro & Simonton, 2003].)

> Joining Mensa means that you are a genius. . . . I worried about the arbitrary 132 cutoff point, until I met someone with an IQ of 131 and, honestly, he was a bit slow on the uptake."
>
> Steve Martin, 1997

The extremes of intelligence Sho Yano was playing Mozart by age 4, aced the SAT at age 8, and graduated *summa cum laude* from Loyola University at age 12, at which age he began combined Ph.D.–M.D. studies at the University of Chicago.

AP Photo/Anne Ryan

These whiz kids remind one of Jean Piaget, who by age 7 was devoting his free time to studying birds, fossils, and machines; who by 15 began publishing scientific articles on mollusks; and who later went on to become the twentieth century's most famous developmental psychologist (Hunt, 1993). Children with extraordinary academic gifts are sometimes more isolated, introverted, and in their own worlds (Winner, 2000). But most thrive.

There are critics who question many of the assumptions of currently popular "gifted child" programs, such as the belief that only 3 to 5 percent of children are gifted and that it pays to identify and "track" these special few—segregating them in special classes and giving them academic enrichment not available to the other 95 percent. Critics note that tracking by aptitude sometimes creates a self-fulfilling prophecy: Those implicitly labeled "ungifted" can be influenced to become so (Lipsey & Wilson, 1993; Slavin & Braddock, 1993). Denying lower-ability students opportunities for enriched education can widen the achievement gap between ability groups and increase their social isolation from one another—one reason there is no tracking in the elementary schools of Japan and China (Carnegie, 1989; Stevenson & Lee, 1990). Because minority and low-income youth are more often placed in lower academic groups, tracking can also promote segregation and prejudice—hardly, note critics, a healthy preparation for working and living in a multicultural society.

Critics and proponents of gifted education do, however, agree on this: Children have differing gifts. Some are especially good at math, others at verbal reasoning, others at art, still others at social leadership. Educating children as if all were alike is as naive as assuming that giftedness is something, like blue eyes, that you either have or do not have. One need not hang labels on children to affirm their special talents and to challenge them all at the frontiers of their own ability and understanding. By providing "appropriate developmental placement" suited to each child's talents, we can promote both equity and excellence for all (Colangelo & others, 2004; Lubinski & Benbow, 2000; Sternberg & Grigorenko, 2000).

"Alpha children wear grey. They work much harder than we do, because they're so frightfully clever. I'm really awfully glad I'm a Beta, because I don't work so hard. And then we are much better than the Gammas and Deltas. Gammas are stupid."

Aldous Huxley, *Brave New World*, 1932

>> LEARNING OUTCOMES

Assessing Intelligence

OBJECTIVE 32-1 | Define *intelligence test*, and discuss the history of intelligence testing.

An *intelligence test* is a method for assessing an individual's mental aptitudes and comparing them with those of others, using numerical scores. More than a century ago in France, Alfred Binet and his collaborator Théodore Simon started the modern intelligence-testing movement by developing questions to predict children's future progress in the Paris school system. Lewis Terman of Stanford University revised Binet's work for use in the United States. Terman believed his Stanford-Binet could help guide people toward appropriate opportunities, but more than Binet, he believed intelligence is inherited. During the early twentieth century, intelligence tests were, regrettably, sometimes used to "document" assumptions about the innate inferiority of certain ethnic and immigrant groups. Intelligence test scores have been expressed as an *intelligence quotient (IQ)*, established by dividing mental age by chronological age times 100.

OBJECTIVE 32-2 | Distinguish between aptitude and achievement tests, and describe modern tests of mental abilities, such as the WAIS.

Aptitude tests are designed to predict what you *can learn*. *Achievement tests* are designed to assess what you *have learned*. The *WAIS (Wechsler Adult Intelligence Scale)*, an aptitude test, is the most widely used intelligence test for adults. Two similar Wechsler scales test intelligence in preschool and older children. The SAT is an aptitude test, and in one study, test-takers' total SAT scores and their score on a test of general intelligence correlated at a very high level: +.82.

OBJECTIVE 32-3 | Discuss the importance of standardizing psychological tests, and describe the distribution of scores in a normal curve.

Standardizing is the process of administering a test to a representative sample of future test-takers to establish a basis for meaningful comparisons of scores. The distribution of many physical and psychological attributes forms a *normal curve* (also known as a *bell-shaped curve*)—a roughly symmetrical shape in which most scores cluster around an average, and increasingly fewer fall at the extremes. Intelligence test scores form such a curve, but in the past six decades, the average score has risen 27 points—a phenomenon known as the Flynn effect.

OBJECTIVE 32-4 | Explain what it means to say that a test is *reliable*.

A test is *reliable* when it yields consistent results. To establish reliability, researchers compare the consistency of test-takers' scores on two halves of the test, alternate forms of the test, or retests on the same test. A test can be reliable but not valid.

OBJECTIVE 32-5 | Explain what it means to say a test is *valid*, and describe two types of validity.

A *valid* test measures or predicts what it is supposed to. *Content validity* is the extent to which a test samples the pertinent behavior (as a driving test measures driving ability). *Predictive validity* is the extent to which the test predicts a behavior it is designed to predict (aptitude tests have predictive ability if they can predict future achievements).

OBJECTIVE 32-6 | Describe the stability of intelligence scores over the life span.

The stability of intelligence test scores increases with age. By age 4, scores fluctuate somewhat but begin to predict adolescent and adult scores. At about age 7, scores become fairly stable and consistent.

OBJECTIVE 32-7 | Discuss the two extremes of the normal distribution of intelligence.

People with scores below 70, the cut-off mark for the diagnosis of mental retardation, vary in their abilities, from near-normal, to (at the very lowest scoring levels) requiring constant aid and supervision. *Down syndrome* is a form of retardation with a physical cause—an extra copy of chromosome 21. High-scoring people tend to be healthy, well-adjusted, and unusually successful academically. School programs that "track" children can become self-fulfilling prophecies as children live up to—or down to—others' perceptions of their ability.

TERMS AND CONCEPTS TO REMEMBER

intelligence test, p. 32-0
mental age, p. 32-0
Stanford-Binet, p. 32-1
intelligence quotient (IQ), p. 32-1
aptitude test, p. 32-2
achievement test, p. 32-2
Wechsler Adult Intelligence Scale (WAIS), p. 32-3

standardization, p. 32-4
normal curve, p. 32-4
reliability, p. 32-5
validity, p. 32-6
content validity, p. 32-6
criterion, p. 32-6
predictive validity, p. 32-6
mental retardation, p. 32-8
Down syndrome, p. 32-8

TEST YOURSELF

1. What was the purpose of Binet's pioneering intelligence test?

2. The Smiths have enrolled their 2-year-old son in a special program that promises to assess his IQ and, if he places in the top 5 percent of test-takers, to create a plan that will guarantee his admission to a top university at age 18. Why is this endeavor of questionable value?

(Answers in Appendix B.)

ASK YOURSELF

1. Are you working to the potential reflected in your college entrance exam scores? What, other than your aptitude, is affecting your college performance?

2. How do you feel about mainstreaming children of all ability levels in the same classroom? What evidence are you using to support your view?

>WEB

Multiple-choice *self-tests* and more may be found at www.worthpublishers.com/myers.

33

Genetic and Environmental Influences on Intelligence

Intelligence runs in families. But why? Are our intellectual abilities mostly inherited? Or are they molded by our environment?

Few issues arouse such passion or have such serious political implications. Consider: If we mainly inherit our differing mental abilities, and if success reflects those abilities, then people's socioeconomic standing will correspond to their inborn differences. This could lead to those on top believing their intellectual birthright justifies their social positions.

But if mental abilities are primarily nurtured by the environments that raise and inform us, then children from disadvantaged environments can expect to lead disadvantaged lives. In this case, people's standing will result from their unequal opportunities.

For now, as best we can, let us set aside such political implications and examine the evidence.

Genetic Influences

OBJECTIVE 33-1 | Discuss the evidence for the genetic contribution to individual intelligence, and explain what psychologists mean by the heritability of intelligence.

"There are more studies addressing the genetics of [general intelligence] than any other human characteristic."

Robert Plomin (1999)

Do people who share the same genes also share comparable mental abilities? As you can see from **FIGURE 33.1,** which summarizes many studies, the answer is clearly yes. In support of the genetic contribution to intelligence, researchers cite three sets of findings:

- Across studies of 10,000 twins, the intelligence test scores of identical twins reared together are virtually as similar as those of the same person taking the same test twice (Lykken, 1999; Plomin, 2001). (The scores of fraternal twins, who typically share only half their genes, are much less similar.) Likewise, the test scores of identical twins reared separately are similar enough to lead twin researcher Thomas Bouchard (1996) to estimate that "about 70 percent" of intelligence score variation "can be attributed to genetic variation." Other researchers have offered estimates from 50 to 75 percent (Devlin & others, 1997; Neisser & others, 1996; Plomin, 2003).
- Brain scans reveal that identical twins have very similar gray matter volume. Moreover, unlike fraternal twins, their brains are virtually the same in areas associated with verbal and spatial intelligence (Thompson & others, 2001).
- Are there genes for genius? Comparisons of the genes of people of high versus average intelligence have produced slow progress in identifying the many genes that contribute to cognitive ability (Plomin, 2003). By inserting an extra gene into fertilized mouse eggs, researchers have, however, produced smarter mice—mice that excel at learning and remembering the location of a hidden underwater platform or at recognizing cues that signal impending shock (Tsien, 2000). The gene helps create a neural receptor involved in memory.

But there is also some evidence pointing to an effect of environment. Fraternal twins, who are genetically no more alike than any other siblings—but who are treated more alike because they are the same age—tend to score more alike than other siblings.

Smart scientist, smart mouse
Working with Ya-Ping Tang and others, Princeton University biologist Joe Z. Tsien genetically engineered a strain of smart mice. Such work may shed new light on the biology of human intelligence.

Courtesy of Laura Pedrick

FIGURE 33.1

Intelligence: Nature and nurture

The most genetically similar people have the most similar intelligence scores. Note: 1.0 indicates a perfect correlation; zero indicates no correlation at all. (Data from McGue & others, 1993.)

Seeking to disentangle genes and environment, researchers have also asked whether adopted children and their siblings, thanks to their shared environment, share similar aptitudes. During childhood, the intelligence test scores of adoptive siblings correlate modestly. Researchers have also compared the intelligence test scores of adopted children with those of (a) their biological parents, the providers of their genes, and (b) their adoptive parents, the providers of their home environment. Over time, adopted children accumulate experience in their differing adoptive families. So would you expect the family environment effect to grow with age and the genetic legacy effect to shrink?

If you would, behavior geneticists have a surprise for you. With age, mental similarities between adopted children and their adoptive families disappear as parental influence wanes; by adulthood, the correlation is roughly zero (McGue & others, 1993). As we accumulate life experience, genetic influences—not environmental ones—become more apparent (Bouchard, 1995, 1996a). Adopted children's intelligence scores become more like those of their biological parents (**FIGURE 33.2**), and identical twins' similarities continue or increase into their eighties (McClearn & others, 1997; Plomin & others, 1997).

"I told my parents that if grades were so important they should have paid for a smarter egg donor."

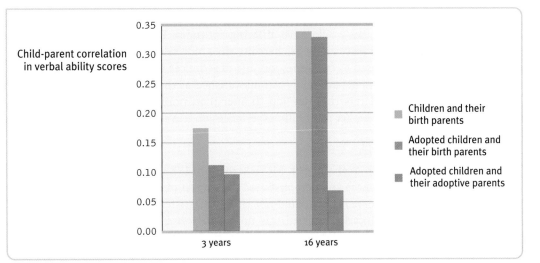

FIGURE 33.2

Who do adopted children resemble?

As the years went by in their adoptive families, children's verbal ability scores became modestly more like their *biological* parents' scores. (Adapted from Plomin & DeFries, 1998.)

■ **heritability** the proportion of variation among individuals that we can attribute to genes. The heritability of a trait may vary, depending on the range of populations and environments studied.

Question: Check your understanding of heritability: If environments become more equal, the heritability of intelligence would
a. increase.
b. decrease.
c. be unchanged.
(See this module's final page.)

"Selective breeding has given me an aptitude for the law, but I still love fetching a dead duck out of freezing water."

Devastating neglect
Romanian orphans who had minimal interaction with caregivers, such as this child in the Lagunul Pentro Copii orphanage in 1990, suffered delayed development.

Given such studies, one might be tempted to make statements about the heritability of intelligence. But be very careful how you use the word **heritability.** To say that the heritability of intelligence—the variation in intelligence test scores attributable to genetic factors—is 50 percent (or a tad more) does *not* mean that your genes are responsible for 50 percent of *your* intelligence and your environment for the rest. It means that we can attribute to heredity 50 percent *of the variation in intelligence* (among those studied). This point is so often misunderstood that I repeat: We can never say what percentage of an *individual's* intelligence is inherited. Heritability refers instead to the extent to which *differences among people* are attributable to genes. Heritability *never* pertains to an individual, only to why people differ.

Even this conclusion must be qualified, because heritability can vary from study to study. For example, environmental differences are more predictive of intelligence scores among children of less-educated parents—among whom family environments may vary widely (Rowe & others, 1999). Mark Twain once proposed that boys should be raised in barrels and fed through a hole until they were 12 years old. Given the boys' equal environments, differences in their individual intelligence test scores at age 12 could be explained only by their heredity. Thus, heritability for their differences would be nearly 100 percent. But if we raise people with similar heredities in drastically different environments (barrels versus advantaged homes), the environment effect will be greater, and heritability—differences due to genes—will therefore be lower. In a world of clones, heritability would be zero.

Genes and environment correlate. If you are just slightly taller and quicker than others, notes James Flynn (2003), you will more likely be picked for a basketball team, will play more, and will get more coaching. The same would be true for your separated identical twin—who might, *not just for genetic reasons,* also come to excel at basketball. Likewise, students with a natural aptitude for mathematics are more likely to select math courses in high school and later to score well on math aptitude tests—thanks *both* to their natural math aptitude *and* to their math experience. If you have a slight genetically disposed intelligence edge, you will more likely stay in school, read books, and ask questions—all of which will amplify your cognitive brain power. Thanks to such gene-environment correlation, modest genetic advantages can be socially multiplied into big performance advantages. Our genes shape the experiences that shape us.

Environmental Influences

OBJECTIVE 33-2 | Discuss the evidence for environmental influences on individual intelligence.

Genes make a difference. Even if we were all raised in the same intellectually stimulating environment, we would have differing aptitudes. But even when we consider the similarities of identical twins, heredity does not tell the whole story. In ways sometimes predisposed by our genes, our life experiences matter.

Human environments are rarely as impoverished as the dark and barren cages inhabited by deprived rats that develop thinner-than-normal brain cortexes (Rosenzweig & others, 1991). Yet severe life experiences do leave footprints on the brain.

Early Intervention Effects

In a destitute Iranian orphanage, J. McVicker Hunt (1982) observed the dramatic effects of early experiences and demonstrated the impact of early intervention. The typical child Hunt observed there could not sit up unassisted at age 2 or walk at age 4. The little care the infants received was not in response to their crying, cooing, or other behaviors, so the children developed little sense of personal control over their environment. They were instead becoming passive "glum lumps." Extreme deprivation was bludgeoning native intelligence.

Aware of the benefits of responsive caregiving, Hunt began a program of "tutored human enrichment." He trained caregivers to play vocal games with the infants. They first imitated the babies' babbling. Then they led the babies in vocal follow-the-leader by shifting from one familiar sound to another. Then they began to teach sounds from the Persian language.

The results were dramatic. By 22 months of age, all 11 infants who received these language-fostering experiences could name more than 50 objects and body parts. So charming had the infants become that most were adopted—an unprecedented success for the orphanage.

Hunt's findings testify to the importance of environment. Severe disadvantage takes a toll (Ramey & Ramey, 1992). Unlike children of affluence, siblings within impoverished families have more similar intelligence scores (Turkheimer & others, 2003). This indicates that among the poor, environmental conditions can override genetic differences. One study of 1450 Virginia schools found that schools with lots of poverty-level children often had less-qualified teachers. And even after controlling for poverty, less-qualified teachers predicted lower achievement scores (Tuerk, 2005). Malnutrition can also influence cognitive development. When the infant malnutrition associated with severe poverty is relieved with nutritional supplements, poverty's effect on physical and cognitive development lessens (Brown & Pollitt, 1996). And improving nutrition helps explain the rising intelligence scores across generations.

Do such findings indicate a way to "give your child a superior intellect"? Some popular books claim that with intensive preschool training such is possible. But most experts are doubtful (Bruer, 1999). Although malnutrition, sensory deprivation, and social isolation can retard normal brain development, the difference between normal and "enriched" environments matters less. There is no environmental recipe for superbabies, beyond normal exposure to sights, sounds, and speech. Sandra Scarr's (1984) verdict still is widely shared: "Parents who are very concerned about providing special educational lessons for their babies are wasting their time."

Hunt would probably have agreed with Scarr that extra instruction has little effect on the intellectual development of children from stimulating environments. But he was optimistic when it came to children from disadvantaged environments. Indeed, his 1961 book, *Intelligence and Experience*, helped launch Project Head Start in 1965. Head Start, a U.S. government-funded preschool program, serves more than 900,000 children, most of whom come from families below the poverty level (Head Start, 2005). It aims to enhance children's chances for success in school and beyond by boosting their cognitive and social skills.

Does it succeed? Researchers study Head Start and other preschool programs by comparing children who experience the program with their counterparts who don't.

"There is a large body of evidence indicating that there is little if anything to be gained by exposing middle-class children to early education."

Developmental psychologist
Edward F. Zigler (1987)

Getting a head start

To increase readiness for schoolwork and expand children's notions of where school might lead them, Project Head Start offers educational activities. Here children in a classroom learn about colors, and children on a field trip prepare for the annual Head Start parade in Boston.

Quality programs, offering individual attention, increase children's school readiness, which decreases their likelihood of repeating a grade or being placed in special education. Generally, the aptitude benefits dissipate over time (reminding us that life experience *after* Head Start matters, too). Psychologist Edward Zigler, the program's first director, nevertheless believes there are long-term benefits (Ripple & Zigler, 2003; Zigler & Styfco, 2001). High-quality preschool programs can provide at least a small boost to emotional intelligence—creating better attitudes toward learning and reducing school dropouts and criminality (Reynolds & others, 2001).

Schooling Effects

Schooling itself is an intervention that pays dividends reflected in intelligence scores. Stephen Ceci and Wendy Williams (1997) have amassed evidence that schooling and intelligence contribute to each other (and that both enhance later income). High intelligence is conducive to prolonged schooling. But intelligence scores tend to rise during the school year and drop over the summer months and when schooling is discontinued. Completing high school elevates intelligence scores over those obtained by comparable children who leave school early. The worldwide rise in intelligence test scores since the 1920s (known as the *Flynn effect* [Flynn, 1987, 1999]) is probably partly due to increasing years of schooling over the last half-century—and to the more stimulating home environments provided by today's better-educated parents.

Group Differences in Intelligence Test Scores

If there were no group differences in aptitude scores, psychologists could politely debate hereditary and environmental influences in their ivory towers. But there are group differences. What are they? And what shall we make of them?

Ethnic Similarities and Differences

OBJECTIVE 33-3 | Describe ethnic similarities and differences in intelligence test scores, and discuss some genetic and environmental factors that might explain them.

Fueling this discussion are two disturbing but agreed-upon facts:

- Racial groups differ in their average scores on intelligence tests.
- High-scoring people (and groups) are more likely to attain high levels of education and income.

A statement by 52 intelligence researchers explained: "The bell curve for Whites is centered roughly around IQ 100; the bell curve for American Blacks roughly around 85; and those for different subgroups of Hispanics roughly midway between those for Whites and Blacks" (Avery & others, 1994). Comparable results come from other academic aptitude tests, such as the SAT. In recent years, the Black-White difference has diminished somewhat, and among children has dropped to 10 points in some studies (Neisser & others, 1996). Yet the test score gap stubbornly persists.

There are differences among other groups as well. European New Zealanders outscore native Maori New Zealanders. Israeli Jews outscore Israeli Arabs. Most Japanese outscore the stigmatized Japanese minority, the Burakumin. And those who can hear outscore those born deaf (Braden, 1994; Steele, 1990; Zeidner, 1990).

Everyone further agrees that such *group* differences provide little basis for judging individuals. Women outlive men by six years, but knowing someone's sex doesn't tell us with any precision how long that person will live. Even Charles Murray and Richard Herrnstein (1994), whose writings drew attention to Black-White differences, reminded us that "millions of Blacks have higher IQs than the average White."

FIGURE 33.3
Group differences and environmental impact
Even if the variation between members within a group reflects genetic differences, the average difference between groups may be wholly due to the environment. Imagine that seeds from the same mixture are sown in poor and fertile soil. Although height differences within each window box will be genetic, the height difference between the two groups will be environmental. (From Lewontin, 1976.)

Swedes and Bantus differ in complexion and language. That first factor is genetic, the second environmental. So what about intelligence scores?

As we have seen, heredity contributes to individual differences in intelligence. Does that mean it also contributes to group differences? Some psychologists believe it does, perhaps because of the world's differing climates and survival challenges (Herrnstein & Murray, 1994; Lynn, 1991, 2001; Rushton, 1998, 2003).

But we have also seen that group differences in a heritable trait may be entirely environmental, as in our earlier barrel-versus-home-reared boys example. Consider one of nature's experiments: Allow some children to grow up hearing their culture's dominant language, while others, born deaf, do not. Then give them an intelligence test rooted in that language, and (no surprise) those with expertise in the test's language will score highest. Although individual performance differences may be substantially genetic, the group difference is not (**FIGURE 33.3**).

Consider: If each identical twin were exactly as tall as his or her co-twin, heritability would be 100 percent. Imagine that we then separated some young twins and gave only half of them a nutritious diet, and that the well-nourished twins all grew to be exactly 3 inches taller than their counterparts—an environmental effect comparable to that actually observed in both Britain and America, where adolescents are several inches taller than their counterparts were a half-century ago (Angoff, 1987; Lynn, 1987). What would the heritability of height now be for our well-nourished twins? Still 100 percent, because the variation in height within the group would remain entirely predictable from the heights of their malnourished identical siblings. So even perfect heritability within groups would not eliminate the possibility of a strong environmental impact on the group differences.

Might the racial gap be similarly environmental? Consider:

Genetics research reveals that under the skin, the races are remarkably alike (Cavalli-Sforza & others, 1994; Lewontin, 1982). Individual differences within a race are much greater than differences between races. The average genetic difference between two Icelandic

Since 1850, the average Dutch man has grown from 5 feet 4 inches to today's 5 feet 10 inches (Bogin, 1998).

In prosperous country X everyone eats all they want. In country Y the rich are well fed, but the semistarved poor are often thin. In which country will the heritability of body weight be greater? (See this module's final page.)

Nature's own morphing
Nature draws no sharp boundaries between races, which blend gradually one into the next around the Earth. Thanks to the human urge to classify, however, people socially define themselves in racial categories, which become catch-all labels for physical features, social identity, and nationality.

© Paul Almasy/Corbis; © Rob Howard/ Corbis;
© Barbara Bannister; Gallo Images/ Corbis; © David Turnley/Corbis;
© Dave Bartruff/Corbis; © Haruyoshi Yamaguchi/Corbis;
© Richard T. Nowitz/Corbis; © Owen Franken/Corbis;
© Paul Almasy/Corbis; © John-Francis Bourke/zefa/Corbis

The culture of scholarship
The children of Indochinese refugee families studied by Nathan Caplan, Marcella Choy, and James Whitmore (1992) typically excel in school. On weekday nights after dinner, the family clears the table and begins homework. Family cooperation is valued, and older siblings help younger ones.

"Do not obtain your slaves from Britain, because they are so stupid and so utterly incapable of being taught."

Cicero, 106–43 B.C.

"African-Americans, from a condition of mass illiteracy 50 years ago, are now among the most educated groups of people in the world, with median years of schooling and college completion rates higher than those of most European nations."

Sociologist Orlando Patterson, *The Ordeal of Integration*, 1997

villagers or between two Kenyans greatly exceeds the group difference between Icelanders and Kenyans. Moreover, looks can deceive. Light-skinned Europeans and dark-skinned Africans are genetically closer than are dark-skinned Africans and dark-skinned Aboriginal Australians.

Race is not a neatly defined biological category. Some scholars argue that there is a reality to race, noting that there are genetic markers for race and that medical risks vary by race. Your vulnerability to skin cancer depends on both sun exposure and who your ancestors were. Behavioral traits may also vary by race. "No runner of Asian or European descent—a majority of the world's population—has broken 10 seconds in the 100-meter dash, but dozens of runners of West African descent have done so," observes psychologist David Rowe (2005). Many more social scientists, though, see race primarily as a social construction without well-defined physical boundaries (Helms & others, 2005; Smedley & Smedley, 2005; Sternberg & others, 2005). People with varying ancestry may categorize themselves in the same race. Moreover, with increasingly mixed ancestries, more and more people defy neat racial categorization. (What race is Tiger Woods?)

Asian students outperform North American students on math achievement and aptitude tests. But this difference appears to be a recent phenomenon and may reflect conscientiousness more than competence. Asian students also attend school 30 percent more days per year and spend much more time in and out of school studying math (Geary & others, 1996; Larson & Verma, 1999; Stevenson, 1992).

The intelligence test performance of today's better-fed, better-educated, and more test-prepared population exceeds that of the 1930s population (the Flynn effect)—by the same margin that the intelligence test score of the average White today exceeds that of the average Black. No one attributes the generational group difference to genetics.

White and black infants have scored equally well on an infant intelligence measure (preference for looking at novel stimuli—a crude predictor of future intelligence scores [Fagan, 1992]).

In different eras, different ethnic groups have experienced golden ages—periods of remarkable achievement. Twenty-five-hundred years ago it was the Greeks and the Egyptians, then the Romans; in the eighth and ninth centuries, genius seemed to reside in the Arab world; 500 years ago it was the Aztec Indians and the peoples of Northern Europe. Today, people marvel at Asians' technological genius. Cultures rise and fall over centuries; genes do not. That fact makes it difficult to attribute a natural superiority to any race.

Moreover, consider the striking results of a national study that looked back over the mental test performances of white and black young adults after graduation from college. From eighth grade through the early high school years, the average aptitude score of the white students increased, while those of the black students decreased—creating a gap that reached its widest point at about the time that high school students take college admissions tests. But during college, the black students' scores increased "more than four times as much" as those of their white counterparts, thus greatly *decreasing* the aptitude gap. "It is not surprising," concluded researcher Joel Myerson and his colleagues (1998), "that as black and white students complete more grades in high school environments that differ in quality, the gap in cognitive test scores widens. At the college level, however, where black and white students are exposed to educational environments of comparable quality . . . many Blacks are able to make remarkable gains, closing the gap in test scores."

Gender Similarities and Differences

OBJECTIVE 33-4 | Describe gender differences in abilities.

In science, as in everyday life, differences, not similarities, excite interest. Compared with the anatomical and physiological similarities between men and women, our sex differences are relatively minor. Yet it is the differences we find exciting. Similarly, in the psychological domain, gender similarities vastly outnumber gender differences, but most people find differences more newsworthy.

Spelling Girls are better spellers: At the end of high school in the United States, only 30 percent of males spell better than the average female (Lubinski & Benbow, 1992). Through 2004, of the 80 U.S. national spelling bee champions, 42 were girls.

Verbal ability Girls are more verbally fluent and more capable of remembering words. And among nearly 200,000 students taking Germany's Test for Medical Studies, young women year after year have surpassed men in remembering facts from short medical cases (Stumpf & Jackson, 1994). (My wife, who remembers many of my experiences for me, tells me that if she died I'd be a man without a past.)

Nonverbal memory Girls have the edge on boys at locating objects (Halpern, 2000). In studies of more than 100,000 American adolescents, girls also modestly surpassed boys in memory for picture associations (Hedges & Nowell, 1995).

Sensation Girls are more sensitive to touch, taste, and odor.

Underachievement Boys outnumber girls at the low extremes and therefore in special education classes (Kleinfeld, 1998; **FIGURE 33.4**). Boys tend to talk later and to stutter more often. In remedial reading classes, boys outnumber girls three to one (Finucci & Childs, 1981). Among U.S. high school underachievers, boys outnumber girls by two to one (McCall & others, 1992).

Despite the gender equivalence in intelligence test scores, males are more likely than females to overestimate their own test scores. Both males and females tend to rate their father's scores higher than their mother's, their brothers' scores higher than their sisters', and their sons' scores higher than their daughters' (Furnham, 2001; Furnham & others, 2002a,b, 2004a,b,c).

Percentage of boys and girls within each IQ score band

IQ score band

Girls   Boys

FIGURE 33.4
Gender and variability
When nearly 80,000 Scottish 11-year-olds were administered an intelligence test in 1932, the average IQ scores for girls (100.6) and boys (100.5) were virtually identical. But boys were overrepresented at the low and high extremes. (Adapted from Deary & others, 2003.)

World math Olympics champs
After outscoring 350,000 of their U.S. peers, these boys all had perfect scores in competition with math whizzes from 68 other countries.

Math and spatial aptitudes In U.S. schools, the average girl's math scores typically equal or surpass the average boy's (ETS, 1992; Kimball, 1989). And on math tests given to more than 3 million representatively sampled people in 100 independent studies, males and females obtained nearly identical average scores (Hyde & others, 1990). But again—despite greater diversity within the genders than between them—group differences make the news. Although females have an edge in math computation, males in 20 of 21 countries scored higher in math problem solving (Bronner, 1998; Hedges & Nowell, 1995). Male U.S. high school seniors, for example, have averaged 45 points higher on the 200- to 800-point SAT math test (literally meaning that they averaged 4 more correct answers on the 60-question test).

The score differences are sharpest at the extremes. Among 12- to 14-year-olds scoring extremely high on SAT math, boys have outnumbered girls 13 to 1, and within that precocious group the boys more often went on to earn a degree in the inorganic sciences and engineering (Benbow & others, 2000). In the United States, males also have an edge in the annual physics and computer science Advanced Placement exams (Stumpf & Stanley, 1998). And in other Western countries, virtually all math prodigies participating in the International Mathematics Olympiad have been males. More female math prodigies have, however, reached the top levels in non-Western countries such as China (Halpern, 1991).

The average male edge seems most reliable in tests like the one shown in **FIGURE 33.5,** which involves speedily rotating three-dimensional objects in one's mind

In the first 56 years of the college Putnam Mathematical Competition, all of the nearly 300 awardees were men (Arenson, 1997). In 1997, a woman broke the male grip by joining 5 men in the winner's circle. In 1998 Melanie Wood became the first female member of a U.S. math Olympics team (Shulman, 2000). Her training began at an early age: When mall-shopping with her then-4-year-old daughter, Melanie's mother would alleviate her child's boredom by giving her linear equations to solve.

Nature or nurture?
At this 2005 Google Inc.-sponsored computer coding competition, programmers competed for cash prizes and possible jobs. What do you think accounted for the fact that only one of the 100 finalists was female?

Which two circles contain a configuration of blocks identical
to the one in the circle at the left?

Standard   Responses

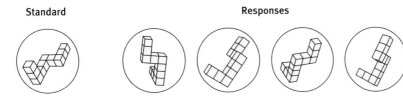

FIGURE 33.5
The mental rotation test
This is a test of spatial abilities. Which two responses show a different view of the standard? (From Vandenberg & Kuse, 1978.) (See this module's final page for answers.)

(Collins & Kimura, 1997; Halpern, 2000). Such spatial ability helps when fitting suitcases into a car trunk, playing chess, or doing certain types of geometry problems.

Working from an evolutionary perspective, David Geary (1995, 1996) and Irwin Silverman and his colleagues (1992, 1998) speculate that skills in navigating within three-dimensional space helped our ancestral fathers in tracking their prey and making their way home. In contrast, the survival of our ancestral mothers was enhanced by keen memory for the location of edible plants—a legacy that lives today in women's superior memory for objects and their location.

Do natural sex differences therefore explain why most mathematicians and more than 9 in 10 rated chess players and American architects, engineers, and mapmakers are men? Or why the world chess body has found it necessary to hold separate competitions for men and women? In 2005, Harvard's president Lawrence Summers caused an uproar when wondering aloud whether the underrepresentation of women in top math and science positions might suggest not only the influence of socialization but also a gender difference in innate abilities.

Exposure to high levels of male sex hormones during the prenatal period does enhance spatial abilities (Berenbaum & others, 1995). Moreover, argues evolutionary psychologist Steven Pinker (2005), there do appear to be biological as well as social influences on gender differences in life priorities (women's greater interest in people versus men's in money and things), in risk-taking (with men more reckless), and in math reasoning and spatial abilities. Such differences are, he notes, observed across cultures, stable over time, observed in genetic boys raised as girls, and influenced by prenatal hormones.

Actually, replied Elizabeth Spelke (2005), it oversimplifies to say that women have more verbal ability and men more math ability. Women excel at verbal fluency, men at verbal analogies. Women excel at rapid math calculations, men at rapid math reasoning. Women excel at remembering objects' spatial positions, men at remembering geometric layouts. And as Summers' other critics emphasized, social expectations and divergent opportunities do shape boys' and girls' interests and abilities (Crawford & others, 1995; Eccles & others, 1990). The male edge in math problem solving grows with age, becoming detectable only after elementary school. Traditionally, math and science have been considered masculine subjects. Many parents send their sons to computer camps and give their daughters more encouragement in English. But as more and more girls are encouraged to develop their abilities in math and science, the gender gap is narrowing (Nowell & Hedges, 1998). In some fields, including psychology, women now earn most of the Ph.D.s. Yet, notes Diane Halpern (2005) with a twinkle in her eye, "no one has asked if men have the innate ability to succeed in those academic disciplines where *they* are underrepresented."

Emotion-detecting ability *Emotional intelligence* is the ability to perceive, understand, manage, and use emotions. Thus, one part of emotional intelligence is empathic accuracy in reading others' emotions. Some of us are more sensitive to emotional cues. Robert Rosenthal, Judith Hall, and their colleagues (1979; McClure, 2000) demonstrated this by showing hundreds of people brief film clips of portions of a person's emotionally expressive face or body, sometimes with a garbled voice added. For example, after showing a 2-second scene revealing only the face of an upset woman, the researchers asked whether the woman was criticizing someone for being late or was talking about her divorce. Rosenthal and Hall found that some people are much better emotion detectors than others are, and that women are better at it than men.

Some psychologists speculate that women's ability to detect emotions helped our ancestral mothers read emotions in their infants and would-be lovers, which may in turn have fueled cultural tendencies to encourage women's empathic skills. Such skills may explain women's somewhat greater responsiveness in both positive and negative emotional situations.

The Question of Bias

OBJECTIVE 33-5 | Discuss whether intelligence tests are biased, and describe the stereotype threat phenomenon.

Knowing there are group differences in intelligence test scores leads us to wonder whether intelligence tests are biased. The answer depends on which of two very different definitions of *bias* are used, and on an understanding of stereotypes.

Two Meanings of Bias

If a test detects not only innate differences in intelligence but also performance differences caused by cultural experiences (as when little David Wechsler scored low), it may be considered biased. In this popular sense, everyone agrees that intelligence tests are biased. An intelligence test measures your developed abilities, which reflect, in part, your education and experiences.

You may have read examples of intelligence test items that make middle-class assumptions (for example, that a cup goes with a saucer, or, as in one of the sample test items from the Wechsler Adult Intelligence Scale, that people buy insurance to protect the value of their homes and possessions). Do such items bias the test against those who do not use saucers or do not have enough possessions to make the cost of insurance relevant? Could such questions explain racial differences in test performance? If so, are tests a vehicle for discrimination, consigning potentially capable children to dead-end classes and jobs?

Defenders of aptitude testing note that racial group differences are at least as great on nonverbal items, such as counting digits backward (Jensen, 1983, 1998). Moreover, they add, blaming the test for a group's lower scores is like blaming a messenger for bad news. Why blame the tests for exposing unequal experiences and opportunities? If, because of malnutrition, people were to suffer stunted growth, would you blame the measuring stick that reveals it? If unequal past experiences predict unequal future achievements, a valid aptitude test will detect such inequalities.

The *scientific* meaning of bias, however, is different. It hinges on whether a test is less valid for some groups than for others—whether it predicts future behavior only for some groups of test-takers. For example, if the U.S. SAT accurately predicted the college achievement of women but not that of men, then the test would be biased. The near-consensus among psychologists, as summarized by the U.S. National Research Council's Committee on Ability Testing and the American Psychological Association's Task Force on Intelligence, is that the major U.S. aptitude tests are *not* biased in this statistical meaning of the term (Neisser & others, 1996; Wigdor & Garner, 1982). The predictive validity of the SAT or of a standard intelligence test is roughly the same for women and men, for Blacks and Whites, and for rich and poor. If an intelligence test score of 95 predicts slightly below average grades, the rough prediction usually applies equally to both genders and all ethnic and economic groups.

Stereotype Threat

To predict school performance accurately, an aptitude test must mirror any gender or racial bias in school teaching and testing. Among students given a difficult math test by Steven Spencer and his colleagues (1997), men outperformed equally capable women—except when the women had been led to expect that women usually do as well as men on the test. Otherwise, the women apparently felt apprehensive, which affected their performance. Claude Steele, Steven Spencer, and Joshua Aronson (2002) have observed the same self-fulfilling effect of negative racial stereotypes. They found this **stereotype threat** phenomenon in black students' verbal aptitude scores, which were lower when they took tests under conditions designed to make black students feel threatened. Stereotype threat also explains why women have scored higher on math tests when no male test-takers were in the group, and why Blacks have scored higher when tested by Blacks than when tested by Whites (Danso & Esses, 2001; Inzlicht & Ben-Zeev, 2000)

Steele (1995, 1997) concluded that if you tell students they probably won't succeed (as remedial "minority support" programs often do), this stereotype will eventually erode their performance both on aptitude tests and in school. Over time, such students may "disidentify" with school achievement. They may detach their self-esteem from academics and look for self-esteem elsewhere—which might help explain why minority students tend to underachieve relative to their abilities. Indeed, as African-American boys progress from eighth to twelfth grade, the disconnect between their grades and their self-esteem becomes pronounced (Osborne, 1997). Minority students in university programs that challenge them to believe in their potential have produced markedly higher grades and had lower dropout rates.

What then can we realistically conclude about aptitude tests and bias? The tests do seem biased (appropriately so, some would say) in one sense—sensitivity to performance differences caused by cultural experience. But they are not biased in the scientific sense of making valid statistical predictions for different groups.

Bottom line: Are the tests discriminatory? Again, the answer can be yes or no. In one sense, yes, their purpose is to discriminate—to distinguish among individuals. In another sense, their purpose is to reduce discrimination by reducing reliance on subjective criteria for school and job placement—criteria such as whom you know, what you look like, or how much the interviewer likes "your kind of person." Civil service aptitude tests, for example, were devised to discriminate more fairly and objectively, by reducing the political, racial, and ethnic discrimination that preceded their use. Banning aptitude tests would lead those who decide on jobs and admissions to rely more on other considerations, such as their personal opinions.

Perhaps, then, our aim should be threefold. First, we should realize the benefits Alfred Binet, the founder of modern-day intelligence testing, foresaw for tests of mental abilities—to enable schools to recognize who might profit most from early intervention. Second, we must remain alert to Binet's fear that intelligence test scores may be misinterpreted as literal measures of a person's worth and fixed potential. And finally, we must remember that *intelligence test scores reflect only one aspect of personal competence.* Our practical intelligence and emotional intelligence matter, too, as do other forms of talent and character. As Madeline L'Engle observed, "Almost all the joyful things of life are outside the measure of IQ tests" (*A Circle of*

■ **stereotype threat** a self-confirming concern that one will be evaluated based on a negative stereotype.

" Math class is tough!"
"Teen talk" talking Barbie doll (introduced February 1992, recalled October 1992)

Untestable compassion
Intelligence test scores are only one part of the picture of a whole person. They don't measure the abilities, talent, and commitment of, for example, people who devote their lives to helping others.

Quiet, 1972). The competence that general intelligence tests sample is important; it helps enable success in some life paths. But it is far from all-important. The carpenter's spatial ability differs from the programmer's logical ability, which differs from the poet's verbal ability. Because there are many ways of being successful, our differences are variations of human adaptability.

>> Learning Outcomes

Genetic and Environmental Influences on Intelligence

Objective 33-1 | Discuss the evidence for the genetic contribution to individual intelligence, and explain what psychologists mean by the heritability of intelligence.

Studies of twins, family members, and adopted children together support the idea that there is a significant genetic contribution to intelligence scores. The most genetically similar people have the most similar scores, ranging from about +.85 for identical twins raised together, to about +.33 for unrelated individuals raised together. No "genius gene" has been discovered yet, but the search is under way. *Heritability of intelligence* refers to the extent to which variation in intelligence test scores in a *group of people* being studied is attributable to genetic factors. Heritability never applies to an individual's intelligence, but only to differences among people.

Objective 33-2 | Discuss the evidence for environmental influences on individual intelligence.

Studies of twins, family members, and adopted children also provide evidence of environmental influence on intelligence. The intelligence test scores of fraternal twins raised together are more similar than those of other siblings, and the scores of identical twins raised apart are less similar (though still very highly correlated) than the scores of identical twins raised together. Studies of children reared in extremely impoverished, enriched, or culturally different environments further indicate the influence of life experiences on test scores.

Objective 33-3 | Describe ethnic similarities and differences in intelligence test scores, and discuss some genetic and environmental factors that might explain them.

As a group, white Americans tend to have an average intelligence test score about 8 to 15 points higher than their Hispanic or African-American counterparts. This gap has narrowed recently among children. Six points suggest that environmental differences are largely responsible for these group differences: (1) The races are remarkably alike genetically. (2) Race is a socially, not biologically, defined category. (3) Asian students outperform North American white students on math achievement and aptitude tests. (4) Intelligence test performance of today's better-fed, better-educated, and more test-prepared population exceeds that of the 1930s population, by the same margin that the score of the average White today exceeds that of the average Black. (5) White and black infants tend to score equally well on tests predicting future intelligence. (6) In different eras, different ethnic groups have experienced periods of remarkable achievement.

Objective 33-4 | Describe gender differences in abilities.

Seven ways males and females differ in their abilities include: (1) Girls are better spellers. (2) Girls are more verbally fluent and can remember more words. (3) Girls are better at locating objects. (4) Girls are more sensitive to touch, taste, and color. (5) Boys outnumber girls in counts of underachievement. (6) Boys outperform girls at math problem solving, though girls outperform boys in math computation. (7) Women detect emotions more easily than men do.

Objective 33-5 | Discuss whether intelligence tests are biased, and describe the stereotype threat phenomenon.

Aptitude tests are necessarily biased in the sense that they are sensitive to performance differences caused by cultural experience. But if by *bias* we mean that these tests predict less accurately for one group than for another, the major aptitude tests are not significantly biased. *Stereotype threat* is a self-confirming concern that one will be evaluated based on a negative stereotype. This phenomenon appears in some instances in intelligence testing among African-Americans and among women of all colors.

TERMS AND CONCEPTS TO REMEMBER

heritability, p. 33-2   stereotype threat, p. 33-11

TEST YOURSELF

1. As society succeeds in creating equality of opportunity, it will also increase the heritability of ability. The heritability of intelligence scores will be greater in a society marked by equal opportunity than in a society of peasants and aristocrats. Why?

(Answer in Appendix B.)

ASK YOURSELF

1. How have genetic and environmental influences shaped *your* intelligence?

ANSWERS TO QUESTIONS WITHIN THE MODULE

Q. If environments became more equal, the heritability of intelligence would
   a. increase.
   b. decrease.
   c. be unchanged.

A. Heritability—variations explained by genetic influences—will *increase* as environmental variation decreases.

Q. In prosperous country X everyone eats all they want. In country Y the rich are well fed, but the semistarved poor are often thin. In which country will the heritability of body weight be greater?

A. Heritability—differences due to genes—will be greater in country X, where environmental differences in nutrition are minimal.

Q. Which two responses in Figure 33.5 (repeated below) show a different view of the standard? (From Vandenberg & Kuse, 1978.)

Standard   **Responses**

A. The first and fourth alternatives are different views of the standard.

>WEB

Multiple-choice *self-tests* and more may be found at www.worthpublishers.com/myers.

ANOTHER VOICE ON: MOTIVATION AND WORK

YANN MARTEL, FROM *THE LIFE OF PI*, 2000

As the cartons of survival rations diminished, I reduced my intake, holding myself to only two biscuits every eight hours. I was continuously hungry. I thought about food obsessively. The less I had to eat, the larger became the portions I dreamed of. My fantasy meals grew to be the size of India. A Ganges of dhal soup. Hot chapattis the size of Rajasthan. Bowls of rice as big as Uttar Pradesh. Sambars to flood all of Tali Nadu. Ice cream heaped as high as the Himalayas. My dreaming became quite expert: All ingredients for my dishes were always in fresh and plentiful supply; the oven or frying pan was always at just the right temperature; the proportion of things was always bang on; nothing was ever burnt or undercooked, nothing too hot or too cold. Every meal was simply perfect—only just beyond the reach of my hands.

By the time the last of the biscuits had disappeared, anything was good to eat, no matter the taste. I could put anything in my mouth, chew it, and swallow it—delicious, foul, or plain—so long as it wasn't salty. My body developed a revulsion for salt that I still experience to this day.

Motivation and Work

"What's my motivation?" the actor asks the director. In our everyday conversation, "What motivated you to do *that*?" is a way of asking "What *caused* your behavior?" To psychologists, a *motivation* is a need or desire that *energizes* behavior and *directs* it toward a goal. Experienced mountaineer Aron Ralston understands the extent to which motivation can energize and direct behavior. Having bagged nearly all of Colorado's tallest peaks, many of them solo and in winter, Ralston, on a Saturday spring morning in 2003, ventured to do some solo canyon hiking that seemed so risk-free he did not bother to tell anyone where he was going. In Utah's narrow Bluejohn Canyon, just 150 yards above his final rappel, he was climbing over an 800-pound rock when it shifted and pinned his right wrist and arm. He was, as the title of his recent book says, caught *Between a Rock and a Hard Place*.

Realizing no one would be rescuing him, Ralston tried with all his might to dislodge the rock. Then with his dull pocket knife he tried chipping away at the rock. When that, too, failed, he rigged up ropes to lift the rock. Alas, nothing worked. Hour after

Motivation personified
Aron Ralston's motivation to live and belong energized and directed his sacrificing half of his arm.

AP Photo / Rocky Mountain News, Judy Walgren

hour, then cold night after cold night, he was stuck. By Tuesday, he had run out of food and water. On Wednesday, as thirst and hunger gnawed, he began saving and sipping his own urine. Using his video recorder, he said his good-byes to family and friends, for whom he now felt intense love: "So again love to everyone. Bring love and peace and happiness and beautiful lives into the world in my honor. Thank you. Love you."

On Thursday, surprised to find himself still alive, Ralston had a seemingly divine insight into his reproductive future, a vision of a preschool boy being scooped up by a one-armed man. With this inspiration, he summoned his remaining strength and his enormous will to live and, over the next hour, willfully broke his bones and then proceeded to use that dull knife to cut off his arm. The moment after putting on a tourniquet, chopping the last piece of skin, and breaking free—and before rappelling with his bleeding half-arm down a 65-foot cliff and hiking 5 miles till finding someone—he was, in his own words, "just reeling with this euphoria . . . having been dead and standing in my grave, leaving my last will and testament, etching 'Rest in peace' on the wall, all of that, gone and then replaced with having my life again. It was undoubtedly the sweetest moment that I will ever experience" (Ralston, 2004).

Aron Ralston's thirst and hunger, his sense of belonging to others, and his underlying will to live and become a father highlight motivation's energizing and directing power. In Modules 35 through 37, we explore motivation by focusing on four motives—hunger, sex, the need to belong, and achievement at work. Although other identifiable motives exist (including thirst and curiosity), a close look at these four reveals the interplay between nature (the physiological "push") and nurture (the cognitive and cultural "pulls"). Before considering specific motivations, we'll take time in Module 34 to see how psychologists have approached the study of motivation.

MODULE

34

Introduction to Motivation

OBJECTIVE 34-1 | Define *motivation* as psychologists use the term today, and name four perspectives useful for studying motivated behaviors.

Psychologists today define **motivation** as a need or desire that energizes and directs behavior. In their attempt to understand motivated behaviors, psychologists have used four perspectives. These include instinct theory (now replaced by the research on genetic predispositions and evolutionary influences), drive-reduction theory (emphasizing the interaction between inner pushes and external pulls), and arousal theory (emphasizing the urge for an optimum level of stimulation). The fourth perspective, Abraham Maslow's hierarchy of needs, describes how some motives are, if unsatisfied, more basic and compelling than others.

Instincts

OBJECTIVE 34-2 | Discuss instinct theory and its misuses.

Early in the twentieth century, as the influence of Charles Darwin's evolutionary theory grew, it became fashionable to classify all sorts of behaviors as instincts. If people criticized themselves, it was because of their "self-abasement instinct." If they boasted, it reflected their "self-assertion instinct." After scanning 500 books, one sociologist compiled a list of 5759 supposed human instincts! Before long, this fad for naming instincts collapsed under its own weight. Rather than *explaining* human behaviors, the early instinct theorists were simply *naming* them. It was like "explaining" a bright child's low grades by labeling the child an "underachiever." To name a behavior is *not* to explain it.

To qualify as an **instinct,** a complex behavior must have a fixed pattern throughout a species and be unlearned (Tinbergen, 1951). Such behaviors are common in other species. Newly hatched ducks and geese form attachments to the first moving object they see. And mature salmon swim hundreds of miles upstream to reach the

"What do you think . . . should we get started on that motivation research or not?"

Same motive, different wiring
The more complex the nervous system, the more adaptable the organism. Both the woman and the weaverbird satisfy their need for shelter in ways that reflect their inherited capacities. The woman's behavior is flexible; she can learn whatever skills she needs to build a house. The bird's behavior pattern is fixed; it can build only this kind of nest.

place they were born, where they will mate and then die. Human behavior, too, exhibits certain innate tendencies, including simple fixed patterns such as an infant's rooting and sucking. Most psychologists, though, view human behavior as directed by physiological needs *and* by psychological wants.

Although instinct theory failed to explain human motives, the underlying assumption that genes predispose species-typical behavior remains as strong as ever. Psychologists may apply this perspective, for example, in explanations of our human similarities, animals' biological predispositions to learn certain behaviors, and the influence of evolution on our phobias, our helping behaviors, and our romantic attractions.

Drives and Incentives

OBJECTIVE 34-3 | Explain how drive-reduction theory views human motivation.

When the original instinct theory of motivation collapsed, it was replaced by **drive-reduction theory**—the idea that a physiological need creates an aroused state that *drives* the organism to reduce the need by, say, eating or drinking. With few exceptions, when a physiological need increases, so does a psychological drive—an aroused, motivated state.

The physiological aim of drive reduction is **homeostasis**—the maintenance of a steady internal state. An example of homeostasis (literally "staying the same") is the body's temperature-regulation system, which works like a thermostat. Both systems operate through feedback loops. Sensors feed room temperature to a control device. If the room temperature cools, the control device switches on the furnace. Likewise, if our body temperature cools, blood vessels constrict to conserve warmth, and we feel driven to put on more clothes or seek a warmer environment. Similarly, if the water level in our cells drops, sensors detect our need for water and we feel thirsty (**FIGURE 34.1**).

Not only are we *pushed* by our "need" to reduce drives, we also are *pulled* by **incentives**—positive or negative stimuli that lure or repel us. This is one way our individual learning histories influence our motives. Depending on our learning, the aroma of good food, whether fresh roasted peanuts or toasted ants, can motivate our behavior. So can the sight of someone we find attractive or the threat of disapproval from family or friends.

When there is both a need and an incentive, we feel strongly driven. The food-deprived person who smells baking bread feels a strong hunger drive. In the presence of that drive, the baking bread becomes a compelling incentive. For each motive, we can therefore ask, "How is it pushed by our inborn physiological needs and pulled by incentives in the environment?"

**FIGURE 34.1
Drive-reduction theory**

- **motivation** a need or desire that energizes and directs behavior.

- **instinct** a complex behavior that is rigidly patterned throughout a species and is unlearned.

- **drive-reduction theory** the idea that a physiological need creates an aroused tension state (a drive) that motivates an organism to satisfy the need.

- **homeostasis** a tendency to maintain a balanced or constant internal state; the regulation of any aspect of body chemistry, such as blood glucose, around a particular level.

- **incentive** a positive or negative environmental stimulus that motivates behavior.

Optimum Arousal

OBJECTIVE 34-4 | Discuss the contribution of arousal theory to the study of motivation.

We are much more than homeostatic systems, however. Some motivated behaviors actually *increase* arousal. Well-fed animals will leave their shelter to explore, seemingly in the absence of any need-based drive. From taking such risks, animals gain information and resources (Renner, 1992).

Curiosity drives monkeys to monkey around trying to figure out how to unlock a latch that opens nothing or how to open a window that allows them to see outside

Driven by curiosity
Baby monkeys and small children are fascinated by things they've never handled before. Their drive to explore the relatively unfamiliar is one of several motives that do not fill any immediate physiological need.

their room (Butler, 1954). It drives the 9-month-old infant who investigates every accessible corner of the house. It drives the scientists whose work this text discusses. And it drives explorers and adventurers such as Aron Ralston. Asked why he wanted to climb Mount Everest, George Mallory answered, "Because it is there." Those who, like Mallory and Ralston, enjoy high arousal are most likely to enjoy intense music, novel foods, and risky behaviors (Zuckerman, 1979).

So, human motivation aims not to eliminate arousal but to seek optimum levels of arousal. Having all our biological needs satisfied, we feel driven to experience stimulation. Lacking stimulation, we feel bored and look for a way to increase arousal to some optimum level. However, with too much stimulation comes stress, and we then look for a way to decrease arousal.

A Hierarchy of Motives

OBJECTIVE 34-5 | Describe Maslow's hierarchy of needs.

Some needs take priority over others. At this moment, with your needs for air and water satisfied, other motives—such as your desire to achieve—are energizing and directing your behavior. Let your need for water go unsatisfied and your thirst will preoccupy you. But if you were deprived of air, your thirst would disappear.

Abraham Maslow (1970) described these priorities as a **hierarchy of needs** (FIGURE 34.2). At the base of this pyramid are our physiological needs, such as those for food and water. Only if these needs are met are we prompted to meet our need for safety, and then to satisfy the uniquely human needs to give and receive love and to enjoy self-esteem. Beyond this, said Maslow (1971), lies the highest of human needs: to actualize one's full potential.

FIGURE 34.2

Maslow's hierarchy of needs
Once our lower-level needs are met, we are prompted to satisfy our higher-level needs. While struggling to meet their basic needs for water, food, safe shelter, and medical attention, these survivors of the 2005 New Orleans hurricane were probably not immediately concerned with the higher-level needs on Maslow's hierarchy, such as esteem and self-actualization. (From Maslow, 1970.)

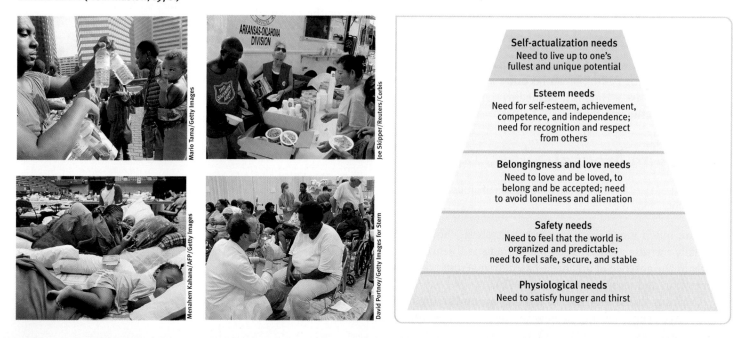

Self-actualization needs
Need to live up to one's fullest and unique potential

Esteem needs
Need for self-esteem, achievement, competence, and independence; need for recognition and respect from others

Belongingness and love needs
Need to love and be loved, to belong and be accepted; need to avoid loneliness and alienation

Safety needs
Need to feel that the world is organized and predictable; need to feel safe, secure, and stable

Physiological needs
Need to satisfy hunger and thirst

Maslow's hierarchy is somewhat arbitrary; the order of such needs is not universally fixed. People have starved themselves to make a political statement. Nevertheless, the simple idea that some motives are more compelling than others provides a framework for thinking about motivation, and life-satisfaction surveys in 39 nations support this basic idea (Oishi & others, 1999). In poorer nations that lack easy access to money and the food and shelter it buys, financial satisfaction more strongly predicts subjective well-being. In wealthy nations, where most are able to meet basic needs, home-life satisfaction is a better predictor. Self-esteem matters most in individualist nations, whose citizens tend to focus more on personal achievements than on family and community identity. So what motives preoccupy you depend on your situation.

> ■ **hierarchy of needs** Maslow's pyramid of human needs, beginning at the base with physiological needs that must first be satisfied before higher-level safety needs and then psychological needs become active.

> "Hunger is the most urgent form of poverty."
> Alliance to End Hunger, 2002

>> Learning Outcomes

Introduction to Motivation

OBJECTIVE 34-1 | **Define** *motivation* **as psychologists use the term today, and name four perspectives useful for studying motivated behavior.**
Motivation is the energizing and directing of behavior. The *instinct, drive-reduction, arousal,* and *hierarchy of needs* perspectives offer insights into motivated behaviors.

OBJECTIVE 34-2 | **Discuss instinct theory and its misuses.**
Instincts are rigidly patterned, complex behaviors found throughout a species. Early instinct theorists, influenced by Darwin's theory of natural selection, tried but failed to classify human behaviors as though they were propelled by such instincts. The underlying idea—that genes predispose species-typical behavior—is still influential.

OBJECTIVE 34-3 | **Explain how drive-reduction theory views human motivation.**
Drive-reduction theory proposes that physiological needs create aroused psychological states that drive us to reduce or satisfy those needs. The physiological aim of drive reduction is internal stability, or *homeostasis.* We are most strongly driven when pushed by the need to reduce a drive (such as satisfying hunger) and pulled by an external incentive (the smell of cooking food, for example). Depending on our personal and cultural histories, we respond more to some stimuli than to others.

OBJECTIVE 34-4 | **Discuss the contribution of arousal theory to the study of motivation.**
Arousal theory helps explain the motivation for behaviors that do not reduce immediate physiological needs or tension states. Curiosity-driven behaviors, for example, suggest that too little stimulation can motivate people to seek a higher level of arousal.

OBJECTIVE 34-5 | **Describe Maslow's hierarchy of needs.**
Maslow's hierarchy of needs proposes a pyramid-shaped sequence in which lower-level needs, such as hunger and thirst, are more compelling than higher-level needs, such as the need to love or to be respected. Maslow's sequence of needs is not universal, but his hierarchy provides a framework for thinking about motivated behaviors.

TERMS AND CONCEPTS TO REMEMBER

motivation, p. 34-0
instinct, p. 34-0
drive-reduction theory, p. 34-1

homeostasis, p. 34-1
incentive, p. 34-1
hierarchy of needs, p. 34-2

TEST YOURSELF

1. While on a long road trip, you suddenly feel very lonely and want to pull over and call a loved one. But the dark, deserted stretch of road is intimidating, so you keep on driving. What motivational perspective would most easily explain this behavior and why?

(Answer in Appendix B.)

ASK YOURSELF

1. Consider your own experiences with Maslow's hierarchy of needs. Have you ever experienced true hunger or thirst that displaced your concern for other, higher-level needs? Do you usually feel safe? Loved? Confident? How often do you feel you are able to address what Maslow called your "self-actualization" needs?

⟩WEB

Multiple-choice *self-tests* and more may be found at www.worthpublishers.com/myers.

Personnel Psychology

Organizational Psychology: Motivating Achievement

Sometimes, notes Gene Weingarten (2002), a humor writer knows "when to just get out of the way." Here are some sample job titles from the U.S. Department of Labor *Dictionary of Occupational Titles:* Animal impersonator, human projectile, banana ripening-room supervisor, impregnator, impregnator helper, dope sprayer, finger waver, rug scratcher, egg smeller, bottom buffer, cookie breaker, brain picker, hand pouncer, bosom presser, mother repairer, and breaker repairer.

Have you ever noticed that when you are immersed in an activity, time flies? And that when you are watching the clock, it seems to move more slowly? French researchers have confirmed that the more we attend to an event's duration, the longer it seems to last (Coull & others, 2004).

Motivation at Work

OBJECTIVE 37-1 | Discuss the importance of flow, and identify the three subfields of industrial-organizational psychology.

The healthy life, said Sigmund Freud, is filled by love and by work. For most of us, work is life's biggest single waking activity. To live is to work. Work helps satisfy several levels of need. Work supports us. Work connects us. Work defines us. Meeting someone for the first time, and wondering "Who are you?" we may ask, "So, what do you do?"

If we feel dissatisfied with our work-related pay, relationships, or identity, we may change where or for whom we work, as 16 percent of Australians did in just the year 2000 (Trewin, 2001). Most people therefore have neither a single vocation nor a predictable career path. Two decades from now, most of you reading this book will be doing work you cannot now imagine. To prepare you and others for this unknown future, many colleges and universities focus less on training your job skills and more on enlarging your capacities for understanding, thinking, and communicating in any work environment.

Amy Wrzesniewski and her colleagues (1997, 2001) have identified person-to-person variations in people's attitudes toward their work. Across various occupations, some people view their work as a *job,* a necessary way to make money but not a positive and fulfilling activity. Others view their work as a *career,* an opportunity to advance from one position to a better position. The rest—those who view their work as a *calling,* a fulfilling and socially useful activity—report the highest satisfaction with their work and their lives.

This finding would not surprise Mihaly Csikszentmihalyi (1990, 1999), who has observed that people's quality of life increases when they are purposefully engaged. Between the anxiety of being overwhelmed and stressed, and the apathy of being underwhelmed and bored, lies a zone in which people experience **flow.** Csikszentmihalyi (chick-SENT-me-hi) formulated the flow concept after studying artists who spent hour after hour painting or sculpting with enormous concentration. Immersed in a project, they worked as if nothing else mattered, and then promptly forgot about it once they finished. The artists seemed driven less by the external rewards of producing art—money, praise, promotion—than by the intrinsic rewards of creating the work. Recognizing that e-mail and other Internet-related distractions can disrupt such flow, Microsoft is developing an *attentional user interface* that aims to "detect when users are available for communication, or when the user is in a state of flow" (Ullman, 2005).

Csikszentmihalyi's later observations—of dancers, chess players, surgeons, writers, parents, mountain climbers, sailors, and farmers; of Australians, North Americans, Koreans, Japanese, and Italians; of people from their teens to their golden years—confirmed an overriding principle: It's exhilarating to flow with an activity that fully engages our skills. Flow experiences boost our sense of self-esteem, competence, and well-being. When the researchers beeped people at random intervals and asked them to report what they were doing and how much they were enjoying themselves, those who were vegetating usually reported little sense of flow and little satisfaction. People reported more positive feelings when interrupted while doing something active, something that engaged their skills, be it play or work. And other research (Inglehart, 1990) indicates that in almost every industrialized nation, people have reported markedly lower well-being if unemployed (**FIGURE 37.1**). Idleness may sound like bliss, but purposeful work enriches our lives.

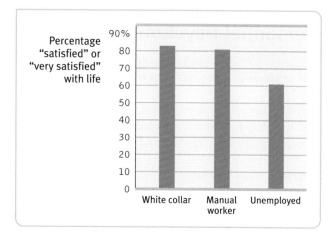

FIGURE 37.1
The bane of unemployment
To want work but not have it is to feel less satisfied with life. Data from 169,776 adults in 16 nations (Inglehart, 1990).

In industrialized nations, work has been changing, from farming to manufacturing to "knowledge work." More and more work is *outsourced* to temporary employees and consultants who communicate electronically from virtual workplaces in remote locations. (This book and its teaching package are developed and produced by a team of people in a dozen cities, from Alaska to Florida.) As work changes, will our attitudes toward our work also change? Will our satisfaction with work increase or decrease? Will the *psychological contract*—the subjective sense of mutual obligations between workers and employers—become more or less trusting and secure? These are among the questions that fascinate psychologists who study work-related behavior.

Industrial-organizational (I/O) psychology is a fast-growing profession that applies psychology's principles to the workplace (see Close-Up: I/O Psychology at Work). Here we consider two subfields: **personnel psychology,** which applies psychology's methods and principles to selecting and evaluating workers, and **organizational psychology,** which considers how work environments and management styles influence worker motivation, satisfaction, and productivity. Personnel psychologists match people with jobs, by identifying and placing well-suited candidates. Organizational psychologists modify jobs and supervision in ways that boost morale and productivity. (A third subfield, *human factors psychology,* explores how machines and environments can be optimally designed to fit human abilities.)

■ **flow** a completely involved, focused state of consciousness, with diminished awareness of self and time, resulting from optimal engagement of one's skills.

■ **industrial-organizational (I/O) psychology** the application of psychological concepts and methods to optimizing human behavior in workplaces.

■ **personnel psychology** a subfield of I/O psychology that focuses on employee recruitment, selection, placement, training, appraisal, and development.

■ **organizational psychology** a subfield of I/O psychology that examines organizational influences on worker satisfaction and productivity and facilitates organizational change.

CLOSE-UP:

I/O PSYCHOLOGY AT WORK

As scientists, consultants, and management professionals, industrial-organizational psychologists are found working in varied areas:

PERSONNEL PSYCHOLOGY

Selecting and placing employees
- Developing and validating assessment tools for selecting, placing and promoting workers
- Analyzing job content
- Optimizing worker placement

Training and developing employees
- Identifying needs

- Designing training programs
- Evaluating training programs

Appraising performance
- Developing criteria
- Measuring individual performance
- Measuring organizational performance

ORGANIZATIONAL PSYCHOLOGY

Developing organizations
- Analyzing organizational structures
- Maximizing worker satisfaction and productivity
- Facilitating organizational change

Enhancing quality of worklife
- Expanding individual productivity
- Identifying elements of satisfaction
- Redesigning jobs

HUMAN FACTORS (ENGINEERING) PSYCHOLOGY
- Designing optimum work environments
- Optimizing person-machine interactions
- Developing systems technologies

Adapted from the Society of Industrial and Organizational Psychology (siop.org)

Artistic strengths
At age 21, Henri Matisse was a sickly and often depressed lawyer's clerk. When his mother gave him a box of paints to cheer him up one day, he felt the darkness lift and his energy surge. He began to fill his days with painting and drawing and went on to art school and a life as one of the world's great painters. For Matisse, doing art felt like "a comfortable armchair." That is how exercising our strengths often feels.

Personnel Psychology

OBJECTIVE 37-2 | Describe how personnel psychologists help organizations with employee selection, work placement, and performance appraisal.

Psychologists can assist organizations at various stages of selecting and assessing employees. They may help identify needed job skills, decide upon selection methods, recruit and evaluate applicants, introduce and train new employees, and appraise their performance.

Harnessing Strengths

As a new AT&T human resource executive, psychologist Mary Tenopyr (1997) was assigned to solve a problem: Customer service representatives were failing at a high rate. After concluding that many of the hires were ill-matched to the demands of their new job, Tenopyr developed a new selection instrument:

1. She asked new applicants to respond to various questions (without as yet making any use of their responses).
2. She followed up later to assess which of the applicants excelled on the job.
3. She identified the individual items on the earlier test that best predicted who would succeed.

The happy result of her data-driven work was a new test that enabled AT&T to identify likely-to-succeed customer representatives.

As this illustrates, personnel selection aims to match people's strengths with work that enables them and their organizations to flourish. Marry the strengths of people with the tasks of organizations and the result is often prosperity and profit.

Your strengths are any enduring qualities that can be productively applied. Are you naturally curious? Persuasive? Charming? Persistent? Competitive? Analytical? Empathic? Organized? Articulate? Neat? Mechanical? Any such trait, if matched with suitable work, can function as a strength. (See Close-Up: Discovering Your Strengths.)

Marcus Buckingham and Donald Clifton (2001) argued that the first step to a stronger organization is instituting a strengths-based selection system. Thus, as a manager, you would first identify a group of the most effective people in any role—

CLOSE-UP:

DISCOVERING YOUR STRENGTHS

You can use some of the techniques personnel psychologists have developed to identify your own strengths and pinpoint types of work that will likely prove satisfying and successful. Buckingham and Clifton (2001) have suggested asking yourself:

- What activities give me pleasure? (Bringing order out of chaos? Playing host? Helping others? Challenging sloppy thinking?)
- What activities leave me wondering, "When can I do this again?" (Rather than "When will this be over?")
- What sort of challenges do I relish? (And which do I dread?)

- What sorts of tasks do I learn easily? (And which do I struggle with?)

Some people find themselves in flow—their skills engaged and time flying—when teaching or selling or writing or cleaning or consoling or creating or repairing. If an activity feels good, if it comes easily, if you look forward to it, then look deeper and see your strengths at work.

Satisfied and successful people devote far less time to correcting their deficiencies than to accentuating their strengths. Top performers are "rarely well rounded," Buckingham and Clifton found (p. 26). Instead, they have sharpened their existing skills.

Given the persistence of our traits and temperaments, we should focus not on our deficiencies, but rather on identifying and employing our talents. Better to recognize the activities we quickly learn and become absorbed in—and to further develop those strengths—than to sign up for assertiveness training if shy, for public speaking courses if nervous and soft-spoken, or for drawing classes if we express our artistic side in stick figures.

As Robert Louis Stevenson said in *Of Men and Books* (1882), "To be what we are, and to become what we are capable of becoming, is the only end of life."

the ones you would want to hire more of—and compare their strengths with those of a group of the least effective people in that role. In defining these groups, you would try to measure performance as objectively as possible. In one Gallup study of more than 5000 telecommunications customer-service representatives, those evaluated most favorably by their managers were strong in "harmony" and "responsibility," while those actually rated most effective by customers were strong in energy, assertiveness, and eagerness to learn. So, for example, if you needed to hire new people in software development, and you had discovered that your best software developers are analytical, disciplined, and eager to learn, you would focus employment ads less on experience than on the identified strengths: "Do you take a logical and systematic approach to problem solving [analytical]? Are you a perfectionist who strives for timely completion of your projects [disciplined]? Do you want to learn to use Java, C++, and PHP [eager to learn]? If you can say yes to these questions, then please call. . . ."

Identifying people's strengths and matching strengths to work is a first step toward workplace effectiveness. To assess applicants' strengths and decide who is best-suited to the job, personnel managers use various tools, including ability tests, personality tests, and behavioral observations in "assessment centers" that simulate job tasks. Here we focus on job interviews.

Do Interviews Predict Performance?

Interviewers tend to feel confident in their ability to predict long-term job performance from an unstructured, get-acquainted interview. What's therefore shocking is how error-prone those predictions are. Whether predicting job or graduate school success, interviewers' judgments are weak predictors. From their review of 85 years of personnel-selection research, I/O psychologists Frank Schmidt and John Hunter (1998; Schmidt, 2002) determined that for all but less-skilled jobs, general mental ability best predicts on-the-job performance. Subjective overall evaluations from informal interviews are more useful than handwriting analysis (which is worthless). But informal interviews are less informative than aptitude tests, work samples, job knowledge tests, and past job performance. If there's a contest between what our gut tells us about someone and what test scores, work samples, and past performance tell us, we should distrust our gut.

The Interviewer Illusion

Interviewers often overrate their discernment, a phenomenon psychologist Richard Nisbett (1987) has labeled the *interviewer illusion*. "I have excellent interviewing skills, and so don't need reference checking as much as someone who doesn't have my ability to read people," is a comment sometimes heard by I/O consultants. Four factors explain this gap between interviewers' intuition and the resulting reality:

- *Interviews disclose the interviewee's good intentions, which are less revealing than habitual behaviors* (Ouellette & Wood, 1998). Intentions matter. People can change. But the best predictor of the person we will be is the person we have been. Wherever we go, we take ourselves along.
- *Interviewers more often follow the successful careers of those they have hired than the successful careers of those they have rejected and lost track of.* This missing feedback prevents interviewers from getting a reality check on their hiring ability.
- *Interviewers presume that people are what they seem to be in the interview situation.* When meeting others, we discount the enormous influence of varying situations and mistakenly presume that what we see is what we will get. But mountains of research on everything from chattiness to conscientiousness reveals that how we behave reflects not only our enduring traits, but the details of the particular situation (wanting to impress in a job interview).
- *Interviewers' preconceptions and moods color how they perceive interviewees' responses* (Cable & Gilovich, 1998; Macan & Dipboye, 1994). If interviewers instantly like a

"Between the idea and reality . . . falls the shadow."

T. S. Eliot, *The Hollow Men*, 1925

■ **structured interviews** interview process that asks the same job-relevant questions of all applicants, each of whom is rated on established scales.

■ **achievement motivation** a desire for significant accomplishment: for mastery of things, people, or ideas; for attaining a high standard.

person who perhaps is similar to themselves, they may interpret the person's assertiveness as indicating "confidence" rather than "arrogance." If told certain applicants have been prescreened, interviewers are disposed to judge them more favorably.

An unstructured interview does provide a sense of someone's personality—their expressiveness, warmth, and verbal ability, for example. But this information reveals less about the person's behavior toward others in different situations than most people suppose. Hoping to improve prediction and selection, personnel psychologists have put people in simulated work situations, scoured sources for information on past performance, aggregated evaluations from multiple interviews, administered tests, and developed job-specific interviews.

Structured Interviews

Unlike casual conversation aimed at getting a feel for someone, **structured interviews** offer a disciplined method of collecting information. A personnel psychologist may analyze a job, script questions, and train interviewers. The interviewers then put the same questions, in the same order, to all applicants, and rate each applicant on established scales.

In an *unstructured* interview, someone might ask, "How organized are you?" "How well do you get along with people?" or "How do you handle stress?" Street-smart applicants know how to score high: "Although I sometimes drive myself too hard, I handle stress by prioritizing and delegating, and by making sure I leave time for sleep and exercise."

By contrast, structured interviews pinpoint strengths (attitudes, behaviors, knowledge, and skills) that distinguish high performers in a particular line of work. The process includes describing job-specific situations and asking candidates to explain how they would handle them, and how they handled similar situations in their prior employment. "Tell me about a time when you were caught between conflicting demands, without time to accomplish both. How did you handle that?"

To reduce memory distortions and bias, the interviewer takes notes and makes ratings as the interview proceeds and avoids irrelevant and follow-up questions. The structured interview therefore feels less warm, but that can be explained to the applicant: "This conversation won't typify how we relate to each other in this organization."

A review of 150 findings revealed that structured interviews had double the predictive accuracy of unstructured seat-of-the-pants interviews (Schmidt & Hunter, 1998; Wiesner & Cronshaw, 1988). Thanks partly to its greater reliability and partly to its job-analysis focus, the predictive power of one structured interview is roughly equal to that of the average judgment from three or four unstructured interviews (Huffcutt & others, 2001; Schmidt & Zimmerman, 2004).

If, instead, we let our intuitions bias the hiring process, notes Malcolm Gladwell (2000), then "all we will have done is replace the old-boy network, where you hired your nephew, with the new-boy network, where you hire whoever impressed you most when you shook his hand. Social progress, unless we're careful, can merely be the means by which we replace the obviously arbitrary with the not so obviously arbitrary."

To recap, personnel psychologists assist organizations in analyzing jobs, recruiting well-suited applicants, selecting and placing employees, and appraising their performance (**FIGURE 37.2**)—the topic we turn to next.

FIGURE 37.2
Personnel psychologists' tasks
Personnel psychologists consult in human resource activities, from job definition to employee appraisal.

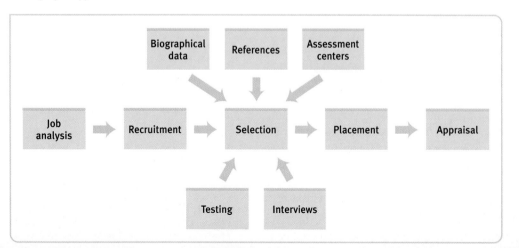

Appraising Performance

Performance appraisal serves organizational purposes: It helps decide who to retain, how to appropriately reward and pay people, and how to better harness employee strengths, sometimes with job shifts or promotions. Performance appraisal also serves individual purposes: Feedback affirms workers' strengths and helps motivate needed improvements.

Performance appraisal methods include

- *checklists* on which supervisors simply check behaviors that describe the worker ("always attends to customers' needs," "takes long breaks").
- *graphic rating scales* on which a supervisor checks the extent to which a worker is dependable, productive, and so forth.
- *behavior rating scales* on which a supervisor checks behaviors that best describe a worker's performance. If rating the extent to which a worker "follows procedures," the supervisor might mark the employee somewhere between "often takes shortcuts" and "always follows established procedures" (Levy, 2003).

In some organizations, performance feedback comes not only from supervisors but also from all organizational levels. If you join an organization that practices *360-degree feedback* (**FIGURE 37.3**) you will rate yourself, your manager, and your other colleagues, and you will be rated by your manager, other colleagues, and customers (Green, 2002). The net result is often more open communication and more complete appraisal.

Performance appraisal, like other social judgments, is vulnerable to bias (Murphy & Cleveland, 1995). *Halo errors* occur when one's overall evaluation of an employee, or of a trait such as their friendliness, biases ratings of their specific work-related behaviors, such as their reliability. *Leniency* and *severity errors* reflect evaluators' tendencies to be either too easy or too harsh on everyone. *Recency errors* occur when raters focus only on easily remembered recent behavior. By encouraging multiple raters and developing objective, job-relevant performance measures, personnel psychologists seek to support their organizations while also helping employees perceive the appraisal process as fair.

Organizational Psychology: Motivating Achievement

OBJECTIVE 37-3 | Define *achievement motivation,* and explain why organizations would employ an I/O psychologist to help motivate employees and foster employee satisfaction.

The appraisal of work and the matching of talents to work matter, but so does overall motivation. Before considering how organizational psychologists assist with efforts to motivate employees and keep them engaged, let's take a closer look at why any employee might want to pursue high standards or difficult goals.

Think of someone you know who strives to succeed by excelling at any task where evaluation is possible. Now think of someone who is less driven. Psychologist Henry Murray (1938) defined the first person's **achievement motivation** as a desire for significant accomplishment, for mastering skills or ideas, for control, and for rapidly attaining a high standard.

As you might expect from their persistence and eagerness for realistic challenges, people with high achievement motivation do achieve more. One study followed the lives of 1528 California children whose intelligence test scores were in the top 1 percent. Forty years later, when researchers compared those who were most and least successful professionally, they found a motivational difference. Those most successful were more ambitious, energetic, and persistent. As children, they had more active hobbies. As adults, they participated in more groups and favored being

FIGURE 37.3
360-degree feedback
With multisource 360-degree feedback, one's knowledge, skills, and behaviors are rated by self and surrounding others. Professors, for example, may be rated by their department chairs, their students, and their colleagues. After receiving all these ratings, professors discuss the 360-degree feedback with their department chair.

Disciplined motivation feeds achievement
Aware that he was far behind other students when beginning his graduate education in psychology, B. F. Skinner devised a daily discipline of rising at 6:00 A.M., studying until breakfast, then going to classes, labs, and the library. After dinner he studied some more, leaving no more than 15 unscheduled minutes each day, and later continued a disciplined daily routine as he became one of the twentieth century's most influential psychologists.

a sports participant to being a spectator (Goleman, 1980). In other studies of both secondary school and university students, self-discipline has been a better predictor of school performance, attendance, and graduation honors than intelligence scores have been. "Discipline outdoes talent," concluded researchers Angela Duckworth and Martin Seligman (2005). By their early twenties, for example, top violinists have accumulated some 10,000 lifetime practice hours—double the practice time of other violin students aiming to be teachers (Ericsson & others, 1993, 2001). From his studies, Herbert Simon (1998), a psychologist who won the Nobel prize for economics, estimates that world-class experts in a field typically have invested "at least 10 years of hard work—say, 40 hours a week for 50 weeks a year."

Similarly, a study of outstanding scholars, athletes, and artists found that all were highly motivated and self-disciplined, willing to dedicate hours every day to the pursuit of their goals (Bloom, 1985). These superstar achievers were distinguished not so much by their extraordinary natural talent as by their extraordinary daily discipline. Great achievement, it seems, mixes a teaspoon of inspiration with a gallon of perspiration.

What distinguishes extremely successful individuals from their equally talented peers, note Duckworth and Seligman, is *grit*—passionate dedication to an ambitious, long-term goal. Although intelligence is distributed like a bell curve, achievements are not. That tells us that achievement involves much more than raw ability. And that is why organizational psychologists seek ways to engage and motivate ordinary people doing ordinary jobs.

Satisfaction and Engagement

Because work is such a big part of life, employee satisfaction is a priority concern for I/O psychologists. Satisfaction with work feeds satisfaction with life (see Close-Up: Doing Well While Doing Good). Moreover, studies confirm that decreased job stress feeds improved health.

Does employee satisfaction also contribute to successful organizations? Positive moods at work do contribute to creativity, persistence, and helpfulness (Brief & Weiss, 2002). But are engaged, happy workers also less often absent? Less likely to quit? Less prone to theft? More punctual? More productive? Conclusive evidence of satisfaction's benefits is, some have said, the holy grail of I/O psychology. Statistical digests of prior research have found a modest positive correlation between individual job satisfaction and performance (Judge & others, 2001; Parker & others, 2003). In one recent analysis of 4500 employees at 42 British manufacturing companies, the most productive workers tended to be those in satisfying work environments (Patterson & others, 2004).

Engaged employees facilitate organizational success
Best Buy's 400 electronic goods stores have nearly identical product layout and operations manuals. Yet some stores have much more engaged employees—and more profitable performance. The store with the highest worker-engagement scores is in the top tenth of stores in having profits beyond budget. And the store with the least-engaged employees is in the bottom tenth (Buckingham, 2001).

CLOSE-UP:

DOING WELL WHILE DOING GOOD: "THE GREAT EXPERIMENT"

At the end of the 1700s, the more than 1000 workers in the cotton mill at New Lanark, Scotland—many of them children drawn from nearby Glasgow poorhouses—worked 13-hour days and lived in grim conditions, with education and sanitation neglected, theft and drunkenness commonplace, and most families occupying just one room.

On a visit to Glasgow, Welsh-born Robert Owen—an idealistic young cotton-mill manager—chanced to meet and fall in love with the mill owner's daughter. After their marriage, Owen, with several partners, purchased the mill and on the first day of the 1800s took control as its manager. Before long, he began what he said was "the most important experiment for the happiness of the human race that had yet been instituted at any time in any part of the world" (Owen, 1814). The exploitation of child and adult labor was, he observed, producing unhappy and inefficient workers. Believing that better working and living conditions could pay economic dividends, he undertook (with some resistance from his partners, whom he ultimately bought out) numerous innovations: a nursery for preschool

Courtesy of New Lanark World Heritage Site

The great experiment
New Lanark Mills, now preserved as a World Heritage Site (www.newlanark.org), provided an influential demonstration of how industries could do well while doing good. In its heyday, New Lanark was visited by many European royals and reformers who came to observe its vibrant workforce and prosperous business.

children, education (with encouragement rather than corporal punishment), Sundays off, health care, paid sick days, unemployment pay for days when the mill could not operate, and a company store selling goods at reduced prices.

Owen also innovated a goals and worker-assessment program that included detailed records of daily productivity and costs. By each employee's workstation, one of four colored boards indicated that person's performance for the previous day. Owen could walk through the mill and at a glance see how individuals were performing. There was, he said, "no beating, no abusive language. . . . I merely looked at the person and then at the color. . . . I could at once see by the expression [which color] was shown."

The commercial success that followed was essential to sustaining what became a movement toward humanitarian reforms. By 1816, with decades of profitability still ahead, Owen believed he had demonstrated "that society may be formed so as to exist without crime, without poverty, with health greatly improved, with little if any misery, and with intelligence and happiness increased a hundredfold." Although his Utopian vision has not been fulfilled, Owen's great experiment did lay the groundwork for employment practices that have today become accepted in much of the world.

In the United States, the *Fortune* "100 Best Companies to Work For" have also produced markedly higher than average returns for their investors (Fulmer & others, 2003). Other positive data come from the biggest-ever study, a recent analysis of Gallup data from more than 198,000 employees (**TABLE 37.1** on the next page) in nearly 8000 business units of 36 large companies (including some 1100 bank branches, 1200 stores, and 4200 teams or departments). James Harter, Frank Schmidt, and Theodore Hayes (2002) explored correlations between various measures of organizational success and *employee engagement*—the extent of workers' involvement, satisfaction, and enthusiasm. They found that engaged workers know what's expected of them, have what they need to do their work, feel fulfilled in their work, have regular opportunities to do what they do best, perceive that they are part of something significant, and have opportunities to learn and develop. They also found that business units with engaged employees have more loyal customers, less

Three types of employees (Crabtree, 2005):
Engaged: working with passion and feeling a profound connection to their company or organization.
Not-engaged: putting in the time, but investing little passion or energy into their work.
Actively disengaged: unhappy workers undermining what their colleagues accomplish.

TABLE 37.1

THE GALLUP WORKPLACE AUDIT

Overall satisfaction—On a 5-point scale, where 5 is extremely satisfied and 1 is extremely dissatisfied, how satisfied are you with *(name of company)* as a place to work? _____

On a scale of 1 to 5, where 1 is strongly disagree and 5 is strongly agree, please indicate your agreement with the following items.

1. I know what is expected from me at work.
2. I have the materials and equipment I need to do my work right.
3. At work, I have the opportunity to do what I do best every day.
4. In the last seven days, I have received recognition or praise for doing good work.
5. My supervisor, or someone at work, seems to care about me as a person.
6. There is someone at work who encourages my development.
7. At work, my opinions seem to count.
8. The mission/purpose of my company makes me feel my job is important.
9. My associates (fellow employees) are committed to doing quality work.
10. I have a best friend at work.
11. In the last six months, someone at work has talked to me about my progress.
12. This last year, I have had opportunities at work to learn and grow.

Note: These statements are proprietary and copyrighted by The Gallup Organization. They may not be printed or reproduced in any manner without the written consent of The Gallup Organization. Reprinted here by permission.

turnover, higher productivity, and greater profits: "Business units above the median on employee engagement had a 70 percent higher success rate than those below the median." Business units in the top quarter on employee engagement averaged about $100,000 more in monthly revenue. A separate analysis for a company with 275 retail stores found that annual turnover was 55 percent among stores whose employee engagement was in the top quarter, and 75 percent among stores with employees in the bottom quarter (Harter, 2000).

Managing Well

OBJECTIVE 37-4 | Describe some effective management techniques.

Every leader dreams of managing in ways that enhance people's satisfaction, engagement, and productivity and their organization's success. Effective leaders harness job-relevant strengths, set goals, and choose an appropriate leadership style.

Harnessing Job-Relevant Strengths

"The major challenge for CEOs over the next 20 years will be the effective deployment of human assets," observes Marcus Buckingham (2001). That challenge is "about psychology. It's about getting [individuals] to be more productive, more focused, more fulfilled than [they were] yesterday." To do so, he and others maintain, effective leaders want first to select the right people. Then, they aim to discern their employees' natural talents, adjust their work roles to suit their talents, and develop those talents into great strengths (**FIGURE 37.4**). For example, should every college professor at a given school be expected to teach the same load, advise the same number of students, serve on the same number of committees, and engage in the same amount of research? Or should each job description be tailored to harness a specific person's unique strengths?

FIGURE 37.4
On the right path
The Gallup Organization path to organizational success (adapted from Fleming, 2001).

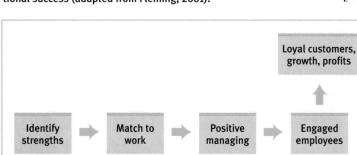

Managers who excel spend less time trying to instill talents that are not there and more time developing and drawing out what is there. Kenneth Tucker (2002) notes that great managers

- start by helping people identify and measure their talents.
- match tasks to talents and then give people freedom to do what they do best.
- care how their people feel about their work.
- reinforce positive behaviors through recognition and reward.

Thus, rather than focusing on weaknesses and packing people off to training seminars to fix those problems, good managers focus training time on educating people about their strengths and building upon them (which means not promoting people into roles ill-suited to their strengths).

Celebrating engaged and productive employees in every organizational role builds upon a basic principle of operant conditioning: To teach a behavior, catch a person doing something right and reinforce it. These principles also apply to reinforcing employees. It sounds simple, but many managers are like parents who, when a child returns home with perfect scores, except for that one troublesome biology class, focus on the biology score and ignore the rest. "Sixty-five percent of Americans received NO praise or recognition in the workplace last year," reported the Gallup Organization (2004).

Positive coaching
Larry Brown, an adviser to "The Positive Coaching Alliance," has been observed during practices to offer his players 4 to 5 positive comments for every negative comment (Insana, 2005). In 2004, his underdog Detroit Pistons won the National Basketball Association championship.

Setting Specific, Challenging Goals

In study after study, people merely asked to do their best do not do so. But more specific, challenging goals do motivate higher achievement, especially when combined with progress reports (Locke & Latham, 2002). Specific, measurable objectives, such as "finish gathering information for the history paper by Friday," serve to direct attention, promote effort, motivate persistence, and stimulate creative strategies. When people share in setting a goal and find the goal challenging yet attainable, reaching it boosts their self-evaluation (White & others, 1995). Moreover, when people state not only goals but also *implementation intentions*—action plans that specify when, where, and how they will march toward achieving those goals—they become more focused in their work and on-time completion becomes more likely (Burgess & others, 2004; Koestner & others, 2002; Koole & Spijker, 2000). (Before beginning each new edition of this book, my editor, my associates, and I *manage by objectives*—we agree on target dates for the completion of each chapter draft.) So, to motivate high productivity, effective leaders work with people to define explicit goals, elicit commitments to implementation plans, and provide feedback on progress.

Choosing an Appropriate Leadership Style

Leadership varies from a boss-focused directive style to a democratic style that empowers workers in setting goals and strategies. Which works best may depend on the situation and the leader. The best leadership style for leading a discussion may not be the best style for leading troops on a charge (Fiedler, 1981). Moreover, different leaders are suited to different styles. Some excel at **task leadership**—setting standards, organizing work, and focusing attention on goals. Being goal-oriented, task leaders are good at keeping a group centered on its mission. Typically, they have a directive style, which can work well if the leader is bright enough to give good orders (Fiedler, 1987).

Other managers excel at **social leadership**—mediating conflicts and building high-achieving teams (Evans & Dion, 1991). Social leaders often have a democratic style: They delegate authority and welcome the participation of team members. Many experiments show that social leadership is good for morale. Subordinates usually feel more satisfied and motivated when they can participate in decision making (Burger, 1987; Spector, 1986).

■ **task leadership** goal-oriented leadership that sets standards, organizes work, and focuses attention on goals.

■ **social leadership** group-oriented leadership that builds teamwork, mediates conflict, and offers support.

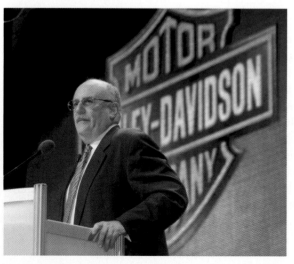

"Good leaders don't ask more than their constituents can give, but they often ask—and get—more than their constituents intended to give or thought it was possible to give."

John W. Gardner, *Excellence*, 1984

Sharing vision and decisions
As CEO, Jeffrey Bleustein helped Harley-Davidson thrive, in part by replacing the organization's command-and-control management style with one based on companywide consensus planning and decision making.

Because effective leadership styles vary with the situation and the person, the once-popular *great person theory of leadership*—that all great leaders share certain traits—now seems overstated. But a leader's personality does matter. Effective leaders of laboratory groups, work teams, and large corporations tend to exude a self-confident *charisma* (House & Singh, 1987; Shamir & others, 1993). Their charisma is a mix of a *vision* of some goal, an ability to *communicate* it clearly and simply, and enough optimism and faith in their group to *inspire* others to follow. In one study of 50 Dutch companies, the highest morale was at those firms with chief executives who most inspired their colleagues "to transcend their own self-interests for the sake of the collective" (de Hoogh & others, 2004). Leadership of this kind—*transformational leadership*—motivates others to identify with and commit themselves to the group's mission. Transformational leaders, many of whom are natural extraverts, articulate high standards, inspire people to share their vision, and offer personal attention (Bono & Judge, 2004). The frequent result is more engaged, trusting, and effective workers (Turner & others, 2002).

Peter Smith and Monir Tayeb (1989) compiled data from studies in India, Taiwan, and Iran indicating that effective managers—whether in coal mines, banks, or government offices—often exhibit a high degree of *both* task and social leadership. As achievement-minded people, effective managers certainly care about how well work is done, yet at the same time they are sensitive to their subordinates' needs. In one national survey of American workers, those in family-friendly organizations offering flexible-time hours reported feeling greater loyalty to their employers (Roehling & others, 2001).

Many successful businesses have also increased employee participation in making decisions, a management style common in Sweden and Japan and increasingly elsewhere (Naylor, 1990; Sundstrom & others, 1990). Although managers often think better of work they have directly supervised, studies reveal a *voice effect*: If given a chance to voice their opinion during a decision-making process, people will respond more positively to the decision (van den Bos & Spruijt, 2002). And as we noted earlier, positive engaged employees are a mark of thriving organizations.

The rags-to-riches Harley-Davidson story illustrates the potential of inviting workers to participate in decision making (Teerlink & Ozley, 2000). In 1987, the struggling company began transforming its *command-and-control* management process to a *joint-vision* process. The aim: "To push decision-making, planning, and strategizing from a handful of people at the top, down throughout the organization. We wanted all the employees to think every day about how to improve the company," reported CEO Jeffrey Bleustein (2002). In the mid-1990s, Harley signed a cooperative agreement with its unions that included them "in decision-making in virtually every aspect of the business." Consensus decision-making can take longer, but "when the decision is made, it gets implemented quickly and the commitment is by the group," says Bleustein. The result has been more engaged workers and also more satisfied stockholders. Every $1 of Harley-Davidson stock purchased at the beginning of 1988 was worth $125 by mid-2005.

Identifiable physiological mechanisms drive some motives, such as hunger (though learned tastes and cultural expectations matter, too). Achievement at work is more obviously driven by psychological factors, such as an intrinsic quest for mastery and the external rewards of recognition. But what unifies these and all other motives is their common effect: the energizing and directing of behavior.

>> LEARNING OUTCOMES

Motivation at Work

OBJECTIVE 37-1 | **Discuss the importance of flow, and identify the three subfields of industrial-organizational psychology.**

People may view their work as a job, a career, or a calling. Those in the last group report the highest satisfaction—a feeling consistent with *flow*, the involved focused state of consciousness in which we have a diminished awareness of ourselves and of passing time. *Industrial-organizational (I/O) psychology* studies behavior in the workplace through the three subfields of *personnel psychology, organizational psychology,* and *human factors psychology.*

OBJECTIVE 37-2 | **Describe how personnel psychologists help organizations with employee selection, work placement, and performance appraisal.**

Personnel psychologists work with organizations to devise selection methods (such as structured interviews) for new employees, to recruit and evaluate applicants, and to design and evaluate training programs. Personnel psychologists also help organizations identify people's strengths, analyze job content, appraise individual and organizational performance, and avoid forms of bias that can affect performance appraisal.

OBJECTIVE 37-3 | **Define *achievement motivation,* and explain why organizations would employ an I/O psychologist to help motivate employees and foster employee satisfaction.**

Achievement motivation is the desire for significant accomplishment; for mastery of things, people, or ideas; and for attaining a high standard. Organizations turn to I/O psychologists because research shows that the most productive and engaged workers are those working in satisfying environments. Employee satisfaction also tends to translate into higher profits, higher productivity, lower turnover, and more loyal customers.

OBJECTIVE 37-4 | **Describe some effective management techniques.**

Effective managers focus training on developing people's strengths, not overcoming their weaknesses. They attempt to "catch the employee doing something right" and reward that behavior. Effective managers also work with employees to set specific, challenging, and measurable objectives and to outline detailed paths to achieving those goals. *Task leadership* sets standards, organizes work, and focuses attention on goals. *Social leadership* builds teamwork, mediates conflict, and offers support. Managers' personalities do matter, and some may be better suited to one leadership style than to the other, or to some combination of the two.

TERMS AND CONCEPTS TO REMEMBER

flow, p. 37-0	structured interviews, p. 37-4
industrial-organizational psychology, p. 37-1	achievement motivation, p. 37-5
personnel psychology, p. 37-1	task leadership, p. 37-9
organizational psychology, p. 37-1	social leadership, p. 37-9

TEST YOURSELF

1. A human resources director explains to you that "I don't bother with tests or references. I can pick employees by my gut." Based on I/O research, what concerns does this raise?

(Answer in Appendix B.)

ASK YOURSELF

1. Are you highly motivated, or not highly motivated, to achieve in school? How has this affected your academic success? How might you improve upon your own achievement levels?

>WEB

Multiple-choice *self-tests* and more may be found at www.worthpublishers.com/myers.

ANOTHER VOICE ON: EMOTION

ADMIRAL DENNIS BLAIR, COMMANDER OF U.S. PACIFIC FORCES (USCINCPAC),
REMARKS AT PACIFIC ISLANDS CONFERENCE OF LEADERS, JANUARY 31, 2001, EAST-WEST CENTER, HONOLULU

On a recent trip to one of your beautiful islands . . . , I had the opportunity to take a break and go fishing, and I overheard a conversation between a Harvard businessman on vacation, and one of the local fishermen. The fisherman had a small boat with several large yellowfin tuna. . . . The businessman complimented the man on the quality of his fish, and asked how long it took to catch them. The fisherman replied only a little while. The businessman asked . . . why didn't he stay out longer and catch more fish? The fisherman said he had enough to support his family's immediate needs.

The businessman then asked, "But what do you do with the rest of your time?"

The fisherman said, "I sleep late, fish a little, play with my children, take a nap with my wife, stroll into the village each evening where I drink a beer and play the ukelele with my friends. I have a full and wonderful life."

The businessman scoffed, "I'm a Harvard MBA, and I could help you. You should spend more time fishing, and with the proceeds, you could buy a bigger boat. With the money from the bigger boat, you could buy several boats. Eventually, you'd own a fleet of fishing boats . . . . You'd make millions of dollars!"

"But what then?" asked the fisherman.

The businessman said, "Then you could retire—move to a small fishing village where you could sleep late . . . fish a little . . . play with your kids . . . take a nap with your wife . . . stroll down to the village in the evenings . . . where you could drink a beer . . . and play the ukelele with your friends!"

Emotion

No one needs to tell you that feelings add color to your life, or that in times of stress they can disrupt your life or save it. Of all the species, we seem the most emotional (Hebb, 1980). More often than any other creature, we express fear, anger, sadness, joy, and love.

We all can recall times when we have been overcome with emotion. I retain a flashbulb memory for the day I went to a huge store to drop off film and brought along Peter, my toddler first-born child. As I set Peter down on his feet and prepared to complete the paperwork, a passerby warned, "You'd better be careful or you'll lose that boy!" Not more than a few breaths later, after dropping the film in the slot, I turned and found no Peter beside me.

With mild anxiety, I peered around one end of the counter. No Peter in sight. With slightly more anxiety, I peered around the other end. No Peter there, either. Now, with my heart accelerating, I circled the neighboring counters. Still no Peter anywhere. As anxiety turned to panic, I began racing up and down the store aisles. He was nowhere to be found. Apprised of my alarm, the store manager used the public-address system to ask customers to assist in looking for a missing child. Soon after, I passed the customer who had warned me. "I told you that you were going to lose him!" he said scornfully. With visions of kidnapping (strangers routinely adored that beautiful child), I braced for the possibility that my negligence had caused me to lose what I loved above all else, and—dread of all dreads—that I might have to return home and face my wife without our only child.

But then, as I passed the customer service counter yet again, there he was, having been found and returned by some obliging customer! In an instant, the arousal of dread spilled into the elation of ecstasy. Clutching my son, with tears suddenly flowing, I found myself unable to speak my thanks and stumbled out of the store awash in joy.

So, how do psychologists think about and study such emotions? In Module 38, we examine three classic theories of emotion that explore the interplay of physiological activation, expressive behavior, and conscious experience. Module 39 then turns to the topic of how we experience and express our emotions. In Module 40, we'll take an in-depth look at fear, anger, and happiness.

MODULE

Theories of Emotion

Embodied Emotion

Not only emotion, but most psychological phenomena (vision, sleep, memory, sex, and so forth) can be approached these three ways—physiologically, behaviorally, and cognitively.

The joys of friendship
According to the James-Lange theory, we don't just smile because we share a friend's joy. We also share the joy because we are smiling with them.

Digital Vision/Getty Images

Introduction to Emotion

OBJECTIVE 38-1 | Identify the three components of emotions, and contrast the James-Lange, Cannon-Bard, and two-factor theories of emotion.

Where do emotions come from? Why do we have them? What are they made of? Emotions are our body's adaptive response. They exist not to give us interesting experiences but to enhance our survival. When we face challenges, emotions focus our attention and energize our action. Our heart races. Our pace quickens. All our senses go on high alert. Receiving unexpected good news, we may find our eyes tearing. We raise our hands triumphantly. We feel exuberance and a newfound confidence. **Emotions** are a mix of (1) physiological arousal (heart pounding), (2) expressive behaviors (quickened pace), and (3) conscious experience, including thoughts (is this a kidnapping?) and feelings (a sense of fear, and later joy). The puzzle for psychologists has been figuring out how these three pieces fit together.

Theories of Emotion

There are two controversies over the interplay of our physiology, expressions, and experience in emotions. The first, a chicken-and-egg debate, is old: Does your physiological arousal precede or follow your emotional experience? (Did I first notice my heart racing and my faster step, and then feel anxious dread about losing Peter? Or did my sense of fear come first, stirring my heart and legs to respond?) The second controversy concerns the interaction between thinking and feeling: Does cognition always precede emotion? (Was I required to make a conscious appraisal of the kidnapping threat before I could react emotionally?)

Common sense tells most of us that we cry because we are sad, lash out because we are angry, tremble because we are afraid. First comes conscious awareness, then the physiological trimmings. But to pioneering psychologist William James, this commonsense view of emotion was 180 degrees out of line. According to James, "We feel sorry because we cry, angry because we strike, afraid because we tremble" (1890, p. 1066). Perhaps you can recall a time when your car skidded on slick pavement. As it careened crazily you hit your brakes and regained control. Just after the fishtail ended, you noticed your racing heart and *then,* shaking with fright, you felt the whoosh of emotion. Your feeling of fear *followed* your body's response. James' idea, also proposed by Danish physiologist Carl Lange, is called the **James-Lange theory.**

The James-Lange theory struck U.S. physiologist Walter Cannon (1871–1943) as implausible. Cannon thought the body's responses were not distinct enough to evoke the different emotions. Does a racing heart signal fear, anger, or love? Also, changes in heart rate, perspiration, and body temperature seemed too slow to trigger sudden emotion. Cannon, and later another physiologist, Philip Bard, concluded that physiological arousal and our emotional experience occur simultaneously: The emotion-triggering stimulus is routed simultaneously to the brain's cortex, causing the subjective awareness of emotion, and to the sympathetic nervous system, causing the body's arousal. This **Cannon-Bard theory** implies that your heart begins pounding *as* you experience fear; one does not cause the other.

Let's check your understanding of the James-Lange and Cannon-Bard theories. Imagine that your brain could not sense your heart pounding or your stomach churning. According to each theory, how would this affect your experienced emotions?

Cannon and Bard would have expected you to experience emotions normally, because they believed emotions occur separately from (though simultaneously with) the body's arousal. James and Lange would have expected greatly diminished emotions because they believed that to experience emotion you must first perceive your body's arousal.

Stanley Schachter and Jerome Singer (1962) proposed a third theory: that our physiology and our cognitions—perceptions, memories, and interpretations—together create emotion. In their **two-factor theory,** emotions therefore have two ingredients: physical arousal and a cognitive label (**FIGURE 38.1**). Like James and Lange, Schachter and Singer presumed that our experience of emotion grows from our awareness of our body's arousal. Yet like Cannon and Bard, Schachter and Singer also believed that emotions are physiologically similar. Thus, in their view, an emotional experience requires a conscious interpretation of the arousal.

To assess the James-Lange, Cannon-Bard, and two-factor theories, we'll consider in the next section the answers researchers have gleaned to three questions:

- Does physiological arousal always precede emotional experience?
- Are different emotions marked by distinct physiological responses?
- What is the connection between what we *think* and how we *feel*?

■ **emotion** a response of the whole organism, involving (1) physiological arousal, (2) expressive behaviors, and (3) conscious experience.

■ **James-Lange theory** the theory that our experience of emotion is our awareness of our physiological responses to emotion-arousing stimuli.

■ **Cannon-Bard theory** the theory that an emotion-arousing stimulus simultaneously triggers (1) physiological responses and (2) the subjective experience of emotion.

■ **two-factor theory** Schachter-Singer's theory that to experience emotion one must (1) be physically aroused and (2) cognitively label the arousal.

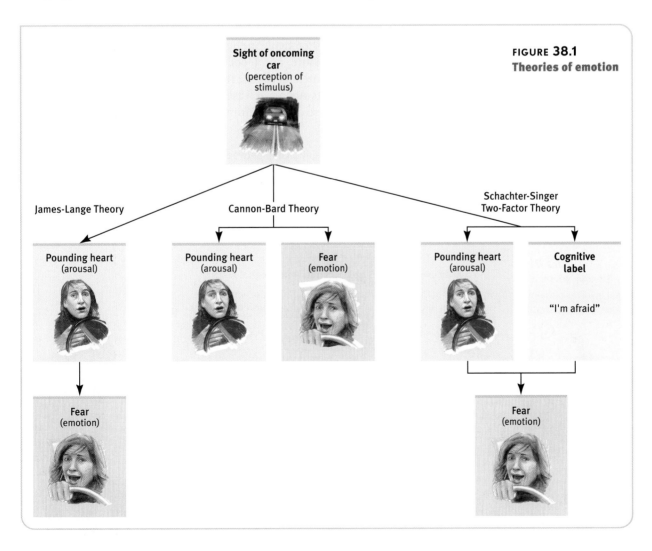

FIGURE 38.1
Theories of emotion

Sight of oncoming car (perception of stimulus)

James-Lange Theory

Pounding heart (arousal)

Fear (emotion)

Cannon-Bard Theory

Pounding heart (arousal)

Fear (emotion)

Schachter-Singer Two-Factor Theory

Pounding heart (arousal)

Cognitive label

"I'm afraid"

Fear (emotion)

Embodied Emotion

Whether you are eagerly anticipating a long-awaited vacation, falling in love, or grieving the death of a loved one, you need little convincing that emotions involve the body. Feeling without a body is like breathing without lungs. Some physical responses are easy to notice, others—many taking place at the level of neurons in your brain—happen without your awareness. As you hear a motorcycle slowing down behind you on a dark street, your muscles tense, your stomach develops butterflies, your mouth becomes dry.

Emotions and the Autonomic Nervous System

OBJECTIVE 38-2 | Describe the role of the autonomic nervous system during emotional arousal.

"Fear lends wings to his feet."
Virgil, Aeneid, 19 B.C.

As your *autonomic nervous system* mobilizes for action, your body also responds for action in less noticeable ways. To provide energy, your liver pours extra sugar into your bloodstream. To help burn the sugar, your respiration increases to supply needed oxygen. Your digestion slows, diverting blood from your internal organs to your muscles. With blood sugar driven into the large muscles, running becomes easier. Your pupils dilate, letting in more light. To cool your stirred-up body, you perspire. If wounded, your blood would clot more quickly. After your next crisis, think of this: Without any conscious effort, your body's response to danger was wonderfully coordinated and adaptive—preparing you to fight or flee.

One explanation of sudden death caused by a voodoo "curse" is that the terrified person's parasympathetic nervous system, which calms the body, overreacts to the extreme arousal by slowing the heart to a stop (Seligman, 1974).

The autonomic nervous system controls our arousal (**FIGURE 38.2**). Its *sympathetic division* directs the adrenal glands atop the kidneys to release the stress hormones epinephrine (adrenaline) and norepinephrine (noradrenaline). This hormonal surge increases heart rate, blood pressure, and blood sugar levels. When the crisis passes, the parasympathetic neural centers become active, calming the body. Even after the *parasympathetic division* inhibits further release of stress hormones, those already in the bloodstream linger awhile, so arousal diminishes gradually.

Arousal and Performance

OBJECTIVE 38-3 | Discuss the relationship between arousal and performance.

Prolonged arousal taxes the body. But in many situations arousal is adaptive. Too little arousal (say, sleepiness) can be as disruptive as extremely high levels. When you're taking an exam, it pays to be moderately aroused—alert but not trembling with nervousness.

FIGURE 38.2
Emotional arousal
Emotional arousal involves autonomic nervous system activation.

Autonomic Nervous System Controls Physiological Arousal		
Sympathetic division (arousing)		Parasympathetic division (calming)
Pupils dilate	EYES	Pupils contract
Decreases	SALIVATION	Increases
Perspires	SKIN	Dries
Increases	RESPIRATION	Decreases
Accelerates	HEART	Slows
Inhibits	DIGESTION	Activates
Secrete stress hormones	ADRENAL GLANDS	Decrease secretion of stress hormones

Although we usually perform best when we feel moderately aroused, the level of arousal for optimal performance varies for different tasks. With easy or well-learned tasks, peak performance comes with relatively high arousal. With more difficult or unrehearsed tasks, optimal arousal is somewhat lower (**FIGURE 38.3**). Runners, who are performing a well-learned task, usually achieve their peak performances when highly aroused by competition. Basketball players shooting free throws—a less automatic skill—may not perform quite as well if a packed fieldhouse makes them hyperaroused (Sokoll & Mynatt, 1984). Likewise, students who feel great anxiety during exams perform more poorly than those equally able but more confident. Teaching anxious students how to relax before an exam often enables them to perform better (Hembree, 1988).

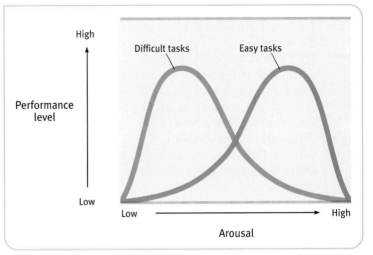

Physiological Similarities Among Specific Emotions

OBJECTIVE 38-4 | Name three emotions that involve similar physiological arousal.

Imagine conducting an experiment measuring the physiological responses of emotion. In each of four rooms, you have someone watching a movie: In the first, the person is viewing a horror show; in the second, an anger-provoking film; in the third, a sexually arousing film; in the fourth, an utterly boring movie. From the control center you monitor each person's physiological responses, measuring perspiration, breathing, and heart rates. Do you think you could tell who is frightened? Who is angry? Who is sexually aroused? Who is bored?

With training, you could probably pick out the bored viewer. But discerning physiological differences among fear, anger, and sexual arousal would be much more difficult (Cacioppo & others, 1997; Zillmann, 1986).

To you and me, sexual arousal, fear, and anger nevertheless *feel* different. If sexually stimulated, you will experience a genital response. If afraid, you may feel a clutching, sinking sensation in your chest and a knot in your stomach. If angry, you may feel "hot under the collar" and experience a pressing inner tension. And, despite similar arousal, fear and anger not only feel different, they also *look* different. People may appear "paralyzed with fear"

or "ready to explode." So, does research pinpoint any distinct physiological or brain pattern indicators of each emotion? Sometimes. Read on.

Physiological Differences Among Specific Emotions

OBJECTIVE 38-5 | Describe some physiological and brain pattern indicators of specific emotions.

The finger temperatures and hormone secretions that accompany fear and rage do sometimes differ (Ax, 1953; Levenson, 1992). And, though fear and joy can prompt similar increased heart rate, they stimulate different facial muscles. During fear, brow muscles tense. During joy, muscles in the cheek and under the eye pull into a smile (Witvliet & Vrana, 1995).

FIGURE 38.3
Arousal and performance
Performance peaks at lower levels of arousal for difficult tasks, and at higher levels for easy or well-learned tasks.

"No one ever told me that grief felt so much like fear. I am not afraid, but the sensation is like being afraid. The same fluttering in the stomach, the same restlessness, the yawning. I keep on swallowing."
C. S. Lewis, *A Grief Observed*, 1961

Emotional arousal
Elated excitement and panicky fear involve similar physiological arousal. That allows us to flip rapidly between the two emotions.

LIE DETECTION

The creators and users of the *lie detector,* or **polygraph** have believed that our physical indicators of emotion can provide a telltale equivalent of Pinocchio's nose. Polygraphs do not literally detect lies, and their accuracy has been increasingly questioned as our understanding of physiological measures of emotion has grown.

Rather, they measure several physical responses that accompany emotion, such as changes in breathing, cardiovascular activity, and perspiration. While you try to relax, an examiner monitors these responses as you answer questions. Some items, called control questions, aim to make anyone a little nervous. If asked, "In the last 20 years, have you ever taken something that didn't belong to you?" many people will tell a white lie and say no, causing arousal the polygraph will detect. If your physiological reactions to critical questions ("Did you ever steal anything from your previous employer?") are weaker than to control questions, the examiner infers you are telling the truth. The assumption has been that only a thief becomes agitated when denying a theft.

Can polygraph tests like this identify liars?
To learn more, read on.

But there are two problems: First, as you have seen, our physiological arousal is much the same from one emotion to another—anxiety, irritation, and guilt all prompt similar physiological reactivity. Second, these tests err about one-third of the time, especially when innocent people respond with heightened tension to the accusations implied by the relevant questions (**FIGURE 38.4**). Many rape victims, for example, "fail" lie detector tests when reacting emotionally while telling the truth about their assailant (Lykken, 1991). Good advice, then, would be never to take a lie detector test if you are innocent.

A 2002 U.S. National Academy of Sciences report noted that "no spy has ever been caught [by] using the polygraph." It is not for lack of trying. The FBI, CIA, and Departments of Defense and Energy in the United States have spent millions of dollars testing tens of thousands of employees. Meanwhile Aldrich Ames, who enjoyed an unexplained lavish life-style as a Russian spy within the CIA, went undetected. Ames "took scores of polygraph tests and passed them all," notes Robert Park (1999). "Nobody thought to investigate the source of his sudden wealth—after all, he was passing the lie detector tests." The truth is, lie detectors can lie.

In one survey, more than 9 in 10 psychophysiologists and research psychologists agreed that savvy criminals and spies could beat the test by augmenting their arousal to control questions, such as by biting their tongues (Iacono & Lykken, 1997). Serial rapist and killer Gary Ridgway, who admitted to 48 Seattle-area murders ("I killed so many women I have a hard time keeping them straight"), was an

Photo credit: Richard T. Nowitz/Photo Researchers, Inc.

In 1966, a young man named Charles Whitman killed his wife and mother and then climbed to the top of a tower at the University of Texas and shot 38 people. An autopsy later revealed a tumor pressing against his amygdala, which may have contributed to his violence.

Emotions differ much more in the brain circuits they use (Kalin, 1993; Panksepp, 1982). Observers watching (and subtly mimicking) fearful faces show more amygdala brain activity than do those watching angry faces (Whalen & others, 2001). The power of the amygdala is also apparent in other research. Stimulate one area of a cat's amygdala and it will pull back in terror at the sight of a mouse. Stimulate another amygdala area and the cat will look enraged—pupils dilated, fur and tail erect, claws out, hissing furiously.

Emotions also activate different areas of the brain's cortex. Experiencing negative emotions such as disgust, people show more activity in the right prefrontal cortex than in the left. Depression-prone people, and those with generally negative personalities also show more right frontal activity (Harmon-Jones, Abramson, & others, 2002). One man, having lost part of his right frontal lobe in brain surgery, became (his not-unhappy wife reported) less irritable and more affectionate (Goleman, 1995). My father, after a right-hemisphere stroke at age 92, lived the last two years of his life with happy gratitude and nary a complaint or negative emotion.

When people experience positive moods—when they are enthusiastic, energized, and happy—brain scans and EEG recordings reveal more left frontal lobe activity.

Given the physical indicators of emotion, might we, like Pinocchio, give some telltale sign whenever we lie? **See Thinking Critically About: Lie Detection.**

early suspect but had been cleared after passing a polygraph test (Johnson, 2003).

A more effective approach to lie detection uses the *guilty knowledge test,* which assesses a suspect's physiological responses to crime-scene details known only to the police and the guilty person (Ben-Shakhar & Elaad, 2003). If a camera and computer had been stolen, for example, presumably only one guilty of the crime would react strongly to the specific brand name of these items. Given enough such specific probes, an innocent person will seldom be wrongly accused.

Several twenty-first century research teams are exploring new ways to nab liars. Some are developing computer software that compares the language of truth-tellers and liars (who use fewer first-person pronouns and more negative-emotion words). Other software analyzes facial microexpressions linked with lying (Adelson, 2004; Newman

FIGURE 38.4

How often do lie detectors lie?
Benjamin Kleinmuntz and Julian Szucko (1984) had polygraph experts study the polygraph data of 50 theft suspects who later confessed to being guilty and 50 suspects whose innocence was later established by someone's confession. Had the polygraph experts been the judges, more than one-third of the innocent would have been declared guilty, and almost one-fourth of the guilty would have been declared innocent.

& others, 2003). Psychologist Paul Ekman (2003) runs training seminars that teach law enforcement officers to detect the fleeting signals of deceit in facial expressions.

Other researchers are going straight to the seat of deceit—the brain. EEG recordings have revealed a brain wave that indicates familiarity with a crime scene, and fMRI scans have shown liars' brains lighting up in places that honest people's brains do not (Faro & others, 2004; Farwell & Smith, 2001; Langleben & others, 2002, 2005). Given the cumbersome and expensive nature of such assessments, researchers are also testing a portable "near-infrared light" that similarly detects brain blood-flow patterns associated with lying (Izzetoglu & others, 2003). Pinocchio's giveaway signal of lying may be not the length of his nose, but rather the telltale activity in places such as his left frontal lobe and anterior cingulate cortex. Skeptics, however, note that we are a long way from commercial reality (Illes, 2004).

People with positive personalities—exuberant infants and alert, energetic, and persistently goal-directed adults—also show more activity in the left frontal lobe than in the right (Davidson, 2000, 2003; Urry & others, 2004). Indeed, the more a person's baseline frontal lobe activity tilts left, the more upbeat the person typically is. (When you're happy and you know it, your brain will surely show it.)

The left frontal lobe's rich supply of dopamine receptors may help explain why a peppy left hemisphere predicts a perky disposition. A neural pathway that increases dopamine levels runs from the frontal lobes to a nearby cluster of neurons, the *nucleus accumbens.* This small region lights up when people experience natural or drug-induced pleasures. In case studies, electrical stimulation of the nucleus accumbens of depressed patients has triggered smiling, laughter, and giddy euphoria (Okun & others, 2004).

To return to our assessment of the James-Lange, Cannon-Bard, and two-factor theories of emotion, we have seen that emotions as varied as fear, joy, and anger involve a similar general autonomic arousal (as in similar heart rate). But we have also seen that real, if subtle, physiological and brain differences help explain why we experience them so differently. As long as the evidence suggested that our physiological

■ **polygraph** a machine, commonly used in attempts to detect lies, that measures several of the physiological responses accompanying emotion (such as perspiration and cardiovascular and breathing changes).

reactions to different emotions were much the same, the James-Lange assumption that we experience our emotions through differing body states seemed improbable. But this new evidence showing subtle physiological distinctions among the emotions makes the James-Lange theory plausible.

The James-Lange theory also finds support in observations of people with severed spinal cords. Psychologist George Hohmann (1966) interviewed 25 soldiers who suffered such injuries in World War II. He asked them to recall emotion-arousing incidents that occurred before and after their spinal injuries. Those with lower-spine injuries, who had lost sensation only in their legs, reported little change in their emotions. Those who could feel nothing below the neck reported a considerable decrease in emotional intensity (as James and Lange would have expected). The anger, as one man confessed, "just doesn't have the heat to it that it used to. It's a mental kind of anger." But emotions expressed mostly in body areas above the neck are felt more intensely by those with high spinal-cord injury. Virtually all the men Hohmann interviewed reported increases in weeping, lumps in the throat, and getting choked up when saying good-bye, worshipping, or watching a touching movie.

Such evidence has breathed new life into the James-Lange theory and has led some researchers to view feelings as "mostly shadows" of our bodily responses and behaviors (Damasio, 2003). But most researchers agree with Cannon and Bard that our experienced emotions also involve cognition (Averill, 1993). Whether we fear the man behind us on the dark street depends entirely on whether we interpret his actions as threatening or friendly. So, with James and Lange we can say that our body's reactions are an important ingredient of emotion. And with Cannon and Bard we can say that there is more to the experience of emotion than reading our body's responses.

> "Every moment is more intense."
> Christopher Reeve (1952–2004) after his paralysis

Cognition and Emotion

What is the connection between what we *think* and how we *feel*? Which is the chicken and which the egg?

We know that our emotions affect our thinking. When we *feel* like singing "Oh, what a beautiful morning!" we *see* the world and the people around us as wonderful. If the following day we find ourselves singing the blues, we perceive the same world and the same people as less than wonderful.

Can we experience emotion apart from thinking? Or do we become what we think? The issue has practical implications for self-improvement: Can we change our emotions by changing our thinking?

Cognition Can Define Emotion

OBJECTIVE 38-6 | Explain how the spillover effect influences our experience of emotions.

Sometimes our arousal response to one event spills over into our response to the next event. Imagine arriving home after an invigorating run and finding a message that you got a longed-for job. With arousal lingering from the run, would you feel more elated than if you received this news after awakening from a nap?

To find out whether this *spillover effect* exists, Stanley Schachter and Jerome Singer (1962) aroused college men with injections of the hormone epinephrine. Picture yourself as one of their participants: After receiving the injection, you go to a waiting room, where you find yourself with another person (actually an accomplice of the experimenters) who is acting either euphoric or irritated. As you observe this person, you begin to feel your heart race, your body flush, and your breathing become more rapid. If told to expect these effects from the injection, what would you feel? Schachter's and Singer's volunteers felt little emotion—because they attributed their arousal to the drug. But if told the injection would produce no effects, what would you feel? Perhaps you would react, as another group of participants did, by "catching" the apparent emotion of the person you are with—becoming happy if the accomplice is acting euphoric, and testy if the accomplice is acting irritated.

This discovery—that a stirred-up state can be experienced as one emotion or another very different one, depending on how we interpret and label it—has been replicated in dozens of experiments. Insult people who have just been aroused by pedaling an exercise bike or watching rock videos and they will find it easy to misattribute their arousal to the provocation. Their feelings of anger will be greater than those of people who were similarly provoked but not previously aroused. Likewise, sexually aroused people react with more hostility in anger-provoking situations. And, vice versa—the arousal that lingers after an intense argument or a frightening experience may intensify sexual passion (Palace, 1995). Just as the Schachter-Singer two-factor theory predicts, arousal + label = emotion. As we have seen, emotional arousal is not as undifferentiated as Schachter and Singer believed. But arousal—from emotions as diverse as anger, fear, and sexual excitement—can indeed spill from one emotion to another (Reisenzein, 1983; Sinclair & others, 1994; Zillmann, 1986). *The point to remember:* Arousal fuels emotion; cognition channels it.

The spillover effect
Arousal from a soccer match (top photo) or a political protest (bottom photo) can fuel anger, which can descend into rioting or other violent confrontations.

Reuters/Corbis

AP Photo/Nati Harnik

Cognition Does Not Always Precede Emotion

OBJECTIVE 38-7 | Distinguish the two alternative pathways that sensory stimuli may travel when triggering an emotional response.

To experience an emotion, must we first label our arousal? Sometimes we experience unlabeled emotion. Imagine receiving some unsettling news. There's a deadline you've forgotten about, or you discover that you've hurt someone's feelings. As the ongoing conversation distracts your attention, you lose awareness of the bad news. Yet as its bodily effects linger, the now-unlabeled feeling still churns. You feel a little bad. You know there's a reason. But for the moment you can't put your finger on it. Robert Zajonc (pronounced ZI-yence; 1980, 1984a) has contended that we actually have many emotional reactions apart from, or even before, our interpretations of a situation. For example, when people repeatedly view stimuli flashed too briefly for them to perceive and recall, they nevertheless come to prefer those stimuli. Without being consciously aware of having seen the stimuli, they rather like them. A subliminally flashed smiling or angry face can also prime us to feel better or worse about a follow-up stimulus (Murphy & others, 1995). In one set of experiments, thirsty people drank about 50 percent more fruit-flavored drink after viewing a subliminally flashed (thus unperceived) happy rather than neutral face (Berridge & Winkielman, 2003). If flashed an angry face, they drank substantially less. Research on neurological processes shows how we can experience emotion unconsciously, before cognition.

Like speedy reflexes that operate apart from the brain's thinking cortex, some emotions take the "low road," via neural pathways that bypass the cortex (which offers the alternative "high road" pathway). One low-road pathway runs from the eye or ear via the thalamus to the *amygdala*, an emotional control center (**FIGURE 38.5** on the next page). This amygdala shortcut, bypassing the cortex, enables our greased-lightning emotional response before our intellect intervenes. So speedy is the amygdala response

Can you recall liking something or someone immediately, without knowing why?

"Oh! ye'll take the high road and I'll take the low road, And I'll be in Scotland afore ye."
Bonnie Banks O' Loch Lomond

FIGURE **38.5**
The brain's shortcut for emotions
Sensory input may be routed (a) directly to the amygdala (via the thalamus) for an instant emotional reaction and (b) to the cortex for analysis.

Thalamus

Amygdala

Fear stimulus

Fear response

(a) The speedy low road

Prefrontal cortex

Sensory cortex

Thalamus

Amygdala

Fear stimulus

Fear response

(b) The thinking high road

The amygdala, notes biologist Robert Sapolsky (2003), "is also central to aggression, underlining the fact that aggression can be rooted in fear—an observation that can explain much sociopolitical behavior."

that we may be unaware of what's transpired (Dimberg & others, 2000). In one fascinating experiment, Paul Whalen and his colleagues (2004) used fMRI scans to observe the amygdala's response to subliminally presented fearful eyes (**FIGURE 38.6**). Compared with a control condition that presented the whites of happy eyes, the fearful eyes triggered increased amygdala activity (despite no one's being aware of seeing them).

The amygdala sends more neural projections up to the cortex than it receives back. This makes it easier for our feelings to hijack our thinking than for our thinking to rule our feelings, note Joseph LeDoux and Jorge Armony (1999). In the forest, we jump at the sound of rustling bushes nearby, leaving the cortex to decide later whether the sound was made by a predator or just the wind. Such an experience supports Zajonc's belief that *some* of our emotional reactions involve no deliberate thinking and that cognition is not always necessary for emotion. The heart is not always subject to the mind.

Emotion researcher Richard Lazarus (1991, 1998) conceded that our brains process and react to vast amounts of information without our conscious awareness, and he willingly granted that some emotional responses do not require *conscious* thinking. But, he noted, even instantaneously felt emotions require some sort of cognitive appraisal of the situation; otherwise, how would we *know* what we are reacting to? The appraisal may be effortless and we may not be conscious of it, but it is still a mental function. Emotions arise when we *appraise* an event as beneficial or harmful to our well-being, whether we truly know it is or not. We appraise the sound of the rustling bushes as the presence of a threat. Later, we learn that it was "just the wind."

FIGURE **38.6**
The brain's sensitivity to threats
Even when fearful eyes (left) were flashed too briefly for people to consciously perceive them, fMRI scans revealed that their hypervigilant amygdala was alerted (Whalen & others, 2004).

Complex emotions such as guilt, happiness, and love most clearly arise from our interpretations and expectations. Highly emotional people are intense partly because of their interpretations. They may *personalize* events as being somehow directed at them, and they may *generalize* their experiences by blowing single incidents out of proportion (Larsen & others, 1987). We may attribute a bad exam grade to an unfair exam and feel angry, to our own inability and feel depressed, or to lack of preparation and feel accepting (Weiner, 1985).

To sum up, as Zajonc and LeDoux have demonstrated, some emotional responses—especially simple likes, dislikes, and fears—involve no conscious thinking (**FIGURE 38.7**). We may fear the spider, even if we "know" it is harmless. Such responses are difficult to alter by changing our thinking.

Fear   Happy

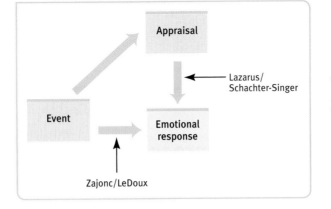

FIGURE 38.7
Two routes to emotion
Zajonc and LeDoux emphasize that some emotional responses are immediate, before any conscious appraisal. Lazarus, Schachter, and Singer emphasized that our appraisal and labeling of events also determines our emotional responses.

Other emotions—including moods such as depression and complex feelings such as hatred and love—are, as Lazarus, Schachter, and Singer predicted, greatly affected by our interpretations, memories, and expectations. For these emotions, learning to *think* more positively about ourselves and the world around us helps us *feel* better.

>> LEARNING OUTCOMES

Introduction to Emotion

OBJECTIVE 38-1 | Identify the three components of emotions, and contrast the James-Lange, Cannon-Bard, and two-factor theories of emotion.

Emotion's three components are (1) physiological arousal, (2) expressive behaviors, and (3) conscious experience. William James and Carl Lange proposed that we feel emotion *after* we notice our physiological responses. Walter Cannon and Philip Bard believed that we feel emotion *at the same time* that our bodies respond. Stanley Schachter and Jerome Singer's two-factor theory of emotion focused on the interplay of thinking and feeling, not on the timing of feelings. They proposed that emotions have two components, physical arousal and a cognitive label.

OBJECTIVE 38-2 | Describe the role of the autonomic nervous system during emotional arousal.

The autonomic nervous system (ANS) controls arousal. Its *sympathetic division* mobilizes us for action by directing the adrenals to release stress hormones, which in turn increase heart rate, blood pressure, and blood sugar levels, and by triggering other defensive physical reactions. The *parasympathetic division* calms us after a crisis has passed, though arousal diminishes gradually.

OBJECTIVE 38-3 | Discuss the relationship between arousal and performance.

Very high or very low arousal can be disruptive. We perform best when arousal is moderate, though this varies with the difficulty of the task. For easy or well-learned tasks, best performance is linked to high arousal. For difficult tasks, performance peaks at lower levels.

OBJECTIVE 38-4 | Name three emotions that involve similar physiological arousal.

We display similar physiological arousal during fear, anger, and sexual arousal, though our emotional experiences (and sometimes our facial expressions) differ during these three states.

OBJECTIVE 38-5 | Describe some physiological and brain pattern indicators of specific emotions.

Some emotions are associated with minute movements of muscles in the brow (during fear) and cheeks (during joy) and under the eyes (during joy). Brain scans also show increased activity in the amygdala during fear. Negative emotions (disgust, for example) trigger more activity in the right prefrontal cortex; positive moods (enthusiasm, for example) register in the left frontal lobe, which has many dopamine receptors.

OBJECTIVE 38-6 | Explain how the spillover effect influences our experience of emotions.

The *spillover effect* occurs when our arousal from one event influences our response to other events. Emotional arousal is sometimes general enough to require us to define the emotion we are experiencing. Arousal fuels emotion; cognition channels it.

OBJECTIVE 38-7 | Distinguish the two alternative pathways that sensory stimuli may travel when triggering an emotional response.

When sensory input goes directly to the amygdala via the thalamus, bypassing the cortex, it triggers an immediate emotional response that may be outside our conscious awareness. Responses to complex emotions (such as guilt, happiness, and love) require interpretation and are routed along the slower route to the cortex for analysis.

TERMS AND CONCEPTS TO REMEMBER

emotion, p. 38-0
James-Lange theory, p. 38-0
Cannon-Bard theory, p. 38-0
two-factor theory, p. 38-1
polygraph, p. 38-4

TEST YOURSELF

1. Christine is holding her 8-month-old baby when a fierce dog appears out of nowhere and, with teeth bared, leaps for the baby's face. Christine immediately ducks for cover to protect the baby, screams at the dog, then notices that her heart is banging in her chest and she's broken out in a cold sweat. How would the James-Lange, Cannon-Bard, and two-factor theories explain Christine's emotional reaction?

2. How do the two divisions of the autonomic nervous system help us respond to and recover from a crisis, and why is this relevant to the study of emotions?

(Answers in Appendix B.)

ASK YOURSELF

1. Can you remember a time when you began to feel upset or uneasy and only later labeled those feelings?

2. Can you think of a recent time when you noticed your body's reactions to an emotionally charged situation, such as a difficult social setting or perhaps even a test or game you were worrying about in advance? Did you perceive the situation as a challenge or a threat? How well did you do?

>WEB

Multiple-choice *self-tests* and more may be found at www.worthpublishers.com/myers.

Expressed Emotion

There is a simple method of deciphering people's emotions: We read their bodies, listen to their tone of voice, and study their faces. People's expressive behavior reveals their emotion. Does this nonverbal language vary with culture, or is it universal? And do our expressions influence our experienced emotions?

Nonverbal Communication

OBJECTIVE 39-1 | Describe some of the factors that affect our ability to decipher nonverbal cues.

All of us communicate nonverbally as well as verbally. To Westerners, a firm handshake immediately conveys an outgoing, expressive personality (Chaplin & others, 2000). With a gaze, an averted glance, or a stare we can communicate intimacy, submission, or dominance (Kleinke, 1986). Among those passionately in love, gazing into one another's eyes is typically prolonged and mutual (Rubin, 1970). Joan Kellerman, James Lewis, and James Laird (1989) wondered if intimate gazes would stir such feelings between strangers. To find out, they asked unacquainted male-female pairs to gaze intently for two minutes either at each other's hands or into each other's eyes. After separating, the eye-gazers reported feeling a tingle of attraction and affection. What if you do not want people to know how you feel, or if you do not even want to feel that way in the first place? Can we suppress our emotional expressions? Sometimes. But as Jane Richards and James Gross (2000) discovered, suppressing expression comes at a cost. Compared with those who simply watched a distressing film, those who diverted mental energy and attention into suppressing their emotional expressions remembered its details less well.

Most of us are good enough at reading nonverbal cues to decipher the emotions in an old silent film. We are especially good at detecting nonverbal threats. When hearing emotions conveyed in another language, people most readily detect anger (Scherer & others, 2001). When viewing subliminally flashed words, we more often sense the presence of a negative word, such as *snake* or *bomb* (Dijksterhuis & Aarts, 2003). In a crowd of faces, a single angry face (**FIGURE 39.1**) will "pop out" faster than a single happy one (Fox & others, 2000; Hansen & Hansen, 1988).

"Your face, my thane, is a book where men may read strange matters."

Lady Macbeth to her husband, in William Shakespeare's *Macbeth*

Injected as part of the war on wrinkles, Botox paralyzes facial muscles that create wrinkles, allowing the overlying skin to relax and smooth. By erasing the subtle expressions of frown lines or twinkling eyes, might this cosmetic procedure hide subtle emotions?

FIGURE 39.1
Radar for threats: An angry face pops out
Our emotion-detecting radar excels at detecting threats, and thus an angry face. Using stimuli such as these, Arne Öhman and his Stockholm colleagues (2001) found that people more speedily detect an angry face than a happy one. In other "Where's Waldo?"-like experiments, people more readily spotted images of threat-relevant snakes than of flowers (Öhman & others, 2001).

Used by permission of S. D. Pollak, D. J. Kistler and the National Academy of Sciences

FIGURE **39.2**
Experience influences how we perceive emotions
Shown one of the morphed middle faces, evenly mixing fear or sadness with anger, physically abused children were more likely than nonabused children to perceive the face as angry (Pollak & Kistler, 2002; Pollak & Tolley-Schell, 2003).

By exposing different parts of emotion-laden faces, Robert Kestenbaum (1992) discovered that we read fear and anger mostly from the eyes, and happiness from the mouth. Fleeting *changes* in expression also help us read a face (Ambadar & others, 2005). Some of us are more sensitive than others to such cues. Robert Rosenthal, Judith Hall, and their colleagues (1979) discovered this by showing hundreds of people brief film clips of portions of a person's emotionally expressive face or body, sometimes accompanied by a garbled voice. For example, after a 2-second scene revealing only the face of an upset woman, the researchers would ask whether the woman was criticizing someone for being late or was talking about her divorce. Rosenthal and Hall reported that, given such "thin slices," some people are much better than others at detecting emotion. Introverts tend to do better at reading others' emotions, although extraverts are themselves easier to read (Ambady & others, 1995).

Experience can sensitize us to particular emotions. Shown a series of faces that morphed from sadness or fear to anger, physically abused children are much quicker than other children to see anger (**FIGURE 39.2**). Shown a face that is 60 percent fear and 40 percent anger, they are as likely to perceive anger as fear. Their perceptions become sensitively attuned to glimmers of danger signals that nonabused children miss.

Gender, Emotion, and Nonverbal Behavior

OBJECTIVE 39-2 | Describe some gender differences in perceiving and communicating emotions.

Is women's intuition, as so many believe, superior to men's? Consider: As Jackie Larsen left her Grand Marais, Minnesota, church prayer group one April 2001 morning, she encountered Christopher Bono, a clean-cut, well-mannered youth. Bono's car had broken down, and he said he was looking for a ride to meet friends in Thunder Bay. When Bono later appeared in Larsen's shop, where she had promised to help him phone his friends, she felt a pain in her stomach. Intuitively sensing that something was very wrong with this young man, she insisted that they talk outside on the sidewalk. "I said, 'I am a mother and I have to talk to you like a mother. . . . I can tell by your manners that you have a nice mother.'" At the mention of his mother, Bono's eyes fixed on her. "I don't know where my mother is," he said.

As the conversation ended, Larsen directed Bono back to the church to meet the pastor. She also called the police and suggested that they trace his license plates. The car was registered to his mother in southern Illinois. When police went to her apartment, they found blood all over and Lucia Bono dead in the bathtub. Christopher Bono, 16, was charged with first-degree murder (Biggs, 2001).

Was it a coincidence that Larsen, who saw through Bono's calm exterior, was a woman? Some psychologists would say no. In her analysis of 125 studies of sensitivity to nonverbal cues, Judith Hall (1984, 1987) discerned that women generally surpass men at reading people's emotional cues. Women's nonverbal sensitivity also gives them an edge in spotting lies (DePaulo, 1994). And women have surpassed men in discerning whether a male-female couple is a genuine romantic couple or a posed phony couple, and in discerning which of two people in a photo is the other's supervisor (Barnes & Sternberg, 1989).

Women's nonverbal sensitivity helps explain their greater emotional literacy. Invited by Lisa Feldman Barrett and her colleagues (2000) to describe how they would feel in certain situations, men described simpler emotional reactions. You might like to try this yourself: Ask some people how they might feel when saying good-bye to friends after graduation. Barrett's work suggests you are more likely to hear men say, simply, "I'll feel bad," and to hear women express more complex emotions: "It will be bittersweet; I'll feel both happy and sad."

Women's skill at decoding others' emotions may also contribute to their greater emotional responsiveness in both positive and negative situations (Grossman & Wood, 1993; Sprecher & Sedikides, 1993; Stoppard & Gruchy, 1993). In studies of 23,000 people from 26 cultures around the world, women more than men reported themselves open to feelings (Costa & others, 2001). That helps explain the extremely strong perception that emotionality is "more true of women"—a perception expressed by nearly 100 percent of 18- to 29-year-old Americans (Newport, 2001).

When surveyed, women are also far more likely than men to describe themselves as empathic. If you have *empathy,* you identify with others and imagine what it must be like to walk in their shoes. You rejoice with those who rejoice and weep with those who weep. Physiological measures of empathy, such as one's heart rate while seeing another's distress, reveal a much smaller gender gap than is reported in surveys (Eisenberg & Lennon, 1983). Nevertheless, females are more likely to *express* empathy—to cry and to report distress when observing someone in distress. Ann Kring and Albert Gordon (1998) observed this gender difference in videotapes of men and women students watching film clips that were sad (children with a dying parent), happy (slapstick comedy), or frightening (a man nearly falling off the ledge of a tall building). As **FIGURE 39.3** shows, the women reacted more visibly to each film type. Women also tend to experience emotional events (such as viewing pictures of mutilation) more deeply—with more brain activation in areas sensitive to emotion—and then to remember the scenes better three weeks later (Canli & others, 2002).

In another exploration of gender and facial expression, Harold Hill and Alan Johnston (2001) animated an image of an average head with expressions (smirks, head tosses, raised eyebrows) that had been digitally captured from the faces of London University students as they read a joke. Despite having no anatomical clues to gender, observers could usually detect gender in the telltale expressions.

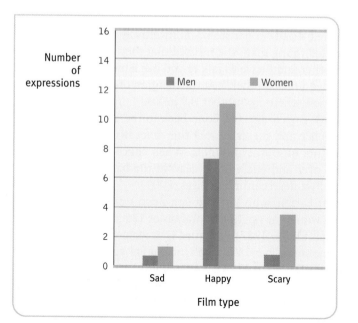

FIGURE 39.3
Gender and expressiveness
Although male and female students did not differ dramatically in self-reported emotions or physiological responses while viewing emotional films, the women's faces *showed* much more emotion. (From Kring & Gordon, 1998.)

Gender differences also appear in the emotions women and men express best. After asking students to recall and talk about times when they were happy, sad, and angry, Erik Coats and Robert Feldman (1996) showed silent 5-second videos of the students' recollections to other participants acting as judges. Nearly two-thirds of the time, the judges correctly discerned women's recall of being happy, but they were able to spot happy recollections less than half the time when observing men. Men, however, slightly surpassed women in conveying their anger.

Detecting and Computing Emotion

OBJECTIVE 39-3 | Discuss the research results on reading and misreading facial and behavioral indicators of emotion.

Hard-to-control facial muscles reveal signs of emotions you may be trying to conceal. Lifting just the inner part of your eyebrows, which few people do consciously, reveals distress or worry. Eyebrows raised and pulled together signal fear. Activated muscles under the eyes and raised cheeks suggest a natural smile. A feigned smile, such as one we make for a photographer, often continues for more than 4 or 5 seconds. Most authentic expressions have faded by that time. Feigned smiles are also switched on and off more abruptly than is a genuine happy smile (Bugental, 1986).

Most people find it difficult to detect deceiving expressions. In one digest of 186 studies of discerning lies from truths, people were just 54 percent accurate—barely better than a coin toss (Bond & DePaulo, 2005). Can we learn how to better detect deceit? Paul Ekman and Maureen O'Sullivan (1991) found that by teaching researchers to watch for telltale signs of lying, such as a rise in voice pitch, they could boost accuracy rates. They had university students watch either a nature film or an upsetting gruesome film. Regardless, the students were instructed to talk and act as if they were watching and enjoying the nature film. Training enabled the researchers to discern lying versus truth-telling with 86 percent accuracy. Using our intuition, could the rest of us do as well? Not likely. Ekman and O'Sullivan challenged 39 college students, 67 psychiatrists, 110 court judges, 126 police officers, and 90 federal polygraphers to spot the liars. All five groups' guesses were, as we noted from other research, near chance (50 percent). Only a sixth group of experienced crowd-scanners—U.S. Secret Service agents—beat chance. But even they were only 64 percent correct.

In a follow-up study, the Ekman team (1999) found three more groups of skilled lie-catchers. When viewing videotapes of people stating their opinions—or the opposite of their opinions—on issues such as the death penalty, federal law officers (mostly CIA agents) spotted the liars 73 percent of the time. Clinical psychologists interested in lying research did so 68 percent of the time, and street-smart Los Angeles County sheriff's interrogators scored an almost equal 67 percent. Experienced British police interrogators exhibit similar accuracy (Mann & others, 2004). With experience—trained intuition—people can often catch the liar's leaking microexpressions of guilt, despair, and fear.

When people aren't seeking to deceive us, we do much better. As we noted earlier, our brains are rather amazing detectors of subtle expressions. Elisha Babad, Frank Bernieri, and Robert Rosenthal (1991) discovered just *how* amazing after videotaping teachers talking to unseen schoolchildren. A mere 10-second clip of either the teacher's voice or face provided enough clues for both young and old viewers to determine whether the teacher liked and admired the child he or she was addressing. Teachers may think they can conceal their feelings and stay objective, but their students can sense what their expressive tones and gestures reveal.

Which of Paul Ekman's smiles is feigned, which natural?
The smile on the right engages the facial muscles of a natural smile.

Dr. Paul Ekman, University of California at San Francisco

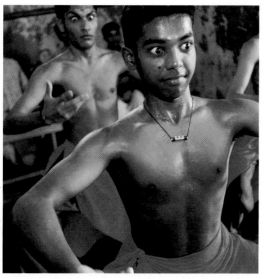

A silent language of emotion
Hindu classic dance uses the face and body to effectively convey 10 different emotions (Hejmadi & others, 2000).

The growing awareness that we communicate through the body's silent language has led to studies of how job applicants and interviewers communicate (or miscommunicate) nonverbally. Popular guidebooks and articles offer advice on how to interpret nonverbal signals when negotiating a business deal, selling a product, or flirting. It pays to be able to read feelings that leak through via subtle facial expressions, body movements, and postures. Fidgeting, for example, may reveal anxiety or boredom. More specific interpretations of postures and gestures are risky, because different expressions may convey the same emotion: Either a cold stare or the avoidance of eye contact may signify hostility. And a single gesture can convey very different emotions: Folded arms, for example, can signify either irritation or relaxation.

Such gestures, facial expressions, and tones of voice are all absent in computer-based communication. E-mail communications sometimes include sideways *emoticons,* such as ;-) for a knowing wink and :-(for a frown. But e-mail letters and Internet discussions otherwise lack nonverbal cues to status, personality, and age. Nobody knows what you look or sound like, or anything about your background; you are judged solely on your words. When first meeting an e-mail pen pal face to face, people are often surprised at the person they encounter.

It's also easy to misread e-mailed communications, where the absence of expressive e-motion can make for ambiguous emotion. So can the absence of those vocal nuances by which we signal that a statement is serious, kidding, or sarcastic. Research by Justin Kruger and his colleagues (1999) shows that communicators often think their "just kidding" intent is equally clear, whether e-mailed or spoken. But they commonly exhibit egocentrism by not foreseeing misinterpretations in the absence of nonverbal cues.

Culture and Emotional Expression

OBJECTIVE 39-4 | Discuss the culture-specific and culturally universal aspects of emotional expression, and explain how emotional expressions could enhance survival.

The meaning of gestures varies with the culture. Some years ago, psychologist Otto Klineberg (1938) observed that in Chinese literature people clapped their hands to express worry or disappointment, laughed a great "Ho-Ho" to express anger, and stuck out their tongues to show surprise. Similarly, the North American "thumbs up" and "A-OK" signs would be insults in certain other cultures. (When former U.S. President Richard Nixon made the latter sign in Brazil, he didn't realize he was saying "Let's have sex.") Just how important cultural definitions of gestures can be was demonstrated in 1968, when North Korea publicized photos of supposedly happy officers from a captured U.S. Navy spy ship. In the photo, three of the men raised their middle fingers; they had told captors it was a "Hawaiian good luck sign" (Fleming & Scott, 1991).

Do facial expressions also have different meanings in different cultures? To find out, two investigative teams—one led by Paul Ekman, Wallace Friesen, and others (1975, 1987, 1994), the other by Carroll Izard (1977, 1994)—showed photographs of different facial expressions to people in different parts of the world and asked them to guess the emotion. You can try this matching task yourself by pairing the six emotions with the six faces of **FIGURE 39.4**.

Regardless of your cultural background, you probably did pretty well. A smile's a smile the world around. Ditto for anger, and to a lesser extent the other basic expressions (Elfenbein & Ambady, 1999). (There is no culture where people frown when they are happy.) Despite some differences, cultures and languages share many similarities in the ways they categorize emotions—as anger, fear, and so on.

Ekman & Matsumoto, Japanese and Caucasian Facial Expression of Emotion

FIGURE 39.4
Culture-specific or culturally universal expressions?
As people of differing cultures and races, do our faces speak differing languages? Which face expresses disgust? Anger? Fear? Happiness? Sadness? Surprise? The answers are on this module's final page. (From Matsumoto and Ekman, 1989.)

Do people from different cultures share these similarities because they share experiences, such as American movies, the BBC, and CNN? Apparently not. Ekman and his team asked isolated people in New Guinea to display various emotions in response to such statements as, "Pretend your child has died." When the researchers showed videotapes of the New Guineans' facial reactions to North American collegians, the students read them easily.

Facial expressions do contain some nonverbal accents that provide clues to one's culture (Marsh & others, 2003). So it is not surprising that data from 182 studies show slightly enhanced accuracy when people judge emotions from their own culture (Elfenbein & Ambady, 2002, 2003a,b). Still, the telltale signs of emotion generally cross cultures.

Children's facial expressions—even those of blind children who have never seen a face—are also universal (Eibl-Eibesfeldt, 1971). People blind from birth spontaneously exhibit the common facial expressions associated with such emotions as joy, sadness, fear, and anger (Galati & others, 1997). The world over, children cry when distressed, shake their heads when defiant, and smile when they are happy.

The discovery that facial muscles speak a fairly universal language would not have surprised pioneering emotion researcher Charles Darwin (1809–1882). He speculated that in prehistoric times, before our ancestors communicated in words, their ability to convey threats, greetings, and submission with facial expressions helped them survive. That shared heritage, he believed, is why all humans express the basic emotions with similar facial expressions. A sneer, for example, retains elements of an animal's baring its teeth in a snarl.

Smiles, too, are social phenomena as well as emotional reflexes. Bowlers don't smile when they score a strike—they smile when they turn to face their companions (Jones & others, 1991; Kraut & Johnston, 1979). Even euphoric winners of Olympic gold medals typically don't smile when they are awaiting their ceremony but do when interacting with officials and facing the crowd and cameras (Fernández-Dols & Ruiz-Belda, 1995).

It has also been adaptive for us to interpret faces in particular contexts. People judge an angry face set in a frightening situation as afraid. They judge a fearful face set in a painful situation as pained (Carroll & Russell, 1996). Movie directors harness this phenomenon by creating contexts and soundtracks that amplify our perceptions of particular emotions.

Emotional expressions may enhance our survival in other ways, too. Surprise raises the eyebrows and widens the eyes, enabling us to take in more information. Disgust wrinkles the nose, closing it from foul odors.

"For news of the heart, ask the face."
Guinean proverb

While weightless, astronauts' fluids move toward their upper body and their faces become puffy. This makes nonverbal communication more difficult, increasing the risks of misunderstanding, especially among multinational crews (Gelman, 1989).

Although cultures share a universal facial language for basic emotions, they differ in how much emotion they express. In cultures that encourage individuality, as in Western Europe, Australia, New Zealand, and North America, emotional displays often are intense and prolonged. People focus on their own goals and attitudes and express themselves accordingly. Watching a film of someone's hand being cut, Americans grimace (whether alone or with other viewers). Japanese viewers hide their emotions when in the presence of others (Triandis, 1994). Cultural differences exist both between and within nations. The Irish and their Irish-American descendants tend to be more expressive than Scandinavians and their Scandinavian-American descendants (Tsai & Chentsova-Dutton, 2003). And that reminds us of a familiar lesson: Like most psychological events, emotion is best understood not only as a biological and cognitive phenomenon, but also as a social-cultural phenomenon.

The Effects of Facial Expressions

OBJECTIVE 39-5 | Discuss the facial feedback and behavior feedback phenomena, and give an example of each.

As William James struggled with feelings of depression and grief, he came to believe that we can control emotions by going "through the outward movements" of any emotion we want to experience. "To feel cheerful," he advised, "sit up cheerfully, look around cheerfully, and act as if cheerfulness were already there."

Recent findings concerning the emotional effects of facial expressions are precisely what James might have predicted. Expressions not only communicate emotion, they also amplify and regulate it. In his 1872 book, *The Expression of the Emotions in Man and Animals,* Darwin contended that "the free expression by outward signs of an emotion intensifies it. . . . He who gives way to violent gestures will increase his rage."

Was Darwin right? I was driving in my car one day when the song "Put On a Happy Face" came on the radio. How phony, I thought. But I tested Darwin's hypothesis anyway, as you can, too. Fake a big grin. Now scowl. Can you feel the "smile therapy" difference?

Participants in dozens of experiments have felt a difference. For example, James Laird and his colleagues (1974, 1984, 1989) subtly induced students to make a frowning expression by asking them to "contract these muscles" and "pull your brows together" (supposedly to help the researchers attach facial electrodes). The results? The students reported feeling a little angry. Students similarly induced to smile felt happier, found cartoons funnier, and recalled happier memories than did the frowners. People instructed to mold their faces in ways that express other basic emotions also experienced those emotions. For example, they reported feeling more fear than anger, disgust, or sadness when made to construct a fearful expression: "Raise your eyebrows. And open your eyes wide. Move your whole head back, so that your chin is tucked in a little bit, and let your mouth relax and hang open a little" (Duclos & others, 1989). The face is more than a billboard that displays our feelings; it also feeds our feelings.

In the absence of competing emotions, this *facial feedback* effect is subtle yet detectable. Consider these findings:

- If manipulated into furrowing their brows (**FIGURE 39.5**), people feel sadder while looking at sad photos.
- Saying the phonemes *e* and *ah,* which activate smiling muscles, puts people—believe it or not—in a better mood than saying the German *ü* (rather like saying the English *e* and *u* together), which activates muscles associated with negative emotions (Zajonc & others, 1989).

"Whenever I feel afraid
I hold my head erect
And whistle a happy tune."

Richard Rodgers and Oscar Hammerstein,
The King and I, 1958

"Refuse to express a passion and it dies. . . .
If we wish to conquer undesirable emotional tendencies in ourselves, we must . . .
go through the outward movements of those contrary dispositions which we prefer to cultivate."

William James, *Principles of Psychology,* 1890

Courtesy of Louis Schakel/Michael Kausman/The New York Times Pictures

FIGURE 39.5

How to make people frown without telling them to frown
Randy Larsen, Margaret Kasimatis, and Kurt Frey's (1992) solution: Attach two golf tees above the eyebrows and ask people to make the tee tips touch. Research participants felt sad while viewing scenes of war, sickness, and starvation, and even sadder with their "sad face" muscles activated.

- Just activating one of the smiling muscles by holding a pen in the teeth (rather than with the lips, which activates a frowning muscle) is enough to make cartoons seem more amusing (Strack & others, 1988). A heartier smile—made not just with the mouth but with raised cheeks that crinkle the eyes—enhances positive feelings even more when you are reacting to something pleasant or funny (Soussignan, 2001). Looking at yourself in a mirror further amplifies the effect (Kleinke & others, 1998). Smile warmly on the outside and you feel better on the inside. Scowl and the whole world seems to scowl back.

Sara Snodgrass and her associates (1986) observed the *behavior feedback* phenomenon with walking. You can duplicate the participants' experience: Walk for a few minutes while taking short, shuffling steps, keeping your eyes downcast. Now walk around taking long strides, with your arms swinging and your eyes looking straight ahead. Can you feel your mood shift? Going through the motions awakens the emotions.

Better yet, report William Flack and his team (1999), manipulate *both* face and posture. To generate an angry feeling, for example, follow the instructions they gave their research participants:

> Push your eyebrows together and down. Clench your teeth tightly and push your lips together. Put your feet flat on the floor directly below your knees, and put your forearms and elbows on the arms of the chair. Now clench your fists tightly and lean your upper body slightly forward.

But let's leave you feeling happier:

> Push the corners of your mouth up and back, letting your mouth open a little. Sit up as straight as you can in your chair. Put your hands at the ends of the armrests, and make sure that your legs are straight in front of you, knees bent, and feet right below your knees.

If assuming emotional expressions and postures triggers a feeling, then would imitating others' expressions help us feel what they are feeling? Again, the laboratory evidence is supportive. Kathleen Burns Vaughn and John Lanzetta (1981) asked some students but not others to make a pained expression whenever an electric shock was apparently delivered to someone they were watching. With each apparent shock, the grimacing observers perspired more and had a faster heart rate than observers who didn't imitate the expression. Just seeing a loved one wince at a light electrical shock also activates a pain-related brain region. This suggests a neural basis for empathy—for literally feeling the other's pain (Singer & others, 2004). So one small way to become more empathic—to feel what others feel—is to let your own face mimic the other person's expression. Acting as another acts helps us feel what another feels. Indeed, natural mimicry of others' emotions helps explain why emotions are contagious (Dimberg & others, 2000; Newmann & Strack, 2000).

A request from your author: Smile often as you read this book.

>> LEARNING OUTCOMES

Expressed Emotion

OBJECTIVE **39-1** | **Describe some of the factors that affect our ability to decipher nonverbal cues.**

Most people can detect nonverbal cues, and we are especially sensitive to nonverbal threats. Experience contributes to our sensitivity to cues, as studies of abused children show.

OBJECTIVE **39-2** | **Describe some gender differences in perceiving and communicating emotions.**

Women generally surpass men at reading deception and other emotional cues, giving detailed descriptions of their emotional reactions, describing themselves as emotional, expressing empathy in words and facial expressions, and conveying happiness. Men communicate anger better.

OBJECTIVE **39-3** | **Discuss the research results on reading and misreading facial and behavioral indicators of emotion.**

Facial muscles reveal signs of emotion. But lie detection methods based on facial expressions don't yet exist, and most of us have difficulty detecting expressions of deceit. The absence of verbal or emotional cues in e-mails deprives us of an important source of information.

OBJECTIVE **39-4** | **Discuss the culture-specific and culturally universal aspects of emotional expression, and explain how emotional expressions could enhance survival.**

Many facial expressions, such as those of happiness and fear, are found all over the world (and among children blind from birth), indicating that they are culturally universal aspects of emotion. Cultures differ, however, in the amount of emotional expression they consider acceptable. In prelinguistic, prehistoric times, emotional expressions could have enhanced survival by enabling communication of threats, greetings, and submission. Some emotional expressions help us to take in more sensory information or to avoid taking in toxic substances.

OBJECTIVE **39-5** | **Discuss the facial feedback and behavior feedback phenomena, and give an example of each.**

The *facial feedback hypothesis* proposes that expressions amplify our emotions by activating muscles associated with specific states (such as happiness) and the muscles signal the body to respond as though we were experiencing those states. Similarly, the *behavior feedback hypothesis* assumes that if we move our body as we would when experiencing some emotion (shuffling along with downcast eyes, as when sad), we are likely to feel that emotion to some degree.

TEST YOURSELF

1. Who tends to express more emotion—men or women? How do we know the answer to that question?

(Answer in Appendix B.)

ASK YOURSELF

1. Can you think of one situation in which you would like to change the way you feel, and create a simple plan for doing so? For instance, if you would like to feel more cheerful on your way to class tomorrow morning rather than dragging yourself there, you might try walking briskly—with head held high and a pleasant expression on your face.

ANSWER TO QUESTION WITHIN THE MODULE

Q. Which of the faces in Figure 39.4 expresses disgust? Anger? Fear? Happiness? Sadness? Surprise?

A. The photos in Figure 39.4, from left to right and top to bottom, express happiness, surprise, fear, sadness, anger, and disgust.

>WEB

Multiple-choice *self-tests* and more may be found at www.worthpublishers.com/myers.

40

Experienced Emotion

OBJECTIVE 40-1 | Name several basic emotions, and describe two dimensions psychologists use to differentiate emotions.

How many distinct emotions are there? Carroll Izard (1977) isolated 10 such basic emotions (joy, interest-excitement, surprise, sadness, anger, disgust, contempt, fear, shame, and guilt), most of which are present in infancy (FIGURE 40.1). Jessica Tracey and Richard Robins (2004) believe that pride is also a distinct emotion, signaled by a small smile, head slightly tilted back, and an open posture. And Phillip Shaver and his colleagues (1996) believe that love, too, may be a basic emotion. But Izard has argued that other emotions are combinations of these 10. Love, he says, is a mixture of joy and interest-excitement.

The ingredients of emotion include not only physiology and expressive behavior but also our conscious experience. We sometimes experience feelings as "obscure and confused," noted Benjamin Constant de Rebecque in 1816. To cut through the obscurity, psychologists have asked people to describe their emotions. Varied people, including Estonians, Poles, Greeks, Chinese, and Canadians, place emotions along the two dimensions illustrated in FIGURE 40.2 (on the next page)—pleasant (or positive) versus unpleasant (or negative) *valence* and low versus high *arousal* (Russell & others, 1989, 1999a,b; Watson & others, 1999).

Successful Olympic gymnasts and high-performing students taking exams label arousal as energizing, as giving them an edge (Raglin, 1992). For them arousal has

(a) Joy (mouth forming smile, cheeks lifted, twinkle in eye)

(b) Anger (brows drawn together and downward, eyes fixed, mouth squarish)

(c) Interest (brows raised or knitted, mouth softly rounded, lips may be pursed)

FIGURE 40.1
Infants' naturally occurring emotions
To identify the emotions present from birth, Carroll Izard analyzed the facial expressions of very young infants.

(d) Disgust (nose wrinkled, upper lip raised, tongue pushed outward)

(e) Surprise (brows raised, eyes widened, mouth rounded in oval shape)

(f) Sadness (brow's inner corner raised, mouth corners drawn down)

(g) Fear (brows level, drawn in and up, eyelids lifted, mouth corners retracted)

FIGURE 40.2
Two dimensions of emotion
James Russell, David Watson, Auke
Tellegen, and others describe emotions as
variations on two dimensions—arousal (low
versus high) and valence (pleasant versus
unpleasant feeling).

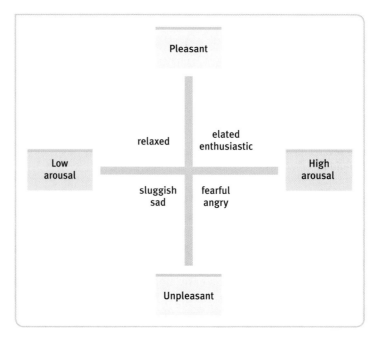

positive valence, while for those suffering stage fright it has negative valence. Experienced professors and public speakers similarly welcome prelecture arousal as meaning they are "up" or "on" rather than flat. On the valence and arousal dimensions, terrified is more frightened (more unpleasant and aroused) than afraid, enraged is angrier than angry, delighted is happier than happy.

Let's take a closer look at three of these emotions: fear, anger, and happiness. What functions do they serve? What influences our experience of each?

Fear

Fear can be poisonous. It can torment us, rob us of sleep, and preoccupy our thinking. People can be literally scared to death. Fear can also be contagious. In 1903, someone yelled "Fire!" as a fire broke out in Chicago's Iroquois Theater. Eddie Foy, the comedian on stage at the time, tried to reassure the crowd by calling out, "Don't get excited. There's no danger. Take it easy!" Alas, the crowd panicked. During the 10 minutes it took the fire department to arrive and quickly extinguish the flames, more than 500 people perished, most of them trampled or smothered in a stampede. Bodies were piled 7 or 8 feet deep in the stairways, and many of the faces bore heel marks (Brown, 1965).

More often, fear is adaptive. It's an alarm system that prepares our bodies to flee from danger. Fear of real or imagined enemies binds people together as families, tribes, and nations. Fear of injury can protect us from harm. Fear of punishment or retaliation can constrain us from harming one another. Fear helps us focus on a problem and rehearse coping strategies.

Learning Fear

OBJECTIVE 40-2 | State two ways we learn our fears.

People can be afraid of almost anything—"afraid of truth, afraid of fortune, afraid of death, and afraid of each other," observed Ralph Waldo Emerson. Why so many fears? Behaviorists John B. Watson and Rosalie Rayner (1920) showed that infants can learn to fear furry objects associated with frightening noises. Child development researchers now know that when infants begin to crawl, they learn from their falls and near-falls—and become increasingly afraid of heights (Campos & others, 1992). Through such conditioning, the short list of naturally painful and frightening events can multiply into a long list of human fears—fear of driving or flying, fear of mice or cockroaches, fear of closed or open spaces, fear of failure or of success, fear of another race or nation.

Learning by observation extends the list. Susan Mineka (1985) sought to explain why nearly all monkeys reared in the wild fear snakes, yet lab-reared monkeys do not. Surely, most wild monkeys do not actually suffer snake bites. Do they learn their fear through observation? To find out, Mineka experimented with six monkeys reared in the wild (all strongly fearful of snakes) and their lab-reared offspring (virtually none of which feared snakes). After repeatedly observing their parents or peers refusing to reach for food in the presence of a snake, the younger monkeys developed a similar strong fear of snakes. When retested three months later, their learned fear persisted, suggesting that our fears may reflect not only our own past traumas but also the fears we learn from our parents and friends.

It did not take direct experience for people to become more fearful after observing the trauma of 9/11. Within New York City, a school system study found tens of thousands of children experiencing nightmares and fears of public places (Goodnough, 2002). Nationally, women responded to the attacks with greater fear, men with greater anger (Lerner & others, 2002). Four weeks after the attack, 27 percent of women and 10 percent of men reported being afraid to fly (ICR, 2001).

The Biology of Fear

OBJECTIVE 40-3 | Discuss some of the biological components of fear.

We may be biologically prepared to learn some fears more quickly than others. Monkeys learn to fear snakes even by watching videotapes of monkeys reacting fearfully to a snake; but they *don't* learn to fear flowers when video splicing transposes the seemingly feared stimulus into a flower (Cook & Mineka, 1991). We humans quickly learn to fear snakes, spiders, and cliffs—fears that probably helped our ancestors survive (Öhman & Mineka, 2003). But our Stone Age fears leave us unprepared for high-tech dangers—cars, electricity, bombs, and global warming—all of which are now far more dangerous (Lumsden & Wilson, 1983; McNally, 1987).

One key to fear learning lies in the amygdala, that limbic system neural center deep in the brain (**FIGURE 40.3**). The amygdala plays a key role in associating various emotions, including fear, with certain situations (Barinaga, 1992b). Rabbits learn to react with fear to a tone that predicts an impending small shock—unless their amygdala is damaged. If rats have their amygdala deactivated by a drug that blocks the strengthening of neural connections, they, too, show no fear learning. The amygdala receives input from regions such as the *anterior cingulate cortex,* a higher-level center for processing emotion. And it sends output to all the parts of the brain that produce the bodily symptoms of extreme fear, such as diarrhea and shortness of breath.

The amygdala is similarly involved in human fears. If an experimenter repeatedly blasts people with a blaring horn after showing a blue slide, they will begin to react emotionally to the slide (as measured by their perspiring skin conducting electricity). If they have suffered damage to the nearby hippocampus, they still show the emotional reaction but won't be able to remember why. If they have suffered amygdala damage, they will remember the conditioning but will show no emotional effect of it (Schacter, 1996).

FIGURE 40.3

The amygdala—a neural key to fear learning

Nerves running out from these knots of neural tissue, one on either side of the brain's center, carry messages that control heart rate, sweating, stress hormones, attention, and other engines that rev up in threatening situations.

Hard-wired fears
Entertainment businesses exploit our survival circuits. Although we can *know* that amusement park deaths are extremely rare, our fear alarm system nevertheless gives us an adrenaline rush and sweaty palms during a free-flying fair ride.

Researchers have been mapping these circuits, showing which activate as humans and other animals learn fears. If people are subjected to an aversive sound while viewing faces, amygdala fear pathways will become active on future viewings of the face (Buchel & others, 1998; Morris & others, 1998). Patients who have lost use of the amygdala are unusually trusting of scary-looking people (Adolphs & others, 1998).

Of course, there are people whose fears seem to fall outside the average range. Some, with *phobias,* have intense fears of specific objects (such as bugs) or situations (such as public speaking) that disrupt their ability to cope. They may be very fearful of threatening or embarrassing situations. To be ever-attentive to potential threats is to be chronically anxious (Mineka & Sutton, 1992). But others—courageous heroes and remorseless criminals—are less fearful than most of us. Astronauts and adventurers who have "the right stuff"—who can keep their wits and function coolly and effectively in times of severe stress—seem to thrive on risk. So, too, do con artists and killers who charm their intended victims without a hint of nervousness. In laboratory tests, they exhibit little fear of a tone that predictably precedes a painful electric shock.

Experience helps shape such fearfulness or fearlessness, but so do our genes. Genes influence our temperament—our emotional reactivity. Among identical twins, one twin's level of fearfulness is similar to the other's—even when they have been reared separately (Lykken, 1982). Scientists have isolated a gene that influences the amygdala's response to frightening situations (Hariri & others, 2002). People with a short version of this gene have less of a protein that speeds the reuptake of the neurotransmitter serotonin. With more serotonin available to activate their amygdala neurons, people with this short gene exhibit a revved-up amygdala response to frightening pictures.

Anger

OBJECTIVE 40-4 | Identify some common triggers and consequences of anger, and assess the catharsis hypothesis.

Anger, the sages have said, is "a short madness" (Horace, 65–8 B.C.) that "carries the mind away" (Virgil, 70–19 B.C.) and can be "many times more hurtful than the injury that caused it" (Thomas Fuller, 1654–1734). But they have also said, "noble anger" (William Shakespeare, 1564–1616) "makes any coward brave" (Cato, 234–149 B.C.) and "brings back . . . strength" (Virgil).

What makes us angry? To find out, James Averill (1983) asked people to recall or keep careful records of their experiences with anger. Most reported becoming at least mildly angry several times a week, some several times a day. The anger was often a response to friends' or loved ones' perceived misdeeds and was especially common when another person's act seemed willful, unjustified, and avoidable. But blameless annoyances—foul odors, high temperatures, a traffic jam, aches and pains—also have the power to make us angry (Berkowitz, 1990).

What do we do with our anger? And what *should* we do with our anger? In a Gallup survey of teens, boys more than girls reported walking away from the situation or working it off with exercise; girls more often reported talking with a friend, listening to music, or writing (Ray, 2005).

When anger fuels physically or verbally aggressive acts we later regret, it becomes maladaptive. Anger also primes prejudice, and after 9/11, Americans who responded with anger more than fear also displayed intolerance for immigrants and Muslims (DeSteno & others, 2004; Skitka & others, 2004). And anger can harm us—chronic hostility is linked to heart disease (Smith & Ruiz, 2002; Williams, 1993). But controlled expressions of

"I thought it would be nice if we had a forum where we could get together and have screaming tantrums."

" Anger will never disappear so long as thoughts of resentment are cherished in the mind."

The Buddha, 500 B.C.

anger are more adaptive than either hostile outbursts or pent-up angry feelings. Participants in Averill's research recalled that when they were angry they often reacted assertively rather than hurtfully. Their anger frequently led them to talk things over with the offender, thereby lessening the aggravation.

Popular books and articles on aggression at times advise that even releasing angry feelings as hostile outbursts can be better than internalizing them. When irritated, should we lash out at the offender? Was Ann Landers (1969) right that "youngsters should be taught to vent their anger"? Are "recovery" therapists right in encouraging us to rage at our dead parents, imaginatively curse the boss, or confront our childhood abuser?

Such encouragement to vent our rage is typical in individualized cultures, but it would seldom be heard in cultures where people's identity is centered more on the group. People who keenly sense their *inter*dependence see anger as a threat to group harmony (Markus & Kitayama, 1991). In Tahiti, for instance, people learn to be considerate and gentle. In Japan, from infancy on, anger expressions are less common than in Western cultures.

The Western "vent your anger" advice presumes that through aggressive action or fantasy we can achieve emotional release, or **catharsis.** Experimenters report that *sometimes* when people retaliate against a provoker, they may indeed calm down. But this tends to be true only *if* their counterattack is directed against the provoker, *if* their retaliation seems justifiable, and *if* their target is not intimidating (Geen & Quanty, 1977; Hokanson & Edelman, 1966). In short, expressing anger can be *temporarily* calming *if* it does not leave us feeling guilty or anxious.

However, despite the afterglow—people sometimes feel better for hours afterward—catharsis usually fails to cleanse one's rage. More often, expressing anger breeds more anger. For one thing, it may provoke further retaliation, thus escalating a minor conflict into a major confrontation. For another, expressing anger can magnify anger. Ebbe Ebbesen and his colleagues (1975) saw this when they interviewed 100 frustrated engineers and technicians just laid off by an aerospace company. They asked some of the workers questions that released hostility, such as, "What instances can you think of where the company has not been fair with you?" When these people later filled out a questionnaire that assessed their attitudes toward the company, did this opportunity to "drain off" their hostility reduce it? Quite the contrary. Compared with those who had not vented their anger, those who had let it all out exhibited *more* hostility. Even when provoked people hit a punching bag *believing* it will be cathartic, the effect is the opposite—leading them to exhibit *more* cruelty (Bushman & others, 1999). And when they wallop a punching bag while ruminating about the person who angered them, they become even more aggressive when given a chance for revenge. "Venting to reduce anger is like using gasoline to put out a fire," concluded the researcher, Brad Bushman (2002).

Ironically, when angry outbursts do temporarily calm us, they may be reinforcing and therefore habit forming. If stressed managers find they can drain off some of their tension by berating an employee, then the next time they feel irritated and tense they may be more likely to explode again. Think about it: The next time you are angry you are likely to do whatever has relieved your anger in the past.

What, then, is the best way to handle our anger? Experts offer two suggestions. First, wait. You can bring down the level of physiological arousal of anger by waiting. "It is true of the body as of arrows," noted Carol Tavris (1982), "what goes up must come down. Any emotional arousal will simmer down if you just wait long enough." Second, deal with anger in a way that involves neither being chronically angry over every little annoyance nor passively sulking, merely rehearsing your reasons for your anger. Ruminating inwardly about the causes of your anger serves only to increase it (Rusting & Nolen-Hoeksema, 1998). Don't join those who stifle their feelings over a series of provocations and then suddenly overreact to a single incident (Baumeister & others, 1990). Calm yourself in other ways, such as by exercising, playing an instrument, or talking it through with a friend.

SIX CHIX

The catharsis myth: Is it true?

■ **catharsis** emotional release. In psychology, the catharsis hypothesis maintains that "releasing" aggressive energy (through action or fantasy) relieves aggressive urges.

A cool culture
Domestic violence is rare in Micronesia. This photo of community life on Pulap Island suggests one possible reason: Family life takes place in the open on this island. Relatives and neighbors who witness angry outbursts can step in before the emotion escalates into child, spouse, or elder abuse.

Anger does communicate strength and competence (Tiedens, 2001). It can benefit a relationship when it expresses a grievance in ways that promote reconciliation rather than retaliation. Civility means not only keeping silent about trivial irritations but also communicating important ones clearly and assertively. A nonaccusing statement of feeling—perhaps letting one's housemate know that "I get irritated when you leave your dirty dishes for me to clean up"—can help resolve the conflicts that cause anger.

What if someone else's behavior really hurts you? Research suggests that the age-old response of forgiveness may be what the doctor ordered. Without letting the offender off the hook or inviting further harm, forgiveness releases anger and can calm the body. To explore the bodily effects of forgiveness, Charlotte Witvliet and her co-researchers (2001) invited college students to recall an incident where someone had hurt them. As the students mentally rehearsed forgiveness, their negative feelings—and their perspiration, blood pressure, heart rate, and facial tension—all were lower than when they rehearsed their grudges.

Happiness

OBJECTIVE 40-5 | Describe how the feel-good, do-good phenomenon works, and discuss the importance of research on subjective well-being.

"How to gain, how to keep, how to recover happiness is in fact for most men at all times the secret motive for all they do," observed William James (1902, p. 76). People everywhere—in 48 countries on six continents in one study—also desire happiness for their children (Diener & Lucas, 2004). Understandably so, for one's state of happiness or unhappiness colors everything. People who are happy perceive the world as safer, make decisions more easily, rate job applicants more favorably, are more cooperative, and live healthier and more energized and satisfied lives (Lyukomirsky & others, 2005; Myers, 1993). When your mood is gloomy and your thinking preoccupied, life as a whole seems depressing. Let your mood brighten and your thinking broadens and becomes more playful and creative (Fredrickson, 2002, 2003). Your relationships, your self-image, and your hopes for the future also seem more promising. Positive emotions fuel upward spirals.

Moreover—and this is one of psychology's most consistent findings—when we feel happy we are more willing to help others. In study after study, a mood-boosting experience (finding money, succeeding on a challenging task, recalling a happy event) has made people more likely to give money, pick up someone's dropped papers, volunteer time, and do other good deeds. Psychologists call it the **feel-good, do-good phenomenon** (Salovey, 1990). Happiness doesn't just feel good, it does good.

■ **feel-good, do-good phenomenon** people's tendency to be helpful when already in a good mood.

■ **subjective well-being** self-perceived happiness or satisfaction with life. Used along with measures of objective well-being (for example, physical and economic indicators) to evaluate people's quality of life.

(Doing good also promotes good feeling, a phenomenon harnessed by some happiness coaches and instructors as they assign people to perform a daily "random act of kindness" and to record the results.)

Despite the significance of happiness, psychology throughout its history has more often focused on negative emotions. Since 1887, *Psychological Abstracts* (a guide to psychology's literature) has included, as of this writing, 12,876 articles mentioning anger, 82,297 mentioning anxiety, and 103,840 mentioning depression. For every 17 articles on these topics, only one dealt with the positive emotions of joy (1450), life satisfaction (5263), or happiness (4727). There is, of course, good reason to focus on negative emotions; they can make our lives miserable and drive us to seek help. But researchers are becoming increasingly interested in **subjective well-being,** assessed either as feelings of happiness (sometimes defined as a high ratio of positive to negative feelings) or as a sense of satisfaction with life. A new *positive psychology* is on the rise.

On this subject, as on so many others, whatever psychological research reveals will have been anticipated by someone. We have inherited many contradictory maxims concerning happiness: that it comes from knowing the truth, or from preserving illusions; from living for the present, or from living for the future; from being with others, or from living in peaceful solitude (Tatarkiewicz, 1976). The list goes on, making the scientific task clear: to ask which of these competing ideas fit reality. Sifting the actual predictors of happiness from the plausible hunches requires research.

The Short Life of Emotional Ups and Downs

OBJECTIVE 40-6 | Discuss some of the daily and longer-term variations in the duration of emotions.

In their happiness research, psychologists have studied influences on both our temporary moods and our long-term life satisfaction. When studying people's hour-by-hour moods, David Watson (2000) and Daniel Kahneman and his colleagues (2004) discovered that positive emotion rises over the early to middle part of most days (**FIGURE 40.4**). Studying people's reports of day-to-day moods confirms that stressful events—an argument, a sick child, a car problem—trigger bad moods. No surprise there. But by the next day, the gloom nearly always lifts (Affleck & others, 1994; Bolger & others, 1989; Stone & Neale, 1984). If anything, people tend to rebound from bad days to a *better*-than-usual good mood the following day. When in a bad mood, can you usually depend on rebounding within a day or two? Are your times of elation similarly hard to sustain? Over the long run, our emotional ups and downs tend to balance.

Apart from prolonged grief over the loss of a loved one or lingering anxiety after a trauma (such as child abuse, rape, or the terrors of war), even tragedy is not permanently depressing. Learning that one is HIV-positive is devastating. But after five weeks of adapting to the grim news, those who tested positive felt less emotionally distraught than they had expected (Sieff & others, 1999). Kidney dialysis patients recognize that their health is relatively poor, yet in their moment-to-moment experiences they report being just as happy as healthy nonpatients (Riis & others, 2005). People who become blind or paralyzed also usually recover near-normal levels of day-to-day happiness (Gerhart & others, 1994; Myers, 1993). Among a sample of Germans incapacitated by ALS (amyotrophic lateral sclerosis, a progressive neurological disease that leads to paralysis), a striking 85 percent rated their quality of life as "satisfactory," "good," or "very good." Moreover, their ratings were not much affected by

FIGURE 40.4

Moods across the day
When psychologist David Watson (2000) sampled nearly 4500 mood reports from 150 people, he found this pattern of variation from the average levels of positive and negative emotions.

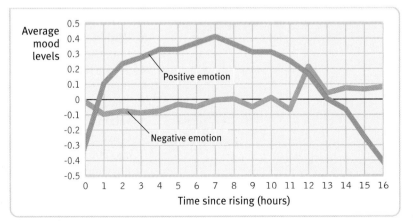

Human resilience

Seven weeks after her 1994 wedding, Anna Putt of South Midlands, England, shown here with her husband, Des, suffered a brain-stem stroke that left her "locked-in." For months afterward, she recalls, "I was paralyzed from the neck down and was unable to communicate. These were VERY frightening times. But with encouragement from family, friends, faith, and medical staff, I tried to keep positive." In the ensuing three years, she became able to "talk" (by nodding at letters), to steer an electric wheelchair with her head, and to use a computer (by nodding while wearing spectacles that guide a cursor). Despite her paralysis, she reports that "I enjoy going out in the fresh air. My motto is 'Don't look back, move forward.' God would not want me to stop trying and I have no intention of doing so. Life is what you make of it!"

whether they were or were not on ventilators or feeding tubes (Kübler & others, 2005). "If you are a paraplegic," explains Daniel Kahneman (2005), "you will gradually start thinking of other things, and the more time you spend thinking of other things the less miserable you are going to be." A major disability often leaves people somewhat less happy than the average person (Lucas, 2005). Yet they reportedly express considerably more happiness than able-bodied people with depression (Schwartz & Estrin, 2004; Kübler & others, in press). Even patients "locked-in" a motionless body "rarely want to die," report Eimar Smith and Mark Delargy (2005), which "counters a popular misconception that such patients would have been better off dead."

In less life-threatening contexts, the pattern continues. Faculty members up for tenure expect their lives would be deflated by a negative decision. Actually, 5 to 10 years later, those denied are not noticeably less happy than those who were awarded tenure, report Daniel Gilbert and colleagues (1998). The same is true of romantic breakups, which feel devastating. The surprising reality: *We overestimate the duration of emotions and underestimate our capacity to adapt.*

Wealth and Well-Being

OBJECTIVE 40-7 | Summarize the findings on the relationship between affluence and happiness.

The emotional impact of dramatically positive events also dissipates sooner than we might expect. Once their rush of euphoria wears off, state lottery winners typically find their overall happiness unchanged (Brickman & others, 1978). Other research confirms that there is much more to well-being than being well-off. Many people (including most German citizens, and most new American collegians, as **FIGURE 40.5** suggests) believe they would be happier if they had more money (Csikszentmihalyi, 1999).

They probably would be—temporarily. Consider:

- Within most affluent countries, people with lots of money are somewhat happier than those who struggle to afford life's basic needs (Di Tella & others, 2001).
- People in rich countries are also somewhat happier than those in poor countries (Steel & Ones, 2002).
- Those who have experienced a recent windfall from a lottery, an inheritance, or a surging economy typically feel some elation (Diener & Oishi, 2000; Gardner & Oswald, 2001). *Losing* money has even more emotional impact (Hobfoll & others, 2003; Kahneman & Tversky, 1979). This illustrates a basic principle, note Roy Baumeister and his colleagues (2001): "Bad is stronger than good." Losses loom larger than gains, cruel words linger longer than kind ones, a bad reputation is more easily acquired than a good one, and pain produces misery more than health produces joy.

"Weeping may tarry for the night, but joy comes with the morning."

Psalms 30:5

"I have a 'fortune cookie maxim' that I'm very proud of: Nothing in life is quite as important as you think it is while you are thinking about it. So, nothing will ever make you as happy as you think it will."

Nobel Laureate psychologist Daniel Kahneman, Gallup interview, "What Were They Thinking?" 2005

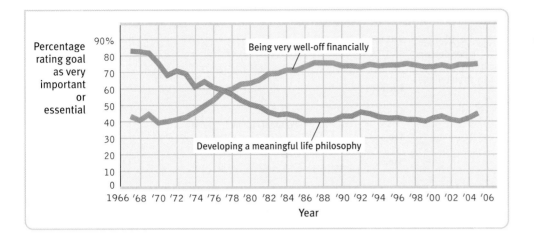

FIGURE 40.5
The changing materialism of entering college students
From 1970 through most of the 1980s, annual surveys of more than 200,000 entering U.S. college students revealed an increasing desire for wealth. (From *The American Freshman* surveys, UCLA, 1966 to 2005.)

Yet in the long run, increased affluence hardly affects happiness. Even in Pakistani and Indian slums, people "are more satisfied than one might expect" (Biswas-Diener & Diener, 2001; Suhail & Chaudry, 2004). Wealth is like health: Its utter absence can breed misery, yet having it is no guarantee of happiness. Growing up poor puts one at risk for certain problems, but so does growing up rich. Children of affluence are at greater-than-normal risk for substance abuse, anxiety, and depression (Luthar & Latendresse, 2005). What matters more than money (assuming one can afford life's necessities with a sense of security) is how you feel about what you have. Those who live with a sense of gratitude—or who cultivate their gratitude by each day writing down what they are grateful for—enjoy greater happiness (McCullough & others, 2004; Watkins, 2004).

Most people agree that money can't buy happiness, but they do believe that a *little* more money would make them a *little* more happy, secure, and comfortable. So, over time, does our happiness grow, little by little, with our paychecks? If his government achieves its 4 percent economic growth-rate goal, noted Australian researcher Richard Eckersley (2001), its people will be twice as rich in 20 years, "and 10 times richer than we were 100 years ago. Can we be sure that this increasing wealth creation is beneficial to personal and social well-being?"

No, we cannot. During the last four decades, the average U.S. citizen's buying power more than doubled. The 1957 after-tax income, inflated to 1995 dollars, was $8500 per person; by 2005, thanks partly to the rich getting richer and to women's increasing employment, it was well above $20,000. Did this more-than-doubled wealth—enabling twice as many cars per person, not to mention iPods, laptops, and camera cell phones—also buy more happiness? Are those of us who enjoy the abundance of the affluent Western world happier with its little levers we can adjust to heat and cool our homes to precisely the desired degree, to release clean water for a warm shower or a cold drink, and to microwave our plentiful food? As **FIGURE 40.6** on the next page shows, the average American, though certainly richer, is not a bit happier. In 1957, some 35 percent said they were "very happy," as did slightly fewer—34 percent—in 2004.

Indeed, if we can judge from statistics—including doubled divorce and teen suicide rates, and mushrooming depression—contemporary Americans seem to be more often miserable. Much the same has been true of the European countries, Australia, and Japan: In these countries, people enjoy better nutrition, health care, education, and science, and they are somewhat happier than those in very poor countries (Diener & Biswas-Diener, 2002; Eckersley, 2000). Yet their increasing real incomes have *not* produced increasing happiness. Such findings lob a bombshell at modern materialism: *Economic growth in affluent countries has provided no apparent boost to morale or social well-being.*

"Money won't make you happy, Waldron. So instead of a raise, I'm giving a Prozac."

"Australians are three times richer than their parents and grandparents were in the 1950s, but they are not happier."
A Manifesto for Well-Being, 2005

"Americans say that money doesn't bring happiness. But it helps you to live with misery in comfort."
Farah Pahlavi, exiled widow of the wealthy Shah of Iran, 2004

FIGURE 40.6

Does money buy happiness?
It surely helps us to avoid certain types of pain. Yet, though buying power has almost tripled since the 1950s, the average American's reported happiness has remained almost unchanged. (Happiness data from National Opinion Research Center surveys; income data from *Historical Statistics of the United States* and *Economic Indicators*.)

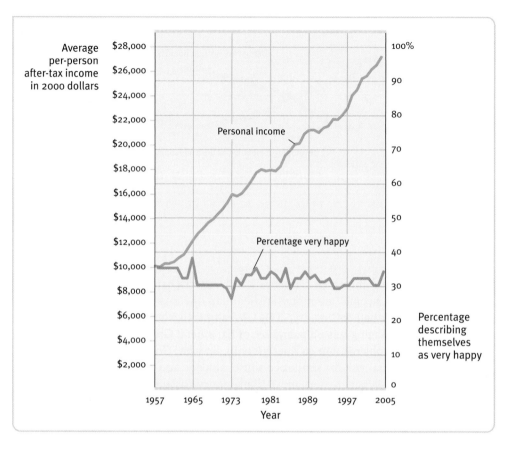

TABLE 40.1

SUBJECTIVE WELL-BEING (COMBINED HAPPINESS AND SATISFACTION) IN 82 SOCIETIES

The Top 10	The Bottom 10
1. Puerto Rico	73. Bulgaria
2. Mexico	74. Belarus
3. Denmark	75. Georgia
4. Ireland	76. Romania
5. Iceland	77. Moldova
6. Switzerland	78. Russia
7. Northern Ireland	79. Armenia
8. Colombia	80. Ukraine
9. Netherlands	81. Zimbabwe
10. Canada	82. Indonesia

(The United States and Australia were in a virtual tie for fifteenth place.)

Source: Ronald Inglehart and others (2004)

The wealthier-but-no-happier phenomenon even appears in China, which in the decade after 1994 enjoyed a dramatic economic advance. Average household incomes more than doubled, enabling households with a color TV to soar from 40 to 82 percent, those with a landline phone to jump from 10 to 63 percent, and those with cell phones to skyrocket from near zero to 48 percent. Despite this dramatic growth in income and consumption, nationwide Gallup surveys revealed that the proportion of Chinese expressing satisfaction with their lives simultaneously *declined* (Burkholder, 2005a,b). Moreover, the better-off urban Chinese were more likely to feel dissatisfaction than were the poorer rural Chinese. And in the latest World Values Surveys of well-being in 82 countries, the happiest two—Puerto Rico and Mexico—were far from the richest (though the unhappiest, mostly in Eastern Europe, were economically stressed—see **TABLE 40.1**).

Equally interesting are studies showing that individuals who strive hardest for wealth tend to live with lower well-being, a finding that "comes through very strongly in every culture I've looked at," reports Richard Ryan (1999). This is especially so for those seeking money to prove themselves, gain power, or show off rather than support their families (Srivastava & others, 2001). Ryan's collaborator, Tim Kasser (2000, 2002), concludes from their studies that those who instead strive for "intimacy, personal growth, and contribution to the community" experience a higher quality of life. This echoes an earlier finding by H. W. Perkins (1991): Among 800 college alumni surveyed, those preferring a high income and occupational success and prestige to having very close friends and a close marriage were twice as likely as their former classmates to describe themselves as "fairly" or "very" *un*happy. A similar correlation appears among 7167 college students

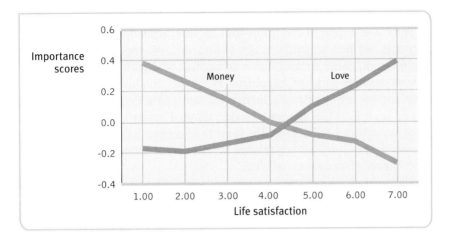

FIGURE 40.7
Values and life satisfaction
Among college and university students worldwide, those who report high life satisfaction give priority to love over money. (From Diener & Oishi, 2000.)

surveyed in 41 countries. Those who value love more than money report much higher satisfaction with life than do their money-hungry peers (**FIGURE 40.7**).

If we are both richer and healthier, but no happier, than our grandparents were at our age, should our national priorities focus more on advancing psychological well-being? In Bhutan, says King Jigme Singye Wangchuk, "gross national happiness is more important than gross national product." Bhutan's prime minister frames his annual report in terms of Bhutan's four pillars of progress toward national happiness: "The promotion of equitable and sustainable socio-economic development, preservation and promotion of cultural values, conservation of the natural environment, and establishment of good governance" (Esty, 2004). Ed Diener and Martin Seligman (2004) have proposed ways in which the U.S. Census Bureau and other national organizations might measure national well-being. "If high well-being is the overarching goal of all nations, national indicators of well-being are crucial to assessing the impact of national and corporate policies," they note.

"But on the positive side, money can't buy happiness—so who cares?"

Two Psychological Phenomena: Adaptation and Comparison

OBJECTIVE 40-8 | Describe how adaptation and relative deprivation affect our appraisals of our achievements.

Two psychological principles explain why, for all but the very poor, more money buys no more than a temporary surge of happiness and why our emotions seem attached to elastic bands that pull us back from highs or lows. In its own way, each principle suggests that happiness is relative.

Happiness and Prior Experience

The **adaptation-level phenomenon** describes our tendency to judge various stimuli relative to those we have previously experienced. As psychologist Harry Helson (1898–1977) explained, we adjust our *neutral* levels—the points at which sounds seem neither loud nor soft, temperatures neither hot nor cold, events neither pleasant nor unpleasant—based on our experience. We then notice and react to variations up or down from these levels.

"No happiness lasts for long."
Seneca, Agamemnon, A.D. 60

■ **adaptation-level phenomenon** our tendency to form judgments (of sounds, of lights, of income) relative to a neutral level defined by our prior experience.

HI & LOIS

CHANCE BROWNE

"Continued pleasures wear off. . . . Pleasure is always contingent upon change and disappears with continuous satisfaction."

Dutch psychologist Nico Frijda (1988)

"Shortly after I realized I had plenty, I realized there was plenty more."

"I have also learned why people work so hard to succeed: It is because they envy the things their neighbors have. But it is useless. It is like chasing the wind. . . . It is better to have only a little, with peace of mind, than be busy all the time with both hands, trying to catch the wind."

Ecclesiastes 4:4

"Our poverty became a reality. Not because of our having less, but by our neighbors having more."

Will Campbell, *Brother to a Dragonfly,* 1977

■ **relative deprivation** the perception that one is worse off relative to those with whom one compares oneself.

Thus, if our current condition—our income, academic average, or social prestige—increases, we feel an initial surge of pleasure. We then adapt to this new level of achievement, come to consider it as normal, and require something even better to give us another surge of happiness. From my childhood, I can recall the thrill of watching my family's first 12-inch, black-and-white TV. Now, if the color goes out on our 27-inch TV, I feel deprived. Having adapted upward, I perceive as negative what I once experienced as positive. *The point to remember:* Satisfaction and dissatisfaction, success and failure—all are relative to our recent experience. Satisfaction, as Ryan (1999) says, "has a short half-life."

So, could we ever create a permanent social paradise? Social psychologist Donald Campbell (1975) answered no: If you woke up tomorrow to your utopia—perhaps a world with no bills, no ills, perfect scores, someone who loves you unreservedly—you would feel euphoric, for a time. But then you would gradually recalibrate your adaptation level. Before long you would again sometimes feel gratified (when achievements surpass expectations), sometimes feel deprived (when they fall below), and sometimes feel neutral. That helps explain why material wants can be insatiable—why many a child "needs" just one more Nintendo game. When the victor belongs to the spoils and the possessor is possessed by possessions, adaptation level has run amuck.

Seeking happiness through material achievement requires an ever-increasing abundance of things (which means depletion of the Earth's resources). At the end of his *Chronicles of Narnia,* C. S. Lewis depicts heaven as a place where good things do continually increase, where life is a never-ending story "in which every chapter is better than the one before." Here on Earth the unavoidable ups and downs of real life preclude a perpetual high.

Happiness and Others' Attainments

Happiness is relative not only to our past experience but also to our comparisons with others (Lyubomirsky, 2001). We are always comparing ourselves with others. And whether we feel good or bad depends on who those others are. We are slow-witted or clumsy only when others are smart or agile.

Two examples: To explain the frustration expressed by U.S. Air Corps soldiers during World War II, researchers formulated the concept of **relative deprivation**—the sense that we are worse off than others with whom we compare ourselves. Despite a relatively rapid promotion rate for the group, many soldiers were frustrated about their own promotion rates (Merton & Kitt, 1950). Apparently, seeing so many others being promoted inflated the soldiers' expectations. And when expectations soar above attainments, the result is disappointment. Alex Rodriguez's $252 million, 10-year baseball contract surely made him temporarily happy, but it also diminished other star players' satisfaction with their lesser, multimillion-dollar contracts. Likewise, the economic surge that has made some urban Chinese newly affluent may have fueled among others a sense of relative deprivation.

Such comparisons help us understand why the middle- and upper-income people in a given country, who can compare themselves with the relatively poor, tend to be slightly more satisfied with life than their less fortunate compatriots. Nevertheless, once people reach a moderate income level, further increases do little to increase their happiness. Why? Because as people climb the ladder of success they mostly compare themselves with peers who are at or above their current level (Gruder, 1977; Suls & Tesch, 1978). "Beggars do not envy millionaires, though of course they will envy other beggars who are more successful," noted Bertrand Russell (1930, p. 90). Thus, "Napoleon envied Caesar, Caesar envied Alexander, and Alexander, I daresay, envied Hercules, who never existed. You cannot, therefore, get away from envy by means of success alone, for there will always be in history or legend some person even more successful than you are" (pp. 68–69).

Just as comparing ourselves with those who are better off creates envy, so counting our blessings as we compare ourselves with those less well off boosts our contentment. Marshall Dermer and his colleagues (1979) demonstrated this by asking University of Wisconsin-Milwaukee women to study others' deprivation and suffering. After viewing vivid depictions of how grim life was in Milwaukee in 1900, or after imagining and then writing about various personal tragedies, such as being burned and disfigured, the women expressed greater satisfaction with their own lives. Similarly, when mildly depressed people read about someone who is even more depressed, they feel somewhat better (Gibbons, 1986). "I cried because I had no shoes," states a Persian saying, "until I met a man who had no feet."

The effect of comparison with others helps explain why students of a given level of academic ability tend to have a higher academic self-concept if they attend a school where most other students are not exceptionally able (Marsh & Parker, 1984). If you were near the top of your high school class, you might feel inferior upon entering a college where everyone was near the top of their class.

Predictors of Happiness

OBJECTIVE 40-9 | Summarize the ways that we can influence our own levels of happiness.

If, as the adaptation-level phenomenon implies, our emotions tend to balance around normal, why do some people seem so filled with joy and others so gloomy day after day? What makes one person normally happy and another less so? The answers vary somewhat by culture. Self-esteem matters more to individualistic Westerners, social acceptance matters more to those in communal cultures (Diener & others, 2003). But across many countries, research does reveal several predictors of happiness (TABLE 40.2)

© The New Yorker Collection, 1996, J. B. Handelsman from cartoonbank.com. All Rights Reserved.

"I could cry when I think of the years I wasted accumulating money, only to learn that my cheerful disposition is genetic."

Although tasks and relationships affect our happiness, genes matter, too. From their study of 254 identical and fraternal twins, David Lykken and Auke Tellegen (1996) estimated that 50 percent of the difference among people's happiness ratings is heritable. Even identical twins raised apart are often similarly happy. Depending on our outlook and recent experiences, our happiness seems to fluctuate around our "happiness set point," which disposes some people to be ever upbeat and others more negative. But when researchers have followed thousands of lives over two decades, they observe that people's satisfaction with life is not fixed (Fujita & Diener, 2005; Mroczek & Spiro, 2005). Satisfaction may rise or fall, and happiness can be influenced by factors that are under our control. (See Close-Up: How to Be Happier, on the next page.)

Studies of chimpanzees in zoos reveal that happiness in chimpanzees, as rated by 200 employees, is also genetically influenced (Weiss & others, 2000, 2002).

TABLE 40.2

HAPPINESS IS . . .

Researchers Have Found That Happy People Tend To	However, Happiness Seems Not Much Related to Other Factors, Such As
Have high self-esteem (in individualistic countries).	Age.
Be optimistic, outgoing, and agreeable.	Gender (women are more often depressed, but also more often joyful).
Have close friendships or a satisfying marriage.	Education levels.
Have work and leisure that engage their skills.	Parenthood (having children or not).
Have a meaningful religious faith.	Physical attractiveness.
Sleep well and exercise.	

Source: Summarized from DeNeve & Cooper (1998), Diener & others (2003), Lucas & others (2004), Myers (1993, 2000), and Myers & Diener (1995, 1996).

The New Yorker Collection, 2001, Pat Byrnes from cartoonbank.com. All Rights Reserved.

"Researchers say I'm not happier for being richer, but do you know how much researchers make?"

CLOSE-UP:

HOW TO BE HAPPIER

Happiness, like cholesterol level, is genetically influenced. Yet as cholesterol is also influenced by diet and exercise, so our happiness is to some extent under our personal control. Here are some research-based suggestions for improving your mood and increasing your satisfaction with life.

1. ***Realize that enduring happiness doesn't come from financial success.*** People adapt to changing circumstances—even to wealth or a disability. Thus wealth is like health: Its utter absence breeds misery, but having it (or any circumstance we long for) doesn't guarantee happiness.

2. ***Take control of your time.*** Happy people feel in control of their lives, often aided by mastering their use of time. It helps to set goals and break them into daily aims. Although we often overestimate how much we will accomplish in any given day (leaving us frustrated), we generally *underestimate* how much we can accomplish in a year, given just a little progress every day.

3. ***Act happy.*** We can sometimes act ourselves into a frame of mind. Manipulated into a smiling expression, people feel better; when they scowl, the whole world seems to scowl back. So put on a happy face. Talk *as if* you feel positive self-esteem, are optimistic, and are outgoing. Going through the motions can trigger the emotions.

4. ***Seek work and leisure that engage your skills.*** Happy people often are in a zone called "flow"—absorbed in a task that challenges them without overwhelming them. The most expensive forms of leisure (sitting on a yacht) often provide less flow experience than gardening, socializing, or craft work.

5. ***Join the "movement" movement.*** An avalanche of research reveals that aerobic exercise not only promotes health and energy, it also is an antidote for mild depression and anxiety. Sound minds reside in sound bodies. Off your duffs, couch potatoes.

6. ***Give your body the sleep it wants.*** Happy people live active vigorous lives yet reserve time for renewing sleep and solitude. Many people suffer from sleep debt, with resulting fatigue, diminished alertness, and gloomy moods.

7. ***Give priority to close relationships.*** Intimate friendships with those who care deeply about you can help you weather difficult times. Confiding is good for soul and body. Resolve to nurture your closest relationships: to *not* take those closest to you for granted, to display to them the sort of kindness that you display to others, to affirm them, to play together and share together.

8. ***Focus beyond self.*** Reach out to those in need. Happiness increases helpfulness (those who feel good do good). But doing good also makes one feel good.

9. ***Be grateful.*** People who keep a gratitude journal—who pause each day to reflect on some positive aspect of their lives (their health, friends, family, freedom, education, senses, natural surroundings, and so on) experience heightened well-being.

10. ***Nurture your spiritual self.*** For many people, faith provides a support community, a reason to focus beyond self, and a sense of purpose and hope. That helps explain why people active in faith communities report greater than average happiness and often cope well with crisis.

Digested from David G. Myers, *The Pursuit of Happiness* (Avon Books)

FIGURE 40.8
Levels of analysis for the study of emotion
As with other psychological phenomena, researchers explore emotion at biological, psychological, and social-cultural levels.

Biological influences:
• physiological arousal
• evolutionary adaptiveness
• response pathways in the brain
• spillover effect

Psychological influences:
• cognitive labeling
• gender differences

Emotion

Social-cultural influences:
• expressiveness
• presence of others
• cultural expectations

Our studies of happiness, regardless of their source and duration, remind us that emotions combine physiological activation (left hemisphere especially), expressive behaviors (huge smile), and conscious experience, including thoughts (I was so ready for that test) and feelings (pride, satisfaction). Fear, anger, happiness, and so much else have this in common: They are biopsychosocial phenomena (**FIGURE 40.8**). Our genetic predispositions, brain activity, outlooks, experiences, relationships, and cultures jointly form us.

>> LEARNING OUTCOMES

Experienced Emotion

OBJECTIVE 40-1 | **Name several basic emotions, and describe two dimensions psychologists use to differentiate emotions.**

Izard's list of 10 basic emotions includes joy, interest-excitement, surprise, sadness, anger, disgust, contempt, fear, shame, and guilt. Other psychologists include pride and love. Emotions can be placed along two dimensions: *arousal* (high versus low) and *valence* (pleasant, or positive, versus unpleasant, or negative).

OBJECTIVE 40-2 | **State two ways we learn our fears.**

We learn specific fears through *conditioning* (associating emotions with specific situations) and through *observational learning* (watching others display fear in response to certain events or surroundings).

OBJECTIVE 40-3 | **Discuss some of the biological components of fear.**

We are biologically prepared to learn some fears (snakes, spiders) but not others (fast driving, electricity). The amygdala plays a key role in fear learning, associating fear with specific situations. The amygdala receives information from cortical areas that process emotion, and it sends information to other areas that produce the bodily symptoms of fear. We may be genetically predisposed to be fearful or fearless.

OBJECTIVE 40-4 | **Identify some common triggers and consequences of anger, and assess the catharsis hypothesis.**

Frustrating or insulting actions we interpret as willful, unjustified, and avoidable may evoke anger. Research does not support the *catharsis hypothesis*—the idea that releasing negative energy will calm aggressive tendencies. Venting rage may calm us temporarily, but in the long run it may actually amplify anger. Anger is better handled by waiting until the level of physical arousal diminishes, calming oneself, and expressing grievances in ways that promote reconciliation. When reconciliation fails, forgiveness can reduce one's anger and its physical symptoms.

OBJECTIVE 40-5 | **Describe how the feel-good, do-good phenomenon works, and discuss the importance of research on subjective well-being.**

The *feel-good, do-good phenomenon* is our increased willingness to help others when we are in a good mood. Research on the causes and consequences of subjective well-being (self-perceived happiness or satisfaction with life) is supplementing psychology's traditional focus on negative emotions.

OBJECTIVE 40-6 | **Discuss some of the daily and longer-term variations in the duration of emotions.**

Negative emotion is highest just after we wake up and before we go to sleep. Positive emotion rises gradually, peaking about seven hours after we rise, then falls gradually. The moods triggered by the day's good or bad events seldom last beyond that day. Even significant bad events, such as a serious illness, seldom destroy happiness permanently.

OBJECTIVE 40-7 | **Summarize the findings on the relationship between affluence and happiness.**

Money can help us avoid pain (and thereby increase happiness) by enabling better nutrition, health care, education, and science. Increases in wealth can also increase happiness in the short term, but in the longer term, affluence does not increase happiness at either the individual or national level.

OBJECTIVE 40-8 | **Describe how adaptation and relative deprivation affect our appraisals of our achievements.**

The *adaptation-level phenomenon* is our tendency to assess stimuli (including material possessions) by contrasting them with a neutral level that changes with our experience. The *relative-deprivation principle* is our perception that we are less well off than others with whom we compare ourselves. Thus, happiness is relative to both our past experience and our comparisons with others.

OBJECTIVE 40-9 | **Summarize the ways that we can influence our own levels of happiness.**

Happiness is in part genetically influenced, and in part under our own control. Research-based suggestions for improving our own happiness are (1) realizing that enduring happiness doesn't come from financial success; (2) taking control of one's time; (3) acting happy; (4) seeking work and leisure that engage one's skills; (5) exercising regularly; (6) getting adequate sleep; (7) giving priority to close relationships; (8) focusing beyond oneself; (9) being grateful for what we have; and (10) nurturing our spiritual selves.

TERMS AND CONCEPTS TO REMEMBER

catharsis, p. 40-5

feel-good, do-good phenomenon, p. 40-6

subjective well-being, p. 40-7

adaptation-level phenomenon, p. 40-11

relative deprivation, p. 40-12

TEST YOURSELF

1. What things do (and do not) predict self-reported happiness?

(Answer in Appendix B.)

ASK YOURSELF

1. If we learn our emotional responses, we may be able to learn new responses to replace old ones. Would you like to change any of your emotional responses? Do you feel you are too easily provoked to anger or fear, for instance? How might you go about changing your behavior or your thinking in order to change your emotional reactions?

>WEB

Multiple-choice **self-tests** and more may be found at www.worthpublishers.com/myers.

ANOTHER VOICE ON: STRESS AND HEALTH

AUDRE LORDE (1934–1992), "LATER," FROM *THE CANCER JOURNALS*, 1980

October 5, 1978

If I said this all didn't matter I would be lying. I see this as a serious break in my work/living, but also as a serious chance to learn something that I can share for use. And I mourn the women who limit their loss to the physical loss alone, who do not move into the whole terrible meaning of mortality as both weapon and power. After all, what could we possibly be afraid of after having admitted to ourselves that we had dealt face to face with death and not embraced it? For once we accept the actual existence of our dying, who can ever have power over us again? Now I am anxious for more living—to sample and partake of the sweetness of each moment . . .

Stress and Health

OBJECTIVE 41-1 | Identify some behavior-related causes of illness and death, and describe health psychology's contribution to the field of behavioral medicine.

No one needs to be told that psychological states cause physical reactions. Nervous about an important encounter, we feel stomach butterflies. Anxious over speaking in public, we frequent the bathroom. Smoldering over a conflict with a family member, we get a splitting headache.

If such stress endures, it may also bring on (in those physiologically predisposed) skin rashes, asthma attacks, or high blood pressure. This mind-body connection was strikingly apparent in an inadvertent experiment conducted by British Airways on an April 23, 1999, flight from San Francisco to London. Three hours after takeoff, a mistakenly played message told passengers the plane was about to crash into the sea. Although the flight crew immediately recognized the error and tried to calm the terrified passengers, several required medical assistance (Associated Press, 1999).

Prolonged stress—together with unhealthy behaviors—can put us at serious risk. Centers for Disease Control researchers have attributed half of the deaths in the United States to people's behavior—to cigarette smoking, alcohol abuse, unprotected sex, ignoring doctors' orders, insufficient exercise, illicit drugs, and poor nutrition (Mokdad & others, 2004). Modify these behavioral sources of illness and we might lessen suffering, increase life expectancy, and enhance quality of life. To pursue these goals, psychologists and physicians created the interdisciplinary field of **behavioral medicine,** integrating behavioral and medical knowledge.

Health psychology provides psychology's contribution to behavioral medicine. Its numbers include many of the 3900 psychologists who were recently counted on the faculties of Canadian and U.S. medical schools (Williams & Kohut, 1999). In the early 1950s, the average medical school had 2 faculty psychologists; at the century's end, each averaged about 30 (Sheridan, 1999).

For psychologists, health is more than "merely the slowest possible rate at which one can die" (Prairie Home Companion, 1999). Health psychologists ask: How do our emotions, personality, attitudes, and behaviors influence our risk of disease (Module 41)? How can we better cope with stress to prevent illness and promote health and well-being, and how do our perceptions of a situation determine the stress we feel (Module 42)? How can we reduce our vulnerability to stress- and behavior-related health problems (Module 43)?

■ **behavioral medicine** an interdisciplinary field that integrates behavioral and medical knowledge and applies that knowledge to health and disease.

■ **health psychology** the application of psychological concepts and research to illness prevention and treatment and to health advancement.

Stress and Illness

Walking along the path toward his mountain campsite, Karl hears a rustle at his feet. As he glimpses a rattlesnake, his body mobilizes: His muscles tense, his adrenaline flows, his heart pounds, and he flees, racing to the security of camp. Once there, Karl's muscles gradually relax and his heart rate and breathing ease.

At about the same time, Karen leaves her suburban apartment and, delayed by road construction, arrives at the parking lot of the commuter train station just in time to see the 8:05 pull away. Catching the next train, she arrives in the city late and elbows her way through crowds of rush-hour pedestrians. Once at her bank office, she apologizes to her first client, who wonders where Karen has been and why his quarterly investment report is not ready. Karen does her best to mollify the client. Afterward, she notices her tense muscles, clenched teeth, and churning stomach.

Karl's response to stress saved his life; Karen's, if chronic, could increase her risk of serious illness or stress-linked health problems. Moreover, feeling under pressure, she might sleep and exercise less and smoke and drink more, further endangering her long-term health.

Stress and Stressors

OBJECTIVE 41-2 | Discuss the role of appraisal in the way we respond to stressful events.

Four in 10 people frequently report experiencing stress (Saad, 2001). What are they talking about? Stress is a slippery concept. It sometimes describes threats or challenges ("Karen was under a lot of stress"), other times our responses ("When Karl saw the rattler, he experienced acute stress"). Karen's missed train was a *stressor,* Karl's physical and emotional responses were a *stress reaction,* and the process by which Karen and Karl related to their environments was *stress.*

Thus, **stress** is not just a stimulus or a response. It is the process by which we appraise and cope with environmental threats and challenges (**FIGURE 41.1**). Stress arises less from events themselves than from how we appraise them (Lazarus, 1998). One person, alone in a house, dismisses its creaking sounds and experiences no stress; someone else suspects an intruder and becomes alarmed. One person regards a new job as a welcome challenge; someone else appraises it as risking failure.

FIGURE 41.1
Stress appraisal
The events of our lives flow through a psychological filter. How we appraise an event influences how much stress we experience and how effectively we respond.

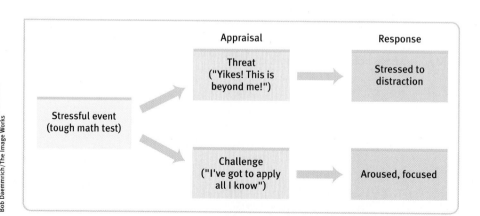

When short-lived, or when perceived as challenges, stressors can have positive effects. A momentary stress can mobilize the immune system for fending off infections and healing wounds (Segerstrom & Miller, 2004). Stress also arouses and motivates us to conquer problems. Championship athletes, successful entertainers, and great teachers and leaders all thrive and excel when aroused by a challenge (Blascovich & others, 2004). Having conquered cancer or rebounded from a lost job, some people emerge with stronger self-esteem and a deepened spirituality and sense of purpose. Indeed, some stress early in life is conducive to later emotional resilience and physical growth (Landauer & Whiting, 1979). Adversity can beget growth. The Chinese character for *crisis*, note Virginia O'Leary and Jeannette Ickovics (1995), combines the symbols for *danger* and *opportunity*.

But stressors can also threaten us. And experiencing severe or prolonged stress may harm us. Children's physiological responses to severe child abuse put them at later risk of chronic disease (Repetti & others, 2002). Those who had post-traumatic stress reactions to heavy combat in the Vietnam War went on to suffer greatly elevated rates of circulatory, digestive, respiratory, and infectious diseases (Boscarino, 1997).

The Stress Response System

OBJECTIVE 41-3 | Describe the dual-track system by which our body responds to stress, and identify the three phases of the general adaptation syndrome.

Medical interest in stress dates back to Hippocrates (460–377 B.C.). But it was not until the 1920s that physiologist Walter Cannon (1929) confirmed that the stress response is part of a unified mind-body system. He observed that extreme cold, lack of oxygen, and emotion-arousing incidents all trigger an outpouring of the stress hormones epinephrine and norepinephrine from the adrenal glands. This outpouring is but one part of the sympathetic nervous system's response. When alerted by any of a number of brain pathways, the sympathetic nervous system increases heart rate and respiration, diverts blood from digestion to the skeletal muscles, dulls pain, and releases sugar and fat from the body's stores—all to prepare the body for the wonderfully adaptive response that Cannon called *fight or flight*.

Since Cannon's time, physiologists have identified an additional stress response system. On orders from the cerebral cortex (via the hypothalamus and pituitary gland), the outer part of the adrenal glands secretes *glucocorticoid* stress hormones such as *cortisol*. The two stress hormone systems work at different speeds, explains biologist Robert Sapolsky (2003): "In a fight-or-flight scenario, epinephrine is the one handing out guns; glucocorticoids are the ones drawing up blueprints for new aircraft carriers needed for the war effort" (FIGURE **41.2**).

There are alternatives to fight-or-flight. One is a common response to the stress of a loved one's death: Withdraw. Pull back. Conserve energy. Another, especially common among women, report Shelley Taylor and her colleagues (2000), is to seek and give support: "Tend and befriend."

■ **stress** the process by which we perceive and respond to certain events, called *stressors*, that we appraise as threatening or challenging.

FIGURE **41.2**
Two-track stress response system
Our body responds to stress with a two-track system. (1) The sympathetic nervous system prompts the release of the stress hormones epinephrine and norepinephrine from nerve endings in the *inner* part of the adrenal glands. (2) The cerebral cortex, by way of the hypothalamus and pituitary gland, directs the release of glucocorticoid stress hormones from the *outer* part of the adrenal glands. Both systems trigger fight-or-flight physiological effects in our bodies, such as faster breathing and tense muscles.

(2) Cerebral cortex orchestrates release of glucocorticoids

Cerebral cortex (perceives stressor)

Hypothalamus
Amygdala
Pituitary gland

(1) Sympathetic nervous system triggers release of epinephrine and norepinephrine.

Arteries widen

Lungs work faster

Heart beats faster

Muscles tense

Adrenal glands release hormones

Stomach, digestion shuts down

Canadian scientist Hans Selye's (1936, 1976) 40 years of research on stress extended Cannon's findings and helped make stress a major concept in both psychology and medicine. The story of how Selye arrived at his concept of the stress response is one worth remembering in times of intellectual discouragement. Hoping to discover a new sex hormone, Selye injected rats with ovarian hormone extract. He detected three effects: enlargement of the adrenal cortex, shrinkage of the thymus gland (which contains disease-fighting white blood cells), and bleeding ulcers. Because no known hormone had ever produced such symptoms, Selye was elated: "At the age of 28, I seemed to be already on the track of a new hormone."

Before long, Selye's elation turned to disappointment. When he injected the rats with other fluids, he observed the same effects: adrenal enlargement, thymus shrinkage, and bleeding ulcers. Alas, he concluded, the effects were *not* due to a new hormone:

> All my dreams of discovering a new hormone were shattered. All the time and all the materials that went into this long study were wasted. . . . I became so depressed that for a few days I could not do any work at all. I just sat in my laboratory, brooding. . . . The ensuing period of introverted contemplation turned out to be the decisive factor in my whole career; it pointed the way for all my subsequent work. . . . As I repetitiously continued to go over my ill-fated experiments and their possible interpretation, it suddenly struck me that one could look at them from an entirely different angle. If there was such a thing as a single nonspecific reaction of the body to damage of any kind, . . . the general medical implications of the syndrome would be enormous! (1976, pp. 24–26)

To verify his hunch, Selye studied animals' reactions to various other stressors, such as electric shock, surgical trauma, and immobilizing restraint. He discovered that the body's adaptive response to stress was so general—like a single burglar alarm that sounds no matter what intrudes—that he called it the **general adaptation syndrome (GAS).**

Selye saw the GAS as having three phases (**FIGURE 41.3**). Let's say you suffer a physical or emotional trauma. In Phase 1, you experience an *alarm reaction* due to the sudden activation of your sympathetic nervous system. Your heart rate zooms. Blood is diverted to your skeletal muscles. You feel the faintness of shock. With your resources mobilized, you are now ready to fight the challenge during Phase 2, *resistance*. Your temperature, blood pressure, and respiration remain high, and there is a sudden outpouring of hormones. If persistent, the stress may eventually deplete your body's

FIGURE 41.3
Selye's general adaptation syndrome
This girl being carried to freedom and medical attention managed to escape her terrorist captors in a 2004, three-day Chechnya school holdup. Experiencing such a trauma, the body enters an alarm phase of temporary shock. From this it rebounds, as stress resistance rises. If the stress is prolonged, as it was for the 400 school hostages and their waiting loved ones, wear and tear may lead to exhaustion.

EPA/Yuri Kochetkov/Landov

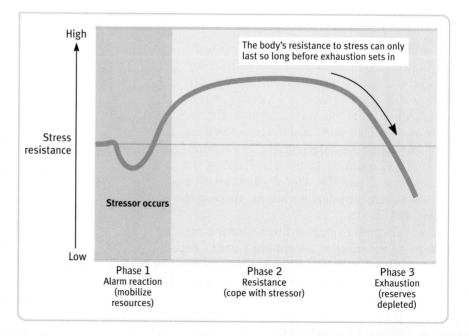

The body's resistance to stress can only last so long before exhaustion sets in

Stress resistance

High

Low

Stressor occurs

Phase 1
Alarm reaction
(mobilize resources)

Phase 2
Resistance
(cope with stressor)

Phase 3
Exhaustion
(reserves depleted)

reserves during Phase 3, *exhaustion*. With exhaustion, you are more vulnerable to illness or even, in extreme cases, collapse and death.

Few medical experts today quarrel with Selye's basic point: Although the human body comes designed to cope with temporary stress, prolonged stress can produce physical deterioration. In one recent study, women who suffered enduring stress as caregivers for children with serious disorders displayed a symptom that is a normal part of the aging process—shorter bits of DNA at the ends of their chromosomes (Epel & others, 2004). When these DNA pieces, called *telomeres,* get too short, the cell can no longer divide, and it ultimately dies. The most stressed women had cells that looked a decade older than their chronological age, which may help explain why severe stress seems to age people. Even fearful, easily stressed rats have been found to die sooner (after about 600 days) than their more confident siblings, which average 700-day life spans (Cavigelli & McClintock, 2003).

Other studies have taken MRI brain scans of people who have experienced a prolonged flood of stress hormones, due to sustained child abuse, combat, or an endocrine disease (Sapolsky, 1999). Most have a shrunken *hippocampus,* the inner brain structure vital to laying down explicit (declarative) memories. In animals, too, various stresses—being subordinate in a group, being physically restrained, being isolated—can cause hippocampal tissue to shrink (McEwen, 1998, 2002). Such findings serve as further incentives to today's *health psychologists,* who have joined with physicians to create the interdisciplinary field of *behavioral medicine.* Health psychologists are actively exploring such questions as What causes stress? And how does stress affect us?

Stressful Life Events

OBJECTIVE 41-4 | Discuss the health consequences of catastrophes, significant life changes, and daily hassles.

Research has focused on our responses to three types of stressors: catastrophes, significant life changes, and daily hassles.

Catastrophes

Catastrophes are unpredictable large-scale events, such as war and natural disasters, that nearly everyone appraises as threatening. Although people often provide one another with aid as well as comfort after such events, the health consequences can be significant. In the three weeks after the 9/11 terrorist attacks, two-thirds of Americans surveyed by University of Michigan researchers said they were having some trouble concentrating and sleeping (Wahlberg, 2001). In another national survey, New Yorkers were especially likely to report such symptoms (NSF, 2001). Sleeping pill prescriptions rose by a reported 28 percent in the New York area (HMHL, 2002).

> **general adaptation syndrome (GAS)** Selye's concept of the body's adaptive response to stress in three stages—alarm, resistance, exhaustion.

Les Stone/Corbis

Toxic stress
On the day of its 1994 earthquake, Los Angeles experienced a fivefold increase in sudden-death heart attacks—especially in the first two hours after the quake and near its epicenter. Physical exertion (running, lifting debris) was a factor in only 13 percent of the deaths, leaving stress as the likely trigger for the others (Muller & Verier, 1996).

■ **coronary heart disease** the clogging of the vessels that nourish the heart muscle; the leading cause of death in many developed countries.

Do other community disasters usually produce effects this great? After digesting data from 52 studies of catastrophic floods, hurricanes, and fires, Anthony Rubonis and Leonard Bickman (1991) found the typical effect more modest but nonetheless genuine. In disaster's wake, rates of psychological disorders such as depression and anxiety rose an average 17 percent. Refugees fleeing their homeland also suffer increased rates of psychological disorder. Their stress stems from the trauma of uprooting and family separation, and from the challenges of adjusting to a foreign culture's new language, ethnicity, climate, and social norms (Pipher, 2002; Williams & Berry, 1991).

Significant Life Changes

The second type of life-event stressor is a significant personal life change—leaving home, the death of a loved one, the loss of a job, a marriage, a divorce. Life transitions and insecurities are often keenly felt during young adulthood. That helps explain why, when 15,000 Canadian adults were asked whether "You are trying to take on too many things at once," responses indicated highest stress levels among the youngest adults (**FIGURE 41.4**). The same is true of Americans: Half of adults under age 50 report "frequent" stress, as do fewer than 30 percent of those over 50 (Saad, 2001).

Some psychologists study the health effects of life changes by following people over time to see if such events precede illnesses. Others compare the life changes recalled by those who have or have not suffered a specific health problem, such as a heart attack. A review of these studies commissioned by the U.S. National Academy of Sciences revealed that people recently widowed, fired, or divorced are more vulnerable to disease (Dohrenwend & others, 1982). A Finnish study of 96,000 widowed people confirmed the phenomenon: Their risk of death doubled in the week following their partner's death (Kaprio & others, 1987). Experiencing a cluster of crises puts one even more at risk.

Daily Hassles

Our happiness stems less from enduring good fortune than from our response to daily events—a perfect exam score, a gratifying e-mail, your team's winning the big game. This principle works for negative events, too. Everyday annoyances—rush-hour traffic, aggravating housemates, long lines at the store, too many things to do, e-mail spam, and obnoxious cell-phone talkers—may be the most significant sources of stress (Kohn & Macdonald, 1992; Lazarus, 1990; Ruffin, 1993). Although some people can simply shrug off such hassles, others are "driven up the wall" by them.

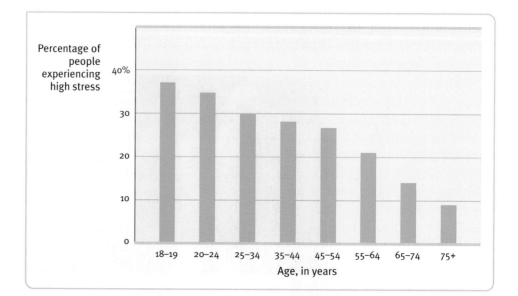

FIGURE 41.4
Chronic stress, by age
As Canadians age, feelings of chronic stress tend to subside. (Data from Statistics Canada, 1999.)

Over time, these little stressors can add up and take a toll on our health and well-being. Hypertension (high blood pressure) rates are high among residents of urban ghettos, where the stresses that accompany poverty, unemployment, solo parenting, and overcrowding are part of daily life for some people. And these daily pressures may be compounded by racism, which—like other stressors—can have both psychological and physical consequences. Thinking that some of the people you encounter each day will distrust you, dislike you, or doubt your abilities makes daily life stressful. Rodney Clark and his colleagues (1999) found that this stress took a toll on the health of many African-Americans, driving up blood pressure levels.

"It's not the large things that send a man to the madhouse . . . no, it's the continuing series of small tragedies . . . not the death of his love but the shoelace that snaps with no time left."

Charles Bukowski, cited by Lazarus in Wallis, 1983

Stress and the Heart

OBJECTIVE 41-5 | Discuss the role of stress in causing coronary heart disease, and contrast Type A and Type B personalities.

In the past century, behavior-related illnesses have emerged as the major causes of death. Stress, it seems, can put us at risk for one of today's four leading causes of serious illness and death: heart disease, cancer, stroke, and chronic lung disease (FIGURE 41.5).

Elevated blood pressure is just one of the factors that increase the risk of **coronary heart disease,** the closing of the vessels that nourish the heart muscle. Although infrequent before 1900, this condition became by the 1950s North America's leading cause of death, and it remains so today. In addition to hypertension and a family history of the disease, many behavioral and physiological factors—smoking, obesity, a high-fat diet, physical inactivity, and an elevated cholesterol level—increase the risk of heart disease. The psychological factors of stress and personality also play a big role.

In 1956, cardiologists Meyer Friedman, Ray Rosenman, and their colleagues stumbled upon an indication of how big that role is (Friedman & Ulmer, 1984). While studying the eating behavior of San Francisco Junior League women and their husbands, Friedman and Rosenman discovered that the women consumed as much cholesterol and fat as their husbands did, yet they were far less susceptible to heart disease. Was it because of their female sex hormones? No, the researchers surmised, because African-American women (with the same sex hormones but facing more stress than the white Junior Leaguers) were as prone to heart disease as their husbands.

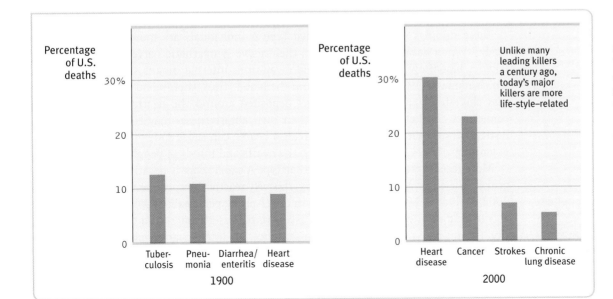

FIGURE 41.5
The four leading causes of death in the United States in 1900 and 2000 With the conquering of the major infectious diseases, diseases influenced by behavior have now emerged as the major causes of death. The story is much the same in Canada, Australia, New Zealand, and most European countries. (From National Center for Health Statistics, *World Health Statistics Annual,* and Statistics Canada, 2002.)

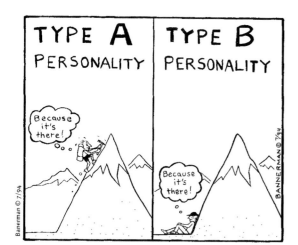

In both India and America, Type A bus drivers are literally hard-driving: They brake, pass, and honk their horns more often than their more easygoing Type B colleagues (Evans & others, 1987).

"The fire you kindle for your enemy often burns you more than him."

Chinese proverb

The Junior League president thought she knew the answer: "It's the stress they have to face in their businesses, day in, day out," she said sadly. "Why, when my husband comes home at night, it takes at least one martini just to unclench his jaws."

To test the idea that stress increases vulnerability to heart disease, Friedman and Rosenman measured the blood cholesterol level and clotting speed of 40 tax accountants. From January through March, both of these coronary warning indicators were completely normal. Then, as the accountants began scrambling to finish their clients' tax returns before the April 15 filing deadline, their cholesterol and clotting measures rose to dangerous levels. In May and June, with the deadline past, the measures returned to normal. The researchers' hunch had paid off: Stress predicted heart attack risk.

The stage was set for Friedman and Rosenman's classic nine-year study of more than 3000 healthy men aged 35 to 59. At the start of the study, they interviewed each man for 15 minutes about his work and eating habits. During the interview, they noted the man's manner of talking and other behavioral patterns. Those who seemed the most reactive, competitive, hard-driving, impatient, time-conscious, supermotivated, verbally aggressive, and easily angered they called **Type A.** The roughly equal number who were more easygoing they called **Type B.** Which group do you suppose turned out to be the most coronary-prone?

By the time the study was complete, 257 men had suffered heart attacks; 69 percent of them were Type A. Moreover, not one of the "pure" Type Bs—the most mellow and laid-back of their group—had suffered a heart attack.

As often happens in science, this exciting discovery provoked enormous public interest. But after the honeymoon period, in which the finding seemed definitive and revolutionary, other researchers began asking: Is the finding reliable? If so, what is the toxic component of the Type A profile: Time-consciousness? Competitiveness? Anger?

In relaxed situations, the arousal of Type As and Type Bs is no different. But when harassed, given a challenge, or threatened with a loss of control, Type A individuals are more physiologically reactive. Their hormonal secretions, pulse rate, and blood pressure soar, while Type Bs remain calm (Lyness, 1993). For example, when Redford Williams (1989) asked Duke University men to do simple math problems (with a prize for the fastest), the Type A students' stress-hormone levels rose to more than double those of their Type B classmates. These hormones accelerate the buildup of plaque (scarlike masses formed by cholesterol deposits) on the artery walls. And that produces atherosclerosis ("hardening" of the arteries), high blood pressure, and increased risk of strokes and heart attacks (Schneiderman & others, 1989).

These findings suggest that reactive Type A individuals are more often "combat ready." When harassed or challenged, their active sympathetic nervous system redistributes bloodflow to the muscles and away from internal organs such as the liver, which removes cholesterol and fat from the blood. Thus, their blood may contain excess cholesterol and fat that later get deposited around the heart. Further stress—sometimes conflicts brought on by their own abrasiveness—may trigger the altered heart rhythms that, in those with weakened hearts, can cause sudden death (Kamarck & Jennings, 1991). In important ways, the hearts and minds of people interact.

More recent research has revealed that Type A's toxic core is negative emotions—especially the anger associated with an aggressively reactive temperament (Smith & Ruiz, 2002; Williams, 1993). The effect of an anger-prone personality appears most noticeably in studies in which interviewers assess verbal assertiveness and emotional intensity. (If you pause in the middle of a sentence, an intense, anger-prone person may jump in and finish it for you.) Among young and middle-aged adults, those who react with anger over little things are the most coronary-prone. One study followed 13,000 middle-aged people for five years. Among those with normal blood pressure, people who had scored high on anger were three times more likely to have had heart attacks, even after researchers controlled for smoking and weight (Williams & others, 2000). Another study followed 1055 male medical students over an average of 36 years. Those who had reported being hot-tempered were five times more likely to have had a heart at-

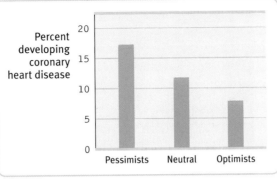

FIGURE 41.6
Pessimism and heart disease
A Harvard School of Public Health team found pessimistic adult men at doubled risk of developing heart disease over a 10-year period. (From Kubzansky & others, 2001.)

tack by age 55 (Chang & others, 2002). As Charles Spielberger and Perry London (1982) put it, rage "seems to lash back and strike us in the heart muscle."

Pessimism seems to be similarly toxic. Laura Kubzansky and her colleagues (2001) studied 1306 initially healthy men who a decade earlier had scored as optimists, pessimists, or neither. Over the decade, pessimists were more than twice as likely as optimists to develop heart disease, even after other risk factors such as smoking had been ruled out (**FIGURE 41.6**).

Depression, too, can be lethal. The accumulated evidence from 57 studies suggests that "depression substantially increases the risk of death, especially death by unnatural causes and cardiovascular disease" (Wulsin & others, 1999). One study of 7406 women age 67 or older found that among those with no depressive symptoms, 7 percent died within six years, as did 24 percent of those with six or more depressive symptoms (Whooley & Browner, 1998). In the years following a heart attack, people with high scores for depression are four times likelier than their low-scoring counterparts to develop further heart problems (Frasure-Smith & Lespérance, 2005). Depression is disheartening.

> "A cheerful heart is a good medicine, but a downcast spirit dries up the bones."
> Proverbs 17:22

Stress and Susceptibility to Disease

OBJECTIVE 41-6 | Distinguish between a psychophysiological illness and hypochondriasis.

Not so long ago, the term *psychosomatic* described psychologically caused physical symptoms. To laypeople, the term implied that the symptoms were unreal—"merely" psychosomatic. To avoid such connotations and to better describe the genuine physiological effects of psychological states, most experts today refer instead to stress-related **psychophysiological illnesses,** such as hypertension and some headaches. Let's take a closer look at some ways stress also affects our resistance to disease.

Stress and the Immune System

OBJECTIVE 41-7 | Describe the effect of stress on immune system functioning.

Hundreds of new experiments reveal the nervous and endocrine systems' influence on the immune system (Sternberg, 2001). Your immune system is a complex surveillance system that defends your body by isolating and destroying bacteria, viruses, and other foreign substances. This system includes two types of white blood cells, called **lymphocytes.** *B lymphocytes* form in the *bone* marrow and release antibodies that fight bacterial infections. *T lymphocytes* form in the *thymus* and other lymphatic tissue and attack cancer cells, viruses, and foreign substances—even "good" ones, such as transplanted organs. Another agent of the immune system is the *macrophage* ("big eater"), which identifies, pursues, and ingests harmful invaders (**FIGURE 41.7** on the next page). Age, nutrition, genetics, body temperature, and stress all influence the immune system's activity.

■ **Type A** Friedman and Rosenman's term for competitive, hard-driving, impatient, verbally aggressive, and anger-prone people.

■ **Type B** Friedman and Rosenman's term for easygoing, relaxed people.

■ **psychophysiological illness** literally, "mind-body" illness; any stress-related physical illness, such as hypertension and some headaches. *Note:* This is distinct from *hypochondriasis*—misinterpreting normal physical sensations as symptoms of a disease.

■ **lymphocytes** the two types of white blood cells that are part of the body's immune system: *B lymphocytes* form in the *bone* marrow and release antibodies that fight bacterial infections; *T lymphocytes* form in the *thymus* and other lymphatic tissue and attack cancer cells, viruses, and foreign substances.

FIGURE 41.7
The immune system in action
A large macrophage (at top) is about to trap and ingest a tiny bacterium (lower right). Macrophages constantly patrol our bodies in search of invaders—such as this *Escherichia coli* bacterium—and debris, such as worn-out red blood cells.

"In the eyes of God or biology or what have you, it is just very important to have women."

Immunologist Normal Talal (1995)

Your immune system can err in two directions. Responding too strongly, it may attack the body's own tissues, causing arthritis or an allergic reaction. Underreacting, it may allow a dormant herpes virus to erupt or cancer cells to multiply. Women are immunologically stronger than men (Morell, 1995), making them less susceptible to infections. But this very strength also makes them more susceptible to self-attacking diseases, such as lupus and multiple sclerosis.

Your immune system is not a headless horseman. The brain regulates the secretion of stress hormones, which suppress the disease-fighting lymphocytes. Thus, when animals are physically restrained, given unavoidable electric shocks, or subjected to noise, crowding, cold water, social defeat, or maternal separation, their immune systems become less active (Maier & others, 1994). One study monitored immune responses in 43 monkeys over six months (Cohen & others, 1992). Twenty-one were stressed by being housed with new roommates—three or four new monkeys—each month. (To empathize with the monkeys, recall the stress of leaving home to attend school or summer camp, and imagine having to repeat this experience monthly.) Compared with monkeys left in stable groups, the socially disrupted monkeys experienced weakened immune systems. Stress similarly depresses the immune system of humans. Consider:

- Surgical wounds heal more slowly in stressed animals and humans. In one experiment, dental students received *punch wounds* (precise small holes punched in the skin). Compared with wounds placed during summer vacation, those placed three days before a major exam healed 40 percent more slowly. In fact, report Janice Kiecolt-Glaser and her co-researchers (1998), "no student healed as rapidly during this stressful period as during vacation."

- In another experiment, 47 percent of participants living stress-filled lives developed colds after a virus was dropped in their noses, as did only 27 percent of those living relatively free of stress (**FIGURE 41.8**). In follow-up research, the happiest and most relaxed people were likewise markedly less vulnerable to an experimentally delivered cold virus (Cohen & others, 2003).

FIGURE 41.8
Stress and colds
In an experiment by Sheldon Cohen and colleagues (1991), people with the highest life stress scores were also most vulnerable when exposed to an experimentally delivered cold virus.

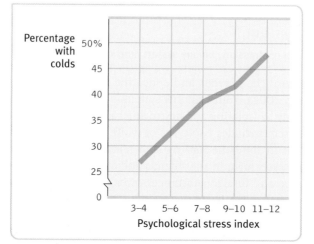

- Data combined from 23 studies reveal that family caregivers of people with dementia exhibit a 15 percent below-normal immune antibody response and a 23 percent increase in stress hormones (Vitaliano & others, 2003). Other data, assembled from 293 studies, confirm that chronic stress causes wear and tear on the immune system (Segerstrom & Miller, 2004).
- Managing stress may be life-sustaining. The one personality trait shared by 169 centenarians (people over 100) was their ability to manage stress well (Perls & others, 1999).

The stress effect on immunity makes physiological sense (Maier & others, 1994). It takes energy to fight infections, produce inflammations, and maintain fevers. Thus, when diseased, our bodies reduce muscular energy output by inactivity and increased sleep. But stress creates a competing energy need. Stress triggers an aroused fight-or-flight response, diverting energy from the disease-fighting system to the muscles and brain, rendering us more vulnerable to illness. The bottom line: Stress does not make us sick, but it does restrain our immune functioning, making us more vulnerable to foreign invaders.

"When the heart is at ease, the body is healthy."

Chinese proverb

Stress and AIDS

OBJECTIVE 41-8 | Discuss the findings on the link between stress and AIDS.

AIDS has become the world's fourth leading cause of death and the number one killer in Africa. AIDS, as its name tells us, is an immune disorder—an *acquired immune deficiency syndrome* caused by the *human immunodeficiency virus (HIV)*, which is spread by the exchange of bodily fluids, primarily semen and blood. If a disease spread by human contact kills slowly, as does HIV, it ironically can be lethal to more people: Those who carry the disease have time to spread it, often without realizing they are infected. When the HIV infection manifests itself as AIDS, some years after the initial infection, the person has difficulty fighting off other diseases, such as pneumonia. Worldwide, reports the United Nations, more than 25 million people have died of AIDS, including 3.1 million in 2005 (UNAIDS, 2005). (In the United States, where "only" a half-million of these fatalities have occurred, AIDS has killed more people than did combat in all the twentieth-century wars.) In 2005, some 40 million—half of them women—were infected with HIV, often without their awareness (UNAIDS, 2005). In Africa, which is ground zero for AIDS, UNAIDS (2005) warns, more than 80 million AIDS deaths are possible by 2025.

In North America and Western Europe, 75 percent of people with AIDS are men. In sub-Saharan Africa, 60 percent of people with AIDS are women (and among 15- to 24-year-olds, 75 percent are women). Girls' thin layer of cervical cells makes them especially vulnerable (Altman, 2004; UNAIDS, 2005).

So if stress serves to suppress immune functioning, could it also exacerbate the course of AIDS? Researchers have found that stress and negative emotions do correlate with a progression from HIV infection to AIDS and with the speed of decline in those infected (Bower & others, 1998; Kiecolt-Glaser & Glaser, 1995; Leserman & others, 1999). HIV-infected men faced with stressful life circumstances, such as the loss of a partner, exhibit somewhat greater immune suppression and a faster disease progression.

Would efforts to reduce stress help control the disease? Although the benefits are small compared with available drug treatments, the answer appears again to be yes. Educational initiatives, bereavement support groups, cognitive therapy, and exercise programs that reduce distress have all had positive consequences for HIV-positive individuals (Baum & Posluszny, 1999; Schneiderman, 1999). Better yet is preventing HIV infection, which is the focus of many educational programs, such as the ABC (abstinence, being faithful, condom use) program used in many countries, with notable success in Uganda (Altman, 2004; USAID, 2004).

Africa is ground zero for AIDS
Lesotho and other African countries have publicized the "ABC" campaign—Abstinence, Be Faithful, and use Condoms.

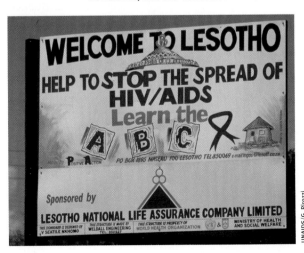

Stress and Cancer

OBJECTIVE 41-9 | Discuss the findings on the link between stress and cancer.

Stress and negative emotions have also been linked to cancer's rate of progression. To explore a possible connection between stress and cancer, experimenters have implanted tumor cells into rodents or given them *carcinogens* (cancer-producing substances). Those rodents also exposed to uncontrollable stress, such as inescapable shocks, were more prone to cancer (Sklar & Anisman, 1981). In rodents with immune systems weakened by stress, tumors developed sooner and grew larger.

Some investigators have reported that people are at increased risk for cancer within a year after experiencing depression, helplessness, or bereavement. One large Swedish study revealed that people with a history of workplace stress had 5.5 times greater risk of colon cancer than those who reported no such problems, a difference not attributable to differing age, smoking, drinking, or physical characteristics (Courtney & others, 1993). Other researchers have found no link between stress and human cancer (Edelman & Kidman, 1997; Fox, 1998; Petticrew & others, 1999, 2002). Concentration camp survivors and former prisoners of war, for example, have not exhibited elevated cancer rates.

One danger in hyping reports on attitudes and cancer is that some patients may be led to blame themselves for their illness—"If only I had been more expressive, relaxed, and hopeful." A corollary danger is a "wellness macho" among the healthy, who take credit for their "healthy character" and lay a guilt trip on the ill: "She has cancer? That's what you get for holding your feelings in and being so nice." Dying thus becomes the ultimate failure.

The emerging view seems to be that stress does not create cancer cells. At worst, it may affect their growth by weakening the body's natural defenses against a few proliferating, malignant cells. Although a relaxed, hopeful state may enhance these defenses, we should be aware of the thin line that divides science from wishful thinking. The powerful biological processes at work in advanced cancer or AIDS are not likely to be derailed by avoiding stress or maintaining a relaxed but determined spirit (Anderson, 2002; Kessler & others, 1991).

"I didn't give myself cancer."
Mayor Barbara Boggs Sigmund, 1939–1990, Princeton, New Jersey

When organic causes of illness are unknown, it is tempting to invent psychological explanations. Before the germ that causes tuberculosis was discovered, personality explanations of TB were popular (Sontag, 1978).

Conditioning the Immune System

OBJECTIVE 41-10 | Describe the impact of learning on immune system functioning.

A seasonal allergy sufferer sees a flower on a restaurant table and, not realizing it is plastic, begins to sneeze. Such experiences hint that stress is not the only psychological influence on the body's ailments. Simple classical conditioning may be an added influence. This raises an intriguing question: If conditioning affects the body's overt physiological responses, might it affect the immune system as well?

Psychologist Robert Ader and immunologist Nicholas Cohen (1985) discovered that the answer is yes. Ader came upon this discovery while researching taste aversion in rats. He paired the rats' drinking of saccharin-sweetened water with injections of a drug that suppresses immune functioning. After repeated pairings, sweetened water alone triggered immune suppression, as if the drug had been given (**FIGURE 41.9**). Such conditioned immune suppression can triple an animal's likelihood of growing a tumor when fed a carcinogen (Blom & others, 1995).

Many questions about the role of the immune system and ways to harness its healing potential remain unanswered. If it is possible to condition the immune system's suppression, should it not also be possible to condition its enhancement? Might this be one way in which *placebos*—treatments that have no biochemical effect—sometimes promote healing? Might negative beliefs—expecting the worst—have an opposite ("nocebo") effect, as people get what they expect? Although results have been mixed, researchers are hoping to answer such questions (Hróbjartsson & Gøtzsche, 2001).

FIGURE **41.9**
The conditioning of immune suppression
After Ader and Cohen (1985) associated sweetened water with a drug that causes immune suppression in rats, the inert substance alone triggered the conditioned immune response.

For now, we can view the stress effect on our disease resistance as a price we pay for the benefits of stress (**FIGURE 41.10**). Stress invigorates our lives by arousing and motivating us. An unstressed life would hardly be challenging or productive. Moreover, it pays to spend our resources in fighting or fleeing an external threat. But we do so at the cost of diminished resources for fighting internal threats to health. When the stress is momentary, the cost is negligible. When uncontrollable aggravations persist, the cost may become considerable.

This behavioral medicine research provides yet another reminder of one of contemporary psychology's overriding themes: *Mind and body interact; everything psychological is simultaneously physiological.* Psychological states are physiological events that influence other parts of our physiological system. Just pausing to *think* about biting into an orange section—the sweet, tangy juice from the pulpy fruit flooding across your tongue—can trigger salivation. As the Indian sage Santi Parva recognized more than 4000 years ago, "Mental disorders arise from physical causes, and likewise physical disorders arise from mental causes." There is an interplay between our heads and our health. We are biopsychosocial systems.

FIGURE **41.10**
Stress can have a variety of health-related consequences
This is especially so when experienced by "disease-prone" angry, depressed, or anxious persons.

Kathleen Finlay/Masterfile

Stress and Illness

OBJECTIVE 41-1 | **Identify some behavior-related causes of illness and death, and describe health psychology's contribution to the field of behavioral medicine.**

Unhealthy behaviors (such as smoking, abuse of alcohol and other drugs, too little exercise, and poor nutrition) and exposure to prolonged stress can make us more vulnerable to some illnesses. *Behavioral medicine* is based on the idea that mind and body interact. *Health psychology* studies the ways our attitudes, emotions, behaviors, and personality influence our health, well-being, and risk of disease.

OBJECTIVE 41-2 | **Discuss the role of appraisal in the way we respond to stressful events.**

Stress is the *process* by which we respond to stressful events (stressors). An important part of that process is our appraisal of an event as threatening, challenging, or unimportant. Our appraisals help determine whether our response will be healthy feelings of energized and directed arousal, or overwhelming feelings of distress.

OBJECTIVE 41-3 | **Describe the dual-track system by which our body responds to stress, and identify the three phases of the general adaptation syndrome.**

The first (and faster) track of the stress-response system is the *fight-or-flight response,* in which the sympathetic nervous system responds to a stressor on several fronts: The inner parts of the adrenal glands pour out epinephrine and norepinephrine, heart and respiration rates increase, blood flows away from digestive organs and toward skeletal muscles, sensations of pain diminish, and the body releases stored sugar and fat. On the slower track of the system, the cerebral cortex, perceiving a stressor, stimulates the hypothalamus and the pituitary gland to trigger the release of glucocorticoid stress hormones, such as cortisol, from the outer part of the adrenals. The three stages of the general adaptation syndrome are *alarm* (temporary shock state in which the body mobilizes resources), *resistance* (period of coping with the stressor), and *exhaustion* (depletion of reserves following prolonged stress).

OBJECTIVE 41-4 | **Discuss the health consequences of catastrophes, significant life changes, and daily hassles.**

Large-scale catastrophic events can increase depression and anxiety and cause problems with concentrating and sleeping. Significant life events, such as personal losses or even changes, may leave people vulnerable to disease. But daily hassles—small, everyday stressors—are the most significant sources of stress for most people and can damage health and well-being.

OBJECTIVE 41-5 | **Discuss the role of stress in causing coronary heart disease, and contrast Type A and Type B personalities.**

Stress can increase the risk of coronary heart disease, a leading cause of death in the United States and other Western countries. The vital link in this stress-disease path is negative emotions—depression, pessimism, but especially anger. Under stress, people with *Type A personalities* (competitive, hard-driving, impatient, and anger-prone) are physiologically more reactive, with an outpouring of hormones that accelerate the buildup of plaque on artery walls, leading to high blood pressure and increased risk of strokes and heart attacks. People with *Type B personalities* (easygoing and relaxed) are at lower risk for these conditions.

OBJECTIVE 41-6 | **Distinguish between a psychophysiological illness and hypochondriasis.**

Psychophysiological illnesses are stress-related physical illnesses, such as hypertension (high blood pressure) and some headaches. *Hypochondriasis* is misinterpreting normal physical sensations as symptoms of a disease.

OBJECTIVE 41-7 | **Describe the effect of stress on immune system functioning.**

The immune system's B lymphocytes (formed in bone marrow) release antibodies that fight bacterial infections. The T lymphocytes (formed in the thymus and lymphatic tissue) fight cancer cells, viruses, and foreign substances. Other immune-system agents, the *macrophages,* ingest harmful invaders, worn-out cells, and other internal debris. Stress does not directly cause disease, but it can divert energy away from immune system activities and make us more vulnerable to infections and disease.

OBJECTIVE 41-8 | **Discuss the findings on the link between stress and AIDS.**

AIDS is caused by the HIV virus, not by stress. But stress and negative emotions may accelerate the progression from viral infection to actual AIDS. HIV-positive individuals benefit more from drug treatments, but programs that reduce stress do seem to help somewhat.

OBJECTIVE 41-9 | **Discuss the findings on the link between stress and cancer.**

Stress does not create cancer cells. Researchers disagree on whether stress influences the disease's progression, but they do agree that avoiding stress and maintaining a hopeful and determined attitude cannot reverse the destructive processes under way in advanced cancer.

OBJECTIVE 41-10 | **Describe the impact of learning on immune system functioning.**

Researchers have conditioned immune system suppression in laboratory experiments and are working on ways to condition immune-system enhancement.

TERMS AND CONCEPTS TO REMEMBER

behavioral medicine, p. P12-1
health psychology, p. P12-1
stress, p. 41-0
general adaptation syndrome
  (GAS), p. 41-2
coronary heart disease, p. 41-5

Type A, p. 41-6
Type B, p. 41-6
psychophysiological illness,
  p. 41-7
lymphocytes, p. 41-7

TEST YOURSELF

1. What are the basic links in our stress response system?

(Answer in Appendix B.)

ASK YOURSELF

1. What are the stresses of your own life? How intensely do you respond to them? Are there changes you could make to avoid the persistent stressors in your life?

≫WEB

Multiple-choice *self-tests* and more may be found at www.worthpublishers.com/myers.

MODULE

42

Coping With Stress

Promoting health begins with implementing strategies that prevent illness and enhance wellness. Traditionally, people have thought about their health only when something goes wrong—visiting a physician for diagnosis and treatment. That, say health psychologists, is like ignoring a car's maintenance and going to a mechanic only when the car breaks down. Now that we realize that our attitudes and behaviors affect our health, attention is turning to health maintenance—ways of coping with stress, preventing illness, and promoting well-being.

Strategies for Alleviating Stress

OBJECTIVE 42-1 | Contrast problem-focused coping and emotion-focused coping.

Stressors are unavoidable. This fact, coupled with the growing awareness that persistent stress correlates with heart disease, lowered immunity, and other bodily ailments, gives us a clear message. We need to learn to **cope** with the stress in our lives by finding emotional, cognitive, or behavioral ways to alleviate it. We address some stressors directly, with **problem-focused coping.** For example, if our impatience leads to a family fight, we may go directly to that family member to work things out. If, despite our best efforts, we cannot get along with that family member, we may also incorporate an **emotion-focused strategy,** such as reaching out to friends to help address our own emotional needs.

We tend to use problem-focused strategies when we feel a sense of control over a situation and think we can change the circumstances, or at least change ourselves to more capably deal with the circumstances. We turn to emotion-focused strategies when we cannot—or *believe* we cannot—change a situation. Sometimes these strategies are movements toward better long-term health, as when we attempt to gain emotional distance from a damaging, discontinued relationship or keep busy with active hobbies to avoid thinking about an old addiction. Emotion-focused strategies can be nonadaptive, however, as when students worried about not keeping up with the reading in class go out to party to get it off their mind. Sometimes a problem-focused strategy (catching up with the reading) more effectively reduces stress and promotes long-term health and satisfaction.

Several factors affect our ability to cope successfully, including our feelings of personal control, our explanatory style, and our supportive connections.

Perceived Control

OBJECTIVE 42-2 | Describe how a perceived lack of control can affect health.

If two rats receive simultaneous shocks, but one can turn a wheel to stop the shocks, the helpless rat becomes more susceptible to ulcers and lowered immunity to disease (Laudenslager & Reite, 1984) (**FIGURE 42.1** on the next page). In humans, too, uncontrollable threats trigger the strongest stress responses (Dickerson & Kemeny, 2004). For example, a bacterial infection often combines with uncontrollable stress to produce the most severe ulcers (Overmier & Murison, 1997). To cure the ulcer, kill the bug with antibiotics and control the acid secretions with reduced stress.

■ **coping** alleviating stress using emotional, cognitive, or behavioral methods.

■ **problem-focused coping** attempting to alleviate stress directly—by changing the stressor or the way we interact with that stressor.

■ **emotion-focused coping** attempting to alleviate stress by avoiding or ignoring a stressor and attending to emotional needs related to one's stress reaction.

FIGURE **42.1**

Health consequences of a loss of control
The "executive" rat at the left can switch off the tail shock by turning the wheel. Because it has control over the shock, it is no more likely to develop ulcers than is the unshocked control rat on the right. The "subordinate" rat in the center receives the same shocks as the executive rat, but with no control over the shocks, it is more likely to develop ulcers. (Adapted from Weiss, 1977.)

"Executive" rat   "Subordinate" rat   Control rat

To shock control   To shock source   No connection to shock source

Perceiving a loss of control, we become vulnerable to ill health. Elderly nursing home residents who have little perceived control over their activities tend to decline faster and die sooner than do those given more control over their activities (Rodin, 1986). Workers given control over their work environment—by being able to adjust office furnishings and control interruptions and distractions—also experience less stress (O'Neill, 1993). This helps explain why British civil service workers at the executive grades outlive those at clerical or laboring grades, and why Finnish workers with low job stress are less than half as likely to die of cardiovascular disease (strokes or heart disease) as those with a demanding job and little control. The more control workers have, the longer they live (Bosma & others, 1997, 1998; Kivimaki & others, 2002; Marmot & others, 1997).

Control may also help explain a well-established link between economic status and longevity. In one study of 843 grave markers in an old graveyard in Glasgow, Scotland, those with the costliest, highest pillars (indicating the most affluence) tended to live the longest (Carroll & others, 1994). Likewise, Scottish regions with the least overcrowding and unemployment have the greatest longevity. There and elsewhere, high economic status predicts a lower risk of heart and respiratory diseases (Sapolsky, 2005). Wealthy predicts healthy among children, too (Chen, 2004). With higher economic status comes lower risks of infant mortality, low birth weight, smoking, and violence. Even among other primates, those at the bottom of the social pecking order are more likely than their higher-status companions to become sick when exposed to a coldlike virus (Cohen & others, 1997). But for those high-status baboons and monkeys who frequently have to physically defend their dominant position, high status also entails stress (Sapolsky, 2005).

Why does perceived loss of control predict health problems? Animal studies show—and human studies confirm—that losing control provokes an outpouring of stress hormones. When rats cannot control shock or when primates or humans feel unable to control their environment, stress hormone levels rise, blood pressure increases, and immune responses drop (Rodin, 1986; Sapolsky, 2005). Captive animals therefore experience more stress and are more vulnerable to disease than are wild animals (Roberts, 1988). The crowding that occurs in high-density neighborhoods, prisons, and college dorms is another source of diminished feelings of control—and of elevated levels of stress hormones and blood pressure (Fleming & others, 1987; Ostfeld & others, 1987).

Explanatory Style

OBJECTIVE 42-3 | Discuss the links among explanatory style, stress, and health.

Another influence on our coping with stress is whether our basic outlook is optimistic or pessimistic. Psychologists Michael Scheier and Charles Carver (1992) report that optimists—people who agree with statements such as, "In uncertain times, I usually expect the best"—perceive more control, cope better with stressful events, and enjoy better health. During the last month of a semester, students previously identified as optimistic report less fatigue and fewer coughs, aches, and pains. And during the stressful first few weeks of law school, those who are optimistic ("It's unlikely that I will fail") enjoy better moods and stronger infection-thwarting immune systems (Segerstrom & others, 1998). Optimists also respond to stress with smaller increases in blood pressure, and they recover more quickly from heart bypass surgery.

One study that followed 2428 middle-aged Finnish men for up to 10 years discovered that the number of deaths among men with a bleak, hopeless outlook was more than double that found among their optimistic counterparts. Another study asked 795 Americans aged 64 to 79 years if they were "hopeful about the future." When the researchers checked up on these folks about five years later, 29 percent of those answering "No" had died—more than double the 11 percent of deaths among those who said "Yes" (Stern & others, 2001). Mayo Clinic research similarly finds that optimists tend to outlive pessimists (Maruta & others, 2002).

Those with a hopeful outlook live longer. At least that was so among 180 Catholic nuns who at about 22 years of age wrote brief autobiographies. Despite living thereafter with similar life-styles and status, those who had expressed happiness, love, and other positive feelings lived an average seven years longer than their more dour counterparts (Danner & others, 2001). By age 80, some 54 percent of those expressing few positive emotions had died, as had only 24 percent of the most positive-spirited.

Those who manage to find humor in life's daily events also seem to benefit. Laughter arouses us, massages muscles, and then leaves us feeling relaxed (Robinson, 1983). There is not yet enough consistent evidence to suggest that "laughter is the best medicine" (Martin, 2001, 2002). But some recent studies suggest that mirthful humor (not hostile sarcasm) may defuse stress and strengthen immune activity (Berk & others, 2001; Kimata, 2001). People who laugh a lot also have exhibited a lower incidence of heart disease (Clark & others, 2001). In one experiment, laughter in response to a hilarious movie clip caused the blood vessels' inner lining to respond with improved tone and increased blood flow, the opposite of what happened after people viewed a stressful movie clip (Miller, 2005). Perhaps future experiments will show that, indeed, those who laugh, last.

> There ain't much fun in medicine, but there's a heck of a lot of medicine in fun."
> Humorist Josh Billings, 1818–1885

Social Support

OBJECTIVE 42-4 | Describe some of the ways that social support acts as a stress buffer.

Social support also matters. Consider Linda and Emily. When interviewed for a study conducted by UCLA social psychologist Shelley Taylor (1989), both Los Angeles women had married, raised three children, suffered comparable breast tumors, and recovered from surgery and six months of chemotherapy. But there was a difference. Linda, a widow in her early fifties, was living alone, her children scattered in Atlanta, Boston, and Europe. "She had become odd in ways that people sometimes do when they are isolated," reported Taylor. "Having no one with whom to share her thoughts on a daily basis, she unloaded them somewhat inappropriately with strangers, including our interviewer."

CLOSE-UP:

PETS ARE FRIENDS, TOO

Jonathan Cavendish /Corbis

Have you ever wished for a friend who would love you just as you are, who is nonjudgmental, and who is always there for you, no matter your mood? For many tens of millions of people that friend exists, and it is a loyal dog or a friendly cat.

Many people describe their pet as a cherished family member who helps them feel calm, happy, and valued. Can pets also help people handle stress? If so, might pets have a

healing power? From her review of research, Karen Allen (2003) reports that, yes, pets have been found to increase the odds of survival after a heart attack, to relieve depression among AIDS patients, and to lower the level of blood lipids that contribute to cardiovascular risk. As nursing pioneer Florence Nightingale (1860) foresaw, "A small pet animal is often an excellent companion for the sick." Allen reports from her own research that women's blood pressure rises as they struggle with challenging math problems in the presence of a best friend or even a spouse, but much less so when accompanied by their dog.

So would pets be good medicine for people who do not have pets? To find out, Allen studied a group of stockbrokers who lived alone, described their work as stressful, and

had high blood pressure. She randomly selected half to adopt an animal shelter cat or dog. When later facing stress, these new pet owners exhibited less than half the blood pressure increase of their counterparts without pets. The effect was greatest for those with few social contacts or friends. Her conclusion: For lowering blood pressure, pets are no substitute for effective drugs and exercise, but they are, for those who enjoy animals and live alone, a healthy pleasure.

Pet Ownership Statistics (in millions)

	Dogs	Cats
Australia	4.0	3.5
Canada	3.5	4.5
United States	65	75
United Kingdom	6.1	7.5

Sources: petnet.com.au, Statistics Canada, U.S. Humane Society, U.K. Cats Protection League

Interviewing Emily was difficult in a different way. Phone calls interrupted. Her children, all living nearby, were in and out of the house, dropping things off with a quick kiss. Her husband called from his office for a brief chat. Two dogs roamed the house, greeting visitors enthusiastically. All in all, Emily "seemed a serene and contented person, basking in the warmth of her family."

Three years later, the researchers tried to reinterview the women. Linda, they learned, had died two years before. Emily was still lovingly supported by her family and friends and was as happy and healthy as ever.

No two cancers are identical, so we cannot be certain that different social situations led to Linda's and Emily's fates. But they do illustrate a conclusion drawn from several large studies: Social support—feeling liked, affirmed, and encouraged by intimate friends and family—promotes not only happiness, but also health. Humans aren't the only source of stress-buffering comfort. After stressful events, Medicare patients who have a dog or other companionable pet are less likely to visit their doctor (Siegel, 1990). (See Close-Up: Pets Are Friends, Too.)

Relationships can sometimes be stressful, especially in crowded living conditions lacking privacy (Evans & others, 1989). "Hell is others," wrote Jean-Paul Sartre. Peter Warr and Roy Payne (1982) asked a representative sample of British adults what, if anything, had emotionally strained them the day before. Their most frequent answer? "Family."

But asked what prompted yesterday's times of pleasure, the same British sample, by an even larger margin, again answered, "Family." For most of us, family relationships provide not only our greatest heartaches (even when well-meaning, family intrusions can be stressful) but also our greatest comfort and joy. Moreover, seven massive investigations, each following thousands of people for several years, revealed that close relationships predict health. Compared with those having few social ties, people are less likely to die prematurely if supported by close relationships with friends, family, fellow workers, members of a faith community, or other support groups (Cohen, 1988; House & others, 1988; Nelson, 1988). Leukemia and heart disease patients also have enjoyed markedly increased survival rates if married or supported by family or friends (Case & others, 1992; Colon & others, 1991; Williams & others, 1992).

Carefully controlled studies indicate that married people live longer, healthier lives than the unmarried (Murray, 2000; Wilson & Oswald, 2002). The National Center for Health Statistics (2004) reports that regardless of people's age, sex, race, and income, they tend to be healthier if married. Married folks experience less pain from headaches and backaches, suffer less stress, drink and smoke less, and, despite being slightly more overweight, are generally healthier. A seven-decades-long Harvard study found that a good marriage at age 50 predicts healthy aging better than does a low cholesterol level at 50 (Vaillant, 2002). But marital functioning also matters. Conflict-laden marriages are not conducive to health; positive, happy, supportive ones are (Kiecolt-Glaser & Newton, 2001). One five-year study following 1532 older married adults found it was even better to give than to receive. After controlling for preexisting health and personality differences, researchers observed a markedly lower risk of dying during the five-year period among those who frequently reached out to help friends and neighbors and who made their spouse feel loved and cared for (Brown & others, 2003).

How can we explain this link between social support and health? Is it just that healthy people are more likely to support others and to marry and stay married? Actually, the research suggests that people with supportive friends and marriage partners eat better, exercise more, sleep better, and smoke less, and therefore cope with stress more effectively (Helgeson & others, 1998).

Environments that support our need to belong also foster stronger immune functioning. Given ample social support, spouses of cancer patients exhibit stronger immune functioning (Baron & others, 1990). Social ties and positive sociability even confer resistance to cold viruses. Sheldon Cohen and his colleagues (1997, 2004) demonstrated this by putting 276 healthy volunteers in quarantine for five days after administering nasal drops laden with a cold virus, and then repeating the experiment with 334 more volunteers. (In both experiments, the volunteers were paid $800 each to endure this experience.) The cold fact is that the effect of social ties is nothing to sneeze at. Age, race, sex, smoking, and other health habits being equal, those with the most social ties were least likely to catch a cold and they produced less mucus. More sociability meant less susceptibility. More than 50 studies further reveal that social support calms the cardiovascular system, lowering blood pressure and stress hormones (Uchino & others, 1996, 1999).

Close relationships also provide the opportunity to *confide* painful feelings, a social support component that has now been extensively studied. In one study, health psychologists James Pennebaker and Robin O'Heeron (1984) contacted the surviving spouses of people who had committed suicide or died in car accidents. Those who bore their grief alone had more health problems than those who could express it openly. Talking about our troubles can be "open heart therapy."

Older people, many of whom have lost a spouse and close friends, are somewhat less likely to enjoy such confiding (**FIGURE 42.2** on the next page), and suppressing emotions is sometimes detrimental to our physical health. When Pennebaker surveyed more than 700 undergraduate women, he found that about 1 in 12 reported a traumatic sexual experience in childhood. Compared with women who had experienced nonsexual traumas, such as parental death or divorce, the sexually abused women—especially those who had kept their secret to themselves—reported more headaches and stomach ailments. Another study, of 437 Australian ambulance drivers, confirmed the ill effects of suppressing one's emotions after witnessing traumas (Wastell, 2002).

"Woe to one who is alone and falls and does not have another to help."
Ecclesiastes 4:10

Friendships are good medicine
Several long-term studies of thousands of people have found that individuals with close supportive relationships are less likely than socially isolated people to die prematurely.

"I get by with a little help from my friends."
John Lennon and Paul McCartney, *Sgt. Pepper's Lonely Hearts Club Band*, 1967

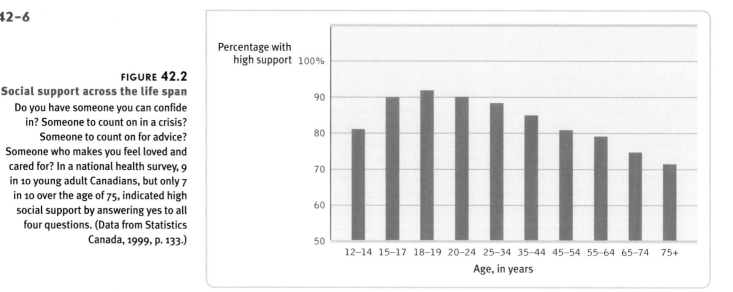

© The New Yorker Collection, 1993, Edward Koren from cartoonbank.com. All Rights Reserved.

FIGURE 42.2

Social support across the life span

Do you have someone you can confide in? Someone to count on in a crisis? Someone to count on for advice? Someone who makes you feel loved and cared for? In a national health survey, 9 in 10 young adult Canadians, but only 7 in 10 over the age of 75, indicated high social support by answering yes to all four questions. (Data from Statistics Canada, 1999, p. 133.)

▩ **aerobic exercise** sustained exercise that increases heart and lung fitness; may also alleviate depression and anxiety.

Actively suppressing thoughts can cause them to bubble up intrusively, preoccupying the person (Wegner, 1990). (In the next five seconds, please *do not* picture a white bear.) Disclosing suppressed thoughts may stop the cycle. In a simulated confessional, Pennebaker asked volunteers to share with a hidden experimenter some upsetting events that had been preying on their minds. He asked some of the volunteers to describe a trivial event before they divulged the troubling one. Physiological measures revealed that their bodies remained tense the whole time they talked about the trivial event; they relaxed only when they later confided the cause of their turmoil.

Writing about personal traumas in a diary can also help (Hemenover, 2003; Lyubomirsky & others, 2006). When volunteers in one experiment did this, they had fewer health problems during the ensuing four to six months (Pennebaker, 1990). As one participant explained, "Although I have not talked with anyone about what I wrote, I was finally able to deal with it, work through the pain instead of trying to block it out. Now it doesn't hurt to think about it."

Pennebaker and his colleagues (1989) also invited 33 Holocaust survivors to spend two hours recalling their experiences. Many did so in intimate detail never before disclosed. In the weeks following, most watched a videotape of their recollections and showed it to family and friends. Those who were most self-disclosing had the most improved health 14 months later. Talking about a stressful event can temporarily arouse people, but in the long run it calms them (Mendolia & Kleck, 1993). Confiding is good for the soul.

Managing Stress

Having a sense of control, developing a more optimistic explanatory style, and building our base of social support can help us *experience* less stress and thus improve our health. But sometimes we cannot alleviate stress and simply need to *manage* our stress in a healthful way. Aerobic exercise, biofeedback, relaxation, meditation, and spirituality may help us gather inner strength and lessen stress.

Aerobic Exercise

OBJECTIVE 42-5 | Discuss the advantages of aerobic exercise as a technique for managing stress and fostering well-being.

Aerobic exercise is sustained exercise that increases heart and lung fitness. Jogging, swimming and biking are common examples. Such exercise strengthens the body. Does it also boost the spirit?

"Is there anyone here who specializes in stress management?"

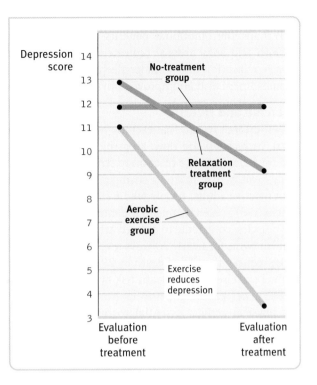

FIGURE 42.3
Aerobic exercise and depression
Mildly depressed college women who participated in an aerobic exercise program showed markedly reduced depression, compared with those who did relaxation exercises or received no treatment. (From McCann & Holmes, 1984).

Exercise and Mood

Many studies suggest that aerobic exercise can reduce stress, depression, and anxiety. For example, 3 in 10 American and Canadian, and 2 in 10 British people who do aerobic exercise three times a week or more also manage stressful events better, exhibit more self-confidence, feel more vigor, and feel depressed and fatigued less often than those who exercise less (McMurray, 2004). In a 2002 Gallup survey, nonexercisers were twice as likely as exercisers to report being "not too happy" (Brooks, 2002). But if we state this observation the other way around—that stressed and depressed people exercise less—cause and effect become unclear.

Experiments have resolved this ambiguity by randomly assigning stressed, depressed, or anxious people either to aerobic exercise or to other treatments. In one such experiment, Lisa McCann and David Holmes (1984) assigned one third of a group of mildly depressed female college students to a program of aerobic exercise and another third to a treatment of relaxation exercises; the remaining third, a control group, received no treatment. As **FIGURE 42.3** shows, 10 weeks later the women in the aerobic exercise program reported the greatest decrease in depression. Many of them had, quite literally, run away from their troubles. Vigorous exercise provides a "substantial" immediate mood boost, reports David Watson (2000) from his monitoring of university students. Even a 10-minute walk stimulates two hours of increased well-being by raising energy levels and lowering tension (Thayer, 1987, 1993).

More than 150 other studies confirm that exercise reduces depression and anxiety and is therefore a useful adjunct to antidepressant drugs and psychotherapy (Arent & others, 2000; Berger & Motl, 2000; Dunn & others, 2005). Not only is exercise about as effective as drugs, some research suggests it better prevents symptom recurrence (Babyak & others, 2000; Salmon, 2001). Researchers are now wondering *why* aerobic exercise alleviates negative emotions. They know that exercise:

- orders up mood-boosting chemicals from our body's internal pharmacy—neurotransmitters such as norepinephrine, serotonin, and the endorphins (Jacobs, 1994; Salmon, 2001).
- modestly enhances cognitive abilities, such as memory (Etnier & others, 1997).
- promotes the growth of new brain cells in mice exercising daily on a running-wheel regimen (Kempermann & Gage, 1999).

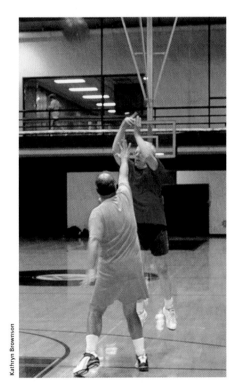

Kathryn Brownson

The mood boost
When one's energy or spirits are sagging, few things reboot the day better than exercising (as I can vouch from my daily noontime basketball). Aerobic exercise appears to counteract depression partly by increasing arousal (replacing depression's low-arousal state) and by doing naturally what Prozac does—increasing the brain's serotonin activity.

Perhaps the emotional benefits of exercise are also a side effect of increased warmth and body arousal (counteracting depression's low arousal state), or of the muscle relaxation and sounder sleep that occur afterward. Or perhaps a sense of accomplishment and an improved physique enhance one's emotional state.

Exercise and Health

Other research reveals that exercise not only boosts our mood, but also strengthens the heart, increases blood flow, keeps blood vessels open, and lowers both blood pressure and the blood pressure reaction to stress (Ford, 2002; Manson, 2002). And being physically healthy may make us stronger and better able to manage our stress. Compared with inactive adults, people who exercise suffer half as many heart attacks (Powell & others, 1987). Exercise makes the muscles hungry for the "bad fats" that, if not used by the muscles, contribute to clogged arteries (Barinaga, 1997). One study following adult Finnish twins for nearly 20 years revealed that, other things being equal, occasional exercise reduced the risk of death by 29 percent, compared with no exercise. Daily conditioning exercise reduced death risk by 43 percent (Kujala & others, 1998).

The genes passed down to us from our distant ancestors were those that enabled the physical activity essential to hunting, foraging, and farming. In muscle cells, those genes, when activated by exercise, respond by producing proteins. In the modern inactive person, note biologists Frank Booth and Darrell Neufer (2005), these genes produce lower quantities of proteins and leave us susceptible to more than 20 chronic diseases, such as type-2 diabetes, cardiovascular disease, and cancer. Inactivity is thus potentially toxic.

By one estimate, moderate exercise adds two years to one's expected life. "Perhaps God does not subtract the time spent exercising from your allotted time on Earth," jests Martin Seligman (1994, p. 193).

Biofeedback, Relaxation, and Meditation

OBJECTIVE 42-6 | Compare the benefits of biofeedback and relaxation training as stress-management techniques, and discuss meditation as a relaxation technique.

Knowing the damaging effects of stress, could we train people to bring their heart rate and blood pressure under conscious control? When a few psychologists started experimenting with this idea, many of their colleagues thought them foolish. After all, these functions are controlled by the autonomic ("involuntary") nervous system. Then, in the late 1960s, experiments by respected psychologists made the skeptics wonder. Neal Miller, for one, found that rats could modify their heartbeat if given pleasurable brain stimulation when their heartbeat increased or decreased. Later research revealed that some paralyzed humans could also learn to control their blood pressure (Miller & Brucker, 1979).

Miller was experimenting with **biofeedback,** a system of recording, amplifying, and feeding back information about subtle physiological responses. Biofeedback instruments mirror the results of a person's own efforts, thereby allowing the person to learn techniques for controlling a particular physiological response (**FIGURE 42.4**).

After a decade of study, however, researchers decided the initial claims for biofeedback were overblown and oversold (Miller, 1985). A 1995 National Institutes of Health panel declared that biofeedback works best on tension headaches. Many have since turned to alternative medicine (for further discussion, turn the page and see Thinking Critically About: Alternative Medicine—New Ways to Health, or Old Snake Oil?) in search of quick relief from stress and illnesses, but simple methods of relaxation, which require no expensive equipment, produce many of the same results biofeedback once promised.

Sixty studies find that relaxation procedures can help alleviate headaches, hypertension, anxiety, and insomnia (Stetter & Kupper, 2002). Such findings would not

biofeedback a system for electronically recording, amplifying, and feeding back information regarding a subtle physiological state, such as blood pressure or muscle tension.

surprise Meyer Friedman and his colleagues. To find out whether teaching Type A heart attack victims (Type A people are, by definition, competitive, hard-driving, impatient, and anger-prone) to relax might reduce their risk of another attack, the researchers randomly assigned hundreds of middle-aged, male heart-attack survivors to one of two groups. The first group received standard advice from cardiologists concerning medications, diet, and exercise habits. The second group received similar advice plus continuing counseling on modifying their life-styles—how to slow down and relax by walking, talking, and eating more slowly; by smiling at others and laughing at themselves; by admitting mistakes; by taking time to enjoy life; and by renewing their religious faith. As **FIGURE 42.5** indicates, during the ensuing three years, the second group experienced half as many repeat heart attacks as the first group. This, wrote the exuberant Friedman, is an unprecedented, spectacular reduction in heart-attack recurrence. A smaller-scale British study similarly divided heart-attack–prone people into control and life-style modification groups (Eysenck & Grossarth-Maticek, 1991). During the next 13 years, it also found a 50 percent reduction in death rate among those trained to alter their thinking and life-style.

Cardiologist Herbert Benson (1996) became intrigued with meditative relaxation when he found that experienced meditators could decrease their blood pressure, heart rate, and oxygen consumption and raise their fingertip temperature. You can experience the essence of this *relaxation response,* as Benson calls it, right now: Assume a comfortable position, breathe deeply, and relax your muscles from foot to face. Now, close your eyes and focus on a single word or a phrase. (About 80 percent of Benson's patients choose to focus on a favorite prayer.) When other thoughts intrude, let them drift away as you silently repeat your phrase continually for 10 to 20 minutes. Tibetan Buddhists deep in meditation and Franciscan nuns deep in centering prayer report a diminished sense of self, space, and time. Brain scans reveal the neural footprints of such spiritual feelings during these mystical experiences: A part of the parietal lobe that tracks where we are in space is less active than usual, and a frontal lobe area involved in focused attention is more active (Newberg & D'Aquili, 2001).

System receives signal   Amplifies signal   Processes signal

Feedback

Displays signal

Patient observes signal

FIGURE 42.4
Biofeedback systems
Biofeedback systems—such as this one, which records tension in the forehead muscle of a headache sufferer—allow people to monitor their subtle physiological responses. As this man relaxes his forehead muscle, the pointer on the display screen (or a tone) may go lower.

Meditation is a modern phenomenon with a long history: "Sit down alone and in silence. Lower your head, shut your eyes, breathe out gently, and imagine yourself looking into your own heart. . . . As you breathe out, say 'Lord Jesus Christ, have mercy on me.' . . . Try to put all other thoughts aside. Be calm, be patient, and repeat the process very frequently" (Gregory of Sinai, died 1346).

FIGURE 42.5
Recurrent heart attacks and life-style modification
The San Francisco Recurrent Coronary Prevention Project offered counseling from a cardiologist to survivors of heart attacks. Those who were also guided in modifying their Type A life-style suffered fewer repeat heart attacks. (From Friedman & Ulmer, 1984.)

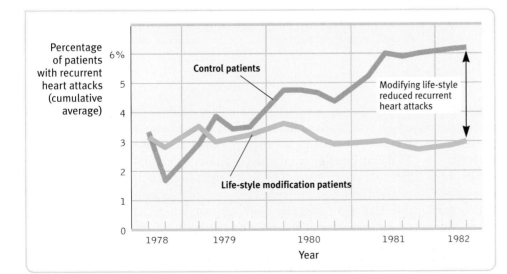

Percentage of patients with recurrent heart attacks (cumulative average)

Control patients

Modifying life-style reduced recurrent heart attacks

Life-style modification patients

Year

THINKING CRITICALLY ABOUT:

ALTERNATIVE MEDICINE—NEW WAYS TO HEALTH, OR OLD SNAKE OIL?

One health care growth market is **complementary and alternative medicine**, which encompasses such methods as acupuncture, massage therapy, homeopathy, spiritual healing, herbal remedies, chiropractic, and aromatherapy. In Germany, herbal remedies and homeopathy are enormously popular. In China, herbal therapies have long flourished, as have acupuncture and acupressure therapies that claim to correct "imbalances of energy flow" (called *Qi* or *Chi*) at identifiable points close to the skin. Andrew Weil's many books on alternative medicine have sold millions of copies, putting him on the cover of *Time* magazine. Facing political pressure to explore such things, the U.S. National Institutes of Health established the National Center for Complementary and Alternative Medicine, which the center defines as health care treatments not taught widely in medical schools, not usually reimbursed by insurance companies, and not used in hospitals (**TABLE 42.1**).

So what shall we make of alternative medicine? Some aspects, such as life-style changes and stress management, have acknowledged validity. Do the other aspects offer, as some believe, a new medical paradigm? Or do they represent, as others maintain, a retreat from rationality and science?

Supporters of alternative medicine offer inspirational cases, such as these from Andrew Weil's books (Relman, 1998):

- A young woman diagnosed with bone cancer starts a vigorous exercise program (biking 500 miles and running 60 miles weekly), becomes vegetarian (consuming fresh fruit, juices, and whole grains), and shucks the alleged cancer.
- A woman uses "respiratory biofeedback" to end her Parkinson's-induced seizures.
- A man with scleroderma, a progressive and fatal disease of the skin and internal organs, cures himself with vinegar, lemons, aloe vera juice, and vitamin E.

Critics point out that people consult physicians for diagnosable, curable diseases and employ alternative medicine when they are either incurably ill or well but feeling subpar. Thus, an otherwise healthy person with a cold may try an herbal remedy and then credit the subsequent return to good health to alternative medicine, rather than to the body's natural return to normal. (Of course, the same may happen when people take traditional medicine for a cold.) Alternative medicine will seem especially effective with cyclical diseases, such as arthritis and allergies, as people seek therapy during the downturn

and presume its effectiveness during the ensuing upturn. Add to this the healing power of belief—the placebo effect—plus the natural disappearance (*spontaneous remission*) of many diseases, and alternative medicine practices are bound to seem effective, whether they are or not. One study of 302 migraine headache patients in Germany found that 51 percent of those receiving acupuncture treatment found relief, as did only 15 percent of those in a waiting list control group. But among a third group that received "sham acupuncture" (needles inserted at nonacupuncture points), 53 percent enjoyed relief. Such results, the investigators suspected, may indicate "a powerful placebo effect" (Linde & others, 2005).

The National Council Against Health Fraud and the editors of leading medical journals and of the *Scientific Review of Alternative Medicine* doubt the efficacy of alternative medicine therapies. "After more than ten years and $200 million," contends Kimball Atwood (2003), government-funded alternative medicine research "has not demonstrated efficacy" for any of the alternative medicine treatments studied.

"Sickness is the manifestation of evil in the body."

Andrew Weil, *Health and Healing*, 1998

Psychologist Richard Davidson reports that Buddhist monks who are experienced in meditation display elevated levels of the left frontal lobe activity associated with positive emotions. To explore whether such activity is a *result* of meditation, Davidson and his colleagues (2003) ran baseline brain scans of all volunteers and then randomly assigned them either to a control group or to an eight-week course in "mindfulness meditation." Compared with both the control group and their own baseline, the meditation participants exhibited noticeably more left-hemisphere activity, and also improved immune functioning, after the training. Such effects may help explain the astonishing results of a study that randomly assigned 73 residents of homes for the elderly either to daily meditation or to none. After three years, one-fourth of the nonmeditators had died, but all the meditators were still alive (Alexander & others, 1989).

TABLE 42.1

SUBFIELDS OF ALTERNATIVE MEDICINE

Alternative Systems of Medical Practice	Health Care Ranging From Self-Care Following Popular Beliefs to Treatments Based on Alternative Traditions or Practices
Bioelectromagnetic applications	The study of how living organisms interact with electromagnetic (EM) fields
Diet, nutrition, life-style changes	The knowledge of how to prevent illness, maintain health, and reverse the effects of chronic disease through dietary or nutritional intervention
Herbal medicine	Employing plant and plant products from folk medicine traditions for pharmacological use
Manual healing	Using touch and manipulation with the hands as a diagnostic and therapeutic tool
Mind-body control	Exploring the mind's capacity to affect the body, based on traditional medical systems that make use of the interconnectedness of mind and body
Pharmacological and biological treatments	Drugs and vaccines not yet accepted by mainstream medicine

Source: Offered without endorsement by the National Center for Complementary and Alternative Medicine (nccam.nih.gov)

"In God we trust. All others must have data."

George Lundberg, Editor, *Journal of the American Medical Association*, 1998

In November 1998, the *Journal of the American Medical Association* published seven new alternative medicine research studies. Three explored treatments that proved useless (chiropractic manipulation for tension headaches, a popular herb for weight loss, and acupuncture to control nerve pain caused by HIV). Four other treatments, however—an herb mixture for inflammatory bowel syndrome, an herbal remedy for bladder problems, yoga for carpal tunnel syndrome pain, and a Chinese method for inducing fetuses in the breech position to turn—showed some benefits. As always, the way to discern what works and what does not is to experiment: Randomly assign patients to receive the therapy or a placebo control. Then ask the critical question: When neither the therapist nor the patient knows who is getting the real therapy, is the real therapy effective?

Much of today's mainstream medicine began as yesterday's alternative medicine. Natural botanical life has given us digitalis (from purple foxglove), morphine (from the opium poppy), and penicillin (from penicillium mold). In each case, the active ingredient was verified in controlled trials. We have medical and public health science to thank for the antibiotics, vaccines, surgical procedures, sanitation, and emergency medicine that helped lengthen our life expectancy by three decades during the last century. If you have acute chest pain, find a lump in your chest, cough up blood, or develop a high fever, you would do well to seek out someone trained in medical science—someone undergirded by research on what treatments really work best for what ailments at what doses for what lengths of time.

Indeed, said *New England Journal of Medicine* editors Marcia Angell and Jerome Kassirer (1998), "There cannot be two kinds of medicine—conventional and alternative. There is only medicine that has been adequately tested and medicine that has not, medicine that works and medicine that may or may not work. Once a treatment has been tested rigorously, it no longer matters whether it was considered alternative at the outset."

■ **complementary and alternative medicine** Unproven health care treatments not taught widely in medical schools, not used in hospitals, and not usually reimbursed by insurance companies.

A more recent study found that hypertension patients assigned to meditation training had (compared with other treatment groups) a 30 percent lower cardiovascular death rate over the ensuing 19-year study period (Schneider & others, 2005).

Spirituality and Faith Communities

OBJECTIVE 42-7 | Discuss the correlation between religiosity and longevity, and offer some possible explanations for this link.

As humans suffered ills and sought healing throughout history, two healing traditions—religion and medicine—have joined hands in caring for them. Often those hands belonged to the same person—the spiritual leader was also the healer. Maimonides was a twelfth-century rabbi and a renowned physician. Hospitals, which were first established in monasteries and then spread by missionaries, often carry the names of saints or faith communities.

As medical science matured, healing and religion diverged. Rather than asking God to spare their children from smallpox, people were able to vaccinate them. Rather than seeking a spiritual healer when burning with bacterial fever, they were able to use antibiotics. Recently, however, religion and healing are converging once again:

- Of America's 135 medical schools, 101 offered spirituality and health courses in 2005, up from 5 in 1992 (Koenig, 2002; Puchalski, 2005).
- Since 1995, Harvard Medical School has annually attracted 1000 to 2000 health professionals to its Spirituality and Healing in Medicine conferences.
- Duke University has established a Center for Spirituality, Theology, and Health.
- A Yankelovich survey (1997) found 94 percent of U.S. HMO professionals and 99 percent of family physicians agreeing that "personal prayer, meditation, or other spiritual and religious practices" can enhance medical treatment.
- Booksellers are featuring such titles as *The Healing Power of Faith* (Simon & Schuster, 1999), *Religion and Health* (Oxford University Press, 2000), and *Faith, Medicine, and Science* (Haworth, 2005).

Is there fire underneath all this smoke? More than a thousand studies have sought to correlate the *faith factor* with health and healing. For example, Jeremy Kark and his colleagues (1996) compared the death rates for 3900 Israelis either in one of 11 religiously orthodox or in one of 11 matched, nonreligious collective settlements (kibbutz communities). The researchers reported that over a 16-year period, "belonging to a religious collective was associated with a strong protective effect" not explained by age or economic differences. In every age group, religious community members were about half as likely to have died as were their nonreligious counterparts. This is roughly comparable to the gender difference in mortality.

In response to such findings, Richard Sloan and his skeptical colleagues (1999, 2000, 2002, 2005) remind us that mere correlations can leave many factors uncontrolled. Consider one obvious possibility: Women are more religiously active than men, and women outlive men. So perhaps religious involvement is merely an expression of the gender effect on longevity.

However, several new studies find the religiosity-longevity correlation among men alone, and even more strongly among women (McCullough & others, 2000, 2005). One study that followed 5286 Californians over 28 years found that, after controlling for age, gender, ethnicity, and education, frequent religious attenders were 36 percent less likely to have died in any year (**FIGURE 42.6**).

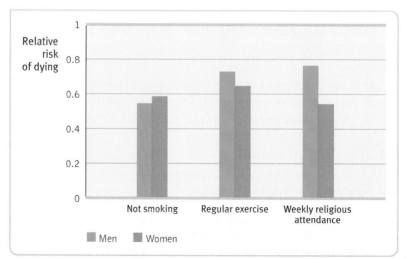

FIGURE 42.6

Predictors of mortality risk: not smoking, frequent exercise, and regular religious attendance
Epidemiologist William Strawbridge and his co-workers (1997, 1999; Oman & others, 2002) followed 5286 Alameda, California, adults over 28 years. After adjusting for age and education, the researchers found that not smoking, regular exercise, and religious attendance all predicted a lowered risk of death in any given year. Women attending weekly religious services, for example, were only 54 percent as likely to die in a typical study year as were nonattenders.

A U.S. National Health Interview Survey (Hummer & others, 1999) followed 21,204 people over 8 years. After controlling for age, sex, race, and region, researchers found that nonattenders were 1.87 times more likely to have died than were those attending more than weekly. This translated into a life expectancy at age 20 of 83 years for frequent attenders and 75 years for infrequent attenders (**FIGURE 42.7**).

These correlational findings do not indicate that nonattenders who start attending services and change nothing else will live 8 years longer. But they do indicate that as a *predictor* of health and longevity, religious involvement rivals nonsmoking and exercise effects. Such findings demand explanation. Can you imagine what intervening variables might account for the correlation?

First, religiously active people have healthier life-styles; for example, they smoke and drink less (Lyons, 2002; Strawbridge & others, 2001). Health-oriented, vegetarian Seventh Day Adventists have a longer-than-usual life expectancy (Berkel & de Waard, 1983). Religiously orthodox Israelis eat less fat than do their nonreligious compatriots. But such differences are not great enough to explain the dramatically reduced mortality in the religious kibbutzim, argued the Israeli researchers. In the recent American studies, too, about 75 percent of the longevity difference remains after controlling for unhealthy behaviors such as inactivity and smoking (Musick & others, 1999).

Social support is another variable that helps explain the faith factor (George & others, 2002). For Judaism, Christianity, and Islam, faith is not solo spirituality but a communal experience that helps satisfy the need to belong. The more than 350,000 faith communities in North America and the millions more elsewhere provide support networks for their active participants—people who are there for one another when misfortune strikes. Moreover, religion encourages another predictor of health and longevity. In the religious kibbutzim, for example, divorce has been almost nonexistent.

But even after controlling for gender, unhealthy behaviors, social ties, and preexisting health problems, the mortality studies find much of the mortality reduction remaining (George & others, 2000; Powell & others, 2003). Researchers therefore speculate that a third set of intervening variables is the stress protection and enhanced well-being associated with a coherent worldview, a sense of hope for the long-term future, feelings of ultimate acceptance, and the relaxed meditation of prayer or Sabbath observance (**FIGURE 42.8**). These variables might also help to explain other recent findings among the religiously active, such as healthier immune functioning

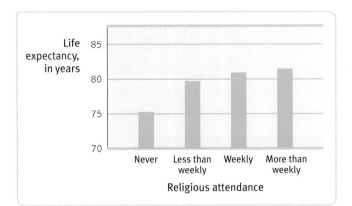

FIGURE 42.7
Religious attendance and life expectancy
In a national health survey financed by the U.S. Centers for Disease Control and Prevention, religiously active people had longer life expectancies. (Data from Hummer & others, 1999.)

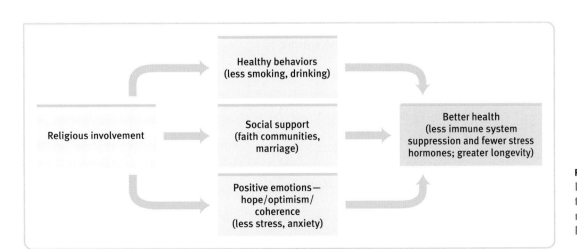

FIGURE 42.8
Possible explanations for the correlation between religious involvement and health/longevity

and fewer hospital admissions and, for AIDS patients, fewer stress hormones and longer survival (Ironson & others, 2002; Koenig & Larson, 1998; Lutgendorf & others, 2004).

Although the religion-health correlation is yet to be fully explained, Harold Pincus (1997), deputy medical director of the American Psychiatric Association, believes these findings "have made clear that anyone involved in providing health care services . . . cannot ignore . . . the important connections between spirituality, religion, and health."

Let's summarize: Sustained emotional reactions to stressful events can be debilitating. However, we can cope with stressors by problem-solving or emotional coping, and we can manage stress by making ourselves emotionally and physically stronger (**FIGURE 42.9**).

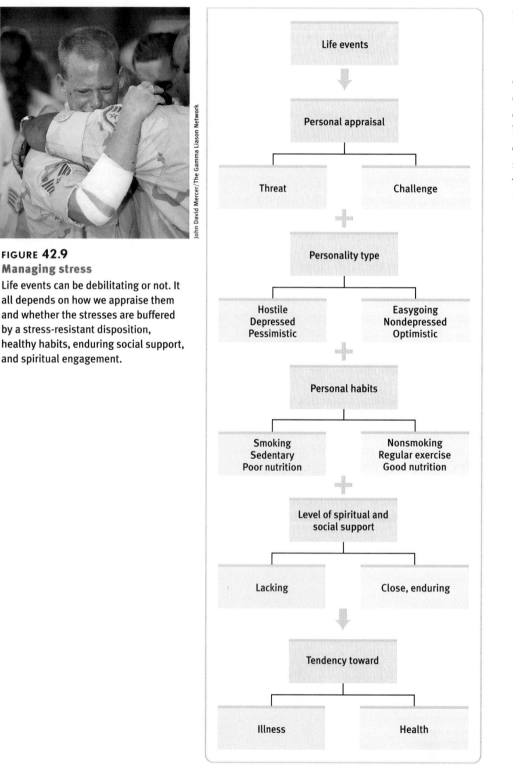

FIGURE 42.9
Managing stress
Life events can be debilitating or not. It all depends on how we appraise them and whether the stresses are buffered by a stress-resistant disposition, healthy habits, enduring social support, and spiritual engagement.

John David Mercer/The Gamma Liason Network

>> Learning Outcomes

Coping With Stress

Objective 42-1 | Contrast problem-focused coping and emotion-focused coping.

When we use *problem-focused coping,* we attempt to reduce stress directly by changing the events that trigger stress reactions or by changing the way we react to those events. We tend to use *emotion-focused coping* (putting distance between ourselves and a stressor, or attending to our own emotional needs) when we believe—rightly or wrongly—that we cannot change a stressful situation.

Objective 42-2 | Describe how a perceived lack of control can affect health.

A perceived lack of control has been associated with higher than normal susceptibility to bacterial infections, cardiovascular disease, and, possibly, a shorter life span due to elevated levels of stress hormones and diminished immune system responses.

Objective 42-3 | Discuss the links among explanatory style, stress, and health.

Compared with people with a pessimistic explanatory style, optimists tend to feel they have more control over stressors, cope better with stressful events, enjoy better moods, have stronger immune systems, and live longer than pessimists.

Objective 42-4 | Describe some of the ways that social support acts as a stress buffer.

Supportive family members, marriage partners, close friends, and companionable pets help people cope with stressful events. Social support fosters stronger immune functioning, calms the cardiovascular system, and lowers blood pressure.

Objective 42-5 | Discuss the advantages of aerobic exercise as a technique for managing stress and fostering well-being.

Aerobic exercise (sustained exercise that increases heart and lung fitness) can raise energy levels, increase self-confidence, lower tension, and alleviate depression and anxiety. Studies have linked aerobic exercise to lowered blood pressure, increased arousal, higher levels of neurotransmitters that boost moods (such as norepinephrine, serotonin, and the endorphins), enhanced cognitive abilities, and (in mice) the growth of new brain cells.

Objective 42-6 | Compare the benefits of biofeedback and relaxation training as stress-management techniques, and discuss meditation as a relaxation technique.

Biofeedback techniques have helped control tension headaches, but simple relaxation exercises have been equally effective in combating hypertension, anxiety, and insomnia, and in lowering rates of recurring heart attacks. Some search for relief from stress and illnesses in complementary and alternative medicine. While meditating, people have shown increased left frontal lobe activity and improved immune functioning, compared with those in control groups.

Objective 42-7 | Discuss the correlation between religiosity and longevity, and offer some possible explanations for this link.

Regular religious attendance has been a reliable predictor of a longer life span. Researchers have isolated three possible influences: (1) Religiously active people have healthy life-styles. (2) Faith communities often function as social support networks and often encourage marriage (which, when happy, is associated with better health and longer life span). (3) Religious attendance—with its accompanying coherent worldview, sense of hope for the future, feelings of acceptance, and relaxed meditative state—may foster positive emotions and decrease feelings of stress and anxiety.

TERMS AND CONCEPTS TO REMEMBER

coping, p. 42-1
problem-focused coping, p. 42-1
emotion-focused coping, p. 42-1
aerobic exercise, p. 42-6
biofeedback, p. 42-8
complementary and alternative medicine, p. 42-10

TEST YOURSELF

1. What are some ways that social support can help us cope with stress?

(Answer in Appendix B.)

ASK YOURSELF

1. In the past month, have you tended toward using more problem-focused or more emotion-focused strategies for coping with stress? Have your methods been effective, or do you think you need to modify your approach?

>WEB

Multiple-choice *self-tests* and more may be found at www.worthpublishers.com/myers.

Personality

OBJECTIVE 44-1 | Define *personality*.

Lord of the Rings hobbit-hero Frodo Baggins knew that throughout his harrowing journey there was one who would never fail him—his loyal and ever-cheerful companion, Sam Gamgee. Even before they left their beloved hometown, Frodo warned Sam that the journey would not be easy:

> "It is going to be very dangerous, Sam. It is already dangerous. Most likely neither of us will come back."
>
> "If you don't come back, sir, then I shan't, that's certain," said Sam. "[The Elves told me] 'Don't you leave him!' Leave him! I said. I never mean to. I am going with him, if he climbs to the Moon; and if any of those Black Riders try to stop him, they'll have Sam Gamgee to reckon with." (Tolkien, *The Fellowship of the Ring*, p. 96)

And so they did! Later in the story, when it became clear that Frodo had to venture into the dreaded land of Mordor without the rest of the company, it was Sam who insisted he would accompany Frodo, come what may. It was Sam who lifted Frodo's flagging spirits with songs and stories from their boyhood, and Sam upon whom Frodo leaned when he could barely take another step. When Frodo was overcome by the evil of the ring he bore, it was Sam who saved Frodo from completely succumbing to it. And in the end, it was Sam who enabled Frodo to successfully reach the end of his journey. Sam Gamgee—the cheerful, conscientious, emotionally stable optimist—never faltered in his faithfulness or his belief that they could overcome the threatening darkness.

J. R. R. Tolkien's character Sam Gamgee, as he appears and reappears throughout the trilogy, exhibits the distinctiveness and consistency that define **personality**—an individual's characteristic pattern of think-

ing, feeling, and acting. Other modules in this book emphasize our similarity—how we all develop, perceive, learn, remember, think, and feel. Modules 44 through 46 emphasize our individuality.

Actually, much of psychology deals with personality. Across the field, psychologists study biological influences on personality; personality development across the life span; personality-related aspects of learning, motivation, emotion, and health; disorders of personality; and social influences on personality.

We begin with two grand theories—historically significant perspectives that helped establish the field of personality psychology and raised key issues still being addressed in today's research and clinical work and that became part of our cultural legacy.

- Sigmund Freud's psychoanalytic theory (Module 44) proposed that childhood sexuality and unconscious motivations influence personality.
- The *humanistic* approach (Module 45) focused on our inner capacities for growth and self-fulfillment.

These historic theories, which offer sweeping perspectives on human nature, are complemented by what Module 46 goes on to explore: today's more focused and down-to-earth scientific research of specific aspects of personality.

Today's personality researchers engage in focused analyses of the basic dimensions of personality and their impact on behavior; on the biological roots of these basic dimensions; on the interaction of persons and environments; and on studies of self-esteem, self-serving bias, and cultural influences on one's sense of self. Along the way, we'll survey some contemporary findings about the unconscious mind—findings that probably would have surprised Freud himself.

■ **personality** an individual's characteristic pattern of thinking, feeling, and acting.

MODULE

The Psychoanalytic Perspective

OBJECTIVE 44-2 | Explain how Freud's experiences in private practice led to his theory of psychoanalysis.

"Sigmund Freud has left an important—and I believe indelible—mark on human self-understanding," observes Drew Westen (1998). Others disagree, noting that Freud's current influence in psychological science has diminished (Robins & others, 1999). But love him or hate him, Freud has profoundly influenced Western culture. Ask 100 people on the street to name a notable deceased psychologist, suggests Keith Stanovich (1996, p. 1), and "Freud would be the winner hands down." In the popular mind, he is to psychology's history what Elvis is to rock music's history. Freud's influence lingers in literary and film interpretation, psychiatry, and clinical psychology. So, who was this early personality theorist, and what did he teach?

Long before entering the University of Vienna in 1873, a youthful Sigmund Freud showed signs of independence and brilliance. He had a prodigious memory and so loved reading plays, poetry, and philosophy that he once ran up a bookstore debt beyond his means. As a teen he often took his evening meal in his tiny bedroom in order to lose no time from his studies.

Freud went to medical school and after graduation set up a private practice, specializing in nervous disorders. Before long, however, he faced patients whose disorders made no neurological sense. For example, a patient might have lost all feeling in a hand—yet there is no sensory nerve that, if damaged, would numb the entire hand and nothing else. Freud's search for a cause for such disorders set his mind running. His views, which evolved as he treated patients and analyzed himself, eventually filled 24 volumes published between 1888 and 1939. Following his first solo book, *The Interpretation of Dreams* (1900), his ideas gradually began to attract both dedicated followers and intense criticism. For now, let's reserve judgment on Freud's theory and instead try to see things as he did. It is impossible to summarize 24 volumes in these few pages, but we can highlight Freud's *psychoanalytic theory*—the first comprehensive theory of personality, which included ideas about an unconscious region of the mind, psychosexual stages, and defense mechanisms for holding anxiety at bay.

Sigmund Freud, 1856–1939
"I was the only worker in a new field."

Culver Pictures

Exploring the Unconscious

OBJECTIVE 44-3 | Discuss Freud's view of the mind as an iceberg, and explain how he used this image to represent conscious and unconscious regions of the mind.

Might some neurological disorders have psychological rather than physiological causes? Observing patients led Freud to his "discovery" of the unconscious. He decided that the peculiar loss of feeling in one's hand might be caused by a fear of touching one's genitals; that unexplained blindness or deafness might be caused by

■ **free association** in psychoanalysis, a method of exploring the unconscious in which the person relaxes and says whatever comes to mind, no matter how trivial or embarrassing.

■ **psychoanalysis** Freud's theory of personality that attributes thoughts and actions to unconscious motives and conflicts; the techniques used in treating psychological disorders by seeking to expose and interpret unconscious tensions.

■ **unconscious** according to Freud, a reservoir of mostly unacceptable thoughts, wishes, feelings, and memories. According to contemporary psychologists, information processing of which we are unaware.

not wanting to see or hear something that aroused intense anxiety. Initially, Freud thought hypnosis might unlock the door to the unconscious, but patients displayed an uneven capacity for hypnosis. He then turned to **free association**—in which he merely told the patient to relax and say whatever came to mind, no matter how embarrassing or trivial. Freud assumed that a line of mental dominoes had fallen from his patients' distant past to their troubled present. Free association, he believed, allowed him to retrace that line, following a chain of thought leading into the patient's unconscious, where painful unconscious memories, often from childhood, could be retrieved and released. Freud called his theory of personality and the associated treatment techniques **psychoanalysis.**

"Good morning, beheaded—uh, I mean beloved."

Basic to Freud's theory was his belief that the mind is like an iceberg—mostly hidden (**FIGURE 44.1**). Our conscious awareness is the part of the iceberg that floats above the surface. Below the surface is the much larger, **unconscious** region containing thoughts, wishes, feelings, and memories, of which we are unaware. Some of these thoughts we store temporarily in a *preconscious* area, from which we can retrieve them into conscious awareness. Of greater interest to Freud was the mass of unacceptable passions and thoughts that he believed we *repress,* or forcibly block from our consciousness because they would be too unsettling to acknowledge. Freud believed that, although we are not consciously aware of them, these troublesome feelings and ideas powerfully influence us, sometimes gaining expression in disguised forms—the work we choose, the beliefs we hold, our daily habits, our troubling symptoms.

For Freud the determinist, nothing was ever accidental. He believed he could glimpse the unconscious seeping not only into people's free associations, beliefs, habits, and symptoms but also into slips of the tongue and pen. He illustrated with a financially stressed patient who, not wanting any large pills, said, "Please do not give me any bills, because I cannot swallow them." Similarly, Freud viewed jokes as expressions of repressed sexual and aggressive tendencies, and dreams as the "royal road to the unconscious." The remembered content of dreams (their *manifest content*) he believed to be a censored expression of the dreamer's unconscious wishes (the dream's *latent content*). In his analysis of dreams, Freud searched for the nature of patients' inner conflicts and their release from inner tensions.

I know how hard it is for you to put food on your family."

George W. Bush, 2000

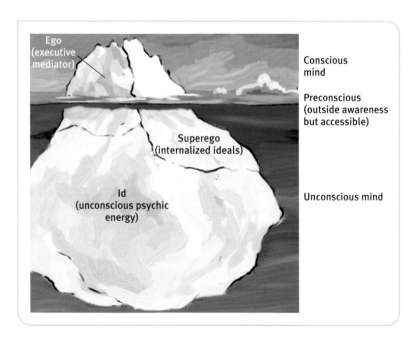

FIGURE **44.1**

Freud's idea of the mind's structure
Consciousness is like an iceberg's visible tip. Note that the id is totally unconscious, but ego and superego operate both consciously and unconsciously. (Adapted from Freud, 1933, p. 111.)

"Fifty is plenty."   "Hundred and fifty."

The ego struggles to reconcile the demands of superego and id, said Freud.

■ **id** contains a reservoir of unconscious psychic energy that, according to Freud, strives to satisfy basic sexual and aggressive drives. The id operates on the *pleasure principle*, demanding immediate gratification.

■ **ego** the largely conscious, "executive" part of personality that, according to Freud, mediates among the demands of the id, superego, and reality. The ego operates on the *reality principle*, satisfying the id's desires in ways that will realistically bring pleasure rather than pain.

■ **superego** the part of personality that, according to Freud, represents internalized ideals and provides standards for judgment (the conscience) and for future aspirations.

■ **psychosexual stages** the childhood stages of development (oral, anal, phallic, latency, genital) during which, according to Freud, the id's pleasure-seeking energies focus on distinct erogenous zones.

■ **Oedipus** [ED-uh-puss] **complex** according to Freud, a boy's sexual desires toward his mother and feelings of jealousy and hatred for the rival father.

■ **identification** the process by which, according to Freud, children incorporate their parents' values into their developing superegos.

■ **fixation** according to Freud, a lingering focus of pleasure-seeking energies at an earlier psychosexual stage, in which conflicts were unresolved.

Personality Structure

OBJECTIVE 44-4 | Describe Freud's view of personality structure, and discuss the interactions of the id, ego, and superego

In Freud's view, human personality—including its emotions and strivings—arises from a conflict between our aggressive, pleasure-seeking biological impulses and the internalized social restraints against them. Freud believed personality is the result of our efforts to resolve this basic conflict—to express these impulses in ways that bring satisfaction without also bringing guilt or punishment. To understand the mind's dynamics during this conflict, Freud proposed three interacting systems: the *id, ego,* and *superego* (see Figure 44.1).

The **id** has a reservoir of unconscious psychic energy constantly striving to satisfy basic drives to survive, reproduce, and aggress. The id operates on the *pleasure principle:* If not constrained by reality, it seeks immediate gratification. To envision an id-dominated person, think of newborn infants, crying out for satisfaction the moment they feel a need, caring nothing for the outside world's conditions and demands. Or think of people with a present rather than future time perspective—those who often use tobacco, alcohol, and other drugs, and would sooner party now than sacrifice today's pleasure for future success and happiness (Keough & others, 1999).

As the **ego** develops, the young child learns to cope with the real world. The ego, operating on the *reality principle,* seeks to gratify the id's impulses in realistic ways that will bring long-term pleasure rather than pain or destruction. (Imagine what would happen if, lacking an ego, we expressed our unrestrained sexual or aggressive impulses whenever we felt them.) The ego contains our partly conscious perceptions, thoughts, judgments, and memories.

Beginning around age 4 or 5, Freud theorized, a child's ego recognizes the demands of the newly emerging **superego,** the voice of conscience that forces the ego to consider not only the real but the ideal, and that focuses solely on how one *ought* to behave. The superego strives for perfection, judging actions and producing positive feelings of pride or negative feelings of guilt. Someone with an exceptionally strong superego may be virtuous yet, ironically, guilt-ridden; another with a weak superego may be wantonly self-indulgent and remorseless.

Because the superego's demands often oppose the id's, the ego struggles to reconcile the two. It is the personality "executive," mediating the impulsive demands of the id, the restraining demands of the superego, and the real-life demands of the external world. If chaste Jane feels sexually attracted to John she may satisfy both id and superego by joining a volunteer organization to which John belongs.

Personality Development

OBJECTIVE 44-5 | Identify Freud's psychosexual stages of development, and describe the effects of fixation on behavior.

Analysis of his patients' histories convinced Freud that personality forms during life's first few years. Again and again his patients' symptoms seemed rooted in unresolved conflicts from early childhood. He concluded that children pass through a series of **psychosexual stages,** during which the id's pleasure-seeking energies focus on distinct pleasure-sensitive areas of the body called *erogenous zones* (TABLE 44.1).

Freud believed that during the *phallic stage* boys seek genital stimulation, and they develop both unconscious sexual desires for their mother and jealousy and hatred for their father, whom they consider a rival. Given these feelings, boys supposedly also feel guilt and a lurking fear of punishment, perhaps by castration, from their father. Freud called this collection of feelings the **Oedipus complex** after the Greek legend of Oedipus, who unknowingly killed his father and married his mother. Some psychoanalysts in Freud's era believed that girls experienced a parallel *Electra complex.* Freud's own thinking seemed to vary on this issue.

TABLE 44.1

FREUD'S PSYCHOSEXUAL STAGES

Stage	Focus
Oral (0–18 months)	Pleasure centers on the mouth—sucking, biting, chewing
Anal (18–36 months)	Pleasure focuses on bowel and bladder elimination; coping with demands for control
Phallic (3–6 years)	Pleasure zone is the genitals; coping with incestuous sexual feelings
Latency (6 to puberty)	Dormant sexual feelings
Genital (puberty on)	Maturation of sexual interests

Children eventually cope with threatening feelings, said Freud, by repressing them and by identifying with (trying to become like) the rival parent. It's as though something inside the child decides, "If you can't beat 'em [the parent of the same sex], join 'em." Through this **identification** process, children's superegos gain strength as they incorporate many of their parents' values. Freud believed that identification with the same-sex parent provides what psychologists now call our *gender identity*—our sense of being male or female. This illustrates what both Freud and today's *object relations theorists* have presumed: that our early childhood relations with parents, caregivers, and everything else influences our developing identity, personality, and frailties.

From the K. Vandervelde private collection

Identification
Freud believed that children cope with threatening feelings of competition with their same-sex parent by identifying with that parent.

In Freud's view, conflicts unresolved during earlier psychosexual stages could surface as maladaptive behavior in the adult years. At any point in the oral, anal, or phallic stages, strong conflict could lock, or **fixate,** the person's pleasure-seeking energies in that stage. A person who had been either orally overindulged or deprived (perhaps by abrupt, early weaning) might fixate at the oral stage, for example. This orally fixated adult could exhibit either passive dependence (like that of a nursing infant) or an exaggerated denial of this dependence—perhaps by acting tough and uttering biting sarcasm. Or the person might continue to seek oral gratification by smoking and eating excessively. In such ways, Freud suggested, the twig of personality is bent at an early age.

Defense Mechanisms

OBJECTIVE 44-6 | Describe the function of defense mechanisms, and identify six of them.

Anxiety, said Freud, is the price we pay for civilization. As members of social groups, we must control our sexual and aggressive impulses, not act them out. But sometimes the ego fears losing control of this inner war between the demands of the id and the superego, and the result is a dark cloud of unfocused anxiety, which leaves us feeling unsettled but unsure why.

"Oh, for goodness' sake! Smoke!"

> "For seven and a half years I've worked alongside President Reagan. We've had triumphs. Made some mistakes. We've had some sex . . . uh . . . setbacks."
>
> George H. W. Bush, 1988

> "The lady doth protest too much, methinks."
>
> William Shakespeare, *Hamlet*, 1600

■ **defense mechanisms** in psychoanalytic theory, the ego's protective methods of reducing anxiety by unconsciously distorting reality.

■ **repression** in psychoanalytic theory, the basic defense mechanism that banishes anxiety-arousing thoughts, feelings, and memories from consciousness.

■ **regression** psychoanalytic defense mechanism in which an individual faced with anxiety retreats to a more infantile psychosexual stage, where some psychic energy remains fixated.

■ **reaction formation** psychoanalytic defense mechanism by which the ego unconsciously switches unacceptable impulses into their opposites. Thus, people may express feelings that are the opposite of their anxiety-arousing unconscious feelings.

Freud proposed that the ego protects itself with **defense mechanisms,** tactics that reduce or redirect anxiety by distorting reality. Here are six examples.

- **Repression** banishes anxiety-arousing thoughts and feelings from consciousness. According to Freud, *repression underlies all the other defense mechanisms,* each of which disguises threatening impulses and keeps them from reaching consciousness. Freud believed that repression explains why we do not remember our childhood lust for our parent of the other sex. However, he also believed that repression is often incomplete, that repressed urges seep out in dream symbols and slips of the tongue.

- **Regression** allows us to retreat to an earlier, more infantile stage of development. Facing the anxious first days of school, a child may regress to the oral comfort of thumb-sucking. Juvenile monkeys, when anxious, retreat to infantile clinging to their mothers or to one another (Suomi, 1987). Even homesick new college students may long for the security and comfort of home.

- In **reaction formation,** the ego unconsciously makes unacceptable impulses look like their opposites. En route to consciousness, the unacceptable proposition "I hate him" becomes "I love him." Timidity becomes daring. Feelings of inadequacy become bravado.

- **Projection** disguises threatening impulses by attributing them to others. Thus, "He doesn't trust me" may be a projection of the actual feeling "I don't trust him" or "I don't trust myself." An El Salvadoran saying captures the idea: "The thief thinks everyone else is a thief."

- **Rationalization** occurs when we unconsciously generate self-justifying explanations to hide from ourselves the real reasons for our actions. Thus, habitual drinkers may say they drink with their friends "just to be sociable." Students who fail to study may rationalize, "All work and no play makes Jack [or Jill] a dull person."

- **Displacement** diverts sexual or aggressive impulses toward an object or person that is psychologically more acceptable than the one that aroused the feelings. Children who fear expressing anger against their parents may displace it by kicking the family pet. Students upset over an exam may snap at a roommate.

Note that all these defense mechanisms function indirectly and unconsciously. They reduce anxiety by disguising our threatening impulses. Just as the body unconsciously defends itself against disease, so also, believed Freud, does the ego unconsciously defend itself against anxiety.

Regression
Faced with a mild stressor, children and young monkeys will regress, retreating to the comfort of earlier behaviors.

The Neo-Freudian and Psychodynamic Theorists

OBJECTIVE 44-7 | Contrast the views of the neo-Freudians and psychodynamic theorists with Freud's original theory.

Freud's writings were controversial, but they soon attracted followers, mostly young, ambitious physicians who formed an inner circle around their strong-minded leader. These pioneering psychoanalysts and others, whom we now call *neo-Freudians,* accepted Freud's basic ideas: the personality structures of id, ego, and superego; the importance of the unconscious; the shaping of personality in childhood; and the dynamics of anxiety and the defense mechanisms. But they veered away from Freud in two important ways. First, they placed more emphasis on the conscious mind's role in interpreting experience and in coping with the environment. And second, they doubted that sex and aggression were all-consuming motivations. Instead, they tended to emphasize loftier motives and social interactions. The following examples illustrate.

Alfred Adler and Karen Horney [HORN-eye] agreed with Freud that childhood is important. But they believed that childhood *social,* not sexual, tensions are crucial for personality formation. Adler (who had proposed the still-popular idea of the *inferiority complex*) himself struggled to overcome childhood illnesses and accidents, and he believed that much of our behavior is driven by efforts to conquer childhood feelings of inferiority, feelings that trigger our strivings for superiority and power. Horney said childhood anxiety, caused by the dependent child's sense of helplessness, triggers our desire for love and security. Horney countered Freud's assumptions that women have weak superegos and suffer "penis envy," and she attempted to balance the bias she detected in this masculine view of psychology.

Unlike other neo-Freudians, Carl Jung—Freud's disciple-turned-dissenter—placed less emphasis on social factors and agreed with Freud that the unconscious exerts a powerful influence. But to Jung (pronounced Yoong), the unconscious contains more than our repressed thoughts and feelings. He believed we also have a **collective unconscious,** a common reservoir of images derived from our species' universal experiences. Jung said that the collective unconscious explains why, for many people, spiritual concerns are deeply rooted and why people in different cultures share certain myths and images, such as mother as a symbol of nurturance. (Today's psychologists discount the idea of inherited experiences. But many do believe that our shared evolutionary history shaped some universal dispositions.)

■ **projection** psychoanalytic defense mechanism by which people disguise their own threatening impulses by attributing them to others.

■ **rationalization** defense mechanism that offers self-justifying explanations in place of the real, more threatening, unconscious reasons for one's actions.

■ **displacement** psychoanalytic defense mechanism that shifts sexual or aggressive impulses toward a more acceptable or less threatening object or person, as when redirecting anger toward a safer outlet.

■ **collective unconscious** Carl Jung's concept of a shared, inherited reservoir of memory traces from our species' history.

The female . . . acknowledges the fact of her castration, and with it, too, the superiority of the male and her own inferiority; but she rebels against this unwelcome state of affairs."

Sigmund Freud, *Female Sexuality,* 1931

Alfred Adler
"The individual feels at home in life and feels his existence to be worthwhile just so far as he is useful to others and is overcoming feelings of inferiority" (*Problems of Neurosis,* 1964).

Karen Horney
"The view that women are infantile and emotional creatures, and as such, incapable of responsibility and independence is the work of the masculine tendency to lower women's self-respect" (*Feminine Psychology,* 1932).

Carl Jung
"We can keep from a child all knowledge of earlier myths, but we cannot take from him the need for mythology" (*Symbols of Transformation,* 1912).

■ **projective test** a personality test, such as the Rorschach or TAT, that provides ambiguous stimuli designed to trigger projection of one's inner dynamics.

■ **Thematic Apperception Test (TAT)** a projective test in which people express their inner feelings and interests through the stories they make up about ambiguous scenes.

■ **Rorschach inkblot test** the most widely used projective test, a set of 10 inkblots, designed by Hermann Rorschach; seeks to identify people's inner feelings by analyzing their interpretations of the blots.

Freud died in 1939. Since then, some of his ideas have been incorporated into *psychodynamic theory*. "Most contemporary dynamic theorists and therapists are not wedded to the idea that sex is the basis of personality," notes Drew Westen (1996). They "do not talk about ids and egos, and do not go around classifying their patients as oral, anal, or phallic characters." What they do assume, with Freud, is that much of our mental life is unconscious, that we often struggle with inner conflicts among our wishes, fears, and values, and that childhood shapes our personalities and ways of becoming attached to others. For example, Freud's idea that early childhood experiences with caregivers were key to the developing personality laid the groundwork for later theory and research on infant attachment and on its long-term consequences.

Assessing Unconscious Processes

OBJECTIVE 44-8 | Describe two projective tests used to assess personality, and discuss some criticisms of them.

Those who study personality or provide therapy need ways to evaluate personality characteristics. Methods of assessment differ because they are tailored to different personality theories. So what might be the tool of choice for clinicians working in the Freudian tradition?

Evaluating personality from this perspective would require a road into the unconscious mind, which contains residues from early childhood experiences. (Recall that Freud believed free association and dream interpretation could reveal the unconscious.) Objective assessment tools, such as agree-disagree or true-false questionnaires would be inadequate because they would merely tap the conscious surface. The tool of choice would be a sort of psychological x-ray—a test that sees through our surface pretensions and reveals our hidden conflicts and impulses.

Projective tests aim to provide such a view by presenting an ambiguous stimulus and then asking test-takers to describe it or tell a story about it. The stimulus has no inherent significance, so any meaning people read into it presumably is a projection of their interests and conflicts. Henry Murray (1933) demonstrated a possible basis for such a test at a party hosted by his 11-year-old daughter. Murray engaged the children in a frightening game called "Murder." When shown some photographs after the game, the children perceived the photos as more malicious than they had before the game. These children, it seemed to Murray, had *projected* their inner feelings into the pictures. A few years later, Murray introduced the **Thematic Apperception Test (TAT),** in which people view ambiguous pictures and then make up stories about them (**FIGURE 44.2**). One use of storytelling has been to assess achievement motiva-

"We don't see things as they are; we see things as we are."

The Talmud

FIGURE 44.2
The TAT
This clinician presumes that the hopes, fears, and interests expressed in this boy's descriptions of a series of ambiguous pictures in the Thematic Apperception Test (TAT) are projections of his inner feelings.

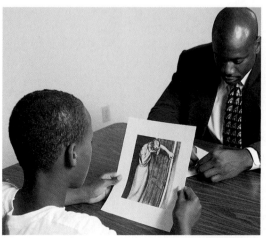

tion. Shown a daydreaming boy, those who imagine he is fantasizing about an achievement are presumed to be projecting their own goals. "As a rule," said Murray, "the subject leaves the test happily unaware that he has presented the psychologist with what amounts to an x-ray of his inner self" (quoted by Talbot, 1999).

Other projective tests ask test-takers to draw a person, to complete sentences ("My mother . . ."), or to provide the first word that comes to mind after the examiner says a test word. Most widely used is the famous **Rorschach inkblot test,** introduced in 1921 by Swiss psychiatrist Hermann Rorschach [ROAR-shock]. The test assumes that what we see in its 10 inkblots reflects our inner feelings and conflicts (**FIGURE 44.3**). If we see predatory animals or weapons, the examiner may infer we have aggressive tendencies.

Is this a reasonable assumption? If so, can a psychologist use the Rorschach to understand one's personality and diagnose an emotional disorder? The two primary criteria of a good test are *reliability* (consistency of results) and *validity* (predicting what it's supposed to). On those criteria, how good is the Rorschach?

By the second half of the twentieth century, critics had pointed out that no universally accepted system existed for scoring and interpreting the Rohrschach tests (Sechrest & others, 1998). Two raters who had been trained in different scoring systems would display only minimal agreement on the results of a given test. Nor was the test very successful at predicting behavior or at discriminating between groups (for example, identifying who is suicidal and who is not). The Rorschach is not an emotional MRI.

Lew Merrim/Photo Researchers, Inc.

With all the criticisms, the Rorschach remains "simultaneously, the most cherished and the most reviled of all psychological assessment tools" (Hunsley & Bailey, 1999). Clinicians—82 percent of whom report administering it at least occasionally—often cherish the Rorschach (Watkins & others, 1995; Lilienfeld & others, 2000). Some offer judges Rorschach-based assessments of criminals' violence potential. Other clinicians view it as a diagnostic tool, a source of suggestive leads, or an ice-breaker and a revealing interview technique. Edward Aronow and his colleagues (1995) report the example of a woman who found "four pink geese" in a Rorschach card, and then, under prompting, recalled that her uncle, a farmer, had molested her, that he had four daughters, and that his white geese became pink when slaughtered. There is now a research-based, computer-aided coding and interpretation tool that aims to improve agreement among raters and enhance the test's validity (Erdberg, 1990; Exner, 2003). For example, a person's seeing lots of reflections in the blots is said to indicate self-centeredness. The Society for Personality Assessment acknowledges that one should not "use Rorschach findings alone to draw a legal conclusion" or to decide whether, for example, child sexual abuse has occurred. But the society contends that "the Rorschach possesses documented reliability and validity" and that its use in personality assessment is "appropriate and justified."

But the evidence is insufficient to its revilers, who argue that the test has very limited validity and who note that inkblot assessments diagnose many normal adults as pathological (Wood & others, 2003, 2006). They argue that only a few of the many Rorschach-derived scores, such as ones for hostility and anxiety, have demonstrated validity. Other critics find "no scientific basis for justifying the use of Rorschach scales in psychological assessments" (Hunsley & Bailey, 1999) and even propose a moratorium on its clinical and forensic use (Garb & others, 2005). "If psychologists used tea leaves instead of the Rorschach, we'd probably be better off," suggests psychologist-critic James Wood (2003), "because then, at least, no one would take the results seriously."

Alternative projective assessment techniques, such as the TAT and the Draw-a-Person test fare little better, conclude Scott Lilienfeld, James Wood, and Howard Garb (2001). "Even seasoned professionals," they warn, "can be fooled by their intuitions and their faith in tools that lack strong evidence of effectiveness. When a substantial body of research demonstrates that old intuitions are wrong, it is time to adopt new ways of thinking." Freud himself probably would have been uncomfortable with trying to diagnose patients based on tests and would have been more interested in the therapist–patient interactions that take place during the test.

FIGURE 44.3
The Rorschach test
In this projective test, people tell what they see in a series of symmetrical inkblots. Some who use this test are confident that the interpretation of ambiguous stimuli will reveal unconscious aspects of the test-taker's personality. Others use it as an icebreaker or to supplement other information.

"If a professional psychologist is 'evaluating' you in a situation in which you are at risk and asks you for responses to ink blots . . . walk out of that psychologist's office."
Robyn Dawes, *House of Cards: Psychology and Psychotherapy Based on Myth*, 1994

© 1983 by Sidney Harris; American Scientist Magazine.

"**The forward thrust of the antlers shows a determined personality, yet the small sun indicates a lack of self-confidence. . . .**"

"The Rorschach Inkblot Test has been resoundingly discredited . . . I call it the Dracula of psychological tests, because no one has been able to drive a stake through the cursed thing's heart."
Carol Tavris, "Mind Games: Psychological Warfare Between Therapists and Scientists," 2003

"Dawkins' law of adversarial debate: 'When two incompatible beliefs are advocated with equal intensity, the truth does not lie halfway between them.'"
Richard Dawkins, 2004

Evaluating the Psychoanalytic Perspective

OBJECTIVE 44-9 | Summarize psychology's current assessment of Freud's theory of psychoanalysis.

Contradictory Evidence from Modern Research

We critique Freud from an early twenty-first–century perspective, a perspective that itself will be subject to revision. Freud did not have access to neurotransmitter or DNA studies, or to all that we have since learned about human development, thinking, and emotion. Thus, to criticize his theories by comparing them with current concepts, some say, is like comparing Henry Ford's Model T with today's Mustang.

But Freud's admirers and his critics agree that recent research contradicts many of his specific ideas. Today's developmental psychologists see our development as lifelong, not fixed in childhood. They doubt that infants' neural networks are mature enough to sustain as much emotional trauma as Freud assumed. Some think Freud overestimated parental influence and underestimated peer influence (and abuse). They also doubt that conscience and gender identity form as the child resolves the Oedipus complex at age 5 or 6. We gain our gender identity earlier and become strongly masculine or feminine even without a same-sex parent present. And they note that Freud's ideas about childhood sexuality arose from his rejection of stories of childhood sexual abuse told by his female patients—stories that some scholars believe he suggested, coerced, or later misremembered and then attributed to their own childhood sexual wishes and conflicts (Esterson, 2001; Powell & Boer, 1994). Today, we understand how Freud's questioning might have created false memories, and we also know that childhood sexual abuse does happen.

New ideas about why we dream dispute Freud's belief that dreams disguise and fulfill wishes. And slips of the tongue can be explained as competition between similar verbal choices in our memory network. Someone who says "I don't want to do that—it's a lot of brothel" may simply be blending *bother* and *trouble* (Foss & Hakes, 1978). Researchers find little support for Freud's idea that defense mechanisms disguise sexual and aggressive impulses (though our cognitive gymnastics do indeed work to protect our self-esteem). History also has failed to support another of Freud's ideas—that suppressed sexuality causes psychological disorders. From Freud's time to ours, sexual inhibition has diminished; psychological disorders have not.

Is Repression a Myth?

Freud's entire psychoanalytic theory rests on his assumption that the human mind often *represses* painful experiences, banishing them into the unconscious until, with the help of a guide, we somehow uncover them, finding them intact, like long-lost books in a dusty attic. Recover and resolve the painful repressed memories of our childhood and emotional healing would follow. Under Freud's influence, repression became a widely accepted concept, used to explain hypnotic phenomena, psychological disorders, and apparent lost and recovered memories of childhood traumas (Cheit, 1998). In one survey, 88 percent of university students believed that painful experiences commonly get pushed out of awareness and into the unconscious (Garry & others, 1994).

Actually, contend many of today's researchers, repression, if it ever occurs, is a rare mental response to terrible trauma. "Repression folklore is . . . partly refuted, partly untested, and partly untestable," says Elizabeth Loftus (1995). Consider: If the human mind indeed commonly banishes painful experiences, how do we explain these odd findings?

- Shouldn't we expect children who have witnessed a parent's murder to repress the experience? A study of sixteen 5- to 10-year-old children who had this horrific experience found that not one repressed the memory (Malmquist, 1986).

"Many aspects of Freudian theory are indeed out of date, and they should be: Freud died in 1939, and he has been slow to undertake further revisions."

Psychologist Drew Westen (1998)

"I remember your name perfectly but I just can't think of your face."

Oxford professor W. A. Spooner, 1844–1930, famous for his linguistic flip-flops (*spoonerisms*). Spooner rebuked one student for "fighting a liar in the quadrangle" and another who "hissed my mystery lecture," adding "You have tasted two worms."

- Shouldn't survivors of Nazi death camps have banished the atrocities from consciousness? With rare exceptions, they remember all too well—although many do benefit from disclosing and talking through their experiences (Helmreich, 1992, 1994; Pennebaker, 1990).
- Shouldn't battle-scarred veterans suffer amnesia for their worst experiences? In one neurological unit in a British hospital, 35 percent of military patients arrived with amnesia after severe combat during World War II (Arrigo & Pezdek, 1997; Karon & Widener, 1997, 1998). But such cases often appear to be either concussion-related or a *false amnesia* tactic for escaping intolerable situations (Holmes, 1990, 1994). Folklore regarding recovered battlefield memories is either unconfirmed or related to therapists' use of suggestive techniques.

There are exceptions—one death camp survivor reportedly forgot for more than 30 years the snatching and shooting of her infant son (Kraft, 1996). Some researchers believe that extreme, prolonged stress, such as the stress some severely abused children experience, might disrupt memory by damaging the hippocampus (Schacter, 1996). But the far more common reality is that high stress (and associated stress hormones) enhances memory. Powerfully negative emotional events are therefore remembered well (Alexander & others, 2005; Shobe & Kihlstrom, 1997).

In fact, too well: Traumatic events, such as rape and torture, haunt survivors, who experience unwanted flashbacks. They are seared onto the soul. "You see the babies," said Holocaust survivor Sally H. (1979). "You see the screaming mothers. You see hanging people. You sit and you see that face there. It's something you don't forget."

The Modern Unconscious Mind

Freud was right about at least one thing: We indeed have limited access to all that goes on in our minds (Erdelyi, 1985, 1988; Kihlstrom, 1990). In fact, our capacity for unconscious learning is quite sophisticated. Pawel Lewicki and his colleagues (1992, 1997) at the University of Tulsa's Nonconscious Information Processing Laboratory discovered that people's nonconscious learning can anticipate patterns "too complex and too confusing to be consciously noticed." In one study, some students watched (others did not) as the numeral 6 jumped around a computer screen from quadrant to quadrant. Although the movement seemed to be in random order—no one consciously detected any rule—it was based on a complex, hidden pattern. And those who had seen the earlier presentations were quicker to find the next 6 when it was hidden among a screen full of numbers. Without knowing how they did it, their ability to track the number from one quadrant to another was improving. When the number's movement became truly random, their performance declined.

Lewicki repeated the experiment with his quick-witted psychology professor colleagues, who knew he was studying nonconscious learning. They, too, gained speed in locating the target's next position, and they, too, did not know why. When the experimenters switched to a random sequence and performance declined, the professors conjectured reasons for the decline (threatening subliminal messages, perhaps?). To students who had displayed nonconscious learning, Lewicki even offered $100 if they could uncover the hidden pattern. Some spent hours trying to decipher the sequence. None succeeded.

Other researchers have confirmed the reality of nonconscious *implicit learning* (Fletcher & others, 2005; Frensch & Rünger, 2003). Such experiments point to a vast realm of out-of-sight information. Nevertheless, the "iceberg" notion held by today's research psychologists differs from Freud's—so much so, argues Anthony Greenwald (1992), that it is time to abandon Freud's view of the unconscious. Many psychologists now think of the unconscious not as seething passions and repressive censoring

■ **terror-management theory** proposes that faith in one's worldview and the pursuit of self-esteem provide protection against a deeply rooted fear of death.

"Two passengers leaned against the ship's rail and stared at the sea. 'There sure is a lot of water in the ocean,' said one. 'Yes,' answered his friend, 'we've only seen the top of it.'"

Psychologist George A. Miller (1962)

"I don't want to attain immortality through my work; I want to attain immortality by not dying."

Woody Allen

"We are arguing like a man who should say, 'If there were an invisible cat in that chair, the chair would look empty; but the chair does look empty; therefore there is an invisible cat in it.'"

C. S. Lewis, *Four Loves*, 1958

but as cooler information processing that occurs without our awareness. To these researchers, the unconscious also involves

- the schemas that automatically control our perceptions and interpretations.
- the priming by stimuli to which we have not consciously attended.
- the right-hemisphere activity that enables the split-brain patient's left hand to carry out an instruction the patient cannot verbalize.
- the parallel processing of different aspects of vision and thinking.
- the implicit memories that operate without conscious recall, even among those with amnesia.
- the emotions that activate instantly, before conscious analysis.
- the self-concept and stereotypes that automatically and unconsciously influence how we process information about ourselves and others.

More than we realize, we fly on autopilot. Our lives are guided by off-screen, out-of-sight, nonconscious information processing. The nonconscious mind is huge. This understanding of nonconscious information processing is more like the pre-Freudian view of an underground stream of thought from which spontaneous creative ideas surface.

Recent history has supported Freud's idea that we defend ourselves against anxiety. Again, however, the contemporary idea differs from Freud's. Jeff Greenberg, Sheldon Solomon, and Tom Pyszczynski (1997) believe that one source of anxiety is "the terror resulting from our awareness of vulnerability and death." More than 130 studies testing their **terror-management theory** show that thinking about one's mortality—for example, by writing a short essay on dying and its associated emotions—provokes enough anxiety to intensify prejudices. Death anxiety motivates contempt for others and esteem for oneself.

Faced with a threatening world, people act not only to enhance their self-esteem but also to adhere more strongly to worldviews that answer questions about life's meaning. Moreover, they cleave to close relationships (Mikulincer & others, 2003). The events of 9/11—a striking experience of the terror of death—led trapped World Trade Center occupants to spend their last moments calling loved ones, and led most Americans to reach out to family and friends.

Recent research has also provided some support for Freud's idea of defense mechanisms (even if they don't work exactly as Freud supposed). For example, Roy Baumeister and his colleagues (1998) found that people tend to see their foibles and attitudes in others, a phenomenon that Freud called projection and that today's researchers call the *false consensus effect,* the tendency to overestimate the extent to which others share our beliefs and behaviors. People who cheat on their taxes or break speed limits tend to think many others do likewise. People falsely told they are high in repressed anger or dishonesty tend more to see such in others (Schimel & others, 2003). Moreover, when trying to suppress thinking about our own faults we become more likely to see them in others (Newman & others, 1997). Supportive evidence is, however, meager for other defenses, such as displacement, that are tied to instinctual energy. More evidence exists for defenses, such as reaction formation, that defend self-esteem. Defense mechanisms, Baumeister concludes, are motivated less by the seething impulses that Freud presumed than by our need to protect our self-image.

Freud's Ideas as Scientific Theory

Psychologists also criticize Freud's theory for its scientific shortcomings, for falling short of the standard that good scientific theories explain observations and offer testable hypotheses. Freud's theory rests on few objective observations and parts of it offer few hypotheses to verify or reject. (For Freud, his own recollections and interpretations of patients' free associations, dreams, and slips were evidence enough.)

What is the most serious problem with Freud's theory? It offers after-the-fact explanations of any characteristic (of one person's smoking, another's fear of horses, another's sexual orientation) yet fails to *predict* such behaviors and traits. If you feel angry at your mother's death, you illustrate his theory because "your unresolved childhood dependency needs are threatened." If you do not feel angry, you again illustrate his theory because "you are repressing your anger." That, said Calvin Hall and Gardner Lindzey (1978, p. 68), "is like betting on a horse after the race has been run." A good theory makes testable predictions.

For such reasons, some of Freud's critics offer harsh words. They see a decaying Freudian edifice built on the swamplands of childhood sexuality, repression, dream analysis, and after-the-fact speculation. "When we stand on [Freud's] shoulders, we only discover that we're looking further in the wrong direction," says John Kihlstrom (1997). Freud's most searing critic, Frederick Crews (1998), likens Freud to Peter Sellers' bumbling Inspector Clouseau, albeit with a unique talent for bamboozling an entire century. What is original about Freud's ideas is not good, and what is good is not original (the unconscious mind is an idea that dates back to Plato).

So, should psychology post a "Do Not Resuscitate" order on this old theory? Freud's supporters object. To criticize Freudian theory for not making testable predictions is, they say, like criticizing baseball for not being an aerobic exercise, something it was never intended to be. Freud never claimed that psychoanalysis was predictive science. He merely claimed that, looking back, psychoanalysts could find meaning in our state of mind (Rieff, 1979).

Freud's supporters also note that some of his ideas *are* enduring. It was Freud who drew our attention to the unconscious and the irrational, to our self-protective defenses, to the importance of human sexuality, and to the tension between our biological impulses and our social well-being. It was Freud who challenged our self-righteousness, punctured our pretensions, and reminded us of our potential for evil.

In science, Darwin's legacy lives while Freud's is waning (Bornstein, 2001). In the popular culture, Freud's legacy lives on. Some ideas that many people assume to be true—that childhood experiences mold personality, that dreams have meaning, that many behaviors have disguised motives—are part of that legacy. His early twentieth-century concepts penetrate our twenty-first-century language. Without realizing their source, we may speak of *ego, repression, projection, complex* (as in "inferiority complex"), *sibling rivalry, Freudian slips,* and *fixation.* "Freud's premises may have undergone a steady decline in currency within academia for many years," noted Martin Seligman (1994), "but Hollywood, the talk shows, many therapists, and the general public still love them."

>> LEARNING OUTCOMES

The Psychoanalytic Perspective

OBJECTIVE 44-1 | Define *personality*.

Psychologists define *personality* as an individual's characteristic pattern of thinking, feeling, and acting. The early grand theories of personality tried to explain human nature, but current theories tend to focus on specific aspects of personality, such as our traits, uniqueness, sense of personal control, and concept of self.

OBJECTIVE 44-2 | Explain how Freud's experiences in private practice led to his theory of psychoanalysis.

As a physician specializing in nervous disorders, Freud encountered patients whose complaints could not be explained in terms of purely physical causes. His attempt to understand these conditions led to his theory of psychoanalysis, the first comprehensive theory of personality.

OBJECTIVE 44-3 | Discuss Freud's view of the mind as an iceberg, and explain how he used this image to represent conscious and unconscious regions of the mind.

Freud believed that most of the mind—the *unconscious*—is hidden from view (as most of an iceberg is hidden below water) because we repress the thoughts, wishes, feelings, and memories that create feelings of anxiety. In his view, this repression is never fully successful, and the troublesome thoughts and feelings express themselves in disguised forms unless we retrieve them into conscious awareness and free ourselves from the tensions they create. He sought to analyze these unconscious dynamics through *free association* and *dream interpretation*.

OBJECTIVE 44-4 | Describe Freud's view of personality structure, and discuss the interactions of the id, ego, and superego.

Freud saw personality as the product of a conflict between our biological impulses and our internalized social restraints on these impulses. Three systems (id, ego, and superego) interact in this conflict. The *id,* which wants immediate gratification, operates in the unconscious and attempts to satisfy basic sexual and aggressive drives. The *superego,* our internalized set of ideals, is the voice of our conscience, judging our actions and producing feelings of pride or guilt. The *ego,* the largely conscious, reality-oriented executive, attempts to reconcile the impulses of the id with the demands of the superego and those of the external world.

OBJECTIVE 44-5 | Identify Freud's psychosexual stages of development, and describe the effects of fixation on behavior.

Freud believed that children develop through psychosexual stages—*oral, anal, phallic, latency,* and *genital*—in which the id is focused on a particular erogenous zone. During the phallic stage, for example, boys may desire their mother and fear punishment for these feelings from their father—a set of reactions Freud called the Oedipus complex. A person who fails to resolve the conflicts associated with a psychosexual stage may remain locked into that stage. This fixation would appear in maladaptive behavior focused on the erogenous zone dominant at that stage.

OBJECTIVE 44-6 | Describe the function of defense mechanisms, and identify six of them.

Freud believed the ego uses defense mechanisms to protect itself from anxiety, the byproduct of the conflict between the id and the superego. The basic defense mechanism, according to Freud, is *repression* (banishing troublesome ideas and feelings into the unconscious); others include *regression* (retreating to an infantile stage), *reaction formation* (transforming unacceptable impulses into acceptable opposites), *projection* (attributing one's unacceptable impulses to others), *rationalization* (explaining one's behavior in terms of self-justifying rather than unacceptable motives), and *displacement* (focusing sexual or aggressive impulses on a person more acceptable than the one who aroused the emotion).

OBJECTIVE 44-7 | Contrast the views of the neo-Freudians and psychodynamic theorists with Freud's original theory.

The *neo-Freudians* accepted many of Freud's basic ideas (the id-ego-superego structure, the importance of the unconscious, the shaping of personality in childhood, and the dynamics of anxiety and the defense mechanisms). But they proposed motives other than sex and aggression, and viewed the ego's conscious control as greater than Freud supposed. Alfred Adler (who coined the term *inferiority complex*) and Karen Horney (who refuted Freud's view of the inferiority of women) argued that social, not sexual, tensions are critical in personality formation. Carl Jung proposed a human collective unconscious containing memory traces from our species' history. Contemporary *psychodynamic* theorists and therapists refute some aspects of Freud's theory, such as the idea that sexual tensions are central to personality formation. They share with Freud the view that much of our mental life is unconscious, that childhood shapes our personality and attachment styles, and that we experience inner conflicts among our wishes, fears, and values.

OBJECTIVE 44-8 | Describe two projective tests used to assess personality, and discuss some criticisms of them.

The *Thematic Apperception Test (TAT)* is a series of ambiguous pictures used to elicit a story in which test-takers express their own inner feelings and interests. The *Rorschach inkblots* are similarly used to evoke test-takers' hidden feelings. Neither test is noted for *reliability* (consistency of results) or *validity* (predicting what it's supposed to predict).

OBJECTIVE 44-9 | Summarize psychology's current assessment of Freud's theory of psychoanalysis.

Recent research has contradicted many of Freud's basic ideas, including the overriding importance of childhood experiences, degree of parental influence, timing of gender-identity formation, importance of sexuality during childhood, existence of hidden content in dreams, frequency of repressed memories, and the existence of the unconscious mind as a reservoir of repressed thoughts and emotions. Critics note that Freud's ideas are not verifiable by scientific methods, and that his theory offers only after-the-fact explanations. Freud's supporters reply that he never viewed psychoanalysis as a predictive science, and that he drew psychology's attention to the unconscious and to the struggle to cope with anxiety. A vast amount of unconscious information processing does occur without our awareness. Current research does not support the concept of defense mechanisms closely tied to defense of the unconscious, but it does support some defenses that protect self-esteem. Finally, Freud is credited with focusing attention on the conflict between biological impulses and social restraints. And without question, his cultural impact has been enormous.

TERMS AND CONCEPTS TO REMEMBER

personality, p. P13-1

free association, p. 44-1

psychoanalysis, p. 44-1

unconscious, p. 44-1

id, p. 44-2

ego, p. 44-2

superego, p. 44-2

psychosexual stages, p. 44-2

Oedipus [ED-uh-puss] complex, p. 44-2

identification, p. 44-3

fixation, p. 44-3

defense mechanisms, p. 44-4

repression, p. 44-4

regression, p. 44-4

reaction formation, p. 44-4

projection, p. 44-4

rationalization, p. 44-4

displacement, p. 44-4

collective unconscious, p. 44-5

projective test, p. 44-6

Thematic Apperception Test (TAT), p. 44-6

Rorschach inkblot test, p. 44-6

terror-management theory, p. 44-10

TEST YOURSELF

1. What, according to Freud, were some of the important defense mechanisms, and what do they defend against? How many of these find support in modern research?

(Answer in Appendix B.)

ASK YOURSELF

1. How would you describe *your* personality? What characteristics make up your typical patterns of thinking, feeling, and acting?

2. What understanding and impressions of Freud did you bring to this chapter? Have they changed in any way after reading this section?

>WEB

Multiple-choice **self-tests** and more may be found at www.worthpublishers.com/myers.

The Humanistic Perspective

By the 1960s, some personality psychologists had become discontented with the negativism of Sigmund Freud's psychoanalytic theory and the mechanistic psychology of B. F. Skinner's behaviorism. In contrast to Freud's study of the base motives of "sick" people, these *humanistic psychologists* focused on the ways "healthy" people strive for self-determination and self-realization. In contrast to behaviorism's scientific objectivity, they studied people through their own self-reported experiences and feelings.

Two pioneering theorists—Abraham Maslow (1908–1970) and Carl Rogers (1902–1987)—offered a *third-force perspective* that emphasized human potential and seeing the world through the person's (not the researcher's) eyes.

Abraham Maslow's Self-Actualizing Person

OBJECTIVE **45-1** | Summarize Abraham Maslow's concept of self-actualization, and explain how his ideas illustrate the humanistic perpective.

Maslow proposed that we are motivated by a hierarchy of needs. If our physiological needs are met, we become concerned with personal safety; if we achieve a sense of security, we then seek to love, to be loved, and to love ourselves; with our love needs satisfied, we seek self-esteem. Having achieved self-esteem, we ultimately seek **self-actualization,** the process of fulfilling our potential.

Abraham Maslow

"Any theory of motivation that is worthy of attention must deal with the highest capacities of the healthy and strong person as well as with the defensive maneuvers of crippled spirits" (*Motivation and Personality*, 1970).

Ted Polumbaum/Time Pix/Getty Images

Maslow (1970) developed his ideas by studying healthy, creative people rather than troubled clinical cases. He based his description of self-actualization on a study of those who seemed notable for their rich and productive lives—among them, Abraham Lincoln, Thomas Jefferson, and Eleanor Roosevelt. Maslow reported that these people shared certain characteristics: Self-aware and self-accepting, open and spontaneous, loving and caring, not paralyzed by others' opinions, they were secure in their sense of who they were. Their interests were problem-centered rather than self-centered. They focused their energies on a particular task, one they often regarded as their mission in life. Most enjoyed a few deep relationships rather than many superficial ones. Many had been moved by spiritual or personal *peak experiences* that surpassed ordinary consciousness.

These, said Maslow, are mature adult qualities, ones found in those who have learned enough about life to be compassionate, to have outgrown their mixed feelings toward their parents, to have found their calling, to have "acquired enough courage to be unpopular, to be unashamed about being openly virtuous, etc." Maslow's work with college students led him to speculate that those likely to become self-actualizing adults were likable, caring, "privately affectionate to those of their elders who deserve it," and "secretly uneasy about the cruelty, meanness, and mob spirit so often found in young people."

Carl Rogers' Person-Centered Perspective

OBJECTIVE 45-2 | Discuss Carl Rogers' person-centered perspective, and explain the importance of unconditional positive regard.

Fellow humanistic psychologist Carl Rogers agreed with much of Maslow's thinking. Rogers believed that people are basically good and are endowed with self-actualizing tendencies. Unless thwarted by an environment that inhibits growth, each of us is like an acorn, primed for growth and fulfillment. Rogers (1980) believed that a growth-promoting climate required three conditions—genuineness, acceptance, and empathy.

According to Rogers, people nurture our growth by being *genuine*—by being open with their own feelings, dropping their facades, and being transparent and self-disclosing.

People also nurture our growth by being *accepting*—by offering us what Rogers called **unconditional positive regard.** This is an attitude of grace, an attitude that values us even knowing our failings. It is a profound relief to drop our pretenses, confess our worst feelings, and discover that we are still accepted. In a good marriage, a close family, or an intimate friendship, we are free to be spontaneous without fearing the loss of others' esteem.

Finally, people nurture our growth by being *empathic*—by sharing and mirroring our feelings and reflecting our meanings. "Rarely do we listen with real understanding, true empathy," said Rogers. "Yet listening, of this very special kind, is one of the most potent forces for change that I know."

Genuineness, acceptance, and empathy are the water, sun, and nutrients that enable people to grow like vigorous oak trees, according to Rogers. For "as persons are accepted and prized, they tend to develop a more caring attitude toward themselves" (Rogers, 1980, p. 116). As persons are empathically heard, "it becomes possible for them to listen more accurately to the flow of inner experiencings."

Rogers believed that genuineness, acceptance, and empathy nurture growth not only in the relationship between therapist and client but also between parent and child, leader and group, teacher and student, administrator and staff member—in fact, between any two human beings.

For Maslow, and even more for Rogers, a central feature of personality is one's **self-concept**—all the thoughts and feelings we have in response to the question, "Who am I?" If our self-concept is positive, we tend to act and perceive the world positively. If it is negative—if in our own eyes we fall far short of our *ideal self*—said Rogers, we feel dissatisfied and unhappy. A worthwhile goal for therapists, parents, teachers, and friends is therefore, he said, to help others know, accept, and be true to themselves.

Assessing the Self

OBJECTIVE 45-3 | Explain how humanistic psychologists assessed personality.

Humanistic psychologists sometimes assessed personality by asking people to fill out questionnaires that would evaluate self-concept. One questionnaire, inspired by Carl Rogers, asked people to describe themselves both as they would *ideally* like to be and as they *actually* are. When the ideal and the actual self are nearly alike, said Rogers, the self-concept is positive. Assessing his clients' personal growth during therapy, he looked for successively closer ratings of actual and ideal self.

Some humanistic psychologists believed that any standardized assessment of personality, even a questionnaire, is depersonalizing. Rather than forcing the person to respond to narrow categories, these humanistic psychologists presumed that interviews and intimate conversation would provide a better understanding of each person's unique experiences.

■ **self-actualization** according to Maslow, the ultimate psychological need that arises after basic physical and psychological needs are met and self-esteem is achieved; the motivation to fulfill one's potential.

■ **unconditional positive regard** according to Rogers, an attitude of total acceptance toward another person.

■ **self-concept** all our thoughts and feelings about ourselves, in answer to the question, "Who am I?"

The picture of empathy
Being open and sharing confidences is easier when the listener shows real understanding. Within such relationships people can relax and fully express their true selves.

"Just remember, son, it doesn't matter whether you win or lose—unless you want Daddy's love."

A father *not* offering unconditional positive regard.

Evaluating the Humanistic Perspective

OBJECTIVE 45-4 | State the major criticisms of the humanistic perspective on personality.

One thing said of Freud can also be said of the humanistic psychologists: Their impact has been pervasive. Their ideas have influenced counseling, education, child-rearing, and management.

They have also influenced—sometimes in ways they did not intend—much of today's popular psychology. Many people have absorbed Maslow's and Rogers' ideas—that a positive self-concept is the key to happiness and success, that acceptance and empathy help nurture positive feelings about oneself, and that people are basically good and capable of self-improvement. One study found that, by a four-to-one margin, Americans believe "human nature is basically good" rather than "fundamentally perverse and corrupt" (NORC, 1985). Humanistic psychologists can also take satisfaction in the changed response to one item on the MMPI (the most widely used personality test): Among those in the 1930s normal standardization sample, only 9 percent agreed that "I am an important person"; by the mid-1980s, more than half agreed (Holden, 1986b). Responding to a 1989 Gallup poll, 85 percent of Americans rated "having a good self-image or self-respect" as *very* important; 0 percent rated it unimportant. And 89 percent of people responding to a 1992 *Newsweek* Gallup poll rated self-esteem as very important for "motivating a person to work hard and succeed." Humanistic psychology's message has been heard.

Perhaps one reason that message has been so well received is that its emphasis on the individual self reflects and reinforces Western cultural values. Movie plots feature rugged individualists who, true to themselves, buck social convention or take the law into their own hands. Popular songs have proclaimed "I Did It My Way" and reminded us that to love yourself is "The Greatest Love of All" (Schoeneman, 1994).

The prominence of the humanistic perspective set off a backlash of criticism. First, said the critics, its concepts are vague and subjective. Consider the description of self-actualizing people as open, spontaneous, loving, self-accepting, and productive. Is this a scientific description? Isn't it merely a description of Maslow's personal values and ideals? Maslow, noted M. Brewster Smith (1978), offered impressions of his own personal heroes. Imagine another theorist who began with a different set of heroes—perhaps Napoleon, Alexander the Great, and John D. Rockefeller, Sr. This theorist would likely describe self-actualizing people as "undeterred by the needs of others," "motivated to achieve," and "obsessed with power."

Critics also objected to the idea that, as Carl Rogers put it, "The only question which matters is, 'Am I living in a way which is deeply satisfying to me, and which truly expresses me?'" (quoted by Wallach & Wallach, 1985). The individualism encouraged by humanistic psychology—trusting and acting on one's feelings, being true to oneself, fulfilling oneself—can, the critics have said, lead to self-indulgence, selfishness, and an erosion of moral restraints (Campbell & Specht, 1985; Wallach & Wallach, 1983). Indeed, it is those who focus beyond themselves who are most likely to experience social support, to enjoy life, and to cope effectively with stress (Crandall, 1984).

Humanistic psychologists have countered that a secure, nondefensive self-acceptance is actually the first step toward loving others. Indeed, people who feel intrinsically liked and accepted—for who they are, not just for their achievements—exhibit less-defensive attitudes (Schimel & others, 2001).

A final accusation leveled against humanistic psychology is that it fails to appreciate the reality of our human capacity for evil. Faced with global warming, overpopulation, terrorism, and the spread of nuclear weapons, we may become apathetic from either of two rationalizations. One is a naive optimism that denies the threat ("People are basically good; everything will work out."). The other is a dark despair ("It's hopeless; why try?"). Action requires enough

"We do pretty well when you stop to think that people are basically good."

realism to fuel concern and enough optimism to provide hope. Humanistic psychology, say the critics, encourages the needed hope but not the equally necessary realism about evil.

Even within humanistic psychology there has been debate over whether people are basically good. Carl Rogers clearly thought so. Although aware of the "incredible amount" of cruel, destructive behavior in the world, he did "not find that this evil is inherent in human nature." He stated that he had never known an individual who—given growth-promoting conditions—had chosen "the cruel or destructive path" (Rogers, 1981). Evil, in his view, springs not from human nature but from toxic cultural influences, including "the constricting, destructive influence of our educational system, the injustice of our distribution of wealth, [and] our cultivated prejudices against individuals who are different."

Fellow humanistic psychologist Rollo May dissented. Of course the cultural context matters, he said. But "who makes up the culture except persons like you and me? The culture is evil as well as good because we, the human beings who constitute it, are evil as well as good." May agreed with the critics who saw people joining the humanistic movement as seekers of "a community of like-minded persons who also are playing possum to the evils about us." Accepting the reality of human evil requires "the age-old religious truths of mercy and forgiveness," he said, "and it leaves no place for self-righteousness" (May, 1982).

>> LEARNING OUTCOMES

The Humanistic Perspective

OBJECTIVE 45-1 | Summarize Abraham Maslow's concept of self-actualization, and explain how his ideas illustrate the humanistic perspective.

Maslow proposed a hierarchy of needs, with physiological needs at the base. He believed that after fulfilling other needs (physiological; safety; belongingness and love; self-esteem), people will be motivated to achieve their highest potential, self-actualization. Maslow typifies humanistic psychology's attempt to turn psychology's attention from baser motives and environmental conditioning to the growth potential of healthy people, believed to be basically good.

OBJECTIVE 45-2 | Discuss Carl Rogers' person-centered perspective, and explain the importance of unconditional positive regard.

Like Maslow, Rogers believed that unless thwarted by their environment, people will grow and realize their self-actualizing tendencies. He advised treating others in a way that is genuine, accepting, and empathic, with an attitude of unconditional positive regard—total acceptance toward the other person. In Rogers' view, a central feature of personality is our self-concept, our thoughts and feelings in response to the question "Who am I?"

OBJECTIVE 45-3 | Explain how humanistic psychologists assessed personality.

Some assessed personality through questionnaires on which people reported their self-concept, for example, by comparing their actual self with their ideal self. Others believed that we could understand a person's subjective personal experiences only through interviews and intimate conversations.

OBJECTIVE 45-4 | State the major criticisms of the humanistic perspective on personality.

Although humanistic psychology helped renew psychology's interest in the self, its critics argue that its concepts were vague and subjective, its values individualist and self-centered, and its assumptions naively optimistic.

TERMS AND CONCEPTS TO REMEMBER

self-actualization, p. 45-0   self-concept, p. 45-1
unconditional positive regard,
    p. 45-1

TEST YOURSELF

1. What does it mean to be "empathic"? To be "self-actualized"?

(Answer in Appendix B.)

ASK YOURSELF

1. Have you had someone in your life who accepted you unconditionally? Do you think this person helped you to know yourself better and to develop a better image of yourself?

>WEB

Multiple-choice *self-tests* and more may be found at www.worthpublishers.com/myers.

MODULE

Contemporary Research on Personality

The Trait Perspective

OBJECTIVE 46-1 | Cite the main difference between the trait and psychoanalytic perspectives on personality.

Trait researchers attempt to define personality in terms of stable and enduring behavior patterns, such as Sam Gamgee's loyalty and optimism. The trait perspective can be traced in part to a remarkable meeting in 1919, when Gordon Allport, a curious 22-year-old psychology student, interviewed Sigmund Freud in Vienna. Allport soon discovered just how preoccupied the founder of psychoanalysis was with finding hidden motives.

> Soon after I had entered the famous red burlap room with pictures of dreams on the wall, he summoned me to his inner office. He did not speak to me but sat in expectant silence, for me to state my mission. I was not prepared for silence and had to think fast to find a suitable conversational gambit. I told him of an episode on the tram car on my way to his office. A small boy about 4 years of age had displayed a conspicuous dirt phobia. He kept saying to his mother, "I don't want to sit there . . . don't let that dirty man sit beside me." To him everything was *schmutzig* (filthy). His mother was a well-starched *Hausfrau*, so dominant and purposive looking that I thought the cause and effect apparent.
>
> When I finished my story Freud fixed his kindly therapeutic eyes upon me and said, "And was that little boy you?" Flabbergasted and feeling a bit guilty, I contrived to change the subject. While Freud's misunderstanding of my motivation was amusing, it also started a deep train of thought (1967, pp. 7–8).

That train of thought ultimately led Allport to do what Freud did not do—to describe personality in terms of fundamental **traits**—people's characteristic behaviors and conscious motives (such as the professional curiosity that actually motivated Allport to see Freud). Meeting Freud, said Allport, "taught me that [psychoanalysis], for all its merits, may plunge too deep, and that psychologists would do well to give full recognition to manifest motives before probing the unconscious." Allport came to define personality in terms of identifiable behavior patterns. He was concerned less with *explaining* individual traits than with *describing* them. How, then, can theorists use traits to describe and classify personalities? One way is describing people using broad personality "types" that signal one's most noteworthy trait and its associated characteristics. An analogy may help. Imagine that you want to describe and classify apples. Someone might correctly say that every apple is unique. Still, you might find it useful to begin by classifying apples as distinct *types*—Granny Smith, MacIntosh, Red or Golden Delicious, and so forth. That is precisely how the ancient Greeks described personality—by classifying people according to four types. Depending on which of one's bodily "humors," or fluids, they believed to predominate, they declared people melancholic (depressed), sanguine (cheerful), phlegmatic (unemotional), or choleric (irritable).

A more recent classification, written by Isabel Briggs Myers (1987) and her mother, Kathleen Briggs, attempts to sort people according to Carl Jung's personality types, based on their responses to 126 questions. The *Myers-Briggs Type Indicator,*

■ **trait** a characteristic pattern of behavior or a disposition to feel and act, as assessed by self-report inventories and peer reports.

which has been taken by 2.5 million Americans a year and used by 89 of the 100 largest corporations, is quite simple (Gladwell, 2004). It offers choices, such as "Do you usually value sentiment more than logic, or value logic more than sentiment?" Then it counts the test-taker's preferences, labels them as indicating, say, a "feeling" or "thinking" type, and feeds them back to the person in complimentary terms. Feeling types, for example, are told they are sensitive to values and "sympathetic, appreciative, and tactful"; thinking types are told they "prefer an objective standard of truth" and are "good at analyzing." (Every type has its strengths, so everyone gets flattered.)

Most people agree with their announced type profile. It mirrors their declared preferences and leaves them feeling good. They may also accept their label as a basis for being matched with work partners and tasks that supposedly suit their temperaments. A National Research Council report noted, however, that despite the test's popularity in business and career counseling, its initial use outran research on its value as a predictor of job performance, and "the popularity of this instrument in the absence of proven scientific worth is troublesome" (Druckman & Bjork, 1991, p. 101; see also Pittenger, 1993). Since those cautionary words, research on the Myers-Briggs has been accumulating, thanks to periodicals such as the *Journal of Psychological Type*.

Exploring Traits

OBJECTIVE 46-2 | Describe some of the ways psychologists have attempted to compile a list of basic personality traits.

Classifying people as one or another distinct personality type fails to capture their full individuality. We are each a unique complex of multiple traits. So how else could we describe our personalities? To return to our apple analogy, we might describe an apple by placing it along several trait dimensions—relatively large or small, red or yellow, sweet or sour. By placing people on several trait dimensions simultaneously, psychologists can describe countless individual personality variations, much as researchers can describe thousands of colors in terms of their variations on just three color dimensions—hue, saturation, and brightness.

What trait dimensions describe personality? If you had an upcoming blind date, what personality traits might give you an accurate sense of the person? Allport and his associate H. S. Odbert (1936) literally counted all the words in an unabridged dictionary with which one could describe people. How many were there? Almost 18,000! How, then, could psychologists condense the list to a manageable number of basic traits?

Factor Analysis

One way has been to propose traits, such as anxiety, that some theory regards as basic. A newer technique is *factor analysis*, a statistical procedure that has been used to identify clusters of related items. Imagine that people who describe themselves as outgoing also tend to say that they like excitement and practical jokes and dislike quiet reading. Such a statistically correlated cluster of behaviors reflects a basic factor, or trait—in this case, *extraversion*.

British psychologists Hans Eysenck and Sybil Eysenck [EYE-zink] believed that we can reduce many of our normal individual variations to two or three dimensions, including *extraversion-introversion* and *emotional stability-instability* (**FIGURE 46.1** on the next page). People in 35 countries around the world, from China to Uganda to Russia, have taken the *Eysenck Personality Questionnaire,* and when their answers are analyzed, the extraversion and emotionality factors inevitably emerged as basic personality dimensions (Eysenck, 1990, 1992). The Eysencks believed that these factors are genetically influenced and recent research supports this belief.

Chris Rock: the extravert
Trait labels such as *extraversion* can describe our temperament and typical behaviors.

AP Photo/Julie Jacobson

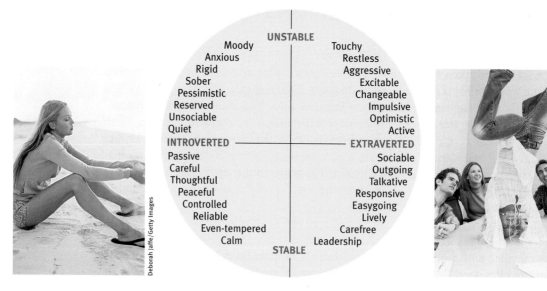

FIGURE 46.1

Two personality factors
Mapmakers can tell us a lot by using two axes (north-south and east-west). Hans Eysenck and Sybil Eysenck use two primary personality factors—extraversion–introversion and stability–instability—as axes for describing personality variation. Varying combinations define other, more specific traits. (From Eysenck & Eysenck, 1963.)

In the figure:

UNSTABLE

Moody, Anxious, Rigid, Sober, Pessimistic, Reserved, Unsociable, Quiet

Touchy, Restless, Aggressive, Excitable, Changeable, Impulsive, Optimistic, Active

INTROVERTED — EXTRAVERTED

Passive, Careful, Thoughtful, Peaceful, Controlled, Reliable, Even-tempered, Calm

Sociable, Outgoing, Talkative, Responsive, Easygoing, Lively, Carefree, Leadership

STABLE

Biology and Personality

Brain-activity scans of extraverts add to the growing list of traits and mental states that have been explored with brain-imaging procedures. (At this writing, that list includes intelligence, impulsivity, addictive cravings, sexual attraction, aggressiveness, empathy, spiritual experience, and even racial and political attitudes [Olson, 2005]). Such studies indicate that extraverts seek stimulation because their normal *brain arousal* is relatively low. For example, PET scans show that a frontal lobe area involved in behavior inhibition is less active in extraverts than in introverts (Johnson & others, 1999).

Our biology influences our personality in other ways as well. Our *genes* have much to say about the *temperament*—our emotional reactivity—and the behavioral style that help define our personality. Jerome Kagan, for example, attributes differences in children's shyness and inhibition to their *autonomic nervous system* reactivity. Given a reactive autonomic nervous system, we respond to stress with greater anxiety and inhibition. The fearless, curious child may become the rock-climbing or fast-driving adult. And studies comparing identical and fraternal twins, comparing identical twins reared apart, and comparing adoptees with their adoptive and biological parents all remind us: Personality forms under the influence of genes.

That fact of life also appears in animal personalities. Samuel Gosling and his colleagues (2003) report that personality differences among dogs (in energy, affection, reactivity, and curious intelligence) are as evident, and as consistently judged, as personality differences among humans. Even birds have stable personalities. Among a European relative of the chickadee, bold birds more quickly inspect new objects and explore trees (Groothuis & Carere, 2005; Verbeek & others, 1994). By selective breeding, researchers can produce bold or shy birds. Both have their place in natural history. In lean years, bold birds are more likely to find food; in abundant years, shy birds feed with less risk.

Assessing Traits

OBJECTIVE 46-3 | Explain how psychologists use personality inventories to assess traits, and discuss the most widely used personality inventory

If stable and enduring traits guide our actions, can we devise valid and reliable tests of them? Several trait assessment techniques exist. Some profile a person's behavior patterns—often providing quick assessments of a single trait, such as extraversion, anxiety, or self-esteem. **Personality inventories**—longer questionnaires covering a wide range of feelings and behaviors—are designed to assess several traits at once.

The most extensively researched personality inventory is the **Minnesota Multiphasic Personality Inventory (MMPI).** Although it assesses "abnormal" personality tendencies rather than normal personality traits, the MMPI illustrates a good way of developing a personality inventory. One of its creators, Starke Hathaway (1960), compared his effort to that of Alfred Binet, who developed the first intelligence test by

■ **personality inventory** a questionnaire (often with true-false or agree-disagree items) on which people respond to items designed to gauge a wide range of feelings and behaviors; used to assess selected personality traits.

■ **Minnesota Multiphasic Personality Inventory (MMPI)** the most widely researched and clinically used of all personality tests. Originally developed to identify emotional disorders (still considered its most appropriate use), this test is now used for many other screening purposes.

■ **empirically derived test** a test (such as the MMPI) developed by testing a pool of items and then selecting those that discriminate between groups.

selecting items that discriminated children who would have trouble progressing normally in French schools. The MMPI items, too, were **empirically derived.** That is, from a large pool of items, Hathaway and his colleagues selected those on which particular diagnostic groups differed. They then grouped the questions into 10 clinical scales.

Hathaway and others initially gave hundreds of true-false statements ("No one seems to understand me"; "I get all the sympathy I should"; "I like poetry") to groups of psychologically disordered patients and to "normal" people. They retained any statement—no matter how silly it sounded—on which the patient group's answer differed from that of the normal group. "Nothing in the newspaper interests me except the comics" may seem senseless, but it just so happened that depressed people were more likely to answer "true." (Nevertheless, people have had fun spoofing the MMPI with their own mock items: "Weeping brings tears to my eyes," "Frantic screams make me nervous," and "I stay in the bathtub until I look like a raisin" [Frankel & others, 1983].) Today's MMPI-2 also has newer scales assessing, for instance, work attitudes, family problems, and anger.

In contrast to the subjectivity of most projective tests favored by psychoanalysts, personality inventories are scored objectively—so objectively that a computer can administer and score them. (The computer can also provide descriptions of people who previously responded similarly.) Objectivity does not, however, guarantee validity. For example, individuals taking the MMPI for employment purposes can give socially desirable answers to create a good impression. But in so doing they may also score high on a "lie scale" that assesses faking (as when people respond "false" to a universally true statement such as "I get angry sometimes"). For better or worse, the objectivity of the MMPI contributes to its popularity and to its translation into more than 100 languages.

The Big Five Factors

OBJECTIVE 46-4 | Identify the Big Five personality factors, and discuss some of the strengths of this approach to studying personality.

Today's trait researchers believe that earlier trait dimensions, such as the Eysencks' introverted-extraverted and unstable-stable dimensions, are important. But they do not tell the whole story. A slightly expanded set of factors—dubbed the *Big Five*—does a better job (John & Srivastava, 1999; McCrae & Costa, 1999). If a test specifies where you are on the five dimensions (conscientiousness, agreeableness, neuroticism, openness, and extraversion; see TABLE **46.1**), it has said

TABLE 46.1

THE "BIG FIVE" PERSONALITY FACTORS (Adapted from McCrae & Costa (1986, p. 1002)

(*Memory tip:* Picturing a **CANOE** will help you recall these.)

Trait Dimension	Endpoints of the Dimension		
Conscientiousness	Organized	←——→	Disorganized
	Careful	←——→	Careless
	Disciplined	←——→	Impulsive
Agreeableness	Soft-hearted	←——→	Ruthless
	Trusting	←——→	Suspicious
	Helpful	←——→	Uncooperative
Neuroticism (emotional stability vs. instability)	Calm	←——→	Anxious
	Secure	←——→	Insecure
	Self-satisfied	←——→	Self-pitying
Openness	Imaginative	←——→	Practical
	Preference for variety	←——→	Preference for routine
	Independent	←——→	Conforming
Extraversion	Sociable	←——→	Retiring
	Fun-loving	←——→	Sober
	Affectionate	←——→	Reserved

HOW TO BE A "SUCCESSFUL" ASTROLOGER OR PALM READER

Can we discern people's traits from the alignment of the stars and planets at the time of their birth? From their handwriting? From lines on their palms?

Astronomers scoff at the naiveté of astrology—the constellations have shifted in the millennia since astrologers formulated their predictions (Kelly, 1997, 1998). Humorists mock it: "No offense," writes Dave Barry, "but if you take the horoscope seriously your frontal lobes are the size of Raisinets." Psychologists instead ask questions: Does it work? Can astrologers surpass chance when given someone's birth date and asked to identify the person from a short lineup of different personality descriptions? Can people pick out their own horoscopes from a lineup of horoscopes?

The consistent answers have been: No, no, and no (British Psychological Society, 1993; Carlson, 1985; Kelly, 1997). Graphologists, who make predictions from handwriting samples, have similarly been found to do no better than chance when trying to discern people's occupations from examining several pages of their handwriting (Beyerstein & Beyerstein, 1992; Dean & others, 1992). Nevertheless, graphologists—and introductory psychology students—will often *perceive* correlations between personality and handwriting even where there are none (King & Koehler, 2000).

If all these perceived correlations evaporate under close scrutiny, how do astrologers and the like persuade thousands of newspapers and millions of people worldwide to buy

© 2000 by Rob Pudim

their advice? Ray Hyman (1981), palm reader turned research psychologist, has revealed the suckering methods of astrologers, palm readers, and crystal-ball gazers.

Their first technique, the "stock spiel," builds on the observation that each of us is in some ways like no one else and in other ways just like everyone. That some things are true of us all enables the "seer" to offer statements that seem impressively accurate: "I sense that you worry about things more than you let on, even to your best friends." A number of such generally true statements can be combined into a personality description. Imagine that you take a personality test and then receive the following character sketch:

> You have a strong need for other people to like and to admire you. You have a

tendency to be critical of yourself. . . . You pride yourself on being an independent thinker and do not accept other opinions without satisfactory proof. You have found it unwise to be too frank in revealing yourself to others. At times you are extraverted, affable, sociable; at other times you are introverted, wary, and reserved. Some of your aspirations tend to be pretty unrealistic (Davies, 1997; Forer, 1949).

In experiments, college students have received stock assessments like this one, drawn from statements in a newsstand astrology book. When they think the bogus, generic feedback was prepared just for them and when it is favorable, they nearly

much of what there is to say about your personality. Around the world, people describe others in terms roughly consistent with this list. But the Big Five is not the last word: Other factor analysis researchers and theorists wonder whether we should add dimensions such as self-consciousness, masculinity-femininity, intellect-imagination, religiosity, or positive-negative emotion (Ashton & others, always rate the description as either "good" or "excellent" (Davies, 1997). Even skeptics of astrology, when given a flattering description attributed to an astrologer, begin to think that "maybe there's something to this astrology stuff after all" (Glick & others, 1989). An astrologer, it has been said, is someone "prepared to tell you what you think of yourself" (Jones, 2000).

French psychologist Michael Gauquelin had similar results when he placed an ad in a Paris newspaper offering a free personal horoscope. Ninety-four percent of those receiving the horoscope praised the description as accurate. Whose horoscope had they all actually received? That of France's Dr. Petiot, a notorious mass murderer (Kurtz, 1983). This acceptance of stock, positive descriptions is called the *Barnum effect,* named in honor of master showman P. T. Barnum's dictum, "There's a sucker born every minute."

A second technique used by seers is to "read" our clothing, physical features, nonverbal gestures, and reactions to what they are saying. Imagine yourself as the character reader visited by a young woman in her late twenties or early thirties. Hyman described the woman as "wearing expensive jewelry, a wedding band, and a black dress of cheap material. The observant reader noted that she was wearing shoes which were advertised for people with foot trouble." Do these clues suggest anything?

Drawing on these observations, the character reader proceeded to amaze his client with his insights.

He assumed the woman had come to see him, as did most of his female customers, because of a love or financial problem. The black dress and the wedding band led him to reason that her husband had died recently. The expensive jewelry suggested she had been financially comfortable during the marriage, but the cheap dress suggested her

"Madame Zelinski can provide an even more accurate reading with your date of birth and Social Security number."

husband's death had left her impoverished. The therapeutic shoes signified she was now on her feet more than she had been used to, implying that she had been working to support herself since her husband's death. Based on these insights, the reader correctly guessed that the woman was wondering if she should remarry in hope of ending her economic hardship. No wonder, say the skeptics, that when mediums cannot see the person who has come to them, their clients cannot recognize the reading that was meant for them from among other readings (O'Keeffe & Wiseman, 2005).

If you are not as shrewd as this character reader, Hyman says it hardly matters. If people seek you out for a reading, start with some safe sympathy: "I sense you're having some problems lately. You seem unsure what to do. I get the feeling another person is involved." Then tell them what they want to hear. Memorize some Barnum statements from astrology and fortune-telling manuals and use them liberally. Tell people it is their responsibility to cooperate by relating your message to their specific experiences. Later they will recall that you predicted those specific details. Phrase statements as questions, and when you detect a positive response assert the statement strongly. Finally, be a good listener, and later, in different words, reveal to people what they earlier revealed to you. If you dupe them, they will come.

Better yet, beware of those who, by exploiting people with these techniques, are fortune takers rather than fortune tellers.

2004). For now, though, the winning number in the personality lottery is five. The Big Five—today's "common currency for personality psychology" (Funder, 2001)—has been the most active personality research topic since the early 1990s and is currently our best approximation of the basic trait dimensions (Endler & Speer, 1998).

The recent wave of Big Five research explores various questions:

- **How stable are these traits?** In adulthood, the Big Five traits are quite stable, with some tendencies (emotional instability, extraversion, and openness) waning a bit in the decades after college, and others (agreeableness and conscientiousness) rising (McCrae & others, 1999; Vaidya & others, 2002). Conscientiousness increases the most during people's twenties, as people mature and learn to manage their jobs and relationships. Agreeableness increases the most during people's thirties and continues to increase through their sixties (Srivastava & others, 2003).
- **How heritable are they?** Heritability of individual differences varies with the diversity of people studied, but it generally runs 50 percent or a tad more for each dimension (Loehlin & others, 1998).
- **How well do they apply to various cultures?** The Big Five dimensions describe personality in various cultures reasonably well (McCrae, 2001; Paunonen & others, 2000). "Features of personality traits are common to all human groups," infer Robert McCrae and 79 co-researchers (2005) from their recent 50-culture study.
- **Do the Big Five traits predict other personal attributes?** Yes again. Two examples: Highly conscientious people are more likely to be morning types (sometimes called "larks"); evening types ("owls") are marginally more extraverted (Jackson & Gerard, 1996). When one's partner scores lower on agreeableness, stability, and openness, marital and sexual satisfaction may suffer (Botwin & others, 1997; Donnellan & others, 2004).

By exploring such questions, Big Five research has sustained trait psychology and renewed appreciation for the importance of personality.

Evaluating the Trait Perspective

Are our personality traits stable and enduring? Or does our behavior depend on where and with whom we find ourselves? J. R. R. Tolkien created characters, like the loyal Sam Gamgee, whose personality traits were consistent across various times and places. The Italian playwright Luigi Pirandello had a different view. For him, personality was ever-changing, tailored to the particular role or situation. In one of Pirandello's plays, Lamberto Laudisi describes himself: "I am really what you take me to be; though, my dear madam, that does not prevent me from also being really what your husband, my sister, my niece, and Signora Cini take me to be—because they also are absolutely right!" To which Signora Sirelli responds, "In other words you are a different person for each of us."

The Person-Situation Controversy

OBJECTIVE 46-5 | Summarize the person-situation controversy, and explain its importance as a commentary on the trait perspective.

Who, then, typifies human personality, Tolkien's consistent Sam Gamgee or Pirandello's inconsistent Laudisi? Both. Our behavior is influenced by the interaction of our inner disposition with our environment. Still, the question lingers: Which is *more* important? Are we *more* as Tolkien or as Pirandello imagined us to be?

When we explore this *person-situation controversy,* we look for genuine personality traits that persist over time *and* across situations. Are some people dependably conscientious and others unreliable, some cheerful and others dour, some friendly and outgoing and others shy? If we are to consider friendliness a trait, friendly people must act friendly at different times and places. Do they? In considering research that has followed lives through time, some scholars (especially those who study infants) are impressed with personality change; others are struck by personality stability during adulthood. As

"There is as much difference between us and ourselves, as between us and others."
Michel de Montaigne, *Essays*, 1588

Roughly speaking, the temporary, external influences on behavior are the focus of social psychology, and the enduring, inner influences are the focus of personality psychology. In actuality, behavior always depends on the interaction of persons with situations.

FIGURE 46.2 illustrates, data from 152 long-term studies reveal that personality trait scores are positively correlated with scores obtained seven years later, and that as people grow older their personality stabilizes. Interests may change—the avid collector of tropical fish may become the avid gardener. Careers may change—the determined salesperson may become a determined social worker. Relationships may change—the hostile spouse may start over with a new partner. But most people recognize their traits as their own, note Robert McCrae and Paul Costa (1994), "and it is well that they do. A person's recognition of the inevitability of his or her one and only personality is . . . the culminating wisdom of a lifetime." So most people—including most psychologists—would probably side with Tolkien's assumption of stability of personality traits.

But the consistency of specific *behaviors* from one situation to the next is another matter. As Walter Mischel (1968, 1984, 2004) has pointed out, people do not act with predictable consistency. Mischel's studies of college students' conscientiousness revealed but a modest relationship between a student's being conscientious on one occasion (say, showing up for class on time) and being similarly conscientious on another occasion (say, turning in assignments on time). Pirandello would not have been surprised. If you've noticed how outgoing you are in some situations and how reserved you are in others, perhaps you're not surprised either (though for certain traits, Mischel reports, you may accurately assess yourself as more consistent).

This inconsistency in behaviors also makes personality test scores weak predictors of behaviors. People's scores on an extraversion test, for example, do not neatly predict how sociable they actually will be on any given occasion. If we remember such results, says Mischel, we will be more cautious about labeling and pigeonholing individuals. We will be more restrained when asked to predict whether someone is likely to violate parole, commit suicide, or be an effective employee. Years in advance, science can tell us the phase of the moon for any given date. A day in advance, meteorologists can often predict the weather. But we are much further from being able to predict how *you* will feel and act tomorrow.

In defense of traits, Seymour Epstein (1983a,b) maintained that trying to predict a specific act on the basis of a personality test result is like trying to predict your answer to a specific aptitude question on the basis of an intelligence test result. Your answer to any given question is unpredictable because it depends on so many variables (your intelligence, yes, but also your reading of the question, your momentary concentration, luck). Your *average* accuracy over many questions on several tests is more predictable. Similarly, people's *average* outgoingness, happiness, or carelessness over *many* situations is predictable, Epstein observed. When rating someone's shyness or agreeableness, this consistency enables people who know someone well to agree (Kenrick & Funder, 1988). As our best friends can verify, we *do* have personality traits—genetically influenced traits, we now know.

"Mr. Coughlin over there was the founder of one of the first motorcycle gangs."

Change and consistency can co-exist. If all people were to become somewhat less shy with age, there would be personality change, but also relative stability and predictability.

FIGURE 46.2
Personality stability
With age, personality traits become more stable, as reflected in the correlation of trait scores with follow-up scores seven years later. (Data from Roberts & DelVecchio, 2000).

Our spaces express our personalities
Even at "zero acquaintance," people can discern something of others' personality from glimpsing their Web site, dorm room, or office. So, what is your read on University of Texas researcher Samuel Gosling?

John Langford Photography

Moreover, our traits are socially significant. They influence our health, our thinking, and our job performance (Deary & Matthews, 1993; Hogan, 1998). Our traits even lurk, report Samuel Gosling and his colleagues in a series of studies, in our

- *music preferences.* Classical, jazz, blues, and folk music lovers tend to be open to experience and verbally intelligent; country, pop, and religious music lovers tend to be cheerful, outgoing, and conscientious (Rentfrow & Gosling, 2003).
- *dorm rooms and offices.* Our personal spaces display our identity and leave a behavioral residue (in our scattered laundry or neat desktop). And that helps explain why just a few minutes' inspection of our living and working spaces can enable someone to assess with reasonable accuracy our conscientiousness, our openness to new experience, and even our emotional stability (Gosling & others, 2002).
- *personal Web sites.* Is a personal Web site also a canvas for self-expression? Or is it an opportunity for people to present themselves in false or misleading ways? It's more the former, report Simine Vazire and Gosling (2004). Visitors to personal Web sites quickly gain important clues to the owner's extraversion, conscientiousness, and openness to experience.

The bottom line: Traits exist. We differ. And our differences matter.

Consistency of Expressive Style

OBJECTIVE 46-6 | Explain why psychologists are interested in the consistency of the trait of expressiveness.

In unfamiliar, formal situations—perhaps as a guest in the home of a person from another culture—our traits may remain hidden as we attend carefully to social cues. In familiar, informal situations—just hanging out with friends—we feel less constrained, allowing our traits to emerge (Buss, 1989). In these informal situations, our expressive styles—our animation, manner of speaking, and gestures—are impressively consistent. Thus, we often form lasting impressions within a few moments of meeting someone. Nalini Ambady and Robert Rosenthal (1992, 1993) videotaped 13 Harvard University graduate students teaching undergraduate courses. Observers then viewed three *thin slices* of each teacher's behavior—mere 10-second clips from the beginning, middle, and end of a class—and rated each teacher's level of confidence, activeness, warmth, and so forth. These behavior ratings, based on 30 *seconds* of teaching from an entire semester, predicted amazingly well the teacher's average student ratings at the semester's end. Observing even thinner slices—three 2-second clips—yielded ratings that still correlated as high as +.72 with the student evaluations. Some people's first impressions, derived from expressive behavior, predicted other people's lasting impressions!

Mere glimpses of someone's behavior can be revealing because of the potency of traits such as expressiveness. In a study of physician malpractice suits, Ambady and her colleagues (2002) filtered four 10-second slices of surgeon-patient conversation, rendering the speech unintelligible while preserving its intonation, pitch, and rhythm. From those remaining clues, listeners were able to sense the surgeons' warmth, hostility, and dominance and to accurately assess which of them had been sued. Knowing nothing of a surgeon's skill or even what was being said, listeners could nonetheless derive from the tone of voice a feeling for whether the doctor was being empathic or overbearing, and that was enough to help predict the patients' responses.

Some people are naturally expressive (and therefore talented at pantomime and charades); others are less expressive (and therefore better poker players). To evaluate people's voluntary control over their expressiveness, Bella DePaulo and her colleagues (1992) asked people to *act* as expressive or inhibited as possible while stating opinions. Their remarkable findings: Inexpressive people, even when feigning expressiveness, were less expressive than expressive people acting naturally. Similarly, expressive people, even when trying to seem inhibited, were less inhibited than inexpressive people acting naturally. It's hard to be someone you're not, or not to be what you are.

The irrepressibility of expressiveness explains why we can size up how outgoing someone is within seconds. Picture this experiment by Maurice Levesque and David Kenny (1993). They seated groups of four university women around a table and asked each woman merely to state her name, year in school, hometown, and college residence. Judging from just these few seconds of verbal and nonverbal behavior, the women were then to guess one another's talkativeness. (How do you think you would do in guessing someone's talkativeness, based on such a small glimpse of their behavior?) When later correlated with how talkative each woman actually was during a series of one-on-one videotaped conversations, the snap judgments proved reasonably accurate. So did the judgments of Peter Borkenau and his co-workers (2004), who videotaped German adults as they engaged in varied behaviors, from making up a story to reading short sentences to introducing someone. Despite situational variations in behavior, personality came shining through. Someone who seemed smart or outgoing in one situation tended to seem (to someone else) smart or outgoing in another. When we judge an expressive trait such as outgoingness, thin slices of behavior can be revealing.

To sum up, we can say that at any moment the immediate situation powerfully influences a person's behavior, especially when the situation makes clear demands. We can better predict drivers' behavior at traffic lights from knowing the color of the lights than from knowing the drivers' personalities. Thus, professors may perceive certain students as subdued (based on their classroom behavior), but friends may perceive them as pretty wild (based on their party behavior). Averaging our behavior across many occasions does, however, reveal distinct personality traits. Moreover, we can, in a flash, perceive individual differences in some traits, such as expressiveness.

The Social-Cognitive Perspective

OBJECTIVE 46-7 | Describe the social-cognitive perspective, and explain how reciprocal determinism illustrates that perspective.

Today's psychological science, as we have noted so often, views persons as biopsychosocial organisms. People's biologically influenced psychological traits interact with their situations. The **social-cognitive perspective** on personality proposed by Albert Bandura (1986, 2001, 2005) emphasizes the interaction of persons and their situations. Much as nature and nurture always work together, so do persons and their situations.

■ **social-cognitive perspective** views behavior as influenced by the interaction between persons (and their thinking) and their social context.

Like learning theorists, social-cognitive theorists believe we learn many of our behaviors either through conditioning or by observing others and modeling our behavior after theirs. (That is the "social" part.) They also emphasize the importance of mental processes: What we *think* about our situations affects our behavior. (That is the "cognitive" part.) Instead of focusing solely on how our environment *controls* us (behaviorism), social-cognitive theorists focus on how we and our environment *interact:* How do we interpret and respond to external events? How do our schemas, our memories, and our expectations influence our behavior patterns?

Reciprocal Influences

Bandura (1986) called the process of interacting with our environment **reciprocal determinism.** "Behavior, internal personal factors, and environmental influences," he said, "all operate as interlocking determinants of each other" (**FIGURE 46.3**). For example, children's TV-viewing habits (past behavior) influence their viewing preferences (internal factor), which influence how television (environmental factor) affects their current behavior. The influences are mutual.

Consider three specific ways in which individuals and environments interact:

1. **Different people choose different environments.** The school you attend, the reading you do, the television programs you watch, the music you listen to, the friends you associate with—all are part of an environment you have chosen, based partly on your dispositions (Ickes & others, 1997). *You choose your environment and it then shapes you.*

2. **Our personalities shape how we interpret and react to events.** Anxious people, for example, are attuned to potentially threatening events (Eysenck & others, 1987). Thus, they perceive the world as threatening, and they react accordingly.

3. **Our personalities help create situations to which we react.** Many experiments reveal that how we view and treat people influences how they in turn treat us. If we expect someone to be angry with us, we may give the person a cold shoulder, touching off the very anger we expect. If we have an easygoing, positive disposition, we will likely enjoy close, supportive friendships (Donnellan & others, 2005; Kendler, 1997).

In such ways, we are both the products and the architects of our environments.

If all this has a familiar ring, it may be because it parallels and reinforces a pervasive theme in psychology and in this book: *Behavior emerges from the interplay of*

FIGURE 46.3
Reciprocal determinism
The social-cognitive perspective proposes that our personalities are shaped by the interaction of personal/cognitive factors (our feelings and thoughts), our environment, and our behaviors.

FIGURE **46.4**
**The biopsychosocial approach
to the study of personality**
As with other psychological phenomena, personality is fruitfully studied at multiple levels.

external and internal influences. Boiling water turns an egg hard and a potato soft. A threatening environment turns one person into a hero, another into a scoundrel. *At every moment,* our behavior is influenced by our biology, our social experiences, and our cognition and personality. And that, again, is why psychology benefits from these multiple levels of analysis (**FIGURE 46.4**).

Personal Control

OBJECTIVE 46-8 | Discuss the effects of a perception of internal or external control, and describe the concept of learned helplessness.

In studying how we interact with our environment, social-cognitive psychologists emphasize our sense of **personal control**—whether we learn to see ourselves as controlling, or as controlled by, our environment. Psychologists have two basic ways to study the effect of personal control (or any personality factor). One: *Correlate* people's feelings of control with their behaviors and achievements. Two: *Experiment,* by raising or lowering people's sense of control and noting the effects. Let's take these one at a time.

Internal Versus External Locus of Control

Consider your own feelings of control. Do you believe that your life is beyond your control? That the world is run by a few powerful people? That getting a good job depends mainly on being in the right place at the right time? Or do you more strongly believe that what happens to you is your own doing? That the average person can influence government decisions? That being a success is a matter of hard work, not luck?

   Hundreds of studies have compared people who differ in their perceptions of control. On the one side are those who have what psychologist Julian Rotter called an **external locus of control**—the perception that chance or outside forces determine their fate. On the other are those who perceive an **internal locus of control** and believe that to a great extent they control their own destiny. In study after study, "internals" achieve more in school, act more independently, enjoy better health, and feel less depressed than do "externals" (Lachman & Weaver, 1998; Lefcourt, 1982; Presson & Benassi, 1996). Moreover, they are better able to delay gratification and cope with various stresses, including marital problems (Miller & others, 1986).

   Self-control—the ability to control impulses and delay gratification—in turn predicts good adjustment, better grades, and social success, report June Tangney and her colleagues (2004). University students who plan their day's activities and then live out their day as planned are also at low risk for depression (Nezlek, 2001).

■ **reciprocal determinism** the interacting influences between personality and environmental factors.

■ **personal control** our sense of controlling our environment rather than feeling helpless.

■ **external locus of control** the perception that chance or outside forces beyond one's personal control determine one's fate.

■ **internal locus of control** the perception that one controls one's own fate.

None of us experiences unvarying self-control. Self-control requires attention and energy. Like a muscle, self-control temporarily weakens after an exertion, replenishes with rest, and becomes stronger with exercise, report Roy Baumeister and Julia Exline (2000). Exercising willpower depletes mental energy. In one experiment, hungry people's resisting temptations to eat chocolate chip cookies led to their giving up sooner on a tedious task.

Learned Helplessness Versus Personal Control

People who feel helpless and oppressed often perceive control as external. This perception may then deepen their feelings of resignation. In fact, this is precisely what researcher Martin Seligman (1975, 1991) and others found in experiments with both animals and people. Dogs strapped in a harness and given repeated shocks, with no opportunity to avoid them, learned a sense of helplessness. Later placed in another situation where they *could* escape the punishment by simply leaping a hurdle, the dogs cowered as if without hope. People, too, when repeatedly faced with traumatic events over which they have no control, come to feel helpless, hopeless, and depressed. Psychologists call this passive resignation **learned helplessness** (**FIGURE 46.5**). In contrast, animals able to escape the shocks in the first situation learned personal control and easily escaped the shocks in the new situation.

Part of the shock we feel in an unfamiliar culture comes from a diminished sense of control when unsure how people in the new environment will respond (Triandis, 1994). Similarly, people given little control over their world in prisons, factories, colleges, and nursing homes experience lower morale and increased stress. Measures that increase control—allowing prisoners to move chairs and control room lights and the TV, having workers participate in decision making, offering nursing home patients choices about their environment—noticeably improve health and morale (Miller & Monge, 1986; Ruback & others, 1986; Wener & others, 1987). In one famous study of nursing home patients, 93 percent of those encouraged to exert more control became more alert, active, and happy (Rodin, 1986). As researcher Ellen Langer (1983, p. 291) concluded, "perceived control is basic to human functioning." She recommended that "for the young and old alike," it is important that we create environments that enhance our sense of control and personal efficacy. No wonder so many people like their iPods and TiVos, which give them control of the content and timing of their entertainment.

The verdict of these studies is reassuring: Under conditions of personal freedom and empowerment, people thrive. Small wonder that the citizens of stable democracies report higher levels of happiness (Inglehart, 1990). Shortly before the democratic revolution in the former East Germany, psychologists Gabriele Oettingen and Martin Seligman (1990) studied the telltale body language of working-class men in East and

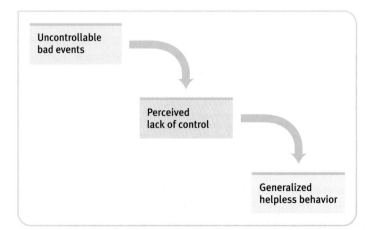

FIGURE 46.5
Learned helplessness
When animals and people experience no control over repeated bad events, they often learn helplessness.

Happy are those who choose their own path
These happy East Berliners, crossing over to West Berlin after the wall came down in 1989, seem to personify this sentiment, from the Roman philosopher Seneca.

West Berlin bars. Compared with their counterparts on the other side of the Wall, the empowered West Berliners much more often laughed, sat upright rather than slumped, and had upward- rather than downward-turned mouths.

Since these data were gathered, democracy movements have increased the personal control enjoyed by many Eastern Europeans. Not so for American collegians, who report feeling more and more *external* control. "The average college student in 2002 had a more external locus of control than 80 percent of college students in the early 1960s," report Jean Twenge and her collaborators (2004).

Some freedom and control is better than none, notes Barry Schwartz (2000, 2004). But does ever-increasing choice breed ever-happier lives? Apparently not. Schwartz notes that the "excess of freedom" in today's Western cultures contributes to decreasing life satisfaction, increased depression, and sometimes paralysis. (One reason I haven't replaced my rusty 12-year-old car is my dread of sorting through all the choices.) Increased consumer choices have not been an unmixed blessing. After choosing among 30 brands of jam or chocolate, people express less satisfaction than those choosing among a half-dozen options (Iyengar & Lepper, 2000). This *tyranny of choice* brings information overload and a greater likelihood that we will feel regret over some of the unchosen options.

Optimism Versus Pessimism

OBJECTIVE 46-9 | Discuss the link between performance and optimistic or pessimistic attributional style, and describe the goals of positive psychology.

One measure of how helpless or effective you feel is where you stand on optimism-pessimism. How do you characteristically explain negative and positive events? Perhaps you have known students whose *attributional style* is negative—who attribute poor performance to their lack of ability ("I can't do this") or to situations enduringly beyond their control ("There is nothing I can do about it"). Such students are more likely to persist in getting low grades than are students who adopt the more hopeful attitude that effort, good study habits, and self-discipline can make a difference (Noel & others, 1987; Peterson & Barrett, 1987). Although mere fantasies tend not to fuel motivation and success, realistic positive expectations do (Oettingen & Mayer, 2002).

In their study of professional achievement, Seligman and Peter Schulman (1986) compared sales made by new life insurance representatives who were more or less optimistic in their outlooks. Those who put an optimistic spin on their setbacks—seeing

■ **learned helplessness** the hopelessness and passive resignation an animal or human learns when unable to avoid repeated aversive events.

Positive expectations often motivate eventual success.

"We just haven't been flapping them hard enough."

them as flukes or as a means to learning a new approach—sold more policies during their first year and were half as likely to quit as were their more pessimistic peers. Seligman's finding came to life for him when Bob Dell, one of the optimistic recruits who began selling for Metropolitan Life after taking Seligman's optimism test, later dialed him up and sold him a policy.

Health, too, benefits from a basic optimism. A depressed hopelessness dampens the body's disease-fighting immune system. In repeated studies, optimists have outlived pessimists or lived with fewer illnesses. Such studies helped point Seligman toward proposing a more positive psychology (see Close-Up).

If positive thinking in the face of adversity pays dividends, so, too, can a dash of realism (Schneider, 2001). Self-disparaging explanations of past failures can depress ambition, but realistic anxiety over possible *future* failures can fuel energetic efforts to avoid the dreaded fate (Norem, 2001; Goodhart, 1986; Showers, 1992). If concerned about bombing the upcoming exam, students may study thoroughly and outperform their equally able but more confident peers. Edward Chang (2001) reports that, compared with European-American students, Asian-American students express somewhat greater pessimism—which he suspects helps explain their impressive academic achievements. Success requires enough optimism to provide hope and enough pessimism to prevent complacency.

Excessive optimism can blind us to real risks. Neil Weinstein (1980, 1982, 1996) has shown how our natural positive-thinking bias can promote "an unrealistic optimism about future life events." Most college students perceive themselves as less likely than their average classmate to develop drinking problems, drop out of school, or have a heart attack by age 40. Most late adolescents see themselves as much less vulnerable than their peers to the AIDS virus (Abrams, 1991).

Our natural positive-thinking bias does seem to vanish, however, when we are bracing ourselves for feedback, such as exam results (Taylor & Shepperd, 1998). (Have you ever noticed that, as a game nears its end, the outcome seems more in doubt when your team is ahead than when it is behind?) Positive illusions also vanish after a traumatic personal experience—as they did for California victims of a catastrophic earthquake, who had to give up their illusions of being less vulnerable than others to earthquakes (Helweg-Larsen, 1999).

Given illusory optimism, documented in some 200 research reports, people may fail to take sensible precautions. Most young Americans know that roughly half of U.S. marriages end in divorce, but they are confident that *theirs* will not (Lehman & Nisbett, 1985). Most cigarette smokers smoke high-tar brands, but only 17 percent believe their brand has a more hazardous tar level than most others (Segerstrom & others, 1993). Compared with other women at their university, sexually active undergraduate women—especially those who do *not* consistently use effective contraception—perceive themselves as *less* vulnerable to unwanted pregnancy (Burger & Burns, 1988). Those who optimistically venture into ill-fated relationships, deny the effects of smoking, or engage in unprotected sex remind us that, like pride, blind optimism may go before a fall.

Ironically, people often are most overconfident when most incompetent. That's because it often takes competence to recognize competence, note Justin Kruger and David Dunning (1999). They found that most students scoring at the low end of tests of grammar and logic believed they had scored in the top half. If you do not know what good grammar is, you may be unaware that your grammar is poor. This "ignorance of

"O God, give us grace to accept with serenity the things that cannot be changed, courage to change the things which should be changed, and the wisdom to distinguish the one from the other."
Reinhold Niebuhr, "The Serenity Prayer," 1943

"I didn't think it could happen to me."
Earvin "Magic" Johnson, *My Life,* 1993 (after contracting HIV)

"Ignorance more freely begets confidence than does knowledge."
Charles Darwin, *The Descent of Man,* 1871

CLOSE-UP:

TOWARD A MORE POSITIVE PSYCHOLOGY

During its first century, psychology understandably focused much of its attention on understanding and alleviating negative states. We have studied abuse and anxiety, depression and disease, prejudice and poverty. Since 1887, articles on selected negative emotions have outnumbered those on positive emotions by 17 to 1.

In ages past, notes 1998 American Psychological Association president Martin Seligman (2002), times of relative peace and prosperity have enabled cultures to turn their attention from repairing weakness and damage to promoting "the highest qualities of life." Prosperous fifth-century Athens nurtured philosophy and democracy. Flourishing fifteenth-century Florence nurtured great art. Victorian England, flush with the bounty of the British empire, nurtured honor, discipline, and duty. In this millennium, Seligman believes, thriving Western cultures have a parallel opportunity to create, as a "humane, scientific monument," a more **positive psychology**— a psychology concerned not only with weakness and damage but also with strength and virtue. Thanks to his own leadership and to some $30 million in new funding, the new positive psychology movement is gaining strength (Seligman, 2004).

Positive psychology shares with humanistic psychology an interest in advancing human fulfillment, but its methodology is scientific. From these roots have grown not only the new

Courtesy of Martin E. P. Seligman, Ph.D. Director, Positive Psychology Center/University of Pennsylvania

Martin E. P. Seligman
"The main purpose of a positive psychology is to measure, understand, and then build the human strengths and the civic virtues."

studies of happiness and health, but also the shift in emphasis from learned helplessness and depression to optimism and thriving. "Positive psychology," say Seligman and colleagues (2005) "is an umbrella term for the study of positive emotions, positive character traits, and enabling institutions."

Taken together, satisfaction with the past, happiness with the present, and optimism about the future define the movement's first pillar: *positive emotions.* Happiness, Seligman argues, is a by-product of a pleasant, engaged, and meaningful life.

Positive psychology is about building not just a pleasant life, says Seligman, but also a *good life* that engages one's skills, and a *meaningful life* that points beyond oneself.

Thus, the second pillar, *positive character,* focuses on exploring and enhancing virtues such as creativity, courage, compassion, integrity, self-control, leadership, wisdom, and spirituality. Current research examines the roots and fruits of such virtues, sometimes by studying individuals who exemplify them in extraordinary ways.

The third pillar, *positive groups, communities, and cultures,* seeks to foster a positive social ecology, including healthy families, communal neighborhoods, effective schools, socially responsible media, and civil dialogue.

Will psychology have a more positive mission in this century? Without slighting the need to repair damage and cure disease, positive psychology's proponents hope so. With *American Psychologist* and *British Psychologist* special issues devoted to positive psychology, with new books (*Authentic Happiness,* 2002; *A Psychology of Human Strengths,* 2003; *Character Strengths and Virtues,* 2004), with 150 networked scientists worldwide working in 50 research groups, and with prizes, research awards, summer institutes, and a new graduate program promoting positive psychology scholarship, these psychologists have reason to be positive.

■ **positive psychology** the scientific study of optimal human functioning; aims to discover and promote strengths and virtues that enable individuals and communities to thrive.

---

one's own incompetence" phenomenon has a parallel, as I can vouch, in hard-of-hearing persons' difficulty recognizing their own hearing loss. We're not so much "in denial" as we are simply unaware of what we don't hear. If I fail to hear my friend calling my name, the friend notices my inattention. But for me it's a nonevent. I hear what I hear—which, to me, seems pretty normal.

The difficulty in recognizing one's own incompetence helps explain why so many low-scoring students are dumbfounded after doing badly on an exam. If you don't know all the Scrabble word possibilities you've overlooked, you may feel pretty smart—until someone points them out. As Deanna Caputo and Dunning (2005) demonstrate in experiments that re-create this phenomenon, our ignorance of what we don't know helps sustain our confidence in our own abilities.

The living-room [Scrabble] player is lucky. . . . He has no idea how miserably he fails with almost every turn, how many possible words or optimal plays slip by unnoticed."

Stephen Fatsis, *Word Freak,* 2001

DOONESBURY

Assessing Behavior in Situations

OBJECTIVE 46-10 | Explain why social-cognitive researchers assess behavior in realistic situations.

Social-cognitive psychologists explore how people interact with situations. To predict behavior, they often observe behavior in realistic situations.

The idea, though effective, is not new. One ambitious example was the U.S. Army's World War II strategy for assessing candidates for spy missions. Rather than using paper-and-pencil tests, army psychologists subjected the candidates to simulated undercover conditions. They tested their ability to handle stress, solve problems, maintain leadership, and withstand intense interrogation without blowing their covers. Although time-consuming and expensive, this assessment of behavior in a realistic situation helped predict later success on actual spy missions (OSS Assessment Staff, 1948).

Military and educational organizations and many Fortune 500 companies are adopting similar strategies in their evaluations of hundreds of thousands of people each year in assessment centers (Bray & Byham, 1991, 1997; Spychalski & others, 1997). AT&T has observed prospective managers doing simulated managerial work. Many colleges assess potential faculty members' teaching abilities by observing them teach, and assess graduate students' potentials via internships and student teaching.

Assessing behavior in situations
Reality TV shows may take "show me" job interviews to the extreme, but they do illustrate a valid point. Seeing how a potential employee behaves in a job-relevant situation helps predict job performance.

Armies assess their soldiers by observing them during military exercises. Most American cities with populations of 50,000 or more use assessment centers in evaluating police and fire officers (Lowry, 1997).

These procedures exploit the principle that the best means of predicting future behavior is neither a personality test nor an interviewer's intuition. Rather, it is the person's past behavior patterns in similar situations (Mischel, 1981; Ouellette & Wood, 1998; Schmidt & Hunter, 1998). As long as the situation and the person remain much the same, the best predictor of future job performance is past job performance; the best predictor of future grades is past grades; the best predictor of future aggressiveness is past aggressiveness; the best predictor of drug use in young adulthood is drug use in high school. If you can't check the person's past behavior, the next-best thing is to create an assessment situation that simulates the task so you can see how the person handles it.

Evaluating the Social-Cognitive Perspective

OBJECTIVE 46-11 | State the major criticism of the social-cognitive perspective.

The social-cognitive perspective on personality sensitizes researchers to how situations affect, and are affected by, individuals. More than other perspectives, it builds from psychological research on learning and cognition.

Critics charge that the social-cognitive perspective focuses so much on the situation that it fails to appreciate the person's inner traits. Where is the person in this view of personality, ask the dissenters (Carlson, 1984), and where are human emotions? True, the situation does guide our behavior. But, say the critics, in many instances our unconscious motives, our emotions, and our pervasive traits shine through. Personality traits have been shown to predict behavior at work, love, and play. Our biologically influenced traits really do matter. Consider Percy Ray Pridgen and Charles Gill. Each faced the same situation: They had jointly won a $90 million lottery jackpot (Harriston, 1993). When Pridgen learned of the winning numbers, he began trembling uncontrollably, huddled with a friend behind a bathroom door while confirming the win, then sobbed. When Gill heard the news, he told his wife and then went to sleep.

Exploring the Self

OBJECTIVE 46-12 | Explain why psychology has generated so much research on the self, and give three examples of current research on the self.

Psychology's concern with people's sense of self dates back at least to William James, who devoted more than 100 pages of his 1890 *Principles of Psychology* to the topic. By 1943, Gordon Allport lamented that the self had become "lost to view." Although humanistic psychology's emphasis on the self did not instigate much scientific research, it did help renew the concept of self and keep it alive. Now, more than a century after James, the self is one of Western psychology's most vigorously researched topics. Every year, new studies galore appear on self-esteem, self-disclosure, self-awareness, self-schemas, self-monitoring, and so forth—more than 220,000 articles in all since 1967. Underlying this research is an assumption that the self, as organizer of our thoughts, feelings, and actions, is a pivotal center of personality.

One example of thinking about self is the concept of *possible selves* put forth by Hazel Markus and her colleagues (Cross & Markus, 1991; Markus & Nurius, 1986). Your possible selves include your visions of the self you dream of becoming—the rich self, the successful self, the loved and admired self. They also include the self you fear becoming—the unemployed self, the lonely self, the academically failed self.

A *New York Times* analysis of 100 rampage murders over the last half-century revealed that 55 of the killers had regularly exploded in anger and 63 had threatened violence (Goodstein & Glaberson, 2000). Most didn't, out of the blue, "just snap."

"The first step to better times is to imagine them."

Chinese fortune cookie

Possible selves
By giving them a chance to try out many possible selves, pretend games offer children important opportunities to grow emotionally, socially, and cognitively. This young boy may or may not grow up to be a physician, but playing adult roles will certainly bear fruit in terms of an expanded vision of what he might become.

Such possible selves motivate us by laying out specific goals and calling forth the energy to work toward them. University of Michigan students in a combined undergraduate/medical school program earn higher grades if they undergo the program with a clear vision of themselves as successful doctors. Dreams do often give birth to achievements.

Our self-focused perspective may motivate us, but it can also lead us to presume too readily that others are noticing and evaluating us. Thomas Gilovich (1996) demonstrated this **spotlight effect** by having individual Cornell University students don Barry Manilow T-shirts before entering a room with other students. Feeling self-conscious, the T-shirt wearers guessed that nearly half of their peers would take note of the shirt as they walked in. In reality, only 23 percent did. This absence of attention applies not only to our dorky clothes and bad hair but also to our nervousness, irritation, or attraction: Fewer people notice than we presume (Gilovich & Savitsky, 1999). Others are also less aware than we suppose of the variability—the ups and downs—of our appearance and performance (Gilovich & others, 2002). Even after a blunder (setting off a library alarm, showing up for dinner in the wrong clothes), we stick out like a sore thumb less than we imagine (Savitsky & others, 2001). Knowing about the spotlight effect can be empowering. Help public speakers to understand that their natural nervousness is not so apparent to their audience, and their speaking performance improves (Savitsky & Gilovich, 2003).

Self-focus affects our recall, too, but in a more constructive way: We remember information better if we encode it in terms of ourselves. Tory Higgins and John Bargh (1987) demonstrated this *self-reference* phenomenon by asking people to consider whether some specific words such as *friendly* described them, and whether the words described someone else. The participants better recalled words they had considered in relation to themselves.

The Benefits of Self-Esteem

OBJECTIVE 46-13 | Give two alternative explanations for the positive correlation between low self-esteem and personal problems.

How we feel about ourselves is also important. High **self-esteem**—a feeling of self-worth—pays dividends. People who feel good about themselves (who strongly agree with self-affirming questionnaire statements) have fewer sleepless nights, succumb less easily to pressures to conform, are more persistent at difficult tasks, are less shy and lonely, and are just plain happier (Crocker & Wolfe, 1999; Leary, 1999; Murray & others, 2002; Watson & others, 2002). Give high–self-esteem people happy news, and they are more likely than low–self-esteem people to savor it rather than dampen it (Wood & others, 2003).

Those whose self-esteem is low do not necessarily see themselves as worthless or wicked, but they seldom say good things about themselves. Low self-esteem often coexists with unhappiness and despair, as psychotherapy researcher Hans Strupp (1982) noted: "As soon as one listens to a patient's story, one encounters unhappiness, frustration, and despair. . . . Basic to all these difficulties are impairments in self-acceptance and self-esteem." When low self-esteem signals social rejection, it may aid survival—by motivating people to behave in ways that restore their inclusion within a supportive group (Leary & others, 1995).

The correlational links between low self-esteem and personal problems have other possible interpretations. Psychologists Roy Baumeister and colleagues (2003, 2005), William Damon (1995), Robyn Dawes (1994), Mark Leary (1999), and Martin Seligman (1994, 2002) all doubt that high self-esteem is really "the armor that protects kids" from life's problems. Maybe self-esteem simply reflects reality. Maybe feeling good *follows* doing well. Maybe it's a side effect of meeting challenges and surmounting difficulties. Maybe self-esteem is a gauge that reads out the state of our relationships

Dear diary,
Sorry to bother you again.

LOW SELF-ESTEEM

with others. If so, isn't pushing the gauge artificially higher akin to forcing a car's low fuel gauge to display "full"? And if problems and failures cause low self-esteem, won't the best boost therefore come not so much from our repeatedly telling children how wonderful they are as from their own effective coping and hard-won achievements?

However, experiments do reveal an *effect* of low self-esteem. Temporarily deflate people's self-image (say, by telling them they did poorly on an aptitude test or by disparaging their personality) and they will be more likely to disparage others or to express heightened racial prejudice (Ybarra, 1999). Those who are negative about themselves also tend to be thin-skinned and judgmental (Baumgardner & others, 1989; Pelham, 1993). Some "love their neighbors as themselves"; others loathe their neighbors as themselves. In experiments, those made to feel insecure often become excessively critical, as if to impress others with their own brilliance (Amabile, 1983). Such findings are consistent with humanistic psychologists Abraham Maslow's and Carl Rogers' presumptions that a healthy self-image pays dividends. Accept yourself and you'll find it easier to accept others. Disparage yourself and you will be prone to the floccinaucinihilipilification[1] of others. Said more simply, people who are down on themselves tend to be down on other things and people.

Maintaining Self-Esteem

OBJECTIVE 46-14 | Discuss some ways that people maintain their self-esteem under conditions of discrimination or low status.

Is it true, as so many assume, that ethnic minorities, people with disabilities, and women live lives handicapped by impoverished self-esteem? The accumulated evidence says no. The National Institute of Mental Health's 1980s study of *Psychiatric Disorders in America* found rates of depression and alcoholism among African- and Hispanic-Americans roughly comparable with those of other Americans (if anything, America's ethnic minorities suffered slightly less depression. More recently, 261 comparisons of more than half a million people have revealed slightly *higher* self-esteem scores for black than for white children, adolescents, and young adults (Gray-Little & Hafdahl, 2000; Twenge & Crocker, 2002).

Some people wonder: How can this be? Some members of stigmatized groups (people of color, those with disabilities, women) have faced discrimination and lower status, yet, according to Jennifer Crocker and Brenda Major (1989), they maintain their self-esteem in three ways:

- They value the things at which they excel.
- They attribute problems to prejudice.
- They do as everyone does—they compare themselves to those in their own group.

These findings help us understand why, despite the realities of prejudice, such groups report levels of happiness roughly comparable to others.

Self-Serving Bias

OBJECTIVE 46-15 | Discuss self-serving bias, and contrast defensive and secure self-esteem.

Humanistic psychologist Carl Rogers (1958) once objected to the religious doctrine that humanity's problems arise from excessive self-love, or pride. He noted that most people he had known "despise themselves, regard themselves as worthless and unlovable." Mark Twain had a similar idea: "No man, deep down in the privacy of his heart, has any considerable respect for himself."

> "There's a lot of talk about self-esteem these days. It seems pretty basic to me. If you want to feel proud of yourself, you've got to do things you can be proud of."
>
> Oseola McCarty, Mississippi washerwoman, after donating $150,000 to the University of Southern Mississippi

- **spotlight effect** overestimating others' noticing and evaluating our appearance, performance, and blunders (as if we presume a spotlight shines on us).

- **self-esteem** one's feelings of high or low self-worth.

---

[1] I couldn't resist throwing that in. But don't worry, you won't be tested on *floccinaucinihilipilification*, which is the act of estimating something as worthless (and was the longest nontechnical word in the first edition of the *Oxford English Dictionary*).

PEANUTS

Actually, most of us have a good reputation with ourselves. In studies of self-esteem, even those who score low respond in the midrange of possible scores. (A low–self-esteem person responds to statements such as "I have good ideas" with qualifying adjectives such as *somewhat* or *sometimes*.) Moreover, one of psychology's most provocative and firmly established recent conclusions concerns our potent **self-serving bias**—our readiness to perceive ourselves favorably (Mezulis & others, 2004; Myers, 2005). Consider these findings:

People accept more responsibility for good deeds than for bad, and for successes than for failures. Athletes often privately credit their victories to their own prowess and their losses to bad breaks, lousy officiating, or the other team's exceptional performance. After receiving poor grades on an exam, most students in a half-dozen studies criticized the exam, not themselves. On insurance forms, drivers have explained accidents in such words as: "An invisible car came out of nowhere, struck my car, and vanished." "As I reached an intersection, a hedge sprang up, obscuring my vision, and I did not see the other car." "A pedestrian hit me and went under my car." The question "What have I done to deserve this?" is one we usually ask of our troubles, not our successes—those, we assume we deserve.

Most people see themselves as better than average. This is true for nearly any subjective and socially desirable dimension. In national surveys, most business executives say they are more ethical than their average counterpart. In several studies, 90 percent of business managers and more than 90 percent of college professors rated their performance as superior to that of their average peer. In Australia, 86 percent of people rate their job performance as above average, and only 1 percent as below average. The phenomenon, which reflects the overestimation of self rather than the underestimation of others (Epley & Dunning, 2000), is less striking in Asia, where people value modesty. Yet self-serving biases have been observed worldwide: among Dutch, Australian, and Chinese students; Japanese drivers; Indian Hindus; and French people of most walks of life. Ironically, people even see themselves as more immune than others to self-serving bias (Pronin & others, 2002). The world, it seems, is Garrison Keillor's Lake Wobegon writ large—a place where "all the women are strong, all the men are good-looking, and all the children are above average."

And who is at least "somewhat likely" to go to heaven? Of Americans surveyed by *U.S. News* (1997), 19 percent thought O. J. Simpson would make it. They were more optimistic about Bill Clinton (52 percent), Princess Diana (60 percent), and Michael Jordan (65 percent). The public figure closest to a perceived heavenly shoo-in was Mother Teresa (79 percent). But she was topped by the survey's respondents, 87 percent of whom believed *they* themselves were destined for eternal bliss.

Self-serving bias flies in the face of pop psychology. "All of us have inferiority complexes," wrote John Powell (1989, p. 15). "Those who seem not to have such a complex are only pretending." But additional findings remove any doubts (Myers, 2005):

- We remember and justify our past actions in self-enhancing ways.
- We exhibit an inflated confidence in our beliefs and judgments.
- We overestimate how desirably *we* would act in situations where most people behave less than admirably.

"To love oneself is the beginning of a life-long romance."

Oscar Wilde, *An Ideal Husband*, 1895

Three in four pet owners believe their pet is smarter than average (Nier, 2004).

"The [self-]portraits that we actually believe, when we are given freedom to voice them, are dramatically more positive than reality can sustain."

Shelley Taylor, *Positive Illusions*, 1989

- We often seek out favorable, self-enhancing information.
- We are quicker to believe flattering descriptions of ourselves than unflattering ones, and we are impressed with psychological tests that make us look good.
- We shore up our self-image by overestimating the commonality of our foibles and by *under*estimating the commonality of our strengths.
- We exhibit group pride—a tendency to see our group (our school, our country, our race) as superior.

■ **self-serving bias** a readiness to perceive oneself favorably.

Moreover, pride does often go before a fall. Self-serving perceptions underlie conflicts ranging from blaming one's spouse for marital discord to arrogantly promoting one's own ethnic superiority. "Aryan pride" fueled Nazi atrocities. No wonder religion and literature so often warn against the perils of excessive pride.

Finding their self-esteem threatened, people with large egos may do more than put others down; they may react violently. Among children, the recipe for frequent fighting mixes high self-esteem with social rejection. The most aggressive children tend to have high self-regard that gets punctured by other kids' dislike (van Boxtel, 2004). An adolescent or adult with a swelled head that gets deflated by insult is potentially dangerous. Brad Bushman and Roy Baumeister (1998) experimented with this "dark side of high self-esteem." They had 540 undergraduate volunteers write a paragraph, in response to which another supposed student gave them either praise ("Great essay!") or stinging criticism ("One of the worst essays I have read!"). Then the essay writers played a reaction-time game against the other student. After wins, they could assault their opponent with noise of any intensity for any duration.

Can you anticipate the result? After criticism, those with unrealistically high self-esteem were "exceptionally aggressive." They delivered three times the auditory torture of those with normal self-esteem. Threatened egotism, more than low self-esteem, it seems, predisposes aggression. "Encouraging people to feel good about themselves when they haven't earned it" poses problems, Baumeister (2001) concludes. "Conceited, self-important individuals turn nasty toward those who puncture their bubbles of self-love."

Despite the demonstrated perils of pride, many people reject the idea of self-serving bias, insisting it overlooks those who feel worthless and unlovable and seem to despise themselves. If self-serving bias prevails, why do so many people disparage themselves? For three reasons: Sometimes self-directed put-downs are *subtly strategic:* They elicit reassuring strokes. Saying "No one likes me" may at least elicit "But not everyone has met you!" Other times, such as before a game or an exam, self-disparaging comments *prepare us for possible failure.* The coach who extols the superior strength of the upcoming opponent makes a loss understandable, a victory noteworthy. And finally, self-disparagement also frequently pertains to one's *old self.* People are much more critical of their distant past selves than of their current selves—even when they have not changed (Wilson & Ross, 2001). "At 18, I was a jerk; today I'm more sensitive." In their own eyes, chumps yesterday, champs today.

Even so, it's true: All of us some of the time, and some of us much of the time, *do* feel inferior—especially when we compare ourselves with those who are a step or two higher on the ladder of status, looks, income, or ability. The deeper and more frequently we have such feelings, the more unhappy, even depressed, we are. But for most people, thinking has a naturally positive bias.

While recognizing the dark side of self-serving bias and self-esteem, some researchers prefer isolating the effects of two types of self-esteem—defensive and secure (Jordan & others, 2003; Kernis, 2003; Ryan & Deci, 2004). *Defensive self-esteem* is fragile. It focuses on sustaining itself, which makes failures and criticism feel threatening. Such egotism exposes one to perceived threats, which feed anger and disorder, note Jennifer Crocker and Lora Park (2004). Thus, like low self-esteem, defensive self-esteem correlates with aggressive and antisocial behavior (Donnellan & others,

> "The enthusiastic claims of the self-esteem movement mostly range from fantasy to hogwash. The effects of self-esteem are small, limited, and not all good."
>
> Roy Baumeister (1996)

> "If you compare yourself with others, you may become vain and bitter; for always there will be greater and lesser persons than yourself."
>
> Max Ehrmann, "Desiderata," 1927

2005). *Secure self-esteem* is less fragile, because it is less contingent on external evaluations. To feel accepted for who we are, and not for our looks, wealth, or acclaim, relieves pressures to succeed and enables us to focus beyond ourselves. By losing ourselves in relationships and purposes larger than self, Crocker and Park add, we may achieve a more secure self-esteem and greater quality of life.

Recognizing both the perils of self-righteousness and the dividends of secure self-esteem, psychologists Baumeister (1989), Jonathan Brown (1991), and Shelley Taylor (1989; Taylor & others, 2003) have all suggested that humans function best with modest self-enhancing illusions. Like the Japanese and European magnetic levitation trains, Brown notes, we function optimally when riding just off the rails—not so high that we gyrate and crash, yet not so in touch that we grind to a halt.

>> LEARNING OUTCOMES

Contemporary Research on Personality

OBJECTIVE 46-1 | Cite the main difference between the trait and psychoanalytic perspectives on personality.
Rather than explain personality in terms of childhood sexuality and unconscious motivations, as Sigmund Freud did, trait researchers have attempted to describe personality in terms of stable and enduring behavior patterns, or predispositions to feel and act. Some psychologists also have attempted to use dominant traits to describe personality "types."

OBJECTIVE 46-2 | Describe some of the ways psychologists have attempted to compile a list of basic personality traits.
Trait researchers attempt to describe personality by placing individuals at points on several trait dimensions simultaneously (sometimes by using *factor analysis*). Hans Eysenck and Sybil Eysenck proposed that two primary, genetically influenced dimensions (extraversion-introversion and emotional stability-instability) explain normal individual variations. Jerome Kagan believes that heredity, by influencing autonomic nervous system reactivity, also influences temperament and behavioral style, which help define personality.

OBJECTIVE 46-3 | Explain how psychologists use personality inventories to assess traits, and discuss the most widely used personality inventory.
Personality inventories are questionnaires on which people respond to items designed to gauge a wide range of feelings and behaviors. Items on the MMPI, the most widely used personality inventory, are empirically derived, and the tests are objectively scored. This does not guarantee *validity* (measuring what it is supposed to measure); people may answer questions in socially appropriate but untruthful ways.

OBJECTIVE 46-4 | Identify the Big Five personality factors, and discuss some of the strengths of this approach to studying personality.
The Big Five personality factors are *conscientiousness, agreeableness, neuroticism, openness,* and *extraversion.* These traits appear to be stable in adulthood, substantially heritable, applicable to all cultures, and good predictors of other personal attributes. Locating an individual on these five dimensions currently offers the most comprehensive picture of personality.

OBJECTIVE 46-5 | Summarize the person-situation controversy, and explain its importance as a commentary on the trait perspective.
Critics of the trait perspective point out that although people's general traits may persist over time, their specific behavior varies as their inner disposition interacts with a particular environment. Trait theorists reply that despite these variations, a person's *average* behavior across many different situations tends to be fairly consistent.

OBJECTIVE 46-6 | Explain why psychologists are interested in the consistency of the trait of expressiveness.
Expressive styles—animation, manner of speaking, and gestures—demonstrate how consistent traits can be, despite situational variations in behavior. Observers have been able to judge expressiveness in video snippets as short as 2 seconds long. We have little voluntary control over our expressiveness.

OBJECTIVE 46-7 | Describe the social-cognitive perspective, and explain how reciprocal determinism illustrates that perspective.
Reciprocal determinism is a term applied to the interacting influences between personality and environmental factors. This interaction is central to the social-cognitive perspective, which applies principles of learning (through conditioning and observation) and cognition (our thinking about our situations) to the study of personality. Such interactions occur when we choose an environment that then shapes us, when our personality shapes how we interpret and react to events, and when our personality helps create situations to which we react.

OBJECTIVE 46-8 | Discuss the effects of a perception of internal or external control, and describe the concept of learned helplessness.
People with an *internal locus of control* (who believe they control their own destiny) tend to experience higher school achievement, better health, less depression, and greater self-control than those with an *external locus of control* (who believe forces beyond their control determine their fate). *Learned helplessness* is an acquired response of hopelessness and passive resignation that animals and humans display after repeated exposure to traumatic events they cannot control.

OBJECTIVE 46-9 | Discuss the link between performance and optimistic or pessimistic attributional style, and describe the goals of positive psychology.

An optimistic or pessimistic *attributional style*—your way of explaining events—can be a window revealing how effective or helpless you feel. Students who express an attitude of hopeful optimism tend to get better grades than those who have a negative attributional style. But excessive optimism can foster feelings of invincibility that expose us to unnecessary risks.

Positive psychology uses scientific methods to study and foster (1) positive subjective well-being; (2) positive character; and (3) positive groups, communities, and cultures.

OBJECTIVE 46-10 | Explain why social-cognitive researchers assess behavior in realistic situations.

Social-cognitive researchers study how people's behaviors and beliefs affect, and are affected by, their surroundings. They observe people in realistic situations because the best way to predict someone's behavior in a given situation is to observe that person's behavior in similar situations.

OBJECTIVE 46-11 | State the major criticism of the social-cognitive perspective.

Critics fault the social-cognitive perspective for focusing so much on the situation that it loses sight of the importance of the influence of unconscious dynamics, emotions, and biologically influenced traits.

OBJECTIVE 46-12 | Explain why psychology has generated so much research on the self, and give three examples of current research on the self.

Psychological research on the self has been accumulating for more than a century. Many psychologists view the self—the organizer of our thoughts, feelings, and actions—as a critical part of personality. Recent research examples include the study of the influence of *possible selves* (the visions of the selves we dream of becoming or fear we may become), the concept of the *spotlight effect* (the assumption that we overestimate the extent to which others notice and evaluate our appearance, performance, and blunders), and the *self-reference effect* (the ability to better recall information if we relate it to our own person or life).

OBJECTIVE 46-13 | Give two alternative explanations for the positive correlation between low self-esteem and personal problems.

Abraham Maslow and Carl Rogers argued that a healthy self-image (high self-esteem) pays dividends in a personally fulfilling and successful life, and some experiments have shown the destructive power of a negative self-image. An alternative explanation of the link between low self-esteem and personal problems is that self-esteem, low or high, reflects reality, and that it is a side effect of one's success or failure in meeting challenges and surmounting difficulties.

OBJECTIVE 46-14 | Discuss some ways that people maintain their self-esteem under conditions of discrimination or low status.

Studies show that under conditions of discrimination or low status, people—often those of color, those with disabilities, and women—maintain their self-esteem by valuing the things at which they excel, by attributing problems to prejudice, and by comparing themselves with people in similar positions.

OBJECTIVE 46-15 | Discuss self-serving bias, and contrast defensive and secure self-esteem.

The *self-serving bias* (our readiness to perceive ourselves favorably) includes our tendencies (1) to more readily accept responsibility for good deeds and for successes than for bad deeds and failures, and (2) to see ourselves as better than average. *Defensive self-esteem* is fragile and takes the form of egotism focused on sustaining itself at any cost. *Secure self-esteem* is less fragile and less dependent on external evaluations.

TERMS AND CONCEPTS TO REMEMBER

trait, p. 46-0
personality inventory, p. 46-2
Minnesota Multiphasic Personality Inventory (MMPI), p. 46-2
empirically derived test, p. 46-3
social-cognitive perspective, p. 46-9
reciprocal determinism, p. 46-10

personal control, p. 46-11
external locus of control, p. 46-11
internal locus of control, p. 46-11
learned helplessness, p. 46-12
positive psychology, p. 46-15
spotlight effect, p. 46-18
self-esteem, p. 46-18
self-serving bias, p. 46-20

TEST YOURSELF

1. How many trait dimensions are currently used to describe personality, and what are those dimensions?

2. How do learned helplessness and optimism influence behavior?

3. In a 1997 Gallup poll, white Americans estimated 44 percent of their fellow white Americans to be high in prejudice (scoring them 5 or higher on a 10-point scale). How many rated themselves similarly high in prejudice? Just 14 percent. What phenomenon does this illustrate?

(Answers in Appendix B.)

ASK YOURSELF

1. Where would you place yourself on the five personality dimensions—stability, extraversion, openness, agreeableness, and conscientiousness? Where would your family and friends place you?

2. Are you a pessimist? Do you readily catastrophize, have low expectations, and attribute bad events to your inability or to circumstances beyond your control? Or are you an optimist, perhaps even someone who frequently exhibits "illusory optimism"? How did either tendency influence your choice of school or major?

3. What possible future selves do you envision? To what extent do these imagined selves motivate you now?

>WEB

Multiple-choice *self-tests* and more may be found at www.worthpublishers.com/myers.

ANOTHER VOICE ON: PSYCHOLOGICAL DISORDERS

CHRISTINE LINCOLN (b. 1966), FROM "SAP RISING"

We share the story about the women called maniacs. Women who lived a long time ago. They were just country women, really, who got tired of cookin' and cleanin', takin' care of their husband and chirrun. Got tired of everybody else usin' up what was supposed to be their lives.

So they met in the woods one night and had this dance. When the men found out, they got angry and tried to put an end to their women's foolishness. But they couldn't. The women rebelled. Started gatherin' every night. Before long, the men started callin' the women crazy, and

started treatin' them like they was, until the women began to believe it. Why is it when a man wants to be free, he's just being a man, but when a woman wants to live life from the position of the birds, the first thing folks say is that she's crazy?

Psychological Disorders

"We are all mad at some time or another."

Baptista Mantuanus, *Eclogues, 1500*

I felt the need to clean my room at home in Indianapolis every Sunday and would spend four to five hours at it. I would take every book out of the bookcase, dust and put it back. At the time I loved doing it. Then I didn't want to do it anymore, but I couldn't stop. The clothes in my closet hung exactly two fingers apart. . . . I made a ritual of touching the wall in my bedroom before I went out because something bad would happen if I didn't do it the right way. I had a constant anxiety about it as a kid, and it made me think for the first time that I might be nuts.

> Marc, diagnosed with obsessive-compulsive disorder (from Summers, 1996)

Whenever I get depressed it's because I've lost a sense of self. I can't find reasons to like myself. I think I'm ugly. I think no one likes me. . . . I become grumpy and short-tempered. Nobody wants to be around me. I'm left alone. Being alone confirms that I am ugly and not worth being with. I think I'm responsible for everything that goes wrong.

> Greta, diagnosed with depression (from Thorne, 1993, p. 21)

Voices, like the roar of a crowd came. I felt like Jesus; I was being crucified. It was dark. I just continued to huddle under the blanket, feeling weak, laid bare and defenseless in a cruel world I could no longer understand.

> Stuart, diagnosed with schizophrenia (from Emmons & others, 1997)

People are fascinated by the exceptional, the unusual, the abnormal. "The sun shines and warms and lights us and we have no curiosity to know why this is so," observed Ralph Waldo Emerson, "but we ask the reason of all evil, of pain, and hunger, and [unusual] people." But why such fascination with disturbed people? Do we see in them something of ourselves? At various moments, all of us feel, think, or act the way disturbed people do much of the time. We, too, get anxious, depressed, withdrawn, suspicious, or deluded, just less intensely and more briefly. It's no wonder then that studying psychological disorders may at times evoke an eerie sense of self-recognition, one that illuminates the dynamics of our own personality. "To study the abnormal is the best way of understanding the normal," proposed William James (1842-1910).

Another reason for our curiosity is that so many of us have felt, either personally or through friends or family members, the bewilderment and pain of a psychological disorder that may bring unexplained physical symptoms, irrational fears, or a feeling that life is not worth living.

Module 47 introduces psychological disorders, explaining the major perspectives and categories and the risks of labeling, and the prevalence of the various disorders. Module 48 describes *anxiety disorders,* which are characterized by persistent distressing anxiety or maladaptive behaviors that reduce anxiety. Module 49 focuses on the rare and controversial *dissociative disorders,* and the problematic *personality disorders,* which impair social functioning. Module 50 examines in depth the emotional extremes of *mood disorders.* And Module 51 outlines the symptoms and characteristics of those suffering from *schizophrenia,* a frightening split from reality.

Introduction to Psychological Disorders

Most people would agree that someone who is too depressed to get out of bed for weeks at a time has a psychological disorder. But what about those who, having experienced a loss, are unable to resume their usual social activities? Where should we draw the line between sadness and depression? Between zany creativity and bizarre irrationality? Between normality and abnormality? Let's start with these questions:

- How should we *define* psychological disorders?
- How should we *understand* disorders—as sicknesses that need to be diagnosed and cured, or as natural responses to a troubling environment?
- How should we *classify* psychological disorders? And can we do so in a way that allows us to help people without stigmatizing them with *labels*?
- How *prevalent* are these disorders, and who is likely to experience them?

Defining Psychological Disorders

OBJECTIVE 47-1 | Identify the criteria for judging whether behavior is psychologically disordered.

■ **psychological disorder** deviant, distressful, and dysfunctional behavior patterns.

Mental health workers view **psychological disorders** as persistently harmful thoughts, feelings, and actions. When behavior is *deviant, distressful,* and *dysfunctional,* psychiatrists and psychologists label it disordered (Comer, 2004).

Being different (deviant) from most other people in one's culture is *part* of what it takes to define a psychological disorder. As the reclusive poet Emily Dickinson observed in 1862,

> Assent—and you are sane—
> Demur—you're straightaway dangerous—
> and handled with a Chain.

Standards for deviant behavior vary by culture and context. In some cultures, people routinely behave in ways (such as going about naked) that in other cultures would be grounds for arrest. In at least one cultural context—wartime—even mass killing may be viewed as normal and even heroic. Stuart claimed to hear voices and people presumed he was deranged. But others may claim to talk with the dead and not be seen as disordered because enough people find them rational (Friedrich, 1987).

Standards for deviance also vary with time. From 1952 through December 9, 1973, homosexuality was classified as an illness. By day's end on December 10, it was not. The American Psychiatric Association had dropped homosexuality as a disorder because more and more of its members no longer viewed being gay as a psychological problem. (Later research has revealed that the stigma and stresses associated with being gay do, however, increase the risk of mental health problems [Meyer, 2003].) In this new century, controversy swirls over the frequent diagnosing of children with *attention-deficit hyperactivity disorder* (see Thinking Critically About: ADHD—Pathologizing Rambunctiousness or Genuine Disorder?).

Culture and normality
Men of the West African Wodaabe tribe put on elaborate makeup and costumes to attract women. In Western society, the same behavior would break behavioral norms and might be judged abnormal.

Carol Beckwith

ADHD—PATHOLOGIZING RAMBUNCTIOUSNESS OR GENUINE DISORDER?

Eight-year-old Todd has always been energetic. At home, he darts from one activity to the next, rarely settling down to read a book or focus on play. At meals, he chatters away and often answers questions before they are fully asked. At play, he is reckless and overreacts to playmates who bump into him or take one of his toys. At school, his exasperated teacher complains that fidgety Todd won't listen or follow instructions and just can't seem to stay seated and do his lessons.

If taken to a psychologist or psychiatrist for an evaluation, Todd is much more likely today than two decades ago to be diagnosed with **attention-deficit hyperactivity disorder (ADHD)**. According to the National Institute of Mental Health (2003), ADHD plagues some 4 percent of children who display one or more of its three key symptoms:

- *Inattention*—distractibility, forgetfulness, disorganization
- *Hyperactivity*—fidgeting, restlessness and not staying seated at school, excessive talking
- *Impulsivity*—difficulty taking turns, interrupting, blurting out answers while questions are being asked

To skeptics, being distractible, fidgety, and impulsive sounds like a "disorder" caused by a single genetic variation: a Y chromosome. And sure enough, ADHD is diagnosed two to three times more often in boys than in girls. Does energetic child + boring school = ADHD overdiagnosis? Is the label being applied to healthy schoolchildren who, in more natural outdoor environments, would seem perfectly normal?

Skeptics think so. In the decade after 1987, they note, the proportion of American children being treated for ADHD nearly quadrupled (Olfson & others, 2003). By 2005, a Gallup survey of 13- to 17-year-olds found that 10 percent reported taking prescribed medication for ADHD (Mason, 2005). In some places, the diagnosis is commonplace, in others it is rare. Toddlers who watch lots of TV are, at age 7, more likely than average to display ADHD symptoms (Christakis & others, 2004). Some teachers refer lots of kids for ADHD assessment, others none. ADHD rates have varied by a factor of 10 in different counties of New York State (Carlson, 2000). Adults, too, now willingly accept the ADHD diagnosis for themselves and, contend the skeptics, find it a handy excuse for their past school failures, vocational difficulties, and lack of self-discipline.

Although acknowledging the diagnostic subjectivity and inconsistency—ADHD is not as objectively defined as is a broken arm—the World Federation for Mental Health (2003) has declared that "there is strong agreement among the international scientific community that ADHD is a real neurobiological disorder whose existence should no longer be debated." ADHD, agrees the National Institute of Mental Health (1999, 2003), is heritable. It is also marked in neuroimaging studies by telltale brain activity, notes a consensus statement by 75 researchers (Barkley & others, 2002). It is *not* caused by too much sugar or poor schools. It often coexists with a learning disorder or with defiant and temper-prone behavior. It is treatable with nonaddictive medications such as Ritalin and Adderall, which are stimulants but help calm the hyperactivity and increase a person's ability to sit and focus on a task. Psychological therapies, such as those focused on shaping behaviors in the classroom and at home, have also helped address the distress of ADHD. And its more frequent diagnosis today may reflect increased awareness of the disorder, especially in areas where the diagnosis is more common.

New research is seeking a more objective assessment of ADHD. Measures include a physical measure of fidgeting, an eye-tracking device that measures ability to focus on and follow spots of light, and more detailed brain imaging (Ashtari & others, 2004; Pavlidis, 2005; Teicher, 2002). Recognizing that about 80 percent of children medicated for ADHD still require medication as teens, as do 50 percent or more as adults, other researchers are exploring the long-term effects of taking stimulant drugs. People appear to tolerate long-term stimulant use with no increased risk of substance abuse (Biederman & others, 1999), but other possible effects are being investigated. In one study, rats were given prolonged exposure to Ritalin early in life, at a dosage comparable to that commonly prescribed for children. When the drug was withdrawn later in life, the rats (compared with others in a control group) were more prone to depressive symptoms and to giving up quickly when facing challenging tasks (Carlezon & others, 2003).

The bottom line: Extreme inattention, hyperactivity, and impulsivity can derail social, academic, and vocational achievements, and these symptoms can be treated with stimulant drugs. But the debate continues over whether normal rambunctiousness is too often diagnosed as a psychiatric disorder, and whether there is a cost to the long-term use of stimulant drugs in treating ADHD.

■ **attention-deficit hyperactivity disorder (ADHD)** a psychological disorder marked by the appearance by age 7 of one or more of three key symptoms: extreme inattention, hyperactivity, and impulsivity.

But there is more to a disorder than being deviant. Olympic gold medalists deviate from the norm in their physical abilities, and society honors them. To be considered disordered, deviant behavior must also cause the person *distress*.

Deviant and distressful behaviors are more likely to be considered disordered when also judged *dysfunctional*. By this measuring stick, even typical behaviors, such as the occasional despondency that many college students feel, may signal a psychological disorder *if* they become disabling. Dysfunction is key to defining a disorder: An intense fear of spiders may be deviant, but if it doesn't impair your life it is not a disorder.

Disordered behavior may also be dangerous. If depression deepens and people develop suicidal thoughts, they may be considered a danger to themselves.

Understanding Psychological Disorders

OBJECTIVE 47-2 | Contrast the medical model of psychological disorders with the biopsychosocial approach to disordered behavior.

To explain puzzling behavior, people in earlier times often presumed that strange forces—the movements of the stars, godlike powers, or evil spirits—were at work. "The devil made him do it," you might have said had you lived during the Middle Ages. The cure might have been to get rid of the evil force—by placating the great powers or exorcising the demon. Until the last two centuries, "mad" people were sometimes caged in zoolike conditions or given "therapies" appropriate to a demon: beatings, burning, or castration. In other times, therapy might have included pulling teeth, removing lengths of intestines, cauterizing the clitoris, or receiving transfusions of animal blood (Farina, 1982).

The Medical Model

In opposition to this brutal treatment, reformers such as Philippe Pinel (1745–1826) in France insisted that madness was not demon possession but a sickness of the mind caused by severe stresses and inhumane conditions. For Pinel and other reformers, "moral treatment" included boosting patients' morale by unchaining them and talking with them, and by replacing brutality with gentleness, isolation with activity, and filth with clean air and sunshine.

When physicians later discovered that syphilis infects the brain and distorts the mind, health reformers and medical workers refocused on physical causes for mental disorders and treatments that would cure them. By the 1800s, the assumption of this **medical model**—that psychological disorders are sicknesses—provided the impetus

Yesterday's "therapy"
In other times and places, psychologically disordered people sometimes received brutal treatments, including the *trephination* evident in this Stone Age skull. Such skull holes may have been drilled in an attempt to release evil spirits and cure those with mental disorders. This patient may or may not have survived the "cure."

John W. Verano

George Wesley Bellows, *Dance in a Madhouse*, 1907. © 1997 The Art Institute of Chicago

"Moral treatment"
Under Philippe Pinel's influence, hospitals sometimes sponsored patient dances, such as the "Lunatic Ball" depicted in this painting by George Bellows (*Dance in a Madhouse*).

for further reform as hospitals replaced asylums. Today, the medical perspective is recognizable in the terminology of the mental *health* movement: A mental *illness* (also called a psycho*pathology*) needs to be *diagnosed* on the basis of its *symptoms* and *cured* through *therapy*, which may include *treatment* in a psychiatric *hospital.*

The medical perspective has gained credibility from recent discoveries. Genetically influenced abnormalities in brain structure and biochemistry contribute to a number of disorders. "Mental illnesses are diagnosable disorders of the brain," declared a U.S. White House fact sheet on mental illness (1999). Two of the most troubling, depression and schizophrenia, often are treated medically. But psychological factors, such as traumatic stress, also play an important role.

The Biopsychosocial Approach

Today's psychologists contend that *all* behavior, whether called normal or disordered, arises from the interaction of nature (genetic and physiological factors) and nurture (past and present experiences). To presume that a person is "mentally ill" attributes the condition solely to an internal problem—to a "sickness" that must be found and cured. But maybe there is no deep, internal problem. Maybe instead there is a growth-blocking difficulty in the person's environment, in the person's current interpretations of events, or in the person's bad habits and poor social skills.

Evidence of environmental effects comes from links between disorder and culture. Some major disorders, such as depression and schizophrenia, occur worldwide. From Asia to Africa and across the Americas, schizophrenia symptoms often include irrationality and incoherent speech (Brislin, 1993; Draguns, 1990b). Other disorders are culture-bound (Beardsley, 1994; Castillo, 1997). Different cultures have different sources of stress, and they produce different ways of coping. Anorexia nervosa and bulimia, for example, are eating disorders that occur mostly in Western cultures. *Susto*, marked by severe anxiety, restlessness, and a fear of black magic, is found in Latin America. *Taijin-kyofusho*, which combines social anxiety about one's appearance with a readiness to blush and a fear of eye contact, appears in Japan. Such disorders may share an underlying dynamic (such as anxiety) while differing in the symptoms (an eating problem or a type of fear) manifested in a particular culture.

Today, most mental health workers assume that disorders are influenced by genetic predispositions and physiological states; by inner psychological dynamics; and by social and cultural circumstances. To get the whole picture, we need to use the biopsychosocial approach (**FIGURE 47.1**), which recognizes that mind and body are inseparable. Negative emotions contribute to physical illness, and physical abnormalities contribute to emotional malaise. We are mind embodied.

■ medical model the concept that diseases have physical causes that can be diagnosed, treated, and, in most cases, cured. When applied to psychological disorders, the medical model assumes that these *mental illnesses* can be diagnosed on the basis of their symptoms and cured through therapy, which may include treatment in a psychiatric hospital.

" Who in the rainbow can draw the line where the violet tint ends and the orange tint begins? Distinctly we see the difference of the colors, but where exactly does the one first blendingly enter into the other? So with sanity and insanity?"
Herman Melville, *Billy Budd, Sailor,* 1924

" It's no measure of health to be well adjusted to a profoundly sick society."
Krishnamurti, 1895–1986

Biological influences:
• evolution
• individual genes
• brain structure and chemistry

Psychological influences:
• stress
• trauma
• learned helplessness
• mood-related perceptions and memories

Psychological disorder

Social-cultural influences:
• roles
• expectations
• definitions of *normality* and *disorder*

FIGURE 47.1
The biopsychosocial approach to psychological disorders
Today's psychology studies how biological, psychological, and social-cultural factors interact to produce specific psychological disorders.

■ **DSM-IV** the American Psychiatric Association's *Diagnostic and Statistical Manual of Mental Disorders* (Fourth Edition), a widely used system for classifying psychological disorders. Presently distributed in an updated "text revision" (DSM-IV-TR).

Classifying Psychological Disorders

OBJECTIVE 47-3 | Describe the goals and content of the DSM-IV.

In biology and the other sciences, classification creates order. To classify an animal as a mammal says a great deal—that it is warm-blooded, has hair or fur, and nourishes its young with milk. In psychiatry and psychology, too, classification orders and describes symptoms. To classify a person's disorder as "schizophrenia" suggests that the person talks incoherently, hallucinates or has delusions (bizarre beliefs), shows either little emotion or inappropriate emotion, or is socially withdrawn. "Schizophrenia" provides a handy shorthand for describing a complex disorder.

In psychiatry and psychology, diagnostic classification aims not only to describe a disorder but also to predict its future course, imply appropriate treatment, and stimulate research into its causes. Indeed, to study a disorder we must first name and describe it. A current authoritative scheme for classifying psychological disorders is the American Psychiatric Association's *Diagnostic and Statistical Manual of Mental Disorders* (Fourth Edition), nicknamed **DSM-IV.** This 1994 volume, now updated as a 2000 "text revision" (DSM-IV-TR), will be more substantially revised as DSM-V, to appear about 2011. (A set of case illustrations accompanying DSM-IV provides several of this book's case examples.) DSM-IV was developed in coordination with the tenth edition of the World Health Organization's *International Classification of Diseases* (ICD-10), which covers both medical and psychological disorders.

The very idea of "diagnosing" people's problems in terms of their "symptoms" presumes a mental "illness." As a result, some practitioners are not enthralled with this medical terminology, but most find the classification to be a helpful and practical tool. It is also financially necessary: Most North American health insurance companies require an ICD diagnosis before they will pay for therapy.

DSM-IV defines a diagnostic process and 16 clinical syndromes (**TABLE 47.1**). Without presuming to explain their causes, it describes various disorders and lists their prevalence. To be helpful and useful, DSM-IV categories and diagnostic guidelines must be reliable, and they are. If one psychiatrist or psychologist diagnoses someone as having, say, catatonic schizophrenia, the chances are good that another mental health worker will independently give the same diagnosis. Following these guidelines, clinicians answer a series of objective questions about observable behaviors, such as, "Is the person afraid to leave home?" In one study, 16 psychologists used this structured-interview procedure to diagnose 75 psychiatric patients as suffering from (1) depression, (2) generalized anxiety, or (3) some other disorder (Riskind & others, 1987). Without knowing the first psychologist's diagnosis, another psychologist viewed a videotape of each interview and offered a second opinion. For 83 percent of the patients, the two opinions agreed.

Some critics have faulted the manual for casting too wide a net and bringing "almost any kind of behavior within the compass of psychiatry" (Eysenck & others, 1983). These critics point to behaviors ranging from irrational fear of humiliation and embarrassment (social phobia) to persistently breaking rules at home or school (conduct disorder). As the number of disorder categories has swelled (from 60 in the 1950s' DSM to 400 in today's), so has the number of adults who meet the criteria for at least one of them—nearly 30 percent in one recent year, according to a U.S. survey (Regier & others, 1998). As a complement to the DSM, some psychologists are offering a manual of human strengths and virtues (see Close-Up: The "un-DSM": A Diagnostic Manual of Human Strengths).

© 1992 by Sidney Harris.

"I'm always like this, and my family was wondering if you could prescribe a mild depressant."

TABLE **47.1**

HOW ARE PSYCHOLOGICAL DISORDERS DIAGNOSED?

Based on assessments, interviews, and observations, many clinicians diagnose by answering the following questions from the five levels, or *axes,* of the DSM-IV-TR.

Axis I Is a *Clinical Syndrome* present?
Using specifically defined criteria, clinicians may select none, one, or more syndromes from the following list:

- Disorders usually first diagnosed in infancy, childhood, and adolescence
- Delirium, dementia, amnesia, and other cognitive disorders
- Mental disorders due to a general medical condition
- Substance-related disorders
- Schizophrenia and other psychotic disorders
- Mood disorders
- Anxiety disorders
- Somatoform disorders
- Factitious disorders (intentionally feigned)
- Dissociative disorders
- Eating disorders
- Sexual disorders and gender identity disorder
- Sleep disorders
- Impulse-control disorders not classified elsewhere
- Adjustment disorders
- Other conditions that may be a focus of clinical attention

Axis II Is a *Personality Disorder* or *Mental Retardation* present?
Clinicians may or may not also select one of these two conditions.

Axis III Is a *General Medical Condition,* such as diabetes, hypertension, or arthritis, also present?

Axis IV Are *Psychosocial or Environmental Problems,* such as school or housing issues, also present?

Axis V What is the *Global Assessment* of this person's functioning?
Clinicians assign a code from 0–100. For example:

91–100 Superior functioning in a wide range of activities; life's problems never seem to get out of hand; is sought out by others because of his or her many positive qualities. No symptoms.
51–60 Moderate symptoms (for example, flat affect or occasional panic attacks) or moderate difficulty in social, occupational, **or** school functioning (for example, few friends, or conflicts with peers or co-workers).
1–10 Persistent danger of severely hurting self or others (for example, recurrent violence) or persistent inability to maintain minimal personal hygiene or serious suicidal act with clear expectation of death.

Labeling Psychological Disorders

OBJECTIVE 47-4 | Discuss the potential dangers and benefits of using diagnostic labels.

The DSM has other critics who register a more fundamental complaint—that these labels are at best arbitrary and at worst value judgments masquerading as science. Once we label a person, we view that person differently (Farina, 1982). Labels create preconceptions that guide our perceptions and our interpretations. It is better, some clinicians say, to study the roots of specific symptoms, such as distorted thoughts or perceptions, than to study catchall categories, such as "schizophrenia" (Persons, 1986).

In the most controversial demonstration of the biasing power of diagnostic labels, David Rosenhan (1973) and seven others went to mental hospital admissions offices, complaining of "hearing voices" that were saying "empty," "hollow," and "thud." Apart from this complaint and giving false names and occupations, they answered questions truthfully. All eight were diagnosed as mentally ill.

That these normal people were misdiagnosed is unsurprising. As one psychiatrist noted, if someone swallowed blood, went to an emergency room, and spat it up, would we fault the doctor for diagnosing a bleeding ulcer? What followed the

> "One of the unpardonable sins, in the eyes of most people, is for a man to go about unlabeled. The world regards such a person as the police do an unmuzzled dog, not under proper control."
>
> T. H. Huxley, *Evolution and Ethics,* 1893

CLOSE-UP:

THE "UN-DSM": A DIAGNOSTIC MANUAL OF HUMAN STRENGTHS

The fast-expanding positive psychology movement, which aims to discover and promote conditions that enable flourishing individuals and communities, has launched an effort, led by psychologists Christopher Peterson and Martin Seligman (2004), to create a classification system for human strengths and virtues. A manual that orders and defines harmful dysfunctions has been helpful, these researchers note. Why not also have a companion manual that would similarly order and define our human strengths—the thinking-feeling-action tendencies that contribute to the *good* life, for self and others?

Like the DSM-IV, *The Values in Action Classification of Strengths* draws insights from many researchers in proposing a common vocabulary that lends itself to cross-cultural understanding and to the budding science of strengths. Also like the DSM, the strengths manual offers assessment strategies and questionnaires that help researchers assess six clusters of 24 strengths:

Wisdom and Knowledge
- curiosity
- love of learning
- critical judgment and open-mindedness
- creativity
- perspective (wisdom)

Courage (overcoming opposition)
- bravery/valor
- industry and perseverance
- integrity and honesty
- vitality (zest and enthusiasm)

Love
- kindness
- intimate attachment
- social intelligence

Justice
- citizenship and teamwork
- fairness and equity
- leadership

Temperance
- humility
- self-control
- prudence and caution
- forgiveness and mercy

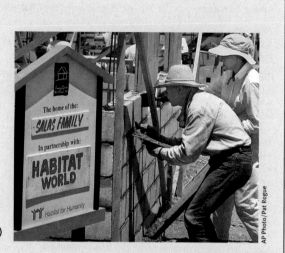

AP Photo/Pat Rogue

Building strengths
In their work for Habitat for Humanity, former U.S. President Jimmy Carter and First Lady Rosalynn Carter model strengths related to love and justice.

Transcendence
- appreciation of beauty, awe/wonder
- gratitude
- hope and optimism
- playfulness and humor
- spirituality and purpose

Labeling effect
Seeing *Asylum* on the shirts of this baseball team (from the State Homeopathic Asylum for the Insane in Middletown, New York), most observers of this 1890s photo will comment on the players' apparent depression or confusion. Actually, all the players were from the asylum's staff.

Elizabeth Eckert, Middletown, NY. From L. Gamwell and N. Tomes, *Madness in America*, 1995, Cornell University Press.

diagnosis *was* startling. Until being released (an average of 19 days later), the "patients" exhibited no further symptoms. Yet the clinicians were able to "discover" the causes of their disorders, such as reacting to mixed emotions about a parent, after analyzing their (quite normal) life histories. Even the routine behavior of taking notes was misinterpreted as a symptom.

Other studies confirm that labels affect how we perceive people. Ellen Langer and her colleagues (1974, 1980) had people watch a videotaped interview. Some were told the interviewee was normal (a job applicant). Others were told the person was out of the ordinary (a psychiatric or cancer patient). Those who watched unlabeled interviewees perceived them as normal; those who watched supposed patients perceived them as "different from most people." Therapists who thought they were evaluating a psychiatric patient perceived the interviewee as "frightened of his own aggressive impulses," a "passive, dependent type," and so forth. A label can, as Rosenhan discovered, have "a life and an influence of its own." (See Thinking Critically About: Insanity and Responsibility.)

INSANITY AND RESPONSIBILITY

My brain . . . my genes . . . my bad upbringing made me do it. Such defenses were anticipated by Shakespeare's *Hamlet*. If I wrong someone when not myself, he explained, "then Hamlet does it not, Hamlet denies it. Who does it then? His madness." Such is the essence of a legal insanity defense, created in 1843 after a deluded Scotsman tried to shoot the prime minister (who he thought was persecuting him) but killed an assistant by mistake. Like U.S. President Reagan's near-assassin, John Hinckley, Scotsman Daniel M'Naughten was sent to a mental hospital rather than to prison.

In both cases, the public was outraged. "Hinckley Insane, Public Mad," declared one headline. And they were mad again when a deranged Jeffrey Dahmer in 1991 admitted murdering 15 young men and eating parts of their bodies. They were mad in 1998 when 15-year-old Kip Kinkel, driven by "those voices in my head," killed his parents and 2 fellow Springfield, Oregon, students and wounded 25 others. And they were mad in 2002 when Andrea Yates, after being taken off her antipsychotic medication, was tried in Texas for drowning her five children. All of these people were sent to jails, not hospitals, following their arrests.

These cases are not uncommon. A 1999 U.S. Justice Department study found that 283,000 jail and prison inmates had severe mental disorders. This is about 16 percent of the U.S. inmate population and considerably more than the 183,000 psychiatric inpatients in all types of U.S. hospitals (Bureau of the Census, 2004; Butterfield, 1999). Many people who have been executed or are on death row have been limited by mental retardation or motivated by delusional voices. Larry Robison (1999) was twice hospitalized for paranoid schizophrenia, as were his

Elaine Thompson/AP Photo

Jail or hospital?
Unabomber Theodore Kaczynski lived in a shack for some 20 years, rarely bathed, sent bombs to strangers (killing 3 and injuring 23), and was diagnosed by his state-appointed psychiatrist with paranoid schizophrenia. One of his early letter bombs was addressed to the author of what was, at the time, psychology's most widely studied text. (The bomb was opened by his assistant, who recovered from injuries.) Should Kaczynski be jailed as a criminal or hospitalized (but also confined) as mentally ill?

brother, sister, uncle, and grandfather. When denied further treatment after insurance coverage ran out, Robison was discharged, killed five people, and was executed by the state of Texas. Four years later, another murderer with schizophrenia, Charles Singleton, was executed by the State of Arkansas after being forcibly medicated with antipsychotic drugs—in order to make him mentally competent, so that he could then be put to death.

Whom should we hold responsible? The people who commit such rare but terrible crimes or the "madness" that clouds their vision? Should we treat or should we punish executives who sexually harass their employees and then claim to have a sexual disorder? If a perpetrator's revolting crime is taken to indicate a disorder, does this create a social basis for evading responsibility (like the person who, having killed his parents, demands mercy because he is an orphan)? Some in Britain believed that is what happened when Brian Blackwell was allowed to plead guilty to a reduced charge of manslaughter after brutally killing his parents. Should he be credited with diminished responsibility because of his "narcissistic personality disorder," as the judicial system agreed, or was the disorder more a description than an explanation of his criminal behavior (*Psychologist*, 2005)? This much seems likely: If some superpsychologist were to understand the biological and environmental basis for everything—from generosity to vandalism—society would still wish to hold people responsible for their actions.

The stigmatizing power of labels was illustrated when a female associate of psychologist Stewart Page (1977) called 180 people in Toronto who were advertising furnished rooms for rent. When she merely asked if the room was still available, the answer was nearly always yes. When she instead said she was about to be released from a mental hospital, the answer three times out of four was no (as it was when

AP Photo/Robert E. Klein

Coping With Disorder
"The only way I knew how to deal with it was to write a song about it," musician Billy Joe Armstrong of Green Day explained, referring to his song "Basket Case," which chronicles a personal struggle with anxiety disorders.

she said she was calling for her brother who was about to be released from jail). Some who said no room was available were later called by a second person who simply asked if the room was still available. Nearly always it was. Surveys in Western Europe have uncovered similar attitudes toward those labeled mentally ill. As we are coming to understand that many psychological disorders are diseases of the brain, not failures of character, the stigma seems to be lifting (Solomon, 1996). Public figures are feeling freer to "come out" and speak with candor about their struggles with disorders such as depression. And the more often people have contact with mental health patients, the more accepting their attitudes are (Kolodziej & Johnson, 1996).

But stereotypes linger. This is hardly surprising, given media images of psychological disorders. Movies sometimes offer reasonably accurate and sympathetic portrayals of disorders, as in the portrayal of mathematician John Nash's schizophrenia in *A Beautiful Mind*. But too often they stereotype mental health patients as homicidal (Hannibal Lecter in *Silence of the Lambs*) or as freaks (Hyler & others, 1991; Wahl, 1992). People with schizophrenia are more likely than others to commit violent crimes, especially if they also abuse alcohol (Citrome & Volavka, 1999; Tiihonen & others, 1997). However, at least 9 in 10 people with disorders are *not* dangerous; instead, they are anxious, depressed, or withdrawn. And *if* they steer clear of alcohol and drugs, those released from mental hospitals are no more prone to violence than are their neighbors (Steadman & others, 1998). Indeed, reports the U.S. Surgeon General's Office (1999, p. 7), "There is very little risk of violence or harm to a stranger from casual contact with an individual who has a mental disorder." (In fact, people with psychological disorders are more likely to be victims of violence, rather than perpetrators [Marley & Bulia, 2001].)

Not only can labels bias perceptions, they can also change reality. When teachers are told certain students are "gifted," when students expect someone to be "hostile," or when interviewers check to see whether someone is "extraverted," they may act in ways that elicit the very behavior expected (Snyder, 1984). Someone who was led to think you are nasty may treat you coldly, leading you to respond as a mean-spirited person would. Labels can serve as self-fulfilling prophecies.

But let us remember the benefits of diagnostic labels. Mental health professionals use labels to communicate about their cases, to comprehend the underlying causes, and to discern effective treatment programs.

Rates of Psychological Disorders

OBJECTIVE 47-5 | Discuss the prevalence of psychological disorders, and summarize the findings on the link between poverty and serious psychological disorders.

No known culture is free of two terrible maladies—depression and schizophrenia (Castillo, 1997; Draguns, 1990a,b, 1997). Some 450 million people worldwide suffer psychological disorders, according to the World Health Organization (WHO, 2004). The WHO also reports that, worldwide, mental disorders have accounted for 15.4 percent of the years of life lost due to death or disability—scoring slightly below cardiovascular conditions and slightly above cancer (Murray & Lopez, 1996). As members of the human family, few of us go through life unacquainted with the reality of psychological disturbance.

So how prevalent are the various disorders? Who is most vulnerable to them? At what times of life? To answer such questions, various countries have conducted lengthy, structured interviews with representative samples of thousands of their citizens. After asking hundreds of questions that probed for symptoms—"Has there ever been a period of two weeks or more when you felt like you wanted to die?"—the researchers have estimated the current, prior year, and lifetime prevalence of various disorders.

Does a full moon trigger "madness" in some people? James Rotton and I. W. Kelly (1985) examined data from 37 studies that related lunar phase to crime, homicides, crisis calls, and mental hospital admissions. Their conclusion: There is virtually no evidence of "moon madness." Nor does lunar phase correlate with suicides, assaults, emergency room visits, or traffic disasters (Martin & others, 1992; Raison & others, 1999).

TABLE **47.2**

PERCENTAGE OF AMERICANS WHO HAVE EXPERIENCED SELECTED PSYCHOLOGICAL DISORDERS IN THE PRIOR YEAR

Disorder	Percentage
Alcohol abuse	5.2
Generalized anxiety	4.0
Phobias	7.8
Obsessive-compulsive disorder	2.1
Mood disorder	5.1
Schizophrenia	1.0
Antisocial personality	1.5
Any mental disorder	14.9

(Some people experience two or more of these disorders, such as depression and alcohol abuse, simultaneously.)

Source: Data from Narrow & others, 2002.

How many people suffer, or have suffered, a psychological disorder? More than most of us suppose:

- Summarizing a U.S. National Institute of Mental Health interview study and a follow-up survey, William Narrow and his colleagues (2002) estimated that 1 in 7 Americans had suffered a clinically significant mental disorder during the prior year (TABLE **47.2**).
- Britain's Office of National Statistics (2002) recently reported a similar 1-in-6 disorder rate.
- An Australian government survey of 10,600 adults found that in any 12 months, slightly less than 1 in 6 "have a mental disorder" (Andrews & others, 1999). Another Australian government study of 4500 children and adolescents concluded that 1 in 7 had "mental health problems" (Sawyer & others, 2000).
- A twenty-first-century World Health Organization (2004) study—based on 90-minute interviews of 60,463 people—estimated the number of prior-year mental disorders in 20 countries. As FIGURE **47.2** displays, the lowest rate of reported mental disorders was in Shanghai, the highest rate in the United States. Moreover, when people immigrate to the United States from Mexico and elsewhere, their mental health and their children's declines as they assimilate over time. For example, compared with people who have recently immigrated from Mexico, Mexican-Americans born in the United States are at greater risk of mental disorder (Grant & others, 2004; Vega & others, 1998).

One predictor of mental disorder is poverty. The incidence of serious psychological disorders is doubly high among those below the poverty line (Centers for Disease Control, 1992). Like so many other correlations, the poverty-disorder association raises a chicken-and-egg question: Does poverty cause disorders? Or do disorders cause poverty? It is both, though the answer varies with the disorder. Schizophrenia understandably leads to poverty. Yet the stresses and demoralization of poverty can also precipitate disorders, especially depression in women and substance abuse in men (Dohrenwend & others, 1992). In one natural experiment on the poverty-pathology link, researchers tracked rates of behavior problems in North Carolina Native American children as economic development enabled a dramatic reduction in their community's poverty rate. As the study began, children of poverty exhibited more deviant and aggressive behaviors. After four years, children whose families had moved above the poverty line exhibited a 40 percent decrease in

FIGURE **47.2**

Prevalence of mental disorders during prior year

From World Health Organization (2004) interviews in 20 countries.

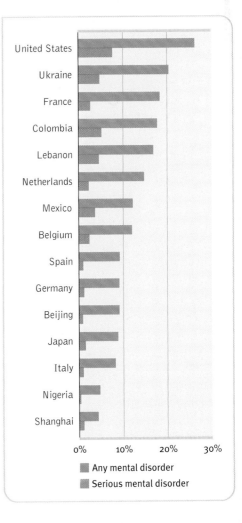

Any mental disorder
Serious mental disorder

TABLE **47.3**

RISK AND PROTECTIVE FACTORS FOR MENTAL DISORDERS

Risk Factors	Protective Factors
Academic failure	Aerobic exercise
Birth complications	Community offering empowerment, opportunity, and security
Caring for chronically ill or patients with dementia	Economic independence
Child abuse and neglect	Feelings of security
Chronic insomnia	Feelings of mastery and control
Chronic pain	Good parenting
Family disorganization or conflict	Literacy
Low birth weight	Positive attachment and early bonding
Low socioeconomic status	Positive parent-child relationships
Medical illness	Problem-solving skills
Neurochemical imbalance	Resilient coping with stress and adversity
Parental mental illness	Self-esteem
Parental substance abuse	Social and work skills
Personal loss and bereavement	Social support from family and friends
Poor work skills and habits	
Reading disabilities	
Sensory disabilities	
Social incompetence	
Stressful life events	
Substance abuse	
Trauma experiences	

Source: World Health Organization (2004a,b)

the behavior problems, while those who continued in their previous positions below or above the poverty line exhibited no change (Costello & others, 2003).

As TABLE **47.3** indicates, there is a wide range of risk and protective factors for mental disorders. Those who experience a psychological disorder usually do so by early adulthood. "Over 75 percent of our sample with any disorder had experienced its first symptoms by age 24," reported Robins and Regier (1991, p. 331). The symptoms of antisocial personality disorder and of phobias are among the earliest to appear, at a median age of 8 and 10, respectively. Symptoms of alcohol abuse, obsessive-compulsive disorder, bipolar disorder (formerly called manic-depressive disorder), and schizophrenia appear at a median age near 20. Major depression often hits somewhat later, at a median age of 25. Such findings make clear the need for research and treatment to help the growing number of people, especially teenagers and young adults, who suffer the bewilderment and pain of a psychological disorder.

Although mindful of the pain, we can also be encouraged by the many successful people—including Leonardo da Vinci, Isaac Newton, and Leo Tolstoy—who pursued brilliant careers while enduring psychological difficulties. The bewilderment, fear, and sorrow caused by psychological disorders are real. But hope, too, is real, as our understanding of these disorders continues to grow.

>> LEARNING OUTCOMES

Introduction to Psychological Disorders

OBJECTIVE 47-1 | **Identify the criteria for judging whether behavior is psychologically disordered.**
Psychologists and psychiatrists consider behavior disordered when it is deviant, distressful, and dysfunctional. The definition of *deviant* varies with context and culture. It also varies with time; for example, some children who might have been judged rambunctious a few decades ago now are being diagnosed with attention-deficit hyperactivity disorder.

OBJECTIVE 47-2 | **Contrast the medical model of psychological disorders with the biopsychosocial approach to disordered behavior.**
The medical model assumes that psychological disorders are mental illnesses that can be diagnosed on the basis of their symptoms and cured through therapy, sometimes in a hospital. The biopsychosocial approach assumes that disordered behavior, like other behavior, arises from genetic predispositions and physiological states; inner psychological dynamics; and social-cultural circumstances.

OBJECTIVE 47-3 | **Describe the goals and content of the DSM-IV.**
The American Psychiatric Association's *Diagnostic and Statistical Manual of Mental Disorders*, Fourth Edition (DSM-IV), currently describes 400 disorders and their prevalence. The manual defines a structured interview technique, in which clinicians answer objective questions, posed at five different levels, or axes, about the individual's observable behaviors. The reliability of the classification is sufficiently high. DSM diagnoses are developed in coordination with International Classification of Diseases (ICD).

OBJECTIVE 47-4 | **Discuss the potential dangers and benefits of using diagnostic labels.**
Critics of the DSM-IV argue that diagnostic labels can stigmatize a person by biasing others' interpretations and perceptions of past and present behaviors and by affecting the ways people react to the labeled person. The benefits of diagnostic labels are that they establish a common vocabulary for mental health professionals giving therapy, and for researchers working on causes and treatments of disorders. Most North American health-care providers require an ICD diagnosis. One label, "insanity"—used in some legal defenses—raises questions about how a society should treat people with disorders who have committed crimes.

OBJECTIVE 47-5 | **Discuss the prevalence of psychological disorders, and summarize the findings on the link between poverty and serious psychological disorders.**
Research indicates that about 1 in 6 people has, or has had, a psychological disorder, usually by early adulthood. Poverty is a predictor of mental illness. Conditions and experiences associated with poverty contribute to the development of mental disorders, but some mental disorders, such as schizophrenia, can drive people into poverty.

TERMS AND CONCEPTS TO REMEMBER

psychological disorder, p. 47-0
attention-deficit hyperactivity disorder (ADHD), p. 47-1

medical model, p. 47-2
DSM-IV, p. 47-6

TEST YOURSELF

1. What is the biopsychosocial approach, and why is it important in our understanding of psychological disorders?
2. Does poverty cause psychological disorders? Explain.

(Answers in Appendix B.)

ASK YOURSELF

1. How would you draw the line between sending disturbed criminals to prisons or to mental hospitals? Would the person's history (for example, having suffered child abuse) influence your decisions?
2. Do you have a family member or friend who has experienced a psychological disorder? If so, has anything you have read in this chapter increased your understanding of the challenges that person has been facing?

>WEB

Multiple-choice *self-tests* and more may be found at www.worthpublishers.com/myers.

Anxiety Disorders

OBJECTIVE 48-1 | Define *anxiety disorders,* and explain how these conditions differ from normal feelings of stress, tension, or uneasiness.

Anxiety is part of life. Speaking in front of a class, peering down from a ledge, or waiting to play in a big game, any one of us might feel anxious. At times many of us feel enough anxiety that we fail to make eye contact or we avoid talking to someone— "shyness," we call it. Fortunately for most of us, our uneasiness is not intense and persistent. If it becomes so, we may have one of the **anxiety disorders,** marked by distressing, persistent anxiety or maladaptive behaviors that reduce anxiety. In this section we focus on four anxiety disorders:

* *Generalized anxiety disorder,* in which a person is unexplainably and continually tense and uneasy
* *Panic disorder,* in which a person experiences sudden episodes of intense dread
* *Phobias,* in which a person feels irrationally and intensely afraid of a specific object or situation
* *Obsessive-compulsive disorder,* in which a person is troubled by repetitive thoughts or actions

Generalized Anxiety Disorder and Panic Disorder

OBJECTIVE 48-2 | Contrast the symptoms of generalized anxiety disorder and panic disorder.

Tom, a 27-year-old electrician, complains of dizziness, sweating palms, heart palpitations, and ringing in his ears. He feels edgy and sometimes finds himself shaking. With reasonable success he hides his symptoms from his family and co-workers. Nevertheless, he has had few social contacts since the symptoms began two years ago. He occasionally has to leave work. His family doctor and a neurologist can find no physical problem.

Tom's unfocused, out-of-control, negative feelings suggest **generalized anxiety disorder.** The symptoms of this disorder are commonplace; their persistence is not. People with this condition (two-thirds are women), are continually tense and jittery, worried about various bad things that might happen, and plagued by muscular tension, agitation, and sleeplessness. The tension and apprehension may leak out through furrowed brows, twitching eyelids, trembling, perspiration, or fidgeting. Concentration is difficult, as attention switches from worry to worry. One of the worst characteristics of generalized anxiety disorder is that the person cannot identify, and therefore cannot deal with or avoid, its cause. To use Sigmund Freud's term, the anxiety is *free-floating.* Generalized anxiety disorder is often accompanied by depression, but even without depression it tends to be disabling (Hunt & others, 2004) and may lead to physical problems, such as ulcers and high blood pressure.

Panic disorder is to anxiety what a tornado is to a windy day. It strikes suddenly, wreaks havoc, and disappears. For the 1 person in 75 with this disorder, anxiety suddenly escalates into a terrifying *panic attack*—a minutes-long episode of intense fear that something horrible is about to happen. Heart palpitations, shortness of breath, choking sensations, trembling, or dizziness typically accompany the panic, which may

Gender and anxiety: Eight months after 9/11, more U.S. women (34 percent) than men (19 percent) told Gallup (2002) they were still less willing than before 9/11 to go into skyscrapers or fly on planes. In early 2003, more women (57 percent) than men (36 percent) were "somewhat worried" about becoming a terrorist victim (Jones, 2003).

be misperceived as a heart attack or other serious physical ailment. Smokers have a two- to fourfold risk of a first-time panic attack (Breslau & Klein, 1999; Goodwin & Hamilton, 2002; Insensee & others, 2003). Because nicotine is a stimulant, lighting up doesn't lighten up.

One woman recalled suddenly feeling "hot and as though I couldn't breathe. My heart was racing and I started to sweat and tremble and I was sure I was going to faint. Then my fingers started to feel numb and tingly and things seemed unreal. It was so bad I wondered if I was dying and asked my husband to take me to the emergency room. By the time we got there (about 10 minutes) the worst of the attack was over and I just felt washed out" (Greist & others, 1986). So unpredictable and frightening is this false-alarm experience that after several attacks, people come to fear the fear itself and to avoid situations where the panic has struck before.

Agoraphobia is fear or avoidance of situations in which escape might be difficult or help unavailable when panic strikes. Given such fear, people may avoid being outside the home, in a crowd, on a bus, or even on an elevator. After spending five years sailing the world, Charles Darwin began suffering panic disorder at age 28. Because of the attacks, he moved to the country, avoided social gatherings, and traveled only in his wife's company. But the relative seclusion did free him to focus on developing his evolutionary theory. "Even ill health," he reflected, "has saved me from the distraction of society and its amusements" (quoted in Ma, 1997).

Phobias

OBJECTIVE 48-3 | Explain how a phobia differs from the fears we all experience.

Phobias *focus* anxiety on a specific object, activity, or situation. (**FIGURE 48.1** ranks some common and less common fears and phobias.) A phobia is an irrational fear that disrupts behavior. Many people accept and live with this common psychological disorder, but some specific phobias can lead to incapacitating efforts to avoid the feared situation. Marilyn, a 28-year-old homemaker, is otherwise healthy and happy, but she so fears thunderstorms that she feels anxious as soon as a weather forecaster mentions possible storms later in the week. If her husband is away and a storm is forecast, she may stay with a close relative. During a storm, she hides from windows and buries her head to avoid seeing the lightning.

Other people suffer from irrational fears of specific animals, insects, heights, blood, or tunnels. Often they avoid the stimulus that arouses the fear, hiding during thunderstorms or avoiding high places. Potentially embarrassing social situations are difficult for those with a *social phobia,* an intense fear of being scrutinized by others. The anxious person may avoid speaking up, eating out, or going to parties—or will sweat, tremble, or have diarrhea when doing so. Social phobia is shyness taken to an extreme.

■ **anxiety disorders** psychological disorders characterized by distressing, persistent anxiety or maladaptive behaviors that reduce anxiety.

■ **generalized anxiety disorder** an anxiety disorder in which a person is continually tense, apprehensive, and in a state of autonomic nervous system arousal.

■ **panic disorder** an anxiety disorder marked by unpredictable minutes-long episodes of intense dread in which a person experiences terror and accompanying chest pain, choking, or other frightening sensations.

■ **phobia** an anxiety disorder marked by a persistent, irrational fear and avoidance of a specific object or situation.

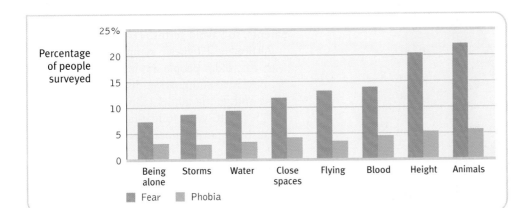

FIGURE 48.1
Some common and uncommon fears
This national interview study identified the commonality of various fears. A strong fear becomes a phobia if it provokes a compelling but irrational desire to avoid the dreaded object or situation.
(From Curtis & others, 1998.)

TABLE **48.1**

COMMON OBSESSIONS AND COMPULSIONS AMONG CHILDREN AND ADOLESCENTS WITH OBSESSIVE-COMPULSIVE DISORDER

Thought or Behavior	Percentage Reporting Symptom
Obsessions (repetitive thoughts)	
Concern with dirt, germs, or toxins	40
Something terrible happening (fire, death, illness)	24
Symmetry, order, or exactness	17
Compulsions (repetitive behaviors)	
Excessive hand washing, bathing, tooth brushing, or grooming	85
Repeating rituals (in/out of a door, up/down from a chair)	51
Checking doors, locks, appliances, car brake, homework	46

Source: Adapted from Rapoport, 1989.

Snapshots

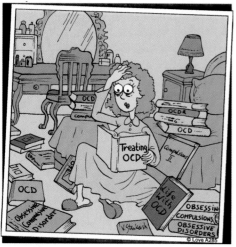

Obsessing about obsessive-compulsive disorder.

Obsessive-Compulsive Disorder

OBJECTIVE 48-4 | Describe the symptoms of obsessive-compulsive disorder.

As with generalized anxiety and phobias, we can see aspects of our own behavior in **obsessive-compulsive disorder (OCD).** We may at times be obsessed with senseless or offensive thoughts that will not go away. Or we may engage in compulsive behaviors, rigidly checking, ordering, and cleaning before guests arrive, or lining up books and pencils "just so" before studying.

Obsessive thoughts and compulsive behaviors cross the fine line between normality and disorder when they become so persistent that they interfere with everyday living and cause the person distress. Checking to see that the door is locked is normal; checking 10 times is not. Washing your hands is normal; washing so often that your skin becomes raw is not. (**TABLE 48.1** offers more examples.) At some time during their lives, often during their late teens or twenties, 2 to 3 percent of people cross that line from normal preoccupations and fussiness to debilitating disorder (Karno & others, 1988). The obsessive thoughts become so haunting, the compulsive rituals so senselessly time-consuming, that effective functioning becomes impossible.

One such person was billionaire aviator Howard Hughes. Hughes compulsively dictated the same phrases over and over again. Under stress, he developed a phobic fear of germs, which led to compulsive behaviors. Hughes became reclusive and insisted his assistants carry out elaborate hand-washing rituals and wear white gloves when handling any document he would later touch. He ordered tape around doors and windows and forbade his staff to touch or even look at him. "Everybody carries germs around with them," he explained. "I want to live longer than my parents, so I avoid germs" (Fowler, 1986).

Although Hughes' symptoms worsened with age, older people are less often plagued by obsessive-compulsive disorder than are teens and young adults (Samuels & Nestadt, 1997). A 40-year follow-up study of 144 Swedish people diagnosed around 1950 found that, for most, the obsessions and compulsions had gradually lessened, though only 1 in 5 had completely recovered (Skoog & Skoog, 1999).

The Aviator
Howard Hughes, and his lifelong struggles with obsessive-compulsive disorder, were portrayed in this 2004 film starring Leonardo DiCaprio.

Post-Traumatic Stress Disorder

OBJECTIVE 48-5 | Describe the symptoms of post-traumatic stress disorder, and discuss survivor resiliency.

During the Iraq war, Jack's platoon was repeatedly under fire. In one ambush, his closest friend was killed while Jack stood a few feet away. Jack himself killed someone in an assault. Years later, images of these events intrude on him as flashbacks and nightmares. He still jumps at the sound of a firecracker or the backfire of a car. When annoyed by his family or friends, he lashes out in ways he seldom did before Iraq. To calm his continuing anxiety, he drinks more than he should.

Traumatic stress—experiencing or witnessing severely threatening, uncontrollable events with a sense of fear, helplessness, or horror—can produce **post-traumatic stress disorder (PTSD),** characterized by lingering symptoms including haunting memories and nightmares, a numbed social withdrawal, jumpy anxiety, and insomnia (Goodman & others, 1993; Kessler, 2000; Wilson & others, 1988). The more frequent and severe the assault experiences are, the more adverse the long-term outcomes tend to be (Golding, 1999). A sensitive limbic system that floods the body with stress hormones also increases vulnerability (Ozer & Weiss, 2004).

Many combat veterans, accident and disaster survivors, and sexual assault victims, including an estimated two-thirds of prostitutes, have experienced the symptoms of PTSD (Brewin & others, 1999; Farley & others, 1998; Taylor & others, 1998). After witnessing atrocities or living in life-threatening circumstances, children of the world's war zones and violent neighborhoods show similar symptoms (Garbarino, 1991, 1992). Their sense of basic trust erodes; many experience fearful wariness, troubled sleep, nightmares, and a sense of hopelessness about their future. This *learned helplessness* on the part of children who have repeatedly suffered abuse appears to make them more vulnerable to post-traumatic stress if assaulted as adults (Mineka & Zinbarg, 1996). Stretch a metal spring and it will snap back—unless stretched too far.

To pin down the frequency of PTSD, the U.S. Centers for Disease Control (1988) compared 7000 Vietnam combat veterans with 7000 noncombat veterans who served during the same years. Combat stress more than doubled a veteran's risk of alcohol abuse, depression, or anxiety. On average, 15 percent of all Vietnam veterans reported PTSD symptoms, but this rate was halved among those who had never seen combat and tripled among those who had experienced heavy combat. And among soldiers held captive in Vietnam, the more torture they suffered, the greater its psychological toll (Mollica & others, 1998). In the more recent Iraq war, one in six U.S. combat infantry has also reported symptoms of PTSD, depression, or severe anxiety in the months after returning home (Hoge & others, 2004).

Civilians, too, exhibit a stress *dose-response relationship.* PTSD rates vary from 4 percent among those who have experienced a natural disaster, to up to 50 percent among those who have been kidnapped, held captive, tortured, or raped (Brewin & others, 2000; Brody, 2000; Kessler, 2000). The greater one's emotional distress during a trauma, the higher the risk for post-traumatic symptoms (Ozer & others, 2003).

A month after the 9/11 terrorist attacks, a survey of Manhattan residents indicated that 8.5 percent were suffering PTSD, most as a result of the attack (Galea & others, 2002). Among those living near the World Trade Center, 20 percent reported such telltale signs as nightmares, severe anxiety, and fear of public places (Susser & others, 2002).

Some psychologists, however, believe that PTSD is overdiagnosed, due partly to a broadening definition of *trauma* (which originally meant direct exposure to serious threat, such as combat or rape [McNally, 2003]). PTSD is actually infrequent, say the

Toxic trauma
Stressed soldiers, such as these in Northern Ireland, are at risk for being diagnosed with PTSD.

■ **obsessive-compulsive disorder (OCD)** an anxiety disorder characterized by unwanted repetitive thoughts (obsessions) and/or actions (compulsions).

■ **post-traumatic stress disorder (PTSD)** an anxiety disorder characterized by haunting memories, nightmares, social withdrawal, jumpy anxiety, and/or insomnia that lingers for four weeks or more after a traumatic experience.

critics, and no good purpose is served by pathologizing normal stress reactions (Wakefield & Spitzer, 2002). "Debriefing" survivors right after a trauma by getting them to revisit the experience and vent emotions has actually proven generally ineffective and sometimes harmful (McNally & others, 2003; Rose & others, 2003). Sometimes reliving the trauma exacerbates one's emotions.

Researchers also point to the impressive *survivor resiliency* most people display (Bonanno, 2004, 2005). About half of adults experience at least one traumatic event in their lifetime, but only about 1 in 10 women and 1 in 20 men develop PTSD (Ozer & Weiss, 2004). More than 9 in 10 New Yorkers, although understandably stunned and grief-stricken by 9/11, did *not* respond pathologically, and by the following January the stress symptoms of the rest had mostly subsided (Galea & others, 2002). Similarly, most combat-stressed veterans and most political dissidents who survive dozens of episodes of torture do *not* later exhibit PTSD (Mineka & Zinbarg, 1996).

Psychologist Peter Suedfeld (1998, 2000), who as a boy survived the Holocaust under conditions of privation while his mother died in Auschwitz, has documented the resilience of Holocaust survivors, most of whom have lived productive lives. The successes of southeast Asians who escaped war and emigrated to America in small boats further testify to the "hardiness and resilience of the survivors," notes Suedfeld. "It is not always true that 'What doesn't kill you makes you stronger,' but it is often true; and, in addition, what doesn't kill you may reveal to you just how strong you really are."

Indeed, suffering can lead to what Richard Tedeschi and Lawrence Calhoun (2004) call *post-traumatic growth*. Tedeschi and Calhoun have found that the struggle with challenging crises often leads people later to report an increased appreciation for life, more meaningful relationships, increased personal strength, changed priorities, and a richer spiritual life. An ancient idea common to Judaism, Christianity, Hinduism, Buddhism, and Islam—that suffering has transformative power—is, they say, borne out in the lives of cancer survivors who take fresh delight in their children and the joy of each new day, and even of bereaved people who report gaining new sensitivities. Reflecting on his son's death, Rabbi Harold Kushner (1986) observed that "I am a more sensitive person, a more effective pastor, a more sympathetic counselor because of Aaron's life and death than I would ever have been without it," though adding that, even so, "I would give up all of those gains in a second if I could have my son back."

Explaining Anxiety Disorders

OBJECTIVE 48-6 | Discuss the contributions of the learning and biological perspectives to our understanding of the development of anxiety disorders.

Anxiety is both a feeling and a cognition—a doubt-laden appraisal of one's safety or social skill. How do these anxious feelings and cognitions arise? Freud's psychoanalytic theory proposed that, beginning in childhood, people repress intolerable impulses, ideas, and feelings and that this submerged mental energy sometimes produces mystifying symptoms such as anxiety. Many of today's psychologists have turned to two contemporary perspectives—learning and biological—for a more complete understanding.

The Learning Perspective

Fear Conditioning

When bad events happen unpredictably and uncontrollably, anxiety often develops (Chorpita & Barlow, 1998). Researchers have linked general anxiety with classical conditioning of fear. In the laboratory, they have created chronically anxious, ulcer-prone rats by giving them unpredictable electric shocks (Schwartz, 1984). Like assault victims who report feeling anxious when returning to the scene of the crime, the rats become apprehensive in their lab environment. For many victims of PTSD, anxiety swells with any reminder of their trauma. Such experiences might help explain why anxious people are hyperattentive to possible threats, and how panic-prone people come to associate anxiety with certain cues (Bouton & others, 2001; Mineka & Zinbarg, 1996). In one survey, 58 percent of those with social phobia experienced their disorder after a traumatic event (Ost & Hugdahl, 1981).

Decades of research on conditioning show that dogs learn to fear neutral stimuli associated with shock, that infants come to fear furry objects associated with frightening noises, and that adults can become terrified of incidental stimuli linked with traumatic experiences. As infants become mobile they experience falls and near-falls—and become increasingly afraid of heights (Campos & others, 1992). Conditioned fears may remain long after we have forgotten the experiences that produced them (Jacobs & Nadel, 1985).

Through such conditioning, the short list of naturally painful and frightening events can multiply into a long list of human fears. My car was once struck by another whose driver missed a stop sign. For months afterward, I felt a twinge of unease when any car approached from a side street. Marilyn's phobia may have been similarly conditioned during a terrifying or painful experience associated with a thunderstorm. Two specific learning processes that might have contributed to her anxiety are stimulus generalization and reinforcement.

Stimulus generalization occurs, for example, when a person fears heights after a fall and later develops a fear of flying in an airplane without ever having flown. Once phobias and compulsions arise, *reinforcement* helps maintain them. Avoiding or escaping the feared situation reduces anxiety, thus reinforcing the phobic behavior. Feeling anxious or fearing a panic attack, a person may go inside and be reinforced by calmed anxiety (Antony & others, 1992). Compulsive behaviors similarly reduce anxiety. If washing your hands relieves your feelings of unease, you may wash your hands again when the feelings return.

Observational Learning

We might also learn fear through observational learning—by observing others' fears. As Susan Mineka (1985) demonstrated, wild monkeys transmit their fear of snakes to their watchful offspring. Human parents similarly transmit fears to their children. Moreover, just observing someone receiving a mild electric shock after a conditioned stimulus produces fear learning similar to that produced by direct experience (Olsson & Phelps, 2004).

The Biological Perspective

There is, however, more to anxiety than simple conditioning or observational learning, as evident from how few people develop lasting phobias after suffering traumas. The biological perspective can broaden our understanding of anxiety disorders. It cannot explain the sharp increase in the anxiety levels of both children and college students over the last half-century, which appears related to such things as fraying social support accompanying family breakup (Twenge, 2000). But the biological perspective does help explain why we learn some fears more readily and why some individuals are more vulnerable.

Natural Selection

We humans seem biologically prepared to fear threats faced by our ancestors. Most of our phobias focus on such objects: spiders, snakes, and other animals; closed spaces and heights; storms and darkness. (Those fearless about these occasional threats were less likely to survive and leave descendants.) It is easy to condition but hard to extinguish fears of such stimuli (Davey, 1995; Öhman, 1986). Many of our modern fears may also have an evolutionary explanation. For example, a fear of flying may also come from our biological past, which predisposes us to fear confinement and heights.

An emotional high
Although we humans seem biologically predisposed to fear heights—certainly an adaptive response—this construction worker seems fearless. The biological perspective helps us understand why most people would be terrified in this situation.

John Coletti/Stock, Boston

Moreover, consider what people tend *not* to learn to fear. World War II air raids produced remarkably few lasting phobias. As the air blitzes continued, the British, Japanese, and German populations became not more panicked, but rather more indifferent to planes outside of their immediate neighborhood (Mineka & Zinbarg, 1996). Evolution has not prepared us to fear bombs dropping from the sky.

Just as our phobias focus on dangers faced by our ancestors, our compulsive acts typically exaggerate behaviors that contributed to our species' survival. Grooming gone wild becomes hair pulling. Washing up becomes ritual hand washing. Checking territorial boundaries becomes checking and rechecking an already locked door (Rapoport, 1989).

Genes

Some people more than others seem genetically predisposed to particular fears and high anxiety. Pair a traumatic event with a sensitive, high-strung temperament and the result may be a new phobia. Among monkeys, fearfulness runs in families. Individual monkeys react more strongly to stress if their close biological relatives are anxiously reactive (Suomi, 1986). The power of genes appears in studies of humans, too. Vulnerability to anxiety disorder rises when the afflicted relative is an identical twin (Barlow, 1988; Hettema & others, 2001; Kendler & others, 1992, 1999, 2002a,b). Identical twins often develop similar phobias, in some cases even when raised separately (Carey, 1990; Eckert & others, 1981). One pair of 35-year-old female identical twins independently developed claustrophobia. They also became so afraid of water that each would gingerly wade backward into the ocean, and then only up to the knees.

The Brain

Generalized anxiety, panic attacks, and even obsessions and compulsions are biologically measurable as an overarousal of brain areas involved in impulse control and habitual behaviors. Brain scans of people with obsessive-compulsive disorder reveal elevated activity in specific brain areas associated with behaviors such as compulsive hand washing, checking, ordering, or hoarding (Mataix-Cols & others, 2004, 2005). As **FIGURE 48.2** shows, the *anterior cingulate cortex,* a brain region that monitors our actions and checks for errors, seems especially likely to be hyperactive in those with OCD (Ursu & others, 2003). When the disordered brain detects that something is amiss, it seems to generate a mental hiccup of repeating thoughts or actions (Gehring & others, 2000).

Fear-learning experiences can traumatize the brain, by creating fear circuits within the amygdala (Armony & others, 1998). Some antidepressant drugs dampen this fear-circuit activity and its associated obsessive-compulsive behavior. All in all, it is clear that biology is part of anxiety.

FIGURE 48.2
An obsessive-compulsive brain
Neuroscientist Stefan Ursu and his colleagues (2003) used functional magnetic resonance imaging (fMRI) scans to compare the brains of those with and without OCD as they engaged in a challenging cognitive task. The fMRI scans showed elevated activity in the anterior cingulate cortex of those with OCD.

S. Ursu, V. A. Stenger, M. K. Shear, M. R. Jones, & C. S. Carter (2003). Overactive action monitoring in obsessive-compulsive disorder. *Psychological Science, 14,* 347–353.

>> LEARNING OUTCOMES

Anxiety Disorders

OBJECTIVE 48-1 | Define *anxiety disorders,* and explain how these conditions differ from normal feelings of stress, tension, or uneasiness.

Anxiety is part of our everyday experience. It is classified as a psychological disorder only when it becomes distressing or persistent or is characterized by maladaptive behaviors intended to reduce it.

OBJECTIVE 48-2 | Contrast the symptoms of generalized anxiety disorder and panic disorder.

People with *generalized anxiety disorder* (two-thirds of whom are women) feel persistently and uncontrollably tense and apprehensive and are in a state of autonomic nervous system arousal. They are unable to identify, or avoid, the cause of these feelings. People with the more extreme *panic disorder* experience periodic minutes-long episodes of intense dread (which may include feelings of terror, chest pains, or choking) and may avoid situations where they have had panic attacks.

OBJECTIVE 48-3 | Explain how a phobia differs from the fears we all experience.

Phobias are more extreme and more disabling than normal fears. People with a *phobia* experience such persistent and irrational fears that they may be incapacitated by their attempts to avoid a specific object, animal, or situation.

OBJECTIVE 48-4 | Describe the symptoms of obsessive-compulsive disorder.

Persistent and repetitive thoughts and actions that characterize *obsessive-compulsive disorder* interfere with everyday living and cause the person distress. The *obsession* is a repetitive thought, such as a concern with dirt or germs; the *compulsion* is a repetitive action, such as excessive hand washing or bathing.

OBJECTIVE 48-5 | Describe the symptoms of post-traumatic stress disorder, and discuss survivor resiliency.

Four or more weeks of haunting memories, nightmares, social withdrawal, jumpy anxiety, and sleep problems are symptoms of *PTSD (post-traumatic stress disorder).* Such symptoms appear following some traumatic event the individual witnessed or experienced but could not control. Some people are more resilient than others. Only about 10 percent of women and 20 percent of men react to trauma by developing PTSD. For those who survive a trauma, the experience can lead to a period of growth.

OBJECTIVE 48-6 | Discuss the contributions of the learning and biological perspectives to our understanding of the development of anxiety disorders.

Those working from the *learning perspective* view anxiety disorders as a product of fear conditioning, stimulus generalization, reinforcement of fearful behaviors, and observational learning of others' fear. Those working from the *biological perspective* consider the evolutionary survival value of fears of life-threatening animals, objects, or situations; inherited predispositions to emotional reactivity; and abnormal responses in the brain's fear circuits.

TERMS AND CONCEPTS TO REMEMBER

anxiety disorders, p. 48-0
generalized anxiety disorder,
   p. 48-0
panic disorder, p. 48-0
phobia, p. 48-1

obsessive-compulsive disorder
   (OCD), p. 48-2
post-traumatic stress disorder
   (PTSD), p. 48-3

TEST YOURSELF

1. How do generalized anxiety disorder, phobias, and obsessive-compulsive disorder differ?

(Answer in Appendix B.)

ASK YOURSELF

1. Can you recall a fear that you have learned? What role, if any, was played by fear conditioning and by observational learning?

>WEB

Multiple-choice *self-tests* and more may be found at www.worthpublishers.com/myers.

MODULE

49

Dissociative and Personality Disorders
Dissociative Disorders

OBJECTIVE **49-1** | Describe the symptoms of dissociative disorders, and explain why some critics are skeptical about dissociative identity disorder.

Among the most bewildering disorders are the rare **dissociative disorders,** in which a person appears to experience a sudden loss of memory or change in identity. When a situation becomes overwhelmingly stressful, people are said to dissociate themselves from it. Their conscious awareness becomes separated from painful memories, thoughts, and feelings. (Note that this explanation presumes the existence of repressed memories, which have recently been questioned.)

Certain symptoms of dissociation are not so rare. Now and then, many people may have a sense of being unreal, of being separated from their body, of watching themselves as if in a movie. Sometimes we may say, "I was not myself at the time." Perhaps you can recall getting in your car and driving to some unintended location while your mind was preoccupied elsewhere. Facing trauma, such detachment may actually protect a person from being overwhelmed by emotion. Only when such experiences are severe and prolonged do they suggest a dissociative disorder.

The king of dissociative disorders is the presumed massive dissociation of self from ordinary consciousness in those with **dissociative identity disorder (DID).** These people are said to have two or more distinct identities that alternately control the person's behavior, with memory impairment across the different personality states. The person with this disorder may be prim and proper one moment and loud and flirtatious the next. Each personality has its own voice and mannerisms, and the original one typically denies any awareness of the other(s).

Although people diagnosed as having multiple personalities are usually not violent, there have been cases in which the person reportedly became dissociated into a "good" and a "bad" (or aggressive) personality—a modest version of the Dr. Jekyll/Mr. Hyde split immortalized in Robert Louis Stevenson's story. One unusual case involved Kenneth Bianchi, who was on trial for the "Hillside Strangler" rapes and murders of 10 California women. During a hypnosis session with Bianchi, psychologist John Watkins (1984) "called forth" a hidden personality: "I've talked a bit to Ken, but I think that perhaps there might be another part of Ken that I haven't talked to, another part that maybe feels somewhat differently from the part that I've talked to. . . . Would you talk with me, Part, by saying, 'I'm here'?" Bianchi answered "Yes" and then claimed to be "Steve."

When speaking as Steve, Bianchi stated that he hated Ken because Ken was nice and that he (Steve), aided by a cousin, had murdered women. He also claimed that Ken knew nothing about his existence and that Ken was innocent of the murders. Was Bianchi's second personality a ruse, simply a way of disavowing responsibility for his actions? Indeed, Bianchi—a practiced liar who had read about multiple personality in psychology books—was later convicted.

Exploring our capacity for personality shifts, Nicholas Spanos (1986, 1994, 1996) asked college students to pretend they were accused murderers being examined by a psychiatrist. When given the same hypnotic treatment Bianchi received, most spontaneously expressed a second personality. This discovery made Spanos wonder: Are dissociative identities simply a more extreme version of our normal human capacity to vary the "selves" we present—as when we might display a goofy, loud self while hanging out with friends, and a subdued, respectful self around grandparents? Are clinicians who discover multiple personalities merely triggering role-playing by fantasy-prone people?

■ **dissociative disorders** disorders in which conscious awareness becomes separated (dissociated) from previous memories, thoughts, and feelings.

■ **dissociative identity disorder (DID)** a rare dissociative disorder in which a person exhibits two or more distinct and alternating personalities. Also called *multiple personality disorder.*

Multiple personalities

Chris Sizemore's story, *The Three Faces of Eve,* gave early visibility to what is now called *dissociative identity disorder.*

Lois Bernstein/Gamma Liaison

If so, can such people then convince themselves of the authenticity of their own role enactments? Are they like actors, who commonly report "losing themselves" in their roles? Spanos was no stranger to this line of thinking. In a related research area, he had also raised these questions about the hypnotic state. Given that most DID patients are highly hypnotizable, whatever explains one condition—dissociation or role playing—may help explain the other.

Those who accept DID as a genuine disorder find support in the distinct brain and body states associated with differing personalities (Putnam, 1991). Handedness, too, sometimes switches with personality (Henninger, 1992). Subtle memories of one personality's experience sometimes fail to transfer to another personality (Eich & others, 1997). In one study, ophthalmologists detected shifting visual acuity and eye-muscle balance as patients switched personalities. These changes did not occur among control subjects trying to simulate DID (Miller & others, 1991).

Skeptics nevertheless find it suspicious that the disorder became so popular in the late twentieth century. In North America, the number of diagnoses exploded from only 2 reported cases per decade from 1930 to 1960, to more than 20,000 in the 1980s—when the DSM contained the first formal code for this disorder (McHugh, 1995a). The average number of displayed personalities also mushroomed—from 3 to 12 per patient (Goff & Simms, 1993). How could such a dramatic disorder have gone unnoticed for so long? Many clinicians have never encountered a case of DID, and the disorder is much less prevalent outside North America, although in other cultures some people are said to be "possessed" by an alien spirit (Aldridge-Morris, 1989; Kluft, 1991). In Britain, the diagnosis—which some consider "a wacky American fad" (Cohen, 1995)—is rare. In India and Japan, it is essentially nonexistent.

To skeptics, these findings point to a cultural phenomenon—a disorder created by therapists in a particular social context (Merskey, 1992). Patients do not enter therapy saying "Allow me to introduce myselves." Rather, note skeptics, some therapists go fishing for multiple personalities: "Have you ever felt like another part of you does things you can't control? Does this part of you have a name? Can I talk to the angry part of you?" Once patients permit a therapist to talk, by name, "to the part of you that says those angry things" they have begun acting out the fantasy. The result may be a real phenomenon, which vulnerable patients may experience as another self. Yet, say skeptics, "It is no coincidence," that multiple personality studies began among practitioners of hypnosis and that symptoms are most dramatic *after* beginning therapy (Goff, 1993; Piper, 1998).

Both psychoanalytic and learning perspectives see the symptoms of dissociative disorders as ways of dealing with anxiety. Psychoanalysts view them as defenses against the anxiety caused by the eruption of unacceptable impulses; a wanton second personality enables the discharge of forbidden impulses. Learning theorists see dissociative disorders as behaviors reinforced by anxiety reduction.

Others view dissociative disorders as post-traumatic disorders—a natural, protective response to "histories of childhood trauma" (Putnam, 1995). Researchers debate whether most people with DID suffered physical, sexual, or emotional abuse as children (Gleaves, 1996; Kihlstrom, 2005; Lilienfeld & others, 1999). One study of 12 murderers diagnosed with DID did find that 11 of them had suffered severe, torturous child abuse (Lewis & others, 1997). One was set afire by his parents. Another was used in child pornography and was scarred from being made to sit on a stove burner. Perhaps, then, multiple personalities are the desperate efforts of the traumatized to detach from a horrific existence.

But then why, wonder the skeptics, did the children of the Holocaust, after enduring boxcars, concentration camps, and their parents' murders, not develop DID? Can the condition sometimes be contrived by fantasy-prone, emotionally vulnerable people, and constructed out of the therapist-patient interaction? If so, predicts psychiatrist Paul McHugh (1995b), "this epidemic will end in the way that the witch craze ended in Salem. The [multiple personality phenomenon] will be seen as manufactured."

Pretense may become reality."
—Chinese proverb

"Would it be possible to speak with the personality that pays the bills?"

Though this be madness, yet there is method in 't."
—William Shakespeare, *Hamlet*, 1600

■ **personality disorders** psychological disorders characterized by inflexible and enduring behavior patterns that impair social functioning.

■ **antisocial personality disorder** a personality disorder in which the person (usually a man) exhibits a lack of conscience for wrongdoing, even toward friends and family members. May be aggressive and ruthless or a clever con artist.

Personality Disorders

OBJECTIVE **49-2** | Contrast the three clusters of personality disorders, and describe the behaviors and brain activity associated with antisocial personality disorder.

Some maladaptive behavior patterns impair people's social functioning without anxiety, depression, or delusions. These disruptive patterns, called **personality disorders,** are inflexible and enduring patterns of behavior that impair one's social functioning. One cluster of disorders expresses anxiety, such as a fearful sensitivity to rejection that predisposes the withdrawn *avoidant personality disorder.* A second cluster expresses eccentric behaviors, such as the emotionless disengagement of the *schizoid personality disorder.*

A third cluster exhibits dramatic or impulsive behaviors. A person with a *histrionic personality disorder* displays shallow, attention-getting emotions and goes to great lengths to gain others' praise and reassurance. Those with self-focused *narcissistic personality disorder* exaggerate their own importance, aided by success fantasies. They find criticism hard to accept, often reacting with rage or shame. Those with *borderline personality disorder* have an unstable identity, unstable relationships, and unstable and impulsive emotions. If personality is one's enduring pattern of thinking, feeling, and acting, then a markedly unstable sense of self defines a borderline personality.

Antisocial Personality Disorder

The most troubling and heavily researched personality disorder is the **antisocial personality disorder.** The person (formerly called a *sociopath* or a *psychopath*) is typically a male whose lack of conscience becomes plain before age 15, as he begins to lie, steal, fight, or display unrestrained sexual behavior (Cale & Lilienfeld, 2002). About half of such children become antisocial adults—unable to keep a job, irresponsible as a spouse and parent, and assaultive or otherwise criminal (Farrington, 1991). When the antisocial personality combines a keen intelligence with amorality, the result may be a charming and clever con artist—or worse.

Despite their antisocial behavior, most criminals do not fit the description of antisocial personality disorder. Why? Because most criminals actually show responsible concern for their friends and family members. Antisocial personalities feel and fear little, and in extreme cases, the results can be horrifyingly tragic. Henry Lee Lucas reported that at age 13 he strangled a woman who refused to have sex with him. He at one time confessed to having bludgeoned, suffocated, stabbed, shot, or mutilated some 360 women, men, and children during his 32 years of crime. During the last 6 years of his reign of terror, Lucas teamed with Elwood Toole, who reportedly slaughtered about 50 people he "didn't think was worth living anyhow." It ended when Lucas confessed to stabbing and dismembering his 15-year-old common-law wife, who was Toole's niece.

The antisocial personality expresses little regret over violating others' rights. "Once I've done a crime, I just forget it," said Lucas. Toole was equally matter-of-fact: "I think of killing like smoking a cigarette, like another habit" (Darrach & Norris, 1984).

Understanding Antisocial Personality Disorder

Antisocial personality disorder is woven of both biological and psychological strands. No single gene codes for a complex behavior such as crime, but twin and adoption studies reveal that biological relatives of those with antisocial and unemotional tendencies are at increased risk for antisocial behavior (Rhee & Waldman, 2002; Viding & others, 2005). Their genetic vulnerability appears as a fearless approach to life. When they await aversive events, such as electric shocks or loud noises, they show little autonomic nervous system arousal (Hare, 1975). Even as youngsters, before committing any crime, they react with lower levels of stress hormones than do others their age (**FIGURE 49.1**).

Antisocial personality?
Dennis Rader, known as the "BTK killer" in Kansas, was convicted in 2005 of killing 10 people over a 30-year span. Rader exhibited the extreme lack of conscience that marks antisocial personality disorder.

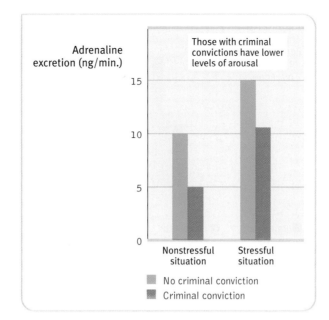

FIGURE **49.1**
Cold-blooded arousability and risk of crime
Levels of the stress hormone adrenaline were measured in two groups of 13-year-old Swedish boys. In both stressful and non-stressful situations, those who were later convicted of a crime (as 18- to 26-year-olds) showed relatively low arousal. (From Magnusson, 1990.)

Some studies have detected the early signs of antisocial behavior in children as young as ages 3 to 6 (Caspi & others, 1996; Tremblay & others, 1994). Boys who later became aggressive or antisocial adolescents tended, as young children, to have been impulsive, uninhibited, unconcerned with social rewards, and low in anxiety. If channeled in more productive directions, such fearlessness may lead to courageous heroism, adventurism, or star-level athleticism (Poulton & Milne, 2002). Lacking a sense of social responsibility, the same disposition produces a cool con artist or killer (Lykken, 1995).

Genetic influences help wire the brain. Adrian Raine (1999) compared PET scans of 41 murderers' brains with those from people of similar age and sex. Raine found reduced activity in the murderers' frontal lobes, an area of the cortex that helps control impulses (**FIGURE 49.2**). This reduction was especially apparent in those who murdered impulsively. In a follow-up study, Raine and his team (2000) found that violent repeat offenders had 11 percent less frontal lobe tissue than normal. This helps explain why people with antisocial personality disorder exhibit marked deficits in frontal lobe cognitive functions, such as planning, organization, and inhibition (Morgan & Lilienfeld, 2000).

Perhaps a biologically based fearlessness, as well as early environment, helps explain the reunion of long-separated sisters Joyce Lott, 27, and Mary Jones, 29—in a South Carolina prison where both were sent on drug charges. After a newspaper story about their reunion, their long-lost half-brother Frank Strickland called. He explained it would be a while before he could come see them—because he, too, was in jail, on drug, burglary, and larceny charges (Shepherd & others, 1990).

Genetics alone is hardly the whole story of antisocial crime, however. Relative to 1960, the average American in 1995 (before the late 1990s crime decline) was twice as likely to be murdered, four times as likely to report being raped, four times as likely to report being robbed, and five times as likely to report being assaulted (FBI, *Uniform Crime Reports*). Violent crime was also surging in other Western nations. Yet the human gene pool had hardly changed. Or consider the British social experiment begun in 1787, exiling 160,000 criminals to Australia. The descendants of these exiles, carrying their ancestors' supposed "criminal genes," have helped create a civilized democracy whose crime rate is similar to Britain's. Genetic predispositions do put some individuals more at risk for antisocial conduct than others; biological as well as environmental influences explain why 5 to 6 percent of offenders commit 50 to 60 percent of crimes (Lyman, 1996). But we must look to sociocultural factors to explain the modern epidemic of violence.

FIGURE **49.2**
Murderous minds
PET scans illustrate reduced activation (less red and yellow) in a murderer's frontal cortex—a brain area that helps brake impulsive, aggressive behavior. (From Raine, 1999.)

Normal   Murderer

FIGURE **49.3**

Biopsychosocial roots of crime
Danish male babies whose backgrounds
were marked *both* by obstetrical complications and social stresses associated with
poverty were twice as likely to be criminal
offenders by ages 20 to 22 as those in either
the biological or social risk groups. (From
Raine & others, 1996.)

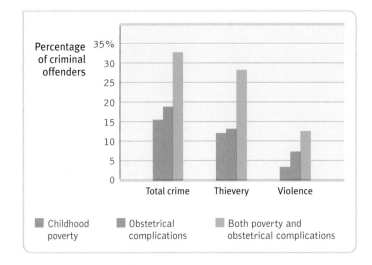

A study of criminal tendencies among young Danish men illustrates the usefulness of a complete biopsychosocial perspective. A research team led by Adrian Raine (1996) checked criminal records on nearly 400 men at ages 20 to 22, knowing that all had experienced either biological risk factors at birth, such as premature birth, or had come from family backgrounds marked by poverty and family instability. The researchers compared each of these groups with a *biosocial* group whose lives were marked by *both* the biological and social risk factors. The biosocial group had double the risk of committing crime (**FIGURE 49.3**). In one quarter-century study that followed 1037 children, two combined factors predicted antisocial problems: childhood maltreatment and a gene that altered neurotransmitter balance (Caspi & others, 2002). Neither "bad" genes nor a "bad" environment alone predisposed later antisocial behavior; rather, genes predisposed some children to be more sensitive to maltreatment. Within "genetically vulnerable segments of the population," environmental influences matter (Moffitt, 2005). With antisocial behavior, as with so much else, nature and nurture interact.

>> LEARNING OUTCOMES

Dissociative and Personality Disorders

OBJECTIVE 49-1 | Describe the symptoms of dissociative disorders, and explain why some critics are skeptical about dissociative identity disorder.

Dissociative disorders are conditions in which conscious awareness seems to become separated from previous memories, thoughts, and feelings. Skeptics note that the diagnosis of *dissociative identity disorder,* commonly known as multiple personality disorder, increased dramatically in the late twentieth century; that it is not found in many countries and is very rare in others; and that it may reflect role-playing by people who are very open to therapists' suggestions. This disorder may be a manifestation of feelings of anxiety or a response learned when behaviors are reinforced by reductions in feelings of anxiety.

OBJECTIVE 49-2 | Contrast the three clusters of personality disorders, and describe the behaviors and brain activity associated with antisocial personality disorder.

Personality disorders are inflexible and enduring patterns of behavior that impair social functioning. The main component of the first cluster is *anxiety;* of the second, *eccentric behaviors;* of the third, *dramatic or impulsive behaviors. Antisocial personality disorder* is characterized by a lack of conscience and, sometimes,

aggressive and ruthless behavior. Brain scans of some murderers with this disorder have shown reduced activity in the frontal lobes, an area of control for impulsive, aggressive behavior. Genetic predisposition may interact with environmental influences to produce antisocial personality disorder.

TERMS AND CONCEPTS TO REMEMBER

dissociative disorders, p. 49-0

dissociative identity disorder
  (DID), p. 49-0

personality disorders, p. 49-2

antisocial personality disorder,
  p. 49-2

TEST YOURSELF

1. Is antisocial personality disorder an inherited condition?

(Answer in Appendix B.)

ASK YOURSELF

1. How would you evaluate the relative contributions of nature and nurture to antisocial personality disorder?

>WEB

Multiple-choice *self-tests* and more may be found at www.worthpublishers.com/myers.

50

MODULE

Mood Disorders

OBJECTIVE 50-1 | Define *mood disorders,* and contrast major depressive disorder and bipolar disorder.

The emotional extremes of **mood disorders** come in two principal forms: (1) *major depressive disorder,* in which the person experiences prolonged hopelessness and lethargy until usually rebounding to normality, and (2) *bipolar disorder* (formerly called *manic depressive disorder*), in which the person alternates between depression and *mania,* an overexcited, hyperactive state.

Major Depressive Disorder

Perhaps you know what depression feels like. If you are like most college students, at some time during this year—more likely the dark months of winter than the bright days of summer—you will probably experience a few of the symptoms of depression. You may feel deeply discouraged about the future, dissatisfied with your life, or isolated from others. You may lack the energy to get things done or even to force yourself out of bed; be unable to concentrate, eat, or sleep normally; or even wonder if you would be better off dead. Perhaps academic success came easily to you in high school, and now you find that disappointing grades jeopardize your goals. Maybe social stresses, such as feeling you don't belong or the breakup of a romance, have plunged you into despair. And maybe brooding has at times only worsened your self-torment.

You are not alone. Depression is the "common cold" of psychological disorders— an expression that effectively describes its pervasiveness but not its seriousness. Although phobias are more common, depression is the number one reason people seek mental health services. Moreover, it is the leading cause of disability worldwide (WHO, 2002). In any given year a depressive episode plagues 5.8 percent of men and 9.5 percent of women, reports the World Health Organization.

As anxiety is a response to the threat of future loss, depression is often a response to past and current loss. To feel bad in reaction to profoundly sad events (such as the death of a loved one) is to be in touch with reality. In such times, depression is like a car's low–oil–pressure light—a signal that warns us to stop and take protective measures. Biologically speaking, life's purpose is not happiness but survival and reproduction, and to this end, coughing, vomiting, and various forms of pain protect the body from dangerous toxins. Similarly, depression is a sort of psychic hibernation: It slows us down, defuses aggression, and restrains risk taking (Allen & Badcock, 2003). To grind temporarily to a halt and ruminate, as depressed people do, is to reassess one's life when feeling threatened, and to redirect energy in more promising ways. From this perspective, there is sense to suffering.

But when does this response become seriously maladaptive? The line separating life's normal "downs" from major depression is difficult to draw. Joy, contentment, sadness, and despair are different points on a continuum, points at which any of us may be found at any given moment.

For some people, recurring depression during winter's dark months constitutes a seasonal affective disorder. For others, winter darkness means more blue moods. When asked "Have you cried today?" Americans answered "yes" more often in the winter:

	Percentage answering yes	
	Men	Women
August	4%	7%
December	8%	21%

Source: Time/CNN survey, 1994

"Depression . . . is well adapted to make a creature guard itself against any great or sudden evil."

Charles Darwin, *The Life and Letters of Charles Darwin,* 1887

■ **mood disorders** psychological disorders characterized by emotional extremes. See *major depressive disorder, mania,* and *bipolar disorder.*

Major depressive disorder occurs when signs of depression (including lethargy, feelings of worthlessness, or loss of interest in family, friends, and activities) last two weeks or more and are not caused by drugs or a medical condition. The difference between a blue mood after bad news and a mood disorder is like the difference between gasping for breath for a few minutes after a hard run and being chronically short of breath. To sense what major depression feels like, suggest some clinicians, imagine combining the anguish of grief with the sluggishness of jet lag.

Between the temporary blue moods we all experience and the crushing impact of major depression is a condition called *dysthymic disorder*—a down-in-the-dumps mood that fills most of the day, nearly every day, for two years or more. Although less disabled than people with major depressions, those with dysthymic disorder tend to experience chronic low energy and self-esteem, have difficulty concentrating or making decisions, and sleep and eat too much or too little.

Bipolar Disorder

With or without therapy, episodes of major depression usually end, and people temporarily or permanently return to their previous behavior patterns. However, some people rebound to, or sometimes start with, the opposite emotional extreme—the euphoric, hyperactive, wildly optimistic state of **mania.** If depression is living in slow motion, mania is fast forward. Alternation between depression and mania signals **bipolar disorder.** During the manic phase of bipolar disorder, the person is typically overtalkative, overactive, and elated (though easily irritated if crossed); has little need for sleep; and shows fewer sexual inhibitions. Speech is loud, flighty, and hard to interrupt.

One of mania's maladaptive symptoms is grandiose optimism and self-esteem, which may lead to reckless investments, spending sprees, and unsafe sex. Although people in a manic state find advice irritating, they need protection from their own poor judgment. In milder forms, however, the energy and free-flowing thinking of mania can fuel creativity. History offers many examples of creative bipolar people, from Walt Whitman and Ernest Hemingway to actress Margot Kidder. Bipolar disorder is especially common among creative artists and poets (Jamison, 1993, 1995; Kaufman & Baer, 2002). George Frideric Handel (1685–1759), who many believe suffered a mild form of bipolar disorder, composed his nearly four-hour-long *Messiah* during three weeks of intense, creative energy (Keynes, 1980). Robert Schumann composed 51 musical works during two years of mania (1840 and 1849) and none during 1844, when he was severely depressed (Slater & Meyer, 1959). Creative professionals who rely on precision and logic (architects, designers, journalists) less often suffer bipolar disorder than those who rely on emotional expression and vivid imagery (poets, novelists, entertainers), reports Arnold Ludwig (1995).

It is as true of emotions as of everything else: What goes up comes down. Before long, the elated mood either returns to normal or plunges into a depression. Though as maladaptive as major depression, bipolar disorder is much less common. Unlike major depression, it afflicts as many men as women.

> "My life had come to a sudden stop. I was able to breathe, to eat, to drink, to sleep. I could not, indeed, help doing so; but there was no real life in me."
>
> Leo Tolstoy, *My Confession*, 1887

> "All the people in history, literature, art, whom I most admire: Mozart, Shakespeare, Homer, El Greco, St. John, Chekhov, Gregory of Nyssa, Dostoevsky, Emily Brontë: not one of them would qualify for a mental-health certificate."
>
> Madeleine L'Engle, *A Circle of Quiet*, 1972

Creativity and bipolar disorders
History has given us many creative artists, composers, and writers with bipolar disorder, including (left to right) Walt Whitman, Virginia Woolf, Samuel Clemens (Mark Twain), and Ernest Hemingway.

Explaining Mood Disorders

OBJECTIVE 50-2 | Discuss the facts that an acceptable theory of depression must explain.

Because depression profoundly affects so many people, it understandably has been the subject of thousands of studies. Psychologists are working to develop a theory of mood disorders that will suggest more effective ways to treat and prevent them. Researcher Peter Lewinsohn and his colleagues (1985, 1998) summarized the facts that any theory of depression must explain. Among them are the following:

- *Many behavioral and cognitive changes accompany depression.* Depressed people are inactive and feel unmotivated. They are sensitive to negative happenings, expect negative outcomes, and more often recall negative information. In a depressed mood, we expect our team to lose, our grades to fall, our love to fail. When the depression lifts, these behavioral and cognitive accompaniments disappear. Nearly half the time, depressed people also exhibit symptoms of another disorder, such as anxiety or substance abuse.
- *Depression is widespread.* Its commonality suggests that its causes, too, must be common.
- *Compared with men, women are nearly twice as vulnerable to major depression* (FIGURE 50.1). In general, women are most vulnerable to disorders involving internalized states, such as depression, anxiety, and inhibited sexual desire. Men's disorders tend to be more external—alcohol abuse, antisocial conduct, lack of impulse control. When women get sad they often get sadder than men do. When men get mad, they often get madder than women do.
- *Most major depressive episodes self-terminate.* Therapy tends to speed recovery, yet most people suffering major depression eventually return to normal even without professional help. The plague of depression comes and, a few weeks or months later, it usually goes, though it sometimes recurs later.
- *Stressful events related to work, marriage, and close relationships often precede depression.* A family member's death, a job loss, a marital crisis, or a physical assault increase one's risk of depression. If stress-related anxiety is a "crackling, menacing brushfire," notes biologist Robert Sapolsky (2003), "depression is a suffocating heavy blanket thrown on top of it." One study followed 2000 people over time. It found that the risk of the onset of depression in the ensuing month ranged from less than 1 percent among those who had experienced no stressful life event to 24 percent among those with three such events (Kendler, 1998). The early loss of a parent due to death or separation also increases later vulnerability to depression (Agid & others, 1999).
- *With each new generation, the rate of depression is increasing, and the disorder is striking earlier (now often in the late teens).* This is true not only in Canada and the United States but also in Germany, Italy, France, Lebanon, New Zealand,

major depressive disorder a mood disorder in which a person experiences, in the absence of drugs or a medical condition, two or more weeks of significantly depressed moods, feelings of worthlessness, and diminished interest or pleasure in most activities.

mania a mood disorder marked by a hyperactive, wildly optimistic state.

bipolar disorder a mood disorder in which the person alternates between the hopelessness and lethargy of depression and the overexcited state of mania. (Formerly called *manic-depressive disorder*.)

About 50 percent of those who recover from depression will suffer another episode within two years. Recovery is more likely to be permanent the later the first episode strikes, the longer the person stays well, the fewer the previous episodes, the less stress experienced, and the more social support received (Belsher & Costello, 1988; Fergusson & Woodward, 2002; Kendler & others, 2001).

" I see depression as the plague of the modern era."

Lewis Judd, former chief, National Institute of Mental Health, 2000

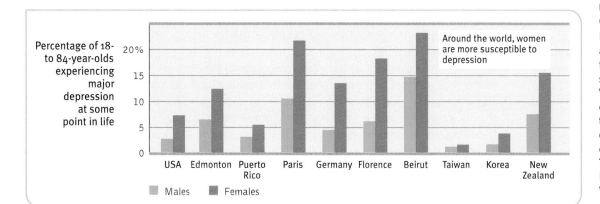

FIGURE **50.1**
Gender and depression
Interviews with 38,000 adults in 10 countries confirm what many smaller studies have found: Women's risk of major depression is nearly double that of men's. Lifetime risk of depression also varies by culture—from 1.5 percent in Taiwan to 19 percent in Beirut. (Data from Weissman & others, 1996.)

Down Came the Rain
Actress Brooke Shields chronicled her disabling postpartum depression in this 2005 book.

Taiwan, and Puerto Rico (Cross-National Collaborative Group, 1992). In Australia, 12 percent of adolescents interviewed reported symptoms of depression. Most hid it from their parents; almost 90 percent of their parents perceived their depressed teen as *not* suffering depression (Sawyer & others, 2000). In North America, today's young adults are three times as likely as their grandparents to report having recently—or ever—suffered depression (despite the grandparents' many more years of being at risk). Asked "Have you ever felt that you were going to have a nervous breakdown?" 17 percent of Americans said "yes" in 1957, as did 24 percent in 1996 (Swindle & others, 2000). The increase appears partly authentic, but may also reflect today's young adults' greater willingness to disclose depression, as well as our tendency to forget many negative experiences over time.

As you might expect, researchers understand and interpret these facts in ways that reflect their different perspectives. Psychoanalytic theory, applying Sigmund Freud's ideas about the importance of early childhood experiences and unconscious impulses, suggested that depression occurs when significant losses evoke feelings associated with losses experienced in childhood. Loss of a romantic relationship or a job might evoke feelings associated with the loss of the intimate relationship with one's mother, for example. Alternatively, unresolved anger toward one's parents might be turned inward against the self. Today's biopsychosocial perspective is broadening our understanding with biological and cognitive explanations.

The Biological Perspective

OBJECTIVE 50-3 | Summarize the contributions of the biological perspective to the study of depression, and discuss the link between suicide and depression.

Most recent mental health research dollars have funded explorations of biological influences on mood disorders. Depression is a whole-body disorder. It involves genetic predispositions, biochemical imbalances, negative thoughts, and melancholy mood.

Genetic Influences

We have long known that mood disorders run in families. The risk of major depression and bipolar disorder increases if you have a depressed parent or sibling (Sullivan & others, 2000). If one identical twin is diagnosed with major depressive disorder, the chances are about 1 in 2 that at some time the other twin will be, too. If one identical twin has bipolar disorder, the chances are 7 in 10 that the other twin will at some point be diagnosed similarly. Among fraternal twins, the corresponding odds are just under 2 in 10 (Tsuang & Faraone, 1990). The greater similarity of identical twins' depressive tendencies also occurs among twins reared apart (DiLalla & others, 1996). Moreover, adopted people who suffer a mood disorder often have close biological relatives who suffer mood disorders, become dependent on alcohol, or commit suicide (Wender & others, 1986). (Turn the page and see Close-Up: Suicide for other research findings on suicide.)

A search for the genes that put people at risk for depression is now under way. To tease out which genes are implicated, researchers use *linkage analysis*. First, they find families that have had the disorder across several generations. Then they draw blood from both affected and unaffected family members and examine their DNA, looking for differences. Linkage analysis points us to a chromosome neighborhood, note behavior genetics researchers Robert Plomin and Peter McGuffin (2003); "a house-to-house search is then needed to find the culprit gene." *Association studies* search for correlations between more specific DNA variation and a population trait. One such DNA variation occurs, for example, in about 40 percent of people with late-onset Alzheimer's disease and about 15 percent of those without Alzheimer's (Plomin &

McGuffin, 2003). The anticipated outcome of linkage and association studies in research on depression is a complex picture: Many genes have small effects that can combine with one another and with nongenetic factors to put some people at greater risk.

The Depressed Brain

Genes act by directing biochemical events that, down the line, influence behavior. The biochemical key is neurotransmitters, those messenger molecules that shuttle signals between nerve cells. *Norepinephrine,* a neurotransmitter that increases arousal and boosts mood, is scarce during depression and overabundant during mania. (Drugs that alleviate mania reduce norepinephrine.) Most people with a history of depression also have a history of habitual smoking. This may indicate an attempt to self-medicate with inhaled nicotine, which can temporarily increase norepinephrine and boost mood (HMHL, 2002).

A second neurotransmitter, *serotonin,* is also scarce during depression. Drugs that relieve depression tend to increase norepinephrine or serotonin supplies by blocking either their reuptake (as Prozac, Zoloft, and Paxil do with serotonin) or their chemical breakdown. Repetitive physical exercise, such as jogging, reduces depression as it increases serotonin (Jacobs, 1994).

Some of the genes under scrutiny provide codes for neurotransmitter systems such as serotonin (Plomin & McGuffin, 2003). One large study identified New Zealand young adults who had experienced several major stresses, such as a relationship breakup or a family death. These stressed individuals were much more likely to suffer depression if they carried a variation of a gene that codes for a protein that controls serotonin activity (Caspi & others, 2003). As we have seen so often throughout this book, genes and environments—nature and nurture—interact to form us.

People with depression have also recently been observed to have lower levels in their diet and blood of a "good" fat, *omega-3 fatty acid,* believed to enhance brain function (Edwards & others, 1998; Maes & others, 1999). Countries such as Japan, where people eat omega-3–rich fish, tend to have low depression rates (Hibbeln, 1998). Future research may determine whether eating more fish, walnuts, and other foods rich in omega-3 supports mental health.

Using modern scanning machines, researchers are also spotting neurological signs of depression. In many recent studies, the brain shows less activity during periods of depression, indicating a slowed-down state, and more activity during periods of mania (**FIGURE 50.2**). The left frontal lobe, which is active during positive emotions, is likely to be inactive during depressed states (Davidson & others, 2002). In one study of people with severe depression, MRI scans found their frontal lobes 7 percent smaller than normal (Coffey & others, 1993). The *hippocampus,* a memory-processing center linked with the brain's emotional circuitry, is vulnerable to stress-related damage. By boosting serotonin, which stimulates hippocampus neuron growth, antidepressant drugs may promote recovery from depression (Jacobs & others, 2000).

Gene-hunters' pursuit of bipolar-DNA links
Linkage studies seek to identify aberrant genes in family members suffering the disorder. These Pennsylvania Amish family members—an isolated population sharing a common life-style and some vulnerability to the disorder—have been among the volunteer participants.

| Depressed state (May 17) | Manic state (May 18) | Depressed state (May 27) |

FIGURE 50.2
The ups and downs of bipolar disorder
PET scans show that brain energy consumption rises and falls with the patient's emotional switches. Red areas are where the brain rapidly consumes glucose.

CLOSE-UP:

SUICIDE

"But life, being weary of these worldly bars, Never lacks power to dismiss itself."
—William Shakespeare, *Julius Caesar*, 1599

Each year some 1 million despairing people worldwide will say no to life by electing a permanent solution to what may be a temporary problem (Mann, 2003; WHO, 2004). Comparing the suicide rates of different groups, researchers have found

- **national differences:** The suicide rates of England, Italy, and Spain are little more than half those of Canada, Australia, and the United States; Austria and Finnish suicide rates are about double (WHO, 2002a). Within Europe, the most suicide-prone people (Lithuanians) have been 15 times more likely to kill themselves than the least (Portuguese).
- **racial differences:** White Americans are nearly twice as likely as black Americans to kill themselves (NIMH, 2002).
- **gender differences:** Women are much more likely than men to attempt suicide. But men are two to

four times more likely (depending on the country) to succeed (**FIGURE 50.3**). (An exception is China, where women account for most suicides [WHO, 2002c]). Men are more likely to use lethal methods, such as firing a bullet into the head, the method of choice in 6 of 10 U.S. suicides. The more lethal a suicide attempt, the more depressed the frontal lobe's serotonin-based activity often is (Mann, 2003).

- **age differences and trends:** The suicide rate surges among older men (Figure 50.2). Across the Western world, suicide rates have also surged since 1960 among older teens, especially males (Eckersley & Dear, 2002). For American, Australian, British, Canadian, and New Zealand 15- to 25-year-olds, suicide rates all doubled or more than doubled in the 30 years after 1960, paralleling the increasing late-teen and early-twenties rates of anxiety and depression.
- **other group differences:** Suicide rates are much higher among the rich, the nonreligious, and those

who are single, widowed, or divorced (Hoyer & Lund, 1993; Stack, 1992; Stengel, 1981). In both the United States and Australia, the teen suicide surge was almost entirely among males (Hassan & Carr, 1989). Gay and lesbian youth much more often suffer distress and attempt suicide than do their heterosexual peers (Goldfried, 2001).

Those who have been depressed have at least five times the general population's risk of suicide (Bostwick & Pankratz, 2000), but people seldom commit suicide while in the depths of depression, when energy and initiative are lacking. It is when they begin to rebound and become capable of following through that the risk increases. Teenage suicides may follow a traumatic event, such as a romantic breakup or a guilt-provoking antisocial act; they are often linked with drug and alcohol abuse (Fowler & others, 1986; Kolata, 1986). Compared with people who suffer no disorder, those addicted to alcohol are roughly 100 times more likely to commit suicide;

The Social-Cognitive Perspective

OBJECTIVE 50-4 | Summarize the contributions of the social-cognitive perspective to the study of depression, and describe the events in the cycle of depression.

Some people slide into depression for no obvious reason, even when life has been going well. But as we have noted, biological risk factors can predispose psychological reactions to stressful experiences (**FIGURE 50.4**). And the mind's negative thoughts somehow influence biological events that in a vicious cycle amplify depressing thoughts.

Depressed people view life through dark glasses. Their intensely negative assumptions about themselves, their situation, and their future lead them to magnify bad experiences and minimize good ones. Listen to Norman, a Canadian college professor, recalling his depression:

> I [despaired] of ever being human again. I honestly felt subhuman, lower than the lowest vermin. Furthermore, I was self-deprecatory and could not understand why anyone would want to associate with me, let alone love me. . . . I was positive that I was a fraud and a phony and that I didn't deserve my Ph.D. I didn't deserve to have tenure; I didn't deserve to be a Full Professor. . . .

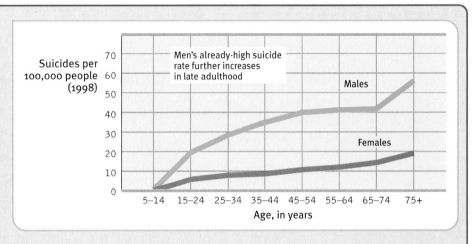

FIGURE **50.3**
Suicide rates by gender and age
Worldwide suicide rates are higher among males than among females. The highest rates of all are found among older men. (From WHO, 2002a.)

some 3 percent of them do (Murphy & Wetzel, 1990). Even among people who have attempted suicide, those who abuse alcohol are five times more likely than others to kill themselves eventually (Beck & Steer, 1989).

Social suggestion may trigger the final act. Following highly publicized suicides and TV programs featuring suicide, known suicides increase. So do fatal auto "accidents" and private airplane crashes.

Suicide is not necessarily an act of hostility or revenge. The elderly sometimes choose death as an alternative to current or future suffering. In people of all ages, suicide may be a way of switching off unendurable pain and relieving the perceived burden on family members (Joiner & others, 2002; Shneidman, 1987).

In retrospect, families and friends may recall signs that they believe should have forewarned them—verbal hints, giving possessions away, or withdrawal and preoccupation with death. But few who talk of suicide or think suicidal thoughts (a number that includes one-third of all adolescents and college students) actually attempt suicide, and few of those who attempt it complete the act (Yip, 1998). The United States, for example, records about 30,000 suicides

annually, but a half-million emergency room visits for attempted suicide (Surgeon General, 1999). One-third of those who kill themselves have tried to kill themselves previously. Most who do commit suicide have talked of it, and anyone who does threaten suicide is at least sending a signal of being desperate or feeling despondent. So, if a friend talks suicide, it's important to listen and to direct the friend to professional help.

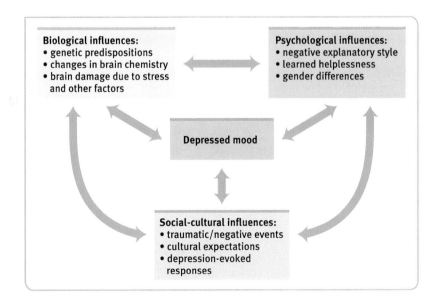

FIGURE **50.4**
Biopsychosocial approach to depression
Seriously depressed moods result from a combination of factors, which affect each other. Altering any one component can alter the others.

I didn't deserve the research grants I had been awarded; I couldn't under-stand how I had written books and journal articles. . . . I must have conned a lot of people. (Endler, 1982, pp. 45–49)

Research reveals how *self-defeating beliefs* and a *negative explanatory style* feed depression's vicious cycle.

Negative Thoughts and Negative Moods Interact

Self-defeating beliefs may arise from *learned helplessness*. Both dogs and humans act depressed, passive, and withdrawn after experiencing uncontrollable painful events (Seligman, 1975, 1991). Gender differences in uncontrollable stress help explain why, beginning in their early teens, women are nearly twice as vulnerable to depression (Kessler, 2001). Women more often than men have been abused or made to feel helpless, and they may respond more strongly to stress (Hankin & Abramson 2001; Mazure & others, 2002; Nolen-Hoeksema, 2001, 2003). Thirty-six percent of women and 16 percent of men entering American colleges feel "frequently overwhelmed by all I have to do" (Sax & others, 2004). (Men report spending more of their time in "light anxiety" activities such as sports, TV watching, and partying, possibly avoiding activities that might make them feel overwhelmed.)

But why do life's unavoidable failures lead some people and not others to become depressed? The difference lies partly with people's *explanatory style*. We have some choice of whom or what to blame for our failures. If you fail a test and blame yourself, you may feel stupid and depressed. If you externalize the blame—perhaps attributing your failure to an unfair test—you are more likely to feel angry.

Depressed people tend to explain bad events in terms that are stable ("It's going to last forever"), global ("It's going to affect everything I do"), and internal ("It's all my fault") (**FIGURE 50.5**). Lyn Abramson, Gerald Metalsky, and Lauren Alloy (1989) theorized that the result of these pessimistic, overgeneralized, self-blaming attributions is a depressing sense of hopelessness. If you tend to see bad grades, social rejection, and work problems as inevitable and your own fault, and if you ruminate about such things, then when bad things happen you will probably experience the blues.

> "I have learned to accept my mistakes by referring them to a personal history which was not of my making."
>
> B. F. Skinner (1983)

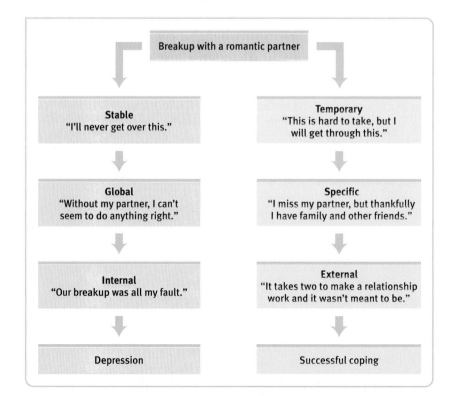

FIGURE 50.5
Explanatory style and depression

PEANUTS

Might Charlie Brown be helped by an optimism-training program?

Reprinted by permission of United Feature Syndicate, Inc.

What might you expect of new college students who are not depressed but do exhibit a pessimistic explanatory style? Lauren Alloy and her collaborators (1999) monitored Temple University and University of Wisconsin students every 6 weeks for 2.5 years. Among those identified as having pessimistic thinking styles, 17 percent had a first episode of major depression, as did only 1 percent of those who began college with optimistic thinking styles. Follow-up research has found that students who exhibit optimism as they begin college develop more social support, which contributes to a lowered risk of depression (Brissette & others, 2002).

Martin Seligman (1991, 1995) argues that depression is common among young Westerners because of epidemic hopelessness stemming from the rise of individualism and the decline of commitment to religion and family. When facing failure or rejection, contends Seligman, the self-focused individual takes on personal responsibility for problems and has nothing to fall back on for hope. In non-Western cultures, where close-knit relationships and cooperation are the norm, major depression is less common and less tied to self-blame over personal failure. In Japan, for example, depressed people instead tend to report feeling shame over letting others down (Draguns, 1990a).

There is, however, a chicken-and-egg problem with the social-cognitive explanation of depression. Self-defeating beliefs, negative attributions, and self-blame surely do support depression. Peter Barnett and Ian Gotlib (1988) note that such cognitions *coincide* with a depressed mood and are *indicators* of depression. But do they *cause* depression, any more than a speedometer's reading 70 mph causes a car's speed? Before or after being depressed, people's thoughts are less negative. Perhaps this is because, in a phenomenon known as *state-dependent memory,* a depressed mood triggers negative thoughts. If you temporarily put people in a bad or sad mood, their memories, judgments, and expectations suddenly become more pessimistic.

Joseph Forgas and his associates (1984) provided a striking demonstration of the mood effect. First, they videotaped people talking to each other. The next day, they put those participants in a good or bad mood via hypnosis and had them watch the videotape of themselves. The happy participants detected in their screen selves more positive than negative behaviors; the unhappy participants more often saw themselves behaving negatively. Thus, even when watching themselves on videotape, mildly depressed people judge themselves more negatively.

Depression's Vicious Cycle

"A recipe for severe depression is preexisting pessimism encountering failure," notes Martin Seligman (1991, p. 78). Depression, as we have seen, is often brought on by stressful experiences—losing a job, getting divorced or rejected, suffering physical trauma—anything that disrupts your sense of who you are and why you are a worthy human being. We have also seen that depression can be adaptive, a time for lying low and gaining insights that can later lead to more effective strategies for interacting with the world. But depression-prone people respond to bad events in an especially self-focused, self-blaming way (Mor & Winquist, 2002; Pyszczynski & others, 1991; Wood & others, 1990a,b). Their self-esteem fluctuates more rapidly up with boosts and down

" Man never reasons so much and becomes so introspective as when he suffers, since he is anxious to get at the cause of his sufferings."

Luigi Pirandello, *Six Characters in Search of an Author, 1922*

Susan Nolen-Hoeksema
"This epidemic of morbid meditation is a disease that women suffer much more than men. Women can ruminate about anything and everything—our appearance, our families, our career, our health." (*Women Who Think Too Much: How to Break Free of Overthinking and Reclaim Your Life,* 2003)

FIGURE 50.6
The vicious cycle of depressed thinking
Cognitive therapists attempt to break this cycle by changing the way depressed people process events. Psychiatrists attempt to alter with medication the biological roots of persistently depressed moods.

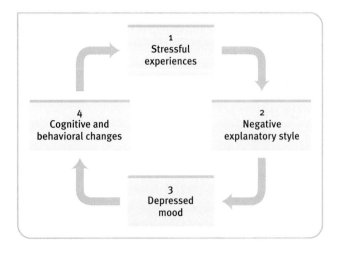

with threats (Butler & others, 1994). When down, their brooding amplifies their negative feelings, which in turn trigger depression's other cognitive and behavioral symptoms.

This cycle also helps explain women's doubled risk of depression. When trouble strikes, men tend to act, women tend to think—and often to *overthink,* as Susan Nolen-Hoeksema (2003) describes their rumination. Women often have vivid recall for both wonderful and horrid experiences; men more vaguely recall such experiences (Seidletz & Diener, 1998). This gender difference in emotional memory may feed women's greater rumination over negative events and explain why fewer men than women reported being "frequently overwhelmed on entering college."

None of us is immune to the dejection, diminished self-esteem, and negative thinking brought on by rejection or defeat. As Edward Hirt and his colleagues (1992) demonstrated, even small losses can temporarily sour our thinking. They studied some avid Indiana University basketball fans who seemed to regard the team as an extension of themselves. After the fans watched their team lose or win, the researchers asked them to predict the team's future performance and their own. After a loss, the morose fans offered bleaker assessments not only of the team's future, but also of their own likely performance at throwing darts, solving anagrams, and getting a date. When things aren't going our way, it may seem as though they never will.

But being withdrawn, self-focused, and complaining can elicit rejection (Furr & Funder, 1998; Gotlib & Hammen, 1992). In one study, researchers Stephen Strack and James Coyne (1983) noted that "depressed persons induced hostility, depression, and anxiety in others and got rejected. Their guesses that they were not accepted were not a matter of cognitive distortion." Weary of the person's fatigue, hopeless attitude, and lethargy, a spouse may threaten to leave or a boss may begin to question the person's competence. Indeed, people in the throes of depression are at high risk for divorce, job loss, and other stressful life events. (This provides another example of genetic-environmental interaction: People genetically disposed to depression more often experience depressing events.) The losses and stress only serve to compound the original depression. Rejection and depression feed each other. Misery may love another's company, but company does not love another's misery.

We can now assemble some of the pieces of the depression puzzle (**FIGURE 50.6**): (1) Negative, stressful events interpreted through (2) a ruminating, pessimistic explanatory style create (3) a hopeless, depressed state that (4) hampers the way the person thinks and acts. This, in turn, fuels (1) negative experiences such as rejection.

It is a cycle we can all recognize. Bad moods feed on themselves: When we *feel* down, we *think* negatively and remember bad experiences. On the brighter side, we can break the cycle of depression at any of these points—by moving to a different environment, by reversing our self-blame and negative attributions, by turning our attention outward, or by engaging in more pleasant activities and more competent behavior.

Winston Churchill called depression a "black dog" that periodically hounded him. Poet Emily Dickinson was so afraid of bursting into tears in public that she spent much of her adult life in seclusion (Patterson, 1951). Abraham Lincoln was so withdrawn and brooding as a young man that his friends feared he might take his own life (Kline, 1974). As each of these lives reminds us, people can and do struggle through depression. Most regain their capacity to love, to work, and even to succeed at the highest levels.

>> Learning Outcomes

Mood Disorders

OBJECTIVE 50-1 | Define *mood disorders*, and contrast major depressive disorder and bipolar disorder.

Mood disorders are characterized by emotional extremes. A person with *major depressive disorder* experiences two or more weeks of seriously depressed moods and feelings of worthlessness, takes little interest in most activities, and derives little pleasure from them. These feelings are not caused by drugs or a medical condition. People with the less common condition of *bipolar disorder* alternate between depression and *mania,* a hyperactive and wildly optimistic impulsive state.

OBJECTIVE 50-2 | Discuss the facts that an acceptable theory of depression must explain.

An acceptable theory of depression must account for the many behavioral and cognitive changes that accompany depression; its widespread occurrence; women's greater susceptibility to the disorder; the tendency of depressive episodes to self-terminate; the link between stressful events and the onset of depression; and the increasing rates and earlier age of onset of depression.

OBJECTIVE 50-3 | Summarize the contributions of the biological perspective to the study of depression, and discuss the link between suicide and depression.

The biological perspective on depression focuses on genetic influences (in part through *linkage analysis* and *association studies*) and on abnormalities in brain structure and function (including those found in neurotransmitter systems). Findings indicate that a predisposition to depression does run in some families, that the neurotransmitters norepinephrine and serotonin are scarce during depression, that activity in the left frontal lobes is slowed during depression, and that stress-related damage to the hippocampus increases the risk of depression. The risk of suicide is greatest when energy returns as depression begins to lift.

OBJECTIVE 50-4 | Summarize the contributions of the social-cognitive perspective to the study of depression, and describe the events in the cycle of depression.

The social-cognitive perspective stresses the power of self-defeating beliefs and negative explanatory styles that view bad events as stable, global, and internally caused. Critics note that these characteristics may coincide with, but not cause, depression. The cycle of depression consists of (1) negative stressful events (2) interpreted through a pessimistic explanatory style, creating a (3) hopeless depressed state, which (4) hampers the way the person thinks and acts, fueling more negative stressful events, such as rejection.

TERMS AND CONCEPTS TO REMEMBER

mood disorders, p. 50-1

major depressive disorder, p. 50-2

mania, p. 50-2

bipolar disorder, p. 50-2

TEST YOURSELF

1. What does it mean to say that "depression is the common cold of psychological disorders"?

(Answer in Appendix B.)

ASK YOURSELF

1. Has your entry into college life been a challenging time for you? What advice would you have for future collegians?

>WEB

Multiple-choice **self-tests** and more may be found at www.worthpublishers.com/myers.

51

Schizophrenia

If depression is the common cold of psychological disorders, chronic schizophrenia is the cancer. Nearly 1 in 100 people will develop schizophrenia, joining the estimated 24 million across the world who suffer one of humanity's most dreaded disorders (WHO, 2002d). It typically strikes as young people are maturing into adulthood, it knows no national boundaries, and it affects both males and females—though men tend to be struck earlier, more severely, and slightly more often (Aleman & others, 2003).

Symptoms of Schizophrenia

OBJECTIVE 51-1 | Describe the symptoms of schizophrenia, and differentiate delusions and hallucinations.

Literally translated, **schizophrenia** means "split mind." It refers not to a multiple-personality split but rather to a split from reality that shows itself in disorganized thinking, disturbed perceptions, and inappropriate emotions and actions.

Disorganized Thinking

Imagine trying to communicate with Maxine, a young woman whose thoughts spill out in no logical order. Her biographer, Susan Sheehan (1982, p. 25), observed her saying aloud to no one in particular, "This morning, when I was at Hillside [Hospital], I was making a movie. I was surrounded by movie stars . . . I'm Mary Poppins. Is this room painted blue to get me upset? My grandmother died four weeks after my eighteenth birthday."

As this strange monologue illustrates, the thinking of a person with schizophrenia is fragmented, bizarre, and distorted by false beliefs, called **delusions** ("I'm Mary Poppins"). Those with *paranoid* tendencies are particularly prone to delusions of persecution. Jumping from one idea to another may occur even within sentences, creating a sort of "word salad." One young man begged for "a little more allegro in the treatment," and suggested that "liberationary movement with a view to the widening of the horizon" will "ergo extort some wit in lectures."

Art by people diagnosed with schizophrenia
Commenting on the kind of artwork shown here, poet and art critic John Ashbery wrote: "The lure of the work is strong, but so is the terror of the unanswerable riddles it proposes."

August Natterer, *Witch's Head*. The Prinzhorn Collection, University of Heidelberg

L. Berthold, *Untitled*. The Prinzhorn Collection, University of Heidelberg

Photos of paintings by Krannert Museum, University of Illinois at Urbana-Champaign

Many psychologists believe disorganized thoughts result from a breakdown in selective attention. We normally have a remarkable capacity for selective attention—for, say, giving our undivided attention to one voice at a party while filtering out competing sensory stimuli. Those with schizophrenia cannot do this. Thus, an irrelevant stimulus or an extraneous part of the preceding thought easily distracts them. Minute stimuli, such as the grooves on a brick or the inflections of a voice, may distract their attention from the whole scene or from the speaker's meaning. As one former patient recalled, "What had happened to me . . . was a breakdown in the filter, and a hodge-podge of unrelated stimuli were distracting me from things which should have had my undivided attention" (MacDonald, 1960, p. 218). This selective attention difficulty is but one of dozens of cognitive differences associated with schizophrenia. Others range from deficiencies in working memory to the ability to smoothly follow a swinging pendulum with the eyes, a task that requires the coordination of several brain regions (Heinrichs, 2005).

Disturbed Perceptions

A person with schizophrenia may perceive things that are not there. Such *hallucinations* (sensory experiences without sensory stimulation) are usually auditory and often take the form of voices making insulting statements or giving orders. The voices may tell the patient that she is bad or that she must burn herself with a cigarette lighter. Less commonly, people see, feel, taste, or smell things that are not there. Hallucinations have been compared to dreams breaking into waking consciousness. When the unreal seems real, the resulting perceptions are at best bizarre, at worst terrifying.

Inappropriate Emotions and Actions

The emotions of schizophrenia are often utterly inappropriate. Maxine's emotions seemed split off from reality. She laughed after recalling her grandmother's death. On occasion, she became angry for no apparent reason or cried when others laughed. Other victims of schizophrenia sometimes lapse into *flat affect,* a zombielike state of apparent apathy.

Motor behavior may also be inappropriate. The person may perform senseless, compulsive acts, such as continually rocking or rubbing an arm. Those who exhibit *catatonia* may remain motionless for hours on end and then become agitated.

As you can imagine, such disorganized thinking, disturbed perceptions, and inappropriate emotions and actions profoundly disrupt social relationships and make it difficult to hold a job. During their most severe periods, people with schizophrenia live in a private inner world, preoccupied with illogical ideas and unreal images. Given a supportive environment, some eventually recover to enjoy a normal life or experience bouts of schizophrenia only intermittently. Others remain socially withdrawn and isolated throughout much of their lives, and their frequent hospitalizations help explain why many countries devote about 2 percent of their national health budget to care and treatment of those with schizophrenia (Knapp & others, 2004).

Subtypes of Schizophrenia

OBJECTIVE 51-2 | Distinguish the five subtypes of schizophrenia, and contrast chronic and acute schizophrenia.

We have thus far described schizophrenia as if it were a single disorder. Actually, it is a cluster of disorders. The subtypes share some common features, but they also have some distinguishing symptoms (**TABLE 51.1** on the next page). Schizophrenia patients

■ **schizophrenia** a group of severe disorders characterized by disorganized and delusional thinking, disturbed perceptions, and inappropriate emotions and actions.

■ **delusions** false beliefs, often of persecution or grandeur, that may accompany psychotic disorders.

TABLE 51.1

SUBTYPES OF SCHIZOPHRENIA

Paranoid:	Preoccupation with delusions or hallucinations, often with themes of persecution or grandiosity
Disorganized:	Disorganized speech or behavior, or flat or inappropriate emotion
Catatonic:	Immobility (or excessive, purposeless movement), extreme negativism, and/or parrotlike repeating of another's speech or movements
Undifferentiated:	Many and varied symptoms
Residual:	Withdrawal, after hallucinations and delusions have disappeared

"When someone asks me to explain schizophrenia I tell them, you know how sometimes in your dreams you are in them yourself and some of them feel like real nightmares? My schizophrenia was like I was walking through a dream. But everything around me was real. At times, today's world seems so boring and I wonder if I would like to step back into the schizophrenic dream, but then I remember all the scary and horrifying experiences."

Stuart Emmons, with Craig Geisler, Kalman J. Kaplan, and Martin Harrow, *Living With Schizophrenia*, 1997

with *positive symptoms* may experience hallucinations, talk in disorganized and deluded ways, and exhibit inappropriate laughter, tears, or rage. Those with *negative symptoms* have toneless voices, expressionless faces, or mute and rigid bodies. Thus, positive symptoms are the *presence* of inappropriate behaviors, and negative symptoms are the *absence* of appropriate behaviors. Because schizophrenia is a cluster of disorders, these varied symptoms could have more than one cause.

Sometimes, as in the case of Maxine, schizophrenia develops gradually, emerging from a long history of social inadequacy (which helps explain why those predisposed to schizophrenia often end up in the lower socioeconomic levels, or even homeless). Other times it appears suddenly, seemingly as a reaction to stress. One rule holds true around the world (World Health Organization, 1979): When schizophrenia is a slow-developing process (called *chronic,* or *process,* schizophrenia), recovery is doubtful. When a previously well-adjusted person develops schizophrenia rapidly (called *acute,* or *reactive,* schizophrenia) in reaction to particular life stresses, recovery is much more likely. Those with chronic schizophrenia often exhibit the negative symptom of withdrawal. Men, whose schizophrenia develops on average four years earlier than women's, more often exhibit negative symptoms and chronic schizophrenia (Räsänen & others, 2000). The outlook is better for those with positive symptoms—they more often have a reactive condition that responds to drug therapy (Fenton & McGlashan, 1991, 1994; Fowles, 1992).

Explaining Schizophrenia

Schizophrenia is not only the most dreaded psychological disorder but also one of the most heavily researched. Most of the new research studies link it with brain abnormalities and genetic predispositions. Schizophrenia is a disease of the brain exhibited in symptoms of the mind.

Brain Abnormalities

OBJECTIVE 51-3 | Outline some abnormal brain chemistry, functions, and structures associated with schizophrenia, and discuss the possible link between prenatal viral infections and schizophrenia.

Might imbalances in brain chemistry underlie schizophrenia? Scientists have long known that strange behavior can have strange chemical causes. The saying "mad as a hatter" refers to the psychological deterioration of British hatmakers whose brains, it was later discovered, were slowly poisoned as they moistened the brims of mercury-laden felt hats with their lips (Smith, 1983). Scientists are clarifying the mechanism by which chemicals such as LSD produce hallucinations. These discoveries hint that schizophrenia symptoms might have a biochemical key.

Dopamine Overactivity

Researchers discovered one such key when they examined schizophrenia patients' brains after death, and found an excess of receptors for *dopamine*—a sixfold excess for the so-called D4 dopamine receptor (Seeman & others, 1993; Wong & others, 1986). They speculate that such a high level may intensify brain signals in schizophrenia, creating positive symptoms such as hallucinations and paranoia. As we might therefore expect, drugs that block dopamine receptors often lessen these symptoms; drugs that increase dopamine levels, such as amphetamines and cocaine, sometimes intensify them (Swerdlow & Koob, 1987). Dopamine overactivity may underlie patients' overreactions to irrelevant external and internal stimuli.

Dopamine-blocking drugs have little effect on persistent negative symptoms of withdrawal. Researchers are now exploring another neurotransmitter, *glutamate,* which directs neurons to pass along an impulse. Impaired glutamate activity appears to be another source of schizophrenia symptoms (Javitt & Coyle, 2004). Drugs that interfere with glutamate receptors can produce schizophrenialike negative symptoms. Moreover, medications that neutralize the effect of such street drugs also seem to alleviate negative symptoms (HMHL, 2001).

Abnormal Brain Activity and Anatomy

Modern brain-scanning techniques reveal that many people with chronic schizophrenia have abnormal activity in multiple brain areas. Some have abnormally low brain activity in the frontal lobes, which are critical for reasoning, planning, and problem solving (Morey & others, 2005; Pettegrew & others, 1993; Resnick, 1992). People diagnosed with schizophrenia also display a noticeable decline in the brain waves that reflect synchronized neural firing in the frontal lobes (Spencer & others, 2004; Symond & others, 2005). Out-of-sync neurons may disrupt the integrated functioning of neural networks, possibly contributing to schizophrenia symptoms.

One study took PET scans of brain activity while people were hallucinating (Silbersweig & others, 1995). When participants heard a voice or saw something, their brains became vigorously active in several core regions, including the thalamus, a structure deep in the brain that filters incoming sensory signals and transmits them to the cortex. Another PET scan study of people with paranoia found increased activity in a fear-processing center, the amygdala (Epstein & others, 1998).

Many studies have found enlarged, fluid-filled areas and a corresponding shrinkage of cerebral tissue in people with schizophrenia (Wright & others, 2000), and one study even found such abnormalities in the brains of people who would *later* develop this disorder (Pantelis & others, 2002). The greater the shrinkage, the more severe the thought disorder (Collinson & others, 2003; Nelson & others, 1998; Shenton, 1992). One smaller-than-normal area is the cortex (**FIGURE 51.1** on the next page). Another is the thalamus, which may explain why people with schizophrenia have difficulty filtering sensory input and focusing attention (Andreasen & others, 1994). The bottom line of various studies, reports Nancy Andreasen (1997, 2001), is that schizophrenia involves not one isolated brain abnormality but problems with several brain regions and their interconnections.

Naturally, scientists wonder what causes these abnormalities. One possibility is some problem during prenatal development or delivery. Low birth weight and birth complications such as oxygen deprivation are known risk factors for schizophrenia (Buka & others, 1999; Zornberg & others, 2000). Famine is also a suspect. People conceived during the peak of the Dutch wartime famine later displayed a doubled rate of schizophrenia, as did those conceived during a 1959–1961 famine in eastern China (St. Clair & others, 2005; Susser & others, 1996).

About 60 percent of schizophrenia patients smoke, often heavily. Nicotine apparently stimulates certain brain receptors, which helps focus attention (Javitt & Coyle, 2004).

Studying the neurophysiology of schizophrenia
Psychiatrist E. Fuller Torrey is collecting the brains of hundreds of those who died as young adults and suffered disorders such as schizophrenia and bipolar disorder. Torrey is making tissue samples available to researchers worldwide.

Chris Usher

FIGURE **51.1**
Schizophrenia and the shrinking brain.
Among adolescents who suffer a relatively rare childhood-onset schizophrenia, MRI scans by Paul Thompson and his colleagues (2001) revealed a much-greater-than-normal loss of cerebral cortex tissue between the ages of 13 and 18.

Maternal Virus During Midpregnancy

Another possible culprit is a midpregnancy viral infection that impairs fetal brain development. Can you imagine some ways to test this fetal-virus idea? Scientists exploring this possibility have asked the following questions:

- *Are people at increased risk of schizophrenia if, during the middle of their fetal development, their country experienced a flu epidemic?* The repeated answer is yes (Mednick & others, 1994; Murray & others, 1992; Wright & others, 1995).
- *Are people born in densely populated areas, where viral diseases spread more readily, at greater risk for schizophrenia?* The answer, confirmed in a study of 1.75 million Danes, is yes (Jablensky, 1999; Mortensen & others, 1999).
- *Are those born during the winter and spring months—after the fall-winter flu season—also at increased risk?* The answer is again yes, at 5 to 8 percent increased risk (Torrey & others, 1997, 2002).
- *In the Southern Hemisphere, where the seasons are the reverse of the Northern Hemisphere, are the months of above-average schizophrenia births similarly reversed?* Again, the answer is yes, though somewhat less so. In Australia, for example, people born between August and October are at greater risk—unless they migrated from the Northern Hemisphere, in which case their risk is greater if they were born between January and March (McGrath & others, 1995, 1999).
- *Are mothers who report being sick with influenza during pregnancy more likely to bear children who develop schizophrenia?* In one study of nearly 8000 women, the answer was yes. The schizophrenia risk increased from the customary 1 percent risk to about 2 percent—but only for infections during the second trimester (Brown & others, 2000).
- *Does blood drawn from pregnant women whose offspring develop schizophrenia show higher-than-normal levels of antibodies that suggest a viral infection?* In one study of 27 women whose children later developed schizophrenia, the answer was yes (Buka & others, 2001). One huge California study collected blood samples from some 20,000 pregnant women during the 1950s and 1960s, some of whose offspring were later diagnosed with schizophrenia. When antibodies in the blood indicated the mother was exposed to influenza during the first half of the pregnancy, the risk of the child's developing schizophrenia tripled. Flu during the second half of the pregnancy produced no such increase (Brown & others, 2004).

Schizophrenia has other causes (as genetics research makes plain). Moreover, the children of some 98 percent of women who catch the flu during their second trimester of pregnancy do *not* develop schizophrenia. Nevertheless, these converging lines of evidence suggest that prenatal viral infections play a contributing role. They also strengthen the U.S. Centers for Disease Control (2003) recommendation that "women who will be more than three months pregnant during the flu season" have a flu shot.

Why might a second-trimester maternal flu bout put fetuses at risk? Is it the virus itself? The mother's immune response to it? Medications taken? (Wyatt & others, 2001). Does the infection weaken the brain's supportive glial cells, leading to reduced synaptic connections (Moises & others, 2002)? In time, answers may become available.

Genetic Factors

OBJECTIVE 51-4 | Discuss the evidence for a genetic contribution to the development of schizophrenia.

Might people also inherit a predisposition to certain brain abnormalities? The evidence strongly suggests that, yes, some do. The nearly 1-in-100 odds of any person's being diagnosed with schizophrenia become about 1 in 10 among those whose sibling or parent has the disorder, and close to 1 in 2 if the affected sibling is an identical twin (FIGURE 51.2). Although there are barely more than a dozen such known cases, it appears that an identical twin of a person with schizophrenia retains that 1-in-2 chance when the twins are reared apart (Plomin & others, 1997).

Even with identical twins, there may be a prenatal environmental component. About two-thirds of identical twins share the same placenta and blood. (They usually also have opposite handedness to their co-twin.) If an identical twin has schizophrenia, the co-twin's chances of being similarly afflicted are 6 in 10 if they shared a single placenta, but only 1 in 10 if the twins had separate placentas (Davis & others, 1995a,b; Phelps & others, 1997). Twins who share a placenta are more likely to experience the same prenatal viruses. So it is possible that shared germs as well as shared genes produce identical twin similarities.

Adoption studies, however, confirm that the genetic link is real (Gottesman, 1991). Children adopted by someone who develops schizophrenia seldom "catch" the disorder. Rather, adopted children have an elevated risk if a biological parent is diagnosed with schizophrenia. One intriguing study of 87,907 Israelis also found that the older the biological father—and thus the more opportunities for the DNA in his sperm cells to have mutated—the greater the risk of offspring with schizophrenia (Malaspina & others, 2001).

With the genetic factor established, researchers are now sleuthing specific genes that, in some combination, might predispose schizophrenia-inducing brain abnormalities (Callicott & others, 2005; Egan & others, 2004). (It is not our genes but our brains that directly control our behavior.) Some of these genes provide the code for proteins involved in the brain's neurotransmission (including one that breaks down dopamine). Other important genes appear to code for proteins used to make the myelin that coats brain cells and influences their impulse transmission. Despite tantalizing findings, the culprit genes have proven elusive. The genetic contribution to schizophrenia is beyond question. But the genetic role is not as straightforward as the

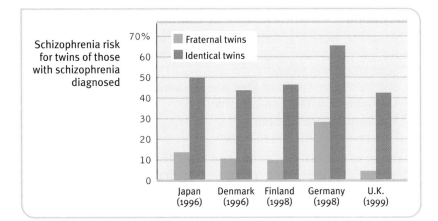

FIGURE 51.2
Risk of developing schizophrenia
The lifetime risk of developing schizophrenia varies with one's genetic relatedness to someone having this disorder. Across countries, barely more than 1 in 10 fraternal twins, but some 5 in 10 identical twins, share a schizophrenia diagnosis. (Adapted from Gottesman, 2001.)

No schizophrenia   Schizophrenia

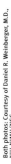

Schizophrenia in identical twins

When twins differ, only the one afflicted with schizophrenia typically has enlarged, fluid-filled cranial cavities (right) (Suddath & others, 1990). The difference between the twins implies some nongenetic factor, such as a virus, is also at work.

The Genain quadruplets

The odds of any four people picked at random all being diagnosed with schizophrenia are 1 in 100 million. But genetically identical sisters Nora, Iris, Myra, and Hester Genain all have the disease. Two of the sisters have more severe forms of the disorder than the others, suggesting the influence of environmental as well as biological factors.

inheritance of eye color. A complex disorder such as schizophrenia is surely influenced by multiple genes with small effects.

Also remember that half the twins who share identical genes with a schizophrenia victim do *not* develop the disorder. Thus, behavior geneticists Susan Nicol and Irving Gottesman (1983) concluded that some people "have a genetic predisposition to the disorder but that this predisposition by itself is not sufficient for the development of schizophrenia." Other factors—including the prenatal viral infections, nutritional deprivation, and oxygen deprivation at birth mentioned earlier—may be ingredients for the disease.

Our knowledge of human genetics and of genetic influences on maladies such as schizophrenia is exploding, thanks partly to millions of new National Institute of Mental Health dollars focused on solving the schizophrenia riddle. So, can scientists develop genetic tests that reveal who is at risk? If so, will people in the future subject their embryos to genetic testing (and gene repair or abortion) if they are at risk for this or some other psychological or physical malady? Might they take their egg and sperm to the genetics lab for screening before combining them to produce an embryo? Or will children be tested for genetic risks and given appropriate preventive treatments? In this brave new twenty-first-century world, such questions await answers.

Psychological Factors

OBJECTIVE 51-5 | Describe some psychological factors that may be early warning signs of schizophrenia in children.

If genetically predisposed physiological abnormalities do not, by themselves, cause schizophrenia, neither do prenatal and psychological factors alone. It remains true, as Nicol and Gottesman (1983) noted more than two decades ago, that "no environmental causes have been discovered that will invariably, or even with moderate probability, produce schizophrenia in persons who are not related to" a person with schizophrenia. Psychologists long ago ceased blaming parents; no longer do they attribute schizophrenia to cold and capricious "refrigerator mothers."

Hoping to identify environmental triggers of schizophrenia, several investigators are now following the development of "high-risk" children, such as those born to a parent with schizophrenia or exposed to prenatal risks (Freedman & others, 1998; Olin & Mednick, 1996; Susser, 1999). One study followed 163 teens and early-twenties adults who had two relatives with schizophrenia. During the 2½-year study, the 20 percent who developed schizophrenia displayed some tendency to withdraw socially and behave oddly in advance of the onset of the disorder (Johnstone & others, 2005). By comparing the experiences of high-risk and low-risk children who do and do not develop schizophrenia, researchers have so far pinpointed the following possible early warning signs:

- A mother whose schizophrenia was severe and long-lasting
- Birth complications, often involving oxygen deprivation and low birth weight
- Separation from parents
- Short attention span and poor muscle coordination
- Disruptive or withdrawn behavior
- Emotional unpredictability
- Poor peer relations and solo play

Few of us can easily relate to the strange thoughts, perceptions, and behaviors of schizophrenia. Sometimes our thoughts do jump around, but we do not talk nonsensically. Occasionally we feel unjustly suspicious of someone, but we do not fear that the world is plotting against us. Often our perceptions err, but rarely do we see or hear things that are not there. We have felt regret after laughing at someone's misfortune, but we rarely giggle in response to bad news. At times we just want to be alone, but we do not live in social isolation. However, millions of people around the world do talk strangely, suffer delusions, hear nonexistent voices, see things that are not there, laugh or cry at inappropriate times, or withdraw into private imaginary worlds. The quest to solve the cruel puzzle of schizophrenia therefore continues, and more vigorously than ever.

>> LEARNING OUTCOMES

Schizophrenia

OBJECTIVE 51-1 | Describe the symptoms of schizophrenia, and differentiate delusions and hallucinations.

Schizophrenia is a group of disorders that typically strike during late adolescence, affect men very slightly more than women, and seem to occur in all cultures. Symptoms of schizophrenia are disorganized and delusional thinking (which may stem from a breakdown of selective attention), disturbed perceptions, and inappropriate emotions and actions. *Delusions* are false beliefs; *hallucinations* are sensory experiences without sensory stimulation.

OBJECTIVE 51-2 | Distinguish the five subtypes of schizophrenia, and contrast chronic and acute schizophrenia.

The subtypes of schizophrenia are *paranoid* (preoccupation with delusions or hallucinations, often of persecution or grandiosity), *disorganized* (disorganized speech or behavior, or flat affect or inappropriate emotions), *catatonic* (immobility, extreme negativism, and/or parrotlike repetition of another's speech or movements), *undifferentiated* (varied symptoms), and *residual* (withdrawal following hallucinations and delusions). *Chronic* (or *process*) *schizophrenia* emerges gradually, is often associated with negative symptoms (absence of appropriate behaviors), and carries a low chance of recovery. *Acute* (or *reactive*) schizophrenia develops rapidly (often in response to stress) in a previously well-adjusted person, may be associated with positive symptoms (presence of inappropriate behaviors), and carries a greater chance of recovery.

OBJECTIVE 51-3 | Outline some abnormal brain chemistry, functions, and structures associated with schizophrenia, and discuss the possible link between prenatal viral infections and schizophrenia.

People with schizophrenia have increased receptors for the neurotransmitter dopamine, which may intensify the positive symptoms of schizophrenia. Research is under way on a possible link between negative symptoms and impaired glutamate activity. Brain abnormalities associated with schizophrenia include enlarged, fluid-filled cerebral cavities and corresponding decreases in the cortex. Brain scans reveal abnormal activity in the frontal lobes, thalamus, and amygdala. Malfunctions in multiple brain regions and their connections apparently interact to produce the symptoms of schizophrenia. Research support is mounting for the causal effects of a virus suffered in mid-pregnancy.

OBJECTIVE 51-4 | Discuss the evidence for a genetic contribution to the development of schizophrenia.

The odds of developing schizophrenia are approximately 1 in 100 in the general population; 1 in 10 if a family member has it; and 1 in 2 if an identical twin has the disorder. Adoption studies show that an adopted child's chances of developing the disorder are greater if the biological parents have schizophrenia, but not if the adopted parents have it. But 50 percent of identical twins whose co-twin has schizophrenia do not develop the condition themselves, demonstrating that genetics is not the sole cause of this disorder.

OBJECTIVE 51-5 | Describe some psychological factors that may be early warning signs of schizophrenia in children.

No environmental event can by itself trigger schizophrenia, but some things may increase the risk in those genetically predisposed to the disorder. Early warning signs of schizophrenia include having a mother whose schizophrenia was severe and long-lasting; birth complications; separation from parents; short attention span and poor muscle coordination; disruptive or withdrawn behavior; emotional unpredictability; and poor peer relations and solo play.

TERMS AND CONCEPTS TO REMEMBER

schizophrenia, p. 51-0   delusions, p. 51-0

TEST YOURSELF

1. What are the five subtypes of schizophrenia?

(Answer in Appendix B.)

ASK YOURSELF

1. Civil libertarians defend the right of schizophrenia patients not to be hospitalized against their will. E. Fuller Torrey (1998), a psychiatrist who views schizophrenia as a brain disorder, objects: "If a person with Alzheimer's wanted to go outside with no shoes in the winter, we wouldn't say, 'That's fine, he should have free choice.'" Do you think patients with schizophrenia should be hospitalized and treated against their will? Or do they always have the right to live free, even if under bridges or in shelters?

>WEB

Multiple-choice *self-tests* and more may be found at www.worthpublishers.com/myers.

ANOTHER VOICE ON: THERAPY

JACK RIDL (b. 1944) FROM "THE HEALERS," POEMS FROM *THE SAME GHOST AND BETWEEN*

My father guessed at work.
He gave me things to do.
We strangled weeds from the flower bed,
Washed the car,
Walked the dog.

My mother guessed at a mother's love.
She went back to tucking sheets
Around me as I lay awake in bed.
She pulled her fingers through my hair.
She turned away. She held me.

My good friend guessed at leaving town.
So we lugged gravel, grinding gears
Up and down the western Pennsylvania
    hills.
We'd raise the bed and listen
To the gravel rush into a silent pile.

My preacher guessed at God.
He knew my answer; spread my sin;
Prayed; asked me to pray;
Sprinkled oil on my head;
Pronounced me of this world.

My doctor guessed at shock.
Strapped me down.
Hooked electrodes to my head.
Baptized me with volts.

I guessed at empty space
And all the breath
That I could spill to fill it up.

Therapy

Today we comprehend deep outer space and can state with certainty the chemical composition of Jupiter's atmosphere. But in understanding and treating the disturbances of deep inner space—the psychological disorders that continue to plague humankind—we are only beginning to make real progress. In the 2200 years since Eratosthenes correctly estimated the Earth's circumference, we have charted the heavens, explored our solar system, reconstructed the basic history of life, cracked the genetic code, and eliminated or found cures for all sorts of diseases. Meanwhile, we have treated psychological disorders with a bewildering variety of harsh and gentle methods: by cutting holes in the head and by giving warm baths and massages; by restraining, bleeding, or "beating the devil" out of people; by placing them in sunny, serene environments; by administering drugs and electric shocks; and by talking—talking about childhood experiences, about current feelings, about maladaptive thoughts and behaviors.

The transition from brutal to gentler treatments occurred thanks to the efforts of reformers such as Philippe Pinel in France and Dorothea Dix in the United States, Canada, and Scotland. Both advocated constructing mental hospitals to offer more humane methods of treatment. However, the introduction of therapeutic drugs and community-based treatment programs has largely emptied mental health hospitals since the mid-1950s.

Dorothea Dix (1802–1887)
"I . . . call your attention to the state of the Insane Persons confined within this Commonwealth, in cages."

Culver Pictures

Mental health therapies can be classified into two main categories: the psychological therapies (Modules 52 and 53) and the biomedical therapies (Module 54). Today, the favored treatment depends on both the disorder and the therapist's viewpoint.

The history of treatment

The engraving (below right) by William Hogarth (1697–1764) of London's St. Mary of Bethlehem hospital (commonly called Bedlam) depicts the treatment of mental disorders in the eighteenth century. Visitors paid to gawk at the patients as if they were viewing zoo animals. The chair on the left was designed by Benjamin Rush (1746–1813) "for the benefit of maniacal patients." Rush, a founder of the movement for more humane treatment of the mentally ill, believed they required restraint to regain their sensibilities.

The Granger Collection

The Granger Collection

MODULES

52

The Psychological Therapies

OBJECTIVE 52-1 | Define *psychotherapy*, and explain what we mean by an *eclectic approach* to therapy.

Psychological therapy, or **psychotherapy** is "a planned emotionally charged, confiding interaction between a trained, socially sanctioned healer and a sufferer" (Frank, 1982). It is often the preferred treatment for disorders that researchers believe are learned, such as phobias. Among the dozens of types of psychotherapy, we will look at only the most influential. Each is built on one or more of psychology's major theories: psychoanalytic, humanistic, behavioral, and cognitive. We will also consider the use of some of these techniques in groups.

Depending on the client and the problem, some therapists—particularly the many using a biopsychosocial approach—draw from a variety of techniques. Indeed, half of all psychotherapists have described themselves as taking an **eclectic approach,** by using a blend of therapies (Beitman & others, 1989; Castonguay & Goldfried, 1994). Closely related to eclecticism is *psychotherapy integration*. Rather than picking and choosing methods, integration advocates aim to combine them into a single, coherent system.

Psychoanalysis

OBJECTIVE 52-2 | Define *psychoanalysis*, and discuss the aims of this form of therapy.

Although few clinicians today practice therapy as Sigmund Freud did, many of his techniques and assumptions survive, especially in the *psychodynamic therapies* (discussed later in this module). Freudian terminology has also crept into our modern vocabulary. Freud's **psychoanalysis** was the first of the psychological therapies.

Aims

Sigmund Freud assumed that many psychological problems are fueled by childhood's residue of repressed impulses and conflicts. It is therefore the psychoanalyst's job to bring these repressed feelings into conscious awareness where the patient can deal with them. By gaining insight into the origins of the disorder—by fulfilling the ancient imperative to "know thyself" in a deep way—patients work through the buried feelings and take responsibility for their own growth. Psychoanalytic theory presumes that healthier, less anxious living becomes possible when people release the energy they had previously devoted to id-ego-superego conflicts.

Freud's consulting room
Freud's office was rich with antiquities from around the world, including artwork related to his ideas about unconscious motives. His famous couch, piled high with pillows, placed patients in a comfortable reclining position facing away from him to help them focus inward.

Methods

OBJECTIVE **52-3** | Describe some of the methods used in psychoanalysis, and list some criticisms of this form of therapy.

Psychoanalysis is historical reconstruction. It aims to unearth the past in hope of unmasking the present. But how?

When Freud discarded hypnosis as unreliable, he turned to *free association*. Imagine yourself as a patient using free association. First, you relax, perhaps by lying on a couch. To help you focus attention on your own thoughts and feelings, the psychoanalyst may sit out of your line of vision. You say aloud whatever comes to your mind from moment to moment, which may be a childhood memory, a dream, or a recent experience. It sounds easy, but soon you notice how often you edit your thoughts as you speak, omitting what seems trivial, irrelevant, or shameful. Even in the safe presence of the analyst, you may pause momentarily before uttering an embarrassing thought. You may make a joking remark or change the subject to something less threatening. Sometimes your mind goes blank or you find yourself unable to remember important details.

To the psychoanalyst, these blocks in the flow of your free associations indicate **resistance.** They hint that anxiety lurks and you are defending against sensitive material. The analyst will want to make you aware of your resistances and then **interpret** their meaning, providing *insight* into your underlying wishes, feelings, and conflicts. This interpretation—of, say, your not wanting to talk about your mother—may, if offered at the right moment, illuminate what you are avoiding and demonstrate how this resistance fits with other pieces of your psychological puzzle.

Freud believed that another clue to unconscious conflicts is your dreams' *latent content*—their underlying but censored meaning. Thus, after inviting you to report a dream, the analyst may offer a dream analysis, suggesting its meaning.

During many such sessions you will probably disclose to your analyst more of yourself than you have ever revealed to anyone else. Because psychoanalytic theory emphasizes the formative power of childhood experiences, much of what you reveal will pertain to your earliest memories. You may find yourself experiencing strong positive or negative feelings for your analyst. Freud would say you are **transferring** to the analyst your strongest feelings from earlier relationships with family members or other important people. Analysts and other therapists believe that transference exposes feelings that a person has previously defended against, such as dependency or mingled love and anger, giving you a belated chance to work through them with your analyst's help. But psychoanalysis is not just about excavating your childhood past. By examining your feelings toward the analyst you may also gain insight into your current relationships.

Critics point out that psychoanalysts' interpretations are hard to refute because they cannot be proven or disproven, a criticism psychoanalysts acknowledge. But they insist that interpretations often are a great help to patients. Psychoanalysis is therapy, not science.

Traditional psychoanalysis takes time, up to several years of several sessions a week, and it is expensive. (Three times a week for just two

- **psychotherapy** an emotionally charged, confiding interaction between a trained therapist and someone who suffers from psychological difficulties.
- **eclectic approach** an approach to psychotherapy that, depending on the client's problems, uses techniques from various forms of therapy.
- **psychoanalysis** Sigmund Freud's therapeutic technique. Freud believed the patient's free associations, resistances, dreams, and transferences—and the therapist's interpretations of them—released previously repressed feelings, allowing the patient to gain self-insight.
- **resistance** in psychoanalysis, the blocking from consciousness of anxiety-laden material.
- **interpretation** in psychoanalysis, the analyst's noting supposed dream meanings, resistances, and other significant behaviors and events in order to promote insight.
- **transference** in psychoanalysis, the patient's transfer to the analyst of emotions linked with other relationships (such as love or hatred for a parent).

"I haven't seen my analyst in 200 years. He was a strict Freudian. If I'd been going all this time, I'd probably almost be cured by now."

Woody Allen, after awakening from suspended animation in the movie *Sleeper*

"In the mental-health profession, we try to avoid negative labels, like 'a hundred and fifty bucks an hour—that's *crazy*!' or 'three fifty-minute sessions a week—that's *insane*!'"

years at more than $100 per hour comes to at least $30,000.) This helps explain why, outside of France, Germany, Quebec, and New York City, relatively few therapists offer it (Goode, 2003). Indeed, in the United States, managed health care has severely limited the types and length of mental health services that may be covered by insurance. This has contributed to a trend toward much shorter treatment periods and many fewer instances of in-patient care.

Psychodynamic Therapy

OBJECTIVE 52-4 | Contrast psychodynamic therapy and interpersonal therapy with traditional psychoanalysis.

Influenced by Freud, *psychodynamic* therapists try to understand a patient's current symptoms by focusing on themes across important relationships, including childhood experiences and the therapist relationship. They also help the person explore and gain perspective on defended-against thoughts and feelings. But these therapists may talk to the patient face to face (rather than out of the line of vision), once a week (rather than several times weekly), and for only a few weeks or months (rather than several years).

No brief excerpt can exemplify the way psychodynamic therapy interprets a patient's conflict. But we can illustrate psychodynamic therapists' goal of enabling insight by looking for common, recurring themes, especially in relationships. In the following interaction, therapist David Malan responds to all he has heard from a depressed patient by suggesting insights into her problems. Note how Malan interprets the woman's earlier remarks (when she did most of the talking) and suggests that her relationship with him reveals a characteristic pattern of behavior (1978, pp. 133–134).

Face-to-face therapy
In this type of therapy session, the couch has disappeared. But the influence of psychoanalytic theory may not have, especially if the therapist probes for the origin of the patient's symptoms by seeking information from the patient's childhood.

Michael Newman/PhotoEdit, Inc.

Malan: *I get the feeling that you're the sort of person who needs to keep active. If you don't keep active, then something goes wrong. Is that true?*
Patient: *Yes.*
Malan: *I get a second feeling about you and that is that you must, underneath all this, have an awful lot of very strong and upsetting feelings. Somehow they're there but you aren't really quite in touch with them. Isn't this right? I feel you've been like that as long as you can remember.*
Patient: *For quite a few years, whenever I really sat down and thought about it I got depressed, so I tried not to think about it.*
Malan: *You see, you've established a pattern, haven't you? You're even like that here with me, because in spite of the fact that you're in some trouble and you feel that the bottom is falling out of your world, the way you're telling me this is just as if there wasn't anything wrong.*

Interpersonal psychotherapy, a brief (12- to 16-session) variation of psychodynamic therapy, has been effective in treating depression (Weissman, 1999). Interpersonal psychotherapy aims to help people gain insight into the roots of their difficulties, but its goal is symptom relief in the here and now, not overall personality change. Rather than focusing mostly on undoing past hurts and offering interpretations, the therapist focuses primarily on current relationships and on helping people improve their relationship skills.

The case of Anna (not her real name), a 34-year-old married professional, illustrates these goals. Five months after receiving a promotion, with accompanying increased responsibilities and longer hours, Anna experienced increased tensions with her husband over his wish for a second child. She began feeling depressed, had trouble sleeping, became irritable, and was gaining weight. A typical psychodynamic therapist might have helped Anna gain insight into her angry impulses and her defenses against anger. An interpersonal therapist similarly wanted Anna to gain these insights, but also engaged her thinking on more immediate issues—how she could balance work and home, resolve the dispute with her husband, and express her emotions more effectively (Markowitz & others, 1998).

"You say, 'Off with her head' but what I'm hearing is, 'I feel neglected.'"

Humanistic Therapies

OBJECTIVE *52-5* | Identify the basic characteristics of the humanistic therapies, and describe the specific goals and techniques of Carl Rogers' client-centered therapy.

The humanistic perspective has emphasized people's inherent potential for self-fulfillment. Not surprisingly, humanistic therapists aim to boost self-fulfillment by helping people grow in self-awareness and self-acceptance. Like psychoanalytic therapies, humanistic therapies attempt to reduce the conflicts that are impeding natural developmental growth. But unlike many psychoanalytic therapists, humanistic therapists tend to focus on

- the *present* and *future* more than the past. They explore feelings as they occur, rather than achieving insights into the childhood origins of the feelings.
- *conscious* rather than unconscious thoughts.
- taking immediate *responsibility* for one's feelings and actions, rather than uncovering hidden determinants.
- promoting growth instead of curing illness. Thus, those in therapy became "clients" rather than "patients" (a label change that many therapists have followed).

One widely used humanistic technique has been Carl Rogers' (1961, 1980) **client-centered therapy.** A client-centered therapist focuses on the person's conscious self-perceptions rather than on the therapist's own interpretations. The therapist listens, without judging or interpreting, and refrains from directing the client toward certain insights, a strategy labeled *nondirective therapy*.

Believing that most people already possess the resources for growth, Rogers encouraged therapists to exhibit *genuineness, acceptance,* and *empathy*. When therapists drop their facades and genuinely express their true feelings, when they enable their

▓ **client-centered therapy** a humanistic therapy, developed by Carl Rogers, in which the therapist uses techniques such as active listening within a genuine, accepting, empathic environment to facilitate clients' growth. (Also called *person-centered therapy*.)

Active listening
Carl Rogers (right) empathized with a client during this group therapy session.

"We have two ears and one mouth that we may listen the more and talk the less."

Zeno, 335–263 B.C., *Diogenes Laertius*

clients to feel unconditionally accepted, and when they empathically sense and reflect their clients' feelings, the clients may deepen their self-understanding and self-acceptance (Hill & Nakayama, 2000). As Rogers (1980, p. 10) explained,

> Hearing has consequences. When I truly hear a person and the meanings that are important to him at that moment, hearing not simply his words, but him, and when I let him know that I have heard his own private personal meanings, many things happen. There is first of all a grateful look. He feels released. He wants to tell me more about his world. He surges forth in a new sense of freedom. He becomes more open to the process of change.
>
> I have often noticed that the more deeply I hear the meanings of the person, the more there is that happens. Almost always, when a person realizes he has been deeply heard, his eyes moisten. I think in some real sense he is weeping for joy. It is as though he were saying, "Thank God, somebody heard me. Someone knows what it's like to be me."

"Hearing" refers to Rogers' technique of **active listening**—echoing, restating, and seeking clarification of what the person expresses (verbally or nonverbally) and acknowledging the expressed feelings. Active listening is now an accepted part of therapeutic counseling practices in many schools, colleges, and clinics. The counselor listens attentively and interrupts only to restate and confirm the client's feelings, to accept what the client is expressing, or to seek clarification. The following brief excerpt between Rogers and a male client illustrates how he sought to provide a psychological mirror that would help clients see themselves more clearly.

> **Client:** *I just ain't no good to nobody, never was, and never will be.*
>
> **Rogers:** *Feeling that now, hm? That you're just no good to yourself, no good to anybody. Never will be any good to anybody. Just that you're completely worthless, huh?—Those really are lousy feelings. Just feel that you're no good at all, hm?*
>
> **Client:** *Yeah. (Muttering in low, discouraged voice) That's what this guy I went to town with just the other day told me.*
>
> **Rogers:** *This guy that you went to town with really told you that you were no good? Is that what you're saying? Did I get that right?*
>
> **Client:** *M-hm.*
>
> **Rogers:** *I guess the meaning of that if I get it right is that here's somebody that—meant something to you and what does he think of you? Why, he's told you that he thinks you're no good at all. And that just really knocks the props out from under you. (Client weeps quietly.) It just brings the tears. (Silence of 20 seconds)*
>
> **Client:** *(Rather defiantly) I don't care though.*
>
> **Rogers:** *You tell yourself you don't care at all, but somehow I guess some part of you cares because some part of you weeps over it. (1984, p. 167 Meador & Rogers)*

Can a therapist be a perfect mirror, without selecting and interpreting what is reflected? Rogers conceded that one cannot be *totally* nondirective. Nevertheless, he believed that the therapist's most important contribution is to accept and understand the client. Given a nonjudgmental, grace-filled environment that provides *unconditional positive regard,* people may accept even their worst traits and feel valued and whole.

If you want to listen more actively in your own relationships, three hints may help:

1. *Paraphrase.* Check your understandings by summarizing the speaker's words in your own words.

2. *Invite clarification.* "What might be an example of that?" may encourage the speaker to say more.

3. *Reflect feelings.* "It sounds frustrating" might mirror what you're sensing from the speaker's body language and intensity.

Behavior Therapies

OBJECTIVE 52-6 | Explain how the basic assumption of behavior therapy differs from those of traditional psychoanalytic and humanistic therapies.

The therapies we have considered so far assume that many psychological problems diminish as self-awareness grows. Traditional psychoanalysts expect problems to subside as people gain insight into their unresolved and unconscious tensions. Humanistic therapists expect problems to abate as people get in touch with their feelings. Behavior therapists, however, doubt the healing power of self-awareness. They assume problem behaviors *are* the problems. For example, you can become aware of why you are highly anxious during exams and still be anxious. **Behavior therapy** applies learning principles to eliminate a troubling behavior. To treat phobias or sexual disorders, behavior therapists do not delve deeply below the surface looking for inner causes. They view maladaptive symptoms, such as anxiety, as learned behaviors that can be replaced with constructive behaviors.

Classical Conditioning Techniques

OBJECTIVE 52-7 | Define *counterconditioning,* and describe the techniques used in exposure therapies and aversive conditioning.

One cluster of behavior therapies derives from principles developed in Ivan Pavlov's early-twentieth-century conditioning experiments. As Pavlov and others showed, we learn various behaviors and emotions through classical conditioning. So, are maladaptive symptoms examples of conditioned responses? If so, might reconditioning be a solution? Learning theorist O. H. Mowrer developed one such conditioning therapy for chronic bed-wetters. The child sleeps on a liquid-sensitive pad connected to an alarm. Moisture on the pad triggers the alarm, waking the child. With sufficient repetition, this association of urinary relaxation with waking up stops the bed-wetting. In three out of four cases the treatment is effective, and the success provides a boost to the child's self-image (Christophersen & Edwards, 1992; Houts & others, 1994).

Another example: If a claustrophobic fear of elevators is a learned aversion to the stimulus of being in a confined space, then might one unlearn the fear by counterconditioning the fear response? **Counterconditioning** pairs the trigger stimulus with a new response that is incompatible with fear. And indeed, behavior therapists have successfully counterconditioned this fear by repeatedly pairing the enclosed space of the elevator with a relaxed response may displace the fear response. In such therapy, two specific counterconditioning techniques—*exposure therapies* and *aversive conditioning* may be used.

Exposure Therapies

Picture this scene reported in 1924 by Mary Cover Jones, an associate of the behaviorist John B. Watson: Three-year-old Peter is petrified of rabbits and other furry objects. Peter's fear arose during the course of his life at home and is quite intense. Jones aims to replace Peter's fear of rabbits with a conditioned response that is incompatible with fear. Her strategy is to associate the fear-evoking rabbit with the pleasurable, relaxed response associated with eating.

As Peter begins his midafternoon snack, Jones introduces a caged rabbit on the other side of the huge room. Peter, eagerly munching away on his crackers and drinking his milk, hardly notices. On succeeding days, she gradually moves the rabbit closer and closer. Within two months, Peter is tolerating the rabbit in his lap, even stroking it while he eats. Moreover, his

■ **behavior therapy** therapy that applies learning principles to the elimination of unwanted behaviors.

■ **counterconditioning** a behavior therapy procedure that conditions new responses to stimuli that trigger unwanted behaviors; based on classical conditioning. Includes *exposure therapy* and *aversive conditioning.*

What might a psychoanalyst say about this therapy for bed-wetting? How might a behavior therapist reply?

Hoping to fly free of fear
Some airlines offer programs that ease fear of flying through education and gradual exposure to simulated and actual air travel. Here a pilot explains the functions of the cockpit equipment to participants.

Professor Gallagher and his controversial technique of simultaneously confronting the fear of heights, snakes, and the dark.

fear of other furry objects subsides as well, having been "countered," or replaced, by a relaxed state that cannot coexist with fear (Fisher, 1984; Jones, 1924).

Unfortunately for those who might have been helped by her counterconditioning procedures, Jones' story of Peter and the rabbit did not immediately become part of psychology's lore. It was not until more than 30 years later that psychiatrist Joseph Wolpe (1958; Wolpe & Plaud, 1997) refined Jones' technique into what has become the most widely used method of behavior therapy: **exposure therapies,** which expose people to what they normally avoid. As people can habituate to the sound of a train passing their new apartment, so, with repeated exposure, can they become less anxiously responsive to things that once petrified them (Deacon & Abramowitz, 2004).

One widely used exposure therapy is **systematic desensitization.** Wolpe assumed, as did Jones, that you cannot be simultaneously anxious and relaxed. Therefore, if you can repeatedly relax when facing anxiety-provoking stimuli, you can gradually eliminate your anxiety. The trick is to proceed gradually.

Let's see how this might work with a common phobia. Imagine yourself afraid of public speaking. A behavior therapist might first ask for your help in constructing a hierarchy of anxiety-triggering speaking situations. Your anxiety hierarchy could range from mildly anxiety-provoking situations, such as speaking up in a small group of friends, to panic-provoking situations, such as having to address a large audience.

Using *progressive relaxation,* the therapist trains you to relax one muscle group after another, until you achieve a drowsy state of complete relaxation and comfort. Then the therapist asks you to imagine, with your eyes closed, a mildly anxiety-arousing situation: You are having coffee with a group of friends and are trying to decide whether to speak up. If imagining the scene causes you to feel any anxiety, you signal your tension by raising your finger, and the therapist instructs you to switch off the mental image and go back to deep relaxation. This imagined scene is repeatedly paired with relaxation until you feel no trace of anxiety.

The therapist progresses up the constructed anxiety hierarchy, using the relaxed state to desensitize you to each imagined situation. After several sessions, you practice what you had imagined in actual situations, beginning with relatively easy tasks and gradually moving to more anxiety-filled ones. Conquering your anxiety in an actual situation, not just in your imagination, raises your self-confidence (Foa & Kozak, 1986; Williams, 1987). Eventually, you may even become a confident public speaker.

When the anxiety-arousing situation is too expensive, difficult, or embarrassing to re-create, **virtual reality exposure therapy** offers an efficient middle ground. Wearing a head-mounted display unit that projects a three-dimensional virtual world, you would view a lifelike series of scenes. As your head turns, motion sensors adjust the scene. Experiments led by several research teams have treated people who fear flying, fear heights, fear particular animals, and fear public speaking (Gershon & others, 2002; Rothbaum & others, 2002). People who fear flying, for example, can peer out a virtual window of a simulated plane, feel vibrations, and hear the engine roar as the plane taxis down the runway and takes off. In initial experiments, those experiencing virtual reality exposure therapy have had greater relief from their fears—in real life—than have those in control groups (Hoffman, 2004; Krijn & others, 2004).

Virtual reality exposure therapy

Within the confines of a room, virtual reality technology exposes people to vivid simulations of feared stimuli, such as a plane's takeoff.

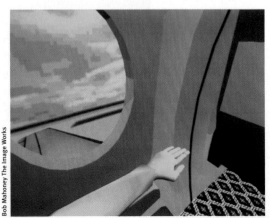

Aversive Conditioning

In systematic desensitization, the goal is substituting a positive (relaxed) response for a negative (fearful) response to a *harmless* stimulus. In **aversive conditioning,** the goal is substituting a negative (aversive) response for a positive response to a *harmful* stimulus (such as alcohol). Thus, aversive conditioning is the reverse of systematic desensitization—it seeks to condition an aversion to something the client *should* avoid.

The procedure is simple: It associates the unwanted behavior with unpleasant feelings. To treat nail biting, one can paint the fingernails with a yucky-tasting nail polish (Baskind, 1997). To treat alcoholism, an aversion therapist offers the client appealing drinks laced with a drug that produces severe nausea. By linking alcohol with violent nausea, the therapist seeks to transform the person's reaction to alcohol from positive to negative (**FIGURE 52.1**).

Does aversive conditioning work? In the short run it may. Arthur Wiens and Carol Menustik (1983) studied 685 patients with alcoholism who completed an aversion therapy program at a Portland, Oregon, hospital. One year later, after returning for several booster treatments of alcohol-sickness pairings, 63 percent were still successfully abstaining. But after three years, only 33 percent had remained abstinent.

The problem is that in therapy (as in research), cognition influences conditioning. People know that outside the therapist's office they can drink without fear of nausea. Their ability to discriminate between the aversive conditioning situation and all other situations can limit the treatment's effectiveness. Thus, aversive conditioning is often used in combination with other treatments.

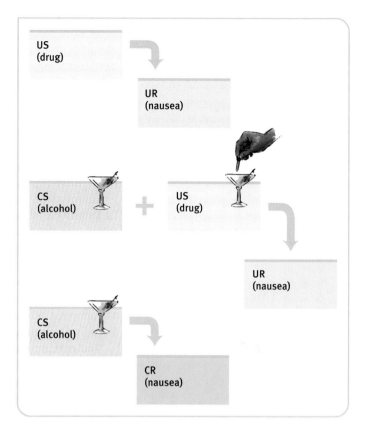

FIGURE 52.1

Aversion therapy for alcoholism
After repeatedly imbibing an alcoholic drink mixed with a drug that produces severe nausea, some people with a history of alcohol abuse develop at least a temporary conditioned aversion to alcohol.

Operant Conditioning

OBJECTIVE 52-8 | State the main premise of therapy based on operant conditioning principles, and describe the views of proponents and critics of behavior modification.

The work of B.F. Skinner and others teaches us a basic principle of operant conditioning: Voluntary behaviors are strongly influenced by their consequences. This simple fact enables behavior therapists to practice *behavior modification*—to reinforce desired behaviors and to withhold reinforcement for undesired behaviors or to punish them. Using operant conditioning to solve specific behavior problems has raised hopes for some cases thought to be hopeless. Children with mental retardation have been taught to care for themselves. Socially withdrawn children with autism have learned to interact. People with schizophrenia have been helped to behave more rationally in their hospital ward. In such cases, therapists use positive reinforcers to shape behavior in a step-by-step manner, rewarding closer and closer approximations of the desired behavior.

In extreme cases, treatment must be intensive. In one study, 19 withdrawn, uncommunicative 3-year-olds with autism participated in a 2-year program in which their parents spent 40 hours each week attempting to shape their behavior (Lovaas, 1987). The combination of positively reinforcing desired behaviors and ignoring or punishing aggressive and self-abusive behaviors worked wonders for some. By first grade, 9 of the 19 children were functioning successfully in school and exhibiting normal intelligence. In a group of 40 comparable children who did not undergo this treatment, only one showed similar improvement.

■ **exposure therapies** behavioral techniques, such as *systematic desensitization,* that treat anxieties by exposing people (in imagination or actuality) to the things they fear and avoid.

■ **systematic desensitization** a type of counterconditioning that associates a pleasant relaxed state with gradually increasing anxiety-triggering stimuli. Commonly used to treat phobias.

■ **virtual reality exposure therapy** An anxiety treatment that progressively exposes people to simulations of their greatest fears, such as airplane flying, spiders, or public speaking.

■ **aversive conditioning** a type of counterconditioning that associates an unpleasant state (such as nausea) with an unwanted behavior (such as drinking alcohol).

■ **token economy** an operant conditioning procedure in which people earn a token of some sort for exhibiting a desired behavior and can later exchange the tokens for various privileges or treats.

■ **cognitive therapy** therapy that teaches people new, more adaptive ways of thinking and acting; based on the assumption that thoughts intervene between events and our emotional reactions.

Rewards used to modify behavior vary. For some people, the reinforcing power of attention or praise is sufficient. Others require concrete rewards, such as food. In institutional settings, therapists may create a **token economy.** When people display appropriate behavior, such as getting out of bed, washing, dressing, eating, talking coherently, cleaning up their rooms, or playing cooperatively, they receive a token or plastic coin as a positive reinforcer. Later, they can exchange their accumulated tokens for various rewards, such as candy, watching television, trips to town, or better living quarters. Token economies have been successfully applied in various settings (homes, classrooms, hospitals, institutions for the delinquent) and among members of various populations (including disturbed children and people with schizophrenia and other mental disabilities).

Critics of behavior modification express two concerns. The first is practical: What happens when the reinforcers stop, as when the person leaves the institution? Could the person become so dependent on extrinsic rewards that the appropriate behaviors quickly disappear? If so, how can therapists make the appropriate behaviors durable? Proponents of behavior modification respond that they may wean patients from the tokens by shifting them toward other rewards, such as social approval, more typical of life outside the institution. They may also train people to behave in ways that are intrinsically rewarding. For example, as a withdrawn person becomes more socially competent, the intrinsic satisfactions of social interaction may help the person maintain the behavior.

The second concern is ethical: Is it right for one human to control another's behavior? Those who set up token economies may deprive people of something they desire and then decide which behaviors they will reinforce. To critics, the whole behavior modification process has an authoritarian taint. So why not reinforce adaptive behavior instead? They argue that treatment with positive rewards is more humane than being institutionalized or punished, and that the right to effective treatment and to an improved life justifies temporary deprivation. Advocates reply that some clients request the therapy. Moreover, control already exists; rewards and punishers are already maintaining destructive behavior patterns.

Cognitive Therapies

OBJECTIVE 52-9 | Contrast cognitive therapy and cognitive-behavior therapy, and give some examples of cognitive therapy for depression.

We have seen how behavior therapists treat specific fears and problem behaviors. But how do they deal with major depression? Or with general anxiety, in which anxiety has no focus and developing a hierarchy of anxiety-triggering situations is difficult? Behavior therapists treating these less clearly defined psychological problems have had help from the same *cognitive revolution* that has profoundly changed other areas of psychology during the last five decades.

Cognitive therapy for eating disorders aided by journaling
Cognitive therapists guide people toward new ways of explaining their good and bad experiences. By recording each day's positive events, and how one enabled them, for example, people may become more mindful of their self-control.

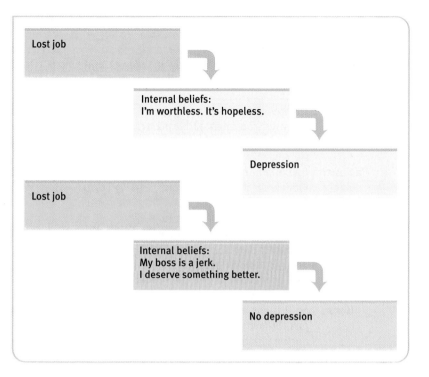

FIGURE 52.2
A cognitive perspective on psychological disorders
The person's emotional reactions are produced not directly by the event but by the person's thoughts in response to the event.

The **cognitive therapies** assume that our thinking colors our feelings (**FIGURE 52.2**), that between the event and our response lies the mind. Self-blaming and over-generalized explanations of bad events are often an integral part of the vicious cycle of depression. The person experiencing depression interprets a suggestion as criticism, disagreement as dislike, praise as flattery, friendliness as pity. Ruminating on such thoughts sustains the bad mood. If depressed thinking patterns can be learned, then surely they can be replaced. Cognitive therapists therefore try in various ways to teach people new, more constructive ways of thinking. If people are miserable, they can be helped to change their minds.

> "Life does not consist mainly, or even largely, of facts and happenings. It consists mainly of the storm of thoughts that are forever blowing through one's mind."
>
> Mark Twain, 1835–1910

Cognitive Therapy for Depression

Cognitive therapist Aaron Beck was originally trained in Freudian techniques. As Beck analyzed the dreams of people with depression, he found recurring negative themes of loss, rejection, and abandonment that extended into their waking thoughts. Such negativity even extends into therapy, as clients recall and rehearse their failings and worst impulses (Kelly, 2000). So with cognitive therapy Beck and his colleagues (1979) instead have sought to reverse clients' catastrophizing beliefs about themselves, their situations, and their futures. With gentle questioning that aims to help people discover their irrationalities, they persuade depressed people to take off the dark glasses through which they view life (Beck & others, 1979, pp. 145–146):

Patient: *I agree with the descriptions of me but I guess I don't agree that the way I think makes me depressed.*

Beck: *How do you understand it?*

Patient: *I get depressed when things go wrong. Like when I fail a test.*

Beck: *How can failing a test make you depressed?*

Patient: *Well, if I fail I'll never get into law school.*

Beck: *So failing the test means a lot to you. But if failing a test could drive people into clinical depression, wouldn't you expect everyone who failed the test to have a depression? . . . Did everyone who failed get depressed enough to require treatment?*

Patient: *No, but it depends on how important the test was to the person.*

Beck: *Right, and who decides the importance?*

Patient: *I do.*

Beck: *And so, what we have to examine is your way of viewing the test (or the way that you think about the test) and how it affects your chances of getting into law school. Do you agree?*

Patient: *Right.*

Beck: *Do you agree that the way you interpret the results of the test will affect you? You might feel depressed, you might have trouble sleeping, not feel like eating, and you might even wonder if you should drop out of the course.*

Patient: *I have been thinking that I wasn't going to make it. Yes, I agree.*

Beck: *Now what did failing mean?*

Patient: *(tearful) That I couldn't get into law school.*

Beck: *And what does that mean to you?*

Patient: *That I'm just not smart enough.*

Beck: *Anything else?*

Patient: *That I can never be happy.*

Beck: *And how do these thoughts make you feel?*

Patient: *Very unhappy.*

Beck: *So it is the meaning of failing a test that makes you very unhappy. In fact, believing that you can never be happy is a powerful factor in producing unhappiness. So, you get yourself into a trap—by definition, failure to get into law school equals "I can never be happy."*

Another variety of cognitive therapy builds on the finding that depressed people do not exhibit the self-serving bias (seeing oneself as better than others) common in nondepressed people. Instead, they often attribute their failures to themselves and attribute their successes to external circumstances. Thus, Adele Rabin and her colleagues (1986) explained to 235 depressed adults the advantages of interpreting events as nondepressed people do. She then trained the participants to reform their habitually negative patterns of thinking and labeling. For example, she had them record each day's positive events and write down how they contributed to each. Compared with people who remained on a waiting list for therapy for depression, those who went through the positive-thinking exercises found their depression dropped dramatically (**FIGURE 52.3**). The more people change their negative thinking styles, the more their mood lifts (Seligman, 1991).

Here is another example: We often think in words. Therefore, getting people to change what they say to themselves is an effective way to change their thinking. Perhaps you can identify with the anxious students who before an exam make matters worse with self-defeating thoughts: "This exam's probably going to be impossible. All these other students seem so relaxed and confident. I wish I were better prepared. Anyhow, I'm so nervous I'll forget everything." To change such negative self-talk, Donald Meichenbaum (1977, 1985) has offered *stress inoculation training,* teaching people to restructure their thinking in stressful situations. Sometimes it may be enough simply to say more positive things to oneself: "Relax. The exam may be hard, but it will be hard for everyone else, too. I studied harder than most people. Besides, I don't need a perfect score to get a good grade." In experiments, depression-prone children and college students exhibit a halved rate of future depression after being trained to dispute their negative thoughts (Seligman, 2002). To a great extent, it *is* the thought that counts.

Knowing that there is two-way traffic between depressed mood and negative thinking, the Penn Optimism Program reached out to 9- to 13-year-old children targeted as at risk for depression. The program puts children through 12 small-group sessions, each lasting two hours, in which they learn to tune into their thoughts when facing tough situations and to imagine alternatives to negative thoughts. The leader might, for example,

FIGURE 52.3

Cognitive therapy for depression
Participants in a program that trained them to think more as nondepressed people do— noticing and taking personal credit for good events and not taking blame for, or overgeneralizing from, bad events—experienced dramatic declines in depression. (From Rabin & others, 1986.)

PEANUTS

present a cartoon depicting a child being called a name and invite the children to brain-storm positive ways to cope. In early experiments, the training halved the proportion of children suffering depression for up to two ensuing years (Gillham & others, 1995).

Cognitive therapists often combine the reversal of self-defeating thinking with efforts to modify behavior. This integrated therapy, called **cognitive-behavior therapy,** aims to alter the way people act (behavior therapy) and to alter the way they think (cognitive therapy). It seeks to make people aware of their irrational negative thinking, to replace it with new ways of thinking, *and* to practice the more positive approach in everyday settings.

In one study, for example, people with obsessive-compulsive behaviors learned to relabel their compulsive thoughts (Schwartz & others, 1996). Feeling the urge to wash their hands again, they would tell themselves, "I'm having a compulsive urge," and attribute it to their brain's abnormal activity, as shown in PET scans. Instead of giving in to the urge, they then engaged for 15 minutes in an enjoyable, alternative behavior, such as practicing an instrument, taking a walk, or gardening. This helped "unstick" the brain by shifting attention and engaging other parts of the brain. For two or three months, the weekly therapy sessions continued, with relabeling and refocusing practice at home. By the study's end, most participants' symptoms had diminished and their PET scans revealed normalized brain activity.

Group and Family Therapies

OBJECTIVE 52-10 | Discuss the rationale and benefits of group therapy, including family therapy.

Except for traditional psychoanalysis, the therapies we have considered may also occur in therapist-led small groups. Group therapy does not provide the same degree of therapist involvement with each client; however, it saves therapists' time and clients' money—and it often is no less effective than individual therapy (Fuhriman & Burlingame, 1994). Therapists frequently suggest group therapy for people experiencing family conflicts or those whose behavior is distressing to others. For up to 90 minutes a week, the therapist guides the interactions of 6 to 10 people as they engage issues and react to one another.

Group sessions also offer a unique benefit: The social context allows people both to discover that others have problems similar to their own and to receive feedback as they try out new ways of behaving. It can be a relief to find that you are not alone—to learn that others, despite their apparent composure, share your problems and your troublesome feelings. It can also be reassuring to hear that you yourself look poised even though you feel anxious and self-conscious.

One special type of group interaction, **family therapy,** assumes that no person is an island, that we live and grow in relation to others, especially our families. We struggle to differentiate ourselves from our families, but we also need to connect with them emotionally. Some of our problem behaviors arise from the tension between these two tendencies, which can create family stress. Clients often come to therapists seeking help in their relationships with family members.

▧ **cognitive-behavior therapy** a popular integrated therapy that combines cognitive therapy (changing self-defeating thinking) with behavior therapy (changing behavior).

▧ **family therapy** therapy that treats the family as a system. Views an individual's unwanted behaviors as influenced by or directed at other family members; attempts to guide family members toward positive relationships and improved communication.

Group therapy
This counselor works with troubled teens in groups, which enables the youths to feel less alone in their troubles and enables the counselor to assist more teens at lower cost.

With an estimated 1.8 million members worldwide, AA is said to be "the largest organization on Earth that nobody wanted to join" (Finlay, 2000).

Unlike most psychotherapy, which focuses on what happens inside the person's own skin, family therapists work with family groups to heal relationships and to mobilize family resources. Their aim is to help family members discover the role they play within their family's social system. A child's rebellion, for example, affects and is affected by other family tensions. Family therapists also attempt—usually with some success, research suggests (Hazelrigg & others, 1987; Shadish & others, 1993)—to open up communication within the family or to help family members discover new ways of preventing or resolving conflicts.

A wide range of people participate in self-help and support groups (Yalom, 1985). One analysis (Davison & others, 2000) of on-line support groups and more than 14,000 self-help groups reports that most support groups focus on stigmatized or hard-to-discuss illnesses. AIDS patients are 250 times more likely than hypertension patients to be in support groups. Those struggling with anorexia and alcoholism often join groups; those with migraines and ulcers do not. People with hearing loss have national organizations with local chapters; people with vision loss more often cope without such.

The grandparent of support groups, Alcoholics Anonymous (AA), reportedly has 87,000 groups worldwide (McKillop & others, 2003). Its famous 12-step strategy, emulated by many other self-help groups, asks members to admit their powerlessness, to seek help from a higher power and from one another, and (the twelfth step) to take the message to others in need of it. In one eight-year, $27 million investigation, people seeking treatment for alcoholism reduced their drinking sharply, although so did those assigned to cognitive-behavior therapy or to a "motivational therapy" (Project Match, 1997). The more AA meetings patients attend, the greater their alcohol abstinence. In one study of 2300 veterans who sought alcoholism treatment, a high level of AA involvement was followed by diminished alcohol problems (McKellar & others, 2003).

In an individualistic age, with more and more people living alone or feeling isolated, the popularity of support groups—for the addicted, the bereaved, the divorced, or simply those seeking fellowship and growth—seems to reflect a longing for community and connectedness. More than 100 million Americans belong to small religious, interest, or self-help groups that meet regularly—and 9 in 10 report that group members "support each other emotionally" (Gallup, 1994).

>> LEARNING OUTCOMES

The Psychological Therapies

OBJECTIVE 52-1 | Define *psychotherapy*, and explain what we mean by an *eclectic approach* to therapy.

Psychotherapy is an emotionally charged, confiding interaction between a trained therapist and someone suffering from psychological difficulties. An *eclectic approach* to psychotherapy uses techniques from various forms of therapy; psychotherapy integration attempts to combine a selection of assorted techniques into a single, coherent system.

OBJECTIVE 52-2 | Define *psychoanalysis*, and discuss the aims of this form of therapy.

Psychoanalysis is Sigmund Freud's therapeutic technique for helping people release previously repressed feelings and gain insight into current conflicts. Clinicians working from the psychoanalytic perspective try to help people gain insight into the unconscious origins of their disorders, work through the accompanying feelings, and take responsibility for their own growth.

OBJECTIVE 52-3 | Describe some of the methods used in psychoanalysis, and list some criticisms of this form of therapy.

Psychoanalysts may ask patients to *free associate* (saying aloud anything that comes to mind) and watch for pauses or diversions that may indicate *resistance* (the defensive blocking from consciousness of anxiety-laden material). Analysts may offer patients their interpretations of these instances of resistance, of dreams, and of other behaviors, such as *transference* (transferring to the therapist the strong feelings harbored against a family member or other significant person). Critics note that traditional psychoanalysis has relied on after-the-fact interpretations and repressed memories, and that it is time-consuming and very costly.

OBJECTIVE 52-4 | Contrast psychodynamic therapy and interpersonal therapy with traditional psychoanalysis.

Psychodynamic therapy has been influenced by traditional psychoanalysis but is briefer and less expensive. A psychodynamic therapist focuses on a patient's current conflicts and defenses by searching for themes common to many past and present important relationships, including (but not limited to) childhood experiences and interactions with the therapist. *Interpersonal therapy* (a brief 12- to 16-session form of psychodynamic therapy) deals primarily with current symptoms (such as depression) rather than the origins of unconscious conflicts.

OBJECTIVE 52-5 | Identify the basic characteristics of the humanistic therapies, and describe the specific goals and techniques of Carl Rogers' client-centered therapy.

Humanistic therapists focus on clients' present and future experiences, on conscious rather than unconscious thoughts, and on taking responsibility for one's feelings and actions. Carl Rogers' *client-centered therapy* proposed that therapists' most important contributions are to function as a psychological mirror through active listening and to provide a growth-fostering environment of unconditional positive regard, characterized by genuineness, acceptance, and empathy.

OBJECTIVE 52-6 | Explain how the basic assumption of behavior therapy differs from those of traditional psychoanalytic and humanistic therapies.

To help people alleviate current conflicts and problems, traditional psychoanalytic therapists attempt to explain the origin of behaviors, and humanistic therapists attempt to promote self-acceptance and self-awareness. Behavior therapists assume the problem behaviors *are* the problem, and they attempt to change them through new learning.

OBJECTIVE 52-7 | Define *counterconditioning*, and describe the techniques used in exposure therapies and aversive conditioning.

Counterconditioning uses classical conditioning techniques to pair new responses with old stimuli that have triggered maladaptive behaviors. *Exposure therapies* (including systematic desensitization and virtual reality exposure therapy) try to substitute a positive response (relaxation) for a negative one (fear). *Aversive conditioning* tries to substitute a negative response (such as nausea) for a positive one (pleasure) to a harmful stimulus (alcohol).

OBJECTIVE 52-8 | State the main premise of therapy based on operant conditioning principles, and describe the views of proponents and critics of behavior modification.

Operant conditioning therapies are based on the principle that voluntary behaviors are strongly influenced by their consequences. *Behavior modification* procedures thus enforce desired behaviors and withhold reinforcement for, or punish, undesired behaviors. In *token economies*, people receive tokens for desired behaviors and can later trade the tokens for privileges or treats. Critics object (1) on the practical grounds that these behaviors may disappear when the tokens are discontinued, and (2) on the ethical grounds that it is not right to control other people's behavior. Proponents counter that (1) social or intrinsic rewards can replace the tokens and continue to be reinforcing, and (2) with or without behavior modification, rewards and punishers already control people's behavior.

OBJECTIVE 52-9 | Contrast cognitive therapy and cognitive-behavior therapy, and give some examples of cognitive therapy for depression.

Cognitive therapy attempts to teach people to think in more adaptive ways, on the assumption that thoughts intervene between an event and our reactions to it. *Cognitive-behavior therapy* attempts to teach people to think in more adaptive ways but also to practice their new ways of thinking. In Aaron Beck's cognitive therapy for depression, therapists try to change self-defeating thinking by training clients to look at themselves in new, more positive ways. In *stress inoculation training,* people with depression learn to dispute their negative thoughts and to restructure their thinking in stressful situations.

OBJECTIVE 52-10 | Discuss the rationale and benefits of group therapy, including family therapy.

Group therapy sessions can help more people and cost less per person than individual therapy would. Clients may benefit from knowing others have similar problems and from getting feedback and reassurance. *Family therapy* views a family as an interactive system and attempts to help members discover the roles they play and to learn to communicate more openly and directly. Millions of people participate in self-help and support groups, such as Alcoholics Anonymous.

TERMS AND CONCEPTS TO REMEMBER

psychotherapy, p. 52-0
eclectic approach, p. 52-0
psychoanalysis, p. 52-0
resistance, p. 52-1
interpretation, p. 52-1
transference, p. 52-1
client-centered therapy, p. 52-3
active listening, p. 52-4
behavior therapy, p. 52-5
counterconditioning, p. 52-5
exposure therapies, p. 52-6

systematic desensitization, p. 52-6
virtual reality exposure therapy, p. 52-6
aversive conditioning, p. 52-7
token economy, p. 52-8
cognitive therapy, p. 52-9
cognitive-behavior therapy, p. 52-11
family therapy, p. 52-11

TEST YOURSELF

1. What is the major distinction between the underlying assumption in psychoanalytic and humanistic therapies and the underlying assumption in behavior therapies?

(Answer in Appendix B.)

ASK YOURSELF

1. Without trying to play therapist, how might you use the helping principles discussed in this module with a friend who is anxious?

>WEB

Multiple-choice *self-tests* and more may be found at www.worthpublishers.com/myers.

53

Evaluating Psychotherapies

OBJECTIVE 53-1 | Define *psychotherapy*.

Advice columnist Ann Landers frequently advised her troubled letter writers to get professional help. One response urged the writer "not to give up. Hang in there until you find [a psychotherapist] who fills the bill. It's worth the effort." On the same day, she advised a second letter writer, "There are many excellent mental health facilities in your city. I urge you to make an appointment at once" (Farina & Fisher, 1982). Many share Ann Landers' confidence in **psychotherapy's** effectiveness.

Before 1950, the primary mental health providers were psychiatrists. Since then, demand has outgrown the psychiatric profession, and now most psychotherapy is done by clinical and counseling psychologists; clinical social workers; pastoral, marital, abuse, and school counselors; and psychiatric nurses. Thus, in addition to 55,000 clinical psychiatrists and 95,000 doctoral-level clinical psychologists in the United States, there are a quarter million other licensed therapists, many with social work training (Glenn, 2003). Much therapy is done through community mental health programs, which provide outpatient therapy, crisis phone lines, and halfway houses for those making the transition from hospitalization to independent living. With such an enormous outlay of time, money, effort, and hope, it is important to ask: Is the faith that Ann Landers and millions of others worldwide place in these therapists justified? And was the *Wall Street Journal* (1999) therefore wrong to suppose that including psychotherapy in health insurance plans would lead to "endless payments for dubious benefits of apparently marginal problems"?

Is Psychotherapy Effective?

The question, though simply put, is not simply answered. For one thing, measuring therapy's effectiveness is not like taking your body's temperature to see if your fever has gone away. If you and I were to undergo psychotherapy, how would we gauge its effectiveness? By how we feel about our progress? How our therapist feels about it? How our friends and family feel about it? How our behavior has changed?

Clients' Perceptions

OBJECTIVE 53-2 | Explain why clients tend to overestimate the effectiveness of psychotherapy.

If clients' testimonials were the only measuring stick, we could strongly affirm the effectiveness of psychotherapy. When 2900 *Consumer Reports* readers (1995; Kotkin & others, 1996; Seligman, 1995) related their experiences with mental health professionals, 89 percent said they were at least "fairly well satisfied." Among those who recalled feeling fair or very poor when beginning therapy, 9 in 10 now were feeling *very good, good,* or at least *so-so.* We have their word for it—and who should know better?

We should not dismiss these testimonials lightly. People enter therapy because they are suffering, and most leave feeling better about themselves. But there are several reasons why client testimonials do not persuade psychotherapy's skeptics:

- ***People often enter therapy in crisis.*** When, with the normal ebb and flow of events, the crisis passes, people may attribute their improvement to the therapy.

■ **psychotherapy** an emotionally charged, confiding interaction between a trained therapist and someone who suffers from psychological difficulties.

- *Clients may need to believe the therapy was worth the effort.* To admit investing time and money in something ineffective is like admitting to having one's car serviced repeatedly by a mechanic who never fixes it. Self-justification is a powerful human motive.
- *Clients generally speak kindly of their therapists.* Even if the clients' problems remain, say the critics, "they work hard to find something positive to say. The therapist had been very understanding, the client had gained a new perspective, he learned to communicate better, his mind was eased, anything at all so as not to have to say treatment was a failure" (Zilbergeld, 1983, p. 117).

Testimonials can be misleading. As research findings continue to document, we are prone to selective and biased recall and to making judgments that confirm our beliefs. Consider a massive experiment with over 500 Massachusetts boys, aged 5 to 13 years, many of whom seemed bound for delinquency. By the toss of a coin, half the boys were assigned to a five-year treatment program. Counselors visited the treated boys twice a month. The boys participated in community programs such as the Boy Scouts. As the need arose, they received academic tutoring, medical attention, and family assistance. Some 30 years after the end of the program, Joan McCord (1978, 1979) located 97 percent of the participants. To assess the treatment's impact, she sent them questionnaires and checked public records from courts, mental hospitals, and other sources.

Assessing the treatment program with client testimonials yielded encouraging results. Many of the men offered glowing reports. Some noted that had it not been for their counselors, "I would probably be in jail," "My life would have gone the other way," or "I think I would have ended up in a life of crime." The court records offered apparent support for these testimonials. Even among the "difficult" boys in the program, *66 percent* had no official juvenile crime record.

But recall psychology's most powerful tool for sorting reality from wishful thinking: the *control group.* For every boy who was counseled, there was a similar boy in a control group who was not. McCord tracked down these untreated people and found that among the predelinquent boys in the control group, *70 percent* had no juvenile record. Moreover, on some measures, such as a record of having committed a second crime, alcoholic tendencies, death rate, and job satisfaction, the untreated men exhibited slightly *fewer* problems. The glowing testimonials of those treated had been unintentionally deceiving.

This shocking finding—that testimonials can badly mislead—was confirmed in the 1990s. Delinquent boys put through "Scared Straight" programs (visiting jails, being taunted by prison inmates) said they were now more likely to be law-abiding. But they weren't. Compared with those not assigned to Scared Straight, boys who were in the program became *more* likely to commit new offenses (Dishion & others, 1999; Petrosino & others, 2000). Testimonials can and do mislead.

Clinicians' Perceptions

OBJECTIVE 53-3 | Give some reasons why clinicians tend to overestimate the effectiveness of psychotherapy, and describe two phenomena that contribute to clients' and clinicians' misperceptions in this area.

If clinicians' perceptions accurately reflected therapeutic effectiveness, we would have even more reason to celebrate. Case studies of successful treatment abound. Furthermore, every therapist treasures compliments from clients as they say good-bye or later express their gratitude. The problem is that clients justify entering psychotherapy by emphasizing their unhappiness, justify leaving therapy by emphasizing their well-being, and stay in touch only if satisfied. Therapists are aware of failures, but they are mostly the failures of *other* therapists—those whose clients, having experienced only temporary relief, are now seeking a new therapist for their recurring problems. Thus, the same person with the same recurring difficulty—the same old anxieties, depression, or marital difficulty—may be a "success" story in several therapists' files.

"REGRESSING" FROM UNUSUAL TO USUAL

Clients' and therapists' perceptions of therapy's effectiveness are vulnerable to inflation from two phenomena. One is the *placebo effect*—the power of *belief* in a treatment. An inert placebo is often used as a control treatment in drug experiments. If you *think* a treatment is going to be effective, it just may be (thanks to the healing power of your positive expectation).

The second phenomenon is **regression toward the mean**—the tendency for unusual events (or emotions) to "regress" (return) toward their average state. Thus, extraordinary happenings (feeling low) tend to be followed by more ordinary ones (a return to our more usual state). Because we returned to that more usual state, anything we tried in the interim may seem to

> "The real purpose of [the] scientific method is to make sure Nature hasn't misled you into thinking you know something that you actually don't."
> Robert Pirsig, *Zen and the Art of Motorcycle Maintenance*, 1974

have been effective. Indeed, when things hit bottom, whatever we try—going to a psychotherapist, starting yoga, doing aerobic exercise—is more likely to be followed by improvement than by further descent.

The point may seem obvious, yet we regularly miss it: We sometimes attribute what may be a normal regression (the expected return to normal) to something we have done. Consider:

- Students who score much lower or higher on an exam than they usually do are likely, when retested, to return toward their average.
- Unusual ESP subjects who defy chance when first tested nearly always lose their "psychic powers" when retested (a phenomenon parapsychologists have called the "decline effect").
- Coaches often yell at their players after an unusually bad first half. They may then feel rewarded for having done so when the team's performance improves (returns to normal) during the second half.

Once you become sensitized to it, you see regression everywhere."
Psychologist Daniel Kahneman (1985)

- Scientists who win a Nobel prize—an extraordinary accomplishment—almost always experience diminished accomplishments thereafter, leading some to believe that winning a Nobel hinders creativity.

In each case, the cause-effect link may be genuine. More likely, however, is that each is an instance of the natural tendency for behavior to regress from the unusual to the more usual. And this defines a task for therapy-efficacy research: discerning whether troubled people's improvement following a particular therapy exceeds what we could expect from the placebo and regression effects, as shown in control groups not receiving the treatment.

■ **regression toward the mean** the tendency for extremes of unusual scores to fall back (regress) toward their average.

Because people enter therapy when they are extremely unhappy, and usually leave when they are less extremely unhappy, most therapists, like most clients, testify to therapy's success—regardless of the treatment (see Thinking Critically About: "Regressing" From Unusual to Usual). Although "treatments" have varied widely, from chains to counseling, every generation views its own approach as enlightened.

Outcome Research

OBJECTIVE 53-4 | Describe the importance of outcome studies in judging the effectiveness of psychotherapies, and discuss some of these findings.

How, then, can we objectively measure the effectiveness of psychotherapy? What types of people and problems are best helped, and by what type of psychotherapy? The questions have both academic and personal relevance. If you or someone you care about feels anxious or depressed, or suffers some psychological disorder, it is crucial for you to understand the likelihood of psychotherapy's being of help.

In hopes of better assessing psychotherapy's effectiveness, psychologists have turned to controlled research studies. Similar research in the 1800s transformed medicine from concocted treatments (bleeding, purging, infusions of plant and metal substances) into a science. The transformation occurred when skeptical physicians began to realize that many patients got better on their own, that most of the fashionable treatments were doing no good, and that sorting fact from superstition required following illnesses closely—with and without a particular treatment. Typhoid fever patients, for example, often improved after being bled, convincing most physicians that the treatment worked. Not until a control group was given mere bed rest—and 70 percent were observed to improve after five weeks of fever—did physicians learn, to their shock, that the blood-letting treatment was worthless (Thomas, 1992).

In psychology, the opening challenge in what became a spirited debate over such research was issued by British psychologist Hans Eysenck (1952). He summarized studies showing that two-thirds of those suffering nonpsychotic disorders improve markedly after undergoing psychotherapy. To this day, no one disputes that optimistic estimate.

So why then are we still debating psychotherapy's effectiveness? Because Eysenck also reported similar improvement among *untreated* persons, such as those who were on waiting lists. With or without psychotherapy, he said, roughly two-thirds improved noticeably. Time was a great healer.

The avalanche of criticism prompted by Eysenck's conclusions revealed shortcomings in his analyses. Also, in 1952 Eysenck could find only 24 studies of psychotherapy outcomes to analyze. Today, there are hundreds. The best of these *randomized clinical trials* randomly assign people on a waiting list to therapy or to no therapy. Afterward, researchers evaluate everyone, using tests and the reports of friends and family or of psychologists who don't know whether therapy was given. The results of many such studies are then digested by a technique called **meta-analysis,** a procedure for statistically combining the conclusions of a large number of different studies as if the results had come from one huge study with thousands of participants. Simply said, meta-analyses give us the bottom-line results of lots of studies.

In the first of more than five dozen meta-analyses of psychotherapy outcome studies, Mary Lee Smith and her colleagues (1980) combined the results of 475 investigations. For psychotherapists, the welcome result was that "the evidence overwhelmingly supports the efficacy of psychotherapy" (p. 183). **FIGURE 53.1** depicts their finding—that the average therapy client ends up better off than 80 percent of the untreated individuals on waiting lists. The claim is more modest than it first appears—by definition, about 50 percent of untreated people also are better off than the average untreated person. Nevertheless, Smith and her collaborators exulted that "psychotherapy benefits people of all ages as reliably as schooling educates them, medicine cures them, or business turns a profit" (p. 183).

■ **meta-analysis** a procedure for statistically combining the results of many different research studies.

"Fortunately, [psycho]analysis is not the only way to resolve inner conflicts. Life itself still remains a very effective therapist."

Karen Horney, *Our Inner Conflicts*, 1945

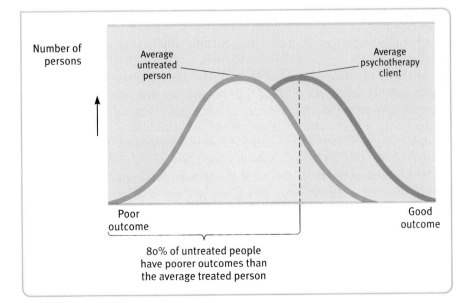

FIGURE **53.1**
Treatment versus no treatment
These two normal distribution curves based on data from 475 studies show the improvement of untreated people and psychotherapy clients. The outcome for the average therapy client surpassed that for 80 percent of the untreated people. (Adapted from Smith & others, 1980.)

Newer research summaries confirm that psychotherapy works (Kopta & others, 1999; Shadish & others, 2000). In one ambitious study, the National Institute of Mental Health compared three depression treatments: cognitive therapy, interpersonal therapy, and a standard drug therapy. Twenty-eight experienced therapists at research sites in Norman, Oklahoma; Washington, DC; and Pittsburgh, Pennsylvania, were trained in one of the three methods and randomly assigned their share of the 239 participants suffering from depression. Clients in all three groups improved more than did those in a control group who received merely an inert medication and supportive attention, encouragement, and advice. Among people who completed a full 16-week treatment program, the depression had lifted for slightly more than half of those in each treatment group—but for only 29 percent of those in the control group (Elkin & others, 1989). This verdict echoes the results of the earlier outcome studies: *Those not undergoing therapy often improve, but those undergoing therapy are more likely to improve.*

Psychotherapy is also cost-effective when compared with the greater costs of medical care for psychologically related complaints. When people seek psychological treatment, their search for medical treatment drops—by 16 percent in one digest of 91 studies (Chiles & others, 1999).

The annual cost of psychological disorders and substance abuse—including crime, accidents, lost work, and treatment—is staggering. Thus, just as an investment in prenatal and well-baby care reduces long-term costs, so will an investment in almost any effective treatment for psychological problems. Anything that boosts employees' psychological well-being will reduce medical costs, improve work efficiency, and diminish absenteeism. Studies by health insurers show that mental health treatment can more than pay for itself with reduced medical costs (American Psychological Association, 1991).

But note that the claim—that psychotherapy, *on average*, is somewhat effective—refers to no one therapy in particular. It is like saying, "Surgery is somewhat effective," or reassuring lung-cancer patients that "on average," medical treatment of health problems is effective. What people want to know is not the average effectiveness of all therapy but the particular effectiveness of a treatment for their specific problems.

The Relative Effectiveness of Different Therapies

OBJECTIVE 53-5 | Summarize the findings on which psychotherapies are most effective for specific disorders.

> "Whatever differences in treatment efficacy exist, they appear to be extremely small, at best."
>
> Bruce Wampold and colleagues (1997)

So what can we tell people considering therapy, and those paying for it, about *which* psychotherapy will be most effective for their problem? Despite claims of superiority by advocates of different types of therapy, the meta-analysis conducted by Mary Lee Smith and her colleagues (1977, 1980) revealed no one type of therapy as generally superior. *Consumer Reports* readers, too, were equally satisfied, no matter what type of therapy they received and whether treated by a psychiatrist, psychologist, or social worker (Seligman, 1995). Moreover—and more astonishing—the group or individual context of the therapy made no discernible difference, nor did the level of training and experience of the therapist. Now, more than two decades after Smith's analysis, newer evidence indicates little if any connection between clinicians' experience, training, supervision, and licensing and their clients' outcomes (Bickman, 1999; Luborsky & others, 2002). Was the dodo bird in *Alice in Wonderland* right: "Everyone has won and all must have prizes"?

A Society of Clinical Psychology task force is answering that question by identifying treatments shown to be beneficial in controlled treatment studies (Chambless &

others, 1997; Norcross, 2002). The task force has pinpointed some elements of effective therapy, such as empathy. And it offers lists of *empirically supported therapies,* including, for example,

- cognitive therapy, interpersonal therapy, and behavior therapy for depression.
- cognitive therapy, exposure therapy, and stress inoculation training for anxiety.
- cognitive-behavior therapy for bulimia.
- behavior modification for bed-wetting.

Behavioral conditioning therapies have also achieved especially favorable results with specific behavior problems such as phobias, compulsions, marital problems, and sexual disorders (Bowers & Clum, 1988; Hunsley & DiGiulio, 2002; Shadish & Baldwin, 2005). And new studies confirm cognitive therapy's effectiveness in coping with depression and reducing suicide risk (Brown & others, 2005; DeRubeis & others, 2005; Hollon & others, 2005).

Moreover, therapy is most effective when the problem is clear-cut (Singer, 1981; Westen & Morrison, 2001). Those who experience phobias or panic, who are unassertive, or who are frustrated by sexual performance problems can hope for improvement. Those who suffer less-focused problems, such as depression and anxiety, usually benefit in the short term but often relapse later. Those who have chronic schizophrenia or who wish to change their whole personality are unlikely to benefit from psychotherapy alone (Zilbergeld, 1983). The more specific the problem, the greater the hope.

Meanwhile, controversy continues—some call it today's civil war in psychology—over the extent to which science should guide both clinical practice and the willingness of health care providers and insurers to pay for psychotherapy. On the one side are science-oriented psychologists working to extend the list of evidence-based practice, with well-defined and validated therapies for various disorders. On the other side are those who view therapy as more art than science, not something amenable to describing in a manual or testing in an experiment. People are too complex and therapy too intuitive for a cookie-cutter approach, say the nonscientist therapists. But by basing practice on evidence and making mental health professionals accountable for effectiveness, say the science-oriented clinicians, therapy stands to gain credibility. Moreover, the public will be protected from pseudotherapies, and therapists will be protected from accusations of sounding like snake-oil salesmen—"Trust me, I know it works, I've seen it work."

Different sores have different salves."

English proverb

Evaluating Alternative Therapies

OBJECTIVE 53-6 | Evaluate the effectiveness of eye movement desensitization and reprocessing (EMDR) and light exposure therapies.

The tendency of abnormal states of mind to "regress" to normal, combined with the placebo effect, creates fertile soil for pseudotherapies. Bolstered by anecdotes, heralded by the media, praised on the Internet, alternative therapies can spread like wildfire. Princess Diana typified the modern fascination with alternative healers by seeking out spiritualists, a hypnotherapist, an "anger-release" therapist, reflexologists, aromatherapists, colonic irrigationists, and a "mind-body" therapist (Smith, 1999). She had much company. In one national survey, 57 percent of those with a history of anxiety attacks and 54 percent of those with a history of depression had used alternative treatments such as herbal medicine, massage, and spiritual healing (Kessler & others, 2001).

What can we say of such alternative therapies? Testimonials aside—every therapy, whether effective or not, will *seem* effective to some—what does the evidence say? Which are empirically validated?

TABLE **53.1**

COMPARISON OF SCIENTIFIC PSYCHOLOGY CITATIONS AND UNFILTERED WEB SITES

Topic	Psychology Journal Citations*	Web Sites**	Ratio
Systematic desensitization	2,301	56,800	1 to 25
Therapeutic touch	94	383,000	1 to 4,074
St. John's wort (herbal remedy)	200	2,590,000	1 to 12,950
Enneagram (personality typing)	32	775,000	1 to 24,218

*Using PsycINFO, January 2006
**Using Google, January 2006

About most, there is no evidence, because their proponents and devotees feel no need for controlled research. For them, personal experience is evidence enough. So which therapies do get systematically evaluated? To gauge scientific versus popular interest in various treatments and assessment techniques, clinical researcher Scott Lilienfeld (1998) suggests comparing the number of times each is mentioned in electronic searches of psychology's scientific literature and on unfiltered Web sources. As TABLE **53.1** shows, some topics exist almost exclusively on the Web.

Let's now evaluate two alternative therapies—eye movement desensitization and reprocessing (EMDR) and light exposure therapy. As we do, remember that sifting sense from nonsense requires the scientific attitude: being skeptical but not cynical, open to surprises but not gullible.

Eye Movement Desensitization and Reprocessing

Walking in a park one day, Francine Shapiro (1989) observed that anxious thoughts vanished as her eyes spontaneously darted about. From this experience she developed a novel anxiety treatment: *eye movement desensitization and reprocessing (EMDR).* While people imagined traumatic scenes, Shapiro triggered eye movements by waving her finger in front of their eyes, supposedly enabling them to unlock and reprocess previously frozen trauma memories. She tried this on 22 people haunted by old traumatic memories, and all reported marked reductions in their distress after just one therapeutic session. This extraordinary result evoked an enormous response from mental health professionals, 40,000 of whom from 52 countries have undergone training (EMDR, 2002). Not since the similarly charismatic Franz Anton Mesmer introduced *animal magnetism* (hypnosis) more than two centuries ago (also after feeling inspired by an outdoor experience) has a new therapy attracted so many devotees so quickly.

Does it work? For 84 to 100 percent of single-trauma victims participating in four recent studies, the answer is yes, reports Shapiro (1999, 2002). (When EMDR did not fare well in other trials, Shapiro argued that the therapists were not properly trained.) Moreover, the treatment need take no more than three 90-minute sessions. The Society of Clinical Psychology task force on empirically validated treatments acknowledges that the treatment is "probably efficacious" for the treatment of nonmilitary post-traumatic stress disorder (Chambless & others, 1997). Encouraged by their seeming successes, EMDR therapists are now applying the technique to other anxiety disorders, such as panic disorder, and, with Shapiro's (1995, 2002) encouragement, to a wide range of complaints, including pain, grief, paranoid schizophrenia, rage, and guilt.

EMDR is a therapy that thousands adore, and thousands more dismiss as a sham—"an excellent vehicle for illustrating the differences between scientific and pseudoscientific therapy techniques," suggest James Herbert and seven others (2000). Why,

"Meta-analyses [indicate that EMDR is] just as effective with fixed eyes. If that conclusion is right, what's useful in the therapy (chiefly behavioral desensitization) is not new, and what's new is superfluous."
Harvard Mental Health Letter, 2002

wondered skeptics, should rapidly moving one's eyes while recalling traumas be therapeutic? Indeed, eye movements, it seems, are not the therapeutic ingredient. When researchers tested the therapy without the eye movements—with finger tapping, for example, or with eyes fixed straight ahead while the therapist's finger wagged—the therapeutic results were the same (Devilly, 2003). What is therapeutic, the skeptics suspect, is the combination of exposure therapy—repeatedly reliving traumatic memories in a safe and reassuring context—and a robust placebo effect. Had Mesmer's pseudotherapy been compared with no treatment at all, notes Richard McNally (1999), it, too (thanks to the healing power of positive belief), could have been found "probably efficacious."

Light Exposure Therapy

Have you ever found yourself oversleeping, gaining weight, and feeling lethargic during the dark mornings and overcast days of winter? For some people, especially women and those living far from the equator, the wintertime blahs constitute a form of depression known as seasonal affective disorder, for which the appropriate acronym is SAD. To counteract these dark spirits, National Institute of Mental Health researchers in the early 1980s had a bright idea: Give SAD people a timed daily dose of intense light. When clinical experience indicated that light exposure could also relieve symptoms associated with wintertime depression, manufacturers produced light boxes that can now be rented or purchased from health supply and lighting stores.

   Is this another placebo effect, attributable to people's expectations? Recent studies shed light on this therapy. One exposed some people with SAD to 90 minutes of bright light and others to a sham placebo treatment—a hissing "negative ion generator" about which the staff expressed similar enthusiasm (but which, unknown to the participants, was not turned on). After four weeks of exposure, 61 percent of those exposed to morning light had greatly improved, as had 50 percent of those exposed to evening light and 32 percent of those exposed to the placebo treatment (Eastman & others, 1998). Two other studies found that 30 minutes of light exposure produced relief for more than half the people receiving morning light therapy and for one-third receiving evening light therapy (Terman & Terman, 1998, 2001). From 20 carefully controlled trials we have a verdict (Golden & others, 2005): For many people, morning bright light does indeed dim SAD symptoms.

Light therapy
To counteract winter depression, some people spend time each morning in front of a box emitting intense light that mimics natural outdoor light.

Courtesy of Christine Brune

Commonalities Among Psychotherapies

OBJECTIVE 53-7 | Describe the three benefits attributed to all psychotherapies.

Good therapists may have differing perspectives, yet share much in common, including compassion, sensitivity, and empathy. Jerome Frank (1982), Marvin Goldfried (Goldfried & Padawer, 1982), Hans Strupp (1986), and Bruce Wampold (2001) studied the common ingredients of various therapies and suggest they all offer at least three benefits: hope for demoralized people; a new perspective on oneself and the world; and an empathic, trusting, caring relationship. These nonspecific factors aren't all that therapy offers, but they are important (Barker & others, 1988; Jones & others, 1988; Roberts & others, 1993). They are part of what the growing numbers of self-help and support groups offer their members. And they have been part of what traditional healers offer (Jackson, 1992). Healers—special people to whom others disclose their suffering—have for centuries listened in order to understand and to empathize, reassure, advise, console, interpret, or explain. (For those thinking about seeking therapy, Close-Up: A Consumer's Guide to Psychotherapists on the next page offers some tips on when to seek help and how to start your search for a therapist.)

CLOSE-UP:

A CONSUMER'S GUIDE TO PSYCHOTHERAPISTS

Life for everyone is marked by a mix of serenity and stress, blessing and bereavement, good moods and bad. So, when should a person seek the help of a mental health professional? When troubling thoughts and emotions interfere with your normal living, you might consider talking to a professional. The American Psychological Association offers these common trouble signals:

- Feelings of hopelessness
- Deep and lasting depression
- Self-destructive behavior, such as alcohol and drug abuse
- Disruptive fears
- Sudden mood shifts
- Thoughts of suicide
- Compulsive rituals, such as hand washing
- Sexual difficulties

In looking for a therapist, you may want to have a preliminary consultation with two or three. You can describe your problem and learn each therapist's treatment approach. You can ask questions about the therapist's values, credentials (**TABLE 53.2**), and fees. And, knowing the importance of the emotional bond between therapist and client, you can assess your own feelings about each of them.

TABLE 53.2

THERAPISTS AND THEIR TRAINING

Type	Description
Counselors	Marriage and family counselors specialize in problems arising from family relations. Pastoral counselors provide counseling to countless people. Abuse counselors work with substance abusers and with spouse and child abusers and their victims.
Clinical or psychiatric social workers	A two-year master of social work graduate program plus postgraduate supervision prepares some social workers to offer psychotherapy, mostly to people with everyday personal and family problems. About half have earned the National Association of Social Workers' designation of clinical social worker.
Clinical psychologists	Most are psychologists with a Ph.D. or Psy.D. and expertise in research, assessment, and therapy, supplemented by a supervised internship and, often, post-doctoral training. About half work in agencies and institutions, half in private practice.
Psychiatrists	Psychiatrists are physicians who specialize in the treatment of psychological disorders. Not all psychiatrists have had extensive training in psychotherapy, but as M.D.s they can prescribe medications. Thus, they tend to see those with the most serious problems. Many have their own private practice.

Hope for Demoralized People

People who seek therapy typically feel anxious, depressed, devoid of self-esteem, and incapable of turning things around. What any therapy offers is the expectation that, with commitment from the therapy seeker, things can and will get better. Apart from the particular therapeutic technique, this belief may itself function as a placebo, promoting improved morale, new feelings of self-efficacy, and diminished symptoms (Prioleau & others, 1983). Similar effects have been found in psychotherapy experiments in which the placebo treatment was listening to inspirational tapes or taking a fake pill.

The finding from meta-analyses that improvement is greater for placebo-treated people than for untreated people (although not as great as for those receiving actual psychotherapy) suggests that one reason therapies help is that they offer hope. Said another way, therapy outcomes vary with the attitude of the person seeking help—the person's motivation, confidence, and commitment. Each therapy, in its individual way, may harness the person's own healing powers. And that, says psychiatrist Jerome Frank, helps us understand why all sorts of treatments—including some folk healing rites that are powerless apart from the participants' belief—may in their own time and place produce cures.

A New Perspective

Every therapy offers people a plausible explanation of their symptoms and an alternative way of looking at themselves or responding to their world. Therapy can offer new experiences as well, ones that help people change their behaviors and their views of themselves. Armed with a believable fresh perspective, they may approach life with a new attitude.

© 1994 by Sidney Harris—"Stress Test," Rutgers University Press.

"I utilize the best from Freud, the best from Jung, and the best from my Uncle Marty, a very smart fellow."

An Empathic, Trusting, Caring Relationship

To say that all therapies are about equally effective is not to say all *therapists* are equally effective. Regardless of their therapeutic technique, effective therapists are empathic people who seek to understand another's experience; who communicate their care and concern to the client; and who earn the client's trust and respect through respectful listening, reassurance, and advice. In a National Institute of Mental Health depression-treatment study, the most effective therapists were those who were perceived as most empathic and caring and who established the closest therapeutic bonds with their clients (Blatt & others, 1996). In another study, Marvin Goldfried and his associates (1998) analyzed taped therapy sessions from 36 recognized master therapists. Some were cognitive-behavior therapists, others were psychodynamic-interpersonal therapists. Regardless, the striking finding was how *similar* the therapists were during the parts of their sessions they considered most significant. At key moments, the empathic therapists of both persuasions would help clients evaluate themselves, link one aspect of their life with another, and gain insight into their interactions with others. Indeed, some believe warmth and empathy are hallmarks of healers everywhere, whether psychiatrists, witch doctors, or shamans (Torrey, 1986). The emotional bond between therapist and client—the *therapeutic alliance*—is a key aspect of effective therapy (Klein & others, 2003; Wampold, 2001).

A caring relationship
Effective therapists form a bond of trust with their patients.

That all therapies offer *hope* through a *fresh perspective* offered by a caring person is supported by a meta-analysis of 39 studies. Each study compared treatment offered by professional therapists with treatment offered by laypeople: friendly professors, people who had had a few hours' training in empathic listening skills, and college students supervised by a professional clinician. The result? The *paraprofessionals,* as these and other briefly trained people are called, typically proved as effective as the professionals (Christensen & Jacobson, 1994). Although most of the problems they treated were mild, the trained paraprofessionals were—believe it or not—as effective as professionals even when dealing with more disturbed adults, such as those diagnosed with serious depression.

To recap, people who seek help usually improve. So do many of those who do not undergo psychotherapy, and that is a tribute to our human resourcefulness and our capacity to care for one another. Nevertheless, though the therapist's orientation and experience appear not to matter much, people who receive some psychotherapy usually improve more than those who do not. People with clear-cut, specific problems tend to improve the most.

Part of what all therapies offer is hope, a fresh way of looking at life, and an empathic, caring relationship. That may explain why the empathy and friendly counsel of paraprofessionals are often as helpful as professional psychotherapy. And that may also explain why people who feel supported by close relationships—who enjoy the fellowship and friendship of caring people—are less likely to need or seek therapy (Frank, 1982; O'Connor & Brown, 1984).

Culture and Values in Psychotherapy

OBJECTIVE 53-8 | Discuss the role of values and cultural differences in the therapeutic process.

All therapies offer hope, and nearly all therapists attempt to enhance their clients' sensitivity, openness, personal responsibility, and sense of purpose (Jensen & Bergin, 1988). But on certain matters of moral and cultural diversity, therapists may differ from one another and from their clients (Kelly, 1990). In Canada and the United States, for example, about 1 person in 25 is a self-proclaimed atheist or agnostic, as are (depending on the survey) one-fifth to one-half of psychiatrists and clinical psychologists (Gallup, 1993; Lukoff & others, 1992). In Britain, two-thirds of psychiatrists say they are atheists

CLOSE-UP:

PREVENTING PSYCHOLOGICAL DISORDERS BY TREATING THE SOCIAL CONTEXTS THAT BREED THEM

OBJECTIVE 53-9 | Explain the rationale of preventive mental health programs.

Psychotherapies and biomedical therapies tend to locate the cause of psychological disorders within the person with the disorder. We infer that people who act cruelly must be cruel and that people who act "crazy" must be "sick." We attach labels to such people, thereby distinguishing them from "normal" folks. It follows, then, that we try to treat "abnormal" people by giving them insight into their problems, by changing their thinking, and/or by helping them gain control with drugs.

There is an alternative viewpoint: We could interpret many psychological disorders as understandable responses to a disturbing and stressful society. According to this view, it is not just the person who needs treatment, but also the person's social context. Better to prevent a problem by reforming a sick situation and by developing people's coping competencies than to wait for a problem to arise and then treat it.

A story about the rescue of a drowning person from a rushing river illustrates this viewpoint: Having successfully administered first aid to the first victim, the rescuer spots another struggling person and pulls her out, too. After a half-dozen repetitions, the rescuer suddenly turns and starts running away while the river sweeps yet another floundering person into view. "Aren't you going to rescue that fellow?" asks a bystander. "Heck no," the rescuer replies. "I'm going upstream to find out what's pushing all these people in."

Preventive mental health is upstream work. It seeks to prevent psychological casualties by identifying and alleviating the conditions that cause them. George Albee (1986) believes there is abundant evidence that poverty, meaningless work, constant criticism, unemployment, racism, and sexism undermine people's sense of competence, personal control, and self-esteem. Such stresses increase their risk of depression, alcoholism, and suicide.

Albee contends that we who care about preventing psychological casualties should therefore support programs

> It is better to prevent than to cure."
> Peruvian folk wisdom

that alleviate poverty, discrimination, and other demoralizing situations. We eliminated smallpox not by treating the afflicted but by inoculating the unafflicted. We conquered yellow fever by controlling mosquitoes. Prevention of psychological problems means empowering those who have learned an attitude of helplessness, changing environments that breed loneliness, renewing the disintegrating family, and bolstering parents' and teachers' skills at nurturing children's achievements and resulting self-esteem. Indeed, "Everything aimed at improving the human condition, at making life more fulfilling and meaningful, may be considered part of primary prevention of mental or emotional disturbance" (Kessler & Albee, 1975, p. 557). That includes such programs as the cognitive training that promotes positive thinking in children at risk for depression.

There is, however, more to the story of psychological disorders than toxic environments and pessimism. Anxiety disorders, major depression, bipolar disorder, and schizophrenia are in part biological events. Yet Albee reminds us again of one of this book's themes: *A human being is an integrated*

Changing in China

These men are listening sympathetically to fellow patients, many of whom are HIV positive, at a support group meeting at a drug rehabilitation center in southwest China.

(Neeleman & Persaud, 1995). That raises an intriguing issue: What values prevail in psychotherapy? What values *should* prevail? Should it matter that highly religious people prefer religiously similar therapists (Worthington & others, 1996)?

Albert Ellis, a well-known therapist, and Allen Bergin, co-editor of the *Handbook of Psychotherapy and Behavior Change,* illustrate how sharply values can differ. Ellis (1980) assumes that "no one and nothing is supreme," that "self-gratification" should be encouraged, and that "unequivocal love, commitment, service, and . . . fidelity to any interpersonal commitment, especially marriage, leads to harmful consequences." Bergin (1980) assumes the opposite—that "because God is supreme, humility and the acceptance of divine authority are virtues," that "self-control and committed love and self-sacrifice are to be encouraged," and that "infidelity to any interpersonal commitment, especially marriage, leads to harmful consequences." Bergin and Ellis disagree more radically than most therapists on what values are healthiest. In so doing, however, they illustrate what they agree on: that psychotherapists' personal beliefs and values influence their practice. Knowing that clients tend to adopt

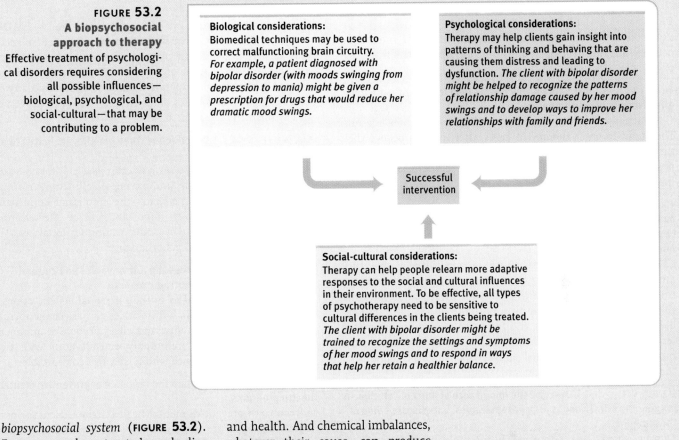

FIGURE **53.2**
A biopsychosocial approach to therapy
Effective treatment of psychological disorders requires considering all possible influences—biological, psychological, and social-cultural—that may be contributing to a problem.

Biological considerations:
Biomedical techniques may be used to correct malfunctioning brain circuitry. *For example, a patient diagnosed with bipolar disorder (with moods swinging from depression to mania) might be given a prescription for drugs that would reduce her dramatic mood swings.*

Psychological considerations:
Therapy may help clients gain insight into patterns of thinking and behaving that are causing them distress and leading to dysfunction. *The client with bipolar disorder might be helped to recognize the patterns of relationship damage caused by her mood swings and to develop ways to improve her relationships with family and friends.*

Successful intervention

Social-cultural considerations:
Therapy can help people relearn more adaptive responses to the social and cultural influences in their environment. To be effective, all types of psychotherapy need to be sensitive to cultural differences in the clients being treated. *The client with bipolar disorder might be trained to recognize the settings and symptoms of her mood swings and to respond in ways that help her retain a healthier balance.*

biopsychosocial system (**FIGURE 53.2**). For years we have trusted our bodies to physicians and our minds to psychiatrists and psychologists. That neat separation no longer seems valid. Stress affects body chemistry and health. And chemical imbalances, whatever their cause, can produce schizophrenia and depression. *"Mens sana in corpore sano,"* says an ancient Latin adage: "A healthy mind in a healthy body."

Mental disorders arise from physical ones, and likewise physical disorders arise from mental ones."

The Mahabharata, c. A.D. 200

their therapists' values (Worthington & others, 1996), Bergin and Ellis also agree that therapists should divulge their values more openly.

Value differences also can become significant when a therapist from one culture meets a client from another. In North America, Europe, and Australia, for example, most therapists reflect their culture's individualism, which often gives priority to personal desires and identity. Clients who are immigrants from Asian countries, which expect people to be more mindful of others' expectations, may have trouble relating to therapies that require them to think only of their own well-being. Such differences help explain the reluctance of some minority populations to use mental health services (Sue, 1990). In one experiment, Asian-American clients matched with counselors who shared their cultural values (rather than mismatched with those who didn't) perceived more counselor empathy and felt more alliance with the counselor (Kim & others, 2005). Recognizing that therapists and clients may differ in their values, communication styles, and language, many therapy training programs now provide training in cultural sensitivity and recruit members of underrepresented cultural groups. (For a social-cultural perspective on disorders and therapy, see the Close-Up: Preventing Psychological Disorders by Treating the Social Contexts That Breed Them.)

>> LEARNING OUTCOMES

Evaluating Psychotherapies

OBJECTIVE 53-1 | Define *psychotherapy.*

Psychotherapy is an emotionally charged, confiding interaction between a trained therapist and someone who suffers from psychological difficulties.

OBJECTIVE 53-2 | **Explain why clients tend to overestimate the effectiveness of psychotherapy.**

Clients judge psychotherapy to be effective for three reasons: They tend to enter therapy in crisis, they need to believe their time and expense were justified, and they try to find something positive to say when asked to evaluate their therapist. Research has not upheld clients' views of therapy's effectiveness.

OBJECTIVE 53-3 | **Give some reasons why clinicians tend to overestimate the effectiveness of psychotherapy, and describe two phenomena that contribute to clients' and clinicians' misperceptions in this area.**

Clients enter therapy when they are unhappy, leave it when they are less unhappy, and stay in touch only if satisfied with the treatment they received. So clinicians are mostly aware of other therapists' failures, not their own. Both the *placebo effect* (the belief a treatment will work) and *regression toward the mean* (the tendency for extreme or unusual scores to fall back toward the mean) contribute to clients' and clinicians' misperceptions of the effectiveness of psychotherapy.

OBJECTIVE 53-4 | **Describe the importance of outcome studies in judging the effectiveness of psychotherapies, and discuss some of these findings.**

Outcome studies are randomized clinical trials in which people on a waiting list receive therapy or no therapy. Statistical digests (*meta-analyses*) of hundreds of these studies reveal that people who remain untreated often improve, but those who receive psychotherapy are more likely to improve and also to spend less time and money seeking other medical treatment later.

OBJECTIVE 53-5 | **Summarize the findings on which psychotherapies are most effective for specific disorders.**

Meta-analyses indicate that no one type of therapy is most effective overall, nor is there any connection between effectiveness and a therapist's training, experience, supervision, or licensing. Some therapies are particularly well-suited to specific disorders, such as cognitive, interpersonal, and behavior therapies for depression; cognitive, exposure, and stress-inoculation therapies for anxiety; cognitive-behavior therapy for bulimia; behavior modification for bed-wetting; and behavior conditioning therapies for phobias, compulsions, and sexual disorders. The more specific the problem, the greater the chances for effective treatment.

OBJECTIVE 53-6 | **Evaluate the effectiveness of eye movement desensitization and reprocessing (EMDR) and light exposure therapies.**

In *EMDR therapy,* a therapist attempts to unlock and reprocess previously frozen traumatic memories by waving a finger in front of the eyes of a person imagining traumatic scenes. EMDR has not held up under scientific testing, and its modest successes may be attributable to the placebo effect. In people with *seasonal affective disorder*, a form of depression linked to periods of decreased sunlight, *light exposure therapy* (exposure to daily timed doses of light that mimics outdoor light) has been proven effective by scientific research.

OBJECTIVE 53-7 | **Describe the three benefits attributed to all psychotherapies.**

All types of psychotherapy seem to offer *new hope* for demoralized people, a *fresh perspective,* and an *empathic, trusting, caring relationship.* The *therapeutic alliance*—the emotional bond between therapist and client—is an important part of effective therapy and may help explain why some paraprofessionals can be as helpful as professional psychotherapists.

OBJECTIVE 53-8 | **Discuss the role of values and cultural differences in the therapeutic process.**

Psychotherapists may differ in their personal beliefs, values, and cultural backgrounds. Such differences can affect the formation of a bond between therapist and client. People searching for a therapist should have preliminary consultations with two or three to find someone with whom they feel comfortable.

OBJECTIVE 53-9 | **Explain the rationale of preventive mental health programs.**

Advocates of preventive mental health argue that many psychological disorders are responses to social conditions. To prevent such disorders, we should change oppressive, esteem-destroying environments into more benevolent, nurturing environments that foster individual growth and self-confidence.

TERMS AND CONCEPTS TO REMEMBER

psychotherapy, p. 53-0
regression toward the mean, p. 53-2
meta-analysis, p. 53-3

TEST YOURSELF

1. How does the placebo effect bias clients' appraisals of the effectiveness of psychotherapies?

2. What are the influences to keep in mind for successful therapeutic intervention?

(Answers in Appendix B.)

ASK YOURSELF

1. Can you think of a time when your positive expectations for improvement may have been self-fulfilling?

2. Can you think of a specific way that improving the environment in your own community might prevent some psychological disorders among its residents?

>WEB

Multiple-choice *self-tests* and more may be found at www.worthpublishers.com/myers.

54

M O D U L E

The Biomedical Therapies

OBJECTIVE 54-1 | Discuss the goals of biomedical therapy, and explain how double-blind studies help researchers evaluate a drug's effectiveness.

The therapy often used to treat serious disorders is **biomedical therapy**—physically changing the brain's functioning by altering its chemistry with drugs, overloading its circuits with electroconvulsive shock, using magnetic impulses to stimulate or dampen its activity, or altering its circuits through psychosurgery.

Drug Therapies

By far the most widely used biomedical treatments today are the drug therapies. Since the 1950s, discoveries in **psychopharmacology** (the study of drug effects on mind and behavior) have revolutionized the treatment of people with severe disorders, liberating hundreds of thousands from hospital confinement. Thanks to drug therapy—and to efforts to minimize involuntary hospitalization and to support people with community mental health programs—the resident population of U.S. state and county mental hospitals is a fraction of what it was a half-century ago (**FIGURE 54.1**). For some unable to care for themselves, however, release from hospitals has meant homelessness, not liberation.

Almost any new treatment, including drug therapy, is greeted by an initial wave of enthusiasm as many people apparently improve. But that enthusiasm often diminishes after researchers subtract the rates of (1) normal recovery among untreated persons and (2) recovery due to the placebo effect, which arises from the positive expectations of patients and mental health workers alike. So, to evaluate the effectiveness of any new drug, researchers use the *double-blind technique*. Half the patients receive the drug, the other half a similar-appearing placebo (an inert substance, such as a suger pill). Neither the staff nor the patients know who gets which. The good news: In double-blind studies, several types of drugs have proven useful in treating psychological disorders.

> " The mentally ill were out of the hospital, but in many cases they were simply out on the streets, less agitated but lost, still disabled but now uncared for."
>
> Lewis Thomas, *Late Night Thoughts on Listening to Mahler's Ninth Symphony*, 1983

■ **biomedical therapy** prescribed medications or medical procedures that act directly on the patient's nervous system.

■ **psychopharmacology** the study of the effects of drugs on mind and behavior.

FIGURE 54.1

The emptying of U.S. mental hospitals

After the widespread introduction of antipsychotic drugs, starting in about 1955, the number of residents in state and county mental hospitals declined sharply. But in the rush to deinstitutionalize the mentally ill, many people who were ill-equipped to care for themselves were left homeless on city streets. (Data from the National Institute of Mental Health and Bureau of the Census, 2004.)

Les Snider/The Image Works

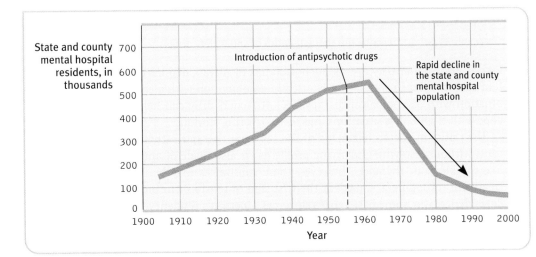

■ **tardive dyskinesia** involuntary movements of the facial muscles, tongue, and limbs; a possible neurotoxic side effect of long-term use of antipsychotic drugs that target D2 dopamine receptors.

Perhaps you can guess an occasional side effect of L-dopa, a drug that *raises* dopamine levels for Parkinson's patients: hallucinations.

Antipsychotic Drugs

OBJECTIVE 54-2 | Describe the characteristics of antipsychotic drugs, and discuss their use in treating schizophrenia.

The revolution in drug therapy for psychological disorders began with the accidental discovery that certain drugs, used for other medical purposes, calmed psychotic patients. These *antipsychotic* drugs, such as chlorpromazine (sold as Thorazine), dampened responsiveness to irrelevant stimuli. Thus they provided the most help to schizophrenia patients experiencing positive symptoms, such as auditory hallucinations and paranoia (Lehman & others, 1998; Lenzenweger & others, 1989). Patients exhibiting negative symptoms, such as apathy and withdrawal, often do not respond well to these antipsychotic drugs. A newer drug, clozapine (marketed since 1989 as Clozaril), does sometimes enable "awakenings" in such people. It also sometimes helps those who have positive symptoms but have not responded to other drugs. Those who take clozapine must have regular blood tests because in 1 percent of cases, it has a toxic effect on white blood cells.

The molecules of antipsychotic drugs are similar enough to molecules of the neurotransmitter dopamine to occupy its receptor sites and block its activity (Pickar & others, 1984; Taubes, 1994). (Clozapine blocks serotonin activity as well.) The finding that most antipsychotic drugs block dopamine receptors reinforces the idea that an overactive dopamine system contributes to schizophrenia.

Antipsychotics are powerful drugs. The first-generation dopamine-blocking drugs (such as Thorazine), which target D2 dopamine receptors, can produce sluggishness, tremors, and twitches similar to those of Parkinson's disease, which is marked by too little dopamine (Kaplan & Saddock, 1989). Long-term use of these medications can also produce **tardive dyskinesia,** a neurotoxic effect, involving involuntary movements of the facial muscles (such as grimacing), tongue, and limbs. In contrast, *new-generation antipsychotic drugs* (such as clozapine, Risperdal, and Zyprexa), which target D1 dopamine receptors, have fewer such side effects. However, these newer medications appear hardly more effective and seem to increase the risk of obesity and diabetes (Leberman & others, 2005). Another complication with both generations of these medications is that one person's effective dose may be another person's overdose or underdose. Only by carefully monitoring the dosage and its effects can psychiatrist and patient tread the fine line between symptom relief and extremely unpleasant side effects. But with the appropriate dosage, combined with life-skills programs and family support, hundreds of thousands of people with schizophrenia who had been consigned to the back wards of mental hospitals have returned to work and to near-normal lives, and relapse rates have been reduced (Leucht & others, 2003).

Antianxiety Drugs

OBJECTIVE 54-3 | Describe the characteristics of antianxiety drugs.

Like alcohol, *antianxiety* agents, such as Xanax or Ativan, depress central nervous system activity (and so should not be used in combination with alcohol). Used in combination with psychological therapy, an antianxiety drug can help a person learn to cope with frightening situations and fear-triggering stimuli.

The criticism sometimes made of the behavior therapies—that they reduce symptoms without resolving underlying problems—is also made of antianxiety drugs. Unlike the behavior therapies, however, these substances may be used as an ongoing treatment. "Popping a Xanax" at the first sign of tension can produce psychological dependence; the immediate relief reinforces a person's tendency to take drugs when anxious. Antianxiety drugs can also cause physiological dependence. When heavy users stop taking them, they may experience withdrawal symptoms, such as increased anxiety and insomnia.

Over the dozen years at the end of the twentieth century, the rate of outpatient treatment for anxiety disorders nearly doubled. The proportion of patients receiving medication during that time increased from 52 to 70 percent (Olfson & others, 2004). And the new standard drug treatment for anxiety disorders? Antidepressants.

Antidepressant Drugs

OBJECTIVE 54-4 | Describe the characteristics of antidepressant drugs, and discuss their use in treating specific disorders.

As the antianxiety drugs can calm people down from a state of anxiety, the *antidepressants* sometimes lift people up from a state of depression. (Their name is a bit of a misnomer now that these drugs are increasingly being used to successfully treat anxiety disorders such as obsessive-compulsive disorder.) This class of drugs works by increasing the availability of norepinephrine or serotonin, neurotransmitters that elevate arousal and mood and appear scarce during depression. Fluoxetine, which tens of million of users worldwide have known as Prozac, partially blocks the reabsorption and removal of serotonin from synapses (**FIGURE 54.2**). Because they slow the synaptic vacuuming up of serotonin, Prozac, and its cousins Zoloft and Paxil, are called *selective-serotonin-reuptake-inhibitors (SSRIs)*. Other dual-action antidepressants work by blocking the reabsorption or breakdown of both norepinephrine and serotonin. Though no less effective, the dual-action drugs have more potential side effects, such as dry mouth, weight gain, hypertension, or dizzy spells (Anderson, 2000; Mulrow, 1999). Administering them by means of a patch, bypassing the intestines and liver, helps reduce such side effects (Bodkin & Amsterdam, 2002).

The greater popularity of SSRI drugs helps explain why 89 percent of patients diagnosed with depression in 2001 received medication from their physicians, up from 70 percent in 1987, the year before SSRIs were introduced (Olfson & others, 2003; Stafford & others, 2001). And that, plus increasing numbers seeking help for depression and anxiety, helps explain a reported tripling in the total number of antidepressant prescriptions since 1992 (Goode, 2002). The drugs account for most of the $19.5 billion in worldwide antidepressant sales in 2000 (Sherman, 2004).

Be advised: Patients with depression who begin taking antidepressants do not wake up the next day singing "Oh, what a beautiful morning!" Although the influence of antidepressants on neurotransmission does occur within hours, their full psychological effect often requires four weeks. One possible reason for the delayed effect is that increased serotonin seems to promote *neurogenesis*—the birth of new brain cells, perhaps reversing stress-induced loss of neurons (Jacobs; 2004; Santarelli & others, 2003).

One side effect of SSRI drugs can be decreased sexual appetite, which has led to their occasional prescription to control sexual behavior (Slater, 2000).

On U.S. college campuses, the 9 percent of counseling center visitors taking psychiatric medication in 1994 nearly tripled, to 24.5 percent in 2004 (Duenwald, 2004).

FIGURE 54.2
Biology of antidepressants
Shown here is the action of Prozac, which partially blocks the reuptake of serotonin.

Message is sent across synaptic gap.

Message is received; excess neurotransmitter molecules are reabsorbed by sending neuron.

Prozac partially blocks normal reuptake of the neurotransmitter serotonin; excess serotonin in synapse enhances its mood-lifting effect.

Sending neuron

Vesicles containing neurotransmitters

Action potential

Synaptic gap

Neurotransmitter molecule

Receptors

Receiving neuron

Reuptake

Serotonin

Prozac

(a)   (b)   (c)

"If this doesn't help you don't worry, it's a placebo."

"No twisted thought without a twisted molecule."

Attributed to psychologist Ralph Gerard

"I think the dosage needs adjusting. I'm not nearly as happy as the people in the ads."

Antidepressant drugs are not the only way to give the body a lift. Aerobic exercise, which helps calm people who feel anxious and energize those who feel depressed, does about as much good for some people with mild to moderate depression, and has additional positive side effects. Cognitive therapy, by helping people reverse their habitual negative thinking style, can boost the drug-aided relief from depression and reduce the post-treatment risk of relapse (Hollon & others, 2002; Keller & others, 2000). Better yet, some studies suggest, is to attack depression from both above and below (Goldapple & others, 2004; TADS, 2004). Use antidepressant drugs (which work, bottom-up, on the emotion-forming limbic system) in conjunction with cognitive behavior therapy (which works, top-down, starting with changed frontal lobe activity).

Everyone agrees that people with depression often improve after a month on antidepressants. But after allowing for natural recovery (the regression to normal called *spontaneous recovery*) and the placebo effect, how big is the drug effect? Not big, report Irving Kirsch and his colleagues (1998, 2002) from their analyses of double-blind clinical trials: Placebos produced improvement comparable to 75 percent or so of the active drug's effect. Another research team analyzed data from 45 studies. Given antidepressants, 41 percent of participants improved; given placebos, 31 percent improved (Khan & others, 2000). Moreover, Kirsch reports, some of the 25 percent difference between the active drug and the placebo in the double-blind trials seems due to an additional placebo effect derived from the drug's side effects, which raise people's expectations because they know they're getting an active drug. Placebos that mimic the side effects of antidepressants are nearly as effective as the drugs themselves (Fisher & Greenberg, 1997).

Many who have witnessed or experienced the healing power of antidepressants question these findings. "It would be very miraculous if all the people I've seen getting better were getting better only by virtue of placebo," said the National Institute of Mental Health's director, Steven Hyman (1999). But this much seems assured: Our expectations have surprisingly powerful effects not only on our perceptions and our responses to such external stimuli as alcohol, hypnosis, and sexual situations (as we saw in earlier modules), but also on our biology and well-being (Kirsch & Lynn, 1999). The mind matters.

Skeptics of the biomedical therapies are unsurprised. Yesterday, says neuroscientist Elliot Valenstein (1998), we blamed mothers and sought to heal their children's inner wounds. Today, hardly wiser, we blame brain chemistry and circuitry and pump in "molecules of the mind." But our knowledge of the biochemical roots of disorder and recovery is elementary, he contends. Psychotherapeutic drugs are not "'smart missiles' that can correct the precise biochemical error responsible for each mental illness" without side effects (1998, p. 5). The chemistry, brain circuitry, and life experiences that underlie behavior are too complex for that.

Although the effects of drug therapy are less exciting than many TV ads suggest, they also are less frightening than other stories have warned. Some people taking Prozac, for example, have committed suicide, but their numbers seem fewer than we would expect from the millions of people with depression who are now taking the medication. Prozac users who commit suicide are like cellular phone users who get brain cancer. Given the millions of people taking Prozac and using cellular phones, alarming anecdotes tell us nothing. The question critical thinkers want answered is this: Do these groups suffer an elevated *rate* of suicide and brain cancer? The answer in each case appears to be no (Paulos, 1995; Tollefson & others, 1993, 1994).

The suicide-risk concern resurfaced in the early twenty-first century with studies indicating that children and adults are at a temporary heightened risk of suicide just after beginning drug treatment (Wessely & Kerwin, 2004; Whittington & others, 2004). One explanation is that the drugs reduce one's lethargy before they lift one's feelings, thus giving formerly inert people enough energy to act on their depression. In Britain, where antidepressant prescriptions for children rose 70 percent from 1992 through 2001, the Department of Health warned against treating mild childhood depression with antidepressant drugs (Alvarez, 2004). In the United States, the Food and Drug Administration began requiring a warning label—that the drugs can cause suicidal behavior in children and teens. But other recent studies indicate that the long-term increase in antidepressant use correlates with a *decline* in the adolescent suicide rate (Grunebaum & others, 2004; Olfson & others, 2003). In U.S. Zip Code areas where antidepressant use increased during the 1990s, teen suicide was most likely to decrease. Such studies suggest that perhaps antidepressants increase suicide risk in the short run, but lower it in the long run.

Mood-Stabilizing Medications

OBJECTIVE 54-5 | Describe the use and effects of mood-stabilizing medications.

"First of all I think you should know that last quarter's sales figures are interfering with my mood-stabilizing drugs."

In addition to antipsychotic, antianxiety, and antidepressant drugs, psychiatrists have *mood-stabilizing drugs* in their arsenal. The simple salt *lithium* can be an effective mood stabilizer for those suffering the manic-depressive swings of bipolar disorder. Australian physician John Cade discovered this in the 1940s when he administered lithium to a patient with severe mania. Although his reason for doing so was misguided—he thought lithium had calmed excitable guinea pigs when actually it had made them sick—Cade found that in less than a week the patient became perfectly well (Snyder, 1986). With continued lithium use, emotional highs and lows typically stabilize. After suffering mood swings for years, about 7 in 10 people with bipolar disorder benefit from a long-term daily dose of this cheap salt (Solomon & others, 1995). Their risk of suicide is but one-sixth that of bipolar patients not taking lithium (Tondo & others, 1997). Although we do not fully understand why, lithium works. And so does Depakote, a drug originally used to treat epilepsy and more recently found effective in the control of manic episodes associated with bipolar disorder.

Brain Stimulation

Electroconvulsive Therapy

OBJECTIVE 54-6 | Describe the use of electroconvulsive therapy in treating severe depression, and discuss some possible alternatives to ECT.

A more controversial brain manipulation occurs through shock treatment, or **electroconvulsive therapy (ECT)** When ECT was first introduced in 1938, the wide-awake patient was strapped to a table and jolted with roughly 100 volts of electricity to the brain, producing racking convulsions and brief unconsciousness. ECT therefore gained a barbaric image, one that lingers still. Today, however, patients first receive a general anesthetic so they are not conscious, and a muscle relaxant to prevent injury from convulsions. Then a psychiatrist momentarily electrically shocks the unconscious patient's brain. Within 30 minutes, the patient awakens and remembers nothing of the treatment or of the hours preceding it (**FIGURE 54.3** on the next page).

Psychiatrists usually limit ECT to treatment of severe depression. (It tends to be ineffective in treating other psychological disorders.) After three such sessions each week for two to four weeks, 80 percent or more of people receiving ECT improve markedly, showing some memory loss for the treatment period but no discernible brain damage (Bergsholm & others, 1989; Coffey, 1993). "A miracle had happened in two weeks," reported noted research psychologist Norman Endler (1982) after ECT alleviated his deep depression. Study after study confirms that ECT is an effective treatment for severe depression in patients who have not responded to drug therapy (Consensus Conference, 1985; UK ECT Review Group, 2003). By 2001, confidence in ECT had further increased, with a *JAMA* (*Journal of the American Medical Association*) editorial concluding that "the results of ECT in treating severe depression are among the most positive treatment effects in all of medicine" (Glass, 2001).

The medical use of electricity is an ancient practice. Physicians treated the Roman Emperor Claudius (10 B.C.–A.D. 54) for headaches by pressing electric eels to his temples.

■ **electroconvulsive therapy (ECT)** a biomedical therapy for severely depressed patients in which a brief electric current is sent through the brain of an anesthetized patient.

How does ECT work? After more than 50 years, no one knows for sure. One recipient likened ECT to the smallpox vaccine, which was saving lives before we knew how it worked. Perhaps the shock-induced seizures cause the brain to react by calming neural centers where overactivity produces depression.

ECT reduces suicidal thoughts and is credited with saving many from suicide (Kellner & others, 2005). It is now administered with briefer pulses that disrupt memory less (Fink, 1998; Kho & others, 2003). Yet its Frankensteinlike image continues. No matter how impressive the results, the idea of electrically shocking people into convulsions still strikes many as barbaric, especially given our ignorance about why ECT works. Moreover, ECT-treated patients, like other patients with a history of depression, are vulnerable to relapse. Nevertheless, electroconvulsive therapy is, in the minds of many psychiatrists and patients, a lesser evil than severe depression's misery, anguish, and risk of suicide.

Alternatives to ECT

Hopes are now rising for gentler alternatives for jump-starting the depressed brain. Some patients with chronic depression have found relief through a chest implant that intermittently stimulates the vagus nerve, which sends signals to the brain's mood-related limbic system (Marangell & others, 2002; Rush & others, 2005). In another study of six patients who had failed to respond even to ECT, four gained "striking and sustained remission of depression" following stimulation through electrodes planted deep in their brains (Mayberg & others, 2005). The stimulation served to reduce activity in a region that is hyperactive in depression, and patients immediately experienced such impressions as a "disappearance of the void" and a sense of "connectedness." This finding will surely inspire further experiments to test the possibility of a brain pacemaker that can buzz people out of depression.

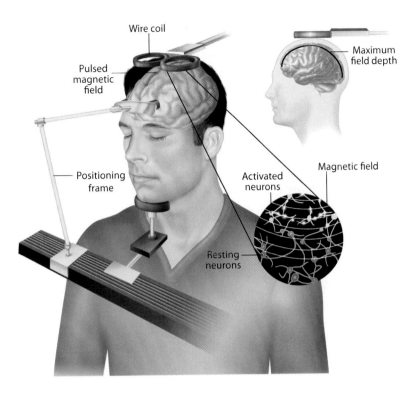

FIGURE **54.4**
Magnets for the mind
Repetitive transcranial magnetic stimulation (rTMS) sends a painless magnetic field through the skull to the cortical surface, where pulses can be used to stimulate or dampen activity in various areas (from George, 2003).

Depressed moods also seem to improve when repeated pulses surge through a magnetic coil held close to a person's skull (**FIGURE 54.4**). Unlike deep brain stimulation, the magnetic energy penetrates only to the brain's surface (though tests are under way with a higher energy field that penetrates more deeply). The painless procedure—called **repetitive transcranial magnetic stimulation (rTMS)**—is performed on wide-awake patients for 20 to 30 minutes for two to four weeks. Unlike ECT, the rTMS procedure produces no seizures, memory loss, or other side effects.

In one double-blind experiment, 67 Israelis with major depression were randomly assigned to two groups (Klein & others, 1999). One group received daily stimulations over a two-week period, while the other received sham treatments (without magnetic stimulation). At the end of the two weeks, half of the stimulated patients showed at least a 50 percent improvement in their scores on a depression scale, as did only a quarter of the placebo group. Newer studies confirmed the therapeutic effect, which inspired the beginning in 2005 of two large, multilocation clinical experiments on rTMS (Cohen & others, 2005; Janicak, 2005; Martin & others, 2003). One possible explanation of this effect is that the stimulation energizes depressed patients' relatively inactive left frontal lobe (Helmuth, 2001). When repeatedly stimulated, nerve cells can form functioning circuits through a process called *long-term potentiation (LTP)*. Before long, conclusive data from the clinical experiments should become available, indicating whether magnetic stimulation is, indeed, a valuable new treatment for depression.

Psychosurgery

OBJECTIVE 54-7 | Summarize the history of the psychosurgical procedure known as a lobotomy, and discuss the use of psychosurgery today.

Because its effects are irreversible, **psychosurgery**—surgery that removes or destroys brain tissue—is the most drastic and the least-used biomedical intervention for changing behavior. In the 1930s, Portuguese physician Egas Moniz developed what

■ **repetitive transcranial magnetic stimulation (rTMS)** the application of repeated pulses of magnetic energy to the brain; used to stimulate or suppress brain activity.

■ **psychosurgery** surgery that removes or destroys brain tissue in an effort to change behavior.

■ **lobotomy** a now-rare psychosurgical procedure once used to calm uncontrollably emotional or violent patients. The procedure cut the nerves that connect the frontal lobes to the emotion-controlling centers of the inner brain.

became the best-known psychosurgical operation: the **lobotomy.** Moniz found that cutting the nerves connecting the frontal lobes with the emotion-controlling centers of the inner brain calmed uncontrollably emotional and violent patients. After shocking the patient into a coma, a neurosurgeon would hammer an icepicklike instrument through each eye socket into the brain, then wiggle it to sever connections running up to the frontal lobes. The whole procedure was crude but easy and inexpensive, and it took only about 10 minutes. During the 1940s and 1950s, tens of thousands of severely disturbed people were "lobotomized," and Moniz was honored with a Nobel prize (Valenstein, 1986).

Although the intention was simply to disconnect emotion from thought, the effect was often more drastic: The lobotomy usually produced a permanently lethargic, immature, impulsive personality. During the 1950s, after some 35,000 people had been lobotomized in the United States alone, calming drugs became available and psychosurgery was largely abandoned. Today, lobotomies are history and other psychosurgery is used only in extreme cases. For example, if a patient suffers uncontrollable seizures, surgeons can deactivate the specific nerve clusters that cause or transmit the convulsions. MRI-guided precision surgery is also occasionally done to cut the circuits involved in severe obsessive-compulsive disorder (Sachdev & Sachdev, 1997). Because these procedures are irreversible, however, neurosurgeons perform them only as a last resort.

Mind-body interaction
The biomedical therapies assume that mind and body are a unit: Affect one and you will affect the other.

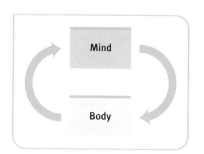

The effectiveness of the biomedical therapies reminds us of a fundamental lesson: We find it convenient to talk of separate psychological and biological influences, but everything psychological is also biological. Every thought and feeling depends on the functioning brain. Every creative idea, every moment of joy or anger, every period of depression emerges from the electrochemical activity of the living brain. The influence is two-way: When psychotherapy relieves obsessive-compulsive behavior, PET scans reveal a calmer brain (Schwartz & others, 1996).

>> Learning Outcomes

The Biomedical Therapies

OBJECTIVE 54-1 | Discuss the goals of biomedical therapy, and explain how double-blind studies help researchers evaluate a drug's effectiveness.

Biomedical therapy attempts to treat disorders with prescribed medications or medical procedures that act directly on a patient's nervous system. Since the 1950s, drug therapy has been used extensively to treat psychological disorders. *Double-blind studies,* in which neither the medical staff nor the patient knows whether the patient is taking the real drug or a placebo, eliminate the bias that can result from clinicians' and patients' expectations of improvement.

OBJECTIVE 54-2 | Describe the characteristics of antipsychotic drugs, and discuss their use in treating schizophrenia.

The antipsychotic drugs dampen responsiveness to irrelevant stimuli, and they have been used effectively to treat schizophrenia accompanied by positive symptoms (the presence of hallucinations and delusions). The first-generation antipsychotic drugs, which block D2 (dopamine) receptors, can produce *tardive dyskinesia,* (involuntary movements of facial muscles, the tongue, and arms and legs). Second-generation antipsychotics, which target D1 receptors, can affect metabolism, increasing the risk of obesity and diabetes.

OBJECTIVE 54-3 | Describe the characteristics of antianxiety drugs.

Antianxiety drugs, which depress central nervous system activity, are often used in combination with psychotherapy for treatment of anxiety disorders. These drugs can be psychologically and physically addictive.

OBJECTIVE 54-4 | Describe the characteristics of antidepressant drugs, and discuss their use in treating specific disorders.

Antidepressant drugs increase the availability of norepinephrine or serotonin, which elevate arousal and mood. *Selective-serotonin-reuptake-inhibitors (SSRIs)* block the reuptake of serotonin. Dual-action antidepressants block the reuptake or absorption of both norepinephrine and serotonin, but they have a greater risk of side effects. Antidepressants may be used to treat depression (often in combination with cognitive therapy) and the anxiety disorders. Their full psychological effects may not appear for several weeks.

OBJECTIVE 54-5 | Describe the use and effects of mood-stabilizing medications.

A few drugs, such as *lithium* for bipolar disorder, have proven very effective in stabilizing moods. Researchers do not yet understand how these medications work.

OBJECTIVE 54-6 | Describe the use of electroconvulsive therapy in treating severe depression, and discuss some possible alternatives to ECT.

In ECT, a brief electric current is sent through the brain of an anesthetized patient. Although controversial, ECT is an effective, last-resort treatment for many people with severe depression who have not responded to drug therapy. How ECT works is unknown. Depression has also been alleviated by some implanted devices that stimulate parts of the brain, and by repetitive transcranial magnetic stimulation (rTMS), in which pulses of magnetic energy sent through the skull to the surface of the cortex stimulate or dampen activity in various brain areas.

OBJECTIVE 54-7 | Summarize the history of the psychosurgical procedure known as a lobotomy, and discuss the use of psychosurgery today.

Lobotomy was a crude and irreversible procedure in which surgical instruments were inserted through a patient's eye sockets to sever connections running to the frontal lobes of the brain, with the intent of calming uncontrollably emotional or violent patients. This surgery disappeared in the 1950s, when its harmful effects (lethargy and an impulsive personality) became known and new and effective drug treatments were introduced. Today, neurosurgeons rarely perform brain surgery to treat psychological disorders.

TERMS AND CONCEPTS TO REMEMBER

biomedical therapy, p. 54-1

psychopharmacology, p. 54-1

tardive dyskinesia, p. 54-2

electroconvulsive therapy (ECT), p. 54-5

repetitive transcranial magnetic stimulation (rTMS), p. 54-7

psychosurgery, p. 54-7

lobotomy, p. 54-8

TEST YOURSELF

1. How do researchers evaluate the effectiveness of particular drug therapies?

(Answer in Appendix B.)

ASK YOURSELF

1. Have your feelings about therapy changed since you entered this course? If so, in what ways?

>WEB

Multiple-choice *self-tests* and more may be found at www.worthpublishers.com/myers.

ANOTHER VOICE ON: SOCIAL PSYCHOLOGY

SEKOU SUNDIATA (b. 1948), "BLINK YOUR EYES," 1995, *THE BLUE ONENESS DREAMS*

I could wake up in the morning
without a warning
and my world could change:

blink your eyes.
All depends, all depends on the skin,
all depends on the skin you're living in.

Social Psychology

OBJECTIVE 55-1 | Describe the three main focuses of social psychology.

On September 11, 2001, shortly after terrorists flew hijacked planes into the World Trade Center, I spoke by phone with my daughter, Laura. She was on the street in her Manhattan neighborhood, describing the tumultuous scene, when suddenly she yelled, "Oh my gosh! Oh my gosh!" as the second massive tower collapsed before her eyes. By almost anyone's definition, this catastrophic violence—accomplished by a mere 19 men with box cutters—was an evil act, to which the communal response was fear mixed with anger. A bully's single kick that collapses a nearly finished sandcastle triggers both fright and outrage. Likewise, for millions of stunned Americans, 9/11 evoked anxiety about what might come next and a lust for revenge.

But the cataclysm also triggered an outpouring of love and compassion. From around the country and the world, money and countless truckloads of food, clothing, and teddy bears—more than New Yorkers could possibly use—poured in. People in Toledo, Fargo, and Stockholm wept for those who wept. There on 6th Avenue and 24th Street, strangers hugged and talked, trying to make sense of senseless destruction. Although few transfusions would be needed, willing donors formed long lines at blood banks. "Everywhere I go I see concern," Laura wrote that evening.

I see compassion. I see people with many differences united. I don't see violence. I don't see impatience. I don't see cruelty. Except when I look at that cloud of smoke, a constant backdrop all day. People are helping each other. People are desperate to do whatever they can.

In the midst of this nightmare, I am utterly filled with love for the people of this city. It is incredible to witness their response. I am covered in goose bumps. My faith in humanity rises over that cloud and I see goodness and respect.

We watch and we wonder: What drives people to feel such hatred and to destroy so many innocent lives? And what motivates the heroic altruism of those who died trying to save others and of the many more who reached out to those coping with loss?

As the 9/11 horror so compellingly demonstrates, we are social animals. Depending on who or what influences our thinking, we may assume the best or the worst in others. And depending on our attitudes, we may approach them with closed fists or open arms.

"We cannot live for ourselves alone," remarked the novelist Herman Melville. "Our lives are connected by a thousand invisible threads." **Social psychologists** explore these connections by scientifically studying how we *think about, influence,* and *relate to* one another. In Modules 55 through 58, we consider these topics.

Social Thinking (Module 55) asks, How do we explain people's behavior? How do we form our beliefs and attitudes? What is the relationship between what we think and what we do? Social Influence (Module 56) asks, What invisible social threads pull us? How strong are they? How do they operate? Antisocial Relations (Module 57) asks, What makes us harm others? And in Prosocial Relations (Module 58): Why do we fall in love? And what can we do to transform the closed fists of aggression into the open arms of compassion?

■ **social psychology** the scientific study of how we think about, influence, and relate to one another.

55

Social Thinking

Especially when the unexpected occurs, we analyze why people act as they do. Does her warmth reflect romantic interest, or is that how she relates to everyone? Does his absenteeism signify illness? Laziness? A stressful work atmosphere? Was the horror of 9/11 the work of crazed evil people, or of ordinary people corrupted by life events? Such questions intrigue social psychologists. Just as personality psychologists study the enduring, inner determinants of behavior that help to explain why different people act differently in a given situation, so *social psychologists* study the social influences that help explain why the same person will act differently in different situations.

Attributing Behavior to Persons or to Situations

OBJECTIVE 55-2 | Contrast dispositional and situational attributions, and explain how the fundamental attribution error can affect our analyses of behavior.

After studying how people explain others' behavior, Fritz Heider (1958) proposed an **attribution theory.** Heider noted that people usually attribute others' behavior either to their internal dispositions or to their external situations. A teacher, for example, may wonder whether a child's hostility reflects an aggressive personality (*a dispositional attribution*) or a reaction to stress or abuse (*a situational attribution*).

In class, we notice that Juliette seldom talks; over coffee, Jack talks nonstop. Attributing their behaviors to their personal dispositions, we decide Juliette is shy and Jack is outgoing. Because people do have enduring personality traits, such attributions are sometimes valid. However, we often fall prey to the **fundamental attribution error,** by overestimating the influence of personality and underestimating the influence of situations. In class, Jack may be as quiet as Juliette. Catch Juliette at a party and you may hardly recognize your quiet classmate.

An experiment by David Napolitan and George Goethals (1979) illustrates the phenomenon. They had Williams College students talk, one at a time, with a young woman who acted either aloof and critical or warm and friendly. Beforehand, they told half the students the woman's behavior would be spontaneous. They told the other half the truth—that she had been instructed to *act* friendly (or unfriendly). What do you suppose was the effect of being told the truth?

There was no effect. The students disregarded the information. If the woman acted friendly, they inferred she really was a warm person. If she acted unfriendly, they inferred she really was a cold person. In other words, they attributed her behavior to her personal disposition *even when told that her behavior was situational*—that she was merely acting that way for the purposes of the experiment. Although the fundamental attribution error occurs in all cultures studied, this tendency to attribute behavior to people's dispositions runs especially strong in individualistic Western countries. In East Asian cultures, for example, people are more sensitive to the power of the situation (Masuda & Kitayama, 2005).

As with other biases, people see themselves as less susceptible than others to the phenomenon (Pronin & others, 2004). The

The fundamental attribution error
If our new colleague at work acts grouchy, we may infer that she's a grouchy person, discounting her having lost sleep over a family worry, having a flat tire on the way to work, and being unable to find a parking place.

B. Busco/The Image Bank/Getty Images

fundamental attribution error is almost irresistible, though. In a high school play, I saw a talented 16-year-old convincingly play the part of a bitter old woman—so convincingly that, although I reminded myself of the fundamental attribution error, I still assumed that the young actress was typecast because she was well-suited for the part. Meeting her later at a cast party, I discovered she actually had a very pleasant disposition. I then remembered that several months earlier I had seen her play the part of a charming 10-year-old in *The Sound of Music*.

You, too, have surely committed the fundamental attribution error. In judging whether your psychology instructor is shy or outgoing, you have perhaps by now inferred that he or she has an outgoing personality. But you know your instructor only from the classroom, a situation that demands outgoing behavior. Catch the instructor in a different situation and you might be surprised (as some of my students have been when confronting me in a pick-up basketball game). Outside their assigned roles, professors seem less professorial, presidents less presidential, servants less servile.

The instructor, on the other hand, observes his or her own behavior in many different situations—in the classroom, in meetings, at home—and so might say, "Me, outgoing? It all depends on the situation. In class or with good friends, yes, I'm outgoing. But at conventions I'm really rather shy." So, when explaining *our own* behavior, or the behavior of those we know well and see in varied situations, we are sensitive to how behavior changes with the situations (Idson & Mischel, 2001).

When explaining *others'* behavior, particularly the behavior of strangers we have observed in only one type of situation, we often commit the fundamental attribution error: We disregard the situation and leap to unwarranted conclusions about their personality traits. Many people initially assumed that Nazi death camp commanders exhibited consistently vile behavior. Actually, many were unremarkable men who went home after the day's brutality and relaxed with a good book and the strains of classical music. Many of us initially assumed the 9/11 terrorists were obviously crazy, when actually they went unnoticed in their neighborhoods, health clubs, and favorite restaurants.

Researchers who have reversed the perspectives of actor and observer—by having each view a videotape replay of the situation from the other's perspective—have also reversed the attributions (Lassiter & Irvine, 1986; Storms, 1973). Seeing the world from the actor's perspective, the observers better appreciate the situation. Taking the observer's point of view, the actors better appreciate their own personal style.

The Effects of Attribution

In everyday life we often struggle to explain others' actions. A jury must decide whether a shooting was malicious or in self-defense. An interviewer must judge whether the applicant's geniality is genuine. When we make such judgments, our attributions—either to the person or to the situation—have important consequences (Fincham & Bradbury, 1993; Fletcher & others, 1990). Happily married couples attribute a spouse's tart-tongued remark to a temporary situation ("She must have had a bad day at work."). Unhappily married persons attribute the same remark to a mean disposition ("Why did I marry such a hostile person?").

Or consider the political effects of attribution: How do you explain poverty or unemployment? Researchers in Britain, India, Australia, and the United States (Furnham, 1982; Pandey & others, 1982; Wagstaff, 1982; Zucker & Weiner, 1993) report that political conservatives tend to attribute such social problems to the personal dispositions of the poor and unemployed themselves: "People generally get what they deserve. Those who don't work are often freeloaders. Anybody who takes the initiative can still get ahead." "Society is not to blame for

■ **attribution theory** suggests how we explain someone's behavior—by crediting either the situation or the person's disposition.

■ **fundamental attribution error** the tendency for observers, when analyzing another's behavior, to underestimate the impact of the situation and to overestimate the impact of personal disposition.

" Calling [9/11] *senseless*, *mindless*, *insane*, or the work of *madmen* is wrong . . . [it] fails to adopt the perspective of the perpetrators, as an act with a clearly defined purpose that we must understand in order to challenge it most effectively."
Psychologist Philip G. Zimbardo, "Fighting Terrorism by Understanding Man's Capacity for Evil," September 16, 2001

"Otis, shout at that man to pull himself together."

An attribution question
Some people blamed the New Orleans residents for not evacuating before the predicted Hurricane Katrina. Others attributed their inaction to the situation—to their not having cars or not being offered bus transportation.

Paul Buck/EPA/Landov

crime, criminals are," said one conservative U.S. presidential candidate (Dole, 1996). Political liberals (and social scientists) are more likely to blame past and present situations: "If you or I had to live with the same poor education, lack of opportunity, and discrimination, would we be any better off?" To understand and prevent terrorism, they say, consider the situations that breed terrorists. Better to drain the swamps than swat the mosquitoes.

Managers also have to make attributions. In evaluating employees, they are likely to attribute poor performance to personal factors, such as low ability or lack of motivation. But remember the actor's viewpoint: Workers doing poorly on a job recognize situational influences, such as inadequate supplies, poor working conditions, difficult co-workers, or impossible demands (Rice, 1985).

The point to remember: Our attributions—to individuals' dispositions or to their situations—have real consequences (**FIGURE 55.1**).

Negative behavior

Situational attribution
"Maybe that driver is ill."

Tolerant reaction
(proceed cautiously, allow driver a wide berth)

Dispositional attribution
"Crazy driver!"

Unfavorable reaction
(speed up and race past the other driver, craning to give a dirty look)

FIGURE 55.1
Attributions and reactions
How we explain someone's behavior affects how we react to it.

Attitudes and Actions

OBJECTIVE 55-3 | Define *attitude*.

Attitudes are feelings, based on our beliefs, that predispose our reactions to objects, people, and events. If we *believe* someone is mean, we may *feel* dislike for the person and *act* unfriendly. "Change the way people think," said South African civil rights martyr Steve Biko, "and things will never be the same." Such is the power of persuasion.

Attitudes Can Affect Actions

OBJECTIVE 55-4 | Describe the conditions under which attitudes can affect actions.

Our attitudes predict our behavior imperfectly because other factors, including the external situation, also influence behavior. Strong social pressures can weaken the attitude-behavior connection (Wallace & others, 2005). For example, the American public's overwhelming support for President George W. Bush's preparation to attack Iraq motivated Democratic leaders to vote to support Bush's war plan, despite their private reservations (Nagourney, 2002). Nevertheless, attitudes may indeed affect behavior when other influences are minimal, when the attitude is specific to the behavior, and when we are keenly aware of our attitudes.

Actions Can Affect Attitudes

OBJECTIVE 55-5 | Explain how the foot-in-the-door phenomenon, role-playing, and cognitive dissonance illustrate the influence of actions on attitudes.

Now consider a more surprising principle: Not only will people sometimes stand up for what they believe, they will also come to believe in what they have stood up for. Many streams of evidence confirm that *attitudes follow behavior* (**FIGURE 55.2**).

The Foot-in-the-Door Phenomenon

Convincing people to act against their beliefs can affect their attitude. During the Korean War, many captured U.S. soldiers were imprisoned in war camps run by Chinese communists. Without using brutality, the captors secured the collaboration of hundreds of their prisoners in various activities. Some merely ran errands or accepted favors. Others made radio appeals and false confessions. Still others informed on fellow prisoners and divulged military information. When the war ended, 21 prisoners chose to stay with the communists. More returned home "brainwashed"—convinced that communism was a good thing for Asia.

A key ingredient of the Chinese "thought-control" program was its effective use of the **foot-in-the-door phenomenon**—a tendency for people who agree to a small action to comply later with a larger one. The Chinese began with harmless requests but gradually escalated their demands on the prisoners (Schein, 1956). Having "trained" the prisoners to speak or write trivial statements, the communists then asked them to copy or create something more important, noting, perhaps, the flaws of capitalism. Then, perhaps to gain privileges, the prisoners participated in group discussions, wrote self-criticisms, or uttered public confessions. After doing so, they often adjusted their beliefs toward consistency with their public acts.

The point is simple, says Robert Cialdini (1993): To get people to agree to something big, "start small and build." And be wary of those who would exploit you with the tactic. This chicken-and-egg spiral, of actions-feeding-attitudes-feeding-actions, enables behavior to escalate. A trivial act makes the next act easier. Succumb to a temptation and you will find the next temptation harder to resist.

■ **attitude** feelings, often based on our beliefs, that predispose us to respond in a particular way to objects, people, and events.

■ **foot-in-the-door phenomenon** the tendency for people who have first agreed to a small request to comply later with a larger request.

FIGURE 55.2
Attitudes follow behavior
Cooperative actions, such as those performed by people on sports teams, feed mutual liking. Such attitudes, in turn, promote positive behavior.

Dozens of experiments have simulated part of the war prisoners' experience by coaxing people into acting against their attitudes or violating their moral standards. The nearly inevitable result: Doing becomes believing. When people are induced to harm an innocent victim—by making nasty comments or delivering electric shocks—they then begin to disparage their victim. If induced to speak or write on behalf of a position they have qualms about, they begin to believe their own words.

> "If the King destroys a man, that's proof to the King it must have been a bad man."
>
> Thomas Cromwell, in Robert Bolt's *A Man for All Seasons*, 1960

Fortunately, the attitudes-follow-behavior principle works as well for good deeds as for bad. The foot-in-the-door tactic has helped boost charitable contributions, blood donations, and product sales. In one experiment, researchers posing as safe-driving volunteers asked Californians to permit the installation of a large, poorly lettered "Drive Carefully" sign in their front yards. Only 17 percent consented. They approached other home owners with a small request first: Would they display a 3-inch-high "Be a Safe Driver" sign? Nearly all readily agreed. When reapproached two weeks later to allow the large, ugly sign in their front yards, 76 percent consented (Freedman & Fraser, 1966).

Racial attitudes likewise follow behavior. In the years immediately following the introduction of school desegregation in the United States and the passage of the Civil Rights Act of 1964, white Americans expressed diminishing racial prejudice. And as Americans in different regions came to act more alike—thanks to more uniform national standards against discrimination—they began to think more alike. Experiments confirm the observation: Moral action strengthens moral convictions.

Role-Playing Affects Attitudes

When you adopt a new role—when you become a college student, marry, or begin a new job—you strive to follow the social prescriptions. At first, your behaviors may feel phony, because you are *acting* a role. The first weeks in the military feel artificial—as if one is pretending to be a soldier. The first weeks of a marriage may feel like "playing house." Before long, however, what began as play-acting in the theater of life becomes *you*.

> "Fake it until you make it."
>
> Alcoholics Anonymous saying

Researchers have confirmed this effect by assessing people's attitudes before and after they adopt a new role, sometimes in laboratory situations, sometimes in everyday situations, such as before and after taking a job. In one well-known laboratory study, male college students volunteered to spend time in a simulated prison devised by psychologist Philip Zimbardo (1972). Some he randomly designated as guards; he gave them uniforms, billy clubs, and whistles and instructed them to enforce certain rules. The remainder became prisoners; they were locked in barren cells and forced to wear humiliating outfits. After a day or two in which the volunteers self-consciously "played" their roles, the simulation became real—too real.

The power of the situation

In Philip Zimbardo's Stanford Prison simulation, a toxic situation triggered degrading behaviors among those assigned to the guard role.

Philip G. Zimbardo, Inc.

Most of the guards developed disparaging attitudes, and some devised cruel and degrading routines. One by one, the prisoners broke down, rebelled, or became passively resigned, causing Zimbardo to call off the study after only six days. More recently, similar situations have played themselves out in the real world—as in Iraq at the Abu Ghraib Prison (see Close-Up).

Greece's military junta during the early 1970s took advantage of the effects of role-playing to train men to become torturers (Staub, 1989). The men's indoctrination into their roles occurred in small steps. First, the trainee stood guard outside the interrogation cells—the "foot in the door." Next, he stood guard inside. Only then was he ready to become actively involved in the questioning and torture. As the nineteenth-century writer Nathaniel Hawthorne noted, "No man, for any considerable period, can wear one face to himself and another to the multitude without finally getting bewildered as to which may be true." What we do, we gradually become.

CLOSE-UP:

ABU GHRAIB PRISON: AN "ATROCITY-PRODUCING SITUATION"?

As the first photos emerged in 2004 from Iraq's Abu Ghraib Prison, the civilized world was shocked. The photos showed U.S. military guards stripping prisoners naked, placing hoods on them, stacking them in piles, prodding them with electricity, taunting them with attack dogs, and subjecting them to sleep deprivation, humiliation, and extreme stress. Was the problem, as so many people initially supposed, a few bad apples—irresponsible or even sadistic guards? That was the U.S. Army's seeming verdict when it court-martialed and imprisoned some of the guards, and then cleared four of the five top commanding officers responsible for Abu Ghraib's policies and operations. The lower-level military guards were "sick bastards," explained the defense attorney for one of the commanding officers (Tarbert, 2004).

Many social psychologists, however, reminded us that a toxic situation can make even good apples go bad

Bad apples or bad barrels?
Both the Stanford Prison Experiment in 1972 and the real-life Abu Ghraib Prison fiasco in 2004 were powerfully toxic situations, contends social psychologist Philip Zimbardo.

(Fiske & others, 2004). "When ordinary people are put in a novel, evil place, such as most prisons, Situations Win, People Lose," offered Philip Zim-

bardo (2004), adding, "That is true for the majority of people in all the relevant social psychological research done over the past 40 years."

Consider the situation, explains Zimbardo. The guards, some of them model soldier-reservists with no prior criminal or sadistic history, were exhausted from working 12-hour shifts, seven days a week, for more than a month at a time. They were dealing with an enemy, and their prejudices were heightened by fears of lethal attacks and by the violent deaths of many fellow soldiers. They were put in an understaffed guard role, given minimal training and oversight, and encouraged to "soften up" for interrogation detainees who had been denied access to the Red Cross. "When you put that set of horrendous work conditions and external factors together, it creates an evil barrel. You could put virtually anybody in it and you're going to get this kind of evil behavior" (Zimbardo, 2005).

Cognitive Dissonance: Relief from Tension

So far we have seen that actions can affect attitudes, sometimes turning prisoners into collaborators, doubters into believers, mere acquaintances into friends, and compliant guards into abusers. But why? One explanation is that when we become aware that our attitudes and actions don't coincide, we experience tension, or *cognitive dissonance*. To relieve this tension, according to the **cognitive dissonance theory** proposed by Leon Festinger, we often bring our attitudes into line with our actions. It is as if we rationalize, "If I chose to do it (or say it), I must believe in it." The less coerced and more responsible we feel for a troubling act, the more dissonance we feel. The more dissonance we feel, the more motivated we are to find consistency, such as changing our attitudes to help justify the act.

The U.S. invasion of Iraq was mainly premised on the presumed threat of Saddam Hussein's weapons of mass destruction (WMD). As the war began, only 38 percent of Americans surveyed said the war was justified even if Iraq did not have WMD (Gallup, 2003), and nearly 80 percent believed such weapons would be found (Duffy, 2003; Newport & others, 2003). When no WMD were found, many Americans felt dissonance, which was heightened by their awareness of the war's financial and human costs, by scenes of chaos in Iraq, and by inflamed anti-American and pro-terrorist sentiments in some parts of the world.

To reduce dissonance, some people revised their memories of the main rationale for going to war, which now became liberating an oppressed people and promoting democracy in the Middle East. Before long, the once-minority opinion became the

cognitive dissonance theory the theory that we act to reduce the discomfort (dissonance) we feel when two of our thoughts (cognitions) are inconsistent. For example, when our awareness of our attitudes and of our actions clash, we can reduce the resulting dissonance by changing our attitudes.

"Look, I have my misgivings, too, but what choice do we have except stay the course?"

majority view: 58 percent of Americans said they supported the war even if there were no WMD (Gallup, 2003). "Whether or not they find weapons of mass destruction doesn't matter," explained Republican pollster Frank Luntz (2003), "because the rationale for the war changed." It was not until late 2004, when hopes for a flourishing peace waned, that Americans' support for the war dropped below 50 percent.

Dozens of experiments have explored cognitive dissonance by making people feel responsible for behavior that is inconsistent with their attitudes and that has foreseeable consequences. As a subject in one of these experiments, you might agree for a measly $2 to help a researcher by writing an essay that supports something you don't believe in (perhaps a tuition increase). Feeling responsible for the statements (which are not consistent with your attitudes), you would probably feel dissonance, especially if you thought an administrator would be reading your essay. How could you reduce the uncomfortable dissonance? One way would be to start believing your phony words. Your pretense would become your reality.

The attitudes-follow-behavior principle has another heartening implication: Although we cannot directly control all our feelings, we can influence them by altering our behavior. Facial expressions and body postures affect our emotions. If we are down in the dumps, we can do as cognitive therapists advise and talk in more positive, self-accepting ways with fewer self-put-downs. If we are unloving, we can become more loving by behaving as if we were so—by doing thoughtful things, expressing affection, giving affirmation. "Assume a virtue, if you have it not," says Hamlet to his mother. "For use can almost change the stamp of nature." *The point to remember:* Evil acts shape the self. But so do acts of good will. Act as though you like someone, and you soon will. Changing our behavior can change how we think about others and how we feel about ourselves.

"Sit all day in a moping posture, sigh, and reply to everything with a dismal voice, and your melancholy lingers. . . . If we wish to conquer undesirable emotional tendencies in ourselves, we must . . . go through the outward movements of those contrary dispositions which we prefer to cultivate."

William James, *Principles of Psychology*, 1890

>> LEARNING OUTCOMES

Social Thinking

OBJECTIVE 55-1 | Describe the three main focuses of social psychology.

Social psychology focuses on three broad topics: how people think about, influence, and relate to one another.

OBJECTIVE 55-2 | Contrast dispositional and situational attributions, and explain how the fundamental attribution error can affect our analyses of behavior.

We usually rely on *situational attributions,* stressing the influence of external events, to explain our own behavior (and often the behavior of those we know well and see in many different contexts). In explaining the actions of people we do not know well, we may resort to *dispositional attributions,* assuming their behavior stems from their personal traits. This *fundamental attribution error* (overestimating the influence of personal factors and underestimating the effect of context) can flaw our judgments of others.

OBJECTIVE 55-3 | Define *attitude.*

Attitudes are positive, negative, or mixed feelings, based on our beliefs, that predispose us to respond in a particular way to objects, people, and events.

OBJECTIVE 55-4 | Describe the conditions under which attitudes can affect actions.

Our attitudes are most likely to affect our behavior when social influences are minimal, the attitude is specific to the behavior, and we are very aware of the attitude.

OBJECTIVE 55-5 | Explain how the foot-in-the-door phenomenon, role-playing, and cognitive dissonance illustrate the influence of actions on attitudes.

The *foot-in-the-door phenomenon* describes people's willingness to agree to a large request after having agreed to a related small request. In *role-playing* studies, such as Philip Zimbardo's prison experiment, people who behaved in certain ways in scripted scenarios have adopted attitudes in keeping with those roles. Leon Festinger's *cognitive dissonance theory* proposes that we feel uncomfortable when we act in ways that conflict with our feelings and beliefs, and we reduce this discomfort by revising our attitudes to align them more closely with our behavior. In all three instances, attitudes adapt to behavior, rather than drive it.

TERMS AND CONCEPTS TO REMEMBER

social psychology, p. P16-1

attribution theory, p. 55-0

fundamental attribution error, p. 55-0

attitude, p. 55-3

foot-in-the-door phenomenon, p. 55-3

cognitive dissonance theory, p. 55-5

TEST YOURSELF

1. Driving to school one wintry day, Marco narrowly misses a car that slides through a red light. "Slow down! What a terrible driver," he thinks to himself. Moments later, Marco himself slips through an intersection and yelps, "Wow! These roads are awful. The city snow plows need to get out here." What social psychology principle has Marco just demonstrated? Explain.

(Answer in Appendix B.)

ASK YOURSELF

1. Do you have an attitude or tendency you would like to change? Using the attitudes-follow-behavior principle, how might you go about changing that attitude?

>WEB

Multiple-choice **self-tests** and more may be found at www.worthpublishers.com/myers.

MODULE

Conformity and Obedience

Group Influence

56

Social Influence

Social psychology's great lesson is the enormous power of social influence. This influence can be seen in our conformity, our compliance, and our group behavior. Suicides, bomb threats, airplane hijackings, and UFO sightings all have a curious tendency to come in clusters. On campus, blue jeans are the dress code; on New York's Wall Street or London's Bond Street, dress suits are the norm. When we know how to act, how to groom, how to talk, life functions smoothly. Armed with principles of social influence, advertisers, fund-raisers, and campaign workers aim to sway our decisions to buy, to donate, to vote. Isolated with others who share their grievances, dissenters may gradually become rebels, and rebels may become terrorists. Let's examine the pull of these social strings. How strong are they? How do they operate?

Conformity and Obedience

OBJECTIVE 56-1 | Describe the chameleon effect, and give an example of it.

Behavior is contagious.

- One person laughs, coughs, or yawns, and others in the group soon do the same. Chimps, too, are more likely to yawn after observing another chimp yawn (Anderson & others, 2004).
- A cluster of people stand gazing upward, and passersby pause to do likewise.
- Bartenders and street musicians know to "seed" their tip containers with money to suggest that others have given.
- "Sickness" can also be psychologically contagious. In the anxious 9/11 aftermath, more than two dozen elementary and middle schools had outbreaks of children reporting red rashes, sometimes causing parents to wonder whether biological terrorism was at work (Talbot, 2002). Some cases may have been stress-related, but mostly, said health experts, people were just noticing normal early acne, insect bites, eczema, and dry skin from overheated classrooms.

We are natural mimics—an effect Tanya Chartrand and John Bargh (1999) call the *chameleon effect*. Unconsciously mimicking others' expressions, postures, and voice tones helps us feel what they are feeling. This helps explain why we feel happier around happy people than around depressed ones, and why studies of groups of British nurses and accountants reveal *mood linkage*—sharing up and down moods (Totterdell & others, 1998). Just hearing someone reading a neutral text in either a happy- or sad-sounding voice creates "mood contagion" in listeners (Neumann & Strack, 2000).

Chartrand and Bargh demonstrated the chameleon effect when they had students work in a room alongside a confederate working for the experimenter. Sometimes the confederates rubbed their face; on other occasions, they shook their foot. Sure enough, participants tended to rub their own face when they were with the face-rubbing person and shake their own foot when they were with the foot-shaking person. Such automatic mimicry is part of empathy. The most empathic people mimic—and are liked—the most. And those most eager to fit in with a group seem intuitively to know this, for they are especially prone to nonconscious mimicry (Lakin & Chartrand, 2003).

Niche conformity

Are these students asserting their individuality or identifying themselves with others of the same microculture?

Yuriko Nakao/Reuters/Corbis

NON SEQUITUR   by WILEY

Sometimes the effects of suggestibility are more serious. In the eight days following the 1999 shooting rampage at Colorado's Columbine High School, every U.S. state except Vermont experienced threats of copycat violence. Pennsylvania alone recorded 60 such threats (Cooper, 1999). Sociologist David Phillips and his colleagues (1985, 1989) found that suicides, too, sometimes increase following a highly publicized suicide. In the wake of Marilyn Monroe's suicide on August 6, 1962, the number of suicides in the United States exceeded the usual August count by 200. Although not all studies have confirmed the copycat suicide phenomenon, suicides have sometimes occurred in local clusters. Within an 18-day span, one 1500-student high school recorded 2 completed suicides, 7 attempted suicides, and 23 students with suicidal thoughts. Within a one-year period, one London psychiatric unit experienced 14 patient suicides (Joiner, 1999).

What causes suicide clusters? Do people act similarly because of their influence on one another? Or because they are simultaneously exposed to the same events and conditions? Seeking answers, social psychologists have conducted experiments on group pressure and conformity.

Group Pressure and Conformity

OBJECTIVE 56-2 | Discuss Asch's experiments on conformity, and distinguish between normative and informational social influence.

Suggestibility is a subtle type of **conformity**—adjusting our behavior or thinking toward some group standard. To study conformity, Solomon Asch (1955) devised a simple test. As a participant in the study, you arrive at the experiment location in time to take a seat at a table where five people are already seated. The experimenter asks which of three comparison lines is identical to a standard line (**FIGURE 56.1**). You see clearly that the answer is Line 2 and await your turn to say so after the others. Your boredom with this experiment begins to show when the next set of lines proves equally easy.

■ **conformity** adjusting one's behavior or thinking to coincide with a group standard.

FIGURE 56.1
Asch's conformity experiments
Which of the three comparison lines is equal to the standard line? What do you suppose most people would say after hearing five others say, "Line 3"? In this photo from one of Asch's experiments, the student in the center shows the severe discomfort that comes from disagreeing with the responses of other group members (in this case, confederates of the experimenter).

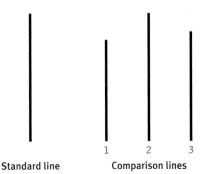

Standard line   Comparison lines

Now comes the third trial, and the correct answer seems just as clear-cut, but the first person gives what strikes you as a wrong answer: "Line 3." When the second person and then the third and fourth give the same wrong answer, you sit up straight and squint. When the fifth person agrees with the first four, you feel your heart begin to pound. The experimenter then looks to you for your answer. Torn between the unanimity of your five fellow respondents and the evidence of your own eyes, you feel tense and much less sure of yourself than you were moments ago. You hesitate before answering, wondering whether you should suffer the discomfort of being the oddball. What answer do you give?

In the experiments conducted by Asch and others after him, thousands of college students have experienced this conflict. Answering such questions alone, they erred less than 1 percent of the time. But the odds were quite different when several others—confederates working for the experimenter—answered incorrectly. Asch reports that more than one-third of the time, these "intelligent and well-meaning" college-student participants were then "willing to call white black" by going along with the group.

Conditions That Strengthen Conformity

Asch's procedure became the model for later investigations. Although experiments have not always found so much conformity, they do reveal that conformity increases when

- one is made to feel incompetent or insecure.
- the group has at least three people.
- the group is unanimous. (The dissent of just one other person greatly increases social courage.)
- one admires the group's status and attractiveness.
- one has made no prior commitment to any response.
- others in the group observe one's behavior.
- one's culture strongly encourages respect for social standards.

Thus, we might predict the behavior of Austin, an enthusiastic but insecure new fraternity member: Noting that the 40 other members appear unanimous in their plans for a fund-raiser, Austin is unlikely to voice his dissent.

Reasons for Conforming

Fish swim in schools. Birds fly in flocks. And humans, too, tend to go with their group, to think what it thinks and do what it does. But why? Why do we clap when others clap, eat as others eat, believe what others believe, even see what others see? Frequently, it is to avoid rejection or to gain social approval. In such cases, we are responding to what social psychologists call **normative social influence.** We are sensitive to social norms—understood rules for accepted and expected behavior—because the price we pay for being different may be severe.

Marco Lokar knows. During the 1991 Persian Gulf War, Lokar, an Italian, was the only Seton Hall University basketball player who chose not to display an American flag on his uniform. As the team traveled, the fans' abusive responses to his nonconforming behavior became unbearable, so he left the team and returned to Italy. Tony Smith also knows. In 2003, when the Manhattanville College basketball player likewise dissented from the impending war with Iraq—by turning sideways and not looking at the flag during the pregame national anthem—similar outrage resulted. In one game at another college, students stood and chanted "Leave the country!"

Respecting norms is not the only reason we conform: Groups may provide valuable information, and only an uncommonly stubborn person will *never* listen to others. When we accept others' opinions about reality, we are responding to **informational social influence.** "Those who never retract their opinions love themselves more than they love truth," observed the eighteenth-century French essayist, Joseph Joubert.

"Have you ever noticed how one example—good or bad—can prompt others to follow? How one illegally parked car can give permission for others to do likewise? How one racial joke can fuel another?"

Marian Wright Edelman,
The Measure of Our Success, 1992

■ **normative social influence** influence resulting from a person's desire to gain approval or avoid disapproval.

■ **informational social influence** influence resulting from one's willingness to accept others' opinions about reality.

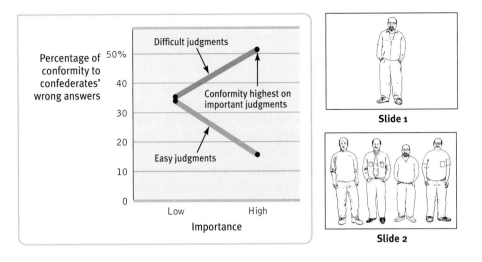

FIGURE 56.2
Informational influence
Sample task: After seeing Slides 1 and 2, participants judged which person in Slide 2 was the same as the person in Slide 1. (From Baron, Vandello, & Brunsman, 1996.)

As Rebecca Denton demonstrated in 2004, sometimes it pays to assume others are right and to follow their lead. Denton set a record for the furthest distance driven on the wrong side of a British divided highway—30 miles, with only one minor sideswipe, before the Welsh motorway ran out and police were able to puncture her tires. Denton later explained that she thought the hundreds of other drivers coming at her were all on the wrong side of the road (Woolcock, 2004).

Robert Baron and his colleagues (1996) cleverly demonstrated our openness to informational influence on tough, important judgments. They modernized the Asch experiment by showing University of Iowa students a slide of a stimulus person, followed by a slide of a four-person lineup (**FIGURE 56.2**). Their experiment made the task either easy (viewing the lineup for five seconds) or difficult (viewing the lineup for but half a second). It also led them to think their judgments as either unimportant (just a preliminary test of some eyewitness identification procedures) or as important (establishing norms for an actual police procedure, with a U.S. $20 award to the most accurate participants). When the accuracy of their judgments seemed important, people rarely conformed when the task was easy, but they conformed half the time when the task was difficult. If we are unsure of what is right, and if being right matters, we are receptive to others' opinions.

Our view of social influence as bad or good depends on our values. When influence supports what we approve, we applaud those who are "open-minded" and "sensitive" enough to be "responsive." When influence supports what we disapprove, we scorn the "submissive conformity" of those who comply with others' wishes. Cultural values also affect our tendency to conform to others' views. Cultures vary in the extent to which they value individualism or collectivism. Western Europeans and people in most English-speaking countries tend to prize individualism more than conformity and obedience. These values are reflected in social influence experiments that have been conducted in 17 countries: In individualist cultures, conformity rates are lower (Bond & Smith, 1996).

Obedience

OBJECTIVE 56-3 | Describe Milgram's experiments on obedience, and outline the conditions in which obedience was highest.

Social psychologist Stanley Milgram (1963, 1974) knew that people often comply with social pressures. But how would they respond to outright commands? To find out, he undertook what have become social psychology's most famous and controversial experiments. Imagine yourself as one of the nearly 1000 participants in Milgram's 20 experiments.

Stanley Milgram (1933–1984)
The late social psychologist's obedience experiments now "belong to the self-understanding of literate people in our age" (Sabini, 1986).

Responding to an advertisement, you come to Yale University's psychology department to participate in an experiment. Professor Milgram's assistant explains that the study concerns the effect of punishment on learning. You and another person draw slips from a hat to see who will be the "teacher" (which your slip says) and who will be the "learner." The learner is then led to an adjoining room and strapped into a chair that is wired through the wall to an electric shock machine. You sit in front of the machine, which has switches labeled with voltages. Your task: to teach and then test the learner on a list of word pairs. You are to punish the learner for wrong answers by delivering brief electric shocks, beginning with a switch labeled "15 Volts—Slight Shock." After each of the learner's errors, you are to move up to the next higher voltage. With each flick of a switch, lights flash, relay switches click on, and an electric buzzing fills the air.

If you comply with the experimenter's instructions, you hear the learner grunt when you flick the third, fourth, and fifth switches. After you activate the eighth switch (labeled "120 Volts—Moderate Shock"), the learner shouts that the shocks are painful. After the tenth switch ("150 Volts—Strong Shock"), he cries, "Get me out of here! I won't be in the experiment anymore! I refuse to go on!" When you hear these pleas, you draw back. But the experimenter prods you: "Please continue—the experiment requires that you continue." If you still resist, he insists, "It is absolutely essential that you continue," or "You have no other choice, you *must* go on."

If you obey, you hear the learner's protests escalate to shrieks of agony as you continue to raise the shock level with each succeeding error. After the 330-volt level, the learner refuses to answer and soon falls silent. Still, the experimenter pushes you toward the final, 450-volt switch, ordering you to ask the questions and, if no correct answer is given, to administer the next shock level.

How far do you think you would follow the experimenter's commands? In a survey Milgram conducted before the experiment, most people declared they would stop playing such a sadistic-seeming role soon after the learner first indicated pain and certainly before he shrieked in agony. This also was the prediction made by each of 40 psychiatrists whom Milgram asked to guess the outcome. When Milgram actually conducted the experiment with men aged 20 to 50, he was astonished to find that 63 percent complied fully—right up to the last switch. Ten later studies that included women found women's compliance rates were similar to men's (Blass, 1999).

Did the "teachers" figure out the hoax—that no shock was being delivered? Did they correctly guess the learner was a confederate who only pretended to feel the shocks? Did they realize the experiment was really testing their willingness to comply with commands to inflict punishment? No, the teachers typically displayed genuine distress: They perspired, trembled, laughed nervously, and bit their lips.

Milgram's use of deception and stress triggered a debate over his research ethics. In his own defense, Milgram pointed out that, after the participants learned of the deception and actual research purposes, virtually none regretted taking part (though perhaps by then the participants had reduced their dissonance). When 40 of the "teachers" who had agonized most were later interviewed by a psychiatrist, none appeared to be suffering emotional aftereffects. All in all, said Milgram, the experiments provoked less enduring stress than university students experience when facing and failing big exams (Blass, 1996).

Wondering whether the participants obeyed because the learners' protests were not convincing, Milgram repeated the experiment, with 40 new teachers. This time his confederate mentioned a "slight heart condition" while being strapped into the chair, and then he complained and screamed more intensely as the shocks became more punishing. Still, 65 percent of the new teachers complied fully (**FIGURE 56.3**).

"Drive off the cliff, James, I want to commit suicide."

Drawing by Mel Yauk.

Percentage of participants who obeyed experimenter

100%
90
80
70
60
50
40
30
20
10
0

The majority of participants continued to obey to the end

Slight (15–60)   Moderate (75–120)   Strong (135–180)   Very strong (195–240)   Intense (255–300)   Extreme intensity (315–360)   Danger: severe (375–420)   XXX (435–450)

Shock levels in volts

FIGURE 56.3
Milgram's follow-up obedience experiment

In a repeat of the earlier experiment, 65 percent of the adult male "teachers" fully obeyed the experimenter's commands to continue. They did so despite the "learner's" earlier mention of a heart condition and despite hearing cries of protest after 150 volts and agonized protests after 330 volts. (Data from Milgram, 1974.)

In later experiments, Milgram discovered that subtle details of a situation powerfully influence people. When he varied the social conditions, the proportion of fully compliant participants varied from 0 to 93 percent. Obedience was highest when

- the person giving the orders was close at hand and was perceived to be a legitimate authority figure. (Such was the case in 2005 when Temple University's basketball coach sent a 250-pound bench player, Nehemiah Ingram, into a game with instructions to commit "hard fouls." Following orders, Ingram fouled out in four minutes after breaking an opposing player's right arm.)
- the authority figure was supported by a prestigious institution. Compliance was somewhat lower when Milgram dissociated his experiments from Yale University.
- the victim was depersonalized or at a distance, even in another room. (Similarly, in combat with an enemy they can see, many soldiers either do not fire their rifles or do not aim them properly. Such refusals to kill are rare among those who operate the more distant weapons of artillery or aircraft [Padgett, 1989].)
- there were no role models for defiance; that is, no other participants were seen disobeying the experimenter.

The power of legitimate, close-at-hand authorities is dramatically apparent in stories of those who complied with orders to carry out the atrocities of the Holocaust, and those who didn't. Obedience alone does not explain the Holocaust; anti-Semitic ideology produced eager killers as well (Mastroianni, 2002). But obedience was a factor. In the summer of 1942 nearly 500 middle-aged German reserve police officers were dispatched to Jozefow, Poland, in German-occupied territory. On July 13, the group's visibly upset commander informed his recruits, mostly family men, that they had been ordered to round up the village's Jews, who were said to be aiding the enemy. Able-bodied men were to be sent to work camps, and all the rest were to be shot on the spot. Given a chance to refuse participation in the executions, only about a dozen immediately did so. Within 17 hours, the remaining 485 officers killed 1500 helpless women, children, and elderly by shooting them in the back of the head as they lay face down. Hearing the pleadings of the victims, and seeing the gruesome results, some 20 percent of the officers did eventually dissent, managing either to miss their victims or to wander away and hide until the slaughter was over (Browning, 1992). But in real life, as in Milgram's experiments, the disobedient were the minority.

Standing up for democracy
Some individuals—roughly one in three in Milgram's experiments—resist social coercion, as did this unarmed man in Beijing, by single-handedly challenging an advancing line of tanks the day after the 1989 Tiananmen Square student uprising was suppressed.

AP/Wide World Photos

Another story was being played out in the French village of Le Chambon, where French Jews destined for deportation to Germany were being sheltered by villagers who openly defied orders to cooperate with the "New Order." The villagers' ancestors had themselves been persecuted and their pastors had been teaching them to "resist whenever our adversaries will demand of us obedience contrary to the orders of the Gospel" (Rochat, 1993). Ordered by police to give a list of sheltered Jews, the head pastor modeled defiance: "I don't know of Jews, I only know of human beings." Without realizing how long and terrible the war would be, or how much punishment and poverty they would suffer, the resisters made an initial commitment to resist. Supported by their beliefs, their role models, their interaction with one another, and their own initial acts, they remained defiant to the war's end.

Lessons From the Conformity and Obedience Studies

OBJECTIVE **56-4** | Explain how the conformity and obedience studies can help us understand our susceptibility to social influence.

What do the Asch and Milgram experiments teach us about ourselves? How does judging the length of a line or flicking a shock switch relate to everyday social behavior? This research, like all psychological experiments, aimed not to re-create the literal behaviors of everyday life but to capture and explore the underlying processes that shape those behaviors. Asch and Milgram devised experiments in which the participants had to choose between adhering to their own standards and being responsive to others, a dilemma we all face frequently.

In Milgram's experiments, participants were also torn between what they should respond to—the pleas of the victim or the orders of the experimenter. Their moral sense warned them not to harm another, yet it also prompted them to obey the experimenter and to be a good research participant. With kindness and obedience on a collision course, obedience usually won.

Such experiments demonstrate that strong social influences can make people conform to falsehoods or capitulate to cruelty. "The most fundamental lesson of our study," Milgram noted, is that "ordinary people, simply doing their jobs, and without any particular hostility on their part, can become agents in a terrible destructive process" (1974, p. 6). Milgram did not entrap his "teachers" by asking them first to zap "learners" with enough electricity to make their hair stand on end. Rather, he exploited the foot-in-the-door effect, beginning with a little tickle of electricity and escalating step by step. In the minds of those throwing the switches, the small action became justified, making the next act tolerable. In Jozefow, in Le Chambon, and in Milgram's experiments, those who resisted usually did so early. After the first acts of compliance or resistance, attitudes began to follow and justify behavior.

So it happens when people succumb, gradually, to evil. In any society, great evils sometimes grow out of people's compliance with lesser evils. The Nazi leaders suspected that most German civil servants would resist shooting or gassing Jews directly, but they

"I was only following orders."
Adolf Eichmann, Director of Nazi deportation of Jews to concentration camps

found them surprisingly willing to handle the paperwork of the Holocaust (Silver & Geller, 1978). Likewise, when Milgram asked 40 men to administer the learning test while someone else did the shocking, 93 percent complied. Contrary to images of devilish villains, evil does not require monstrous characters; all it takes is ordinary people corrupted by an evil situation—ordinary soldiers who follow orders to torture prisoners, ordinary students who follow orders to haze initiates into their group, ordinary employees who follow orders to produce and market harmful products. Before leading the 9/11 attacks, Mohamed Atta reportedly was a sane, rational person who had been a "good boy" and an excellent student from a close-knit family—not someone who fits our image of evil monster.

> "The normal reaction to an abnormal situation is abnormal behavior."
> James Waller, *Becoming Evil: How Ordinary People Commit Genocide and Mass Killing*, 2006

Group Influence

How do groups affect our behavior? To find out, social psychologists study the various influences that operate in the simplest of groups—one person in the presence of another—and those that operate in more complex groups, such as families, teams, and committees.

Individual Behavior in the Presence of Others

OBJECTIVE 56-5 | Describe the conditions in which the presence of others is likely to result in social facilitation, social loafing, or deindividuation.

Appropriately, social psychology's first experiments focused on the simplest of all questions about social behavior: How are we influenced by the mere presence of others—by people watching us or joining us in various activities?

Social Facilitation

Having noticed that cyclists' racing times were faster when they competed against each other than when they competed with a clock, Norman Triplett (1898) hypothesized that the presence of others boosts performance. To test his hypothesis, Triplett had adolescents wind a fishing reel as rapidly as possible. He discovered that they wound the reel faster in the presence of someone doing the same thing. This phenomenon of stronger performance in others' presence is called **social facilitation.** For example, after a light turns green, drivers take about 15 percent less time to travel the first 100 yards when another car is beside them at the intersection than when they are alone (Towler, 1986).

But now things get tricky. On tougher tasks (learning nonsense syllables or solving complex multiplication problems), people perform *less* well when observers or others working on the same task are present. Further studies revealed why the presence of others sometimes helps and sometimes hinders performance (Guerin, 1986; Zajonc, 1965). When others observe us, we become aroused. This arousal strengthens the most *likely* response—the correct one on an easy task, an incorrect one on a difficult task. Thus, when we are being observed, we perform well-learned tasks more quickly and accurately, and unmastered tasks less quickly and accurately. James Michaels and his associates (1982) found that expert pool players who made 71 percent of their shots when alone made 80 percent when four people came to watch them. Poor shooters, who made 36 percent of their shots when alone, made only 25 percent when watched. The energizing effect of an enthusiastic audience probably contributes to the home advantage enjoyed by various sports teams. Studies of more than 80,000 college and professional athletic events in Canada, the United States, and England reveal that home teams win about 6 in 10

Michelle Agins/NYT Pictures

Social facilitation
Skilled athletes often find they are "on" before an audience. What they do well, they do even better when people are watching.

◼ **social facilitation** stronger responses on simple or well-learned tasks in the presence of others.

TABLE 56.1

HOME ADVANTAGE IN MAJOR TEAM SPORTS

Sport	Games Studied	Home Team Winning Percentage
Baseball	23,034	53.5%
Football	2,592	57.3
Ice hockey	4,322	61.1
Basketball	13,596	64.4
Soccer	37,202	69.0

From Courneya & Carron, 1992

games (somewhat fewer for baseball and football, somewhat more for basketball and soccer—see **TABLE 56.1**).

The point to remember: What you do well, you are likely to do even better in front of an audience, especially a friendly audience; what you normally find difficult may seem all but impossible when you are being watched.

Social facilitation also helps explain a funny effect of crowding: Comedy records that are mildly amusing to people in an uncrowded room seem funnier in a densely packed room (Aiello & others, 1983; Freedman & Perlick, 1979). As comedians and actors know, a "good house" is a full one. The arousal triggered by crowding amplifies other reactions, too. If sitting close to one another, participants in experiments like a friendly person even more, an unfriendly person even less (Schiffenbauer & Schiavo, 1976; Storms & Thomas, 1977). The practical lesson: If choosing a room for a class or setting up chairs for a gathering, have barely enough seating.

Social Loafing

Social facilitation experiments test the effect of others' presence on performance on an individual task, such as shooting pool. But what happens to performance when people perform the task as a group? In a team tug-of-war, for example, do you suppose the effort a person puts forth would be more than, less than, or the same as the effort he or she would exert in a one-on-one tug-of-war? To find out, Alan Ingham and his fellow researchers (1974) asked blindfolded University of Massachusetts students to "pull as hard as you can" on a rope. When Ingham fooled the students into believing three others were also pulling behind them, they exerted only 82 percent as much effort as when they knew they were pulling alone.

To describe this diminished effort, Bibb Latané (1981; Jackson & Williams, 1988) coined the term **social loafing.** In 78 experiments conducted in the United States, India, Thailand, Japan, China, and Taiwan, social loafing occurred on various tasks, though it was especially common among men in individualistic cultures (Karau & Williams, 1993). In one of Latané's experiments, blindfolded people seated in a group clapped or shouted as loud as they could while listening through headphones to the sound of loud clapping or shouting. When told they were doing it with the others, the participants produced about one-third less noise than when they thought their individual efforts were identifiable.

Why this social loafing? First, people acting as part of a group feel less accountable and therefore worry less about what others think. Second, they may view their contribution as dispensable (Harkins & Szymanski, 1989; Kerr & Bruun, 1983). As many leaders of organizations know—and as you have perhaps observed on student group assignments—if group members share equally in the benefits regardless of how much they contribute, some may slack off. Unless highly motivated and identified with their group, they may free-ride on the other group members' efforts.

Deindividuation

So, the presence of others can arouse people (as in the social facilitation experiments) or can diminish their feelings of responsibility (as in the social loafing experiments). But sometimes the presence of others both arouses people *and* diminishes their sense of responsibility. The result can be uninhibited behavior ranging from a food fight in the dining hall or screaming at a basketball referee to vandalism or rioting. Abandoning normal restraints to the power of the group is termed **deindividuation.** To be deindividuated is to be less self-conscious and less restrained when in a group situation.

Deindividuation often occurs when group participation makes people feel aroused and anonymous. In one experiment, New York University women dressed in depersonalizing Ku Klux Klan-style hoods delivered twice as much electric shock to a victim as did identifiable women (Zimbardo, 1970). (As in all such experiments, the "victim" did not actually receive the shocks.) Similarly, tribal warriors who depersonalize

■ **social loafing** the tendency for people in a group to exert less effort when pooling their efforts toward attaining a common goal than when individually accountable.

■ **deindividuation** the loss of self-awareness and self-restraint occurring in group situations that foster arousal and anonymity.

■ **group polarization** the enhancement of a group's prevailing inclinations through discussion within the group.

themselves with face paints or masks are more likely than those with exposed faces to kill, torture, or mutilate captured enemies (Watson, 1973). Whether in a mob, at a rock concert, at a ballgame, or at worship, to lose self-consciousness (to become deindividuated) is to become more responsive to the group experience.

Effects of Group Interaction

OBJECTIVE 56-6 | Discuss how group interaction can facilitate group polarization and groupthink.

We have examined the conditions under which being in the *presence* of others can

- motivate people to exert themselves or tempt them to free-ride on the efforts of others.
- make easy tasks easier and difficult tasks harder.
- enhance humor or fuel mob violence.

Research shows that *interacting* with others can similarly have both bad and good effects.

Group Polarization

Educational researchers have noted that, over time, initial differences between groups of college students tend to grow. If the first-year students at College X tend to be more intellectually oriented than those at College Y, that difference will probably be amplified by the time they are seniors. Similarly, if the political conservatism of students who join fraternities and sororities is greater than that of students who do not, the gap in the political attitudes of the two groups will probably widen as they progress through college (Wilson & others, 1975). Likewise, notes Eleanor Maccoby (2002) from her decades of observing gender development, girls talk more intimately than boys do and play and fantasize less aggressively—and these gender differences widen over time as they interact mostly with their own gender.

This enhancement of a group's prevailing tendencies—called **group polarization**—occurs when people within a group discuss an idea that most of them either favor or oppose. Group polarization can have beneficial results, as when it amplifies a sought-after spiritual awareness or reinforces the resolve of those in a self-help group, or strengthens feelings of tolerance in a low-prejudice group. But it can also have dire consequences. George Bishop and I discovered that when high-prejudice students discussed racial issues, they became *more* prejudiced (**FIGURE 56.4**). (Low-prejudice students became even more accepting.) The experiment's ideological separation and polarization finds a seeming parallel in the growing polarization of American politics. The percentage of landslide counties—voting 60 percent or more for one presidential candidate—increased from 26 percent in 1976 to 48 percent in 2004 (Bishop, 2004). More and more, people are living near and learning from others who think as they do.

The polarizing effect of interaction among the like-minded applies not only to U.S. "red" and "blue" states, but also to suicide terrorists. After analyzing terrorist organizations around the world, psychologists Clark McCauley and Mary Segal (1987; McCauley, 2002) noted that the terrorist mentality does not erupt suddenly. Rather, it usually arises among people who get together because of a grievance and then become more and more extreme as they interact in isolation from any moderating influences. Increasingly, group members (who may be isolated with other "brothers" and "sisters" in camps) categorize the world as "us" and "them" (Moghaddam, 2005; Qirko, 2004). Suicide terrorism virtually never is done on a personal whim, reports researcher Ariel Merari (2002).

FIGURE 56.4
Group polarization
If a group is like-minded, discussion strengthens its prevailing opinions. Talking over racial issues increased prejudice in a high-prejudice group of high school students and decreased it in a low-prejudice group (Myers & Bishop, 1970).

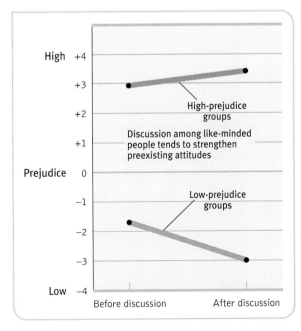

The Internet provides a medium for group polarization. Its tens of thousands of virtual groups enable bereaved parents, peacemakers, and teachers to find solace and support from kindred spirits. But the Internet also enables people who share interests in government cover-ups, extraterrestrial visitors, white supremacy, or citizen militias to find one another and to find support for their shared suspicions (McKenna & Bargh, 1998).

Groupthink

Does group interaction ever distort important decisions? Social psychologist Irving Janis began to think so as he read historian Arthur M. Schlesinger, Jr.'s account of how President John F. Kennedy and his advisers blundered into an ill-fated plan to invade Cuba with 1400 CIA-trained Cuban exiles. When the invaders were easily captured and soon linked to the U.S. government, Kennedy wondered in hindsight, "How could we have been so stupid?"

To find out, Janis (1982) studied the decision-making procedures that led to the fiasco. He discovered that the soaring morale of the recently elected president and his advisers fostered undue confidence in the plan. To preserve the good group feeling, any dissenting views were suppressed or self-censored, especially after President Kennedy voiced his enthusiasm for the scheme. Since no one spoke strongly against the idea, everyone assumed consensus support. To describe this harmonious but unrealistic group thinking, Janis coined the term **groupthink.**

Janis and others then examined other historical fiascos—the failure to anticipate the 1941 Japanese attack on Pearl Harbor, the escalation of the Vietnam War, the U.S. Watergate cover-up, the Chernobyl nuclear reactor accident (Reason, 1987), and the U.S. space shuttle *Challenger* explosion (Esser & Lindoerfer, 1989). They discovered that in these cases, too, groupthink was fed by overconfidence, conformity, self-justification, and group polarization.

Groupthink surfaced again, reported the U.S. Senate Intelligence Committee (2004), when "personnel involved in the Iraq WMD issue demonstrated several aspects of groupthink: examining few alternatives, selective gathering of information, pressure to conform within the group or withhold criticism, and collective rationalization." This groupthink led analysts to "interpret ambiguous evidence as conclusively indicative of a WMD program as well as ignore or minimize evidence that Iraq did not have [WMD] programs."

Despite such fiascos and tragedies, two heads are better than one in solving some types of problems. Knowing this, Janis also studied instances in which U.S. presidents and their advisers collectively made good decisions, such as when the Truman administration formulated the Marshall Plan, which offered assistance to Europe after World War II, and when the Kennedy administration worked to keep the Soviets from installing missiles in Cuba. In such instances—and in the business world, too, Janis believed—groupthink is prevented when a leader welcomes various opinions, invites experts' critiques of developing plans, and assigns people to identify possible problems. Just as the suppression of dissent bends a group toward bad decisions, so open debate often shapes good ones. None of us is as smart as all of us.

The Power of Individuals

OBJECTIVE 56-7 | Identify the characteristic common to minority positions that sway majorities.

In affirming the power of social influence, we must not overlook our power as individuals. *Social control* (the power of the situation) and *personal control* (the power of the individual) interact. People aren't billiard balls. When feeling pressured, we may react by doing the opposite of what is expected, thereby reasserting our sense of freedom (Brehm & Brehm, 1981).

"One's impulse to blow the whistle on this nonsense was simply undone by the circumstances of the discussion."
Arthur M. Schlesinger, Jr., *A Thousand Days*, 1965

"Truth springs from argument among friends."
Philosopher David Hume, 1711–1776

■ **groupthink** the mode of thinking that occurs when the desire for harmony in a decision-making group overrides a realistic appraisal of alternatives.

Such was the experience of three individual soldiers at the Abu Ghraib prison (O'Connor, 2004). Lt. David Sutton put an end to one incident, which he reported to his commanders. Navy dog-handler William Kimbro refused pressure to participate in improper interrogations using his attack dogs. Specialist Joseph Darby brought visual images of the horrors into the light of day, providing incontestable evidence of the atrocities. Each risked ridicule or even court-martial for not following orders.

As these three soldiers discovered, committed individuals can sway the majority and make social history. Were this not so, communism would have remained an obscure theory, Christianity would be a small Middle Eastern sect,

Margaret Bourke-White/Life Magazine. © 1946 Time Warner, Inc.

Gandhi
As the life of Mahatma Gandhi powerfully testifies, a consistent and persistent minority voice can sometimes sway the majority. The nonviolent appeals and fasts of the Hindu nationalist and spiritual leader were instrumental in winning India's independence from Britain in 1947.

and Rosa Parks' refusal to sit at the back of the bus would not have ignited the civil rights movement. Technological history, too, is often made by innovative minorities who overcome the majority's resistance to change. To many, the railroad was a nonsensical idea; some farmers even feared that train noise would prevent hens from laying eggs. People derided Robert Fulton's steamboat as "Fulton's Folly." As Fulton later said, "Never did a single encouraging remark, a bright hope, a warm wish, cross my path." Much the same reaction greeted the printing press, the telegraph, the incandescent lamp, and the typewriter (Cantril & Bumstead, 1960).

European social psychologists have sought to better understand *minority influence*—the power of one or two individuals to sway majorities (Moscovici, 1985). They investigated groups in which one or two individuals consistently expressed a controversial attitude or an unusual perceptual judgment. They repeatedly found that a minority that unswervingly holds to its position is far more successful in swaying the majority than is a minority that waffles. Holding consistently to a minority opinion will not make you popular, but it may make you influential. This is especially so if your self-confidence stimulates others to consider why you react as you do. Although people often follow the majority view publicly, they may privately develop sympathy for the minority view. Even when a minority's influence is not yet visible, it may be persuading some members of the majority to rethink their views (Wood & others, 1994). The powers of social influence are enormous, but so are the powers of the committed individual.

>> LEARNING OUTCOMES

Social Influence

OBJECTIVE 56-1 | **Describe the chameleon effect, and give an example of it.**

The *chameleon effect* is our tendency to unconsciously mimic those around us, as when we pick up the mood of a happy or sad person. Automatic mimicry is an ingredient in the ability to empathize with others.

OBJECTIVE 56-2 | **Discuss Asch's experiments on conformity, and distinguish between normative and informational social influence.**

Solomon Asch found that people will conform to a group's judgment even when it is clearly incorrect. Conformity increases when we feel incompetent or insecure, admire the group's status and attractiveness, have made no prior commitment to a response, are being observed by members of the group, come from a culture that strongly encourages respect for group standards, and are in a group with at least three members, all unanimous in their decision. We may conform either to gain social approval (*normative social influence*—especially likely when we are unsure of what is right and being right matters) or because we welcome the information that others provide (*informational social influence*).

OBJECTIVE 56-3 | **Describe Milgram's experiments on obedience, and outline the conditions in which obedience was highest.**

In Stanley Milgram's experiments, people torn between obeying an experimenter and responding to another's pleas to stop the shocks usually chose to obey orders, even though obedience supposedly meant harming the other person. People were most likely to obey when the person giving orders was nearby and was perceived as a legitimate authority figure; the person giving orders was supported by a prestigious institution; the victim was depersonalized or at a distance; and no other person modeled defiance by disobeying.

OBJECTIVE 56-4 | **Explain how the conformity and obedience studies can help us understand our susceptibility to social influence.**

In the conformity studies, randomly chosen ordinary people conformed in spite of their own beliefs. In the obedience studies, randomly chosen people obeyed instructions to deliver punishments that, if real, would have harmed total strangers. People who resisted instructions did so early; after that, attitudes followed behavior. Understanding these tendencies could make us less susceptible to powerful social influences in our own lives.

OBJECTIVE 56-5 | **Describe the conditions in which the presence of others is likely to result in social facilitation, social loafing, or deindividuation.**

The presence of either observers or co-actors boosts arousal, strengthening our most likely response. This *social facilitation* tends to increase performance on easy or well-learned tasks but decrease it on difficult or newly learned ones. In the presence of others pooling their efforts toward a group goal, *social loafing* may occur, as some individuals ride free on the efforts of others. *Deindividuation,* a psychological state in which people become less self-aware and self-restrained, may result when a group experience arouses people and makes them feel anonymous.

OBJECTIVE 56-6 | **Discuss how group interaction can facilitate group polarization and groupthink.**

Discussion among like-minded people often produces *group polarization,* an enhancement of the group's prevailing opinions. This process fosters *groupthink,* as groups pressure members to conform, suppress dissenting information, and fail to consider alternatives. To prevent groupthink, leaders can welcome a variety of opinions, invite experts' critiques, and assign people to identify possible problems in developing plans.

OBJECTIVE 56-7 | **Identify the characteristic common to minority positions that sway majorities.**

Minorities that successfully sway group opinions usually express their views consistently.

TERMS AND CONCEPTS TO REMEMBER

conformity, p. 56-1
normative social influence, p. 56-1
informational social influence, p. 56-1
social facilitation, p. 56-7
social loafing, p. 56-8
deindividuation, p. 56-8
group polarization, p. 56-9
groupthink, p. 56-10

TEST YOURSELF

1. You are organizing a Town Hall–style meeting of fiercely competitive political candidates. To add to the fun, friends have suggested handing out masks of the candidates' faces for supporters to wear. What phenomenon might these masks engage?

(Answer in Appendix B.)

ASK YOURSELF

1. What two examples of social influence have you experienced this week? (Remember, influence may be informational.)

>WEB

Multiple-choice *self-tests* and more may be found at www.worthpublishers.com/myers.

57

MODULE

Antisocial Relations

Social psychology studies how we think about and influence one another, and also how we *relate* to one another. What causes us to harm or to help or to fall in love? How can we transform the closed fists of aggression into the open arms of compassion? In this module we ponder insights into *antisocial* relations gleaned by researchers who have studied prejudice, aggression, and conflict.

Prejudice

OBJECTIVE 57-1 | Identify the three components of prejudice.

Prejudice means "prejudgment." It is an unjustifiable and usually negative attitude toward a group—often a different cultural, ethnic, or gender group. Like all attitudes, **prejudice** is a mixture of *beliefs* (called **stereotypes**), *emotions* (hostility, envy, or fear), and predispositions to *action* (to discriminate). To *believe* that overweight people are gluttonous, to *feel* antipathy for an overweight person, and to be hesitant to hire or date an overweight person is to be prejudiced. Prejudice is a negative *attitude;* **discrimination** is a negative *behavior.*

Like other forms of prejudgment, prejudices are schemas that influence how we notice and interpret events. In one 1970s study, most white participants perceived a white man shoving a black man as "horsing around." When they saw a black man shove a white man, they interpreted the act as "violent" (Duncan, 1976). Our preconceived ideas about people bias our impressions of their behavior. Prejudgments color perceptions.

How Prejudiced Are People?

OBJECTIVE 57-2 | Contrast overt and subtle forms of prejudice, and give examples of each.

To learn about levels of prejudice, we can assess what people say and what they do. To judge by what Americans say, gender and racial attitudes have changed dramatically in the last half-century. The one-third of Americans who in 1937 said they would vote for a qualified woman whom their party nominated for president soared to 87 percent in 2003 (Jones & Moore, 2003). Support for all forms of racial contact, including interracial marriage (**FIGURE 57.1** on the next page), has also dramatically increased. Nearly everyone agrees that children of all races should attend the same schools and that women and men should receive the same pay for the same job.

Yet as overt prejudice wanes, subtle prejudice lingers. Despite increased verbal support for interracial marriage, many people admit that in socially intimate settings (dating, dancing, marrying) they would feel uncomfortable with someone of another race. And in Western Europe, where many "guest workers" and refugees settled at the end of the twentieth century, "modern prejudice"—rejecting immigrant minorities as job applicants for supposedly nonracial reasons—has been replacing blatant prejudice (Jackson & others, 2001; Pettigrew, 1998). A slew of recent experiments illustrate that prejudice can be not only subtle but also automatic and unconscious (see Close-Up: Automatic Prejudice two pages from here).

■ **prejudice** an unjustifiable (and usually negative) attitude toward a group and its members. Prejudice generally involves stereotyped beliefs, negative feelings, and a predisposition to discriminatory action.

■ **stereotype** a generalized (sometimes accurate but often overgeneralized) belief about a group of people.

■ **discrimination** unjustifiable negative behavior toward a group or its members.

FIGURE **57.1**
Prejudice over time
Americans' approval of interracial marriage has soared over the past half-century. (Gallup surveys reported by Ludwig, 2004.)

> "Unhappily the world has yet to learn how to live with diversity."
>
> Pope John Paul II, Address to the United Nations, 1995

But prejudice still surfaces in public settings. In a 2004 survey of Europeans, 6 in 10 people in both Britain and Germany said immigrants are a bad influence on their country (Lester, 2004). In most places in the world, gays and lesbians cannot comfortably acknowledge who they are and whom they love. In several U.S. states where black motorists are a minority of the drivers and speeders on interstate highways, they have been the majority of those stopped and searched by state police (Lamberth, 1998; Staples, 1999a,b). In one New Jersey turnpike study, African-Americans were 13.5 percent of the car occupants, 15 percent of the speeders, and 35 percent of the drivers stopped. Elmo Randolph, a New Jersey dentist, knew it all along. After being stopped more than 100 times over four years while driving his gold BMW from his home to his office, Dr. Randolph, guilty of nothing more than "driving while black," sold the car.

Gender prejudice and discrimination persist, too. Despite gender equality in intelligence scores, people tend to perceive their fathers as more intelligent than their mothers (Furnham & Rawles, 1995). In Saudi Arabia, women are not allowed to drive. In Western countries, we pay more to those (usually men) who drive machines that take care of our streets than to those (usually women) who take care of our children. Worldwide, women are more likely to live in poverty (Lipps, 1999), and their 69 percent literacy rate is well below men's 83 percent (PRB, 2002).

Female infants are no longer left out on a hillside to die of exposure, as was the practice in ancient Greece. Yet even today boys are often valued more than their sisters. During the 1970s Bangladesh famine, preschool girls were more malnourished than boys were, and in many developing countries death rates are higher for girls than for boys (Bairagi, 1987). With testing that enables sex-selective abortions, several south Asian countries, including certain regions of China and India, have experienced a shortfall in female births. Natural female mortality and the normal 105-to-100 male-to-female birth ratio hardly explains the world's estimated 101 million (say that number slowly) "missing women" (Sen, 2003). In 2005, China announced that the newborn sex ratio had reached 119 boys for every 100 girls (Yardley, 2005). With demographic predictions of 40 million Chinese bachelors unable to find mates, China has declared that sex-selective abortions—gender genocide—are now a criminal offense.

Suppose that you could only have one child. Would you prefer that it be a boy or a girl? When Gallup asked that question of Americans, two-thirds expressed a gender preference, and for two-thirds of those—in 2003 as in 1941—it was for a boy (Lyons, 2003). But the news isn't all bad for girls and women. Most people *feel* more positively about women in general than they do about men (Eagly, 1994;

AUTOMATIC PREJUDICE

As we have seen throughout this book, we process information on two levels: conscious and unconscious. To some extent, our thinking, our memories, and our attitudes are *explicit*—on the radar screen of our awareness. And to an even greater extent, today's researchers believe, they are *implicit*—below the radar, out-of-sight. Modern studies of implicit, automatic attitudes indicate that prejudice is often more of an unthinking knee-jerk response than a decision. Consider these findings on U.S. racial prejudice:

Implicit racial associations Anthony Greenwald and his colleagues (1998) showed that even people who deny harboring racial prejudice may carry negative associations. For example, 9 in 10 white respondents took longer to identify pleasant words (such as *peace* and *paradise*) as "good" when good was presented with black rather than white faces. Moreover, report Kurt Hugenberg and Galen Bodenhausen (2003), people who displayed the most *implicit prejudice* on this test also were the quickest to perceive anger and apparent threat in black faces.

Unconscious patronization Kent Harber (1998) asked white university women to evaluate a flawed essay said to be written by a black or a white fellow student. When they believed the

writer was black, the women gave markedly *higher* ratings and never expressed the harsh criticisms they assigned to white-authored essays, such as "When I read college work this bad I just want to lay my head down on the table and cry." Did the evaluators calibrate their evaluations to their racial stereotypes, Harber wondered, leading them to patronize the black writers with less exacting standards? If used in real-world evaluations, such low expectations and the resulting "inflated praise and insufficient criticism" could hinder minority student achievement. (To preclude such bias, many teachers read essays while "blind" to their authors.)

Race-influenced perceptions Two research teams were curious about the shooting of an unarmed man in the doorway of his Bronx apartment building by officers who mistook his wallet for a gun. Each research team reenacted the situation, asking people to press buttons quickly to "shoot" or not shoot men who suddenly appeared on screen holding either a gun or a harmless object such as a flashlight or bottle (Correll & others, 2002; Greenwald & others, 2003). People (both Blacks and Whites, in one of the studies) more often mistakenly shot targets who were black.

Seeing black Several studies show that the more a person's features are perceived as typical of their racial category, the more likely they are to elicit race-based responding (Maddox, 2004). In one study of 182 police officers, Jennifer Eberhardt and her collaborators (2004) found that "black faces looked more criminal to police officers; the more black, the more criminal."

Reflexive bodily responses Today's biopsychosocial approach has stimulated neuroscience studies that measure people's instant responses to viewing white and black faces. These studies have detected implicit prejudice in people's facial-muscle responses and in the activation of their amygdala, an emotion-processing center (Cunningham & others, 2004; Eberhardt, 2005; Vanman & others, 2004). Even people who consciously express little prejudice may give off telltale signals as their body responds selectively to another's race.

If your own gut check sometimes reveals feelings you would rather not have about other people, be assured that you are not alone. It is what we do with our feelings that matters. By monitoring our feelings and actions, and by replacing old habits with new ones based on new friendships, we can free ourselves from prejudice.

Haddock & Zanna, 1994). People worldwide see women as having some traits, such as nurturance, sensitivity, and less aggressiveness, that most people prefer (Glick & others, 2004; Swim, 1994). That may explain why women tend to like women more than men like men (Rudman & Goodwin, 2004). And perhaps that is also why peo-

ple prefer slightly feminized computer-generated faces—men's and women's—to slightly masculinized faces. Researcher David Perrett and his colleagues (1998) speculate that a slightly feminized male face connotes kindness, cooperativeness, and other traits of a good father. When the British Broadcasting Company invited 18,000 women to guess which of the men in **FIGURE 57.2** was most likely to place a personal ad seeking a "special lady to love and cherish forever," 66 percent guessed the slightly feminized face (b).

(a)   (b)

Professor Dave Perrett, St. Andrews University

FIGURE 57.2
Who do you like best?
Which one placed an ad seeking a special lady to love and cherish forever? (See this module's final page.)

Social Roots of Prejudice

OBJECTIVE 57-3 | Discuss the social factors that contribute to prejudice.

Why does prejudice arise? Inequalities, social divisions, and emotional scapegoating are partly responsible.

Social Inequalities

When some people have money, power, and prestige and others do not, the "haves" usually develop attitudes that justify things as they are. In the extreme case, slave owners perceived slaves as innately lazy, ignorant, and irresponsible—as having the very traits that "justified" enslaving them. More commonly, women are perceived as unassertive but sensitive and therefore suited for the caretaking tasks they have traditionally performed (Hoffman & Hurst, 1990). In short, prejudice rationalizes inequalities.

Discrimination also increases prejudice through the reactions it provokes in its victims. In his classic 1954 book, *The Nature of Prejudice*, Gordon Allport noted that being a victim of discrimination can produce either self-blame or anger. Both reactions may create new grounds for prejudice through the classic *blame-the-victim* dynamic. If the circumstances of poverty breed a higher crime rate, someone can then use the higher crime rate to justify continuing the discrimination against those who live in poverty.

Us and Them: Ingroup and Outgroup

Thanks to our ancestral need to belong, we are a group-bound species. We cheer for our groups, kill for them, die for them. Indeed, we define who we are—our identities—partly in terms of our groups. Australian psychologists John Turner (1987) and Michael Hogg (1996) note that through our *social identities* we associate ourselves with certain groups and contrast ourselves with others. When Ian identifies himself as a man, an Aussie, a Labourite, a University of Sydney student, a Catholic, and a MacGregor, he knows who he is, and so do we.

The social definition of who you are also implies who you are not. Mentally drawing a circle that defines "us" (the **ingroup**) excludes "them" (the **outgroup**). Such group identifications typically promote an **ingroup bias**—a favoring of one's own group. Even arbitrarily creating an us-them distinction—by grouping people with the toss of a coin—leads people to show favoritism to their own group when dividing any rewards (Tajfel, 1982; Wilder, 1981).

The ingroup
Scotland's famed "Tartan Army" football fans, shown here during a match against archrival England, share a social identity that defines "us" (the Scottish ingroup) and "them" (the English outgroup).

Mike Hewitt/Getty Images

Eric Travers/EPA/Landov

French fury
Members of France's marginalized ethnic groups reached the tipping point for tolerance in 2005, when they began destructive rioting.

The urge to distinguish enemies from friends and to have one's group be dominant predisposes prejudice against strangers (Whitley, 1999). To Greeks of the classical era, all non-Greeks were "barbarians." Most children believe their own school is better than the other schools in town. Many high school students form cliques—jocks, goths, skaters, gangsters, freaks, geeks—and disparage those outside their group. Even chimpanzees have been seen to wipe clean the spot where they were touched by a chimp from another group (Goodall, 1986).

Emotional Roots of Prejudice

OBJECTIVE 57-4 | Explain how scapegoating illustrates the emotional component of prejudice.

Prejudice springs not only from the divisions of society but also from the passions of the heart. Facing the terror of death tends to heighten patriotism and produce loathing and aggression toward "them"—those who threaten one's worldview (Pyszczynski & others, 2002). Recalling such terror may alter attitudes, as happened to participants when Mark Landau and eight others (2004) reminded them of their own mortality or of the terror of 9/11. This reminder of terror led to their expressing increased support for President Bush (a phenomenon harnessed by the president's 2004 campaign).

Prejudice may also express anger: When things go wrong, finding someone to blame can provide a target, a scapegoat, for one's anger. In the late 1600s, New England settlers, after suffering devastating losses at the hands of Native Americans and their French allies, lashed out by hanging people as supposed witches (Norton, 2002). Following 9/11, some outraged people lashed out at innocent Arab-Americans, about whom negative stereotypes blossomed. Calls to eliminate Saddam Hussein, whom Americans had been grudgingly tolerating, also increased. "Fear and anger create aggression, and aggression against citizens of different ethnicity or race creates racism and, in turn, new forms of terrorism," noted Philip Zimbardo (2001).

Evidence for this **scapegoat theory** of prejudice comes from high prejudice levels among economically frustrated people and from experiments in which a temporary frustration intensifies prejudice. In experiments, students who experience failure or are made to feel insecure will often restore their self-esteem by disparaging a rival school or another person (Cialdini & Richardson, 1980; Crocker & others, 1987). To boost our own sense of status, it helps to have others to denigrate. That is why a rival's misfortune sometimes provides a twinge of pleasure. By contrast, those made to feel loved and supported become more open to and accepting of others who differ (Mikulincer & Shaver, 2001).

> All good people agree,
> And all good people say
> All nice people, like us, are We
> And everyone else is They.
> But if you cross over the sea
> Instead of over the way
> You may end by (think of it)
> Looking on We
> As only a sort of They."
>
> Rudyard Kipling, "We and They," 1926

> If the Tiber reaches the walls, if the Nile does not rise to the fields, if the sky doesn't move or the Earth does, if there is famine, if there is plague, the cry is at once: 'The Christians to the lions!'"
>
> Tertullian, *Apologeticus*, A.D. 197

■ **ingroup** "Us"—people with whom one shares a common identity.

■ **outgroup** "Them"—those perceived as different or apart from one's ingroup.

■ **ingroup bias** the tendency to favor one's own group.

■ **scapegoat theory** the theory that prejudice offers an outlet for anger by providing someone to blame.

Cognitive Roots of Prejudice

OBJECTIVE 57-5 | Cite four ways that cognitive processes help create and maintain prejudice.

Prejudice springs from the divisions of society, the passions of the heart, and also from the mind's natural workings. Stereotyped beliefs are a by-product of how we cognitively simplify the world.

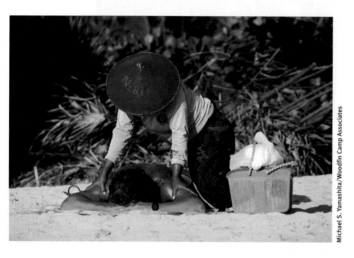

Do people of another race look alike?
Foreign sunbathers on Bali's beaches may think they do. Balinese masseuses wear identifying numbers on their hats, enabling visitors to recognize them easily.

Categorization

One way we simplify our world is to categorize. A chemist categorizes molecules as organic and inorganic. A mental health professional categorizes psychological disorders by types. In categorizing people into groups, however, we often stereotype them, biasing our perceptions of their diversity. We recognize how greatly we differ from other individuals in our groups. But we overestimate the similarity of those within other groups. "They"—the members of some other group—seem to look and act alike, but "we" are diverse (Bothwell & others, 1989). To those in one ethnic group, members of another often seem more alike in appearance, personality, and attitudes than they are. With experience, however, people get better at recognizing individual faces from another group. For example, people of European descent more accurately identify individual African faces if they have watched a great deal of basketball on television, exposing them to many African-heritage faces (Li & others, 1996).

Vivid Cases

We often judge the frequency of events by instances that readily come to mind. In a classic experiment, Myron Rothbart and his colleagues (1978) demonstrated this ability to overgeneralize from vivid, memorable cases. They divided University of Oregon student volunteers into two groups, then showed them information about 50 men. The first group's list included 10 men arrested for nonviolent crimes, such as forgery. The second group's list included 10 men arrested for violent crimes, such as assault. Later when both groups recalled how many men on their list had committed any sort of crime, the second group overestimated the number. Vivid (violent) cases are readily available to our memory and therefore influence our judgments of a group (**FIGURE 57.3**).

FIGURE 57.3
Vivid cases feed stereotypes
The 9/11 Muslim terrorists created, in many minds, an exaggerated stereotype of Muslims as terror-prone. Actually, reported a National Research Council panel on terrorism, when offering the inexact illustration at right, most terrorists are not Muslim and "the vast majority of Islamic people have no connection with and do not sympathize with terrorism" (Smelser & Mitchell, 2002).

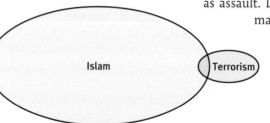

The Just-World Phenomenon

As we noted earlier, people often justify their prejudice by blaming its victims. Bystanders, too, may blame victims by assuming the world is just and therefore "people get what they deserve." In experiments, merely observing someone receive painful shocks has led many people to think less of the victim (Lerner, 1980). This **just-world phenomenon** reflects an idea we commonly teach our children—that good is rewarded and evil is punished. From this it is but a short leap to assume that those who succeed must be good and those who suffer must be bad. Such reasoning enables the rich to see both their own wealth and the poor's misfortune as justly deserved. As one German civilian is said to have remarked when visiting the Bergen-Belsen concentration camp shortly after World War II, "What terrible criminals these prisoners must have been to receive such treatment."

Hindsight bias is also at work here (Carli & Leonard, 1989). Have you ever heard people say that rape victims, abused spouses, or people with AIDS got what they deserved? In some countries, women who have been raped have been sentenced to severe punishment for having violated a law against adultery (Mydans, 2002). An experiment by Ronnie Janoff-Bulman and her collaborators (1985) illustrates this phenomenon of blaming the victim. When given a detailed account of a date that ended with the woman's being raped, people perceived the woman's behavior as at least partly to blame. In hindsight, they thought, "She should have known better." (Blaming the victim also serves to reassure people that it couldn't happen to them.) Others, given the same account with the rape ending deleted, did not perceive the woman's behavior as inviting rape.

Aggression

OBJECTIVE 57-6 | Explain how psychology's definition of *aggression* differs from everyday usage.

The most destructive force in our social relations is aggression. In psychology, *aggression* has a more precise meaning than it does in everyday usage. The assertive, persistent salesperson is not aggressive. Nor is the dentist who makes you wince with pain. But the person who passes along a vicious rumor about you, the person who verbally assaults you, and the attacker who mugs you are aggressive. In psychology, **aggression** is any physical or verbal behavior intended to hurt or destroy, whether done reactively out of hostility or proactively as a calculated means to an end. Thus, murders and assaults that occurred as hostile outbursts are aggression. So were the 110 million war-related deaths that took place during the last century, many of which were cool and calculated.

Aggression research affirms that behavior emerges from the interaction of biology and experience. For a gun to fire, the trigger must be pulled; with some people, as with hair-trigger guns, it doesn't take much to trip an explosion. Let us look first at biological factors that influence our thresholds for aggressive behavior, then at the psychological factors that pull the trigger.

The Biology of Aggression

OBJECTIVE 57-7 | Describe three levels of biological influences on aggression.

Aggression varies too widely from culture to culture, era to era, and person to person to be considered an unlearned instinct. But biology does *influence* aggression. Stimuli that trigger aggressive behavior operate through our biological system. We can look for biological influences at three levels—genetic, neural, and biochemical. Our genes engineer our individual nervous systems, which operate electrochemically.

Genetic Influences
Animals have been bred for aggressiveness—sometimes for sport, sometimes for research. Twin studies suggest that genes influence human aggression as well (Miles & Carey, 1997; Rowe & others, 1999). If one identical twin admits to "having a violent temper," the other twin will often independently admit the same. Fraternal twins are much less likely to respond similarly. Researchers are now searching for genetic markers found in those who commit the most violence. (One is already well known and is carried by half the human race: the Y chromosome.)

In the last 25 years in the United States, guns have caused some 800,000 suicidal, homicidal, and accidental deaths. Compared with people of the same sex, race, age, and neighborhood, those who keep a gun in the home (ironically, often for protection) are nearly three times more likely to be murdered in the home—nearly always by a family member or close acquaintance. For every self-defense use of a gun in the home, there are 4 unintentional shootings, 7 criminal assaults or homicides, and 11 attempted or completed suicides (Kellermann & others, 1993, 1997, 1998).

■ **just-world phenomenon** the tendency of people to believe the world is just and that people therefore get what they deserve and deserve what they get.

■ **aggression** any physical or verbal behavior intended to hurt or destroy.

"It's a guy thing."

Neural Influences

Animal and human brains have neural systems that, when stimulated, either inhibit or produce aggressive behavior (Moyer, 1983). Consider:

- The domineering leader of a caged monkey colony had a radio-controlled electrode implanted in a brain area that, when stimulated, inhibits aggression. When researchers placed the button that activated the electrode in the colony's cage, one small monkey learned to push it every time the boss became threatening.
- A mild-mannered woman had an electrode implanted in her brain's limbic system (in the amygdala) by neurosurgeons seeking to diagnose a disorder. Because the brain has no sensory receptors, she was unable to feel the stimulation. But at the flick of a switch she snarled, "Take my blood pressure. Take it now," then stood up and began to strike the doctor.
- Intensive evaluation of 15 death-row inmates revealed that all 15 had suffered a severe head injury. Although most neurologically impaired people are not violent, researcher Dorothy Lewis and her colleagues (1986) inferred that unrecognized neurological disorders may be one ingredient in the violence recipe. Other studies of violent criminals have revealed diminished activity in the frontal lobes, which play an important role in controlling impulses (Amen & others, 1996; Davidson & others, 2000; Raine, 1999).

So, does the brain have a "violence center" that produces aggression when stimulated? Actually, no one spot in the brain controls aggression, because aggression is a complex behavior that occurs in particular contexts. Rather, the brain has neural systems that *facilitate* aggression, given provocation. And it has a frontal lobe system for inhibiting aggression, making aggression more likely if this system is damaged, inactive, disconnected, or not yet fully mature.

Biochemical Influences

Hormones, alcohol, and other substances in the blood influence the neural systems that control aggression. A raging bull will become a gentle Ferdinand when castration reduces its testosterone level. The same is true of castrated mice. When injected with testosterone, the castrated mice once again become aggressive.

Although humans are less sensitive to hormonal changes, violent criminals tend to be muscular young males with lower-than-average intelligence scores, low levels of the neurotransmitter serotonin, and higher-than-average testosterone levels (Dabbs & others, 2001a; Pendick, 1994). Drugs that sharply reduce their testosterone levels also subdue their aggressive tendencies. High testosterone correlates with irritability, low

> "We could avoid two-thirds of all crime simply by putting all able-bodied young men in cryogenic sleep from the age of 12 through 28."
>
> David T. Lykken, *The Antisocial Personalities*, 1995

A lean, mean fighting machine—the testosterone-laden female hyena
The hyena's unusual embryology pumps testosterone into female fetuses. The result is revved-up young female hyenas who seem born to fight.

Misuaki Iwago/Minden Pictures

tolerance for frustration, assertiveness, and impulsiveness—qualities that predispose somewhat more aggressive responses to provocation (Dabbs & others, 2001b; Harris, 1999). Among both teenage boys and adult men, high testosterone levels correlate with delinquency, hard drug use, and aggressive-bullying responses to frustration (Berman & others, 1993; Dabbs & Morris, 1990; Olweus & others, 1988). With age, testosterone levels—and aggressiveness—diminish.

The traffic between hormones and behavior is two-way. Testosterone heightens dominance and aggressiveness. But dominating behavior also boosts testosterone levels (Mazur & Booth, 1998). One study measured testosterone levels in the saliva of male college basketball fans before and after a big game. Testosterone levels swelled among the victorious fans and sank among the dejected ones (Bernhardt & others, 1998).

For both biological and psychological reasons, alcohol unleashes aggressive responses to frustration (Bushman, 1993; Ito & others, 1996; Taylor & Chermack, 1993). (Just *thinking* you've imbibed alcohol has some effect; but so, too, does unknowingly ingesting alcohol slipped into a drink.) Police data and prison surveys reinforce conclusions drawn from experiments on alcohol and aggression. Aggression-prone people are more likely to drink and to become violent when intoxicated (White & others, 1993). People who have been drinking commit 4 in 10 violent crimes and 3 in 4 acts of spousal abuse (Greenfeld, 1998).

The Psychology of Aggression

OBJECTIVE 57-8 | Outline four psychological triggers of aggression.

Biological factors influence the ease with which aggression is triggered. But what psychological factors pull the trigger?

Aversive Events

Although suffering sometimes builds character, it may also bring out the worst in us. Studies in which animals or humans experience unpleasant events reveal that those made miserable often make others miserable (Berkowitz, 1983, 1989).

Being blocked short of a goal also increases people's readiness to aggress. This phenomenon is called the **frustration-aggression principle:** Frustration creates anger, which may in some people generate aggression, especially in the presence of an aggressive cue, such as a gun. Organisms often respond to stress with a *fight-or-flight reaction*. After the frustration and stress of 9/11, Americans responded with a readiness to fight. Terrorism similarly may spring from a desire for revenge, sometimes after a friend or family member has been killed or injured.

Like frustration, other aversive stimuli—physical pain, personal insults, foul odors, hot temperatures, cigarette smoke, and a host of others—can also evoke hostility. For example, violent crime and spousal abuse rates are higher during hotter years, seasons, months, and days (**FIGURE 57.4** on the next page). When people are hotter than usual, they think, feel, and act more aggressively. From the available data, Craig Anderson and his colleagues (2000) project that, other things being equal, global warming of 4 degrees Fahrenheit (about 2 degrees centigrade) would induce more than 50,000 additional assaults and murders in the United States alone.

Ostracism can also be a real pain. In a series of studies, Jean Twenge and her collaborators (2001, 2002, 2003) told some people that others whom they had met didn't want them in their group, or that a personality test indicated they "were likely to end up alone later in life." Those led to feel socially excluded were later more likely to disparage or even deliver a blast of noise to someone who insulted

■ **frustration-aggression principle** the principle that frustration—the blocking of an attempt to achieve some goal—creates anger, which can generate aggression.

Recipe for aggression
When Indiana Pacers' Ron Artest attacked Detroit Pistons basketball fans, many influences appeared to create the perfect storm for aggression. The young male Pacer players, who were dominating the Pistons, were likely flush with testosterone. The Pistons' frustration had led one of its players to aggressively shove Artest. The high arousal level of the players and of the frustrated fans (many of whom were disinhibited by alcohol consumption) was easily channeled into aggression when one deindividuated fan threw a cup of beer at Artest.

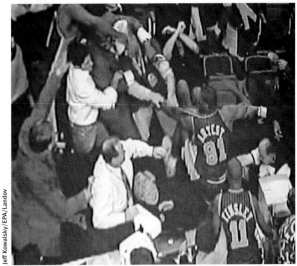

Jeff Kowalsky/EPA/Landow

FIGURE 57.4
Uncomfortably hot weather and aggressive reactions
Between 1980 and 1982 in Houston, murders and rapes were more common on days over 91 degrees Fahrenheit (33 degrees centigrade), as shown in the graph. This finding is consistent with those from laboratory experiments in which people working in a hot room react to provocations with greater hostility. (From Anderson & Anderson, 1984.)

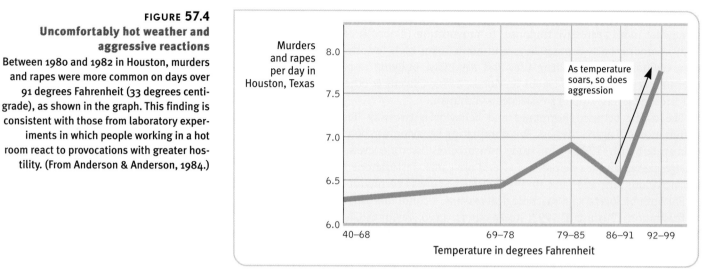

them. This rejection-induced aggression brings to mind various North American and European school shootings, committed by youth who had been shunned and mocked by peers. Other studies confirm that rejection often intensifies aggression (Catanese & Tice, 2005; Gaertner & Iuzzini, 2005).

Learning That Aggression Is Rewarding

Aggression may be a natural response to aversive events, but learning can alter natural reactions. Animals naturally eat when they are hungry. But if appropriately rewarded or punished, they can be taught either to overeat or to starve.

Our reactions are more likely to be aggressive in situations where experience has taught us that aggression pays. Children whose aggression successfully intimidates other children may become more aggressive. Animals that have successfully fought to get food or mates become increasingly ferocious.

Different cultures model, reinforce, and evoke different tendencies toward violence. For example, crime rates are higher (and average happiness is lower) in countries marked by a great disparity between rich and poor (Triandis, 1994). Richard Nisbett and Dov Cohen (1996) show how violence can vary by culture within a country. They analyzed violence among white Americans in southern U.S. towns settled by Scots-Irish herders whose tradition emphasized "manly honor," the use of arms to protect one's flock, and a history of coercive slavery. Their cultural descendants have triple the homicide rates and are more supportive of physically punishing children, of warfare initiatives, and of uncontrolled gun ownership than are their white counterparts in New England towns settled by Puritan, Quaker, and Dutch farmer-artisans.

Social influence also appears in high violence rates among cultures and families that experience minimal father care (Triandis, 1994). For example, the U.S. Bureau of Justice Statistics has reported that 70 percent of imprisoned juveniles did not grow up with two parents (Beck & others, 1988). (An absent parent is usually a father.) The correlation between father absence and violence in the United States holds for all races, income levels, and locations (Myers, 2000).

It is important, however, to note how many individuals are leading gentle, even heroic lives amid social stresses, reminding us again that individuals differ. The person matters. That people differ over time and place reminds us that environments differ. Yesterday's plundering Vikings have become today's peace-promoting Scandinavians. Situations matter. Like all behavior, aggression arises from the interaction of persons and situations.

"Why do we kill people who kill people to show that killing people is wrong?"

National Coalition to Abolish the Death Penalty, 1992

Once established, however, aggressive behavior patterns are difficult to change. To foster a kinder, gentler world we had best model and reward sensitivity and cooperation from an early age, perhaps by training parents to discipline without modeling violence. Modeling violence—screaming and hitting—is precisely what exasperated parents often do. Parents of delinquent youngsters typically discipline with beatings, thus modeling aggression as a method of dealing with problems (Patterson & others, 1982, 1992). They also frequently cave into (reward) their children's tears and temper tantrums.

Parent-training programs advise a more positive approach. They encourage parents to reinforce desirable behaviors and to frame statements positively ("When you finish loading the dishwasher you can go play," rather than "If you don't load the dishwasher, there'll be no playing"). One *aggression-replacement program* that brought down re-arrest rates of juvenile offenders and gang members taught the youths and their parents communication skills, trained them in how to control anger, and encouraged more thoughtful moral reasoning (Goldstein & others, 1998).

Observing Models of Aggression

Parents are hardly the only aggression models. Observing TV violence tends to desensitize people to cruelty and prime them to respond aggressively when provoked. Does this media effect extend to sexual violence?

A woman's risk of rape has varied across cultures and times and was greater at the last century's end than half a century previous (Koss & others, 1994; Tjaden & Thoennes, 2000). In surveys, about one-fifth of women have reported that a man has forced them to do something sexually, about one-half have reported some form of unwanted sexual coercion, and most have reported experiencing verbal sexual harassment (Craig & others, 1989; Laumann & others, 1994; Sandberg & others, 1985). Similar levels of sexual coercion have been found in Canadian, Australian, and New Zealand surveys (Koss & others, 1994; Patton & Mannison, 1995).

What factors might explain this increased sexual aggression? Alcohol consumption—often linked with aggression—has not increased. We do know that sexually coercive men typically are sexually promiscuous and hostile in their relationships with women (**FIGURE 57.5**). Might changes in the media have contributed to such tendencies?

Coinciding with the increase in sexual aggression was the rise of the home video business, giving easier access to R-rated "slasher films" and X-rated films. Content analyses reveal that most X-rated films depict quick, casual sex between strangers, but that scenes of rape and sexual exploitation of women by men are also common (Cowan & others, 1988; NCTV, 1987; Yang & Linz, 1990). In just the United States, video, pay-per-view, and Internet pornography have combined to create a $10 billion- to $14-billion business—a bigger business than professional football, basketball, and baseball, put together," noted the *New York Times* (Rich, 2001). In one survey of collegians, 10 percent of women and 28.4 percent of men acknowledged accessing sexually explicit material on the Internet more often than "rarely" (Goodson & others, 2001). Although the explosion in Internet pornography has not been accompanied by a further increase in reported rapes, researchers nevertheless wonder whether images of sexual exploitation influence sexual aggression.

Rape scenes often portray the victim at first fleeing and resisting her attacker, but then becoming aroused and finally driven to ecstasy. In less graphic form, the same unrealistic script—she resists, he persists, she melts—is commonplace on TV and in romance novels. In *Gone With the Wind*, Scarlett O'Hara is carried to bed screaming and wakes up singing. Most rapists accept this *rape myth*—the idea that some women invite or enjoy rape and get "swept away" while being "taken" (Brinson, 1992). (In actuality, rape is traumatic, and it frequently harms women's reproductive and sexual health [Golding, 1996].)

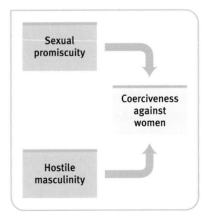

FIGURE 57.5

Men who sexually coerce women
The recipe for coercion against women combines an impersonal approach to sex with a hostile masculinity. (Adapted from Malamuth, 1996.)

Pornography means different things to different people. Following Webster's dictionary, some define pornography as erotic depictions intended to excite sexual arousal. Others define it as sexual materials that exploit, degrade, or subordinate women.

In follow-up studies, Zillmann (1989) found that after massive exposure to X-rated sexual films, men and women became more accepting of extramarital sex, of women's sexual submission to men, and of a man's seducing a 12-year-old girl. As people heavily exposed to televised crime perceive the world as more dangerous, so people heavily exposed to pornography see the world as more sexual.

As U.S. First Lady, Hillary Rodham Clinton voiced concerns shared by many when she worried about media models of an "impulsive sexuality" that encourage uncommitted sex (a predictor of sexual violence) and father-absent families (a predictor of juvenile violence).

" What we're trying to do is raise the level of awareness of violence against women and pornography to at least the level of awareness of racist and Ku Klux Klan literature."

Gloria Steinem (1988)

When interviewed, Canadian and U.S. sex offenders (rapists, child molesters, and serial killers) do report a greater-than-usual appetite for sexually explicit and sexually violent materials—materials typically labeled as pornography (Marshall, 1989; Ressler & others, 1988; Oddone-Paolucci & others, 2000). For example, the Los Angeles Police Department has reported that pornography was "conspicuously present" in 62 percent of its extrafamilial child sexual abuse cases during the 1980s (Bennett, 1991). But are the sexual offenders merely, as sex researcher John Money (1988) suspected, using pornography "as an alibi to explain to themselves and their captors what otherwise is inexplicable"?

Laboratory experiments reveal that repeatedly watching X-rated films (even if nonviolent) later makes one's own partner seem less attractive, makes a woman's friendliness seem more sexual, and makes sexual aggression seem less serious (Harris, 1994). In one such experiment, Dolf Zillmann and Jennings Bryant (1984) showed undergraduates six brief, sexually explicit films each week for six weeks. A control group viewed nonerotic films during the same six-week period. Three weeks later, both groups read a newspaper report about a man convicted but not yet sentenced for raping a hitchhiker. When asked to suggest an appropriate prison term, those who had viewed sexually explicit films recommended sentences half as long as those recommended by the control group.

Experiments cannot elicit actual sexual violence, but they can assess a man's willingness to hurt a woman. Often the research gauges the effect of violent versus nonviolent erotic films on men's willingness to deliver supposed electric shocks to women who had earlier provoked the men. These experiments suggest that it's not the eroticism but rather the depictions of sexual *violence* (whether in R-rated slasher films or X-rated films) that most directly affect men's acceptance and performance of aggression against women. A conference of 21 social scientists, including many of the researchers who conducted these experiments, produced a consensus (Surgeon General, 1986): "Pornography that portrays sexual aggression as pleasurable for the victim increases the acceptance of the use of coercion in sexual relations." Contrary to much popular opinion, viewing such depictions does not provide an outlet for bottled-up impulses. Rather, "in laboratory studies measuring short-term effects, exposure to violent pornography increases punitive behavior toward women."

Acquiring Social Scripts

Significant behaviors, such as violence, usually have many determinants, making any single explanation an oversimplification. Asking what causes violence is therefore like asking what causes cancer. Those who study the effects of asbestos exposure on cancer rates may remind us that asbestos is indeed a cancer cause, albeit only one among many. Likewise, report Neil Malamuth and his colleagues (1991, 1995), several factors can create a predisposition to sexual violence. They include the media but also dominance motives, disinhibition by alcohol, and a history of child abuse. Still, if media depictions of violence can disinhibit and desensitize; if viewing sexual violence fosters hostile, domineering attitudes and behaviors; and if viewing pornography leads viewers to trivialize rape, devalue their partners, and engage in uncommitted sex, then media influence is not a minor issue.

Social psychologists attribute the media's influence partly to the *social scripts* (mental tapes for how to act, provided by our culture) they portray. When we find ourselves in new situations, uncertain how to act, we rely on social scripts. After so many action films, youngsters may acquire a script that gets played when they face real-life conflicts. Challenged, they may "act like a man" by intimidating or eliminating the threat. Likewise, after viewing multiple sexual innuendoes and acts in most prime-time TV hours—often involving impulsive or short-term relationships—youths may acquire sexual scripts they later enact in real-life relationships (Kunkel & others, 2001; Sapolsky & Tabarlet, 1991).

CLOSE-UP:

PARALLELS BETWEEN SMOKING EFFECTS AND MEDIA VIOLENCE EFFECTS

Researchers Brad Bushman and Craig Anderson (2001) note that the correlation between viewing violence and behaving aggressively nearly equals the correlation between smoking and lung cancer. They also note other parallels:

1. Not everyone who smokes gets lung cancer.
2. Smoking is only one cause of lung cancer, although an important one.
3. The first cigarette can nauseate, but the sickening effect lessens with repetition.
4. The short-term effect of one cigarette is minor and dissipates within an hour or so.
5. The long-term, cumulative effect of smoking can be severe.
6. Corporate interests have denied the smoking–lung cancer link.

1. Not everyone who watches violence becomes aggressive.
2. Viewing violence is only one cause of aggression, although an important one.
3. The first violence exposure can upset, but the upset lessens with repetition.
4. One violent TV program can prime aggressive thoughts and behaviors, but the effect dissipates within an hour or so.
5. The long-term, cumulative effect of viewing violence is increased likelihood of habitual aggression.
6. Corporate interests have denied the viewing violence–aggression link.

Might public consciousness be raised by making people aware of the information you have just been reading (see Close-Up: Parallels Between Smoking Effects and Media Violence Effects)? In the 1940s, movies often depicted African-Americans as childlike superstitious buffoons. Today, we would not tolerate such images. In the 1960s and 1970s, some rock music and movies glamorized drug use. Responding to a tidal change in cultural attitudes, the entertainment industry now more often portrays the dark side of drug use. In response to growing public concern about violence in the media, television violence levels declined in the early 1990s (Gerbner & others, 1993). The growing sensitivity to violence has raised hopes that entertainers, producers, and audiences might someday look back with embarrassment on the days when movies "entertained" people with scenes of torture, mutilation, and sexual coercion.

Do Video Games Teach or Release Violence?

OBJECTIVE 57-9 | Discuss the effects of violent video games on social attitudes and behavior.

Violent video games became an issue for public debate after teen assassins in Paducah, Kentucky; Littleton, Colorado; and more than a dozen other places seemed to mimic the carnage in the splatter games they had so often played (Anderson, 2004). In 2002, two Grand Rapids, Michigan, teens and a man in his early twenties spent part of a night drinking beer and playing Grand Theft Auto III, using cars to run down simulated pedestrians, then beating them with fists, leaving a bloody body behind (Kolker, 2002). Then they went driving on a real drive, spotted a 38-year-old man on a bicycle, ran him down with their car, got out, stomped and punched him, and returned home to play the game some more. (The man, a father of three, died six days later.)

When youths play such games, do they learn social scripts? Interactive games transport the player into their own vivid reality. When youths play Grand Theft Auto: San

Densensitizing people to violence

Mark C. Burnett/Stock, Boston

"It'll be like the LA riots, the Oklahoma bombing, WWI, Vietnam, Duke, and Doom all mixed together."

Journal entry by Columbine killer Eric Harris, 1998

"We are what we repeatedly do."

Aristotle

FIGURE 57.6

Biopsychosocial understanding of aggression

Many factors contribute to aggressive behavior, but there are many ways to combat these influences, including learning anger management and communication skills, and avoiding violent media and video games.

Andreas, they can carjack vehicles; run down pedestrians; do drive-by shootings; pick up a prostitute, have sex with her, and then kill her. What scripts are being learned?

Most abused children don't become abusive adults. And most youths who spend hundreds of hours in these mass murder simulators won't become teen assassins. Still, we wonder: If passively viewing violence elevates aggressive responses to provocation and lowers sensitivity to cruelty, what will be the effect of actively role-playing aggression? Although very few will commit slaughter, how many will become desensitized to violence and more open to violent acts?

Thirty-eight recent studies of more than 7000 people offer some answers (Anderson & others, 2004). Mary Ballard and Rose Wiest (1998) observed a rising level of arousal and feelings of hostility in college men as they played Mortal Kombat. Other studies have found that video games can prime aggressive thoughts and increase aggression. Consider this report from Craig Anderson and Karen Dill (2000): University men who have spent the most hours playing violent video games tend to be the most physically aggressive (for example, to acknowledge having hit or attacked someone else). In one experiment, people randomly assigned to play a game involving bloody murders with groaning victims (rather than to play nonviolent Myst) became more hostile. On a follow-up task, they also were more likely to blast intense noise at a fellow student.

Studies of young adolescents by Douglas Gentile and his co-researchers (2004) further reveal that kids who play a lot of violent video games see the world as more hostile, get into more arguments and fights, and get worse grades (those hours aren't spent reading or studying). Ah, but is this merely because naturally hostile kids are drawn to such games? No, says Gentile. Even among violent-game players who scored low in hostility, the 38 percent who had been in fights was nearly 10 times the 4 percent involved in fights among their nongaming counterparts. Moreover, over time, the nongamers become more likely to have fights only if they start playing the violent games. Anderson (2004a) believes that, due partly to the more repetitive and active participation of game play, violent video games have even greater effects "than the well-documented effects of exposure to violent television and movies."

Although much remains to be learned, these studies disconfirm the *catharsis hypothesis*—the idea that we feel better if we "blow off steam" by venting our emotions. Playing violent video games *increases* aggressive thoughts, emotions, and behaviors. One video game company's CEO rationalizes that we are "violent by nature [and] need release valves." "It's a way to process violent feelings and anxieties through a fantasy medium," adds a prominent civil liberties lawyer in explaining her hunch that playing violent games calms violent tendencies (Heins, 2004). Actually, expressing anger breeds more anger, and practicing violence breeds more violence. Tomorrow's games may have even greater effects. Social psychologists Susan Persky and Jim Blascovich (2005) created a violent video game for students to play on either a desktop computer or by putting on a headset and stepping into a virtual reality. As they predicted, the virtual reality more dramatically heightened aggressive feelings and behavior during and after the play.

To sum up, research reveals biological, psychological, and social influences on aggressive behavior. Like so much else, aggression is a biopsychosocial phenomenon (**FIGURE 57.6**).

Biological influences:
- genetic influences
- biochemical influences, such as testosterone and alcohol
- neural influences, such as severe head injuries

Psychological influences:
- dominating behavior (which boosts testosterone levels in the blood)
- believing you've drunk alcohol (whether you actually have or not)
- frustration
- aggressive role models
- rewards for aggressive behavior

Aggressive behavior

Social-cultural influences:
- deindividuation from being in a crowd
- challenging environmental factors, such as crowding, heat, and direct provocations
- parental models of aggression
- minimal father involvement
- being rejected from a group
- exposure to violent media

Conflict

OBJECTIVE 57-10 | Explain how social traps and mirror-image perceptions fuel social conflict.

We live in surprising times. With astonishing speed, late-twentieth-century democratic movements swept away totalitarian rule in Eastern European countries, and hopes for a new world order displaced the Cold War chill. And yet, the twenty-first century began with terrorist acts and war, and the world continued to spend $2 billion every day for arms and armies—money that could have been used for housing, nutrition, education, and health. Knowing that wars begin in human minds, psychologists have wondered: What in the human mind causes destructive conflict? How might the perceived threats of social diversity be replaced by a spirit of cooperation?

To a social psychologist, a **conflict** is a seeming incompatibility of actions, goals, or ideas. The elements of conflict are much the same at all levels, from nations at war, to cultural disputes within a society, to individuals in a marital dispute. In each situation, people become enmeshed in a potentially destructive social process that can produce results no one wants. Among the destructive processes are social traps and distorted perceptions.

Social Traps

In some situations, we support our collective well-being by pursuing our personal interests. As capitalist Adam Smith wrote in *The Wealth of Nations* (1776), "It is not from the benevolence of the butcher, the brewer, or the baker that we expect our dinner, but from their regard to their own interest." In other situations, we harm our collective well-being by pursuing our personal interests. Such situations are **social traps.**

Consider the simple game matrix in FIGURE 57.7, which is similar to those used in experiments with countless thousands of people. In this game, both sides can win or both can lose, depending on the players' individual choices. Pretend you are Person 1, and that you and Person 2 will each receive the amount shown after you separately choose either *A* or *B*. (You might invite someone to look at the matrix with you and take the role of Person 2.) Which do you choose—*A* or *B*?

As you ponder the game, you will discover that you and Person 2 are caught in a dilemma. If you both choose *A*, you both benefit, making $5 each. Neither of you benefits if you both choose *B*, for neither of you makes anything. Nevertheless, on any single trial you serve your own interests if you choose *B*: You can't lose, and you might make $10. But the same is true for the other person. Hence, the social trap: As long as you both pursue your own immediate best interest and choose *B*, you will both end up with nothing—the typical result—when you could have made $5.

Many real-life situations similarly pit our individual interests against our communal well-being. Individual whalers reasoned that the few whales they took would not threaten the species and that if they didn't take them other whalers would anyway. The result: Some species of whales became endangered. The individual car owner and home owner reasons, "It would cost me comfort or money to buy a more fuel-efficient car and furnace. Besides, the fossil fuels I burn don't noticeably add to the greenhouse gases." When enough others reason similarly, the collective result threatens disaster—global warming and the threat of rising seas and more extreme weather.

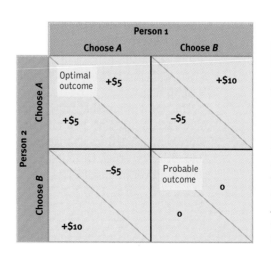

> **conflict** a perceived incompatibility of actions, goals, or ideas.
>
> **social trap** a situation in which the conflicting parties, by each rationally pursuing their self-interest, become caught in mutually destructive behavior.

FIGURE 57.7
Social-trap game matrix
By pursuing our self-interest and not trusting others, we can end up losers. To illustrate this, imagine playing the game to the left. The pink triangles show the outcomes for Person 1, which depend on the choices made by both players. If you were Person 1, would you choose *A* or *B*? (This game is called a *non-zero-sum game* because the outcomes need not add up to zero; both sides can win or both can lose.)

Not in my ocean!
Many people support alternative energy sources, including windmills. But proposals to construct windmill farms in real-world neighborhoods elicit less support. One such proposal, for locating windmills off the coast of Massachusetts' Nantucket Island, has produced heated debate over the future benefits of clean energy versus the costs of altering treasured ocean views and, possibly, migratory bird routes.

AP Photo/Lisa Poole

Social traps challenge us to find ways of reconciling our right to pursue our personal well-being with our responsibility for the well-being of all. Psychologists are therefore exploring ways to convince people to cooperate for their mutual betterment—through agreed-upon *regulations,* through better *communication,* and through promoting *awareness* of our responsibilities toward community, nation, and the whole of humanity (Dawes, 1980, Linder, 1982, Sato, 1987). Under such conditions, people more often cooperate, whether it be in playing a laboratory game or the real game of life.

Enemy Perceptions

Psychologists have noted that those in conflict have a curious tendency to form diabolical images of one another. These distorted images are ironically similar, so similar in fact that we call them *mirror-image perceptions:* As we see "them"—as untrustworthy and evil intentioned—so "they" see us. Each demonizes the other.

Mirror-image perceptions often feed a vicious cycle of hostility. If Juan believes Maria is annoyed with him, he may snub her, causing her to act in ways that justify his perception. As with individuals, so with countries. Perceptions can become self-fulfilling prophecies. They may confirm themselves by influencing the other country to react in ways that seem to justify them.

In the early twenty-first century, many Americans came to loathe Saddam Hussein. Like the "evil" Saddam Hussein, declared George W. Bush (2001), "some of today's tyrants are gripped by an implacable hatred of the United States of America. They hate our friends, they hate our values, they hate democracy and freedom and individual liberty. Many care little for the lives of their own people." Hussein (2002) reciprocated the perception, seeing the United States as "an evil tyrant" that, with Satan as its protector, lusted for oil and aggressively attacked those who "defend what is right."

The point is not that truth must lie midway between two such views (one may be more accurate). The point is that enemy perceptions often form mirror images. Moreover, as enemies change, so do perceptions. In American minds and media, the "bloodthirsty, cruel, treacherous" Japanese of World War II later became our "intelligent, hardworking, self-disciplined, resourceful allies" (Gallup, 1972).

>> Learning Outcomes

Antisocial Relations

OBJECTIVE 57-1 | Identify the three components of prejudice.

Prejudice is an attitude composed of *beliefs, emotions,* and *predispositions to action.* The beliefs are frequently *stereotypes* (sometimes accurate but often overgeneralized beliefs). The emotions are most often negative, and the action is usually *discrimination* (unjustifiable negative behavior).

OBJECTIVE 57-2 | Contrast overt and subtle forms of prejudice, and give examples of each.

Overt prejudice, such as denying a particular ethnic group the right to vote, is discrimination that *explicitly* (openly and consciously) expresses negative beliefs and emotions. *Subtle prejudice,* such as feeling fearful in the presence of a stranger with a particular ethnic background, is an *implicit* (often unconscious) expression of negative beliefs and emotions.

OBJECTIVE 57-3 | Discuss the social factors that contribute to prejudice.

One contributing factor is *inequality* (unequal distribution of money, power, and prestige) within a group; in such conditions, the "haves" usually develop negative attitudes toward the "have-nots" to justify their more privileged positions. Definitions of *social identity* ("we" the ingroup versus "they" the outgroup) are another source of prejudice because they promote ingroup bias (a tendency to favor one's own group) and discrimination.

OBJECTIVE 57-4 | Explain how scapegoating illustrates the emotional component of prejudice.

Troubled times, especially those that remind us of our own mortality, produce feelings of fear and anger. As in-group loyalty and out-group prejudice intensify, people may boost their self-esteem by searching for a *scapegoat*—someone to blame for the troubling event.

OBJECTIVE 57-5 | Cite four ways that cognitive processes help create and maintain prejudice.

We simplify the world around us by *creating categories,* but when we categorize people, we often stereotype them, overgeneralizing their characteristics and underestimating their differences. We also tend to judge the frequency of events by *vivid cases* that come to mind more readily than the long string of less vivid events involving the same group. We may justify people's less-privileged or punished position by the *just-world phenomenon,* assuming that the world is just and people get what they deserve. *Hindsight bias* (the tendency to believe, after learning an outcome, that we would have predicted it beforehand) may also contribute.

OBJECTIVE 57-6 | Explain how psychology's definition of *aggression* differs from everyday usage.

Psychology's definition of *aggression* as "any physical or verbal behavior intended to harm or destroy" includes behaviors (such as killing in combat) that might not be included in everyday usage.

OBJECTIVE 57-7 | Describe three levels of biological influences on aggression.

Genes influence aggression, for example by influencing temperament. *Neural systems* in the brain facilitate or inhibit aggression. Hormones (such as testosterone), alcohol (which releases inhibitions), and other substances are *biochemical influences* that contribute to aggression. Biological conditions set the threshold for aggressiveness, but psychological factors trigger aggressive behaviors.

OBJECTIVE 57-8 | Outline four psychological triggers of aggression.

Aversive events (such as environmental conditions or social rejection) can create frustration, leading to feelings of anger and hostility. *Reinforcement for aggressive behavior* can establish learned patterns of aggression that are difficult to change. People can also learn aggression and become desensitized to violence by *observing models act aggressively* in person or in the media. Media depictions of violence can also trigger aggression by providing *social scripts* (culturally sanctioned ways of acting in a given situation).

OBJECTIVE 57-9 | Discuss the effects of violent video games on social attitudes and behavior.

Playing violent video games can provide opportunities to observe modeled aggression and to role-play aggression; increase arousal and feelings of hostility; prime aggressive thoughts and increase aggression; and (in adolescents) lead to increased participation in arguments and fights and to falling grades. Virtual reality games may heighten these effects.

OBJECTIVE 57-10 | Explain how social traps and mirror-image perceptions fuel social conflict.

Social conflicts are situations in which people perceive their actions, goals, or ideas to be incompatible. In *social traps,* two or more individuals rationally pursue their own personal interests without regard for the well-being of others. People in conflict tend to perceive the worst in each other, producing *mirror-images* of identical demons. The perceptions can become self-fulfilling prophecies, triggering reactions that confirm the images. Helping people to agree on regulations, communicate better, and be more aware of responsibilities toward others can foster cooperation and avoid social traps.

TERMS AND CONCEPTS TO REMEMBER

prejudice, p. 57-1

stereotype, p. 57-1

discrimination, p. 57-1

ingroup, p. 57-4

outgroup, p. 57-4

ingroup bias, p. 57-4

scapegoat theory, p. 57-5

just-world phenomenon, p. 57-6

aggression, p. 57-7

frustration-aggression principle, p. 57-9

conflict, p. 57-15

social trap, p. 57-15

TEST YOURSELF

1. Horace says, "I have no prejudice within me toward anyone. I believe everyone deserves equal opportunity in housing and employment." Even if Horace indeed expresses no obvious prejudice, what sort of prejudice might nonetheless exist?

(Answer in Appendix B.)

ASK YOURSELF

1. Recent court rulings established that U.S. cities could seize private property and sell it to businesses that would increase taxes, benefiting the collective well-being. Do you agree with the ruling?

ANSWER TO QUESTION WITHIN THE MODULE

Q. Which face in Figure 57.2 do you like best? Which one placed an ad seeking a long-term relationship?

A. Research suggests that subtly feminized features convey a likeable image, which people tend to associate more with committed dads than with promiscuous cads. Thus, if you responded as others did to these questions, you would have picked computer-generated face (b) in response to both questions.

❯WEB

Multiple-choice *self-tests* and more may be found at www.worthpublishers.com/myers.

58

MODULE

Prosocial Relations

Social psychology studies how we think about and influence one another, and also how we *relate* to one another. Social psychologists focus not only on the dark side of social relationships, but also on the bright side, by studying *prosocial* behavior—behavior that intends to help or benefit someone. Our positive behaviors toward others are evident from explorations of attraction, altruism, and peacemaking.

Attraction

Pause a moment and think about your relationships with two people—a close friend, and someone who stirs in you feelings of romantic love. What is the psychological chemistry that binds us together in these special sorts of attachments that help us cope with all other relationships? Social psychology suggests some answers.

■ **mere exposure effect** the phenomenon that repeated exposure to novel stimuli increases liking of them.

The Psychology of Attraction

OBJECTIVE 58-1 | Describe the influence of proximity, physical attractiveness, and similarity on interpersonal attraction.

We endlessly wonder how we can win others' affection and what makes our own affections flourish or fade. Does familiarity breed contempt, or does it intensify our affection? Do birds of a feather flock together, or do opposites attract? Is beauty only skin deep, or does attractiveness matter greatly? Consider three ingredients of our liking for one another: proximity, physical attractiveness, and similarity.

Proximity

Before friendships become close, they must begin. *Proximity*—geographic nearness—is friendship's most powerful predictor. Proximity provides opportunities for aggression, but much more often it breeds liking. Study after study reveals that people are most likely to like, and even to marry, those who live in the same neighborhood, who sit nearby in class, who work in the same office, who share the same parking lot, who eat in the same dining hall. Look around.

Why is proximity so conducive to liking? Obviously, part of the answer is the greater availability of those we often meet. But there is more to it than that. For one thing, repeated exposure to novel stimuli—be they nonsense syllables, musical selections, geometric figures, Chinese characters, human faces, or the letters of our own name—increases our liking for them (Moreland & Zajonc, 1982; Zajonc, 2001; Nuttin, 1987). People are even somewhat more likely to marry someone whose first or last name resembles their own (Jones & others, 2004).

This phenomenon, exploited by advertisers, we call the **mere exposure effect**. Within certain limits (Bornstein, 1989, 1999), familiarity breeds fondness. Richard Moreland and Scott Beach (1992) demonstrated this by having four equally attractive women silently attend a 200-student class for zero, 5, 10, or 15 class sessions. At the end of the course, students were shown slides of each woman and asked to rate each one's attractiveness. The most attractive? The ones they'd seen most often. The phenomenon will come as no surprise to the young Taiwanese man who wrote more than 700 letters to his girlfriend, urging her to marry him. She did marry—the mail carrier (Steinberg, 1993).

Familiarity breeds acceptance
When this rare white penguin was born in the Sydney, Australia, zoo, his tuxedoed peers ostracized him. Zookeepers thought they would need to dye him black to gain acceptance. But after three weeks of contact, the other penguins came to accept him.

Rex USA

The mere exposure effect
The mere exposure effect applies even to ourselves. Because the human face is not perfectly symmetrical, the face we see in the mirror is not the same as the one our friends see. Most of us prefer the familiar mirror image, while our friends like the reverse (Mita & others, 1977). The Prime Minister Junichiro Koizumi known to the Japanese people is shown at left. The person Koizumi sees in the mirror each morning is shown at right, and that's the photo he would probably prefer.

"I'm going to have to recuse myself."

"Personal beauty is a greater recommendation than any letter of introduction."

Aristotle, *Apothegems*, 330 B.C.

No face is more familiar than one's own. And that explains why, when Lisa De-Bruine (2002) had McMaster University students play a social trap–type game with a supposed other player, they were more trusting and cooperative when the other person's image had some features of their own face morphed into it. In me I trust. In a follow-up study, DeBruine (2004) found that men also *liked* other men (and women liked other women) whose faces incorporated some morphed features of their own.

For our ancestors, the mere exposure phenomenon was adaptive. What was familiar was generally safe and approachable. What was unfamiliar was more often dangerous and threatening. Robert Zajonc (1998) concludes that evolution has hard-wired into us the tendency to bond with those who are familiar and to be wary of those who are unfamiliar. Gut-level prejudice against those culturally different may thus be a primitive, automatic emotional response (Devine, 1995).

Physical Attractiveness

Once proximity affords you contact, what most affects your first impressions: The person's sincerity? Intelligence? Personality? Hundreds of experiments reveal that it is something far more superficial: Appearance. For people taught that "beauty is only skin deep" and that "appearances can be deceiving," the power of physical attractiveness is unnerving. In one early study, Elaine Hatfield and her co-workers (Walster & others, 1966) randomly matched new University of Minnesota students for a Welcome Week dance. Before the dance, each student took a battery of personality and aptitude tests. On the night of the blind date, the couples danced and talked for more than two hours and then took a brief intermission to rate their dates. What determined whether they liked each other? As far as the researchers could determine, only one thing mattered: Physical attractiveness (which had been rated by the researchers

Good looks help people get good jobs
In the 2004 presidential election, many Americans found the face on the left more likeable and trustworthy.

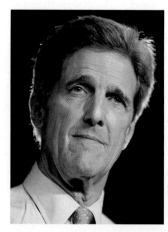

beforehand). Both the men and the women liked good-looking dates best. Although women are more likely than men to *say* that another's looks don't affect them, a man's looks do affect women's behavior (Feingold, 1990; Sprecher, 1989; Woll, 1986).

People's physical attractiveness has wide-ranging effects. It predicts their frequency of dating, their feelings of popularity, and others' initial impressions of their personalities. We perceive attractive people to be healthier, happier, more sensitive, more successful, and more socially skilled, though not more honest or compassionate (Eagly & others, 1991; Feingold, 1992; Hatfield & Sprecher, 1986).

When Neanderthals fall in love.

Attractive, well-dressed people are more likely to make a favorable impression on potential employers and to enjoy occupational success (Cash & Janda, 1984; Langlois & others, 2000; Solomon, 1987). Income analyses show a penalty for plainness or obesity and a premium for beauty (Engemann & Owyang, 2005).

An analysis of 100 top-grossing films since 1940 found that attractive characters were portrayed as morally superior to unattractive characters (Smith & others, 1999). But Hollywood modeling doesn't explain why, to judge from their gazing times, even babies prefer attractive over unattractive faces (Langlois & others, 1987). So do some blind people, discovered University of Birmingham professor John Hull (1990, p. 23) after going blind. A colleague's remarking on a woman's beauty would strangely affect his feelings. He finds this "deplorable . . . but I still feel it. . . . What can it matter to me what sighted men think of women . . . yet I do care what sighted men think, and I do not seem able to throw off this prejudice."

The importance of looks seems unfair and unenlightened. Why should it matter? Two thousand years ago the Roman statesman Cicero felt the same way: "The final good and the supreme duty of the wise person is to resist appearance." Cicero might be reassured by two other findings about attractiveness.

First, people's attractiveness is surprisingly unrelated to their self-esteem and happiness (Diener & others, 1995; Major & others, 1984). One reason may be that, except after comparing themselves with superattractive people, few people (thanks, perhaps, to the mere exposure effect) view themselves as unattractive (Thornton & Moore, 1993). Another reason is that strikingly attractive people are sometimes suspicious that praise for their work may simply be a reaction to their looks. When less attractive people are praised, they are more likely to accept it as sincere (Berscheid, 1981).

Love comes in at the eye."
William Butler Yeats, "A Drinking Song," 1909

Percentage of Men and Women Who "Constantly Think About Their Looks"

	Men	Women
Canada	18%	20%
United States	17	27
Mexico	40	45
Venezuela	47	65

From Roper Starch survey, reported by McCool (1999).

Extreme makeover
In affluent, beauty-conscious cultures, increasing numbers of people, such as this woman from the American TV show *Extreme Makeover*, have turned to cosmetic surgery to improve their looks. If money were no concern, might you ever do the same?

In the eye of the beholder
Conceptions of attractiveness vary by culture. Moreover, the current concept of attractiveness in Kenya, Morocco, and Scandinavia may well change in the future.

New York Times columnist Maureen Dowd on liposuction (January 19, 2000): "Women in the 50's vacuumed. Women in the oo's *are* vacuumed. Our Hoovers have turned on us!"

Cicero might also find comfort in knowing that attractiveness judgments are relative. The standards by which judges crown Miss Universe hardly apply to the whole planet. Rather, beauty is in the eye of the culture—beauty standards reflect one's place and time. Hoping to look attractive, people in different cultures have pierced their noses, lengthened their necks, bound their feet, and dyed or painted their skin and hair. They have gorged themselves to achieve a full figure or liposuctioned fat to achieve a slim one, applied chemicals hoping to rid themselves of unwanted hair or to regrow wanted hair, strapped on leather garments to make their breasts seem smaller or surgically filled their breasts with silicone and put on Wonder Bras to make them look bigger. In North America, the ultra-thin ideal of the Roaring Twenties gave way to the soft, voluptuous Marilyn Monroe ideal of the 1950s, only to be replaced by today's lean yet busty ideal. Americans now spend more on beauty supplies than on education and social services combined and, when still not satisfied, undergo millions of cosmetic medical treatments each year, including plastic surgery, Botox skin smoothing, teeth-capping or whitening, and laser hair removal (Wall, 2002). But the beauty race is like the arms race, with the result that since 1970 more and more women have become *un*happy with their appearance (Feingold & Mazella, 1998).

Some aspects of attractiveness, however, do cross place and time (Cunningham & others, 1995; Langlois & others, 2000). Men in 37 cultures, from Australia to Zambia, judge women as more attractive if they have a youthful appearance. Women feel attracted to healthy-looking men, but especially to those who seem mature, dominant, and affluent.

People everywhere also seem to prefer physical features—noses, legs, physiques—that are neither unusually large nor small. An averaged face is attractive (**FIGURE 58.1**). In one clever demonstration of this, Judith Langlois and Lori Roggman (1990) digitized the faces of up to 32 college students and used a computer to average them. Students judged the averaged, composite faces as more attractive than 96 percent of the individual faces. One reason is that averaged faces are symmetrical, and people with symmetrical faces and bodies are more sexually attractive (Rhodes & others, 1999; Singh, 1995; Thornhill & Gangestad, 1994). Merge either half of your face with its mirror image and your symmetrical new face would boost your attractiveness a notch.

FIGURE 58.1
Average is attractive
Which of these faces offered by University of St. Andrews psychologist David Perrett (2002) is most attractive? Most people say it's the face on the right—of a nonexistent person that is the average composite of these three plus 57 other actual faces.

Cultural standards aside, attractiveness also depends on our feelings about the person. In a Rodgers and Hammerstein musical, Prince Charming asks Cinderella, "Do I love you because you're beautiful, or are you beautiful because I love you?" Chances are it's both. As we see our loved ones again and again, their physical imperfections grow less noticeable and their attractiveness grows more apparent (Beaman & Klentz, 1983; Gross & Crofton, 1977). Shakespeare said it in *A Midsummer Night's Dream:* "Love looks not with the eyes, but with the mind." Come to love someone and watch beauty grow.

Similarity

Let's say that proximity has brought you into contact with someone and that your appearance has made a favorable first impression. What now influences whether acquaintances develop into friends? For example, as you get to know someone better, is the chemistry better if you are opposites or if you are alike?

It makes a good story—extremely different types living in harmonious union: Rat, Mole, and Badger in *The Wind in the Willows,* Frog and Toad in Arnold Lobel's books. The stories delight us by expressing what we seldom experience, for we tend *not* to like dissimilar people (Rosenbaum, 1986). In real life, opposites retract. Birds that flock together usually *are* of a feather. Friends and couples are far more likely to share common attitudes, beliefs, and interests (and, for that matter, age, religion, race, education, intelligence, smoking behavior, and economic status) than are randomly paired people. Much as you and I may dismiss such differences, seeing ourselves as one human family in a global village, we can't hang out with 6 billion people. Moreover, the more alike people are, the more their liking endures (Byrne, 1971). Journalist Walter Lippmann was right to suppose that love is best sustained "when the lovers love many things together, and not merely each other." That is also the assumption of one psychologist-founded Internet dating site, which claims to use the similarities that mark happy couples to match singles, some 10,000 of whom are known to have married (Carter & Snow, 2004; Warren, 2005). Similarity breeds content.

Proximity, attractiveness, and similarity are not the only determinants of attraction. We also like those who like us, especially when our self-image is low. When we believe someone likes us, we respond to them more warmly, which leads them to like us even more (Curtis & Miller, 1986). To be liked is powerfully rewarding.

Indeed, a simple *reward theory of attraction*—that we will like those whose behavior is rewarding to us and that we will continue relationships that offer more rewards than costs—can explain all the findings we have considered so far. When a person lives or works in close proximity with someone else, it costs less time and effort to develop the friendship and enjoy its benefits. Attractive people are aesthetically pleasing, and associating with them can be socially rewarding. Those with similar views reward us by validating our own.

Romantic Love

OBJECTIVE 58-2 | Describe the effect of physical arousal on passionate love, and identify two predictors of enduring companionate love.

Occasionally, people move quickly from initial impressions, to friendship, to the more intense, complex, and mysterious state of romantic love. Elaine Hatfield (1988) distinguishes two types of love: temporary passionate love and a more enduring companionate love.

Beauty grows with mere exposure
Herman Miller, Inc.'s famed Aeron chair initially received high comfort ratings but abysmal beauty ratings. To some it looked like "lawn furniture" or "a giant prehistoric insect" (Gladwell, 2005). But then, with design awards, media visibility, and imitators, the ugly duckling came to be the company's best-selling chair ever and to be seen as beautiful. With people, too, beauty lies partly in the beholder's eye and can grow with exposure.

"I can't wait to see what you're like on line."

HI & LOIS

Reprinted with special permission of King Features Syndicate.

Passionate Love

Noting that arousal is a key ingredient of **passionate love,** Hatfield suggests that Stanley Schachter's two-factor theory of emotion can help us understand this intense positive absorption in another. The theory assumes that (1) emotions have two ingredients—physical arousal plus cognitive appraisal—and that (2) arousal from any source can enhance one emotion or another, depending on how we interpret and label the arousal.

In tests of this theory, college men have been aroused by fright, by running in place, by viewing erotic materials, or by listening to humorous or repulsive monologues. They were then introduced to an attractive woman and asked to rate her (or their girlfriend). Unlike unaroused men, those who were stirred up attributed some of their arousal to the woman or girlfriend and felt more attracted to her (Carducci & others, 1978; Dermer & Pyszczynski, 1978; White & Kight, 1984).

Outside the laboratory, Donald Dutton and Arthur Aron (1974, 1989) went to two bridges across British Columbia's rocky Capilano River. One, a swaying footbridge, was 230 feet above the rocks; the other was low and solid. An attractive young female accomplice intercepted men coming off each bridge, sought their help in filling out a short questionnaire, and then offered her phone number in case they wanted to hear more about her project. Far more of those who had just crossed the high bridge—which left their hearts pounding—accepted the number and later called the woman. To be revved up and to associate some of that arousal with a desirable person is to feel the pull of passion. Adrenaline makes the heart grow fonder.

Companionate Love

Although the spark of romantic love often endures, the intense absorption in the other, the thrill of the romance, the giddy "floating on a cloud" feeling typically fades. Does this mean the French are correct in saying that "love makes the time pass and time makes love pass"? Or can friendship and commitment keep a relationship going after the passion cools? In Leo Tolstoy's *Family Happiness,* a young woman walks with a man she loves and realizes "that from that day he was mine, and I should never lose him now." Later, after their marriage, she reflects while sitting at home that their romantic courtship has been replaced by something quieter and more secure. "That day ended the romance of our marriage," she explains. "The old feeling became a precious irrecoverable remembrance; but a new feeling of love for my children and the father of my children laid the foundation of a new life and a quite different happiness; and that life and happiness have lasted to the present time."

Hatfield agrees, noting that as love matures it becomes a steadier **companionate love**—a deep, affectionate attachment. There may be adaptive wisdom to this change from passion to affection. Passionate love often produces children, whose survival is aided by the parents' waning obsession with one another. Social psychologist Ellen Berscheid and her colleagues (1984) noted that the failure to appreciate passionate love's limited half-life can doom a relationship: "If the inevitable odds against eternal passionate love in a relationship were better understood, more people might choose to be satisfied with the quieter feelings of satisfaction and contentment." Indeed, recognizing the short duration of passionate love, some societies have deemed such feelings an irrational reason for marrying.

> When two people are under the influence of the most violent, most insane, most delusive, and most transient of passions, they are required to swear that they will remain in that excited, abnormal, and exhausting condition continuously until death do them part."
>
> George Bernard Shaw, "Getting Married," 1908

Better, such cultures say, to choose (or have someone choose for you) a partner with a compatible background and interests. Non-Western cultures, where people rate love less important for marriage, do have lower divorce rates (Levine & others, 1995).

One key to a gratifying and enduring relationship is **equity:** Both partners receive in proportion to what they give. When equity exists—when both partners freely give and receive, when they share decision making—their chances for sustained and satisfying companionate love are good (Gray-Little & Burks, 1983; Van Yperen & Buunk, 1990). Mutually sharing self and possessions, giving and getting emotional support, promoting and caring about one another's welfare are at the core of every type of loving relationship (Sternberg & Grajek, 1984). It's true for lovers, for parent and child, and for intimate friends.

Another vital ingredient of loving relationships is **self-disclosure,** the revealing of intimate details about ourselves—our likes and dislikes, our dreams and worries, our proud and shameful moments. "When I am with my friend," noted the Roman statesman Seneca, "me thinks I am alone, and as much at liberty to speak anything as to think it." Self-disclosure breeds liking, and liking breeds self-disclosure (Collins & Miller, 1994). As one person reveals a little, the other reciprocates, the first then reveals more, and on and on, as friends or lovers move to deeper intimacy. Each increase in intimacy rekindles passion (Baumeister & Bratslavsky, 1999).

One experiment marched pairs of volunteer students through 45 minutes of increasingly self-disclosing conversation—from "When did you last sing to yourself" to "When did you last cry in front of another person? By yourself?" By the experiment's end, those experiencing the escalating intimacy felt remarkably close to their conversation partner, much closer than others who had spent the time with small-talk questions, such as "What was your high school like?" (Aron & others, 1997). Given self-disclosing intimacy plus mutually supportive equality, the odds favor enduring companionate love.

MATRIMONY

COURTSHIP

Courtship and Matrimony (From the collection of Werner Nekes)

Sometimes passionate love becomes enduring companionate love, sometimes not *(invert the picture)* What, in addition to similar attitudes and interests, predicts long-term loving attachment?

" When a match has equal partners then I fear not."

Aeschylus, *Prometheus Bound*, 478 B.C.

Altruism

OBJECTIVE 58-3 | Define *altruism,* and give an example.

Carl Wilkens, a Seventh Day Adventist missionary, was living with his family in Kigali, Rwanda, when Hutu militia began to slaughter the Tutsi in 1994. The U.S. government, church leaders, and friends all implored Wilkens to leave. He refused. After evacuating his family, and even after every other American had left Kigali, he alone stayed and contested the 800,000-person genocide. When the militia came to kill him and his Tutsi servants, his Hutu neighbors deterred them. Despite repeated death threats, he spent his days risking roadblocks to take food and water to orphanages and to negotiate, plead, and bully his way through the bloodshed, saving lives time and again. "It just seemed the right thing to do," he later explained (Kristof, 2004). Elsewhere in Kigali, Paul Rusesabagina, a Hutu married to a Tutsi

▪ **passionate love** an aroused state of intense positive absorption in another, usually present at the beginning of a love relationship.

▪ **companionate love** the deep affectionate attachment we feel for those with whom our lives are intertwined.

▪ **equity** a condition in which people receive from a relationship in proportion to what they give to it.

▪ **self-disclosure** revealing intimate aspects of oneself to others.

and the acting manager of a luxury hotel, was sheltering more than 1200 terrified Tutsis and moderate Hutus. When international peacemakers abandoned the city and hostile militia threatened his guests in the "Hotel Rwanda" (as it became called in a 2004 movie), the courageous Rusesabagina began cashing in past favors, bribing the militia, and telephoning influential persons abroad to bring pressure on local authorities, thereby sparing the lives of the hotel's occupants from the surrounding chaos.

Such selfless goodness exemplifies **altruism**—the unselfish regard for the welfare of others. Altruism became a major concern of social psychologists after an especially vile act of sexual violence. On March 13, 1964, a stalker repeatedly stabbed Kitty Genovese, then raped her as she lay dying outside her Queens, New York, apartment at 3:30 A.M. "Oh, my God, he stabbed me!" Genovese screamed into the early morning stillness. "Please help me!" Windows opened and lights went on as 38 of her neighbors heard her screams. Her attacker fled and then returned to stab her eight more times and rape her again. Not until he had fled for good did anyone so much as call the police, at 3:50 A.M.

> "Probably no single incident has caused social psychologists to pay as much attention to an aspect of social behavior as Kitty Genovese's murder."
>
> R. Lance Shotland (1984)

Bystander Intervention

OBJECTIVE 58-4 | Describe the steps in the decision-making process involved in bystander intervention.

Reflecting on the Genovese murder and other such tragedies, most commentators were outraged by the bystanders' "apathy" and "indifference." Rather than blaming the onlookers, social psychologists John Darley and Bibb Latané (1968b) attributed their inaction to an important situational factor—the presence of others. Given certain circumstances, they suspected, most of us might behave similarly.

After staging emergencies under various conditions, Darley and Latané assembled their findings into a decision scheme: We will help only if the situation enables us first to *notice* the incident, then to *interpret* it as an emergency, and finally to *assume responsibility* for helping (**FIGURE 58.2**). At each step, the presence of other bystanders turns people away from the path that leads to helping. In the laboratory and on the street, people in a group of strangers are more likely than solitary individuals to keep their eyes focused on what they themselves are doing or where they are going. If they notice an unusual situation, they may infer from the blasé reactions of the other passersby that the situation is not an emergency. "The person lying on the sidewalk must be drunk," they think, and move on.

But sometimes, as with the Genovese murder, the emergency is unambiguous and people still fail to help. The witnesses looking out through their windows noticed the incident, correctly interpreted the emergency, and yet failed to assume responsibility. Why? To find out, Darley and Latané (1968a) simulated a physical emergency in their laboratory. University students participated in a discussion over an intercom.

FIGURE 58.2

The decision-making process for bystander intervention

Before helping, one must first notice an emergency, then correctly interpret it, and then feel responsible. (From Darley & Latané, 1968b.)

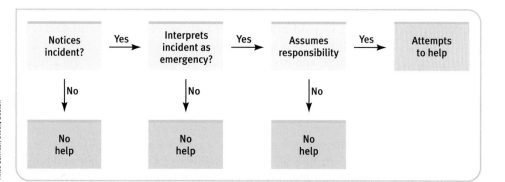

Each student was in a separate cubicle, and only the person whose microphone was switched on could be heard. One of the students was an accomplice of the experimenters. When his turn came, he made sounds as though he were having an epileptic seizure and called for help.

How did the other students react? As FIGURE **58.3** shows, those who believed only they could hear the victim—and therefore thought they bore total responsibility for helping him—usually went to his aid. Those who thought others also could hear were more likely to react as did Kitty Genovese's neighbors. When more people shared responsibility for helping—when there was diffusion of responsibility—any single listener was less likely to help.

In hundreds of additional experiments, psychologists have studied the factors that influence bystanders' willingness to relay an emergency phone call, aid a stranded motorist, donate blood, pick up dropped books, contribute money, and give time. For example, Latané, James Dabbs (1975), and 145 collaborators took 1497 elevator rides in three cities and "accidentally" dropped coins or pencils in front of 4813 fellow passengers. The women coin droppers were more likely to receive help than were the men—a gender difference often reported by other researchers (Eagly & Crowley, 1986). But the major finding was the **bystander effect**—any particular bystander was less likely to give aid with other bystanders present. When alone with the person in need, 40 percent helped; in the presence of five other bystanders, only 20 percent helped.

From their observations of behavior in tens of thousands of such "emergencies," altruism researchers have discerned some additional patterns. The *best* odds of our helping someone occur when

- the victim appears to need and deserve help.
- the victim is in some way similar to us.
- we have just observed someone else being helpful.
- we are not in a hurry.
- we are in a small town or rural area.
- we are feeling guilty.
- we are focused on others and not preoccupied.
- we are in a good mood.

■ **altruism** unselfish regard for the welfare of others.

■ **bystander effect** the tendency for any given bystander to be less likely to give aid if other bystanders are present.

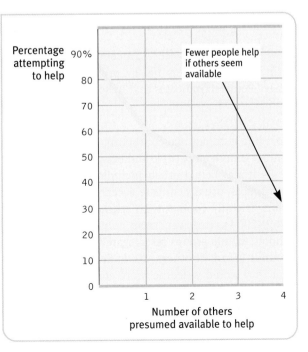

FIGURE 58.3

Responses to a simulated physical emergency

When people thought they alone heard the calls for help from a person they believed to be having an epileptic seizure, they usually helped. But when they thought four others were also hearing the calls, fewer than a third responded. (From Darley & Latané, 1968a.)

This last result, that happy people are helpful people, is one of the most consistent findings in all of psychology. No matter how people are cheered—whether by being made to feel successful and intelligent, by thinking happy thoughts, by finding money, or even by receiving a posthypnotic suggestion—they become more generous and more eager to help (Carlson & others, 1988).

The Norms for Helping

OBJECTIVE 58-5 | Explain altruistic behavior from the perspective of social exchange theory and social norms.

Why do we help? One widely held view is that self-interest underlies all human interactions, that our constant goal is to maximize rewards and minimize costs. Accountants call it cost-benefit analysis. Philosophers call it utilitarianism. Social psychologists call it **social exchange theory.** If you are pondering whether to donate blood, you may weigh the costs of doing so (time, discomfort, and anxiety) against the benefits (reduced guilt, social approval, good feelings). If you anticipate rewards from helping that exceed the costs, you help.

But why do we leave tips for people we will never see again and give directions to strangers? In part because we have been socialized to do so, through norms that prescribe how we *ought* to behave, often to our mutual benefit. Through socialization, we learn the **reciprocity norm,** the expectation that we should return help, not harm, to those who have helped us. In our relations with others of similar status, the reciprocity norm compels us to give (in favors, gifts, or social invitations) about as much as we receive. We also learn a **social-responsibility norm:** that we should help those who need our help—young children and others who cannot give as much as they receive—even if the costs outweigh the benefits. In repeated Gallup surveys, people who each week attend religious services often exhibit the social-responsibility norm: They report volunteering more than twice as many hours in helping the poor and infirm than do those who rarely or never attend religious services (Hodgkinson & Weitzman, 1992; Independent Sector, 2002). They also give away three times as much money.

Peacemaking

OBJECTIVE 58-6 | Discuss effective ways of encouraging peaceful cooperation and reducing social conflict.

How can we make peace? Can cooperation, communication, and conciliation transform the antagonisms fed by prejudice and conflicts into attitudes that promote peace? Research indicates that in some cases, they can.

Cooperation

Does it help to put two conflicting parties into close contact? It depends. When such contact is noncompetitive and between parties with equal status, such as fellow store clerks, it may help. Initially prejudiced co-workers of different races have, in such circumstances, usually come to accept one another. Among North Americans and Europeans, friendly contact with ethnic minorities has led to less prejudice (Pettigrew, 1969, 2004). However, mere contact is not always enough. In most desegregated schools, ethnic groups resegregate themselves in the lunchrooms and on the school grounds (Clark & others, 2005; Schofield, 1986). People in each group often think that they would welcome more contact with the other group, but they assume the other group does not reciprocate the wish (Shelton & Richeson, 2005). "I don't reach out to them, because I don't want to be rebuffed; they don't reach out to me, because they're just not interested." When such mirror-image misperceptions are corrected, friendships may then form and prejudices melt.

Oh, make us happy and you make us good!"

Robert Browning, *The Ring and the Book*, 1868

You cannot shake hands with a clenched fist."

Indira Gandhi, 1971

To see if enemies could overcome their differences, researcher Muzafer Sherif (1966) first instigated conflict. He placed 22 Oklahoma City boys in two separate areas of a Boy Scout camp. He then put the two groups through a series of competitive activities, with prizes going to the victors. Before long, each group became intensely proud of itself and hostile to the other group's "sneaky," "smart-alecky stinkers." Food wars broke out during meals. Cabins were ransacked. Fistfights had to be broken up by members of the camp staff. When Sherif brought the two groups together, they avoided one another, except to taunt and threaten.

Nevertheless, within a few days Sherif transformed these young enemies into jovial comrades. He gave them **superordinate goals**—shared goals that overrode their differences and that could be achieved only through cooperation. A planned disruption of the camp water supply necessitated that all 22 boys work together to restore water. Renting a movie in those pre-VCR days required their pooled resources. A stalled truck needed the combined force of all the boys pulling and pushing together to get it moving. Having used isolation and competition to make strangers into enemies, Sherif used shared predicaments and goals to reconcile the enemies and make them friends. What reduced conflict was not mere contact, but *cooperative* contact.

A shared predicament—a fearsome external threat and a superordinate desire to overcome it—likewise had a powerfully unifying effect in the weeks after 9/11. Nothing breeds solidarity quite like a common enemy. As suicide attacks in Israel can unify partisan Jews, and as Israeli military attacks on Palestinians can unify diverse Muslims, so Americans immediately felt that "we" were under attack. Gallup-surveyed approval of "our President" shot up from 51 percent the week before the attack to a highest-ever level of 90 percent 10 days after, just surpassing the previous approval-rating record of 89 percent enjoyed by his father, George Bush, at the climax of the 1991 Persian Gulf War (Newport, 2002). In chat groups and everyday speech, even the word *we* (relative to *I*) surged in the immediate aftermath (Pennebaker, 2002).

John Dovidio and Samuel Gaertner (1999) report that cooperation has especially positive effects when it leads people to define a new, inclusive group that dissolves their former subgroups. Seat the members of two groups not on opposite sides, but alternately around the table. Give them a new, shared name. Have them work together. Such experiences change "us and them" into "we." Those once perceived as being in another group now are seen as part of one's own group. One 18-year-old New Jersey man would not be surprised. After 9/11, he explained a shift in his social identity: "I just thought of myself as black. But now I feel like I'm an American, more than ever" (Sengupta, 2001). In one experiment by Dovidio and his colleagues (2004), white Americans who read a newspaper article about a terrorist threat against all Americans subsequently expressed reduced prejudice against African-Americans.

During the 1970s, several teams of educational researchers simultaneously wondered: If cooperative contacts between members of rival groups encourage positive attitudes, could we apply this principle in multicultural schools? Could we promote interracial friendships by replacing competitive classroom situations with cooperative ones? And could cooperative learning maintain or even enhance student achievement? Many experiments confirm that in all three cases, the answer is yes (Johnson & Johnson, 1989, 1994; Slavin & others, 2003). Members of interracial groups who work together on projects and play together on athletic teams typically come to feel friendly toward those of the other race. So do those who engage in cooperative classroom learning. So encouraging are these results that thousands of teachers have introduced interracial cooperative learning into their classrooms. Working with fellow students in all their diversity sets the stage, declared the Carnegie Council on Adolescent Development (1989), for "adult work life and for citizenship in a multicultural society."

■ **social exchange theory** the theory that our social behavior is an exchange process, the aim of which is to maximize benefits and minimize costs.

■ **reciprocity norm** an expectation that people will help, not hurt, those who have helped them.

■ **social-responsibility norm** an expectation that people will help those dependent upon them.

■ **superordinate goals** shared goals that override differences among people and require their cooperation.

Most of us have overlapping identities which unite us with very different groups. We *can* love what we are, without hating what—and who—we are *not*. We can thrive in our own tradition, even as we learn from others."

U.N. Secretary General Kofi Annan, Nobel Prize Lecture, 2001

**Superordinate goals
override differences**
Cooperative efforts to achieve shared
goals are an effective way to break down
social barriers.

Syracuse Newspapers/ The Image Works

"I am prepared this day to declare myself
a citizen of the world, and to invite everyone everywhere to embrace this broader
vision of our interdependent world, our
common quest for justice, and ultimately
for Peace on Earth."

Father Theodore Hesburgh, *The Human Imperative*,
1974

The power of cooperative activity to make friends of former enemies has led psychologists to urge increased international exchange and cooperation (Klineberg,
1984). As we engage in mutually beneficial trade, as we work to protect our common
destiny on this fragile planet, and as we become more aware that our hopes and fears
are shared, we can change misperceptions that lead to fragmentation and conflict
into a solidarity based on common interests.

Working toward shared goals enables diverse peoples to discover unity in their
common values and superordinate identity. "Common values," are what we need, declared the chair of Britain's Commission for Racial Equality as ethnic tensions recently flared (Phillips, 2004). And today's Rwandan government policy proclaims,
"There is no ethnicity here. We are all Rwandan," as it seeks to resolve historic ani-
mosities between Tutsis and Hutus (Lacey, 2004). Western democracies have largely
been spared ethnic tribal warfare because their different racial groups share so many
of the very same goals, notes sociologist Amitai Etzioni (1999). In the United States,
these shared goals include fair treatment for all, higher moral standards, and a wish
that all high school graduates "understand the common history and ideas that tie all
Americans together." Although diversity commands attention, we are—as working toward shared goals reminds us—more alike than different.

Communication

In experiments featuring a game known as the *social-trap*, distrusting people pursue
their individual interests as a defense against exploitation. But when they are allowed to discuss the dilemma and negotiate, cooperation increases (Jorgenson &
Papciak, 1981).

When real-life conflicts become intense, a third-party mediator—a marriage
counselor, labor mediator, diplomat, community volunteer—may likewise facilitate
much-needed communication (Rubin & others, 1994). Mediators help each party
to voice its viewpoint and to understand the other's. By leading each side to think
about the other's underlying needs and goals, the mediator aims to replace a competitive *win-lose* orientation with a cooperative *win-win* orientation that aims at a
mutually beneficial resolution. A classic example: Two friends, after quarreling
over an orange, agreed to split it. One squeezed his half for juice. The other used
the peel from her half to make a cake. If only the two had understood each other's
motives, they could have hit on the win-win solution of one having all the juice,
the other all the peel.

Such understanding and cooperative resolution is most needed, yet least likely, in
times of anger or crisis (Bodenhausen & others, 1994; Tetlock, 1988). When conflicts intensify, images become more stereotyped, communication more difficult, and
judgments more rigid.

Conciliation

When tension and suspicion peak, cooperation and communication may become impossible. Each party is likely to threaten, coerce, or retaliate. In the weeks before the Persian Gulf War, President George Bush threatened, in the full glare of publicity, to "kick Saddam's ass." Saddam Hussein communicated in kind, threatening to make Americans "swim in their own blood."

Under such conditions, is there an alternative to war or surrender? Social psychologist Charles Osgood (1962, 1980) has advocated a strategy of "Graduated and Reciprocated Initiatives in Tension-Reduction," nicknamed **GRIT.** In applying GRIT, one side first announces its recognition of mutual interests and its intent to reduce tensions. It then initiates one or more small, conciliatory acts. Without weakening one's retaliatory capability, this modest beginning opens the door for reciprocation by the other party. Should the enemy respond with hostility, one reciprocates in kind. But so, too, with any conciliatory response. Thus, President Kennedy's gesture of stopping atmospheric nuclear tests began a series of reciprocated conciliatory acts that culminated in the 1993 atmospheric test-ban treaty.

"To begin with, I would like to express my sincere thanks and deep appreciation for the opportunity to meet with you. While there are still profound differences between us, I think the very fact of my presence here today is a major breakthrough."

In laboratory experiments, GRIT has been the most effective strategy known for increasing trust and cooperation (Lindskold & others, 1978, 1988). Even during intense personal conflict, when communication has been nonexistent, a small conciliatory gesture—a smile, a touch, a word of apology—may work wonders. Conciliations allow both parties to begin edging down the tension ladder to a safer rung where communication and mutual understanding can begin.

And how good that such can happen, for civilization advances not by cultural isolation—maintaining walls around ethnic enclaves—but by tapping the knowledge, the skills, and the arts that are each culture's legacy to the whole human race. Thomas Sowell (1991) observed that, thanks to cultural sharing, every modern society is enriched by a cultural mix. We have China to thank for paper and printing, and for the magnetic compass that opened the great explorations. We have Egypt to thank for trigonometry. We have the Islamic world and India's Hindus to thank for our Arabic numerals. While celebrating and claiming these diverse cultural legacies, we can also welcome the enrichment of today's social diversity. We can view ourselves as instruments in a human orchestra. And we can therefore affirm our own culture's heritage while building bridges of communication, understanding, and cooperation across cultural traditions as we think about, influence, and relate to one another.

■ **GRIT** Graduated and Reciprocated Initiatives in Tension-Reduction—a strategy designed to decrease international tensions.

>> LEARNING OUTCOMES

Prosocial Relations

OBJECTIVE 58-1 | **Describe the influence of proximity, physical attractiveness, and similarity on interpersonal attraction.**

Proximity—geographical nearness—promotes attraction, in part because it increases the opportunities for interaction and in part because of the mere exposure effect (repeated exposure to novel stimuli enhances liking). People prefer being with *physically attractive* people and perceive them as healthier, happier, more sensitive, more successful, and more socially skilled. Judgments of attractiveness vary by culture, and as time goes by we find those we care about to be more attractive. *Similarity of attitudes and interests* greatly increases liking after people make it past the first impression.

OBJECTIVE 58-2 | **Describe the effect of physical arousal on passionate love, and identify two predictors of enduring companionate love.**

Associating arousal with a desirable person is a key ingredient of *passionate love,* the intense absorption we cognitively label as love. Passionate love often matures into the deep affectionate attachment of *companionate love.* This transition is most likely in relationships characterized by *equality* and *intimate self-disclosure.*

OBJECTIVE 58-3 | **Define *altruism,* and give an example.**

Altruism is the unselfish regard for the welfare of others. Examples of altruism include helping victims of a natural disaster or giving blood with no expectation of personal reward.

OBJECTIVE 58-4 | **Describe the steps in the decision-making process involved in bystander intervention.**

The *bystander effect* is the tendency, identified by John Darley and Bibb Latané, for any given observer to be less likely to help if others are present. To offer help, a person must notice the incident, interpret it as an emergency, and assume responsibility for offering help. Diffusion of responsibility lowers the likelihood of helping. Odds of helping are highest when the victim is similar to us and appears to need and deserve help, and when we observe others helping, are feeling guilty, are not in a hurry or preoccupied, are in a small town or rural area, and are in a good mood.

OBJECTIVE 58-5 | **Explain altruistic behavior from the perspective of social exchange theory and social norms.**

Social exchange theory proposes that our social behaviors—even altruistic, helpful acts—are based on self-interest: maximizing our benefits (which may include our own good feelings) and minimizing our costs. *Social norms* influence altruistic behaviors by telling us how we *should* behave. The *reciprocity norm* is the expectation that we will help those who help us, and the *social-responsibility norm* is the expectation that we will help those who are dependent on us.

OBJECTIVE 58-6 | **Discuss effective ways of encouraging peaceful cooperation and reducing social conflict.**

Friendly contact between prejudiced people can change attitudes. But social conflict is most likely to be reduced when the circumstances favor cooperation to achieve superordinate goals (especially if subgroups disappear), understanding through communication (sometimes with the help of a third party), and reciprocated conciliatory gestures (such as the *GRIT* strategy).

TERMS AND CONCEPTS TO REMEMBER

mere exposure effect, p. 58-1
passionate love, p. 58-6
companionate love, p. 58-6
equity, p. 58-7
self-disclosure, p. 58-7
altruism, p. 58-8
bystander effect, p. 58-9

social exchange theory,
  p. 58-10
reciprocity norm, p. 58-10
social-responsibility norm,
  p. 58-10
superordinate goals, p. 58-11
GRIT, p. 58-13

TEST YOURSELF

1. Why didn't anybody help Kitty Genovese? What social relations principle did this incident illustrate?

(Answer in Appendix B.)

ASK YOURSELF

1. Do you regret not getting along with some friend or family members? How might you go about reconciling that relationship?

>WEB

Multiple-choice *self-tests* and more may be found at www.worthpublishers.com/myers.

Careers in Psychology

Jennifer Lento
University of San Diego

What can you do with a degree in psychology? Lots!

As a psychology major, you will graduate with a scientific mindset and an awareness of basic principles of human behavior (biological mechanisms, development, cognition, psychological disorders, social interaction). This background will prepare you for success in many areas, including business, helping professions, health services, marketing, law, sales, and teaching. You may even go on to graduate school for specialized training to become a psychology professional. This appendix describes the various levels of psychology education and some jobs available at those levels; psychology's specialized subfields; and ways you can improve your chances of admission to graduate school.[1]

Preparing for a Career in Psychology

Psychology is the second most popular major in the United States, second only to business (*Princeton Review,* 2005). More than 70,000 psychology majors graduate from U.S. colleges and universities each year. An undergraduate degree in psychology can prepare you for a broad array of jobs after graduation. For other jobs, you will need a graduate degree.

The Bachelor's Degree

Psychology majors graduate with a valuable skill set that increases their marketability in many fields. About 42 percent of U.S. psychology majors go on to graduate school in psychology (Fogg, Harrington, & Harrington, 2004). What happens to the rest? Most work in for-profit organizations after graduation, especially in management, sales, and administration. **TABLE A.1** on the next page shows the top 10 occupations that employ people with a bachelor's degree in psychology.

Clearly, psychology majors are marketable beyond the boundaries of psychology. Their sought-after skills and abilities include an ability to work and get along with others, a desire and willingness to learn new skills, adaptability to changing situations, and good critical-thinking and problem-solving skills (Landrum, 2001). There are some things that all psychology majors can do to maximize success in the job market. Employers that hire people with only a bachelor's degree tend to favor individuals with positive explanatory styles and practical experience as well as a good education (Cannon, 2005). Betsy Morgan and Ann Korschgen (1998) offer the following helpful tips for increasing your chances of getting a job after graduation:

1. Get to know your instructors.
2. Take courses that support your interests.

---

[1] Although this text covers the world of psychology for students in many countries, this appendix draws primarily from available U.S. data. Its description of psychology's subfields and its suggestions for preparing to enter the profession are, however, also applicable in many other countries.

TABLE A.1

TOP 10 U.S. OCCUPATIONS THAT EMPLOY PEOPLE WITH A BACHELOR'S DEGREE IN PSYCHOLOGY

1. Top- and mid-level managers, executives, administrators
2. Sales occupations, including retail
3. Social workers
4. Other management-related occupations
5. Personnel, training, labor relations specialists
6. Other administrative (record clerks, telephone operators)
7. Insurance, securities, real estate, business services
8. Other marketing and sales occupations
9. Registered nurses, pharmacists, therapists, physician assistants
10. Accountants, auditors, other financial specialists

Source: Fogg, Harrington, & Harrington (2004).

3. Familiarize yourself with available resources, such as campus career services and alumni.
4. Participate in at least one internship experience.
5. Volunteer some of your time and talent to campus or community organizations, such as Psi Chi or Psi Beta (psychology's national honor societies) or your school's psychology club.

Postgraduate Degrees

A graduate degree in psychology will give you proficiency in an area of psychological specialization. According to the U.S. Bureau of Labor Statistics (2004), psychologists with advanced degrees held approximately 139,000 jobs in 2000. Such jobs are expected to increase 21 to 35 percent (depending on the subfield of psychology) through 2012 because of the need for psychological services in a variety of settings. The work settings for psychologists vary somewhat by type of graduate degree. As shown in **FIGURE A.1,** psychologists with a doctorate work primarily in universities and colleges; most people with a master's degree work in other educational institutions (such as elementary and middle schools) and in for-profit companies. Among those seeking advanced training in psychology in the United States, 29 percent earn a master's degree, 7 percent earn a doctoral degree, and 6 percent earn some other professional degree (e.g., law or health professions) (Fogg, Harrington, & Harrington, 2004).

The Master's Degree

A master's degree in psychology requires at least two years of full-time graduate study in a specific subfield of psychology. In addition to specialized course work in psychology, requirements usually include practical experience in an applied setting and/or a master's thesis reporting on an original research project. You might acquire a master's degree to do specialized work in psychology. As a graduate with a master's degree, you might handle research and data collection and analysis in a university, government, or private industry setting. You might work under the supervision of a psychologist with a doctorate, providing some clinical service such as therapy or testing. Or you might find a job in the health, government, industry,

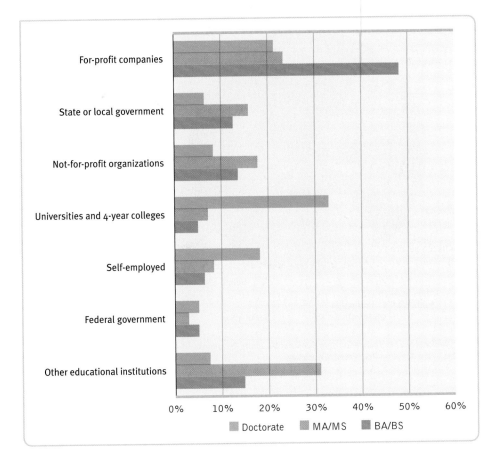

FIGURE **A.1**
Work settings for psychology-degree recipients
(Fogg, Harrington, & Harrington, 2004)

or education fields. You might also acquire a master's degree as a stepping stone for more advanced study in a doctoral program in psychology, which will considerably expand the number of employment opportunities available to you (Super & Super, 2001).

Doctoral Degrees

You will probably need five to seven years of graduate study in a specific subfield of psychology to get your doctoral degree. The *doctor of philosophy (Ph.D.)* in psychology culminates in a *dissertation* (an extensive research paper you will be required to defend orally) based on original research. Courses in quantitative research methods, which include the use of computer-based analysis, are an important part of graduate study and are necessary to complete the dissertation. The *doctor of psychology (Psy.D.)* may be based on clinical (therapeutic) work and examinations rather than a dissertation. If you pursue clinical and counseling psychology programs, you should expect at least a one-year internship in addition to the regular course work, clinical practice, and research.

FIGURE A.2 (on the next page) lists by subfield the Ph.D.s earned in the United States in a recent year. Clinical psychology is the most popular specialty area among holders of doctorates in psychology. The largest employment growth areas for doctoral graduates have been in the for-profit and self-employment sectors, including health services providers, industrial/organizational psychology, and educational psychology. About one-third of doctoral-level psychologists are employed in academic settings (Fogg, Harrington, & Harrington, 2004).

In 2001, a total of 73 percent of new doctoral respondents and 55 percent of new master's respondents indicated that their primary occupational position was their

FIGURE **A.2**
U.S. Ph.D.s by subfield, 2001

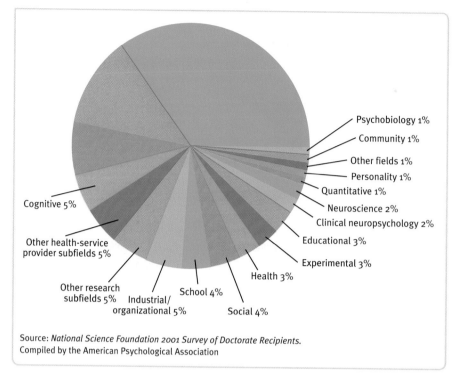

Psychobiology 1%
Community 1%
Other fields 1%
Personality 1%
Quantitative 1%
Neuroscience 2%
Clinical neuropsychology 2%
Educational 3%
Experimental 3%
Health 3%
Social 4%
School 4%
Industrial/organizational 5%
Other research subfields 5%
Other health-service provider subfields 5%
Cognitive 5%

Source: *National Science Foundation 2001 Survey of Doctorate Recipients.*
Compiled by the American Psychological Association

Prescription privileges
Many psychologists would like the opportunity to prescribe therapeutic drugs in order to expand the scope of clinical practice and to meet the need for psychiatric services in many parts of the United States. Psychologists in the U.S. military and in the states of New Mexico and Louisiana currently have prescription privileges.

first choice. Most new graduates with a master's degree or a Ph.D. are fairly satisfied with their current positions overall in terms of salary, benefits, opportunities for personal development, supervisors, colleagues, and working conditions (Kohout & Wicherski, 2004; Singleton, Tate, & Kohout, 2003).

Subfields of Psychology

If you are like most psychology students, you may be unaware of the wide variety of specialties and work settings available in psychology (Terre & Stoddart, 2000). To date, the American Psychological Association (APA) has 53 divisions (TABLE **A.2**). The following paragraphs (arranged alphabetically) describe some careers in the main specialty areas of psychology, most of which require a graduate degree in psychology.

Clinical psychologists promote psychological health in individuals, groups, and organizations. Some clinical psychologists specialize in specific psychological disorders. Others treat a range of disorders, from adjustment difficulties to severe psychopathology. Clinical psychologists might engage in research, teaching, assessment, and consultation. Some hold workshops and lectures on psychological issues for other professionals or for the public. Clinical psychologists work in a variety of settings, including private practice, mental health service organizations, schools, universities, industries, legal systems, medical systems, counseling centers, government agencies, and military services.

To become a clinical psychologist, you will need to earn a doctorate from a clinical psychology program. The APA sets the standards for clinical psychology graduate programs, offering *accreditation* (official recognition) to those who meet their standards. Unlike practitioners in most other subfields of psychology, clinical psychologists must, in all U.S. states, obtain a license to offer services such as therapy and testing.

Cognitive psychologists primarily do research to add to psychology's store of knowledge. Cognitive psychologists study thought processes and focus on such topics as

TABLE **A.2**

APA DIVISIONS BY NUMBER AND NAME

1. Society for General Psychology	29. Psychotherapy
2. Society for the Teaching of Psychology	30. Society of Psychological Hypnosis
3. Experimental Psychology	31. State, Provincial, and Territorial Psychological Association Affairs
4. *There is no Division 4.*	32. Humanistic Psychology
5. Evaluation, Measurement, and Statistics	33. Mental Retardation and Developmental Disabilities
6. Behavioral Neuroscience and Comparative Psychology	34. Population and Environmental Psychology
7. Developmental Psychology	35. Society for the Psychology of Women
8. Society for Personality and Social Psychology	36. Psychology of Religion
9. Society for the Psychological Study of Social Issues (SPSSI)	37. Child, Youth, and Family Services
10. Society for the Psychology of Aesthetics, Creativity, and the Arts	38. Health Psychology
11. *There is no Division 11.*	39. Psychoanalysis
12. Society of Clinical Psychology	40. Clinical Neuropsychology
13. Society of Consulting Psychology	41. American Psychology-Law Society
14. Society for Industrial and Organizational Psychology	42. Psychologists in Independent Practice
15. Educational Psychology	43. Family Psychology
16. School Psychology	44. Society for the Psychological Study of Lesbian, Gay, and Bisexual Issues
17. Society of Counseling Psychology	45. Society for the Psychological Study of Ethnic Minority Issues
18. Psychologists in Public Service	46. Media Psychology
19. Society for Military Psychology	47. Exercise and Sport Psychology
20. Adult Development and Aging	48. Society for the Study of Peace, Conflict, and Violence: Peace Psychology Division
21. Applied Experimental and Engineering Psychology	49. Group Psychology and Group Psychotherapy
22. Rehabilitation Psychology	50. Addictions
23. Society for Consumer Psychology	51. Society for the Psychological Study of Men and Masculinity
24. Society for Theoretical and Philosophical Psychology	52. International Psychology
25. Behavior Analysis	53. Society of Clinical Child and Adolescent Psychology
26. Society for the History of Psychology	54. Society of Pediatric Psychology
27. Society for Community Research and Action: Division of Community Psychology	55. American Society for the Advancement of Pharmacotherapy
28. Psychopharmacology and Substance Abuse	

Source: American Psychological Association

Karen Moskowitz/Getty Images

Cognitive consulting
Cognitive psychologists may advise businesses on how to operate more effectively by understanding the human factors involved.

perception, language, attention, problem solving, memory, judgment and decision making, forgetting, and intelligence. Recent areas of research interest include designing computer-based models of thought processes and identifying biological correlates of cognition. As a cognitive psychologist, you might work as a professor, industrial consultant, or human factors specialist in an educational or business setting.

Community psychologists move beyond focusing on specific individuals or families and deal with broad problems of mental health in community settings. These psychologists believe that human behavior is powerfully influenced by the interaction between people and their physical, social, political, and economic environments. They seek to improve individual functioning by enhancing environmental settings that promote psychological health. Community psychologists focus on prevention, promotion of positive mental health, and crisis intervention, with special attention to the problems of underserved groups and ethnic minorities. As a community psychologist, your work settings could include federal, state, and local departments of mental health, corrections, and welfare. You might conduct research or help evaluate research in health service settings, serve as an independent consultant for a private or government agency, or teach and consult as a college or university faculty member.

Counseling psychologists help people adjust to life transitions or make life-style changes. This field is very similar to clinical psychology, except that counseling psychologists typically help people with adjustment problems rather than severe psychopathology. Like clinical psychologists, counseling psychologists conduct therapy and provide assessments to individuals and groups. As a counseling psychologist, you would emphasize your clients' strengths, helping clients cope during a transitional time using their own skills, interests, and abilities. You might find yourself working in an academic setting as a faculty member or administrator or in a university counseling center, community mental health center, business, or private practice. As with clinical psychology, you will need to obtain a state license to provide counseling services to the public.

Developmental psychologists conduct research in age-related behavioral changes and apply their scientific knowledge to educational, child care, policy, and related settings. As a developmental psychologist, you would investigate change across a broad range of topics, including the biological, social, psychological, and cognitive aspects of development. Developmental psychology informs a number of applied fields, including educational psychology, school psychology, child psychopathology, and gerontology. You will probably specialize in behavior during infancy, childhood, adolescence, or middle or late adulthood. Your work setting could be an educational institution, day-care center, youth group program, or senior center.

Educational psychologists study the relationship between learning and our physical and social environments. They study the psychological processes involved in learning and develop strategies for enhancing the learning process. As an educational psychologist, you might work in a university—in a psychology department or a school of education. You might conduct basic research on topics related to learning or develop innovative methods of teaching to enhance the learning process. You might be employed by a school or government agency or charged with designing and implementing effective employee-training programs in a business setting.

Experimental or *research psychologists* are a diverse group of scientists who investigate a variety of basic behavioral processes in research involving humans and/or other animals. Prominent areas of study in experimental research include motivation, thought, attention, learning, memory, perception, and language. As an experimental psychologist, you would most likely work in an academic setting, teaching courses and supervising students' research in addition to conducting your own research. Or you might be employed by a research institution, business, industry affiliate, or government agency.

Health psychologists are researchers and practitioners concerned with psychology's contribution to promoting health and preventing disease. As applied psychologists or clinicians, they may help individuals lead healthier lives by designing, conducting, and evaluating programs to stop smoking, lose weight, improve sleep, or prevent the spread of sexually transmitted diseases. As researchers and clinicians, they identify conditions and practices associated with health and illness to help create effective interventions. In public service, health psychologists study and work to improve government policies and health-care systems. As a health psychologist, you could be employed in a hospital, medical school, rehabilitation center, public health agency, college or university, or, if you are also a clinical psychologist, in private practice.

Forensic psychologists apply psychological principles to legal issues. They conduct research on the interface of law and psychology, help to create public policies related to mental health, and help law-enforcement agencies in criminal investigations. They also provide therapy and assessment to assist the legal community. Some forensic psychologists hold law degrees and provide clients with legal services as well. Although most forensic psychologists are clinical psychologists, they might have expertise in other areas of psychology, such as social or cognitive psychology. As a forensic psychologist, you might work in a university psychology department, law school, research organization, community mental health agency, law-enforcement agency, court, or correctional setting.

Industrial/organizational (I/O) psychologists study the relationship between people and their working environments. They may develop new ways to increase productivity, improve personnel selection, or promote job satisfaction in a business setting. Their interests include organizational structure and change, consumer behavior, and personnel selection and training. As an I/O psychologist, you might conduct workplace training or provide organizational analysis and development. You may find yourself working in business, industry, the government, or a college or university. Or you may be self-employed as a consultant or work for a management counseling firm.

Neuropsychologists investigate the relationship between neurological processes (structure and function of the brain) and behavior. As a neuropsychologist you might assess, diagnose, or treat disorders related to the central nervous system, such as Alzheimer's disease or stroke. If you are a *clinical neuropsychologist,* you might work in the neurology, neurosurgery, or psychiatric unit of a hospital. Neuropsychologists also work in academic settings, where they conduct research and teach.

Psychometric and *quantitative psychologists* study the methods and techniques used to acquire psychological knowledge. A psychometrician may update existing neurocognitive or personality tests or devise new tests for use in clinical and school settings or in business and industry. These psychologists also administer, score, and interpret such tests. Quantitative psychologists collaborate with researchers to design, analyze, and interpret the results of research programs. As a psychometric or quantitative psychologist, you will need to be well trained in research methods, statistics, and computer technology. You will most likely be employed by a university or college, testing company, private research firm, or government agency.

Rehabilitation psychologists are researchers and practitioners who work with people who have lost optimal functioning after an accident, illness, or other event. As a rehabilitation psychologist, you would probably work in a medical rehabilitation institution or hospital. You might also work in a medical school, university, state or federal vocational rehabilitation agency, or in private practice serving people with physical disabilities.

School psychologists are involved in the assessment of and intervention for children in educational settings. They diagnose and treat cognitive, social, and emotional

Criminal profiling
On the popular TV show *Law and Order, Special Victims Unit,* Dr. George Huang (played by B.D. Wong) is an FBI agent and psychiatrist who uses his background in forensic psychology to conduct criminal investigations.

problems that may negatively influence children's learning or overall functioning at school. As a school psychologist, you would collaborate with teachers, parents, and administrators, making recommendations to improve student learning. You would work in an academic setting, a mental health clinic, a federal or state government agency, a child guidance center, or a behavioral research laboratory.

Social psychologists are interested in our interactions with others. Social psychologists study how our beliefs, feelings, and behaviors are affected by and influence other people. They study topics such as attitudes, aggression, prejudice, interpersonal attraction, group behavior, and leadership. As a social psychologist, you might work in organizational consultation, marketing research, or other applied psychology fields. You would probably also be a college or university faculty member. Some social psychologists work for hospitals, federal agencies, or businesses performing applied research.

Sports psychologists are interested in how participation in sports and other physical activities can enhance personal development and well-being throughout the life span. As a sports psychologist, you would study the psychological factors that influence, and are influenced by, participation in sports and other physical activities, and you would apply this knowledge to everyday settings. You would most likely work as part of a team or organization, but you might also work in a private capacity.

Preparing Early for Graduate Study in Psychology

Competition for the openings for advanced degrees in psychology is keen. If you choose to go to graduate school, there a number of things you can do now to maximize your chances of gaining admission to the school of your choice.

If possible, begin preparing during your first year on campus to maximize opportunities and obtain the experience needed to gain admission to a competitive program. Kristy Arnold and Kelly Horrigan (2002) offer a number of suggestions to facilitate this process:

1. *Network.* Get to know faculty members and the psychology department by attending activities and meetings. Become involved in psychology clubs and in Psi Chi or Psi Beta, the national honor societies in psychology. These meetings connect students with similar interests and expose them to a broader study of the field.

2. *Become actively involved in research as early as possible.* Start by doing simple tasks such as data entry and data collection, and over time you will be prepared to conduct your own research project under the supervision of a research mentor.

3. *Volunteer or get a job in a psychology-related field.* Getting involved will show your willingness to apply psychological concepts to real-world settings. Further, it will showcase your ability to juggle a number of tasks successfully, such as work and school—an important skill for graduate school success.

4. *Maintain good grades.* Demonstrate the ability to do well in graduate school by demonstrating successful completion of challenging courses, especially those related to your interests in graduate school.

In your junior year, you should begin studying for the Graduate Record Exam (GRE), the standardized test that applicants to graduate school must complete. If you start preparing early, you will be ready for success in your graduate school application and study.

Membership benefits
Members of the Psi Chi Honor Society, such as those meeting here, enjoy educational and professional benefits. So do members of Psi Beta, the psychology honor society at two-year colleges. Members may attend special sessions at psychological conventions, apply for research grants and awards, and read about new findings and new opportunities in their society's newsletter.

Stephen Simpson/Getty Images

So, the next time someone asks you what you will do with your psychology degree, tell them you have a lot of options. You might use your acquired skills and understanding to get a job and succeed in any number of fields, or you might pursue graduate school and then career opportunities in psychology or other associated professions. In any case, what you have learned about behavior and mental processes will surely enrich your life (Hammer, 2003).

For More Information

American Psychological Association (2003). *Careers for the twenty-first century.* Washington, DC.

American Psychological Association (2005). *Graduate study in psychology.* Washington, DC.

Appleby, D. C. (2002). *The savvy psychology major.* Dubuque, IA: Kendall/Hunt.

Arnold, K., & Horrigan, K. (2002). Gaining admission into the graduate program of your choice. *Eye on Psi Chi*, 30–33.

Actkinson, T. R. (2000). Master's and myths. *Eye on Psi Chi, 4,* 19–25.

Aubrecht, L. (2001). What can you do with a BA in psychology? *Eye on Psi Chi, 5,* 29–31.

Huss, M. (1996). Secrets to standing out from the pile: Getting into graduate school. *Psi Chi Newsletter,* 6–7.

Lammers, B. (2000). Quick tips for applying to graduate school in psychology. *Eye on Psi Chi, 4,* 40–42.

Landrum, E. (2001). I'm getting my bachelor's degree in psychology. What can I do with it? *Eye on Psi Chi, 6,* 22–24.

Morgan, B., & Korschgen, A. (2001). Psychology career exploration made easy. *Eye on Psi Chi,* 35–36.

Sternberg, R. (Ed.) (2002). *Career paths in psychology: Where your degree can take you.* Washington, DC: APA.

Answers to
Test Yourself Questions

MODULE 1 The History and Scope of Psychology

1. What events defined the founding of scientific psychology?

ANSWER: The most outstanding event defining the founding of scientific psychology was Wilhelm Wundt's opening of the University of Leipzig psychology laboratory in 1879. The new science of psychology was soon organized into different schools of thought, including structuralism (founded by Edward Bradford Titchener, using introspection to explore the elemental structure of the human mind) and functionalism (founded by William James, focusing on how mental and behavioral processes enable organisms to adapt, survive, and flourish). James also wrote an important psychology textbook, completed in 1890.

2. What are psychology's major levels of analysis?

ANSWER: Psychology's three major levels of analysis are the biological, psychological, and social-cultural. The complementary insights of psychologists studying behavior and mental processes from the neuroscience, evolutionary, behavior genetics, psychodynamic, behavioral, cognitive, and social-cultural perspectives offer a richer understanding than could usually be gained from any one viewpoint alone.

MODULE 2 Thinking Critically With Psychological Science

1. What is the scientific attitude, and why is it important for critical thinking?

ANSWER: The scientific attitude combines *skeptical* testing of various claims and ideas with *humility* about ones' own unexamined presumptions. Examining assumptions, searching for hidden values, evaluating evidence, and assessing conclusions are essential parts of critical thinking.

2. How are human and animal research subjects protected?

ANSWER: Animal protection legislation, laboratory regulation and inspection, and local ethics committees serve to protect human and animal welfare.

MODULE 3 Research Strategies: How Psychologists Ask and Answer Questions

1. What are the strengths and weaknesses of the three different methods psychologists use to describe behavior—case studies, surveys, and naturalistic observation?

ANSWER: *Case studies* offer in-depth insights that may offer clues to what's true of others—or may, if the case is atypical, mislead. *Surveys* can accurately reveal the tendencies of large populations. But if the questions are leading, or if nonrandom samples are queried, the results can again mislead us. *Naturalistic observation* enables study of behavior undisturbed by researchers. But the lack of control may leave cause and effect ambiguous.

2. **Here are some recently reported correlations, with interpretations drawn by journalists. Further research, often including experiments, has clarified cause and effect in each case. Knowing just these correlations, can you come up with other possible explanations for each of these?**

   a. *Alcohol use is associated with violence. (One interpretation: Drinking triggers or unleashes aggressive behavior.)* Perhaps anger triggers drinking, or perhaps the same genes or rearing predispose both drinking and aggression. (Here researchers have learned that drinking does indeed trigger aggressive behavior.)

   b. *Educated people live longer, on average, than less-educated people. (One interpretation: Education lengthens life and enhances health.)* Perhaps richer people can afford more education *and* better health care. (Research supports *this* conclusion.)

   c. *Teens engaged in team sports are less likely to use drugs, smoke, have sex, carry weapons, and eat junk food than are teens who do not engage in team sports. (One interpretation: Team sports encourage healthy living.)* Perhaps some third factor explains this correlation—teens who use drugs, smoke, have sex, carry weapons, and eat junk food may be "loners" who do not enjoy playing on any team.

   d. *Adolescents who frequently see smoking in movies are more likely to smoke. (One interpretation: Movie stars' behavior influences impressionable teens.)* Perhaps adolescents who smoke and attend movies frequently have less parental supervision and more access to spending money than other adolescents.

3. **Why, when testing a new drug for blood pressure, would we learn more about its effectiveness from giving it to half of the participants in a group of 1000 than to all 1000 participants?**

   ANSWER: To determine whether this drug is medically effective, we must compare its effect on those randomly assigned to receive it (the experimental condition) with those who receive a placebo (the control condition). The only difference between the groups is whether they received the actual drug. So, if blood pressure is lower in the experimental group, then we know that the drug itself has produced this effect, not just the participants' knowledge that they are being treated (placebo effect).

4. **Consider a question posed by Christopher Jepson, David Krantz, and Richard Nisbett (1983) to University of Michigan introductory psychology students:**

   The registrar's office at the University of Michigan has found that usually about 100 students in Arts and Sciences have perfect marks at the end of their first term at the University. However, only about 10 to 15 students graduate with perfect marks. What do you think is the most likely explanation for the fact that there are more perfect marks after one term than at graduation?

   ANSWER: Most students in the study came up with plausible causes for the drop in marks, such as, "Students tend to work harder at the beginning of their college careers than toward the end." Fewer than a third recognized the statistical phenomenon clearly at work: Averages based on fewer courses are more variable, which guarantees a greater number of extremely low and high marks at the end of the first term.

(MODULE 4) Neural and Hormonal Systems

1. **How do neurons communicate with one another?**

   ANSWER: A neuron fires when excitatory inputs exceed inhibitory inputs by a sufficient threshold. When the resulting impulse reaches the axon's end, it triggers the release of chemical neurotransmitters. After crossing a tiny gap, these molecules activate receptor sites on neighboring neurons. So, the brief answer to how neurons communicate with one another is *chemically*.

2. **How does information flow through your nervous system as you pick up a fork? Can you summarize this process?**

   ANSWER: Your central nervous system's hungry brain activates and guides the muscles of your arm and hand via your peripheral nervous system's motor neurons. As you pick up the fork, your brain processes the information from your sensory nervous system, enabling it to continue to guide the fork to your mouth. The functional circle starts with sensory input, continues with interneuron processing by the central nervous system, and finishes with motor output.

3. **Why is the pituitary gland called the "master gland"?**
   ANSWER: The pituitary gland, responding to signals from the hypothalamus, releases hormones that act as triggers. In response, other endocrine glands release their own hormones, which in turn influence brain and behavior.

MODULE 5 The Brain

1. **Within what brain region would damage be most likely to disrupt your ability to skip rope? Your ability to sense tastes or sounds? In what brain region would damage perhaps leave you in a coma? Without the very breath and heartbeat of life?**
   ANSWER: These regions are, respectively, the *cerebellum,* the *thalamus,* the *reticular formation,* and the *medulla.* These questions assess your understanding of the essential functions of the lower-level brain areas.

MODULE 6 Behavior Genetics and Evolutionary Psychology

1. **What is *heritability*?**
   ANSWER: *Heritability* is the proportion of variation among individuals that we can attribute to genes. Note: Heritability is *not* the extent to which an *individual's* traits are genetically determined. Rather, it is the extent to which variation *among* individuals is due to their differing genes. For any trait, heritability can vary, depending on the population and range of environments studied.

2. **What are the three main criticisms of the evolutionary explanation of human sexuality?**
   ANSWER: Critics of the evolutionary explanation of human sexuality point out that (1) it starts with an effect and works backward to propose an explanation; (2) unethical and immoral men could use such explanations to rationalize their behavior toward women; and (3) this explanation overlooks the effects of cultural expectations and socialization.

MODULE 7 Environmental Influences on Behavior

1. **To predict whether a teenager smokes, ask how many of the teen's friends smoke. One explanation for this correlation is peer influence. What's another?**
   ANSWER: There may also be a *selection effect.* Adolescents tend to sort themselves into likeminded groups—the jocks, the geeks, the druggies, and so forth. Those who smoke may similarly seek out other teenagers who also smoke.

2. **How do individualist and collectivist cultures differ?**
   ANSWER: A culture that favors individualism gives priority to personal goals over group goals; people in that culture will tend to define their identity in terms of their own personal attributes. A culture that favors collectivism gives priority to group goals over individual goals; people in collectivist cultures tend to define their identity in terms of group identifications. Cultures vary in the extent to which they favor individualism or collectivism.

3. **What are gender roles, and what do their variations tell us about our human capacity for learning and adaptation?**
   ANSWER: *Gender roles* are social rules or norms for accepted and expected behavior for females and males. The norms associated with various roles, including gender roles, vary widely in different cultural contexts, which is proof that we are very capable of learning and adapting to the social demands of different environments.

MODULE 8 Prenatal Development and the Newborn

1. **Your friend—a heavy smoker—hopes to become pregnant soon and has stopped smoking. Why is this a good idea? What negative effects does smoking during pregnancy have on the fetus?**

   ANSWER: If a woman smokes during her pregnancy, the fetus may receive fewer nutrients and be born underweight and at risk for health problems. Your friend is wise to quit smoking before there is a chance that the pregnancy has begun. The most harmful effects of teratogens, such as cigarette smoke, occur during the first trimester of pregnancy—often before a woman even knows she is pregnant.

MODULE 9 Infancy and Childhood

1. **Use Piaget's first three stages of cognitive development to explain why young children are *not* just miniature adults in the way they think.**

   ANSWER: Infants in the *sensorimotor stage* tend to be focused only on their own perceptions of the world and may, for example, be unaware that objects continue to exist when unseen. A *preoperational* child is still egocentric and incapable of appreciating simple logic, such as the reversibility of operations. A preteen in the *concrete operational stage* is beginning to think logically about concrete events but not about abstract concepts.

MODULE 10 Adolescence

1. **How has the transition from childhood to adulthood changed in Western cultures in the last 100 years?**

   ANSWER: In the last 100 years, the transition to adulthood has started earlier and lasted longer, so that adolescence has lengthened from a period of about 7 years in 1890 to about 12 years in the 1990s.

MODULE 11 Adulthood, and Reflections on Developmental Issues

1. **Research has shown that living together before marriage predicts an increased likelihood of future divorce. Can you imagine two possible explanations for this correlation?**

   ANSWER: William Axinn and Arland Thornton (1992) report data that support two explanations. (1) The first explanation is an example of a *selection effect*—our tendency to seek out others who are similar to us. Cohabitation attracts people who are more open to terminating unsatisfying relationships. People who cohabit bring a more individualistic ethic to marriage, are more likely to see close relationships as temporary and fragile, are more accepting of divorce, and are about three times more likely after marriage to have an affair (Forste & Tanfer, 1996). (2) Axinn and Thornton's second explanation illustrates the *causal effect* of the experience of cohabitation. Over time, those who cohabit tend to become more approving of dissolving an unfulfilling union. This divorce-accepting attitude increases the odds of later divorce.

2. **What findings in psychology support the stage theory of development and the idea of stability in personality across the life span? What findings challenge these ideas?**

   ANSWER: Stage theory is supported by the work of Piaget (cognitive development), Kohlberg (moral development), and Erikson (psychosocial development), but it is challenged by findings that change is more gradual and less culturally universal than these theorists supposed. Some traits, such as temperament, do exhibit remarkable stability across many years. But we do change in other ways, such as in our social attitudes, especially during life's early years.

MODULE 12 Introduction to Sensation and Perception

1. What is the rough distinction between sensation and perception?

ANSWER: *Sensation* is the bottom-up process by which the physical sensory system receives and represents stimuli. *Perception* is the top-down mental process of organizing and interpreting sensory input. But in our everyday experiences, sensation and perception are different aspects of one continuous process.

2. Your friend insists that he *did* call you to dinner as you intently watched TV. What principle explains your not perceiving him?

ANSWER: This example illustrates *selective attention*—focusing conscious awareness on a particular stimulus. Your not perceiving the voice probably indicates that you were selectively focusing your attention on the TV.

MODULE 13 Vision

1. What is the rapid sequence of events that occurs when you see and recognize someone you know?

ANSWER: Light waves reflect off the person and travel into your eye, where the rods and cones convert the light waves' energy into neural impulses sent to your brain. Your brain then processes the subdimensions of this visual input—including color, depth, movement, and form—separately but simultaneously, and integrates this information (along with previously stored information) into a conscious perception of the person you know.

MODULE 14 Hearing

1. In a nutshell, how do we transform sound waves into perceived sound?

ANSWER: A simple figure offers a synopsis:

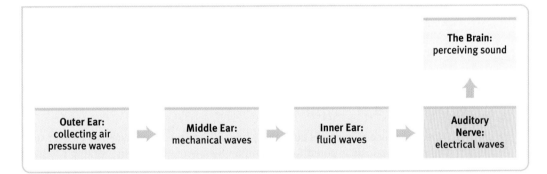

MODULE 15 Other Important Senses

1. What does the biopsychosocial approach to pain teach us?

ANSWER: Considering the biological, psychological, and social-cultural influences on the perception of pain teaches us that our experience of pain is much more than neural messages sent to the brain.

2. How does our system for sensing smell differ from our sensory systems for vision, touch, and taste?

ANSWER: We have three types of color receptors, four basic touch senses, and five taste sensations. But we have no basic smell receptors. Instead, 350 receptor proteins, individually and in combination, recognize some 10,000 discernible odors.

MODULE 16 Perceptual Organization

1. How does the study of illusions inform our understanding of normal perceptions?

ANSWER: Perceptual illusions reveal the ways we organize and interpret sensory information. Our occasional misperceptions demonstrate the workings of our normally effective perceptual processes. For example, the perceived relationship between distance and size is generally valid, but under special circumstances it can lead us astray—as when it helps create the Moon illusion.

2. **What do we mean when we say that, in perception, the whole is greater than the sum of its parts?**
ANSWER: Gestalt psychologists used this saying to describe our perceptual tendency to organize clusters of sensations into meaningful forms or coherent groups.

MODULE 17 Perceptual Interpretation

1. **What type of evidence shows that, indeed, "there is more to perception than meets the senses"?**
ANSWER: We construct our perceptions based on both sensory input and—experiments show—on our assumptions, expectations, schemas, and perceptual sets, often influenced by the surrounding context.

MODULE 18 Waking and Sleeping Rhythms

1. **During psychology's history, what were the ups and downs of "consciousness"?**
ANSWER: Psychology began as the study of consciousness, but during the behaviorist era (for much of the first half of the twentieth century) psychologists focused on observations of behavior. After 1960, driven by discoveries in cognitive psychology and neuroscience, the study of consciousness (our awareness of ourselves and our environment) reemerged as a major topic in psychology.

2. **Are you getting enough sleep? What might you ask yourself to answer this question?**
ANSWER: You could start with the true/false questions in James Mass' sleep deprivation quiz in Table 18.1. Also, William Dement (1999, p. 73) invites you to consider these questions: "How often do you think about taking a quick snooze? How often do you rub your eyes and yawn during the day? How often do you feel like you really need some coffee?" Dement concludes that "each of these is a warning of a sleep debt that you ignore at your peril."

MODULE 19 Hypnosis

1. **When is the use of hypnosis potentially harmful, and when can hypnosis be used to help?**
ANSWER: Hypnosis is potentially harmful when some therapists, seeking to "hypnotically refresh" memories, plant false memories. But posthypnotic suggestions have helped alleviate some ailments, and hypnosis can also help control pain.

MODULE 20 Drugs and Consciousness

1. **A U.S. government survey of 27,616 current or former alcohol drinkers found that 40 percent of those who began drinking before age 15 grew dependent on alcohol. The same was true of only 10 percent of those who first imbibed at ages 21 or 22 (Grant & Dawson, 1998). What possible explanations might there be for this correlation between early use and later abuse?**
ANSWER: Possible explanations include (1) a biological predisposition to both early use and later abuse, (2) brain changes and taste preferences induced by early use, and (3) enduring habits, attitudes, activities, and/or peer relationships that are conducive to alcohol use.

2. **In what ways are near-death experiences similar to drug-induced hallucinations?**
ANSWER: Reports of near-death experiences and drug-induced hallucinations feature similar experiences: replay of old memories, out-of-body sensations, and visions of tunnels or funnels of bright light or beings of light.

MODULE 21 Classical Conditioning

1. **As we develop, we learn cues that lead us to expect and prepare for good and bad events. We learn to repeat behaviors that bring rewards. And we watch others and learn. What do psychologists call these three types of learning?**

   Answer: Through *classical conditioning*, we learn cues that lead us to expect and prepare for good and bad events. Through *operant conditioning*, we learn to repeat behaviors that bring rewards. Through *observational learning*, we watch others and learn.

2. **In slasher movies, sexually arousing images of women are sometimes paired with violence against women. Based on classical conditioning principles, what might be an effect of this pairing?**

   Answer: If viewing an attractive nude or semi-nude woman (a US) elicits sexual arousal (a UR), then pairing the US with a new stimulus (violence) could turn the violence into a conditioned stimulus (CS) that also becomes sexually arousing, a conditioned response (CR).

MODULE 22 Operant Conditioning

1. *Positive reinforcement, negative reinforcement,* and *punishment* are tricky concepts for many students. Can you fit the right term in the four boxes in this table? (I've done the first one—positive reinforcement—for you.)

Type of Stimulus	Give It	Take It Away
Desired (for example, a compliment):	Positive reinforcement	*Punishment (e.g., time-out)*
Undesired/aversive (for example, an insult):	*Punishment*	*Negative reinforcement*

MODULE 23 Learning by Observation

1. **Jason's parents and older friends all smoke, but they advise him not to. Juan's parents and friends don't smoke, but they say nothing to deter him from doing so. Will Jason or Juan be more likely to start smoking?**

   Answer: Although both saying and doing can influence people, experiments suggest that children more often do as others do and say as they say. Generalizing this finding to smoking, we can expect that Jason will be more likely to start smoking.

MODULE 24 Introduction to Memory

1. **Memory includes (in alphabetical order) long-term memory, sensory memory, and working/short-term memory. What's the correct order of these three memory stores?**

   Answer: Sensory memory, working/short-term memory, long-term memory.

MODULE 25 Encoding: Getting Information In

1. **What would be the most effective strategy to learn and retain a list of names of key historical figures for a week? For a year?**

   Answer: For a week: Make the names personally meaningful. For a year: Overlearn the list and space out rehearsals over the course of several weeks.

MODULE 26 Storage: Retaining Information

1. **Your friend tells you that her father experienced brain damage in an accident. She wonders if psychology can explain why he can still play checkers very well but has a hard time holding a sensible conversation. What can you tell her?**

ANSWER: Our *explicit* (declarable) memories differ from our *implicit* memories of skills and procedures, such as checkers. Our implicit memories are processed by more ancient brain areas, which apparently escaped damage during the accident.

MODULE 27 Retrieval: Getting Information Out

1. What is priming?

ANSWER: *Priming* is the activation (often without our awareness) of associations. Seeing a gun, for example, might temporarily predispose someone to interpret an ambiguous face as threatening or to recall a boss as nasty. Although the person might not consciously remember the gun, it may prime how that individual interprets or recalls events.

MODULE 28 Forgetting, Memory Construction, and Memory Improvement

1. Can you offer an example of proactive interference?

ANSWER: *Proactive* (forward-acting) interference occurs when earlier learning disrupts your recall of a later experience. Proactive interference has occurred if learning the names of new classmates in your first class makes it more difficult to learn the new names in your second class.

2. What—given the commonality of source amnesia—might life be like if we remembered all our waking experiences and all our dreams?

ANSWER: Real experiences would be confused with those we dreamed. When meeting someone, we might therefore be unsure whether we were reacting to something they previously had done or to something we dreamed they had done. William Dement (1999, p. 298) thinks this "would put a great burden on your sanity. . . . I truly believe that the wall of memory is a blessed protection."

3. What are the recommended memory strategies you just read about? (One advised rehearsing to-be-remembered material. What were the others?)

ANSWER: Study repeatedly to boost long-term recall. Spend more time rehearsing or actively thinking about the material. Make the material personally meaningful. To remember a list of unfamiliar items, use mnemonic devices. Refresh your memory by activating retrieval cues. Recall events while they are fresh, before you encounter possible misinformation. Minimize interference. Test your own knowledge, both to rehearse it and to help determine what you do not yet know.

MODULE 29 Thinking

1. The availability heuristic is a quick-and-easy but sometimes misleading guide to judging reality. What is the availability heuristic?

ANSWER: The *availability heuristic* is our tendency to judge the likelihood of an event by how easily we can recall instances of it. Like all heuristics, this guide is efficient. But it can mislead, as it does when we attempt to judge various risks (for example, of plane travel).

MODULE 30 Language and Thought

1. If children are not yet speaking, is there any reason to think they would benefit from parents and other caregivers reading to them?

ANSWER: Indeed there is, because well before age 1 children are learning to detect words among the stream of spoken sounds, and to discern grammatical rules. Before age 1, they also are babbling with the phonemes of their own language. More than many parents realize, their infants are soaking up language. As researcher Peter Jusczyk reminds us, "Little ears are listening."

2. **To say that "words are the mother of ideas" assumes the truth of what concept?**
   ANSWER: This phrase supports the linguistic determinism hypothesis, which asserts that language determines thought. Research indicates that this position is too extreme, but language does *influence* what we perceive and think.

3. **If your dog barks at a stranger at the front door, does this qualify as language? What if the dog yips in a telltale way to let you know she needs to go out?**
   ANSWER: These are definitely communications. But if language consists of words and the grammatical rules we use to combine them to communicate meaning, few scientists would label a dog's barking and yipping as language.

MODULE 31 Introduction to Intelligence

1. **Joseph is a straight-A student at Harvard Law School, writes a small column for the *Harvard Law Review*, and will be working for a Supreme Court justice next year. Judith is very proud of her grandson and says he is way more intelligent than she ever was. But Joseph is also very proud of his grandmother, who had been imprisoned by the Nazis. When the war ended, she walked out of Germany, contacted a relief agency, traveled to the United States, and began a new life. According to the definition of intelligence in this module, is Joseph the only intelligent person in this story? Why or why not?**
   ANSWER: Joseph is not the only intelligent person in this story. *Intelligence* is the ability to learn from experience, solve problems, and use knowledge to adapt to new situations. Judith certainly fits this description, given all that she accomplished after her release.

MODULE 32 Assessing Intelligence

1. **What was the purpose of Binet's pioneering intelligence test?**
   ANSWER: Binet's original test was designed to predict school achievement.

2. **The Smiths have enrolled their 2-year-old son in a special program that promises to assess his IQ and, if he places in the top 5 percent of test-takers, to create a plan that will guarantee his admission to a top university at age 18. Why is this endeavor of questionable value?**
   ANSWER: The Smiths would be wasting their time and money. Two years is too young an age for reliably predicting future intelligence.

MODULE 33 Genetic and Environmental Influences on Intelligence

1. **As society succeeds in creating equality of opportunity, it will also increase the heritability of ability. The heritability of intelligence scores will be greater in a society marked by equal opportunity than in a society of peasants and aristocrats. Why?**
   ANSWER: Perfect environmental equality would create 100 percent heritability—because genes alone would account for any remaining human differences.

MODULE 34 Introduction to Motivation

1. **While on a long road trip, you suddenly feel very lonely and want to pull over and call a loved one. But the dark, deserted stretch of road is intimidating, so you keep on driving. What motivational perspective would most easily explain this behavior and why?**
   ANSWER: *Drive-reduction theory*—the idea that physical needs create an aroused state that drives us to reduce the need—helps explain your behavior.

MODULE 35 Hunger

1. **You are traveling and have not eaten anything in eight hours. As your long-awaited favorite dish is placed in front of you, your mouth waters. Even imagining this may set your mouth to watering. What triggers this anticipatory drooling?**

ANSWER: You, like Pavlov's dogs, have learned through *classical conditioning* to respond to the cues—the sight and aroma—that signal the food about to enter your mouth. Both *physiological cues* (eight hours of deprivation have left you with low blood sugar) and *psychological cues* (the anticipation of the tasty meal) have heightened your experienced hunger.

MODULE 36 Sexual Motivation and the Need to Belong

1. How might the evolutionary psychology perspective explain sexual motivation and our need to affiliate?

ANSWER: Evolutionary psychologists attempt to explain behaviors in terms of their survival value. From this perspective, sexual motivation and the need to affiliate can be interpreted as behaviors that help ensure the transmission (and therefore survival) of our DNA to future generations.

MODULE 37 Motivation at Work

1. A human resources director explains to you that "I don't bother with tests or references. I can pick employees by my gut." Based on I/O research, what concerns does this raise?

ANSWER: Personnel interviewers feel very confident in their ability to predict long-term job performance from informal interviews. Unfortunately, this ability goes astray so often that I/O psychologists have labeled the gap between interviewers' intuition and workplace reality the *interviewer illusion*. Four factors contribute: (1) interviews disclose prospective workers' good intentions, not their habitual behaviors; (2) interviewers tend to track the successful careers of those they hire, not the successful careers of those they reject; (3) interviewers presume people are what they seem to be in interviews; and (4) interviewers' preconceptions and moods color how they perceive interviewees' responses.

MODULE 38 Introduction to Emotion

1. Christine is holding her 8-month-old baby when a fierce dog appears out of nowhere and, with teeth bared, leaps for the baby's face. Christine immediately ducks for cover to protect the baby, screams at the dog, then notices that her heart is banging in her chest and she's broken out in a cold sweat. How would the James-Lange, Cannon-Bard, and two-factor theories explain Christine's emotional reaction?

ANSWER: The James-Lange theory would say that Christine's emotional reaction consists of her awareness of her physiological responses to the dog attack. The Cannon-Bard theory would say that her fear experience happened simultaneously with her physiological arousal. Schacter's two-factor theory would presume that her emotional reaction stemmed from her interpreting and labeling the arousal.

2. How do the two divisions of the autonomic nervous system help us respond to and recover from a crisis, and why is this relevant to the study of emotions?

ANSWER: The sympathetic division of the ANS arouses us in a crisis, and the parasympathetic division of the ANS calms us when the crisis has passed. Researchers study these physiological responses, in combination with brain pattern indicators, to reach a more complete understanding of the feeling component of emotions.

MODULE 39 Expressed Emotion

1. Who tends to express more emotion—men or women? How do we know the answer to that question?

ANSWER: Women tend to surpass men not only as emotion detectors but also at expressing certain emotions (though men have slightly surpassed women in conveying anger). Researchers discovered this by showing people brief, silent clips of men's and women's faces expressing various emotions and by observing who is most skilled at reading and sending emotions.

MODULE 40 Experienced Emotion

1. What things do (and do not) predict self-reported happiness?
ANSWER: People's age, gender, education level, parenthood, and physical attractiveness are not closely related to their happiness. Predictors of happiness include high self-esteem; optimism and an agreeable, outgoing personality; close friendships or a satisfying marriage; satisfying work and leisure activities; a meaningful religious faith; and adequate sleep and exercise.

MODULE 41 Stress and Illness

1. What are the basic links in our stress response system?
ANSWER: When alerted to a threat (to negative, uncontrollable events), our sympathetic nervous system arouses us. Heart rate and respiration increase. Blood is diverted from digestion to the skeletal muscles. The body releases sugar and fat to prepare for fight or flight. Simultaneously, the brain (via the hypothalamus and adjacent pituitary gland) orders the adrenal glands to secrete the stress hormone cortisol. The system is wonderfully adaptive. But if stress is continuous, health consequences and exhaustion may result.

MODULE 42 Coping With Stress

1. What are some ways that social support can help us cope with stress?
ANSWER: Several large studies show that social support can buffer stress and predict health. Social support seems to foster stronger immune functioning and to lower blood pressure. These effects may stem from a healthier life style, as well as an opportunity to confide in others.

MODULE 43 Modifying Illness-Related Behaviors

1. Nonsmokers, the text reports, are less likely to become depressed and get divorced. What type of research finding is this, and what explanations might it have?
ANSWER: This is a correlational finding. Like other correlational findings, it can be interpreted in several ways:

- Not smoking may be just one part of a generally healthy life-style that includes healthy emotions and relationships.
- Depressed people and those with troubled relationships may be drawn to smoking.
- Smoking, depression, and divorce may share common roots. Perhaps certain genes predispose a temperament that is prone to smoking, depression, and divorce. Or perhaps a certain upbringing or peer environment is conducive to smoking, depression, and divorce.

MODULE 44 The Psychoanalytic Perspective

1. What, according to Freud, were some of the important defense mechanisms, and what do they defend against? How many of these find support in modern research?
ANSWER: Freud believed repression to be the basic defense mechanism. Others include regression, reaction formation, projection, rationalization, and displacement. All supposedly serve to reduce anxiety. Modern research supports the phenomenon Freud called *projection* and current researchers call the *false consensus effect*. Some evidence also supports self-esteem defenses, such as reaction formation. But there is little support for the others.

MODULE 45 The Humanistic Perspective

1. What does it mean to be "empathic"? To be "self-actualized"?

ANSWER: To be *empathic* is to share and mirror another person's feelings. Carl Rogers believed that people nurture growth in others by being empathic. Abraham Maslow viewed *self-actualization* as the ultimate psychological need—the motivation to fulfill one's potential.

MODULE 46 Contemporary Research on Personality

1. How many trait dimensions are currently used to describe personality, and what are those dimensions?

ANSWER: "The Big Five" trait dimensions—*emotional stability, extraversion, openness, agreeableness,* and *conscientiousness*—provide a reasonably complete personality description.

2. How do learned helplessness and optimism influence behavior?

ANSWER: Learned helplessness produces passive resignation after organisms find themselves unable to avoid aversive events. Nursing homes, prisons, colleges, and autocratic companies and countries have all been observed to produce symptoms of learned helplessness. Optimism has the opposite effect, leading to better moods, more persistence, and better health. Excessive optimism, however, can expose us to risks.

3. In a 1997 Gallup poll, white Americans estimated 44 percent of their fellow white Americans to be high in prejudice (scoring them 5 or higher on a 10-point scale). How many rated themselves similarly high in prejudice? Just 14 percent. What phenomenon does this illustrate?

ANSWER: This illustrates the general tendency to see oneself as superior to the average other, which is one example of the *self-serving bias.*

MODULE 47 Introduction to Psychological Disorders

1. What is the biopsychosocial approach, and why is it important in our understanding of psychological disorders?

ANSWER: This contemporary approach assumes that biological, psychological, and social-cultural influences combine to produce psychological disorders. Genes matter. The brain matters. Inner thoughts and feelings matter. Social and cultural influences matter. To get the whole integrated picture, a biopsychosocial perspective helps.

2. Does poverty cause psychological disorders? Explain.

ANSWER: Poverty-related stresses can indeed help trigger disorders. But disabling disorders can also contribute to poverty. Thus, poverty and disorders are often a chicken-and-egg situation, and it's hard to know which came first.

MODULE 48 Anxiety Disorders

1. How do generalized anxiety disorder, phobias, and obsessive-compulsive disorder differ?

ANSWER: *Generalized anxiety disorder* is unfocused tension, apprehension, and arousal. *Phobias* focus anxiety on specific feared objects or situations. *Obsessive-compulsive disorders* express anxiety through unwanted repetitive thoughts (obsessions) or actions (compulsions).

MODULE 49 Dissociative and Personality Disorders

1. Is antisocial personality disorder an inherited condition?

ANSWER: *Antisocial personality disorder*—in which a person exhibits a lack of conscience for wrongdoing—seems to have both biological and psychological components. Twin and adoption studies show that biological relatives of people with this disorder are at increased risk for antisocial behavior. But the tendency to be fearless, when combined with a sense of social responsibility, can lead to heroism, adventurism, or athletic success.

MODULE 50 Mood Disorders

1. What does it mean to say that "depression is the common cold of psychological disorders"?
ANSWER: Saying that "depression is the common cold of psychological disorders" is a quick way to state that this serious disorder is the most common condition in those seeking mental health treatment—with almost 6 percent of men and nearly 10 percent of women reporting a depressive episode each year. Worldwide, depression is the leading cause of disability.

MODULE 51 Schizophrenia

1. What are the five subtypes of schizophrenia?
ANSWER: They are *paranoid* (marked by delusions or hallucinations), *disorganized* (disorganized speech, flat emotion), *catatonic* (immobility or repetitive purposeless movements), *undifferentiated* (varied symptoms), and *residual* (withdrawal, after hallucinations and delusions have disappeared).

MODULE 52 The Psychological Therapies

1. What is the major distinction between the underlying assumption in psychoanalytic and humanistic therapies and the underlying assumption in behavior therapies?
ANSWER: Psychoanalytic and humanistic therapies seek to relieve problems by providing insight into their origins. Behavior therapies assume the problem behavior *is* the problem and treat it directly, paying less attention to its origins.

MODULE 53 Evaluating Psychotherapies

1. How does the placebo effect bias clients' appraisals of the effectiveness of psychotherapies?
ANSWER: The *placebo effect* is the healing power of *belief* in a treatment. Patients who expect a treatment to be effective may believe it was.

2. What are the influences to keep in mind for successful therapeutic intervention?
ANSWER: Successful therapeutic intervention—or prevention—can intervene at many different levels because biological, psychological, and social-cultural influences can combine and interact to produce psychological disorders. Bodily (for example, neurochemical) imbalances can affect mental states, and both biochemical and mental states may be affected by environmental conditions.

MODULE 54 The Biomedical Therapies

1. How do researchers evaluate the effectiveness of particular drug therapies?
ANSWER: Ideally, researchers assign people to treatment and no-treatment conditions to see if those who receive therapy improve more than those who don't. In many studies, the no-treatment comparison includes a placebo condition, which allows a double-blind controlled study. If neither the therapist nor the client knows for sure whether the client has received the experimental treatment (for example, a drug), then any difference between the treated and untreated groups will reflect the treatment's actual effect.

MODULE 55 Social Thinking

1. **Driving to school one wintry day, Marco narrowly misses a car that slides through a red light. "Slow down! What a terrible driver," he thinks to himself. Moments later, Marco himself slips through an intersection and yelps, "Wow! These roads are awful. The city snow plows need to get out here." What social psychology principle has Marco just demonstrated? Explain.**

   ANSWER: By attributing the other person's behavior to the person ("he's a terrible driver") and his own to the situation ("these roads are awful"), Marco has exhibited the *fundamental attribution error*.

MODULE 56 Social Influence

1. **You are organizing a Town Hall–style meeting of fiercely competitive political candidates. To add to the fun, friends have suggested handing out masks of the candidates' faces for supporters to wear. What phenomenon might these masks engage?**

   ANSWER: The anonymity provided by the masks, combined with the arousal of the contentious setting, might create *deindividuation* (lessened self-awareness and self-restraint in a group setting).

MODULE 57 Antisocial Relations

1. **Horace says, "I have no prejudice within me toward anyone. I believe everyone deserves equal opportunity in housing and employment." Even if Horace indeed expresses no obvious prejudice, what sort of prejudice might nonetheless exist?**

   ANSWER: Horace exhibited no overt, conscious prejudice. He could nevertheless harbor implicit, unconscious prejudice that surfaces in subtle and automatic ways, including assumed racial associations, race-influenced perceptions, and telltale bodily responses to encountering someone of a different race.

MODULE 58 Prosocial Relations

1. **Why didn't anybody help Kitty Genovese? What social relations principle did this incident illustrate?**

   ANSWER: The incident illustrated the *bystander effect*. In the presence of others, an individual is less likely to notice a situation, correctly interpret it as an emergency, and then take responsibility for offering help. Many of Kitty Genovese's neighbors noticed the situation and recognized it as an emergency but they apparently assumed others would help, and they did not feel responsible for offering help.

GLOSSARY

absolute threshold the minimum stimulation needed to detect a particular stimulus 50 percent of the time.

accommodation adapting one's current understandings (schemas) to incorporate new information.

accommodation the process by which the eye's lens changes shape to focus near or far objects on the retina.

acetylcholine [ah-seat-el-KO-leen] **(ACh)** a neurotransmitter that enables learning and memory and also triggers muscle contraction.

achievement motivation a desire for significant accomplishment: for mastery of things, people, or ideas; for attaining a high standard.

achievement test a test designed to assess what a person has learned.

acoustic encoding the encoding of sound, especially the sound of words.

acquisition the initial stage in classical conditioning; the phase associating a neutral stimulus with an unconditioned stimulus so that the neutral stimulus comes to elicit a conditioned response. In operant conditioning, the strengthening of a reinforced response.

action potential a neural impulse; a brief electrical charge that travels down an axon. The action potential is generated by the movement of positively charged atoms in and out of channels in the axon's membrane.

active listening empathic listening in which the listener echoes, restates, and clarifies. A feature of Rogers' client-centered therapy.

acuity the sharpness of vision.

adaptation-level phenomenon our tendency to form judgments (of sounds, of lights, of income) relative to a neutral level defined by our prior experience.

addiction compulsive drug craving and use.

adolescence the transition period from childhood to adulthood, extending from puberty to independence.

adrenal [ah-DREEN-el] **glands** a pair of endocrine glands just above the kidneys. The adrenals secrete the hormones epinephrine (adrenaline) and norepinephrine (noradrenaline), which help to arouse the body in times of stress.

aerobic exercise sustained exercise that increases heart and lung fitness; may also alleviate depression and anxiety.

aggression any physical or verbal behavior intended to hurt or destroy.

algorithm a methodical, logical rule or procedure that guarantees solving a particular problem. Contrasts with the usually speedier—but also more error-prone—use of *heuristics*.

alpha waves the relatively slow brain waves of a relaxed, awake state.

altruism unselfish regard for the welfare of others.

Alzheimer's disease a progressive and irreversible brain disorder characterized by gradual deterioration of memory, reasoning, language, and, finally, physical functioning.

amnesia the loss of memory.

amphetamines drugs that stimulate neural activity, causing speeded-up body functions and associated energy and mood changes.

amygdala [uh-MIG-duh-la] two lima bean-sized neural clusters that are components of the limbic system and are linked to emotion.

anorexia nervosa an eating disorder in which a normal-weight person (usually an adolescent female) diets and becomes significantly (15 percent or more) underweight, yet, still feeling fat, continues to starve.

antisocial personality disorder a personality disorder in which the person (usually a man) exhibits a lack of conscience for wrongdoing, even toward friends and family members. May be aggressive and ruthless or a clever con artist.

anxiety disorders psychological disorders characterized by distressing, persistent anxiety or maladaptive behaviors that reduce anxiety.

aphasia impairment of language, usually caused by left hemisphere damage either to Broca's area (impairing speaking) or to Wernicke's area (impairing understanding).

applied research scientific study that aims to solve practical problems.

aptitude test a test designed to predict a person's future performance; *aptitude* is the capacity to learn.

assimilation interpreting one's new experience in terms of one's existing schemas.

association areas areas of the cerebral cortex that are not involved in primary motor or sensory functions; rather, they are involved in higher mental functions such as learning, remembering, thinking, and speaking.

associative learning learning that certain events occur together. The events may be two stimuli (as in classical conditioning) or a response and its consequences (as in operant conditioning).

attachment an emotional tie with another person; shown in young children by their seeking closeness to the caregiver and showing distress on separation.

attention-deficit hyperactivity disorder (ADHD) a psychological disorder marked by the appearance by age 7 of one or more of three key symptoms: extreme inattention, hyperactivity, and impulsivity.

attitude feelings, often based on our beliefs, that predispose us to respond in a particular way to objects, people, and events.

attribution theory suggests how we explain someone's behavior—by crediting either the situation or the person's disposition.

audition the sense or act of hearing.

autism a disorder that appears in childhood and is marked by deficient communication, social interaction, and understanding of others' states of mind.

automatic processing unconscious encoding of incidental information, such as space, time, and frequency, and of well-learned information, such as word meanings.

autonomic [aw-tuh-NAHM-ik] **nervous system** the part of the peripheral nervous system that controls the glands and the muscles of the internal organs (such as the heart). Its sympathetic division arouses; its parasympathetic division calms.

availability heuristic estimating the likelihood of events based on their availability in memory; if instances come readily to mind (perhaps because of their vividness), we presume such events are common.

aversive conditioning a type of counterconditioning that associates an unpleasant state (such as nausea) with an unwanted behavior (such as drinking alcohol).

axon the extension of a neuron, ending in branching terminal fibers, through which messages pass to other neurons or to muscles or glands.

babbling stage at about 4 months, the stage of speech development in which the infant spontaneously utters various sounds at first unrelated to the household language.

barbiturates drugs that depress the activity of the central nervous system, reducing anxiety but impairing memory and judgment.

basal metabolic rate the body's resting rate of energy expenditure.

basic research pure science that aims to increase the scientific knowledge base.

basic trust according to Erik Erikson, a sense that the world is predictable and trustworthy; said to be formed during infancy by appropriate experiences with responsive caregivers.

behavior genetics the study of the relative power and limits of genetic and environmental influences on behavior.

behavior therapy therapy that applies learning principles to the elimination of unwanted behaviors.

behavioral medicine an interdisciplinary field that integrates behavioral and medical knowledge and applies that knowledge to health and disease.

behaviorism the view that psychology (1) should be an objective science that (2) studies behavior without reference to mental processes. Most research psychologists today agree with (1) but not with (2).

belief bias the tendency for one's preexisting beliefs to distort logical reasoning, sometimes by making invalid conclusions seem valid, or valid conclusions seem invalid.

belief perseverance clinging to one's initial conceptions after the basis on which they were formed has been discredited.

binocular cues depth cues, such as retinal disparity and convergence, that depend on the use of two eyes.

biofeedback a system for electronically recording, amplifying, and feeding back information regarding a subtle physiological state, such as blood pressure or muscle tension.

biological psychology a branch of psychology concerned with the links between biology and behavior. (Some biological psychologists call themselves *behavioral neuroscientists, neuropsychologists, behavior geneticists, physiological psychologists,* or *biopsychologists.*)

biological rhythms periodic physiological fluctuations.

biomedical therapy prescribed medications or medical procedures that act directly on the patient's nervous system.

biopsychosocial approach an integrated perspective that incorporates biological, psychological, and social-cultural levels of analysis.

bipolar disorder a mood disorder in which the person alternates between the hopelessness and lethargy of depression and the overexcited state of mania. (Formerly called manic-depressive disorder.)

blind spot the point at which the optic nerve leaves the eye, creating a "blind" spot because no receptor cells are located there.

bottom-up processing analysis that begins with the sensory receptors and works up to the brain's integration of sensory information.

brainstem the oldest part and central core of the brain, beginning where the spinal cord swells as it enters the skull; the brainstem is responsible for automatic survival functions.

Broca's area controls language expression—an area of the frontal lobe, usually in the left hemisphere, that directs the muscle movements involved in speech.

bulimia nervosa an eating disorder characterized by episodes of overeating, usually of high-calorie foods, followed by vomiting, laxative use, fasting, or excessive exercise.

bystander effect the tendency for any given bystander to be less likely to give aid if other bystanders are present.

Cannon-Bard theory the theory that an emotion-arousing stimulus simultaneously triggers (1) physiological responses and (2) the subjective experience of emotion.

case study an observation technique in which one person is studied in depth in the hope of revealing universal principles.

catharsis emotional release. In psychology, the catharsis hypothesis maintains that "releasing" aggressive energy (through action or fantasy) relieves aggressive urges.

central nervous system (CNS) the brain and spinal cord.

cerebellum [sehr-uh-BELL-um] the "little brain" attached to the rear of the brainstem; its functions include processing sensory input and coordinating movement output and balance.

cerebral [seh-REE-bruhl] **cortex** the intricate fabric of interconnected neural cells that covers the cerebral hemispheres; the body's ultimate control and information-processing center.

chromosomes threadlike structures made of DNA molecules that contain the genes.

chunking organizing items into familiar, manageable units; often occurs automatically.

circadian [ser-KAY-dee-an] **rhythm** the biological clock; regular bodily rhythms (for example, of temperature and wakefulness) that occur on a 24-hour cycle.

classical conditioning a type of learning in which an organism comes to associate stimuli. A neutral stimulus that signals an unconditioned stimulus (US) begins to produce a response that anticipates and prepares for the unconditioned stimulus. Also called *Pavlovian* or *respondent conditioning.*

client-centered therapy a humanistic therapy, developed by Carl Rogers, in which the therapist uses techniques such as active listening within a genuine, accepting, empathic environment to facilitate clients' growth. (Also called *person-centered therapy.*)

clinical psychology a branch of psychology that studies, assesses, and treats people with psychological disorders.

cochlea [KOHK-lee-uh] a coiled, bony, fluid-filled tube in the inner ear through which sound waves trigger nerve impulses.

cochlear implant a device for converting sounds into electrical signals and stimulating the auditory nerve through electrodes threaded into the cochlea

cognition all the mental activities associated with thinking, knowing, remembering, and communicating.

cognitive-behavior therapy a popular integrated therapy that combines cognitive therapy (changing self-defeating thinking) with behavior therapy (changing behavior).

cognitive dissonance theory the theory that we act to reduce the discomfort (dissonance) we feel when two of our thoughts (cognitions) are inconsistent. For example, when our awareness of our attitudes and of our actions clash, we can reduce the resulting dissonance by changing our attitudes.

cognitive map a mental representation of the layout of one's environment. For example, after exploring a maze, rats act as if they have learned a cognitive map of it.

cognitive therapy therapy that teaches people new, more adaptive ways of thinking and acting; based on the assumption that thoughts intervene between events and our emotional reactions.

collective unconscious Carl Jung's concept of a shared, inherited reservoir of memory traces from our species' history.

collectivism giving priority to the goals of one's group (often one's extended family or work group) and defining one's identity accordingly.

color constancy perceiving familiar objects as having consistent color, even if changing illumination alters the wavelengths reflected by the object.

companionate love the deep affectionate attachment we feel for those with whom our lives are intertwined.

complementary and alternative medicine Unproven health care treatments not taught widely in medical schools, not used in hospitals, and not usually reimbursed by insurance companies.

concept a mental grouping of similar objects, events, ideas, or people.

concrete operational stage in Piaget's theory, the stage of cognitive development (from about 6 or 7 to 11 years of age) during which children gain the mental operations that enable them to think logically about concrete events.

conditioned reinforcer a stimulus that gains its reinforcing power through its association with a primary reinforcer; also known as *secondary reinforcer.*

conditioned response (CR) in classical conditioning, the learned response to a previously neutral (but now conditioned) stimulus (CS).

conditioned stimulus (CS) in classical conditioning, an originally irrelevant stimulus that, after association with an unconditioned stimulus (US), comes to trigger a conditioned response.

conduction hearing loss hearing loss caused by damage to the mechanical system that conducts sound waves to the cochlea.

cones retinal receptor cells that are concentrated near the center of the retina and that function in daylight or in well-lit conditions. The cones detect fine detail and give rise to color sensations.

confirmation bias a tendency to search for information that confirms one's preconceptions.

conflict a perceived incompatibility of actions, goals, or ideas.

conformity adjusting one's behavior or thinking to coincide with a group standard.

consciousness our awareness of ourselves and our environment.

conservation the principle (which Piaget believed to be a part of concrete operational reasoning) that properties such as mass, volume, and number remain the same despite changes in the forms of objects.

content validity the extent to which a test samples the behavior that is of interest (such as a driving test that samples driving tasks).

continuous reinforcement reinforcing the desired response every time it occurs.

control condition the condition of an experiment that contrasts with the experimental condition and serves as a comparison for evaluating the effect of the treatment.

convergence a binocular cue for perceiving depth; the extent to which the eyes converge inward when looking at an object. The greater the inward strain, the closer the object.

coping alleviating stress using emotional, cognitive, or behavioral methods.

coronary heart disease the clogging of the vessels that nourish the heart muscle; the leading cause of death in many developed countries.

corpus callosum [KOR-pus kah-LOW-sum] the large band of neural fibers connecting the two brain hemispheres and carrying messages between them.

correlation a measure of the extent to which two factors vary together, and thus of how well either factor predicts the other. The *correlation coefficient* is the mathematical expression of the relationship, ranging from −1 to +1.

counseling psychology a branch of psychology that assists people with problems in living (often related to school, work, or marriage) and in achieving greater well-being.

counterconditioning a behavior therapy procedure that conditions new responses to stimuli that trigger unwanted behaviors; based on classical conditioning. Includes *exposure therapies* and *aversive conditioning.*

creativity the ability to produce novel and valuable ideas.

criterion the behavior (such as future college grades) that a test (such as the SAT) is designed to predict; thus, the measure used in defining whether the test has predictive validity.

critical period an optimal period shortly after birth when an organism's exposure to certain stimuli or experiences produces proper development.

critical thinking thinking that does not blindly accept arguments and conclusions. Rather, it examines assumptions, discerns hidden values, evaluates evidence, and assesses conclusions.

cross-sectional study a study in which people of different ages are compared with one another.

crystallized intelligence one's accumulated knowledge and verbal skills; tends to increase with age.

culture the enduring behaviors, ideas, attitudes, and traditions shared by a large group of people and transmitted from one generation to the next.

defense mechanisms in psychoanalytic theory, the ego's protective methods of reducing anxiety by unconsciously distorting reality.

deindividuation the loss of self-awareness and self-restraint occurring in group situations that foster arousal and anonymity.

déjà vu that eerie sense that "I've experienced this before." Cues from the current situation may subconsciously trigger retrieval of an earlier experience.

delta waves the large, slow brain waves associated with deep sleep.

delusions false beliefs, often of persecution or grandeur, that may accompany psychotic disorders.

dendrite the bushy, branching extensions of a neuron that receive messages and conduct impulses toward the cell body.

dependent variable the outcome factor; the variable that may change in response to manipulations of the independent variable.

depressants drugs (such as alcohol, barbiturates, and opiates) that reduce neural activity and slow body functions.

depth perception the ability to see objects in three dimensions although the images that strike the retina are two-dimensional; allows us to judge distance.

developmental psychology a branch of psychology that studies physical, cognitive, and social change throughout the life span.

difference threshold the minimum difference between two stimuli required for detection 50 percent of the time. We experience the difference threshold as a just noticeable difference. (Also called *just noticeable difference* or *jnd*.)

discrimination in classical conditioning, the learned ability to distinguish between a conditioned stimulus and stimuli that do not signal an unconditioned stimulus.

discrimination unjustifiable negative behavior toward a group or its members.

displacement psychoanalytic defense mechanism that shifts sexual or aggressive impulses toward a more acceptable or less threatening object or person, as when redirecting anger toward a safer outlet.

dissociation a split in consciousness, which allows some thoughts and behaviors to occur simultaneously with others.

dissociative disorders disorders in which conscious awareness becomes separated (dissociated) from previous memories, thoughts, and feelings.

dissociative identity disorder (DID) a rare dissociative disorder in which a person exhibits two or more distinct and alternating personalities. Also called *multiple personality disorder*.

DNA (deoxyribonucleic acid) a complex molecule containing the genetic information that makes up the chromosomes.

double-blind procedure an experimental procedure in which both the research participants and the research staff are ignorant (blind) about whether the research participants have received the treatment or a placebo. Commonly used in drug-evaluation studies.

Down syndrome a condition of retardation and associated physical disorders caused by an extra chromosome in one's genetic makeup.

dream a sequence of images, emotions, and thoughts passing through a sleeping person's mind. Dreams are notable for their hallucinatory imagery, discontinuities, and incongruities, and for the dreamer's delusional acceptance of the content and later difficulties remembering it.

drive-reduction theory the idea that a physiological need creates an aroused tension state (a drive) that motivates an organism to satisfy the need.

DSM-IV the American Psychiatric Association's *Diagnostic and Statistical Manual of Mental Disorders* (Fourth Edition), a widely used system for classifying psychological disorders. Presently distributed in an updated "text revision" (DSM-IV-TR).

dualism the presumption that mind and body are two distinct entities that interact.

echoic memory a momentary sensory memory of auditory stimuli; if attention is elsewhere, sounds and words can still be recalled within 3 or 4 seconds.

eclectic approach an approach to psychotherapy that, depending on the client's problems, uses techniques from various forms of therapy.

Ecstasy (MDMA) a synthetic stimulant and mild hallucinogen. Produces euphoria and social intimacy, but with short-term health risks and longer-term harm to serotonin-producing neurons and to mood and cognition.

effortful processing encoding that requires attention and conscious effort.

ego the largely conscious, "executive" part of personality that, according to Freud, mediates among the demands of the id, superego, and reality. The ego operates on the *reality principle*, satisfying the id's desires in ways that will realistically bring pleasure rather than pain.

egocentrism in Piaget's theory, the preoperational child's difficulty in taking another's point of view.

electroconvulsive therapy (ECT) a biomedical therapy for severely depressed patients in which a brief electric current is sent through the brain of an anesthetized patient.

electroencephalogram (EEG) an amplified recording of the waves of electrical activity that sweep across the brain's surface. These waves are measured by electrodes placed on the scalp.

embryo the developing human organism from about 2 weeks after fertilization through the second month.

emotion a response of the whole organism, involving (1) physiological arousal, (2) expressive behaviors, and (3) conscious experience.

emotion-focused coping attempting to alleviate stress by avoiding or ignoring a stressor and attending to emotional needs related to one's stress reaction.

emotional intelligence the ability to perceive, understand, manage, and use emotions.

empirically derived test a test (such as the MMPI) developed by testing a pool of items and then selecting those that discriminate between groups.

empiricism the view that (a) knowledge comes from experience via the senses, and (b) science flourishes through observation and experiment.

encoding the processing of information into the memory system—for example, by extracting meaning.

endocrine [EN-duh-krin] **system** the body's "slow" chemical communication system; a set of glands that secrete hormones into the bloodstream.

endorphins [en-DOR-fins] "morphine within"—natural, opiatelike neurotransmitters linked to pain control and to pleasure.

environment every nongenetic influence, from prenatal nutrition to the people and things around us.

equity a condition in which people receive from a relationship in proportion to what they give to it.

estrogen a sex hormone, secreted in greater amounts by females than by males. In nonhuman female mammals, estrogen levels peak during ovulation, promoting sexual receptivity.

evolutionary psychology the study of the evolution of behavior and the mind, using principles of natural selection.

experiment a research method in which an investigator manipulates one or more factors (independent variables) to observe the effect on some behavior or mental process (the dependent variable). By random assignment of participants, the experimenter aims to control other relevant factors.

experimental condition the condition of an experiment that exposes participants to the treatment, that is, to one version of the independent variable.

explicit memory memory of facts and experiences that one can consciously know and "declare." (Also called *declarative memory*.)

exposure therapies behavioral techniques, such as systematic desensitization, that treat anxieties by exposing people (in imagination or actuality) to the things they fear and avoid.

external locus of control the perception that chance or outside forces beyond one's personal control determine one's fate.

extinction the diminishing of a conditioned response; occurs in classical conditioning when an unconditioned stimulus (US) does not follow a conditioned stimulus (CS); occurs in operant conditioning when a response is no longer reinforced.

extrasensory perception (ESP) the controversial claim that perception can occur apart from sensory input. Said to include *telepathy, clairvoyance,* and *precognition*.

extrinsic motivation a desire to perform a behavior due to promised rewards or threats of punishment.

factor analysis a statistical procedure that identifies clusters of related items (called *factors*) on a test; used to identify different dimensions of performance that underlie one's total score.

false consensus effect the tendency to overestimate the extent to which others share our beliefs and behaviors.

family therapy therapy that treats the family as a system. Views an individual's unwanted behaviors as influenced by or directed at other family members; attempts to guide family members toward positive relationships and improved communication.

farsightedness a condition in which faraway objects are seen more clearly than near objects because the image of near objects is focused behind the retina.

feature detectors nerve cells in the brain that respond to specific features of the stimulus, such as shape, angle, or movement.

feel-good, do-good phenomenon people's tendency to be helpful when already in a good mood.

fetal alcohol syndrome (FAS) physical and cognitive abnormalities in children caused by a pregnant woman's heavy drinking. In severe cases, symptoms include noticeable facial misproportions.

fetus the developing human organism from 9 weeks after conception to birth.

figure-ground the organization of the visual field into objects (the *figures*) that stand out from their surroundings (the *ground*).

fixation according to Freud, a lingering focus of pleasure-seeking energies at an earlier psychosexual stage in which conflicts were unresolved.

fixation the inability to see a problem from a new perspective; an impediment to problem solving.

fixed-interval schedule in operant conditioning, a reinforcement schedule that reinforces a response only after a specified time has elapsed.

fixed-ratio schedule in operant conditioning, a reinforcement schedule that reinforces a response only after a specified number of responses.

flashbulb memory a clear memory of an emotionally significant moment or event.

flow a completely involved, focused state of consciousness, with diminished awareness of self and time, resulting from optimal engagement of one's skills.

fluid intelligence one's ability to reason speedily and abstractly; tends to decrease during late adulthood.

fMRI (functional magnetic resonance imaging) a technique for revealing blood flow and, therefore, brain activity by comparing successive MRI scans. MRI scans show brain anatomy; fMRI scans show brain function.

foot-in-the-door phenomenon the tendency for people who have first agreed to a small request to comply later with a larger request.

formal operational stage in Piaget's theory, the stage of cognitive development (normally beginning about age 12) during which people begin to think logically about abstract concepts.

fovea the central focal point in the retina, around which the eye's cones cluster.

framing the way an issue is posed; how an issue is framed can significantly affect decisions and judgments.

fraternal twins twins who develop from separate fertilized eggs. They are genetically no closer than brothers and sisters, but they share a fetal environment.

free association in psychoanalysis, a method of exploring the unconscious in which the person relaxes and says whatever comes to mind, no matter how trivial or embarrassing.

frequency the number of complete wavelengths that pass a point in a given time (for example, per second).

frequency theory in hearing, the theory that the rate of nerve impulses traveling up the auditory nerve matches the frequency of a tone, thus enabling us to sense its pitch.

frontal lobes the portion of the cerebral cortex lying just behind the forehead; involved in speaking and muscle movements and in making plans and judgments.

frustration-aggression principle the principle that frustration—the blocking of an attempt to achieve some goal—creates anger, which can generate aggression.

functional fixedness the tendency to think of things only in terms of their usual functions; an impediment to problem solving.

functionalism a school of psychology that focused on how mental and behavioral processes function—how they enable the organism to adapt, survive, and flourish.

fundamental attribution error the tendency for observers, when analyzing another's behavior, to underestimate the impact of the situation and to overestimate the impact of personal disposition.

gate-control theory the theory that the spinal cord contains a neurological "gate" that blocks pain signals or allows them to pass on to the brain. The "gate" is opened by the activity of pain signals traveling up small nerve fibers and is closed by activity in larger fibers or by information coming from the brain.

gender in psychology, the biologically and socially influenced characteristics by which people define *male* and *female.*

gender-typing the acquisition of a traditional masculine or feminine role.

gender identity one's sense of being male or female.

gender role a set of expected behaviors for males and for females.

gender schema theory the theory that children learn from their cultures a concept of what it means to be male and female and that they adjust their behavior accordingly.

general adaptation syndrome (GAS) Selye's concept of the body's adaptive response to stress in three stages—alarm, resistance, exhaustion.

general intelligence (*g*) a general intelligence factor that according to Spearman and others underlies specific mental abilities and is therefore measured by every task on an intelligence test.

generalization the tendency, once a response has been conditioned, for stimuli similar to the conditioned stimulus to elicit similar responses.

generalized anxiety disorder an anxiety disorder in which a person is continually tense, apprehensive, and in a state of autonomic nervous system arousal.

genes the biochemical units of heredity that make up the chromosomes; a segment of DNA capable of synthesizing a protein.

genome the complete instructions for making an organism, consisting of all the genetic material in that organism's chromosomes.

gestalt an organized whole. Gestalt psychologists emphasized our tendency to integrate pieces of information into meaningful wholes.

glial cells (glia) cells in the nervous system that support, nourish, and protect neurons.

glucose the form of sugar that circulates in the blood and provides the major source of energy for body tissues. When its level is low, we feel hunger.

grammar in a language, a system of rules that enables us to communicate with and understand others.

GRIT Graduated and Reciprocated Initiatives in Tension-Reduction—strategy designed to decrease international tensions.

group polarization the enhancement of a group's prevailing inclinations through discussion within the group.

grouping the perceptual tendency to organize stimuli into coherent groups.

groupthink the mode of thinking that occurs when the desire for harmony in a decision-making group overrides a realistic appraisal of alternatives.

habituation decreasing responsiveness with repeated stimulation. As infants gain familiarity with repeated exposure to a visual stimulus, their interest wanes and they look away sooner.

hallucinations false sensory experiences, such as seeing something in the absence of an external visual stimulus.

hallucinogens psychedelic ("mind-manifesting") drugs, such as LSD, that distort perceptions and evoke sensory images in the absence of sensory input.

health psychology the application of psychological concepts and research to illness prevention and treatment and to health advancement.

heritability the proportion of variation among individuals that we can attribute to genes. The heritability of a trait may vary, depending on the range of populations and environments studied.

heuristic a simple thinking strategy that often allows us to make judgments and solve problems efficiently; usually speedier but also more error-prone than *algorithms.*

hierarchy of needs Maslow's pyramid of human needs, beginning at the base with physiological needs that must first be satisfied before higher-level safety needs and then psychological needs become active.

hindsight bias the tendency to believe, after learning an outcome, that one would have foreseen it. (Also known as the I-knew-it-all-along phenomenon.)

hippocampus a neural center located in the limbic system that helps process explicit memories for storage.

homeostasis a tendency to maintain a balanced or constant internal state; the regulation of any aspect of body chemistry, such as blood glucose, around a particular level.

hormones chemical messengers, mostly those manufactured by the endocrine glands, that are produced in one tissue and affect another.

hue the dimension of color that is determined by the wavelength of light; what we know as the color names *blue, green,* and so forth.

human factors psychology a branch of psychology that explores how people and machines interact and how machines and physical environments can be made safe and easy to use.

humanistic psychology historically significant perspective that emphasized the growth potential of healthy people; used personalized methods to study personality in hopes of fostering personal growth.

hypnosis a social interaction in which one person (the hypnotist) suggests to another (the subject) that certain perceptions, feelings, thoughts, or behaviors will spontaneously occur.

hypothalamus [hi-po-THAL-uh-muss] a neural structure lying below (*hypo*) the thalamus; it directs several maintenance activities (eating, drinking, body temperature), helps govern the endocrine system via the pituitary gland, and is linked to emotion.

hypothesis a testable prediction, often implied by a theory.

iconic memory a momentary sensory memory of visual stimuli; a photographic or picture-image memory lasting no more than a few tenths of a second.

id contains a reservoir of unconscious psychic energy that, according to Freud, strives to satisfy basic sexual and aggressive drives. The id operates on the pleasure principle, demanding immediate gratification.

identical twins twins who develop from a single fertilized egg that splits in two, creating two genetically identical organisms.

identification the process by which, according to Freud, children incorporate their parents' values into their developing superegos.

identity one's sense of self; according to Erikson, the adolescent's task is to solidify a sense of self by testing and integrating various roles.

illusory correlation the perception of a relationship where none exists.

imagery mental pictures; a powerful aid to effortful processing, especially when combined with semantic encoding.

implicit memory retention independent of conscious recollection. (Also called *procedural memory*.)

imprinting the process by which certain animals form attachments during a critical period very early in life.

inattentional blindness failing to see visible objects when our attention is directed elsewhere.

incentive a positive or negative environmental stimulus that motivates behavior.

independent variable the experimental factor that is manipulated; the variable whose effect is being studied.

individualism giving priority to one's own goals over group goals, and defining one's identity in terms of personal attributes rather than group identifications.

industrial-organizational (I/O) psychology the application of psychological concepts and methods to optimizing human behavior in workplaces.

informational social influence influence resulting from one's willingness to accept others' opinions about reality.

ingroup "Us"—people with whom one shares a common identity.

ingroup bias the tendency to favor one's own group.

inner ear the innermost part of the ear, containing the cochlea, semicircular canals, and vestibular sacs

insight a sudden and often novel realization of the solution to a problem; it contrasts with strategy-based solutions.

insomnia recurring problems in falling or staying asleep.

instinct a complex behavior that is rigidly patterned throughout a species and is unlearned.

intelligence mental quality consisting of the ability to learn from experience, solve problems, and use knowledge to adapt to new situations.

intelligence quotient (IQ) defined originally as the ratio of mental age (*ma*) to chronological age (*ca*) multiplied by 100 (thus, IQ = $ma/ca \times 100$). On contemporary intelligence tests, the average performance for a given age is assigned a score of 100.

intelligence test a method for assessing an individual's mental aptitudes and comparing them with those of others, using numerical scores.

intensity the amount of energy in a light or sound wave, which we perceive as brightness or loudness, as determined by the wave's amplitude.

interaction the effect of one factor (such as environment) depends on another factor (such as heredity).

internal locus of control the perception that one controls one's own fate.

interneurons central nervous system neurons that internally communicate and intervene between the sensory inputs and motor outputs.

interpretation in psychoanalysis, the analyst's noting supposed dream meanings, resistances, and other significant behaviors and events in order to promote insight.

intimacy in Erikson's theory, the ability to form close, loving relationships; a primary developmental task in late adolescence and early adulthood.

intrinsic motivation a desire to perform a behavior for its own sake.

iris a ring of muscle tissue that forms the colored portion of the eye around the pupil and controls the size of the pupil opening.

James-Lange theory the theory that our experience of emotion is our awareness of our physiological responses to emotion-arousing stimuli.

just-world phenomenon the tendency of people to believe the world is just and that people therefore get what they deserve and deserve what they get.

kinesthesis [kin-ehs-THEE-sehs] the system for sensing the position and movement of individual body parts.

language our spoken, written, or signed words and the ways we combine them to communicate meaning.

latent content according to Freud, the underlying meaning of a dream (as distinct from its manifest content). Freud believed that a dream's latent content functions as a safety valve.

latent learning learning that occurs but is not apparent until there is an incentive to demonstrate it.

law of effect Thorndike's principle that behaviors followed by favorable consequences become more likely, and that behaviors followed by unfavorable consequences become less likely.

learned helplessness the hopelessness and passive resignation an animal or human learns when unable to avoid repeated aversive events.

learning a relatively permanent change in an organism's behavior due to experience.

lens the transparent structure behind the pupil that changes shape to help focus images on the retina.

lesion [LEE-zhuhn] tissue destruction. A brain lesion is a naturally or experimentally caused destruction of brain tissue.

levels of analysis the differing complementary views, from biological to psychological to social-cultural, for analyzing any given phenomenon.

limbic system a doughnut-shaped system of neural structures at the border of the brainstem and cerebral hemispheres; associated with emotions such as fear and aggression and drives such as those for food and sex. Includes the hippocampus, amygdala, and hypothalamus.

linguistic determinism Whorf's hypothesis that language determines the way we think.

lobotomy a now-rare psychosurgical procedure once used to calm uncontrollably emotional or violent patients. The procedure cut the nerves that connect the frontal lobes to the emotion-controlling centers of the inner brain.

long-term memory the relatively permanent and limitless storehouse of the memory system. Includes knowledge, skills, and experiences.

long-term potentiation (LTP) an increase in a synapse's firing potential after brief, rapid stimulation. Believed to be a neural basis for learning and memory.

longitudinal study research in which the same people are restudied and retested over a long period.

LSD a powerful hallucinogenic drug; also known as *acid* (*lysergic acid diethylamide*).

lymphocytes the two types of white blood cells that are part of the body's immune system: *B lymphocytes* form in the *b*one marrow and release antibodies that fight bacterial infections; *T lymphocytes* form in the *t*hymus and other lymphatic tissue and attack cancer cells, viruses, and foreign substances.

major depressive disorder a mood disorder in which a person experiences, in the absence of drugs or a medical condition, two or more weeks of significantly depressed moods, feelings of worthlessness, and diminished interest or pleasure in most activities.

mania a mood disorder marked by a hyperactive, wildly optimistic state.

manifest content according to Freud, the remembered story line of a dream (as distinct from its latent, or hidden, content).

maturation biological growth processes that enable orderly changes in behavior, relatively uninfluenced by experience.

mean the arithmetic average of a distribution, obtained by adding the scores and then dividing by the number of scores.

median the middle score in a distribution; half the scores are above it and half are below it.

medical model the concept that diseases have physical causes that can be diagnosed, treated, and, in most cases, cured. When applied to psychological disorders, the medical model assumes that these *mental illnesses* can be diagnosed on the basis of their symptoms and cured through therapy, which may include treatment in a psychiatric hospital.

medulla [muh-DUL-uh] the base of the brainstem; controls heartbeat and breathing.

memory the persistence of learning over time through the storage and retrieval of information.

menarche [meh-NAR-key] the first menstrual period.

menopause the time of natural cessation of menstruation; also refers to the biological changes a woman experiences as her ability to reproduce declines.

mental age a measure of intelligence test performance devised by Binet; the chronological age that most typically corresponds to a given level of performance. Thus, a child who does as well as the average 8-year-old is said to have a mental age of 8.

mental retardation a condition of limited mental ability, indicated by an intelligence score of 70 or below and difficulty in adapting to the demands of life; varies from mild to profound.

mental set a tendency to approach a problem in a particular way, often a way that has been successful in the past.

mere exposure effect the phenomenon that repeated exposure to novel stimuli increases liking of them.

meta-analysis a procedure for statistically combining the results of many different research studies.

methamphetamine a powerfully addictive drug that stimulates the central nervous system, with speeded-up body functions and associated energy and mood changes; over time, appears to reduce baseline dopamine levels.

middle ear the chamber between the eardrum and cochlea containing three tiny bones (hammer, anvil, and stirrup) that concentrate the vibrations of the eardrum on the cochlea's oval window.

Minnesota Multiphasic Personality Inventory (MMPI) the most widely researched and clinically used of all personality tests. Originally developed to identify emotional disorders (still considered its most appropriate use), this test is now used for many other screening purposes.

mirror neurons frontal lobe neurons that fire when performing certain actions or when observing another doing so. The brain's mirroring of another's action may enable imitation, language learning, and empathy.

misinformation effect incorporating misleading information into one's memory of an event.

mnemonics [nih-MON-iks] memory aids, especially those techniques that use vivid imagery and organizational devices.

mode the most frequently occurring score(s) in a distribution.

modeling the process of observing and imitating a specific behavior.

molecular genetics the subfield of biology that studies the molecular structure and function of genes.

monism the presumption that mind and body are different aspects of the same thing.

monocular cues depth cues, such as interposition and linear perspective, available to either eye alone.

mood-congruent memory the tendency to recall experiences that are consistent with one's current good or bad mood.

mood disorders psychological disorders characterized by emotional extremes. See *major depressive disorder, mania,* and *bipolar disorder.*

morpheme in a language, the smallest unit that carries meaning; may be a word or a part of a word (such as a prefix).

motivation a need or desire that energizes and directs behavior.

motor cortex an area at the rear of the frontal lobes that controls voluntary movements.

motor neurons neurons that carry outgoing information from the central nervous system to the muscles and glands.

MRI (magnetic resonance imaging) a technique that uses magnetic fields and radio waves to produce computer-generated images that distinguish among different types of soft tissue; allows us to see structures within the brain.

mutation a random error in gene replication that leads to a change.

myelin [MY-uh-lin] **sheath** a layer of fatty tissue segmentally encasing the fibers of many neurons; enables vastly greater transmission speed of neural impulses as the impulse hops from one node to the next.

narcolepsy a sleep disorder characterized by uncontrollable sleep attacks. The sufferer may lapse directly into REM sleep, often at inopportune times.

natural selection the principle that, among the range of inherited trait variations, those that lead to increased reproduction and survival will most likely be passed on to succeeding generations.

naturalistic observation observing and recording behavior in naturally occurring situations without trying to manipulate and control the situation.

nature-nurture issue the longstanding controversy over the relative contributions that genes and experience make to the development of psychological traits and behaviors.

near-death experience an altered state of consciousness reported after a close brush with death (such as through cardiac arrest); often similar to drug-induced hallucinations.

nearsightedness a condition in which nearby objects are seen more clearly than distant objects because distant objects focus in front of the retina.

negative reinforcement increasing behaviors by stopping or reducing negative stimuli, such as shock. A negative reinforcer is any stimulus that, when *removed* after a response, strengthens the response. (*Note:* Negative reinforcement is *not* punishment.)

nerves neural "cables" containing many axons. These bundled axons, which are part of the peripheral nervous system, connect the central nervous system with muscles, glands, and sense organs.

nervous system the body's speedy, electrochemical communication network, consisting of all the nerve cells of the peripheral and central nervous systems.

neural networks interconnected neural cells. With experience, networks can learn, as feedback strengthens or inhibits connections that produce certain results. Computer simulations of neural networks show analogous learning.

neuron a nerve cell; the basic building block of the nervous system.

neurotransmitters chemical messengers that traverse the synaptic gaps between neurons. When released by the sending neuron, neurotransmitters travel across the synapse and bind to receptor sites on the receiving neuron, thereby influencing whether that neuron will generate a neural impulse.

night terrors a sleep disorder characterized by high arousal and an appearance of being terrified; unlike nightmares, night terrors occur during Stage 4 sleep, within two or three hours of falling asleep, and are seldom remembered.

norm an understood rule for accepted and expected behavior. Norms prescribe "proper" behavior.

normal curve the symmetrical bell-shaped curve that describes the distribution of many physical and psychological attributes. Most scores fall near the average, and fewer and fewer scores lie near the extremes.

normative social influence influence resulting from a person's desire to gain approval or avoid disapproval.

object permanence the awareness that things continue to exist even when not perceived.

observational learning learning by observing others.

obsessive-compulsive disorder (OCD) an anxiety disorder characterized by unwanted repetitive thoughts (obsessions) and/or actions (compulsions).

occipital [ahk-SIP-uh-tuhl] **lobes** the portion of the cerebral cortex lying at the back of the head; includes the visual areas, which receive visual information from the opposite visual field.

Oedipus [ED-uh-puss] **complex** according to Freud, a boy's sexual desires toward his mother and feelings of jealousy and hatred for the rival father.

one-word stage the stage in speech development, from about age 1 to 2, during which a child speaks mostly in single words.

operant behavior behavior that operates on the environment, producing consequences.

operant chamber a chamber also known as a *Skinner box*, containing a bar or key that an animal can manipulate to obtain a food or water reinforcer, with attached devices to record the animal's rate of bar pressing or key pecking. Used in operant conditioning research.

operant conditioning a type of learning in which behavior is strengthened if followed by a reinforcer or diminished if followed by a punisher.

operational definition a statement of the procedures (operations) used to define research variables. For example, *human intelligence* may be operationally defined as what an intelligence test measures.

opiates opium and its derivatives, such as morphine and heroin; they depress neural activity, temporarily lessening pain and anxiety.

opponent-process theory the theory that opposing retinal processes (red-green, yellow-blue, white-black) enable color vision. For example, some cells are stimulated by green and inhibited by red; others are stimulated by red and inhibited by green.

optic nerve the nerve that carries neural impulses from the eye to the brain.

organizational psychology a subfield of I/O psychology that examines organizational influences on worker satisfaction and productivity and facilitates organizational change.

outgroup "Them"—those perceived as different or apart from one's ingroup.

overconfidence the tendency to be more confident than correct—to overestimate the accuracy of one's beliefs and judgments.

panic disorder an anxiety disorder marked by unpredictable minutes-long episodes of intense dread in which a person experiences terror and accompanying chest pain, choking, or other frightening sensations.

parallel processing the processing of several aspects of a problem simultaneously; the brain's natural mode of information processing for many functions, including vision. Contrasts with the step-by-step (serial) processing of most computers and of conscious problem solving.

parapsychology the study of paranormal phenomena, including ESP and psychokinesis.

parasympathetic nervous system the division of the autonomic nervous system that calms the body, conserving its energy.

parietal [puh-RYE-uh-tuhl] **lobes** the portion of the cerebral cortex lying at the top of the head and toward the rear; receives sensory input for touch and body position.

partial (intermittent) reinforcement reinforcing a response only part of the time; results in slower acquisition of a response but much greater resistance to extinction than does continuous reinforcement.

passionate love an aroused state of intense positive absorption in another, usually present at the beginning of a love relationship.

perception the process of organizing and interpreting sensory information, enabling us to recognize meaningful objects and events.

perceptual adaptation in vision, the ability to adjust to an artificially displaced or even inverted visual field.

perceptual constancy perceiving objects as unchanging (having consistent lightness, color, shape, and size) even as illumination and retinal images change.

perceptual set a mental predisposition to perceive one thing and not another.

peripheral nervous system (PNS) the sensory and motor neurons that connect the central nervous system (CNS) to the rest of the body.

personal control our sense of controlling our environment rather than feeling helpless.

personal space the buffer zone we like to maintain around our bodies.

personality an individual's characteristic pattern of thinking, feeling, and acting.

personality disorders psychological disorders characterized by inflexible and enduring behavior patterns that impair social functioning.

personality inventory a questionnaire (often with true-false or agree-disagree items) on which people respond to items designed to gauge a wide range of feelings and behaviors; used to assess selected personality traits.

personnel psychology a subfield of I/O psychology that focuses on employee recruitment, selection, placement, training, appraisal, and development.

PET (positron emission tomography) scan a visual display of brain activity that detects where a radioactive form of glucose goes while the brain performs a given task.

phi phenomenon an illusion of movement created when two or more adjacent lights blink on and off in quick succession.

phobia an anxiety disorder marked by a persistent, irrational fear and avoidance of a specific object or situation.

phoneme in a language, the smallest distinctive sound unit.

physical dependence a physiological need for a drug, marked by unpleasant withdrawal symptoms when the drug is discontinued.

pitch a tone's experienced highness or lowness; depends on frequency.

pituitary gland the endocrine system's most influential gland. Under the influence of the hypothalamus, the pituitary regulates growth and controls other endocrine glands.

place theory in hearing, the theory that links the pitch we hear with the place where the cochlea's membrane is stimulated.

placebo [pluh-SEE-bo; Latin for "I shall please"] **effect** experimental results caused by expectations alone; any effect on behavior caused by the administration of an inert substance or condition, which is assumed to be an active agent.

plasticity the brain's capacity for modification, as evident in brain reorganization following damage (especially in children) and in experiments on the effects of experience on brain development.

polygraph a machine, commonly used in attempts to detect lies, that measures several of the physiological responses accompanying emotion (such as perspiration and cardiovascular and breathing changes).

population all the cases in a group, from which samples may be drawn for a study. (*Note*: Except for national studies, this does not refer to a country's whole population.)

positive psychology the scientific study of optimal human functioning; aims to discover and promote strengths and virtues that enable individuals and communities to thrive.

positive reinforcement increasing behaviors by presenting positive stimuli, such as food. A positive reinforcer is any stimulus that, when *presented* after a response, strengthens the response.

post-traumatic stress disorder (PTSD) an anxiety disorder characterized by haunting memories, nightmares, social withdrawal, jumpy anxiety, and/or insomnia that lingers for four weeks or more after a traumatic experience.

posthypnotic suggestion a suggestion, made during a hypnosis session, to be carried out after the subject is no longer hypnotized; used by some clinicians to help control undesired symptoms and behaviors.

predictive validity the success with which a test predicts the behavior it is designed to predict; it is assessed by computing the correlation between test scores and the criterion behavior. (Also called *criterion-related validity*.)

prejudice an unjustifiable (and usually negative) attitude toward a group and its members. Prejudice generally involves stereotyped beliefs, negative feelings, and a predisposition to discriminatory action.

preoperational stage in Piaget's theory, the stage (from about 2 to 6 or 7 years of age) during which a child learns to use language but does not yet comprehend the mental operations of concrete logic.

primary reinforcer an innately reinforcing stimulus, such as one that satisfies a biological need.

primary sex characteristics the body structures (ovaries, testes, and external genitalia) that make sexual reproduction possible.

priming the activation, often unconsciously, of certain associations, thus predisposing one's perception, memory, or response.

proactive interference the disruptive effect of prior learning on the recall of new information.

problem-focused coping attempting to alleviate stress directly—by changing the stressor or the way we interact with that stressor.

projection psychoanalytic defense mechanism by which people disguise their own threatening impulses by attributing them to others.

projective test a personality test, such as the Rorschach or TAT, that provides ambiguous stimuli designed to trigger projection of one's inner dynamics.

prosocial behavior positive, constructive, helpful behavior. The opposite of antisocial behavior.

prototype a mental image or best example of a category. Matching new items to the prototype provides a quick and easy method for including items in a category (as when comparing feathered creatures to a prototypical bird, such as a robin).

psychiatry a branch of medicine dealing with psychological disorders; practiced by physicians who sometimes provide medical (for example, drug) treatments as well as psychological therapy.

psychoactive drug a chemical substance that alters perceptions and mood.

psychoanalysis Freud's theory of personality and therapeutic technique that attributes thoughts and actions to unconscious motives and conflicts. Freud believed the patient's free associations, resistances, dreams, and transferences—and the therapist's interpretations of them—released previously repressed feelings, allowing the patient to gain self-insight.

psychological dependence a psychological need to use a drug, such as to relieve negative emotions.

psychological disorder deviant, distressful, and dysfunctional behavior patterns.

psychology the scientific study of behavior and mental processes.

psychopharmacology the study of the effects of drugs on mind and behavior.

psychophysics the study of relationships between the physical characteristics of stimuli, such as their intensity, and our psychological experience of them.

psychophysiological illness literally, "mind-body" illness; any stress-related physical illness, such as hypertension and some headaches. *Note:* This is distinct from *hypochondriasis*—misinterpreting normal physical sensations as symptoms of a disease.

psychosexual stages the childhood stages of development (oral, anal, phallic, latency, genital) during which, according to Freud, the id's pleasure-seeking energies focus on distinct erogenous zones.

psychosurgery surgery that removes or destroys brain tissue in an effort to change behavior.

psychotherapy an emotionally charged, confiding interaction between a trained therapist and someone who suffers from psychological difficulties.

puberty the period of sexual maturation, during which a person becomes capable of reproducing.

punishment an event that *decreases* the behavior that it follows.

pupil the adjustable opening in the center of the eye through which light enters.

random assignment assigning participants to experimental and control conditions by chance, thus minimizing preexisting differences between those assigned to the different groups.

random sample a sample that fairly represents a population because each member has an equal chance of inclusion.

range the difference between the highest and lowest scores in a distribution.

rationalization defense mechanism that offers self-justifying explanations in place of the real, more threatening, unconscious reasons for one's actions.

reaction formation psychoanalytic defense mechanism by which the ego unconsciously switches unacceptable impulses into their opposites. Thus, people may express feelings that are the opposite of their anxiety-arousing unconscious feelings.

recall a measure of memory in which the person must retrieve information learned earlier, as on a fill-in-the-blank test.

reciprocal determinism the interacting influences between personality and environmental factors.

reciprocity norm an expectation that people will help, not hurt, those who have helped them.

recognition a measure of memory in which the person need only identify items previously learned, as on a multiple-choice test.

reflex a simple, automatic, inborn response to a sensory stimulus, such as the knee-jerk response.

refractory period a resting period after orgasm, during which a man cannot achieve another orgasm.

regression psychoanalytic defense mechanism in which an individual faced with anxiety retreats to a more infantile psychosexual stage, where some psychic energy remains fixated.

regression toward the mean the tendency for extremes of unusual scores to fall back (regress) toward their average.

rehearsal the conscious repetition of information, either to maintain it in consciousness or to encode it for storage.

reinforcer in operant conditioning, any event that *strengthens* the behavior it follows.

relative deprivation the perception that one is worse off relative to those with whom one compares oneself.

relearning a memory measure that assesses the amount of time saved when learning material for a second time.

reliability the extent to which a test yields consistent results, as assessed by the consistency of scores on two halves of the test, on alternate forms of the test, or on retesting.

REM rebound the tendency for REM sleep to increase following REM sleep deprivation (created by repeated awakenings during REM sleep).

REM sleep rapid eye movement sleep, a recurring sleep stage during which vivid dreams commonly occur. Also known as *paradoxical sleep*, because the muscles are relaxed (except for minor twitches) but other body systems are active.

repetitive transcranial magnetic stimulation (rTMS) the application of repeated pulses of magnetic energy to the brain; used to stimulate or suppress brain activity.

replication repeating the essence of a research study, usually with different participants in different situations, to see whether the basic finding extends to other participants and circumstances.

representativeness heuristic judging the likelihood of things in terms of how well they seem to represent, or match, particular prototypes; may lead one to ignore other relevant information.

repression in psychoanalytic theory, the basic defense mechanism that banishes anxiety-arousing thoughts, feelings, and memories from consciousness.

resistance in psychoanalysis, the blocking from consciousness of anxiety-laden material.

respondent behavior behavior that occurs as an automatic response to some stimulus; Skinner's term for behavior learned through classical conditioning.

reticular formation a nerve network in the brainstem that plays an important role in controlling arousal.

retina the light-sensitive inner surface of the eye, containing the receptor rods and cones plus layers of neurons that begin the processing of visual information.

retinal disparity a binocular cue for perceiving depth: By comparing images from the two eyeballs, the brain computes distance—the greater the disparity (difference) between the two images, the closer the object.

retrieval the process of getting information out of memory storage.

retroactive interference the disruptive effect of new learning on the recall of old information.

rods retinal receptors that detect black, white, and gray; necessary for peripheral and twilight vision, when cones don't respond.

role a set of expectations (norms) about a social position, defining how those in the position ought to behave.

rooting reflex a baby's tendency, when touched on the cheek, to turn toward the touch, open the mouth, and search for the nipple.

Rorschach inkblot test the most widely used projective test, a set of 10 inkblots, designed by Hermann Rorschach; seeks to identify people's inner feelings by analyzing their interpretations of the blots.

savant syndrome a condition in which a person otherwise limited in mental ability has an exceptional specific skill, such as in computation or drawing.

scapegoat theory the theory that prejudice offers an outlet for anger by providing someone to blame.

scatterplot a graphed cluster of dots, each of which represents the values of two variables. The slope of the points suggests the direction of the relationship between the two variables. The amount of scatter suggests the strength of the correlation (little scatter indicates high correlation). (Also called a *scattergram* or *scatter diagram*.)

schema a concept or framework that organizes and interprets information.

schizophrenia a group of severe disorders characterized by disorganized and delusional thinking, disturbed perceptions, and inappropriate emotions and actions.

secondary sex characteristics nonreproductive sexual characteristics, such as female breasts and hips, male voice quality, and body hair.

selective attention the focusing of conscious awareness on a particular stimulus, as in the cocktail party effect.

self-actualization according to Maslow, the ultimate psychological need that arises after basic physical and psychological needs are met and self-esteem is achieved; the motivation to fulfill one's potential.

self-concept (1) a sense of one's identity and personal worth. (2) all our thoughts and feelings about ourselves, in answer to the question, "Who am I?"

self-disclosure revealing intimate aspects of oneself to others.

self-esteem one's feelings of high or low self-worth.

self-serving bias a readiness to perceive oneself favorably.

semantic encoding the encoding of meaning, including the meaning of words.

semantics the set of rules by which we derive meaning from morphemes, words, and sentences in a given language; also, the study of meaning.

sensation the process by which our sensory receptors and nervous system receive and represent stimulus energies from our environment.

sensorimotor stage in Piaget's theory, the stage (from birth to about 2 years of age) during which infants know the world mostly in terms of their sensory impressions and motor activities.

sensorineural hearing loss hearing loss caused by damage to the cochlea's receptor cells or to the auditory nerves; also called *nerve deafness*.

sensory adaptation diminished sensitivity as a consequence of constant stimulation.

sensory cortex the area at the front of the parietal lobes that registers and processes body touch and movement sensations.

sensory interaction the principle that one sense may influence another, as when the smell of food influences its taste.

sensory memory the immediate, very brieg recording of sensory information in the memory system.

sensory neurons neurons that carry incoming information from the sense receptors to the central nervous system.

serial position effect our tendency to recall best the last and first items in a list.

set point the point at which an individual's "weight thermostat" is supposedly set. When the body falls below this weight, an increase in hunger and a lowered metabolic rate may act to restore the lost weight.

sexual disorder a problem that consistently impairs sexual arousal or functioning.

sexual orientation an enduring sexual attraction toward members of either one's own sex (homosexual orientation) or the other sex (heterosexual orientation).

sexual response cycle the four stages of sexual responding described by Masters and Johnson—excitement, plateau, orgasm, and resolution.

shaping an operant conditioning procedure in which reinforcers guide behavior toward closer and closer approximations of the desired behavior.

short-term memory activated memory that holds a few items briefly, such as the seven digits of a phone number while dialing, before the information is stored or forgotten.

signal detection theory a theory predicting how and when we detect the presence of a faint stimulus ("signal") amid background stimulation ("noise"). Assumes there is no single absolute threshold and detection depends partly on a person's experience, expectations, motivation, and level of fatigue.

sleep periodic, natural, reversible loss of consciousness—as distinct from unconsciousness resulting from a coma, general anesthesia, or hibernation. (Adapted from Dement, 1999.)

sleep apnea a sleep disorder characterized by temporary cessations of breathing during sleep and repeated momentary awakenings.

social-cognitive perspective views behavior as influenced by the interaction between persons (and their thinking) and their social context.

social-responsibility norm an expectation that people will help those dependent upon them.

social clock the culturally preferred timing of social events such as marriage, parenthood, and retirement.

social exchange theory the theory that our social behavior is an exchange process, the aim of which is to maximize benefits and minimize costs.

social facilitation stronger responses on simple or well-learned tasks in the presence of others.

social leadership group-oriented leadership that builds teamwork, mediates conflict, and offers support.

social learning theory the theory that we learn social behavior by observing and imitating and by being rewarded or punished.

social loafing the tendency for people in a group to exert less effort when pooling their efforts toward attaining a common goal than when individually accountable.

social psychology the scientific study of how we think about, influence, and relate to one another.

social trap a situation in which the conflicting parties, by each rationally pursuing their self-interest, become caught in mutually destructive behavior.

somatic nervous system the division of the peripheral nervous system that controls the body's skeletal muscles. Also called the *skeletal nervous system.*

source amnesia attributing to the wrong source an event we have experienced, heard about, read about, or imagined. (Also called *source misattribution.*) Source amnesia, along with the misinformation effect, is at the heart of many false memories.

spacing effect the tendency for distributed study or practice to yield better long-term retention than is achieved through massed study or practice.

split brain a condition in which the two hemispheres of the brain are isolated by cutting the connecting fibers (mainly those of the corpus callosum) between them.

spontaneous recovery the reappearance, after a pause, of an extinguished conditioned response.

spotlight effect overestimating others' noticing and evaluating our appearance, performance, and blunders (as if we presume a spotlight shines on us).

standard deviation a computed measure of how much scores vary around the mean score.

standardization defining meaningful scores by comparison with the performance of a pretested standardization group.

Stanford-Binet the widely used American revision (by Terman at Stanford University) of Binet's original intelligence test.

statistical significance a statistical statement of how likely it is that an obtained result occurred by chance.

stereotype a generalized (sometimes accurate but often overgeneralized) belief about a group of people.

stereotype threat a self-confirming concern that one will be evaluated based on a negative stereotype.

stimulants drugs (such as caffeine, nicotine, and the more powerful amphetamines, cocaine, and Ecstasy) that excite neural activity and speed up body functions.

storage the retention of encoded information over time.

stranger anxiety the fear of strangers that infants commonly display, beginning by about 8 months of age.

structuralism an early school of psychology that used introspection to explore the elemental structure of the human mind.

stress the process by which we perceive and respond to certain events, called *stressors,* that we appraise as threatening or challenging.

structured interviews interview process that asks the same job-relevant questions of all applicants, each of whom is rated on established scales.

subjective well-being self-perceived happiness or satisfaction with life. Used along with measures of objective well-being (for example, physical and economic indicators) to evaluate people's quality of life.

subliminal below one's absolute threshold for conscious awareness.

superego the part of personality that, according to Freud, represents internalized ideals and provides standards for judgment (the conscience) and for future aspirations.

superordinate goals shared goals that override differences among people and require their cooperation.

survey a technique for ascertaining the self-reported attitudes or behaviors of people, usually by questioning a representative, random sample of them.

sympathetic nervous system the division of the autonomic nervous system that arouses the body, mobilizing its energy in stressful situations.

synapse [SIN-aps] the junction between the axon tip of the sending neuron and the dendrite or cell body of the receiving neuron. The tiny gap at this junction is called the *synaptic gap* or *cleft.*

syntax the rules for combining words into grammatically sensible sentences in a given language.

systematic desensitization a type of counterconditioning that associates a pleasant relaxed state with gradually increasing anxiety-triggering stimuli. Commonly used to treat phobias.

tardive dyskinesia involuntary movements of the facial muscles, tongue, and limbs; a possible neurotoxic side effect of long-term use of antipsychotic drugs that target D2 dopamine receptors.

task leadership goal-oriented leadership that sets standards, organizes work, and focuses attention on goals.

telegraphic speech early speech stage in which a child speaks like a telegram—"go car"—using mostly nouns and verbs and omitting auxiliary words.

temperament a person's characteristic emotional reactivity and intensity.

temporal lobes the portion of the cerebral cortex lying roughly above the ears; includes the auditory areas, each of which receives auditory information primarily from the opposite ear.

teratogens agents, such as chemicals and viruses, that can reach the embryo or fetus during prenatal development and cause harm.

terror-management theory proposes that faith in one's worldview and the pursuit of self-esteem provide protection against a deeply rooted fear of death.

testosterone the most important of the male sex hormones. Both males and females have it, but the additional testosterone in males stimulates the growth of the male sex organs in the fetus and the development of the male sex characteristics during puberty.

thalamus [THAL-uh-muss] the brain's sensory switchboard, located on top of the brainstem; it directs messages to the sensory receiving areas in the cortex and transmits replies to the cerebellum and medulla.

THC the major active ingredient in marijuana; triggers a variety of effects, including mild hallucinations.

Thematic Apperception Test (TAT) a projective test in which people express their inner feelings and interests through the stories they make up about ambiguous scenes.

theory an explanation using an integrated set of principles that organizes and predicts observations.

theory of mind people's ideas about their own and others' mental states—about their feelings, perceptions, and thoughts and the behavior these might predict.

threshold the level of stimulation required to trigger a neural impulse.

token economy an operant conditioning procedure in which people earn a token of some sort for exhibiting a desired behavior and can later exchange the tokens for various privileges or treats.

tolerance the diminishing effect with regular use of the same dose of a drug, requiring the user to take larger and larger doses before experiencing the drug's effect.

top-down processing information processing guided by higher-level mental processes, as when we construct perceptions drawing on our experience and expectations.

trait a characteristic pattern of behavior or a disposition to feel and act, as assessed by self-report inventories and peer reports.

transduction conversion of one form of energy into another. In sensation, the transforming of stimulus energies, such as sights, sounds, and smells, into neural impulses our brains can interpret.

transference in psychoanalysis, the patient's transfer to the analyst of emotions linked with other relationships (such as love or hatred for a parent).

two-factor theory Schachter-Singer's theory that to experience emotion one must (1) be physically aroused and (2) cognitively label the arousal.

two-word stage beginning about age 2, the stage in speech development during which a child speaks mostly two-word statements.

Type A Friedman and Rosenman's term for competitive, hard-driving, impatient, verbally aggressive, and anger-prone people.

Type B Friedman and Rosenman's term for easygoing, relaxed people.

unconditional positive regard according to Rogers, an attitude of total acceptance toward another person.

unconditioned response (UR) in classical conditioning, the unlearned, naturally occurring response to the unconditioned stimulus (US), such as salivation when food is in the mouth.

unconditioned stimulus (US) in classical conditioning, a stimulus that unconditionally—naturally and automatically—triggers a response.

unconscious according to Freud, a reservoir of mostly unacceptable thoughts, wishes, feelings, and memories. According to contemporary psychologists, information processing of which we are unaware.

validity the extent to which a test measures or predicts what it is supposed to. (See also *content validity* and *predictive validity*.)

variable-interval schedule in operant conditioning, a reinforcement schedule that reinforces a response at unpredictable time intervals.

variable-ratio schedule in operant conditioning, a reinforcement schedule that reinforces a response after an unpredictable number of responses.

vestibular sense the sense of body movement and position, including the sense of balance.

virtual reality exposure therapy An anxiety treatment that progressively exposes people to simulations of their greatest fears, such as airplane flying, spiders, or public speaking.

visual capture the tendency for vision to dominate the other senses.

visual cliff a laboratory device for testing depth perception in infants and young animals.

visual encoding the encoding of picture images.

wavelength the distance from the peak of one light or sound wave to the peak of the next. Electromagnetic wavelengths vary from the short blips of cosmic rays to the long pulses of radio transmission.

Weber's law the principle that, to be perceived as different, two stimuli must differ by a constant minimum percentage (rather than a constant amount).

Wechsler Adult Intelligence Scale (WAIS) the WAIS is the most widely used intelligence test; contains verbal and performance (nonverbal) subtests.

Wernicke's area controls language reception—a brain area involved in language comprehension and expression; usually in the left temporal lobe.

withdrawal the discomfort and distress that follow discontinuing the use of an addictive drug.

working memory a newer understanding of short-term memory that involves conscious, active processing of incoming auditory and visual-spatial information, and of information retrieved from long-term memory.

X chromosome the sex chromosome found in both men and women. Females have two X chromosomes; males have one. An X chromosome from each parent produces a female child.

Y chromosome the sex chromosome found only in males. When paired with an X chromosome from the mother, it produces a male child.

Young-Helmholtz trichromatic (three-color) theory the theory that the retina contains three different color receptors—one most sensitive to red, one to green, one to blue—which when stimulated in combination can produce the perception of any color.

zygote the fertilized egg; it enters a 2-week period of rapid cell division and develops into an embryo.

REFERENCES

Aas, H., & Klepp, K-I. (1992). Adolescents' alcohol use related to perceived norms. *Scandinavian Journal of Psychology, 33*, 315–325.

Abbey, A. (1987). Misperceptions of friendly behavior as sexual interest: A survey of naturally occurring incidents. *Psychology of Women Quarterly, 11*, 173–194.

Abbey, A. (1991). Acquaintance rape and alcohol consumption on college campuses: How are they linked? *Journal of American College Health, 39*, 165–169.

Abbott, R. D., White, L. R., Ross, G. W., Masaki, K. H., Curb, J. D., & Petrovitch, H. (2004). Walking and dementia in physically capable elderly men. *Journal of the American Medical Association, 292*, 1447–1453.

Abrams, D. (1991). AIDS: What young people believe and what they do. Paper presented at the British Association for the Advancement of Science conference.

Abrams, D. B., & Wilson, G. T. (1983). Alcohol, sexual arousal, and self-control. *Journal of Personality and Social Psychology, 45*, 188–198.

Abrams, M. (2002, June). Sight unseen—Restoring a blind man's vision is now a real possibility through stem-cell surgery. But even perfect eyes cannot see unless the brain has been taught to use them. *Discover, 23*, 54–60.

Abramson, L. Y., Metalsky, G. I., & Alloy, L. B. (1989). Hopelessness depression: A theory-based subtype. *Psychological Review, 96*, 358–372.

Ackerman, D. (2004). *An alchemy of mind: The marvel and mystery of the brain.* New York: Scribner.

Adelmann, P. K., Antonucci, T. C., Crohan, S. F., & Coleman, L. M. (1989). Empty nest, cohort, and employment in the well-being of midlife women. *Sex Roles, 20*, 173–189.

Adelson, R. (2004, August). Detecting deception. *APA Monitor*, pp. 70–73.

Ader, R., & Cohen, N. (1985). CNS-immune system interactions: Conditioning phenomena. *Behavioral and Brain Sciences, 8*, 379–394.

Adolphs, R., Tranel, D., & Damasio, A. R. (1998). The human amygdala in social judgment. *Nature, 393*, 470–474.

Affleck, G., Tennen, H., Urrows, S., & Higgins, P. (1994). Person and contextual features of daily stress reactivity: Individual differences in relations of undesirable daily events with mood disturbance and chronic pain intensity. *Journal of Personality and Social Psychology, 66*, 329–340.

Aggleton, J. P., Kentridge, R. W., & Neave, N. J. (1993). Evidence for longevity differences between left handed and right handed men: An archival study of cricketers. *Journal of Epidemiology and Community Health, 47*, 206–209.

Agid, O., Shapira, B., Zislin, J., Ritsner, M., Hanin, B., Murad, H., Troudart, T., Bloch, M., Heresco-Levy, U., & Lerer, B. (1999). Environment and vulnerability to major psychiatric illness: A case control study of early parental loss in major depression, bipolar disorder and schizophrenia. *Molecular Psychiatry, 4*, 163–172.

Agnati, L. F., Bjelke, B., & Fuxe, K. (1992). Volume transmission in the brain. *American Scientist, 80*, 362–373.

Aiello, J. R., Thompson, D. D., & Brodzinsky, D. M. (1983). How funny is crowding anyway? Effects of room size, group size, and the introduction of humor. *Basic and Applied Social Psychology, 4*, 193–207.

Ainsworth, M. D. S. (1973). The development of infant-mother attachment. In B. Caldwell & H. Ricciuti (Eds.), *Review of child development research* (Vol. 3). Chicago: University of Chicago Press.

Ainsworth, M. D. S. (1979). Infant-mother attachment. *American Psychologist, 34*, 932–937.

Ainsworth, M. D. S. (1989). Attachments beyond infancy. *American Psychologist, 44*, 709–716.

Albee, G. W. (1986). Toward a just society: Lessons from observations on the primary prevention of psychopathology. *American Psychologist, 41*, 891–898.

Albert, B., Brown, S., & Flanigan, C. M. (Eds.) (2003). *14 and younger: The sexual behavior of young adolescents.* Washington, DC: National Campaign to Prevent Teen Pregnancy.

Alcock, J. E. (1981). *Parapsychology: Science or magic?* Oxford: Pergamon.

Alcock, J. E. (1985, Spring). Parapsychology: The "spiritual" science. *Free Inquiry*, pp. 25–35.

Aldrich, M. S. (1989). Automobile accidents in patients with sleep disorders. *Sleep, 12*, 487–494.

Aldridge-Morris, R. (1989). *Multiple personality: An exercise in deception.* Hillsdale, NJ: Erlbaum.

Aleman, A., Kahn, R. S., & Selten, J-P. (2003). Sex differences in the risk of schizophrenia: Evidence from meta-analysis. *Archives of General Psychiatry, 60*, 565–571.

Alexander, C. N., Langer, E. J., Newman, R. I., Chandler, H. M., & Davies, J. L. (1989). Transcendental meditation, mindfulness, and longevity: An experimental study with the elderly. *Journal of Personality and Social Psychology, 57*, 950–964.

Alexander, K. W., Quas, J. A., Goodman, G. S., Ghetti, S., Edelstein, R. S., Redlich, A. D., Cordon, I. M., & Jones, D. P. H. (2005). Traumatic impact predicts long-term memory for documented child sexual abuse. *Psychological Science, 16*, 33–40.

Allard, F., & Burnett, N. (1985). Skill in sport. *Canadian Journal of Psychology, 39*, 294–312.

Allen, J. B., Repinski, D. J., Ballard, J. C., & Griffin, B. W. (1996). Beliefs about the etiology of homosexuality may influence attitudes toward homosexuals. Paper presented to the American Psychological Society convention.

Allen, K. (2003). Are pets a healthy pleasure? The influence of pets on blood pressure. *Current Directions in Psychological Science, 12*, 236–239.

Allen, L. S., & Gorski, R. A. (1992). Sexual orientation and the size of the anterior commisure in the human brain. *Proceedings of the National Academy of Sciences, 89*, 7199–7202.

Allen, N. B., & Badcock, P. B. T. (2003). The social risk hypothesis of depressed mood: Evolutionary, psychosocial, and neurobiological perspectives. *Psychological Bulletin, 129,* 887–913.

Alloy, L. B., Abramson, L. Y., Whitehouse, W. G., Hogan, M. E., Tashman, N. A., Steinberg, D. L., Rose, D. T., & Donovan, P. (1999). Depressogenic cognitive styles: Predictive validity, information processing and personality characteristics, and developmental origins. *Behaviour Research and Therapy, 37,* 503–531.

Allport, G. W. (1954). *The nature of prejudice.* New York: Addison-Wesley.

Allport, G. W. (1967). Gordon W. Allport. In E. G. Boring & G. Lindzey (Eds.), *A history of psychology in autobiography* (Vol. V). New York: Appleton-Century-Crofts.

Allport, G. W., & Odbert, H. S. (1936). Trait-names: A psycho-lexical study. *Psychological Monographs, 47*(1).

Altman, L. K. (2004, November 24). Female cases of HIV found rising worldwide. *New York Times* (www.nytimes.com).

Altmeyer, B. (2001). Changes in attitudes toward homosexuals. *Journal of Homosexuality, 42,* 63–75.

Alvarez, L. (2004, December 21). Therapy? or pills? A quandary in Britain. *New York Times* (www.nytimes.com).

Alwin, D. F. (1990). Historical changes in parental orientations to children. In N. Mandell (Ed.), *Sociological studies of child development* (Vol. 3). Greenwich, CT: JAI Press.

Amabile, T. M. (1983). *The social psychology of creativity.* New York: Springer-Verlag.

Amabile, T. M. (1987). The motivation to be creative. In S. Isaksen (Ed.), *Frontiers in creativity: Beyond the basics.* Buffalo, NY: Bearly Limited.

Amabile, T. M. (1988). From individual creativity to organizational innovation. In K. Gronhaug & G. Kaufmann (Eds.), *Innovation: A crossdisciplinary perspective.* Oslo: Norwegian University Press.

Amabile, T. M., & Hennessey, B. A. (1992). The motivation for creativity in children. In A. K. Boggiano & T. S. Pittman (Eds.), *Achievement and motivation: A social-developmental perspective.* New York: Cambridge University Press.

Ambadar, Z., Schooler, J. W., & Cohn, J. F. (2005). Deciphering the enigmatic face: The importance of facial dynamics in interpreting subtle facial expressions. *Psychological Science, 16,* 403–410.

Ambady, N., Hallahan, M., & Rosenthal, R. (1995). On judging and being judged accurately in zero-acquaintance situations. *Journal of Personality and Social Psychology, 69,* 518–529.

Ambady, N., LaPlante, D., Nguyen. T., Rosenthal, R., & Levinson, W. (2002). Surgeon's tone of voice: A clue to malpractice history. *Surgery, 132,* 5–9.

Ambady, N., & Rosenthal, R. (1992). Thin slices of expressive behavior as predictors of interpersonal consequences: A meta-analysis. *Psychological Bulletin, 111,* 256–274.

Ambady, N., & Rosenthal, R. (1993). Half a minute: Predicting teacher evaluations from thin slices of nonverbal behavior and physical attractiveness. *Journal of Personality and Social Psychology, 64,* 431–441.

Amedi, A., Floel, A., Knect, S., Zohary, E., & Cohen, L. (2004). Transcranial magnetic stimulation of the occipital pole interferes with verbal processing in blind subjects. *Nature Neuroscience, 7,* 1266–1270.

Amen, D. G., Stubblefield, M., Carmichael, B., & Thisted, R. (1996). Brain SPECT findings and aggressiveness. *Annals of Clinical Psychiatry, 8,* 129–137.

American Enterprise (1992, January/February). Women, men, marriages & ministers, p.106.

American Psychiatric Association. (1994). *Diagnostic and statistical manual of mental disorders (Fourth Edition).* Washington, DC: American Psychiatric Press.

American Psychological Association. (1991). Medical cost offset. Washington, DC: American Psychological Association Practice Directorate.

American Psychological Association. (1992). Ethical principles of psychologists and code of conduct. *American Psychologist, 47,* 1597–1611.

American Psychological Association. (2002). *Ethical principles of psychologists and code of conduct.* Washington, DC: American Psychological Association.

American Psychological Association. (2003). *Careers for the twenty-first century.* Washington, DC: Author.

American Psychological Association. (2004). Roper v. Simmons. Synopsis at http://www.apa.org/psyclaw/roper-v-simmons.html.

American Psychological Association. (2005). *Graduate study in psychology.* Washington, DC: Author.

Andersen, R. E., Crespo, C. J., Bartlett, S. J., Cheskin, L. J., & Pratt, M. (1998). Relationship of physical activity and television watching with body weight and level of fatness among children. *Journal of the American Medical Association, 279,* 938–942.

Andersen, S. M. (1998). Service Learning: A National Strategy for Youth Development. A position paper issued by the Task Force on Education Policy. Washington, DC: Institute for Communitarian Policy Studies, George Washington University.

Anderson, A. K., & Phelps, E. A. (2000). Expression without recognition: Contributions of the human amygdala to emotional communication. *Psychological Science, 11,* 106–111.

Anderson, B. L. (2002). Biobehavioral outcomes following psychological interventions for cancer patients. *Journal of Consulting and Clinical Psychology, 70,* 590–610.

Anderson, C. A. (2004). An update on the effects of playing violent video games. *Journal of Adolescence, 27,* 113–122.

Anderson, C. A., & Anderson, D. C. (1984). Ambient temperature and violent crime: Tests of the linear and curvilinear hypotheses. *Journal of Personality and Social Psychology, 46,* 91–97.

Anderson, C. A., Anderson, K. B., Dorr, N., DeNeve, K. M., & Flanagan, M. (2000). Temperature and aggression. In M. P. Zanna (Ed.), *Advances in Experimental Social Psychology.* San Diego: Academic Press.

Anderson, C. A., Berkowitz, L., Donnerstein, E., Huesmann, L. R., Johnson, J. D., Linz, D., Malamuth, N. M., & Wartella, E. (2003). The influence of media violence on youth. *Psychological Science in the Public Interest, 4*(3), 81–110.

Anderson, C. A., Carnagey, N. L., Flanagan, M., Benjamin, A. J., Jr., Eubanks, J., & Valentine, J. C. (2004). Violent video games: Specific effects of violent content on aggressive thoughts and behavior. *Advances in Experimental Social Psychology, 36,* 199–249.

Anderson, C. A., & Dill, K. E. (2000). Video games and aggressive thoughts, feelings, and behavior in the laboratory and in life. *Journal of Personality and Social Psychology, 78,* 772–790.

Anderson, C. A., Lindsay, J. J., & Bushman, B. J. (1999). Research in the psychological laboratory: Truth or triviality? *Current Directions in Psychological Science, 8,* 3–9.

Anderson, I. M. (2000). Selective serotonin reuptake inhibitors versus tricyclic antidepressants: A meta-analysis of efficacy and tolerability. *Journal of Affective Disorders, 58,* 19–36.

Anderson, J. R., Myowa-Yamakoshi, M., & Matsuzawa, T. (2004). Contagious yawning in chimpanzees. *Biology Letters, 271,* S468–S470.

Anderson, R. C., Pichert, J. W., Goetz, E. T., Schallert, D. L., Stevens, K. V., & Trollip, S. R. (1976). Instantiation of general terms. *Journal of Verbal Learning and Verbal Behavior, 15,* 667–679.

Anderson, S. R. (2004). *Doctor Dolittle's delusion: Animals and the uniqueness of human language.* New Haven: Yale University Press.

Andreasen, N. C. (1997). Linking mind and brain in the study of mental illnesses: A project for a scientific psychopathology. *Science, 275,* 1586–1593.

Andreasen, N. C. (2001). *Brave new brain: Conquering mental illness in the era of the genome.* New York: Oxford University Press.

Andreasen, N. C., Arndt, S., Swayze, V., II, Cizadlo, T., & Flaum, M. (1994). Thalamic abnormalities in schizophrenia visualized through magnetic resonance image averaging. *Science, 266*, 294–298.

Andrews, G., Hall, W., Teesson, M., & Henderson, S. (1999, April). *The mental health of Australians.* Canberra: Mental Health Branch, Commonwealth Department of Health and Aged Care.

Angell, M., & Kassirer, J. P. (1998). Alternative medicine: The risks of untested and unregulated remedies. *New England Journal of Medicine, 17*, 839–841.

Angelsen, N. K., Vik, T., Jacobsen, G., & Bakketeig, L. S. (2001). Breast feeding and cognitive development at age 1 and 5 years. *Archives of Disease in Childhood, 85*, 183–188.

Angoff, W. H. (1987). The nature-nurture debate, aptitudes, and group differences. Presidential address to American Psychological Association Division 5.

Angoff, W. H. (1988, Winter). A philosophical discussion: The issues of test and item bias. *ETS Developments*, pp. 10–11.

Anthony, J. C., Warner, L. A., & Kessler, R. C. (1994). Comparative epidemiology of dependence on tobacco, alcohol, controlled substances, and inhalants: Basic findings from the national comorbidity survey. *Experimental and Clinical Psychopharmacology, 2*, 244–268.

Antony, M. M., Brown, T. A., & Barlow, D. H. (1992). Current perspectives on panic and panic disorder. *Current Directions in Psychological Science, 1*, 79–82.

Antrobus, J. (1991). Dreaming: Cognitive processes during cortical activation and high afferent thresholds. *Psychological Review, 98*, 96–121.

APA. (2003, November). *Psychology careers for the twenty-first century.* Washington, DC: American Psychological Association.

Appleby, D. C. (2002). *The savvy psychology major.* Dubuque, IA: Kendall/Hunt.

Archer, J. (2004). Sex differences in aggression in real-world settings: A meta-analytic review. *Review of General Psychology, 8*, 291–322.

Arendt, H. (1963). *Eichmann in Jerusalem: A report on the banality of evil.* New York: Viking Press.

Arenson, K. W. (1997, May 4). Romanian woman breaks male grip on top math prize. *New York Times* News Service (in *Grand Rapids Press*, p. A7).

Arent, S. M., Landers, D. M., & Etnier, J. L. (2000). The effects of exercise on mood in older adults: A meta-analytic review. *Journal of Aging and Physical Activity, 8*, 407–430.

Aries, E. (1987). Gender and communication. In P. Shaver & C. Henrick (Eds.), *Review of Personality and Social Psychology, 7*, 149–176.

Armel, K. C., & Ramachandran, V. S. (2003). Projecting sensations to external objects: Evidence from skin conductance response. *Proceedings of the Royal Society of London. Series B. Biological Sciences, 270*, 1499–1506.

Armony, J. L., Quirk, G. J., & LeDoux, J. E. (1998). Differential effects of amygdala lesions on early and late plastic components of auditory cortex spike trains during fear conditioning. *Journal of Neuroscience, 18*, 2592–2601.

Arnett, J. J. (1999). Adolescent storm and stress, reconsidered. *American Psychologist, 54*, 317–326.

Arnett, J. J. (2000). Emerging adulthood: A theory of development from the late teens through the twenties. *American Psychologist, 55*, 469–480.

Arnold, K., & Horrigan, K. (2002). Gaining admission into the graduate program of your choice. *Eye on Psi Chi*, 30–33.

Aron, A., Melinat, E., Aron, E. N., Vallone, R. D., & Bator, R. J. (1997). The experimental generation of interpersonal closeness: A procedure and some preliminary findings. *Personality and Social Psychology Bulletin, 23*, 363–377.

Aronow, E., Reznikoff, M., & Moreland, K. (1995). The Rorschach: Projective technique or psychometric test? *Journal of Personality Assessment, 64*, 213–228.

Aronson, E. (2001, April 13). Newsworthy violence. E-mail to SPSP discussion list, drawing from *Nobody Left to Hate*. New York: Freeman, 2000.

Arrigo, J. M., & Pezdek, K. (1997). Lessons from the study of psychogenic amnesia. *Current Directions in Psychology, 6*, 148–152.

Arseneault, L., Cannon, M., Poulton, R., Murray, R., Caspi, A., & Moffitt, T. E. (2002). Cannabis use in adolescence and risk for adult psychosis: Longitudinal prospective study. *British Medical Journal, 325*, 1212–1213.

Asch, S. E. (1955). Opinions and social pressure. *Scientific American, 193*, 31–35.

Aserinsky, E. (1988, January 17). Personal communication.

ASHA. (2003). STD statistics. American Social Health Association (www.ashastd.org/stdfaqs/statistics.html).

Ashtari, M., Kumra, S., Clarke, T., Ardekani, B., Bhaskar, S., & Rhinewine, J. (2004, November 29). Diffusion tensor imaging of children with attention deficit/hyperactivity disorder. Paper presented to the Radiological Society of North America convention.

Ashton, M. C., Lee, K., & Goldberg, L. R. (2004). A hierarchical analysis of 1,710 English personality-descriptive adjectives. *Journal of Personality and Social Psychology, 87*, 707–721.

Assanand, S., Pinel, J. P. J., & Lehman, D. R. (1998). Personal theories of hunger and eating. *Journal of Applied Social Psychology, 28*, 998–1015.

Associated Press. (1999, April 26). Airline passengers mistakenly told plane would crash. *Grand Rapids Press*, p. A3.

Astin, A. W., Parrott, S. A., Korn, W. S., & Sax, L. J. (1997). *The American freshman: Thirty-year trends, 1966–1996.* Los Angeles, CA: Higher Education Research Institute, UCLA.

Atkinson, R. (1988). *The teenage world: Adolescent self-image in ten countries.* New York: Plenum Press.

Atkinson, R. C., & Shiffrin, R. M. (1968). Human memory: A control system and its control processes. In K. Spence (Ed.), *The psychology of learning and motivation* (Vol. 2). New York: Academic Press.

Atkinson, T. (2000). Master's and myths. *Eye on Psi Chi*, 19–25.

Atwell, R. H. (1986, July 28). Drugs on campus: A perspective. *Higher Education & National Affairs*, p. 5.

Atwood, K. C., IV (2003, September/October). The ongoing problem with the National Center for Complementary and Alternative Medicine. *Skeptical Inquirer*, pp. 23–29.

Au, T. K., Knightly, L. M., Jun, S-A., & Oh, J. S. (2002). Overhearing a language during childhood. *Psychological Science, 13*, 238–242.

Aubrecht, L. (2001). What can you do with a BA in psychology? *Eye on Psi Chi, 29*–31.

August, D., & Hakuta, K. (Ed.) (1998). *Educating language-minority children.* Washington, DC: National Academy of Sciences.

Austin, E. J., Deary, I. J., Whiteman, M. C., Fowkes, F. G. R., Pedersen, N. L., Rabbitt, P., Bent, N., & McInnes, L. (2002). Relationships between ability and personality: Does intelligence contribute positively to personal and social adjustment? *Personality and Individual Differences, 32*, 1391–1411.

Australian Bureau of Statistics. (1999). *Australia now—A statistical profile: Health—overweight and obesity* (www.abs.gov.au).

***Australian Social Trends*,** (1995). Health risk factors: Alcohol use. Australian Bureau of Statistics, 4102.

Averill, J. R. (1983). Studies on anger and aggression: Implications for theories of emotion. *American Psychologist, 38*, 1145–1160.

Averill, J. R. (1993). William James's other theory of emotion. In M. E. Donnelly (Ed.), *Reinterpreting the legacy of William James*. Washington, DC: American Psychological Association.

Avery, R. D., & others. (1994, December 13). Mainstream science on intelligence. *Wall Street Journal*, p. A-18.

Avis, N. E. (2003). Depression during the menopausal transition. *Psychology of Women Quarterly, 27,* 91–100.

Ax, A. F. (1953). The physiological differentiation of fear and anger in humans. *Psychosomatic Medicine, 15,* 433–442.

Azar, B. (1998, June). Why can't this man feel whether or not he's standing up? *APA Monitor* (www.apa.org/monitor/jun98/touch.html).

Babad, E., Bernieri, F., & Rosenthal, R. (1991). Students as judges of teachers' verbal and nonverbal behavior. *American Educational Research Journal, 28,* 211–234.

Babyak, M., Blumenthal, J. A., Herman, S., Khatri, P., Doraiswamy, M., Moore, K., Craighead, W. W., Baldewics, T. T., & Krishnan, K. R. (2000). Exercise treatment for major depression: Maintenance of therapeutic benefit at ten months. *Psychosomatic Medicine, 62,* 633–638.

Bachman, J., Wadsworth, K., O'Malley, P., Johnston, L., & Schulenberg, J. (1997). *Smoking, drinking, and drug use in young adulthood: The impact of new freedoms and new responsibilities.* Mahwah, NJ: Erlbaum.

Backman, L., & Dixon, R. A. (1992). Psychological compensation: A theoretical framework. *Psychological Bulletin, 112,* 259–283.

Backus, J. (1977). *The acoustical foundations of music* (2nd ed.). New York: Norton.

Baddeley, A. (1992). Working memory. *Science, 255,* 556–569.

Baddeley, A. (1998). *Human memory: Theory and practice, revised edition.* Boston: Allyn and Bacon.

Baddeley, A. D. (1982). *Your memory: A user's guide.* New York: Macmillan.

Baddeley, A. D. (2001). Is working memory still working? *American Psychologist, 56,* 849–864.

Baddeley, A. D. (2002, June). Is working memory still working? *European Psychologist, 7,* 85–97.

Bagemihl, B. (1999). *Biological exuberance: Animal homosexuality and natural diversity.* New York: St. Martins.

Bahrick, H. P. (1984). Semantic memory content in permastore: 50 years of memory for Spanish learned in school. *Journal of Experimental Psychology: General, 111,* 1–29.

Bahrick, H. P., Bahrick, L. E., Bahrick, A. S., & Bahrick, P. E. (1993). Maintenance of foreign language vocabulary and the spacing effect. *Psychological Science, 4,* 316–321.

Bahrick, H. P., Bahrick, P. O., & Wittlinger, R. P. (1975). Fifty years of memory for names and faces: A cross-sectional approach. *Journal of Experimental Psychology: General, 104,* 54–75.

Bailey, J. M., Gaulin, S., Agyei, Y., & Gladue, B. A. (1994). Effects of gender and sexual orientation on evolutionary relevant aspects of human mating psychology. *Journal of Personality and Social Psychology, 66,* 1081–1093.

Bailey, J. M., Kirk, K. M., Zhu, G., Dunne, M. P., & Martin, N. G. (2000). Do individual differences in sociosexuality represent genetic or environmentally contingent strategies? Evidence from the Australian twin registry. *Journal of Personality and Social Psychology, 78,* 537–545.

Bailey, J. M., & Zucker, K. J. (1995). Childhood sex-typed behavior and sexual orientation: A conceptual analysis and quantitative review. *Developmental Psychology, 31,* 43–55.

Baillargeon, R. (1995). A model of physical reasoning in infancy. In C. Rovee-Collier & L. P. Lipsitt (Eds.), *Advances in infancy research* (Vol. 9). Stamford, CT: Ablex.

Baillargeon, R. (1998). Infants' understanding of the physical world. In M. Sabourin, F. I. M. Craik, & M. Roberts (Eds.), *Advances in psychological science, Vol. 2: Biological and cognitive aspects.* Hove, England: Psychology Press.

Baillargeon, R. (2004). Infants' physical world. *Current Directions in Psychological Science, 13,* 89–94.

Bairagi, R. (1987). Food crises and female children in rural Bangladesh. *Social Science, 72,* 48–51.

Baker, E. L. (1987). The state of the art of clinical hypnosis. *International Journal of Clinical and Experimental Hypnosis, 35,* 203–214.

Baker, M. C. (2001). *The atoms of language: The mind's hidden rules of grammar.* New York: Basic Books.

Baker, T. B., Piper, M. E., McCarthy, D. E., Majeskie, M. R., & Fiore, M. C. (2004). Addiction motivation reformulated: An affective processing model of negative reinforcement. *Psychological Review, 111,* 33–51.

Baker-Ward, L., Gordon, B. N., Ornstein, P. A., Larus, D. M., & Clubb, P. A. (1993). Young children's long-term retention of a pediatric examination. *Child Development, 64,* 1519–1533.

Bakermans-Kranenburg, M. J., van Ijzendoorn, M. H., & Juffer, F. (2003). Less is more: Meta-analyses of sensitivity and attachment interventions in early childhood. *Psychological Bulletin, 129,* 195–215.

Ballard, M. E., & Wiest, J. R. (1998). Mortal Kombat: The effects of violent videogame play on males' hostility and cardiovascular responding. *Journal of Applied Social Psychology, 26,* 717–730.

Baltes, P. B. (1993). The aging mind: Potential and limits. *The Gerontologist, 33,* 580–594.

Baltes, P. B. (1994). Life-span developmental psychology: On the overall landscape of human development. Invited address, American Psychological Association convention.

Baltes, P. B., & Baltes, M. M. (1999, September-October). Harvesting the fruits of age: Growing older, growing wise. *Science and the Spirit,* pp. 11–14.

Bancroft, J., Loftus, J., & Long, J. S. (2003). Distress about sex: A national survey of women in heterosexual relationships. *Archives of Sexual Behavior, 32,* 193–208.

Bandura, A. (1982). The psychology of chance encounters and life paths. *American Psychologist, 37,* 747–755.

Bandura, A. (1986). *Social foundations of thought and action: A social-cognitive theory.* Englewood Cliffs, NJ: Prentice-Hall.

Bandura, A. (2001). Social cognitive theory: An agentic perspective. *Annual Review of Psychology, 52,* 1–26.

Bandura, A. (2005). The evolution of social cognitive theory. In K. G. Smith & M. A. Hitt (Eds.), *Great minds in management: The process of theory development.* Oxford: Oxford University Press.

Bandura, A., Ross, D., & Ross, S. A. (1961). Transmission of aggression through imitation of aggressive models. *Journal of Abnormal and Social Psychology, 63,* 575–582.

Barber, T. X. (2000). A deeper understanding of hypnosis: Its secrets, its nature, its essence. *American Journal of Clinical Hypnosis, 42,* 208–272.

Barbour, D. L., & Wang, X. (2003). Contrast tuning in auditory cortex. *Science, 299,* 1073–1075.

Barinaga, M. (1991). How long is the human life-span? *Science, 254,* 936–938.

Barinaga, M. (1992a). The brain remaps its own contours. *Science, 258,* 216–218.

Barinaga, M. (1992b). How scary things get that way. *Science, 258,* 887–888.

Barinaga, M. (1997). Visual system provides clues to how the brain perceives. *Science, 275,* 1583–1585.

Barinaga, M. (1999). Salmon follow watery odors home. *Science, 286,* 705–706.

Barinaga, M. B. (1997). How exercise works its magic. *Science, 276,* 1325.

Barker, S. L., Funk, S. C., & Houston, B. K. (1988). Psychological treatment versus nonspecific factors: A meta-analysis of conditions that engender comparable expectations for improvement. *Clinical Psychology Review, 8,* 579–594.

Barkley, R. A., & 74 others (2002). International consensus statement (January 2002). *Clinical Child and Family Psychology Review, 5,* 2.

Barlow, D. H. (1988). *Anxiety and its disorders: The nature and treatment of anxiety and panic.* New York: Guilford.

Barnes, M. L., & Sternberg, R. J. (1989). Social intelligence and decoding of nonverbal cues. *Intelligence, 13,* 263–287.

Barnett, P. A., & Gotlib, I. H. (1988). Psychosocial functioning and depression: Distinguishing among antecedents, concomitants, and consequences. *Psychological Bulletin, 104,* 97–126.

Barnier, A. J., & McConkey, K. M. (2004). Defining and identifying the highly hypnotizable person. In M. Heap, R. J. Brown, & D. A. Oakley (Eds.), *High hypnotisability: Theoretical, experimental and clinical issues.* London: Brunner-Routledge.

Baron, R. A. (1988). Negative effects of destructive criticism: Impact on conflict, self-efficacy, and task performance. *Journal of Applied Psychology, 73,* 199–207.

Baron, R. S., Cutrona, C. E., Hicklin, D., Russell, D. W., & Lubaroff, D. M. (1990). Social support and immune function among spouses of cancer patients. *Journal of Personality and Social Psychology, 59,* 344–352.

Baron, R. S., Vandello, J. A., & Brunsman, B. (1996). The forgotten variable in conformity research: Impact of task importance on social influence. *Journal of Personality and Social Psychology, 71,* 915–927.

Baron-Cohen, S. (2004). *The essential difference: Men, women, and the extreme male brain.* London: Penguin Books.

Baron-Cohen, S. (2005, April 6 and May 19). The assortative mating theory: A talk with Simon Baron-Cohen. *The Edge* (www.edge.org).

Baron-Cohen, S., Leslie, A. M., & Frith, U. (1985). Does the autistic child have a "theory of mind"? *Cognition, 21,* 37–46.

Barr, R. (1991, October). In *The Evening Standard, 9.*

Barrett, L. F., Lane, R. D., Sechrest, L., & Schwartz, G. E. (2000). Sex differences in emotional awareness. *Personality and Social Psychology Bulletin, 26,* 1027–1035.

Barry, D. (1995, September 17). Teen smokers, too, get cool, toxic, waste-blackened lungs. *Asbury Park Press,* p. D3.

Barry, D. (1996, August 11). The power to embarrass (syndicated column).

Bartoshuk, L. M. (1993). The wisdom of the body: Using case studies to teach sensation and perception. Paper presented to the National Institute on the Teaching of Psychology, St. Petersburg Beach, Florida.

Baruch, G. K., & Barnett, R. (1986). Role quality, multiple role involvement, and psychological well-being in midlife women. *Journal of Personality and Social Psychology, 51,* 578–585.

Bashore, T. R., Ridderinkhof, K. R., & van der Molen, M. W. (1997). The decline of cognitive processing speed in old age. *Current Directions in Psychological Science, 6,* 163–169.

Baskind, D. E. (1997, December 14). Personal communication, from Delta College.

Bass, L. E., & Kane-Williams, E. (1993). Stereotype or reality: Another look at alcohol and drug use among African American children. U.S. Department of Health and Human Services, *Public Health Reports, 108* (Supplement 1), 78–84.

Bassett, D. R., Schneider, P. L., & Huntington, G. E. (2004). Physical activity in an Old Order Amish community. *Medicine and Science in Sports and Exercise, 36,* 79–85.

Bat-Chava, Y. (1993). Antecedents of self-esteem in deaf people: A meta-analytic review. *Rehabilitation Psychology, 38*(4), 221–234.

Bat-Chava, Y. (1994). Group identification and self-esteem of deaf adults. *Personality and Social Psychology Bulletin, 20,* 494–502.

Bauer, P. J. (2002). Long-term recall memory: Behavioral and neuro-developmental changes in the first 2 years of life. *Current Directions in Psychology, 11,* 137–141.

Baum, A., & Posluszny, D. M. (1999). Health psychology: Mapping biobehavioral contributions to health and illness. *Annual Review of Psychology, 50,* 137–163.

Baumeister, R. (2005). *The cultural animal: Human nature, meaning, and social life.* New York: Oxford University Press.

Baumeister, R. F. (1989). The optimal margin of illusion. *Journal of Social and Clinical Psychology, 8,* 176–189.

Baumeister, R. F. (1996). Should schools try to boost self-esteem? Beware the dark side. *American Educator, 20,* 14019, 43.

Baumeister, R. F. (2000). Gender differences in erotic plasticity: The female sex drive as socially flexible and responsive. *Psychological Bulletin, 126,* 347–374.

Baumeister, R. F. (2001, April). Violent pride: Do people turn violent because of self-hate, or self-love? *Scientific American,* pp. 96–101.

Baumeister, R. F., & Bratslavsky, E. (1999). Passion, intimacy, and time: Passionate love as a function of change in intimacy. *Personality and social Psychology Review, 3,* 49–67.

Baumeister, R. F., Bratslavsky, E., Finkenauer, C., & others. (2001). Bad is stronger than good. *Review of General Psychology, 5,* 323–370.

Baumeister, R. F., Campbell, J., Krueger, J. I., & Vohs, K. D. (2003). Does high self-esteem cause better performance, interpersonal success, happiness, or healthier lifestyles? *Psychological Science in the Public Interest, 4*(1), 1–44.

Baumeister, R. F., Campbell, J. D., Krueger, J. I., & Vohs, K. D. (2005, January). Exploding the self-esteem myth. *Scientific American,* pp. 84–91.

Baumeister, R. F., Catanese, K. R., & Vohs, K. D. (2001). Is there a gender difference in strength of sex drive? Theoretical views, conceptual distinctions, and a review of relevant evidence. *Personality and Social Psychology Review, 5,* 242–273.

Baumeister, R. F., Dale, K., & Sommer, K. L. (1998). Freudian defense mechanisms and empirical findings in modern personality and social psychology: Reaction formation, projection, displacement, undoing, isolation, sublimation, and denial. *Journal of Personality, 66,* 1081–1125.

Baumeister, R. F., & Exline, J. J. (2000). Self-control, morality, and human strength. *Journal of Social and Clinical Psychology, 19,* 29–42.

Baumeister, R. F., & Leary, M. R. (1995). The need to belong: Desire for interpersonal attachments as a fundamental human motivation. *Psychological Bulletin, 117,* 497–529.

Baumeister, R. F., Stillwell, A., & Wotman, S. R. (1990). Victim and perpetrator accounts of interpersonal conflict: Autobiographical narratives about anger. *Journal of Personality and Social Psychology, 59,* 994–1005.

Baumeister, R. F., & Tice, D. M. (1986). How adolescence became the struggle for self: A historical transformation of psychological development. In J. Suls & A. G. Greenwald (Eds.), *Psychological perspectives on the self* (Vol. 3). Hillsdale, NJ: Erlbaum.

Baumeister, R. F., Twenge, J. M., & Nuss, C. K. (2002). Effects of social exclusion on cognitive processes: Anticipated aloneness reduces intelligent thought. *Journal of Personality and Social Psychology, 83,* 817–827.

Baumgardner, A. H., Kaufman, C. M., & Levy, P. E. (1989). Regulating affect interpersonally: When low esteem leads to greater enhancement. *Journal of Personality and Social Psychology, 56,* 907–921.

Baumrind, D. (1982). Adolescent sexuality: Comment on Williams' and Silka's comments on Baumrind. *American Psychologist, 37,* 1402–1403.

Baumrind, D. (1996). The discipline controversy revisited. *Family Relations, 45,* 405–414.

Baumrind, D., Larzelere, R. E., & Cowan, P. A. (2002). Ordinary physical punishment: Is it harmful? Comment on Gershoff (2002). *Psychological Bulletin, 128,* 602–611.

Bavelier, D., Newport, E. L., & Supalla, T. (2003). Children need natural languages, signed or spoken. *Cerebrum, 5*(1), 19–32.

Bavelier, D., Tomann, A., Hutton, C., Mitchell, T., Corina, D., Liu, G., & Neville, H. (2000). Visual attention to the periphery is enhanced in congenitally deaf individuals. *Journal of Neuroscience, 20,* 1–6.

Bayley, P. J., Gold, J. J., Hopkins, R. O., & Squire, L. R. (2005). The neuroanatomy of remote memory. *Neuron, 46,* 799–810.

BBC. (2005, July). Japanese breaks pi memory record. http://news.bbc.co.uk/2/hi/asia-pacific/4644103.stm.

Beaman, A. L., & Klentz, B. (1983). The supposed physical attractiveness bias against supporters of the women's movement: A meta-analysis. *Personality and Social Psychology Bulletin, 9,* 544–550.

Beardsley, L. M. (1994). Medical diagnosis and treatment across cultures. In W. J. Lonner & R. Malpass (Eds.), *Psychology and culture.* Boston: Allyn & Bacon.

Beardsley, T. (1996, July). Waking up. *Scientific American,* pp. 14, 18.

Beauchamp, G. K. (1987). The human preference for excess salt. *American Scientist, 75,* 27–33.

Beck, A. J., Kline, S. A., & Greenfeld, L. A. (1988). Survey of youth in custody, 1987. U.S. Department of Justice, Bureau of Justice Statistics Special Report.

Beck, A. T., Rush, A. J., Shaw, B. F., & Emery, G. (1979). *Cognitive therapy of depression.* New York: Guilford Press.

Beck, A. T., & Steer, R. A. (1989). Clinical predictors of eventual suicide: A 5- to 10-year prospective study of suicide attempters. *Journal of Affective Disorders, 17,* 203–209.

Becklen, R., & Cervone, D. (1983). Selective looking and the noticing of unexpected events. *Memory and Cognition, 11,* 601–608.

Beckman, M. (2004). Crime, culpability, and the adolescent brain. *Science, 305,* 596–599.

Beeman, M. J., & Chiarello, C. (1998). Complementary right- and left-hemisphere language comprehension. *Current Directions in Psychological Science, 7,* 2–8.

Beitman, B. D., Goldfried, M. R., & Norcross, J. C. (1989). The movement toward integrating the psychotherapies: An overview. *American Journal of Psychiatry, 146,* 138–147.

Bell, A. P., Weinberg, M. S., & Hammersmith, S. K. (1981). *Sexual preference: Its development in men and women.* Bloomington: Indiana University Press.

Bell, R. Q., & Waldrop, M. F. (1989). Achievement and cognitive correlates of minor physical anomalies in early development. In M. G. Bornstein & N. A. Krasnegor (Eds.), *Stability and continuity in mental development: Behavioral and biological perspectives.* Hillsdale, NJ: Erlbaum.

Bellugi, U. (1994, August). Quoted in P. Radetsky, Silence, signs, and wonder. *Discover,* pp. 60–68.

Beloff, J. (1985, Spring). Science, religion and the paranormal. *Free Inquiry,* pp. 36–41

Belsher, G., & Costello, C. G. (1988). Relapse after recovery from unipolar depression: A critical review. *Psychological Bulletin, 104,* 84–96.

Belsky, J. (1990). Parental and nonparental child care and children's socioemotional development: A decade in review. *Journal of Marriage and the Family, 52,* 885–903.

Belsky, J. (2003). The politicized science of day care: A personal and professional odyssey. *Family Policy Review 1(2),* 23–40.

Bem, D. J. (1984). Quoted in *The Skeptical Inquirer, 8,* 194.

Bem, D. J. (1996). Exotic becomes erotic: A developmental theory of sexual orientation. *Psychological Review, 103,* 320–335.

Bem, D. J. (1998). Is EBE theory supported by the evidence? Is it androcentric? A reply to Peplau et al. (1998). *Psychological Review, 105,* 395–398.

Bem, D. J. (2000). Exotic becomes erotic: Interpreting the biological correlates of sexual orientation. *Archives of Sexual Behavior, 29,* 531–548.

Bem, D. J., & Honorton, C. (1994). Does psi exist? Replicable evidence for an anomalous process of information transfer. *Psychological Bulletin, 115,* 4–18.

Bem, D. J., Palmer, J., & Broughton, R. S. (2001). Updating the Ganzfeld database: A victim of its own success? *Journal of Parapsychology, 65,* 207–218.

Bem, S. L. (1987). Masculinity and femininity exist only in the mind of the perceiver. In J. M. Reinisch, L. A. Rosenblum, & S. A. Sanders (Eds.), *Masculinity/femininity: Basic perspectives.* New York: Oxford University Press.

Bem, S. L. (1993). *The lenses of gender.* New Haven: Yale University Press.

Ben-Shakhar, G., & Elaad, E. (2003). The validity of psychophysiological detection of information with the guilt knowledge test: A meta-analytic review. *Journal of Applied Psychology, 88,* 131–151.

Benbow, C. P., Lubinski, D., Shea, D. L., & Eftekhari-Sanjani, H. (2000). Sex differences in mathematical reasoning ability at age 13: Their status 20 years later. *Psychological Science, 11,* 474–2000.

Bennett, R. (1991, February). Pornography and extrafamilial child sexual abuse: Examining the relationship. Unpublished manuscript, Los Angeles Police Department Sexually Exploited Child Unit.

Bennett, W. I. (1995). Beyond overeating. *New England Journal of Medicine, 332,* 673–674.

Benson, H. (1996). *Timeless healing: The power and biology of belief.* New York: Scribner.

Benson, K., & Feinberg, I. (1977). The beneficial effect of sleep in an extended Jenkins and Dallenbach paradigm. *Psychophysiology, 14,* 375–384.

Benson, P. L. (1992, Spring). Patterns of religious development in adolescence and adulthood. *PIRI Newsletter,* 2–9.

Benson, P. L., Sharma, A. R., & Roehlkepartain, E. C. (1994). *Growing up adopted: A portrait of adolescents and their families.* Minneapolis: Search Institute.

Berenbaum, S. A., & Bailey, J. M. (2003). Effects on gender identity of prenatal androgens and genital appearance: Evidence from girls with congenital adrenal hyperplasia. *Journal of Clinical Endocrinology and Metabolism, 88,* 1102–1106.

Berenbaum, S. A., & Hines, M. (1992). Early androgens are related to childhood sex-typed toy preferences. *Psychological Science, 3,* 203–206.

Berenbaum, S. A., Korman, K., & Leveroni, C. (1995). Early hormones and sex differences in cognitive abilities. *Learning and Individual Differences, 7,* 303–321.

Berger, B. G., & Motl, R. W. (2000). Exercise and mood: A selective review and synthesis of research employing the profile of mood states. *Journal of Applied Sports Psychology, 12,* 69–92.

Bergin, A. E. (1980). Psychotherapy and religious values. *Journal of Consulting and Clinical Psychology, 48,* 95–105.

Bergsholm, P., Larsen, J. L., Rosendahl, K., & Holsten, F. (1989). Electroconvulsive therapy and cerebral computed tomography. *Acta Psychiatrica Scandinavia, 80,* 566–572.

Berk, L. E. (1994, November). Why children talk to themselves. *Scientific American,* pp. 78–83.

Berk, L. S., Felten, D. L., Tan, S. A., Bittman, B. B., & Westengard, J. (2001). Modulation of neuroimmune parameters during the eustress of humor-associated mirthful laughter. *Alternative Therapies, 7,* 62–76.

Berkel, J., & de Waard, F. (1983). Mortality pattern and life expectancy of Seventh-Day Adventists in the Netherlands. *International Journal of epidemiology, 12,* 455–459.

Berkowitz, L. (1983). Aversively stimulated aggression: Some parallels and differences in research with animals and humans. *American Psychologist, 38,* 1135–1144.

Berkowitz, L. (1989). Frustration-aggression hypothesis: Examination and reformulation. *Psychological Bulletin, 106,* 59–73.

Berkowitz, L. (1990). On the formation and regulation of anger and aggression: A cognitive-neoassociationistic analysis. *American Psychologist, 45,* 494–503.

Berman, M., Gladue, B., & Taylor, S. (1993). The effects of hormones, Type A behavior pattern, and provocation on aggression in men. *Motivation and Emotion, 17,* 125–138.

Berndt, T. J. (1992). Friendship and friends' influence in adolescence. *Current Directions in Psychological Science, 1,* 156–159.

Bernhardt, P. C., Dabbs, J. M., Jr., Fielden, J. A., & Lutter, C. D. (1998). Testosterone changes during vicarious experiences of winning and losing among fans at sporting events. *Physiology and Behavior, 65,* 59–62.

Bernstein, D. M., Atance, C., Loftus, G. R., & Meltzoff, A. (2004). We saw it all along: Visual hindsight bias in children and adults. *Psychological Science, 15,* 264–267.

Berntsen, D., & Thomsen, D. K. (2005). Personal memories for remote historical events: Accuracy and clarity of flashbulb memories related to World War II. *Journal of Experimental Psychology: General, 134,* 242–257.

Berridge, K. C., & Winkielman, P. (2003). What is an unconscious emotion? (The case of unconscious "liking"). *Cognition and Emotion, 17,* 181–211.

Berry, D. S., & McArthur, L. Z. (1986). Perceiving character in faces: The impact of age-related craniofacial changes on social perception. *Psychological Bulletin, 100,* 3–18.

Berscheid, E. (1981). An overview of the psychological effects of physical attractiveness and some comments upon the psychological effects of knowledge of the effects of physical attractiveness. In G. W. Lucker, K. Ribbens, & J. A. McNamara (Eds.), *Psychological aspects of facial form* (Craniofacial growth series). Ann Arbor: Center for Human Growth and Development, University of Michigan.

Berscheid, E. (1985). Interpersonal attraction. In G. Lindzey & E. Aronson (Eds.), *The handbook of social psychology.* New York: Random House.

Berscheid, E., Gangestad, S. W., & Kulakowski, D. (1984). Emotion in close relationships: Implications for relationship counseling. In S. D. Brown & R. W. Lent (Eds.), *Handbook of counseling psychology.* New York: Wiley.

Bértolo, H., Paiva, T., Pessoa, L., Mestre, T., Marques, R., & Santos, R. (2003). Visual dream content, graphical representation and EEG alpha activity in congenitally blind subjects. *Cognitive Brain Research, 15,* 277–284.

Besson, M., Faita, F., Peretz, I., Bonnel, A.-M., & Requin, J. (1998). Singing in the brain: Independence of lyrics and tunes. *Psychological Science, 9,* 494–498.

Bettencourt, B. A., & Dorr, N. (1997). Collective self-esteem as a mediator of the relationship between allocentrism and subjective well-being. *Personality and Social Psychology Bulletin, 23,* 955–964.

Bettencourt, B. A., & Kernahan, C. (1997). A meta-analysis of aggression in the presence of violent cues: Effects of gender differences and aversive provocation. *Aggressive Behavior, 23,* pp. 447–457.

Beyerstein, B., & Beyerstein, D. (Eds.) (1992). *The write stuff: Evaluations of graphology.* Buffalo, NY: Prometheus Books.

Bhatt, R. S., Wasserman, E. A., Reynolds, W. F., Jr., & Knauss, K. S. (1988). Conceptual behavior in pigeons: Categorization of both familiar and novel examples from four classes of natural and artificial stimuli. *Journal of Experimental Psychology: Animal Behavior Processes, 14,* 219–234.

Bialystok, E. (2001). *Bilingualism in development, language, literacy, and cognition.* New York: Cambridge University Press.

Bickman, L. (1999). Practice makes perfect and other myths about mental health services. *American Psychologist, 54,* 965–978.

Biederman, J., Wilens, T., Mick, E., Spencer, T., & Faraone, S. V. (1999). Pharmacotherapy of Attention-Deficit/Hyperactivity Disorder reduces risk for substance use disorder. *Pediatrics, 104,* 1–5.

Biello, S. M., & Dafters, R. I. (2001). MDMA and fenfluramine alter the response of the circadian clock to a serotonin agonist in vitro. *Brain Research, 920,* 202–209.

Biggs, V. (2001, April 13). Murder suspect captured in Grand Marais. *Cook County News-Herald.*

Bigler, E. D., Johnson, S. C., Jackson, C., & Blatter, D. D. (1995). Aging, brain size, and IQ. *Intelligence, 21,* 109–119.

Binet, A., & Simon, T. (1905; reprinted 1916). New methods for the diagnosis of the intellectual level of subnormals. In A. Binet & T. Simon, *The development of intelligence in children.* Baltimore: Williams & Wilkins.

Birch, S. A. J. (2005). When knowledge is a curse: Children's and adults' reasoning about mental states. *Current Directions in Psychological Science, 14,* 25–29.

Birnbaum, S. G., Yuan, P. X., Wang, M., Vijayraghavan, S., Bloom, A. K., Davis, D. J., Gobeski, K. T., Sweatt, J. D., Manhi, H. K., & Arnsten, A. F. T. (2004). Protein kinase C overactivity impairs prefrontal cortical regulation of working memory. *Science, 306,* 882–884.

Bishop, B. (2004, November 22). Personal correspondence, and earlier articles on "The great divide" in the *Austin Statesman.*

Bishop, G. D. (1991). Understanding the understanding of illness: Lay disease representations. In J. A. Skelton & R. T. Croyle (Eds.), *Mental representation in health and illness.* New York: Springer-Verlag.

Biswas-Diener, R., & Diener, E. (2001). Making the best of a bad situation: Satisfaction in the slums of Calcutta. *Social Indicators Research, 55,* 329–352.

Bjork, R. A. (1999). Assessing our own competence: Heuristics and illusions. In D. Gopher & A. Koriat (Eds.), *Attention and performance XVII. Cognitive regulation of performance: Interaction of theory and application.* Cambridge, MA: MIT Press.

Bjork, R. A. (2000, July/August). Toward one world of psychological science. *APS Observer,* p. 3.

Bjorklund, D. F., & Green, B. L. (1992). The adaptive nature of cognitive immaturity. *American Psychologist, 47,* 46–54.

Blackmore, S. (1991, Fall). Near-death experiences: In or out of the body? *Skeptical Inquirer,* pp. 34–45.

Blackmore, S. (1993). *Dying to live.* Amherst, NY: Prometheus Books.

Blackmore, S. (1999). *The meme machine.* Oxford: Oxford University Press.

Blackmore, S. (2000, October). The power of memes. *Scientific American,* pp. 63–73.

Blakemore, S-J., Wolpert, D. M., & Frith, C. D. (1998). Central cancellation of self-produced tickle sensation. *Nature Neuroscience, 1,* 635–640.

Blakeslee, S. (2005, February 8). Focus narrows in search for autism's cause. *New York Times* (www.nytimes.com).

Blanchard, R. (1997). Birth order and sibling sex ratio in homosexual versus heterosexual males and females. *Annual Review of Sex Research, 8,* 27–67.

Blanchard, R. (2001). Fraternal birth order and the maternal immune hypothesis of male homosexuality. *Hormones and Behavior, 40,* 105–114.

Blanke, O., Landis, T., & Spinelli, L. (2004). Out-of-body experience and autoscopy of neurological origin. *Brain: Journal of Neurology, 127,* 243–258.

Blanke, O., Ortigue, S., Landis, T., & Seeck, M. (2002). Stimulating illusory own-body perceptions. *Nature, 419,* 269–270.

Blankenburg, F., Taskin, B., Ruben, J., Moosmann, M., Ritter, P., Curio, G., & Villringer, A. (2003). Imperceptive stimuli and sensory processing impediment. *Science, 299,* 1864.

Blascovich, J., Seery, M. D., Mugridge, C. A., Norris, R. K., & Weisbuch, M. (2004). Predicting athletic performance from cardiovascular indexes of challenge and threat. *Journal of Experimental Social Psychology, 40,* 683–688.

Blass, T. (1996). Stanley Milgram: A life of inventiveness and controversy. In G. A. Kimble, C. A. Boneau, & M. Wertheimer (Eds.), *Portraits of pioneers in psychology* (Vol. II). Washington, DC, and Mahwah, NJ: American Psychological Association and Lawrence Erlbaum Publishers.

Blass, T. (1999). The Milgram paradigm after 35 years: Some things we now know about obedience to authority. *Journal of Applied Social Psychology, 29,* 955–978.

Blatt, S. J., Sanislow, C. A., III, Zuroff, D. C., & Pilkonis, P. (1996). Characteristics of effective therapists: Further analyses of data from the National Institute of Mental Health Treatment of Depression Collaborative

Research Program. *Journal of Consulting and Clinical Psychology, 64,* 1276–1284.

Bleustein, J. (2002, June 15). Quoted in "Harley retooled," by S. S. Smith, *American Way Magazine.*

Blizzard, R. (2004, August 31). Smoking: Will education overpower addiction? Gallup Poll (www.gallup.com).

Blom, J. M. C., Tamarkin, L., Shiber, J. R., & Nelson, R. J. (1995). Learned immunosuppression is associated with an increased risk of chemically-induced tumors. *Neuroimmunomodulation, 2,* 92–99.

Bloom, B. J. (1964). *Stability and change in human characteristics.* New York: Wiley.

Bloom, B. S. (Ed.). (1985). *Developing talent in young people.* New York: Ballantine.

Bloom, F. E. (1993, January/February). What's new in neurotransmitters. *BrainWork,* pp. 7–9.

Bloom, P. (2000). *How children learn the meanings of words.* Cambridge, MA: MIT Press.

Bloom, S. R. (2002, September/October). Quoted in Researchers identify natural appetite suppressant. *Brain Work.*

Blum, K., Cull, J. G., Braverman, E. R., & Comings, D. E. (1996). Reward deficiency syndrome. *American Scientist, 84,* 132–145.

Boahen, K. (2005, May). Neuromorphic microchips. *Scientific American,* pp. 56–63.

Bock, B. C., Marcus, B. H., King. T. E., Borrelli, B., & Roberts, M. R. (1999). Exercise effects on withdrawal and mood among women attempting smoking cessation. *Addictive Behavior, 24,* 399–410.

Bodenhausen, G. V., Sheppard, L. A., & Kramer, G. P. (1994). Negative affect and social judgment: The differential impact of anger and sadness. *European Journal of Social Psychology, 24,* 45–62.

Bodkin, J. A., & Amsterdam, J. D. (2002). Transdermal selegiline in major depression: A double-blind, placebo-controlled, parallel-group study in outpatients. *American Journal of Psychiatry, 159,* 1869–1875.

Boehm, K. E., Schondel, C. K., Marlowe, A. L., & Manke-Mitchell, L. (1999). Teens' concerns: A national evaluation. *Adolescence, 34,* 523–528.

Boesch-Achermann, H., & Boesch, C. (1993). Tool use in wild chimpanzees: New light from dark forests. *Current Directions in Psychological Science, 2,* 18–21.

Bogaert, A. F. (2003). Number of older brothers and sexual orientation: New texts and the attraction/behavior distinction in two national probability samples. *Journal of Personality and Social Psychology, 84,* 644–652.

Bogaert, A. F. (2004). Asexuality: Prevalence and associated factors in a national probability sample. *Journal of Sex Research, 41,* 279–287.

Bogaert, A. F., Friesen, C., & Klentrou, P. (2002). Age of puberty and sexual orientation in a national probability sample. *Archives of Sexual Behavior, 31,* 73–81.

Boggiano, A. K., Barrett, M., Weiher, A. W., McClelland, G. H., & Lusk, C. M. (1987). Use of the maximal-operant principle to motivate children's intrinsic interest. *Journal of Personality and Social Psychology, 53,* 866–879.

Boggiano, A. K., Harackiewicz, J. M., Bessette, M. M., & Main, D. S. (1985). Increasing children's interest through performance-contingent reward. *Social Cognition, 3,* 400–411.

Bogin, B. (1998, February). The tall and the short of it (range of height in humans demonstrates plasticity of human species). *Discover.*

Bohman, M., & Sigvardsson, S. (1990). Outcome in adoption: Lessons from longitudinal studies. In D. Brodzinsky & M. Schechter (Eds.), *The psychology of adoption.* New York: Oxford University Press.

Bolger, N., DeLongis, A., Kessler, R. C., & Schilling, E. A. (1989). Effects of daily stress on negative mood. *Journal of Personality and Social Psychology, 57,* 808–818.

Bonanno, G. A. (2001). Grief and emotion: Experience, expression, and dissociation. In M. Stroebe, W. Stroebe, R. O. Hansson, & H. Schut (Eds.), *New handbook of bereavement: Consciousness, coping, and care.* Cambridge: Cambridge University Press.

Bonanno, G. A. (2004). Loss, trauma, and human resilience: Have we underestimated the human capacity to thrive after extremely aversive events? *American Psychologist, 59,* 20–28.

Bonanno, G. A. (2005). Adult resilience to potential trauma. *Current Directions in Psychological Science, 14,* 135–137.

Bonanno, G. A., & Kaltman, S. (1999). Toward an integrative perspective on bereavement. *Psychological Bulletin, 125,* 760–777.

Bond, C. F., Jr., & DePaulo, B. M. (in press). Accuracy of deception judgments. Unpublished manuscript, Texas Christian University.

Bond, C. F., Jr., Pitre, U., & Van Leeuwen, M. D. (1991). Encoding operations and the next-in-line effect. *Personality and Social Psychology Bulletin, 17,* 435–441.

Bond, M. H. (1988). Finding universal dimensions of individual variation in multi-cultural studies of values: The Rokeach and Chinese values surveys. *Journal of Personality and Social Psychology, 55,* 1009–1015.

Bond, R., & Smith, P. B. (1996). Culture and conformity: A meta-analysis of studies using Asch's (1952b, 1956) line judgment task. *Psychological Bulletin, 119,* 111–137.

Boneva, B. S., & Frieze, I. H. (2001). Toward a concept of a migrant personality. *Journal of Social Issues, 57,* 477–491.

Bono, J. E., & Judge, T. A. (2004). Personality and transformational and transactional leadership: A meta-analysis. *Journal of Applied Psychology, 89,* 901–910.

Bookheimer, S. H., Strojwas, M. H., Cohen, M. S., Saunders, A. M., Pericak-Vance, M. A., Mazziotta, J. C., & Small, G. W. (2000). Patterns of brain activation in people at risk for Alzheimer's disease. *New England Journal of Medicine, 343,* 450–456.

Booth, F. W., & Neufer, P. D. (2005). Exercise controls gene expression. *American Scientist, 93,* 28–35.

Boring, E. G. (1930). A new ambiguous figure. *American Journal of Psychology, 42,* 444–445.

Borkenau, P., Mauer, N., Riemann, R., Spinath, F. M., & Angleitner, A. (2004). Thin slices of behavior as cues of personality and intelligence. *Journal of Personality and Social Psychology, 86,* 599–614.

Bornstein, M. H., Cote, L. R., Maital, S., Painter, K., Park, S-Y., Pascual, L., Pecheux, M-G., Ruel, J., Venute, P., & Vyt, A. (2004). Cross-linguistic analysis of vocabulary in young children: Spanish, Dutch, French, Hebrew, Italian, Korean, and American English. *Child Development, 75,* 1115–1139.

Bornstein, M. H., Tal, J., Rahn, C., Galperin, C. Z., Pecheux, M-G., Lamour, M., Toda, S., Azuma, H., Ogino, M., & Tamis-LeMonda, C. S. (1992a). Functional analysis of the contents of maternal speech to infants of 5 and 13 months in four cultures: Argentina, France, Japan, and the United States. *Developmental Psychology, 28,* 593–603.

Bornstein, M. H., Tamis-LeMonda, C. S., Tal, J., Ludemann, P., Toda, S., Rahn, C. W., Pecheux, M-G., Azuma, H., Vardi, D. (1992b). Maternal responsiveness to infants in three societies: The United States, France, and Japan. *Child Development, 63,* 808–821.

Bornstein, R. F. (1989). Exposure and affect: Overview and meta-analysis of research, 1968–1987. *Psychological Bulletin, 106,* 265–289.

Bornstein, R. F. (1999). Source amnesia, misattribution, and the power of unconscious perceptions and memories. *Psychoanalytic Psychology, 16,* 155–178.

Bornstein, R. F. (2001). The impending death of psychoanalysis. *Psychoanalytic Psychology, 18,* 3–20.

Bornstein, R. F., Galley, D. J., Leone, D. R., & Kale, A. R. (1991). The temporal stability of ratings of parents: Test-retest reliability and influence of parental contact. *Journal of Social Behavior and Personality, 6,* 641–649.

Boroditsky, R., Fisher, W., & Sand, M. (1995, July). Teenagers and contraception. Section of The Canadian contraception study. *Journal of the Society of Obstetricians and Gynaecologists of Canada*, Special Supplement, pp. 22–25.

Bortfeld, H., Morgan, J. L., Golinkoff, R. M., & Rathbun, K. (2005). Mommy and me: Familiar names help launch babies into speech-stream segmentation. *Psychological Science, 16*, 298–304.

Boscarino, J. A. (1997). Diseases among men 20 years after exposure to severe stress: Implications for clinical research and medical care. *Psychosomatic Medicine, 59*, 605–614.

Bosma, H., Marmot, M. G., Hemingway, H., Nicolson, A. C., Brunner, E., & Stansfeld, S. A. (1997). Low job control and risk of coronary heart disease in Whitehall II (prospective cohort) study. *British Medical Journal, 314*, 558–565.

Bosma, H., Peter, R., Siegrist, J., & Marmot, M. (1998). Two alternative job stress models and the risk of coronary heart disease. *American Journal of Public Health, 88*, 68–74.

Bostwick, J. M., & Pankratz, V. S. (2000). Affective disorders and suicide risk: A re-examination. *American Journal of Psychiatry, 157*, 1925–1932.

Bosworth, R. G., & Dobkins, K. R. (1999). Left-hemisphere dominance for motion processing in deaf signers. *Psychological Science, 10*, 256–262.

Bothwell, R. K., Brigham, J. C., & Malpass, R. S. (1989). Cross-racial identification. *Personality and Social Psychology Bulletin, 15*, 19–25.

Bothwell, R. K., Deffenbacher, K. A., & Brigham, J. C. (1987). Correlation of eyewitness accuracy and confidence: Optimality hypothesis revised. *Journal of Applied Psychology, 72*, 691–695.

Botwin, M. D., Buss, D. M., & Shackelford, T. K. (1997). Personality and mate preferences: Five factors in mate selection and marital satisfaction. *Journal of Personality, 65*, 107–136.

Bouchard, T. J., Jr. (1981, December 6). Interview on *Nova: Twins* [program broadcast by the Public Broadcasting Service].

Bouchard, T. J., Jr. (1995). Longitudinal studies of personality and intelligence: A behavior genetic and evolutionary psychology perspective. In D. H. Saklofske & M. Zeidner (Eds.), *International handbook of personality and intelligence*. New York: Plenum.

Bouchard, T. J., Jr. (1996a). IQ similarity in twins reared apart: Finding and responses to critics. In R. Sternberg & C. Grigorenko (Eds.), *Intelligence: Heredity and environment*. New York: Cambridge University Press.

Bouchard, T. J., Jr. (1996b). Behavior genetic studies of intelligence, yesterday and today: The long journey from plausibility to proof. *Journal of Biosocial Science, 28*, 527–555.

Bouchard, T. J., Jr. (2004). Genetic influence on human psychological traits. *Current Directions in Psychological Science, 13*, 148–151.

Bouchard, T. J., Jr., & McGue, M. (1990). Genetic and rearing environmental influences on adult personality: An analysis of adopted twins reared apart. *Journal of Personality, 58*, 263.

Bouton, M. E., Mineka, S., & Barlow, D. H. (2001). A modern learning theory perspective on the etiology of panic disorder. *Psychological Review, 108*, 4–32.

Bowden, E. M., & Beeman, M. J. (1998). Getting the right idea: Semantic activation in the right hemisphere may help solve insight problems. *Psychological Science, 9*, 435–440.

Bower, B. (2003, November 22). Vision seekers. *Science News, 164*, pp. 331, 332.

Bower, G. H. (1983). Affect and cognition. *Philosophical Transaction: Royal Society of London, Series B, 302*, 387–402.

Bower, G. H. (1986). Prime time in cognitive psychology. In P. Eelen (Ed.), *Cognitive research and behavior therapy: Beyond the conditioning paradigm*. Amsterdam: North Holland Publishers.

Bower, G. H., Clark, M. C., Lesgold, A. M., & Winzenz, D. (1969). Hierarchical retrieval schemes in recall of categorized word lists. *Journal of Verbal Learning and Verbal Behavior, 8*, 323–343.

Bower, G. H., & Morrow, D. G. (1990). Mental models in narrative comprehension. *Science, 247*, 44–48.

Bower, J. E., Kemeny, M. E., Taylor, S. E., & Fahey, J. L. (1998). Cognitive processing, discovery of meaning, CD4 decline, and AIDS-related mortality among bereaved HIV-seropositive men. *Journal of Consulting and Clinical Psychology, 66*, 979–986.

Bower, J. M., & Parsons, L. M. (2003, August). Rethinking the "lesser brain." *Scientific American*, pp. 50–57.

Bowers, K. S. (1984). Hypnosis. In N. Endler & J. M. Hunt (Eds.), *Personality and behavioral disorders* (2nd ed.). New York: Wiley.

Bowers, K. S. (1987, July). Personal communication.

Bowers, T. G., & Clum, G. A. (1988). Relative contribution of specific and nonspecific treatment effects: Meta-analysis of placebo-controlled behavior therapy research. *Psychological Bulletin, 103*, 315–323.

Bowlby, J. (1973). *Separation: Anxiety and anger*. New York: Basic Books.

Bowles, S., & Kasindorf, M. (2001, March 6). Friends tell of picked-on but "normal" kid. *USA Today*, p. 4A.

Bowman, H. (2003, Fall). Interactions between chimpanzees and their human caregivers in captive settings: The effects of gestural communication on reciprocity. *Friends of Washoe, 25*(1), 7–16.

Boyatzis, C. J., Matillo, G. M., & Nesbitt, K. M. (1995). Effects of the "Mighty Morphin Power Rangers" on children's aggression with peers. *Child Study Journal, 25*, 45–55.

Boynton, R. M. (1979). *Human color vision*. New York: Holt, Rinehart & Winston.

Braden, J. P. (1994). *Deafness, deprivation, and IQ*. New York: Plenum.

Bradley, D. R., Dumais, S. T., & Petry, H. M. (1976). Reply to Cavonius. *Nature, 261*, 78.

Bradshaw, J. (1990). *Homecoming: Reclaiming and championing your inner child*. New York: Bantam Books.

Brainerd, C. J. (1996). Piaget: A centennial celebration. *Psychological Science, 7*, 191–195.

Brainerd, C. J., & Poole, D. A. (1997). Long-term survival of children's memories: A review. *Learning and Individual Differences, 9*, 125–151.

Brainerd, C. J., & Reyna, V. F. (1998). When things that were never experienced are easier to "remember" than things that were. *Psychological Science, 9*, 484–489.

Brainerd, C. J., & Reyna, V. F. (2002). Fuzzy-trace theory and false memory. *Current Directions in Psychological Science, 11*, 164–169.

Brainerd, C. J., Reyna, V. F., & Brandse, E. (1995). Are children's false memories more persistent than their true memories? *Psychological Science, 6*, 359–364.

Brandon, S., Boakes, J., Glaser, & Green, R. (1998). Recovered memories of childhood sexual abuse: Implications for clinical practice. *British Journal of Psychiatry, 172*, 294–307.

Brannon, L. A., & Brock, T. C. (1994). Perilous underestimation of sex partners' sexual histories in calculating personal AIDS risk. Paper presented to the American Psychological Society convention.

Bransford, J. D., & Johnson, M. K. (1972). Contextual prerequisites for understanding: Some investigations of comprehension and recall. *Journal of Verbal Learning and Verbal Behavior, 11*, 717–726.

Braun, S. (1996). New experiments underscore warnings on maternal drinking. *Science, 273*, 738–739.

Braun, S. (2001, Spring). Seeking insight by prescription. *Cerebrum*, pp. 10–21.

Bray, D. W., & Byham, W. C. (1991, Winter). Assessment centers and their derivatives. *Journal of Continuing Higher Education*, pp. 8–11.

Bray, D. W., Byham, W. (1997). Insights into the history and future of assessment centers: An interview with Dr. Douglas W. Bray and Dr. William Byham. *Journal of Social Behavior and Personality, 12*, 3–12.

Bray, G. A. (1969). Effect of caloric restriction on energy expenditure in obese patients. *Lancet, 2,* 397–398.

Brayne, C., Spiegelhalter, D. J., Dufouil, C., Chi, L-Y., Dening, T. R., Paykel, E. S., O'Connor, D. W., Ahmed, A., McGee, M. A., & Huppert, F. A. (1999). Estimating the true extent of cognitive decline in the old old. *Journal of the American Geriatrics Society, 47,* 1283–1288.

Breedlove, S. M. (1997). Sex on the brain. *Nature, 389,* 801.

Brehm, S., & Brehm, J. W. (1981). *Psychological reactance: A theory of freedom and control.* New York: Academic Press.

Breland, K., & Breland, M. (1961). The misbehavior of organisms. *American Psychologist, 16,* 661–664.

Brenner, M. (1973). The next-in-line effect. *Journal of Verbal Learning and Verbal Behavior, 12,* 320–323.

Breslau, N., & Klein, D. F. (1999). Smoking and panic attacks: An epidemiologic investigation. *Archives of General Psychiatry, 56,* 1141–1147.

Bressan, P., & Dal Martello, M. F. (2002). Talis pater, talis filius: Perceived resemblance and the belief in genetic relatedness. *Psychological Science, 13,* 213–218.

Bretz, R. D. (1989). College grade point average as a predictor of adult success: A meta-analytic review and some additional evidence. *Public Personnel Management, 18,* 11–22.

Brewer, C. L. (1990). Personal correspondence.

Brewer, C. L. (1996). Personal communication.

Brewer, W. F. (1977). Memory for the pragmatic implications of sentences. *Memory & Cognition, 5,* 673–678.

Brewin, C. R., Andrews, B., Rose, S., & Kirk, M. (1999). Acute stress disorder and posttraumatic stress disorder in victims of violent crime. *American Journal of Psychiatry, 156,* 360–366.

Brewin, C. R., Andrews, B., & Valentine, J. D. (2000). Meta-analysis of risk factors for posttraumatic stress disorder in trauma-exposed adults. *Journal of Consulting and Clinical Psychology, 68,* 748–766.

Brickman, P., Coates, D., & Janoff-Bulman, R. J. (1978). Lottery winners and accident victims: Is happiness relative? *Journal of Personality and Social Psychology, 36,* 917–927.

Brief, A. P., & Weiss, H. M. (2002). Organizational behavior: Affect in the workplace. *Annual Review of Psychology, 53,* 279–307.

Brinson, S. L. (1992). The use and opposition of rape myths in prime-time television dramas. *Sex Roles, 27,* 359–375.

Briscoe, D. (1997, February 16). Women lawmakers still not in charge. Associated Press (in *Grand Rapids Press,* p. A23).

Brislin, R. (1993). *Understanding culture's influence on behavior.* Fort Worth, TX: Harcourt Brace.

Brislin, R. W. (1988). Increasing awareness of class, ethnicity, culture, and race by expanding on students' own experiences. In I. Cohen (Ed.), *The G. Stanley Hall Lecture Series.* Washington, DC: American Psychological Association.

Brissette, I., & Cohen, S. (2002). The contribution of individual differences in hostility to the associations between daily interpersonal conflict, affect, and sleep. *Personality and Social Psychology Bulletin, 28,* 1265–1274.

Brissette, I., Scheier, M. F., & Carver, C. S. (2002). The role of optimism in social network development, coping, and psychological adjustment during a life transition. *Journal of Personality and Social Psychology, 82,* 102–111.

British Psychological Society. (1993). Ethical principles for conducting research with human participants. *The Psychologist: Bulletin of the British Psychological Society, 6,* 33–36.

Britton, W. B., & Bootzin, R. R. (2004). Near-death experiences and the temporal lobe. *Psychological Science, 15,* 254–258.

Broadbent, D. E. (1978). The current state of noise research: Reply to Poulton. *Psychological Bulletin, 85,* 1052–1067.

Brody, J. E. (1999, November 30). Yesterday's precocious puberty is norm today. *New York Times* (www.nytimes.com).

Brody, J. E. (2000, March 21). When post-traumatic stress grips youth. *New York Times* (www.nytimes.com).

Brody, J. E. (2001, December 11). An old enemy, smoking, hangs tough. *New York Times* (www.nytimes.com).

Brody, J. E. (2002, November 26). When the eyelids snap shut at 65 miles an hour. *New York Times* (www.nytimes.com).

Brody, J. E. (2003, August 19). Skipping a college course: Weight gain 101. *New York Times* (www.nytimes.com).

Brody, J. E. (2003, September). Addiction: A brain ailment, not a moral lapse. *New York Times* (www.nytimes.com).

Brody, J. E. (2003, December 23). Stampede of diabetes as U.S. races to obesity. *New York Times* (www.nytimes.com).

Brody, N. (1992). *Intelligence,* 2nd ed. San Diego: Academic Press.

Brody, N. (1997). Dispositional paradigms: Comment on Eysenck (1997) and the biosocial science of individual differences. *Journal of Personality and Social Psychology, 73*(6), 1242–1245.

Brody, N. (2001). Inspection time: Past, present, and future. *Intelligence, 29,* 537–541.

Brody, N. (2003). Construct validation of the Sternberg Triarchic Abilities Test: Comment and reanalysis. *Intelligence, 31,* 319–329.

Brodzinsky, D. M., & Schechter, M. D. (Eds.) (1990). *The psychology of adoption.* New York: Oxford University Press.

Broman, S. H. (1989). Infant physical status and later cognitive development. In M. G. Bornstein & N. A. Krasnegor (Eds.), *Stability and continuity in mental development: Behavioral and biological perspectives.* Hillsdale, NJ: Erlbaum.

Bronner, E. (1998, February 25). U.S. high school seniors among worst in math and science. *New York Times* (www.nytimes.com).

Brooke, J. (2000, January 20). Canada proposes scaring smokers with pictures on the pack. *New York Times* (www.nytimes.com)

Brooks, D. (2005, April 28). Mourning Mother Russia. *New York Times* (www.nytimes.com).

Brooks, D. J. (2002, October 8). Running down the road to happiness. *Gallup Tuesday Briefing* (www.gallup.com).

Brooks, G. (1960). "The Bean Eaters," *The World of Gwendolyn Brooks,* Harper & Row.

Brown, A. S. (2003). A review of the déjà vu experience. *Psychological Bulletin, 129,* 394–413.

Brown, A. S. (2004). *The déjà vu experience.* Hove, England: Psychology Press.

Brown, A. S., Begg, M. D., Gravenstein, S., Schaefer, C. A., Wyatt, R. J., Bresnahan, M., Babulas, V. P., & Susser, E. S. (2004). Serologic evidence of prenatal influenza in the etiology of schizophrenia. *Archives of General Psychiatry, 61,* 774–780.

Brown, A. S., Bracken, E., Zoccoli, S., & Douglas, K. (2004). Generating and remembering passwords. *Applied Cognitive Psychology, 18,* 641–651.

Brown, A. S., Schaefer, C. A., Wyatt, R. J., Goetz, R., Begg, M. D., Gorman, J. M., & Susser, E. S. (2000). Maternal exposure to respiratory infections and adult schizophrenia spectrum disorders: A prospective birth cohort study. *Schizophrenia Bulletin, 26,* 287–295.

Brown, E. L., & Deffenbacher, K. (1979). *Perception and the senses.* New York: Oxford University Press.

Brown, G. K., Ten Have, T., Henriques, G. R., Xie, S. X., Hollander, J. E., & Beck, A. T. (2005). Cognitive therapy for the prevention of suicide attempts. *JAMA: Journal of the American Medical Association, 294,* 563–570.

Brown, J. D. (1991). Accuracy and bias in self-knowledge. In C. R. Snyder & D. F. Forsyth (Eds.), *Handbook of social and clinical psychology: The health perspective.* New York: Pergamon Press.

Brown, J. D., Steele, J. R., & Walsh-Childers, K. (2002). Sexual teens, sexual media: Investigating media's influence on adolescent sexuality. Mahwah, NJ: Erlbaum.

Brown, J. L., & Pollitt, E. (1996, February). Malnutrition, poverty and intellectual development. *Scientific American*, pp. 38–43.

Brown, L. R., Kane, H., & Ayres, E. (1993). *Vital signs 1993: The trends that are shaping our future.* New York: Norton.

Brown, R. (1965). *Social psychology.* New York: Free Press.

Brown, R. (1973). *A first language: The early stages.* Cambridge, MA: Harvard University Press.

Brown, R. (1986). Linguistic relativity. In S. H. Hulse & B. F. Green, Jr. (Eds.), *One hundred years of psychological research in America.* Baltimore: Johns Hopkins University Press.

Brown, R., & Kulik, J. (1982). Flashbulb memories. In U. Neisser (Ed.), *Memory observed.* San Francisco: Freeman.

Brown, S. L., Nesse, R. M., Vinokur, A. D., & Smith, D. M. (2003). Providing social support may be more beneficial than receiving it: Results from a prospective study of mortality. *Psychological Science, 14,* 320–327.

Brown, S. W., Garry, M., Loftus, E., Silver, B., DuBois, K., & DuBreuil, S. (1996). People's beliefs about memory: Why don't we have better memories? Paper presented at the American Psychological Society convention.

Brownell, K. D. (1997, March). We must be more militant about food. *APA Monitor,* p. 48.

Brownell, K. D. (2002). Public policy and the prevention of obesity. In C. G. Fairburn & K. D. Brownell (Eds.), *Eating disorders and obesity: A comprehensive handbook* (2nd ed.). New York: Guilford.

Brownell, K. D., & Wadden, T. A. (1992). Etiology and treatment of obesity: Understanding a serious, prevalent, and refractory disorder. *Journal of Consulting and Clinical Psychology, 60,* 505–517.

Browning, C. (1992). *Ordinary men: Reserve police battalion 101 and the final solution in Poland.* New York: HarperCollins.

Brownmiller, S. (1975). *Against our will: Men, women, and rape.* New York: Simon and Schuster.

Bruce, D., Dolan, A., & Phillips-Grant, K. (2000). On the transition from childhood amnesia to the recall of personal memories. *Psychological Science, 11,* 360–364.

Bruck, M., & Ceci, S. J. (1999). The suggestibility of children's memory. *Annual Review of Psychology, 50,* 419–439.

Bruck, M., & Ceci, S. J. (2004). Forensic developmental psychology: Unveiling four common misconceptions. *Current Directions in Psychological Science, 15,* 229–232.

Bruer, J. T. (1999). *The myth of the first three years: A new understanding of early brain development and lifelong learning.* New York: Free Press.

Brumberg, J. J. (2000). *Fasting girls: The history of anorexia nervosa.* New York: Vintage.

Brune, K., & Handwerker, H. (2004). *Hyperalgesia: Molecular mechanisms and clinical implications.* Special issue of *Progress in Pain Research and Management, 30.* Seattle, WA: International Association for the Study of Pain, IASP Press.

Bryant, R. A. (2001). Posttraumatic stress disorder and traumatic brain injury: Can they co-exist? *Clinical Psychology Review, 21,* 931–948.

Buchel, C., Morris, J., Dolan, R. J., & Friston, K. J. (1998). Brain systems mediating aversive conditioning: An event-related fMRI study. *Neuron, 20,* 947–957.

Buck, L., & Axel, R. (1991). A novel multigene family may encode odorant receptors: A molecular basis for odor recognition. *Cell, 65,* 175–187.

Buckingham, M. (2001, August). Quoted by P. LaBarre, "Marcus Buckingham thinks your boss has an attitude problem." *The Magazine* (fastcompany.com/online/49/buckingham.html).

Buckingham, M., & Clifton, D. O. (2001). *Now, discover your strengths.* New York: Free Press.

Buckley, K. E., & Leary, M. R. (2001). Perceived acceptance as a predictor of social, emotional, and academic outcomes. Paper presented at the Society of Personality and Social Psychology annual convention.

Buehler, R., Griffin, D., & Ross, M. (1994). Exploring the "planning fallacy": Why people underestimate their task completion times. *Journal of Personality and Social Psychology, 67,* 366–381.

Bugelski, B. R., Kidd, E., & Segmen, J. (1968). Image as a mediator in one-trial paired-associate learning. *Journal of Experimental Psychology, 76,* 69–73.

Bugental, D. B. (1986). Unmasking the "polite smile": Situational and personal determinants of managed affect in adult-child interaction. *Personality and Social Psychology Bulletin, 12,* 7–16.

Buka, S. L., Goldstein, J. M., Seidman, L. J., Zornberg, G., Donatelli, J-A. A., Denny, L. R., & Tsuang, M. T. (1999). Prenatal complications, genetic vulnerability, and schizophrenia: The New England longitudinal studies of schizophrenia. *Psychiatric Annals, 29,* 151–156.

Buka, S. L., Tsuang, M. T., Torrey, E. F., Klebanoff, M. A., Wagner, R. L., & Yolken, R. H. (2001). Maternal infections and subsequent psychosis among offspring. *Archives of General Psychiatry, 58,* 1032–1037.

Bullough, V. (1990). The Kinsey scale in historical perspective. In D. P. McWhirter, S. A. Sanders, & J. M. Reinisch (Eds.), *Homosexuality/heterosexuality: Concepts of sexual orientation.* New York: Oxford University Press.

Buquet, R. (1988). Le rêve et les déficients visuels (Dreams and the visually impaired). *Psychanalyse-à-l'Université, 13,* 319–327.

Bureau of the Census. (2004). *Statistical abstract of the United States 2004.* Washington, DC: U.S. Government Printing Office.

Bureau of Labor Statistics. (2004, September 14). American time-user survey summary. Washington, DC: United States Department of Labor (www.bls.gov).

Bureau of Labor Statistics, U.S. Department of Labor. (2004–2005). Occupational Outlook Handbook, 2004–05 Edition.

Bureau of the Census. (2004). *Statistical abstract of the United States 2004.* Washington, DC: U.S. Government Printing Office.

Burger, J. M. (1987). Increased performance with increased personal control: A self-presentation interpretation. *Journal of Experimental Social Psychology, 23,* 350–360.

Burger, J. M., & Burns, L. (1988). The illusion of unique invulnerability and the use of effective contraception. *Personality and Social Psychology Bulletin, 14,* 264–270.

Burgess, M., Enzle, M. E., & Schmaltz, R. (2004). Defeating the potentially deleterious effects of externally imposed deadlines: Practitioners' rules-of-thumb. *Personality and Social Psychology Bulletin, 30,* 868–877.

Buri, J. R., Louiselle, P. A., Misukanis, T. M., & Mueller, R. A. (1988). Effects of parental authoritarianism and authoritativeness on self-esteem. *Personality and Social Psychology Bulletin, 14,* 271–282.

Burish, T. G., & Carey, M. P. (1986). Conditioned aversive responses in cancer chemotherapy patients: Theoretical and developmental analysis. *Journal of Counseling and Clinical Psychology, 54,* 593–600.

Burke, D. M., & Shafto, M. A. (2004). Aging and language production. *Current Directions in Psychological Science, 13,* 21–24.

Burkholder, R. (2005a, January 11). Chinese far wealthier than a decade ago—but are they happier? *Gallup Poll News Service* (www.gallup.com).

Burkholder, R. (2005b, January 18). China's citizens optimistic, yet not entirely satisfied. *Gallup Poll News Service* (www.gallup.com).

Burns, B. C. (2004). The effects of speed on skilled chess performance. *Psychological Science, 15,* 442–447.

Burrell, B. (2005). *Postcards from the brain museum: The improbable search for meaning in the matter of famous minds.* New York: Broadway Books.

Burt, D. M., & Perrett, D. I. (1995). Perception of age in adult Caucasian male faces: Computer graphic manipulation of shape and colour information. *Proceedings of the Royal Society, 259,* 137–143.

Bush, G. W. (2001, May 1). Speech to the National Defense University, Washington, DC.

Bushman, B. J. (1993). Human aggression while under the influence of alcohol and other drugs: An integrative research review. *Current Directions in Psychological Science, 2,* 148–152.

Bushman, B. J. (2002). Does venting anger feed or extinguish the flame? Catharsis, rumination, distraction, anger, and aggressive responding. *Personality and Social Psychology Bulletin, 28,* 724–731.

Bushman, B. J., & Anderson, C. A. (2001). Media violence and the American public: Scientific facts versus media misinformation. *American Psychologist, 56,* 477–489.

Bushman, B. J., & Baumeister, R. F. (1998). Threatened egotism, narcissism, self-esteem, and direct and displaced aggression: Does self-love or self-hate lead to violence? *Journal of Personality and Social Psychology, 75,* 219–229.

Bushman, B. J., Baumeister, R. F., & Stack, A. D. (1999). Catharsis, aggression, and persuasive influence: Self-fulfilling or self-defeating prophecies? *Journal of Personality and Social Psychology, 76,* 367–376.

Bushman, B. J., & Bonaci, A. M. (2002). Violence and sex impair memory for television ads. *Journal of Applied Psychology, 87,* 557–564.

Busnel, M. C., Granier-Deferre, C., & Lecanuet, J. P. (1992, October). Fetal audition. *New York Academy of Sciences, 662,* 118–134.

Buss, A. H. (1989). Personality as traits. *American Psychologist, 44,* 1378–1388.

Buss, D. M. (1991). Evolutionary personality psychology. *Annual Review of Psychology, 42,* 459–491.

Buss, D. M. (1994). The strategies of human mating: People worldwide are attracted to the same qualities in the opposite sex. *American Scientist, 82,* 238–249.

Buss, D. M. (1995). Evolutionary psychology: A new paradigm for psychological science. *Psychological Inquiry, 6,* 1–30.

Buss, D. M. (1996). Sexual conflict: Evolutionary insights into feminism and the "battle of the sexes." In D. M. Buss & N. M. Malamuth (Eds.), *Sex, power, conflict: Evolutionary and feminist perspectives.* New York: Oxford University Press.

Buss, D. M. (1996). Sexual conflict: Evolutionary insights into feminism and the "battle of the sexes." In D. M. Buss & N. M. Malamuth (Eds.), *Sex, power, conflict: Evolutionary and feminist perspectives.* New York: Oxford University Press.

Butler, A. C., Hokanson, J. E., & Flynn, H. A. (1994). A comparison of self-esteem lability and low trait self-esteem as vulnerability factors for depression. *Journal of Personality and Social Psychology, 66,* 166–177.

Butler, J., & Rovee-Collier, C. (1989). Contextual gating of memory retrieval. *Developmental Psychobiology, 22,* 533–552.

Butler, R. A. (1954, February). Curiosity in monkeys. *Scientific American,* pp. 70–75.

Butterfield, F. (1999, July 12). Experts say study confirms prison's new role as mental hospital. *New York Times* (www.nytimes.com).

Butterworth, G. (1992). Origins of self-perception in infancy. *Psychological Inquiry, 3,* 103–111.

Byne, W., & Parsons, B. (1993). Human sexual orientation: The biologic theories reappraised. *Archives of General Psychiatry, 50,* 228–239.

Bynum, R. (2004, November 1). Associated Press article.

Byrne, D. (1971). *The attraction paradigm.* New York: Academic Press.

Byrne, D. (1982). Predicting human sexual behavior. In A. G. Kraut (Ed.), *The G. Stanley Hall Lecture Series* (Vol. 2). Washington, DC: American Psychological Association.

Byrne, J. (2003, September 21). From correspondence reported by Michael Shermer, "E-Skeptic for September 21, 2003, from The Skeptics Society."

Byrne, R. W. (1991, May/June). Brute intellect. *The Sciences,* pp. 42–47.

Byrne, R. W., & Russon, A. E. (1998). Learning by imitation: A hierarchical approach. *Behavioral and Brain Sciences, 21,* 667–721.

Byrnes, J. P., Miller, D. C., & Schafer, W. C. (1999). Gender differences in risk taking: A meta-analysis. *Psychological Bulletin 125,* 367–383.

Cable, D. M., & Gilovich, T. (1998). Looked over or overlooked? Prescreening decisions and postinterview evaluations. *Journal of Personality and Social Psychology, 83,* 501–508.

Cacioppo, J. T., Berntson, G. G., Klein, D. J., & Poehlmann, K. M. (1997). The psychophysiology of emotion across the lifespan. *Annual Review of Gerontology and Geriatrics, 17,* 27.

Cahill, L. (1994). (Beta)-adrenergic activation and memory for emotional events. *Nature, 371,* 702–704.

Cahill, L. (2005, May). His brain, her brain. *Scientific American,* pp. 40–47.

Cale, E. M., & Lilienfeld, S. O. (2002). Sex differences in psychopathy and antisocial personality disorder: A review and integration. *Clinical Psychology Review, 22,* 1179–1207.

Call, K. T., Riedel, A. A., Hein, K., McLoyd, V., Petersen, A., & Kipke, M. (2002). Adolescent health and well-being in the twenty-first century: A global perspective. *Journal of Research on Adolescence, 12,* 69–98.

Callaghan, T., Rochat, P., Lillard, A., Claux, M. L., Odden, H., Itakura, S., Tapanya, S., & Singh, S. (2005). Synchrony in the onset of mental-state reasoning. *Psychological Science, 16,* 378–384.

Calle, E. E., Thun, M. J., Petrelli, J. M., Rodriguez, C., & Health, C. W., Jr. (1999). Body-mass index and mortality in a prospective cohort of U.S. adults. *New England Journal of Medicine, 341,* 1097–1105.

Callicott, J. H., & 11 others (2005). Variation in DISC1 affects hippocampal structure and function and increased risk for schizophrenia. *Proceedings of the National Academy of Sciences, 102,* 8627–8632.

Calvin, W. H. (1996). *The cerebral code: Thinking a thought in the mosaics of the mind.* Cambridge, MA: MIT Press.

Calvo-Merino, B., Glaser, D. E., Grèzes, J., Passingham, R. E., & Haggard, P. (2004). Action observation and acquired motor skills: An fMRI study with expert dancers. *Cerebral Cortex, 15,* 1243–1249.

Camerer, C. F., Loewenstein, G., & Weber, M. (1989). The curse of knowledge in economic settings: An experimental analysis. *Journal of Political Economy, 97,* 1232–1254.

Campbell, D. T. (1975). On the conflicts between biological and social evolution and between psychology and moral tradition. *American Psychologist, 30,* 1103–1126.

Campbell, D. T., & Specht, J. C. (1985). Altruism: Biology, culture, and religion. *Journal of Social and Clinical Psychology, 3*(1), 33–42.

Campbell, S. (1986). *The Loch Ness Monster: The evidence.* Willingborough: Acquarian Press.

Camper, J. (1990, February 7). Drop pompom squad, U. of I. rape study says. *Chicago Tribune,* p. 1.

Camperio-Ciani, A., Corna, F., & Capiluppi, C. (2004). Evidence for maternally inherited factors favouring male homosexuality and promoting female fecundity. *Proceedings of the Royal Society of London B, 271,* 2217–2221.

Campos, J. J., Bertenthal, B. I., & Kermoian, R. (1992). Early experience and emotional development: The emergence of wariness and heights. *Psychological Science, 3,* 61–64.

Canli, T., Desmond, J. E., Zhao, Z., & Gabrieli, J. D. E. (2002). Sex differences in the neural basis of emotional memories. *Proceedings of the National Academy of Sciences, 99,* 10789–10794.

Cannon, J. (2005). Career planning and opportunities: The bachelor's degree in psychology. *Eye on Psi Chi, 26–28.*

Cannon, W. B. (1929). *Bodily changes in pain, hunger, fear, and rage.* New York: Branford.

Cannon, W. B., & Washburn, A. (1912). An explanation of hunger. *American Journal of Physiology, 29,* 441–454.

Cantor, N., & Kihlstrom, J. F. (1987). *Personality and social intelligence.* Englewood Cliffs, NJ: Prentice Hall.

Cantril, H., & Bumstead, C. H. (1960). *Reflections on the human venture.* New York: New York University Press.

Caplan, N., Choy, M. H., & Whitmore, J. K. (1992, February). Indochinese refugee families and academic achievement. *Scientific American,* pp. 36–42.

Caputo, D., & Dunning, D. (2005). What you don't know: The role played by errors of omission in imperfect self-assessments. *Journal of Experimental Social Psychology,* 488–505.

Carducci, B. J., Cosby, P. C., & Ward, D. D. (1978). Sexual arousal and interpersonal evaluations. *Journal of Experimental Social Psychology, 14,* 449–457.

Carey, G. (1990). Genes, fears, phobias, and phobic disorders. *Journal of Counseling and Development, 68,* 628–632.

Carlezon, W. A., Jr., Mague, S. D., & Andersen, S. L. (2003). Enduring behavioral effects of early exposure to methylphenidate in rats. *Biological Psychiatry, 54,* 1330–1337.

Carli, L. L., & Leonard, J. B. (1989). The effect of hindsight on victim derogation. *Journal of Social and Clinical Psychology, 8,* 331–343.

Carlson, C. L. (2000). ADHD is overdiagnosed. In R. L. Atkinson, R. C. Atkinson, E. E. Smith, D. J. Bem, & S. Nolen-Hoeksema (Eds.), *Hilgard's introduction to psychology,* 13th ed. Fort Worth: Harcourt.

Carlson, D. K. (2002, February 19). Acceptance of homosexuality: A youth movement. The Gallup Organization (www.gallup.com/poll/tb/educaYouth/200220219.asp).

Carlson, M. (1995, August 29). Quoted by S. Blakeslee, In brain's early growth, timetable may be crucial. *New York Times,* pp. C1, C3.

Carlson, M., Charlin, V., & Miller, N. (1988). Positive mood and helping behavior: A test of six hypotheses. *Journal of Personality and Social Psychology, 55,* 211–229.

Carlson, R. (1984). What's social about social psychology? Where's the person in personality research? *Journal of Personality and Social Psychology, 47,* 1304–1309.

Carlson, S. (1985). A double-blind test of astrology. *Nature, 318,* 419–425.

Carnegie Council on Adolescent Development. (1989, June). *Turning points: Preparing American youth for the 21st century.* (The report of the Task Force on Education of Young Adolescents.) New York: Carnegie Corporation.

Carrière, G. (2003). Parent and child factors associated with youth obesity. *Statistics Canada, Catalogue 82-003, Supplement to Health Reports, 2003.*

Carroll, D., Davey Smith, G., & Bennett, P. (1994, March). Health and socio-economic status. *The Psychologist,* pp. 122–125.

Carroll, J. (2005, January 14). Terrorism concerns fade. *The Gallup Organization* (www.gallup.com).

Carroll, J. M., & Russell, J. A. (1996). Do facial expressions signal specific emotions? Judging emotion from the face in context. *Journal of Personality and Social Psychology, 70,* 205–218.

Carskadon, M. (2002). *Adolescent sleep patterns: Biological, social, and psychological influences.* New York: Cambridge University Press.

Carter, R. (1998). *Mapping the mind.* Berkeley, CA: University of California Press.

Carter, S., & Snow, C. (2004, May). Helping singles enter better marriages using predictive models of marital success. Presented to the American Psychological Society convention.

Cartwright, R. D. (1978). *A primer on sleep and dreaming.* Reading, MA: Addison-Wesley.

Caryl, P. G. (1994). Early event-related potentials correlate with inspection time and intelligence. *Intelligence, 18,* 15–46.

CASA. (2003). *The formative years: Pathways to substance abuse among girls and young women ages 8–22.* New York: National Center on Addiction and Substance Use, Columbia University.

Case, R. B., Moss, A. J., Case, N., McDermott, M., & Eberly, S. (1992). Living alone after myocardial infarction: Impact on prognosis. *Journal of the American Medical Association, 267,* 515–519.

Cash, T., & Janda, L. H. (1984, December). The eye of the beholder. *Psychology Today,* pp. 46–52.

Cash, T. F., & Henry, P. E. (1995). Women's body images: The results of a national survey in the U.S.A. *Sex Roles, 33,* 19–28.

Caspi, A. (2000). The child is father of the man: Personality continuities from childhood to adulthood. *Journal of Personality and Social Psychology, 78,* 158–172.

Caspi, A., Harrington, H., Milne, B., Amell, J. W., Theodore, R. F., & Moffitt, T. E. (2003). Children's behavioral styles at age 3 are linked to their adult personality traits at age 26. *Journal of Personality, 71,* 496–513.

Caspi, A., McClay, J., Moffitt, T., Mill, J., Martin, J., Craig, I. W., Taylor, A., & Poulton, R. (2002). Role of genotype in the cycle of violence in maltreated children. *Science, 297,* 851–854.

Caspi, A., Moffitt, T. E., Newman, D. L., & Silva, P. A. (1996). Behavioral observations at age 3 years predict adult psychiatric disorders: Longitudinal evidence from a birth cohort. *Archives of General Psychiatry, 53,* 1033–1039.

Caspi, A., Sugden, K., Moffitt, T. E., Taylor, A., Craig, I. W., Harrington, H. L., McClay, J., Mill, J., Martin, J., Braithwaite, A., & Poulton, R. (2003). Influence of life stress on depression: Moderation by a polymorphism in the 5-HTT gene. *Science, 30,* 386–389.

Cassandro, V. J., & Simonton, D. K. (2003). Creativity and genius. In C. L. M. Keyes & J. Haidt (Eds.), *Flourishing: Positive psychology and the life well-lived.* Washington, DC: American Psychological Association.

Cassidy, J., & Shaver, P. R. (1999). *Handbook of attachment.* New York: Guilford.

Castillo, R. J. (1997). *Culture and mental illness: A client-centered approach.* Pacific Grove, CA: Brooks/Cole.

Castonguay, L. G., & Goldfried, M. R. (1994). Psychotherapy integration: An idea whose time has come. *Applied & Preventive Psychology, 3,* 159–172.

Catanese, K. R., & Tice, D. M. (2005). The effect of rejection on anti-social behaviors: Social exclusion produces aggressive behaviors. In K. D. Williams, J. P. Forgas, & W. Von Hippel (Eds.), *The social outcast: Ostracism, social exclusion, rejection, and bullying.* New York: Psychology Press.

Cattell, R. B. (1963). Theory of fluid and crystallized intelligence: A critical experiment. *Journal of Educational Psychology, 54,* 1–22.

Cavalli-Sforza, L., Menozzi, P., & Piazza, A. (1994). *The history and geography of human genes.* Princeton, NJ: Princeton University Press.

Cavigelli, S. A., & McClintock, M. K. (2003). Fear of novelty in infant rats predicts adult corticosterone dynamics and an early death. *Proceedings of the National Academy of Sciences, 100,* 16131–16136.

CDC. (2004). Teenagers in the United States: Sexual activity, contraceptive use, and childbearing, 2002. A fact sheet for series 23, number 24. DHHS Publication (PHS) 2005–1976.

CDC. (2004, December 16). Prevalence of overweight and obesity among adults: United States, 1999–2002. Centers for Disease Control and Prevention, National Center for Health Statistics (www.cdc.gov).

Ceci, S. J. (1993). Cognitive and social factors in children's testimony. Master Lecture, American Psychological Association convention.

Ceci, S. J., & Bruck, M. (1993). Child witnesses: Translating research into policy. *Social Policy Report* (Society for Research in Child Development), *7*(3), 1–30.

Ceci, S. J., & Bruck, M. (1995). *Jeopardy in the courtroom: A scientific analysis of children's testimony.* Washington, DC: American Psychological Association.

Ceci, S. J., Huffman, M. L. C., Smith, E., & Loftus, E. F. (1994). Repeatedly thinking about a non-event: Source misattributions among preschoolers. *Consciousness and Cognition, 3,* 388–407.

Ceci, S. J., & Liker, J. K. (1986). A day at the races: A study of IQ, expertise, and cognitive complexity. *Journal of Experimental Psychology: General, 115,* 255–266.

Ceci, S. J., & Williams, W. M. (1997). Schooling, intelligence, and income. *American Psychologist, 52,* 1051–1058.

Centers for Disease Control. (1992, September 16). Serious mental illness and disability in the adult household population: United States, 1989. *Advance Data No. 218 from Vital and Health Statistics,* National Center for Health Statistics.

Centers for Disease Control. (2003). Who should get a flu shot (influenza vaccine). National Center for Infectious Diseases (http://www.cdc.gov/ncidod/diseases/flu/who.htm).

Centers for Disease Control Vietnam Experience Study. (1988). Health status of Vietnam veterans. *Journal of the American Medical Association, 259,* 2701–2709.

Centerwall, B. S. (1989). Exposure to television as a risk factor for violence. *American Journal of Epidemiology, 129,* 643–652.

Cerella, J. (1985). Information processing rates in the elderly. *Psychological Bulletin, 98,* 67–83.

CFI. (2003, July). International developments. *Report.* Amherst, NY: Center for Inquiry International.

Chambless, D. L., Baker, M. J., Baucom, D. H., Beutler, L. E., Calhoun, K. S., Crits-Christoph, P., Daiuto, A., DeRubeis, R., Detweiler, J., Haaga, D. A. F., Johnson, S. B., McCurry, S., Mueser, K. T., Pope, K. S., Sanderson, W. C., Shoham, V., Stickle, T., Williams, D. A., & Woody, S. R. (1997). Update on empirically validated therapies, II. *The Clinical Psychologist, 51*(1), 3–16.

Chamove, A. S. (1980). Nongenetic induction of acquired levels of aggression. *Journal of Abnormal Psychology, 89,* 469–488.

Chance News (1999, July 15). National Lottery and death rates. From *Daily Express,* 13 August 1998.

Chang, E. C. (2001). Cultural influences on optimism and pessimism: Differences in Western and Eastern construals of the self. In E. C. Chang (Ed.), *Optimism and pessimism.* Washington, DC: APA Books.

Chang, P. P., Ford, D. E., Meoni, L. A., Wang, N.-Y., & Klag, M. J. (2002). Anger in young men and subsequent premature cardiovascular disease: The precursors study. *Archives of Internal Medicine, 162,* 901–906.

Chaplin, W. F., Phillips, J. B., Brown, J. D., Clanton, N. R., & Stein, J. L. (2000). Handshaking, gender, personality, and first impressions. *Journal of Personality and Social Psychology, 79,* 110–117.

Charles, S. T., Reynolds, C. A., & Gatz, M. (2001). Age-related differences and change in positive and negative affect over 23 years. *Journal of Personality and Social Psychology, 80,* 136–151.

Charpak, G., & Broch, H. (2004). *Debunked! ESP, telekinesis, and other pseudoscience.* Baltimore, MD: Johns Hopkins University Press.

Chartrand, T. L., & Bargh, J. A. (1999). The chameleon effect: The perception-behavior link and social interaction. *Journal of Personality and Social Psychology, 76,* 893–910.

Chase, M. H., & Morales, F. R. (1983). Subthreshold excitatory activity and motorneuron discharge during REM periods of active sleep. *Science, 221,* 1195–1198.

Chase, W. G., & Simon, H. A. (1973). Perception in chess. *Cognitive Psychology, 4,* 55–81.

Chase-Lansdale, P. L., Moffitt, R. A., Lohman, B. J., Cherlin, A. J., Coley, R. L., Pittman, L. D., Roff, J., & Votruba-Drzal, E. (2003). Mothers' transitions from welfare to work and the well-being of preschoolers and adolescents. *Science, 299,* 1548–1552.

Chassin, L., Presson, C. C., Sherman, S. J., & McGrew, J. (1987). The changing smoking environment for middle and high school students: 1980–1983. *Journal of Behavioral Medicine, 10,* 581–593.

Chaudhari, N., Landin, A. M., & Roper, S. D. (2000). A metabotropic glutamate receptor variant functions as a taste receptor. *Nature Neuroscience, 3,* 113–119.

Chaves, J. F. (1989). Hypnotic control of clinical pain. In N. P. Spanos & J. F. Chaves (Eds.), *Hypnosis: The cognitive-behavioral perspective.* Buffalo, NY: Prometheus Books.

Cheek, J. M., & Melchior, L. A. (1990). Shyness, self-esteem, and self-consciousness. In H. Leitenberg (Ed.), *Handbook of social and evaluation anxiety.* New York: Plenum.

Cheit, R. E. (1998). Consider this, skeptics of recovered memory. *Ethics & Behavior, 8,* 141–160.

Chen, E. (2004). Why socioeconomic status affects the health of children: A psychosocial perspective. *Current Directions in Psychological Science, 13,* 112–115.

Cheng, C. (2001). Assessing coping flexibility in real-life and laboratory settings: A multimethod approach. *Journal of Personality and Social Psychology, 80,* 814–833.

Cheng, T. O. (1999). Teenage smoking in China. *Journal of Adolescence, 22,* 607–620.

Chess, S., & Thomas, A. (1987). *Know your child: An authoritative guide for today's parents.* New York: Basic Books.

Child Trends. (2001, August). Facts at a glance. (www.childtrends.org).

Chiles, J. A., Lambert, M. J., & Hatch, A. L. (1999). The impact of psychological interventions on medical cost offset: A meta-analytic review. *Clinical Psychology: Science and Practice, 6,* 204–220.

Chisholm, K. (1998). A three year follow-up of attachment and indiscriminate friendliness in children adopted from Romanian orphanages. *Child Development, 69,* 1092–1106.

Choi, I., & Choi, Y. (2002). Culture and self-concept flexibility. *Personality and Social Psychology Bulletin, 28,* 1508–1517.

Chomsky, N. (1959). Review of B. F. Skinner's *Verbal behavior. Language, 35,* 26–58.

Chomsky, N. (1972). *Language and mind.* New York: Harcourt Brace Jovanovich.

Chomsky, N. (1987). Language in a psychological setting. Sophia Linguistic Working Papers in Linguistics, No. 22, Sophia University, Tokyo.

Chorpita, B. F., & Barlow, D. H. (1998). The development of anxiety: The role of control in the early environment. *Psychological Bulletin, 124,* 3–21.

Christakis, D. S., Zimmerman, F. J., DiGiuseppe, D. L., & McCarty, C. A. (2004). Early television exposure and subsequent attentional problems in children. *Pediatrics, 113,* 708–713.

Christensen, A., & Jacobson, N. S. (1994). Who (or what) can do psychotherapy: The status and challenge of nonprofessional therapies. *Psychological Science, 5,* 8–14.

Christophersen, E. R., & Edwards, K. J. (1992). Treatment of elimination disorders: State of the art 1991. *Applied & Preventive Psychology, 1,* 15–22.

Chugani, H. T., & Phelps, M. E. (1986). Maturational changes in cerebral function in infants determined by [18]FDG Positron Emission Tomography. *Science, 231,* 840–843.

CIA. (2005). Life expectancy at birth. *The world fact book.* www.cia.gov.

Cialdini, R. B. (1993). *Influence: Science and practice* (3rd ed.). New York: HarperCollins.

Cialdini, R. B., & Richardson, K. D. (1980). Two indirect tactics of image management: Basking and blasting. *Journal of Personality and Social Psychology, 39,* 406–415.

Citrome, L., & Volavka, J. (1999). Schizophrenia: Violence and comorbidity. *Current Opinion in Psychiatry, 12,* 47–51.

Clack, B., Dixon, J., & Tredoux, C. (2005). Eating together apart: Patterns of segregation in a multi-ethnic cafeteria. *Journal of Community and Applied Social Psychology, 15,* 1-16.

Clancy, S. A., McNally, R. J., Schachter, D. L., Lenzenweger, M. F., & Pitman, R. K. (2002). Memory distortion in people reporting abduction by aliens. *Journal of Abnormal Psychology, 111,* 455-461.

Clancy, S. A., Schacter, D. L., McNally, R. J., & Pitman, R. K. (2000). False recognition in women reporting recovered memories of sexual abuse. *Psychological Science, 11,* 26-31.

Clark, A., Seidler, A., & Miller, M. (2001). Inverse association between sense of humor and coronary heart disease. *International Journal of Cardiology, 80,* 87-88.

Clark, K. B., Chein, I., & Cook, S. W. (1952; reprinted 2004). The effects of segregation and the consequences of desegregation: A (September 1952) social science statement in the *Brown v Board of Education of Topeka* Supreme Court Case. *American Psychologist, 59,* 495-501.

Clark, K. B., & Clark, M. P. (1947). Racial identification and preference in Negro children. In T. M.. Newcomb and E. L. Hartley (Eds.), *Readings in social psychology.* New York: Holt.

Clark, R., Anderson, N. B., Clark, V. R., & Williams, D. R. (1999). Racism as a stressor for African Americans: A biopsychosocial model. *American Psychologist, 54,* 805-816.

Clark, R. D. (1990, May). The impact of AIDS on gender differences in willingness to engage in casual sex. *Journal of Applied Social Psychology, 20,* 771-782.

Clark, R. D., III, & Hatfield, E. (1989). Gender differences in willingness to engage in casual sex. *Journal of Psychology and Human Sexuality, 2,* 39-55.

Coats, E. J., & Feldman, R. S. (1996). Gender differences in nonverbal correlates of social status. *Personality and Social Psychology Bulletin, 22,* 1014-1022.

Cofer, J. O., (1992). *The Latin Deli,* New York: W. W. Norton and Company.

Coffey, C. E. (Ed.) (1993). *Clinical science of electroconvulsive therapy.* Washington, DC: American Psychiatric Press.

Coffey, C. E., Lucke, J. F., Saxton, J. A., Ratcliff, G., Unitas, L. J., Billig, B., & Bryan, R. N. (1998). Sex differences in brain aging: A quantitative magnetic resonance imagine study. *Archives of Neurology, 55,* 169-179.

Coffey, C. E., Wilkinson, W. E., Weiner, R. D., Parashos, I. A., Djang, W. T., Webb, M. C., Figiel, G. S., & Spritzer, C. E. (1993). Quantitative cerebral anatomy in depression: A controlled magnetic resonance imaging study. *Archives of General Psychiatry, 50,* 7-16.

Cogan, J. C., Bhalla, S. K., Sefa-Dedeh, A., & Rothblum, E. D. (1996). A comparison study of United States and African students on perceptions of obesity and thinness. *Journal of Cross-Cultural Psychology, 27,* 98-113.

Cogan, J. C., & Ernsberger, P. (1999). Dieting, weight, and health: Reconceptualizing research and policy. *Journal of Social Issues, 55,* 187-205.

Cohen, D. (1995, June 17). Now we are one, or two, or three. *New Scientist,* pp. 14-15.

Cohen, G., Conway, M. A., & Maylor, E. A. (1994, September). Flashbulb memories in older adults. *Psychology & Aging, 9(3),* 454-463.

Cohen, H., Kaplan, Z., Kotler, M., Kouperman, I., Moisa, R., & Grisaru, N. (2005). Repetitive transcranial magnetic stimulation of the right dorsolateral prefrontal cortex in posttraumatic stress disorder: A double-blind, placebo-controlled study. *American Journal of Psychiatry, 16,* 515-524.

Cohen, K. M. (2002). Relationships among childhood sex-atypical behavior, spatial ability, handedness, and sexual orientation in men. *Archives of Sexual Behavior, 31,* 129-143.

Cohen, S. (1988). Psychosocial models of the role of social support in the etiology of physical disease. *Health Psychology, 7,* 269-297.

Cohen, S. (2004). Social relationships and health. *American Psychologist, 59,* 676-684.

Cohen, S., Doyle, W. J., Skoner, D. P., Rabin, B. S., & Gwaltney, J. M., Jr. (1997). Social ties and susceptibility to the common cold. *Journal of the American Medical Association, 277,* 1940-1944.

Cohen, S., Doyle, W. J., Turner, R., Alper, C. M., & Skoner, D. P. (2003). Sociability and susceptibility to the common cold. *Psychological Science, 14,* 389-395.

Cohen, S., Kaplan, J. R., Cunnick, J. E., Manuck, S. B., & Rabin, B. S. (1992). Chronic social stress, affiliation, and cellular immune response in nonhuman primates. *Psychological Science, 3,* 301-304.

Cohen, S., Line, S., Manuck, S. B., Rabin, B. S., Heise, E. R., & Kaplan, J. R. (1997). Chronic social stress, social status, and susceptibility to upper respiratory infections in nonhuman primates. *Psychosomatic Medicine, 59,* 213-221.

Cohen, S., Tyrrell, D. A. J., & Smith, A. P. (1991). Psychological stress and susceptibility to the common cold. *New England Journal of Medicine, 325,* 606-612.

Colangelo, N., Assouline, S. G., & Gross, M. U. M. (2004). *A nation deceived: How schools hold back America's brightest students,* Volumes I and II. The Templeton National Report on Acceleration. Iowa City, IA: College of Education, University of Iowa.

Colapinto, J. (2000). *As nature made him: The boy who was raised as a girl.* New York: HarperCollins.

Colarelli, S. M., & Dettman, J. R. (2003). Intuitive evolutionary perspectives in marketing. *Psychology and Marketing, 20,* 837-865.

Colarelli, S. M., Spranger, J. L., & Hechanova, M. R. (2006). Women, power, and sex composition in small groups: An evolutionary perspective. *Journal of Organizational Behavior, 27,* 163-184.

Colcombe, S., & Kramer, A. F. (2003). Fitness effects on the cognitive function of older adults: A meta-analytic study. *Psychological Science, 14,* 125-130.

Colcombe, S. J., Kramer, A. F., Erickson, K. I., Scalf, P., McAuley, E., Cohen, N. J., Webb, A., Jerome, G. J., Marquex, D. X., & Elavsky, S. (2004). Cardiovascular fitness, cortical plasticity, and aging. *Proceedings of the National Academy of Sciences, 101,* 3316-3321.

Cole, K. C. (1998). *The universe and the teacup: The mathematics of truth and beauty.* New York: Harcourt Brace.

Coleman, J. (1997, June 30). Cigarette industry thriving in Japan. Associated Press (in *Grand Rapids Press,* p. A14).

Coleman, J. C. (1980). *The nature of adolescence.* London: Methuen.

Coleman, P. D., & Flood, D. G. (1986). Dendritic proliferation in the aging brain as a compensatory repair mechanism. In D. F. Swaab, E. Fliers, M. Mirmiram, W. A. Van Gool, & F. Van Haaren (Eds.), *Progress in brain research* (Vol. 20). New York: Elsevier.

Collins, D. W., & Kimura, D. (1997). A large sex difference on a two-dimensional mental rotation task. *Behavioral Neuroscience, 111,* 845-849.

Collins, N. L., & Miller, L. C. (1994). Self-disclosure and liking: A meta-analytic review. *Psychological Bulletin, 116,* 457-475.

Collins, R. L., Elliott, M. N., Berry, S. H., Danouse, D. E., Kunkel, D., Hunter, S. B., & Miu, A. (2004). Watching sex on television predicts adolescent initiation of sexual behavior. *Pediatrics, 114,* 280-289.

Collins, W. A., Maccoby, E. E., Steinberg, L., Hetherington, E. M., & Bornstein, M. H. (2000). Contemporary research on parenting: The case for nature and nurture. *American Psychologist, 55,* 218-232.

Collinson, S. L., MacKay, C. E., James, A. C., Quested, D. J., Phillips, T., Roberts, N., & Crow, T. J. (2003). Brain volume, asymmetry and intellectual impairment in relation to sex in early-onset schizophrenia. *British Journal of Psychiatry, 183,* 114-120.

Colom, R., Lluis-Font, J. M., & Andrés-Pueyo, A. (2005). The generational intelligence gains are caused by decreasing variance in the lower half of the distribution: Supporting evidence for the nutrition hypothesis. *Intelligence, 33,* 83–91.

Colombo, J. (1982). The critical period concept: Research, methodology, and theoretical issues. *Psychological Bulletin, 91,* 260–275.

Colon, E. A., Callies, A. L., Popkin, M. K., & McGlave, P. B. (1991). Depressed mood and other variables related to bone marrow transplantation survival in acute leukemia. *Psychosomatics, 32,* 420–425.

Comer, R. J. (2004). *Abnormal psychology.,* 5th ed. New York: Worth Publishers.

Commissioner of Official Languages. (1999). *Annual Report 1998.* Minister of Public Works and Government Services Canada, Cat. No. SF1-1998.

Conner, M., & McMillan, B. (1999). Interaction effects in the theory of planned behaviour: Studying cannabis use. *British Journal of Social Psychology, 38,* 195–222.

Consensus Conference. (1985). Electroconvulsive therapy. *Journal of the American Medical Association, 254,* 2103–2108.

Consumer Reports. (1995, November). Does therapy help? Pp. 734–739.

Conway, M., & Ross, M. (1984). Getting what you want by revising what you had. *Journal of Personality and Social Psychology, 47,* 738–748.

Conway, M. A., Wang, Q., Hanyu, K., & Haque, S. (2005). A cross-cultural investigation of autobiographical memory. On the universality and cultural variation of the reminiscence bump. *Journal of Cross-Cultural Psychology, 36,* 739–749.

Cook, E. W., III, Hodes, R. L., & Lang, P. J. (1986). Preparedness and phobia: Effects of stimulus content on human visceral conditioning. *Journal of Abnormal Psychology, 95,* 195–207.

Cook, M., & Mineka, S. (1991). Selective associations in the origins of phobic fears and their implications for behavior therapy. In P. Martin (Ed.), *Handbook of behavior therapy and psychological science: An integrative approach.* New York: Pergamon Press.

Cooke, L. J., Wardle, J., & Gibson, E. L. (2003). Relationship between parental report of food neophobia and everyday food consumption in 2–6-year-old children. *Appetite, 41,* 205–206.

Cooper, K. J. (1999, May 1). This time, copycat wave is broader. *Washington Post* (www.washingtonpost.com).

Coopersmith, S. (1967). *The antecedents of self-esteem.* San Francisco: Freeman.

Corballis, M. C. (1989). Laterality and human evolution. *Psychological Review, 96,* 492–505.

Corballis, M. C. (2002). *From hand to mouth: The origins of language.* Princeton: Princeton University Press.

Corballis, M. C. (2003). From mouth to hand: Gesture, speech, and the evolution of right-handedness. *Behavioral and Brain Sciences, 26,* 199–260.

Coren, S. (1993a). Failure to find statistical significance in left-handedness and pathology studies: A forgotten consideration. *Bulletin of the Psychonomic Society, 31,* 443–446.

Coren, S. (1993b). *The left-hander syndrome: The causes and consequences of left-handedness.* New York: Vintage Books.

Coren, S. (1996). *Sleep thieves: An eye-opening exploration into the science and mysteries of sleep.* New York: Free Press.

Corey, D. P., & 15 others (2004). TRPA1 is a candidate for the mechanosensitive transduction channel of vertebrate hair cells. *Nature* (advance online publication, October 13, at www.nature.com).

Corina, D. P. (1998). The processing of sign language: Evidence from aphasia. In B. Stemmer & H. A. Whittaker (Eds.), *Handbook of neurolinguistics.* San Diego: Academic Press.

Corina, D. P., Vaid, J., & Bellugi, U. (1992). The linguistic basis of left hemisphere specialization. *Science, 255,* 1258–1260.

Corneille, O., Huart, J., Becquart, E., & Brédart, S. (2004). When memory shifts toward more typical category exemplars: Accentuation effects in the recollection of ethnically ambiguous faces. *Journal of Personality and Social Psychology, 86,* 236–250.

Correll, J., Park, B., Judd, C. M., & Wittenbrink, B. (2002). The police officer's dilemma: Using ethnicity to disambiguate potentially threatening individuals. *Journal of Personality and Social Psychology, 83,* 1314–1329.

Costa, P. T., Jr., Terracciano, A., & McCrae, R. R. (2001). Gender differences in personality traits across cultures: Robust and surprising findings. *Journal of Personality and Social Psychology, 81,* 322–331.

Costa, P. T., Jr., Zonderman, A. B., McCrae, R. R., Cornoni-Huntley, J., Locke, B. Z., & Barbano, H. E. (1987). Longitudinal analyses of psychological well-being in a national sample: Stability of mean levels. *Journal of Gerontology, 42,* 50–55.

Costanzo, M. (1997). *Just revenge: Costs and consequences of the death penalty.* New York: St. Martins.

Costello, E. J., Compton, S. N., Keeler, G., & Angold, A. (2003). Relationships between poverty and psychopathology: A natural experiment. *Journal of the American Medical Association, 290,* 2023–2029.

Coughlin, J. F., Mohyde, M., D'Ambrosio, L. A., & Gilbert, J. (2004). Who drives older driver decisions? Cambridge, MA: MIT Age Lab.

Couli, J. T., Vidal, F., Nazarian, B., & Macar, F. (2004). Functional anatomy of the attentional modulation of time estimation. *Science, 303,* 1506–1508.

Courage, M. L., & Howe, M. L. (2002). From infant to child: The dynamics of cognitive change in the second year of life. *Psychological Bulletin, 128,* 250–277.

Courneya, K. S., & Carron, A. V. (1992). The home advantage in sports competitions: A literature review. *Journal of Sport and Exercise Psychology, 14,* 13–27.

Courtney, J. G., Longnecker, M. P., Theorell, T., & de Verdier, M. G. (1993). Stressful life events and the risk of colorectal cancer. *Epidemiology, 4,* 407–414.

Cousins, N. (1989). *Head first: The biology of hope.* New York: Dutton.

Covington, M. V., & Omelich, C. L. (1988). I can resist anything but temptation: Adolescent expectations for smoking cigarettes. *Journal of Applied Social Psychology, 18,* 203–227.

Cowan, G., Lee, C., Levy, D., & Snyder, D. (1988). Dominance and inequality in X-rated videocassettes. *Psychology of Women Quarterly, 12,* 299–311.

Cowan, N. (1988). Evolving conceptions of memory storage, selective attention, and their mutual constraints within the human information-processing system. *Psychological Bulletin, 104,* 163–191.

Cowan, N. (1994). Mechanisms of verbal short-term memory. *Current Directions in Psychological Science, 3,* 185–189.

Cowan, N. (2001). The magical number 4 in short-term memory: A reconsideration of mental storage capacity. *Behavioral and Brain Sciences, 24,* 87–185.

Cowart, B. J. (1981). Development of taste perception in humans: Sensitivity and preference throughout the life span. *Psychological Bulletin, 90,* 43–73.

Crabbe, J. C. (2002). Genetic contributions to addiction. *Annual Review of Psychology, 53,* 435–462.

Crabtree, S. (2002, January 22). Gender roles reflected in teen tech use. *Gallup Tuesday Briefing* (www.gallup.com).

Crabtree, S. (2005, January 13). Engagement keeps the doctor away. *Gallup Management Journal* (gmj.gallup.com).

Craig, M. E., Kalichman, S. C., & Follingstad, D. R. (1989). Verbal coercive sexual behavior among college students. *Archives of Sexual Behavior, 18,* 421–434.

Craik, F. I. M. (1986). A functional account of age differences in memory. In F. Klix & H. Hagendorf (Eds.), *Human memory and cognitive capabilities.* Amsterdam: Elsevier.

Craik, F. I. M., & Tulving, E. (1975). Depth of processing and the retention of words in episodic memory. *Journal of Experimental Psychology: General, 104,* 268–294.

Craik, F. I. M., & Watkins, M. J. (1973). The role of rehearsal in short-term memory. *Journal of Verbal Learning and Verbal Behavior, 12,* 599–607.

Crain-Thoreson, C., & Dale, P. S. (1992). Do early talkers become early readers? Linguistic precocity, preschool language, and emergent literacy. *Developmental Psychology, 28,* 421–429.

Crandall, C. S. (1988). Social contagion of binge eating. *Journal of Personality and Social Psychology, 55,* 588–598.

Crandall, C. S. (1994). Prejudice against fat people: Ideology and self-interest. *Journal of Personality and Social Psychology, 66,* 882–894.

Crandall, C. S. (1995). Do parents discriminate against their heavyweight daughters? *Personality and Social Psychology Bulletin, 21,* 724–735.

Crandall, J. E. (1984). Social interest as a moderator of life stress. *Journal of Personality and Social Psychology, 47,* 164–174.

Crawford, M., Chaffin, R., & Fitton, L. (1995). *Learning and Individual Differences, 7,* 341–362.

Crews, F. (Ed.) (1998). *Unauthorized Freud: Doubters confront a legend.* New York: Viking.

Crocker, J., & Major, B. (1989). Social stigma and self-esteem: The self-protective properties of stigma," *Psychological Review, 89,* 608–630.

Crocker, J., & Park, L. E. (2004). The costly pursuit of self-esteem. *Psychological Bulletin, 130,* 392–414.

Crocker, J., Thompson, L. L., McGraw, K. M., & Ingerman, C. (1987). Downward comparison, prejudice, and evaluation of others: Effects of self-esteem and threat. *Journal of Personality and Social Psychology, 52,* 907–916.

Crocker, J., & Wolfe, C. (1999). Rescuing self-esteem: A contingencies of worth perspective. Unpublished manuscript, University of Michigan.

Croft, R. J., Klugman, A., Baldeweg, T., & Gruzelier, J. H. (2001). Electrophysiological evidence of serotonergic impairment in long-term MDMA ("Ecstasy") users. *American Journal of Psychiatry, 158,* 1687–1692.

Crombie, A. C. (1964, May). Early concepts of the senses and the mind. *Scientific American,* pp. 108–116.

Crook, T. H., & West, R. L. (1990). Name recall performance across the adult life-span. *British Journal of Psychology, 81,* 335–340.

Cross, S., & Markus, H. (1991). Possible selves across the life span. *Human Development, 34,* 230–255.

Cross-National Collaborative Group. (1992). The changing rate of major depression. *Journal of the American Medical Association, 268,* 3098–3105.

Crossen, C. (1994). *Tainted truth: The manipulation of fact in America.* New York: Simon & Schuster.

Crowell, J. A., & Waters, E. (1994). Bowlby's theory grown up: The role of attachment in adult love relationships. *Psychological Inquiry, 5,* 1–22.

Croyle, R. T., & Ditto, P. H. (1990). Illness cognition and behavior: An experimental approach. *Journal of Behavioral Medicine, 13,* 31–52.

Csikszentmihalyi, M. (1990). *Flow: The psychology of optimal experience.* New York: Harper & Row.

Csikszentmihalyi, M. (1999). If we are so rich, why aren't we happy? *American Psychologist, 54,* 821–827.

Csikszentmihalyi, M., & Hunter, J. (2003). Happiness in everyday life: The uses of experience sampling. *Journal of Happiness Studies, 4,* 185–199.

Csikszentmihalyi, M., & Larson, R. (1984). *Being adolescent: Conflict and growth in the teenage years.* New York: Basic Books.

Cunningham, M. R., Roberts, A. R., Barbee, A. P., Druen, P. B., & Wu, C. H. (1995). "Their ideas of beauty are, on the whole, the same as ours": Consistency and variability in the cross-cultural perception of female physical attractiveness. *Journal of Personality and Social Psychology, 68,* 261–279.

Cunningham, W. A., Johnson, M. K., Raye, C. L., Gatenby, J. C., Gore, J. C., & Banaji, M. R. (2004). Separable neural components in the processing of Black and White faces. *Psychological Science, 15,* 806–813.

Curtis, G. C., Magee, W. J., Eaton, W. W., Wittchen, H-U., & Kessler, R. C. (1998). Specific fears and phobias: Epidemiology and classification. *British Journal of Psychiatry, 173,* 212–217.

Curtis, R. C., & Miller, K. (1986). Believing another likes or dislikes you: Behaviors making the beliefs come true. *Journal of Personality and Social Psychology, 51,* 284–290.

Cutler, B. L., & Penrod, S. D. (1989). Forensically relevant moderators of the relation between eyewitness identification accuracy and confidence. *Journal of Applied Psychology, 74,* 650–652.

Czeisler, C. A., Allan, J. S., Strogatz, S. H., Ronda, J. M., Sanchez, R., Rios, C. D., Freitag, W. O., Richardson, G. S., & Kronauer, R. E. (1986). Bright light resets the human circadian pacemaker independent of the timing of the sleep-wake cycle. *Science, 233,* 667–671.

Czeisler, C. A., Duffy, J. F., Shanahan, T. L., Brown, E. N., Mitchell, J. F., Rimmer, D. W., Ronda, J. M., Silva, E. J., Allan, J. S., Emens, J. S., Dijk, D-J., & Kronauer, R. E. (1999). Stability, precision, and near-24-hour period of the human circadian pacemaker. *Science, 284,* 2177–2181.

Czeisler, C. A., Kronauer, R. E., Allan, J. S., & Duffy, J. F. (1989). Bright light induction of strong (type O) resetting of the human circadian pacemaker. *Science, 244,* 1328–1333.

Dabbs, J. M., Jr. (2000). Heroes, rogues, and lovers: Testosterone and behavior. New York: McGraw-Hill.

Dabbs, J. M., Jr., Bernieri, F. J., Strong, R. K., Campo, R., & Milun, R. (2001b). Going on stage: Testosterone in greetings and meetings. *Journal of Research in Personality, 35,* 27–40.

Dabbs, J. M., Jr., & Morris, R. (1990). Testosterone, social class, and antisocial behavior in a sample of 4,462 men. *Psychological Science, 1,* 209–211.

Dabbs, J. M., Jr., Riad, J. K., & Chance, S. E. (2001a). Testosterone and ruthless homicide. *Personality and Individual Differences, 31,* 599–603.

Dabbs, J. M., Jr., Ruback, R. B., & Besch, N. F. (1987). Male saliva testosterone following conversations with male and female partners. Paper presented at the American Psychological Association convention.

Daley, T. C., Whaley, S. E., Sigman, M. D., Espinosa, M. P., & Neumann, C. (2003). IQ on the rise: The Flynn effect in rural Kenyan children. *Psychological Science, 14,* 215–219.

Dalton, M. A., Ahrens, M. B., Sargent, J. D., Mott, L. A., Beach, M. L., Tickle, J. J., & Heatherton, T. F. (2002). Relation between parental restrictions on movies and adolescent use of tobacco and alcohol. *Effective Clinical Practice, 5,* 1–9.

Damasio, A. (2003). *Looking for Spinoza: Joy, sorrow, and the feeling brain.* New York: Harcourt.

Damasio, A. R. (1994). *Descartes' error: Emotion, reason, and the human brain.* New York: Grossett/Putnam & Sons.

Damasio, H., Grabowski, T., Frank, R., Galaburda, A. M., & Damasio, A. R. (1994). The return of Phineas Gage: Clues about the brain from the skull of a famous patient. *Science, 264,* 1102–1105.

Damon, W. (1995). *Greater expectations: Overcoming the culture of indulgence in America's homes and schools.* New York: Free Press.

Damon, W., & Hart, D. (1982). The development of self-understanding from infancy through adolescence. *Child Development, 53,* 841–864.

Damon, W., & Hart, D. (1988). *Self-understanding in childhood and adolescence.* Cambridge: Cambridge University Press.

Damon, W., Menon, J., & Bronk, K. (2003). The development of purpose during adolescence. *Applied Developmental Science, 7,* 119–128.

Dannenberg, A. L., Burton, D., & Jackson, R. J. (2004). Economic and environmental costs of obesity: The impact on airlines. *American Journal of Preventive Medicine, 27,* 264.

Danner, D. D., Snowdon, D. A., & Friesen, W. V. (2001). Positive emotions in early life and longevity: Findings from the Nun Study. *Journal of Personality and Social Psychology, 80*, 804–813.

Danso, H., & Esses, V. (2001). Black experimenters and the intellectual test performance of white participants: The tables are turned. *Journal of Experimental Social Psychology, 37*, 158–165.

Darley, J. M., & Latané, B. (1968a). Bystander intervention in emergencies: Diffusion of responsibility. *Journal of Personality and Social Psychology, 8*, 377–383.

Darley, J. M., & Latané, B. (1968b, December). When will people help in a crisis? *Psychology Today*, pp. 54–57, 70–71.

Darley, J. M., Seligman, C., & Becker, L. J. (1979, April). The lesson of twin rivers: Feedback works. *Psychology Today*, pp. 16, 23–24.

Darrach, B., & Norris, J. (1984, August). An American tragedy. *Life*, pp. 58–74.

Daum, I., & Schugens, M. M. (1996). On the cerebellum and classical conditioning. *Psychological Science, 5*, 58–61.

Dauvilliers, Y., Carlander, B., Moinari, N., Desautels, A., Okun, M., Tafti, M., Montplaisir, J., Mignot, E., & Billard, M. (2003). Month of birth as a risk factor for narcolepsy. *Sleep, 26*, 663–665.

Davey, G. C. L. (1992). Classical conditioning and the acquisition of human fears and phobias: A review and synthesis of the literature. *Advances in Behavior Research and Therapy, 14*, 29–66.

Davey, G. C. L. (1995). Preparedness and phobias: Specific evolved associations or a generalized expectancy bias? *Behavioral and Brain Sciences, 18*, 289–297.

Davidoff, J. (2004). Coloured thinking. *The Psychologist, 17*, 570–572.

Davidson, R. (2000). Affective style, psychopathology, and resilience: Brain mechanisms and plasticity. *American Psychologist, 55*, 1196–1209.

Davidson, R. J. (2003). Affective neuroscience and psychophysiology: Toward a synthesis. *Psychophysiology, 40*, 655–665.

Davidson, R. J., Kabat-Zinn, J., Schumacher, J., Rosenkranz, M., Muller, D., Santorelli, S. F., Urbanowski, F., Harrington, A., Bonus, K., & Sheridan, J. F. (2003). Alterations in brain and immune function produced by mindfulness meditation. *Psychosomatic Medicine, 65*, 564–570.

Davidson, R. J., Pizzagalli, D., Nitschke, J. B., & Putnam, K. (2002). Depression: Perspectives from affective neuroscience. *Annual Review of Psychology, 53*, 545–574.

Davidson, R. J., Putnam, K. M., & Larson, C. L. (2000). Dysfunction in the neural circuitry of emotion regulation—a possible prelude to violence. *Science, 289*, 591–594.

Davies, D. R., Matthews, G., & Wong, C. S. K. (1991). Aging and work. *International Review of Industrial and Organizational Psychology, 6*, 149–211.

Davies, M. F. (1997). Positive test strategies and confirmatory retrieval processes in the evaluation of personality feedback. *Journal of Personality and Social Psychology, 73*, 574–583.

Davies, P. (1992). *The mind of God: The scientific basis for a rational world.* New York: Simon & Schuster.

Davies, P. (1999). *The fifth miracle: The search for the origin and meaning of life.* New York: Simon & Schuster.

Davies, P. (2004, April 14). Into the 21st century. *Metaviews* (www.metanexus.net).

Davis, B. E., Moon, R. Y., Sachs, H. C., & Ottolini, M. C. (1998). Effects of sleep position on infant motor development. *Pediatrics, 102*, 1135–1140.

Davis, J. O., & Phelps, J. A. (1995a). Twins with schizophrenia: Genes or germs? *Schizophrenia Bulletin, 21*, 13–18.

Davis, J. O., Phelps, J. A., & Bracha, H. S. (1995b). Prenatal development of monozygotic twins and concordance for schizophrenia. *Schizophrenia Bulletin, 21*, 357–366.

Davis, S., Rees, M., Ribot, J., Moufarege, A., Rodenberg, C., & Purdie, D. (2003). Efficacy and safety of testosterone patches for the treatment of low sexual desire in surgically menopausal women. Presented to the American Society for Reproductive Medicine, San Antonio, October 11–15.

Davison, K. P., Pennebaker, J. W., & Dickerson, S. S. (2000). Who talks? The social psychology of illness support groups. *American Psychologist, 55*, 205–217.

Dawes, R. M. (1980). Social dilemmas. *Annual Review of Psychology, 31*, 169–193.

Dawes, R. M. (1994). *House of cards: Psychology and psychotherapy built on myth.* New York: Free Press.

Dawkins, R. (1998). *Unweaving the rainbow.* Boston: Houghton Mifflin.

Dawkins, R. (1999, April 8). Is science killing the soul (a discussion with Richard Dawkins and Steven Pinker). www.edge.org

Dawkins, R. (2004). edge.org.

Dawson, N. V., Arkes, H. R., Siciliano, C., Blinkhorn, R., Lakshmanan, M., & Petrelli, M. (1988). Hindsight bias: An impediment to accurate probability estimation in clinicopathologic conferences. *Medical Decision Making, 8*, 259–264.

Deacon, B. J., & Abramowitz, J. S. (2004). Cognitive and behavioral treatments for anxiety disorders: A review of meta-analytic findings. *Journal of Clinical Psychology, 60*, 429–441.

Dean, G. A., Kelly, I. W., Saklofske, D. H., & Furnham, A. (1992). Graphology and human judgment. In B. Beyerstein & D. Beyerstein (Eds.), *The write stuff: Evaluations of graphology.* Buffalo, NY: Prometheus Books.

Deary, I. J., & Caryl, P. G. (1993). Intelligence, EEG and evoked potentials. In P. A. Vernon (Ed.), *Biological approaches to the study of human intelligence.* Norwood, NJ: Ablex.

Deary, I. J., & Der, G. (2005). Reaction time explains IQ's association with death. *Psychological Science, 16*, 64–69.

Deary, I. J., & Matthews, G. (1993). Personality traits are alive and well. *The Psychologist: Bulletin of the British Psychological Society, 6*, 299–311.

Deary, I. J., & Stough, C. (1997). Looking down on human intelligence. *American Psychologist, 52*, 1148–1149.

Deary, I. J., Thorpe, G., Wilson, V., Starr, J. M., & Whalley, L. J. (2003). Population sex differences in IQ at age 11: The Scottish mental survey 1932. *Intelligence, 31*, 533–541.

Deary, I. J., Whiteman, M. C., Starr, J. M., Whalley, L. J., & Fox, H. C. (2004). The impact of childhood intelligence on later life: Following up the Scottish mental surveys of 1932 and 1947. *Journal of Personality and Social Psychology, 86*, 130–147.

de Beyer, J. (1999). Why is tobacco control a public health priority around the world? Washington, DC: World Bank.

de Beyer, J. (2005, February 4). Tobacco: How trade policy affects health. Annual Conference: Health in Foreign Policy. Panel II: Global Commerce and Health.

de Boysson-Bardies, B., Halle, P., Sagart, L., & Durand, C. (1989). A cross linguistic investigation of vowel formats in babbling. *Journal of Child Language, 16*, 1–17.

DeBruine, L. M. (2002). Facial resemblance enhances trust. *Proceedings of the Royal Society of London, 269*, 1307–1312.

DeBruine, L. M. (2004). Facial resemblance increases the attractiveness of same-sex faces more than other-sex faces. *Proceedings of the Royal Society of London B, 271*, 2085–2090.

DeCasper, A. J., Lecanuet, J-P., Busnel, M-C., & others. (1994). Fetal reactions to recurrent maternal speech. *Infant Behavior and Development, 17*, 159–164.

DeCasper, A. J., & Prescott, P. A. (1984). Human newborns' perception of male voices: Preference, discrimination and reinforcing value. *Developmental Psychobiology, 17*, 481–491.

DeCasper, A. J., & Spence, M. J. (1986). Prenatal maternal speech influences newborns' perception of speech sounds. *Infant Behavior and Development, 9,* 133–150.

Deci, E. L., Koestner, R., & Ryan, R. M. (1999, November). A meta-analytic review of experiments examining the effects of extrinsic rewards on intrinsic motivation. *Psychological Bulletin, 125(6),* 627–668.

Deci, E. L., & Ryan, R. M. (1985). *Intrinsic motivation and self-determination in human behavior.* New York: Plenum Press.

Deci, E. L., & Ryan, R. M. (1992). The initiation and regulation of intrinsically motivated learning and achievement. In A. K. Boggiano & T. S. Pittman (Eds.), *Achievement and motivation: A social-developmental perspective.* New York: Cambridge University Press.

Deci, E. L., & Ryan, R. M. (2000). The "what" and "why" of goal pursuits: Human needs and the self-determination of behavior. *Psychological Inquiry, 11,* 227–268.

de Courten-Myers, G. (2005, February 4). Personal correspondence (estimating total brain neurons, extrapolating from her carefully estimated 20 to 23 billion cortical neurons).

de Courten-Myers, G. M. (2002, May 9). Personal correspondence.

de Cuevas, J. (1990, September–October). "No, she holded them loosely." *Harvard Magazine,* pp. 60–67.

de Hoogh, A. H. B., den Hartog, D. N., Koopman, P. L., Thierry, H., van den Berg, P. T., van der Weide, J. G., & Wilderom, C. P. M. (2004). Charismatic leadership, environmental dynamism, and performance. *European Journal of Work and Organisational Psychology, 13,* 447–471.

De Houwer, J., Thomas, S., & Baeyens, F. (2001). Associative learning of likes and dislikes: A review of 25 years of research on human evaluative conditioning. *Psychological Bulletin, 127,* 853–869.

De Koninck, J. (2000). Waking experiences and dreaming. In M. Kryger, T. Roth, & W. Dement (Eds.), *Principles and practice of sleep medicine, 3rd ed.* Philadelphia: Saunders.

Delaney, P. F., Ericsson, K. A., Weaver, G. E., & Mahadevan, S. (1999). Accounts of the memorist Rajan's exceptional performance: Comparing three theoretical proposals. Paper presented to the American Psychological Society convention.

Delgado, J. M. R. (1969). *Physical control of the mind: Toward a psychocivilized society.* New York: Harper & Row.

DeLoache, J. S. (1995). Early understanding and use of symbols: The model model. *Current Directions in Psychological Science, 4,* 109–113.

DeLoache, J. S., & Brown, A. L. (1987, October–December). Differences in the memory-based searching of delayed and normally developing young children. *Intelligence, 11(4),* 277–289.

DeLoache, J. S., Uttal, D. H., & Rosengren, K. S. (2004). Scale errors offer evidence for a perception-action dissociation early in life. *Science, 304,* 1027–1029.

Dement, W. (1997, September). What all undergraduates should know about how their sleeping lives affect their waking lives. Stanford University: www.leland.stanford.edu/~dement/sleepless.html

Dement, W. C. (1978). *Some must watch while some must sleep.* New York: Norton.

Dement, W. C. (1999). *The promise of sleep.* New York: Delacorte Press.

Dement, W. C., & Wolpert, E. A. (1958). The relation of eye movements, body mobility, and external stimuli to dream content. *Journal of Experimental Psychology, 55,* 543–553.

Demir, E., & Dickson, B. J. (2005). *Fruitless* splicing specifies male courtship behavior in *Drosophila. Cell, 121,* 785–794.

Dempster, F. N. (1988). The spacing effect: A case study in the failure to apply the results of psychological research. *American Psychologist, 43,* 627–634.

Denes-Raj, V., Epstein, S., & Cole, J. (1995). The generality of the ratio-bias phenomenon. *Personality and Social Psychology Bulletin, 21,* 1083–1092.

DeNeve, K. M., & Cooper, H. (1998). The happy personality: A meta-analysis of 137 personality traits and subjective well-being. *Psychological Bulletin, 124,* 197–229.

Dennerstein, L., Dudley, E., Guthrie, J., & Barrett-Connor, E. (2000). Life satisfaction, symptoms, and the menopausal transition. *Medscape Women's Health, 5(4)* (www.medscape.com).

Dennett, D. (1996, September 9). Quoted by Ian Parker, Richard Dawkins' evolution. *The New Yorker,* pp. 41–45.

Denton, K., & Krebs, D. (1990). From the scene to the crime: The effect of alcohol and social context on moral judgment. *Journal of Personality and Social Psychology, 59,* 242–248.

D'Eon, J. L. (1989). Hypnosis in the control of labor pain. In N. P. Spanos & J. F. Chaves (Eds.), *Hypnosis: The cognitive-behavioral perspective.* Buffalo, NY: Prometheus Books.

DePaulo, B. M. (1994). Spotting lies: Can humans learn to do better? *Current Directions in Psychological Science 3,* 83–86.

DePaulo, B. M., Blank, A. L., Swaim, G. W., & Hairfield, J. G. (1992). Expressiveness and expressive control. *Personality and Social Psychology Bulletin, 18,* 276–285.

De Quervain, D. J.-F., Roozendaal, B., & McGaugh, J. L. (1998). Stress and glucocorticoids impair retrieval of long-term spatial memory. *Nature, 394,* 787–790.

Deregowski, J. (1972, November). Pictorial perception and culture. *Scientific American,* pp. 82–88.

Dermer, M., Cohen, S. J., Jacobsen, E., & Anderson, E. A. (1979). Evaluative judgments of aspects of life as a function of vicarious exposure to hedonic extremes. *Journal of Personality and Social Psychology, 37,* 247–260.

Dermer, M., & Pyszczynski, T. A. (1978). Effects of erotica upon men's loving and liking responses for women they love. *Journal of Personality and Social Psychology, 36,* 1302–1309.

Deroche-Garmonet, V., Belin, D., & Piazza, P. V. (2004). Evidence for addiction-like behavior in the rat. *Science, 305,* 1014–1017.

DeRubeis, R. J., & 10 others. (2005). Cognitive therapy vs. medications in the treatment of moderate to severe depression. *Archives of General Psychiatry, 62,* 409–416.

DeSteno, D., Dasgupta, N., Bartlett, M. Y., & Cajdric, A. (2004). Prejudice from thin air: The effect of emotion on automatic intergroup attitudes. *Psychological Science, 15,* 319–324.

DeSteno, D., Petty, R. E., Wegener, D. T., & Rucker, D. D. (2000). Beyond valence in the perception of likelihood: The role of emotion specificity. *Journal of Personality and Social Psychology, 78,* 397–416.

Deutsch, J. A. (1972, July). Brain reward: ESP and ecstasy. *Psychology Today,* 46–48.

Deutsch, M. (1991). Egalitarianism in the laboratory and at work. In R. Vermunt & H. Steensma (Eds.), *Social justice in human relations.* New York: Plenum.

DeValois, R. L., & DeValois, K. K. (1975). Neural coding of color. In E. C. Carterette & M. P. Friedman (Eds.), *Handbook of perception: Vol. V. Seeing.* New York: Academic Press.

Devilly, G. J. (2003). Eye movement desensitization and reprocessing: A chronology of its development and scientific standing. *Scientific Review of Mental Health Practice, 1,* 113–118.

Devine, P. G. (1995). Prejudice and outgroup perception. In A. Tesser (Ed.), *Advanced social psychology.* New York: McGraw-Hill.

Devlin, B., Daniels, M., & Roeder, K. (1997). The heritability of IQ. *Nature, 388,* 468–471.

Dew, M. A., Hoch, C. C., Buysse, D. J., Monk, T. H., Begley, A. E., Houck, P. R., Hall, M., Kupfer, D. J., Reynolds, C. F., III (2003). Healthy older adults' sleep predicts all-cause mortality at 4 to 19 years of follow-up. *Psychosomatic Medicine, 65,* 63–73.

de Waal, F. B. M. (1999, December). The end of nature versus nurture. *Scientific American,* pp. 94–99.

de Waal, F. B. M., Dindo, M., Freeman, C. A., & Hall, M. J. (2005). The monkey in the mirror: Hardly a stranger. *Proceedings of the National Academy of Sciences, 102,* 11140–11147.

de Waal, F. B. M., & Johanowicz, D. L. (1993). Modification of reconciliation behavior through social experience: An experiment with two macaque species. *Child Development, 64,* 897–908.

De Wolff, M. S., & van IJzendoorn, M. H. (1997). Sensitivity and attachment: A meta-analysis on parental antecedents of infant attachment. *Child Development, 68,* 571–591.

Dey, E. L., Astin, A. W., & Korn, W. S. (1991). *The American freshman: Twenty-five year trends.* Los Angeles: Higher Education Research Institute, UCLA.

Dhawan, N., Roseman, I. J., Naidu, R. K., Thapa, K., & Rettek, S. I. (1995). Self-concepts across two cultures: India and the United States. *Journal of Cross-Cultural Psychology, 26,* 606–621.

Diaconis, P. (2002, August 11). Quoted by L. Belkin, The odds of that. *New York Times* (www.nytimes.com).

Diaconis, P., & Mosteller, F. (1989). Methods for studying coincidences. *Journal of the American Statistical Association, 84,* 853–861.

Diamond, J. (1989, May). The great leap forward. *Discover,* pp. 50–60.

Diamond, J. (2001, February). A tale of two reputations: Why we revere Darwin and give Freud a hard time. *Natural History,* pp. 20–24.

Diamond, L. M. (2000). Sexual identity, attractions, and behavior among young sexual-minority women over a 2-year period. *Developmental Psychology, 36,* 241–250.

Diamond, L. M. (2003). Was it a phase? Young women's relinquishment of lesbian/bisexual identities over a 5-year period. *Journal of Personality and Social Psychology, 84,* 352–364.

Diamond, R. (1993). Genetics and male sexual orientation (letter). *Science, 261,* 1258.

Dickerson, S. S., & Kemeny, M. E. (2004). Acute stressors and cortisol responses: A theoretical integration and synthesis of laboratory research. *Psychological Bulletin, 130,* 355–391.

Dickson, B. (2005, June 3). Quoted in E. Rosenthal, For fruit flies, gene shift tilts sex orientation. *New York Times* (www.nytimes.com).

Diener, E., & Biswas-Diener, R. (2002). Will money increase subjective well-being? A literature review and guide to needed research. *Social Indicators Research, 57,* 119–169.

Diener, E., Diener, M., & Diener, C. (1995). Factors predicting the subjective well-being of nations. *Journal of Personality and Social Psychology, 69,* 851–864.

Diener, E., Emmons, R. A., & Sandvik, E. (1986). The dual nature of happiness: Independence of positive and negative moods. Unpublished manuscript, University of Illinois.

Diener, E., & Oishi, S. (2000). Money and happiness: Income and subjective well-being across nations. In E. Diener & E. M. Suh (Eds.), *Subjective well-being across cultures.* Cambridge, MA: MIT Press.

Diener, E., Oishi, S., & Lucas, R. E. (2003). Personality, culture, and subjective well-being: Emotional and cognitive evaluations of life. *Annual Review of Psychology, 54,* 403–425.

Diener, E., & Seligman, M. E. P. (2002). Very happy people. *Psychological Science, 13,* 81–84.

Diener, E., & Seligman, M. E. P. (2004). Beyond money: Toward an economy of well-being. *Psychological Science in the Public Interest, 5,* 1–31.

Diener, E., Wirtz, D., & Oishi, S. (2001). End effects of rated life quality: The James Dean effect. *Psychological Science, 12,* 124–128.

Diener, E., Wolsic, B., & Fujita, F. (1995). Physical attractiveness and subjective well-being. *Journal of Personality and Social Psychology, 69,* 120–129.

Diener, M. L., & Lucas, R. E. (2004). Adults' desires for children's emotions across 48 countries: Associations with individual and national characteristics. *Journal of Cross-Cultural Psychology, 35,* 525–547.

Dietz, W. H., Jr., & Gortmaker, S. L. (1985). Do we fatten our children at the television set? Obesity and television viewing in children and adolescents. *Pediatrics, 75,* 807–812.

Dijksterhuis, A., & Aarts, H. (2003). On wildebeests and humans: The preferential detection of negative stimuli. *Psychological Science, 14,* 14–18.

DiLalla, D. L., Carey, G., Gottesman, I. I., & Bouchard, T. J., Jr. (1996). Heritability of MMPI personality indicators of psychopathology in twins reared apart. *Journal of Abnormal Psychology, 105,* 491–499.

Dimberg, U., Thunberg, M., & Elmehed, K. (2000). Unconscious facial reactions to emotional facial expressions. *Psychological Science, 11,* 86–89.

Dimberg, U., Thunberg, M., & Grunedal, S. (2002). Facial reactions to emotional stimuli: Automatically controlled emotional responses. *Cognition and Emotion, 16,* 449–472.

Dindia, K., & Allen, M. (1992). Sex differences in self-disclosure: A meta-analysis. *Psychological Bulletin, 112,* 106–124.

Dinges, N. G., & Hull, P. (1992). Personality, culture, and international studies. In D. Lieberman (Ed.), *Revealing the world: An interdisciplinary reader for international studies.* Dubuque, IA: Kendall-Hunt.

Dion, K. K., & Dion, K. L. (1993). Individualistic and collectivistic perspectives on gender and the cultural context of love and intimacy. *Journal of Social Issues, 49,* 53–69.

Dion, K. K., & Dion, K. L. (2001). Gender and cultural adaptation in immigrant families. *Journal of Social Issues, 57,* 511–521.

DiPietro, J. A. (2004). The role of prenatal maternal stress in child development. *Current Directions in Psychological Science, 13,* 71–74.

Discover (1996, May). A fistful of risks. Pp. 82–83.

Dishion, T. J., McCord, J., & Poulin, F. (1999). When interventions harm: Peer groups and problem behavior. *American Psychologist, 54,* 755–764.

Di Tella, R., MacCulloch, R. J., & Oswald, A. J. (2001). The macroeconomics of happiness. Warwick Economic Research Paper No. 615, Department of Economics, University of Warwick.

Doherty, E. W., & Doherty, W. J. (1998). Smoke gets in your eyes: Cigarette smoking and divorce in a national sample of American adults. *Families, Systems, and Health, 16,* 393–400.

Dohrenwend, B. P., Levav, I., Shrout, P. E., Schwartz, S., Naveh, G., Link, B. G., Skodol, A. E., & Stueve, A. (1992). Socioeconomic status and psychiatric disorders: The causation-selection issue. *Science, 255,* 946–952.

Dohrenwend, B., Pearlin, L., Clayton, P., Hamburg, B., Dohrenwend, B. P., Riley, M., & Rose, R. (1982). Report on stress and life events. In G. R. Elliott & C. Eisdorfer (Eds.), *Stress and human health: Analysis and implications of research* (A study by the Institute of Medicine/National Academy of Sciences). New York: Springer.

Dolan, R. J. (1999). On the neurology of morals. *Nature Neuroscience, 2,* 927–929.

Dolcos, F., LaBar, K. S., & Cabeza, R. (2004). Interaction between the amygdala and the medial temporal lobe memory system predicts better memory for emotional events. *Neuron, 42,* 855–863.

Dole, R. (1996, April 20). Quoted by M. Duffy, Look who's talking. *Time,* p. 48.

Dolezal, H. (1982). *Living in a world transformed.* New York: Academic Press.

Domhoff, G. W. (1996). *Finding meaning in dreams: A quantitative approach.* New York: Plenum.

Domhoff, G. W. (1999). New directions in the study of dream content using the Hall and Van de Castle coding system. *Dreaming, 9,* 115–137.

Domhoff, G. W. (2000). Moving dream theory beyond Freud and Jung. Paper presented to the symposium "Beyond Freud and Jung?" Graduate Theological Union, Berkeley, CA, 9/23/2000.

Domhoff, G. W. (2003). *The scientific study of dreams: Neural networks, cognitive development, and content analysis.* Washington, DC: APA Books.

Domjan, M. (1992). Adult learning and mate choice: Possibilities and experimental evidence. *American Zoologist, 32,* 48–61.

Domjan, M. (1994). Formulation of a behavior system for sexual conditioning. *Psychonomic Bulletin & Review, 1,* 421–428.

Domjan, M. (2005). Pavlovian conditioning: A functional perspective. *Annual Review of Psychology, 56.*

Domjan, M., Blesbois, E., & Williams, J. (1998). The adaptive significance of sexual conditioning: Pavlovian control of sperm release. *Psychological Science, 9,* 411–415.

Domjan, M., Cusato, B., & Krause, M. (2004). Learning with arbitrary versus ecological conditioned stimuli: Evidence from sexual conditioning. *Psychonomic Bulletin & Review, 11,* 232–246.

Donahoe, J. W., & Vegas, R. (2004). Pavlovian conditioning: The CS-UR relation. *Journal of Experimental Psychology: Animal Behavior, 30,* 17–33.

Donnellan, M. B., Conger, R. D., & Bryant, C. M. (2004). The Big Five and enduring marriages. *Journal of Research in Personality, 38,* 481–504.

Donnellan, M. B., Trzesniewski, K. H., Robins, R. W., Moffitt, T. E., & Caspi, A. (2005). Low self-esteem is related to aggression, antisocial behavior, and delinquency. *Psychological Science, 16,* 328–335.

Donnerstein, E. (1998). Why do we have those new ratings on television? Invited address to the National Institute on the Teaching of Psychology.

Donnerstein, E., Linz, D., & Penrod, S. (1987). *The question of pornography.* New York: Free Press.

Dorman, M. F., & Wilson, B. S. (2004). The design and function of cochlear implants. *American Scientist, 92,* 436–445.

Dorner, G. (1976). *Hormones and brain differentiation.* Amsterdam: Elsevier Scientific.

Dorner, G. (1988). Neuroendocrine response to estrogen and brain differentiation in heterosexuals, homosexuals, and transsexuals. *Archives of Sexual Behavior, 17,* 57–75.

Dorozyaski, A. (1993, January/February). Maternal alcoholism: Grapes of wrath. *Psychology Today,* p. 18.

Dorris, M. (1989). *The Broken Cord.* New York: HarperCollins.

Doty, R. L. (2001). Olfaction. *Annual Review of Psychology, 52,* 423–452.

Doty, R. L., Shaman, P., Applebaum, S. L., Giberson, R., Siksorski, L., & Rosenberg, L. (1984). Smell identification ability: Changes with age. *Science, 226,* 1441–1443.

Doty, R. W. (1998). The five mysteries of the mind, and their consequences. *Neuropsychologia, 36,* 1069–1076.

Dovidio, J. F., & Gaertner, S. L. (1999). Reducing prejudice: Combating intergroup biases. *Current Directions in Psychological Science, 8,* 101–105.

Dovidio, J. F., ten Vergert, M., Stewart, T. L., Gaertner, S. L., Johnson, J. D., Esses, V. M., Riek, B. M., & Pearson, A. R. (2004). Perspective and prejudice: Antecedents and mediating mechanisms. *Personality and Social Psychology Bulletin, 30,* 1537–1549.

Downing, P. E., Jiang, Y., & Shuman, M. (2001). A cortical area selective for visual processing of the human body. *Science, 293,* 2470–2473.

Doyle, R. (2005, March). Gay and lesbian census. *Scientific American,* p. 28.

Draguns, J. G. (1990a). Normal and abnormal behavior in cross-cultural perspective: Specifying the nature of their relationship. *Nebraska Symposium on Motivation 1989, 37,* 235–277.

Draguns, J. G. (1990b). Applications of cross-cultural psychology in the field of mental health. In R. W. Brislin (Ed.), *Applied cross-cultural psychology.* Newbury Park, CA: Sage.

Draguns, J. G. (1997). Abnormal behavior patterns across cultures: Implications for counseling and psychotherapy. *International Journal of Intercultural Relations, 21,* 213–248.

Druckman, D., & Bjork, R. A. (1991). *In the mind's eye: Enhancing human performance.* National Academy Press: Washington, DC.

Druckman, D., & Bjork, R. A. (Eds.) (1994). *Learning, remembering, believing: Enhancing human performance.* Washington, DC: National Academy Press.

Duckworth, A. L., & Seligman, M. E. P. (2005). Discipline outdoes talent: Self-discipline predicts academic performance in adolescents. *Psychological Science, 12,* 939–944.

Duclos, S. E., Laird, J. D., Sexter, M., Stern, L., & Van Lighten, O. (1989). Emotion-specific effects of facial expressions and postures on emotional experience. *Journal of Personality and Social Psychology, 57,* 100–108.

Duenwald, M. (2004, October 26). The dorms may be great, but how's the counseling? *New York Times* (www.nytimes.com).

Duffy, M. (2003, June 9). Weapons of mass disappearance. *Time,* pp. 28–33.

Dugatkin, L. A. (2002, Winter). Watching culture shape even guppy love. *Cerebrum,* pp. 51–66.

Duggan, J. P., & Booth, D. A. (1986). Obesity, overeating, and rapid gastric emptying in rats with ventromedial hypothalamic lesions. *Science, 231,* 609–611.

Dugger, C. W. (2005, January 18). U.N. proposes doubling of aid to cut poverty. *New York Times* (www.nytimes.com).

Duncan, B. L. (1976). Differential social perception and attribution of intergroup violence: Testing the lower limits of stereotyping of blacks. *Journal of Personality and Social Psychology, 34,* 590–598.

Duncan, G. J., Hill, M. S., & Hoffman, S. D. (1988). Welfare dependence within and across generations. *Science, 239,* 467–471.

Duncan, J. (2000, July 21). Quoted by N. Angier, Study finds region of brain may be key problem solver. *New York Times* (www.nytimes.com).

Duncan, J., Seitz, R. J., Kolodny, J., Bor, D., Herzog, H., Ahmed, A., Newell, F. N., & Emslie, H. (2000). A neural basis of general intelligence. *Science, 289,* 457–460.

Duncker, K. (1945). On problem solving. *Psychological Monographs, 58* (Whole no. 270).

Dunn, A. L., Trivedi, M. H., Kampert, J. B., Clark, C. G., & Chambliss, H. O. (2005). Exercise treatment for depression: Efficacy and dose response. *American Journal of Preventive Medicine, 28,* 1–8.

Dunson, D. B., Colombo, B., & Baird, D. D. (2002). Changes with age in the level and duration of fertility in the menstrual cycle. *Human Reproduction, 17,* 1399–1403.

Durston, S., Hulshoff, P., Hilleke, E., Casey, B. J., Giedd, J. N., Buitelaar, J. K., & van Engeland, H. (2001). Anatomical MRI of the developing human brain: What have we learned? *Journal of the American Academy of Child and Adolescent Psychiatry, 40,* 1012–1020.

Dush, C. M. K, Cohan, C. L., & Amato, P. R. (2003). The relationship between cohabitation and marital quality and stability: Change across cohorts? *Journal of Marriage and Family, 65,* 539–549.

Dutton, D. G., & Aron, A. (1989). Romantic attraction and generalized liking for others who are sources of conflict-based arousal. *Canadian Journal of Behavioural Sciences, 21,* 246–257.

Dutton, D. G., & Aron, A. P. (1974). Some evidence for heightened sexual attraction under conditions of high anxiety. *Journal of Personality and Social Psychology, 30,* 510–517.

Dye, D. A., & Reck, M. (1989). College grade point average as a predictor of adult success: A reply. *Public Personnel Management, 18,* 235–241.

Eagly, A. (1994). Are people prejudiced against women? Donald Campbell Award invited address, American Psychological Association convention.

Eagly, A. H., Ashmore, R. D., Makhijani, M. G., & Kennedy, L. C. (1991). What is beautiful is good, but . . .: A meta-analytic review of research on the physical attractiveness stereotype. *Psychological Bulletin, 110,* 109–128.

Eagly, A. H., & Crowley, M. (1986). Gender and helping behavior: A meta-analytic review of the social psychological literature. *Psychological Bulletin, 100,* 283–308.

Eagly, A. H., & Johnson, B. T. (1990). Gender and leadership style: A meta-analysis. *Psychological Bulletin, 108,* 233–256.

Eagly, A. H., & Wood, W. (1999). The origins of sex differences in human behavior: Evolved dispositions versus social roles. *American Psychologist, 54,* 408–423.

Eastman, C. L., Boulos, Z., Terman, M., Campbell, S. S., Dijk, D-J., & Lewy, A. J. (1995). Light treatment for sleep disorders: Consensus report. VI. Shift work. *Journal of Biological Rhythms, 10,* 157–164.

Eastman, C. L., Young, M. A., Fogg, L. F., Liu, L., & Meaden, P. M. (1998). Bright light treatment of winter depression: A placebo-controlled trial. *Archives of General Psychiatry, 55,* 883–889.

Ebbesen, E. B., Duncan, B., & Konecni, V. J. (1975). Effects of content of verbal aggression on future verbal aggression: A field experiment. *Journal of Experimental Social Psychology, 11,* 192–204.

Ebbinghaus, H. (1885). *Über das Gedächtnis.* Leipzig: Duncker & Humblot. Cited in R. Klatzky (1980), *Human memory: Structures and processes.* San Francisco: Freeman.

Ebbinghaus, H. (1885/1964). *Memory: A contribution to experimental psychology* (tr. by H. A. Ruger & C. E. Bussenius). New York: Dover.

Eberhardt, J. L. (2005). Imaging race. *American Psychologist, 60,* 181–190.

Eberhardt, J. L., Goff, P. A., Purdie, V. J., & Davies, P. G. (2004). Seeing Black: Race, crime, and visual processing. *Journal of Personality and Social Psychology, 87,* 876–893.

Eccles, J. S., Jacobs, J. E., & Harold, R. D. (1990). Gender role stereotypes, expectancy effects, and parents' socialization of gender differences. *Journal of Social Issues, 46,* 183–201.

Eckensberger, L. H. (1994). Moral development and its measurement across cultures. In W. J. Lonner & R. Malpass (Eds.), *Psychology and culture.* Boston: Allyn and Bacon.

Eckersley, R. (2000). The mixed blessings of material progress: Diminishing returns in the pursuit of happiness. *Journal of Happiness Studies, 1,* 267–292.

Eckersley, R. (2001, March 23). Wealthier, but poorer for all that. *The Australian,* p. 13.

Eckersley, R., & Dear, K. (2002). Correlates of youth suicide. *Social Science and Medicine, 55,* 1891–1935.

Eckert, E. D., Heston, L. L., & Bouchard, T. J., Jr. (1981). MZ twins reared apart: Preliminary findings of psychiatric disturbances and traits. In L. Gedda, P. Paris, & W. D. Nance (Eds.), *Twin research: Vol. 3. Pt. B. Intelligence, personality, and development.* New York: Alan Liss.

Ecklund-Flores, L. (1992). The infant as a model for the teaching of introductory psychology. Paper presented to the American Psychological Association annual convention.

Economist. (2001, December 20). An anthropology of happiness. *The Economist* (www.economist.com/world/asia).

Economist. (2004, September 16). Supercharging the brain (www.economist.co.uk).

Edelman, S., & Kidman, A. D. (1997). Mind and cancer: Is there a relationship? A review of the evidence. *Australian Psychologist, 32,* 1–7.

Edison, T. A. (1948). *The diary and sundry observations of Thomas Alva Edison,* edited by D. D. Runes. New York: Philosophical Library. Cited by S. Coren (1996). *Sleep Thieves.* New York: Free Press.

Edwards, C. P. (1981). The comparative study of the development of moral judgment and reasoning. In R. H. Munroe, R. L. Munroe, & B. B. Whiting (Eds.), *Handbook of cross-cultural human development.* New York: Garland Press.

Edwards, C. P. (1982). Moral development in comparative cultural perspective. In D. A. Wagner & H. W. Stevenson (Eds.), *Cultural perspectives on child development.* San Francisco: Freeman.

Edwards, R., Peet, M., Shay, J., & Horrobin, D. (1998). Omega-3 polyunsaturated fatty acid levels in the diet and in red blood cell membranes of depressed patients. *Journal of Affective Disorders, 48,* 149–155.

Egan, M. F., & 16 others. (2004). Variation in *GRM3* affects cognition, prefrontal glutamate, and risk for schizophrenia. *Proceedings of the National Academy of Sciences, 101,* 12604–12609.

Ehrhardt, A. A. (1987). A transactional perspective on the development of gender differences. In J. M. Reinisch, L. A. Rosenblum, & S. A. Sanders (Eds.), *Masculinity/femininity: Basic perspectives.* New York: Oxford University Press.

Ehrlichman, H., & Halpern, J. N. (1988). Affect and memory: Effects of pleasant and unpleasant odors on retrieval of happy and unhappy memories. *Journal of Personality and Social Psychology, 55,* 769–779.

Eibl-Eibesfeldt, I. (1971). *Love and hate: The natural history of behavior patterns.* New York: Holt, Rinehart & Winston.

Eich, E. (1990). Learning during sleep. In R. B. Bootzin, J. F. Kihlstrom, & D. L. Schacter (Eds.), *Sleep and cognition.* Washington, DC: American Psychological Association.

Eich, E., Macaulay, D., Loewenstein, R. J., & Dihle, P. H. (1997). Memory, amnesia, and dissociative identity disorder. *Psychological Science, 8,* 417–422.

Einstein, G. O., & McDaniel, M. A. (1990). Normal aging and prospective memory. *Journal of Experimental Psychology: Learning, Memory, and Cognition, 16,* 717–726.

Einstein, G. O., McDaniel, M. A., Richardson, S. L., Guynn, M. J., & Cunfer, A. R. (1995). Aging and prospective memory: Examining the influences of self-initiated retrieval processes. *Journal of Experimental Psychology: Learning, Memory, and Cognition, 21,* 996–1007.

Einstein, G. O., McDaniel, M. A., Smith, R. E., & Shaw, P. (1998). Habitual prospective memory and aging: Remembering intentions and forgetting actions. *Psychological Science, 9,* 284–288.

Eisenberg, N., Cumberland A., & Spinrad, T. L. (1998a). Parental socialization of emotion. *Psychological Inquiry, 9,* 241–271.

Eisenberg, N., & Lennon, R. (1983). Sex differences in empathy and related capacities. *Psychological Bulletin, 94,* 100–131.

Eisenberg, N., Spinrad, T. L., & Cumberland, A. (1998b). The socialization of emotion: Reply to commentaries. *Psychological Inquiry, 9,* 317–333.

Eisenberger, N. I., Lieberman, M. D., & Williams, K. D. (2003). Does rejection hurt? An fMRI study of social exclusion. *Science, 302,* 290–292.

Eisenberger, R., & Rhoades, L. (2001). Incremental effects of reward on creativity. *Journal of Personality and Social Psychology, 81,* 728–741.

Eiser, J. R. (1985). Smoking: The social learning of an addiction. *Journal of Social and Clinical Psychology, 3,* 446–457.

Ekman, P. (1994). Strong evidence for universals in facial expressions: A reply to Russell's mistaken critique. *Psychological Bulletin, 115,* 268–287.

Ekman, P. (2003). *Emotions revealed: Recognizing faces and feelings to improve communication and emotional life.* New York: Times Books.

Ekman, P., Friesen, W. V., O'Sullivan, M., Chan, A., Diacoyanni-Tarlatzis, I., Heider, K., Krause, R., LeCompte, W. A., Pitcairn, T., Ricci-Bitti, P. E., Scherer, K., Tomita, M., & Tzavaras, A. (1987). Universals and cultural differences in the judgments of facial expressions of emotion. *Journal of Personality and Social Psychology, 53,* 712–717.

Ekman, P., & O'Sullivan, M. (1991). Who can catch a liar? *American Psychologist, 46,* 913–920.

Ekman, P., O'Sullivan, M. O., & Frank, M. G. (1999). A few can catch a liar. *Psychological Science, 10,* 263–266.

Elbert, T., Pantev, C., Wienbruch, C., Rockstroh, B., & Taub, E. (1995). Increased cortical representation of the fingers of the left hand in string players. *Science, 270,* 305–307.

Elfenbein, H. A., & Ambady, N. (1999). Does it take one to know one? A meta-analysis of the universality and cultural specificity of emotion recognition. Unpublished manuscript, Harvard University.

Elfenbein, H. A., & Ambady, N. (2002). On the universality and cultural specificity of emotion recognition: A meta-analysis. *Psychological Bulletin, 128,* 203–235.

Elfenbein, H. A., & Ambady, N. (2003a). When familiarity breeds accuracy: Cultural exposure and facial emotion recognition. *Journal of Personality and Social Psychology, 85,* 276–290.

Elfenbein, H. A., & Ambady, N. (2003b). Universals and cultural differences in recognizing emotions. *Current Directions in Psychological Science, 12,* 159–164.

Elkin, I., Shea, T., Watkins, J. T., Imber, S. D., Sotsky, S. M., Collins, J. F., Glass, D. R., Pilkonis, P. A., Leber, W. R., Docherty, J. P., Fiester, S. J., & Parloff, M. B. (1989). National Institute of Mental Health treatment of depression collaborative research program. *Archives of General Psychiatry, 46,* 971–983.

Elkind, D. (1970). The origins of religion in the child. *Review of Religious Research, 12,* 35–42.

Elkind, D. (1978). *The child's reality: Three developmental themes.* Hillsdale, NJ: Erlbaum.

Ellis, A. (1980). Psychotherapy and atheistic values: A response to A. E. Bergin's "Psychotherapy and religious values." *Journal of Consulting and Clinical Psychology, 48,* 635–639.

Ellis, A., & Becker, I. M. (1982). *A guide to personal happiness.* North Hollywood, CA: Wilshire Book Co.

Ellis, B. J. (2004). Timing of pubertal maturation in girls: An integrated life history approach. *Psychological Bulletin, 130,* 920–958.

Ellis, B. J., Bates, J. E., Dodge, K. A., Fergusson, D. M., John, H. L., Pettit, G. S., & Woodward, L. (2003). Does father absence place daughters at special risk for early sexual activity and teenage pregnancy? *Child Development, 74,* 801–821.

Ellis, L., & Ames, M. A. (1987). Neurohormonal functioning and sexual orientation: A theory of homosexuality-heterosexuality. *Psychological Bulletin, 101,* 233–258.

Emde, R. N., Plomin, R., Robinson, J., Corley, R., DeFries, J., Fulker, D. W., Reznick, J. S., Campos, J., Kagan, J., & Zahn-Waxler, C. (1992). Temperament, emotion, and cognition at fourteen months: The MacArthur Longitudinal Twin Study. *Child Development, 63,* 1437–1455.

EMDR. (2002, September 19). Description for professionals. (www.emdr.org).

Emerging Trends. (1997, September). Teens turn more to parents than friends on whether to attend church. Princeton, NJ: Princeton Religion Research Center, p. 5.

Emery, G. (2004). Psychic predictions 2004. Committee for the Scientific Investigation of Claims of the Paranormal (www.csicop.org).

Emery, N. J., & Clayton, N. S. (2004). The mentality of crows: Convergent evolution of intelligence in corvids and apes. *Science, 306,* 1903–1907.

Emmons, S., Geisler, C., Kaplan, K. J., & Harrow, M. (1997). *Living with schizophrenia.* Muncie, IN: Taylor and Francis (Accelerated Development).

Emmorey, K., Allen, J. S., Bruss, J., Schenker, N., & Damasio, H. (2003). A morphometric analysis of auditory brain regions in congenitally deaf adults. *Proceedings of the National Academy of Sciences, 100,* 10049–10054.

Empson, J. A. C., & Clarke, P. R. F. (1970). Rapid eye movements and remembering. *Nature, 227,* 287–288.

Emslie, C., Hunt, K., & Macintyre, S. (2001). Perceptions of body image among working men and women. *Journal of Epidemiology and Community Health, 55,* 406–407.

Endler, N. S. (1982). *Holiday of darkness: A psychologist's personal journey out of his depression.* New York: Wiley.

Endler, N. S., & Speer, R. L. (1998). Personality psychology: Research trends for 1993–1995. *Journal of Personality, 66,* 621–669.

Engemann, K. M., & Owyang, M. T. (2005, April). So much for that merit raise: The link between wages and appearance. *Regional Economist* (www.stlouisfed.org).

Engen, T. (1987). Remembering odors and their names. *American Scientist, 75,* 497–503.

Engle, R. W. (2002). Working memory capacity as executive attention. *Current Directions in Psychological Science, 11,* 19–23.

Epel, E. S., Blackburn, E. H., Lin, J., Dhabhar, F. S., Adler, N. E., Morrow, J. D., & Cawthon, R. M. (2004). Accelerated telomere shortening in response to life stress. *Proceedings of the National Academy of Sciences, 101,* 17312–17315.

Epley, N., & Dunning, D. (2000). Feeling "holier than thou": Are self-serving assessments produced by errors in self- or social prediction? *Journal of Personality and Social Psychology, 79,* 861–875.

Epley, N., Keysar, B., Van Boven, L., & Gilovich, T. (2004). Perspective taking as egocentric anchoring and adjustment. *Journal of Personality and Social Psychology, 87,* 327–339.

EPOCH. (2000). *Legal reforms: Corporal punishment of children in the family* (www.stophitting.com/laws/legalReform.php).

Epstein, J., Stern, E., & Silbersweig, D. (1998). Mesolimbic activity associated with psychosis in schizophrenia: Symptom-specific PET studies. In J. F. McGinty (Ed.), *Advancing from the ventral striatum to the extended amygdala: Implications for neuropsychiatry and drug use: In honor of Lennart Heimer. Annals of the New York Academy of Sciences, 877,* 562–574.

Epstein, S. (1983a). Aggregation and beyond: Some basic issues on the prediction of behavior. *Journal of Personality, 51,* 360–392.

Epstein, S. (1983b). The stability of behavior across time and situations. In R. Zucker, J. Aronoff, & A. I. Rabin (Eds.), *Personality and the prediction of behavior.* San Diego: Academic Press.

Epstein, S., & Meier, P. (1989). Constructive thinking: A broad coping variable with specific components. *Journal of Personality and Social Psychology, 57,* 332–350.

Erdberg, P. (1990). Rorschach assessment. In G. Goldstein & M. Hersen (Eds.), *Handbook of psychological assessment,* 2nd ed. New York: Pergamon.

Erdelyi, M. H. (1985). *Psychoanalysis: Freud's cognitive psychology.* New York: Freeman.

Erdelyi, M. H. (1988). Repression, reconstruction, and defense: History and integration of the psychoanalytic and experimental frameworks. In J. Singer (Ed.), *Repression: Defense mechanism and cognitive style.* Chicago: University of Chicago Press.

Erel, O., & Burman, B. (1995). Interrelatedness of marital relations and parent-child relations: A meta-analytic review. *Psychological Bulletin, 118,* 108–132.

Erel, O., Oberman, Y., & Yirmiya, N. (2000). Maternal versus nonmaternal care and seven domains of children's development. *Psychological Bulletin, 126,* 727–747.

Erickson, M. F., & Aird, E. G. (2005). *The motherhood study: Fresh insights on mothers' attitudes and concerns.* New York: The Motherhood Project, Institute for American Values.

Ericsson, K. A. (2001). Attaining excellence through deliberate practice: Insights from the study of expert performance. In M. Ferrari (Ed.), *The pursuit of excellence in education.* Hillsdale, NJ: Erlbaum.

Ericsson, K. A. (2002). Attaining excellence through deliberate practice: Insights from the study of expert performance. In C. Desforges & R. Fox (Eds.), *Teaching and learning: The essential readings.* Malden, MA: Blackwell Publishers.

Ericsson, K. A., & Chase, W. G. (1982). Exceptional memory. *American Scientist, 70,* 607–615.

Ericsson, K. A., Krampe, R. T., & Heizman, S. (1993). Can we create gifted people? In G. R. Bock & K. Ackrill (Eds.), *Ciba Foundation Symposium 178: The origins and development of high ability.* New York: Wiley. Cited by M. J. A. Howe, J. W. Davison, & J. A. Sioboda (1998). Innate talents: Reality or myth? *Behavioral and Brain Sciences, 21,* 399–442.

Ericsson, K. A., & Lehmann, A. C. (1996). Expert and exceptional performance: Evidence of maximal adaptations to task constraints. *Annual Review of Psychology, 47,* 273–305.

Erikson, E. H. (1963). *Childhood and society.* New York: Norton.

Erikson, E. H. (1983, June). A conversation with Erikson (by E. Hall). *Psychology Today,* pp. 22–30.

Ernsberger, P., & Koletsky, R. J. (1999). Biomedical rationale for a wellness approach to obesity: An alternative to a focus on weight loss. *Journal of Social Issues, 55,* 221–260.

Eron, L. D. (1987). The development of aggressive behavior from the perspective of a developing behaviorism. *American Psychologist, 42,* 435–442.

ESPAD. (2003). Summary of the 2003 findings. European School Survey Project on Alcohol and Other Drugs (www.espad.org).

Esser, J. K., & Lindoerfer, J. S. (1989). Groupthink and the space shuttle *Challenger* accident: Toward a quantitative case analysis. *Journal of Behavioral Decision Making, 2,* 167–177.

Esterson, A. (2001). The mythologizing of psychoanalytic history: Deception and self-deception in Freud's accounts of the seduction theory episode. *History of Psychiatry, 12,* 329–352.

Esty, A. (2004). The new wealth of nations. *American Scientist, 92,* 513.

Eszterhas, J. (2002, August 9). Hollywood's responsibility for smoking deaths. *New York Times* (www.nytimes.com).

Etcoff, N. L., Ekman, P., Magee, J. J., & Frank, M. G. (2000). Lie detection and language comprehension. *Nature, 405,* 139.

Etnier, J. L., Salazar, W., Landers, D. M., Petruzzello, S. J., Han, M., & Nowell, P. (1997). The influence of physical fitness and exercise upon cognitive functioning: A meta-analysis. *Journal of Sport & Exercise Psychology, 19,* 249–277.

ETS. (1992). Three reports shed new light on gender differences in testing. *ETS Developments, 37*(3), 4–7.

Etzioni, A. (1999). The monochrome society. *The Public Interest, 137* (Fall), 42–55.

Evans, C. R., & Dion, K. L. (1991). Group cohesion and performance: A meta-analysis. *Small Group Research, 22,* 175–186.

Evans, G. W. (2004). The environment of childhood poverty. *American Psychologist, 59,* 77–92.

Evans, G. W., Hygge, S., & Bullinger, M. (1995). Chronic noise and psychological stress. *Psychological Science, 6,* 333–338.

Evans, G. W., Palsane, M. N., & Carrere, S. (1987). Type A behavior and occupational stress: A cross-cultural study of blue-collar workers. *Journal of Personality and Social Psychology, 52,* 1002–1007.

Evans, G. W., Palsane, M. N., Lepore, S. J., & Martin, J. (1989). Residential density and psychological health: The mediating effects of social support. *Journal of Personality and Social Psychology, 57,* 994–999.

Evans, R. I., Dratt, L. M., Raines, B. E., & Rosenberg, S. S. (1988). Social influences on smoking initiation: Importance of distinguishing descriptive versus mediating process variables. *Journal of Applied Social Psychology, 18,* 925–943.

Ewing, R., Schmid, T., Killingsworth, R., Zlot, A., & Raudenbush, S. (2003). Relationship between urban sprawl and physical activity, obesity, and morbidity. *American Journal of Health Promotion, 18,* 47–57.

Exner, J. E. (2003). *The Rorschach: A comprehensive system,* 4th edition. Hoboken, NJ: Wiley.

Eysenck, H. J. (1952). The effects of psychotherapy: An evaluation. *Journal of Consulting Psychology, 16,* 319–324.

Eysenck, H. J. (1990, April 30). An improvement on personality inventory. *Current Contents: Social and Behavioral Sciences, 22*(18), 20.

Eysenck, H. J. (1992). Four ways five factors are *not* basic. *Personality and Individual Differences, 13,* 667–673.

Eysenck, H. J., & Grossarth-Maticek, R. (1991). Creative novation behaviour therapy as a prophylactic treatment for cancer and coronary heart disease: Part II—Effects of treatment. *Behaviour Research and Therapy, 29,* 17–31.

Eysenck, H. J., Wakefield, J. A., Jr., & Friedman, A. F. (1983). Diagnosis and clinical assessment: The DSM-III. *Annual Review of Psychology, 34,* 167–193.

Eysenck, M. W., MacLeod, C., & Mathews, A. (1987). Cognitive functioning and anxiety. *Psychological Research, 49,* 189–195.

Eysenck, S. B. G., & Eysenck, H. J. (1963). The validity of questionnaire and rating assessments of extraversion and neuroticism, and their factorial stability. *British Journal of Psychology, 54,* 51–62.

Faber, N. (1987, July). Personal glimpse. *Reader's Digest,* p. 34.

Fagan, J. F., III (1992). Intelligence: A theoretical viewpoint. *Current Directions in Psychological Science, 1,* 82–86.

Fairburn, C. G., Cowen, P. J., & Harrison, P. J. (1999). Twin studies and the etiology of eating disorders. *International Journal of Eating Disorders, 26,* 349–358.

Fantz, R. L. (1961, May). The origin of form perception. *Scientific American,* pp. 66–72.

Farah, M. J., Rabinowitz, C., Quinn, G. E., & Liu, G. T. (2000). Early commitment of neural substrates for face recognition. *Cognitive Neuropsychology, 17,* 117–124.

Farina, A. (1982). The stigma of mental disorders. In A. G. Miller (Ed.), *In the eye of the beholder.* New York: Praeger.

Farina, A., & Fisher, J. D. (1982). Beliefs about mental disorders: Findings and implications. In G. Weary & H. L. Mirels (Eds.), *Integrations of clinical and social psychology.* New York: Oxford University Press.

Farley, M, Baral, I., Kiremire, M., & Sezgin, U. (1998). Prostitution in five countries: Violence and post-traumatic stress disorder. *Feminism and Psychology, 8,* 405–426.

Farley, T., & Cohen, D. (2001, December). Fixing a fat nation. *Washington Monthly* (www.washingtonmonthly.com/features/2001/0112.farley.cohen.html).

Faro, S. (2004). Presentation to the Radiological Society of North America, Chicago.

Farrington, D. P. (1991). Antisocial personality from childhood to adulthood. *The Psychologist: Bulletin of the British Psychological Society, 4,* 389–394.

Farwell, L. A., & Smith, S. S. (2001). Using brain MERMER testing to detect concealed knowledge despite efforts to conceal. *Journal of Forensic Sciences, 46* (1), 1–9.

FBI. (2004). Crime in the United States 2003, Five-Year Arrest Trends by Sex, 1999–2003. Table 35.

Feder, H. H. (1984). Hormones and sexual behavior. *Annual Review of Psychology, 35,* 165–200.

Feeney, J. A., & Noller, P. (1990). Attachment style as a predictor of adult romantic relationships. *Journal of Personality and Social Psychology, 58,* 281–291.

Feigenson, L., Carey, S., & Spelke, E. (2002). Infants' discrimination of number vs. continuous extent. *Cognitive psychology, 44,* 33–66.

Feingold, A. (1990). Gender differences in effects of physical attractiveness on romantic attraction: A comparison across five research paradigms. *Journal of Personality and Social Psychology, 59,* 981–993.

Feingold, A. (1992). Good-looking people are not what we think. *Psychological Bulletin, 111,* 304–341.

Feingold, A., & Mazzella, R. (1998). Gender differences in body image are increasing. *Psychological Science, 9*, 190–195.

Feminist Psychologist. (2002, Winter). Justice for Mary Whiton Calkins, p. 11.

Fenn, K. M., Nusbaum, H. C., & Margoliash, D. (2003). Consolidation during sleep of perceptual learning of spoken language. *Nature, 425*, 614–616.

Fenton, W. S., & McGlashan, T. H. (1991). Natural history of schizophrenia subtypes: II. Positive and negative symptoms and long-term course. *Archives of General Psychiatry, 48*, 978–986.

Fenton, W. S., & McGlashan, T. H. (1994). Antecedents, symptom progression, and long-term outcome of the deficit syndrome in schizophrenia. *American Journal of Psychiatry, 151*, 351–356.

Ferguson, E. D. (1989). Adler's motivational theory: An historical perspective on belonging and the fundamental human striving. *Individual Psychology, 45*, 354–361.

Fergusson, D. M., & Woodward, L. G. (2002). Mental health, educational, and social role outcomes of adolescents with depression. *Archives of General Psychiatry, 59*, 225–231.

Fernandez, E., & Turk, D. C. (1989). The utility of cognitive coping strategies for altering pain perception: A meta-analysis. *Pain, 38*, 123–135.

Fernández-Ballesteros, R., & Caprara, M. (2003). Psychology of aging in Europe. *European Psychologist, 8*, 129–130.

Ferris, C. F. (1996, March). The rage of innocents. *The Sciences*, pp. 22–26.

Fiedler, F. E. (1981). Leadership effectiveness. *American Behavioral Scientist, 24*, 619–632.

Fiedler, F. E. (1987, September). When to lead, when to stand back. *Psychology Today*, pp. 26–27.

Fiedler, K., Nickel, S., Muehlfriedel, T., & Unkelbach, C. (2001). Is mood congruency an effect of genuine memory or response bias? *Journal of Experimental Social Psychology, 37*, 201–214.

Field, T. (1996). Attachment and separation in young children. *Annual Review of Psychology, 47*, 541–561.

Field, T. (2001). Massage therapy facilitates weight gain in preterm infants. *Current Directions in Psychological Science, 10*, 51–54.

Field, T., Hernandez-Reif, M., Diego, M., Feijo, L., Vera, Y., & Gil, K. (2004). Massage therapy by parents improves early growth and development. *Infant Behaviour and Development, 27*, 435–442.

Fields, R. D. (2004, April). The other half of the brain. *Scientific American*, pp. 54–61.

Fields, R. D. (2005, February). Making memories stick. *Scientific American*, pp. 75–81.

Fincham, F. D., & Bradbury, T. N. (1993). Marital satisfaction, depression, and attributions: A longitudinal analysis. *Journal of Personality and Social Psychology, 64*, 442–452.

Fink, G. R., Markowitsch, H. J., Reinkemeier, M., Bruckbauer, T., Kessler, J., & Heiss, W-D. (1996). Cerebral representation of one's own past: Neural networks involved in autobiographical memory. *Journal of Neuroscience, 16*, 4275–4282.

Fink, M. (1998). ECT and managed care. *Journal Watch Psychiatry, 4*, 73, 76.

Finkel, L. H., & Sajda, P. (1994). Constructing visual perception. *American Scientist, 82*, 224–237.

Finlay, S. W. (2000). Influence of Carl Jung and William James on the origin of alcoholics anonymous. *Review of General Psychology, 4*, 3–12.

Finney, E. M., Fine, I., & Dobkins, K. R. (2001). Visual stimuli activate auditory cortex in the deaf. *Nature Neuroscience, 4*, 1171–1173.

Finucci, J. M., & Childs, B. (1981). Are there really more dyslexic boys than girls? In A. Ansara, N. Geschwind, A. Galaburda, M. Albert, & N. Gartrell (Eds.), *Sex differences in dyslexia*. Towson, MD: The Orton Dyslexia Society.

Fischhoff, B. (1982). Debiasing. In D. Kahneman, P. Slovic, & A. Tversky (Eds.), *Judgment under uncertainty: Heuristics and biases*. New York: Cambridge University Press.

Fischhoff, B., Slovic, P., & Lichtenstein, S. (1977). Knowing with certainty: The appropriateness of extreme confidence. *Journal of Experimental Psychology: Human Perception and Performance, 3*, 552–564.

Fisher, H. E. (1993, March/April). After all, maybe it's biology. *Psychology Today*, pp. 40–45.

Fisher, H. E., Aron, A., Mashek, D., Li, H., & Brown, L. L. (2002). Defining the brain systems of lust, romantic attraction, and attachment. *Archives of Sexual Behavior, 31*, 413–419.

Fisher, H. T. (1984). Little Albert and Little Peter. *Bulletin of the British Psychological Society, 37*, 269.

Fisher, R. P., & Geiselman, R. E. (1992). *Memory-enhancing techniques for investigative interviewing: The cognitive interview*. Springfield, IL: Charles C. Thomas.

Fisher, R. P., Geiselman, R. E., & Raymond, D. S. (1987). Critical analysis of police interview techniques. *Journal of Police Science and Administration, 15*, 177–185.

Fisher, S., & Greenberg, R. (Eds.) (1997). *From placebo to panacea: Putting psychiatric drugs to the test*. New York: Wiley.

Fiske, S. T., Harris, L. T., & Cuddy, A. J. C. (2004). Why ordinary people torture enemy prisoners. *Science, 306*, 1482–1483.

Flack, W. F., Jr., Laird, J. D., & Cavallaro, L. A. (1999). Separate and combined effects of facial expressions and bodily postures on emotional feelings. *European Journal of Social Psychology, 29*, 203–217.

Flavell, J. H., Flavell, E. R., & Green, F. L. (2001). Development of children's understanding of connections between thinking and feeling. *Psychological Science, 12*, 430–432.

Fleming, I., Baum, A., & Weiss, L. (1987). Social density and perceived control as mediator of crowding stress in high-density residential neighborhoods. *Journal of Personality and Social Psychology, 52*, 899–906.

Fleming, J. H. (2001, Winter/Spring). Introduction to the special issue on linkage analysis. *The Gallup Research Journal*, pp. i–vi.

Fleming, J. H., & Scott, B. A. (1991). The costs of confession: The Persian Gulf War POW tapes in historical and theoretical perspective. *Contemporary Social Psychology, 15*, 127–138.

Fletcher, G. J. O., Fitness, J., & Blampied, N. M. (1990). The link between attributions and happiness in close relationships: The roles of depression and explanatory style. *Journal of Social and Clinical Psychology, 9*, 243–255.

Fletcher, P. C., Zafiris, O., Frith, C. D., Honey, R. A. E., Corlett, P. R., Zilles, K., & Fink, G. R. (2005). On the benefits of not trying: Brain activity and connectivity reflecting the interactions of explicit and implicit sequence learning. *Cerebral Cortex, 7*, 1002–1015.

Flora, S. R. (2004). *The power of reinforcement*. Albany, NY: SUNY Press.

Flouri, E., & Buchanan, A. (2004). Early father's and mother's involvement and child's later educational outcomes. *British Journal of Educational Psychology, 74*, 141–153.

Flynn, J. R. (1987). Massive IQ gains in 14 nations: What IQ tests really measure. *Psychological Bulletin, 101*, 171–191.

Flynn, J. R. (1999). Searching for justice: The discovery of IQ gains over time. *American Psychologist, 54*, 5–20.

Flynn, J. R. (2003). Movies about intelligence: The limitations of g. *Current Directions in Psychological Science, 12*, 95–99.

Foa, E. B., & Kozak, M. J. (1986). Emotional processing of fear: Exposure to corrective information. *Psychological Bulletin, 99*, 20–35.

Fogg, N. P., Harrington P. E., & Harrington T. F. (1999). *The College Majors Handbook*. Indianapolis, IN: JIST Works, Inc.

Fong, G. T., Frantz, D. H., & Nisbett, R. E. (1986). The effects of statistical training on thinking about everyday problems. *Cognitive Psychology, 18*, 253–292.

Ford, E. S. (2002). Does exercise reduce inflammation? Physical activity and C-reactive protein among U.S. adults. *Epidemiology, 13*, 561–569.

Foree, D. D., & LoLordo, V. M. (1973). Attention in the pigeon: Differential effects of food-getting versus shock-avoidance procedures. *Journal of Comparative and Physiological Psychology, 85*, 551–558.

Forer, B. R. (1949). The fallacy of personal validation: A classroom demonstration of gullibility. *Journal of Abnormal and Social Psychology, 44*, 118–123.

Forgas, J. P., Bower, G. H., & Krantz, S. E. (1984). The influence of mood on perceptions of social interactions. *Journal of Experimental Social Psychology, 20*, 497–513.

Forge, A., Li, L., Corwin, J. T., & Nevill, G. (1993). Ultrastructural evidence for hair cell regeneration in the mammalian inner ear. *Science, 259*, 1616–1619.

Forman, D. R., Aksan, N., & Kochanska, G. (2004). Toddlers' responsive imitation predicts preschool-age conscience. *Psychological Science, 15*, 699–704.

Foss, D. J., & Hakes, D. T. (1978). *Psycholinguistics: An introduction to the psychology of language.* Englewood Cliffs, NJ: Prentice-Hall.

Fosse, R., Stickgold, R., & Hobson, J. A. (2001). Brain-mind states: Reciprocal variation in thoughts and hallucinations. *Psychological Science, 12*, 30–36.

Foster, J. D., Campbell, W. K., & Twenge, J. M. (2003). Individual differences in narcissism: Inflated self-views across the lifespan and around the world. *Journal of Research in Personality, 37*, 469–486.

Foster, R. G. (2004). Are we trying to banish biological time? *Cerebrum, 6*(2), 7–26.

Foulkes, D. (1999). *Children's dreaming and the development of consciousness.* Cambridge, MA: Harvard University Press.

Fouts, R. S. (1992). Transmission of a human gestural language in a chimpanzee mother-infant relationship. *Friends of Washoe, 12/13*, pp. 2–8.

Fouts, R. (1997). *Next of kin: What chimpanzees have taught me about who we are.* New York: Morrow.

Fouts, R. S., & Bodamer, M. (1987). Preliminary report to the National Geographic Society on: "Chimpanzee intrapersonal signing." *Friends of Washoe, 7*(1), 4–12.

Fowler, M. J., Sullivan, M. J., & Ekstrand, B. R. (1973). Sleep and memory. *Science, 179*, 302–304.

Fowler, R. C., Rich, C. L., & Young, D. (1986). San Diego suicide study: II. Substance abuse in young cases. *Archives of General Psychiatry, 43*, 962–965.

Fowler, R. D. (1986, May). Howard Hughes: A psychological autopsy. *Psychology Today*, pp. 22–33.

Fowles, D. C. (1992). Schizophrenia: Diathesis-stress revisited. *Annual Review of Psychology, 43*, 303–336.

Fox, B. H. (1998). Psychosocial factors in cancer incidence and prognosis. In P. M. Cinciripini & others (Eds.), *Psychological and behavioral factors in cancer risk.* New York: Oxford University Press.

Fox, E., Lester, V., Russo, R., Bowles, R. J., Pichler, A., & Dutton, K. (2000). Facial expression of emotion: Are angry faces detected more efficiently? *Cognition and Emotion, 14*, 61–92.

Fox, J. L. (1984). The brain's dynamic way of keeping in touch. *Science, 225*, 820–821.

Fox, N. C., Crum, W. R., Scahill, R. I., Stevens, J. M., Janssen, J. C., Rossor, M. N. (2001). Imaging of onset and progression of Alzheimer's disease with voxel-compression mapping of serial magnetic resonance images. *Lancet, 358*, 201–205.

Fozard, J. L., & Popkin, S. J. (1978). Optimizing adult development: Ends and means of an applied psychology of aging. *American Psychologist, 33*, 975–989.

Fracassini, C. (2000, August 27). Holidaymakers led by the nose in sales quest. *Scotland on Sunday.*

Fraley, R. C. (2002). Attachment stability from infancy to adulthood: Meta-analysis and dynamic modeling of developmental mechanisms. *Personality and Social Psychology Review, 6*, 123–151.

Francis, D., Diorio, J., Liu, D., & Meaney, M. J. (1999). Nongenomic transmission across generations of maternal behavior and stress responses in the rat. *Science, 286*, 1155–1158.

Frank, J. D. (1982). Therapeutic components shared by all psychotherapies. In J. H. Harvey & M. M. Parks (Eds.), *The Master Lecture Series: Vol. 1. Psychotherapy research and behavior change.* Washington, DC: American Psychological Association.

Frank, R. (1999). *Luxury fever: Why money fails to satisfy in an era of excess.* New York: Free Press.

Frank, S. J. (1988). Young adults' perceptions of their relationships with their parents: Individual differences in connectedness, competence, and emotional autonomy. *Developmental Psychology, 24*, 729–737.

Frankel, A., Strange, D. R., & Schoonover, R. (1983). CRAP: Consumer rated assessment procedure. In G. H. Scherr & R. Liebmann-Smith (Eds.), *The best of The Journal of Irreproducible Results.* New York: Workman Publishing.

Frankenburg, W., Dodds, J., Archer, P., Shapiro, H., & Bresnick, B. (1992). The Denver II: A major revision and restandardization of the Denver Developmental Screening Test. *Pediatrics, 89*, 91–97.

Franz, E. A., Waldie, K. E., & Smith, M. J. (2000). The effect of callosotomy on novel versus familiar bimanual actions: A neural dissociation between controlled and automatic processes? *Psychological Science, 11*, 82–85.

Frasure-Smith, N., & Lespérance, F. (2005). Depression and coronary heart disease: Complex synergism of mind, body, and environment. *Current Directions in Psychological Science, 14*, 39–43.

Fredrickson, B. L. (2002). Positive emotions. In C. R. Snyder & S. J. Lopez (Eds.), *Handbook of positive psychology.* New York: Oxford.

Fredrickson, B. L. (2003). The value of positive emotions. *American Scientist, 91*, 330–335.

Fredrickson, B. L., & Kahneman, D. (1993). Duration neglect in retrospective evaluations of affective episodes. *Journal of Personality and Social Psychology, 65*, 45–55.

Fredrickson, B. L., Roberts, T-A., Noll, S. M., Quinn, D. M., & Twenge, J. M. (1998). That swimsuit becomes you: Sex differences in self-objectification, restrained eating, and math performance. *Journal of Personality and Social Psychology, 75*, 269–284.

Freedman, D. J., Riesenhuber, M., Poggio, T., & Miller, E. K. (2001). Categorical representation of visual stimuli in the primate prefrontal cortex. *Science, 291*, 312–316.

Freedman, J. L. (1978). *Happy people.* San Diego: Harcourt Brace Jovanovich.

Freedman, J. L. (1988). Television violence and aggression: What the evidence shows. In S. Oskamp (Ed.), *Television as a social issue.* Newbury Park, CA: Sage.

Freedman, J. L., & Fraser, S. C. (1966). Compliance without pressure: The foot-in-the-door technique. *Journal of Personality and Social Psychology, 4*, 195–202.

Freedman, J. L., & Perlick, D. (1979). Crowding, contagion, and laughter. *Journal of Experimental Social Psychology, 15*, 295–303.

Freedman, L. R., Rock, D., Roberts, S. A., Cornblatt, B. A., & Erlenmeyer-Kimling, L. (1998). The New York high-risk project: Attention, anhedonia and social outcome. *Schizophrenia Research, 30*, 1–9.

Freeman, W. J. (1991, February). The physiology of perception. *Scientific American*, pp. 78–85.

Frensch, P. A., & Rünger, D. (2003). Implicit learning. *Current Directions in Psychological Science, 12* , 13–18.

Freud, S. (1933). *New introductory lectures on psychoanalysis.* New York: Carlton House.

Freud, S. (1935; reprinted 1960). *A general introduction to psychoanalysis.* New York: Washington Square Press.

Frey, M. C., & Detterman, D. K. (2004). Scholastic assessment or *g*? The relationship between the Scholastic Assessment Test and general cognitive ability. *Psychological Science, 15,* 373–378.

Freyd, J. J., Putnam, F. W., Lyon, T. D., Becker-Blease, K. A., Cheit, R. E., Siegel, N. B., & Pezdek, K. (2005). The science of child sexual abuse. *Science, 308,* 501.

Friedman, M., & Ulmer, D. (1984). *Treating Type A behavior—and your heart.* New York: Knopf.

Friedrich, O. (1987, December 7). New age harmonies. *Time,* pp. 62–72.

Friend, T. (2004). *Animal talk: Breaking the codes of animal language.* New York: Free Press.

Frith, U., & Frith, C. (2001). The biological basis of social interaction. *Current Directions in Psychological Science, 10,* 151–155.

Fritsch, G., & Hitzig, E. (1870; reprinted 1960). On the electrical excitability of the cerebrum. In G. Von Bonin (Trans.), *Some papers on the cerebral cortex.* Springfield, IL: Charles C. Thomas.

Fromkin, V., & Rodman, R. (1983). *An introduction to language* (3rd ed.). New York: Holt, Rinehart & Winston.

Fry, A. F., & Hale, S. (1996). Processing speed, working memory, and fluid intelligence: Evidence for a developmental cascade. *Psychological Science, 7,* 237–241.

Fuhriman, A., & Burlingame, G. M. (1994). Group psychotherapy: Research and practice. In A. Fuhriman & G. M. Burlingame (Eds.), *Handbook of group psychotherapy.* New York: Wiley.

Fujiki, N., Yoshida, Y., Ripley, B., Mignot, E., & Nishino, S. (2003). Effects of IV and ICV hypocretin-1 (Orexin A) in hypocretin receptor-2 gene mutated narcoleptic dogs and IV hypocretin-1 replacement therapy in a hypocretin-ligand-deficient narcoleptic dog. *Sleep, 26,* 953–959.

Fujita, F., & Diener, E. (2005). Life satisfaction set point: Stability and change. *Journal of Personality and Social Psychology, 88,* 158–164.

Fuller, M. J., & Downs, A. C. (1990). Spermarche is a salient biological marker in men's development. Poster presented at the American Psychological Society convention.

Fulmer, I. S., Gerhart, B., & Scott, K. S. (2003). Are the 100 best better? An empirical investigation fo the relationship between being a "great place to work" and firm performance. *Personnel Psychology, 56,* 965–993.

Funder, D. C. (2001). Personality. *Annual Review of Psychology, 52,* 197–221.

Funder, D. C., & Block, J. (1989). The role of ego-control, ego-resiliency, and IQ in delay of gratification in adolescence. *Journal of Personality and Social Psychology, 57,* 1041–1050.

Furlow, F. B., & Thornhill, R. (1996, January/February). The orgasm wars. *Psychology Today,* pp. 42–46.

Furnham, A. (1982). Explanations for unemployment in Britain. *European Journal of Social Psychology, 12,* 335–352.

Furnham, A. (2001). Self-estimates of intelligence: Culture and gender difference in self and other estimates of both general (g) and multiple intelligences. *Personality and Individual Differences, 31,* 1381–1405.

Furnham, A., & Baguma, P. (1994). Cross-cultural differences in the evaluation of male and female body shapes. *International Journal of Eating Disorders, 15,* 81–89.

Furnham, A., Callahan, I., & Akande, D. (2004). Self-estimates of intelligence: A study in two African countries. *Journal of Psychology, 138,* 265–285.

Furnham, A., Callahan, I., & Rawles, R. (2003). Adults' knowledge of general psychology. *European Psychologist, 8,* 101–116.

Furnham, A., Hosoe, T., & Tang, T. L-P. (2002a). Male hubris and female humility? A cross-cultural study of ratings of self, parental, and sibling multiple intelligence in American, Britain, and Japan. *Intelligence, 30,* 101–115.

Furnham, A., & Mottabu, R. (2004). Sex and culture differences in the estimates of general and multiple intelligence: A study comparing British and Egyptian students. *Individual Differences Research, 3,* 82–96.

Furnham, A., & Rawles, R. (1995). Sex differences in the estimation of intelligence. *Journal of Social Behavior and Personality, 10,* 741–748.

Furnham, A., Reeves, E., & Bughani, S. (2002b). Parents think their sons are brighter than their daughters: Sex differences in parental self-estimations and estimations of their children's multiple intelligences. *Journal of Genetic Psychology, 163,* 24–39.

Furnham, A., & Taylor, L. (1990). Lay theories of homosexuality: Aetiology, behaviours, and 'cures.' *British Journal of Social Psychology, 29,* 135–147.

Furnham, A., & Thomas, C. (2004). Parents' gender and personality and estimates of their own and their children's intelligence. *Personality and Individual Differences, 37,* 887–903.

Furr, R. M., & Funder, D. C. (1998). A multimodal analysis of personal negativity. *Journal of Personality and Social Psychology, 74,* 1580–1591.

Gabbay, F. H. (1992). Behavior-genetic strategies in the study of emotion. *Psychological Science, 3,* 50–55.

Gabrieli, J. D. E., Desmond, J. E., Demb, J. E., Wagner, A. D., Stone, M. V., Vaidya, C. J., & Glover, G. H. (1996). Functional magnetic resonance imaging of semantic memory processes in the frontal lobes. *Psychological Science, 7,* 278–283.

Gaertner, L., & Iuzzini, J. (2005). Rejection and entitativity: A synergistic model of mass violence. In K. D. Williams, J. P. Forgas, & W. von Hippel (Eds.). *The social outcast: Ostracism, social exclusion, rejection, and bullying.* New York: Psychology Press.

Gage, F. H. (2003, September). Repair yourself. *Scientific American,* pp. 46–53.

Galambos, N. L. (1992). Parent-adolescent relations. *Current Directions in Psychological Science, 1,* 146–149.

Galanter, E. (1962). Contemporary psychophysics. In R. Brown, E. Galanter, E. H. Hess, & G. Mandler (Eds.), *New directions in psychology.* New York: Holt Rinehart, & Winston.

Galati, D., Scherer, K. R., & Ricci-Bitti, P. E. (1997). Voluntary facial expression of emotion: Comparing congenitally blind with normally sighted encoders. *Journal of Personality and Social Psychology, 73,* 1363–1379.

Galea, S., Boscarino, J., Resnick, H., & Vlahov, D. (2002). Mental health in New York City after the September 11 terrorist attacks: Results from two population surveys. Chapter 7. In *Mental-Health, United States, 2001,* R. W. Manderscheid, & M. J. Henderson (Eds.). Washington, DC: Superintendent of Documents, U.S. Government Printing Office.

Gallup. (2002, February 21). Homosexual relations. The Gallup Organization (www.gallup.com/poll/topics/homosexual.asp).

Gallup. (2002, June 11). Poll insights: The gender gap—post Sept. 11th fear. The Gallup Organization (www.gallup.com/poll/pollInsights).

Gallup. (2002). Alcohol and drinking (results of November 8–11, 2001 survey) (www.gallup.com/poll/topics/alcohol.asp).

Gallup. (2005, May 5). The gender gap: President Bush's handling of Iraq. The Gallup Poll (www.gallup.com).

Gallup, G., Jr. (1982). *Adventures in immortality.* New York: McGraw-Hill.

Gallup, G., Jr. (1998). Can animals empathize? *Scientific American, 4,* 66.

Gallup, G., Jr. (2002, April 30). Education and youth. *Gallup Tuesday Briefing* (www.gallup.com/poll/tb/educaYouth/20020430.asp).

Gallup, G. G., Jr., & Suarez, S. D. (1986). Self-awareness and the emergence of mind in humans and other primates. In J. Suls & A. G. Greenwald (Eds.), *Psychological perspectives on the self* (Vol. 3.). Hillsdale, NJ: Erlbaum.

Gallup, G. H. (1972). *The Gallup poll: Public opinion 1935–1971* (Vol. 3). New York: Random House.

Gallup, G. H., Jr. (1994, October). Millions finding care and support in small groups. *Emerging Trends*, pp. 2–5.

Gallup Organization. (1993). Other hemispheres may think our religion is alien and exotic. *PRRC Emerging Trends, 15*, 1–3.

Gallup Organization. (2003, July 8). American public opinion about Iraq. Gallup Poll News Service (www.gallup.com)

Gallup Organization. (2004, August 16). 65% of Americans receive NO praise or recognition in the workplace. E-mail from Tom Rath: bucketbook@gallup.com.

Gangestad, S. W., & Simpson, J. A. (2000). The evolution of human mating: Trade-offs and strategic pluralism. *Behavioral and Brain Sciences, 23.*

Garb, H. N., Wood, J. M., Lilienfeld, S. O., & Nezworski, M. T. (2005). Roots of the Rorschach controversy. *Clinical Psychology Review, 25*, 97–118.

Garbarino, J., Dubrow, N., & Kostelny, K. (1992). *Children in danger: Coping with the consequences of community violence.* San Francisco: Jossey-Bass Inc.

Garbarino, J., Kostelny, K., & Dubrow, N. (1991). What children can tell us about living in danger. *American Psychologist, 46*, 376–383.

Garcia, J., & Gustavson, A. R. (1997, January). Carl R. Gustavson (1946–1996): Pioneering wildlife psychologist. *APS Observer*, pp. 34–35.

Garcia, J., & Koelling, R. A. (1966). Relation of cue to consequence in avoidance learning. *Psychonomic Science, 4*, 123–124.

Gardner, H. (1983). *Frames of mind: The theory of multiple intelligences.* New York: Basic Books.

Gardner, H. (1998, March 19). An intelligent way to progress. *The Independent* (London), p. E4.

Gardner, H. (1998, November 5). Do parents count? *New York Review of Books* (www.nybooks.com).

Gardner, H. (1999, February). Who owns intelligence? *Atlantic Monthly*, pp. 67–76.

Gardner, H. (1999). *Multiple views of multiple intelligence.* New York: Basic Books.

Gardner, J., & Oswald, A. (2001). Does money buy happiness? A longitudinal study using data on windfalls. Working paper, Department of Economics, Cambridge University.

Gardner, R. A., & Gardner, B. I. (1969). Teaching sign language to a chimpanzee. *Science, 165*, 664–672.

Gardner, R. M., & Tockerman, Y. R. (1994). A computer-TV video methodology for investigating the influence of somatotype on perceived personality traits. *Journal of Social Behavior and Personality, 9*, 555–563.

Garfield, C. (1986). *Peak performers: The new heroes of American business.* New York: Morrow.

Garlick, D. (2002). Understanding the nature of the general factor of intelligence: The role of individual differences in neural plasticity as an explanatory mechanism. *Psychological Review, 109*, 116–136.

Garlick, D. (2003). Integrating brain science research with intelligence research. *Current Directions in Psychological Science, 12*, 185–189.

Garner, D. M., & Wooley, S. C. (1991). Confronting the failure of behavioral and dietary treatments for obesity. *Clinical Psychology Review, 11*, 729–780.

Garnets, L., & Kimmel, D. (1990). Lesbian and gay dimensions in the psychological study of human diversity. Master lecture, American Psychological Association convention.

Garry, M., & Loftus, E. F., & Brown, S. W. (1994). Memory: A river runs through it. *Consciousness and Cognition, 3*, 438–451.

Garry, M., Manning, C. G., Loftus, E. F., & Sherman, S. J. (1996). Imagination inflation: Imagining a childhood event inflates confidence that it occurred. *Psychonomic Bulletin & Review, 3*, 208–214.

Garza, D. L., & Feltz, D. L. (1998). Effects of selected mental practice on performance, self-efficacy, and competition confidence of figure skaters. *The Sports Psychologist, 12*, 1–15.

Gates, G. A., & Miyamoto, R. T. (2003). Cochlear implants. *New England Journal of Medicine, 349*, 421–423.

Gates, W. (1998, July 20). Charity begins when I'm ready (interview). *Fortune* (www.pathfinder.com/fortune/1998/980720/bil7.html).

Gawande, A. (1998, September 21). The pain perplex. *The New Yorker*, pp. 86–94.

Gawin, F. H. (1991). Cocaine addiction: Psychology and neurophysiology. *Science, 251*, 1580–1586.

Gazzaniga, M. S. (1967, August). The split brain in man. *Scientific American*, pp. 24–29.

Gazzaniga, M. S. (1983). Right hemisphere language following brain bisection: A 20-year perspective. *American Psychologist, 38*, 525–537.

Gazzaniga, M. S. (1988). Organization of the human brain. *Science, 245*, 947–952.

Gazzaniga, M. S. (1992). *Nature's mind: The biological roots of thinking, emotions, sexuality, language, and intelligence.* New York: Basic Books.

Gazzaniga, M. S. (1997). Brain, drugs, and society. *Science, 275*, 459.

Geary, D. C. (1995). Sexual selection and sex differences in spatial cognition. *Learning and Individual Differences, 7*, 289–301.

Geary, D. C. (1996). Sexual selection and sex differences in mathematical abilities. *Behavioral and Brain Sciences, 19*, 229–247.

Geary, D. C. (1998). *Male, female: The evolution of human sex differences.* Washington, DC: American Psychological Association.

Geary, D. C., Salthouse, T. A., Chen, G-P., & Fan, L. (1996). Are East Asian versus American differences in arithmetical ability a recent phenomenon? *Developmental Psychology, 32*, 254–262.

Geen, R. G., & Quanty, M. B. (1977). The catharsis of aggression: An evaluation of a hypothesis. In L. Berkowitz (Ed.), *Advances in experimental social psychology* (Vol. 10). New York: Academic Press.

Geen, R. G., & Thomas, S. L. (1986). The immediate effects of media violence on behavior. *Journal of Social Issues, 42*(3), 7–28.

Gehring, W. J., Wimke, J., & Nisenson, L. G. (2000). Action monitoring dysfunction in obsessive-compulsive disorder. *Psychological Science, 11*(1), 1–6.

Geldard, F. A. (1972). *The human senses* (2nd ed.). New York: Wiley.

Gelman, D. (1989, May 15). Voyages to the unknown. *Newsweek*, pp. 66–69.

Genesee, F., & Gándara, P. (1999). Bilingual education programs: A cross-national perspective. *Journal of Social Issues, 55*, 665–685.

Genevro, J. L. (2003). *Report on bereavement and grief research.* Washington, DC: Center for the Advancement of Health.

Genovese, J. E. C. (2004). The ten percent solution. *Skeptic, 10*(4), 55–57.

Gentile, D. A., Lynch, P. J., Linder, J. R., & Walsh, D. A. (2004). The effects of violent video game habits on adolescent hostility, aggressive behaviors, and school performance. *Journal of Adolescence, 27*, 5–22.

Gentile, D. A., Walsh, D. A., Ellison, P. R., Fox, M., & Cameron, J. (2004). Media violence as a risk factor for children: A longitudinal study. Paper presented at the American Psychological Society Convention.

Gentry, J., & Eron, L. D. (1993). American Psychological Association Commission on Violence and Youth. *American Psychological Association, 48*, 89.

George, L. K., Ellison, C. G., & Larson, D. B. (2002). Explaining the relationships between religious involvement and health. *Psychological Inquiry, 13*, 190–200.

George, L. K., Larson, D. B., Koenig, H. G., & McCullough, M. E. (2000). Spirituality and health: What we know, what we need to know. *Journal of Social and Clinical Psychology, 19*, 102–116.

George, M. S. (2003, September). Stimulating the brain. *Scientific American*, pp. 67–73.

Gerard, R. W. (1953, September). What is memory? *Scientific American*, pp. 118–126.

Gerbner, G. (1990). Stories that hurt: Tobacco, alcohol, and other drugs in the mass media. In H. Resnik (Ed.), *Youth and drugs: Society's mixed messages*. Rockville, MD: Office for Substance Abuse Prevention, U.S. Department of Health and Human Services.

Gerbner, G. (1993, June). Women and minorities on television: A study in casting and fate. A report to the Screen Actors Guild and the American Federation of Radio and Television Artists.

Gerbner, G., Gross, L., Morgan, M., & Signorielli, N. (1994). Growing up with television: The cultivation perspective. In J. Bryant, & D. Zillman (Eds.), *Media Effects: Advances in theory and research*. Hillsdale, NJ: Erlbaum.

Gerbner, G., Morgan, M., & Signorielli, N. (1993). Television violence profile No. 16: The turning point from research to action. Annenberg School for Communication, University of Pennsylvania.

Gerhart, K. A., Koziol-McLain, J., Lowenstein, S. R., & Whiteneck, G. G. (1994). Quality of life following spinal cord injury: Knowledge and attitudes of emergency care providers. *Annals of Emergency Medicine, 23*, 807–812.

Gerrard, M., & Luus, C. A. E. (1995). Judgments of vulnerability to pregnancy: The role of risk factors and individual differences. *Personality and Social Psychology Bulletin, 21*, 160–171.

Gershoff, E. T. (2002). Parental corporal punishment and associated child behaviors and experiences: A meta-analytic and theoretical review. *Psychological Bulletin, 128*, 539–579.

Gershon, J., Anderson, P., Graap, K., Zimand, E., Hodges, L., & Rothbaum, B. O. (2002). Virtual reality exposure therapy in the treatment of anxiety disorders, *Scientific Review of Mental Health Practice, 1*, 76–81.

Geschwind, N. (1979, September). Specializations of the human brain. *Scientific American*, pp. 180–199.

Geschwind, N., & Behan, P. O. (1984). Laterality, hormones, and immunity. In N. Geschwind & A. M. Galaburda (Eds.), *Cerebral dominance: The biological foundations*. Cambridge, MA: Harvard University Press.

Gfeller, J. D., Lynn, S. J., & Pribble, W. E. (1987). Enhancing hypnotic susceptibility: Interpersonal and rapport factors. *Journal of Personality and Social Psychology, 52*, 586–595.

Gibbons, F. X. (1986). Social comparison and depression: Company's effect on misery. *Journal of Personality and Social Psychology, 51*, 140–148.

Gibbs, W. W. (1996, June). Mind readings. *Scientific American*, pp. 34–36.

Gibbs, W. W. (2002, August). Saving dying languages. *Scientific American*, pp. 79–85.

Gibbs, W. W. (2005, June). Obesity: An overblown epidemic? *Scientific American*, pp. 70–77.

Gibson, E. J., & Walk, R. D. (1960, April). The "visual cliff." *Scientific American*, pp. 64–71.

Gibson, H. B. (1995, April). Recovered memories. *The Psychologist*, pp. 153–154.

Gigerenzer, G. (2004). Dread risk, September 11, and fatal traffic accidents. *Psychological Science, 15*, 286–287.

Gigerenzer, G. (2004). Fast and frugal heuristics: The tools of bounded rationality. In D. Koehler & N. Harvey (Eds.), *Handbook of judgment and decision making*. Oxford, UK: Blackwell.

Gignac, G., Vernon, P. A., & Wickett, J. C. (2003). Factors influencing the relationship between brain size and intelligence. In H. Nyborg, *The scientific study of general intelligence*. Amsterdam: Pergamon.

Gilbert, D. T., Pelham, B. W., & Krull, D. S. (2003). The psychology of good ideas. *Psychological Inquiry, 14*, 258–260.

Gilbert, D. T., Pinel, E. C., Wilson, T. D., Blumberg, S. J., & Wheatley, T. P. (1998). Immune neglect: A source of durability bias in affective forecasting. *Journal of Personality and Social Psychology, 75*, 617–638.

Giles, D. E., Dahl, R. E., & Coble, P. A. (1994). Childbearing, developmental, and familial aspects of sleep. In J. M. Oldham & M. B. Riba (Eds.), *Review of Psychiatry*, (Vol. 13). Washington, DC: American Psychiatric Press.

Gillham, J. E., Reivich, K. J., Jaycox, L. H., & Seligman, M. E. P. (1995). Preventing depressive symptoms in schoolchildren: Two year follow-up. *Psychological Science, 6*, 343–351.

Gilligan, C. (1982). *In a different voice: Psychological theory and women's development*. Cambridge, MA: Harvard University Press.

Gilligan, C., Lyons, N. P., & Hanmer, T. J. (Eds.). (1990). *Making connections: The relational worlds of adolescent girls at Emma Willard School*. Cambridge, MA: Harvard University Press.

Gilovich, T. (1991). *How we know what isn't so: The fallibility of human reason in everyday life*. New York: Free Press.

Gilovich, T. D. (1996). The spotlight effect: Exaggerated impressions of the self as a social stimulus. Unpublished manuscript, Cornell University.

Gilovich, T., Kruger, J., & Medvec, V. H. (2002). The spotlight effect revisted: Overestimating the manifest variability of our actions and appearance. *Journal of Experimental Social Psychology, 38*, 93–99.

Gilovich, T., & Medvec, V. H. (1995). The experience of regret: What, when, and why. *Psychological Review, 102*, 379–395.

Gilovich, T., & Savitsky, K. (1999). The spotlight effect and the illusion of transparency: Egocentric assessments of how we are seen by others. *Current Directions in Psychological Science, 8*, 165–168.

Gilovich, T., Vallone, R., & Tversky, A. (1985). The hot hand in basketball: On the misperception of random sequences. *Cognitive Psychology, 17*, 295–314.

Gingerich, O. (1999, February 6). Is there a role for natural theology today? *The Real Issue* (www.origins.org/real/n9501/natural.html).

Giuliano, T. A., Barnes, L. C., Fiala, S. E., & Davis D. M. (1998a). An empirical investigation of male answer syndrome. Paper presented at the Southwestern Psychological Association convention.

Giuliano, T. A., Fiala, S. E., Davis, D. M., Barnes, L. C., & Patrick, E. C. (1998b). The reluctance to admit "I don't know": Exploring "male answer syndrome." Paper presented to the American Psychological Society convention.

Gladue, B. A. (1990). Hormones and neuroendocrine factors in atypical human sexual behavior. In J. R. Feierman (Ed.), *Pedophilia: Biosocial dimensions*. New York: Springer-Verlag.

Gladue, B. A. (1994). The biopsychology of sexual orientation. *Current Directions in Psychological Science, 3*, 150–154.

Gladwell, M. (2000, May 9). The new-boy network: What do job interviews really tell us? *New Yorker*, pp. 68–86.

Gladwell, M. (2004, September 20). Personality plus. *New Yorker*, pp. 42–48.

Gladwell, M. (2005). *Blink: The power of thinking without thinking*. New York: Little Brown.

Glass, D. C., & Singer, J. E. (1972). *Urban stress*. New York: Academic Press.

Glass, R. I. (2004). Perceived threats and real killers. *Science, 304*, 927.

Glass, R. M. (2001). Electroconvulsive therapy: Time to bring it out of the shadows. *Journal of the American Medical Association, 285*, 1346–1348.

Glater, J. D. (2001, March 26). Women are close to being majority of law students. *New York Times* (www.nytimes.com).

Gleaves, D. H. (1996). The sociocognitive model of dissociative identity disorder: A reexamination of the evidence. *Psychological Bulletin, 120*, 42–59.

Glenn, N. D. (1975). Psychological well-being in the postparental stage: Some evidence from national surveys. *Journal of Marriage and the Family, 37,* 105–110.

Glick, P., & 15 others (2004). Bad but bold: Ambivalent attitudes toward men predict gender inequality in 16 nations. *Journal of Personality and Social Psychology, 86,* 713–728.

Glick, P., Gottesman, D., & Jolton, J. (1989). The fault is not in the stars: Susceptibility of skeptics and believers in astrology to the Barnum effect. *Personality and Social Psychology Bulletin, 15,* 572–583.

Gluhoski, V. L., & Wortman, C. B. (1996). The impact of trauma on world views. *Journal of Social and Clinical Psychology, 15,* 417–429.

Godden, D. R., & Baddeley, A. D. (1975). Context-dependent memory in two natural environments: On land and underwater. *British Journal of Psychology, 66,* 325–331.

Goel, M. S., McCarthy, E. P., Phillips, R. S., & Wee, C. C. (2004). Obesity among U.S. immigrant subgroups by duration of residence. *Journal of the American Medical Association, 292,* 2860–2867.

Goel, V., & Dolan, R. J. (2001). The functional anatomy of humor: Segregating cognitive and affective components. *Nature Neuroscience, 4,* 237–238.

Goff, D. C. (1993). Reply to Dr. Armstrong. *Journal of Nervous and Mental Disease, 181,* 604–605.

Goff, D. C., & Simms, C. A. (1993). Has multiple personality disorder remained consistent over time? *Journal of Nervous and Mental Disease, 181,* 595–600.

Goff, L. M., & Roediger, III, H. L. (1998). Imagination inflation for action events: Repeated imaginings lead to illusory recollections. *Memory and Cognition, 26,* 20–33.

Gold, M., & Yanof, D. S. (1985). Mothers, daughters, and girlfriends. *Journal of Personality and Social Psychology, 49,* 654–659.

Goldapple, K., Segal, Z., Garson, C., Lau, M., Bieling, P., Kennedy, S., & Mayberg, H. (2004). Modulation of cortical-limbic pathways in major depression. *Archives of General Psychiatry, 61,* 34–41.

Golden, R. N., Gaynes, B. N., Ekstrom, R. D., Hamer, R. M., Jacobsen, F. M., Suppes, T., Wisner, K. L., & Nemeroff, C. B. (2005). The efficacy of light therapy in the treatment of mood disorders: A review and meta-analysis of the evidence. *American Journal of Psychiatry, 162,* 656–662.

Goldfried, M. R. (2001). Integrating gay, lesbian, and bisexual issues into mainstream psychology. *American Psychologist, 56,* 977–988.

Goldfried, M. R., & Padawer, W. (1982). Current status and future directions in psychotherapy. In M. R. Goldfried (Ed.), *Converging themes in psychotherapy: Trends in psychodynamic, humanistic, and behavioral practice.* New York: Springer.

Goldfried, M. R., Raue, P. J., & Castonguay, L. G. (1998). The therapeutic focus in significant sessions of master therapists: A comparison of cognitive-behavioral and psychodynamic-interpersonal interventions. *Journal of Consulting and Clinical Psychology, 66,* 803–810.

Goldin-Meadow, S., Nusbaum, H., Kelly, S. D., & Wagner, S. (2001). Explaining math: Gesturing lightens the load. *Psychological Science, 12,* 516–522.

Golding, J. M. (1996). Sexual assault history and women's reproductive and sexual health. *Psychology of Women Quarterly, 20,* 101–121.

Golding, J. M. (1999). Sexual-assault history and the long-term physical health problems: Evidence from clinical and population epidemiology. *Current Directions in Psychological Science, 8,* 191–194.

Goldstein, A. P., Glick, B., & Gibbs, J. C. (1998). *Aggression replacement training: A comprehensive intervention for aggressive youth* (rev. ed.). Champaign, IL: Research Press.

Goldstein, I. (2000, August). Male sexual circuitry. *Scientific American,* pp. 70–75.

Goldstein, I., Lue, T. F., Padma-Nathan, H., Rosen, R. C., Steers, W. D., & Wicker, P. A. (1998). Oral sildenafil in the treatment of erectile dysfunction. *New England Journal of Medicine, 338,* 1397–1404.

Goleman, D. (1980, February). 1,528 little geniuses and how they grew. *Psychology Today,* pp. 28–53.

Goleman, D. (1995). *Emotional intelligence.* New York: Bantam.

Gonsalves, B., Reber, P. J., Gitelman, D. R., Parrish, T. B., Mesulam, M-M., & Paller, K. A. (2004). Neural evidence that vivid imagining can lead to false remembering. *Psychological Science, 15,* 655–659.

Goodall, J. (1968). The behaviour of free-living chimpanzees in the Gombe Stream Reserve. *Animal Behaviour Monographs, 1,* 161–311.

Goodall, J. (1986). *The chimpanzees of Gombe: Patterns of behavior.* Cambridge, MA: Harvard University Press.

Goodall, J. (1998). Learning from the chimpanzees: A message humans can understand. *Science, 282,* 2184–2185.

Goodchilds, J. (1987). Quoted by Carol Tavris, Old age is not what it used to be. *The New York Times Magazine: Good Health Magazine,* September 27, pp. 24–25, 91–92.

Goode, E. (1999, February 16). Tales of midlife crisis found greatly exaggerated. *New York Times* (www.nytimes.com).

Goode, E. (1999, April 13). If things taste bad, 'phantoms' may be at work. *New York Times* (www.nytimes.com).

Goode, E. (2002, June 30). Antidepressants life clouds, but lose 'miracle drug' label. *New York Times* (www.nytimes.com).

Goode, E. (2003, January 28). Even in the age of Prozac, some still prefer the couch. *New York Times* (www.nytimes.com).

Goodhart, D. E. (1986). The effects of positive and negative thinking on performance in an achievement situation. *Journal of Personality and Social Psychology, 51,* 117–124.

Goodman, E. (2000). Depressive symptoms and cigarette smoking among teens. *Pediatrics, 106,* 4. 748–756.

Goodman, G. S., Ghetti, S., Quas, J. A., Edelstein, R. S., Alexander, K. W., Redlich, A. D., Cordon, I. M., & Jones, D. P. H. (2003). A prospective study of memory for child sexual abuse: New findings relevant to the repressed-memory controversy. *Psychological Science, 14,* 113–118.

Goodman, G. S., Rudy, L., Bottoms, B. L., & Aman, B. (1990). Children's concerns and memory: Issues of ecological validity in the study of children's eyewitness testimony. In R. Fivush & J. A. Hudson (Eds.), *Knowing and remembering in young children.* New York: Cambridge University Press.

Goodman, L. A., Koss, M. P., & Russo, N. F. (1993). Violence against women: Mental health effects. Part II. Conceptualizations of posttraumatic stress. *Applied & Preventive Psychology, 2,* 123–130.

Goodnough, A. (2002, May 2). Post-9/11 pain found to linger in young minds. *New York Times* (www.nytimes.com).

Goodson, P., McCormick, D., & Evans, A. (2001). Searching for sexually explicit materials on the Internet: An exploratory study of college students' behavior and attitudes. *Archives of Sexual Behavior, 30,* 101–118.

Goodstein, L., & Glaberson, W. (2000, April 9). The well-marked roads to homicidal rage. *New York Times* (www.nytimes.com).

Goodwin, F. K., & Morrison, A. R. (1999). Scientists in bunkers: How appeasement of animal rights activism has failed. *Cerebrum, 1*(2), 50–62.

Goodwin, R., & Hamilton, S. P. (2002). Cigarette smoking and panic: The role of neuroticism. *American Journal of Psychiatry, 159,* 1208–1213.

Gopnik, A., & Meltzoff, A. N. (1986). Relations between semantic and cognitive development in the one-word stage: The specificity hypothesis. *Child Development, 57,* 1040–1053.

Goranson, R. E. (1978). *The hindsight effect in problem solving.* Unpublished manuscript, cited by G. Wood (1984), Research methodology: A decision-making perspective. In A. M. Rogers & C. J. Scheirer (Eds.), *The G. Stanley Hall Lecture Series* (Vol. 4). Washington, DC: American Psychological Association.

Gordon, P. (2004). Numerical cognition without words: Evidence from Amazonia. *Science, 306,* 496–499.

Gore, A., Jr. (1992). *Earth in the balance: Ecology and the human spirit.* Boston: Houghton-Mifflin.

Gore-Felton, C., Koopman, C., Thoresen, C., Arnow, B., Bridges, E., & Spiegel, D. (2000). Psychologists' beliefs and clinical characteristics: Judging the veracity of childhood sexual abuse memories. *Professional Psychology: Research and Practice, 31,* 372–377.

Gortmaker, S. L., Must, A., Perrin, J. M., Sobol, A. M., & Dietz, W. H. (1993). Social and economic consequences of overweight in adolescence and young adulthood. *New England Journal of Medicine, 329,* 1008–1012.

Gosling, S. D., Ko, S. J., Mannarelli, T., & Morris, M. E. (2002). A room with a cue: Personality judgments based on offices and bedrooms. *Journal of Personality and Social Psychology, 82,* 379–398.

Gosling, S. D., Kwan, V. S. Y., & John, O. P. (2003). A dog's got personality: A cross-species comparative approach to personality judgments in dogs and humans. *Journal of Personality and Social Psychology, 85,* 1161–1169.

Gotlib, I. H., & Hammen, C. L. (1992). *Psychological aspects of depression: Toward a cognitive-interpersonal integration.* New York: Wiley.

Gottesman, I. I. (1991). *Schizophrenia genesis: The origins of madness.* New York: Freeman.

Gottesman, I. I. (2001). Psychopathology through a life span—genetic prism. *American Psychologist, 56,* 867–881.

Gottfredson, L. S. (2002a). Where and why *g* matters: Not a mystery. *Human Performance, 15,* 25–46.

Gottfredson, L. S. (2002b). *g:* Highly general and highly practical. In R. J. Sternberg & E. L. Grigorenko (Eds.), *The general factor of intelligence: How general is it?* Mahwah, NJ: Erlbaum.

Gottfredson, L. S. (2003a). Dissecting practical intelligence theory: Its claims and evidence. *Intelligence, 31,* 343–397.

Gottfredson, L. S. (2003b). On Sternberg's "Reply to Gottfredson." *Intelligence, 31,* 415–424.

Gottfried, J. A., O'Doherty, J., & Dolan, R. J. (2003). Encoding predictive reward value in human amygdala and orbitofrontal cortex. *Science, 301,* 1104–1108.

Gottman, J., with Silver N. (1994). *Why marriages succeed or fail.* New York: Simon & Schuster.

Gougoux, F., Zatorre, R., Lassonde, M., Voss, P., & Lepore, F. (2005). A functional neuroimaging study of sound localization: Visual cortex activity predicts performance in early-blind individuals. *PloS Biology, 3*(2): e27.

Gould, E., Reeves, A. J., Graziano, M. S. A., & Gross, C. G. (1999). Neurogenesis in the neocortex of adult primates. *Science, 286,* 548–552.

Gould, S. J. (1981). *The mismeasure of man.* New York: Norton.

Gould, S. J. (1997, June 12). Darwinian fundamentalism. *The New York Review of Books, XLIV*(10), 34–37.

Grady, C. L., & McIntosh, A. R., Horwitz, B., Maisog, J. M., Ungeleider, L. G., Mentis, M. J., Pietrini, P., Schapiro, M. B., & Haxby, J. V. (1995). Age-related reductions in human recognition memory due to impaired encoding. *Science, 269,* 218–221.

Graf, P. (1990). Life-span changes in implicit and explicit memory. *Bulletin of the Psychonomic Society, 28,* 353–358.

Graham, J. W., Marks, G., & Hansen, W. B. (1991). Social influence processes affecting adolescent substance use. *Journal of Applied Psychology, 76,* 291–298.

Grant, B. F., & Dawson, D. A. (1998). Age of onset of drug use and its association with DSM-IV drug abuse and dependence: Results from the national Longitudinal Alcohol Epidemiologic Survey. *Journal of Substance Abuse, 10,* 163–173.

Grant, B. F., Stinson, F. S., Hasin, D. S., Dawson, D. A., Chou, S. P., & Anderson, K. (2004). Immigration and lifetime prevalence of DSM-IV psychiatric disorders among Mexican Americans and non-Hispanic Whites in the United States. *Archives of General Psychiatry, 61,* 1226–1233.

Gray-Little, B., & Burks, N. (1983). Power and satisfaction in marriage: A review and critique. *Psychological Bulletin, 93,* 513–538.

Gray-Little, B., & Hafdahl, A. R. (2000). Factors influencing racial comparisons of self-esteem: A quantitative review. *Psychological Bulletin, 126,* 26–54.

GRE. (1990). *GRE guide to the use of the Graduate Record Examinations Program.* Princeton, NJ: Graduate Record Examinations Board, Educational Testing Service.

Green, B. (2002). Listening to leaders: Feedback on 360-degree feedback one year later. *Organizational Development Journal, 20,* 8–16.

Green, C. S., & Bavelier, D. (2003). Action video game modifies visual selective attention. *Nature, 423,* 534–537.

Green, J. T., & Woodruff-Pak, D. S. (2000). Eyeblink classical conditioning: Hippocampal formation is for neutral stimulus associations as cerebellum is for association-response. *Psychological Bulletin, 126,* 138–158.

Greenberg, D. L. (2004). President Bush's false 'flashbulb' memory of 9/11/01. *Applied Cognitive Psychology, 18,* 363–370.

Greenberg, J., Solomon, S., & Pyszczynski, T. (1997). Terror management theory of self-esteem and cultural worldviews: Empirical assessments and conceptual refinements. *Advances in Social Psychology, 29,* 61–142.

Greene, J., Sommerville, R. B., Nystrom, L. E., Darley, J. M., & Cohen, J. D. (2001). An fMRI investigation of emotional engagement in moral judgment. *Science, 293,* 2105.

Greene, R. L. (1987). Effects of maintenance rehearsal on human memory. *Psychological Bulletin, 102,* 403–413.

Greenfeld, L. A. (1998). *Alcohol and crime: An analysis of national data on the prevalence of alcohol involvement in crime.* Washington, DC: Document NCJ-168632, Bureau of Justice Statistics (www.ojp.usdoj.gov/bjs).

Greenough, W. T., Black, J. E., & Wallace, C. S. (1987). Experience and brain development. *Child Development, 58,* 539–559.

Greenwald, A. G. (1992). New look 3: Unconscious cognition reclaimed. *American Psychologist, 47,* 766–779.

Greenwald, A. G. (1992). Subliminal semantic activation and subliminal snake oil. Paper presented to the American Psychological Association Convention, Washington, DC.

Greenwald, A. G., McGhee, D. E., & Schwartz, J. L. K. (1998). Measuring individual differences in implicit cognition: The implicit association test. *Journal of Personality and Social Psychology, 74,* 1464–1480.

Greenwald, A. G., Oakes, M. A., & Hoffman, H. (2003). Targets of discrimination: Effects of race on responses to weapons holders. *Journal of Experimental Social Psychology, 39,* 399.

Greenwald, A. G., Spangenberg, E. R., Pratkanis, A. R., & Eskenazi, J. (1991). Double-blind tests of subliminal self-help audiotapes. *Psychological Science, 2,* 119–122.

Greenwood, M. R. C. (1989). Sexual dimorphism and obesity. In A. J. Stunkard & A. Baum (Eds.). *Perspectives in behavioral medicine: Eating, sleeping, and sex.* Hillsdale, NJ: Erlbaum.

Greers, A. E. (2004). Speech, language, and reading skills after early cochlear implantation. *Archives of Otolaryngology—Head & Neck Surgery, 130,* 634–638.

Gregory, R. L. (November, 1968). Visual illusions. *Scientific American, 219*(5), 66–76.

Gregory, R. L. (1978). *Eye and brain: The psychology of seeing* (3rd ed.). New York: McGraw-Hill.

Gregory, R. L., & Gombrich, E. H. (Eds.). (1973). *Illusion in nature and art.* New York: Charles Scribner's Sons.

Greif, E. B., & Ulman, K. J. (1982). The psychological impact of menarche on early adolescent females: A review of the literature. *Child Development, 53,* 1413–1430.

Greist, J. H., Jefferson, J. W., & Marks, I. M. (1986). *Anxiety and its treatment: Help is available.* Washington, DC: American Psychiatric Press.

Grewal, D., & Salovey, P. (2005). Feeling smart: The science of emotional intelligence. *American Scientist, 93,* 330–339.

Grèzes, J., & Decety, J. (2001). Function anatomy of execution, mental simulation, observation, and verb generation of actions: A meta-analysis. *Human Brain Mapping, 12,* 1–19.

Griffiths, M. (2001). Sex on the Internet: Observations and implications for Internet sex addiction. *Journal of Sex Research, 38,* 333–342.

Grill-Spector, K., & Kanwisher, N. (2005). Visual recognition: As soon as you know it is there, you know what it is. *Psychological Science, 16,* 152–160.

Grilo, C. M., & Pogue-Geile, M. F. (1991). The nature of environmental influences on weight and obesity: A behavior genetic analysis. *Psychological Bulletin, 110,* 520–537.

Grobstein, C. (1979, June). External human fertilization. *Scientific American,* pp. 57–67.

Groothuis, T. G. G., & Carere, C. (2005). Avian personalities: Characterization and epigenesis. *Neuroscience and Biobehavioral Reviews, 29,* 137–150.

Gross, A. E., & Crofton, C. (1977). What is good is beautiful. *Sociometry, 40,* 85–90.

Grossberg, S. (1995). The attentive brain. *American Scientist, 83,* 438–449.

Grossman, M., & Wood, W. (1993). Sex differences in intensity of emotional experience: A social role interpretation. *Journal of Personality and Social Psychology, 65,* 1010–1022.

Gruder, C. L. (1977). Choice of comparison persons in evaluating oneself. In J. M. Suls & R. L. Miller (Eds.), *Social comparison processes.* New York: Hemisphere.

Grudnik, J., & Kranzler, J. H. (2001). Meta-analysis of the relationship between intelligence and inspection time. *Intelligence, 13,* 523–537.

Grunebaum, M. F., Ellis, S. P., Li, S., O(quendo, M. A., Mann, J. J. (2004). Antidepressants and suicide risk in the United States, 1985–1999. *Journal of Clinical Psychiatry, 65,* 1456–1462.

Guerin, B. (1986). Mere presence effects in humans: A review. *Journal of Personality and Social Psychology, 22,* 38–77.

Guerin, B. (2003). Language use as social strategy: A review and an analytic framework for the social sciences. *Review of General Psychology, 7,* 251–298.

Guilbault, R. L., Bryant, F. B., Brockway, J. H., & Posavac, E. J. (2004). A meta-analysis of research on hindsight bias. *Basic and Applied Social Psychology, 26,* 103–117.

Guisinger, S. (2004). Adapted to flee famine: Adding an evolutionary perspective on anorexia nervosa. *Psychological Review, 110,* 745–761.

Gundersen, E. (2001, August 1). MTV is a many splintered thing. *USA Today,* pp. D1, D2.

Güntürkün, O. (2003). Adult persistence of head-turning asymmetry. *Nature, 421,* 711.

Gura, T. (2004). New data on appetite-suppressing peptide challenges critics. *Science, 306,* 1453–1454.

Gustafson, D., Lissner, L., Bengtsson, C., Björkelund, C., & Skoog, I. (2004). A 24-year follow-up of body mass index and cerebral atrophy. *Neurology, 63,* 1876–1881.

Gustafson, D., Rothenberg, E., Blennow, K., Steen, B., & Skoog, I. (2003). An 18-year follow-up of overweight and risk of Alzheimer disease. *Archives of Internal Medicine, 163,* 1524–1528.

Gustavson, C. R., Garcia, J., Hankins, W. G., & Rusiniak, K. W. (1974). Coyote predation control by aversive conditioning. *Science, 184,* 581–583.

Gustavson, C. R., Kelly, D. J., & Sweeney, M. (1976). Prey-lithium aversions I: Coyotes and wolves. *Behavioral Biology, 17,* 61–72.

Guttmacher Institute. (1994). *Sex and America's teenagers.* New York: Alan Guttmacher Institute.

Guttmacher Institute. (2000). *Fulfilling the promise: Public policy and U.S. family planning clinics.* New York: Alan Guttmacher Institute.

H., Sally (1979, August). Videotape recording number T-3, Fortunoff Video Archive of Holocaust Testimonies. New Haven, CT: Yale University Library.

Haber, R. N. (1970, May). How we remember what we see. *Scientific American,* pp. 104–112.

Haddock, G., & Zanna, M. P. (1994). Preferring "housewives" to "feminists." *Psychology of Women Quarterly, 18,* 25–52.

Haidt, J. (2000). The positive emotion of elevation. *Prevention and Treatment, 3,* article 3 (journals.apa.org/prevention/volume3).

Haidt, J. (2001). The emotional dog and its rational tail: A social intuitionist approach to moral judgment. *Psychological Review, 108,* 814–834.

Haidt, J. (2002). The moral emotions. In R. J. Davidson, K. Scherer, & H. H. Goldsmith (Eds.), *Handbook of Affective Sciences.* New York: Oxford University Press.

Haier, R. J., Jung, R. E., Yeo, R. A., Head, K., & Alkire, M. T. (2004). Structural brain variation and general intelligence. *NeuroImage, 23,* 425–433.

Haines, R. F. (1991). A breakdown in simultaneous information processing. In G. Obrecht & L. W. Stark (Eds.), *Presbyopia research.* New York: Plenum Press.

Hakuta, K., Bialystok, E., & Wiley, E. (2003). Critical evidence: A test of the critical-period hypothesis for second-language acquisition. *Psychological Science, 14,* 31–38.

Halberstadt, J. B., & Niedenthal, P. M. (2001). Effects of emotion concepts on perceptual memory for emotional expressions. *Journal of Personality and Social Psychology, 81,* 587–598.

Halberstadt, J. B., & Niedenthal, P. M., & Kushner, J. (1995). Resolution of lexical ambiguity by emotional state. *Psychological Science, 6,* 278–281.

Haldeman, D. C. (1994). The practice and ethics of sexual orientation conversion therapy. *Journal of Consulting and Clinical Psychology, 62,* 221–227.

Haldeman, D. C. (2002). Gay rights, patient rights: The implications of sexual orientation conversion therapy. *Professional Psychology: Research and Practice, 33,* 260–264.

Hall, C. S. (1984). "A ubiquitous sex difference in dreams" revisited. *Journal of Personality and Social Psychology, 46,* 1109–1117.

Hall, C. S., Dornhoff, W., Blick, K. A., & Weesner, K. E. (1982). The dreams of college men and women in 1950 and 1980: A comparison of dream contents and sex differences. *Sleep, 5,* 188–194.

Hall, C. S., & Lindzey, G. (1978). *Theories of personality* (2nd ed.). New York: Wiley.

Hall, G. (1997). Context aversion, Pavlovian conditioning, and the psychological side effects of chemotherapy. *European Psychologist, 2,* 118–124.

Hall, G. S. (1904). *Adolescence: Its psychology and its relations to physiology, anthropology, sex, crime, religion and education* (Vol. I). New York: Appleton-Century-Crofts.

Hall, J. A. (1984). *Nonverbal sex differences: Communication accuracy and expressive style.* Baltimore: Johns Hopkins University Press.

Hall, J. A. (1987). On explaining gender differences: The case of nonverbal communication. In P. Shaver & C. Hendrick (Eds.), *Review of Personality and Social Psychology, 7,* 177–200.

Hall, J. A. Y., & Kimura, D. (1994). Dermatoglyphic assymetry and sexual orientation in men. *Behavioral Neuroscience, 108,* 1203–1206.

Hall, J. G. (2003). Twinning. *Lancet, 362,* 735–743.

Hall, S. S. (2004, May). The good egg. *Discover,* pp. 30–39.

Halpern, C. T., Joyner, K., Udry, J. R., & Suchindran, C. (2000). Smart teens don't have sex (or kiss much either). *Journal of Adolescent Health, 26,* 213–225.

Halpern, D. F. (1991). Cognitive sex differences: Why diversity is a critical research issue. Paper presented to the American Psychological Association convention.

Halpern, D. F. (2000). *Sex-related ability differences: Changing perspectives, changing minds.* Mahwah, NJ: Erlbaum.

Halpern, D. F. (2005, May 20). Response to Drs. Pinker and Spelke. www.edge.org.

Halpern, D. F., & Coren, S. (1988). Do right-handers live longer? *Nature, 333,* 213.

Halpern, D. F., & Coren, S. (1990). Laterality and longevity: Is left-handedness associated with a younger age at death? In S. Coren (Ed.), *Left-handedness: Behavioral implications and anomalies.* Amsterdam: North-Holland.

Halpern, D. F., & Coren, S. (1991). Lateral preference and life span. *New England Journal of Medicine, 324,* 998.

Halpern, D. F., & Coren, S. (1993). Left-handedness and life span: A reply to Harris. *Psychological Bulletin, 114,* 235–241.

Halpern, D. F., Gilbert, R., & Coren, S. (1996). PC or not-PC? Contemporary challenges to unpopular research. *Journal of Social Distress and the Homeless, 5,* 251–271.

Halsey, A. H., & Webb, J. (2000). *Twentieth-century British social trends.* Basingstoke: Macmillan.

Hamann, S., Herman, R. A., Nolan, C. L., & Wallen, K. (2004). Men and women differ in amygdala response to visual sexual stimuli. *Nature Neuroscience, 7,* 411–416.

Hamann, S., Monarch, E. S., & Goldstein, F. C. (2002). Impaired fear conditioning in Alzheimer's disease. *Neuropsychologica, 40,* 1187–1195.

Hamill, R., Wilson, T. D., & Nisbett, R. E. (1980). Insensitivity to sample bias: Generalizing from atypical cases. *Journal of Personality and Social Psychology, 39,* 578–589.

Hamilton, G. (2001, July 11). Family sues Coca-Cola over son's death. *National Post.*

Hamilton, R. H. (2000, November). Increased prevalence of absolute pitch in blind musicians (Abstract 739.13). Society for Neuroscience meeting, New Orleans.

Hammer, E. (2003). How lucky you are to be a psychology major. *Eye on Psi Chi,* 4–5.

Hammersmith, S. K. (1982, August). *Sexual preference: An empirical study from the Alfred C. Kinsey Institute for Sex Research.* Paper presented at the meeting of the American Psychological Association, Washington, DC.

Hampson, R. (2000, April 10). In the end, people just need more room. *USA Today,* p. 19A.

Haney, C., & Logan, D. D. (1994). Broken promise: The Supreme Court's response to social science research on capital punishment. *Journal of Social Issues, 50,* 75–101.

Hankin, B. L., & Abramson, L. Y. (2001). Development of gender differences in depression: An elaborated cognitive vulnerability-transactional stress theory. *Psychological Bulletin, 127,* 773–796.

Hansen, C. H., & Hansen, R. D. (1988). Finding the face-in-the-crowd: An anger superiority effect. *Journal of Personality and Social Psychology, 54,* 917–924.

Harber, K. D. (1998), Feedback to minorities: Evidence of a positive bias. *Journal of Personality and Social Psychology, 74,* 622–628.

Hardin, C., & Banaji, M. R. (1993). The influence of language on thought. *Social Cognition, 11,* 277–308.

Hare, R. D. (1975). Psychophysiological studies of psychopathy. In D. C. Fowles (Ed.), *Clinical applications of psychophysiology.* New York: Columbia University Press.

Hariri, A. R., Mattay, V. S., Tessitore, A., Kolachana, B., Fera, F., Goldman, D., Egan, M. F., & Weinberger, D. R. (2002). Serotonin transporter genetic variation and the response of the human amygdala. *Science, 297,* 400–403.

Harkins, S. G., & Szymanski, K. (1989). Social loafing and group evaluation. *Journal of Personality and Social Psychology, 56,* 934–941.

Harlow, H. F., Harlow, M. K., & Suomi, S. J. (1971). From thought to therapy: Lessons from a primate laboratory. *American Scientist, 59,* 538–549.

Harlow, R. E., & Cantor, N. (1996). Still participating after all these years: A study of life task participation in later life. *Journal of Personality and Social Psychology, 71,* 1235–1249.

Harmon-Jones, E., Abramson, L. Y., Sigelman, J., Bohlig, A., Hogan, M. E., & Harmon-Jones, C. (2002). Proneness to hypomania/mania symptoms or depression symptoms and asymmetrical frontal cortical responses to an anger-evoking event. *Journal of Personality and Social Psychology, 82,* 610–618.

Harris, B. (1979). Whatever happened to Little Albert? *American Psychologist, 34,* 151–160.

Harris, J. A. (1999). Review and methodological considerations in research on testosterone and aggression. *Aggression and Violent Behavior, 4,* 273–291.

Harris, J. R. (1998). *The nurture assumption.* New York: Free Press.

Harris, J. R. (2000b). Socialization, personality development, and the child's environments: Comment on Vandell (2000). *Developmental Psychology, 36,* 711–723.

Harris, J. R. (2006). *No two are alike: Human nature and human individuality.* New York: Norton.

Harris, L. J. (1993). Do left-handers die sooner than right-handers? Commentary on Coren and Halpern's (1991) "Left-handedness: A marker for decreased survival fitness." *Psychological Bulletin, 114,* 203–234.

Harris, R. J. (1994). The impact of sexually explicit media. In J. Brant & D. Zillmann (Eds.), *Media effects: Advances in theory and research.* Hillsdale, NJ: Erlbaum.

Harrison, Y., & Horne, J. A. (2000). The impact of sleep deprivation on decision making: A review. *Journal of Experimental Psychology: Applied, 6,* 236–249.

Harriston, K. A. (1993, December 24). 1 shakes, 1 snoozes; both win $45 million. *Washington Post* release (in *Tacoma News Tribune*).

Hart, C. L., Taylor, M. D., Smith, G. D., Whalley, L. J., Starr, J. M., Hole, D. J., Wilson, V., & Deary, I. J. (2003). Childhood IQ, social class, deprivation, and their relationships with mortality and morbidity risk in later life: Prospective observational study linking the Scottish Mental Survey 1932 and the Midspan Studies. *Psychosomatic Medicine, 65,* 877–883.

Hart, D. (1988). The development of personal identity in adolescence: A philosophical dilemma approach. *Merrill-Palmer Quarterly, 34,* 105–114.

Harter, J. K. (2000, Winter/Spring). The linkage of employee perceptions to outcomes in a retail environment—cause and effect? *Gallup Research Journal,* pp. 25–38.

Harter, J. K., Schmidt, F. L., & Hayes, T. L. (2002). Business-unit-level relationship between employee satisfaction, employee engagement, and business outcomes: A meta-analysis. *Journal of Applied Psychology, 87,* 268–279.

Hartmann, E. (1981, April). The strangest sleep disorder. *Psychology Today,* pp. 14, 16, 18.

Hartmann, E. (1984). *The nightmare: The psychology and biology of terrifying dreams.* New York: Basic Books.

Harvey, F. (2002, February). Surrounded by sound. *Scientific American,* pp. 94–95.

Hassan, R., & Carr, J. (1989). Changing patterns of suicide in Australia. *Australian and New Zealand Journal of Psychiatry, 23,* 226–234.

Hatfield, E. (1988). Passionate and companionate love. In R. J. Sternberg & M. L. Barnes (Eds.), *The psychology of love.* New Haven: Yale University Press.

Hatfield, E., & Sprecher, S. (1986). *Mirror, mirror . . . The importance of looks in everyday life.* Albany: State University of New York Press.

Hathaway, S. R. (1960). *An MMPI Handbook* (Vol. 1, Foreword). Minneapolis: University of Minnesota Press. (Revised edition, 1972).

Hauser, M. D., Chomsky, N., & Fitch, W. T. (2002). The faculty of language: What is it, who has it, and how did it evolve? *Science, 298,* 1569–1579.

Hawkes, N. (2002, September 10). Fat children may die before their parents (report on presentation to the British Association for the Advancement of Science). *Times of London,* p. 3.

Haxby, J. V. (2001, July 7). Quoted by B. Bower, Faces of perception. *Science News,* pp. 10–12. See also J. V. Haxby, M. I. Gobbini, M. L. Furey, A. Ishai, J. L. Schouten & P. Pietrini, Distributed and overlapping representations of faces and objects in ventral temporal cortex. *Science, 293,* 2425–2430.

Hayne, H. (2004). Infant memory development: Implications for childhood amnesia. *Developmental Review, 24,* 33–73.

Hazan, C., & Shaver, P. R. (1994). Attachment as an organizational framework for research on close relationships. *Psychological Inquiry, 5,* 1–22.

Hazelrigg, M. D., Cooper, H. M., & Borduin, C. M. (1987). Evaluating the effectiveness of family therapies: An integrative review and analysis. *Psychological Bulletin, 101,* 428–442.

Head Start. (2005). Head Start program fact sheet. www.acf.hhs.gov/programs/hsb/research/2005.htm

Healey, J. (2004). *Overweight and obesity.* Thirroul, NSW, Australia: Spinney Press.

Heaps, C. M., & Nash, M. (2001). Comparing recollective experience in true and false autobiographical memories. *Journal of Experimental Psychology: Learning, Memory, and Cognition, 27,* 920–930.

Heath, A. C., & Madden, P. A. F. (1995). Genetic influences on smoking behavior. In J. R. Turner & L. R. Cardon (Eds.), *Behavior genetic approaches in behavioral medicine.* New York: Plenum Press, 45–66.

Hebb, D. O. (1980). *Essay on mind.* Hillsdale, NJ: Erlbaum. 9–16.

Hebert, R. (2001, September). Doing a number on memory. *APS Observer,* pp. 1, 7–11.

Hebl, M. R., & Mannix, L. M. (2003). The weight of obesity in evaluating others: A mere proximity effect. *Personality and Social Psychology Bulletin, 29,* 28–38.

Hedges, L. V., & Nowell, A. (1995). Sex differences in mental test scores, variability, and numbers of high-scoring individuals. *Science, 269,* 41–45.

Heider, F. (1958). *The psychology of interpersonal relations.* New York: Wiley.

Heiman, J. R. (1975, April). The physiology of erotica: Women's sexual arousal. *Psychology Today,* 90–94.

Heinrichs, R. W. (2005). The primacy of cognition in schizophrenia. *American Psychologist, 60,* 229–242.

Heins, M. (2004, December 14). Quoted by B. Kloza, Violent Christmas games. *ScienCentralNews* (www.sciencecentral.com).

Heishman, S. J., Kozlowski, L. T., & Henningfield, J. E. (1997). Nicotine addiction: Implications for public health policy. *Journal of Social Issues, 53,* 13–33.

Hejmadi, A., Davidson, R. J., & Rozin, P. (2000). Exploring Hindu Indian emotion expressions: Evidence for accurate recognition by Americans and Indians. *Psychological Science, 11,* 183–187.

Helgeson, V. S., Cohen, S., & Fritz, H. L. (1998). Social ties and cancer. In P. M. Cinciripini & others (Eds.), *Psychological and behavioral factors in cancer risk.* New York: Oxford University Press.

Heller, W. (1990, May/June). Of one mind: Second thoughts about the brain's dual nature. *The Sciences,* pp. 38–44.

Helmreich, W. B. (1992). *Against all odds: Holocaust survivors and the successful lives they made in America.* New York: Simon & Schuster.

Helmreich, W. B. (1994). Personal correspondence. Department of Sociology, City University of New York.

Helms, J. E., Jernigan, M., & Mascher, J. (2005). The meaning of race in psychology and how to change it: A methodological perspective. *American Psychologist, 60,* 27–36.

Helmuth, L. (2001). Boosting brain activity from the outside in. *Science, 292,* 1284–1286.

Helweg-Larsen, M. (1999). (The lack of) optimistic biases in response to the 1994 Northridge earthquake: The role of personal experience. *Basic and Applied Social Psychology, 21,* 119–129.

Hembree, R. (1988). Correlates, causes, effects, and treatment of test anxiety. *Review of Educational Research, 58,* 47–77.

Hemenover, S. H. (2003). The good, the bad, and the healthy: Impacts of emotional disclosure of trauma on resilient self-concept and psychological distress. *Personality and Social Psychology Bulletin, 29,* 1236–1244.

Henderlong, J., & Lepper, M. R. (2002). The effects of praise on children's intrinsic motivation: A review and synthesis. *Psychological Bulletin, 128,* 774–795.

Henkel, L. A., Franklin, N., & Johnson, M. K. (2000, March). Cross-modal source monitoring confusions between perceived and imagined events. *Journal of Experimental Psychology: Learning, Memory, & Cognition, 26,* 321–335.

Henley, N. M. (1989). Molehill or mountain? What we know and don't know about sex bias in language. In M. Crawford & M. Gentry (Eds.), *Gender and thought: Psychological perspectives.* New York: Springer-Verlag.

Henninger, P. (1992). Conditional handedness: Handedness changes in multiple personality disordered subject reflect shift in hemispheric dominance. *Consciousness and Cognition, 1,* 265–287.

Henry, J. D., MacLeod, M. S., Phillips, L. H., & Crawford, J. R. (2004). A meta-analytic review of prospective memory and aging. *Psychology and Aging, 19,* 27–39.

Hepper, P. G., Shahidullah, S., & White, R. (1990). Origins of fetal handedness. *Nature, 347,* 431.

Hepper, P. G., Wells, D. L., & Lynch, C. (2004). Prenatal thumb sucking is related to postnatal handedness. *Neuropsychologia, 43,* 313–315.

Herbert, B. (2001, July 23). Economics 202 at Big Tobacco U. *New York Times* (www.nytimes.com).

Herbert, J. D., Lilienfeld, S. O., Lohr, J. M., Montgomery, R. W., O'Donohue, W. T., Rosen, G. M., & Tolin, D. F. (2000). Science and pseudoscience in the development of eye movement desensitization and reprocessing: Implications for clinical psychology. *Clinical Psychology Review, 20,* 945–971.

Herek, G. M., & Capitanio, J. P. (1996). "Some of my best friends": Intergroup contact, concealable stigma, and heterosexuals' attitudes toward gay men and lesbians. *Personality and Social Psychology Bulletin, 22,* 412–424.

HERI. (2005, April 13). Spirituality in higher education: A national study of college students' search for meaning and purpose. Press release from Higher Education Research Institute, UCLA.

Herman, C. P., & Polivy, J. (1980). Restrained eating. In A. J. Stunkard (Ed.), *Obesity.* Philadelphia: Saunders.

Herman, C. P., & Polivy, J. (2003). Realistic and unrealistic self-change efforts. *American Psychologist, 58,* 823.

Herman-Giddens, M. E., Wang, L., & Koch, G. (2001). Secondary sexual characteristics in boys: Estimates from the National Health and Nutrition Examination Survey III, 1988–1994. *Archives of Pediatrics and Adolescent Medicine, 155,* 1022–1028.

Herrmann, D. (1982). Know thy memory: The use of questionnaires to assess and study memory. *Psychological Bulletin, 92,* 434–452.

Herrnstein, R. J., & Loveland, D. H. (1964). Complex visual concept in the pigeon. *Science, 146,* 549–551.

Hershenson, M. (1989). *The moon illusion.* Hillsdale, NJ: Erlbaum.

Hertenstein, M. J. (2002). Touch: Its communicative functions in infancy. *Human Development, 45,* 70–94.

Herz, R. S. (2001). Ah sweet skunk! Why we like or dislike what we smell. *Cerebrum, 3*(4), 31–47.

Herz, R. S., Schankler, C., & Beland, S. (2004). Olfaction, emotion and associative learning: Effects on motivated behavior. *Motivation and Emotion, 28*(4), 363–383.

Hess, E. H. (1956, July). Space perception in the chick. *Scientific American,* pp. 71–80.

Hettema, J. M., Neale, M. C., & Kendler, K. S. (2001). A review and meta-analysis of the genetic epidemiology of anxiety disorders. *American Journal of Psychiatry, 158,* 1568–1578.

Hewlett, B. S. (1991). *Intimate fathers: The nature and context of Aka Pygmy.* Ann Arbor: University of Michigan Press.

Hibbeln, J. R. (1998). Fish consumption and major depression. *Lancet, 351,* 1213.

Hickok, G., Bellugi, U., & Klima, E. S. (2001, June). Sign language in the brain. *Scientific American,* pp. 58–65.

Higgins, E. T., & Bargh, J. A. (1987). Social cognition and social perception. *Annual Review of Psychology, 38,* 369–425.

Hilgard, E. R. (1986). *Divided consciousness: Multiple controls in human thought and action.* New York: Wiley.

Hilgard, E. R. (1992). Dissociation and theories of hypnosis. In E. Fromm & M. R. Nash (Eds.), *Contemporary hypnosis research.* New York: Guilford.

Hill, C. E., & Nakayama, E. Y. (2000). Client-centered therapy: Where has it been and where is it going? A comment on Hathaway. *Journal of Clinical Psychology, 56,* 961–875.

Hill, H., & Johnston, A. (2001). Categorizing sex and identity from the biological motion of faces. *Current Biology, 11,* 880–885.

Hines, M. (2004). *Brain gender.* New York: Oxford University Press.

Hines, M., & Green, R. (1991). Human hormonal and neural correlates of sex-typed behaviors. *Review of Psychiatry, 10,* 536–555.

Hingson, R. W., Heeren, T., Zakocs, R. C., Kopstein, A., & Wechsler, H. (2002). Magnitude of alcohol-related mortality and morbidity among U.S. college students ages 18–24. *Journal of Studies on Alcohol, 63,* 136–144.

Hintzman, D. L. (1978). *The psychology of learning and memory.* San Francisco: Freeman.

Hinz, L. D., & Williamson, D. A. (1987). Bulimia and depression: A review of the affective variant hypothesis. *Psychological Bulletin, 102,* 150–158.

Hirsch, J. (2003). Obesity: Matter over mind? *Cerebrum, 5*(1), 7–18.

Hirst, W., Neisser, U., & Spelke, E. (1978, June). Divided attention. *Human Nature,* pp. 54–61.

Hirt, E. R., Zillmann, D., Erickson, G. A., & Kennedy, C. (1992). Costs and benefits of allegiance: Changes in fans' self-ascribed competencies after team victory versus defeat. *Journal of Personality and Social Psychology, 63,* 724–738.

HMHL. (2001, February). How schizophrenia develops: New evidence and new ideas. *Harvard Mental Health Letter,* pp. 1–4.

HMHL. (2002, January). Disaster and trauma. *Harvard Mental Health Letter,* pp. 1–5.

HMHL. (2002, August). Smoking and depression. *Harvard Mental Health Letter,* pp. 6–7.

Hobfoll, S. E., Johnson, R. J., Ennis, E., & Jackson, A. P. (2003). Resource loss, resource gain, and emotional outcomes among inner city women. *Journal of Personality, 84,* 632–643.

Hobson, J. A. (1989). *Sleep.* New York: Scientific American Library.

Hobson, J. A. (1995, September). Quoted by C. H. Colt, The power of dreams. *Life,* pp. 36–49.

Hobson, J. A. (2003). *Dreaming: An introduction to the science of sleep.* New York: Oxford.

Hobson, J. A. (2004). *13 dreams Freud never had: The new mind science.* New York: Pi Press.

Hodgkinson, V. A., & Weitzman, M. S. (1992). *Giving and volunteering in the United States.* Washington, DC: Independent Sector.

Hoebel, B. G., & Teitelbaum, P. (1966). Effects of forcefeeding and starvation on food intake and body weight in a rat with ventromedial hypothalamic lesions. *Journal of Comparative and Physiological Psychology, 61,* 189–193.

Hoffman, C., & Hurst, N. (1990). Gender stereotypes: Perception or rationalization? *Journal of Personality and Social Psychology, 58,* 197–208.

Hoffman, D. D. (1998). *Visual intelligence: How we create what we see.* New York: Norton.

Hoffman, H. G. (2004, August). Virtual-reality therapy. *Scientific American,* pp. 58–65.

Hofstede, G. (1980). *Culture's consequences: International differences in work-related values.* Beverly Hills: Sage.

Hogan, J. (1995, November). Get smart, take a test. *Scientific American,* pp. 12, 14.

Hogan, R. (1998). Reinventing personality. *Journal of Social and Clinical Psychology, 17,* 1–10.

Hoge, C. W., Castro, C. A., Messer, S. C., McGurk, D., Cotting, D. I., & Koffman, R. L. (2004). Combat duty in Iraq and Afghanistan, mental health problems, and barriers to care. *New England Journal of Medicine, 35,* 13–22.

Hogg, M. A. (1996). Intragroup processes, group structure and social identity. In W. P. Robinson (Ed.), *Social groups and identities: Developing the legacy of Henri Tajfel.* Oxford: Butterworth Heinemann.

Hohmann, G. W. (1966). Some effects of spinal cord lesions on experienced emotional feelings. *Psychophysiology, 3,* 143–156.

Hokanson, J. E., & Edelman, R. (1966). Effects of three social responses on vascular processes. *Journal of Personality and Social Psychology, 3,* 442–447.

Holahan, C. K., & Sears, R. R. (1995). *The gifted group in later maturity.* Stanford, CA: Stanford University Press.

Holden, C. (1980a). Identical twins reared apart. *Science, 207,* 1323–1325.

Holden, C. (1980b, November). Twins reunited. *Science, 80,* 55–59.

Holden, C. (1986b). Researchers grapple with problems of updating classic psychological test. *Science, 233,* 1249–1251.

Holden, C. (1993). Wake-up call for sleep research. *Science, 259,* 305.

Holden, G. W., & Miller, P. C. (1999). Enduring and different: A meta-analysis of the similarity in parents' child rearing. *Psychological Bulletin, 125,* 223–254.

Holliday, R. E., & Albon, A. J. (2004). Minimizing misinformation effects in young children with cognitive interview mnemonics. *Applied Cognitive Psychology, 18,* 263–281.

Hollis, K. L. (1997). Contemporary research on Pavlovian conditioning: A "new" functional analysis. *American Psychologist, 52,* 956–965.

Hollon, S. D., & 10 others (2005). Prevention of relapse following cognitive therapy vs. medications in moderate to severe depression. *Archives of General Psychiatry, 62,* 417–422.

Hollon, S. D., Thase, M. E., & Markowitz, J. C. (2002). Treatment and prevention of depression. *Psychological Science in the Public Interest, 3,* 39–77.

Holloway, K. (2000, June 22). Among the deaf, sign language faces a challenge. *New York Times* (www.nytimes.com).

Holmes, D. (1990). The evidence for repression: An examination of sixty years of research. In J. Singer (Ed.), *Repression and dissociation: Implications for personality theory, psychopathology, and health.* Chicago: University of Chicago Press.

Holmes, D. S. (1994). Is there evidence for repression? No. (Unexpurgated version on an article which was rewritten by the *Harvard Mental Health Letter* and published as "Is there evidence for repression? Doubtful," June, 1994, pp. 4–6.)

Holstege, G., Georgiadis, J. R., Paans, A. M. J., Meiners, L. C., van der Graaf, F. H. C. E., & Reinders, A. A. T. S. (2003a). Brain activation during male ejaculation. *Journal of Neuroscience, 23,* 9185–9193.

Holstege, G., Reinders, A. A. T., Paans, A. M. J., Meiners, L. C., Pruim, J., & Georgiadis, J. R. (2003b). Brain activation during female sexual orgasm. Program No. 727.7. Washington, DC: Society for Neuroscience.

Holt, L. (2002, August). Reported in "Sounds of speech," p. 26, and in personal correspondence, July 18, 2002.

Holzman, P. S., & Matthysse, S. (1990). The genetics of schizophrenia: A review. *Psychological Science, 1,* 279–286.

Home Office. (2003). Prevalence of drug use: Key findings from the 2002/2003 British Crime Survey. London: Research, Development and Statistics Directorate, Home Office.

Hooper, J., & Teresi, D. (1986). *The three-pound universe.* New York: Macmillan.

Hooykaas, R. (1972). *Religion and the rise of modern science.* Grand Rapids, MI: Eerdmans.

Hopkins, W. D., Russell, J., Freeman, H., Buehler, N., Reynolds, E., & Schapiro, S. J. (2005). The distribution and development of handedness for manual gestures in captive chimpanzees *(Pan troglodytes). Psychological Science, 16,* 487–493.

Horn, J. L. (1982). The aging of human abilities. In J. Wolman (Ed.), *Handbook of developmental psychology.* Englewood Cliffs, NJ: Prentice-Hall.

Horowitz, T. S., Cade, B. E., Wolfe, J. M., & Czeisler, C. A. (2003). Searching night and day: A dissociation of effects of circadian phase and time awake on visual selective attention and vigilance. *Psychological Science, 14,* 549–557.

Horwood, L. J., & Fergusson, D. M. (1998). Breastfeeding and later cognitive and academic outcomes. *Pediatrics, 101*(1).

Hötting, K, & Röder, B. (2004). Hearing cheats touch, but less in congenitally blind than in sighted individuals. *Psychological Science, 15,* 60–64.

House, J. S., Landis, K. R., & Umberson, D. (1988). Social relationships and health. *Science, 241,* 540–545.

House, R. J., & Singh, J. V. (1987). Organizational behavior: Some new directions for I/O psychology. *Annual Review of Psychology, 38,* 669–718.

Houts, A. C., Berman, J. S., & Abramson, H. (1994). Effectiveness of psychological and pharmacological treatments for nocturnal enuresis. *Journal of Consulting and Clinical Psychology, 62,* 737–745.

Howe, M. L. (1997). Children's memory for traumatic experiences. *Learning and Individual Differences, 9,* 153–174.

Howe, M. L. (2003). Memories from the cradle. *Current Directions in Psychological Science, 12,* 62–65.

Hoyer, G., & Lund, E. (1993). Suicide among women related to number of children in marriage. *Archives of General Psychiatry, 50,* 134–137.

Hróbjartsson, A., & Gøtzsche, P. C. (2001). Is the placebo powerless? An analysis of clinical trials comparing placebo with no treatment. *New England Journal of Medicine, 344,* 1594–602.

Hu, F. B., Li, T. Y., Colditz, G. A., Willett, W. C., & Manson, J. E. (2003). Television watching and other sedentary behaviors in relation to risk of obesity and type 2 diabetes mellitus in women. *Journal of the American Medical Association, 289,* 1785–1791.

Huart, J., Corneille, O., & Becquart, E. (2005). Face-based categorization, context-based categorization, and distortions in the recollection of gender ambiguous faces. *Journal of Experimental Social Psychology, 41,* 598–608.

Hubbard, E. M., Arman, A. C., Ramachandran, V. S., & Boynton, G. M. (2005). Individual differences among grapheme-color synesthetes: Brain-behavior correlations. *Neuron, 45,* 975–985.

Hubel, D. H. (1979, September). The brain. *Scientific American,* pp. 45–53.

Hubel, D. H., & Wiesel, T. N. (1979, September). Brian mechanisms of vision. *Scientific American,* pp. 150–162.

Hublin, C., Kaprio, J., Partinen, M., Heikkila, K., & Koskenvuo, M. (1997). Prevalence and genetics of sleepwalking—A population-based twin study. *Neurology, 48,* 177–181.

Hublin, C., Kaprio, J., Partinen, M., & Koskenvuo, M. (1998). Sleeptalking in twins: Epidemiology and psychiatric comorbidity. *Behavior Genetics, 28,* 289–298.

Hucker, S. J., & Bain, J. (1990). Androgenic hormones and sexual assault. In W. Marshall, R. Law, & H. Barbaree (Eds.), *The handbook on sexual assault.* New York: Plenum.

Hudson, W. (1960). Pictorial depth perception in sub-cultural groups in Africa. *Journal of Social Psychology, 52,* 183–208.

Huffcutt, A. I., Conway, J. M., Roth, P. L., & Stone, N. J. (2001). Identification and meta-analytic assessment of psychological constructs measured in employment interviews. *Journal of Applied Psychology, 86,* 897–913.

Hugenberg, K., & Bodenhausen, G. V. (2003). Facing prejudice: Implicit prejudice and the perception of facial threat. *Psychological Science, 14,* 640–643.

Hughes, H. C. (1999). *Sensory exotica: A world beyond human experience.* Cambridge, MA: MIT Press.

Hugick, L. (1989, July). Women play the leading role in keeping modern families close. *Gallup Report,* No. 286, pp. 27–34.

Huizink, A. C., Mulder, E. J. H., & Buitelaar, J. K. (2004). Prenatal stress and risk for psychopathology: Specific effects or indication of general susceptibility? *Psychological Bulletin, 130,* 115–142.

Hull, J. G., & Bond, C. F., Jr. (1986). Social and behavioral consequences of alcohol consumption and expectancy: A meta-analysis. *Psychological Bulletin, 99,* 347–360.

Hull, J. G., Young, R. D., & Jouriles, E. (1986). Applications of the self-awareness model of alcohol consumption: Predicting patterns of use and abuse. *Journal of Personality and Social Psychology, 51,* 790–796.

Hull, J. M. (1990). *Touching the rock: An experience of blindness.* New York: Vintage Books.

Hulme, C., & Tordoff, V. (1989). Working memory development: The effects of speech rate, word length, and acoustic similarity on serial recall. *Journal of Experimental Child Psychology, 47,* 72–87.

Hummer, R. A., Rogers, R. G., Nam, C. B., & Ellison, C. G. (1999). Religious involvement and U.S. adult mortality. *Demography, 36,* 273–285.

Humphreys, L. G., & Davey, T. C. (1988). Continuity in intellectual growth from 12 months to 9 years. *Intelligence, 12,* 183–197.

Hunsley, J., & Bailey, J. M. (1999). The clinical utility of the Rorschach: Unfulfilled promises and an uncertain future. *Psychological Assessment, 11*(3), 266–277.

Hunsley, J., & Di Giulio, G. (2002). Dodo bird, phoenix, or urban legend? The question of psychotherapy equivalence. *Scientific Review of Mental Health Practice, 1,* 11–22.

Hunt, C., Slade, T., & Andrews, G. (2004). Generalized anxiety disorder and major depressive disorder comorbidity in the National Survey of Mental Health and Well-Being. *Depression and Anxiety, 20,* 23–31.

Hunt, E. (1983). On the nature of intelligence. *Science, 219,* 141–146.

Hunt, J. M. (1982). Toward equalizing the developmental opportunities of infants and preschool children. *Journal of Social Issues, 38*(4), 163–191.

Hunt, M. (1974). *Sexual behavior in the 1970s.* Chicago: Playboy Press.

Hunt, M. (1982). *The universe within.* New York: Simon and Schuster.

Hunt, M. (1990). *The compassionate beast: What science is discovering about the humane side of humankind.* New York: William Morrow.

Hunt, M. (1993). *The story of psychology.* New York: Doubleday.

Hunter, J. E. (1997). Needed: A ban on the significance test. *Psychological Science, 8,* 3–7.

Hunter, S., & Sundel, M. (Eds.). (1989). *Midlife myths: Issues, findings, and practice implications.* Newbury Park, CA: Sage.

Huss, M. (1996). Secrets to standing out from the pile: Getting into graduate school. *Psi Chi Newsletter,* 6–7.

Hussein, S. (2002, July 17 and August 28). Speeches to the Iraqi people as reported by various media.

Huston, A. C., & Aronson, S. R. (2005). Mothers' time with infant and time in employment as predictors of mother-child relationships and children's early development. *Child Development, 76,* 467–482.

Huston, A. C., Donnerstein, E., Fairchild, H., Feshbach, N. D., Katz, P. A., & Murray, J. P. (1992). *Big world, small screen: The role of television in American society.* Lincoln, NE: University of Nebraska Press.

Hyde, J. S. (1983, November). *Bem's gender schema theory.* Paper presented at GLCA Women's Studies Conference, Rochester, IN.

Hyde, J. S., Fennema, E., & Lamon, S. J. (1990). Gender differences in mathematics performance: A meta-analysis. *Psychological Bulletin, 107,* 139–155.

Hygge, S., Evans, G. W., & Bullinger, M. (2002). A prospective study of some effects of aircraft noise on cognitive performance in schoolchildren. *Psychological Science, 13,* 469–474.

Hyler, S., Gabbard, G. O., & Schneider, I. (1991). Homicidal maniacs and narcissistic parasites: Stigmatization of mentally ill persons in the movies. *Hospital and Community Psychiatry, 42,* 1044–1048.

Hyman, R. (1981). Cold reading: How to convince strangers that you know all about them. In K. Frazier (Ed.), *Paranormal borderlands of science.* Buffalo, NY: Prometheus.

Hyman, S. (1999). Quoted by M. Enserink, Can the placebo be the cure? *Science, 284,* 238–240.

Iacono, W. G., & Lykken, D. T. (1997). The validity of the lie detector: Two surveys of scientific opinion. *Journal of Applied Psychology, 82,* 426–433.

Ickes, W., Snyder, M., & Garcia, S. (1997). Personality influences on the choice of situations. In R. Hogan, J. Johnson, & S. Briggs (Eds.). *Handbook of Personality Psychology.* San Diego, CA: Academic Press.

ICR. (2001, October 12). Women fear flying; pill sales rise (survey by ICR of Media, PA). Associated Press (in *Grand Rapids Press*), p. A3.

Idson, L. C., & Mischel, W. (2001). The personality of familiar and significant people: The lay perceiver as a social-cognitive theorist. *Journal of Personality and Social Psychology, 80,* 585–596.

Ikonomidou, C., Bittigau, P., Ishimaru, M. J., Wozniak, D. F., Koch, C., Genz, K., Price, M. T., Stefovska, V., Hoerster, F., Tenkova, T., Dikranian, K., & Olney, J. W. (2000). Ethanol-induced apoptotic neurodegeneration and fetal alcohol syndrome. *Science, 287,* 1056–1060.

Illes, J. (2004, Fall). A fish story? Brain maps, lie detection, and personhood. *Cerebrum,* pp. 73–80.

Immen, W. (1995, July 16). Canadians ignore 'safe sex' warning. *Toronto Globe and Mail* (in *Grand Rapids Press,* p. A22).

Independent Sector. (2002). *Faith and philanthropy: The connection between charitable giving behavior and giving to religion.* Washington, DC: Independent Sector.

Ingham, A. G., Levinger, G., Graves, J., & Peckham, V. (1974). The Ringelmann effect: Studies of group size and group performance. *Journal of Experimental Social Psychology, 10,* 371–384.

Inglehart, R. (1990). *Culture shift in advanced industrial society.* Princeton, NJ: Princeton University Press.

Inglehart, R., Basañez, M., Diez-Medrano, J., Halman, L., & Luijkx, R. (Eds.). (2004). *Human beliefs and values: A sourcebook based on the 1999-2001 values surveys.* Mexico City: Siglo XXI.

Ingram, V. (2003). Alzheimer's disease. *American Scientist, 91,* 312–321.

Inman, M. L., & Baron, R. S. (1996). Influence of prototypes on perceptions of prejudice. *Journal of Personality and Social Psychology, 70,* 727–739.

Insana, R. (2005, February 21). Coach says honey gets better results than vinegar (interview with Larry Brown). *USA Today,* p. 4B.

Inzlicht, M., & Ben-Zeev, T. (2000). A threatening intellectual environment: Why females are susceptible to experiencing problem-solving deficits in the presence of males. *Psychological Science, 11,* 365–371.

IPU. (2005). Women in national parliaments: Situation as of 28 February 2005. Inter-Parliamentary Union (www.ipu.org).

Ireland, T. O., Smith, C. A., & Thornberry, T. P. (2002). Developmental issues in the impact of child maltreatment on later delinquency and drug use. *Criminology, 40,* 359–399.

Ironson, G., Solomon, G. F., Balbin, E. G., O'Cleirigh, C., George, A., Kumar, M., Larson, D., & Woods, T. E. (2002). The Ironson-Woods spiritual/religiousness index is associated with long survival, health behaviors, less distress, and low cortisol in people with HIV/AIDS. *Annals of Behavioral Medicine, 24,* 34–48.

Irwin, M., Mascovich, A., Gillin, J. C., Willoughby, R., Pike, J., & Smith, T. L. (1994). Partial sleep deprivation reduces natural killer cell activity in humans. *Psychosomatic Medicine, 56,* 493–498.

Isensee, B., Wittchen, H-U., Stein, M. B., Hofler, M., & Lieb, R. (2003). Smoking increases the risk of panic: Findings from a prospective community study. *Archives of General Psychiatry, 60,* 692–700.

Isham, W. P., & Kamin, L. J. (1993). Blackness, deafness, IQ, and *g. Intelligence, 17,* 37–46.

ISR. (2003, Spring). Drug use: Religion plays role for White as well as Black teens (data from 70,000 seniors surveyed 1997-2001, *ISR Monitoring the Future Study*). Ann Arbor, MI: Institute for Social Research Newsletter, University of Michigan.

Ito, T. A., Miller, N., & Pollock, V. E. (1996). Alcohol and aggression: A meta-analysis on the moderating effects of inhibitory cues, triggering events, and self-focused attention. *Psychological Bulletin, 120,* 60–82.

Iversen, L. L. (2000). *The science of marijuana.* New York: Oxford.

Iverson, J. M., & Goldin-Meadow, S. (1998). Why people gesture when they speak. *Nature, 396,* 228.

Iyengar, S. S., & Lepper, M. R. (2000). When choice is demotivating: Can one desire too much of a good thing? *Journal of Personality and Social Psychology, 79,* 995–1006.

Iyer, P. (1993, April). The soul of an intercontinental wanderer. *Harper's, 286,* 13–17.

Izard, C. E. (1977). *Human emotions.* New York: Plenum Press.

Izard, C., Fine, S., Schultz, D., Mostow, A., Ackerman, B., & Younstrom, E. (2001). Emotion knowledge as a predictor of social behavior and academic competence in children at risk. *Psychological Science, 12,* 18–23.

Izzetoglu, K., Yurtsever, G., Bozkurt, A., Yazici, B., Bunce, S., Pourrezaei, K., Onaral, B. (2003). NIR spectroscopy measurements of cognitive load elicited by GKT and target categorization. System Sciences, Proceedings of the 36th Hawaii International Conference on System Sciences, 129–134.

Jablensky, A. (1999). Schizophrenia: Epidemiology. *Current Opinion in Psychiatry, 12,* 19–28.

Jackson, J. M., & Williams, K. D. (1988). Social loafing: A review and theoretical analysis. Unpublished manuscript, Fordham University.

Jackson, J. S., Brown, K. T., Brown, T. N., & Marks, B. (2001). Contemporary immigration policy orientations among dominant-group members in western Europe. *Journal of Social Issues, 57,* 431–456.

Jackson, L. A., & Gerard, D. A. (1996). Diurnal types, the "Big Five" personality factors and other personal characteristics. *Journal of Social Behavior and Personality, 11,* 273–283.

Jackson, S. W. (1992). The listening healer in the history of psychological healing. *American Journal Psychiatry, 149,* 1623–1632.

Jacobe, D. (2003, December 2). Why the gender gap in investor optimism? Gallup Poll Tuesday Briefing (www.gallup.com).

Jacobi, C., Hayward, C., deZwaan, M., Kraemer, H. C., & Agras, W. S. (2004). Coming to terms with risk factors for eating disorders: Application of risk terminology and suggestions for a general taxonomy. *Psychological Bulletin, 130,* 19–65.

Jacobs, B. L. (1987). How hallucinogenic drugs work. *American Scientist, 75,* 386–392.

Jacobs, B. L. (1994). Serotonin, motor activity, and depression-related disorders. *American Scientist, 82,* 456–463.

Jacobs, B. L. (2004). Depression: The brain finally gets into the act. *Current Directions in Psychological Science, 13,* 103–106.

Jacobs, B., van Praag, H., & Gage, F. H. (2000). Adult brain neurogenesis and psychiatry: A novel theory of depression. *Molecular Psychiatry, 5,* 262–269.

Jacobs, W. J., & Nadel, L. (1985). Stress-induced recovery of fears and phobias. *Psychological Bulletin, 92,* 512–531.

Jacoby, L. L., Bishara, A. J., Hessels, S., & Toth, J. P. (2005). Aging, subjective experience, and cognitive control: Dramatic false remembering by older adults. *Journal of Experimental Psychology: General, 154,* 131–148.

Jaffe, E. (2004, October). Peace in the Middle East may be impossible: Lee D. Ross on naive realism and conflict resolution. *APS Observer,* pp. 9–11.

Jakicic, J. M., Winters, C., Lang, W., & Wing R. R. (1999). Effects of intermittent exercise and use of home exercise equipment on adherence, weight loss, and fitness in overweight women. *Journal of the American Medical Association, 282,* 1554–1560.

James, K. (1986). Priming and social categorizational factors: Impact on awareness of emergency situations. *Personality and Social Psychology Bulletin, 12,* 462–467.

James, W. (1890). *The principles of psychology* (Vol. 2). New York: Holt.

James, W. (1902; reprinted 1958). *Varieties of religious experience.* New York: Mentor Books.

Jameson, D. (1985). Opponent-colors theory in light of physiological findings. In D. Ottoson & S. Zeki (Eds.), *Central and peripheral mechanisms of color vision.* New York: Macmillan.

Jamison, K. R. (1993). *Touched with fire: Manic-depressive illness and the artistic temperament.* New York: Free Press.

Jamison, K. R. (1995, February). Manic-depressive illness and creativity. *Scientific American,* pp. 62–67.

Janicak, P. G. (2005). Treating psychiatric disorders using transcranial magnetic stimulation. *Psychiatric Annals, 35,* 102–108.

Janis, I. L. (1982). *Groupthink: Psychological studies of policy decisions and fiascoes.* Boston: Houghton Mifflin.

Janis, I. L. (1986). Problems of international crisis management in the nuclear age. *Journal of Social Issues, 42(2),* 201–220.

Janoff-Bulman, R., Timko, C., & Carli, L. L. (1985). Cognitive biases in blaming the victim. *Journal of Experimental Social Psychology, 21,* 161–177.

Javitt, D. C., & Coyle, J. T. (2004, January). Decoding schizophrenia. *Scientific American,* pp. 48–55.

Jeffery, R. W., Drewnowski, A., Epstein, L. H., Stunkard, A. J., Wilson, G. T., Wing, R. R., & Hill, D. R. (2000). Long-term maintenance of weight loss: Current status. *Health Psychology, 19,* No. 1 (Supplement), 5–16.

Jenkins, J. G., & Dallenbach, K. M. (1924). Obliviscence during sleep and waking. *American Journal of Psychology, 35,* 605–612.

Jenkins, J. M., & Astington, J. W. (1996). Cognitive factors and family structure associated with theory of mind development in young children. *Developmental Psychology, 32,* 70–78.

Jensen, A. R. (1980). *Bias in mental testing.* New York: The Free Press.

Jensen, A. R. (1983, August). The nature of the black-white difference on various psychometric tests: Spearman's hypothesis. Paper presented at the meeting of the American Psychological Association, Anaheim, CA.

Jensen, A. R. (1989). New findings on the intellectually gifted. *New Horizons, 30,* 73–80.

Jensen, A. R. (1998). *The g factor: The science of mental ability.* Westport, CT: Praeger/Greenwood.

Jensen, J. P., & Bergin, A. E. (1988). Mental health values of professional therapists: A national interdisciplinary survey. *Professional Psychology: Research and Practice, 19,* 290–297.

Jepson, C., Krantz, D. H., & Nisbett, R. E. (1983). Inductive reasoning: Competence or skill. *The Behavioral and Brain Sciences, 3,* 494–501.

Jervis, R. (1985, April 2). Quoted in D. Goleman, Political forces come under new scrutiny of psychology. *The New York Times,* pp. C1, C4.

Jing, H. (1999, Summer). China faces myriad psychological challenges of modernization. *Psychology International* (APA newsletter), p. 7.

Johansson, P., Hall, L., Sikström, S., & Olsson, A. (2005). Failure to detect mismatches between intention and outcome in a simple decision task. *Science, 310,* 116–119.

John, O. P., & Srivastava, S. (1999). The Big Five trait taxonomy: History, measurement, and theoretical perspectives. In L. A. Pervin & O. P. John (Eds.), *Handbook of personality: Theory and research.* New York: Guilford.

Johnson, C. B., Stockdale, M. S., & Saal, F. E. (1991). Persistence of men's misperceptions of friendly cues across a variety of interpersonal encounters. *Psychology of Women Quarterly, 15,* 463–475.

Johnson, D. F. (1997, Winter). Margaret Floy Washburn. *Psychology of Women Newsletter,* pp. 17, 22.

Johnson, D. L., Wiebe, J. S., Gold, S. M., Andreasen, N. C., Hichwa, R. D., Watkins, G. L., & Ponto, L. L. B. (1999). Cerebral blood flow and personality: A Positron Emission Tomography study. *American Journal of Psychiatry, 156,* 252–257.

Johnson, D. W., & Johnson, R. T. (1989). *Cooperation and competition: Theory and research.* Edina, MN: Interaction Book.

Johnson, D. W., & Johnson, R. T. (1994). Constructive conflict in the schools. *Journal of Social Issues, 50(1),* 117–137.

Johnson, G. (2003, November 5). Suspect admits 48 Seattle-area killings. Associated Press release.

Johnson, J. G., Cohen, P., Kotler, L., Kasen, S., & Brook, J. S. (2002). Psychiatric disorders associated with risk for the development of eating disorders during adolescence and early adulthood. *Journal of Consulting and Clinical Psychology, 70,* 1119–1128.

Johnson, J. S., & Newport, E. L. (1991). Critical period effects on universal properties of language: The status of subjacency in the acquisition of a second language. *Cognition, 39,* 215–258.

Johnson, L. C. (2001, July 10). The declining terrorist threat. *New York Times* (www.nytimes.com).

Johnson, M. E., & Hauck, C. (1999). Beliefs and opinions about hypnosis held by the general public: A systematic evaluation. *American Journal of Clinical Hypnosis, 42,* 10–20.

Johnson, M. H. (1992). Imprinting and the development of face recognition: From chick to man. *Current Directions in Psychological Science, 1,* 52–55.

Johnson, M. H., & Morton, J. (1991). *Biology and cognitive development: The case of face recognition.* Oxford: Blackwell Publishing.

Johnson, W., McGue, M., & Krueger, R. F. (2005). Personality stability in late adulthood: A behavioral genetic analysis. *Journal of Personality, 73,* 523–552.

Johnston, L. D., O'Malley, P. M., Bachman, J. G., & Schulenberg, J. E. (2005). *Monitoring the future: National results on adolescent drug use: Overview of key findings, 2004.* Bethesda, MD: National Institute on Drug Abuse.

Johnston, L. D., O'Malley, P. M., Bachman, J. G., & Schulenberg, J. E. (2005). *Teen drug use down but progress halts among youngest teens.* University of Michigan News and Information Services: Ann Arbor, MI. www.monitoringthefuture.org.

Johnstone, E. C., Ebmeier, K. P., Miller, P., Owens, D. G. C., & Lawrie, S. M. (2005). Predicting schizophrenia: Findings from the Edinburgh High-Risk Study. *British Journal of Psychiatry, 186,* 18–25.

Joiner, T. E., Jr. (1999). The clustering and contagion of suicide. *Current Directions in Psychological Science, 8,* 89–92.

Joiner, T. E., Pettit, J. W., Walker, R. L., Voelz, Z. R., Cruz, J., Rudd, M. D., & Lester, D. (2002). Perceived burdensomeness and suicidality: Two studies on the suicide notes of those attempting and those completing suicide. *Journal of Social and Clinical Psychology, 21,* 531–545.

Jones, E. E., Cumming, J. D., & Horowitz, M. J. (1988). Another look at the nonspecific hypothesis of therapeutic effectiveness. *Journal of Consulting and Clinical Psychology, 56,* 48–55.

Jones, J. M. (2003, February 12). Fear of terrorism increases amidst latest warning. *Gallup News Service* (www.gallup.com/releases/pr030212.asp).

Jones, J. M., & Moore, D. W. (2003, June 17). Generational differences in support for a woman president. The Gallup Organization (www.gallup.com).

Jones, J. T., Pelham, B. W., Carvallo, M., & Mirenberg, M. C. (2004). How do I love thee? Let me count the Js: Implicit egotism and interpersonal attraction. *Journal of Personality and Social Psychology, 87,* 665–683.

Jones, L. (2000, December). Skeptics New Year quiz. *Skeptical Briefs,* p. 11.

Jones, M. C. (1924). A laboratory study of fear: The case of Peter. *Journal of Genetic Psychology, 31,* 308–315.

Jones, M. V., Paull, G. C., & Erskine, J. (2002). The impact of a team's aggressive reputation on the decisions of association football referees. *Journal of Sports Sciences, 20,* 991–1000.

Jones, S. S., Collins, K., & Hong, H-W. (1991). An audience effect on smile production in 10-month-old infants. *Psychological Science, 2,* 45–49.

Jones, W. H., Carpenter, B. N., & Quintana, D. (1985). Personality and interpersonal predictors of loneliness in two cultures. *Journal of Personality and Social Psychology, 48,* 1503–1511.

Jonides, J., Lacey, S. C., & Nee, D. E. (2005). Processes of working memory in mind and brain. *Psychological Science, 14,* 2–5.

Jordan, C. H., Spencer, S. J., Zanna, M. P., Hoshino-Browne, E., & Correll, J. (2003). Secure and defensive high self-esteem. *Journal of Personality and Social Psychology, 85,* 969–978.

Jorgenson, D. O., & Papciak, A. S. (1981). The effects of communication, resource feedback, and identifiability on behavior in a simulated commons. *Journal of Experimental Social Psychology, 17,* 373–385.

Joseph, J. (2001). Separated twins and the genetics of personality differences: A critique. *American Journal of Psychology, 114,* 1–30.

Judge, T. A., Thoresen, C. J., Bono, J. E., & Patton, G. K. (2001). The job satisfaction/job performance relationship: A qualitative and quantitative review. *Psychological Bulletin, 127,* 376–407.

Jung-Beeman, M., Bowden, E. M., Haberman, J., Frymiare, J. L., Arambel-Liu, S., Greenblatt, R., Reber, P. J., & Kounios, J. (2004). Neural activity when people solve verbal problems with insight. *PloS Biology 2*(4): e111.

Kagan, J. (1976). Emergent themes in human development. *American Scientist, 64,* 186–196.

Kagan, J. (1984). *The nature of the child.* New York: Basic Books.

Kagan, J. (1990). Interview with M. V. Ellis & E. S. Robbins, In Celebration of nature: A dialogue with Jerome Kagan. *Journal of Counseling and Development, 68,* 623–627.

Kagan, J. (1995). On attachment. *Harvard Review of Psychiatry, 3,* 104–106.

Kagan, J. (1998). *Three seductive ideas.* Cambridge, MA: Harvard University Press.

Kagan, J., Arcus, D., Snidman, N., Feng, W. Y., Hendler, J., & Greene, S. (1994). Reactivity in infants: A cross-national comparison. *Developmental Psychology, 30,* 342–345.

Kagan, J., Lapidus, D. R., & Moore, M. (December, 1978). Infant antecedents of cognitive functioning: A longitudinal study. *Child Development, 49*(4), 1005–1023.

Kagan, J., & Snidman, N. (2004). *The long shadow of temperament.* Cambridge, MA: Belknap Press.

Kagan, J., Snidman, N., & Arcus, D. M. (1992). Initial reactions to unfamiliarity. *Current Directions in Psychological Science, 1,* 171–174.

Kahneman, D. (1985, June). Quoted by K. McKean, Decisions, decisions. *Discover,* pp. 22–31.

Kahneman, D. (1999). Assessments of objective happiness: A bottom-up approach. In D. Kahneman, E. Diener, & N. Schwartz (Eds.), *Understanding well-being: Scientific perspectives on enjoyment and suffering.* New York: Russell Sage Foundation.

Kahneman, D. (2005, January 13). What were they thinking? Q&A with Daniel Kahneman. *Gallup Management Journal* (gmj.gallup.com).

Kahneman, D. (2005, February 10). Are you happy now? *Gallup Management Journal* interview (www.gmj.gallup.com).

Kahneman, D., Fredrickson, B. L., Schreiber, C. A., & Redelmeier, D. A. (1993). When more pain is preferred to less: Adding a better end. *Psychological Science, 4,* 401–405.

Kahneman, D., Krueger, A. B., Schkade, D. A., Schwarz, N., & Stone, A. A. (2004). A survey method for characterizing daily life experience: The day reconstruction method. *Science, 306,* 1776–1780.

Kahneman, D., & Tversky, A. (1972). Subjective probability: A judgment of representativeness. *Cognitive Psychology, 3,* 430–454.

Kahneman, D., & Tversky, A. (1979). Intuitive prediction: Biases and corrective procedures. *Management Science, 12,* 313–327.

Kail, R. (1991). Developmental change in speed of processing during childhood and adolescence. *Psychological Bulletin, 109,* 490–501.

Kaiser (2001). Inside-out: A report on the experiences of lesbians, gays and bisexuals in America and the public's views on issues and policies related to sexual orientation. The Henry J. Kaiser Foundation (www.kff.org).

Kaiser Family Foundation. (2003, October 28). New study finds children age zero to six spend as much time with TV, computers and video games as playing outside. www.kff.org/entmedia/entmedia102803nr.cfm

Kalff, A. C., Kroes, M., Vles, J. S. H., Hendriksen, J. G. M., Feron, F. J. M., Steyaert, J., van Zeban, T. M. C. B., Jolles, J., & van Os, J. (2001). Neighbourhood level and individual level SES effects on child problem behaviour: a multilevel analysis. *Journal of Epidemiology and Community Health, 55,* 246–250.

Kalin, N. H. (1993, May). The neurobiology of fear. *Scientific American,* pp. 94–101.

Kamarck, T., & Jennings, J. R. (1991). Biobehavioral factors in sudden cardiac death. *Psychological Bulletin, 109,* 42–75.

Kamena, M. (1998). Repressed/false childhood sexual abuse memories: A survey of therapists. Paper presented to the Sexual Abuse memories Symposium at the American Psychological Association convention.

Kaminski, J., Cali, J., & Fischer, J. (2004). Word learning in a domestic dog: Evidence for "fast mapping." *Science, 304,* 1682–1683.

Kanaya, T., Scullin, M. H., & Ceci, S. J. (2003). The Flynn effect and U.S. policies: The impact of rising IQ scores on American society via mental retardation diagnoses. *American Psychologist, 58,* 778–790.

Kanazawa, S. (2004). General intelligence as a domain-specific adaptation. *Psychological Review, 111,* 512–523.

Kandel, D. B., & Raveis, V. H. (1989). Cessation of illicit drug use in young adulthood. *Archives of General Psychiatry, 46,* 109–116.

Kandel, E. R., & Schwartz, J. H. (1982). Molecular biology of learning: Modulation of transmitter release. *Science, 218,* 433–443.

Kann, L., Warren, W., Collins, J. L., Ross, J., Collins, B., Kolbe, L. J. (1993). Results from the national school-based 1991 Youth Risk Behavior Survey and progress toward achieving related health objectives for the nation. U.S. Department of Health and Human Services, *Public Health Reports, 108* (Supplement 1), 47–55.

Kapitza, S. (1991, August). Antiscience trends in the U.S.S.R. *Scientific American,* pp. 32–38.

Kaplan, A. (2004). Exploring the gene-environment nexus in anorexia, bulimia. *Psychiatric Times, 21* (www.psychiatrictimes.com/p040801b.html).

Kaplan, H. I., & Saddock, B. J. (Eds.). (1989). *Comprehensive textbook of psychiatry, V.* Baltimore, MD: Williams and Wilkins.

Kaprio, J., Koskenvuo, M., & Rita, H. (1987). Mortality after bereavement: A prospective study of 95,647 widowed persons. *American Journal of Public Health, 77,* 283–287.

Karacan, I., Aslan, C., & Hirshkowitz, M. (1983). Erectile mechanisms in man. *Science, 220,* 1080–1082.

Karacan, I., Goodenough, D. R., Shapiro, A., & Starker, S. (1966). Erection cycle during sleep in relation to dream anxiety. *Archives of General Psychiatry, 15,* 183–189.

Karau, S. J., & Williams, K. D. (1993). Social loafing: A meta-analytic review and theoretical integration. *Journal of Personality and Social Psychology, 65,* 681–706.

Kark, J. D., Shemi, G., Friedlander, Y., Martin, O., Manor, O., & Blondheim, S. H. (1996). Does religious observance promote health? Mortality in secular vs. religious kibbutzim in Israel. *American Journal of Public Health, 86,* 341–346.

Karni, A., Meyer, G., Rey-Hipolito, C., Jezzard, P., Adams, M. M., Turner, R., & Ungerleider, L. G. (1998). The acquisition of skilled motor performance: Fast and slow experience-driven changes in primary motor cortex. *Proceedings of the National Academy of Sciences, 95,* 861–868.

Karni, A., & Sagi, D. (1994). Dependence on REM sleep for overnight improvement of perceptual skills. *Science, 265,* 679–682.

Karno, M., Golding, J. M., Sorenson, S. B., & Burnam, A. (1988). The epidemiology of obsessive-compulsive disorder in five US communities. *Archives of General Psychiatry, 45,* 1094–1099.

Karon, P. B., & Widener, A. (1998). Repressed memories: The real story. *Professional Psychology: Research and Practice, 29,* 482–487.

Karon, P. B., & Widener, A. J. (1997). Repressed memories and World War II: Lest we forget. *Professional Psychology: Research and Practice, 28,* 338–340.

Kashima, Y., Siegal, M., Tanaka, K., & Kashima, E. S. (1992). Do people believe behaviours are consistent with attitudes? Towards a cultural psychology of attribution processes. *British Journal of Social Psychology, 31,* 111–124.

Kassel, J. D., Stroud, L. R., & Paronis, C. A. (2003). Smoking, stress, and negative affect: Correlation, causation, and context across stages of smoking. *Psychological Bulletin, 129,* 270–304.

Kasser, T. (2000). Two version of the American dream: Which goals and values make for a high quality of life? In E. Diener (Ed.), *Advances in quality of life theory and research.* Dordrecht, Netherlands: Kluwer.

Kasser, T. (2002). *The high price of materialism.* Cambridge, MA: MIT Press.

Kaufman, J. C., & Baer, J. (2002). I bask in dreams of suicide: Mental illness, poetry, and women. *Review of General Psychology, 6,* 271–286.

Kaufman, J., & Zigler, E. (1987). Do abused children become abusive parents? *American Journal of Orthopsychiatry, 57,* 186–192.

Kaufman, L., & Kaufman, J. H. (2000). Explaining the moon illusion. *Proceedings of the National Academy of Sciences, 97,* 500–505.

Kavšek, M. (2004). Predicting later IQ from infant visual habituation and dishabituation: A meta-analysis. *Journal of Applied Developmental Psychology, 25,* 369–393.

Kazdin, A. E., & Benjet, C. (2003). Spanking children: Evidence and issues. *Current Directions in Psychological Science, 12,* 99–103.

Keenan, J. P., Nelson, A., O'Connor, M., & Pascual-Leone, A. (2001). Self-recognition and the right hemisphere. *Nature, 409,* 305.

Keesey, R. E., & Corbett, S. W. (1983). Metabolic defense of the body weight set-point. In A. J. Stunkard & E. Stellar (Eds.), *Eating and its disorders.* New York: Raven Press.

Kellehear, A. (1996). *Experiences near death: Beyond medicine and religion.* New York: Oxford University Press.

Keller, H. (2003). "Before the Soul Dawn," *The World I Live In,* New York Review Books.

Keller, M. B., McCullough, J. P., Klein, D. N., Arnow, B., Dunner, D. L., Gelenberg, A. J., Markowitz, J. C., Nemeroff, C. B., Russell, J. M., Thase, M. E., Trivedi, M. H., & Zajecka J. (2000), A comparison of nefazodone, the cognitive behavioral-analysis system of psychotherapy, and their combination for the treatment of chronic depression. *New England Journal of Medicine, 342,* 1462–1470.

Kellerman, J., Lewis, J., & Laird, J. D. (1989). Looking and loving: The effects of mutual gaze on feelings of romantic love. *Journal of Research in Personality, 23,* 145–161.

Kellermann, A. L. (1997). Comment: Gunsmoke—changing public attitudes toward smoking and firearms. *American Journal of Public Health, 87,* 910–913.

Kellermann, A. L., Rivara, F. P., Rushforth, N. B., Banton, H. G., Feay, D. T., Francisco, J. T., Locci, A. B., Prodzinski, J., Hackman, B. B., & Somes, G. (1993). Gun ownership as a risk factor for homicide in the home. *New England Journal of Medicine, 329,* 1084–1091.

Kellermann, A. L., Somes, G. Rivara, F. P., Lee, R. K., & Banton, J. G. (1998). Injuries and deaths due to firearms in the home. *Journal of Trauma, 45,* 263–267.

Kelley, J., & De Graaf, N. D. (1997). National context, parental socialization, and religious belief: Results from 15 nations, *American Sociological Review, 62,* 639–659.

Kelling, S. T., & Halpern, B. P. (1983). Taste flashes: Reaction times, intensity, and quality. *Science, 219,* 412–414.

Kellner, C. H., & 15 others (2005). Relief of expressed suicidal intent by ECT: A consortium for research in ECT study. *American Journal of Psychiatry, 162,* 977–982.

Kelly, A. E. (2000). Helping construct desirable identities: A self-presentational view of psychotherapy. *Psychological Bulletin, 126,* 475–494.

Kelly, I. W. (1997). Modern astrology: A critique. *Psychological Reports, 81,* 1035–1066.

Kelly, I. W. (1998). Why astrology doesn't work. *Psychological Reports, 82,* 527–546.

Kelly, T. A. (1990). The role of values in psychotherapy: A critical review of process and outcome effects. *Clinical Psychology Review, 10,* 171–186.

Kempe, R. S., & Kempe, C. C. (1978). *Child abuse.* Cambridge, MA: Harvard University Press.

Kempermann, G., & Gage, F. H. (1999, May). New nerve cells for the adult brain. *Scientific American,* pp. 48–53.

Kempermann, G., Kuhn, H. G., & Gage, F. H. (May, 1998). *Journal of Neuroscience, 18*(9), 3206–3212.

Kendall-Tackett, K. A., Williams, L. M., & Finkelhor, D. (1993). Impact of sexual abuse on children: A review and synthesis of recent empirical studies. *Psychological Bulletin, 113,* 164–180.

Kendler, K. S. (1996). Parenting: A genetic-epidemiologic perspective. *The American Journal of Psychiatry, 153,* 11–20.

Kendler, K. S. (1997). Social support: A genetic-epidemiologic analysis. *American Journal of Psychiatry, 154,* 1398–1404.

Kendler, K. S. (1998, January). Major depression and the environment: A psychiatric genetic perspective. *Pharmacopsychiatry, 31*(1), 5–9.

Kendler, K. S., Jacobson, K. C., Myers, J., & Prescott, C. A. (2002a). Sex differences in genetic and environmental risk factors for irrational fears and phobias. *Psychological Medicine, 32*, 209–217.

Kendler, K. S., Karkowski, L. M., & Prescott, C. A. (1999). Fears and phobias: Reliability and heritability. *Psychological Medicine, 29*, 539–553.

Kendler, K. S., Myers, J., & Prescott, C. A. (2002b). The etiology of phobias: An evaluation of the stress-diathesis model. *Archives of General Psychiatry, 59*, 242–248.

Kendler, K. S., Neale, M. C., Kessler, R. C., Heath, A. C., & Eaves, L. J. (1992). Generalized anxiety disorder in women: A population-based twin study. *Archives of General Psychiatry, 49*, 267–272.

Kendler, K. S., Neale, M. C., Thornton, L. M., Aggen, S. H., Gilman, S. E., & Kessler, R. C. (2002). Cannabis use in the last year in a U.S. national sample of twin and sibling pairs. *Psychological Medicine, 32*, 551–554.

Kendler, K. S., Thornton, L. M., & Gardner, C. O. (2001). Genetic risk, number of previous depressive episodes, and stressful life events in predicting onset of major depression. *American Journal of Psychiatry, 158*, 582–586.

Kendler, K. S., Thornton, L. M., Gilman, S. E., & Kessler, R. C. (2000). Sexual orientation in a U.S. national sample of twin and nontwin sibling pairs. *American Journal of Psychiatry, 157*, 1843–1846.

Kennedy, S., & Over, R. (1990). Psychophysiological assessment of male sexual arousal following spinal cord injury. *Archives of Sexual Behavior, 19*, 15–27.

Kenrick, D. T., & Funder, D. C. (1988). Profiting from controversy: Lessons from the person-situation debate. *American Psychologist, 43*, 23–34.

Kenrick, D. T., & Gutierres, S. E. (1980). Contrast effects and judgments of physical attractiveness: When beauty becomes a social problem. *Journal of Personality and Social Psychology, 38*, 131–140.

Kenrick, D. T., Gutierres, S. E., & Goldberg, L. L. (1989). Influence of popular erotica on judgments of strangers and mates. *Journal of Experimental Social Psychology, 25*, 159–167.

Kenrick, D. T., & Trost, M. R. (1987). A biosocial theory of heterosexual relationships. In K. Kelly (Ed.), *Females, males, and sexuality*. Albany: State University of New York Press.

Keough, K. A., Zimbardo, P. G., & Boyd, J. N. (1999). Who's smoking, drinking, and using drugs? Time perspective as a predictor of substance use. *Basic and Applied Social Psychology, 2*, 149–164.

Kernis, M. H. (2003). Toward a conceptualization of optimal self-esteem. *Psychological Inquiry, 14*, 1–26.

Kerr, N. L., & Bruun, S. E. (1983). Dispensability of member effort and group motivation losses: Free-rider effects. *Journal of Personality and Social Psychology, 44*, 78–94.

Kessler, M., & Albee, G. (1975). Primary prevention. *Annual Review of Psychology, 26*, 557–591.

Kessler, R. C. (2000). Posttraumatic stress disorder: The burden to the individual and to society. *Journal of Clinical Psychiatry, 61*(suppl. 5), 4–12.

Kessler, R. C. (2001). Epidemiology of women and depression. *Journal of Affective Disorders, 74*, 5–13.

Kessler, R. C., Foster, C., Joseph, J., Ostrow, D., Wortman, C., Phair, J., & Chmiel, J. (1991). Stressful life events and symptom onset in HIV infection. *American Journal of Psychiatry, 148*, 733–738.

Kessler, R. C., Soukup, J., Davis, R. B., Foster, D. F., Wilkey, S. A., Van Rompay, M. I., & Eisenberg, D. M. (2001). The use of complementary and alternative therapies to treat anxiety and depression in the United States. *American Journal of Psychiatry, 158*, 289–294.

Kestenbaum, R. (1992). Feeling happy versus feeling good: The processing of discrete and global categories of emotional expressions by children and adults. *Developmental Psychology, 28*, 1132–1142.

Keynes, M. (1980, December 20/27). Handel's illnesses. *The Lancet*, pp. 1354–1355.

Keys, A., Brozek, J., Henschel, A., Mickelsen, O., & Taylor, H. L. (1950). *The biology of human starvation*. Minneapolis: University of Minnesota Press.

Keys, L. (2001, May 27). Once isolated nation falls for TV. Associated Press (*Grand Rapids Press*, p. A14).

Khan, A., Warner, H. A., & Brown, W. A. (2000). Symptom reduction and suicide risk inpatients treated with placebo in antidepressant clinical trials. *Archives of General Psychiatry, 57*, 311–317.

Kho, K. H., van Vreeswijk, M. F., Simpson, S., & Zwinderman, A. H. (2003). A meta-analysis of electroconvulsive therapy efficacy in depression. *Journal of ECT, 19*, 139–147.

Kiecolt-Glaser, J. K., & Glaser, R. (1995). Psychoneuroimmunology and health consequences: Data and shared mechanisms. *Psychosomatic Medicine, 57*, 269–274.

Kiecolt-Glaser, J. K., & Newton, T. L. (2001). Marriage and health: His and hers. *Psychological Bulletin, 127*, 472–503.

Kiecolt-Glaser, J. K., Page, G. G., Marucha, P. T., MacCallum, R. C., & Glaser, R. (1998). Psychological influences on surgical recovery: Perspectives from psychoneuroimmunology. *American Psychologist, 53*, 1209–1218.

Kihlstrom, J. F. (1990). Awareness, the psychological unconscious, and the self. Address to the American Psychological Association convention.

Kihlstrom, J. F. (1990). The psychological unconscious. In L. A. Pervin (Ed.), *Handbook of personality: Theory and research*. New York: Guilford Press.

Kihlstrom, J. F. (1994). The social construction of memory. Paper presented at the American Psychological Society convention.

Kihlstrom, J. F. (1997, November 11). Freud as giant pioneer on whose shoulders we should stand. Social Psychology listserv posting (spsp@stolaf.edu).

Kihlstrom, J. F. (2005). Dissociative disorders. *Annual Review of Clinical Psychology, 1*, 227–253.

Kihlstrom, J. F., & McConkey, K. M. (1990). William James and hypnosis: A centennial reflection. *Psychological Science, 1*, 174–177.

Killeen, P. R., & Nash, M. R. (2003). The four causes of hypnosis. *Internal Journal of Clinical and Experimental Hypnosis, 51*, 195–231.

Kim, B. S. K., Ng, G. F., & Ahn, A. J. (2005). Effects of client expectation for counseling success, client-counselor worldview match, and client adherence to Asian and European American cultural values on counseling process with Asian Americans. *Journal of Counseling Psychology, 52*, 67–76.

Kim, H., & Markus, H. R. (1999). Deviance or uniqueness, harmony or conformity? A cultural analysis. *Journal of Personality and Social Psychology, 77*, 785–800.

Kim, K. H. S., Relkin, N. R., Lee, K-M., & Hirsch, J. (1997). Distinct cortical areas associated with native and second languages. *Nature, 388*, 171–174.

Kim, Y., & Lee, S-H. (1994). The Confucian model of morality, justice, selfhood and society: Implications for modern society. In *The universal and particular natures of Confucianism*. The Academy of Korean Studies.

Kimata, H. (2001). Effect of humor on allergen-induced wheal reactions. *Journal of the American Medical Association, 285*, 737.

Kimball, M. M. (1989). A new perspective on women's math achievement. *Psychological Bulletin, 105*, 198–214.

Kimble, G. A. (1956). *Principles of general psychology*. New York: Ronald.

Kimble, G. A. (1981). *Biological and cognitive constraints on learning*. Washington, DC: American Psychological Association.

King, R. N., & Koehler, D. J. (2000). Illusory correlations in graphological interference. *Journal of Experimental Psychology: Applied, 6*, 336–348.

Kinnier, R. T., & Metha, A. T. (1989). Regrets and priorities at three stages of life. *Counseling and Values, 33*, 182–193.

Kinsey, A. C., Pomeroy, W., & Martin, C. (1948). *Sexual behavior in the human male*. Philadelphia: Saunders.

Kinsey, A. C., Pomeroy, W., Martin, C., & Gebhard, P. (1953). *Sexual behavior in the human female.* Philadelphia: Saunders.

Kirby, D. (2002). Effective approaches to reducing adolescent unprotected sex, pregnancy, and childbearing. *Journal of Sex Research, 39,* 51–57.

Kirkpatrick, L. (1999). Attachment and religious representations and behavior. In J. Cassidy & P. R. Shaver (Eds.), *Handbook of attachment.* New York: Guilford.

Kirsch, I. (1996). Hypnotic enhancement of cognitive-behavioral weight loss treatments: Another meta-reanalysis. *Journal of Consulting and Clinical Psychology, 64,* 517–519.

Kirsch, I., & Braffman, W. (2001). Imaginative suggestibility and hypnotizability. *Current Directions in Psychological Science, 10,* 57–61.

Kirsch, I., & Lynn, S. J. (1995). The altered state of hypnosis. *American Psychologist, 50,* 846–858.

Kirsch, I., & Lynn, S. J. (1998a). Dissociation theories of hypnosis. *Psychological Bulletin, 123,* 100–115.

Kirsch, I., & Lynn, S. J. (1998b). Social-cognitive alternatives to dissociation theories of hypnotic induction. *Review of General Psychology, 2,* 66–80.

Kirsch, I., & Lynn, S. J. (1999). Automaticity in clinical psychology. *American Psychologist, 54,* 504–515.

Kirsch, I., Montgomery, G., & Sapirstein, G. (1995). Hypnosis as an adjunct to cognitive-behavioral psychotherapy: A meta-analysis. *Journal of Consulting and Clinical Psychology, 63,* 214–220.

Kirsch, I., Moore, T. J., Scoboria, A., & Nicholls, S. S. (2002, July 15). New study finds little difference between effects of antidepressants and placebo. *Prevention and Treatment* (journals.apa.org/prevention).

Kirsch, I., & Sapirstein, G. (1998). Listening to Prozac but hearing placebo: A meta-analysis of antidepressant medication. *Prevention and Treatment, 1,* posted June 26 at (journals.apa.org/prevention/volume1).

Kisor, H. (1990). *What's that pig outdoors.* New York: Hill and Wang.

Kitayama, S., & Markus, H. R. (2000). The pursuit of happiness and the realization of sympathy: Cultural patterns of self, social relations, and well-being. In E. Diener & E. M. Suh (Eds.), *Subjective well-being across cultures.* Cambridge, MA: MIT Press.

Kite, M. E., & Whitley, B. E., Jr. (1996). Sex differences in attitudes toward homosexual persons, behaviors, and civil rights: A meta-analysis. *Personality and Social Psychology Bulletin, 22,* 336–353.

Kivimaki, M., Leino-Arjas, P., Luukkonen, R., Rihimaki, H., & Kirjonen, J. (2002). Work stress and risk of cardiovascular mortality: Prospective cohort study of industrial employees. *British Medical Journal, 325,* 857.

Klayman, J., & Ha, Y-W. (1987). Confirmation, disconfirmation, and information in hypothesis testing. *Psychological Review, 94,* 211–228.

Klein, D. N., & 16 others (2003). Therapeutic alliance in depression treatment: Controlling for prior change and patient characteristics. *Journal of Consulting and Clinical Psychology, 71,* 997–1006.

Klein, E., Kreinin, I., Chistyakov, A., Koren, D., Mecz, L., Marmur, S., Ben-Shachar, D., & Feinsod, M. (1999). Therapeutic efficacy of right prefrontal slow repetitive transcranial magnetic stimulation in major depression. *Archives of General Psychiatry, 56,* 315–320.

Klein, S. B., & Kihlstrom, J. F. (1998). On bridging the gap between social-personality psychology and neuropsychology. *Personality and Social Psychology Review, 2,* 228–242.

Kleinfeld, J. (1998). The myth that schools shortchange girls: Social science in the service of deception. Washington, DC: Women's Freedom Network. Available from ERIC, Document ED423210, and via www.uaf.edu/northern/schools/myth.html

Kleinke, C. L., Peterson, T. R., & Rutledge, T. R. (1998). Effects of self-generated facial expressions on mood. *Journal of Personality and Social Psychology, 74,* 272–279.

Kleinmuntz, B., & Szucko, J. J. (1984). A field study of the fallibility of polygraph lie detection. *Nature, 308,* 449–450.

Kleitman, N. (1960, November). Patterns of dreaming. *Scientific American,* pp. 82–88.

Klemm, W. R. (1990). Historical and introductory perspectives on brain-stem-mediated behaviors. In W. R. Klemm & R. P. Vertes (Eds.), *Brainstem mechanisms of behavior.* New York: Wiley.

Kline, D., & Schieber, F. (1985). Vision and aging. In J. E. Birren & K. W. Schaie (Eds.), *Handbook of the psychology of aging.* New York: Van Nostrand Reinhold.

Kline, G. H., Stanley, S. M., Markman, J. H., Olmos-Gallo, P. A., St. Peters, M., Whitton, S. W., & Prado, L. M. (2004). Timing is everything: Pre-engagement cohabitation and increased risk for poor marital outcomes. *Journal of Family Psychology, 18,* 311–318.

Kline, N. S. (1974). *From sad to glad.* New York: Ballantine Books.

Klineberg, O. (1938). Emotional expression in Chinese literature. *Journal of Abnormal and Social Psychology, 33,* 517–520.

Klineberg, O. (1984). Public opinion and nuclear war. *American Psychologist, 39,* 1245–1253.

Klinke, R., Kral, A., Heid, S., Tillein, J., & Hartmann, R. (1999). Recruitment of the auditory cortex in congenitally deaf cats by long-term cochlear electrostimulation. *Science, 285,* 1729–1733.

Kluft, R. P. (1991). Multiple personality disorder. In A. Tasman & S. M. Goldfinger (Eds.), *Review of Psychiatry,* (Vol. 10). Washington, DC: American Psychiatric Press.

Klüver, H., & Bucy, P. C. (1939). Preliminary analysis of functions of the temporal lobes in monkeys. *Archives of Neurology and Psychiatry, 42,* 979–1000.

Knapp, M., Mangalore, R., & Simon, J. (2004). The global costs of schizophrenia. *Schizophrenia Bulletin, 30,* 279–293.

Knapp, S., & VandeCreek, L. (2000, August). Recovered memories of childhood abuse: Is there an underlying professional consensus? *Professional Psychology: Research and Practice, 31,* 365–371.

Knecht, S., Floeel, A., Draeger, B., Breitenstein, C., Sommer, J., Henningsen, H., Ringelstein, E. F., & Pascual-Leone, A. (2002). Degree of language lateralization determines susceptibility to unilateral brain lesions. *Nature Neuroscience, 5,* 695–699.

Knickmeyer, E. (2001, August 7). In Africa, big is definitely better. Associated Press (*Seattle Times,* p. A7).

Knight, W. (2004, August 2). Animated face helps deaf with phone chat. *NewScientist.com.*

Koenig, H. (2002, October 9). Personal communication, from Director of Center for the Study of Religion/Spirituality and Health, Duke University.

Koenig, H. G., & Larson, D. B. (1998). Use of hospital services, religious attendance, and religious affiliation. *Southern Medical Journal, 91,* 925–932.

Koenig, L. B., McGue, M., Krueger, R. F., & Bouchard, T. J., Jr. (2005). Genetic and environmental influences on religiousness: Findings for retrospective and current religiousness ratings. *Journal of Personality, 73,* 471–488.

Koestner, R., Lekes, N., Powers, T. A., & Chicoine, E. (2002). Attaining personal goals: Self-concordance plus implementation intentions equals success. *Journal of Personality and Social Psychology, 83,* 231–244.

Kohlberg, L. (1981). *The philosophy of moral development: Essays on moral development* (Vol. I). San Francisco: Harper & Row.

Kohlberg, L. (1984). *The psychology of moral development: Essays on moral development* (Vol. II). San Francisco: Harper & Row.

Kohler, I. (1962, May). Experiments with goggles. *Scientific American,* pp. 62–72.

Köhler, W. (1925; reprinted 1957). *The mentality of apes.* London: Pelican.

Kohn, P. M., & Macdonald, J. E. (1992). The survey of recent life experiences: A decontaminated hassles scale for adults. *Journal of Behavioral Medicine, 15,* 221–236.

Kohout, J., & Wicherski, M. (2004). *2001 Doctorate employment survey,* Washington, DC: American Psychological Association.

Kolata, G. (1986). Youth suicide: New research focuses on a growing social problem. *Science, 233,* 839–841.

Kolata, G. (1987). Metabolic catch-22 of exercise regimens. *Science, 236,* 146–147.

Kolata, G. (2004, September 30). Health and money issues arise over who pays for weight loss. *New York Times* (www.nytimes.com).

Kolb, B. (1989). Brain development, plasticity, and behavior. *American Psychologist, 44,* 1203–1212.

Kolb, B., & Whishaw, I. Q. (1998). Brain plasticity and behavior. *Annual Review of Psychology, 49,* 43–64.

Kolb, B., & Whishaw, I. Q. (2006). *An introduction to brain and behavior, 2nd* edition. New York: Worth Publishers.

Kolker, K. (2002, December 8). Video violence disturbs some; others scoff at influence. *Grand Rapids Press,* pp. A1, A12.

Kolodziej, M. E., & Johnson, B. T. (1996). Interpersonal contact and acceptance of persons with psychiatric disorders: A research synthesis. *Journal of Consulting and Clinical Psychology, 64,* 1387–1396.

Konishi, M. (1993, April). Listening with two ears. *Scientific American,* pp. 66–73.

Koole, S., & Spijker, M. (2000). Overcoming the planning fallacy through willpower: Effects of implementation intentions on actual and predicted task-completion times. *European Journal of Social Psychology, 30,* 873–888.

Kopta, S. M., Lueger, R. J., Saunders, S. M., & Howard, K. I. (1999). Individual psychotherapy outcome and process research: Challenges leading to greater turmoil or a positive transition? *Annual Review of Psychology, 30,* 441–469.

Koriat, A., Goldsmith, M., & Pansky, A. (2000). Toward a psychology of memory accuracy. *Annual Review of Psychology, 51,* pp. 481–537.

Koss, M. P., Heise, L., & Russo, N. P. (1994). The global health burden of rape. *Psychology of Women Quarterly, 18,* 509–537.

Kosslyn, S. M., & Koenig, O. (1992). *Wet mind: The new cognitive neuroscience.* New York: Free Press.

Kosslyn, S. M., Thompson, W. L., Costantini-Ferrando, M. F., Alpert, N. M., & Spiegel, D. (2000). Hypnotic visual illusion alters color processing in the brain. *American Journal of Psychiatry, 157,* 1279–1284.

Kotchick, B. A., Shaffer, A., & Forehand, R. (2001). Adolescent sexual risk behavior: A multi-system perspective. *Clinical Psychology Review, 21,* 493–519.

Kotkin, M., Daviet, C., & Gurin, J. (1996). The *Consumer Reports* mental health survey. *American Psychologist, 51,* 1080–1082.

Kotva, H. J., & Schneider, H. G. (1990). Those "talks"—general and sexual communication between mothers and daughters. *Journal of Social Behavior and Personality, 5,* 603–613.

Kraft, C. (1978). A psychophysical approach to air safety: Simulator studies of visual illusions in night approaches. In H. L. Pick, H. W. Leibowitz, J. E. Singer, A. Steinschneider, & H. W. Stevenson (Eds.), *Psychology: From research to practice.* New York: Plenum Press.

Kraft, R. (1996, December 2, and 1994, July 20). Personal correspondence (from Otterbein College) regarding Holocaust memories.

Kraus, N., Malmfors, T., & Slovic, P. (1992). Intuitive toxicology: Expert and lay judgments of chemical risks. *Risk Analysis, 12,* 215–232.

Krauss, C. (2002, August 11). A well-rounded Canada. *New York Times* (in *Grand Rapids Press,* p. E5).

Krauss, R. M. (1998). Why do we gesture when we speak? *Current Directions in Psychology, 7,* 54–60.

Kraut, R. E., & Johnston, R. E. (1979). Social and emotional messages of smiling: An ethological approach. *Journal of Personality and Social Psychology, 37,* 1539–1553.

KRC Research & Consulting. (2001, August 7). Memory isn't quite what it used to be (survey for General Nutrition Centers). *USA Today,* p. D1.

Krebs, D. L., & Van Hesteren, F. (1994). The development of altruism: Toward an integrative model. *Developmental Review, 14,* 103–158.

Kreitner, R. (1992). *Management,* 5th ed. Boston: Houghton Mifflin.

Krijn, M., Emmelkamp, P. M. G., Olafsson, R. P., & Biemond, R. (2004). Virtual reality exposure therapy of anxiety disorders: A review. *Clinical Psychology Review, 24,* 259–281.

Kring, A. M., & Gordon, A. H. (1998). Sex differences in emotion: Expression, experience, and physiology. *Journal of Personality and Social Psychology, 74,* 686–703.

Kristof, N. D. (2004, July 21). Saying no to killers. *New York Times* (www.nytimes.com).

Kroenke, K., & Mangelsdorff, A. D. (1989). Common symptoms in ambulatory care: Incidence, evaluation, therapy, and outcome. *American Journal of Medicine, 86,* 262–266.

Kroll, R., Danis, S., Moreau, M., Waldbaum, A., Shifren, J., & Wekselman, K. (2004). Testosterone transdermal patch (TPP) significantly improved sexual function in naturally menopausal women in a large Phase III study. Presented to the American Society of Reproductive Medicine annual meeting, Philadelphia, October.

Krosnick, J. A., & Alwin, D. F. (1989). Aging and susceptibility to attitude change. *Journal of Personality and Social Psychology, 57,* 416–425.

Krosnick, J. A., Betz, A. L., Jussim, L. J., & Lynn, A. R. (1992). Subliminal conditioning of attitudes. *Personality and Social Psychology Bulletin, 18,* 152–162.

Kruger, J., & Dunning, D. (1999). Unskilled and unaware of it: How difficulties in recognizing one's own incompetence lead to inflated self-assessments. *Journal of Personality and Social Psychology, 77,* 1121–1134.

Kruger, J., Epley, N., & Gilovich, T. (1999). Egocentrism over email. Paper presented to the American Psychological Society meeting.

Krugman, P. (2003, September 14). The tax-cut con. *New York Times* (www.nytimes.com).

Krugman, P. (2005, July 4). Girth of a nation. *New York Times* (www.nytimes.com).

Krupa, D. J., Thompson, J. K., & Thompson, R. F. (1993). Localization of a memory trace in the mammalian brain. *Science, 260,* 989–991.

Krützen, M., Mann, J., Heithaus, M. R., Connor, R. C., Bejder, L., & Sherwin,, W. B. (2005). Cultural transmission of tool use in bottlenose dolphins. *Proceedings of the National Academy of Sciences, 102,* 8939–8943.

Kubey, R., & Csikszentmihalyi, M. (2002, February). Television addiction is no mere metaphor. *Scientific American,* pp. 74–80.

Kübler, A., Winter, S., Ludolph, A. C., Hautzinger, M., & Birbaumer, N. (2005). Severity of depressive symptoms and quality of life in patients with amyotrophic lateral sclerosis. *Neurorehabilitation and Neural Repair, 19*(3), 182–193.

Kubzansky, L. D., Sparrow, D., Vokanas, P., Kawachi, I. (2001). Is the glass half empty or half full? A prospective study of optimism and coronary heart disease in the normative aging study. *Psychosomatic Medicine, 63,* 910–916.

Kuhl, P. K., & Meltzoff, A. N. (1982). The bimodal perception of speech in infancy. *Science, 218,* 1138–1141.

Kujala, U. M., Kaprio, J., Sarna, S., & Koskenvuo, M. (1998). Relationship of leisure-time physical activity and mortality: The Finnish twin cohort. *Journal of the American Medical Association, 279,* 440–444.

Kulkin, H. S., Chauvin, E. A., & Percle, G. A. (2000). Suicide among gay and lesbian adolescents and young adults: A review of the literature. *Journal of Homosexuality, 40,* 1–29.

Kuncel, N. R., Nezlett, S. A., & Ones, D. S. (2004). Academic performance, career potential, creativity, and job performance: Can one construct predict them all? *Journal of Personality and Social Psychology, 86,* 148–161.

Kunkel, D. (2001, February 4). *Sex on TV.* Menlo Park, CA: Henry J. Kaiser Family Foundation (www.kff.org).

Kunkel, D., Cope-Farrar, K., Biely, E., Farinola, W. J. M., & Donnerstein, E. (2001). *Sex on TV (2): A biennial report to the Kaiser Family Foundation.* Menlo Park, CA: Kaiser Family Foundation.

Kurtz, P. (1983, Spring). Stars, planets, and people. *The Skeptical Inquirer,* pp. 65–68.

Kushner, H. (1986). Quoted by J. Viorst, *Necessary losses.* New York: Fawcett, p. 295.

Kutas, M. (1990). Event-related brain potential (ERP) studies of cognition during sleep: Is it more than a dream? In R. R. Bootzin, J. F. Kihlstrom, & D. Schacter (Eds.), *Sleep and cognition.* Washington, DC: American Psychological Association.

Kvavilashvili, L., Mirani, J., Schlagman, S., & Kornbrot, D. E. (2003). Comparing flashbulb memories of September 11 and the death of Princess Diana: Effects of time delays and nationality. *Applied Cognitive Psychology, 17,* 1017–1031.

Labouvie-Vief, G., & Schell, D. A. (1982). Learning and memory in later life. In B. B. Wolman (Ed.), *Handbook of developmental psychology.* Englewood Cliffs, NJ: Prentice-Hall.

Lacayo, R. (1995, June 12). Violent reaction. *Time,* pp. 25–39.

Lacey, M. (2004. April 9). A decade after massacres, Rwanda outlaws ethnicity. *New York Times* (www.nytimes.com).

Lachman, M. E. (2004). Development in midlife. *Annual Review of Psychology, 55,* 305–331.

Lachman, M. E., & Weaver, S. L. (1998). The sense of control as a moderator of social class differences in health and well-being. *Journal of Personality and Social Psychology, 74,* 763–773.

Ladd, E. C. (1998, August/September). The tobacco bill and American public opinion. *The Public Perspective,* pp. 5–19.

Ladd, G. T. (1887). *Elements of physiological psychology.* New York: Scribner's.

Laird, J. D. (1974). Self-attribution of emotion: The effects of expressive behavior on the quality of emotional experience. *Journal of Personality and Social Psychology, 29,* 475–486.

Laird, J. D. (1984). The real role of facial response in the experience of emotion: A reply to Tourangeau and Ellsworth, and others. *Journal of Personality and Social Psychology, 47,* 909–917.

Laird, J. D., Cuniff, M., Sheehan, K., Shulman, D., & Strum, G. (1989). Emotion specific effects of facial expressions on memory for life events. *Journal of Social Behavior and Personality, 4,* 87–98.

Lakin, J. L., & Chartrand, T. L. (2003). Using nonconscious behavioral mimicry to create affiliation and rapport. *Psychological Science, 14,* 334–339.

Lalumière, M. L., Blanchard, R., & Zucker, K. J. (2000). Sexual orientation and handedness in men and women: A meta-analysis. *Psychological Bulletin, 126,* 575–592.

Lambert, W. E. (1992). Challenging established views on social issues: The power and limitations of research. *American Psychologist, 47,* 533–542.

Lambert, W. E., Genesee, F., Holobow, N., & Chartrand, L. (1993). Bilingual education for majority English-speaking children. *European Journal of Psychology of Education, 8,* 3–22.

Lamberth, J. (1998, August 6). Driving while black: A statistician proves that prejudice still rules the road. *Washington Post,* p. C1.

Lammers, W. (2000). Quick tips for applying to graduate school in psychology. *Eye on Psi Chi, 4*(3), 40–42.

Lampinen, J. M. (2002). What exactly is déjà vu? *Scientific American* (scieam.com/askexpert/biology/biology63).

Landau, M. J., Solomon, S., Greenberg, J., Cohen, F., Pyszczynski, T., Arndt, J., Miller, C. H., Ogilvie, D. M., & Cook, A. (2004). Deliver us from evil: The effects of mortality salience and reminders of 9/11 on support for President George W. Bush. *Personality and Social Psychology Bulletin, 30,* 1136–1150.

Landauer, T. (2001, September). Quoted by R. Herbert, You must remember this. *APS Observer,* p. 11.

Landauer, T. K. (1986). How much do people remember? Some estimates of the quantity of learned information in long-term memory. *Cognitive Science, 10,* 477–493.

Landauer, T. K., & Whiting, J. W. M. (1979). Correlates and consequences of stress in infancy. In R. Munroe, B. Munroe & B. Whiting (Eds.), *Handbook of Cross-Cultural Human Development.* New York: Garland.

Landers, A. (1969, April 8). Syndicated newspaper column. Cited by L. Berkowitz, The case for bottling up rage. *Psychology Today,* September, 1973, pp. 24–31.

Landrum, E. (2001). I'm getting my bachelor's degree in psychology. What can I do with it? *Eye on Psi Chi, 22–24.*

Landry, M. J. (2002). MDMA: A review of epidemiologic data. *Journal of Psychoactive Drugs, 34,* 163–169.

Lang, E. V., Benotsch, E. G., Fick, L. J., Lutgendorf, S., Berbaum, M. L., Logan, H., & Spiegel, D. (2000). Adjunctive non-pharmacological analgesia for invasive medical procedures: A randomised trial. *Lancet, 355,* 1486–1490.

Langer, E. J. (1983). *The psychology of control.* Beverly Hills, CA: Sage.

Langer, E. J., & Abelson, R. P. (1974). A patient by any other name . . . : Clinician group differences in labeling bias. *Journal of Consulting and Clinical Psychology, 42,* 4–9.

Langer, E. J., & Imber, L. (1980). The role of mindlessness in the perception of deviance. *Journal of Personality and Social Psychology, 39,* 360–367.

Langleben, D. D., Schroeder, L., Maldjian, J. A., Gur, R. C., McDonald, S., Ragland, J. D., O'Brien, C. P., & Childress, A. R. (2002). Brain activity during simulated deception: An event-related functional magnetic resonance study. *NeuroImage, 15,* 727–732.

Langlois, J. H., Kalakanis, L., Rubenstein, A. J., Larson, A., Hallam, M., & Smoot, M. (2000). Maxims or myths of beauty? A meta-analytic and theoretical review. *Psychological Bulletin, 126,* 390–423.

Langlois, J. H., & Roggman, L. A. (1990). Attractive faces are only average. *Psychological Science, 1,* 115–121.

Langlois, J. H., Roggman, L. A., Casey, R. J., Ritter, J. M., Rieser-Danner, L. A., & Jenkins, V. Y. (1987). Infant preferences for attractive faces: Rudiments of a stereotype? *Developmental Psychology, 23,* 363–369.

Larkin, K., Resko, J. A., Stormshak, F., Stellflug, J. N., & Roselli, C. E. (2002). Neuroanatomical correlates of sex and sexual partner preference in sheep. Society for Neuroscience convention.

Larrance, D. T., & Twentyman, C. T. (1983). Maternal attributions and child abuse. *Journal of Abnormal Psychology, 92,* 449–457.

Larsen, R. J. (2004). Emotion and cognition: The case of automatic vigilance. *Psychological Science Agenda, 18* (www.apa.org/science/psa/sb-larsenprt.html).

Larsen, R. J., & Diener, E. (1987). Affect intensity as an individual difference characteristic: A review. *Journal of Research in Personality, 21,* 1–39.

Larsen, R. J., Diener, E., & Cropanzano, R. S. (1987). Cognitive operations associated with individual differences in affect intensity. *Journal of Personality and Social Psychology, 53,* 767–774.

Larsen, R. J., Kasimatis, M., & Frey, K. (1992). Facilitating the furrowed brow: An unobtrusive test of the facial feedback hypothesis applied to unpleasant affect. *Cognition and Emotion, 6,* 321–338.

Larson, R. W. (2001). How U.S. children and adolescents spend time: What it does (and doesn't) tell us about their development. *Current Directions in Psychological Science, 10,* 160-164.

Larson, R. W., & Verma, S. (1999). How children and adolescents spend time across the world: Work, play, and developmental opportunities. *Psychological Bulletin, 125,* 701-736.

Larzelere, R. E. (1996). A review of the outcomes of parental use of nonabusive or customary physical punishment. *Pediatrics, 78,* 824-828.

Larzelere, R. E. (1999). The intervention selection bias. Unpublished manuscript. Boys Town, NE: Boys Town.

Larzelere, R. E. (2000). Child outcomes of non-abusive and customary physical punishment by parents: An updated literature review. *Clinical Child and Family Psychology Review, 3,* 199-221.

Larzelere, R. E., Kuhn, B. R., & Johnson, B. (2004). The intervention selection bias: An underrecognized confound in intervention research. *Psychological Bulletin, 130,* 289-303.

Lashley, K. S. (1950). In search of the engram. In *Symposium of the Society for Experimental Biology* (Vol. 4). New York: Cambridge University Press.

Lassiter, G. D., & Irvine, A. A. (1986). Video-taped confessions: The impact of camera point of view on judgments of coercion. *Journal of Personality and Social Psychology, 16,* 268-276.

Latané, B. (1981). The psychology of social impact. *American Psychologist, 36,* 343-356.

Latané, B., & Dabbs, J. M., Jr. (1975). Sex, group size and helping in three cities. *Sociometry, 38,* 180-194.

Laudenslager, M. L., & Reite, M. L. (1984). Losses and separations: Immunological consequences and health implications. *Review of Personality and Social Psychology, 5,* 285-312.

Laumann, E. O., Gagnon, J. H., Michael, R. T., & Michaels, S. (1994). *The social organization of sexuality: Sexual practices in the United States.* Chicago: University of Chicago Press.

Lazarus, R. S. (1990). Theory-based stress measurement. *Psychological Inquiry, 1,* 3-13.

Lazarus, R. S. (1991). Progress on a cognitive-motivational-relational theory of emotion. *American Psychologist, 46,* 352-367.

Lazarus. R. S. (1998). *Fifty years of the research and theory of R. S. Lazarus: An analysis of historical and perennial issues.* Mahwah, NJ: Erlbaum.

Lea, S. E. G. (2000). Towards an ethical use of animals. *The Psychologist, 13,* 556-557.

Leach, P. (1993). Should parents hit their children? *The Psychologist: Bulletin of the British Psychological Society, 6,* 216-220.

Leach, P. (1994). *Children first.* New York: Knopf.

Leary, M. R. (1999). The social and psychological importance of self-esteem. In R. M. Kowalski & M. R. Leary (Eds.), *The social psychology of emotional and behavioral problems.* Washington, DC: APA Books.

Leary, M. R., Haupt, A. L., Strausser, K. S., & Chokel, J. T. (1998). Calibrating the sociometer: The relationship between interpersonal appraisals and state self-esteem. *Journal of Personality and Social Psychology, 74,* 1290-1299.

Leary, M. R., Schreindorfer, L. S., & Haupt, A. L. (1995). The role of low self-esteem in emotional and behavioral problems: Why is low self-esteem dysfunctional? *Journal of Social and Clinical Psychology, 14,* 297-314.

Leary, W. E. (1998, September 28). Older people enjoy sex, survey says. *New York Times* (www.nytimes.com).

LeDoux, J. (1996). *The emotional brain: The mysterious underpinnings of emotional life.* New York: Simon & Schuster.

LeDoux, J. E. (2002). *The synaptic self.* London: Macmillan.

LeDoux, J. E., & Armony, J. (1999). Can neurobiology tell us anything about human feelings? In D. Kahneman, E. Diener, & N. Schwartz (Eds.), *Well-being: The foundations of hedonic psychology.* New York: Sage.

Lee, K., Byatt, G., & Rhodes, G. (2000). Caricature effects, distinctiveness, and identification: Testing the face-space framework. *Psychological Science, 11,* 379-385.

Lefcourt, H. M. (1982). *Locus of control: Current trends in theory and research.* Hillsdale, NJ: Erlbaum.

Legrand, L. N., Iacono, W. G., & McGue, M. (2005). Predicting addiction. *American Scientist, 93,* 140-147.

Le Grand, R., Mondloch, C. J., Maurer, D., & Brent, H. P. (2004). Impairment in holistic face processing following early visual deprivation. *Psychological Science, 15,* 762-768.

Lehman, A. F., Steinwachs, D. M., Dixon, L. B., Goldman, H. H., Osher, F., Postrado, L., Scott, J. E., Thompson, J. W., Fahey, M., Fischer, P., Kasper, J. A., Lyles, A., Skinner, E. A., Buchanan, R., Carpenter, W. T., Jr., Levine, J., McGlynn, E. A., Rosenheck, R., & Zito, J. (1998). Translating research into practice: The schizophrenia patient outcomes research team (PORT) treatment recommendations. *Schizophrenia Bulletin, 24,* 1-10.

Lehman, D. R., Lempert, R. O., & Nisbett, R. E. (1988). The effects of graduate training on reasoning: Formal discipline and thinking about everyday-life events. *American Psychologist, 43,* 431-442.

Lehman, D. R., & Nisbett, R. E. (1985). Effects of higher education on inductive reasoning. Unpublished manuscript, University of Michigan.

Lehman, D. R., Wortman, C. B., & Williams, A. F. (1987). Long-term effects of losing a spouse or child in a motor vehicle crash. *Journal of Personality and Social Psychology, 52,* 218-231.

Leibowitz, H. W. (1985). Grade crossing accidents and human factors engineering. *American Scientist, 73,* 558-562.

Leigh, B. C. (1989). In search of the seven dwarves: Issues of measurement and meaning in alcohol expectancy research. *Psychological Bulletin, 105,* 361-373.

Leitenberg, H., & Henning, K. (1995). Sexual fantasy. *Psychological Bulletin, 117,* 469-496.

Lemonick, M. D. (2002, June 3). Lean and hungrier. *Time,* p. 54.

L'Engle, M. (1972). *A wind in the door.* Bantam Doubleday Dell Books for Young Readers.

Lennox, B. R., Bert, S., Park, G., Jones, P. B., & Morris, P. G. (1999). Spatial and temporal mapping of neural activity associated with auditory hallucinations. *Lancet, 353,* 644.

Lenzenweger, M. F., Dworkin, R. H., & Wethington, E. (1989). Models of positive and negative symptoms in schizophrenia: An empirical evaluation of latent structures. *Journal of Abnormal Psychology, 98,* 62-70.

Leonhardt, D. (2004, August 17). Top athletes may be running into a tall hurdle: Themselves. *New York Times* (www.nytimes.com).

Lerman, C., Caporaso, N. E., Audrain, J., Main, D., Bowman, E. D., Lockshin, B., Boyd, N. R., & Shields, P. G. (1999). Evidence suggesting the role of specific genetic factors in cigarette smoking. *Health Psychology, 18,* 14-20.

Lerner, J. S, Gonzalez, R. M., Small, D. A., & Fischhoff, B. (2002). Effects of Fear and Anger on Perceived Risks of Terrorism: A National Field Experiment. *Psychological Science, 14*(2), 144-150.

Lerner, M. J. (1980). *The belief in a just world: A fundamental delusion.* New York: Plenum Press.

Leserman, J., Jackson, E. D., Petitto, J. M., Golden, R. N., Silva, S. G., Perkins, D. O., Cai, J., Folds, J. D., & Evans, D. L. (1999). Progression to AIDS: The effects of stress, depressive symptoms, and social support. *Psychosomatic Medicine, 61,* 397-406.

Lessard, N., Pare, M., Lepore, F., & Lassonde, M. (1998). Early-blind human subjects localize sound sources better than sighted subjects. *Nature, 395,* 278-280.

Lester, W. (2004, May 26). AP polls: Nations value immigrant workers. Associated Press release.

Leucht, S., Barnes, T. R. E., Kissling, W., Engel, R. R., Correll, C., & Kane, J. M. (2003). Relapse prevention in schizophrenia with new-generation antipsychotics: A systematic review and exploratory meta-analysis of randomized, controlled trials. *American Journal of Psychiatry, 160,* 1209–1222.

LeVay, S. (1991). A difference in hypothalamic structure between heterosexual and homosexual men. *Science, 253,* 1034–1037.

LeVay, S. (1994, March). Quoted in D. Nimmons, Sex and the brain. *Discover,* pp. 64–71.

Levenson, R. W. (1992). Autonomic nervous system differences among emotions. *Psychological Science, 3,* 23–27.

Leventhal, T., & Brooks-Gunn, J. (2000). The neighborhoods they live in: The effects of neighborhood residence on child and adolescent outcomes. *Psychological Bulletin, 126,* 309–337.

Lever, J. (2003, November 11). Personal correspondence reporting data responses volunteered to *Elle/MSNBC.com* survey of weight perceptions.

Levesque, M. J., & Kenny, D. A. (1993). Accuracy of behavioral predictions at zero acquaintance: A social relations analysis. *Journal of Personality and Social Psychology, 65,* 1178–1187.

Levin, I. P., & Gaeth, G. J. (1988). How consumers are affected by the framing of attribute information before and after consuming the product. *Journal of Consumer Research, 15,* 374–378.

Levine, J. A., Eberhardt, N. L., & Jensen, M. D. (1999). Role of nonexercise activity thermogenesis in resistance to fat gain in humans. *Science, 283,* 212–214.

Levine, J. A., Lanningham-Foster, L. M., McCrady, S. K., Krizan, A. C., Olson, L. R., Kane, P. H., Jensen, M. D., & Clark, M. M. (2005). Interindividual variation in posture allocation: Possible role in human obesity. *Science, 307,* 584–586.

Levine, R., Sato, S., Hashimoto, T., & Verma, J. (1995). Love and marriage in eleven cultures. *Journal of Cross-Cultural Psychology, 26,* 554–571.

Levine, R. V., & Norenzayan, A. (1999). The pace of life in 31 countries. *Journal of Cross-Cultural Psychology, 30,* 178–205.

Levy, B., & Langer, E. (1992). Avoidance of the memory loss stereotype: Enhanced memory among the elderly deaf. American Psychological Association convention, Washington, DC.

Levy, P. E. (2003). *Industrial/organizational psychology: Understanding the workplace.* Boston: Houghton Mifflin.

Lewicki, P., Hill, T., & Czyzewska, M. (1992). Nonconscious acquisition of information. *American Psychologist, 47,* 796–801.

Lewicki, P., Hill, T., & Czyzewska, M. (1997). Hidden covariation detection: A fundamental and ubiquitous phenomenon. *Journal of Experimental Psychology: Learning, Memory, and Cognition, 23,* 221–228.

Lewinsohn, P. M., Hoberman, H., Teri, L., & Hautziner, M. (1985). An integrative theory of depression. In S. Reiss & R. Bootzin (Eds.), *Theoretical issues in behavior therapy.* Orlando, FL: Academic Press.

Lewinsohn, P. M., Rohde, P., & Seeley, J. R. (1998). Major depressive disorder in older adolescents: Prevalence, risk factors, and clinical implications. *Clinical Psychology Review, 18,* 765–794.

Lewinsohn, P. M., & Rosenbaum, M. (1987). Recall of parental behavior by acute depressives, remitted depressives, and nondepressives. *Journal of Personality and Social Psychology, 52,* 611–619.

Lewis, C. S. (1960). *Mere Christianity.* New York: Macmillan.

Lewis, C. S. (1967). *Christian reflections.* Grand Rapids, MI: Eerdmans.

Lewis, D. O., Pincus, J. H., Bard, B., Richardson, E., Prichep, L. S., Feldman, M., & Yeager, C. (1988). Neuropsychiatric, psychoeducational, and family characteristics of 14 juveniles condemned to death in the United States. *American Journal of Psychiatry, 145,* 584–589.

Lewis, D. O., Pincus, J. H., Feldman, M., Jackson, L., & Bard, B. (1986). Psychiatric, neurological, and psychoeducational characteristics of 15 death row inmates in the United States. *American Journal of Psychiatry, 143,* 838–845.

Lewis, D. O., Yeager, C. A., Swica, Y., Pincus, J. H., & Lewis, M. (1997). Objective documentation of child abuse and dissociation in 12 murderers with dissociative identity disorder. *American Journal of Psychiatry, 154,* 1703–1710.

Lewis, M. (1992). Commentary. *Human Development, 35,* 44–51.

Lewontin, R. (1976). Race and intelligence. In N. J. Block & G. Dworkin (Eds.), *The IQ controversy: Critical readings.* New York: Pantheon.

Lewontin, R. (1982). *Human diversity.* New York: Scientific American Library.

Li, J. C., Dunning, D., & Malpass, R. L. (1996). Cross-racial identification among European-Americans Basketball fandom and the contact hypothesis. Unpublished manuscript, Cornell University.

Li, J., Laursen, T. M., Precht, D. H., Olsen, J., & Mortensen, P. B. (2005). Hospitalization for mental illness among parents after the death of a child. *New England Journal of Medicine, 352,* 1190–1196.

Libet, B. (1985). Unconscious cerebral initiative and the role of conscious will in voluntary action. *Behavioral and Brain Sciences, 12,* 181–187.

Libet, B. (2004). Mind time: The temporal factor in consciousness. Cambridge, MA: Harvard University Press.

Licata, A., Taylor, S., Berman, M., & Cranston, J. (1993). Effects of cocaine on human aggression. *Pharmacology Biochemistry and Behavior, 45,* 549–552.

Lichtman, S. W., Pisarska, K., Berman, E. R., Pestone, M., Dowling, H., Offenbacher, E., Weisel, H., Heshka, S., Matthews, D. E., & Heymsfield, S. B. (1992). Discrepancy between self-reported and actual caloric intake and exercise in obese subjects. *New England Journal of Medicine, 327,* 1893–1898.

Lieberman, J. A., & 11 others (2005). Effectiveness of antipsychotic drugs in patients with chronic schizophrenia. *New England Journal of Medicine, 353,* 1209–1223.

Lilienfeld, S. O. (1998). Pseudoscience in contemporary clinical psychology: What it is and what we can do about it. *The Clinical Psychologist, 51*(4), 3–5.

Lilienfeld, S. O., Lynn, S. J., Kirsch, I., Chaves, J. F., Sarbin, T. R., Ganaway, G. K., & Powell, R. A. (1999). Dissociative identity disorder and the sociocognitive model: Recalling the lessons of the past. *Psychological Bulletin, 125,* 507–523.

Lilienfeld, S. O., Wood, J. M., & Garb, H. N. (2000). The scientific status of projective techniques. *Psychological Science in the Public Interest, 1,* 27–66.

Lilienfeld, S. O., Wood, J. M., & Garb, H. N. (2001, May). What's wrong with this picture? *Scientific American,* pp. 81–87.

Lin, L., Faraco, J., Li, R., Kadotani, H., Rogers, W., Lin, X., Qiu, X., de Jong, P. J., Nishino, S., & Mignot E. (1999). The sleep disorder canine narcolepsy is caused by a mutation in the hypocretin (orexin) receptor 2 gene. *Cell, 98,* 365–376.

Lincoln, C. (2001). *Sap Rising,* Pantheon Books.

Linde, K., & 10 others (2005). Acupuncture for patients with migraine: A randomized controlled trial. *Journal of the American Medical Association, 293,* 2118–2125.

Linder, D. (1982). Social trap analogs: The tragedy of the commons in the laboratory. In V. J. Derlega & J. Grzelak (Eds.), *Cooperative and helping behavior: Theories and research.* New York: Academic Press.

Lindskold, S. (1978). Trust development, the GRIT proposal, and the effects of conciliatory acts on conflict and cooperation. *Psychological Bulletin, 85,* 772–793.

Lindskold, S., & Han, G. (1988). GRIT as a foundation for integrative bargaining. *Personality and Social Psychology Bulletin, 14,* 335–345.

Linville, P. W., Fischer, G. W., & Fischhoff, B. (1992). AIDS risk perceptions and decision biases. In J. B. Pryor & G. D. Reeder (Eds.), *The social psychology of HIV infection.* Hillsdale, NJ: Erlbaum.

Lippa, R. A. (2002). Gender-related traits of heterosexual and homosexual men and women. *Archives of Sexual Behavior, 31,* 83–98.

Lippman, J. (1992, October 25). Global village is characterized by a television in every home. *Los Angeles Times* Syndicate (in *Grand Rapids Press*, p. F9).

Lipps, H. M. (1999). *A new psychology of women: Gender, culture, and ethnicity.* Mountain View, CA: Mayfield Publishing.

Lipsey, M. W., & Wilson, D. B. (1993). The efficacy of psychological, educational, and behavioral treatment: Confirmation from meta-analyses. *American Psychologist, 48,* 1181–1209.

Lipsitt, L. P. (2003). Crib death: A biobehavioral phenomenon? *Current Directions in Psychological Science, 12,* 164–170.

Lipton, J. S., & Spelke, E. S. (2003). Origins of number sense: Large-number discrimination in human infants. *Psychological Science, 14,* 296–401.

Livingstone, M., & Hubel, D. (1988). Segregation of form, color, movement, and depth: Anatomy, physiology, and perception. *Science, 240,* 740–749.

Lock, M. (1998). Menopause: Lessons from anthropology. *Psychosomatic Medicine, 60,* 410–419.

Locke, E. A., & Latham, G. P. (2002). Building a practically useful theory of goal setting and task motivation. *American Psychologist, 57,* 705–717.

Loehlin, J. C., McCrae, R. R., & Costa, P. T., Jr. (1998). Heritabilities of common and measure-specific components of the Big Five personality factors. *Journal of Research in Personality, 32,* 431–453.

Loehlin, J. C., & Nichols, R. C. (1976). *Heredity, environment, and personality.* Austin: University of Texas Press.

Loewenstein, G., & Furstenberg, F. (1991). Is teenage sexual behavior rational? *Journal of Applied Social Psychology, 21,* 957–986.

Loftus, E. F. (1979). The malleability of human memory. *American Scientist, 67,* 313–320.

Loftus, E. (1995, March/April). Remembering dangerously. *Skeptical Inquirer,* pp. 20–29.

Loftus, E. F. (1980). *Memory: Surprising new insights into how we remember and why we forget.* Reading, MA: Addison-Wesley.

Loftus, E. F. (1993). The reality of repressed memories. *American Psychologist, 48,* 518–537.

Loftus, E. F. (2001, November). Imagining the past. *The Psychologist, 14,* 584–587.

Loftus, E. F., Coan, J., & Pickrell, J. E. (1996). Manufacturing false memories using bits of reality. In L. Reder (Ed.), *Implicit memory and metacognition.* Mahway, NJ: Erlbaum.

Loftus, E. F., & Kaufman, L. (1992). Why do traumatic experiences sometimes produce good memory (flashbulbs) and sometimes no memory (repression)? In E. Winograd & U. Neisser (Eds.), *Affect and accuracy in recall: Studies of "flashbulb" memories.* New York: Cambridge University Press.

Loftus, E. F., & Ketcham, K. (1994). *The myth of repressed memory.* New York: St. Martin's Press.

Loftus, E. F., Levidow, B., & Duensing, S. (1992). Who remembers best? Individual differences in memory for events that occurred in a science museum. *Applied Cognitive Psychology, 6,* 93–107.

Loftus, E. F., & Loftus, G. R. (1980). On the permanence of stored information in the human brain. *American Psychologist, 35,* 409–420.

Loftus, E. F., Milo, E. M., & Paddock, J. R. (1995). The accidental executioner: Why psychotherapy must be informed by science. *The Counseling Psychologist, 23,* 300–309.

Loftus, E. F., & Palmer, J. C. (October, 1974). Reconstruction of automobile destruction: An example of the interaction between language and memory. *Journal of Verbal Learning & Verbal Behavior, 13*(5), 585–589.

Loftus, E. F. (1992). When a lie becomes memory's truth: Memory distortion after exposure to misinformation. *Current Directions in Psychological Science, 1,* 121–123.

Logan, T. K., Walker, R., Cole, J., & Leukefeld, C. (2002). Victimization and substance abuse among women: Contributing factors, interventions, and implications. *Review of General Psychology, 6,* 325–397.

Logothetis, N. K., & Schall, J. D. (1989). Neuronal correlates of subjective visual perception. *Science, 245,* 761–763.

Logue, A. W. (1998a). Laboratory research on self-control: Applications to administration. *Review of General Psychology, 2,* 221–238.

Logue, A. W. (1998b). Self-control. In W. T. O'Donohue, (Ed.), *Learning and behavior therapy.* Boston, MA: Allyn & Bacon.

London, P. (1970). The rescuers: Motivational hypotheses about Christians who saved Jews from the Nazis. In J. Macaulay & L. Berkowitz (Eds.), *Altruism and helping behavior.* New York: Academic Press.

Looy, H. (2001). Sex differences: Evolved, constructed, and designed. *Journal of Psychology and Theology, 29,* 301–313.

Lopes, P. N., Brackett, M. A., Nezlek, J. B., Sch_tz, A., Sellin, Il, & Salovey, P. (2004). Emotional intelligence and social interaction. *Personality and Social Psychology Bulletin, 30,* 1018–1034.

Lopez, A. D. (1999). Measuring the health hazards of tobacco: Commentary. *Bulletin of the World Health Organization, 77*(1), 82–83.

Lopez, D. J. (2002, January/February). Snaring the fowler: Mark Twain debunks phrenology. *Skeptical Inquirer* (www.csicop.org).

Lord, C. G., Lepper, M. R., & Preston, E. (1984). Considering the opposite: A corrective strategy for social judgment. *Journal of Personality and Social Psychology, 47,* 1231–1247.

Lord, C. G., Ross, L., & Lepper, M. (1979). Biased assimilation and attitude polarization: The effects of prior theories on subsequently considered evidence. *Journal of Personality and Social Psychology, 37,* 2098–2109.

Lorenz, K. (1937). The companion in the bird's world. *Auk, 54,* 245–273.

Los Angeles Times (1998, 14 March). Daughters give birth on same day, p. A15.

Louie, K., & Wilson, M. A. (2001). Temporally structured replay of awake hippocampal ensemble activity during rapid eye movement sleep. *Neuron, 29,* 145–156.

Lourenco, O., & Machado, A. (1996). In defense of Piaget's theory: A reply to 10 common criticisms. *Psychological Review, 103,* 143–164.

Lovaas, O. I. (1987). Behavioral treatment and normal educational and intellectual functioning in young autistic children. *Journal of Consulting and Clinical Psychology, 55,* 3–9.

Love, J. M., & 13 others (2003). Child care quality matters: How conclusions may vary with context. *Child Development, 74,* 1021–1033.

Love, S. M. (2002, July 16). Preventive medicine, properly practiced. *New York Times* (www.nytimes.com).

Lowry, P. E. (1997). The assessment center process: New directions. *Journal of Social Behavior and Personality, 12,* 53–62.

Lu, Z.-L., Williamson, S. J., & Kaufman, L. (1992). Behavioral lifetime of human auditory sensory memory predicted by physiological measures. *Science, 258,* 1668–1670.

Lubinski, D., & Benbow, C. P. (1992). Gender differences in abilities and preferences among the gifted: Implications for the math-science pipeline. *Current Directions in Psychological Science, 1,* 61–66.

Lubinski, D., & Benbow, C. P. (2000). States of excellence. *American Psychologist, 137*–150.

Luborsky, L., Rosenthal, R., Diguer, L., Andrusyna, T. P., Berman, J. S., Levitt, J. T., Seligman, D. A., & Krause, E. D. (2002). The dodo bird verdict is alive and well—mostly. *Clinical Psychology: Science and Practice, 9,* 2–34.

Lucas, A., Morley, R., Cole, T. J., Lister, G., & Leeson-Payne, C. (1998). Breast milk and subsequent intelligence quotient in children born preterm. *Lancet, 339,* 261–264.

Lucas, R. E. (2005). Long-term disability has lasting effects on subjective well-being: Evidence from two nationally representative longitudinal studies. Unpublished manuscript, Michigan State University.

Lucas, R. E., Clark, A. E., Georgellis, Y., & Diener, E. (2003). Re-examining adaptation and the setpoint model of happiness: Reactions to changes in marital status. *Journal of Personality and Social Psychology, 84,* 527–539. (Figure courtesy of R. E. Lucas.)

Lucas, R. E., Clark, A. E., Georgellis, Y., & Diener, E. (2004). Unemployment alters the set point for life satisfaction. *Psychological Science, 15,* 8–13.

Ludwig, A. M. (1995). *The price of greatness: Resolving the creativity and madness controversy.* New York: Guilford Press.

Ludwig, J. (2004, June 1). Acceptance of interracial marriage at record high. Gallup Poll Tuesday Briefing (www.gallup.com).

Lukoff, D., Lu, F., & Turner, R. (1992). Toward a more culturally sensitive DSM-IV: Psychoreligious and psychospiritual problems. *Journal of Nervous and Mental Disease, 180,* 673–682.

Lumsden, C. J., & Wilson, E. O. (1983). *Promethean fire: Reflections on the origin of mind.* Cambridge, MA: Harvard University Press.

Luntz, F. (2003, June 10). Quoted by T. Raum, "Bush insists banned weapons will be found." Associated Press (story.news.yahoo.com).

Luria, A. M. (1968). In L. Solotaroff (Trans.), *The mind of a mnemonist.* New York: Basic Books.

Lustig, C., & Buckner, R. L. (2004). Preserved neural correlates of priming in old age and dementia. *Neuron, 42,* 865–875.

Lutgendorf, S. K., Russell, D., Ullrich, P., Harris, T. B., & Wallace, R. (2004). Religious participation, Interleukin-6, and mortality in older adults. *Health Psychology, 23,* 465–475.

Luthar, S. S., & Latendresse, S. J. (2005). Children of the affluent: Challenges to well-being. *Current Directions in Psychological Science, 14,* 49–53.

Lykken, D. T. (1982, September). Fearlessness: Its carefree charm and deadly risks. *Psychology Today,* pp. 20–28.

Lykken, D. T. (1991). Science, lies, and controversy: An epitaph for the polygraph. Invited address upon receipt of the Senior Career Award for Distinguished Contribution to Psychology in the Public Interest, American Psychological Association convention.

Lykken, D. T. (1995). *The antisocial personalities.* Hillsdale, NJ: Erlbaum.

Lykken, D. T. (1999). *Happiness.* New York: Golden Books.

Lykken, D. T. (2001). Happiness—stuck with what you've got? *The Psychologist, 14,* 470–473.

Lykken, D. T., & Tellegen, A. (1993). Is human mating adventitious or the result of lawful choice? A twin study of mate selection. *Journal of Personality and Social Psychology, 65,* 56–68.

Lykken, D. T., & Tellegen, A. (1996). Happiness is a stochastic phenomenon. *Psychological Science, 7,* 186–189.

Lyman, D. R. (1996). Early identification of chronic offenders: Who is the fledgling psychopath? *Psychological Bulletin, 120,* 209–234.

Lynch, G. (2002). Memory enhancement: The search for mechanism-based drugs. *Nature Neuroscience, 5* (suppl.), 1035–1038.

Lynch, G., & Staubli, U. (1991). Possible contributions of long-term potentiation to the encoding and organization of memory. *Brain Research Reviews, 16,* 204–206.

Lyness, S. A. (1993). Predictors of differences between Type A and B individuals in heart rate and blood pressure reactivity. *Psychological Bulletin, 114,* 266–295.

Lynn, M. (1988). The effects of alcohol consumption on restaurant tipping. *Personality and Social Psychology Bulletin, 14,* 87–91.

Lynn, R. (1987). Japan: Land of the rising IQ. A reply to Flynn. *Bulletin of the British Psychological Society, 40,* 464–468.

Lynn, R. (1991, Fall/Winter). The evolution of racial differences in intelligence. *The Mankind Quarterly, 32,* 99–145.

Lynn, R. (2001). *Eugenics: A reassessment.* Westport, CT: Praeger/Greenwood.

Lynn, S. J., Rhue, J. W., & Weekes, J. R. (1990). Hypnotic involuntariness: A social cognitive analysis. *Psychological Review, 97,* 169–184.

Lyons, L. (2002, June 25). Are spiritual teens healthier? *Gallup Tuesday Briefing,* Gallup Organization (www.gallup.com/poll/tb/religValue/20020625b.asp).

Lyons, L. (2003, September 23). Oh, boy: Americans still prefer sons. *Gallup Poll Tuesday Briefing* (www.gallup.com).

Lyons, L. (2004, February 3). Growing up lonely: Examining teen alienation. Gallup Poll Tuesday Briefing (www.gallup.com).

Lyons, L. (2005, January 4). Teens stay true to parents' political perspectives. Gallup Poll News Service (www.gallup.com).

Lytton, H., & Romney, D. M. (1991). Parents' differential socialization of boys and girls: A meta-analysis. *Psychological Bulletin, 109,* 267–296.

Lyubomirsky, S. (2001). Why are some people happier than others? The role of cognitive and motivational processes in well-being. *American Psychologist, 56,* 239–249.

Lyubomirsky, S., King, L., & Diener, E. (2005). The benefits of frequent positive affect: Does happiness lead to success? *Psychological Bulletin, 131,* 803–855.

Lyubomirsky, S., Sousa, L., & Dickerhoof, R. (2006). The costs and benefits of writing, talking, and thinking about life's triumphs and defeats. *Journal of Personality and Social Psychology,* in press.

Ma, L. (1997, September). On the origin of Darwin's ills. *Discover,* p. 27.

Maas, J. B. (1999). *Power sleep. The revolutionary program that prepares your mind for peak performance.* New York: HarperCollins.

Maass, A., & Russo, A. (2003). Directional bias in the mental representation of spatial events: Nature or culture? *Psychological Science, 14,* 296–301.

Macaluso, E., Frith, C. D., & Driver, J. (2000). Modulation of human visual cortex by crossmodal spatial attention. *Science, 289,* 1206–1208.

Macan, T. H., & Dipboye, R. L. (1994). The effects of the application on processing of information from the employment interview. *Journal of Applied Social Psychology, 24,* 1291.

Macaskill, P., Pierce, J. P., Simpson, J. M., & Lyle, D. M. (1992). Mass media-led antismoking campaign can remove the education gap in quitting behavior. *American Journal of Public Health, 82,* 96–98.

Maccoby, E. (1980). *Social development: Psychological growth and the parent-child relationship.* New York: Harcourt Brace Jovanovich.

Maccoby, E. E. (1990). Gender and relationships: A developmental account. *American Psychologist, 45,* 513–520.

Maccoby, E. E. (1995). Divorce and custody: The rights, needs, and obligations of mothers, fathers, and children. *Nebraska Symposium on Motivation, 42,* 135–172.

Maccoby, E. E. (1998). *The paradox of gender.* Cambridge, MA: Harvard University Press.

Maccoby, E. E. (2002). Gender and group process: A developmental perspective. *Current Directions in Psychological Science, 11,* 54–58.

Maccoby, E. E. (2003, July 22). In Susan Gilbert, Turning a mass of data on child care into advice for parents. *New York Times* (www.nytimes.com).

MacDonald, G., & Leary, M. R. (2005). Why does social exclusion hurt? The relationship between social and physical pain. *Psychological Bulletin, 131,* 202–223.

MacDonald, N. (1960). Living with schizophrenia. *Canadian Medical Association Journal, 82,* 218–221.

MacDonald, T. K., Fong, G. T., Zanna, M. P., & Martineau, A. M. (2000). Alcohol myopia and condom use: Can alcohol intoxication be associated with more prudent behavior? *Journal of Personality and Social Psychology, 78,* 605–619.

MacDonald, T. K., Zanna, M. P., & Fong, G. T. (1995). Decision making in altered states: Effects of alcohol on attitudes toward drinking and driving. *Journal of Personality and Social Psychology, 68*, 973–985.

MacDonald, T. K., Zanna, M. P., & Fong, G. T. (1996). Why common sense goes out the window: The effects of alcohol on intentions to use condoms. *Personality and Social Psychology Bulletin, 22*, 763–775.

Macfarlane, J. W. (1964). Perspectives on personality consistency and change from the guidance study. *Vita Humana, 7*, 115–126.

MacFarlane, A. (1978, February). What a baby knows. *Human Nature,* pp. 74–81.

MacKay, D. G. (1983). Prescriptive grammar and the pronoun problem. In B. Thorne, C. Kramarae, & N. Henley (Eds.), *Language, gender and society.* Rowley, MA: Newbury House.

MacKinnon, D. W., & Hall, W. B. (1972). Intelligence and creativity. In *Proceedings, XVIIth International Congress of Applied Psychology* (Vol. 2). Brussels: Editest.

MacLeod, C., & Campbell, L. (1992). Memory accessibility and probability judgments: An experimental evaluation of the availability heuristic. *Journal of Personality and Social Psychology, 63*, 890–902.

MacNeilage, P. F., & Davis, B. L. (2000). On the origin of internal structure of word forms. *Science, 288*, 527–531.

Maddieson, I. (1984). *Patterns of sounds.* Cambridge: Cambridge University Press.

Maddox, K. B. (2004). Perspectives on racial phenotypicality bias. *Personality and Social Psychology Review, 8*, 383–401.

Maes, H. H. M., Neale, M. C., & Eaves, L. J. (1997). Genetic and environmental factors in relative body weight and human adiposity. *Behavior Genetics, 27*, 325–351.

Maes, M., Armand, C., Delanghe, J., Altamura, C., Neels, H., & Meltzer, H. Y. (1999). Lowered omega3 polyunsaturated fatty acids in serum phospholipids and cholesteryl esters of depressed patients. *Psychiatry Residency, 85*, 275–291.

Maestripieri, D. (2003). Similarities in affiliation and aggression between cross-fostered rhesus macaque females and their biological mothers. *Developmental Psychobiology, 43*, 321–327.

Magnusson, D. (1990). Personality research—challenges for the future. *European Journal of Personality, 4*, 1–17.

Maguire, E. A., Spiers, H. J., Good, C. D., Hartley, T., Frackowiak, R. S. J., & Burgess, N. (2003a). Navigation expertise and the human hippocampus: A structural brain imaging analysis. *Hippocampus, 13*, 250–259.

Maguire, E. A., Valentine, E. R., Wilding, J. M., & Kapur, N. (2003b). Routes to remembering: The brains behind superior memory. *Nature Neuroscience, 6*, 90–95.

Mahowald, M. W., & Ettinger, M. G. (1990). Things that go bump in the night: The parsomias revisited. *Journal of Clinical Neurophysiology, 7*, 119–143.

Maier, S. F., Watkins, L. R., & Fleshner, M. (1994). Psychoneuroimmunology: The interface between behavior, brain, and immunity. *American Psychologist, 49*, 1004–1017.

Major, B., Carrington, P. I., & Carnevale, P. J. D. (1984). Physical attractiveness and self-esteem: Attribution for praise from an other-sex evaluator. *Personality and Social Psychology Bulletin, 10*, 43–50.

Major, B., Schmidlin, A. M., & Williams, L. (1990). Gender patterns in social touch: The impact of setting and age. *Journal of Personality and Social Psychology, 58*, 634–643.

Malamuth, N. M. (1996). Sexually explicit media, gender differences, and evolutionary theory. *Journal of Communication, 46*, 8–31.

Malamuth, N. M., & Check, J. V. P. (1981). The effects of media exposure on acceptance of violence against women: A field experiment. *Journal of Research in Personality, 15*, 436–446.

Malamuth, N. M., Linz, D., Heavey, C. L., Barnes, G., & Acker, M. (1995). Using the confluence model of sexual aggression to predict men's conflict with women: A 10-year follow-up study. *Journal of Personality and Social Psychology, 69*, 353–369.

Malamuth, N. M., Sockloskie, R. J., Koss, M. P., & Tanaka, J. S. (1991). Characteristics of aggressors against women: Testing a model using a national sample of college students. *Journal of Consulting and Clinical Psychology, 59*, 670–681.

Malan, D. H. (1978). "The case of the secretary with the violent father." In H. Davanloo (Ed.), *Basic principles and techniques in short-term dynamic psychotherapy.* New York: Spectrum.

Malaspina, D., Harlap, S., Fennig, S., Heiman, D., Nahon, D., Feldman, D., & Susser, E. S. (2001). Advancing paternal age and the risk of schizophrenia. *Archives of General Psychiatry, 58*, 361–367.

Malinosky-Rummell, R., & Hansen, D. J. (1993). Long-term consequences of childhood physical abuse. *Psychological Bulletin, 114*, 68–79.

Malkiel, B. G. (1989). Is the stock market efficient? *Science, 243*, 1313–1318.

Malkiel, B. G. (1995, June). Returns from investing in equity mutual funds 1971 to 1991. *Journal of Finance,* pp. 549–572.

Malkiel, B. (2004). *A random walk down Wall Street* (8th ed.). New York: Norton.

Malloy, E. A. (1994, June 7). Report of the Commission on Substance Abuse at Colleges and Universities, reported by *Associated Press.*

Malmquist, C. P. (1986). Children who witness parental murder: Posttraumatic aspects. *Journal of the American Academy of Child Psychiatry, 25*, 320–325.

Malnic, B., Hirono, J., Sato, T., & Buck, L. B. (1999). Combinatorial receptor codes for odors. *Cell, 96*, 713–723.

Manber, R., Bootzin, R. R., Acebo, C., & Carskadon, M. A. (1996). The effects of regularizing sleep-wake schedules on daytime sleepiness. *Sleep, 19*, 432–441.

Mandel, D. (1983, March 13). One man's holocaust: Part II. The story of David Mandel's journey through hell as told to David Kagan. *Wonderland Magazine (Grand Rapids Press),* pp. 2–7.

Mann, J. J. (2003). Neurobiology of suicidal behaviour. *Nature Reviews Neuroscience, 4*, 819–828.

Mann, S., Vrij, A., & Bull, R. (2004). Detecting true lies: Police officers' ability to detect suspects' lies. *Journal of Applied Psychology, 89*, 137–149.

Manning, A. (2002, May 17). Teenage smoking rates drop. *USA Today* (story.news.yahoo.com).

Manson, J. E. (2002). Walking compared with vigorous exercise for the prevention of cardiovascular events in women. *New England Journal of Medicine, 347*, 716–725.

Maquet, P. (2001). The role of sleep in learning and memory. *Science, 294*, 1048–1052.

Maquet, P., Peters, J-M., Aerts, J., Delfiore, G., Degueldre, C., Luxen, A., & Franck, G. (1996). Functional neuroanatomy of human rapid-eye-movement sleep and dreaming. *Nature, 383*, 163–166.

Marangell, L. B., Rush, A. J., George, M. S., Sackeim, H. A., Johnson, C. R., Husain, M. M., Nahas, Z., & Lisanby, S. H. (2002). Vagus nerve stimulation (VNS) for major depressive episodes: One year outcomes. *Biological Psychiatry, 51*, 280–287.

Marcus, G. (2004). *The birth of the mind: How a tiny number of genes creates the complexity of human thought.* New York: Basic Books.

Marcus, G. F., Vijayan, S., Rao, S. B., & Vishton, P. M. (1999). Rule learning by seven-month-old infants. *Science, 283*, 77–80.

Margolis, M. L. (2000). Brahms' lullaby revisited: Did the composer have obstructive sleep apnea? *Chest, 118*, 210–213.

Marino, L. A., Reiss, D., & Gallup, G. G., Jr. (1994). Mirror self-recognition in bottlenose dolphins: Implications for comparative investigations of highly dissimilar species. In S. P. Parker, R. Mitchell, & M. Boccia (Eds.), *Self-awareness in animals and humans: Developmental perspectives.* New York: Cambridge University Press.

Mark, V., & Ervin, F. (1970). *Violence and the brain.* New York: Harper & Row.

Markowitsch, H. J. (1995). Which brain regions are critically involved in the retrieval of old episodic memory? *Brain Research Reviews, 21,* 117–127.

Markowitz, J. C., Svartberg, M., & Swartz, H. A. (1998). Is IPT time-limited psychodynamic psychotherapy? *Journal of Psychotherapy Practice and Research, 7,* 185–195.

Markus, G. B. (1986). Stability and change in political attitudes: Observe, recall, and "explain." *Political Behavior, 8,* 21–44.

Markus, H. (2001, October 7). Culture and the good life. Address to the Positive Psychology Summit conference, Washington, DC.

Markus, H., & Kitayama, S. (1991). Culture and the self: Implications for cognition, emotion, and motivation. *Psychological Review, 98,* 224–253.

Markus, H., & Nurius, P. (1986). Possible selves. *American Psychologist, 41,* 954–969.

Marlatt, G. A. (1991). Substance abuse: Etiology, prevention, and treatment issues. Master lecture, American Psychological Association convention.

Marley, J., & Bulia, S. (2001). Crimes against people with mental illness: Types, perpetrators and influencing factors. *Social Work, 46,* 115–124.

Marmot, M. G., Bosma, H., Hemingway, H., Brunner, E., & Stansfeld, S. (1997). Contribution of job control and other risk factors to social variations in coronary heart disease incidents. *Lancet, 350,* 235–239.

Marr, D. (1982). *Vision.* San Francisco: W. H. Freeman.

Marschark, M., Richman, C. L., Yuille, J. C., & Hunt, R. R. (1987). The role of imagery in memory: On shared and distinctive information. *Psychological Bulletin, 102,* 28–41.

Marsh, A. A., Elfenbein, H. A., & Ambady, N. (2003). Nonverbal "accents": Cultural differences in facial expressions of emotion. *Psychological Science, 14,* 373–376.

Marsh, H. W., & Parker, J. W. (1984). Determinants of student self-concept: Is it better to be a relatively large fish in a small pond even if you don't learn to swim as well? *Journal of Personality and Social Psychology, 47,* 213–231.

Marshall, E. (2004). A star-studded search for memory-enhancing drugs. *Science, 304,* 36–38.

Marshall, M. J. (2002). *Why spanking doesn't work.* Springville, UT: Bonneville Books.

Marshall, W. L. (1989). Pornography and sex offenders. In D. Zillmann & J. Bryant (Eds.), *Pornography: Research advances and policy considerations.* Hillsdale, NJ: Erlbaum.

Marteau, T. M. (1989). Framing of information: Its influences upon decisions of doctors and patients. *British Journal of Social Psychology, 28,* 89–94.

Marti, M. W., Robier, D. M., & Baron, R. S. (2000). Right before our eyes: The failure to recognize non-prototypical forms of prejudice. *Group Processes and Intergroup Relations, 3,* 403–418.

Martin, A., Wiggs, C. L., Ungerleider, L. G., & Haxby, J. V. (1996). Neural correlates of category-specific knowledge. *Nature, 379,* 649–652.

Martin, C. L., & Ruble, D. (2004). Children's search for gender cues. *Current Directions in Psychological Science, 13,* 67–70.

Martin, C. L., Ruble, D. N., & Szkrybalo, J. (2002). Cognitive theories of early gender development. *Psychological Bulletin, 128,* 903–933.

Martin, J. L. R., Barbanojh, M. J., Schlaepfer, T. E., Thompson, E., Perez, V., & Kulisevsky, J. (2003). Repetitive transcranial magnetic stimulation for the treatment of depression: Systematic review and meta-analysis. *British Journal of Psychiatry, 182,* 480–491.

Martin, R. A. (2001). Humor, laughter, and physical health: Methodological issues and research findings. *Psychological Bulletin, 127,* 504–519.

Martin, R. A. (2002). Is laughter the best medicine? Humor, laughter, and physical health. *Current Directions in Psychological Science, 11,* 216–220.

Martin, R. J., White, B. D., & Hulsey, M. G. (1991). The regulation of body weight. *American Scientist, 79,* 528–541.

Martin, S. J., Kelly, I. W., & Saklofske, D. H. (1992). Suicide and lunar cycles: A critical review over 28 years. *Psychological Reports, 71,* 787–795.

Martins, Y., Preti, G., Crabtree, C. R., & Wysocki, C. J. (2005). Preference for human body odors is influenced by gender and sexual orientation. *Psychological Science, 16,* 694–701.

Maruta, T., Colligan, R. C., Malinchoc, M., & Offord, K. P. (2002). Optimists vs. pessimists: Survival rate among medical patients over a 30-year period. *Mayo Clinic Proceedings, 75,* 140–143.

Marx, J. (2005). Preventing Alzheimer's: A lifelong commitment? *Science, 309,* 864–866.

Maslow, A. H. (1970). *Motivation and personality* (2nd ed.). New York: Harper & Row.

Maslow, A. H. (1971). *The farther reaches of human nature.* New York: Viking Press.

Mason, C., & Kandel, E. R. (1991). Central visual pathways. In E. R. Kandel, J. H. Schwartz, & T. M. Jessell (Eds.), *Principles of neural science* (3rd ed.). New York: Elsevier.

Mason, H. (2003, March 25). Wake up, sleepy teen. *Gallup Poll Tuesday Briefing* (www.gallup.com).

Mason, H. (2003, September 2). Americans, Britons at odds on animal testing. Gallup Poll News Service (www.gallup.com).

Mason, H. (2004, September 28). Support for smoking bans smoldering in Britain, Canada. *Gallup Poll* (www.gallup.com).

Mason, H. (2005, January 25). Who dreams, perchance to sleep? Gallup Poll News Service (www.gallup.com).

Mason, H. (2005, February 22). How many teens are on mood medication? The Gallup Organization (www.gallup.com).

Mason, R. A., & Just, M. A. (2004). How the brain processes causal inferences in text. *Psychological Science, 15,* 1–7.

Masse, L. C., & Tremblay, R. E. (1997). Behavior of boys in kindergarten and the onset of substance use during adolescence. *Archives of General Psychiatry, 54,* 62–68.

Massimini, M., Ferrarelli, F., Huber, R., Esser, S. K., Singh, H., & Tononi, G. (2005). Breakdown of cortical effective connectivity during sleep. *Science, 309,* 2228–2232.

Masten, A. S. (2001). Ordinary magic: Resilience processes in development. *American Psychologist, 56,* 227–238.

Masters, W. H., & Johnson, V. E. (1966). *Human sexual response.* Boston: Little, Brown.

Masuda, T., & Kitayama, S. (2005). Perceiver-induced constraint and attitude attribution in Japan and the US: A case for the cultural dependence of the correspondence bias. *Journal of Experimental Social Psychology, 40,* 409–416.

Mataix-Cols, D., Rosario-Campos, M. C., & Leckman, J. F. (2005). A multidimensional model of obsessive-compulsive disorder. *American Journal of Psychiatry, 162,* 228–238.

Mataix-Cols, D., Wooderson, S., Lawrence, N., Brammer, M. J., Speckens, A., & Phillips, M. L. (2004). Distinct neural correlates of washing, checking, and hoarding symptom dimensions in obsessive-compulsive disorder. *Archives of General Psychiatry, 61,* 564–576.

Mather, M., Canli, T., English, T., Whitfield, S., Wais, P., Ochsner, K., Gabrieli, J. D. E., & Carstensen, L. L. (2004). Amygdala responses to emotionally valenced stimuli in older and younger adults. *Psychological Science, 15,* 259–263.

Mather, M., & Carstensen, L. L. (2003). Aging and attentional biases for emotional faces. *Psychological Science, 14,* 409–415.

Matsumoto, D. (1994). *People: Psychology from a cultural perspective*. Pacific Grove, CA: Brooks/Cole.

Matsumoto, D., & Ekman, P. (1989). American-Japanese cultural differences in intensity ratings of facial expressions of emotion. *Motivation and Emotion, 13*, 143–157.

Maurer, D., Lewis, T. L., Brent, H. P., & Levin, A. V. (1999). Rapid improvement in the acuity of infants after visual input. *Science, 286*, 108–110.

Maurer, D., & Maurer, C. (1988). *The world of the newborn*. New York: Basic Books.

May, C., & Hasher, L. (1998). Synchrony effects in inhibitory control over thought and action. *Journal of Experimental Psychology: Human Perception and Performance, 24*, 363–380.

May, C. P., Hasher, L., & Stoltzfus, E. R. (1993). Optimal time of day and the magnitude of age differences in memory. *Psychological Science, 4*, 326–330.

May, R. (1982). The problem of evil: An open letter to Carl Rogers. *Journal of Humanistic Psychology, 22*, 10–21.

Mayberg, H. S., Lozano, A. M., Voon, V., McNeely, H. E., Seminowicz, D., Hamani, C., Schwalb, J. M., & Kennedy, S. H. (2005). Deep brain stimulation for treatment-resistant depression. *Neuron, 45*, 651–660.

Mayberry, R. I., Lock, E., & Kazmi, H. (2002). Linguistic ability and early language exposure. *Nature, 417*, 38.

Mayer, J. D. Salovey, P., & Caruso, D. (2002). *The Mayer-Salovey-Caruso emotional intelligence test (MSCEIT)*. Toronto: Multi-Health Systems, Inc.

Mazur, A., & Booth, A. (1998). Testosterone and dominance in men. *Behavioral and Brain Sciences, 21*, 353–363.

Mazure, C., Keita, G., & Blehar, M. (2002). *Summit on women and depression: Proceedings and recommendations*. Washington, DC: American Psychological Association (www.apa.org/pi/wpo/women&depression.pdf).

Mazzoni, G., & Memon, A. (2003). Imagination can create false autobiographical memories. *Psychological Science, 14*, 186–188.

Mazzuca, J. (2002, July 2). Same-sex parenting: Does public back Rosie? The Gallup Organization (www.gallup.com/poll/tb/religValue/20020702.asp).

Mazzuca, J. (2002, August 20). Teens shrug off movie sex and violence. *Gallup Tuesday Briefing* (www.gallup.com/poll/tb/educayouth/20020820b.asp).

McAneny, L. (1996, September). Large majority think government conceals information about UFO's. *Gallup Poll Monthly*, pp. 23–26.

McBeath, M. K., Shaffer, D. M., & Kaiser, M. K. (1995). How baseball outfielders determine where to run to catch fly balls. *Science, 268*, 569–572.

McBurney, D. H. (1996). *How to think like a psychologist: Critical thinking in psychology*. Upper Saddle River, NJ: Prentice-Hall.

McBurney, D. H., & Collings, V. B. (1984). *Introduction to sensation and perception* (2nd ed.). Englewood Cliffs, NJ: Prentice-Hall.

McBurney, D. H., & Gent, J. F. (1979). On the nature of taste qualities. *Psychological Bulletin, 86*, 151–167.

McCall, R. B., Evahn, C., & Kratzer, L. (1992). High school underachievers. Newbury Park, CA: Sage.

McCann, I. L., & Holmes, D. S. (1984). Influence of aerobic exercise on depression. *Journal of Personality and Social Psychology, 46*, 1142–1147.

McCann, U. D., Eligulashvili, V., & Ricaurte, G. A. (2001). (+-)3,4-Methylenedioxymethamphetamine ('Ecstasy')-induced serotonin neurotoxicity: Clinical studies. *Neuropsychobiology, 42*, 11–16.

McCarthy, P. (1986, July). Scent: The tie that binds? *Psychology Today*, pp. 6, 10.

McCaul, K. D., & Malott, J. M. (1984). Distraction and coping with pain. *Psychological Bulletin, 95*, 516–533.

McCauley, C. R. (2002). Psychological issues in understanding terrorism and the response to terrorism. In C. E. Stout (Ed.), *The psychology of terrorism, Vol. 3*. Westport, CT: Praeger/Greenwood.

McCauley, C. R., & Segal, M. E. (1987). Social psychology of terrorist groups. In C. Hendrick (Ed.), *Group processes and intergroup relations*. Beverly Hills, CA: Sage.

McClearn, G. E., Johansson, B., Berg, S., Pedersen, N. L., Ahern, F., Petrill, S. A., & Plomin, R. (1997). Substantial genetic influence on cognitive abilities in twins 80 or more years old. *Science, 276*, 1560–1563.

McClintock, M. K., & Herdt, G. (December, 1996). Rethinking puberty: The development of sexual attraction. *Current Directions in Psychological Science, 5(6)*, 178–183.

McClure, E. B. (2000). A meta-analytic review of sex differences in facial expression processing and their development in infants, children, and adolescents. *Psychological Bulletin, 126*, 424–453.

McClure, S. M., Laibson, D. I., Loewenstein, G., & Cohen, J. D. (2004). Separate neural systems value immediate and delayed monetary rewards. *Science, 306*, 503–507.

McConkey, K. M. (1995). Hypnosis, memory, and the ethics of uncertainty. *Australian Psychologist, 30*, 1–10.

McConnell, R. A. (1991). National Academy of Sciences opinion on parapsychology. *Journal of the American Society for Psychical Research, 85*, 333–365.

McCool, G. (1999, October 26). Mirror-gazing Venezuelans top of vanity stakes. *Toronto Star* (via web.lexis-nexis.com).

McCord, J. (1978). A thirty-year follow-up on treatment effects. *American Psychologist, 33*, 284–289.

McCord, J. (1979). Following up on Cambridge-Somerville. *American Psychologist, 34*, 727.

McCormick, C. M., & Witelson, S. F. (1991). A cognitive profile of homosexual men compared to heterosexual men and women. *Psychoneuroendocrinology, 16*, 459–473.

McCrae, R. R. (2001). Trait psychology and culture. *Journal of Personality, 69*, 819–846.

McCrae, R. R., & Costa, P. T., Jr. (1986). Clinical assessment can benefit from recent advances in personality psychology. *American Psychologist, 41*, 1001–1003.

McCrae, R. R., & Costa, P. T., Jr. (1990). *Personality in adulthood*. New York: Guilford.

McCrae, R. R., & Costa, P. T., Jr. (1994). The stability of personality: Observations and evaluations. *Current Directions in Psychological Science, 3*, 173–175.

McCrae, R. R., & Costa, P. T., Jr. (1999). A five-factor theory of personality. In L. A. Pervin & O. P. John (Eds.), *Handbook of personality: Theory and research*. New York: Guilford.

McCrae, R. R., Costa, P. T., Jr., de Lirna, M. P., Simoes, A., Ostendorf, F., Angleitner, A., Marusic, I., Bratko, D., Caprara, G. V., Barbaranelli, C., Chae, J-H., & Piedmont, R. L. (1999). Age differences in personality across the adult life span: Parallels in five cultures. *Developmental Psychology, 35*, 466–477.

McCrae, R. R., Costa, P. T., Jr., Ostendorf, F., Angleitner, A., Hrebickova, M., Avia, M. D., Sanz, J., Sanchez-Bernardos, M. L., Kusdil, M. E., Woodfield, R., Saunders, P. R., & Smith, P. B. (2000). Nature over nurture: Temperament, personality, and life span development. *Journal of Personality and Social Psychology, 78*, 173–186.

McCrae, R. R., Terracciano, A., & 78 others (2005). Universal features of personality traits from the observer's perspective: Data from 50 cultures. *Journal of Personality and Social Psychology, 88*, 547–561.

McCrink, K., & Wynn, K. (2004). Large-number addition and subtraction by 9-month-old infants. *Psychological Science, 15*, 776–781.

McCullough, M. E., Hoyt, W. T., Larson, D. B., Koenig, H. G., & Thoresen, C. (2000). Religious involvement and mortality: A meta-analytic review. *Health Psychology, 19*, 211–222.

McCullough, M. E., & Laurenceau, J-P. (2005). Religiousness and the trajectory of self-rated health across adulthood. *Personality and Social Psychology Bulletin, 31,* 560–573.

McCullough, M. E., Tsang, J-A., & Emmons, R. A. (2004). Gratitude in intermediate affective terrain: Links of grateful moods to individual differences and daily emotional experience. *Journal of Personality and Social Psychology, 86,* 295–309.

McEwen, B. S. (1998). Protective and damaging effects of stress mediators. *Seminars in Medicine of the Beth Israel Deaconess Medical Center, 338,* 171–179.

McEwen, B. S. (2002). Sex, stress and the hippocampus: Allostasis, allostatic load and the aging process. *Neurobiology of Aging, 23,* 921–939.

McFadden, D. (2002). Masculinization effects in the auditory system. *Archives of Sexual Behavior, 31,* 99–111.

McFarland, C., & Ross, M. (1987). The relation between current impressions and memories of self and dating partners. *Psychological Bulletin, 13,* 228–238.

McFarland, C., Ross, M., & DeVourville, N. (1989). Women's theories of menstruation and biases in recall of menstrual symptoms. *Journal of Personality and Social Psychology, 57,* 522–531.

McFarland, C., White, K., & Newth, S. (2003). Mood acknowledgment and correction for the mood-congruency bias in social judgment. *Journal of Experimental Social Psychology, 39,* 483–491.

McGarry-Roberts, P. A., Stelmack, R. M., & Campbell, K. B. (1992). Intelligence, reaction time, and event-related potentials. *Intelligence, 16,* 289–313.

McGaugh, J. I. (2003). *Memory and emotion: The making of lasting memories.* New York: Columbia University Press.

McGaugh, J. L. (1994). Quoted by B. Bower, Stress hormones hike emotional memories. *Science News, 146,* p. 262.

McGaugh, J. L. (2000). Memory—a century of consolidation. *Science, 287,* 248–251.

McGhee, P. E. (June, 1976). Children's appreciation of humor: A test of the cognitive congruency principle. *Child Development, 47*(2), 420–426.

McGlone, M. S., & Tofighbakhsh, J. (2000). Birds of a feather flock conjointly (?): Rhyme as reason in aphorisms. *Psychological Science, 11,* 424–428.

McGrath, J. J., & Welham, J. L. (1999). Season of birth and schizophrenia: A systematic review and meta-analysis of data from the Southern hemisphere. *Schizophrenia Research, 35,* 237–242.

McGrath, J., Welham, J., & Pemberton, M. (1995). Month of birth, hemisphere of birth and schizophrenia. *British Journal of Psychiatry, 167,* 783–785.

McGrath, M. J., & Cohen, D. B. (1978). REM sleep facilitation of adaptive waking behavior: A review of the literature. *Psychological Bulletin, 85,* 24–57.

McGue, M., & Bouchard, T. J., Jr. (1998). Genetic and environmental influences on human behavioral differences. *Annual Review of Neuroscience, 21,* 1–24.

McGue, M., Bouchard, T. J., Jr., Iacono, W. G., & Lykken, D. T. (1993). Behavioral genetics of cognitive ability: A life-span perspective. In R. Plomin & G. E. McClearn (Eds.), *Nature, nurture and psychology.* Washington, DC: American Psychological Association.

McGue, M., & Lykken, D. T. (1992). Genetic influence on risk of divorce. *Psychological Science, 3,* 368–373.

McGuire, M. T., Wing, R. R., Klem, M. L., Lang, W., & Hill, J. O. (1999). What predicts weight regain in a group of successful weight losers? *Journal of Consulting and Clinical Psychology, 67,* 177–185.

McGuire, W. J. (1986). The myth of massive media impact: Savings and salvagings. In G. Comstock (Ed.), *Public communication and behavior.* Orlando, FL: Academic Press.

McGuire, W. J., McGuire, C. V., Child, P., & Fujioka, T. (1978). Salience of ethnicity in the spontaneous self-concept as a function of one's ethnic distinctiveness in the social environment. *Journal of Personality and Social Psychology, 36,* 511–520.

McGurk, H., & MacDonald, J. (1976). Hearing lips and seeing voices. *Nature, 264,* 746–748.

McHugh, P. R. (1995a). Witches, multiple personalities, and other psychiatric artifacts. *Nature Medicine, 1*(2), 110–114.

McHugh, P. R. (1995b). Resolved: Multiple personality disorder is an individually and socially created artifact. *Journal of the American Academy of Child and Adolescent Psychiatry, 34,* 957–959.

McHugh, P. R., & Moran, T. H. (1978). Accuracy of the regulation of caloric ingestion in the rhesus monkey. *American Journal of Physiology, 235,* R29–34.

McKellar, J., Stewart, E., & Humphreys, K. (2003). Alcoholics Anonymous involvement and positive alcohol-related outcomes: Cause, consequence, or just a correlate? A prospective 2-year study of 2,319 alcohol-dependent men. *Journal of Consulting and Clinical Psychology, 71,* 302–308.

McKenna, K. Y. A., & Bargh, J. A. (1998). Coming out in the age of the Internet: Identity "demarginalization" through virtual group participation. *Journal of Personality and Social Psychology, 75,* 681–694.

McKillop, J., Lisman, S. A., Weinstein, A., & Rosenbaum, D. (2003). Controversial treatments for alcoholism. In S. O. Lilienfeld, S. J. Lynn, & J. M. Lohr (Eds.), *Science and pseudoscience in clinical psychology.* New York: Guilford Press.

McLaughlin, C. S., Chen, C., Greenberger, E., & Biermeier, C. (1997). Family, peer, and individual correlates of sexual experience among Caucasian and Asian American late adolescents. Journal of Personality and Social Psychology, *Journal of Research on Adolescence, 7,* 33–53.

McMurray, C. (2004, January 13). U.S., Canada, Britain: Who's getting in shape? *Gallup Poll Tuesday Briefing* (www.gallup.com).

McMurray, C. (2004, February 24). Current smoking trends in U.S., Canada, Britain. *Gallup Poll Tuesday Briefing* (www.gallup.com).

McNally, R. J. (1987). Preparedness and phobias: A review. *Psychological Bulletin, 101,* 283–303.

McNally, R. J. (1999). EMDR and Mesmerism: A comparative historical analysis. *Journal of Anxiety Disorders, 13,* 225–236.

McNally, R. J. (2003). *Remembering trauma.* Cambridge, MA: Harvard University Press.

McNally, R. J., Bryant, R. A., & Ehlers, A. (2003). Does early psychological intervention promote recovery from posttraumatic stress? *Psychological Science in the Public Interest, 4,* 45–79.

McNeil, B. J., Pauker, S. G., & Tversky, A. (1988). On the framing of medical decisions. In D. E. Bell, H. Raiffa, & A. Tversky (Eds.), *Decision making: Descriptive, normative, and prescriptive interactions.* New York: Cambridge, 1988.

Meador, B. D., & Rogers, C. R. (1984). Person-centered therapy. In R. J. Corsini (Ed.), *Current psychotherapies* (3rd ed.). Itasca, IL: Peacock.

Medical Institute for Sexual Health. (1994, April). Condoms ineffective against human papilloma virus. *Sexual Health Update, 2.*

Medland, S. E., Perelle, I., De Monte, V., & Ehrman, L. (2004). Effects of culture, sex, and age on the distribution of handedness: An evaluation of the sensitivity of three measures of handedness. *Laterality: Asymmetries of Body, Brain, and Cognition, 9,* 287–297.

Mednick, S. A., Huttunen, M. O., & Machon, R. A. (1994). Prenatal influenza infections and adult schizophrenia. *Schizophrenia Bulletin, 20,* 263–267.

Mehl, M. R., & Pennebaker, J. W. (2003). The sounds of social life: A psychometric analysis of students' daily social environments and natural conversations. *Journal of Personality and Social Psychology, 84,* 857–870.

Meichenbaum, D. (1977). *Cognitive-behavior modification: An integrative approach.* New York: Plenum Press.

Meichenbaum, D. (1985). *Stress inoculation training.* New York: Pergamon.

Meltzoff, A. N. (1988). Infant imitation after a 1-week delay: Long-term memory for novel acts and multiple stimuli. *Developmental Psychology, 24,* 470–476.

Meltzoff, A. N., & Moore, M. K. (1989). Imitation in newborn infants: Exploring the range of gestures imitated and the underlying mechanisms. *Developmental Psychology, 25,* 954–962.

Meltzoff, A. N., & Moore, M. K. (1997). Explaining facial imitation: A theoretical model. *Early Development and Parenting, 6,* 179–192.

Melzack, R. (1984). The myth of painless childbirth. *Pain, 19,* 321–337.

Melzack, R. (1990, February). The tragedy of needless pain. *Scientific American,* pp. 27–33.

Melzack, R. (1992, April). Phantom limbs. *Scientific American,* pp. 120–126.

Melzack, R. (1993). Distinguished contribution series. *Canadian Journal of Experimental Psychology, 47,* 615–629.

Melzack, R. (1998, February). Quoted in Phantom limbs. *Discover,* p. 20.

Melzack, R. (1999). Pain and Stress: A new perspective. In R. J. Gatchel, & D. C. Turk (Eds.), *Psychosocial factors in pain: Critical perspectives.* New York: Guilford Press.

Melzack, R., & Wall, P. D. (1965). Pain mechanisms: A new theory. *Science, 150,* 971–979.

Melzack, R., & Wall, P. D. (1983). *The challenge of pain.* New York: Basic Books.

Mendolia, M., & Kleck, R. E. (1993). Effects of talking about a stressful event on arousal: Does what we talk about make a difference? *Journal of Personality and Social Psychology, 64,* 283–292.

Merari, A. (2002). Explaining suicidal terrorism: Theories versus empirical evidence. Invited address to the American Psychological Association.

Merriman, J. (1999, May 13). These pounds aren't sterling. *Reuters* (www.abcnews.go.com).

Merskey, H. (1992). The manufacture of personalities: The production of multiple personality disorder. *British Journal of Psychiatry, 160,* 327–340.

Merton, R. K. (1938; reprinted 1970). *Science, technology and society in seventeenth-century England.* New York: Fertig.

Merton, R. K., & Kitt, A. S. (1950). Contributions to the theory of reference group behavior. In R. K. Merton & P. F. Lazarsfeld (Eds.), *Continuities in social research: Studies in the scope and method of the American soldier.* Glencoe, IL: Free Press.

Messer, D. (2000). Language acquisition. *The Psychologist, 13,* 138–143.

Messer, W. S., & Griggs, R. A. (1989). Student belief and involvement in the paranormal and performance in introductory psychology. *Teaching of Psychology, 16,* 187–191.

Mestel, R. (1997, April 26). Get real, Siggi. *New Scientist* (www.newscientist.com/ns/970426/siggi.html).

Meston, C. M., & Frohlich, P. F. (2000). The neurobiology of sexual function. *Archives of General Psychiatry, 57,* 1012–1030.

Meston, C. M., Trapnell, P. D., & Gorzalka, B. B. (1996). Ethnic and gender differences in sexuality: Variations in sexual behavior between Asian and non-Asian university students. *Archives of Sexual Behavior, 25,* 33–72.

Metcalfe, J. (1998). Cognitive optimism: Self-deception or memory-based processing heuristics. *Personality and Social Psychology Review, 2,* 100–110.

Meyer, I. H. (2003). Prejudice, social stress, and mental health in lesbian, gay, and bisexual populations: Conceptual issues and research evidence. *Psychological Bulletin, 129,* 674–697.

Meyer-Bahlburg, H. F. L. (1995). Psychoneuroendocrinology and sexual pleasure: The aspect of sexual orientation. In P. R. Abramson & S. D. Pinker-

ton (Eds.), *Sexual nature/sexual culture.* Chicago: University of Chicago Press.

Mezulis, A. M., Abramson, L. Y., Hyde, J. S., & Hankin, B. L. (2004). Is there a universal positivity bias in attributions? A meta-analytic review of individual, developmental, and cultural differences in the self-serving attributional bias. *Psychological Bulletin, 130,* 711–747.

Michaels, J. W., Bloomel, J. M., Brocato, R. M., Linkous, R. A., & Rowe, J. S. (1982). Social facilitation and inhibition in a natural setting. *Replications in Social Psychology, 2,* 21–24.

Michel, G. F. (1981). Right-handedness: A consequence of infant supine head-orientation preference? *Science, 212,* 685–687.

Middlebrooks, J. C., & Green, D. M. (1991). Sound localization by human listeners. *Annual Review of Psychology, 42,* 135–159.

Mikkelsen, T. S., & 66 others (2005). Initial sequence of the chimpanzee genome and comparison with the human genome. *Nature, 437,* 69–87.

Mikulincer, M., Babkoff, H., Caspy, T., & Sing, H. (1989). The effects of 72 hours of sleep loss on psychological variables. *British Journal of Psychology, 80,* 145–162.

Mikulincer, M., Florian, V., & Hirschberger, G. (2003). The existential function of close relationships: Introducing death into the science of love. *Personality and Social Psychology Review, 7,* 20–40.

Mikulincer, M., & Shaver, P. R. (2001). Attachment theory and intergroup bias: Evidence that priming the secure base schema attenuates negative reactions to our-groups. *Journal of Personality and Social Psychology, 81,* 97–115.

Mikulincer, M., & Shaver, P. R. (2005). Attachment theory and emotions in close relationships: Exploring the attachment-related dynamics of emotional reactions to relational events. *Personal Relationships, 12,* 149–168.

Milan, R. J., Jr., & Kilmann, P. R. (1987). Interpersonal factors in premarital contraception. *Journal of Sex Research, 23,* 289–321.

Miles, D. R., & Carey, G. (1997). Genetic and environmental architecture of human aggression. *Journal of Personality and Social Psychology, 72,* 207–217.

Milgram, S. (1963). Behavioral study of obedience. *Journal of Abnormal & Social Psychology, 67*(4), 371–378.

Milgram, S. (1974). *Obedience to authority.* New York: Harper & Row.

Miller, E. J., Smith, J. E., & Trembath, D. L. (2000). The "skinny" on body size requests in personal ads. *Sex Roles, 43,* 129–141.

Miller, G. (2004). Axel, Buck share award for deciphering how the nose knows. *Science, 306,* 207.

Miller, G. A. (1956). The magical number seven, plus or minus two: Some limits on our capacity for processing information. *Psychological Review, 63,* 81–97.

Miller, G. A. (1962). *Psychology: The science of mental life.* New York: Harper & Row.

Miller, J. G., & Bersoff, D. M. (1995). Development in the context of everyday family relationships: Culture, interpersonal morality and adaptation. In M. Killen and D. Hart (Eds.), *Morality in everyday life: A developmental perspective.* New York: Cambridge University Press.

Miller, K. I., & Monge, P. R. (1986). Participation, satisfaction, and productivity: A meta-analytic review. *Academy of Management Journal, 29,* 727–753.

Miller, L. (2005, January 4). U.S. airlines have 34 deaths in 3 years. Associated Press.

Miller, L. C., Putcha-Bhagavatula, A., & Pedersen, W. C. (2002). Men's and women's mating preferences: Distinct evolutionary mechanisms? *Current Directions in Psychological Science, 11,* 88–93.

Miller, L. K. (1999). The Savant Syndrome: Intellectual impairment and exceptional skill. *Psychological Bulletin, 125,* 31–46.

Miller, M. (2005, March 7). Effects of laughter and mental stress on endothelial function: Potential impact of entertainment. Paper presented to the Scientific Session of the American College of Cardiology, Orlando.

Miller, N. E. (1985, February). Rx: biofeedback. *Psychology Today,* pp. 54–59.

Miller, N. E. (1995). Clinical-experimental interactions in the development of neuroscience: A primer for nonspecialists and lessons for young scientists. *American Psychologist, 50,* 901–911.

Miller, N. E., & Brucker, B. S. (1979). A learned visceral response apparently independent of skeletal ones in patients paralyzed by spinal lesions. In N. Birbaumer & H. D. Kimmel (Eds.), *Biofeedback and self-regulation.* Hillsdale, NJ: Erlbaum.

Miller, P. A., Eisenberg, N., Fabes, R. A., & Shell, R. (1996). Relations of moral reasoning and vicarious emotion to young children's prosocial behavior toward peers and adults. *Developmental Psychology, 32,* 210–219.

Miller, P. C., Lefcourt, H. M., Holmes, J. G., Ware, E. E., & Saleh, W. E. (1986). Marital locus of control and marital problem solving. *Journal of Personality and Social Psychology, 51,* 161–169.

Miller, S. D., Blackburn, T., Scholes, G., White, G. L., & Mamalis, N. (1991). Optical differences in multiple personality disorder: A second look. *Journal of Nervous and Mental Disease, 179,* 132–135.

Mills, M., & Melhuish, E. (1974). Recognition of mother's voice in early infancy. *Nature, 252,* 123–124.

Milner, D. A. (2003). Visual awareness and the primate brain. In M. A. Jeeves (Ed.), *Human nature.* London: Routledge.

Milton, J., & Wiseman, R. (2001). Does psi exist? Reply to Storm and Ertel (2001). *Psychological Bulletin, 127,* 434–438.

Milton, J., & Wiseman, R. (2002). A response to Storm and Ertel (2002). *Journal of Parapsychology, 66,* 183–185.

Mineka, S. (1985). The frightful complexity of the origins of fears. In F. R. Brush & J. B. Overmier (Eds.), *Affect, conditioning and cognition: Essays on the determinants of behavior.* Hillsdale, NJ: Erlbaum.

Mineka, S., & Suomi, S. J. (1978). Social separation in monkeys. *Psychological Bulletin, 85,* 1376–1400.

Mineka, S., & Sutton, S. K. (1992). Cognitive biases and the emotional disorders. *Psychological Science, 3,* 65–69.

Mineka, S., & Zinbarg, R. (1996). Conditioning and ethological models of anxiety disorders: Stress-in-dynamic-context anxiety models. In D. Hope (Ed.), *Perspectives on anxiety, panic, and fear. Nebraska symposium on motivation.* Lincoln, NE: University of Nebraska Press.

Miner-Rubino, K., & Winter, D. G., & Stewart, A. J. (2004). Gender, social class, and the subjective experience of aging: Self-perceived personality change from early adulthood to late midlife. *Personality and Social Psychology Bulletin, 30,* 1599–1610.

Mingroni, M. A. (2004). The secular rise in IQ: Giving heterosis a closer look. *Intelligence, 32,* 65–83.

Mirescu, C., Peters, J. D., & Gould, E. (2004). Early life experience alters response of adult neurogenesis to stress. *Nature Neuroscience, 7,* 841–846.

Mischel, W. (1968). *Personality and assessment.* New York: Wiley.

Mischel, W. (1981). Current issues and challenges in personality. In L. T. Benjamin, Jr. (Ed.), *The G. Stanley Hall Lecture Series* (Vol. 1). Washington, DC: American Psychological Association.

Mischel, W. (1984). Convergences and challenges in the search for consistency. *American Psychologist, 39,* 351–364.

Mischel, W. (2004). Toward an integrative science of the person. *Annual Review of Psychology, 55,* 1–22.

Mischel, W., Shoda, Y., & Peake, P. K. (1988). The nature of adolescent competencies predicted by preschool delay of gratification. *Journal of Personality and Social Psychology, 54,* 687–696.

Mischel, W., Shoda, Y., & Rodriguez, M. L. (1989). Delay of gratification in children. *Science, 244,* 933–938.

Miserandino, M. (1991). Memory and the seven dwarfs. *Teaching of Psychology, 18,* 169–171.

Mita, T. H., Dermer, M., & Knight, J. (1977). Reversed facial images and the mere-exposure hypothesis. *Journal of Personality and Social Psychology, 35,* 597–601.

Mitchell, T. R., Thompson, L., Peterson, E., & Cronk, R. (1997). Temporal adjustments in the evaluation of events: The "rosy view." *Journal of Experimental Social Psychology, 33,* 421–448.

MMWR. (1999, April 2). Tobacco use among middle and high school students—Florida, 1998 and 1999. *Morbidity and Mortality Weekly Report, 48,* 248–253.

Moffitt, T. E. (2005). The new look of behavioral genetics in developmental psychopathology: Gene-environment interplay in antisocial behaviors. *Psychological Bulletin, 131,* 533–554.

Moffitt, T. E., Caspi, A., Harrington, H., & Milne, B. J. (2002). Males on the life-course-persistent and adolescence-limited antisocial pathways: Follow-up at age 26 years. *Development and Psychopathology, 14,* 179–207.

Moghaddam, F. M. (2005). The staircase to terrorism: A psychological exploration. *American Psychologist, 60,* 161–169.

Mohn, J. K., Tingle, L. R., & Finger, R. (2003). An analysis of the causes of the decline in non-marital birth and pregnancy rates for teens from 1991 to 1995. *Adolescent and Family Health, 3,* 39–47.

Moises, H. W., Zoega, T., & Gottesman, I. I. (2002, 3 July). The glial growth factors deficiency and synaptic destabilization hypothesis of schizophrenia. *BMC Psychiatry, 2*(8) (www.biomedcentral.com/1471-244X/2/8).

Mokdad, A. H., Marks, J. S., Stroup, D. F., & Gerberding, J. L. (2004). Actual causes of death in the United States, 2000. *Journal of the American Medical Association, 291,* 1238–1245.

Mollica, R. F., McInnes, K., Pham, T., Fawzi, M. C. S., Murphy, E., & Lin, L. (1998). The dose-effect relationships between torture and psychiatric symptoms in Vietnamese ex-political detainees and a comparison group. *Journal of Nervous and Mental Diseases, 186,* 543–553.

Monaghan, P. (1992, September 23). Professor of psychology stokes a controversy on the reliability and repression of memory. *Chronicle of Higher Education,* pp. A9–A10.

Mondloch, C. J., Lewis, T. L., Budreau, D. R., Maurer, D., Dannemiller, J. L., Stephens, B. R., & Kleiner-Gathercoal, K. A. (1999). Face perception during early infancy. *Psychological Science, 10,* 419–422.

Money, J. (1987). Sin, sickness, or status? Homosexual gender identity and psychoneuroendocrinology. *American Psychologist, 42,* 384–399.

Money, J. (1988). *Gay, straight, and in-between.* New York: Oxford University Press.

Money, J., Berlin, F. S., Falck, A., & Stein, M. (1983). *Antiandrogenic and counseling treatment of sex offenders.* Baltimore: Department of Psychiatry and Behavioral Sciences, The Johns Hopkins University School of Medicine.

Moody, R. (1976). *Life after life.* Harrisburg, PA: Stackpole Books.

Mook, D. G. (1983). In defense of external invalidity. *American Psychologist, 38,* 379–387.

Moorcroft, W. (1993). *Sleep, dreaming, and sleep disorders: An introduction* (2nd ed.). Landam, MD: University Press of America.

Moorcroft, W. H. (2003). *Understanding sleep and dreaming.* New York: Kluwer/Plenum.

Moore, D. W. (2003, November 23). Many Americans deluding themselves about weight. *Gallup Poll* (poll.gallup.com).

Moore, D. W. (2004, December 17). Sweet dreams go with a good night's sleep. *Gallup News Service* (www.gallup.com).

Mor, N., & Winquist, J. (2002). Self-focused attention and negative affect: A meta-analysis. *Psychological Bulletin, 128,* 638–662.

Moreland, R. L., & Beach, S. R. (1992). Exposure effects in the classroom: The development of affinity among students. *Journal of Experimental Social Psychology, 28,* 255–276.

Moreland, R. L., & Zajonc, R. B. (1982). Exposure effects in person perception: Familiarity, similarity, and attraction. *Journal of Experimental Social Psychology, 18,* 395–415.

Morell, V. (1995a). Attacking the causes of "silent" infertility. *Science, 269,* 775–776.

Morell, V. (1995b). Zeroing in on how hormones affect the immune system. *Science, 269,* 773–775.

Morelli, G. A., Rogoff, B., Oppenheim, D., & Goldsmith, D. (1992). Cultural variation in infants' sleeping arrangements: Questions of independence. *Developmental Psychology, 26,* 604–613.

Morey, R. A., Inan, S., Mitchell, T. V., Perkins, D. O., Lieberman, J. A., & Belger, A. (2005). Imaging frontostriatal function in ultra-high-risk, early, and chronic schizophrenia during executive processing. *Archives of General Psychiatry, 62,* 254–262.

Morgan, A. B., & Lilienfeld, S. O. (2000). A meta-analytic review of the relation between antisocial behavior and neuropsychological measures of executive function. *Clinical Psychology Review, 20,* 113–136.

Morgan, B., & Korschgen, A. (2001). Psychology career exploration made easy. *Eye on Psi Chi,* 35–36.

Morin, R., & Brossard, M. A. (1997, March 4). Communication breakdown on drugs. *Washington Post,* pp. A1, A6.

Morris, J. S., Ohman, A., & Dolan, R. (1998). Conscious and unconscious emotional learning in the human amygdala. *Nature, 393,* 467–470.

Morrison, A. R. (2003). The brain on night shift. *Cerebrum, 5*(3), 23–36.

Mortensen, E. L., Michaelsen, K. F., Sanders, S. A., & Reinisch, J. M. (2002). The association between duration of breastfeeding and adult intelligence. *Journal of the American Medical Association, 287,* 2365–2371.

Mortensen, P. B. (1999). Effects of family history and place and season of birth on the risk of schizophrenia. *New England Journal of Medicine, 340,* 603–608.

Moruzzi, G., & Magoun, H. W. (1949). Brain stem reticular formation and activation of the EEG. *Electroencephalography and Clinical Neurophysiology, 1,* 455–473.

Moscovici, S. (1985). Social influence and conformity. In G. Lindzey & E. Aronson (Eds.), *The handbook of social psychology* (3rd ed). Hillsdale, N.J.: Erlbaum.

Moser, P. W. (1987, May). Are cats smart? Yes, at being cats. *Discover,* pp. 77–88.

Mosher, D. L., & Anderson, R. D. (1986). Macho personality, sexual aggression, and reactions to guided imagery of realistic rape. *Journal of Research in Personality, 20,* 77–94.

Moss, A. J., Allen, K. F., Giovino, G. A., & Mills, S. L. (1992, December 2). Recent trends in adolescent smoking, smoking-update correlates, and expectations about the future. *Advance Data* No. 221 (from Vital and Health Statistics of the Centers for Disease Control and Prevention).

Moss, H. A., & Susman, E. J. (1980). Longitudinal study of personality development. In O. G. Brim, Jr., & J. Kagan (Eds.), *Constancy and change in human development.* Cambridge, MA: Harvard University Press.

Moyer, K. E. (1983). The physiology of motivation: Aggression as a model. In C. J. Scheier & A. M. Rogers (Eds.), *G. Stanley Hall Lecture Series* (Vol. 3). Washington, DC: American Psychological Association.

Mroczek, D. K. (2001). Age and emotion in adulthood. *Current Directions in Psychological Science, 10,* 87–90.

Mroczek, D. K., & Kolarz, D. M. (1998). The effect of age on positive and negative affect: A developmental perspective on happiness. *Journal of Personality and Social Psychology, 75,* 1333–1349.

Mroczek, D. K., & Spiro, A., III (2005). Change in life satisfaction during adulthood: Findings from the Veterans Affairs normative aging study. *Journal of Personality and Social Psychology, 88,* 189–202.

Muhlnickel, W. (1998). Article on tinnitus processing in the brain *Proceedings of the National Academy of Sciences, 95,* 10340–10343.

Muller, J. E., Mittleman, M. A., Maclure, M., Sherwood, J. B., & Tofler, G. H. (1996). Triggering myocardial infarction by sexual activity. *Journal of the American Medical Association, 275,* 1405–1409.

Muller, J. E., & Verrier, R. L. (1996). Triggering of sudden death—Lessons from an earthquake. *New England Journal of Medicine, 334,* 461.

Mullin, C. R., & Linz, D. (1995). Desensitization and resensitization to violence against women: Effects of exposure to sexually violent films on judgments of domestic violence victims. *Journal of Personality and Social Psychology, 69,* 449–459.

Mulrow, C. D. (1999, March). Treatment of depression—newer pharmacotherapies, summary. *Evidence Report/Technology Assessment, 7.* Agency for Health Care Policy and Research, Rockville, MD. (http://www.ahrq.gov/clinic/deprsumm.htm).

Murphy, G. E., & Wetzel, R. D. (1990). The lifetime risk of suicide in alcoholism. *Archives of General Psychiatry, 47,* 383–392.

Murphy, K. R., & Cleveland, J. N. (1995). *Understanding performance appraisal: Social, organizational, and goal-based perspectives.* Thousand Oaks, CA: Sage.

Murphy, S. T., Monahan, J. L., & Miller, L. C. (1998). Inference under the influence: The impact of alcohol and inhibition conflict on women's sexual decision making. *Personality and Social Psychology Bulletin, 24,* 517–528.

Murphy, S. T., Monahan, J. L., & Zajonc, R. B. (1995). Additivity of nonconscious affect: Combined effects of priming and exposure. *Journal of Personality and Social Psychology, 69,* 589–602.

Murphy, T. N. (1982). Pain: Its assessment and management. In R. J. Gatchel, A. Baum, & J. E. Singer (Eds.), *Handbook of psychology and health: Vol. I. Clinical psychology and behavioral medicine: Overlapping disciplines.* Hillsdale, NJ: Erlbaum.

Murray, B. (1998, May). Psychology is key to airline safety at Boeing. *The APA Monitor,* p. 36.

Murray, C., & Herrnstein, R. J. (1994, October 31). Race, genes and I.Q.—An apologia. *New Republic,* pp. 27–37.

Murray, C. J., & Lopez, A. D. (Eds.) (1996). *The global burden of disease: A comprehensive assessment of mortality and disability from diseases, injuries, and risk factors in 1990 and projected to 2020.* Cambridge, MA: Harvard University Press.

Murray, H. (1938). *Explorations in personality.* New York: Oxford University Press.

Murray, H. A. (1933). The effect of fear upon estimates of the maliciousness of other personalities. *Journal of Social Psychology, 4,* 310–329.

Murray, H. A., & Wheeler, D. R. (1937). A note on the possible clairvoyance of dreams. *Journal of Psychology, 3,* 309–313.

Murray, J. E. (2000). Marital protection and marital selection: Evidence from a historical-prospective sample of American men. *Demography, 37,* 511–521.

Murray, R., Jones, P., O'Callaghan, E., Takei, N., & Sham, P. (1992). Genes, viruses, and neurodevelopmental schizophrenia. *Journal of Psychiatric Research, 26,* 225–235.

Murray, S. L., Bellavia, G. M., Rose, P., & Griffin, D. W. (2003). Once hurt, twice hurtful: How perceived regard regulates daily marital interactions. *Journal of Personality and Social Psychology, 84,* 126–147.

Murray, S. L., Rose, P., Bellavia, G. M., Holmes, J. G., & Kusche, A. G. (2002). When rejection stings: How self-esteem constrains relationship-enhancement processes. *Journal of Personality and Social Psychology, 83,* 556–573.

Musallam, S., Corneil, B. D., Greger, B., Scherberger, H., & Andersen, R. A. (2004). Cognitive control signals for neural prosthetics. *Science, 305,* 258–262.

Musick, M. A., Herzog, A. R., & House, J. S. (1999). Volunteering and mortality among older adults: Findings from a national sample. *Journals of Gerontology, 54B,* 173–180.

Mustanski, B. S., & Bailey, J. M. (2003). A therapist's guide to the genetics of human sexual orientation," *Sexual and Relationship Therapy 18,* 1468–1479.

Mustanski, B. S., Bailey, J. M., & Kaspar, S. (2002). Dermatoglyphics, handedness, sex, and sexual orientation. *Archives of Sexual Behavior, 31,* 113–122.

Mydans, S. (2002, May 17). In Pakistan, rape victims are the 'criminals.' *New York Times* (www.nytimes.com).

Myers, D. G. (1993). *The pursuit of happiness.* New York: Avon Books.

Myers, D. G. (2000). *The American paradox: Spiritual hunger in an age of plenty.* New Haven: Yale University Press.

Myers, D. G. (2001, December). Do we fear the right things? *American Psychological Society Observer,* p. 3.

Myers, D. G. (2002). *Intuition: Its powers and perils.* New Haven: Yale University Press.

Myers, D. G. (2005). *Social psychology,* 8th edition. New York: McGraw-Hill.

Myers, D. G., & Bishop, G. D. (1970). Discussion effects on racial attitudes. *Science, 169,* 78–779.

Myers, D. G., & Diener, E. (1995). Who is happy? *Psychological Science, 6,* 10–19.

Myers, D. G., & Diener, E. (1996, May). The pursuit of happiness. *Scientific American,* p. 545)

Myers, D. G., & Scanzoni, L. D. (2005). *What God has joined together? A Christian case for gay marriage.* San Francisco: HarperSanFrancisco.

Myers, I. B. (1987). *Introduction to type: A description of the theory and applications of the Myers-Briggs Type Indicator.* Palo Alto, CA: Consulting Psychologists Press.

Myerson, J., Rank, M. R., Raines, F. Q., & Schnitzler, M. A. (1998). Race and general cognitive ability: The myth of diminishing returns to education. *Psychological Science, 9,* 139–142.

Nagourney, A. (2002, September 25). For remarks on Iraq, Gore gets praise and scorn. *New York Times* (www.nytimes.com).

Napolitan, D. A., & Goethals, G. R. (1979). The attribution of friendliness. *Journal of Experimental Social Psychology, 15,* 105–113.

Narrow, W. E., Rae, D. S., Robins, L. N., & Regier, D. A. (2002). Revised prevalence estimates of mental disorders in the United States. *Archives of General Psychiatry, 59,* 115–123.

Nash, M. R. (2001, July). The truth and the hype of hypnosis. *Scientific American,* pp. 47–55.

National Academy of Sciences. (1999). *Marijuana and medicine: Assessing the science base* (by J. A. Benson, Jr. & S. J. Watson, Jr.). Washington, DC: National Academy Press.

National Academy of Sciences. (2001). *Exploring the biological contributions to human health: Does sex matter?* Washington, DC: Institute of Medicine, National Academy Press.

National Academy of Sciences. (2002). *The polygraph and lie detection.* Washington, DC: Committee to Review the Scientific Evidence on the Polygraph, National Research Council.

National Academy of Sciences, Institute of Medicine. (1982). *Marijuana and health.* Washington, DC: National Academic Press.

National Center for Health Statistics. (1990). *Health, United States, 1989.* Washington, DC: U.S. Department of Health and Human Services.

National Center for Health Statistics. (1991). Family structure and children's health: United States, 1988, *Vital and Health Statistics, Series 10, No. 178,* CHHS Publication No. PHS 91-1506 by Deborah A. Dawson.

National Center for Health Statistics. (1992, May). *Health United States 1991.* Hyattsville, MD: Department of Health and Human Services Pub. No. (PHS) 92-1232, Table 27.

National Center for Health Statistics. (2002, September 16). Deaths: Leading Causes for 2000. *National Vital Statistics Reports, 50,* 16. Hyattsville, MD: National Center for Health Statistics.

National Center for Health Statistics. (2004, December 15). Marital status and health: United States, 1999–2002 (by Charlotte A. Schoenborn). *Advance Data from Vital and Human Statistics,* number 351. Centers for Disease Control and Prevention.

National Institute of Mental Health. (1982). *Television and behavior: Ten years of scientific progress and implications for the eighties.* Washington, DC: U. S. Government Printing Office.

National Institute of Mental Health. (1999). *ADHD: Attention deficit hyperactivity disorder.* Bethesda, MD: National Institute of Health Publication No 96–3572, 1994, update July 1, 1999.

National Institute of Mental Health. (2003). *Attention deficit hyperactivity disorder.* Bethesda, MD: National Institute of Mental Health.

National Institute on Drug Abuse. (2004). NIDA InfoFacts: Marijuana. www.nida.nih.gov/Infofax/marijuana.html.

National Institutes of Health. (1998). Clinical guidelines on the identification evaluation and treatment of overweight and obesity in adults. Executive summary, Obesity Education Initiative, National Heart, Lung, and Blood Institute.

National Research Council. (1987). *Risking the future: Adolescent sexuality, pregnancy, and childbearing.* Washington, DC: National Academy Press.

National Research Council. (1990). *Human factors research needs for an aging population.* Washington, DC: National Academy Press.

National Safety Council. (2005, October 3). Passenger deaths and death rates, from *Injury Facts* (via correspondence with Kevin T. Fearn, Research & Statistical Services Department).

Naylor, T. H. (1990). Redefining corporate motivation, Swedish style. *Christian Century, 107,* 566–570.

NCTV News. (1987, July-August). More research links harmful effects to non-violent porn, p. 12.

Neeleman, J., & Persaud, R. (1995). Why do psychiatrists neglect religion? *British Journal of Medical Psychology, 68,* 169–178.

Neese, R. M. (1991, November/December). What good is feeling bad? The evolutionary benefits of psychic pain. *The Sciences,* pp. 30–37.

Neisser, U. (1979). The control of information pickup in selective looking. In A. D. Pick (Ed.), *Perception and its development: A tribute to Eleanor J. Gibson.* Hillsdale, NJ: Erlbaum.

Neisser, U. (1997). The ecological study of memory. *Philosophical Transactions of the Royal Society of London, 352,* 1697–1701.

Neisser, U. (1998). *The rising curve: Long-term gains in IQ and related measures.* Washington, DC: American Psychological Association.

Neisser, U., Boodoo, G., Bouchard, T. J., Jr., Boykin, A. W., Brody, N., Ceci, S. J., Halpern, D. F., Loehlin, J. C., Perloff, R., Sternberg, R. J., & Urbina, S. (1996). Intelligence: Knowns and unknowns. *American Psychologist, 51,* 77–101.

Neisser, U., Winograd, E., & Weldon, M. S. (1991). Remembering the earthquake: "What I experienced" vs. "How I heard the news." Paper presented to the Psychonomic Society convention.

Neitz, J., Geist, T., & Jacobs, G. H. (1989). Color vision in the dog. *Visual Neuroscience, 3,* 119–125.

Nell, V. (2002). Why young men drive dangerously: Implications for injury prevention. *Current Directions in Psychological Science, 11,* 75–79.

Nelson, E. C., Heath, A. C., Madden, P. A. F., Cooper, M. L., Dinwiddie, S. H., Bucholtz, K. K., Glowinski, A., McLaughlin, T., Dunne, M. P., Statham, D. J., & Martin, N. G. (2002). Association between self-reported childhood sexual abuse and adverse psychosocial outcomes. *Archives of General Psychiatry, 59,* 139–145.

Nelson, G., Hoon, M. A., Chandrashekar, J., Zhang, Y., Ryba, N. J., Nicholas, J. P., & Zuker, C. S. (2001). Mammalian sweet taste receptors. *Cell, 106,* 381–390.

Nelson, M. D., Saykin, A. J., Flashman, L. A., & Riordan, H. J. (1998). Hippocampal volume reduction in schizophrenia as assessed by magnetic resonance imaging. *Archives of General Psychiatry, 55,* 433–440.

Nelson, N. (1988). *A meta-analysis of the life-event/health paradigm: The influence of social support.* Philadelphia: Temple University Ph.D. dissertation.

Nephew, T. M., Williams, G. D., Stinson, F. S., Nguyen, K., & Dufour, M. C. (1999). Surveillance report #51: Apparent per capita alcohol consumption: National, state, and regional trends, 1977–1997. Bethesda, MD: National Institute on Alcohol Abuse and Alcoholism.

Nesca, M., & Koulack, D. (1994). Recognition memory, sleep and circadian rhythms. *Canadian Journal of Experimental Psychology, 48,* 359–379.

Nestler, E. J., & Malenka, R. C. (2004, March). The addicted brain. *Scientific American,* pp. 79–83.

Neubauer, P. B., & Neubauer, A. (1990). *Nature's thumbprint: The new genetics of personality.* Reading, MA: Addison-Wesley.

Neugarten, B. L., Wood, V., Kraines, R. J., & Loomis, B. (1963). Women's attitudes toward the menopause. *Vita Humana, 6,* 140–151.

Neumann, R., & Strack, F. (2000). "Mood contagion": The automatic transfer of mood between persons. *Journal of Personality and Social Psychology, 79,* 211–223.

Nevin, J. A. (1988). Behavioral momentum and the partial reinforcement effect. *Psychological Bulletin, 103,* 44–56.

Newberg, A., & D'Aquili, E. (2001). *Why God won't go away: Brain science and the biology of belief.* New York: Simon and Schuster.

Newcomb, M. D., & Harlow, L. L. (1986). Life events and substance use among adolescents: Mediating effects of perceived loss of control and meaninglessness in life. *Journal of Personality and Social Psychology, 51,* 564–577.

Newcombe, N. S., Drummey, A. B., Fox, N. A., Lie, E., & Ottinger-Alberts, W. (2000). Remembering early childhood: How much, how, and why (or why not). *Current Directions in Psychological Science, 9,* 55–58.

Newman, A. J., Bavelier, D., Corina, D., Jezzard, P., & Neville, H. J. (2002). A critical period for right hemisphere recruitment in American Sign Language processing. *Nature Neuroscience, 5,* 76–80.

Newman, L. S., & Baumeister, R. F. (1996). Toward an explanation of the UFO abduction phenomenon: Hypnotic, elaboration, extraterrestrial sadomasochism, and spurious memories. *Psychological Inquiry, 7,* 99–126.

Newman, L. S., Duff, K. J., & Baumeister, R. F. (1997). A new look at defensive projection: Thought suppression, accessibility, and biased person perception. *Journal of Personality and Social Psychology, 72,* 980–1001.

Newman, L. S., & Ruble, D. N. (1988). Stability and change in self-understanding: The early elementary school years. *Early Child Development and Care, 40,* 77–99.

Newman, M. L., Pennebaker, J. W., Berry, D. S., & Richards, J. M. (2003). Lying words: Predicting deception from linguistic style. *Personality and Social Psychology Bulletin, 29,* 665–675.

Newport, E. L. (1990). Maturational constraints on language learning. *Cognitive Science, 14,* 11–28.

Newport, F. (2001, February). Americans see women as emotional and affectionate, men as more aggressive. *The Gallup Poll Monthly,* pp. 34–38.

Newport, F. (2002, July 29). Bush job approval update. Gallup News Service (www.gallup.com/poll/releases/pr020729.asp).

Newport, F., Moore, D. W., Jones, J. M., & Saad, L. (2003, March 21). Special release: American opinion on the war. *Gallup Poll Tuesday Briefing* (www.gallup.com).

Newton, I. (1704). *Opticks, or a treatise of the reflections, refractions, inflections & colours of light.* Oxford, England Whittlesey House, McGraw-Hill, 1931.

Neylan, T. C., Metzler, T. J., Best, S. R., Weiss, D. S., Fagan, J. A., Liberman, A., Rogers, C., Vedantham, K., Brunet, A., Lipsey, T. L., & Marmar, C. R. (2002). Critical incident exposure and sleep quality in police officers. *Psychosomatic Medicine, 64,* 345–352.

Nezlek, J. B. (2001). Daily psychological adjustment and the planfulness of day-to-day behavior. *Journal of Social and Clinical Psychology, 20,* 452–475.

Ng, S. H. (1990). Androcentric coding of *man* and *his* in memory by language users. *Journal of Experimental Social Psychology, 26,* 455–464.

NHTSA. (2000). Traffic safety facts 1999: Older population. Washington, DC: National Highway Traffic Safety Administration (National Transportation Library: www.ntl.bts.gov).

Niccols, G. A. (1994). Fetal alcohol syndrome: Implications for psychologists. *Clinical Psychology Review, 14,* 91–111.

NICHHD Early Child Care Research Network. (2002). Structure/process/outcome: Direct and indirect effects of caregiving quality on young children's development. *Psychological Science, 13,* 199–206.

NICHHD Early Child Care Research Network. (2003). Does amount of time spent in child care predict socioemotional adjustment during the transition to kindergarten? *Child Development, 74,* 976–1005.

Nickell, J. (1996, May/June). A study of fantasy proneness in the thirteen cases of alleged encounters in John Mack's *Abduction. Skeptical Inquirer,* pp. 18–20, 54.

Nickerson, R. S. (1998). Applied experimental psychology. *Applied Psychology: An International Review, 47,* 155–173.

Nickerson, R. S. (1999). How we know—and sometimes misjudge—what others know: Imputing one's own knowledge to others. *Psychological Bulletin, 125,* 737–759.

Nickerson, R. S., & Adams, M. J. (1979). Long-term memory for a common object. *Cognitive Psychology, 11,* 287–307.

Nicol, S. E., & Gottesman, I. I. (1983). Clues to the genetics and neurobiology of schizophrenia. *American Scientist, 71,* 398–404.

Nicolaus, L. K., Cassel, J. F., Carlson, R. B., & Gustavson, C. R. (1983). Taste-aversion conditioning of crows to control predation on eggs. *Science, 220,* 212–214.

Nicolelis, M. A. L., & Chapin, J. K. (2002, October). Controlling robots with the mind. *Scientific American,* pp. 46–53.

NIDA. (2002). Methamphetamine abuse and addiction. *Research Report Series.* National Institute on Drug Abuse, NIH Publication Number 02-4210.

NIDA. (2005, May). Methamphetamine. *NIDA Info Facts.* National Institute on Drug Abuse.

Nier, J. A. (2004). Why does the "above average effect" exist? Demonstrating idiosyncratic trait definition. *Teaching of Psychology, 31,* 53–54.

Nightingale, F. (1860/1969). *Notes on nursing.* Mineola, NY: Dover.

Nigro, G. (1984). Cited by U. Neisser, The role of invariant structures in the control of movement. In M. Frese & J. Sabini (Eds.), *Goal directed behavior: The concept of action in psychology.* Hillsdale, NJ: Erlbaum.

NIH. (2001, July 20). Workshop summary: Scientific evidence on condom effectiveness for sexually transmitted disease (STD) prevention. Bethesda: National Institute of Allergy and Infectious Diseases, National Institutes of Health.

NIMH. (2002, April 26). U.S. suicide rates by age, gender, and racial group. National Institute of Mental Health (www.nimh.nih.gov/research/suichart.cfm).

Nisbett, R. E. (1987). Lay personality theory: Its nature, origin, and utility. In N. E. Grunberg, R. E. Nisbett, & others, *A distinctive approach to psychological research: The influence of Stanley Schachter* (Hillsdale, NJ: 1987).

Nisbett, R. E., & Borgida, E. (1975). Attribution and the psychology of prediction. *Journal of Personality and Social Psychology, 32,* 932–943.

Nisbett, R. E., & Cohen, D. (1996). *Culture of honor: The psychology of violence in the South.* Boulder, CO: Westview Press.

Nisbett, R. E., & Ross, L. (1980). *Human inference: Strategies and shortcomings of social judgment.* Englewood Cliffs, NJ: Prentice-Hall.

Noel, J. G., Forsyth, D. R., & Kelley, K. N. (1987). Improving the performance of failing students by overcoming their self-serving attributional biases. *Basic and Applied Social Psychology, 8,* 151–162.

Nolen-Hoeksema, S. (2001). Gender differences in depression. *Current Directions in Psychological Science, 10,* 173–176.

Nolen-Hoeksema, S. (2003). *Women who think too much: How to break free of overthinking and reclaim your life.* New York: Holt.

Nolen-Hoeksema, S., & Larson, J. (1999). *Coping with loss.* Mahwah, NJ: Erlbaum.

NORC (National Opinion Research Center). (1985, October/November). Images of the world. *Public Opinion,* p. 38.

NORC (National Opinion Research Center). (2002). Percent saying sex with person other than spouse is always or almost always wrong. National Opinion Research Center General Social Survey of 2000 (www.csa.berkeley.edu:7502).

Norcross, J. C. (Ed.). (2002). *Psychotherapy relationships that work: Therapist contributions and responsiveness to patient needs.* New York: Oxford University Press.

Norem, J. K. (2001). *The positive power of negative thinking: Using defensive pessimism to harness anxiety and perform at your peak.* Basic Books.

Norman, D. A. (1988). *The psychology of everyday things.* New York: Basic Books.

Norman, D. A. (2001). The perils of home theater (www.jnd.org/dn.mss/ProblemsOfHomeTheater.html).

Noroozian, M., Lofti, J., Gassemzadeh, H., Emami, H., & Mehrabi, Y. (2003). Academic achievement and learning abilities in left-handers: Guilt or gift? *Cortex, 38,* 779–785.

Norton, K. L., Olds, T. S., Olive, S., & Dank, S. (1996). Ken and Barbie at life size. *Sex Roles, 34,* 287–294.

Norton, M. B. (2002, October 31). *They called it witchcraft. New York Times* (www.nytimes.com).

Nowak, R. (1994). Nicotine scrutinized as FDA seeks to regulate cigarettes. *Science, 263,* 1555–1556.

Nowell, A., & Hedges, L. V. (1998). Trends in gender differences in academic achievement from 1960 to 1994: An analysis of differences in mean, variance, and extreme scores. *Sex Roles, 39,* 21–43.

NSF. (2001, October 24). Public bounces back after Sept. 11 attacks, national study shows. *NSF News,* National Science Foundation (www.nsf.gov/od/lpa/news/press/ol/pr0185.htm).

Nuttin, J. M., Jr. (1987). Affective consequences of mere ownership: The name letter effect in twelve European languages. *European Journal of Social Psychology, 17,* 381–402.

Oakhill, J., Garnham, A., & Johnson-Laird, P. N. (1990). Belief bias effects in syllogistic reasoning. In D. J. Gilhooly, M. T. G. Keane, R. H. Logie, & G. Erdos (Eds.), *Lines of thinking* (Vol. 1). Chichester, England: Wiley.

Oakhill, J. V., Johnson-Laird, P. N., & Garnham, A. (1989). Believability and syllogistic reasoning. *Cognition, 31,* 117–140.

O'Connor, A. (2004, February 6). Study details 30-year increase in calorie consumption. *New York Times* (www.nytimes.com).

O'Connor, A. (2004, May 14). Pressure to go along with abuse is strong, but some soldiers find strength to refuse. *New York Times* (www.nytimes.com).

O'Connor, P., & Brown, G. W. (1984). Supportive relationships: Fact or fancy? *Journal of Social and Personal Relationships, 1,* 159–175.

Oddone-Paolucci, E., Genuis, M., & Violato, C. (2000). A meta-analysis of the published research on the effects of pornography. In C. Violato, E. Oddone-Paolucci, & M. Genuis (Eds.), *The changing family and child development.* Aldershot, England: Ashgate.

O'Donnell, L., Stueve, A., O'Donnell, C., Duran, R., San Doval, A., Wilson, R. F., Haber, D., Perry, E., & Pleck, J. H. (2002). Long-term reduction in sexual initiation and sexual activity among urban middle schoolers in the reach for health service learning program. *Journal of Adolescent Health, 31,* 93–100.

Oetting, E. R., & Beauvais, F. (1987). Peer cluster theory, socialization characteristics, and adolescent drug use: A path analysis. *Journal of Counseling Psychology, 34,* 205–213.

Oetting, E. R., & Beauvais, F. (1990). Adolescent drug use: Findings of national and local surveys. *Journal of Social and Personal Relationships, 1,* 159–175.

Oettingen, G., & Mayer, D. (2002). The motivating function of thinking about the future: Expectations versus fantasies. *Journal of Personality and Social Psychology, 83,* 1198–1212.

Oettingen, G., & Seligman, M. E. P. (1990). Pessimism and behavioural signs of depression in East versus West Berlin. *European Journal of Social Psychology, 20,* 207–220.

Offer, D., Kaiz, M., Howard, K. I., & Bennett, E. S. (2000). The altering of reported experiences. *Journal of the American Academy of Child and Adolescent Psychiatry, 39,* pp. 735–742.

Offer, D., Ostrov, E., Howard, K. I., & Atkinson, R. (1988). *The teenage world: Adolescents' self-image in ten countries.* New York: Plenum.

Office of National Statistics. (2002). *The social and economic circumstances of adults with mental disorders* (report based on the analysis of the ONS Survey of Psychiatric Morbidity Among Adults in Great Britain carried out in 2000). Norwich: HMSO.

Ogden, C. L., Fryar, C. D., Carroll, M. D., & Flegal, K. M. (2004, October 27). Mean body weight, heights, and body mass index, Unites States 1960–2002. *Advance Data from Vital and Health Statistics,* No. 347.

Öhman, A. (1986). Face the beast and fear the face: Animal and social fears as prototypes for evolutionary analyses of emotion. *Psychophysiology, 23,* 123–145.

Öhman, A., Lundqvist, D., & Esteves, F. (2001). The face in the crowd revisited: A threat advantage with schematic stimuli. *Journal of Personality and Social Psychology, 80,* 381–396.

Öhman, A., & Mineka, S. (2003). The malicious serpent: Snakes as a prototypical stimulus for an evolved module of fear. *Current Directions in Psychological Science, 12,* 5–9.

Oishi, S., Diener, E. F., Lucas, R. E., & Suh, E. M. (1999). Cross-cultural variations in predictors of life satisfaction: Perspectives from needs and values. *Personality and Social Psychology Bulletin, 25,* 980–990.

O'Keeffe, C., & Wiseman, R. (2005). Testing alleged mediumship: Methods and results. *British Journal of Psychology, 96,* 165–179.

Okun, M. S., & 12 others (2004). What's in a "smile?" Intra-operative observations of contralateral smiles induced by deep brain stimulation. *Neurocase, 10,* 271–279.

Olds, J. (1958). Self-stimulation of the brain. *Science, 127,* 315–324.

Olds, J. (1975). Mapping the mind onto the brain. In F. G. Worden, J. P. Swazey, & G. Adelman (Eds.), *The neurosciences: Paths of discovery.* Cambridge, MA: MIT Press.

Olds, J., & Milner, P. (1954). Positive reinforcement produced by electrical stimulation of the septal area and other regions of rat brain. *Journal of Comparative and Physiological Psychology, 47,* 419–427.

O'Leary, V. E., & Ickovics, J. R. (1995). Resilience and thriving in response to challenge: An opportunity for a paradigm shift in women's health. *Women's Health: Research on Gender, Behavior, and Policy, 1,* 121–142.

Olfson, M., Gameroff, M. J., Marcus, S. C., & Jensen, P. S. (2003). National trends in the treatment of attention deficit hyperactivity disorder. *American Journal of Psychiatry, 160,* 1071–1077.

Olfson, M., Marcus, S. C., Wan, G. J., & Geissler, E. C. (2004). National trends in the outpatient treatment of anxiety disorders. *Journal of Clinical Psychiatry, 65,* 1166–1173.

Olfson, M., Shaffer, D., Marcus, S. C., & Greenberg, T. (2003). Relationship between antidepressant medication treatment and suicide in adolescents. *Archives of General Psychiatry, 60,* 978–982.

Olin, S. S., & Mednick, S. A. (1996). Risk factors of psychosis: Identifying vulnerable populations premorbidly. *Schizophrenia Bulletin, 22,* 223–240.

Oliner, S. P., & Oliner, P. M. (1988). *The altruistic personality: Rescuers of Jews in Nazi Europe.* New York: Free Press.

Oliver, M. B. (1994). Portrayals of crime, race, and aggression in "reality-based" police shows: A content analysis. *Journal of Broadcasting and Electronic Media, 38,* 179–192.

Olshansky, S. J., Carnes, B. A., & Cassel, C. K. (1993, April). The aging of the human species. *Scientific American,* pp. 46–52.

Olshansky, S. J., Passaro, D. J., Hershow, R. C., Layden, J., Carnes, B. A., Brody, J., Hayflick, L., Butler, R. N., Allison, D. B., & Ludwig, D. S. (2005). A potential decline in life expectancy in the United States in the 21st century. *New England Journal of Medicine, 352,* 1138–1145.

Olson, M. A., & Fazio, R. H. (2001). Implicit attitude formation through classical conditioning. *Psychological Science, 12,* 413–417.

Olson, S. (2005). Brain scans raise privacy concerns. *Science, 307,* 1548–1550.

Olsson, A., & Phelps, E. A. (2004). Learned fear of "unseen" faces after Pavlovian, observational, and instructed fear. *Psychological Science, 15,* 822–828.

Olweus, D., Mattsson, A., Schalling, D., & Low, H. (1988). Circulating testosterone levels and aggression in adolescent males: A causal analysis. *Psychosomatic Medicine, 50,* 261–272.

Oman, D., Kurata, J. H., Strawbridge, W. J., & Cohen, R. D. (2002). Religious attendance and cause of death over 31 years. *International Journal of Psychiatry in Medicine, 32,* 69–89.

O'Neil, J. (2002, September 3). Vital Signs: Behavior: Parent smoking and teenage sex. *New York Times.*

O'Neill, M. J. (1993). The relationship between privacy, control, and stress responses in office workers. Paper presented at the Human Factors and Ergonomics Society convention.

Oren, D. A., & Terman, M. (1998). Tweaking the human circadian clock with light. *Science, 279,* 333–334.

Orlovskaya, D. D., Uranova, N. A., Zimina, I. S., Kolomeets, N. S., Vikhreva, O. V., Rachmanova, V. I., Black, J. E., Klintsova, A. Y., & Greenough, W. T. (1999). Effect of professional status on the number of synapses per neuron in the prefrontal cortex of normal human and schizophrenic brain. *Society for Neuroscience Abstracts, 329.11, 25,* 818, 1999.

Orne, M. T., & Evans, F. J. (1965). Social control in the psychological experiment: Antisocial behavior and hypnosis. *Journal of Personality and Social Psychology, 1,* 189–200.

Osborne, J. W. (1997). Race and academic disidentification. *Journal of Educational Psychology, 89,* 728–735.

Osborne, L. (1999, October 27). A linguistic big bang. *New York Times Magazine* (www.nytimes.com).

Osgood, C. E. (1962). *An alternative to war or surrender.* Urbana: University of Illinois Press.

Osgood, C. E. (1980). *GRIT: A strategy for survival in mankind's nuclear age?* Paper presented at the Pugwash Conference on New Directions in Disarmament.

OSS Assessment Staff. (1948). *The assessment of men.* New York: Rinehart.

Ost, L. G., & Hugdahl, K. (1981). Acquisition of phobias and anxiety response patterns in clinical patients. *Behaviour Research and Therapy, 16,* 439–447.

Ostfeld, A. M., Kasl, S. V., D'Atri, D. A., & Fitzgerald, E. F. (1987). *Stress, crowding, and blood pressure in prison.* Hillsdale, NJ: Erlbaum.

Ouellette, J. A., & Wood, W. (1998). Habit and intention in everyday life: The multiple processes by which past behavior predicts future behavior. *Psychological Bulletin, 124,* 54–74.

Overmier, J. B., & Murison, R. (1997). Animal models reveal the "psych" in the psychosomatics of peptic ulcers. *Current Directions in Psychological Science, 6,* 180–184.

Owen, R. (1814). First essay in *New view of society or the formation of character.* Quoted in *The story of New Lanark.* New Lanark Mills, Lanark, Scotland: New Lanark Conservation Trust, 1993.

Oxfam (2005, March 26). Three months on: New figures show tsunami may have killed up to four times as many women as men. Oxfam Press Release (www.oxfam.org.uk).

Oyserman, D., Coon, H. M., & Kemmelmeier, M. (2002a). Rethinking individualism and collectivism: Evaluation of theoretical assumptions and meta-analyses. *Psychological Bulletin, 128,* 3–72.

Oyserman, D., Kemmelmeier, M., & Coon, H. M. (2002b). Cultural psychology, a new look: Reply to Bond (2002), Fiske (2002), Kitayama (2002), and Miller (2002). *Psychological Bulletin, 128,* 110–117.

Ozer, E. J., Best, S. R., Lipsey, T. L., & Weiss, D. S. (2003). Predictors of posttraumatic stress disorder and symptoms in adults: A meta-analysis. *Psychological Bulletin, 129,* 52–73.

Ozer, E. J., & Weiss, D. S. (2004). Who develops posttraumatic stress disorder. *Current Directions in Psychological Science, 13,* 169–172.

Özgen, E. (2004). Language, learning, and color perception. *Current Directions in Psychological Science, 13,* 95–98.

Pacifici, R., Zuccaro, P., Farre, M., Pichini, S., Di Carlo, S., Roset, P. N., Ortuno, J., Pujadus, M., Bacosi, A., Menoyo, E., Segura, J., & de la Torre, R. (2001). Effects of repeated doses of MDMA ("Ecstasy") on cell-mediated immune response in humans. *Life Sciences, 69,* 2931–2941.

Padgett, V. R. (1989). Predicting organizational violence: An application of 11 powerful principles of obedience. Paper presented to the American Psychological Association convention.

Padilla, R. V., & Benavides, A. H. (Eds.) (1992). *Critical perspectives on bilingual education research.* Tempe, AZ: Bilingual Press.

Page, S. (1977). Effects of the mental illness label in attempts to obtain accommodation. *Canadian Journal of Behavioral Science, 9,* 84–90.

Paikoff, R. L., & Brooks-Gunn, J. (1991). Do parent-child relationships change during puberty? *Psychological Bulletin, 110,* 47–66.

Paivio, A. (1986). *Mental representations: A dual coding approach.* New York: Oxford University Press.

Palace, E. M. (1995). Modification of dysfunctional patterns of sexual response through autonomic arousal and false physiological feedback. *Journal of Consulting and Clinical Psychology, 63,* 604–615.

Palladino, J. J., & Carducci, B. J. (1983). *"Things that go bump in the night": Students' knowledge of sleep and dreams.* Paper presented at the meeting of the Southeastern Psychological Association.

Paller, K. A. (2004). Electrical signals of memory and of the awareness of remembering. *Current Directions in Psychological Science, 13,* 49–55.

Pallier, C., Colomé, A., & Sebastián-Gallés, N. (2001). The influence of native-language phonology on lexical access: Exemplar-based versus abstract lexical entries. *Psychological Science, 12,* 445–448.

Palmer, S., Schreiber, C., & Box, C. (1991). Remembering the earthquake: "Flashbulb" memory for experienced vs. reported events. Paper presented to the Psychonomic Society convention.

Paltrow, S. J. (2004, March 22). Detailed picture of U.S. actions on Sept. 22 remains elusive. *Wall Street Journal,* pp. A1, A9.

Pandey, J., Sinha, Y., Prakash, A., & Tripathi, R. C. (1982). Right-left political ideologies and attribution of the causes of poverty. *European Journal of Social Psychology, 12,* 327–331.

Panksepp, J. (1982). Toward a general psychobiological theory of emotions. *Behavioral and Brain Sciences, 5,* 407–467.

Pantelis, C., Velakoulis, D., McGorry, P. D., Wood, S. J., Suckling, J., Phillips, L. J., Yung, A. R., Bullmore, E. T., Brewer, W., Soulsby, B., Desmond, P., & McGuire, P. K. (2002). Neuroanatomical abnormalities before and after onset of psychosis: A cross-sectional and longitudinal MRI comparison. *The Lancet,* published online at image.thelancet.com/extras/01art9092web.pdf.

Pantev, C., Oostenveld, R., Engelien, A., Ross, B., Roberts, L. R., & Hoke, M. (1998). Increased auditory cortical representation in musicians. *Nature, 392,* 811–814.

Park, D. C., Lautenschlager, G., Hedden, T., Davidson, N. S., Smith, A. D., & Smith, P. K. (2002). Models of visuospatial and verbal memory across the adult life span. *Psychology and Aging, 17,* 299–320.

Park, R. L. (1999). Liars never break a sweat. *New York Times,* July 12, 1999 (www.nytimes.com).

Parker, C. P., Baltes, B. B., Young, S. A., Huff, J. W., Altmann, R. A., LaCost, H. A., & Roberts, J. E. (2003). Relationships between psychological climate perceptions and work outcomes: A meta-analytic review. *Journal of Organizational Behavior, 24,* 389–416.

Parker, S., Nichter, M., Nichter, M., & Vuckovic, N. (1995). Body image and weight concerns among African American and white adolescent females: Differences that make a difference. *Human Organization, 54,* 103–114.

Passell, P. (1993, March 9). Like a new drug, social programs are put to the test. *New York Times,* pp. C1, C10.

Pate, J. E., Pumariega, A. J., Hester, C., & Garner, D. M. (1992). Cross-cultural patterns in eating disorders: A review. *Journal of the American Academy of Child and Adolescent Psychiatry, 31,* 802–809.

Patoine, B. (2005, January-February). Imagine that! Neural prosthetics harness thoughts to control computers and robotics. *Brain Work,* pp. 1–3.

Patterson, D. R. (2004). Treating pain with hypnosis. *Current Directions in Psychological Science, 13,,* 252–255.

Patterson, D. R., & Jensen, M. (2003). Hypnosis for clinical pain control. *Psychological Bulletin, 129,* 495–521.

Patterson, F. (1978, October). Conversations with a gorilla. *National Geographic,* pp. 438–465.

Patterson, G. R., Chamberlain, P., & Reid, J. B. (1982). A comparative evaluation of parent training procedures. *Behavior Therapy, 13,* 638–650.

Patterson, G. R., Reid, J. B., & Dishion, T. J. (1992). *Antisocial boys.* Eugene, OR: Castalia.

Patterson, M., Warr, P., & West, M. (2004). Organizational climate and company productivity: The role of employee affect and employee level. *Journal of Occupational and Organizational Psychology, 77,* 193–216.

Patterson, R. (1951). *The riddle of Emily Dickinson.* Boston: Houghton Mifflin.

Patton, G. C., Coffey, C., Carlin, J. B., Degenhardt, L., Lynskey, M., & Hall, W. (2002). Cannabis use and mental health of young people: Cohort study. *British Medical Journal, 325,* 1195–1198.

Patton, W., & Mannison, M. (1995). Sexual coercion in dating situations among university students: Preliminary Australian data. *Australian Journal of Psychology, 47,* 66–72.

Paulesu, E., Demonet, J-F., Fazio, F., McCrory, E., Chanoine, V., Brunswick, N., Cappa, S. F., Cossu, G., Habib, M., Frith, C. D., & Frith, U. (2001). Dyslexia: Cultural diversity and biological unity. *Science, 291,* 2165–2167.

Paulos, J. A. (1995). *A mathematician reads the newspaper.* New York: Basic Books.

Paunonen, S. V., Zeidner, M., Engvik, H. A., Oosterveld, P., & Maliphant, R. (2000). The nonverbal assessment of personality in five cultures. *Journal of Cross-Cultural Psychology, 31,* 220–239.

Paus, T., Zijdenbos, A., Worsley, K., Collins, D. L., Blumenthal, J., Giedd, J. N., Rapoport, J. L., & Evans, A. C. (1999) Structural maturation of neural pathways in children and adolescents: In vivo study. *Science, 283,* 1908–1911.

Pavlidis, G. T. (2005, January 17). Eye movements can diagnose preschoolers at high risk for attention deficit/hyperactivity disorder (ADHD). Press release, Brunel University (www.brunel.ac.uk).

Pavlov, I. (1927). *Conditioned reflexes: An investigation of the physiological activity of the cerebral cortex.* Oxford: Oxford University Press.

Pedersen, N. L., Plomin, R., McClearn, G. E., & Friberg, L. (1988). Neuroticism, extraversion, and related traits in adult twins reared apart and reared together. *Journal of Personality and Social Psychology, 55,* 950–957.

Peeters, A., Barendregt, J. J., Willekens, F., Mackenbach, J. P., & Mamum, A. A. (2003). Obesity in adulthood and its consequences for life expectancy: A life-table analysis. *Annals of Internal Medicine, 138,* 24–32.

Peigneux, P., Laureys, S., Fuchs, S., Collette, F., Perrin, F., Reggers, J., Phillips, C., Degueldre, C., Del Fiore, G., Aerts, J., Luxen, A., & Maquet, P. (2004). Are spatial memories strengthened in the human hippocampus during slow wave sleep? *Neuron, 44,* 535–545.

Pekkanen, J. (1982, June). Why do we sleep? *Science, 82,* p. 86.

Pelham, B. W. (1993). On the highly positive thoughts of the highly depressed. In R. F. Baumeister (Ed.), *Self-esteem: The puzzle of low self-regard.* New York: Plenum.

Pendick, D. (1994, January/February). The mind of violence. *Brain Work: The Neuroscience Newsletter,* pp. 1–3, 5.

Penfield, W. (1969). Consciousness, memory, and man's conditioned reflexes. In K. Pigram (Ed.), *On the biology of learning.* New York: Harcourt, Brace & World.

Penhune, V. B., Cismaru, R., Dorsaint-Pierre, R., Petitto, L-A., & Zatorre, R. J. (2003). The morphometry of auditory cortex in the congenitally deaf measured using MRI. *NeuroImage, 20,* 1215–1225.

Pennebaker, J. (1990). *Opening up: The healing power of confiding in others.* New York: William Morrow.

Pennebaker, J. W. (2002, January 28). Personal communication.

Pennebaker, J. W., Barger, S. D., & Tiebout, J. (1989). Disclosure of traumas and health among Holocaust survivors. *Psychosomatic Medicine, 51,* 577–589.

Pennebaker, J. W., & O'Heeron, R. C. (1984). Confiding in others and illness rate among spouses of suicide and accidental death victims. *Journal of Abnormal Psychology, 93,* 473–476.

Pennebaker, J. W., & Stone, L. D. (2003). Words of wisdom: Language use over the life span. *Journal of Personality and Social Psychology, 85,* 291–301.

Peplau, L. A. (1982). Research on homosexual couples: An overview. *Journal of Homosexuality, 8*(2), 3–8.

Peplau, L. A., & Garnets, L. D. (2000). A new paradigm for understanding women's sexuality and sexual orientation. *Journal of Social Issues, 56,* 329–350.

Pepperberg, I. M. (2002). Cognitive and communicative abilities of grey parrots. *Current Directions in Psychological Science, 11,* 83–87.

Perkins, A., & Fitzgerald, J. A. (1997). Sexual orientation in domestic rams: Some biological and social correlates. In L. Ellis and L. Ebertz (Eds.), *Sexual orientation: Toward biological understanding.* Westport, CT: Praeger Publishers.

Perkins, H. W. (1991). Religious commitment, Yuppie values, and well-being in post-collegiate life. *Review of Religious Research, 32,* 244–251.

Perlmutter, M. (1983). Learning and memory through adulthood. In M. W. Riley, B. B. Hess, & K. Bond (Eds.), *Aging in society: Selected reviews of recent research.* Hillsdale, NJ: Erlbaum.

Perls, T., & Silver, M. H., with Lauerman, J. F. (1999). *Living to 100: Lessons in living to your maximum potential.* Thorndike, ME: Thorndike Press.

Perrett, D. (2002, October 1). Perception laboratory, Department of Psychology, University of St. Andrews, Scotland (www.perception.st-and.ac.uk).

Perrett, D. I., Harries, M., Misflin, A. J., & Chitty, A. J. (1988). Three stages in the classification of body movements by visual neurons. In H. B. Barlow, C. Blakemore, & M. Weston Smith (Eds.), *Images and understanding.* Cambridge: Cambridge University Press.

Perrett, D. I., Hietanen, J. K., Oram, M. W., & Benson, P. J. (1992). Organization and functions of cells responsive to faces in the temporal cortex.

Philosophical Transactions of the Royal Society of London: Series B, 335, 23–30.

Perrett, D. I., Lee, K. J., Penton-Voak, I., Rowland, D., Yoshikawa, S., Burt, D. M., Henzi, S. P., Castles, D. L., Akamatsu, S. (1998, August). Effects of sexual dimorphism on facial attractiveness. *Nature, 394,* 884–887.

Perrett, D. I., May, K. A., & Yoshikawa, S. (1994). Facial shape and judgments of female attractiveness. *Nature, 368,* 239–242.

Persky, S., & Blascovich, J. (2005). Consequences of playing violent video games in immersive virtual environments, In A. Axelsson & Ralph Schroeder (Eds.). *Work and Play in Shared Virtual Environments.* New York: Springer.

Persons, J. B. (1986). The advantages of studying psychological phenomena rather than psychiatric diagnoses. *American Psychologist, 41,* 1252–1260.

Pert, C. (1986). Quoted in J. Hooper & D. Teresi, *The three-pound universe.* New York: Macmillan.

Pert, C. B. (1986, Summer). The wisdom of the receptors: Neuropeptides, the emotions, and bodymind. *Advances* (Institute for the Advancement of Health), 3, 8–16.

Pert, C. B., & Snyder, S. H. (1973). Opiate receptor: Demonstration in nervous tissue. *Science, 179,* 1011–1014.

Perugini, E. M., Kirsch, I., Allen, S. T., Coldwell, E., Meredith, J., Montgomery, G. H., & Sheehan, J. (1998). Surreptitious observation of responses to hypnotically suggested hallucinations: A test of the compliance hypothesis. *International Journal of Clinical and Experimental Hypnosis, 46,* 191–203.

Peschel, E. R., & Peschel, R. E. (1987). Medical insights into the castrati in opera. *American Scientist, 75,* 578–583.

Peters, T. J., & Waterman, R. H., Jr. (1982). *In search of excellence: Lessons from America's best-run companies.* New York: Harper & Row.

Peterson, C., & Barrett, L. C. (1987). Explanatory style and academic performance among university freshmen. *Journal of Personality and Social Psychology, 53,* 603–607.

Peterson, C., Peterson, J., & Skevington, S. (1986). Heated argument and adolescent development. *Journal of Social and Personal Relationships, 3,* 229–240.

Peterson, C., & Seligman, M. E. P. (2004). *Character strengths and virtues: A handbook and classification.* New York: Oxford.

Peterson, C. C., & Siegal, M. (1999). Representing inner worlds: Theory of mind in autistic, deaf, and normal hearing children. *Psychological Science, 10,* 126–129.

Peterson, L. R., & Peterson, M. J. (1959). Short-term retention of individual verbal items. *Journal of Experimental Psychology, 58,* 193–198.

Petitto, L. A., & Marentette, P. F. (1991). Babbling in the manual mode: Evidence for the ontogeny of language. *Science, 251,* 1493–1496.

Petrosino, A., Turpin-Petrosino, C., & Finckenauer, J. O. (2000). Well-meaning programs can have harmful effects! Lessons from experiments of programs such as Scared Straight. *Crime and Delinquency, 46,* 354–379.

Pettegrew, J. W., Keshavan, M. S., & Minshew, N. J. (1993). 31P nuclear magnetic resonance spectroscopy: Neurodevelopment and schizophrenia. *Schizophrenia Bulletin, 19,* 35–53.

Petticrew, C., Bell, R., & Hunter, D. (2002). Influence of psychological coping on survival and recurrence in people with cancer: Systematic review. *British Medical Journal, 325,* 1066.

Petticrew, M., Fraser, J. M., & Regan, M. F. (1999). Adverse life events and risk of breast cancer: A meta-analysis. *British Journal of Health Psychology, 4,* 1–17.

Pettigrew, T. F. (1969). Racially separate or together? *Journal of Social Issues, 25,* 43–69.

Pettigrew, T. F. (1998). Reactions toward the new minorities of western Europe. *Annual Review of Sociology, 24,* 77–103.

Pettigrew, T. F. (2004). Justice deferred a half century after Brown v. Board of Education. *American Psychologist, 59,* 521–529.

Pew. (2003). Views of a changing world 2003. The Pew Global Attitudes Project. Washington, DC: Pew Research Center for the People and the Press (http://people-press.org/reports/pdf/185.pdf).

Phelps, J. A., Davis J. O., & Schartz, K. M. (1997). Nature, nurture, and twin research strategies. *Current Directions in Psychological Science 6,* 117–120.

Philip Morris. (2003). Philip Morris USA youth smoking prevention. Teenage attitudes and behavior study, 2002. In "Raising kids who don't smoke," vol. 1(2).

Phillips, D. P. (1985). Natural experiments on the effects of mass media violence on fatal aggression: Strengths and weaknesses of a new approach. In L. Berkowitz (Ed.), *Advances in experimental social psychology* (Vol. 19). Orlando, FL: Academic Press.

Phillips, D. P., Carstensen, L. L., & Paight, D. J. (1989). Effects of mass media news stories on suicide, with new evidence on the role of story content. In D. R. Pfeffer (Ed.), *Suicide among youth: Perspectives on risk and prevention.* Washington, DC: American Psychiatric Press.

Phillips, J. L. (1969). *Origins of intellect: Piaget's theory.* San Francisco: Freeman.

Phillips, T. (2004, April 3). Quoted by T. Baldwin & G. Rozenberg, Britain 'must scrap multiculturalism.' *The Times,* p. 1.

Piaget, J. (1932). *The moral judgment of the child.* New York: Harcourt, Brace & World.

Picchioni, D., Mignot, E. J., & Harsh, J. R. (2004). The month-of-birth pattern in narcolepsy is moderated by cataplexy severity and may be independent of HLA-DQB1*0602. *Sleep, 27,* 1471–1475.

Pickar, D., Labarca, R., Linnoila, M., Roy, A., Hommer, D., Everett, D., & Payl, S. M. (1984). Neuroleptic-induced decrease in plasma homovanillic acid and antipsychotic activity in schizophrenic patients. *Science, 225,* 954–957.

Pike, K. M., & Rodin, J. (1991). Mothers, daughters, and disordered eating. *Journal of Abnormal Psychology, 100,* 198–204.

Piliavin, J. A. (2003). Doing well by doing good: Benefits for the benefactor. In C. L. M. Keyes & J. Haidt (Eds.), *Flourishing: Positive psychology and the life well-lived.* Washington, DC: American Psychological Association.

Pillemer, D. (1998). *Momentous events, vivid memories.* Cambridge: Harvard University Press, 1998.

Pillemer, D. G. (1995). What is remembered about early childhood events? Invited paper presentation to the American Psychological Society convention.

Pillsworth, M. G., Haselton, M. G., & Buss, D. M. (2004). Ovulatory shifts in female desire. *Journal of Sex Research, 41,* 55–65.

Pincus, H. A. (1997) Commentary: Spirituality, religion, and health: Expanding, and using the knowledge base. *Mind/Body Medicine, 2,* 49.

Pinel, J. P. J. (1993). *Biopsychology* (2nd ed). Boston: Allyn & Bacon.

Pingitore, R., Dugoni, B. L., Tindale, R. S., & Spring, B. (1994). Bias against overweight job applicants in a simulated employment interview. *Journal of Applied Psychology, 79,* 909–917.

Pinker, S. (1990, September-October). Quoted by J. de Cuevas, "No, she holded them loosely." *Harvard Magazine,* pp. 60–67.

Pinker, S. (1995). The language instinct. *The General Psychologist, 31,* 63–65.

Pinker, S. (1998). Words and rules. *Lingua, 106,* 219–242.

Pinker, S. (1999, June 24). His brain measured up. *New York Times* (www.nytimes.com).

Pinker, S. (2002, September 9). A biological understanding of human nature: A talk with Steven Pinker. The Edge Third Culture Mail List (www.edge.org).

Pinker, S. (2002). *The blank slate.* New York: Viking.

Pinker, S. (2005, April 22). The science of gender and science: A conversation with Elizabeth Spelke. Harvard University (www.edge.org).

Pinkerton, S. D., & Abramson, P. R. (1997). Condoms and the prevention of AIDS. *American Scientist, 85,* 364–373.

Pipe, M-E. (1996). Children's eyewitness memory. *New Zealand Journal of Psychology, 25,* 36–43.

Pipe, M-E., Lamb, M. E., Orbach, Y., & Esplin, P. W. (2004). Recent research on children's testimony about experienced and witnessed events. *Developmental Review, 24,* 440–468.

Piper, A., Jr. (1998, Winter). Multiple personality disorder: Witchcraft survives in the twentieth century. *Skeptical Inquirer,* pp. 44–50.

Pipher, M. (2002). *The middle of everywhere: The world's refugees come to our town.* New York: Harcourt Brace.

Pittenger, D. J. (1993). The utility of the Myers-Briggs Type Indicator. *Review of Eduational Research, 63,* 467–488.

Pleck, J. H., Sonenstein, F. L., & Ku, L. C. (1993). Masculinity ideology: Its impact on adolescent males' heterosexual relationships. *Journal of Social Issues, 49,* 11–29.

Pliner, P. (1982). The effects of mere exposure on liking for edible substances. *Appetite: Journal for Intake Research, 3,* 283–290.

Pliner, P., & Pelchat, M. L. (1991). Neophobia in humans and the special status of foods of animal origin. *Appetite, 16,* 205–218.

Plomin, R. (1997). Identifying genes for cognitive abilities and disabilities. In R. Sternberg, & E. Grigorenko (Eds.), *Intelligence, heredity, and environment.* New York: Cambridge University Press.

Plomin, R. (1999). Genetics and general cognitive ability. *Nature, 402* (Suppl), C25–C29.

Plomin, R. (2001). Genetics and behaviour. *The Psychologist, 14,* 134–139.

Plomin, R. (2003). General cognitive ability. In R. Plomin, J. C. DeFries, I. W. Craig, & P. McGuffin (Eds.), *Behavioral genetics in a postgenomic world.* Washington, DC: APA Books.

Plomin, R., & Bergeman, C. S. (1991). The nature of nurture: Genetic influence on "environmental" measures. *Behavioral and Brain Sciences, 14,* 373–427.

Plomin, R., Corley, R., Caspi, A., Fulker, D. W., & DeFries, J. (1998). Adoption results for self-reported personality: Evidence for nonadditive genetic effects? *Journal of Personality and Social Psychology, 75,* 211–219.

Plomin, R., & Crabbe, J. (2000). DNA. *Psychological Bulletin, 126,* 806–828.

Plomin, R., & Daniels, D. (1987). Why are children in the same family so different from one another? *Behavioral and Brain Sciences, 10,* 1–60.

Plomin, R., & DeFries, J. C. (1998, May). The genetics of cognitive abilities and disabilities. *Scientific American,* pp. 62–69.

Plomin, R., DeFries, J. C., McClearn, G. E., & Rutter, M. (1997a). *Behavioral genetics.* New York: Freeman.

Plomin, R., Fulker, D. W., Corley, R., & DeFries, J. C. (1997b). Nature, nurture and cognitive development from 1 to 16 years: A parent-offspring adoption study. *Psychological Science, 8,* 442–447.

Plomin, R., McClearn, G. E., Pedersen, N. L., Nesselroade, J. R., & Bergeman, C. S. (1988). Genetic influence on childhood family environment perceived retrospectively from the last half of the life span. *Developmental Psychology, 24,* 37–45.

Plomin, R., & McGuffin, P. (2003). Psychopathology in the postgenomic era. *Annual Review of Psychology, 54,* 205–228.

Plomin, R., Reiss, D., Hetherington, E. M., & Howe, G. W. (January, 1994). Nature and nurture: Genetic contributions to measures of the family environment. *Developmental Psychology, 30*(1), 32–43.

Plous, S. (1993). Psychological mechanisms in the human use of animals. *Journal of Social Issues, 49*(1), 11–52.

Plous, S., & Herzog, H. A. (2000). Poll shows researchers favor lab animal protection. *Science, 290,* 711.

Poldrack, R. A., & Wagner, A. D. (2004). What can neuroimaging tell us about the mind? *Current Directions in Psychological Science, 13,* 177–181.

Polivy, J., & Herman, C. P. (1985). Dieting and binging: A causal analysis. *American Psychologist, 40,* 193–201.

Polivy, J., & Herman, C. P. (1987). Diagnosis and treatment of normal eating. *Journal of Personality and Social Psychology, 55,* 635–644.

Polivy, J., & Herman, C. P. (2002). Causes of eating disorders. *Annual Review of Psychology, 53,* 187–213.

Pollack, A. (2004, April 13). With tiny brain implants, just thinking may make it so. *New York Times* (www.nytimes.com).

Pollak, S., Cicchetti, D., & Klorman, R. (1998). Stress, memory, and emotion: Developmental considerations from the study of child maltreatment. *Developmental Psychopathology, 10,* 811–828.

Pollak, S. D., & Kistler, D. J. (2002). Early experience is associated with the development of categorical representations for facial expressions of emotion. *Proceedings of the National Academy of Sciences, 99,* 9072–9076.

Pollak, S. D., & Tolley-Schell, S. A. (2003). Selective attention to facial emotion in physically abused children. *Journal of Abnormal Psychology, 112,* 323–328.

Pollard, R. (1992). 100 years in psychology and deafness: A centennial retrospective. Invited address to the American Psychological Association convention, Washington, DC.

Polusny, M. A., & Follette, V. M. (1995). Long-term correlates of child sexual abuse: Theory and review of the empirical literature. *Applied & Preventive Psychology, 4,* 143–166.

Pomerleau, O. F., Collins, A. C., Shiffman, S., & Pomerleau, C. S. (1993). Why some people smoke and others do not: New perspectives. *Journal of Consulting and Clinical Psychology, 61,* 723–731.

Poole, D. A., & Lindsay, D. S. (1995). Interviewing preschoolers: Effects of nonsuggestive techniques, parental coaching and leading questions on reports of nonexperienced events. *Journal of Experimental Child Psychology, 60,* 129–154.

Poole, D. A., & Lindsay, D. S. (2001). Children's eyewitness reports after exposure to misinformation from parents. *Journal of Experimental Psychology: Applied, 7,* 27–50.

Poole, D. A., & Lindsay, D. S. (2002). Reducing child witnesses' false reports of misinformation from parents. *Journal of Experimental Child Psychology, 81,* 117–140.

Poole, D. A., Lindsay, D. S., Memon, A., & Bull, R. (1995). Psychotherapy and the recovery of memories of childhood sexual abuse: U.S. and British practitioners' opinions, practices, and experiences. *Journal of Consulting and Clinical Psychology, 63,* 426–437.

Poon, L. W. (1987). Myths and truisms: Beyond extant analyses of speed of behavior and age. Address to the Eastern Psychological Association convention.

Pope, H. G., & Yurgelun-Todd, D. (1996). The residual cognitive effects of heavy marijuana use in college students. *Journal of the American Medical Association, 275,* 521–527.

Popenoe, D. (1993). The evolution of marriage and the problem of stepfamilies: A biosocial perspective. Paper presented at the National Symposium on Stepfamilies, Pennsylvania State University.

Popenoe, D., & Whitehead, B. D. (2002). *Should We Live Together?,* 2nd Ed. New Brunswick, NJ: The National Marriage Project, Rutgers University.

Porac, C., Coren, S., & Duncan, P. (1980). Life-span age trends in laterality. *Journal of Gerontology, 35,* 715–721.

Poremba, A., & Gabriel, M. (2001). Amygdalar efferents initiate auditory thalamic discriminative training-induced neuronal activity. *Journal of Neuroscience, 21,* 270–278.

Porkka-Heiskanen, T., Strecker, R. E., Thakkar, M., Bjorkum, A. A., Greene, R. W., & McCarley, R. W. (1997). Adenosine: A mediator of the sleep-inducing effects of prolonged wakefulness. *Science, 276,* 1265–1268.

Porter, D., & Neuringer, A. (1984). Music discriminations by pigeons. *Journal of Experimental Psychology: Animal Behavior Processes, 10,* 138–148.

Porter, R. P. (1998). Twisted tongues: The failure of bilingual education. Washington, DC: The Communitarian Network (www.gwu.edu/~ccps/pop_biling.html).

Porter, S., Birt, A. R., Yuille, J. C., & Lehman, D. R. (2000, Nov.). Negotiating false memories: Interviewer and rememberer characteristics relate to memory distortion. *Psychological Science, 11,* 507–510.

Porter, S., Yuille, J. C., & Lehman, D. R. (1999). The nature of real, implanted, and fabricated memories for childhood events: Implications for the recovered memory debate. *Law and Human Behavior, 23,* 517–537.

Posavac, H. D., Posavac, S. S., & Posavac, E. J. (1998). Exposure to media images of female attractiveness and concern with body weight among young women. *Sex Roles, 38,* 187–201.

Posner, M. I., & Carr, T. H. (1992). Lexical access and the brain: Anatomical constraints on cognitive models of word recognition. *American Journal of Psychology, 105,* 1–26.

Poulton, R., & Milne, B. J. (2002). Low fear in childhood is associated with sporting prowess in adolescence and young adulthood. *Behaviour Research and Therapy, 40,* 1191–1197.

Povinelli, D. J., & Bering, J. M. (2002). The mentality of apes revisited. *Current Directions in Psychological Science, 11,* 115–119.

Powell, J. (1989). *Happiness is an inside job.* Valencia, CA: Tabor.

Powell, K. E., Thompson, P. D., Caspersen, C. J., & Kendrick, J. S. (1987). Physical activity and the incidence of coronary heart disease. *Annual Review of Public Health, 8,* 253–287.

Powell, L. H., Schahabi, L., & Thoresen, C. E. (2003). Religion and spirituality: Linkages to physical health. *American Psychologist, 58,* 36–52.

Powell, R. A., & Boer, D. P. (1994). Did Freud mislead patients to confabulate memories of abuse? *Psychological Reports, 74,* 1283–1298.

Prairie Home Companion. (1999). *The Prairie Home Companion's Pretty Good Joke Book* (Vol. 4). St. Paul, MN: Prairie Home Companion.

Pratkanis, A. R. (1992). The cargo-cult science of subliminal persuasion. *Skeptical Inquirer, 16,* 260–272.

Pratkanis, A. R., & Greenwald, A. G. (1988). Recent perspectives on unconscious processing: Still no marketing applications. *Psychology and Marketing, 5,* 337–353.

PRB. (2002). *2002 Women of our World.* Population Reference Bureau (www.prb.org).

PRB. (2004). *2004 world population data sheet.* Washington, DC: Population Reference Bureau.

Prentice, D. A., & Miller, D. T. (1993). Pluralistic ignorance and alcohol use on campus: Some consequences of misperceiving the social norm. *Journal of Personality and Social Psychology, 64,* 243–256.

Presley, C. A., Meilman, P. W., & Lyerla, R. (1997). *Alcohol and drugs on American college campuses: Issues of violence and harrassment.* Carbondale, IL: Core Institute, Southern Illinois University.

Presson, P. K., & Benassi, V. A. (1996). Locus of control orientation and depressive symptomatology: A meta-analysis. *Journal of Social Behavior and Personality, 11,* 201–212.

Pringle, P. J., Geary, M. P., Rodeck, C. H., Kingdom, J. C., Kayamba-Kay's, S., & Hindmarsh, P. C. (2005). The influence of cigarette smoking on antenatal growth, birth size, and the insulin-like growth factor axis. *Journal of Clinical Endocrinology and Metabolism, 90,* 2556–2562.

Prioleau, L., Murdock, M., & Brody, N. (1983). An analysis of psychotherapy versus placebo studies. *The Behavioral and Brain Sciences, 6,* 275–310.

Project Match Research Group. (1997). Matching alcoholism treatments to client heterogeneity: Project MATCH posttreatment drinking outcomes. *Journal of Studies on Alcohol, 58,* 7–29.

Project on Redefining the Meaning and Purpose of Baccalaureate Degrees. (1985). *Integrity in the college curriculum.* Washington, DC: Association of American Colleges.

Pronin, E., Gilovich, T., & Ross, L. (2004). Objectivity in the eye of the beholder: Divergent perceptions of bias in self versus others. *Psychological Review, 111,* 781–799.

Pronin, E., Lin, D. Y., & Ross, L. (2002). The bias blind spot: Perceptions of bias in self versus others. *Personality and Social Psychology Bulletin, 28,* 369–381.

Provine, R. R. (2001). *Laughter: A scientific investigation.* New York: Penguin.

Psychologist (2003, April). Who's the greatest? *The Psychologist, 16,* 17.

Psychologist (2005, August). Description or explanation? *The Psychologist, 18,* 460–461.

Puchalski, C. (2005, March 12). Personal correspondence from Director, George Washington Institute for Spirituality and Health.

Putnam, F. W. (1991). Recent research on multiple personality disorder. *Psychiatric Clinics of North America, 14,* 489–502.

Putnam, F. W. (1995). Rebuttal of Paul McHugh. *Journal of the American Academy of Child and Adolescent Psychiatry, 34,* 963.

Putnam, R. (2000). *Bowling alone.* New York: Simon and Schuster.

Pyszczynski, T., Hamilton, J. C., Greenberg, J., & Becker, S. E. (1991). Self-awareness and psychological dysfunction. In C. R. Snyder & D. O. Forsyth (Eds.), *Handbook of social and clinical psychology: The health perspective.* New York: Pergamon.

Pyszczynski, T. A., Solomon, S., & Greenberg, J. (2002). *In the wake of 9/11: The psychology of terror.* Washington, DC: American Psychological Association.

Qirko, H. N. (2004). "Fictive kin" and suicide terrorism. *Science, 304,* 49–50.

Quasha, S. (1980). *Albert Einstein: An intimate portrait.* New York: Forest.

Quinn, P. C. (2002). Category representation in young infants. *Current Directions in Psychological Science, 11,* 66–70.

Quinn, P. C., Bhatt, R. S., Brush, D., Grimes, A., & Sharpnack, H. (2002). Development of form similarity as a Gestalt grouping principle in infancy. *Psychological Science, 13,* 320–328.

Quinn, P. J., Williams, G. M., Najman, J. M., Andersen, M. J., & Bor, W. (2001). The effect of breastfeeding on child development at 5 years: A cohort study. *Journal of Pediatrics & Child Health, 3,* 465–469.

Rabin, A. S., Kaslow, N. J., & Rehm, L. P. (1986). Aggregate outcome and follow-up results following self-control therapy for depression. Paper presented at the American Psychological Association convention.

Rabinowicz, T., Dean, D. E., Petetot, J. M., & de Courten-Myers, G. M. (1999). Gender differences in the human cerebral cortex: More neurons in males; more processes in females. *Journal of Child Neurology, 14,* 98–107.

Rabinowicz, T., de Courten-Myers, G. M., Petetot, J. M., Xi, G., & de los Reyes, E. (1996). Human cortex development: Estimates of neuronal numbers indicate major loss late during gestation. *Journal of Neuropathology and Experimental Neurology, 55,* 320–328.

Radford, B. (2002, November/December). Psychics wrong about Chandra Levy. *Skeptical Inquirer,* p. 9.

Raglin, J. S. (1992). Anxiety and sport performance. In J. O. Holloszy (Ed.), *Exercise and sports sciences reviews* (Vol. 20). Baltimore: Williams & Wilkins.

Rahman, Q., & Wilson, G. D. (2003). Born gay? The psychobiology of human sexual orientation. *Personality and Individual Differences, 34,* 1337–1382.

Rahman, Q., Wilson, G. D., & Abrahams, S. (2004). Biosocial factors, sexual orientation and neurocognitive functioning. *Psychoneuroendocrinology, 29,* 867–881.

Raine, A. (1999). Murderous minds: Can we see the mark of Cain? *Cerebrum: The Dana Forum on Brain Science 1*(1), 15–29.

Raine, A., Brennan, P., Mednick, B., & Mednick, S. A. (1996). High rates of violence, crime, academic problems, and behavioral problems in males with both early neuromotor deficits and unstable family environments. *Archives of General Psychiatry, 53,* 544–549.

Raine, A., Lencz, T., Bihrle, S., LaCasse, L., & Colletti, P. (2000). Reduced prefrontal gray matter volume and reduced autonomic activity in antisocial personality disorder. *Archives of General Psychiatry, 57,* 119–127.

Rainville, P., Duncan, G. H., Price, D. D., Carrier, B., & Bushnell, M. C. (1997). Pain affect encoded in human anterior cingulate but not somatosensory cortex. *Science, 277,* 968–971.

Raison, C. L., Klein, H. M., & Steckler, M. (1999). The mood and madness reconsidered. *Journal of Affective Disorders, 53,* 99–106.

Ralston, A. (2004). Enough rope. Interview for ABC TV, Australia, by Andrew Denton (www.abc.net.au/enoughrope/stories/s1227885.htm).

Ramachandran, V. S., & Blakeslee, S. (1998). *Phantoms in the brain: Probing the mysteries of the human mind.* New York: Morrow.

Ramey, S. L., & Ramey, C. T. (1992). Early educational intervention with disadvantaged children—To what effect? *Applied and Preventive Psychology, 1,* 131–140.

Rand, C. S. W., & Macgregor, A. M. C. (1990). Morbidly obese patients' perceptions of social discrimination before and after surgery for obesity. *Southern Medical Journal, 83,* 1390–1395.

Rand, C. S. W., & Macgregor, A. M. C. (1991). Successful weight loss following obesity surgery and perceived liability or morbid obesity. *Internal Journal of Obesity, 15,* 577–579.

Randi, J. (1999, February 4). 2000 Club mailing list e-mail letter.

Rapoport, J. L. (1989, March). The biology of obsessions and compulsions. *Scientific American,* pp. 83–89.

Räsänen, S., Pakaslahti, A., Syvalahti, E., Jones, P. B., & Isohanni, M. (2000). Sex differences in schizophrenia: A review. *Nordic Journal of Psychiatry, 54,* 37–45.

Ray, J. (2005, April 12). U.S. teens walk away from anger: Boys and girls manage anger differently. The Gallup Organization (www.gallup.com).

Ray, O., & Ksir, C. (1990). *Drugs, society, and human behavior* (5th ed.). St. Louis: Times Mirror/Mosby.

Raynor, H. A., & Epstein, L. H. (2001). Dietary variety, energy regulation, and obesity. *Psychological Bulletin, 127,* 325–341.

Reason, J. (1987). The Chernobyl errors. *Bulletin of the British Psychological Society, 40,* 201–206.

Reason, J., & Mycielska, K. (1982). *Absent-minded? The psychology of mental lapses and everyday errors.* Englewood Cliffs, NJ: Prentice-Hall.

Redelmeier, D. A., & Tversky, D. A. (1996). On the belief that arthritis pain is related to the weather. *Proceedings of the National Academy of Sciences, 93,* 2895–2896.

Redish, A. D. (2004). Addiction as a computational process gone awry. *Science, 306,* 1944–1947.

Reed, P. (2000). Serial position effects in recognition memory for odors. *Journal of Experimental Psychology: Learning, Memory, and Cognition, 26,* 411–422.

Reed, T. E., & Jensen, A. R. (1992). Conduction velocity in a brain nerve pathway of normal adults correlates with intelligence level. *Intelligence, 16,* 259–272.

Reeve, C. L., & Hakel, M. D. (2002). Asking the right questions about *g. Human Performance, 15,* 47–74.

Regier, D. A., Kaelber, C. T., Rae, D. S., Farmer, M. E., Knauper, B., Kessler, R. C., & Norquist, G. S. (1998). Limitations of diagnostic criteria and assessment instruments for mental disorders: Implications for research and policy. *Archives of General Psychiatry, 55,* 109–115.

Reichman, J. (1998). *I'm not in the mood: What every woman should know about improving her libido.* New York: Morrow.

Reiner, W. G., & Gearhart, J. P. (2004). Discordant sexual identity in some genetic males with cloacal exstrophy assigned to female sex at birth. *New England Journal of Medicine, 350,* 333–341.

Reisenzein, R. (1983). The Schachter theory of emotion: Two decades later. *Psychological Bulletin, 94,* 239–264.

Reiser, M. (1982). *Police psychology.* Los Angeles: LEHI.

Reiss, D., & Marino, L. (2001). Mirror self-recognition in the bottlenose dolphin: A case of cognitive convergence. *Proceedings of the National Academy of Sciences, 98,* 5937–5942.

Relman, A. S. (1998, December 14). A trip to stonesville. *New Republic* (www.thenewrepublic.com).

Remafedi, G. (1999). Suicide and sexual orientation: Nearing the end of controversy? *Archives of General Psychiatry, 56,* 885–886.

Remley, A. (1988, October). From obedience to independence. *Psychology Today,* pp. 56–59.

Remondes, M., & Schuman, E. M. (2004). Role for a cortical input to hippocampal area CA1 in the consolidation of a long-term memory. *Nature, 431,* 699–703.

Reneman, L., Lavalaye, J., Schmand, B., De Wolff, F. A., Van Den Brink, W., Den Heeten, G., & Booij, J. (2001). Cortical serotonin transporter density and verbal memory in individuals who stopped using 3, 4-methylenedioxy-methampetamine. *Archives of General Psychiatry, 58,* 901–908.

Renner, M. J. (1992). Curiosity and exploration. In L. R. Squire (Ed.), *Encyclopedia of Learning and Memory.* New York: Macmillan.

Renner, M. J., & Renner, C. H. (1993). Expert and novice intuitive judgments about animal behavior. *Bulletin of the Psychonomic Society, 31,* 551–552.

Renner, M. J., & Rosenzweig, M. R. (1987). *Enriched and impoverished environments: Effects on brain and behavior.* New York: Springer-Verlag.

Rentfrow, P. J., & Gosling, S. D. (2003). The Do Re Mi's of everyday life: The structure and personality correlates of music preferences. *Journal of Personality and Social Psychology, 84,* 1236–1256.

Repetti, R. L., Taylor, S. E., & Seeman, T. E. (2002). Risky families: Family social environments and the mental and physical health of offspring. *Psychological Bulletin, 128,* 330–366.

Rescorla, R. A. (1988, March). Pavlovian conditioning: It's not what you think it is. *American Psychologist, 43,* 151–160.

Rescorla, R. A., & Wagner, A. R. (1972). A theory of Pavlovian conditioning: Variations in the effectiveness of reinforcement and nonreinforcement. In A. H. Black & W. F. Perokasy (Eds.), *Classical conditioning II: Current theory.* New York: Appleton-Century-Crofts.

Resnick, M. D., Bearman, P. S., Blum, R. W., Bauman, K. E., Harris, K. M., Jones, J., Tabor, J., Beuhring, T., Sieving, R., Shew, M., Bearinger, L. H., & Udry, J. R. (1997). Protecting adolescents from harm: Findings from the National Longitudinal Study on Adolescent Health. *Journal of the American Medical Association, 278,* 823–832.

Resnick, R. A., O'Regan, J. K., & Clark, J. J. (1997). To see or not to see: The need for attention to perceive changes in scenes. *Psychological Science, 8,* 368–373.

Resnick, S. M. (1992). Positron emission tomography in psychiatric illness. *Current Directions in Psychological Science, 1,* 92–98.

Responsive Community. (1996, Fall). Age vs. weight. Page 83 (reported from a *Wall Street Journal* survey).

Ressler, R. K., Burgess, A. W., & Douglas, J. E. (1988). *Sexual homicide patterns.* Boston: Lexington Books.

Reynolds, A. J., Temple, J. A., Robertson, D. L., & Manri, E. A. (2001). Long-term effects of an early childhood intervention on educational achievement and juvenile arrest. *Journal of the American Medical Association, 285,* 2339–2346.

Rhee, S. H., & Waldman, I. D. (2002). Genetic and environmental influences on antisocial behavior: A meta-analysis of twin and adoption studies. *Psychological Bulletin, 128,* 490–529.

Rhodes, G., Sumich, A., & Byatt, G. (1999). Are average facial configurations attractive only because of their symmetry? *Psychological Science, 10,* 52–58.

Rhodes, S. R. (1983). Age-related differences in work attitudes and behavior: A review and conceptual analysis. *Psychological Bulletin, 93,* 328–367.

Rholes, W. S., & Simpson, J. A. (Eds.) (2004). *Adult attachment: Theory, research, and clinical implications.* New York: Guilford.

Ribeio, S., Gervasoni, D., Soares, E. S., Zhou, Y., & Lin S-C., Pantoja, J., Lavine, M., & Nicolelis, M. A. L. (2004). Long-lasting novelty-induced neuronal reverberation during slow-wave sleep in multiple forebrain areas. *PloS Biology, 2*(1), e37 (www.plosbiology.org).

Ricciardelli, L. A., & McCabe, M. P. (2004). A biopsychosocial model of disordered eating and the pursuit of muscularity in adolescent boys. *Psychological Bulletin, 130,* 179–205.

Riccio, D. C., Millin, P. M., & Gisquet-Verrier, P. (2003). Retrograde amnesia: Forgetting back. *Current Directions in Psychological Science, 12,* 41–44.

Rice, B. (1985, September). Performance review: The job nobody likes. *Psychology Today,* pp. 30–36.

Rice, M. E., & Grusec, J. E. (1975). Saying and doing: Effects on observer performance. *Journal of Personality and Social Psychology, 32,* 584–593.

Rich, F. (2001, May 20). Naked capitalists: there's no business like porn business. *New York Times* (www.nytimes.com).

Richards, J. M., & Gross, J. J. (2000). Emotion regulation and memory: The cognitive costs of keeping one's cool. *Journal of Personality and Social Psychology, 79,* 410–424.

Richardson, J. (1993). The curious case of coins: Remembering the appearance of familiar objects. *The Psychologist: Bulletin of the British Psychological Society, 6,* 360–366.

Richardson, J. T. E., & Zucco, G. M. (1989). Cognition and olfaction: A review. *Psychological Bulletin, 105,* 352–360.

Rieff, P. (1979). *Freud: The mind of a moralist* (3rd ed.). Chicago: University of Chicago Press.

Rieger, G., Chivers, M. L., & Bailey, J. M. (2005). Sexual arousal patterns of bisexual men. *Psychological Science, 16,* 579–584.

Riis, J., Loewenstein, G., Baron, J., Jepson, C., Fagerlin, A., & Ubel, P. A. (2005). Ignorance of hedonic adaptation to hemodialysis: A study using ecological momentary assessment. *Journal of Experimental Psychology: General, 134,* 3–9.

Ring, K. (1980). *Life at death: A scientific investigation of the near-death experience.* New York: Coward, McCann & Geoghegan.

Ripple, C. H., & Zigler, E. (2003). Research, policy, and the federal role in prevention initiatives for children. *American Psychologist, 58,* 482–490.

Riskind, J. H., Beck, A. T., Berchick, R. J., Brown, G., & Steer, R. A. (1987). Reliability of DSM-III diagnoses for major depression and generalized anxiety disorder using the structured clinical interview for DSM-III. *Archives of General Psychiatry, 44,* 817–820.

Rizzolatti, G., Fadiga, L., Fogassi, L., & Gallese, V. (2002). From mirror neurons to imitation: Facts and speculations. In A. N. Meltzoff & W. Prinz (Eds.), *The imitative mind: Development, evolution, and brain bases.* Cambridge: Cambridge University Press, 2002.

Roberson, D., Davidoff, J., Davies, I. R. L., & Shapiro, L. R. (2004). The development of color categories in two languages: A longitudinal study. *Journal of Experimental Psychology: General, 133,* 554–571.

Roberts, A. H., Kewman, D. G., Mercier, L., & Hovell, M. (1993). The power of nonspecific effects in healing: Implications for psychosocial and biological treatments. *Clinical Psychology Review, 13,* 375–391.

Roberts, B. W., Caspi, A., & Moffitt, T. E. (2001). The kids are alright: Growth and stability in personality development from adolescence to adulthood. *Journal of Personality and Social Psychology, 81,* 670–683.

Roberts, B. W., Caspi, A., & Moffitt, T. E. (2003). Work experiences and personality development in young adulthood. *Journal of Personality and Social Psychology, 84,* 582–593.

Roberts, B. W., & DelVecchio, W. F. (2000). The rank-order consistency of personality traits from childhood to old age: A quantitative review of longitudinal studies. *Psychological Bulletin, 126,* 3–25.

Roberts, B. W., O'Donnell, M., & Robins, R. W. (2004). Goal and personality trait development in emerging adulthood. *Journal of Personality and Social Psychology, 87,* 541–550.

Roberts, L. (1988). Beyond Noah's ark: What do we need to know? *Science, 242,* 1247.

Roberts, T-A. (1991). Determinants of gender differences in responsiveness to others' evaluations. *Dissertation Abstracts International, 51*(8–B).

Robins, L. N., Davis, D. H., & Goodwin, D. W. (1974). Drug use by U.S. Army enlisted men in Vietnam: A follow-up on their return home. *American Journal of Epidemiology, 99,* 235–249.

Robins, L., & Regier, D. (Eds.). (1991). *Psychiatric disorders in America.* New York: Free Press.

Robins, R. W., Gosling, S. D., & Craik, K. H. (1999). An empirical analysis of trends in psychology. *American Psychologist, 54,* 117–128.

Robins, R. W., & Trzesniewski, K. H. (2005). Self-esteem development across the lifespan. *Current Directions in Psychological Science, 14*(3), 158–162.

Robins, R. W., Trzesniewski, K. H., Tracy, J. L., Gosling, S. D., & Potter, J. (2002). Global self-esteem across the lifespan. *Psychology and Aging, 17,* 423–434.

Robinson, J. (2002, October 8). What percentage of the population is gay? *Gallup Tuesday Briefing* (www.gallup.com/poll/tb/religValue/20021008b.asp).

Robinson, J. L., Kagan, J., Reznick, J. S., & Corley, R. (1992). The heritability of inhibited and uninhibited behavior: A twin study. *Developmental Psychology, 28,* 1030–1037.

Robinson, T. E., & Berridge, K. C. (2003). Addiction. *Annual Review of Psychology, 54,* 25–53.

Robinson, T. N. (1999). Reducing children's television viewing to prevent obesity. *Journal of the American Medical Association, 282,* 1561–1567.

Robinson, V. M. (1983). Humor and health. In P. E. McGhee & J. H. Goldstein (Eds.), *Handbook of humor research: Vol. II. Applied studies.* New York: Springer-Verlag.

Robison, J., & Mason, H. (2002, July 2). Getting between teens and tobacco. *Gallup Tuesday Briefing,* Gallup Organization (www.gallup.com/poll/tb/healthcare/20020702.asp).

Robison, L. (1999). Why our MENTALLY ILL son is on DEATH ROW. www.swuuc.org/fjuuc/Courier/robison.htm. See also www.larryrobison.org

Rochat, F. (1993). How did they resist authority? Protecting refugees in Le Chambon during World War II. Paper presented at the American Psychological Association convention.

Rock, I., & Palmer, S. (1990, December). The legacy of Gestalt psychology. *Scientific American,* pp. 84–90.

Rodin, J. (1986). Aging and health: Effects of the sense of control. *Science, 233,* 1271–1276.

Rodriguez, E., George, N., Lachaux, J-P., Martinerie, J., Renault, B., & Varela, F. J. (1999). Perception's shadow: Long-distance synchronization of human brain activity. *Nature, 297,* 430–433.

Roediger, H. (2001, September). Quoted by R. Herbert, Doing a number on memory. *APS Observer,* pp. 1, 7–11.

Roediger, H. L., III, & McDermott, K. B. (1995). Creating false memories: Remembering words not presented in lists. *Journal of Experimental Psychology: Learning, Memory, and Cognition, 21,* 803–814.

Roediger, H. L., III, Wheeler, M. A., & Rajaram, S. (1993). Remembering, knowing, and reconstructing the past. In D. L. Medin (Ed.), *The psychology of learning and motivation: Advances in research and theory* (Vol. 30). Orlando, FL: Academic Press.

Roehling, M. V. (1999). Weight-based discrimination in employment: Psychological and legal aspects. *Personnel Psychology, 52,* 969–1016.

Roehling, P. V., Roehling, M. V., & Moen, P. (2001). The relationship between work-life policies and practices and employee loyalty: A life course perspective. *Journal of Family and Economic Issues, 22,* 141–170.

Roenneberg, T., Kuehnle, T., Pramstaller, P. P., Ricken, J., Havel, M., Guth, A., Merrow, M. (2004). A marker for the end of adolescence. *Current Biology, 14,* R1038–9.

Roesser, R. (1998). What you should know about hearing conservation. Better Hearing Institute (www.betterhearing.org).

Rogers, C. R. (1958). Reinhold Niebuhr's *The self and the dramas of history:* A criticism. *Pastoral Psychology, 9,* 15–17.

Rogers, C. R. (1961). *On becoming a person: A therapist's view of psychotherapy.* Boston: Houghton Mifflin.

Rogers, C. R. (1980). *A way of being.* Boston: Houghton Mifflin.

Rogers, C. R. (1981, Summer). Notes on Rollo May. *Perspectives, 2*(1), p. 16.

Rogers, L. J. (2003, Fall). Seeking the right answers about right brain-left brain. *Cerebrum, 5*(4), 55–68.

Rogers, S. (1992-1993, Winter). How a publicity blitz created the myth of subliminal advertising. *Public Relations Quarterly,* pp. 12–17.

Rogers, S. (1994). Subliminal advertising: Grand scam of the 20th century. Paper presented to the American Academy of Advertising convention.

Rogerson, P. A. (1994). On the relationship between handedness and longevity. *Social Biology, 40,* 283–287.

Rohan, M. J., & Zanna, M. P. (1996). Value transmission in families," in C. Seligman, J. M. Olson, & M. P. Zanna (Eds.), *The psychology of values: The Ontario Symposium* (Vol. 8). Malwah, NJ: Erlbaum.

Rohner, R. P. (1986). *The warmth dimension: Foundations of parental acceptance-rejection theory.* Newbury Park, CA: Sage.

Rohner, R. P., & Veneziano, R. A. (2001). The importance of father love: History and contemporary evidence. *Review of General Psychology, 5,* 382–405.

Roiser, J. P., Cook, L. J., Cooper, J. D., Rubinsztein, D. C., & Sahakian, B. J. (2005). Association of a functional polymorphism in the serotonin transporter gene with abnormal emotional processing in ecstasy users. *American Journal of Psychiatry, 162,* 609–612.

Rokach, A., Orzeck, T., Moya, M., & Exposito, F. (2002). Causes of loneliness in North America and Spain. *European Psychologist, 7,* 70–79.

Rosch, E. (1974). Linguistic relativity. In A. Silverstein (Ed.), *Human communication: Theoretical perspectives.* New York: Halsted Press.

Rosch, E. (1978). Principles of categorization. In E. Rosch & B. L. Lloyd (Eds.), *Cognition and categorization.* Hillsdale, NJ: Erlbaum.

Rose, J. S., Chassin, L., Presson, C. C., & Sherman, S. J. (1999). Peer influences on adolescent cigarette smoking: A prospective sibling analysis. *Merrill-Palmer Quarterly, 45,* 62–84.

Rose, R. J., Kaprio, J., Winter, T., Dick, D. M., Viken, R. J., Pulkkinen, L., & Koskenvuo, M. (2002). Femininity and fertility in sisters with twin brothers: Prenatal androgenization? Cross-sex socialization? *Psychological Science, 13,* 263–266.

Rose, R. J., Viken, R. J., Dick, D. M., Bates, J. E., Pulkkinen, L., & Kaprio, J. (2003a). It *does* take a village: Nonfamiliar environments and children's behavior. *Psychological Science, 14,* 273–277.

Rose, S. (1999). Precis of *Lifelines: Biology, freedom, determinism. Behavioral and Brain Sciences, 22,* 871–921.

Rose, S., Bisson, J., & Wessely, S. (2003b). A systematic review of single-session psychological interventions ('debriefing') following trauma. *Psychotherapy and Psychosomatics, 72,* 176–184.

Roselli, C. E., Resko, J. A., & Stormshak, F. (2002). Hormonal influences on sexual partner preference in rams. *Archives of Sexual Behavior, 31,* 43–9.

Rosenbaum, M. (1986). The repulsion hypothesis: On the nondevelopment of relationships. *Journal of Personality and Social Psychology, 51,* 1156–1166.

Rosenberg, N. A., Pritchard, J. K., Weber, J. L., Cann, H. M., Kidd, K. K., Zhivotosky, L. A., & Feldman, M. W. (2002). Genetic structure of human populations. *Science, 298,* 2381–2385.

Rosenhan, D. L. (1973). On being sane in insane places. *Science, 179,* 250–258.

Rosenthal, R., Hall, J. A., Archer, D., DiMatteo, M. R., & Rogers, P. L. (1979). The PONS test: Measuring sensitivity to nonverbal cues. In S. Weitz (Ed.), *Nonverbal communication* (2nd ed.). New York: Oxford University Press.

Rosenzweig, M. R. (1984). Experience, memory, and the brain. *American Psychologist, 39,* 365–376.

Ross, L., Greene, D., & House, P. (1977). The false consensus effect: An egocentric bias in social perception and attribution process. *Journal of Experimental Social Psychology, 13,* 279–301.

Ross, M., McFarland, C., & Fletcher, G. J. O. (1981). The effect of attitude on the recall of personal histories. *Journal of Personality and Social Psychology, 40,* 627–634.

Ross, M., Xun, W. Q. E., & Wilson, A. E. (2002). Language and the bicultural self. *Personality and Social Psychology Bulletin, 28,* 1040–1050.

Rossi, A. S., & Rossi, P. H. (1993). *Of human bonding: Parent-child relations across the life course.* Hawthorne, NY: Aldine de Gruyter.

Rossi, P. J. (1968). Adaptation and negative after effect to lateral optical displacement in newly hatched chicks. *Science, 160,* 430–432.

Rostosky, S. S., Wilcox, B. L., Wright, M. L. C., & Randall, B. A. (2004). The impact of religiosity on adolescent sexual behavior: A review of the evidence. *Journal of Adolescent Research, 19,* 677–697.

Roth, T., Roehrs, T., Zwyghuizen-Doorenbos, A., Stpeanski, E., & Witting, R. (1988). Sleep and memory. In I. Hindmarch & H. Ott (Eds.), *Benzodiazepine receptor ligans, memory and information processing.* New York: Springer-Verlag.

Rothbart, M., Fulero, S., Jensen, C., Howard, J., & Birrell, P. (1978). From individual to group impressions: Availability heuristics in stereotype formation. *Journal of Experimental Social Psychology, 14,* 237–255.

Rothbart, M. K., Ahadi, S. A., & Evans, D. E. (2000). Temperament and personality: Origins and outcomes. *Journal of Personality and Social Psychology, 78,* 122–135.

Rothbaum, B. O., Hodges, L., Anderson, P. L., Price, L., & Smith, S. (2002). Twelve-month followup of virtual reality and standard exposure therapies for the fear of flying. *Journal of Consulting and Clinical Psychology, 70,* 428–432.

Rothbaum, F., & Tsang, B. Y-P. (1998). Lovesongs in the United States and China: On the nature of romantic love. *Journal of Cross-Cultural Psychology, 29,* 306–319.

Rothman, A. J., & Salovey, P. (1997). Shaping perceptions to motivate healthy behavior: The role of message framing. *Psychological Bulletin, 121,* 3–19.

Rothstein, W. G. (1980). The significance of occupations in work careers: An empirical and theoretical review. *Journal of Vocational Behavior, 17,* 328–343.

Rotton, J., & Kelly, I. W. (1985). Much ado about the full moon: A meta-analysis of lunar-lunacy research. *Psychological Bulletin, 97,* 286–306.

Rovee-Collier, C. (1989). The joy of kicking: Memories, motives, and mobiles. In P. R. Solomon, G. R. Goethals, C. M. Kelley, & B. R. Stephens (Eds.), *Memory: Interdisciplinary approaches.* New York: Springer-Verlag.

Rovee-Collier, C. (1993). The capacity for long-term memory in infancy. *Current Directions in Psychological Science, 2,* 130–135.

Rovee-Collier, C. (1997). Dissociations in infant memory: Rethinking the development of implicit and explicit memory. *Psychological Review, 104,* 467–498.

Rowe, D. C. (1990). As the twig is bent? The myth of child-rearing influences on personality development. *Journal of Counseling and Development, 68,* 606–611.

Rowe, D. C. (2005). Under the skin: On the impartial treatment of genetic and environmental hypotheses of racial differences. *American Psychologist, 60,* 60–70.

Rowe, D. C., Almeida, D. M., & Jacobson, K. C. (1999). School context and genetic influences on aggression in adolescence. *Psychological Science, 10,* 277–280.

Rowe, D. C., Jacobson, K. C., & Van den Oord, E. J. C. G. (1999). Genetic and environmental influences on vocabulary IQ: Parental education level as moderator. *Child Development, 70*(5), 1151–1162.

Rowe, D. C., Vazsonyi, A. T., & Flannery, D. J. (1994). No more than skin deep: Ethnic and racial similarity in developmental process. *Psychological Review, 101*(3), 396.

Rowe, D. C., Vazsonyi, A. T., & Flannery, D. J. (1995). Ethnic and racial similarity in developmental process: A study of academic achievement. *Psychological Science, 6,* 33–38.

Rozin, P., Dow, S., Mosovitch, M., & Rajaram, S. (1998). What causes humans to begin and end a meal? A role for memory for what has been eaten, as evidenced by a study of multiple meal eating in amnesic patients. *Psychological Science, 9,* 392–396.

Rozin, P., Millman, L., & Nemeroff, C. (1986). Operation of the laws of sympathetic magic in disgust and other domains. *Journal of Personality and Social Psychology, 50,* 703–712.

Ruback, R. B., Carr, T. S., & Hopper, C. H. (1986). Perceived control in prison: Its relation to reported crowding, stress, and symptoms. *Journal of Applied Social Psychology, 16,* 375–386.

Rubenstein, J. S., Meyer, D. E., & Evans, J. E. (2001). Executive control of cognitive processes in task switching. *Journal of Experimental Psychology: Human Perception and Performance, 27,* 763–797.

Rubin, D. C., Rahhal, T. A., & Poon, L. W. (1998). Things learned in early adulthood are remembered best. *Memory and Cognition, 26,* 3–19.

Rubin, J. Z., Pruitt, D. G., & Kim, S. H. (1994). *Social conflict: Escalation, stalemate, and settlement.* New York: McGraw-Hill.

Rubin, L. B. (1985). *Just friends: The role of friendship in our lives.* New York: Harper & Row.

Rubin, Z. (1970). Measurement of romantic love. *Journal of Personality and Social Psychology, 16,* 265–273.

Rubonis, A. V., & Bickman, L. (1991). Psychological impairment in the wake of disaster: The disaster-psychopathology relationship. *Psychological Bulletin, 109,* 384–399.

Ruchlis, H. (1990). *Clear thinking: A practical introduction.* Buffalo, NY: Prometheus Books.

Rudman, L. A., & Goodwin, S. A. (2004). Gender differences in automatic in-group bias: Why do women like women more than men like men? *Journal of Personality and Social Psychology, 87,* 494–509.

Ruffin, C. L. (1993). Stress and health—little hassles vs. major life events. *Australian Psychologist, 28,* 201–208.

Rule, B. G., & Ferguson, T. J. (1986). The effects of media violence on attitudes, emotions, and cognitions. *Journal of Social Issues, 42*(3), 29–50.

Rumbaugh, D. M. (1977). *Language learning by a chimpanzee: The Lana project.* New York: Academic Press.

Rumbaugh, D. M. (1994, February 15). Remarks on *Nova: Can chimps talk?* PBS Television.

Rumbaugh, D. M., & Savage-Rumbaugh, S. (1978). Chimpanzee language research: Status and potential. *Behavior Research Methods & Instrumentation, 10,* 119–131.

Rumbaugh, D. M., & Savage-Rumbaugh, S. (1994, January/February). Language and apes. *Psychology Teacher Network,* pp. 2–5, 9.

Rumbaugh, D. M., & Washburn, D. A. (2003). *Intelligence of apes and other rational beings.* New Haven, CT: Yale University Press.

Rupp, R. (1998). *How we remember and why we forget.* New York: Three Rivers Press.

Rush, A. J., & 15 others (2005). Vagus nerve stimulation for treatment-resistant depression: A randomized, controlled acute phase trial. *Biological Psychiatry, 58,* 347–354.

Rushton, J. P. (1975). Generosity in children: Immediate and long-term effects of modeling, preaching, and moral judgment. *Journal of Personality and Social Psychology, 31,* 459–466.

Rushton, J. P. (1998). The "Jensen effect" and the "Spearman-Jensen hypothesis" of black-white IQ differences. *Intelligence, 26,* 217–225.

Rushton, J. P. (2003). Race, brain size, and IQ: The case for consilience. *Behavioral and Brain Sciences, 26,* 648–649.

Rushton, J. P., & Ankney, C. D. (1996). Brain size and cognitive ability: Correlations with age, sex, social class, and race. *Psychonomic Bulletin & Review, 3,* 21–36.

Russell, B. (1930/1985). *The conquest of happiness.* London: Unwin Paperbacks.

Russell, J. A., & Carroll, J. M. (January, 1999a). On the bipolarity of positive and negative affect. *Psychological Bulletin, 125,* 3–30.

Russell, J. A., & Carroll, J. M. (1999b). The phoenix of bipolarity: Reply to Watson and Tellegan (1999). *Psychological Bulletin, 125,* 611–614.

Russell, J. A., Lewicka, M., & Niit, T. (1989). A cross-cultural study of a circumplex model of affect. *Journal of Personality and Social Psychology, 57,* 848–856.

Rusting, C. L., & Nolen-Hoeksema, S. (1998). Regulating responses to anger: Effects of rumination and distraction on angry mood. *Journal of Personality and Social Psychology, 74,* 790–803.

Rutter, M., and the English and Romanian Adoptees (ERA) study team. (1998). Developmental catch-up, and deficit, following adoption after severe global early privation. *Journal of Child Psychology and Psychiatry, 39,* 465–476.

Ryan, L., Hatfield, C., & Hofstetter, M. (2002). Caffeine reduces time-of-day effects on memory performance in older adults. *Psychological Science, 13,* 68–71.

Ryan, R. (1999, February 2). Quoted by Alfie Kohn, In pursuit of affluence, at a high price. *New York Times* (www.nytimes.com).

Ryan, R. M., & Deci, E. L. (2004). Avoiding death or engaging life as accounts of meaning and culture: Comment on Pyszczynski et al. (2004). *Psychological Bulletin, 130,* 473–477.

Ryckman, R. M., Robbins, M. A., Kaczor, L. M., & Gold J. A. (1989). Male and female raters' stereotyping of male and female physiques. *Personality and Social Psychology Bulletin, 15,* 244–251.

Saad, L. (2001, December 17). Americans' mood: Has Sept. 11 made a difference? Gallup Poll News Service (www.gallup.com/poll/releases/pr011217.asp).

Saad, L. (2002, July 30). Dieter's dilemma: Bagel or bacon? *Gallup Tuesday Briefing,* Gallup Organization (www.gallup.com/poll/tb/healthcare/20020730.asp).

Saad, L. (2002, November 21). Most smokers wish they could quit. Gallup News Service (www.gallup.com).

Saad, L. (2003, December 9). Religion is very important to majority of Americans. Gallup News Service (www.gallup.com).

Sabini, J. (1986). Stanley Milgram (1933–1984). *American Psychologist, 41,* 1378–1379.

Sabol, S. Z., Nelson, M. L., Fisher, C., Gunzerath, L., Brody, C. L., Hu, S., Sirota, L. A., Marcus, S. E., Greenberg, B. D., Lucas, F. R., IV, Benjamin, J. Murphy, D. L., & Hamer, D. H. (1999). A genetic association for cigarette smoking behavior. *Health Psychology, 18,* 7–13.

Sachdev, P., & Sachdev, J. (1997). Sixty years of psychosurgery: Its present status and its future. *Australian and New Zealand Journal of Psychiatry, 31,* 457–464.

Sacks, O. (1985). *The man who mistook his wife for a hat.* New York: Summit Books.

Sacks, O. (1990). *Seeing voices: A journey into the world of the deaf.* New York: HarperCollins.

Sadato, N., Pascual-Leone, A., Grafman, J., Ibanez, V., Deiber, M-P., Dold, G., & Hallett, M. (1996). Activation of the primary visual cortex by Braille reading in blind subjects. *Nature, 380,* 526–528.

Saffran, J. R., Aslin, R. N., & Newport, E. L. (1996). Statistical learning by 8-month-old infants. *Science, 274,* 1926–1928.

Sagan, C. (1979). *Broca's brain.* New York: Random House.

Sagan, C. (1987, February 1). The fine art of baloney detection. *Parade.*

Sagan, C., & Druyan, A. (1992). *Shadows of forgotten ancestors: A search for who we are.* New York: Random House.

Sage, C., Huang, M., Karimi, K., Gutierrez, G., Vollrath, M. A., Zhang, D-S., Garcia-Anoveros, J., Hinds, P. W., Corwin, J. T., Coren, D. P., & Chen, Z-Y. (2005). Proliferation of functional hair cells in vivo in the absence of the retinoblastoma protein. *Science, 307,* 1114–1118.

Sakurai, T., Amemiya, A., Ishii, M., Matsuzaki, I., Chemelli, R. M., Tanaka, H., Williams, S. C., Richardson, J. A., Kozlowski, G. P., Wilson, S., Arch, J. R. S., Buckingham, R. E., Haynes, A. C., Carr, S. A., Annan, R. S., McNulty, D. E., Liu, W-S., Terrett, J. A., Elshourbagy, N. A., Bergsma, D. J., Yanagisawa, M. (1998). Orexins and orexin receptors: A family of hypothalamic neuropeptides and G protein-coupled receptors that regulate feeding behavior. *Cell, 92,* 573–585.

Salive, M. E., Guralnik, J. M., & Glynn, R. J. (1993). Left-handedness and mortality. *American Journal of Public Health, 83,* 265–267.

Salmon, P. (2001). Effects of physical exercise on anxiety, depression, and sensitivity to stress: A unifying theory. *Clinical Psychology Review, 21,* 33–61.

Salovey, P. (1990, January/February). Interview. *American Scientist,* pp. 25–29.

Salovey, P., & Birnbaum, D. (1989). Influence of mood on health-relevant cognitions. *Journal of Personality and Social Psychology, 57,* 539–551.

Salovey, P., & Mayer, J. D. (1990). Emotional intelligence. *Imagination, Cognition, and Personality, 9,* 185–211.

Salovey, P., Mayer, J. D., & Caruso, D. (2002). The positive psychology of emotional intelligence. In C. R. Snyder & S. J. Lopez (Eds.), *Handbook of positive psychology.* New York: Oxford.

Salthouse, T. A. (2004). What and when of cognitive aging. *Current Directions in Psychological Science, 13,* 140–144.

Sampson, E. E. (2000). Reinterpreting individualism and collectivism: Their religious roots and monologic versus dialogic person–other relationship. *American Psychologist, 55,* 1425–1432.

Samuels, J., & Nestadt, G. (1997). Epidemiology and genetics of obsessive-compulsive disorder. *International Review of Psychiatry, 9,* 61–71.

Samuels, S., & McCabe, G. (1989). Quoted by P. Diaconis & F. Mosteller, Methods for studying coincidences. *Journal of the American Statistical Association, 84,* 853–861.

Sandberg, G. G., Jackson, T. L., & Petretic-Jackson, P. (1985). *Sexual aggression and courtship violence in dating relationships.* Paper presented at the meeting of the Midwestern Psychological Association.

Sanders, G., Sjodin, M., & de Chastelaine, M. (2002). On the elusive nature of sex differences in cognition hormonal influences contributing to within-sex variation. *Archives of Sexual Behavior, 31,* 145–152.

Sanders, G., & Wright, M. (1997). Sexual orientation differences in cerebral asymmetry and in the performance of sexually dimorphic cognitive and motor tasks. *Archives of Sexual Behavior, 26,* 463–479.

Sandfort, T. G. M., de Graaf, R., Bijl, R., & Schnabel, P. (2001). Same-sex sexual behavior and psychiatric disorders. *Archives of General Psychiatry, 58,* 85–91.

Sandler, W., Meir, I., Padden, C., & Aronoff, M. (2005). The emergence of grammar: Systematic structure in a new language. *Proceedings of the National Academy of Sciences, 102,* 2261–2265.

Sanford, A. J., Fray, N., Stewart, A., & Moxey, L. (2002). Perspective in statements of quantity, with implications for consumer psychology. *Psychological Science, 13,* 130–134.

Santarelli, L., & 11 others (2003). Requirement of hippocampal neurogenesis for the behavioral effects of antidepressants. *Science, 301,* 805–809.

Sanz, C., Blicher, A., Dalke, K., Gratton-Fabri, L., McClure-Richards, T., & Fouts, R. (1998, Winter-Spring). Enrichment object use: Five chimpanzees' use of temporary and semi-permanent enrichment objects. *Friends of Washoe, 19*(1,2), 9–14.

Sanz, C., Morgan, D., Gulick, S. (2004). New insights into chimpanzees, tools, and termites from the Congo Basin. *American Naturalist, 164,* 567–581.

Sapadin, L. A. (1988). Friendship and gender: Perspectives of professional men and women. *Journal of Social and Personal Relationships, 5,* 387–403.

Sapolsky, B. S., & Tabarlet, J. O. (1991). Sex in primetime television: 1979 versus 1989. *Journal of Broadcasting and Electronic Media, 35,* 505–516.

Sapolsky, R. (1999, March). Stress and your shrinking brain. *Discover,* pp. 116–120.

Sapolsky, R. (2003, September). Taming stress. *Scientific American,* pp. 87–95.

Sapolsky, R. (2005). The influence of social hierarchy on primate health. *Science, 308,* 648–652.

Sapolsky, R. M., & Finch, C. E. (1991, March/April). On growing old. *The Sciences,* pp. 30–38.

Sato, K. (1987). Distribution of the cost of maintaining common resources. *Journal of Experimental Social Psychology, 23,* 19–31.

Saudino, K. J., Wertz, A. E., Gagne, J. R., & Chawla, S. (2004). Night and day: Are siblings as different in temperament as parents say they are? *Journal of Personality and Social Psychology, 87,* 698–706.

Savage-Rumbaugh, E. S., Murphy, J., Sevcik, R. A., Brakke, K. E., Williams, S. L., & Rumbaugh, D. M., with commentary by Bates, E. (1993). Language comprehension in ape and child. *Monographs of the Society for Research in Child Development, 58* (no. 233), 1–254.

Savic, I., Berglund, H., & Lindstrom, P. (2005). Brain response to putative pheromones in homosexual men. *Proceedings of the National Academy of Sciences, 102,* 7356–7361.

Savitsky, K., Epley, N., & Gilovich, T. (2001). Do others judge us as harshly as we think? Overestimating the impact of our failures, shortcomings, and mishaps. *Journal of Personality and Social Psychology, 81,* 44–56.

Savitsky, K., & Gilovich, T. (2003). The illusion of transparency and the alleviation of speech anxiety. *Journal of Experimental Social Psychology, 39,* 618–625.

Savoy, C., & Beitel, P. (1996). Mental imagery for basketball. *International Journal of Sport Psychology, 27*, 454–462.

Sawyer, M. G., Arney, F. M., Baghurst, P. A., Clark, J. J., Graetz, B. W., Kosky, R. J., Nurcombe, B., Patton, G. C., Prior, M. R., Raphael, B., Rey, J., Whaites, L. C., & Zubrick, S. R. (2000). *The mental health of young people in Australia.* Canberra: Mental Health and Special Programs Branch, Commonwealth Department of Health and Aged Care.

Sax, L. J., Hurtado, S., Lindholm, J A., Astin, A. W., Korn, W. S., & Mahoney, K. M. (2004). *The American freshman: National norms for Fall, 2004.* Los Angeles: Cooperative Institutional Research Program, UCLA.

Sax, L. J., Lindholm, J. A., Astin, A. W., Korn, W. S., & Mahoney, K. M. (2002). *The American freshman: National norms for Fall 2002.* Los Angeles, CA: Higher Education Research Institute, UCLA.

Sayre, R. F. (1979). The parents' last lessons. In D. D. Van Tassel (Ed.), *Aging, death, and the completion of being.* Philadelphia: University of Pennsylvania Press.

Sbraga, T. P., & O'Donohue, W. (2003). Post hoc reasoning in possible cases of child sexual abuse: Symptoms of inconclusive origins. *Clinical Psychology: Science and Practice, 10*, 320–334.

Scarborough, E., & Furumoto, L. (1987). *Untold lives: The first generation of American women psychologists.* New York: Columbia University Press.

Scarr, S. (1984, May). What's a parent to do? A conversation with E. Hall. *Psychology Today,* pp. 58–63.

Scarr, S. (1986). *Mother care/other care.* New York: Basic Books.

Scarr, S. (1989). Protecting general intelligence: Constructs and consequences for interventions. In R. J. Linn (Ed.), *Intelligence: Measurement, theory, and public policy.* Champaign: University of Illinois Press.

Scarr, S. (1990). Back cover comments on J. Dunn & R. Plomin (1990). *Separate lives: Why siblings are so different.* New York: Basic Books.

Scarr, S. (1993, May/June). Quoted by *Psychology Today,* Nature's thumbprint: So long, superparents, p. 16.

Scarr, S. (1997). Why child care has little impact on most children's development. *Current Directions in Psychological Science, 6*, 143–148.

Schab, F. R. (1991). Odor memory: Taking stock. *Psychological Bulletin, 109*, 242–251.

Schachter, S. (1982). Recidivism and self-cure of smoking and obesity. *American Psychologist, 37*, 436–444.

Schachter, S., & Singer, J. E. (1962). Cognitive, social and physiological determinants of emotional state. *Psychological Review, 69*, 379–399.

Schacter, D. L. (1992). Understanding implicit memory: A cognitive neuroscience approach. *American Psychologist, 47*, 559–569.

Schacter, D. L. (1996). *Searching for memory: The brain, the mind, and the past.* New York: Basic Books.

Schacter, D. L. (1999). The seven sins of memory: Insights from psychology and cognitive neuroscience. *American Psychologist, 54*, 182–201.

Schafer, G. (2005). Infants can learn decontextualized words before their first birthday. *Child Development, 76*, 87–96.

Schaie, K. W. (1994). The life course of adult intellectual abilities. *American Psychologist, 49*, 304–313.

Schaie, K. W., & Geiwitz, J. (1982). *Adult development and aging.* Boston: Little, Brown.

Schall, T., & Smith, G. (2000, Fall). Career trajectories in baseball. *Chance,* pp. 35–38.

Scheier, M. F., & Carver, C. S. (1992). Effects of optimism on psychological and physical well-being: Theoretical overview and empirical update. *Cognitive Therapy and Research, 16*, 201–228.

Schein, E. H. (1956). The Chinese indoctrination program for prisoners of war: A study of attempted brainwashing. *Psychiatry, 19*, 149–172.

Schelling, T. C. (1992). Addictive drugs: The cigarette experience. *Science, 255*, 430–433.

Scherer, K. R., Banse, R., & Wallbott, H. G. (2001). Emotion inferences from vocal expression correlate across languages and cultures. *Journal of Cross-Cultural Psychology, 32*, 76–92.

Schiavi, R. C., & Schreiner-Engel, P. (1988). Nocturnal penile tumescence in healthy aging men. *Journal of Gerontology: Medical Sciences, 43*, M146–150.

Schiffenbauer, A., & Schiavo, R. S. (1976). Physical distance and attraction: An intensification effect. *Journal of Experimental Social Psychology, 12*, 274–282.

Schimel, J., Arndt, J., Pyszczynski, T., & Greenberg, J. (2001). Being accepted for who we are: Evidence that social validation of the intrinsic self reduces general defensiveness. *Journal of Personality and Social Psychology, 80*, 35–52.

Schimel, J., Greenberg, J., & Martens, A. (2003). Evidence that projection of a feared trait can serve a defensive function. *Personality and Social Psychology Bulletin, 29*, 969–979.

Schlaug, G., Jancke, L., Huang, Y., & Steinmetz, H. (1995). In vivo evidence of structural brain asymmetry in musicians. *Science, 267*, 699–701.

Schmidt, F. L. (2002). The role of general cognitive ability and job performance: Why there cannot be a debate. *Human Performance, 15*, 187–210.

Schmidt, F. L., & Hunter, J. E. (1998). The validity and utility of selection methods in personnel psychology: Practical and theoretical implications of 85 years of research findings. *Psychological Bulletin, 124*, 262–274.

Schmidt, F. L., & Zimmerman, R. D. (2004). A counterintuitive hypothesis about employment interview validity and some supporting evidence. *Journal of Applied Psychology, 89*, 553–561.

Schmitt, D. P., & Pilcher, J. J. (2004). Evaluating evidence of psychological adaptation: How do we know one when we see one? *Psychological Science, 15*, 643–649.

Schnaper, N. (1980). Comments germane to the paper entitled "The reality of death experiences" by Ernst Rodin. *Journal of Nervous and Mental Disease, 168*, 268–270.

Schneider, R. H., Alexander, C. N., Staggers, F., Rainforth, M., Salerno, J. W., Hartz, A., Arndt, S., Barnes, V. A., & Nidich, S. (2005). Long-term effects of stress reduction on mortality in persons > or = 55 years of age with systemic hypertension. *American Journal of Cardiology, 95*, 1060–1064.

Schneider, S. L. (2001). In search of realistic optimism: Meaning, knowledge, and warm fuzziness. *American Psychologist, 56*, 250–263.

Schneiderman, N. (1999). Behavioral medicine and the management of HIV/AIDS. *International Journal of Behavioral Medicine, 6*, 3–12.

Schneiderman, N., Chesney, M. A., & Krantz, D. S. (1989). Biobehavioral aspects of cardiovascular disease: Progress and prospects. *Health Psychology, 8*, 649–676.

Schoeneman, T. J. (1994). *Individualism.* In V. S. Ramachandran (Ed.), *Encyclopedia of Human Behavior.* San Diego: Academic Press.

Schofield, J. W. (1986). Black-White contact in desegregated schools. In M. Hewstone & R. Brown (Eds.), *Contact and conflict in intergroup encounters.* Oxford: Basil Blackwell.

Schonfield, D., & Robertson, B. A. (1966). Memory storage and aging. *Canadian Journal of Psychology, 20*, 228–236.

Schooler, J. W., Gerhard, D., & Loftus, E. F. (1986). Qualities of the unreal. *Journal of Experimental Psychology: Learning, Memory, and Cognition, 12*, 171–181.

Schulenberg, J., Bachman, J. G., O'Malley, P. M., & Johnston, L. D. (March, 1994). High school educational success and subsequent substance use: A panel analysis following adolescents into young adulthood. *Journal of Health & Social Behavior, 35*(1), 45–62.

Schuman, H., & Scott, J. (June, 1989). Generations and collective memories. *American Sociological Review, 54*(3), 359–381.

Schwartz, B. (1984). *Psychology of learning and behavior* (2nd ed.). New York: Norton.

Schwartz, B. (2000). Self-determination: The tyranny of freedom. *American Psychologist, 55,* 79–88.

Schwartz, B. (2004). *The paradox of choice: Why more is less.* New York: Ecco/HarperCollins.

Schwartz, J., & Estrin, J. (2004, November 7). Living for today, locked in a paralyzed body. *New York Times* (www.nytimes.com).

Schwartz, J., & Pomfret, J. (1998, November 20). Smoking-related deaths in China are up sharply. *Washington Post* (www.washingtonpost.com).

Schwartz, J. M., Stoessel, P. W., Baxter, L. R., Jr., Martin, K. M., & Phelps, M. E. (1996). Systematic changes in cerebral glucose metabolic rate after successful behavior modification treatment of obsessive-compulsive disorder. *Archives of General Psychiatry, 53,* 109–113.

Schwarz, N., Strack, F., Kommer, D., & Wagner, D. (1987). Soccer, rooms, and the quality of your life: Mood effects on judgments of satisfaction with life in general and with specific domains. *European Journal of Social Psychology, 17,* 69–79.

Science (2004). Obesity drugs. *Science, 306,* 2014.

Sclafani, A. (1995). How food preferences are learned: Laboratory animal models. *Proceedings of the Nutrition Society, 54,* 419–427.

Scott, D. J., & others. (2004, November 9). U-M team reports evidence that smoking affects human brain's natural "feel good" chemical system (press release by Kara Gavin). University of Michigan Medical School (www.med.umich.edu).

Scott, W. A., Scott, R., & McCabe, M. (1991). Family relationships and children's personality: A cross-cultural, cross-source comparison. *British Journal of Social Psychology, 30,* 1–20.

Sechrest, L., Stickle, T. R., & Stewart, M. (1998). The role of assessment in clinical psychology. In A. Bellack, M. Hersen (Series eds.) & C. R. Reynolds (Vol. ed.), *Comprehensive clinical psychology: Vol 4: Assessment.* New York: Pergamon.

Seeman, P., Guan, H-C., & Van Tol, H. H. M. (1993). Dopamine D4 receptors elevated in schizophrenia. *Nature, 365,* 441–445.

Segal, N. L. (1999). *Entwined lives: Twins and what they tell us about human behavior.* New York: Dutton.

Segal, N. L. (2000). Virtual twins: New findings on within-family environmental influences on intelligence. *Journal of Educational Psychology, 92,* 442–448.

Segall, M. H., Dasen, P. R., Berry, J. W., & Poortinga, Y. H. (1990). *Human behavior in global perspective: An introduction to cross-cultural psychology.* New York: Pergamon.

Segerstrom, S. C., McCarthy, W. J., Caskey, N. H., Gross, T. D., & Jarvik, M. E. (1993). Optimistic bias among cigarette smokers. *Journal of Applied Social Psychology, 23,* 1606–1618.

Segerstrom, S. C., Taylor, S. E., Kemeny, M. E., & Fahey, J. L. (1998). Optimism is associated with mood, coping, and immune change in response to stress. *Journal of Personality and Social Psychology, 74,* 1646–1655.

Segerstrom, S., & Miller, G. E. (2004). Psychological stress and the human immune system: A meta-analytic study of 30 years of inquiry. *Psychological Bulletin, 130,* 601–630.

Seidlitz, L., & Diener, E. (1998). Sex differences in the recall of affective experiences. *Journal of Personality and Social Psychology, 74,* 262–271.

Self, C. E. (1994). *Moral culture and victimization in residence halls.* Dissertation: Thesis (M.A.). Bowling Green University.

Seligman, M. E. P. (1974, May). Submissive death: Giving up on life. *Psychology Today,* pp. 80–85.

Seligman, M. E. P. (1975). *Helplessness: On depression, development and death.* San Francisco: Freeman.

Seligman, M. E. P. (1991). *Learned optimism.* New York: Knopf.

Seligman, M. E. P. (1994). *What you can change and what you can't.* New York: Knopf.

Seligman, M. E. P. (1995). The effectiveness of psychotherapy: The *Consumer Reports* study. *American Psychologist, 50,* 965–974.

Seligman, M. E. P. (2002). *Authentic happiness: Using the new positive psychology to realize your potential for lasting fulfillment.* New York: Free Press.

Seligman, M. E. P. (2004). Eudaemonia, the good life. A talk with Martin Seligman. www.edge.org.

Seligman, M. E. P., & Schulman, P. (1986). Explanatory style as a predictor of productivity and quitting among life insurance sales agents. *Journal of Personality and Social Psychology, 50,* 832–838.

Seligman, M. E. P., Steen, T. A., Park, N., & Peterson, C. (2005). Positive psychology progress: Empirical validation of interventions. *American Psychologist, 60,* 410–421.

Seligman, M. E. P., & Yellen, A. (1987). What is a dream? *Behavior Research and Therapy, 25,* 1–24.

Selye, H. (1936). A syndrome produced by diverse nocuous agents. *Nature, 138,* 32.

Selye, H. (1976). *The stress of life.* New York: McGraw-Hill.

Sen, A. (2003). Missing women—revisited. *British Medical Journal, 327,* 1297–1298.

Senghas, A., & Coppola, M. (2001). Children creating language: How Nicaraguan Sign Language acquired a spatial grammar. *Psychological Science, 12,* 323–328.

Sengupta, S. (2001, October 10). Sept. 11 attack narrows the racial divide. *New York Times* (www.nytimes.com).

Serdula, M. K., Mokdad, A., Williamson, D. F., Galuska, D. A., Mendlein, J. M., & Heath, G. W. (1999). Prevalence of attempting weight loss and strategies for controlling weight. *Journal of the American Medical Association, 282,* 1353–1358.

Sergent, C., & Dehaene, S. (2004). Is consciousness a gradual phenomenon? *Psychological Science, 15,* 720–728.

Serruya, M. D., Hatsopoulos, N. G., Paninski, L., Fellow, M. R., & Donoghue, J. P. (2002). Instant neural control of a movement signal. *Nature, 416,* 141–142.

Service, R. F. (1994). Will a new type of drug make memory-making easier? *Science, 266,* 218–219.

Seto, M. C., & Barbaree, H. E. (1995). The role of alcohol in sexual aggression. *Clinical Psychology Review, 15,* 545–566.

Shadish, W. R., Baldwin, S. A. (2005). Effects of behavioral marital therapy: A meta-analysis of randomized controlled trials. *Journal of Consulting and Clinical Psychology, 73,* 6–14.

Shadish, W. R., Matt, G. E., Navarro, A. M., & Phillips, G. (2000). The effects of psychological therapies under clinically representative conditions: A meta-analysis. *Psychological Bulletin, 126,* 512–529.

Shadish, W. R., Montgomery, L. M., Wilson, P., Wilson, M. R., Bright, I., & Okwumabua, T. (1993). Effects of family and marital psychotherapies: A meta-analysis. *Journal of Consulting and Clinical Psychology, 61,* 992–1002.

Shaffer, D. M., Krauchunas, S. M., Eddy, M., & McBeath, M. K. (2004). How dogs navigate to catch frisbees. *Psychological Science, 15,* 437–441.

Shafir, E., & LeBoeuf, R. A. (2002). Rationality. *Annual Review of Psychology, 53,* 491–517.

Shamir, B., House, R. J., & Arthur, M. B. (1993). The motivational effects of charismatic leadership: A self-concept based theory. *Organizational Science, 4*(4), 577–594.

Shapiro, F. (1989). Efficacy of the eye movement desensitization procedure in the treatment of traumatic memories. *Journal of Traumatic Stress, 2,* 199–223.

Shapiro, F. (1995). *Eye movement desensitization and reprocessing: Basic principles, protocols, and procedures.* New York: Guilford.

Shapiro, F. (1999). Eye movement desensitization and reprocessing (EMDR) and the anxiety disorders: Clinical and research implications of an integrated psychotherapy treatment. *Journal of Anxiety Disorders, 13,* 35–67.

Shapiro, F. (Ed.) (2002). *EMDR as an integrative psychotherapy approach: Experts of diverse orientations explore the paradigm prism.* Washington, DC: APA Books.

Sharma, A. R., McGue, M. K., & Benson, P. L. (1998). The psychological adjustment of United States adopted adolescents and their nonadopted siblings. *Child Development, 69,* 791–802.

Shaughnessy, J., & Zechmeister, E. (1992). Memory monitoring accuracy as influenced by the distribution of retrieval practice. *Bulletin of the Psychonomic Society, 30,* 125–128.

Shaver, P. R., Morgan, H. J., & Wu, S. (1996). Is love a basic emotion? *Personal Relationships, 3,* 81–96.

Shaw, H. L. (1989–90). Comprehension of the spoken word and ASL translation by chimpanzees (Pan troglodytes). *Friends of Washoe, 9*(1/2), 8–19.

Sheehan, S. (1982). *Is there no place on earth for me?* Boston: Houghton Mifflin.

Sheldon, K. M., Elliot, A. J., Kim, Y., & Kasser, T. (2001). What is satisfying about satisfying events? Testing 10 candidate psychological needs. *Journal of Personality and Social Psychology, 80,* 325–339.

Shelton, J. N., & Richeson, J. A. (2005). Intergroup contact and pluralistic ignorance. *Journal of Personality and Social Psychology, 88,* 91–107.

Shenton, M. E. (1992). Abnormalities of the left temporal lobe and thought disorder in schizophrenia: A quantitative magnetic resonance imaging study. *New England Journal of Medicine, 327,* 604–612.

Shepard, R. N. (1990). *Mind sights.* New York: Freeman.

Shepherd, C. (1997, April). News of the weird. *Funny Times,* p. 15.

Shepherd, C. (1999, June). News of the weird. *Funny Times,* p. 21.

Shepherd, C., Kohut, J. J., & Sweet, R. (1990). *More news of the weird.* New York: Penguin/Plume Books.

Sheridan, E. P. (1999). Psychology's future in medical schools and academic health care centers. *American Psychologist, 54,* 267–271.

Sherif, M. (1966). *In common predicament: Social psychology of intergroup conflict and cooperation.* Boston: Houghton Mifflin.

Sherman, D. (2004, May 30). Doctors peer into brains to gauge antidepressants. Reuters News Service.

Sherman, P. W., & Flaxman, S. M. (2001). Protecting ourselves from food. *American Scientist, 89,* 142–151.

Shermer, M. (1999). *How we believe: The search for God in an age of science.* New York: Freeman.

Sherry, D., & Vaccarino, A. L. (1989). Hippocampus and memory for food caches in black-capped chickadees. *Behavioral Neuroscience, 103,* 308–318.

Shettleworth, S. J. (1973). Food reinforcement and the organization of behavior in golden hamsters. In R. A. Hinde & J. Stevenson-Hinde (Eds.), *Constraints on learning.* London: Academic Press.

Shettleworth, S. J. (1993). Where is the comparison in comparative cognition? Alternative research programs. *Psychological Science, 4,* 179–184.

Shneidman, E. (1987, March). At the point of no return. *Psychology Today,* pp. 54–58.

Shobe, K. K., & Kihlstrom, J. F. (June, 1997). Is traumatic memory special? *Current Directions in Psychological Science, 6*(3), 70–74.

Shotland, R. L. (1984, March 12). Quoted in Maureen Dowd, 20 years after the murder of Kitty Genovese, the question remains: Why? *The New York Times,* p. B1.

Showers, C. (1992). The motivational and emotional consequences of considering positive or negative possibilities for an upcoming event. *Journal of Personality and Social Psychology, 63,* 474–484.

Shulman, P. (2000, June). The girl who loved math. *Discover,* pp. 67–70.

Sieff, E. M., Dawes, R. M., & Loewenstein, G. (1999). Anticipated versus actual reaction to HIV test results. *The American Journal of Psychology, 112,* 297–313.

Siegel, J. M. (1990). Stressful life events and use of physician services among the elderly: The moderating role of pet ownership. *Journal of Personality and Social Psychology, 58,* 1081–1086.

Siegel, J. (2000, Winter). Recent developments in narcolepsy research: An explanation for patients and the general public. *Narcolepsy Network Newsletter,* pp. 1–2.

Siegel, J. M. (2002). Sleep. *Encarta encyclopedia* (www.bol.ucla.edu/~jsiegel/encarta/Article.htm).

Siegel, J. M. (2003, November). Why we sleep. *Scientific American,* pp. 92–97.

Siegel, R. K. (1977, October). Hallucinations. *Scientific American,* pp. 132–140.

Siegel, R. K. (1980). The psychology of life after death. *American Psychologist, 35,* 911–931.

Siegel, R. K. (1982, October). Quoted by J. Hooper, Mind tripping. *Omni,* pp. 72–82, 159–160.

Siegel, R. K. (1984, March 15). Personal communication.

Siegel, R. K. (1990). *Intoxication.* New York: Pocket Books.

Siegler, R. S., & Ellis, S. (1996). Piaget on childhood. *Psychological Science, 7,* 211–215.

Silbersweig, D. A., Stern, E., Frith, C., Cahill, C., Holmes, A., Grootoonk, S., Seaward, J., McKenna, P., Chua, S. E., Schnorr, L., Jones, T., & Frackowiak, R. S. J. (1995). A functional neuroanatomy of hallucinations in schizophrenia. *Nature, 378,* 176–179.

Silva, A. J., Stevens, C. F., Tonegawa, S., & Wang, Y. (1992). Deficient hippocampal long-term potentiation in alpha-calcium-calmodulin kinase II mutant mice. *Science, 257,* 201–206.

Silva, C. E., & Kirsch, I. (1992). Interpretive sets, expectancy, fantasy proneness, and dissociation as predictors of hypnotic response. *Journal of Personality and Social Psychology, 63,* 847–856.

Silver, M., & Geller, D. (1978). On the irrelevance of evil: The organization and individual action. *Journal of Social Issues, 34,* 125–136.

Silverman, I., & Eals, M. (1992). Sex differences in spatial abilities: Evolutionary theory and data. In J. H. Barkow, L. Cosmides, & J. Tooby (Eds.), *The adapted mind: Evolutionary psychology and the generation of culture.* New York: Oxford University Press.

Silverman, I., & Phillips, K. (1998). The evolutionary psychology of spatial sex differences. In C. Crawford & D. L. Krebs (Eds.), *Handbook of Evolutionary Psychology: Ideas, Issues, and Applications.* Mahwah, NJ: Erlbaum.

Silverman, K., Evans, S. M., Strain, E. C., & Griffiths, R. R. (1992). Withdrawal syndrome after the double-blind cessation of caffeine consumption. *New England Journal of Medicine, 327,* 1109–1114.

Silverman, P. S., & Retzlaff, P. D. (1986). Cognitive stage regression through hypnosis: Are earlier cognitive stages retrievable? *International Journal of Clinical and Experimental Hypnosis, 34,* 192–204.

Simek, T. C., & O'Brien, R. M. (1981). *Total golf: A behavioral approach to lowering your score and getting more out of your game.* Huntington, NY: B-MOD Associates.

Simek, T. C., & O'Brien, R. M. (1988). A chaining-mastery, discrimination training program to teach Little Leaguers to hit a baseball. *Human Performance, 1,* 73–84.

Simon, H. (1998, November 16). Flash of genius (interview with P. E. Ross). *Forbes,* pp. 98–104.

Simon, H. (2001, February). Quoted by A. M. Hayashi, "When to trust your gut." *Harvard Business Review,* pp. 59–65.

Simons, D. J. (1996). In sight, out of mind: When object representations fail. *Psychological Science, 7,* 301–305.

Simons, D. J., & Ambinder, M. S. (2005). Change blindness: Theory and consequences. *Current Directions in Psychological Science, 14,* 44–48.

Simons, D. J., & Chabris, C. F. (1999). Gorillas in our midst: Sustained inattentional blindness for dynamic events. *Perception, 28,* 1059–1074.

Simonton, D. K. (1988). Age and outstanding achievement: What do we know after a century of research? *Psychological Bulletin, 104,* 251–267.

Simonton, D. K. (1990). Creativity in the later years: Optimistic prospects for achievement. *The Gerontologist, 30,* 626–631.

Simonton, D. K. (1992). The social context of career success and course for 2,026 scientists and inventors. *Personality and Social Psychology Bulletin, 18,* 452–463.

Simonton, D. K. (2000). Creativity: Cognitive, personal, developmental, and social aspects. *American Psychologist, 55,* 151–158.

Sinclair, R. C., Hoffman, C., Mark, M. M., Martin, L. L., & Pickering, T. L. (1994). Construct accessibility and the misattribution of arousal: Schachter and Singer revisited. *Psychological Science, 5,* 15–18.

Singelis, T. M., Bond, M. H., Sharkey, W. F., & Lai, C. S. Y. (1999). Unpackaging culture's influence on self-esteem and embarrassability: The role of self-construals. *Journal of Cross-Cultural Psychology, 30,* 315–341.

Singelis, T. M., & Sharkey, W. F. (1995). Culture, self-construal, and embarrassability. *Cross-Cultural Psychology, 26,* 622–644.

Singer, J. L. (1981). Clinical intervention: New developments in methods and evaluation. In L. T. Benjamin, Jr. (Ed.), *The G. Stanley Hall Lecture Series* (Vol. 1). Washington, DC: American Psychological Association.

Singer, T., Seymour, B., O'Doherty, J., Kaube, H., Dolan, R. J., & Frith, C. (2004). Empathy for pain involves the affective but not sensory components of pain. *Science, 303,* 1157–1162.

Singh, D. (1993). Adaptive significance of female physical attractiveness: Role of waist-to-hip ratio. *Journal of Personality and Social Psychology, 65,* 293–307.

Singh, D. (1995). Female health, attractiveness, and desirability for relationships: Role of breast asymmetry and waist-to-hip ratio. *Ethology and Sociobiology, 16,* 465–481.

Singh, S. (1997). *Fermat's enigma: The epic quest to solve the world's greatest mathematical problem.* New York: Bantam Books.

Singh, S., & Riber, K. A. (1997, November). Fermat's last stand. *Scientific American,* pp. 68–73.

Singleton, D., Tate, A., & Kohout, J. (2003). *2002 Master's, specialist's, and related degrees employment survey.* Washington, DC: American Psychological Association.

Sipski, M. L., & Alexander, C. J. (1999). Sexual response in women with spinal cord injuries: Implications for our understanding of the able bodied. *Journal of Sex and Marital Therapy, 25,* 11–22.

Sirenteanu, R. (1999). Switching on the infant brain. *Science, 286,* 59, 61.

Sivard, R. L. (1996). *World military and social expenditures 1996,* 16th edition. Washington, DC: World Priorities.

Sjöstrum, L. (1980). Fat cells and body weight. In A. J. Stunkard (Ed.), *Obesity.* Philadelphia: Saunders.

Skinner, B. F. (1953). *Science and human behavior.* New York: Macmillan.

Skinner, B. F. (1956). A case history in scientific method. *American Psychologist, 11,* 221–233.

Skinner, B. F. (1957). *Verbal behavior.* Englewood Cliffs, NJ: Prentice-Hall.

Skinner, B. F. (1961, November). Teaching machines. *Scientific American,* pp. 91–102.

Skinner, B. F. (1983, September). Origins of a behaviorist. *Psychology Today,* pp. 22–33.

Skinner, B. F. (1985). *Cognitive science and behaviorism.* Unpublished manuscript, Harvard University.

Skinner, B. F. (1986). What is wrong with daily life in the western world? *American Psychologist, 41,* 568–574.

Skinner, B. F. (1988). The school of the future. Address to the American Psychological Association convention.

Skinner, B. F. (1989). Teaching machines. *Science, 243,* 1535.

Skinner, B. F. (1990). Address to the American Psychological Association convention.

Skitka, L. J., Bauman, C. W., & Mullen, E. (2004). Political tolerance and coming to psychological closure following the September 11, 2001, terrorist attacks: An integrative approach. *Personality and Social Psychology Bulletin, 30,* 743–756.

Sklar, L. S., & Anisman, H. (1981). Stress and cancer. *Psychological Bulletin, 89,* 369–406.

Skoog, G., & Skoog, I. (1999). A 40-year follow-up of patients with obsessive-compulsive disorder. *Archives of General Psychiatry, 56,* 121–127.

Skov, R. B., & Sherman, S. J. (1986). Information-gathering processes: Diagnosticity, hypothesis-confirmatory strategies, and perceived hypothesis confirmation. *Journal of Experimental Social Psychology, 22,* 93–121.

Slater, A. (1994, February 15). Personal correspondence.

Slater, E., & Meyer, A. (1959). *Confinia Psychiatra.* Basel: S. Karger AG.

Slater, L. (2000, November 19). How do you cure a sex addict? *New York Times Magazine* (www.nytimes.com).

Slavin, R. E., & Braddock, J. H., III (1993, Summer). Ability grouping: On the wrong track. *The College Board Review,* pp. 11–18.

Slavin, R. E., Hurley, E. A., & Chamberlain, A. (2003). Cooperative learning and achievement: Theory and research. In W. M. Reynolds & G. E. Miller (Eds.), *Handbook of psychology: Educational psychology, Vol. 7.* New York: Wiley.

Sloan, R. P. (2005). Field analysis of the literature on religion, spirituality, and health. Columbia University (available at www.metanexus.net/tarp).

Sloan, R. P., & Bagiela E. (2002). Claims about religious involvement and health outcomes. *Annals of Behavioral Medicine, 24,* 14–21.

Sloan, R. P., Bagiella, E., & Powell, T. (1999). Religion, spirituality, and medicine. *Lancet, 353,* 664–667.

Sloan, R. P., Bagiella, E., VandeCreek, L., & Poulos, P. (2000). Should physicians prescribe religious activities? *New England Journal of Medicine, 342,* 1913–1917.

Slovic, P. (2000). What does it mean to know a cumulative risk? Adolescents' perceptions of short-term and long-term consequences of smoking. *Journal of Behavioral Decision Making, 13,* 259–266.

Slovic, P. (2001). Cigarette smokers: Rational actors or rational fools? In P. Slovic (Ed.), *Smoking risk, perception and policy.* Thousand Oaks, CA: Sage.

Slovic, P., Finucane, M., Peters, E., & MacGregor, D. G. (2002). The affect heuristic. In T. Gilovich, D. Griffin, & D. Kahneman (Eds.), *Intuitive judgment: Heuristics and biases.* New York: Cambridge University Press.

Slovic, P., & Fischhoff, B. (1977). On the psychology of experimental surprises. *Journal of Experimental Psychology: Human Perception and Performance, 3,* 544–551.

Slutske, W. S. (2005). Alcohol use disorders among U.S. college students and their non-college-attending peers. *Archives of General Psychiatry, 62,* 321–327.

Small, M. F. (1997). Making connections. *American Scientist, 85,* 502–504.

Small, M. F. (2002, July). What you can learn from drunk monkeys. *Discover,* pp. 40–45.

Smart, R. G., Adlaf, E. M., & Walsh, G. W. (1991). The Ontario student drug use survey: Trends between 1977 and 1991. Toronto: Addiction Research Foundation.

Smedley, A., & Smedley, B. D. (2005). Race as biology is fiction, racism as a social problem is real: Anthropological and historical perspectives on the social construction of race. *American Psychologist, 60*, 16–26.

Smelser, N. J., & Mitchell, F. (Eds.) (2002). *Terrorism: Perspectives from the behavioral and social sciences.* Washington, DC: National Research Council, National Academies Press.

Smith, A. (1983). Personal correspondence.

Smith, D. V., & Margolskee, R. F. (2001, March). Making sense of taste. *Scientific American*, pp. 32–39.

Smith, E., & Delargy, M. (2005). Locked-in syndrome. *British Medical Journal, 330*, 406–409.

Smith, J. E., Waldorf, V. A., & Trembath, D. L. (1990). "Single white male looking for thin, very attractive . . ." *Sex Roles, 23*, 675–685.

Smith, M. B. (1978). Psychology and values. *Journal of Social Issues, 34*, 181–199.

Smith, M., Franz, E. A., Joy, S. M., & Whitehead, K. (2005). Superior performance of blind compared with sighted individuals on bimanual estimations of object size. *Psychological Science, 16*, 11–14.

Smith, M. L., & Glass, G. V. (1977). Meta-analysis of psychotherapy outcome studies. *American Psychologist, 32*, 752–760.

Smith, M. L., Glass, G. V., & Miller, R. L. (1980). *The benefits of psychotherapy.* Baltimore: Johns Hopkins Press.

Smith, P. B., & Tayeb, M. (1989). Organizational structure and processes. In M. Bond (Ed.), *The cross-cultural challenge to social psychology.* Newbury Park, CA: Sage.

Smith, P. F. (1995). Cannabis and the brain. *New Zealand Journal of Psychology, 24*, 5–12.

Smith, S. B. (1999). *Diana in search of herself: Portrait of a troubled princess.* New York: Times Books.

Smith, S. M., McIntosh, W. D., & Bazzini, D. G. (1999). Are the beautiful good in Hollywood? An investigation of the beauty-and-goodness stereotype on film. *Basic and Applied Social Psychology, 21*, 69–80.

Smith, T. W. (1998, December). American sexual behavior: Trends, sociodemographic differences, and risk behavior. National Opinion Research Center GSS Topical Report No. 25.

Smith, T. W., & Ruiz, J. M. (2002). Psychosocial influences on the development and course of coronary heart disease: Current status and implications for research and practice. *Journal of Consulting and Clinical Psychology, 70*, 548–568.

Smolak, L., & Murnen, S. K. (2002). A meta-analytic examination of the relationship between child sexual abuse and eating disorders. *International Journal of Eating Disorders, 31*, 136–150.

Smoreda, Z., & Licoppe, C. (2000). Gender-specific use of the domestic telephone. *Social Psychology Quarterly, 63*, 238–252.

Snarey, J. R. (1985). Cross-cultural universality of social-moral development: A critical review of Kohlbergian research. *Psychological Bulletin, 97*, 202–233.

Snarey, J. R. (1987, June). A question of morality. *Psychology Today*, pp. 6–7.

Snodgrass, S. E., Higgins, J. G., & Todisco, L. (1986). The effects of walking behavior on mood. Paper presented at the American Psychological Association convention.

Snowdon, D. A., Kemper, S. J., Mortimer, J. A., Greiner, L. H., Wekstein, D. R., & Markesbery, W. R. (1996). Linguistic ability in early life and cognitive function and Alzheimer's disease in late life: Finds from the Nun Study. *Journal of the American Medical Association, 275*, 528–532.

Snyder, F., & Scott, J. (1972). The psychophysiology of sleep. In N. S. Greenfield & R. A. Sterbach (Eds.), *Handbook of psychophysiology.* New York: Holt, Rinehart & Winston.

Snyder, M. (1984). When belief creates reality. In L. Berkowitz (Ed.), *Advances in experimental social psychology* (Vol. 18). New York: Academic Press.

Snyder, S. H. (1984). Neurosciences: An integrative discipline. *Science, 225*, 1255–1257.

Snyder, S. H. (1986). *Drugs and the brain.* New York: Scientific American Library.

Society for Personality Assessment. (2005). The status of the Rorschach in clinical and forensic practice: An official statement by The Board of Trustees of the Society for Personality Assessment (www.personality.org).

Sokol, D. K., Moore, C. A., Rose, R. J., Williams, C. J., Reed, T., & Christian, J. C. (1995). Intrapair differences in personality and cognitive ability among young monozygotic twins distinguished by chorion type. *Behavior Genetics, 25*, 457–466.

Sokoll, G. R., & Mynatt, C. R. (1984). *Arousal and free throw shooting.* Paper presented at the meeting of the Midwestern Psychological Association.

Solomon, D. A., Keitner, G. I., Miller, I. W., Shea, M. T., & Keller, M. B. (1995). Course of illness and maintenance treatments for patients with bipolar disorder. *Journal of Clinical Psychiatry, 56*, 5–13.

Solomon, J. (1996, May 20). Breaking the silence. *Newsweek*, pp. 20–22.

Solomon, M. (1987, December). Standard issue. *Psychology Today*, pp. 30–31.

Sommer, R. (1969). *Personal space.* Englewood Cliffs, NJ: Prentice-Hall.

Sonenstein, F. L. (1992). Condom use. *Science, 257*, 861.

Sontag, S. (1978). *Illness as metaphor.* New York: Farrar, Straus, & Giroux.

Soussignan, R. (2001). Duchenne smile, emotional experience, and autonomic reactivity: A test of the facial feedback hypothesis. *Emotion, 2*, 52–74.

Sowell, T. (1991, May/June). Cultural diversity: A world view. *American Enterprise*, pp. 44–55.

Spanos, N. P. (1982). A social psychological approach to hypnotic behavior. In G. Weary & H. L. Mirels (Eds.), *Integrations of clinical and social psychology.* New York: Oxford.

Spanos, N. P. (1986). Hypnosis, nonvolitional responding, and multiple personality: A social psychological perspective. *Progress in Experimental Personality Research, 14*, 1–62.

Spanos, N. P. (1991). Hypnosis, hypnotizability, and hypnotherapy. In C. R. Snyder & D. R. Forsyth (Eds.), *Handbook of social and clinical psychology: The health perspective.* New York: Pergamon Press.

Spanos, N. P. (1994). Multiple identity enactments and multiple personality disorder: A sociocognitive perspective. *Psychological Bulletin, 116*, 143–165.

Spanos, N. P. (1996). *Multiple identities and false memories: A sociocognitive perspective.* Washington, DC: American Psychological Association Books.

Spanos, N. P., & Coe, W. C. (1992). A Social-psychological approach to hypnosis. In E. Fromm & M. R. Nash (Eds.), *Contemporary hypnosis research.* New York: Guilford.

Spector, P. E. (1986). Perceived control by employees: A meta-analysis of studies concerning autonomy and participation at work. *Human Relations, 39*, 1005–1016.

Spelke, E. (2005, April 22). The science of gender and science. Harvard University (www.edge.org).

Spelke, E. S. (2000). Core knowledge. *American Psychologist, 55*, 1233–1243.

Spencer, J., Quinn, P. C., Johnson, M. H., & Karmiloff-Smith, A. (1997). Heads you win, tails you lose: Evidence for young infants categorizing mammals by head and facial attributes. *Early Development & Parenting, 6*, 113–126.

Spencer, K. M., Nestor, P. G., Perlmutter, R., Niznikiewicz, M. A., Klump, M. C., Frumin, M., Shenton, M. E., & McCarley, R. W. (2004). Neural synchrony indexes disordered perception and cognition in schizophrenia. *Proceedings of the National Academy of Sciences, 101,* 17288–17293.

Spencer, S. J., Steele, C. M., & Quinn, D. M. (1997). Stereotype threat and women's math performance. Unpublished manuscript, Hope College.

Sperling, G. (1960). The information available in brief visual presentations. *Psychological Monographs, 74* (Whole No. 498).

Sperry, R. W. (1964). *Problems outstanding in the evolution of brain function.* James Arthur Lecture, American Museum of Natural History, New York. Cited by R. Ornstein (1977), *The psychology of consciousness* (2nd ed.). New York: Harcourt Brace Jovanovich.

Sperry, R. W. (1982). Some effects of disconnecting the cerebral hemispheres. *Science, 217,* 1223–1226.

Sperry, R. W. (1985). Changed concepts of brain and consciousness: Some value implications. *Zygon, 20,* 41–57.

Sperry, R. W. (1992, Summer). Turnabout on consciousness: A mentalist view. *Journal of Mind & Behavior, 13*(3), 259–280.

Spiegel, K., Leproult, R., & Van Cauter, E. (1999). Impact of sleep debt on metabolic and endrocrine function. *Lancet, 354,* 1435–1439.

Spielberger, C., & London, P. (1982). Rage boomerangs. *American Health, 1,* 52–56.

Spradley, J. P., & Phillips, M. (1972). Culture and stress: A quantitative analysis. *American Anthropologist, 74,* 518–529.

Sprecher, S. (1989). The importance to males and females of physical attractiveness, earning potential, and expressiveness in initial attraction. *Sex Roles, 21,* 591–607.

Sprecher, S., & Sedikides, C. (1993). Gender differences in perceptions of emotionality: The case of close heterosexual relationships. *Sex Roles, 28,* 511–530.

Spring, B., Pingitore, R., Bourgeois, M., Kessler, K. H., & Bruckner, E. (1992). The effects and non-effects of skipping breakfast: Results of three studies. Paper presented at the American Psychological Association convention.

Springer, S. P., & Deutsch, G. (1985). *Left brain, right brain.* San Francisco: Freeman.

Spychalski, A., Quinones, M. A., & Gaugler, B. B. (1997). A survey of assessment center practices in the United States. *Personnel Psychology, 50,* 71–90.

Squire, L. R. (1992). Memory and the hippocampus: A synthesis from findings with rats, monkeys, and humans. *Psychological Review, 99,* 195–231.

Srivastava, S., John, O. P., Gosling, S. D., & Potter, J. (2003). Development of personality in early and middle adulthood: Set like plaster or persistent change? *Journal of Personality & Social Psychology, 84,* 1041–1053.

Srivastava, A., Locke, E. A., & Bartol, K. M. (2001). Money and subject well-being: It's not the money, it's the motives. *Journal of Personality and Social Psychology, 80,* 959–971.

St. Clair, D., Xu, M., Wang, P., Yu, Y., Fang, Y., Zhang, F., Zheng, X., Gu, N., Feng, G., Sham, P., & He, L. (2005). Rates of adult schizophrenia following prenatal exposure to the Chinese famine of 1959–1961. *Journal of the American Medical Association, 294,* 557–562.

Stack, S. (1992). Marriage, family, religion, and suicide. In R. Maris, A. Berman, J. Maltsberger, & R. Yufit (Eds.), *Assessment and prediction of suicide.* New York: Guilford Press.

Stafford, R. S., MacDonald, E. A., & Finkelstein, S. N. (2001). National patterns of medication treatment for depression, 1987 to 2001. *Primary Care Companion Journal of Clinical Psychiatry, 3,* 232–235.

Stanford University Center for Narcolepsy. (2002). Narcolepsy is a serious medical disorder and a key to understanding other sleep disorders (www.med.stanford.edu/school/Psychiatry/narcolepsy).

Stanley, J. C. (1997). Varieties of intellectual talent. *Journal of Creative Behavior, 31,* 93–119.

Stanovich, K. (1996). *How to think straight about psychology.* New York: HarperCollins.

Staples, B. (1999a, May 2). When the 'paranoids' turn out to be right. *New York Times* (www.nytimes.com).

Staples, B. (1999b, May 24). Why 'racial profiling' will be tough to fight. *New York Times* (www.nytimes.com).

Stark, R. (2002). Physiology and faith: Addressing the "universal" gender difference in religious commitment. *Journal for the Scientific Study of Religion, 41,* 495–507.

Stark, R. (2003a). *For the glory of God: How monotheism led to reformations, science, witch-hunts, and the end of slavery.* Princeton, NJ: Princeton University Press.

Stark, R. (2003b, October-November). False conflict: Christianity is not only compatible with science—it created it. *American Enterprise,* pp. 27–33.

Starr, J. M., Deary, I. J., Lemmon, H., & Whalley, L. J. (2000). Mental ability age 11 years and health status age 77 years. *Age and Ageing, 29,* 523–528.

Statistics Canada. (1999). *Statistical report on the health of Canadians.* Prepared by the Federal, Provincial and Territorial Advisory Committee on Population Health for the Meeting of Ministers of Health, Charlottetown, PEI, September 16–17, 1999.

Statistics Canada. (2002). (www.statcan.ca).

Statistics Canada. (2003). Victims and persons accused of homicide, by age and sex. Table 253-0003. www.statcan.ca

Staub, E. (1989). *The roots of evil: The psychological and cultural sources of genocide.* New York: Cambridge University Press.

Steadman, H. J., Mulvey, E. P., Monahan, J., Robbins, P. C., Appelbaum, P. S., Grisso, T., Roth, L. H., & Silver, E. (1998). Violence by people discharged from acute psychiatric inpatient facilities and by others in the same neighborhoods. *Archives of General Psychiatry, 55,* 393–401.

Steel, P., & Ones, D. S. (2002). Personality and happiness: A national-level analysis. *Journal of Personality and Social Psychology, 83,* 767–781.

Steele, C. (1990, May). A conversation with Claude Steele. *APS Observer,* pp. 11–17.

Steele, C. M. (1995, August 31). Black students live down to expectations. *New York Times.*

Steele, C. M. (1997). A threat in the air: How stereotypes shape intellectual identity and performance. *American Psychologist, 52,* 613–629.

Steele, C. M., & Josephs, R. A. (1990). Alcohol myopia: Its prized and dangerous effects. *American Psychologist, 45,* 921–933.

Steele, C. M., Spencer, S. J., & Aronson, J. (2002). Contending with group image: The psychology of stereotype and social identity threat. *Advances in Experimental Social Psychology, 34,* 379–440.

Steele, J. (2000). Handedness in past human population: Skeletal markers. *Laterality, 5,* 193–220.

Steenhuysen, J. (2002, May 8). Bionic retina gives six patients partial sight. Reuters News Service. (See also www.optobionics.com/artificialretina.htm.)

Steinberg, L. (1987, September). Bound to bicker. *Psychology Today,* pp. 36–39.

Steinberg, L., & Morris, A. S. (2001). Adolescent development. *Annual Review of Psychology, 52,* 83–110.

Steinberg, L., & Scott, E. S. (2003). Less guilty by reason of adolescence: Developmental immaturity, diminished responsibility, and the juvenile death penalty. *American Psychologist, 58,* 1009–1018.

Steinberg, N. (1993, February). Astonishing love stories (from an earlier United Press International report). *Games,* p. 47.

Steinem, G. (1988). Six great ideas that television is missing. In G. Comstock (Ed.), *Public communication and behavior.* New York: Academic Press.

Steinhauer, J. (1999). More traffic in the double-stroller lane: Twin births surge, and the parents face special, and costly challenges. *New York Times* (www.nytimes.com).

Steinhauer, J. (1999, November 29). Number of twins rises; so does parental stress. *New York Times* (www.nytimes.com).

Steinmetz, J. E. (1999). The localization of a simple type of learning and memory: The cerebellum and classical eyeblink conditioning. *Contemporary Psychology, 7,* 72–77.

Stengel, E. (1981). Suicide. In *The new encyclopaedia britannica, macropaedia* (Vol. 17, pp. 777–782). Chicago: Encyclopaedia Britannica.

Stern, M., & Karraker, K. H. (1989). Sex stereotyping of infants: A review of gender labeling studies. *Sex Roles, 20,* 501–522.

Stern, S. L., Dhanda, R., & Hazuda, H. P. (2001). Hopelessness predicts mortality in older Mexican and European Americans. *Psychosomatic Medicine, 63,* 344–351.

Sternbach, H. (1998). Age-associated testosterone decline in men: Clinical issues for psychiatry. *American Journal of Psychiatry, 155,* 1310–1318.

Sternberg, E. M. (2001). *The balance within: The science connecting health and emotions.* New York: Freeman.

Sternberg, R. (Ed.), (2002). *Career paths in psychology: Where your degree can take you.* Washington, DC: APA.

Sternberg, R. J. (1985). *Beyond IQ: A triarchic theory of human intelligence.* New York: Cambridge University Press.

Sternberg, R. J. (1988). Applying cognitive theory to the testing and teaching of intelligence. *Applied Cognitive Psychology, 2,* 231–255.

Sternberg, R. J. (1998). Principles of teaching for successful intelligence. *Educational Psychologist, 33,* 65–72.

Sternberg, R. J. (1999). The theory of successful intelligence. *Review of General Psychology, 3,* 292–316.

Sternberg, R. J. (2000). Presidential aptitude in Science.

Sternberg, R. J. (2003). Our research program validating the triarchic theory of successful intelligence: Reply to Gottfredson. *Intelligence, 31,* 399–413.

Sternberg, R. J., & Grajek, S. (1984). The nature of love. *Journal of Personality and Social Psychology, 47,* 312–329.

Sternberg, R. J., & Grigorenko, E. L. (2000). Theme-park psychology: A case study regarding human intelligence and its implications for education. *Educational Psychology Review, 12,* 247–268.

Sternberg, R. J., Grigorenko, E. L., & Kidd, K. K. (2005). Intelligence, race, and genetics. *American Psychologist, 60,* 46–59.

Sternberg, R. J., & Kaufman, J. C. (1998). Human abilities. *Annual Review of Psychology, 49,* 479–502.

Sternberg, R. J., & Lubart, T. I. (1991). An investment theory of creativity and its development. *Human Development,* 1–31.

Sternberg, R. J., & Lubart, T. I. (1992). Buy low and sell high: An investment approach to creativity. *Psychological Science, 1,* 1–5.

Sternberg, R. J., & Wagner, R. K. (1993). The *g*-ocentric view of intelligence and job performance is wrong. *Current Directions in Psychological Science, 2,* 1–5.

Sternberg, R. J., Wagner, R. K., Williams, W. M., & Horvath, J. A. (1995). Testing common sense. *American Psychologist, 50,* 912–927.

Stetter, F., & Kupper, S. (2002). Autogenic training: A meta-analysis of clinical outcome studies. *Applied Psychophysiology and Biofeedback, 27,* 45–98.

Stevenson, H. W. (1992, December). Learning from Asian schools. *Scientific American,* pp. 70–76.

Stevenson, H. W., & Lee, S-Y. (1990). Contexts of achievement: A study of American, Chinese, and Japanese children. *Monographs of the Society for Research in Child Development, 55* (Serial No. 221, Nos. 1–2).

Stewart, B. (2002, April 6). Recall of the wild. *New York Times* (www.nytimes.com).

Stewart, D. (2000, February). Driving the wrong way. *The Psychologist,* pp. 64–65.

Stice, E. (2002). Risk and maintenance factors for eating pathology: A meta-analytic review. *Psychological Bulletin, 128,* 825–848.

Stice, E., & Shaw, H. E. (1994). Adverse effects of the media portrayed thin-ideal on women and linkages to bulimic symptomatology. *Journal of Social and Clinical Psychology, 13,* 288–308.

Stice, E., Spangler, D., & Agras, W. S. (2001). Exposure to media-portrayed thin-ideal images adversely affects vulnerable girls: A longitudinal experiment. *Journal of Social and Clinical Psychology, 20,* 270–288.

Stickgold, R. (2000, March 7). Quoted by S. Blakeslee, For better learning, researchers endorse "sleep on it" adage. *New York Times,* p. F2.

Stickgold, R., Hobson, J. A., Fosse, R., & Fosse, M. (2001). Sleep, learning, and dreams: Off-line memory processing. *Science, 294,* 1052–1057.

Stickgold, R., James, L., & Hobson, J. A. (2000). Visual discrimination learning requires sleep after training. *Nature Neuroscience, 3,* 1237–1238.

Stickgold, R., Malia, A., Maquire, D., Roddenberry, D., & O'Connor, M. (2000, October 13). Replaying the game: Hypnagogic images in normals and amnesics. *Science, 290,* 350–353.

Stipek, D. (1992). The child at school. In M. H. Bornstein & M. E. Lamb (Eds.), *Developmental psychology: An advanced textbook.* Hillsdale, NJ: Erlbaum.

Stith, S. M., Rosen, K. H., Middleton, K. A., Busch, A. L., Lunderberg, K., & Carlton, R. P. (2000). The intergenerational transmission of spouse abuse: A meta-analysis. *Journal of Marriage and the Family, 62,* 640–654.

Stockton, M. C., & Murnen, S. K. (1992). Gender and sexual arousal in response to sexual stimuli: A meta-analytic review. Presented at the American Psychological Society convention.

Stone, A. A., & Neale, J. M. (1984). Effects of severe daily events on mood. *Journal of Personality and Social Psychology, 46,* 137–144.

Stoolmiller, M. (1999). Implications of the restricted range of family environments for estimates of heritability and nonshared environment in behavior-genetic adoption studies. *Psychological Bulletin, 125,* 392–409.

Stoppard, J. M., & Gruchy, C. D. G. (1993). Gender, context, and expression of positive emotion. *Personality and Social Psychology Bulletin, 19,* 143–150.

Storm, L. (2000). Research note: Replicable evidence of psi: A revision of Milton's (1999) meta-analysis of the ganzfeld data bases. *Journal of Parapsychology, 64,* 411–416.

Storm, L. (2003). Remote viewing by committee: RV using a multiple agent/multiple percipient design. *Journal of Parapsychology, 67,* 325–342.

Storms, M. D. (1973). Videotape and the attribution process: Reversing actors' and observers' points of view. *Journal of Personality and Social Psychology, 27,* 165–175.

Storms, M. D. (1981). A theory of erotic orientation development. *Psychological Review, 88,* 340–353.

Storms, M. D. (1983). *Development of sexual orientation.* Washington, DC: Office of Social and Ethical Responsibility, American Psychological Association.

Storms, M. D., & Thomas, G. C. (1977). Reactions to physical closeness. *Journal of Personality and Social Psychology, 35,* 412–418.

Strack, F., Martin, L., & Stepper, S. (1988). Inhibiting and facilitating conditions of the human smile: A nonobtrusive test of the facial feedback hypothesis. *Journal of Personality and Social Psychology, 54,* 768–777.

Strack, S., & Coyne, J. C. (1983). Social confirmation of dysphoria: Shared and private reactions to depression. *Journal of Personality and Social Behavior, 44,* 798–806.

Strahan, E. J., Spencer, S. J., & Zanna, M. P. (2002). Subliminal priming and persuasion: Striking while the iron is hot. *Journal of Experimental Social Psychology, 38,* 556–568.

Strange, B. A., & Dolan, R. J. (2004). b-Adrenergic modulation of emotional memory-evoked human amygdala and hippocampal responses. *Proceedings of the National Academy of Sciences, 101,* 11454–11458.

Stratton, G. M. (1896). Some preliminary experiments on vision without inversion of the retinal image. *Psychological Review, 3,* 611–617.

Straub, R. O., Seidenberg, M. S., Bever, T. G., & Terrace, H. S. (1979). Serial learning in the pigeon. *Journal of the Experimental Analysis of Behavior, 32,* 137–148.

Straus, M. A., & Gelles, R. J. (1980). *Behind closed doors: Violence in the American family.* New York: Anchor/Doubleday.

Straus, M. A., Sugarman, D. B., & Giles-Sims, J. (1997). Spanking by parents and subsequent antisocial behavior of children. *Archives of Pediatric Adolescent Medicine, 151,* 761–767.

Strawbridge, W. J. (1999). Mortality and religious involvement: A review and critique of the results, the methods, and the measures. Paper presented at a Harvard University conference on religion and health, sponsored by the National Institite for Healthcare Research and the John Templeton Foundation.

Strawbridge, W. J., Cohen, R. D., & Shema, S. J. (1997). Frequent attendance at religious services and mortality over 28 years. *American Journal of Public Health, 87,* 957–961.

Strawbridge, W. J., Shema, S. J., Cohen, R. D., & Kaplan, G. A. (2001). Religious attendance increases survival by improving and maintaining good health behaviors, mental health, and social relationships. *Annals of Behavioral Medicine, 23,* 68–74.

Strayer, D. L., Drews, F. A., & Johnston, W. A. (2003). Cell phone-induced failures of visual attention during simulated driving. *Journal of Experimental Psychology: Applied, 9,* 23–32.

Strayer, D. L., & Johnston, W. A. (2001). Driven to distraction: Dual-task studies of simulated driving and conversing on a cellular telephone. *Psychological Science, 12,* 462–466.

Streissguth, A. P., Aase, J. M., Clarren, S. K., Randels, S. P., LaDue, R. A., & Smith, D. F. (1991). Fetal alcohol syndrome in adolescents and adults. *Journal of the American Medical Association, 265,* 1961–1967.

Strickland, B. (1992, February 20). Gender differences in health and illness. Sigma Xi national lecture delivered at Hope College.

Striegel-Moore, R. H., Silberstein, L. R., & Rodin, J. (1993). The social self in bulimia nervosa: Public self-consciousness, social anxiety, and perceived fraudulence. *Journal of Abnormal Psychology, 102,* 297–303.

Stroebe, M., Stroebe, W., & Schut, H. (2001). Gender differences in adjustment to bereavement: An empirical and theoretical review. *Review of General Psychology, 5,* 62–83.

Stroebe, M., Stroebe, W., Schut, H., Zech, E., & van den Bout, J. (2002). Does disclosure of emotions facilitate recovery from bereavement? Evidence from two prospective studies. *Journal of Consulting and Clinical Psychology, 70,* 169–178.

Stroebe, W., Schut, H., & Stroebe, M. S. (2005). Grief work, disclosure and counseling: Do they help the bereaved? *Clinical Psychology Review, 25,* 395–414.

Strupp, H. H. (1982). The outcome problem in psychotherapy: Contemporary perspectives. In J. H. Harvey & M. M. Parks (Eds.), *The master lecture series: Vol. 1. Psychotherapy research and behavior change.* Washington, DC: American Psychological Association.

Strupp, H. H. (1986). Psychotherapy: Research, practice, and public policy (How to avoid dead ends). *American Psychologist, 41,* 120–130.

Stumpf, H., & Jackson, D. N. (1994). Gender-related differences in cognitive abilities: Evidence from a medical school admissions testing program. *Personality and Individual Differences, 17,* 335–344.

Stumpf, H., & Stanley, J. C. (1998). Stability and change in gender-related differences on the college board advanced placement and achievement tests. *Current Directions in Psychology, 7,* 192–196.

Stunkard, A. J., Harris, J. R., Pedersen, N. L., & McClearn, G. E. (1990). A separated twin study of the body mass index. *New England Journal of Medicine, 322,* 1483–1487.

Sturm, R. (2003). Increases in clinically severe obesity in the United States, 1986–2000. *Archives of Internal Medicine, 163,* 2146–2148.

Subiaul, F., Cantlon, J. F., Holloway, R. L., & Terrace, H. S. (2004). Cognitive imitation in rhesus macaques. *Science, 305,* 407–410.

Suddath, R. L., Christison, G. W., Torrey, E. F., Casanova, M. F., & Weinberger, D. R. (1990). Anatomical abnormalities in the brains of monozygotic twins discordant for schizophrenia. *New England Journal of Medicine, 322,* 789–794.

Suddendorf, T., & Whiten, A. (2001). Mental evolution and development: Evidence for secondary representation in children, great apes, and other animals. *Psychological Bulletin, 137,* 629–650.

Sue, D. W. (1990). Culture-specific strategies in counseling: A conceptual framework. *Professional Psychology: Research and Practice, 21,* 424–433.

Suedfeld, P. (1998). Homo invictus: The indomitable species. *Canadian Psychology, 38,* 164–173.

Suedfeld, P. (2000). Reverberations of the Holocaust fifty years later: Psychology's contributions to understanding persecution and genocide. *Canadian Psychology, 41,* 1–9.

Suedfeld, P., & Mocellin, J. S. P. (1987). The "sensed presence" in unusual environments. *Environment and Behavior, 19,* 33–52.

Sugita, Y. (2004). Experience in early infancy is indispensable for color perception. *Current Biology. 14,* 1267–1271.

Suhail, K., & Chaudry, H. R. (2004). Predictors of subjective well-being in an Eatern Muslim Cultre. *Journal of Social and Clinical Psychology, 23,* 359.

Suinn, R. M. (1997). Mental practice in sports psychology: Where have we been, Where do we go? *Clinical Psychology: Science and Practice.*

Sullivan, P. F., Neale, M. C., & Kendler, K. S. (2000). Genetic epidemiology of major depression: Review and meta-analysis. *American Journal of Psychiatry, 157,* 1552–1562.

Suls, J. M., & Tesch, F. (1978). Students' preferences for information about their test performance: A social comparison study. *Journal of Experimental Social Psychology, 8,* 189–197.

Summers, M. (1996, December 9). Mister clean. *People Weekly,* pp. 139–142.

Sundet, J. M., Barlaug, D. G., & Torjussen, T. M. (2004). The end of the Flynn effect? A study of secular trends in mean intelligence test scores of Norwegian conscripts during half a century. *Intelligence, 32,* 349–362.

Sundstrom, E., De Meuse, K. P., & Futrell, D. (1990). Work teams: Applications and effectiveness. *American Psychologist, 45,* 120–133.

Suomi, S. J. (1986). Anxiety-like disorders in young nonhuman primates. In R. Gettleman (Ed.), *Anxiety disorders of childhood.* New York: Guilford Press.

Suomi, S. J. (1987). Genetic and maternal contributions to individual differences in rhesus monkey biobehavioral development. In N. A. Krasnegor & others (Eds.), *Perinatal development: A psychobiological perspective.* Orlando, FL: Academic Press.

Super, C., & Super, D. (2001). Education and Training. *Opportunities in psychology careers* (pp. 68–80). Chicago, IL: VGM Career Books.

Suppes, P. Quoted by R. H. Ennis (1982). Children's ability to handle Piaget's propositional logic: A conceptual critique. In S. Modgil & C. Modgil (Eds.), *Jean Piaget: Consensus and controversy.* New York: Praeger.

Surgeon General. (1986). *The Surgeon General's workshop on pornography and public health,* June 22–24. Report prepared by E. P. Mulvey & J. L. Haugaard and released by Office of the Surgeon General on August 4, 1986.

Surgeon General. (1999). *Mental health: A report of the Surgeon General.* Rockville, MD: U.S. Department of Health and Human Services.

Susser, E. (1999). Life course cohort studies of schizophrenia. *Psychiatric Annals, 29,* 161–165.

Susser, E., Neugenbauer, R., Hoek, H. W., Brown, A. S., Lin, S., Labovitz, D., & Gorman, J. M. (1996). Schizophrenia after prenatal famine. *Archives of General Psychiatry, 53*(1), 25–31

Susser, E. S., Herman, D. B., & Aaron, B. (2002, August). Combating the terror of terrorism. *Scientific American,* pp. 70–77.

Svirsky, M. A., Robbins, A. M., Kirk, K. I., Pisoni, D. B., & Miyamoto, R. T. (2000). Language development in profoundly deaf children with cochlear implants. *Psychological Science, 11,* 153–158.

Sweat, J. A., & Durm, M. W. (1993). Psychics: Do police departments really use them? *Skeptical Inquirer, 17,* 148–158.

Swerdlow, N. R., & Koob, G. F. (1987). Dopamine, schizophrenia, mania, and depression: Toward a unified hypothesis of cortico-stiato-pallido-thalamic function (with commentary). *Behavioral and Brain Sciences, 10,* 197–246.

Swim, J. K. (1994). Perceived versus meta-analytic effect sizes: An assessment of the accuracy of gender stereotypes. *Journal of Personality and Social Psychology, 66,* 21–36.

Swindle, R., Jr., Heller, K., Bescosolido, B., & Kikuzawa, S. (2000). Responses to nervous breakdowns in America over a 40-year period: Mental health policy implications. *American Psychologist, 55,* 740–749.

Symbaluk, D. G., Heth, C. D., Cameron, J., & Pierce, W. D. (1997). Social modeling, monetary incentives, and pain endurance: The role of self-efficacy and pain perception. *Personality and Social Psychology Bulletin, 23,* 258–269.

Symond, M. B., Harris, A. W. F., Gordon, E., & Williams, L. M. (2005). "Gamma synchrony" in first-episode schizophrenia: A disorder of temporal connectivity? *American Journal of Psychiatry, 162,* 459–465.

Symons, C. S., & Johnson, B. T. (1997). The self-reference effect in memory: A meta-analysis. *Psychological Bulletin, 121*(3), 371–394.

TADS (Treatment for Adolescents with Depression Study Team). (2004). Fluoxetine, cognitive-behavioral therapy, and their combination for adolescents with depression: Treatment for adolescents with depression study (TADS) randomized controlled trial. *Journal of the American Medical Association, 292,* 807–820.

Taha, F. A. (1972). A comparative study of how sighted and blind perceive the manifest content of dreams. *National Review of Social Sciences, 9*(3), 28.

Taheri, S. (2004). The genetics of sleep disorders. *Minerva Medica, 95,* 203–212.

Taheri, S., Lin, L., Austin, D., Young, T., & Mignot, E. (2004). Short sleep duration is associated with reduced leptin, elevated ghrelin, and increased body mass index. *PloS Medicine, 1*(3), e62 (www.plosmedicine.org).

Taheri, S., Zeitzer, J. M., & Mignot, E. (2002). The role of hypocretins (orexins) in sleep regulation and narcolepsy. *Annual Review of Neuroscience, 25,* 283–313.

Tajfel, H. (Ed.). (1982). *Social identity and intergroup relations.* New York: Cambridge University Press.

Talal, N. (1995). Quoted by V. Morell, Zeroing in on how hormones affect the immune system. *Science, 269,* 773–775.

Talarico, J. M., & Rubin, D. C. (2003). Confidence, not consistency, characterizes flashbulb memories. *Psychological Science, 14,* 455–461.

Talbot, M. (1999, October 31). The Rorschach chronicles. *New York Times* (www.nytimes.com).

Talbot, M. (2002, June 2). Hysteria hysteria. *New York Times* (www.nytimes.com).

Talwar, S. K., Xu, S., Hawley, E. S., Weiss, S. A., Moxon, K. A., & Chapin, J. K. (2002). Rat navigation guided by remote control. *Nature, 417,* 37–38.

Tamres, L. K., Janicki, D., & Helgeson, V. S. (2002). Sex differences in coping behavior: A meta-analytic review and an examination of relative coping. *Personality and Social Psychology Review, 6,* 2–30.

Tang, S-H., & Hall, V. C. (1995). The overjustification effect: A meta-analysis. *Applied Cognitive Psychology, 9,* 365–404.

Tangney, J. P., Baumeister, R. F., & Boone, A. L. (2004). High self-control predicts good adjustment, less pathology, better grades, and interpersonal success. *Journal of Personality, 72,* 271–324.

Tannen, D. (1990). *You just don't understand: Women and men in conversation.* New York: Morrow.

Tannenbaum, P. (2002, February). Quoted by R. Kubey & M. Csikszentmihalyi, Television addiction is no mere metaphor. *Scientific American,* pp. 74–80.

Tanner, J. M. (1978). *Fetus into man: Physical growth from conception to maturity.* Cambridge, MA: Harvard University Press.

Tarbert, J. (2004, May 14). Bad apples, bad command, or both? Dart Center for Journalism and Trauma (www.dartcenter.org).

Tarmann, A. (2002, May/June). Out of the closet and onto the Census long form. *Population Today, 30,* pp. 1, 6.

Tasbihsazan, R., Nettelbeck, T., & Kirby, N. (2003). Predictive validity of the Fagan Test of Infant Intelligence. *British Journal of Developmental Psychology, 21,* 585–597.

Tatarkiewicz, W. (1976). *Analysis of happiness.* The Hague: Martinus Nijhoff, 1976.

Taubes, G. (1994). Will new dopamine receptors offer a key to schizophrenia? *Science, 265,* 1034–1035.

Taubes, G. (2001). The soft science of dietary fat. *Science, 291,* 2536–2545.

Taubes, G. (2002, July 7). What if it's all been a big fat lie? *New York Times* (www.nytimes.com).

Tavris, C. (1982, November). Anger defused. *Psychology Today,* pp. 25–35.

Taylor, H. (2003, February 26). The religious and other beliefs of Americans 2003. *The Harris Poll #11* (www.harrisinteracctive.com).

Taylor, K. M., Shepperd, J. A. (1998). Bracing for the worst: Severity, testing, and feedback timing as moderators of the optimistic bias. *Personality and Social Psychology Bulletin, 24,* 915–926.

Taylor, S. E. (1989). *Positive illusions.* New York: Basic Books.

Taylor, S. E. (2002). *The tending instinct: How nurturing is essential to who we are and how we live.* New York: Times Books.

Taylor, S. E., Cousino, L. K., Lewis, B. P., Gruenewald, T. L., Gurung, R. A. R., & Updegraff, J. A. (2000). Biobehavioral responses to stress in females: Tend-and-befriend, not fight-or-flight. *Psychological Review, 107,* 411–430.

Taylor, S. E., Lerner, J. S., Sherman, D. K., Sage, R. M., & McDowell, N. K. (2003). Portrait of the self-enhancer: Well adjusted and well liked or maladjusted and friendless? *Journal of Personality and Social Psychology, 84,* 165–176.

Taylor, S. E., Pham, L. B., Rivkin, I. D., & Armor, D. A. (1998). Harnessing the imagination: Mental simulation, self-regulation, and coping. *American Psychologist, 53,* 429–439.

Taylor, S., Kuch, K., Koch, W. J., Crockett, D. J., & Passey, G. (1998). The structure of posttraumatic stress symptoms. *Journal of Abnormal Psychology, 107,* 154–160.

Taylor, S. P., & Chermack, S. T. (1993). Alcohol, drugs and human physical aggression. *Journal of Studies on Alcohol,* Supplement No. 11, 78–88.

Teasdale, T. W., & Owen, D. R. (2000). Forty-year secular trends in cognitive abilities. *Intelligence, 28,* 115–120.

Tedeschi, R. G., & Calhoun, L. G. (2004). Posttraumatic growth: Conceptual foundations and empirical evidence. *Psychological Inquiry, 15,* 1–18.

Teerlink, R., & Ozley, L. (2000). *More than a motorcycle: The leadership journey at Harley-Davidson.* Cambridge, MA: Harvard Business School Press.

Teghtsoonian, R. (1971). On the exponents in Stevens' law and the constant in Ekinan's law. *Psychological Review, 78,* 71–80.

Teicher, M. (2002). McLean motion and attention test (M-MAT): A new test to diagnose a troubling disorder. McLean Hospital Annual Report (www.mclean.harvard.edu).

Teicher, M. H. (2002, March). The neurobiology of child abuse. *Scientific American,* pp. 68–75.

Tenopyr, M. L. (1997). Improving the workplace: Industrial/organizational psychology as a career. In R. J. Sternberg (Ed.), *Career paths in psychology: Where your degree can take you.* Washington, DC: American Psychological Association.

Teran-Santos, J., Jimenez-Gomez, A., & Cordero-Guevara, J. (1999). The association between sleep apnea and the risk of traffic accidents. *New England Journal of Medicine, 340,* 847–851.

Terman, J. S., Terman, M., Lo, E-S., & Cooper, T. B. (2001). Circadian time of morning light administration and therapeutic response in winter depression. *Archives of General Psychiatry, 58,* 69–73.

Terman, L. M. (1916). *The measurement of intelligence.* Boston: Houghton Mifflin.

Terman, M., Terman, J. S., & Ross, D. C. (1998). A controlled trial of timed bright light and negative air ionization for treatment of winter depression. *Archives of General Psychiatry, 55,* 875–882.

Terrace, H. S. (1979, November). How Nim Chimpsky changed my mind. *Psychology Today,* pp. 65–76.

Terre, L., & Stoddart, R. (2000). Cutting edge specialties for graduate study in psychology. *Eye on Psi Chi, 23,* 26.

Tesser, A., Forehand, R., Brody, G., & Long, N. (1989). Conflict: The role of calm and angry parent-child discussion in adolescent development. *Journal of Social and Clinical Psychology, 8,* 317–330.

Tetlock, P. E. (1988). Monitoring the integrative complexity of American and Soviet policy rhetoric: What can be learned? *Journal of Social Issues, 44,* 101–131.

Tetlock, P. E. (1998). Close-call counterfactuals and belief-system defenses: I was not almost wrong but I was almost right. *Journal of Personality and Social Psychology, 75,* 639–652.

Thannickal, T. C., Moore, R. Y., Nienhuis, R., Ramanathan, L., Gulyani, S., Aldrich, M., Cornford, M., & Siegel, J. M. (2000). Reduced number of hypocretin neurons in human narcolepsy. *Neuron, 27,* 469–474.

Thatcher, R. W., Walker, R. A., & Giudice, S. (1987). Human cerebral hemispheres develop at different rates and ages. *Science, 236,* 1110–1113.

Thayer, R. E. (1987). Energy, tiredness, and tension effects of a sugar snack versus moderate exercise. *Journal of Personality and Social Psychology, 52,* 119–125.

Thayer, R. E. (1993). Mood and behavior (smoking and sugar snacking) following moderate exercise: A partial test of self-regulation theory. *Personality and Individual Differences, 14,* 97–104.

Thomas, A., & Chess, S. (1986). The New York Longitudinal Study: From infancy to early adult life. In R. Plomin & J. Dunn (Eds.), *The study of temperament: Changes, continuities, and challenges.* Hillsdale, NJ: Erlbaum.

Thomas, L. (1974). *The lives of a cell.* New York: Viking Press.

Thomas, L. (1979). *The medusa and the snail.* New York: Viking.

Thomas, L. (1983). *The youngest science: Notes of a medicine watcher.* New York: Viking Press.

Thomas, L. (1992). *The fragile species.* New York: Scribner's.

Thomas, W. P., & Collier, V. P. (1998). Two languages are better than one. *Educational Leadership, 55,* 23–36.

Thompson, C. P., Frieman, J., & Cowan, T. (1993). Rajan's memory. Paper presented at the American Psychological Society convention.

Thompson, G. (1998, December 14). As obesity in children increases, so do cases of adult-onset diabetes. *New York Times* (www.nytimes.com).

Thompson, J. K., Jarvie, G. J., Lahey, B. B., & Cureton, K. J. (1982). Exercise and obesity: Etiology, physiology, and intervention. *Psychological Bulletin, 91,* 55–79.

Thompson, J. K., & Stice, E. (2001). Thin-ideal internalization: Mounting evidence for a new risk factor for body-image disturbance and eating pathology. *Current Directions in Psychological Science, 10,* 181–183.

Thompson, P. (1980). Margaret Thatcher: A new illusion. *Perception, 9,* 483–484.

Thompson, P. M., Cannon, T. D., Narr, K. L., van Erp, T., Poutanen, V-P., Huttunen, M., Lönnqvist, J., Standerskjöld-Nordenstam, C-G., Kaprio, J., Khaledy, M., Dail, R., Zoumalan, C. I., & Toga, A. W. (2001). Genetic influences on brain structure. *Nature Neuroscience, 4,* 1253–1258.

Thompson, P. M., Giedd, J. N., Woods, R. P., MacDonald, D., Evans, A. C., & Toga, A. W. (2000). Growth patterns in the developing brain detected by using continuum mechanical tensor maps. *Nature, 404,* 190–193.

Thompson, R., Emmorey, K., & Gollan, T. H. (2005). "Tip of the fingers" experiences by Deaf signers. *Psychological Science, 16,* 856–860.

Thomson, R., & Murachver, T. (2001). Predicting gender from electronic discourse. *British Journal of Social Psychology, 40,* 193–208 (and personal correspondence from T. Murachver, May 23, 2002).

Thorndike, A. L., & Hagen, E. P. (1977). *Measurement and evaluation in psychology and education.* New York: Macmillan.

Thorndike, E. L. (1898). Animal intelligence: An experimental study of associative processes in animals. *Psychological Review Monograph Supplements, 2,* 4–160.

Thorne, J., with Larry Rothstein (1993). *You are not alone: Words of experience and hope for the journey through depression.* New York: HarperPerennial.

Thornhill, R., & Gangestad, S. W. (1994). Human fluctuating asymmetry and sexual behavior. *Psychological Science, 5,* 297–302.

Thornton, B., & Moore, S. (1993). Physical attractiveness contrast effect: Implications for self-esteem and evaluations of the social self. *Personality and Social Psychology Bulletin, 19,* 474–480.

Thorpe, W. H. (1974). *Animal nature and human nature.* London: Metheun.

Tiedens, L. Z. (2001). Anger and advancement versus sadness and subjugation: The effect of negative emotion expressions on social status conferral. *Journal of Personality and Social Psychology, 80,* 86–94.

Tiihonen, J., Isohanni, M., Rasanen, P, Koiranen, M., & Moring, J. (1997). Specific major mental disorders and criminality: A 26-year prospective study of the 1966 northern Finland birth cohort. *American Journal of Psychiatry, 154,* 840–845.

Tikkanen, T. (2001). Psychology in Europe: A growing profession with high standards and a bright future. *European Psychologist, 6,* 144–146.

Time. (1997, December 22). Greeting card association data, p.19.

Tinbergen, N. (1951). *The study of instinct.* Oxford: Clarendon.

Tirrell, M. E. (1990). Personal communication.

Tjaden, P., & Thoennes, N. (2000b). Full report of the prevalence, incidence, and consequences of violence against women: Findings from the National Violence Against Women Survey (NCJ 183781). Washington, DC: U.S. Department of Justice, National Institute of Justice.

Todes, D. P. (1997). From the machine to the ghost within: Pavlov's transition from digestive physiology to conditional reflexes. *American Psychologist, 52,* 947–955.

Tolchin, M. (1994, April 17). Major airlines go two years without a fatality. *New York Times* report (in *Grand Rapids Press,* p. A10).

Tolkien, J. R. R. (1965). *The fellowship of the ring.* Boston: Houghton Mifflin Co.

Tollefson, G. D., Fawcett, J., Winokur, G., Beasley, C. M., et al. (1993). Evaluation of suicidality during pharmacologic treatment of mood and non-mood disorders. *Annals of Clinical Psychiatry, 5*(4), 209–224.

Tollefson, G. D., Rampey, A. H., Beasley, C. M., & Enas, G. G. (1994). Absence of a relationship between adverse events and suicidality during pharmacotherapy for depression. *Journal of Clinical Psychopharmacology, 14,* 163–169.

Tolman, E. C., & Honzik, C. H. (1930). Introduction and removal of reward, and maze performance in rats. *University of California Publications in Psychology, 4,* 257–275.

Tolstoy, L. (1904). *My confessions.* Boston: Dana Estes.

Tondo, L., Jamison, K. R., & Baldessarini, R. J. (1997). Effect of lithium maintenance on suicidal behavior in major mood disorders. In D. M. Stoff & J. J. Mann (Eds.), *The neurobiology of suicide: From the bench to the clinic.* New York: New York Academy of Sciences.

Toni, N., Buchs, P.-A., Nikonenko, I., Bron, C. R., & Muller, D. (1999). LTP promotes formation of multiple spine synapses between a single axon terminal and a dendrite. *Nature, 402,* 421–42.

Torrey, E. F. (1986). *Witchdoctors and psychiatrists.* New York: Harper & Row.

Torrey, E. F. (1998, February 22). Quoted by M. Winerip, Schizophrenia's most zealous foe. *New York Times Magazine,* pp. 26–28.

Torrey, E. F., & Miller, J. (2002). The invisible plague: The rise of mental illness from 1750 to the present. New Brunswick, NJ: London: Rutgers University Press.

Torrey, E. F., Miller, J., Rawlings, R., & Yolken, R. H. (1997). Seasonality of births in schizophrenia and bipolar disorder: A review of the literature. *Schizophrenia Research, 28,* 1–38.

Totterdell, P., Kellett, S., Briner, R. B., & Teuchmann, K. (1998). Evidence of mood linkage in work groups. *Journal of Personality and Social Psychology, 74,* 1504–1515.

Tovee, M. J., Mason, S. M., Emery, J. L., McCluskey, S. E., & Cohen-Tovee, E. M. (1997). Supermodels: Stick insects or hourglasses? *The Lancet, 350,* 1474–1475.

Towler, G. (1986). From zero to one hundred: Coaction in a natural setting. *Perceptual and Motor Skills, 62,* 377–378.

Tracey, J. L., & Robins, R. W. (2004). Show your pride: Evidence for a discrete emotion expression. *Psychological Science, 15,* 194–197.

Tramontana, M. G., Hooper, S. R., & Selzer, S. C. (1988). Research on the preschool prediction of later academic achievement: A review. *Developmental Review, 8,* 89–146.

Tranel, D., Bechara, A., & Denburg, N. L. (2002). Asymmetric functional roles of right and left ventromedial prefrontal cortices in social conduct, decision-making and emotional processing. *Cortex, 38,* pp. 589–613.

Travis, J. (1994). Glia: The brain's other cells. *Science, 266,* 970–972.

Treffert, D. A., & Wallace, G. L. (2002). Island of genius—The artistic brilliance and dazzling memory that sometimes accompany autism and other disorders hint at how all brains work. *Scientific American, 286,* 76–86.

Treisman, A. (1987). Properties, parts, and objects. In K. R. Boff, L. Kaufman, & J. P. Thomas (Eds.), *Handbook of perception and human performance.* New York: Wiley.

Tremblay, R. E., Pihl, R. O., Vitaro, F., & Dobkin, P. L. (1994). Predicting early onset of male antisocial behavior from preschool behavior. *Archives of General Psychiatry, 51,* 732–739.

Trewin, D. (2001). *Australian social trends 2001.* Canberra: Australian Bureau of Statistics.

Triandis, H. C. (1981). Some dimensions of intercultural variation and their implications for interpersonal behavior. Paper presented at the American Psychological Association convention.

Triandis, H. C. (1989a). The self and social behavior in differing cultural contexts. *Psychological Review, 96,* 506–520.

Triandis, H. C. (1989b). Cross-cultural studies of individualism and collectivism. In J. J. Berman (Ed.), *Nebraska symposium on motivation 1989* (Vol. 37). Lincoln, NE: University of Nebraska Press.

Triandis, H. C. (1994). *Culture and social behavior.* New York: McGraw-Hill.

Triandis, H. C., Bontempo, R., Villareal, M. J., Asai, M., & Lucca, N. (1988). Individualism and collectivism: Cross-cultural perspectives on self-ingroup relationships. *Journal of Personality and Social Psychology, 54,* 323–338.

Trickett, P. K., & McBride-Chang, C. (1995). The developmental impact of different forms of child abuse and neglect. *Developmental Review, 15,* 311–337.

Trimble, J. E. (1994). Cultural variations in the use of alcohol and drugs. In W. J. Lonner & R. Malpass (Eds.), *Psychology and culture.* Boston: Allyn & Bacon.

Triplett, N. (1898). The dynamogenic factors in pacemaking and competition. *American Journal of Psychology, 9,* 507–533.

Trolier, T. K., & Hamilton, D. L. (1986). Variables influencing judgments of correlational relations. *Journal of Personality and Social Psychology, 50,* 879–888.

Trut, L. N. (1999). Early canid domestication: The farm-fox experiment. *American Scientist, 87,* 160–169.

Tsai, J. L., & Chentsova-Dutton, Y. (2003). Variation among European Americans in emotional facial expression. *Journal of Cross-Cultural Psychology, 34,* 650–657.

Tsang, Y. C. (1938). Hunger motivation in gastrectomized rats. *Journal of Comparative Psychology, 26,* 1–17.

Tsien, J. Z. (April, 2000). Building a brainier mouse. *Scientific American,* 62–68.

Tsuang, M. T., & Faraone, S. V. (1990). *The genetics of mood disorders.* Baltimore, MD: Johns Hopkins University Press.

Tuber, D. S., Miller, D. D., Caris, K. A., Halter, R., Linden, F., & Hennessy, M. B. (1999). Dogs in animal shelters: Problems, suggestions, and needed expertise. *Psychological Science, 10,* 379–386.

Tucker, K. A. (2002). I believe you can fly. *Gallup Management Journal* (www.gallupjournal.com/CA/st/20020520.asp).

Tuerk, P. W. (2005). Research in the high-stakes era: Achievement, resources, and no child left behind. *Psychological Science, 16,* 419–425.

Tulving, E. (1996, August 18). Quoted in J. Gatehouse, Technology revealing brain's secrets. *Montreal Gazette,* p. A3.

Turkheimer, E., Haley, A., Waldron, M., D'Onofrio, B., & Gottesman, I. I. (2003). Socioeconomic status modifies heritability of IQ in young mothers. *Psychological Science, 14,* 623–628.

Turner, C. W., Hesse, B. W., & Peterson-Lewis, S. (1986). Naturalistic studies of the long-term effects of television violence. *Journal of Social Issues, 42*(3), 7–28.

Turner, J. C. (1987). *Rediscovering the social group: A self-categorization theory.* New York: Basil Blackwell.

Turner, N., Barling, J., & Zacharatos, A. (2002). Positive psychology at work. In C. R. Snyder & S. J. Lopez (Eds.), *The handbook of positive psychology.* New York: Oxford University Press.

Turpin, A. (2005, April 3). The science of psi. *FT Weekend,* pp. W1, W2.

Tutu, D. (1999). *No future without forgiveness.* New York: Doubleday.

Tversky, A. (1985, June). Quoted in K. McKean, Decisions, decisions. *Discover,* pp. 22–31.

Tversky, A., & Kahneman, D. (1974). Judgment under uncertainty: Heuristics and biases. *Science, 185,* 1124–1131.

Twenge, J. M. (1997). Changes in masculine and feminine traits over time: A meta-analysis. *Sex Roles 36*(5–6), 305–325.

Twenge, J. M. (2000). The age of anxiety? Birth cohort change in anxiety and neuroticism, 1952–1993. *Journal of Personality and Social Psychology, 79,* 1007–1021.

Twenge, J. M. (2001). Changes in women's assertiveness in response to status and roles: A cross-temporal meta-analysis, 1931–1993. *Journal of Personality and Social Psychology, 8,* 133–145.

Twenge, J. M., Baumeister, R. F., Tice, D. M., & Stucke, T. S. (2001). If you can't join them, beat them: Effects of social exclusion on aggressive behavior. *Journal of Personality and Social Psychology, 81,* 1058–1069.

Twenge, J. M., & Campbell, W. K. (2001). Age and birth cohort differences in self-esteem: A cross-temporal meta-analysis. *Personality and Social Psychology Review, 5,* 321–344.

Twenge, J. M., Catanese, K. R., & Baumeister, R. F. (2002). Social exclusion causes self-defeating behavior. *Journal of Personality and Social Psychology, 83,* 606–615.

Twenge, J. M., Catanese, K. R., & Baumeister, R. F. (2003). Social exclusion and the deconstructed state: Time perception, meaninglessness, lethargy, lack of emotion, and self-awareness. *Journal of Personality and Social Psychology, 85,* 409–423.

Twenge, J. M., & Crocker, J. (2002). Race and self-esteem: Meta-analyses comparing Whites, Blacks, Hispanics, Asians, and American Indians and comment on Gray-Little and Hafdahl (2000). *Psychological Bulletin, 128,* 371–408.

Twenge, J. M., & Nolen-Hoeksema, S. (2002). Age, gender, race, socioeconomic status, and birth cohort differences on the children's depression inventory: A meta-analysis. *Journal of Abnormal Psychology, 111,* 578–588.

Twenge, J. M., Zhang, L., & Im, C. (2004). It's beyond my control: A cross-temporal meta-analysis of increasing externality in locus of control, 1960–2002. *Personality and Social Psychology Review, 8,* 308–319.

Twiss, C., Tabb, S., & Crosby, F. (1989). Affirmative action and aggregate data: The importance of patterns in the perception of discrimination. In F. Blanchard & F. Crosby (Eds.), *Affirmative action: Social psychological perspectives.* New York: Springer-Verlag.

Tyler, C. (1998). An eye-placement principle in 500 years of portraits. San Francisco: Smith-Kettlewell Eye Reseach Institute (http://www.ski.org/CWTyler_lab/ARVO/cwtarvo.html).

Tyler, K. A. (2002). Social and emotional outcomes of childhood sexual abuse: A review of recent research. *Aggression and Violent Behavior, 7,* 567–589.

Uchino, B. N., Cacioppo, J. T., & Kiecolt-Glaser, J. K. (1996). The relationship between social support and physiological processes: A review with emphasis on underlying mechanisms and implications for health. *Psychological Bulletin, 119,* 488–531.

Uchino, B. N., Uno, D., & Holt-Lunstad, J. (1999). Social support, physiological processes, and health. *Current Directions in Psychological Science, 8,* 145–148.

Udry, J. R. (2000). Biological limits of gender construction. *American Sociological Review, 65,* 443–457.

Uehling, M. C. (1998, August). A brief history of Stephen Hawking. *Biography Magazine,* pp. 61–65, 116–117.

UK ECT Review Group. (2003). Efficacy and safety of electroconvulsive therapy in depressive disorders: A systematic review and meta-analysis. *Lancet, 361,* 799–808.

Ullman, E. (2005, October 19). The boss in the machine. *New York Times* (www.nytimes.com).

Ulrich, R. E. (1991). Animal rights, animal wrongs and the question of balance. *Psychological Science, 2,* 197–201.

Ulrich, R. S. (1984). View through a window may influence recovery from surgery. *Science, 224,* 420–421.

UNAIDS. (2004, July). *UNAIDS 2004 report on the global AIDS epidemic* (www.unaids.org).

UNAIDS. (2004). *AIDS epidemic update 2004.* United Nations (www.unaids.org).

UNAIDS. (2004). Sub-Saharan Africa. Joint United Nations Programme on HIV/AIDS (www.unaids.org).

UNAIDS. (2005). *AIDS epidemic update, December 2005.* United Nations (www.unaids.org).

UNAIDS. (2005). *AIDS in Africa: Three scenarios to 2025.* United Nations (www.unaids.org).

UNAIDS. (2005). Epidemiology. Joint United Nations Programme on HIV/AIDS (www.unaids.org).

Underwood, B. J. (1957). Interference and forgetting. *Psychological Review, 64,* 49–60.

United Nations. (1992). *1991 demographic yearbook.* New York: United Nations.

Urbany, J. E., Bearden, W. O., & Weilbaker, D. C. (1988). The effect of plausible and exaggerated reference prices on consumer perceptions and price search. *Journal of Consumer Research, 15,* 95–110.

Urry, H. L., Nitschke, J. B., Dolski, I., Jackson, D. C., Dalton, K. M., Mueller, C. J., Rosenkranz, M. A., Ryff, C. D., Singer, B. H., & Davidson, R. J. (2004). Making a life worth living: Neural correlates of well-being. *Psychological Science, 15,* 367–372.

Ursu, S., Stenger, V. A., Shear, M. K., Jones, M. R., & Carter, C. S. (2003). Overactive action monitoring in obsessive-compulsive disorder: Evidence from functional magnetic resonance imaging. *Psychological Science, 14,* 347–353.

USAID. (2004, January). The ABCs of HIV prevention. www.usaid.gov.

U.S. News & World Report. (1997, March 31). Oprah: A heavenly body? Survey finds talk-show host a celestial shoo-in. P. 18.

U.S. Senate Select Committee on Intelligence (2004, July 9). *Report of the U.S. Intelligence Community's prewar intelligence assessments on Iraq.* www.gpoaccess.gov/serialset/creports/iraq.html

Vaidya, J. G., Gray, E. K., Haig, J., & Watson, D. (2002). On the temporal stability of personality: Evidence for differential stability and the role of life experiences. *Journal of Personality and Social Psychology, 83,* 1469–1484.

Vaillant, G. E. (1977). *Adaptation to life.* New York: Little, Brown.

Vaillant, G. E. (2002). *Aging well: Surprising guideposts to a happier life from the landmark Harvard study of adult development.* Boston: Little, Brown.

Vaitl, D., & 14 others (2005). Psychobiology of altered states of consciousness. *Psychological Bulletin, 131,* 98–127.

Valenstein, E. (1998). *Blaming the brain: The truth about drugs and mental health.* Free Press.

Valenstein, E. S. (1986). *Great and desperate cures: The rise and decline of psychosurgery.* New York: Basic Books.

Vallone, R. P., Griffin, D. W., Lin, S., & Ross, L. (1990). Overconfident prediction of future actions and outcomes by self and others. *Journal of Personality and Social Psychology, 58,* 582–592.

van Boxtel, H. W., Orobio de Castro, B., & Goossens, F. A. (2004). High self-perceived social competence in rejected children is related to frequent fighting. *European Journal of Developmental Psychology, 1,* 205–214.

Vance, E. B., & Wagner, N. N. (1976). Written descriptions of orgasm: A study of sex differences. *Archives of Sexual Behavior, 5,* 87–98.

Vandell, D. L. (2000). Parents, peer groups, and other socializing influences. *Developmental Psychology, 36,* 699–710.

Vandello, J. A., & Cohen, D. (1999). Patterns of individualism and collectivism across the United States. *Journal of Personality and Social Psychology, 77,* 279–292.

Vandenberg, S. G., & Kuse, A. R. (1978). Mental rotations: A group test of three-dimensional spatial visualization. *Perceptual and Motor Skills, 47,* 599–604.

van den Boom, D. (1990). Preventive intervention and the quality of mother-infant interaction and infant exploration in irritable infants. In W. Koops, H. J. G. Soppe, J. L. van der Linden, P. C. M. Molenaar, & J. J. F. Schroots (Eds.), *Developmental psychology behind the dikes: An outline of developmental psychology research in The Netherlands.* The Netherlands: Uitgeverij Eburon. Cited by C. Hazan & P. R. Shaver (1994). Deeper into attachment theory. *Psychological Inquiry, 5,* 68-79.

van den Bos, K., & Spruijt, N. (2002). Appropriateness of decisions as a moderator of the psychology of voice. *European Journal of Social Psychology, 32,* 57-72.

VanderStoep, S. W., & Shaughnessy, J. J. (1997). Taking a course in research methods improves reasoning about real-life events. *Teaching of Psychology, 24,* 122-124.

Van Dyke, C., & Byck, R. (1982, March). Cocaine. *Scientific American,* pp. 128-141.

van Engen, M. L., & Willemsen, T. M. (2004). Sex and leadership styles: A meta-analysis of research published in the 1990s. *Psychological Reports, 94,* 3-18.

van IJzendoorn, M. H., & De Wolff, M. S. (1997). In search of the absent father—Meta-analyses of infant-father attachment: A rejoinder to our discussants. *Child Development, 68,* 604-610.

van IJzendoorn, M. H., & Kroonenberg, P. M. (1988). Cross-cultural patterns of attachment: A meta-analysis of the strange situation. *Child Development, 59,* 147-156.

Van Leeuwen, M. S. (1978). A cross-cultural examination of psychological differentiation in males and females. *International Journal of Psychology, 13,* 87-122.

Van Leeuwen, M. S. (1982). IQism and the just society: Historical background. *Journal of the American Scientific Affiliation, 34,* 193-201.

van Lommel, P., van Wees, R., Meyers, V., & Elfferich, I. (2001). Near-death experience in survivors of cardiac arrest: A prospective study in the Netherlands. *Lancet, 358,* 2039-2045.

Vanman, E. J., Saltz, J. L., Nathan, L. R., & Warren, J. A. (2004). Racial discrimination by low-prejudiced Whites. *Psychological Science, 15,* 711-714.

Van Praag, H., Schinder, A. F., Christie, B. R., Toni, N., Palmer, T. D., & Gage, F. H. (2002). Neurogenesis: Functional neurons in adult hippocampus. *Nature, 415,* 1030-1034.

Van Rooy, D. L., & Viswesvaran, C. (2004). Emotional intelligence: A meta-analytic investigation of predictive validity and nomological net. *Journal of Vocational Behavior, 65,* 71-95.

van Schaik, C. P., Ancrenaz, M., Borgen, G., Galdikas, B., Knott, C. D., Singleton, I., Suzuki, A., Utami, S. S., & Merrill, M. (2003). Orangutan cultures and the evolution of material culture. *Science, 299,* 102-105.

VanTassel-Baska, J. (1983). Profiles of precocity: The 1982 Midwest Talent Search finalists. *Gifted Child Quarterly, 27,* 139-145.

Van Yperen, N. W., & Buunk, B. P. (1990). A longitudinal study of equity and satisfaction in intimate relationships. *European Journal of Social Psychology, 20,* 287-309.

Vaughn, K. B., & Lanzetta, J. T. (1981). The effect of modification of expressive displays on vicarious emotional arousal. *Journal of Experimental Social Psychology, 17,* 16-30.

Vazire, S., & Gosling, S. D. (2004). e-Perceptions: Personality impressions based on personal websites. *Journal of Personality and Social Psychology, 87,* 123-132.

Vecera, S. P., Vogel, E. K., & Woodman, G. F. (2002). Lower region: A new cue for figure-ground assignment. *Journal of Experimental Psychology: General, 13,* 194-205.

Vega, W. A., Kolody, B., Aguilar-Gaxiola, S., Alderete, E., Catalano, R., & Caraveo-Anduaga, J. (1998). Lifetime prevalence of DSM-III-R psychiatric disorders among urban and rural Mexican Americans in California. *Archives of General Psychiatry, 55,* 771-778.

Vekassy, L. (1977). Dreams of the blind. *Magyar Pszichologiai Szemle, 34,* 478-491.

Vemer, E., Coleman, M., Ganong, L. H., & Cooper, H. (1989). Marital satisfaction in remarriage: A meta-analysis. *Journal of Marriage and the Family, 51,* 713-725.

Venn, J. (1986). Hypnosis and the Lamaze method: A reply to Wideman and Singer. *American Psychologist, 41,* 475-476.

Verbeek, M. E. M., Drent, P. J., & Wiepkema, P. R. (1994). Consistent individual differences in early exploratory behaviour of male great tits. *Animal Behaviour, 48,* 1113-1121.

Verhaeghen, P., & Salthouse, T. A. (1997). Meta-analyses of age-cognition relations in adulthood: Estimates of linear and nonlinear age effects and structural models. *Psychological Bulletin, 122,* 231-249.

Vernon, P. A. (1983). Speed of information processing and general intelligence. *Intelligence, 7,* 53-70.

Viding, E., Blair, R., James, R., Moffitt, T. E., & Plomin, R. (2005). Evidence for substantial genetic risk for psychopathy in 7-year-olds. *Journal of Child Psychology & Psychiatry, 46,* 592-597.

Vigliocco, G., & Hartsuiker, R. J. (2002). The interplay of meaning, sound, and syntax in sentence production. *Psychological Bulletin, 128,* 442-472.

Vining, E. P. G., Freeman, J. M., Pillas, D. J., Uematsu, S., Carson, B. S., Brandt, J., Boatman, D., Pulsifer, M. B., & Zukerberg, A. (1997). Why would you remove half a brain? The outcome of 58 children after hemispherectomy—The Johns Hopkins Experience: 1968 to 1996. *Pediatrics, 100,* 163-171.

Vita, A. J., Terry, R. B., Hubert, H. B., & Fries, J. F. (1998). Aging, health risks, and cumulative disability. *New England Journal of Medicine, 338,* 1035-1041.

Vitaliano, P. P., Zhang, J., & Scanlan, J. M. (2003). Is caregiving hazardous to one's physical health? A meta-analysis. *Psychological Bulletin, 129,* 946-972.

Vitevitch, M. S. (2003). Change deafness: The inability to detect changes between two voices. *Journal of Experimental Psychology: Human Perception and Performance, 29,* 333-342.

Vogel, S. (1999). *The skinny on fat: Our obsession with weight control.* New York: W. H. Freeman.

Vohs, K., Voelz, Z., Pettit, J., Bardone, A., Katz, J., Abramson, L., Heatherton, T., & Joiner, T. (2001). Perfectionism, body dissatisfaction, and self-esteem: An interactive model of bulimic symptom development. *Journal of Social and Clinical Psychology, 20,* 476-497.

Vokey, J. R. (2002). Subliminal messages. In J. R. Vokey and S.W. Allen (Eds.), *Psychological sketches* (6th Edition). Lethbridge, Alberta: Psyence Ink, pp. 223-246.

von Békésy, G. (1957, August). The ear. *Scientific American,* pp. 66-78.

von Senden, M. (1932; reprinted 1960). In P. Heath (Trans.), *Space and sight: The perception of space and shape in the congenitally blind before and after operation.* Glencoe, IL: Free Press.

Vreeland, C. N., Gallagher, B. J., III, & McFalls, J. A., Jr. (1995). The beliefs of members of the American Psychiatric Association on the etiology of male homosexuality: A national survey. *Journal of Psychology, 129,* 507-517.

Wadden, T. A., Vogt, R. A., Foster, G. D., & Anderson, D. A. (1998). Exercise and the maintenance of weight loss: 1-year follow-up of a controlled clinical trial. *Journal of Consulting and Clinical Psychology, 66,* 429-433.

Wager, T. D., Rilling, J. K., Smith, E. E., Sokolik, A., Casey, K. L., Davidson, R. J., Kosslyn, S. M., Rose, R. M., & Cohen, J. D. (2004). Placebo-induced changes in fMRI in the anticipation and experience of pain. *Science, 303,* 1162-1167.

Wagner, A. D., Schacter, D. L., Rotte, M., Koutstaal, W., Maril, A., Dale, A. M., Rosen, B. R., & Buckner, R. L. (1998). Building memories: Remembering and forgetting of verbal experiences as predicted by brain activity. *Science, 281,* 1188-1191.

Wagner, U., Gais, S., Haider, H., Verleger, R., & Born, J. (2004). Sleep inspires insight. *Nature, 427,* 352–355.

Wagstaff, G. (1982). Attitudes to rape: The "just world" strikes again? *Bulletin of the British Psychological Society, 13,* 275–283.

Wahl, O. F. (1992). Mass media images of mental illness: A review of the literature. *Journal of Community Psychology, 20,* 343–352.

Wahlberg, D. (2001, October 11). We're more depressed, patriotic, poll finds. *Grand Rapids Press,* p. A15.

Wakefield, J. C., & Spitzer, R. L. (2002). Lowered estimates—but of what? *Archives of General Psychiatry, 59,* 129–130.

Waldrop, M. M. (1987). The workings of working memory. *Science, 237,* 1564–1567.

Walker, W. R., Skowronski, J. J., Gibbons, J. A., Vogl, R. J., & Thompson, C. P. (2003). On the emotions that accompany autobiographical memories: Dysphoria disrupts the fading affect bias. *Cognition and Emotion, 17,* 703–723.

Walker, W. R., Skowronski, J. J., & Thompson, C. P. (2003). Life is pleasant—and memory helps to keep it that way! *Review of General Psychology, 7,* 203–210.

Wall, B. (2002, August 24–25). Profit matures along with baby boomers. *International Herald Tribune,* p. 13.

Wall, P. (2000). *Pain: The science of suffering.* New York: Columbia University Press.

Wall Street Journal. (1999, December 17). Money and misery. Editorial, p. A14.

Wallace, D. S., Paulson, R. M., Lord, C. G., & Bond, C. F., Jr. (2005). Which behaviors do attitudes predict? Meta-analyzing the effects of social pressure and perceived difficulty. *Review of General Psychology, 9*(3), 214–227.

Wallach, M. A., & Wallach, L. (1983). *Psychology's sanction for selfishness: The error of egoism in theory and therapy.* New York: Freeman.

Wallach, M. A., & Wallach, L. (1985, February). How psychology sanctions the cult of the self. *Washington Monthly,* pp. 46–56.

Wallbott, H. G. (1988). In and out of context: Influences of facial expression and context information on emotion attributions. *British Journal of Social Psychology, 27,* 357–369.

Wallis, C. (1983, June 6). Stress: Can we cope? *Time,* pp. 48–54.

Walster (Hatfield), E., Aronson, V., Abrahams, D., & Rottman, L. (1966). Importance of physical attractiveness in dating behavior. *Journal of Personality and Social Psychology, 4,* 508–516.

Wampold, B. E. (2001). *The great psychotherapy debate: Models, methods, and findings.* Mahwah, NJ: Erlbaum.

Wampold, B. E., Mondin, G. W., Moody, M., & Ahn, H. (1997). The flat earth as a metaphor for the evidence for uniform efficacy of bona fide psychotherapies: Reply to Crits-Christoph (1997) and Howard et al. (1997). *Psychological Bulletin, 122,* 226–230.

Wang, Y., Liu, D., & Wang, Y. (2003). Discovering the capacity of human memory. *Brain and Mind, 4,* 189–198.

Wansink, B., & van Ittersum, K. (2003). Bottoms up! The influence of elongation on pouring and consumption volume. *Journal of Consumer Research, 30,* 455–464.

Warchol, M. E., Lambert, P. R., Goldstein, B. J., Forge, A., & Corwin, J. T. (1993). Regenerative proliferation in inner ear sensory epithelia from adult guinea pigs and humans. *Science, 259,* 1619–1622.

Ward, A., & Mann, T. (2000). Don't mind if I do: Disinhibited eating under cognitive load. *Journal of Personality and Social Psychology, 78,* 753–763.

Ward, C. (1994). Culture and altered states of consciousness. In W. J. Lonner & R. Malpass (Eds.), *Psychology and culture.* Boston: Allyn & Bacon.

Ward, J. (2003). State of the art synaesthesia. *The Psychologist, 16,* 196–199.

Ward, K. D., Klesges, R. C., & Halpern, M. T. (1997). Predictors of smoking cessation and state-of-the-art smoking interventions. *Journal of Socies Issues, 53,* 129–145.

Wardle, J., Cooke, L. J., Gibson, L., Sapochnik, M., Sheiham, A., Lawson, M. (2003). Increasing children's acceptance of vegetables; a randomized trial of parent-led exposure. *Appetite, 40,* 155–162.

Warm, J. S., & Dember, W. N. (1986, April). Awake at the switch. *Psychology Today,* pp. 46–53.

Warner, J., McKeown, E., Johnson, K., Ramsay, A., Cort, C., & King, M. (2004). Rates and predictors of mental illness in gay men, lesbians and bisexual men and women. *British Journal of Psychiatry, 185,* 479–485.

Warr, P., & Payne, R. (1982). Experiences of strain and pleasure among British adults. *Social Science and Medicine, 16,* 1691–1697.

Warren, N. C. (2005, March 4). Personal correspondence from founder of eHarmony.com.

Wason, P. C. (1960). On the failure to eliminate hypotheses in a conceptual task. *Quarterly Journal of Experimental Psychology, 12,* 129–140.

Wason, P. C. (1981). The importance of cognitive illusions. *The Behavioral and Brain Sciences, 4,* 356.

Wasserman, E. A. (1993). Comparative cognition: Toward a general understanding of cognition in behavior. *Psychological Science, 4,* 156–161.

Wasserman, E. A. (1995). The conceptual abilities of pigeons. *American Scientist, 83,* 246–255.

Wastell, C. A. (2002). Exposure to trauma: The long-term effects of suppressing emotional reactions. *Journal of Nervous and Mental Disorders, 190,* 839–845.

Watamura, S. E., Donzella, B., Alwin, J., & Gunnar, M. R. (2003). Morning-to-afternoon increases in cortisol concentrations for infants and toddlers at child care: Age differences and behavioral correlates. *Child Development, 74,* 1006–1020.

Waterhouse, R. (1993, July 19). Income for 62 percent is below average pay. *The Independent,* p. 4.

Waterman, A. S. (1988). Identity status theory and Erikson's theory: Commonalities and differences. *Developmental Review, 8,* 185–208.

Watkins, C. E., Campbell, V. L., Nieberding, R., & Hallmark, R. (1995). Contemporary practice of psychological assessment by clinical psychologists. *Professional Psychology: Research and Practice, 26,* 54–60.

Watkins, J. G. (1984). The Bianchi (L. A. Hillside Strangler) case: Sociopath or multiple personality? *International Journal of Clinical and Experimental Hypnosis, 32,* 67–101.

Watkins, P. C. (2004). Gratitude and subjective well-being. In R. A. Emmons and M. E. McCullough (Eds.), *The psychology of gratitude.* New York: Oxford University Press.

Watson, D. (2000). *Mood and temperament.* New York: Guilford Press.

Watson, D. (2003). To dream, perchance to remember: Individual differences in dream recall. *Personality and Individual Differences, 34,* 1271–1286.

Watson, D., Suls, J., & Haig, J. (2002). Global self-esteem in relation to structural models of personality and affectivity. *Journal of Personality and Social Psychology, 83,* 185–197.

Watson, D., Wiese, D., Vaidya, J., & Tellegen, A. (1999). The two general activation systems of affect: Structured findings, evolutionary considerations, and psychobiological evidence. *Journal of Personality and Social Psychology, 76,* 820–838.

Watson, J. B. (1913). Psychology as the behaviorist views it. *Psychological Review, 20,* 158–177.

Watson, J. B. (1924). The unverbalized in human behavior. *Psychological Review, 31,* 339–347.

Watson, J. B., & Rayner, R. (1920). Conditioned emotional reactions. *Journal of Experimental Psychology, 3,* 1–14.

Watson, R. I., Jr. (1973). Investigation into deindividuation using a cross-cultural survey technique. *Journal of Personality and Social Psychology, 25,* 342–345.

Watson, S. J., Benson, J. A., Jr., & Joy, J. E. (2000). NEWS AND VIEWS—Marijuana and medicine: Assessing the science base: A summary of the 1999 Institute of Medicine report. *Archives of General Psychiatry, 57,* 547–553.

Wayment, H. A., & Peplau, L. A. (1995). Social support and well-being among lesbian and heterosexual women: A structural modeling approach. *Personality and Social Psychology Bulletin, 21,* 1189–1199.

Weaver, J. B., Masland, J. L., & Zillmann, D. (1984). Effect of erotica on young men's aesthetic perception of their female sexual partners. *Perceptual and Motor Skills, 58,* 929–930.

Webb, W. B. (1992). *Sleep: The gentle tyrant.* Bolton, MA: Anker Publishing.

Webb, W. B., & Campbell, S. S. (1983). Relationships in sleep characteristics of identical and fraternal twins. *Archives of General Psychiatry, 40,* 1093–1095.

Wechsler, D. (1972). "Hold" and "Don't Hold" tests. In S. M. Chown (Ed.), *Human aging.* New York: Penguin.

Wechsler, H., Davenport, A., Dowdall, G., Moeykens, B., & Castillo, S. (1994). Health and behavioral consequences of binge drinking in college. *Journal of the American Medical Association, 272,* 1672–1677.

Wechsler, H., Lee, J. E., Kuo, M., Seibring, M., Nelson, T. F., & Lee, H. (2002). Trends in college binge drinking during a period of increased prevention efforts. *Journal of American College Health, 50,* 203–217.

Wee, C. C., Phillips, R. S., Legedza, A. T. R., Davis, R. B., Soukup, J. R., Colditz, G. A., & Hamel, M. B. (2005). Health care expenditures associated with overweight and obesity among US adults: Importance of age and race. *American Journal of Public Health, 95,* 159–165.

Weed, W. S. (2001, May). Can we go to Mars without going crazy? *Discover,* pp. 31–43.

Wegner, D. M. (1990). *White bears and other unwanted thoughts: Suppression, obsession, and the psychology of mental control.* New York: Penguin Books.

Wegner, D. M. (2002). *The illusion of conscious will.* Cambridge, MA: MIT Press.

Weigel, G. (2005, March-April). Is Europe dying? Notes on a crisis of civilizational morale. *New Atlantic Initiative,* American Enterprise Institute for Public Policy Research (www.aei.org/nai).

Weinberg, M. S., & Williams, C. (1974). *Male homosexuals: Their problems and adaptations.* New York: Oxford University Press.

Weinberger, N. M. (2004, November). Music and the brain. *Scientific American,* pp. 89–95.

Weiner, B. (1985). An attributional theory of achievement motivation and emotion. *Psychological Review, 92,* 548–573.

Weingarten, G. (2002, March 10). Below the beltway. *Washington Post,* p. W03.

Weinstein, N. D. (1980). Unrealistic optimism about future life events. *Journal of Personality and Social Psychology, 39,* 806–820.

Weinstein, N. D. (1982). Unrealistic optimism about susceptibility to health problems. *Journal of Behavioral Medicine, 5,* 441–460.

Weinstein, N. D. (1987). Unrealistic optimism about susceptibility to health problems: Conclusions from a community-wide sample. *Journal of Behavioral Medicine, 10,* 481–500.

Weinstein, N. D. (1996, October 4). 1996 optimistic bias bibliography. Distributed via internet (weinstein_c@aesop.rutgers.edu).

Weiskrantz, L. (1986). *Blindsight: A case study and implications.* Oxford, UK: Oxford University Press.

Weiss, A., King, J. E., & Enns, R. M. (2002). Subjective well-being is heritable and genetically correlated with dominance in chimpanzees (*Pan troglodytes*). *Journal of Personality and Social Psychology, 83,* 1141–1149.

Weiss, A., King, J. E., & Figueredo, A. J. (2000). The heritability of personality factors in chimpanzees (*Pan troglodytes*). *Behavior Genetics, 30,* 213–221.

Weiss, J. M. (1977). Psychological and behavioral influences on gastrointestinal lesions in animal models. In J. D. Maser & M. E. P. Seligman (Eds.), *Psychopathology: Experimental models.* San Francisco: Freeman.

Weissman, M. M. (1999). Interpersonal psychotherapy and the health care scene. In D. S. Janowsky (Ed.), *Psychotherapy indications and outcomes.* Washington, DC: American Psychiatric Press.

Weissman, M. M., Bland, R. C., Canino, G. J., Faravelli, C., Greenwald, S., Hwu, H-G., Joyce, P. R., Karam, E. G., Lee, C-K., Lellouch, J., Lepine, J-P., Newman, S. C., Rubio-Stepic, M., Wells, J. E., Wickramaratne, P. J., Wittchen, H-U., & Yeh, E-K. (1996). Cross-national epidemiology of major depression and bipolar disorder. *Journal of the American Medical Association, 276,* 293–299.

Weisz, J. R., Rothbaum, F. M., & Blackburn, T. C. (1984). Standing out and standing in: The psychology of control in America and Japan. *American Psychologist, 39,* 955–969.

Wellman, H. M., Cross, D., & Watson, J. (2001). Meta-analysis of theory-of-mind development: The truth about false belief. *Child Development, 72,* 655–684.

Wellman, H. M., & Gelman, S. A. (1992). Cognitive development: Foundational theories of core domains. *Annual Review of Psychology, 43,* 337–375.

Wells, B. L. (1986). Predictors of female nocturnal orgasms: A multivariate analysis. *Journal of Sex Research, 22,* 421–437.

Wells, C. (1983, March). Teaching the brain new tricks. *Esquire,* 49–57.

Wells, G. L. (1981). Lay analyses of causal forces on behavior. In J. Harvey (Ed.), *Cognition, social behavior and the environment.* Hillsdale, NJ: Erlbaum.

Wells, G., & Murray, D. M. (1984). Eyewitness confidence. In G. L. Wells & E. F. Loftus (Eds.), *Eyewitness testimony: Psychological perspectives.* New York: Cambridge University Press.

Wender, P. H., Kety, S. S., Rosenthal, D., Schulsinger, F., Ortmann, J., & Lunde, I. (1986). Psychiatric disorders in the biological and adoptive families of adopted individuals with affective disorders. *Archives of General Psychiatry, 43,* 923–929.

Wener, R., Frazier, W., & Farbstein, J. (1987, June). Building better jails. *Psychology Today,* pp. 40–49.

Wessely, S., & Kerwin, R. (2004). Suicide risk and the SSRIs. *Journal of the American Medical Association, 292,* 379–381.

West, P. D. B., & Evans, E. F. (1990). Early detection of hearing damage in young listeners resulting from exposure to amplified music. *British Journal of Audiology, 24,* 89–103.

Westen, D. (1996). Is Freud really dead? Teaching psychodynamic theory to introductory psychology. Presentation to the Annual Institute on the Teaching of Psychology, St. Petersburg Beach, Florida.

Westen, D. (1998). The scientific legacy of Sigmund Freud: Toward a psychodynamically informed psychological science. *Psychological Bulletin, 124,* 333–371.

Westen, D., & Morrison, K. (2001). A multidimensional meta-analysis of treatments for depression, panic, and generalized anxiety disorder: An empirical examination of the status of empirically supported therapies. *Journal of Consulting and Clinical Psychology, 69,* 875–899.

Wetter, D. W., Fiore, M. C., Gritz, E. R., Lando, H. A., Stitzer, M. L., Hasselblad, V., & Baker, T. B. (1998). The Agency for Health Care Policy and Research. *Smoking cessation clinical practice guideline: Findings and implications for psychologists. American Psychologist, 53,* 657–669.

Weuve, J., Kang, J. H., Manson, J. E., Breteler, M. M. B., Ware, J. H., & Grodstein, F. (2004). Physical activity, including walking, and cognitive function in older women. *Journal of the American Medical Association, 292,* 1454–1460.

Wever, E. G. (1949). Theory of hearing. New York: Wiley.

Whalen, P. J., Kagan, J., Cook, R. G., Davis, F. C., Kim, H., Polis, S., McLaren, D. G., Somerville, L. H., McLean, A. A., Maxwell, J. S., & Johnstone, T. (2004). Human amygdala responsibility to masked fearful eye whites. *Science, 302,* 2061.

Whalen, P. J., Shin, L. M., McInerney, S. C., Fisher, H., Wright, C. I., & Rauch, S. L. (2001). A functional MRI study of human amygdala responses to facial expressions of fear versus anger. *Emotion, 1,* 70–83.

Whaley, S. E., Sigman, M., Beckwith, L., Cohen, S. E., & Espinosa, M. P. (2002). Infant-caregiver interaction in Kenya and the United States: The importance of multiple caregivers and adequate comparison samples. *Journal of Cross-Cultural Psychology, 33,* 236–247.

Whalley, L. J., & Deary, I. J. (2001). Longitudinal cohort study of childhood IQ and survival up to age 76. *British Medical Journal, 322,* 1–5.

Whalley, L., Starr, J. M. Athawes, R., Hunter, D., Pattie, A., & Deary, I. J. (2000). Childhood mental ability and dementia. *Neurology, 55,* 1455–1459.

Wheelwright, J. (2004, August). Study the clones first. *Discover,* pp. 44–50.

White, G. L., & Kight, T. D. (1984). Misattribution of arousal and attraction: Effects of salience of explanations for arousal. *Journal of Experimental Social Psychology, 20,* 55–64.

White, H. R., Brick, J., & Hansell, S. (1993). A longitudinal investigation of alcohol use and aggression in adolescence. *Journal of Studies on Alcohol,* Supplement No. 11, 62–77.

White House. (1999, June 7). White House fact sheet on myths and facts about mental illness. Washington, DC: White House Press Office.

White, K. M. (1983). Young adults and their parents: Individuation to mutuality. *New Directions for Child Development, 22,* 61–76.

White, L., & Edwards, J. (1990). Emptying the nest and parental well-being: An analysis of national panel data. *American Sociological Review, 55,* 235–242.

White, P. H., Kjelgaard, M. M., & Harkins, S. G. (1995). Testing the contribution of self-evaluation to goal-setting effects. *Journal of Personality and Social Psychology, 69,* 69–79.

White, R. A. (1998). Intuition, heart knowledge, and parapsychology. *Journal of the American Society for Psychical Research, 92,* 158–171.

Whitehead, B. D., & Popenoe, D. (2001). *The state of our unions 2001: The social health of marriage in America.* Rutgers University: The National Marriage Project.

Whiten, A., & Boesch, C. (2001, January). Cultures of chimpanzees. *Scientific American,* pp. 60–67.

Whiten, A., & Byrne, R. W. (1988). Tactical deception in primates. *Behavioral and Brain Sciences, 11,* 233–244, 267–273.

Whiting, B. B., & Edwards, C. P. (1988). *Children of different worlds: The formation of social behavior.* Cambridge, MA: Harvard University Press.

Whitley, B. E., Jr. (1990). The relationships of heterosexuals' attributions for the causes of homosexuality to attitudes toward lesbians and gay men. *Personality and Social Psychology Bulletin, 16,* 369–377.

Whitley, B. E., Jr. (1999). Right-wing authoritarianism, social dominance orientation, and prejudice. *Journal of Personality and Social Psychology, 77,* 126–134.

Whitley, B. E., Jr. (2002). Gender-role variables and attitudes toward homosexuality. *Sex Roles, 45,* 691–720.

Whittington, C. J., Kendall, T., Fonagy, P., Cottrell, D., Cotgrove, A., & Boddington, E. (2004). Selective serotonin reuptake inhibitors in childhood depression: Systematic review of published versus unpublished data. *Lancet, 363,* 1341–1345.

WHO. (2002). The global burden of disease. Geneva: World Health Organization (www.who.int/msa/mnh/ems/dalys/intro.htm).

WHO. (2002a, September 4). Suicide rates. World Health Organization (www5.who.int/mental_health).

WHO. (2002c, December 9). China: WHO lauds launch of nation's first suicide prevent center: Xinhua news. World Health Organization (www5.who.int/mental_health).

WHO. (2002d). Schizophrenia. World Health Organization (www5.who.int/mental_health).

WHO. (2004). Prevalence, severity, and unmet need for treatment of mental disorders in the World Health Organization World Mental Health Surveys. *Journal of the American Medical Association, 291,* 2581–2590.

WHO. (2005, February 24). Global tobacco treaty enters into force with 57 countries already committed. World Health Organization media centre (www.who.int).

Whooley, M. A., & Browner, W. S. (1998). Association between depressive symptoms and mortality in older women. *Archives of Internal Medicine, 158,* 2129–2135.

Whorf, B. L. (1956). Science and linguistics. In J. B. Carroll (Ed.), *Language, thought, and reality: Selected writings of Benjamin Lee Whorf.* Cambridge, MA: MIT Press.

Wichman, H. (1992). *Human factors in the design of spacecraft.* Stony Brook, NY: State University of New York.

Wickelgren, I. (2005). Autistic brains out of sync? *Science, 308,* 1856–1858.

Wickelgren, W. A. (1977). *Learning and memory.* Englewood Cliffs, NJ: Prentice-Hall.

Widom, C. S. (1989a). Does violence beget violence? A critical examination of the literature. *Psychological Bulletin, 106,* 3–28.

Widom, C. S. (1989b). The cycle of violence. *Science, 244,* 160–166.

Wiens, A. N., & Menustik, C. E. (1983). Treatment outcome and patient characteristics in an aversion therapy program for alcoholism. *American Psychologist, 38,* 1089–1096.

Wierson, M., & Forehand, R. (1994). Parent behavioral training for child noncompliance: Rationale, concepts, and effectiveness. *Current Directions in Psychological Science, 3,* 146–149.

Wiertelak, E. P., Smith K. P., Furness, L., Mooney-Heiberger, K., Mayr, T., Maier, S. F., & Watkins, L. R. (1994). Acute and conditioned hyperalgesic responses to illness. *Pain, 56,* 227–234.

Wierzbicki, M. (1993). Psychological adjustment of adoptees: A meta-analysis. *Journal of Clinical Child Psychology, 22,* 447–454.

Wiesel, T. N. (1982). Postnatal development of the visual cortex and the influence of environment. *Nature, 299,* 583–591.

Wiesner, W. H., & Cronshow, S. P. (1988). A meta-analytic investigation of the impact of interview format and degree of structure on the validity of the employment interview. *Journal of Occupational Psychology, 61,* 275–290.

Wigdor, A. K., & Garner, W. R. (1982). *Ability testing: Uses, consequences, and controversies.* Washington, DC: National Academy Press.

Wilcox, A. J., Baird, D. D., Dunson, D. B., McConnaughey, D. R., Kesner, J. S., & Weinberg, C. R. (2004). On the frequency of intercourse around ovulation: Evidence for biological influences. *Human Reproduction, 19,* 1539–1543.

Wilder, D. A. (1981). Perceiving persons as a group: Categorization and intergroup relations. In D. L. Hamilton (Ed.), *Cognitive processes in stereotyping and intergroup behavior.* Hillsdale, NJ: Erlbaum.

Wildman, D. E., Uddin, M., Liu, G., Grossman, L. I., & Goodman, M. (2003). Implications of natural selection in shaping 99.4% nonsynonymous DNA identity between humans and chimpanzees: Enlarging genus *Homo. Proceedings of the National Academy of Sciences, 100,* 7181–7188.

Wilford, J. N. (1999, February 9). New findings help balance the cosmological books. *New York Times* (www.nytimes.com).

Williams, C. L., & Berry, J. W. (1991). Primary prevention of acculturative stress among refugees. *American Psychologist, 46,* 632–641.

Williams, J. E., & Best, D. L. (1990). *Measuring sex stereotypes: A multination study.* Newbury Park, CA: Sage.

Williams, J. E., Paton, C. C., Siegler, I. C., Eigenbrodt, M. L., Nieto, F. J., & Tyroler, H. A. (2000). Anger proneness predicts coronary heart disease risk: Prospective analysis from the artherosclerosis risk in communities (ARIC) study. *Circulation, 101,* 17, 2034–2040.

Williams, K. D. (2002). *Ostracism: The power of silence.* New York: Guilford.

Williams, K. D., & Zadro, L. (2001). Ostracism: On being ignored, excluded and rejected. In M. Leary (Ed.), *Rejection.* New York: Oxford University Press.

Williams, R. (1989). *The trusting heart: Great news about Type A behavior.* New York: Random House.

Williams, R. (1993). *Anger kills.* New York: Times Books.

Williams, R. B., Barefoot, J. C., Califf, R. M., Haney, T. L., Saunders, W. B., Pryor, D. B., Hlatky, M. A., Siegler, I. C., & Mark, D. B. (1992). Prognostic importance of social and economic resources among medically treated patients with angiographically documented coronary artery disease. *Journal of the American Medical Association, 267,* 520–524.

Williams, S., & Kohut, J. L. (1999). Psychologists in medical schools in 1997: Research brief. *American Psychologist, 54,* 272–276.

Williams, S. L. (1987). Self-efficacy and mastery-oriented treatment for severe phobias. Paper presented to the American Psychological Association convention.

Willingham, W. W., Lewis, C., Morgan, R., & Ramist, L. (1990). *Predicting college grades: An analysis of institutional trends over two decades.* Princeton: Educational Testing Service.

Willmuth, M. E. (1987). Sexuality after spinal cord injury: A critical review. *Clinical Psychology Review, 7,* 389–412.

Wilson, A. E., & Ross, M. (2001). From chump to champ: People's appraisals of their earlier and present selves. *Journal of Personality and Social Psychology, 80,* 572–584.

Wilson, C. M., & Oswald, A. J. (2002). How does marriage affect physical and psychological health? A survey of the longitudinal evidence. Working paper, University of York and Warwick University.

Wilson, J. P., Harel, Z., & Kahana, B. (1988). *Human adaptation to extreme stress: From the Holocaust to Vietnam.* New York: Plenum Press.

Wilson, R. C., Gaft, J. G., Dienst, E. R., Wood, L., & Bavry, J. L. (1975). *College professors and their impact on students.* New York: Wiley.

Wilson, R. S. (1979). Analysis of longitudinal twin data: Basic model and applications to physical growth measures. *Acta Geneticae medicae et Gemellologiae, 28,* 93–105.

Wilson, R. S., & Bennett, D. A. (2003). Cognitive activity and risk of Alzheimer's disease. *Current Directions in Psychological Science, 12,* 87–91.

Wilson, R. S., & Matheny, A. P., Jr. (1986). Behavior-genetics research in infant temperament: The Louisville twin study. In R. Plomin & J. Dunn (Eds.), *The study of temperament: Changes, continuities, and challenges.* Hillsdale, NJ: Erlbaum.

Wilson, T. D. (2002). *Strangers to ourselves: Discovering the adaptive unconscious.* Cambridge: Harvard University Press.

Windholz, G. (1989, April-June). The discovery of the principles of reinforcement, extinction, generalization, and differentiation of conditional reflexes in Pavlov's laboratories. *Pavlovian Journal of Biological Science, 26,* 64–74.

Windholz, G. (1997). Ivan P. Pavlov: An overview of his life and psychological work. *American Psychologist, 52,* 941–946.

Wingo, P. A., Ries, L. A. G., Giovino, G. A., Miller, D. S., Rosenberg, H. M., Shopland, D. R., Thun, M. J., & Edwards, B. K. (1999) The annual report to the nation on the status of cancer, 1973-1996, with a special section on lung cancer and tobacco smoking. *Journal of the National Cancer Institute, 91,* 675–690.

Wink, P., & Dillon, M. (2002). Spiritual development across the adult life course: Findings from a longitudinal study. *Journal of Adult Development, 9,* 79–94.

Winner, E. (2000). The origins and ends of giftedness. *American Psychologist, 55,* 159–169.

Wirtz, D., Kruger, J., Scollon, C. N., & Diener, E. (2003). What to do on Spring break? The role of predicted, on-line, and remembered experience in future choice. *Psychological Science, 14,* 520–524.

Wiseman, R. (2002). Laugh Lab—final results. University of Hertfordshire (www.laughlab.co.uk).

Wiseman, R., Jeffreys, C., Smith, M., & Nyman, A. (1999). The psychology of the seance. *The Skeptical Inquirer, 23*(2), 30–33.

Wisman, A., & Goldenberg, J. L. (2005). From the grave to the cradle: Evidence that mortality salience engenders a desire for offspring. *Journal of Personality and Social Psychology, 89,* 46–61.

Witelson, S. F., Kigar, D. L., & Harvey, T. (1999). The exceptional brain of Albert Einstein. *The Lancet, 353,* 2149–2153.

Witvliet, C. V. O., Ludwig, T., & Vander Laan, K. (2001). Granting forgiveness or harboring grudges: Implications for emotions, physiology, and health. *Psychological Science, 12,* 117–123.

Witvliet, C. V. O., & Vrana, S. R. (1995). Psychophysiological responses as indices of affective dimensions. *Psychophysiology, 32,* 436–443.

Wixted, J. T., & Ebbesen, E. B. (1991). On the form of forgetting. *Psychological Science, 2,* 409–415.

Woehr, D. J., & Cavell, T. A. (1993). Self-report measures of ability, effort, and nonacademic activity as predictors of introductory psychology test scores. *Teaching of Psychology, 20,* 156–160.

Woerlee, G. M. (2004, May/June). Darkness, tunnels, and light. *Skeptical Inquirer,* pp. 28–32.

Wolfson, A. R., & Carskadon, M. A. (1998). Sleep schedules and daytime functioning in adolescents. *Child Development, 69,* 875–887.

Woll, S. (1986). So many to choose from: Decision strategies in videodating. *Journal of Social and Personal Relationships, 3,* 43–52.

Wolpe, J. (1958). *Psychotherapy by reciprocal inhibition.* Stanford, CA: Stanford University Press.

Wolpe, J., & Plaud, J. J. (1997). Pavlov's contributions to behavior therapy: The obvious and the not so obvious. *American Psychologist, 52,* 966–972.

Wong, D. F., Wagner, H. N., Tune, L. E., Dannals, R. F., & others. (1986). Positron emission tomography reveals elevated D_2 dopamine receptors in drug-naive schizophrenics. *Science, 234,* 1588–1593.

Wong, M. M., & Csikszentmihalyi, M. (1991). Affiliation motivation and daily experience: Some issues on gender differences. *Journal of Personality and Social Psychology, 60,* 154–164.

Wood, C. J, & Aggleton, J. P. (1989). Handedness in "fast ball" sports: Do left-handers have an innate advantage? *British Journal of Psychology, 80,* 227–240.

Wood, J. (2003, May 19). Quoted by R. Mestel, Rorschach tested: Blot out the famous method? Some experts say it has no place in psychiatry. *Los Angeles Times* (www.latimes.com).

Wood, J. M., Bootzin, R. R., Kihlstrom, J. F., & Schacter, D. L. (1992). Implicit and explicit memory for verbal information presented during sleep. *Psychological Science, 3,* 236–239.

Wood, J. M., Nezworski, M. T., Garb, H. N., & Lilienfeld, S. O. (2006). The controversy over the Exner Comprehensive System and the Society for Personality Assessment's white paper on the Rorschach. *Independent Practitioner,* in press.

Wood, J. V., Heimpel, S. A., & Michela, J. L. (2003). Savoring versus dampening: Self-esteem differences in regulating positive affect. *Journal of Personality and Social Psychology, 85,* 566–580.

Wood, J. V., Saltzberg, J. A., & Goldsamt, L. A. (1990a). Does affect induce self-focused attention? *Journal of Personality and Social Psychology, 58,* 899–908.

Wood, J. V., Saltzberg, J. A., Neale, J. M., Stone, A. A., & Rachmiel, T. B. (1990b). Self-focused attention, coping responses, and distressed mood in everyday life. *Journal of Personality and Social Psychology, 58,* 1027–1036.

Wood, W. (1987). Meta-analytic review of sex differences in group performance. *Psychological Bulletin, 102,* 53–71.

Wood, W., & Eagly, A. (2002). A cross-cultural analysis of the behavior of women and men: Implications for the origins of sex differences. *Psychological Bulletin, 128,* 699–727.

Wood, W., Lundgren, S., Ouellette, J. A., Busceme, S., & Blackstone, T. (1994). Minority influence: A meta-analytic review of social influence processes. *Psychological Bulletin, 115,* 323–345.

Woodruff-Pak, D. S. (1989). Aging and intelligence: Changing perspectives in the twentieth century. *Journal of Aging Studies, 3,* 91–118.

Woods, N. F., Dery, G. K., & Most, A. (1983). Recollections of menarche, current menstrual attitudes, and premenstrual symptoms. In S. Golub (Ed.), *Menarche: The transition from girl to woman.* Lexington, MA: Lexington Books.

Woody, E. Z., & McConkey, K. M. (2003). What we don't know about the brain and hypnosis, but need to: A view from the Buckhorn Inn. *International Journal of Clinical and Experimental Hypnosis, 51,* 309–338.

Woolcock, N. (2004, September 3). Driver thought everyone else was on wrong side. *The Times,* p. 22.

World Federation for Mental Health. (2005). ADHD: The hope behind the hype. www.wfmh.org

World Health Organization. (1979). *Schizophrenia: An international follow-up study.* Chicester, England: Wiley.

World Health Organization. (2004a). *Prevention of mental disorders: Effective interventions and policy options. Summary report.* Geneva: World Health Organization, Department of Mental Health and Substance Abuse.

World Health Organization. (2004b). *Promoting mental health: Concepts, emerging evidence, practice. Summary report.* Geneva: World Health Organization, Department of Mental Health and Substance Abuse.

Worobey, J., & Blajda, V. M. (1989). Temperament ratings at 2 weeks, 2 months, and 1 year: Differential stability of activity and emotionality. *Developmental Psychology, 25,* 257–263.

Worthington, E. L., Jr. (1989). Religious faith across the life span: Implications for counseling and research. *The Counseling Psychologist, 17,* 555–612.

Worthington, E. L., Jr., Kurusu, T. A., McCullogh, M. E., & Sandage, S. J. (1996). Empirical research on religionand psychotherapeutic processes and outcomes: A 10-year review and research prospectus. *Psychological Bulletin, 119,* 448–487.

Wortman, C. B., & Silver, R. C. (1989). The myths of coping with loss. *Journal of Consulting and Clinical Psychology, 57,* 349–357.

Wren, C. S. (1999, April 8). Drug survey of children finds middle school a pivotal time. *New York Times* (www.nytimes.com).

Wright, I. C., Rabe-Hesketh, S., Woodruff, P. W. R., David, A. S., Murray, R. M., & Bullmore, E. T. (2000). Meta-analysis of regional brain volumes in schizophrenia. *American Journal of Psychiatry, 157,* 16–25.

Wright, K. (November, 1996). The Tarzan syndrome. *Discover, 17*(11), 88–94, 96, 98.

Wright, P. H. (1989). Gender differences in adults' same- and cross-gender friendships. In R. G. Adams & R. Blieszner (Eds.), *Older adult friendships: Structure and process.* Newbury Park, CA: Sage.

Wright, P., Takei, N., Rifkin, L., & Murray, R. M. (1995). Maternal influenza, obstetric complications, and schizophrenia. *American Journal of Psychiatry, 152,* 1714–1720.

Wright, R. (1999, January 11). Who gets the good genes? *Time,* p. 67.

Wright, W. (1998). *Born that way: Genes, behavior, personality.* New York: Knopf.

Wrzesniewski, A., & Dutton, J. E. (2001). Crafting a job: Revisioning employees as active crafters of their work. *Academy of Management Review, 26,* 179–201.

Wrzesniewski, A., McCauley, C. R., Rozin, P., & Schwartz, B. (1997). Jobs, careers, and callings: People's relations to their work. *Journal of Research in Personality, 31,* 21–33.

Wuethrich, B. (2001, March). Features—GETTING STUPID—Surprising new neurological behavioral research reveals that teenagers who drink too much may permanently damage their brains and seriously compromise their ability to learn. *Discover, 56,* 56–64.

Wulsin, L. R., Vaillant, G. E., & Wells, V. E. (1999). A systematic review of the mortality of depression. *Psychosomatic Medicine, 61,* 6–17.

Wyatt, J. K., & Bootzin, R. R. (1994). Cognitive processing and sleep: Implications for enhancing job performance. *Human Performance, 7,* 119–139.

Wyatt, R. J., Henter, I., & Sherman-Elvy, E. (2001). Tantalizing clues to preventing schizophrenia. *Cerebrum: The Dana Forum on Brain Science, 3,* pp. 15–30.

Wynn, K. (1992). Addition and subtraction by human infants. *Nature, 358,* 749–759.

Wynn, K. (2000). Findings of addition and subtraction in infants are robust and consistent: reply to Wakeley, Rivera, and Langer. *Child Development, 71,* 1535–1536.

Wynn, K., Bloom, P., & Chiang, W-C. (2002). Enumeration of collective entities by 5-month-old infants. *Cognition, 83,* B55-B62.

Wynn, V., & Gilhooly, K. (1999). The veracity of memories for what you were doing and who you were with when you heard of the death of Diana. *British Psychological Society 1999 Proceedings, 71,* p. 47.

Wynne, C. D. L. (2004). *Do animals think?* Princeton, NJ: Princeton University Press.

Wysocki, C. J., & Gilbert, A. N. (1989). *National Geographic* survey: Effects of age are heterogeneous. *Annals of the New York Academy of Sciences, 561,* 12–28.

Xu, Y., & Corkin, S. (2001). H.M. revisits the Tower of Hanoi puzzle. *Neuropsychology, 15,* 69–79.

Yalom, I. D. (1985). *The theory and practice of group psychotherapy* (3rd ed.). New York: Basic Books.

Yang, N., & Linz, D. (1990). Movie ratings and the content of adult videos: The sex-violence ratio. *Journal of Communication, 40*(2), 28–42.

Yankelovich Partners. (1995, May/June). Growing old. *American Enterprise,* p. 108.

Yankelovich Partners. (1997, December 15). Ability of spirituality to help people who are sick. (Press release.)

Yardley, J. (2005, January 31). Fearing future, China starts to give girls their due. *New York Times* (www.nytimes.com).

Yarnell, P. R., & Lynch, S. (1970, April 25). Retrograde memory immediately after concussion. *Lancet,* pp. 863–865.

Yarrow, L. J., Goodwin, M. S., Manheimer, H., & Milowe, I. D. (1973). Infancy experience and cognitive and personality development at ten years. In L. J. Stone, H. T. Smith, & L. B. Murphy (Eds.), *The competent infant.* New York: Basic Books.

Yates, A. (1989). Current perspectives on the eating disorders: I. History, psychological and biological aspects. *Journal of the American Academy of Child and Adolescent Psychiatry, 28,* 813–828.

Yates, A. (1990). Current perspectives on the eating disorders: II. Treatment, outcome, and research directions. *Journal of the American Academy of Child and Adolescent Psychiatry, 29,* 1–9.

Yates, W. R. (2000). Testosterone in psychiatry. *Archives of General Psychiatry, 57,* 155–156.

Ybarra, O. (1999). Misanthropic person memory when the need to self-enhance is absent. *Personality and Social Psychology Bulletin, 25,* 261–269.

Yip, P. S. F. (1998). Age, sex, marital status and suicide: An empirical study of east and west. *Psychological Reports, 82,* 311–322.

Yirmiya, N., Erel, O., Shaken, M., & Solomonica-Levi, D. (1998). Meta-analyses comparing theory of mind abilities of individuals with autism, individuals with mental retardation, and normally developing individuals. *Psychological Bulletin, 124,* 283–307.

Zajonc, R. B. (1965). Social facilitation. *Science, 149,* 269–274.

Zajonc, R. B. (1980). Feeling and thinking: Preferences need no inferences. *American Psychologist, 35,* 151–175.

Zajonc, R. B. (1984a). On the primacy of affect. *American Psychologist, 39,* 117–123.

Zajonc, R. B. (1984b, July 22). Quoted by D. Goleman, Rethinking IQ tests and their value. *The New York Times,* p. D22.

Zajonc, R. B. (1998). Emotions. In D. Gilbert, S. T. Fiske, & G. Lindzey (Eds.), *Handbook of social psychology,* 4th ed. New York: McGraw-Hill.

Zajonc, R. B. (2001). Mere exposure: A gateway to the subliminal. *Current Directions in Psychological Science, 10,* 224–228.

Zajonc, R. B., & Markus, G. B. (1975). Birth order and intellectual development. *Psychological Review, 82,* 74–88.

Zajonc, R. B., Murphy, S. T., & Inglehart, M. (1989). Feeling and facial efference: Implications of the vascular theory of emotions. *Psychological Review, 96,* 395–416.

Zammit, S., Allebeck, P., Andreasson, S., Lundberg, I., & Lewis, G. (2002). Self reported cannabis use as a risk factor for schizophrenia in Swedish conscripts of 1969: Historical cohort study. *British Medical Journal, 325,* 1199.

Zauberman, G., & Lynch, J. G., Jr. (2005). Resource slack and propensity to discount delayed investments of time versus money. *Journal of Experimental Psychology: General, 134,* 23–37.

Zeidner, M. (1990). Perceptions of ethnic group modal intelligence: Reflections of cultural stereotypes or intelligence test scores? *Journal of Cross-Cultural Psychology, 21,* 214–231.

Zeineh, M. M., Engel, S. A., Thompson, P. M., & Bookheimer, S. Y. (2003). Dynamics of the hippocampus during encoding and retrieval of face-name pairs. *Science, 299,* 577–580.

Zigler, E. F. (1987). Formal schooling for four-year-olds? No. *American Psychologist, 42,* 254–260.

Zigler, E., & Styfco, S. J. (2001). Extended childhood intervention prepared children for school and beyond. *Journal of the American Medical Association, 285,* 2378–2380.

Zilbergeld, B. (1983). *The shrinking of America: Myths of psychological change.* Boston: Little, Brown.

Zillmann, D. (1986). Effects of prolonged consumption of pornography. Background paper for *The Surgeon General's workshop on pornography and public health,* June 22–24. Report prepared by E. P. Mulvey & J. L. Haugaard and released by Office of the Surgeon General on August 4, 1986.

Zillmann, D. (1989). Effects of prolonged consumption of pornography. In D. Zillmann & J. Bryant (Eds.), *Pornography: Research advances and policy considerations.* Hillsdale, NJ: Erlbaum.

Zillmann, D., & Bryant, J. (1984). Effects of massive exposure to pornography. In N. Malamuth & E. Donnerstein (Eds.), *Pornography and sexual aggression.* Orlando, FL: Academic Press.

Zimbardo, P. G. (1970). The human choice: Individuation, reason, and order versus deindividuation, impulse, and chaos. In W. J. Arnold & D. Levine (Eds.), *Nebraska Symposium on Motivation, 1969.* Lincoln, NE: University of Nebraska Press.

Zimbardo, P. G. (1972, April). Pathology of imprisonment. *Transaction/Society,* pp. 4–8.

Zimbardo, P. G. (2001, September 16). Fighting terrorism by understanding man's capacity for evil. Op Ed Essay distributed by spsp-discuss@stolaf.edu.

Zimbardo, P. G. (2004, May 25). Journalist interview re: Abu Ghraib prison abuses: Eleven answers to eleven questions. Unpublished manuscript, Stanford University.

Zimbardo, P. G. (2005, January 18). You can't be a sweet cucumber in a vinegar barrel. *The Edge* (www.edge.org).

Zimmer, C. (2003). How the mind reads other minds. *Science, 300,* 1079–1080.

Zornberg, G. L., Buka, S. L., & Tsuang, M. T. (2000). At issue: The problem of obstetrical complications and schizophrenia. *Schizophrenia Bulletin, 26,* 249–256.

Zubieta, J-K., Heitzeg, M. M., Smith, Y. R., Bueller, J. A., Xu, K., Xu, Y., Koeppe, R. A., Stohler, C. S., & Goldman, D. (2003). COMT val[158]met genotype affects μ-opioid neurotransmitter responses to a pain stressor. *Science, 299,* 1240–1243.

Zucco, G. M. (2003). Anomalies in cognition: Olfactory memory. *European Psychologist, 8,* 77–86.

Zucker, G. S., & Weiner, B. (1993). Conservatism and perceptions of poverty: An attributional analysis. *Journal of Applied Social Psychology, 23,* 925–943.

Zuckerman, M. (1979). *Sensation seeking: Beyond the optimal level of arousal.* Hillsdale, NJ: Erlbaum.

Name Index

SUBJECT INDEX